The Development of Children

For our grandparents, parents, children, and grandchildren, who have been the family medium of our development. And for our editors, Jonathan Cobb, Moira Lerner, and Peter Deane, who have seen us safely through the labyrinth.

The Development of Children

FOURTH EDITION

Michael Cole
University of California, San Diego
Sheila R. Cole

WORTH PUBLISHERS

The Development of Children, Fourth edition

Manufactured in the United States of America

ISBN: 0-7167-3833-3

Printing: 1 2 3 4   04 03 02 01

Sponsoring Editor: Jessica Bayne
Development Editor: Peter Deane
Project Editor: Margaret Comaskey
Production Manager: Barbara Anne Seixas
Art Director/Cover Design: Barbara Reingold
Cover Photograph: Marks Productions/Image Bank
Designer: Paul Lacy
Illustration Coordinator: Lou Capaldo
Illustrations: Chris Notarile, Fineline Inc., Tomo Narashima
Photo Research: Elyse Rieder, Vikii Wong
Composition: Progressive Information Technologies
Printing and Binding: R. R. Donnelley & Sons Company

Library of Congress Cataloging-in-Publication Data

Cole, Michael, 1938-
The development of children / Michael Cole, Sheila R. Cole.--4th ed.
p. cm.
Includes bibliographical references and indexes.
ISBN 0-7167-3833-3
1. Child development. I. Cole, Sheila. II. Title.

RJ131.C585 2000
305.231--dc21

99-087966

Worth Publishers
41 Madison Avenue
New York, NY 10010
http://www.worthpublishers.com

Brief Contents

Contents

Preface

The task of writing a textbook to introduce students to the topic of human development poses a special challenge. On the one hand, everyone who opens such a book has had extensive firsthand experience with the process of growing up. In addition, each reader has had many opportunities to witness and to think about the development of other people who are older, the same age, and younger. So, in one sense at least, readers are already experts on the topic of human development. On the other hand, their expertise is subjective, intuitive, and, correspondingly, relatively narrow in scope.

The challenge, and our goal, in writing this book has been to show students that a broad scientific framework for understanding children's development can enrich their understanding of their own lives and of the processes of development in general. Our greatest aspiration is to bring intellectual excitement to their learning about human development so that the research and theorizing we write about will guide the practical applications of scientific knowledge for students who will become parents and practitioners.

In our view, development is best understood as a fusion of biological, social, and psychological processes interacting in the unique medium of human culture. We have tried to show, not only the role each of these factors considered separately, but also how they interact in diverse cultural contexts to create whole, unique, human beings. Development also consists of transformations that take place over time, and in our view it is best examined and described chronologically. We begin our presentation with the phenomenon of conception and trace the sequence of developmental changes from that instant into infancy, childhood, and adolescence.

Throughout, we have been guided by the belief that it is a mistake to make sharp distinctions between practical, theoretical, and research orientations in studying development. Truly fundamental knowledge must draw on and illuminate all three orientations.

A PRACTICAL ORIENTATION

The authors of *The Development of Children* have known each other since adolescence. We have shared a personal interest in children's development from the time we were teenagers, first as camp counselors working with young children, then as parents raising children of our own, and now as grandparents, regularly called upon to play the role. We each have a deep professional interest in child development, as well. Michael Cole is a specialist in the study of children's learning and cognitive development. Sheila Cole is a journalist who has written articles about children and books for children.

Both personally and professionally, we are actively interested in discovering practical approaches for fostering the development of children. So it is natural that our book should focus continually on issues such as the benefits of special nutrition programs for children who have experienced malnutrition early in life; methods for assessing the quality of out-of-home care for young children; the importance of extended families in ameliorating the problems facing poor children; the challenges of learning to read and to do arithmetic in school; ways to foster emotional self-regulation and reduce aggression among children; the special hazards of teenage pregnancy; and effective means of parenting teenagers. We also include many examples drawn from the everyday lives of children to show how a society's beliefs influence its children's development by shaping both the laws and the social norms that govern child-rearing practices.

A THEORETICAL ORIENTATION

There is much truth to the saying that nothing is so practical as a good theory. A deep understanding of how children develop requires familiarity not only with the everyday lives of children but also with theories that provide coherent interpretations of the facts derived from scientific research. Such understanding is an essential foundation for attempts to create and guide practical courses of action.

A major difficulty for students of child development is the number and diversity of theories that compete to provide an understanding of basic issues and phenomena. We have adopted two strategies to deal with this problem. First, we frame our presentation in terms of the enduring issues that all theories of development must resolve: how biological and environmental contributions (nature and nurture) are woven together; the extent to which the interaction of these factors results in continuities and discontinuities in the dynamic process of development; and the reasons for the individual differences among people. Second, we present competing theories in a constant dialogue with one another, with data from contemporary research, and with the practical issues the theories were designed to address. Rather than gloss over differences among theories, we have attempted to build an appreciation of the bases for the competing interpretations the theories offer. Then we have tried to move beyond the differences to show how each theory contributes to an overall understanding of development.

A RESEARCH ORIENTATION

The dialogue between theory and practice leads naturally to disputes about the facts of development as well as about the methodologies used to marshal facts in support of one perspective or another. Therefore it is essential that students understand research methods both as a means of judging the merits of the evidence that psychologists and other developmentalists gather and as a means of thinking critically about the conclusions they draw. What is the evidence that sparing the rod spoils the child? How might we determine whether the differences between boys' and girls' games result from social forces or from deep-seated biological predispositions? Are the links that have been found between watching violent programs on television and subsequent aggressive behavior necessarily causal? And why is it so difficult for developmentalists to answer enduring questions about development once and for all? Only through an awareness of the logic, methods, and, indeed, the shortcomings of developmental research can students come away from a course on development with the ability to evaluate for themselves the relative merits of different scientists' conclusions.

The kind of critical thinking students need to evaluate evidence and to appreciate the process of research does not develop spontaneously. It requires careful explanation and repeated exposure. Consequently, we have made detailed and probing discussions of relevant research a constant feature of the book.

A FOCUS ON CULTURE

Over the years, our work has taken us to live in many parts of the world: West Africa, Mexico, Russia, Israel, Japan, and Great Britain. Within the United States, we have lived and worked in affluent suburbs and inner-city ghettos. Often our children have accompanied us, providing us with even richer opportunities for getting to know children in a wide variety of circumstances. Such experiences have led us to believe that culture is a fundamental constituent of any comprehensive theory of development.

For students to appreciate this truth fully, it is necessary for them to overcome as much as possible any ethnocentrism they may have in their view of children's development. The task is by no means an easy one. For many Americans, the initial reaction to daily life in an African village, an Asian metropolis, or the impoverished neighborhoods of a large U.S. city is likely to be "culture shock," a sense of disorientation that stems from the difficulty of understanding the way of life of people in other cultures or foreign circumstances. Very often, culture shock is accompanied by a sense of cultural superiority; the way "we" do it (prepare our food, build our houses, care for our children) seems superior to the way "they" do it. In addition, appreciation of culture's contribution to development requires more than attention to the ways people far away raise their children. Culture is fundamental to children's experience in any society—not something added on to the process of development, but an essential part of that process.

Recognizing how difficult it is to think objectively about the nature of development in unfamiliar cultures, we have tried to keep our readers constantly aware of the diversity of the cultural contexts in which children grow up and of the variations that exist in human child-rearing practices. Only by considering their culture as but one alternative design among many designs for living can students arrive at a valid understanding of the principles that guide the development of all human beings.

A FOCUS ON BIOLOGY

It may seem surprising that authors who profess a special interest in culture would simultaneously underscore, as we do, the importance of biological factors to human development. Often the two sources of human variability are discussed as opposing each other, as if somehow, by virtue of living within a culture, human beings ceased to be biologically evolving creatures. However, modern research on development has shown this to be a false opposition. Not only is the ability to create and use culture one of the most striking biological facts about our species, but there would be no development at all without biological maturation. Advances in the biological sciences have profoundly influenced human development through improved health care and advanced medical procedures. In addition, the biological sciences have increased our understanding of development by shedding light on critical issues such as the intimate links between biological changes in the brain and changes in children's cognitive capacities. The importance of the biological domain in development is made clear throughout this book.

A FOCUS ON THE DYNAMIC INTERACTION OF DOMAINS

The Development of Children combines traditional chronological and topical approaches to development in a deliberate attempt to make as clear as possible the idea that development is a process involving the whole child in a dynamically changing set of cultural contexts. Although the book is chronological in its overall structure, and adopts traditional stage boundaries for each of its major sections, the organization of the text is also topical in two respects. First, within broad, conventionally defined stages, it describes developments as occurring in the biological domain, the social domain, or the psychological domain (including emotion and cognition), while at the same time tracing the ways in which these developments interweave with development in other domains. Second, it focuses on the way stagelike changes emerge from the convergence of events in the various developmental domains.

Chronological and topical perspectives correspond to the warp and the woof of development. The pattern that is woven from their combination is the story of development. It is that story we have attempted to tell in this book.

NEW TO THE FOURTH EDITION

It has been almost 20 years since we undertook the first edition of this book. Over that period of time there has been a constantly increasing stream of scientific research that has made each revision a real challenge. Some topics that were of central interest to developmentalists have receded from the spotlight to be replaced by new and exciting findings. For example, 20 years ago research on middle childhood was particularly dominant, while both infancy and adolescence were relatively neglected areas of research. Today the study of infancy and adolescence draw the lion's share of interest.

In attempting to ensure that the presentation in this edition is as up to date as possible, we have carefully documented major new developments in the field as the 700 or more new references attest. We have also used the vantage point of our long experience in surveying the field to weed out research that, while authoritative in earlier decades, has been superseded owing to more powerful methods or new theoretical insights that have rendered earlier approaches less interesting.

Readers familiar with the third edition will find that each of the distinctive features of earlier editions has been built upon, streamlined, and better integrated. These include

- **Additions to our already extensive discussions of practical issues.** These include discussions of genetic counseling, the consequences of maternal depression, the controversy over day care, the problem of bullying, organizing classrooms to take advantage of children's home cultures, childhood obesity and adolescent eating disorders, learning disabilities, the use of computers in schools, adolescent risk taking, the creation of special rituals to promote ethnic identity formation, and many other topics of current concern.
- **A special focus on linking theory and practice.** Throughout the text, applications of developmental research are closely linked to their research base. In addition, the Epilogue specifically addresses the many ways in which the principles and scientific knowledge of developmental study can be used as a guide to everyday practice.
- **Increased attention to linkages among the social, emotional, and cognitive developmental events from which the whole child emerges.** In this edition we have devoted additional attention to examining how changes in social, biological, emotional, and cognitive domains occur as part of a single life process.
- **Increased treatment of key traditional topics.** Continuing a trend already in evidence in the third edition, we have expanded our coverage

of several traditional topics, including perceptual, socioemotional, and physical development, gender and ethnic identity formation, and post-Piagetian approaches to cognitive development.

- **Valuing diversity.** Like its predecessors, this edition of *The Development of Children* places special emphasis on the importance of understanding and appreciating the diversity of development as it occurs in many parts of the world and among different populations within North America. We are gratified that concern with cultural diversity has found a growing place in the study of child development, but we believe the urgency of understanding and appreciating the role of diversity in human development is greater today than ever before. The fourth edition reflects this increased concern.
- **Accessibility.** In preparing this edition we have made a special effort to increase the accessibility of our presentation without reducing its rigor. Every discussion, holdover and new alike, has been closely scrutinized with an eye to streamlining, sharpening focus, and making the linkages among key points more apparent. It is an effort from which, we think, students of all levels of ability will benefit.

A NOTE TO INSTRUCTORS

The Development of Children has been designed to be taught within either a quarter or a semester system. For classes taught on the quarter system in which the curriculum is restricted to childhood, the final section of the book can be left to students to read or not, as they choose, and the remainder can be fitted comfortably into a 10-week course. For 10-week courses that include adolescence, sections rather than whole chapters in Part I can be read; Chapter 7 (on the way infant experience shapes later development) and Chapter 8 (on language) could also be skipped or assigned selectively without disrupting the general flow of the presentation.

Instructors who prefer to organize this course in a topical fashion may also wish to assign segments rather than entire chapters in Part I: these chapters present important foundational issues that can be explored to any depth that is deemed appropriate. Chapters 4 through 6 can be read in sequence, or topical issues from each can be abstracted for reading in connection with corresponding chapters in Parts III, IV, and V. The natural sequence of chapters for the remainder of the course then becomes 9, 12, 13, and 16, which emphasize cognitive development, and 10, 14, and 15, which emphasize social and personality development. Instructors planning to use this textbook in conjunction with a topical course will find it helpful to turn to the Appendix on page A-1, "Guide to Discussions of Specific Aspects of Development."

SUPPLEMENTS

An extensive package of supplements has been prepared, each corresponding to the fourth edition of *The Development of Children* in content, level, and organization.

READINGS ON THE DEVELOPMENT OF CHILDREN, THIRD EDITION

This reader, by Mary Gauvain, University of California at Riverside, and Michael Cole, is newly updated for this edition of the text and includes seventeen new articles.

INSTRUCTOR'S RESOURCE MANUAL

The *Instructor's Resource Manual* by Jennifer Coots, University of California at Long Beach, features chapter-by-chapter previews and lecture guides, learning objectives, topics for discussion and debate, handouts for student projects, and supplementary readings from journals. Course planning suggestions and ideas for term projects are also included.

STUDY GUIDE

The carefully crafted *Study Guide* by Stephanie Stolarz-Fantino, University of California at San Diego, helps students to read and retain the text material at a higher level than they are likely to achieve by reading the text alone. Each chapter includes a variety of practice tests and exercises to help integrate themes that reappear in various chapters. Each chapter also includes a review of key concepts, guided study questions, and section reviews that encourage students' active participation in the learning process.

TEST BANK

Thoroughly revised, the *Test Bank* by Jennifer Coots, University of California at Long Beach, includes approximately 60 multiple-choice and 70 fill-in, true-false, matching, and essay questions for every chapter. Each question is keyed to the textbook by topic, page number, and level of difficulty.

COMPUTERIZED TEST BANK CD-ROM

This computerized test bank CD-ROM, on dual platform for Windows and Macintosh, offers an easy-to-use test-generation system, allowing instructors to select specific questions, generate a random assortment from one or more chapters, and even add questions to the system. The CD-ROM is also the access point for online testing.

ONLINE TESTING

Diploma is a program from the Brownstone Research Group that allows you to create and administer examinations on paper, over a network, and now, over the Internet. You will also be able to incorporate multimedia, graphics, movies, sound, or interactive activities within the questions. Security features allow you to restrict tests to specific computers or time blocks. The package also includes an impressive suite of grade book and question-analysis features.

TRANSPARENCY SET

A set of 50 full-color transparencies offers key illustrations, charts, graphs, and tables from the textbook.

COLE COMPANION WEB SITE

The *Cole and Cole Companion Web Site* at www.worthpublishers.com/coledevelopmentofchildren4e offers a variety of simulations, tutorials, and study aids organized by chapter with periodic updates (that is, new Web links, exercises, and new developments in developmental psychology). In addition to the on-line testing, syllabus posting, and Web site building services, the *Companion Web Site* offers the following features:

- **Psychology Updates:** *Psychology in the News* updates instructors and students about current events and research in developmental psychology.

- **Web Links:** Over 150 annotated Web links related to the study of developmental psychology are organized by chapter.
- **Online Quizzes:** Instructors can easily and securely quiz students online. The site features prewritten, multiple-choice quizzes for each of the book's chapters (not from the test bank). Students receive instant feedback and can take the quizzes multiple times. Answers are stored and instructors can view results by quiz, student, or question, or can get weekly results via email.
- **Interactive Animations:** Animations of psychological processes are based on the text art and include a quizzing function.
- **Flashcards:** Interactive flashcards tutor students on all chapter/text terminology and allow them to then quiz themselves on the terms.

IMAGE AND LECTURE GALLERY

Worth's *Image and Lecture Gallery* at www.worthpublishers.com/ILG provides access to electronic versions of lecture materials. Registered users can browse, search, and download illustrations from Worth titles and prebuilt PowerPoint presentation files for specific chapters, containing all chapter art or all chapter section headings in text form. Users can also create personal folders on a personalized home page for easy organization of the materials.

WEBCT AND BLACKBOARD ONLINE ARCHITECTURE

With WebCT "architecture," instructors can create a course Web site and/or online course, with content, threaded discussions, quizzing, an online gradebook, course calendar, and more! We have placed *The Development of Children, Fourth Edition* graphic and media content in the WebCT format. Worth Publishers is happy to provide instructors with Cole/Cole content for Blackboard architecture as well.

JOURNEY THROUGH CHILDHOOD DEVELOPMENTAL PSYCHOLOGY VIDEO SERIES

Designed for both in-class demonstration and at-home viewing, these two videos with accompanying student/instructor workbooks will enable development students to observe the activities, responses, and behaviors of children of various ages and ethnicities in a variety of naturalistic environments—including school, home, day-care, and health-care settings. The videos include interviews with noted researchers and child development experts, including Patricia Greenfield, Barbara Rogoff, and Gilda Morelli. The instructor's observation guide offers teaching and activity suggestions, while the student observation guide directs students on observational skills and links between segments.

THE SCIENTIFIC AMERICAN FRONTIERS VIDEO COLLECTION FOR DEVELOPMENTAL PSYCHOLOGY

This renowned collection is comprised of seventeen video segments of approximately 15 minutes each covering topics ranging from language development to nature–nurture issues. The videos can be used to launch classroom lectures or to emphasize and clarify course material. The accompanying *Faculty Guide* by Richard O. Straub, University of Michigan, describes and relates each segment to specific topics in *The Development of Children, Fourth Edition.*

ACKNOWLEDGMENTS

A book of this scope and complexity could not be produced without the help of others. A great many people gave generously of their time and experience to deepen our treatment of various areas of development, particularly the many scholars who consented to review drafts of our manuscript and make suggestions for improvement. The remaining imperfections exist despite their best efforts.

For the foundations laid in earlier editions, we gratefully acknowledge the help of **Curt Acredolo,** University of California, Davis; **Karen Adolph,** Carnegie Mellon University; **Margarita Azmitia,** University of California, Santa Cruz; **MaryAnn Baenninger,** Trenton State College; **Ann E. Bigelow,** St. Francis Xavier University; **Gay L. Bisanz,** University of Alberta, Edmonton; **Jeffrey Bisanz,** University of Alberta; **Kathryn N. Black,** Purdue University; **Patricia C. Broderick,** Villanova University; **Urie Bronfenbrenner,** Cornell University; **Gordon Bronson,** University of California, Berkeley; **Ann L. Brown,** University of California, Berkeley; **Michaelanthony Brown-Cheatham,** San Diego State University; **Angela Buchanan,** De Anza College; **Tara C. Callaghan,** St. Francis Xavier University; **Richard Canfield,** Cornell University; **William B. Carey,** Children's Hospital of Philadelphia; **Robbie Case,** OISE; **David B. Conner,** Northeast Missouri State University; **Andrew C. Coyne,** Ohio State University; **William E. Cross, Jr.,** Cornell University; **Frank Curcio,** Boston University; **David M. Day,** University of Toronto; **Anthony De Casper,** University of North Carolina, Greensboro; **Judy S. DeLoache,** University of Illinois at Urbana-Champaign; **Cathy Dent-Read,** University of California, Irvine; **Don Devers,** North Virginia Community College, Annandale; **Rosanne K. Dlugosz,** Scottsdale Community College; **Rebecca Eder,** University of California, Davis; **Gregory T. Eells,** Oklahoma State University; **Peter Eimas,** Brown University; **Jeffrey W. Elias,** Texas Tech University; **Beverly Fagot,** University of Oregon; **Sylvia Farnham-Diggory,** University of Delaware; **David H. Feldman,** Tufts University; **Mark Feldmen,** Stanford University; **Kurt Fischer,** Harvard University; **Brenda K. Fleming,** Family Service Agency, Phoenix; **Herbert P. Ginsburg,** Teachers College, Columbia University; **Sam Glucksberg,** Princeton University; **Kathleen S. Gorman,** University of Vermont; **Mark Grabe,** University of North Dakota; **Steve Greene,** Princeton University; **Harold D. Grotevant,** University of Minnesota; **William S. Hall,** University of Maryland, College Park; **Paul Harris,** University of Oxford; **Janis E. Jacobs,** University of Nebraska, Lincoln; **Jeannette L. Johnson,** University of Maryland, College Park; **Daniel P. Keating,** Ontario Institute for Studies in Education; **Claire Kopp,** University of California, Los Angeles; **Gisela Labouvie-Vief,** Wayne State University; **Alan W. Lanning,** College of DuPage; **Kathleen L. Lemanek,** University of Kansas; **Jacqueline Lerner,** Michigan State University; **Elizabeth Levin,** Laurentian University; **Zella Luria,** Tufts University; **Sandra Machida,** California State University, Chico; **Jean Mandler,** University of California, San Diego; **Sarah Mangelsdorf,** University of Illinois at Urbana-Champaign; **Michael Maratsos,** University of Minnesota; **Patricia H. Miller,** University of Florida; **Shitala P. Mishra,** University of Arizona; **Joan Moyer,** Arizona State University; **Frank B. Murray,** University of Delaware; **Sharon Nelson-LeGall,** University of Pittsburgh; **Nora Newcombe,** Temple University; **Ageliki Nicolopoulou,** Smith College; **Elizabeth Pemberton,** University of Delaware; **Herbert L. Pick, Jr.,** University of Minnesota; **Ellen F. Potter,** University of South Carolina, Columbia; **David E. Powley,** University of Mobile; **Thomas M. Randall,** Rhode Island College; **LeRoy P. Richardson,** Montgomery County Community College; **Christine M. Roberts,** University of Connecticut; **Barbara Rogoff,** University of California, Santa Cruz; **Marnie Roosevelt,** Santa Monica Community College; **Karl Rosengren,** University of Illinois at Urbana-Champaign; **Carolyn Saarni,**

Sonoma State University; **Arnold Sameroff,** University of Michigan; **Sylvia Scribner,** City University of New York; **Felicísima C. Seráfica,** Ohio State University; **Robert S. Siegler,** Carnegie Mellon University; **Jerome L. Singer,** Yale University; **Elizabeth Spelke,** Cornell University; **Catherine Sophion,** University of Hawaii at Manoa; **Doreen Steg,** Drexel University; **Stephanie Stolarz-Fantino,** San Diego State University; **Evelyn Thoman,** University of Connecticut; **Michael Tomasello,** Emory University; **Katherine Van Giffen,** California State University, Long Beach; **Terrie Varga,** Oklahoma State University; **Billy E. Vaughn,** California School of Professional Psychology, San Diego; **Lawrence J. Walker,** University of British Columbia; **Harriet S. Waters,** State University of New York at Stony Brook; **Nanci Weinberger,** Bryant College; **Thomas S. Weisner,** University of California, Los Angeles; **Patricia E. Worden,** California State University at San Marcos; **Phillip Sanford Zeskind,** Virginia Polytechnic University; **Patricia Zukow-Goldring,** University of California, Irvine.

Paul Baltes (Max Planck Institute for Human Development, Berlin), **Joe Campos** (University of California, Berkeley), **Robbie Case** (Stanford University), **Carol Izard** (University of Delaware), and **Larry Nucci** (University of Illinois, Chicago) merit special thanks for providing us with valuable illustrative material and special advice for our various editions.

For the fourth edition, we thank **Mike Anderson,** The University of Western Australia; **Jeremy M. Anglin,** University of Waterloo; **Janet Wilke Astington,** University of Toronto; **Ruth Ault,** Davidson College; **Simon Baron-Cohen,** University of Cambridge; **Bill Barowy,** Lesley College; **Elizabeth Bates,** University of California, San Diego; **Richard Beach,** University of Minnesota; **Ann Benjamin,** University of Massachusetts, Lowell; **Marc Bornstein,** National Institutes of Health; **Sandra Leane Bosacki,** University of Toronto; **Mary Bryson,** University of British Columbia; **David W. Carroll,** University of Wisconsin, Superior; **P. Lindsay Chase-Lansdale,** University of Chicago; **Paul Cobb,** Vanderbilt University; **Leslie B. Cohen,** University of Texas; **Jennifer Coots,** University of California, Long Beach; **Brian Cox,** Hofstra University; **Charles Crook,** Loughborough University; **James L. Dannemiller,** University of Wisconsin; **Pierre R. Dasen,** University of Geneva; **Natacha M. De Genna,** Concordia University; **Adele Diamond,** Eunice Kennedy Shriver Center; **Timothy Dickel,** Creighton University; **Carol Dweck,** Columbia University; **Shari Ellis,** University of Florida; **William Fabricus,** Arizona State University; **Jo Ann Farver,** University of Southern California; **Tiffany Field,** Nova Southeastern University; **Robyn Fivush,** Emory University; **Constance Flanagan,** Pennsylvania State University; **Peter Fonagy,** University College, London; **Elice Forman,** University of Pittsburgh; **Eugene E. Garcia,** University of California, Berkeley; **Janet Gates,** Geneva College; **Brenda O. Gilbert,** Southern Illinois University; **Mary Gauvain,** University of California, Riverside; **Katherine Goff,** University of Colorado at Denver; **Roberta Golinkoff,** University of Delaware; **Artin Goncu,** University of Illinois at Chicago; **Alison Gopnik,** University of California, Berkeley; **Sandra Graham-Bermann,** University of Michigan; **Koeno Gravemeijer,** The Freudenthal Institute; **Patricia Greenfield,** University of California, Los Angeles; **Christine Happle,** University of Bern; **Catherine L. Harris,** Boston University; **Susan Harter,** University of Denver; **Sara Harkness,** University of Connecticut; **Gail Heyman,** University of California, San Diego; **Carolee Howes,** University of California, Los Angeles; **Fergus Hughes,** University of Wisconsin, Green Bay; **Michael Hughes,** University of California, San Diego; **Kedmon Hungwe,** University of Zimbabwe; **Yo Jackson,** University of Kansas; **Barbara Kisilevsky,** Queens University; **Grazyna Kochanska,** University of Iowa; **Gary W. Ladd,** University of Illinois; **Ann L. Law,** Rider University; **Jay L. Lemke,** City University of New York; **Michael Lewis,** Robert Wood Johnson Medical School; **Lynn S. Libern,** Pennsylvania State University; **Cynthia Lightfoot,** Pennsylvania State University; **Lewis Lipsitt,** Brown University; **Marguerite Malakoff,** Harvey Mudd College; **Guiseppe**

Mantovani, University of Padova; **Ann McGillicuddy-DeLisi,** Lafayette College; **Shirley McGuire,** University of California, San Diego; **Bud Mehan,** University of California, San Diego; **Andrew Meltzoff,** University of Washington; **Luis C. Moll,** University of Arizona; **Gilda Morelli,** Boston College; **Elsa Nownes,** University of Tennessee; **Larry Nucci,** University of Illinois at Chicago; **D. Kimbrough Oller,** University of Maine; **Willis Overton,** Temple University; **Martin Packer,** Dusquesne University; **Josef Perner,** University of Salzburg; **Robert Plomin,** Institute of Psychiatry, London; **Paul Quinn,** University of Pittsburgh; **Jane Rankin,** Drake University; **Mary Jo Ratterman,** Franklin & Marshall College; **J. Steven Reznick,** Yale University; **Mary Rothbart,** University of Oregon; **Carolyn Rovee-Collier,** Rutgers University; **Stephanie Rowley,** University of North Carolina at Chapel Hill; **Diane Ruble,** New York University; **Cristina Saccuman,** University of California, San Diego; **Ian St James-Roberts,** Thomas Coram Research Unit; **Robert Serpell,** University of Maryland, Baltimore County; **Ellen Seiter,** University of California, San Diego; **Daniel Smothergill,** Syracuse University; **Romy V. Spitz,** Rutgers University; **Charles M. Super,** University of Connecticut; **Laura Thompson,** New Mexico State University; **Terri Thorkildsen,** University of Illinois, Chicago; **Marion Underwood,** University of Texas at Dallas; **S. Stavros Valenti,** Hofstra University; **Douglas Wahlsten,** University of Alberta; **Marsha Walton,** Rhodes College; **Sandra Waxman,** Northwestern University; **Gordon Wells,** University of Toronto; **Mara Welsh,** University of California, Berkeley; **Patricia Zukow-Goldring,** University of California, Los Angeles.

We are also grateful to Stacey Alexander, Jessica Bayne, Megan Burns, Margaret Comaskey, Peter Deane, Craig Donini, Yuna Lee, Barbara Anne Seixas, and Catherine Woods of Worth Publishers.

Michael Cole

Sheila Cole

CHAPTER 1

The Study of Human Development

EARLY BEGINNINGS
- The Rise of a New Discipline

MODERN DEVELOPMENTAL PSYCHOLOGY

THE CENTRAL QUESTIONS OF DEVELOPMENTAL PSYCHOLOGY
- Questions about Continuity
- Questions about the Sources of Development
- Questions about Individual Differences

THE DISCIPLINE OF DEVELOPMENTAL PSYCHOLOGY
- Criteria of Scientific Description
- Methods of Data Collection
- Research Designs
- Research Designs and Data-Collection Methods in Perspective
- The Role of Theory

THIS BOOK AND THE FIELD OF DEVELOPMENTAL PSYCHOLOGY

The mature person is one of the most remarkable products that any society can bring forth. He or she is a living cathedral, the handiwork of many individuals over many years.

David W. Plath, *Long Engagements*

The study of child development is the study of the physical, cognitive, and psychosocial changes that children undergo from the moment of conception onward. Each of us begins life as a single cell, no larger than the head of a pin. By the time we are born 9 months later, we are incredibly complex organisms made up of billions of cells of many different kinds. We breathe on our own, explore the world with our senses, eat, and begin to take our place in the family and community that created us. But we are totally helpless. We cannot roll over, feed ourselves, keep ourselves clean and warm, or communicate, except to make our distress known by crying and thrashing about.

Two years later we can walk, talk, feed ourselves (with help, to be sure), and play pretend games. By the time we are 7 to 8 years old we can run errands, play organized games without adult supervision, and begin to learn the specialized skills we will need as adults. A few years later we can reason hypothetically, take responsibility for ourselves and others, and even produce children of our own.

The basic scientific task of developmental psychology is to understand how this remarkable process comes about.

EARLY BEGINNINGS

Victor, the Wild Boy of Aveyron.

Jean-Marc Itard, who tried to transform the Wild Boy into a civilized Frenchman.

Although many events could be identified as the starting point of the study of child development, our story begins early one morning in France in the winter of 1800, when a naked, dirty boy wandered into a hamlet in the province of Aveyron looking for food. Some of the people in the area had caught glimpses of the boy in the months before as he dug for roots, climbed trees, and ran about on all fours. They said he was a wild beast. Word spread quickly when the boy appeared in the village, and everyone came to see him.

Among the curious was a government commissioner, who took the boy home and fed him. The child, who appeared to be about 12 years old, seemed ignorant of civilized customs and comforts. When clothes were put on him, he tore them off. He refused to eat anything but raw potatoes, roots, and nuts. He urinated and defecated whenever and wherever the need arose. The only sounds he made were meaningless cries, and he seemed indifferent to human voices. In his report, the commissioner concluded that the boy had lived alone since early childhood, "a stranger to social needs and practices. . . . [T]here is . . . something extraordinary in his behavior, which makes him seem close to the state of wild animals" (quoted in Lane, 1976, pp. 8–9).

When the commissioner's report reached Paris, it caused a sensation. People were fascinated by the bizarre story of the child that newspapers hailed as the "Wild Boy of Aveyron." Scholars hoped that by studying how this uncivilized creature changed once he had participated in society, they could resolve long-standing questions about the nature and development of human beings—questions such as: How do we differ from other animals? What would we be like if we grew up totally isolated from human society? To what degree are we products of our upbringing and experience and to what degree is our character an expression of inborn traits?

Plans to study the Wild Boy nearly ran aground, however. The first physicians to examine him diagnosed him as mentally deficient and speculated that he had been put out to die by his parents for that reason. They recommended that he be placed in an asylum. Initially, he was, until Jean-Marc Itard (1744–1838), a young physician, disputed the diagnosis of retardation. Itard argued that the boy only appeared to be defective because he had been isolated from society and thereby prevented from developing normally. In France in the late eighteenth century, as many as one in three normal children were abandoned by their parents, usually because the family was too poor to support another child (Kessen, 1965). Itard believed that the boy was such a child. The fact that he had been able to survive on his own in the forests of Aveyron argued against his being mentally impaired.

Itard took personal charge of the boy. He thought that he could teach him to become a fully competent Frenchman, master of the French language and the best of civilized knowledge. France had recently overthrown its monarchy and had embraced the political ideals of liberty, equality, and brotherhood. Itard and other supporters of the republic wanted to demonstrate that it was possible to improve the course of peasant children's development by educating them. To test his theory that it is the social environment that shapes children's development, Itard devised an elaborate set of experimental training procedures to teach the Wild Boy how to categorize objects, to reason, and to communicate (Itard, 1801/1982).

At first, Victor, as Itard named the Wild Boy, made rapid progress. He learned to communicate simple needs as well as to recognize and write a few words. He learned to use a chamber pot. He also developed affection for the people who took care of him. But Victor never learned to speak and interact with other people normally.

After 5 years of intense work, Itard abandoned his experiment. Victor had not made enough progress to satisfy Itard's superiors, and Itard himself was unsure about how much more progress the boy could make. Victor was sent to live with a woman who was paid to care for him. He died in 1828, still referred to as the Wild Boy of Aveyron. His unusual experiences in life left unanswered the large questions about human nature, the influence of civilized society, and the degree to which individuals are shaped by one or other of these forces that scholars had hoped would be answered by his discovery.

Most physicians and scholars of the time eventually concluded that Victor had indeed been mentally defective from birth. But doubts remain to this day. Some modern scholars think that Itard may have been right in his belief that Victor was normal at birth but was stunted in his development as a result of his social isolation (Lane, 1976). When he was found, Victor had spent many of his formative years alone. He had already passed the age that is currently thought to be the upper boundary for normal language acquisition. Others believe that Victor suffered from autism, a pathological mental condition whose symptoms include a deficit in language and an inability to interact normally with others (Frith, 1989). It is also possible that Itard's teaching methods failed where different approaches might have succeeded. We cannot be sure.

Itard's attempts to educate Victor mark the beginning point for the science of developmental psychology because Itard was among the first scholars to go beyond speculation to conduct experiments to test his ideas.

THE RISE OF A NEW DISCIPLINE

Although there was no scientific specialty called developmental psychology in Itard's day, interest in children and their development was beginning to grow among social reformers as well as scientists (Cairns, 1998). During the nineteenth century, the industrialization of Europe and North America transformed the social organization of people's lives. Industrialization also transformed the role of children in society and the settings within which they developed. Instead of growing up on farms, where they contributed their labor and were cared for by their mothers and fathers until they reached adulthood, many children were employed in factories in sprawling industrial cities, alongside, and sometimes in place of, their parents (Clement, 1997).

It was at this time that schooling became widespread. Urban children who did not work were usually regarded as a liability by the community, which saw them as rowdy nuisances. Public schools were established as much to increase social control over children as for any academic reasons. They provided places to supervise children's development when neither parents nor employers were supervising them.

For those children who were in the labor force, work often involved long hours in factories or mines, under dangerous and unhealthy conditions. As these conditions became a matter of social concern, they sparked increased social attention and scientific activity. The Factories Inquiries Committee in England, for instance, conducted a study in 1833 to discover whether children could work 12 hours a day without suffering damage. The majority of the committee members decided that 12 hours was an acceptable workday for children. Others who thought a 10-hour workday would be preferable were concerned less with small children's intellectual or emotional well-being than with their morals. They recommended that the remaining 2 hours be devoted to the children's religious and moral education (Lomax et al., 1978).

This early research involved more than a practical response to social concerns. Early developmental psychologists and physicians used the data they collected to clarify basic questions about human development and how to study it. The early studies of children's growth and work capacity, for example, made the important theoretical point that the environment affects development in measurable ways. Researchers found that because of their long hours and inadequate rest and nutrition, children who worked in textile mills

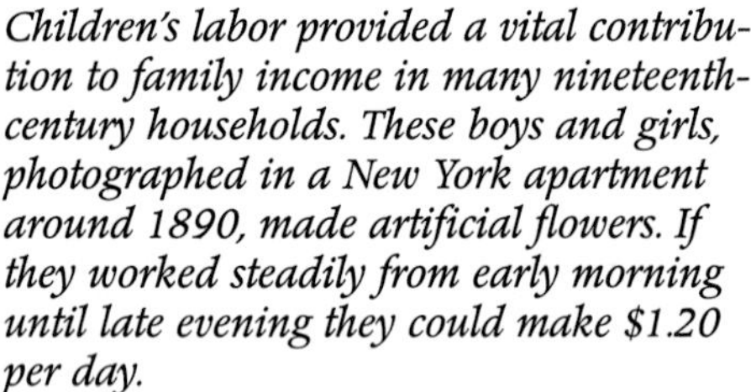

Children's labor provided a vital contribution to family income in many nineteenth-century households. These boys and girls, photographed in a New York apartment around 1890, made artificial flowers. If they worked steadily from early morning until late evening they could make $1.20 per day.

Children provided essential labor in many industries well into the twentieth century. These boys worked in the coal mines of Pennsylvania in 1911. Some of them were as young as six.

were shorter and weighed less than local nonworking children of corresponding ages. Surveys of intellectual growth showed wide variations in children's achievements that seemed to depend on family background and individual experience. These findings fueled the continuing scientific and social debate about the factors that are primarily responsible for development.

A crucial event that spurred further interest in the scientific study of children was the publication of Charles Darwin's *The Origin of Species,* in 1859. Darwin's thesis that human beings have evolved from earlier species fundamentally changed the way people thought about children. Instead of imperfect adults to be seen and not heard, children came to be viewed as scientifically interesting because their behavior provided clues to the ways in which human beings are related to other species. It became fashionable, for example, to compare the behavior of children with the behavior of higher primates to see if individual children went through a "chimpanzee stage" similar to the one through which the human species was thought to have evolved (see Figure 1.1). Although such parallels between species proved oversimplified, the idea that human development must be studied as a part of human evolution has won general acceptance.

Late in the nineteenth century, developmental psychology became an institutionalized form of research and practice. Special institutes and departments devoted to the study of development began to spring up in major U.S. universities, and both government agencies and philanthropic foundations began to support research efforts in child development as well as specialized magazines on infant care and parenting. Today there is broad popular acceptance of the idea that conducting scientific research on children is a good way "to make this a better world through developing better people" (Young, 1990, p. 17).

MODERN DEVELOPMENTAL PSYCHOLOGY

The core concern of contemporary developmental psychologists is to acquire a systematic understanding of **child development,** that is, the sequence of physical, cognitive, and psychosocial changes that children undergo as they

child development The sequence of physical, cognitive, and psychological and social changes that children undergo as they grow older.

(a)

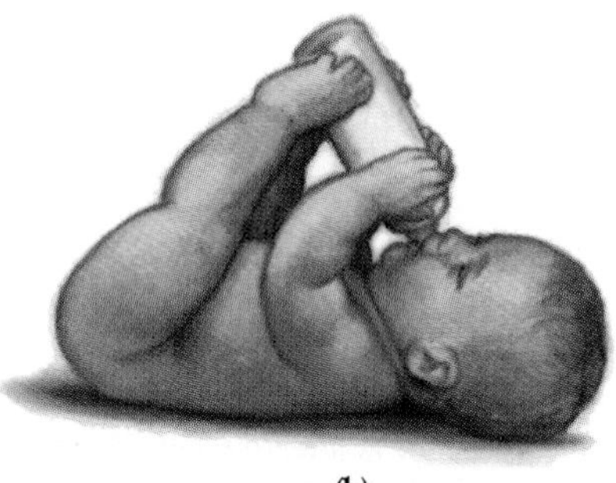

(b)

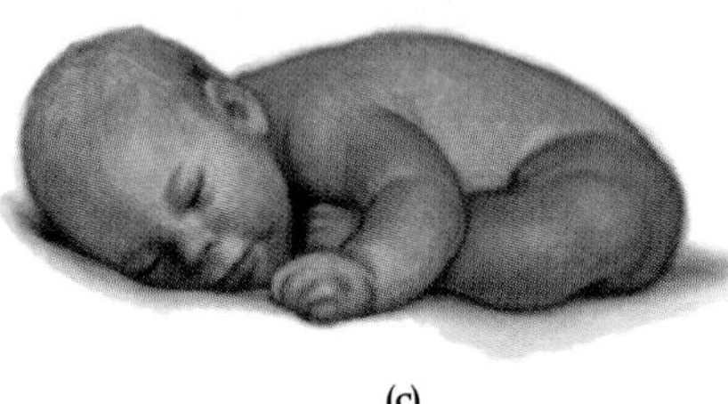

(c)

FIGURE 1.1

Early evolutionists scrutinized the motor development of children for evidence that it recapitulated evolutionary stages. Here an infant (a) crawls about on all fours like many animals, (b) uses its feet for grasping as primates do, and (c) sleeps in an animal-like crouch. (After Hrdlicka, 1931.)

grow older—changes that begin with conception and continue throughout life. Interest in child development rests on the ancient intuition that, if we can understand our roots and the history of changes that brought us to the present moment, we can better understand ourselves in order to anticipate the future and to prepare to meet it on our own terms.

The discipline of developmental psychology translates these personal goals into systematic procedures for studying, predicting, and shaping the process of development. Developmental psychologists are also amassing knowledge that contributes to, and profits from, the insights of neighboring disciplines, such as biology, anthropology, linguistics, and sociology.

In the century since they began to concern themselves with the systematic study of human development, psychologists have discovered a great deal about human beings at every age level, starting even before birth. During the past two decades, the pace of this work, aided by important advances in technology, has accelerated greatly. Psychologists are currently investigating a vast array of interesting questions, such as the following:

- Can changes in diet and upbringing compensate for genetic abnormalities?
- How are fetuses in the womb influenced by the events occurring in the outside world, and how do such influences shape their development after birth?
- What makes it possible for infants to acquire their native language so rapidly with no special training?
- In what ways is brain development affected by experience?
- What leads to the marked differences in levels and forms of aggression between boys and girls early in childhood?
- When do children become aware that other people have thought processes of their own, and what makes this awareness possible?
- Why is there little pretend play among young children in many societies, and what difference does this make in later development?
- When do children begin to reason systematically, and what makes this form of thought possible?
- What causes some children to be bullies?
- Why do some children learn to read with little effort, while others require extensive help?
- Is parent–child conflict a necessary part of adolescence?

In addition to searching for the answers to such questions, developmental psychologists are active in promoting the healthy development of children. They work in hospitals, child-care centers, schools, recreational facilities, and clinics. They assess children's developmental status and prescribe measures for assisting children who are in difficulty. They design special environments, such as cribs that allow premature babies to develop normally outside the womb. They devise therapies for children who have difficulty controlling their tempers, and they develop more effective techniques for teaching children to read.

The detailed knowledge that developmental psychologists have accumulated in the course of their research is important, as are the research methods themselves. But as we investigate the findings and methods of developmental science, it is essential to keep in mind that the more general goal of developmental inquiry is just as important: to assemble the accumulating facts into larger patterns, called theories or frameworks, which increase our understanding of human nature and its development as a whole.

THE CENTRAL QUESTIONS OF DEVELOPMENTAL PSYCHOLOGY

Despite great variety in the work they do and the theories that guide their research, developmental psychologists share an interest in three fundamental questions about the process of development:

1. *Continuity.* Is development a gradual process of change, or is it punctuated by periods of rapid change and the sudden emergence of new forms of thought and behavior?
2. *Sources of development.* What are the contributions of genetic heredity and the environment to the process of developmental change?
3. *Individual differences.* No two human beings are exactly alike. How does a person come to have stable individual characteristics that make him or her different from all other people?

Psychologists are deeply divided on many aspects of these three fundamental issues. Their differing assumptions about continuity, sources of change, and individual differences give rise to competing theoretical frameworks.

QUESTIONS ABOUT CONTINUITY

Developmental psychologists ask three basic questions about continuity: (1) How similar are the principles of development in humans to those in other species? In other words, how much continuity is there between human beings and other animal life? (2) Is individual development continuous, consisting of the gradual accumulation of small quantitative changes, or is it discontinuous, involving a series of qualitative transformations as we grow older? (3) Is the way in which the environment affects development continuous, or are there periods in a person's life during which certain experiences are critical for continued normal development?

Although chimpanzees and human beings share more than 99 percent of their genetic material, the differences between the two species are enormous.

phylogeny The evolutionary history of a species.

culture A people's design for living as encoded in their language, and seen in the physical artifacts, beliefs, values, customs, and activities that have been passed down from one generation to the next.

Are the Principles of Human Development Distinctive?

For centuries people have debated the extent to which we humans differ from other creatures and the extent to which we are subject to the same natural laws as other forms of life. The study of human uniqueness concerns **phylogeny,** the evolutionary history of a species.

The question of continuities and discontinuities between humans and other species is central to how psychologists think about the laws governing human development. Insofar as the relation of *Homo sapiens* to other species is continuous, the study of other animals can provide useful evidence about the processes of human development because the same principles of development are at work. To the extent that human beings are distinctive, research findings concerning the development of other species may be misleading when they are applied to them.

When Charles Darwin (1809–1882) published *The Origin of Species,* the idea of evolution was already a subject of widespread speculation. Darwin was a firm believer in continuity among species. He saw evolution as a process of accumulating change. As he put it, the difference between *Homo sapiens* and our near evolutionary neighbors is "one of degree, not of kind" (Darwin, 1859/1958, p. 107).

To test Darwin's claim that our species evolved continuously as a part of the natural order, scientists have searched for evidence of *evolutionary links*—intermediate forms that connect us with other forms of life—and have compared our genetic makeup and behavior with those of other organisms. On the side of continuity between ourselves and other animals, it has been established that we share as much as 99 percent of our genetic material with chimpanzees (D'Andrade & Morin, 1996). It is nevertheless clear that there is something distinctive about our species' characteristics. The difficult question is: What is that something?

Several characteristics that distinguish humans from other primates have been noted by Michael Tomasello (1999). In their natural habitats, nonhuman primates

- do not point out objects to others,
- do not hold objects up to show them to others,
- do not try to bring others to locations to observe things there,
- do not actively offer objects to other individuals by holding them out, and
- do not intentionally teach others.

These characteristics appear to be closely related to two general phenomena that have long been associated with human distinctiveness. First, *Homo sapiens* develop in a unique environment that has been shaped by countless earlier generations of people in their struggle for survival (Bruner, 1996; Cole, 1996). This special environment consists of *artifacts* (such as tools, clothing, words), *knowledge* about how to construct and use those artifacts, *beliefs* about the world, and *values* (ideas about what is worthwhile), all of which guide adults' interactions with the physical world and with each other and their children. Anthropologists call this accumulation of artifacts, knowledge, beliefs, and values *culture.* **Culture** is the "man-made" part of the environment that greets us at birth (Herskovitz, 1948) and the "design for living" that we acquire from our community (Kluckhohn & Kelly, 1945).

Second, *Homo sapiens* shape and pass on their culture to succeeding generations largely through language. It is not surprising, then, that since antiquity, language has been proposed as a defining characteristic of our species. In the seventeenth century the philosopher René Descartes stated the traditional view eloquently:

> Language is in effect the sole sure sign of latent thought in the body; all men use it, even those who are dull or deranged, who are missing a tongue, or who lack the voice organs, but no animal can use it, and this is why it is permissible to take language as the true difference between man and beast. (Quoted in Lane, 1976, p. 23)

Even Darwin, who believed strongly in the continuity of species, agreed that our distinctiveness, insofar as *Homo sapiens* is distinct, is the result of our capacity to communicate through language. In recent years, scientists have demonstrated that chimpanzees and other primates have rudiments of culture and language (Savage-Rumbaugh, Shanker, & Taylor, 1998; Tomasello, 1999). However, as we shall see in later chapters, the capacities for using culture and language, considered as an ensemble, are far greater in humans than in other species.

Is Individual Development Continuous?

The second major question about continuity concerns **ontogeny,** the development of an individual organism during its lifetime. As a rule, psychologists who believe that ontogeny is primarily a process of continuous, gradual accumulation of small changes emphasize *quantitative change,* such as growth in vocabulary or memory capacity. Those who view ontogeny as a process punctuated by abrupt, discontinuous changes emphasize the emergence of *qualitatively* new patterns at specific points in development, such as the change from babbling to talking. Qualitatively new patterns that emerge during development are referred to as **developmental stages.** The contrast between the continuity and discontinuity views is illustrated in Figure 1.2.

ontogeny The development of an individual organism during its lifetime.

developmental stage A qualitatively distinctive, coherent pattern of behavior that emerges during the course of development.

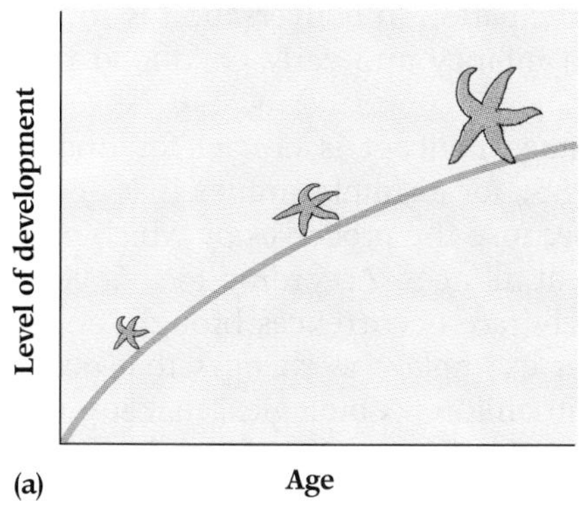

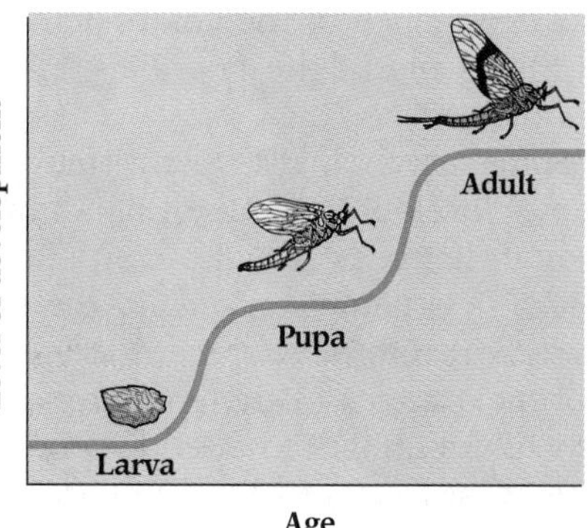

FIGURE 1.2

(a) The contrasting courses of development of starfish and insects provide idealized examples of continuous and discontinuous development. In the continuity view, development is a process of gradual growth (small starfish, medium-sized starfish, large starfish). In the discontinuity view, development is a series of stagelike transformations (larva, pupa, adult). (b) Human development includes elements of both continuity and discontinuity.

The psychologist John Flavell (1971) suggests four criteria that are central to the concept of a developmental stage:

1. *Stages of development are distinguished by qualitative changes.* The change in motor activity associated with the transition from crawling to walking upright illustrates what is meant by a qualitative change to a new stage of development. Walking does not arise from the perfection of the movements used to crawl. Rather, the child undergoes a total reorganization of movement, using different muscles in different combinations.
2. *The transition from one stage to the next is marked by simultaneous changes in a great many, if not all, aspects of a child's behavior.* The transition from crawling to walking is accompanied by a new quality of emotional attachment between children and their caregivers as well as the new forms of child–caregiver relations that the child's greater mobility requires.
3. *When the change from one stage to the next occurs, it is rapid.* The transition from crawling to walking typically takes place within the space of about 90 days.
4. *The numerous behavioral and physical changes that mark the appearance of a stage form a coherent pattern.* Walking occurs at about the same time as pointing, the ability to follow the gaze of another, the child's first words, and a new relationship between children and their parents.

Proponents of the stage concept argue that a stage view is crucial to understanding development, for insofar as development is characterized by discontinuous qualitative changes, the way the child experiences the world and the way the world influences the child will differ from one stage to the next. For example, infants are especially sensitive to differences in the sounds of language (Aslin, Jusczyk, & Pisoni, 1998), but they do not understand what is being said. Once they begin to understand and produce language themselves, the way they learn about the world appears to change fundamentally, and so does the nature of their interaction with others. The discontinuity represented by the emergence of the child's active participation in conversation is so notable that it marks the boundary between infancy and early childhood in a great range of societies.

Some psychologists deny that the stage concept is crucial for understanding development. Albert Bandura (1986), for example, argues that developmental change is basically continuous because the processes by which people learn new behaviors remain the same at all ages. According to this view, discontinuities in development are relatively rare occurrences brought about by abrupt changes in the environment (for example, the changes that occur when children begin to attend school) or in children's biological makeup (for example, the changes associated with sexual maturation). Robert Siegler, a psychologist who specializes in studying the development of children's thinking, makes a similar argument: "Children's thinking," he writes, "is continually changing, and most of the changes seem to be gradual rather than sudden" (1991, p. 8).

During most of the twentieth century, stage theories of development have been more numerous and more influential than continuity theories. Yet stage theories are confronted with a variety of facts that appear to violate one or more of the criteria for developmental stages proposed by Flavell.

One acute problem for modern stage theories is that, contrary to their depiction of qualitatively consistent, across-the-board shifts in behavior and thinking, children often appear to be in one stage on one occasion and in a different stage on another. According to one influential stage theory of cognitive development, for example, 4-year-olds are in a stage in which their thinking is largely egocentric, making it very difficult for them to see anything from a point of view other than their own. And in fact, 4-year-olds frequently do seem limited to their own perspective—they often fail to appreciate that someone looking at an object from a location different from their own may not see the object as they themselves see it or that someone who has just returned to the room doesn't know, as they do, what has transpired while he or she was gone. Yet when they are speaking to a 2-year-old, they usually simplify their speech, apparently taking the younger child's perspective and realizing that he or she might otherwise have difficulty understanding them. At 4 years of age, children are also likely to ignore the needs of a younger sibling, but they frequently become solicitous when the younger child appears to be upset (Dunn, 1988; Eisenberg, 1992). The fact that at a given point in development a child can exhibit behaviors associated with different stages seems to undercut the idea that being in a particular stage defines the child's *general* capabilities and psychological makeup.

critical period A period during which specific biological or environmental events are required for normal development to occur.

sensitive period An optimal time for certain developments to occur because environmental events are most effective for fostering their development at that time.

Are There "Critical" or "Sensitive" Periods of Development?

Another question about the continuity of individual human development is whether there are periods of growth during which specific environmental or biological events *must* occur if development is to proceed normally. In certain animals, such periods of biological readiness and sensitivity to environmental input are referred to as **critical periods** because they often take place over the course of a few hours. For example, in certain birds that can walk at birth and thus could become separated from their mother, there is a critical period just after hatching during which the chicks become attached to the first moving object they see—which, of course, is usually their mother—and thereafter follow the object wherever it goes. The critical nature of this period is illustrated by the fact that if the first moving object they see happens to be a human (such as the ethologist Konrad Lorenz, shown in Figure 1.3), the chicks become attached to that person just as they would to their mother. If they are prevented from seeing any moving object for a certain number of hours after hatching, they fail to become attached to anything.

While the notion of "all-or-nothing" *critical* periods seems too restrictive with regard to human development, many developmental psychologists support the idea of "sensitive" periods. A **sensitive period** is a time when it is optimal for certain developments to occur and when environmental influences

FIGURE 1.3
Ethologist Konrad Lorenz proposed the existence of a critical period in the development of newly hatched geese during which they form an attachment to the first moving thing they see. These goslings, which were allowed to see Lorenz rather than an adult goose when they hatched, follow him in the water as he swims.

BOX 1.1

Philosophical Forefathers of Developmental Psychology

When Europeans first became conscious of the peoples of Africa and Asia, in the fifteenth and sixteenth centuries, they debated the source of the obvious physical and behavioral differences between those people and themselves. Were these creatures human, they wondered. Were they also God's children, and if so, why did they look and act so differently? In modern terms, this debate asked whether these foreign peoples were different in their basic nature or were different because of the conditions of their nurture.

Europeans asked similar questions about one another. Were peasants and princes different because God willed them so? Or were they different because they had been exposed to different experiences after they entered the world? These were not abstract questions, of interest only to philosophers. They were questions of deep political significance. For centuries kings and nobles had claimed that they had a God-given right to rule over others because they were naturally superior by virtue of their birth.

At the beginning of the modern era, two philosophers whose writings were to have great influence on the history of child development, John Locke and Jean-Jacques Rousseau, challenged the view that human differences were determined primarily by birth. Their views of human differences and social inequality were directly connected to their beliefs about children's development.

John Locke

The English philosopher John Locke (1632–1704) proposed that the child's mind is a tabula rasa, a blank slate upon which experience writes its story. In *Some Thoughts Concerning Education* (1699/1938), Locke expressed the central intuition that guided his thinking:

> The little, and almost insensible Impressions on our tender Infancies, have very important and lasting Consequences: And there 'tis, as in the Fountains of some Rivers, where a gentle Application of the Hand turns the flexible waters into Chanels, that make them take quite contrary Courses, and by this little Direction given them at first in the Source, they receive different Tendencies, and arrive at last, at very remote and distant Places. (pp. 1–2)

Locke did not deny that there are limits to what the "Application of the Hand" can achieve. One cannot make water run uphill. He believed that children are born with different "temperaments and propensities," and he advised that instruction be tailored to fit these differences, a view that remains central to modern theories of education. But Locke clearly asserted that nurture, in the form of adults who "channel" children's initial impulses, is the key factor in the creation of the main differences between people.

Jean-Jacques Rousseau

The French philosopher Jean-Jacques Rousseau (1712–1778) also argued that differences among people are primarily the result of experience, but his view of children and the role of adults in their training differed from Locke's. Rousseau asserted that children are born neither as blank slates nor—as was commonly held by many thinkers of the time—as innately sinful beings. Rather, Rousseau maintained that, in a natural state, man is born pure, only to be corrupted by exposure to modern civilization. Further, he asserted, children are born with an innate understanding of virtue that would

are likely to be most effective in fostering their occurrence. For example, in order for children to develop normal language abilities, it is essential that they be exposed to language during childhood, but there is no specific period during childhood in which language input is known to be essential. Children seem to be most sensitive to language input in the first few years of life, but even if they are not regularly exposed to language until the age of 6 or 7, it appears that they are still capable of acquiring it. Thereafter, the risk of failing to acquire language increases (Grimshaw et al., 1998; Johnson & Newport, 1989).

Sensitive periods may not be limited to development that involves biological readiness. Yasuko Minoura (1992) reports the existence of a "cultural sensitive period." She found that Japanese children who had resided in the United States for the 4 years between the ages of 9 and 13 had great difficulty reincorporating themselves into Japanese society when they returned to their native land as teenagers. They had learned and accepted an American way of thinking and feeling that made the Japanese way of interacting and thinking seem strange. For example, the returnees reported that they found it difficult to avoid being open and explicit about their feelings, and this got them into trouble with the Japanese children they met. The same was not true of the younger children who had spent an equal amount of time in the United States gradually emerge over time were it not for their exposure to civilization.

In *Emile* (1762/1911), a book that was part novel and part treatise on education, Rousseau indicated his opinion of adults' attempts to bring the child "up" to virtue:

> God makes all things good. Man meddles with them and they become evil. He forces one soil to yield the products of another, one tree to bear another's fruit. He confuses and confounds time, place, and natural conditions. He mutilates his dog, his horse, and his slave. He destroys and defaces all things; . . . he will have nothing as nature made it, not even man himself, who must learn his paces like a saddlehorse, and be shaped to his master's taste like the trees in his garden. (p. 5)

In his tale of Emile's education, Rousseau provided a vision of childhood and education in which the role of the caretaker is to protect the child from the pressures of adult society. Emile, who stands for Everychild, is depicted not as an incomplete adult who must be perfected through instruction but as a whole human being whose capabilities are suited to his age. Emile passes through several natural stages of development. In each, his activities are appropriate to his needs at the time, and they are guided by an adult who uses suitably paced educational practices. As William Kessen (1965) points out, these ideas about stages of development were later taken up by developmental psychologists, and they remain influential to this day.

Locke, Rousseau, and the Modern World

Locke's notion of a tabula rasa and Rousseau's vision of natural man have been rightly criticized and sometimes ridiculed in the centuries that have passed since the two philosophers died. Modern research makes it clear that we are not blank slates when we are born; we enter the world with brains that are highly structured. Nor is it plausible that there ever existed a purely "natural" state of humankind, which the modern world corrupts. When Victor, the Wild Boy who really did grow up in a "state of nature," misbehaved outrageously during one of his outings with Itard, people joked, "If only Rousseau could see his noble savage now!"

The common wisdom underlying Locke's and Rousseau's views on the crucial role of experience in the shaping of human behavior remains valid, however. In 1776 the United States of America was founded as a republic based on a profound faith in the "self-evident" truth that "all men are created equal." In an earlier era, when kings and nobles ruled by "divine right," the open expression of such ideas would have been unthinkable. A clear indication of the political significance of the belief that human beings can shape the course of their development by arranging their environments is the fact that when the archbishop of Paris read *Emile,* he sought to have Rousseau arrested. Alerted by friends, Rousseau fled from France.

With the acceptance of the idea that children are born good, or at least not evil, came a deep obligation to confront obvious inequalities in the conditions of developing children's lives. Eventually, most people came to accept the idea that society must take some responsibility for children's welfare—and indeed, for the welfare of all people.

but returned to Japan before they were 11 years old. The younger children's reentry into Japanese culture, while not trouble free, was rapid and thorough.

QUESTIONS ABOUT THE SOURCES OF DEVELOPMENT

The second major issue that preoccupies developmental psychologists is the way in which genetically directed biological factors interact with environmental factors to produce developmental outcomes. This issue is often posed as a debate about the relative importance of "nature" and "nurture." **Nature** refers to the inherited biological predispositions of the individual; **nurture** refers to the influences of the social environment on the individual, particularly those of the family and the community. Much of the argument about Victor, the Wild Boy of Aveyron, was about the relative influences of nature and nurture: Was Victor incapable of speech and other behaviors normal for a boy his age because of a defective biological endowment (nature) or because of inadequate nurturing? (Early formulations of this issue are discussed in Box 1.1.)

Beliefs about the relative contributions of nature and nurture to development can have far-reaching effects on the way society treats children. If, for example, it is assumed that girls, by *nature,* lack interest and ability in mathematics and science, they are not likely to be encouraged by their parents,

nature The inherited biological predispositions of the individual.

nurture The influence of the social and cultural environment on the individual.

teachers, and other members of society to become mathematicians or scientists. If, on the other hand, it is assumed that mathematical and scientific talent are largely a result of *nurture,* a society may train girls and boys equally in these activities.

Modern psychologists emphasize that we cannot adequately describe development by considering nature or nurture in isolation from each other because the organism and its environment constitute a single life process (Gottlieb, 1997). Nonetheless, it is common practice to study living systems by trying to separate out the effects of these two influences and analyze them independently. The problem, then, is twofold: (1) to determine the relative contributions of nature and nurture to various kinds of behavior and (2) to discover how the developing child is created from the interaction of nature and nurture.

QUESTIONS ABOUT INDIVIDUAL DIFFERENCES

Every person is, in some respects, like all other people, like some other people, and like no other person. All humans are alike because we are all members of the same species; all humans are like some people but not others insofar as they share important biological characteristics (males are like each other and different from females) or cultural characteristics (Australian Aborigines are alike in comparison with the Inuit people of North America); and every person is psychologically and physically unique. Even identical twins, who have exactly the same genetic constitutions, are not alike in every respect.

Two questions about individual differences must be taken into account in trying to understand the nature of development: (1) What makes individuals different from one another and (2) to what extent are individual characteristics stable over time?

The question of what makes individuals different from one another is really another form of the question about the sources of development: Are we different from one another primarily because of our nature or because of our nurture? If baby Sam is unusually fussy, is it because he inherited a tendency to be easily upset or because his parents continually overstimulate him? If baby Georgia is unusually plump, is it because she inherited a tendency to obesity or because her parents give her food that contains too much fat and sugar? Although powerful statistical techniques and ingenious methods of data collection have been used in an effort to tease apart the fundamental sources of variation among individuals, disagreements of theory and fact remain (Gottlieb et al., 1998; Lewontin, 1994; Plomin et al., 1997).

Insofar as individual characteristics are innate and stable, they provide a glimpse of what children will be like in the future. If baby Sam is innately fussy, perhaps he will be an irritable child. If baby Georgia has inherited a low metabolism rate, maybe she will be overweight as a teenager. Determining the extent to which the past provides a guide to the future is a major task facing developmentalists.

The idea that some of our psychological characteristics remain stable over extended periods of time is an appealing one. Parents sometimes remark that their children have been friendly, or shy, or intent since infancy. However, demonstrating such stability scientifically—at least from an early age—has proved difficult. The problem is that measures that seem appropriate for assessing psychological traits such as memory or affability during infancy are not likely to be appropriate for assessing the same traits in an 8-year-old or in a teenager. Perhaps for this reason, many studies have failed to observe stable psychological traits in childhood (Eaton, 1994). The refinement of research techniques in recent years, however, has allowed some investigators to find moderately stable individual differences in a number of psychological characteristics. There is evidence, for example, that children who were shy and uncertain at 21 months of age are still likely to be timid and cautious at age 12 or later (Kagan, 1994) and that infants who rapidly processed visual information at 7 months of age display rapid perceptual processing when tested at the age of 11 years (Rose & Feldman, 1997).

The stability of children's psychological characteristics over time depends on stability in their environment in addition to any stability that might be attributed to their genetic makeup (Asendorpf & Valsiner, 1992). Studies have found that children who remain in an orphanage that provides only minimal care from infancy through adolescence are lethargic and unintelligent. They are also at risk for intellectual and emotional difficulties as adults. But if the environment of young orphanage children is changed—that is, if they are given extra, stimulating care by the orphanage staff or if they are adopted into caring families—their condition improves markedly, and many of them become intellectually normal adults (Clarke & Clarke, 1986).

THE DISCIPLINE OF DEVELOPMENTAL PSYCHOLOGY

Among the sciences that study development, psychology focuses on the individual human being. By contrast, sociology and anthropology focus on human groups, while the biological sciences encompass our species as a whole, viewing it in relation to other forms of life. This division of scientific labor creates a paradox. On the one hand, psychologists try to understand development in terms of the individual person; on the other hand, the natural-sciences tradition, which has dominated psychology during this century, studies people in general or as members of groups, not as specific individuals (Danzinger, 1990). This paradox is eloquently described by the novelist-philosopher Walker Percy:

> There is a secret about the scientific method which every scientist knows and takes as a matter of course, but which the layman does not know. . . . The secret is this: Science cannot utter a single word about an individual molecule, thing, or creature insofar as it is an individual but only insofar as it is like other individuals. (1975, p. 22)

The difference between these two ways of knowing—one based on intimate knowledge of individuals and their biographies, the other based on characteristics common to many people—is a source of constant tension in psychologists' attempts to understand development. The more psychologists want to know about individuals, the more they need to know about each person's life history and current circumstances. But the more they concentrate on unique histories and patterns of influence, the less they can generalize their findings to other individuals.

If, for example, the goal of a particular research project is to create a beneficial environment for infants born prematurely or to understand the role of symbolic play in toddlers' intellectual development, it may be appropriate to treat all children as equivalent with respect to the issue in question. But if the goal is to help Johnny, who suddenly has started to fail in school and to misbehave in class, the psychologist may want to know about the circumstances of Johnny's birth, recent changes in his family life, and perhaps even the specific mix of children and activities Johnny is dealing with at school. Uncertainties about how to draw correct conclusions concerning the relationship between general trends and individual cases occur across the broad spectrum of methods that psychologists use in their research.

CRITERIA OF SCIENTIFIC DESCRIPTION

Whether dealing with an individual or a group of children, developmental psychologists, like any other scientists, begin their research with common-sense observation and speculation. Then they attempt to test their ideas in

objectivity The requirement that scientific knowledge not be distorted by the investigator's preconceptions.

reliability The scientific requirement that when the same behavior is measured on two or more occasions by the same or different observers, the measurements be consistent with each other.

validity The scientific requirement that data being collected actually reflect the phenomenon being studied.

replicability The scientific requirement that other researchers can use the same procedures as an initial investigator did and obtain the same results.

representative sample A sample of people that reflects all the characteristics of the overall population that the researcher is interested in learning about.

ways that provide clear answers and that allow others to check their reasoning and procedures. Psychologists use four general criteria to judge the conclusions derived from investigations of children's behavior: *objectivity, reliability, validity,* and *replicability.*

To be useful in constructing a disciplined account of human development, data should be collected and analyzed with **objectivity;** that is, they should not be biased by the investigators' preconceptions. Total objectivity is impossible to achieve in practice because all human beings—psychologists included—come to the study of behavior with beliefs that influence their interpretations of what they see. But objectivity remains an important ideal toward which to work.

Research data should exhibit the property of **reliability** in two senses. First, each time the conditions that yielded the original data are repeated, they should yield the same results. Second, independent observers should agree in their descriptions of the results. Suppose that one wants to know how upset infants become when a pacifier is taken from them while they are sucking on it (Goldsmith & Campos, 1982). Statements about the degree of an infant's distress are considered reliable in the first sense if the level of distress (measured in terms of crying or thrashing about) is found to be more or less the same on successive occasions when the baby's sucking is interrupted. The statements are considered reliable in the second sense if independent observers agree on how distressed the baby becomes each time the pacifier is taken away.

Validity means that the data being collected actually reflect the phenomenon that the researcher claims to be studying. Say, for example, that a researcher hypothesized that the distress infants display when sucking is interrupted reflects an enduring predisposition to become irritable when frustrated. To test this hypothesis, the researcher might see how infants react when a rattle is removed from their grasp or when they are not fed on time. If they do not become distressed under these conditions, this may mean that the hypothesis is incorrect. However, it could also mean that taking away a rattle or failing to keep to a feeding schedule is not a valid measure of infant frustration.

In scientific research, **replicability,** the fourth requirement, means that other researchers can use the same procedures as an initial investigator did and obtain the same results. In studies of newborns' ability to imitate, for example, some researchers report that newborns will imitate certain exaggerated facial expressions that they see another person making directly in front of them. However, using the same methods, other investigators have failed to find evidence of such imitation in newborns (see Chapter 4, pp. 160–161). Only if the same finding, under the same conditions, is obtained repeatedly by different investigators is it likely to be considered firmly established by the scientific community.

When developmentalists are studying groups, a fifth criterion, *representative sampling,* usually comes into play. Most often, the populations that developmentalists are interested in learning about are too large to be studied in their entirety, so researchers must study samples of these populations. In such a case it is important that they study a **representative sample** of the population of interest, that is, a sample that reflects all the characteristics—including age, sex, socioeconomic status, ethnicity, and so on—of the overall population of interest. This is because conclusions drawn from data collected from one group of people may not be applicable to other groups with different characteristics. For example, a study of the amount of distress infants display when briefly separated from their mothers might yield one set of results if the study looks at infants from middle-class families in Denver and a different set of results if it looks at infants from working-class homes in Denver or middle-class homes in Tokyo.

METHODS OF DATA COLLECTION

Over the past century, psychologists have refined a variety of methods for gathering information about the development of children. Among the most widely used are self-reports, naturalistic observations, experiments, and clinical interviews. No one method can answer every question about human development. Each has a strategic role to play, depending on the topic. Often researchers use two or more methods in combination to confirm their conclusions.

self-report A method of gathering data in which people report on their own psychological states and behavior.

naturalistic observation Observation of the actual behavior of people in the course of their everyday lives.

baby biography A parent's detailed record of an infant's behavior over an extended period of time.

Self-Reports

Perhaps the most direct way to obtain information about psychological development is through **self-reports,** people's answers to questions about themselves. Psychologists usually conduct interviews to obtain self-reports, but they can also use written questionnaires or a behavioral check sheet (a list of behaviors that the subject checks off as they occur). Topics as diverse as adolescents' developing thoughts and feelings about themselves (Harter, 1998) and parents' disciplinary techniques (McGillicuddy-DeLisi & Sigel, 1995) have been investigated in this manner. Some researchers provide teenagers with beepers, which sound at random intervals throughout the day, signaling the teenagers to fill out a questionnaire about what they were doing and feeling when the beeper sounded (Larson & Richards, 1998).

Self-reports obtained through interviews and questionnaires can provide detailed accounts of the person's life experiences that might otherwise escape the investigator's notice. However, they are also highly susceptible to inaccuracies. This difficulty is obvious in the case of very young children who may not understand the questions they are asked. But it is also a serious difficulty with adults, who are likely to be selective in what they are willing to report about themselves and their children (Brewin, Andrews, & Gotlib, 1993). Parents' selective memory is also a problem in long-term retrospective reports, in which parents recall what their children's behavior was like at earlier ages and what their own responses to it were.

Naturalistic Observations

The most direct way to gather objective information about children is to study them through **naturalistic observations,** that is, to observe them in the course of their everyday lives and record what happens. Since the presence of a stranger (that is, the researcher) is likely to be intrusive in many situations, the ideal strategy is to arrange to have the children observed by someone who ordinarily spends time with them—a parent or a teacher, for example.

In the nineteenth century, several scientists began to write **baby biographies,** diaries in which they recorded observations of their own children. The most famous of these accounts is Darwin's (1877) daily record of the early development of his eldest son (Figure 1.4). By documenting the development of his son and determining what characteristics he shared with other species at different ages, Darwin hoped to find support for his thesis of human evolution. Jean Piaget (1952b, 1954), a developmental psychologist, also kept a diary of the development of his children that served as the foundation of his influential theory of cognitive development. (We will encounter excerpts from this work several times in the course of this book). Another form of diary-keeping, in which parents carefully document their children's developing language skills, has been extremely useful in the study of language acquisition (Fenson et al., 1994; Tomasello, 1992).

A major virtue of baby biographies written by family members is that the authors spend a great deal of time with their subjects and have the opportunity to observe them in both routine and unusual circumstances. For

FIGURE 1.4
The naturalist Charles Darwin became famous for his theory of evolution. His observations of his son, which he recorded in a baby biography, provide one of the first systematic descriptions of infant development.

ethology An interdisciplinary science that studies the biological and evolutionary foundations of behavior.

ethnographers Scholars who study the cultural organization of behavior.

ecology The range of situations in which people are actors, the roles they play, the predicaments they encounter, and the consequences of those encounters.

developmental niche The physical and social context in which a child lives, including the child-rearing and educational practices of the society and the psychological characteristics of the parents.

example, Marilyn Shatz (1994) was able to document her grandson's developing understanding of other people's thought processes because she spent time caring for him and he knew her well. One of the many telling bits of evidence she uncovered arose when she mistakenly thought he had wet his pajamas. Reading her reaction, he said, "You thought these were wet." His comment clearly indicated that he had achieved a milestone in children's cognitive development—the understanding that people can hold ideas that are contrary to fact. A subtle finding such as this one might not be revealed in tests conducted by a stranger.

Despite their virtues, especially when written by well-trained developmentalists, baby biographies must be used with great caution because even scientists usually cannot maintain objectivity when they describe their own children. As the psychologist William Kessen comments, "No one can distort as convincingly as a loving parent" (1965, p. 117).

Other forms of naturalistic observation are more commonly used. For ethologists, for example, naturalistic observation is a major research tool. **Ethology** is an interdisciplinary science that studies the biological, evolutionary foundations of behavior (Hinde, 1987a, b). Ethologists place great emphasis on naturalistic observation because they believe that biologically important behaviors affecting human development are best studied in the settings that are significant to people's daily lives (Savin-Williams, 1987).

F. Francis Strayer and A. J. Santos (1996) carried out naturalistic observations in this tradition when they studied the way children interact in preschool classrooms. By observing and recording who interacted with whom and the nature of the interactions, Strayer and Santos discovered that social hierarchies develop spontaneously in preschool classes much as they do in certain species of social animals. Once developed, these social hierarchies regulate the interactions that children engage in with each other.

Naturalistic observation is also favored by **ethnographers,** who study the cultural organization of behavior. In the hands of developmentalists, ethnographic descriptions provide detailed knowledge of the ways that children's experiences are organized by parents and communities, as well as the many ways that children respond to such organization. Edward Tronick and his colleagues, for example, have documented how young infants born to the Efe foragers of the Congo's Ituri forest are routinely cared for by several people and are likely to be nursed by several women. This pattern, which seems so at odds with Western ideas about child rearing, is essential to the Efe's foraging way of life and is accepted by Efe children as a matter of course (Tronick, Winn, & Morelli, 1985).

Observation in Many Contexts Naturalistic observations can be confined to a single context or can be employed to gather data in many contexts. The latter type of observational strategy is often used to study a child's *ecology,* a term derived from the Greek word for "house." In the biological sciences, the "house" is the habitat of a population of plants or animals, and the ecology of that population is the pattern of its relationship with its environment. In psychology, **ecology** has come to refer to the range of situations in which people are actors, the roles they play, the predicaments they encounter, and the consequences of those encounters (see Figure 1.5) (Bronfenbrenner & Morris, 1998).

Charles Super and Sarah Harkness (1997), who have studied children's development in several countries, emphasize the links between children's development and the community within which they are born. They refer to the child's place within the community as a **developmental niche.** They suggest that every developmental niche be analyzed in terms of three components: (1) the physical and social context in which the child lives, (2) the culturally determined child-rearing and educational practices of the child's society, and (3) the psychological characteristics of the child's parents. Thorough descriptions of children's real-life experiences in their sociocultural contexts provide a

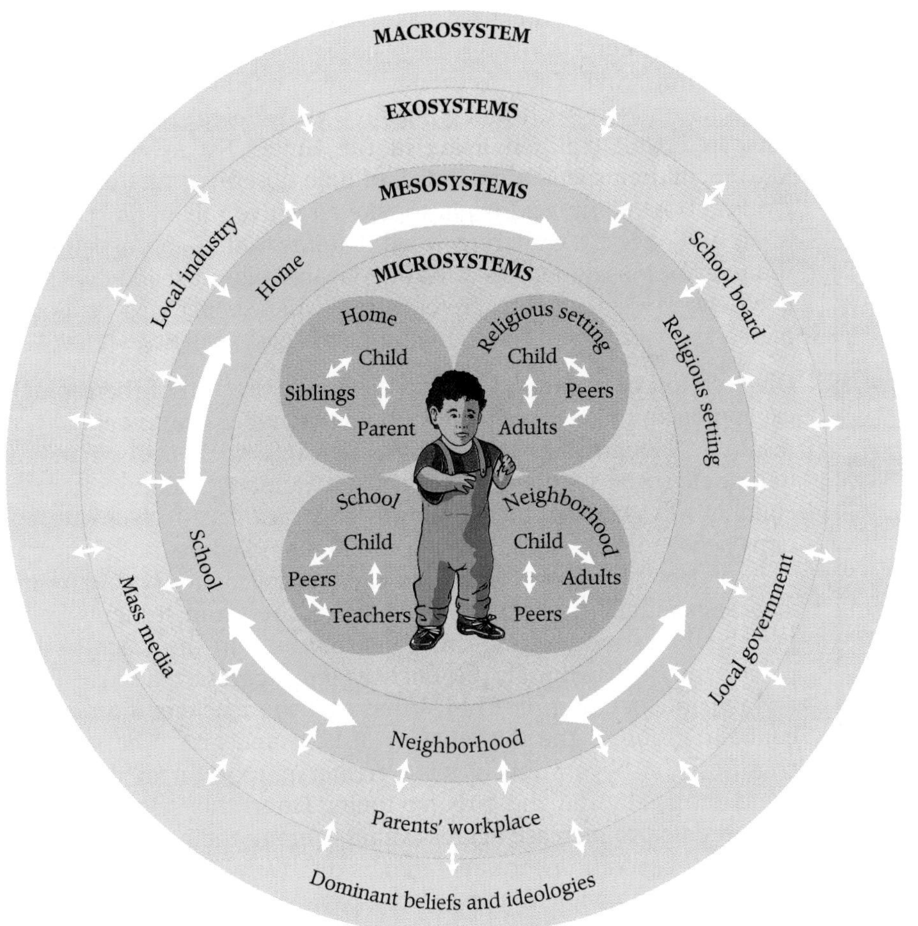

FIGURE 1.5
The ecological approach sees children in the context of all the various settings they inhabit on a daily basis (microsystems). These settings are related to one another in a variety of ways (mesosystems), which are in turn linked to settings and social institutions where the children are not present but which have an important influence on their development (exosystems). All of these systems are organized in terms of the culture's dominant beliefs and ideologies (the macrosystem).

sense of the whole child and the many influences that act on children. Such descriptions can tell us what opportunities and difficulties children face in their lives and how circumstances might be changed to foster children's development.

Probably the most ambitious study of the ecology of human development ever to be undertaken was conducted by Roger Barker and Herbert Wright (1951, 1955). These researchers spent hundreds of hours observing and describing the natural ecology of schoolchildren in various communities in the United States and abroad. In one such study, they observed a 7-year-old American boy from the time he awoke on April 26, 1949, until he went to sleep that night. Barker and Wright found that in this single day the boy participated in approximately 1300 distinct activities in a wide variety of settings involving hundreds of objects and dozens of people. These observations gave some idea of the wide range of skills children possess by the age of 7 and of the many social demands that are routinely made on children. (You will learn more about this study in Chapter 12.)

For a variety of practical reasons, few ecological studies approach the scope of Barker and Wright's. Most investigators who study children across a range of contexts are forced to be more selective. They usually decide in advance to observe a particular type of behavior in different contexts, or they choose a few important contexts and observe the various behaviors that children exhibit within them. For example, in a study of the role of play in the lives of young Mayan children of different ages living in a remote farming village in southeastern Mexico, Susan Gaskins (1999) used the latter approach, observing children for a total of several hours spread across several days. She made "spot observations," recording what the children were doing at different

DOONESBURY By Garry Trudeau

Cartoonist Gary Trudeau comments on the phenomenon, established in observational research, that teachers respond differently to boys and girls in their classrooms.

times of the day in order to make sure that she captured the full range of children's activities. Each observation period lasted for an hour, during which Gaskins tried to provide a detailed record of who the children were with and what they were doing. She found that compared with children living in the United States, young rural Mayan children spend a great deal of time observing the routine activities of the adults and begin to take an active role in daily chores at an early age by gathering wood, hauling water, and assisting in the preparation of food. As a result, Mayan children spend considerably less time engaged in pretend play, which is perhaps *the* dominant activity of young children in industrialized societies.

Observation in a Single Context The very breadth of the ecological approach makes it time-consuming and expensive to apply. As a result, developmental psychologists often restrict their observations to a single social setting that is widely encountered and important in children's lives, observing in minute detail the face-to-face interactions between children or between children and adults.

A classic study by Lisa Serbin and her colleagues (1973), for instance, examined interactions between teachers and students in 15 preschool classrooms to see whether anything in the teacher's behavior might unwittingly be encouraging aggressiveness in boys and dependence in girls. They found that the teachers did not pay equal attention to the misbehavior of boys and girls. The teachers chastised the boys publicly for a greater proportion of their misdeeds than they did the girls for theirs. Often this selective treatment seemed to increase aggressiveness among the boys. In a parallel set of observations, the researchers discovered that the teachers rewarded dependent behavior in the girls by paying more attention to the girls who were sitting closest to them; they paid equal amounts of attention to all boys no matter where they were sitting in the classroom. Such findings have been confirmed in a large number of studies (Ruble & Martin, 1998). Once such practices are discovered, new patterns of interaction can be suggested to the teachers that might foster more appropriate behavior in schoolchildren of both sexes. An important outgrowth of this line of research has been the introduction in some schools of all-girl classes in certain curriculum areas, such as mathematics, as a way of improving girls' educational performance.

Limitations of Naturalistic Observations Observational studies are a keystone of child development research and a crucial source of data about children's development. What we can learn from them, however, is limited. Observers enter the scene with expectations about what they are going to see, and we all tend to observe selectively in accordance with our expectations. An observer cannot write down everything, so information is inevitably lost. In some studies, prearranged note-taking schemes specify what to look for and how to report it. The drawback of such schemes is that they are not flexible enough to take account of unexpected events, so details are often lost in this way, too. If time elapses between an event and note taking, observations may be further distorted because people's selective remembering accentuates the problem of selective observing (D'Andrade, 1974). Recordings of behavior on videotape or film are useful, but they are extremely time-consuming to analyze.

Another difficulty with observational research is that, when people know they are being watched, they often behave differently than they normally would (Hoff-Ginsberg & Tardiff, 1995). This problem was clearly demonstrated by a laboratory study in which Zoe Graves and Joseph Glick (1978) asked mothers to help their 18- to 25-month-old children put together a simple jigsaw puzzle. To determine the influence that being observed had on the mothers' behavior, Graves and Glick told half of the mothers that the video equipment that would have been used to record their interactions was not working. They found that the mothers who believed they were off camera were less helpful to their children than the mothers who believed that their actions were being recorded.

Perhaps the major problem with naturalistic observation is that it rarely allows researchers to establish the existence of *causal* relationships between phenomena, a basic aim of science. Naturalistic observations can establish whether a **correlation** exists between two factors, that is, whether changes in one factor vary with changes in another. But a correlation cannot tell us whether one factor causes the other or whether both factors are caused by a third, undetermined factor (see Box 1.2). In their ecological study, for example, Barker and Wright found that children acted more grown up in church than they did in a drugstore. But there was no way to know, for example, if this was because the nature of the church setting evoked mature behavior or because the children's parents were there to observe them. Similar questions arise in the study by Serbin and her colleagues. Did the teachers chastise the boys for their misbehavior more often than they chastised the girls because they had stereotyped the boys as troublemakers who needed discipline to be kept in line or because they simply noticed the boys' misbehavior more often than the girls'? Similar questions can be raised about almost any observational study of behavior. To attempt to resolve such questions, psychologists turn to experimental methods.

correlation The condition that exists between two factors when changes in one factor are associated with changes in the other.

experiment In psychology, research in which a change is introduced in a person's experience and the effect of that change is measured.

scientific hypothesis An assumption that is precise enough to be tested and can be shown to be incorrect.

Experimental Methods

A psychological **experiment** usually consists of introducing some change in a person's or animal's experience and then measuring any effect that the change has on the person's or animal's behavior. Ideally, all other possible causal influences are held constant while the factor of interest is made to vary to determine if that factor makes a difference. If an experiment is well designed and executed, it should provide a means of confirming or disconfirming a scientific hypothesis about the causes of the behavior observed. A **scientific hypothesis** is an assumption that is precise enough to be tested and can be shown to be incorrect. If there is no way to disprove the hypothesis, it has little scientific value.

An investigation of the emergence of infants' fear of high places demonstrates how the experimental method can help resolve uncertainties about causal factors in development. For many years it was believed that the fear of heights is innate in the human infant, emerging in accordance with a maturational schedule around the time infants begin to locomote, or move about under their own steam (Richards & Rader, 1983). Joseph Campos and his colleagues disagreed with this hypothesis (Bertenthal et al., 1984; Campos et al., 1992). They believed that infants' fear of heights is a result of experience, especially the experience that infants acquire as they crawl around their environment.

To test their hypothesis, Campos and his colleagues initially studied a group of 6-to-8-month-olds who had been crawling for a week or two. The researchers began by seeing if the infants would cross a laboratory "visual cliff," a transparent platform that gives the illusion of a sharp drop in elevation (Figure 1.6). In the first few trials, all the infants did crawl across the cliff, without hesitation. On subsequent trials over the next several weeks, however, the infants became increasingly reluctant to cross over the visual cliff, even though nothing bad had happened when they crossed over it before. Something seemed to be building up in the infants' minds as they gained experience. But what was building up, and what experience was causing it?

FIGURE 1.6
A baby hesitates at the edge of a visual cliff, a transparent platform that makes it appear to the baby that there is a sharp drop just ahead.

BOX 1.2

Correlation and Causation

In their attempts to identify the specific factors that influence a particular aspect of development, psychologists often begin by determining if there is a correlation between factors that appear to be associated with the development in question. Two factors are said to be *correlated* with each other when changes in one are related to changes in the other. As children grow older, for example, they display increased ability to remember lists of words; that is, children's age is correlated with their ability to remember. Similarly, the higher the social class of parents, the greater the achievement of their children in school; that is, school achievement is correlated with social class. Correlations such as these can provide important hints about causal factors in development, but as we will see momentarily, they fall short of specifying actual causation.

The first step in determining the possible importance of a correlation is to establish its strength. To do this, researchers use a *correlation coefficient* (symbolized as r), which provides a quantitative index of the degree of association between two factors. A correlation coefficient enables psychologists to distinguish between relationships that occur with significant regularity and those that occur by chance.

A correlation coefficient that describes the relationship between factor X and factor Y can vary in both size and direction. When $r = 1.00$, there is a perfect positive correlation between the two factors, meaning that as factor X changes, factor Y changes in the *same* direction. When $r = -1.00$, there is a perfect *negative* correlation between factor X and factor Y, meaning that as factor X changes, factor Y changes in the *opposite* direction. If every increase in age in a population were accompanied by an increase in weight, for example, the correlation between age and weight would be 1.00. If, instead, people always lost weight as they aged, the correlation would be −1.00. If age and weight were not related at all, the correlation would be .00. Intermediate positive or negative values of a coefficient of correlation indicate intermediate levels of association. For example, there is a correlation of approximately .50 between the heights of parents and their offspring, indicating that tall parents tend to have tall offspring (Tanner, 1990).

A correlation may point to a causal relationship between two events, but, as noted above, correlation is not the same as causation. That is, correlation does not establish that the occurrence of one event *causes* the occurrence of the other. In some cases it may be just as likely that factor X is caused by factor Y as it is that factor X is causing factor Y. In other cases, it may be that the correlated changes in X and Y are being caused by some third factor.

The difficulty of distinguishing correlation from causation is often a source of scientific controversy. In a case such as the heights of parents and their children, the problem is not serious. The child's height obviously does not cause the height of the parents. Nor is confusion likely to arise about the relationship between a child's age and his or her weight. Age by itself cannot cause increases in weight because "age" is simply another term for the time that has elapsed since an agreed-upon starting point; and certainly, weight cannot cause an increase in age.

Other cases are less clear-cut. Among schoolchildren, for example, a correlation of about .30 has been found between height and scores on tests of mental ability; that is, taller chil-

experimental group The persons in an experiment whose experience is changed as part of the experiment.

control group The group in an experiment that is treated as much as possible like the experimental group except that it does not participate in the experimental manipulation.

To confirm their hypothesis that the onset of infants' fear of heights results from the experience of moving about on their own, Campos and his colleagues conducted an experiment (Bertenthal et al., 1984). They located 92 infants who were near the age when they might be expected to start crawling and begin showing a fear of heights. The infants were randomly assigned to one of two groups. One group was designated as the **experimental group**–the group in an experiment whose environment is changed. Over several days the infants in this group were given more than 40 hours of experience moving about in special baby walkers before they learned to crawl (see Figure 1.7). The other children, called the **control group**–the group in an experiment that is treated as much as possible like the experimental group except that it does not participate in the experimental manipulation–were provided with no special experience in locomoting. If Campos and his colleagues were correct, the babies in the experimental group should respond differently to the visual cliff than would the babies in the control group because the experimental group had more experience moving around on their own.

Forty hours of careening around a room in a walker may not seem like a lot of experience, but it apparently made a big difference in the way the infants in the experimental group responded to the visual cliff. Although responses varied somewhat, in general, the infants in the experimental group showed fear on their first exposure to the visual cliff, whereas the infants in the control group did not.

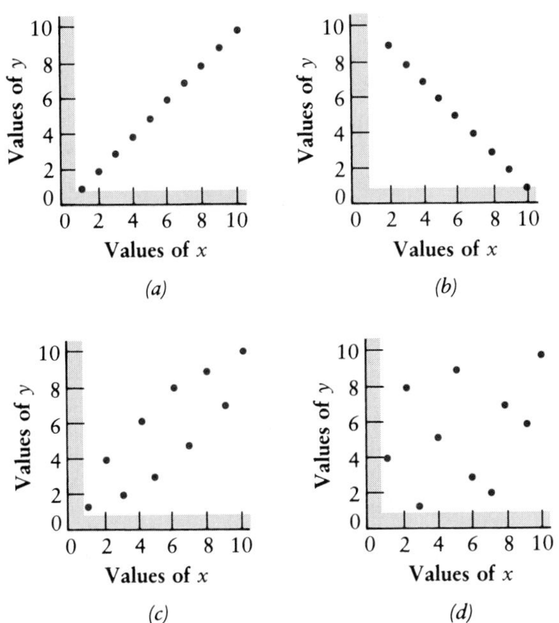

Four possible relationships between two variables: (a) As values of x increase, values of y increase, producing a correlation of 1.00. (b) As values of x increase, values of y decrease, producing a correlation of – 1.00. (c) As values of x increase, values of y often increase, but there are some exceptions, producing a correlation of .84. (d) As values of x increase, values of y show a weak but noticeable tendency to increase, producing a correlation of .33.

dren tend to score higher on intelligence tests than do their shorter age-mates (Tanner, 1990). Since nothing about children's height can plausibly be said to be a cause of their intelligence, and nothing about children's intelligence can be said to cause their heights, some other factor (such as nutrition, for example) must be the cause of both.

The slipperiest cases are those in which the possible cause-and-effect relationship between two variables could plausibly work in either direction. For example, there is a correlation of .50 between children's current grades in school and their scores on standard IQ tests (Minton & Schneider, 1980). On the basis of this association, it might be tempting to conclude that intelligence causes school achievement. Although that explanation fits many people's notions about school achievement, it can just as plausibly be argued that students who get good grades do so by working hard and learning more, thereby boosting their IQ scores.

The use of correlation coefficients to describe relationships among phenomena is important in the study of human development because so many of the factors of interest to developmentalists (such as social class, ethnic origin, and genetic constitution) cannot be controlled experimentally. Because correlations often suggest causal relationships but do not provide crucial evidence of causation, controversies that have no clear resolution may arise, requiring developmentalists to exercise caution in interpreting their data.

This experiment provided strong support for the hypothesis that the development of the ability to locomote plays a large role in the development of the fear of heights. Additional research would be useful to rule out other possible factors that this research did not delve into. Suppose, for example, children were moved around in little vehicles that permitted them to explore the environment without any movement on their part. Would they still become fearful when placed on the visual cliff? Such uncertainties about research results are almost inevitable. It is often necessary to carry out a series of experiments to isolate specific causes because the complexities of human behavior exceed the researcher's ability to control all the relevant factors in a single experiment (Cole & Means, 1981).

In general, the clear strength of the experimental method is its ability to isolate causal factors in a way no other method of investigation can. However, two main factors limit its usefulness as a source of information about development: (1) for ethical reasons, many kinds of experiments cannot be performed, and (2) the very control of the environment that experiments require may distort the validity of the results obtained.

Ethics and Experimentation The easiest way to find out if experience hearing a language is necessary to learn to talk would be to create rearing conditions in which a child is cared for but never spoken to. Obviously, such an experiment might cause harm to the participants and should not be performed. Indeed, the central ethical tenet of all psychological research is that if a

FIGURE 1.7
A walker exposes infants to the experience of locomotion before they learn to walk or crawl. How does using a walker influence performance on the visual cliff?

research procedure may harm anyone, it should not be carried out. Ethical issues in psychological research are not always so clear-cut as this tenet suggests, however. What is harmful, and how do we assess the risks? Practically any intervention in another person's life may involve some risk, so the judgment can be a difficult one.

To protect the rights of others, modern researchers are closely monitored by their own institutions and by government agencies. Before they can carry out their research, they must satisfy a committee of their peers that they will not harm the people who participate in their investigations and that the research promises some benefits to those people in the long run (see Box 1.3).

Experiments and Artificiality Sometimes people behave differently in an artificial, experimental situation than they would normally. Children are particularly likely to behave unnaturally in an unfamiliar laboratory setting with researchers they have never met before. This, of course, raises doubts about the value of experimental results. Indeed, this problem is so pervasive that the psychologist Urie Bronfenbrenner (1979) has described typical laboratory experiments involving children as studies of "the strange behavior of children in strange situations with strange adults for the briefest possible periods of time" (p. 19).

Researchers usually have to live with the artificiality of the experimental setting because the factors being studied arise too seldom to be studied systematically in real life. In some cases, however, researchers have partially overcome the problem of artificiality by introducing experimental variation in naturally occurring situations without significantly disrupting the usual course of events. For example, to investigate how young children add new words to their vocabularies in ordinary circumstances, Elsa Bartlett (1977) and Susan Carey (1978) had a preschool teacher introduce an unusual color, olive, to her charges in the course of her normal classroom routine. To avoid the possibility that some children already knew the name of the color, the teacher referred to it as "chromium." The researchers found that when the new word was introduced casually—"Please pass the chromium crayon"—the children acquired the word after very few exposures. This finding is in sharp contrast with laboratory studies of word acquisition, which typically find that children require extensive instruction by an adult to learn a new word. Thus, by introducing new words to children in a natural way, Bartlett and Carey brought about a basic change in psychologists' understanding of a vitally important aspect of development. (We will return to their findings in Chapter 8.)

clinical method A research method in which questions are tailored to the individual, with each question depending on the answer to the preceding one.

Clinical Interview Methods

With the exception of diary studies, all the research methods discussed thus far are designed to apply uniform procedures of data collection to every individual observed. In this respect, clinical interview methods differ fundamentally from the others. The essence of the **clinical method** is to tailor questions to the individual subject. Each question depends on the answer to the one that precedes it, allowing the researcher to follow up on any given question, verify his or her understanding of the subject's responses, and probe more deeply into the subject's thoughts and feelings.

John B. Watson and Rosalie Rayner experimenting with infant fears.

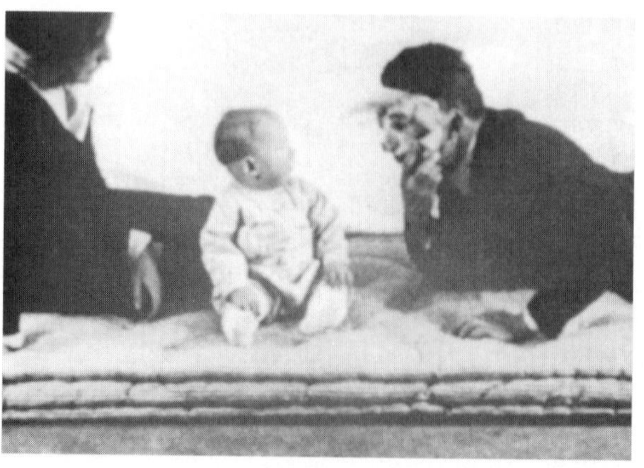

As the term "clinical" implies, clinical interview methods are often used to investigate the problems of persons who are troubled or unwell. When developmental psychologists use clinical interview methods in this way, they, like medical clinicians, are seeking a set of appropriate remedies. The most famous application of clinical interview methods in developmental psychology is found in the work of Sigmund Freud, who believed the early family history of the child is essential to later personality development. From a patient's account of his or her life events, fantasies, fears, and dreams, Freud sought to

BOX 1.3

Ethical Standards for Research with Children

The following guidelines are adapted and condensed from the Ethical Standards for Research with Children issued by the Society for Research in Child Development.

Children as research subjects present ethical problems for the investigator that are different from those presented by adult subjects. Not only are children often viewed as more vulnerable to stress, but, having less knowledge and experience, they are less able to evaluate what participation in research may mean. Consent of the parent for the study of the child, moreover, must be obtained in addition to the child's consent. These are some of the major differences between research with children and research with adults.

- No matter how young the children, their rights supersede the rights of the investigator.
- The final responsibility to establish and maintain ethical practices in research remains with the individual investigator.
- The investigator is responsible for the ethical practices of collaborators, assistants, students, and employees, all of whom, however, incur parallel obligations.
- The investigator should inform children of all features of the research that may affect their willingness to participate and should answer children's questions in terms appropriate to their comprehension.
- The investigator should respect children's freedom to choose to participate in research or not, as well as to discontinue participation at any time.
- Informed consent of parents or those who act in loco parentis (for example, teachers, superintendents of institutions) similarly should be obtained, preferably in writing. Informed consent requires that parents or other responsible adults be told all features of the research that may affect their willingness to allow children to participate.
- The informed consent of any person whose interaction with the child is the subject of the study should also be obtained.
- The investigator may use no research operation that may harm children either physically or psychologically.
- Although we accept the ethical idea of full disclosure of information, a particular study may necessitate concealment or deception. Whenever concealment or deception is thought to be essential to the conduct of the study, investigators should satisfy a committee of their peers that their judgment is correct.
- The investigator should keep in confidence all information obtained about research participants.
- Immediately after the data are collected, the investigator should clarify for the research participant any misconceptions that may have arisen. The investigator also recognizes a duty to report general findings to participants in terms appropriate to their understanding. When scientific or humane values may justify withholding information, every effort should be made so that withholding the information has no damaging consequences for the participant.
- When, in the course of research, information comes to the investigator's attention that may seriously affect the child's well-being, the investigator has a responsibility to discuss the information with those expert in the field in order that the parents may arrange the necessary assistance for their child.
- When it is learned that research procedures may result in undesirable consequences for the participant, the investigator should employ appropriate measures to correct these consequences, and should consider redesigning the procedure.
- Investigators should be mindful of the social, political, and human implications of their research and should be especially careful in the presentation of their findings. This standard, however, in no way denies investigators the right to pursue any area of research or the right to observe proper standards of scientific reporting.
- When an experimental treatment under investigation is believed to be of benefit to children, control groups should be offered other beneficial alternative treatments, if available, instead of no treatment.

identify the crucial factors that produced the difficulty from which that person was suffering.

Clinical methods are not restricted to pathology. In addition to the diaries he kept of his children's development, the developmental psychologist Jean Piaget often used clinical interview techniques to explore children's developing understandings of the world. In one of his early studies in the development of children's thinking, he used a clinical interview procedure to focus on children's understanding of the idea of "thinking." In the examples that follow, note that it would have been impossible for Piaget to anticipate exactly how the children would respond. Therefore, he adapted his questions to the flow of the conversation.

7 year old

> *Piaget:* . . . *You know what it means to think?*
> *Child:* Yes
> *Piaget:* Then think of your house. What do you think with?
> *Child:* With the mouth.
>
> (Adapted from Piaget, 1929/1979, p. 39)

11 year old

> *Piaget:* Where is thought?
> *Child:* In the head.
> *Piaget:* If someone opened your head, would he see your thought?
> *Child:* No.

(At this point Piaget changes his line of questioning to get at the child's conception of thinking from a different direction.)

> *Piaget:* What is a dream?
> *Child:* It's a thought.
> *Piaget:* What do you dream with?
> *Child:* With the head.
> *Piaget:* Are the eyes open or shut?
> *Child:* Shut.
> *Piaget:* Where is the dream whilst you are dreaming?
> *Child:* In the head.
> *Piaget:* Not in front of you?
> *Child:* It's as if (!) you could see it.
>
> (From Piaget, 1929/1979, p. 54)

Piaget's probing interviews of these children revealed two age-related patterns of understanding what thinking is. For the younger child, thinking is a bodily process—the act of speaking. You can see it happening. In contrast, the older child conceives of thinking as something invisible and unobservable, a mental process. Piaget used such data to argue for the existence of a stagelike developmental change in the way children understand and experience the world. He believed that about the age of 10 to 11 is when children first become able to think about thinking as a mental process that cannot be seen.

Alexander Luria (1902–1977), a Russian psychologist, used the clinical interview method to uncover qualitative differences in thinking in different cultural environments. It was his belief, for example, that people living in preindustrialized societies where there is little or no literacy and schooling would categorize objects according to the way they are used in everyday life rather than according to some abstract criterion. In one study he presented drawings of four objects—a hammer, a saw, a log, and a hatchet—to a group of pastoralist cow-herders, and asked them which of the objects were similar and which did not fit with the others. Most of us would see two obvious criteria by which these objects could be categorized: either as "things needed to get firewood" (which excludes the hammer) or as tools (which excludes the log). Luria's subjects saw the objects in quite different terms, as indicated by the following typical exchange:

> *Subject:* They all fit here! The saw has to saw the log, the hammer has to hammer it, and the hatchet has to chop it. And if you want to saw the log up really good, you need the hammer. You can't take any of these things away. There isn't any you don't need.
> *Luria:* But one fellow told me that the log didn't belong here.
> *Subject:* Why'd he say that? If we say the log isn't like the other things and put it off to one side, we'd be making a mistake. All these things are needed for the log.

> *Luria:* But that other fellow said that the saw, hammer, and hatchet are all alike in some way, while the log isn't.
> *Subject:* So what if they're not alike? They all work together and chop the log. Here everything works right, here everything's just fine.
> (Luria, 1976, p. 58)

Luria's approach is a classic use of the clinical interview. The investigator probes the subject's understanding by challenging his or her responses to questions and suggesting alternative (sometimes incorrect) viewpoints. As indicated by the interview above, for Luria's subjects, "similar" with respect to the presented objects seemed to mean "enters into the same activity." By contrasting his subjects' answers with the answers given by people who had gone to school and begun to participate in industrialized forms of economic activity and social relations, Luria was led to the conclusion that traditional pastoralists organize their thinking in terms of concepts that closely relate objects to their functions, and they do not develop thinking based on objects' membership in the same abstract category.

The strong point of clinical interview methods is that they provide insight into the dynamics of individual development. Every person interviewed provides a distinctive pattern of responses that corresponds to his or her individual experiences. But the clinical interview method has its limitations. First, to arrive at general conclusions on the interview topic, the clinician must ignore individual differences across interviews in order to distill the general pattern. But as the general pattern appears, the individual picture disappears. Second, because the method relies heavily on verbal expression, it is inappropriate for use with very young children, who have difficulty expressing themselves fully or precisely. This is especially the case in trying to assess children's cognitive abilities, since young children often understand things well before they can explain their understanding.

Margaret Beale Spencer has used the interview and observation methods extensively in her work on children's self-esteem. Here she works with high school special education students who are participating in a computer-based learning program.

RESEARCH DESIGNS

If research is to illuminate the process of developmental change, it must be designed to reveal how the factors responsible for change work over time—that is, how change is brought about at different ages. There are two basic research designs that psychologists use for this purpose, *longitudinal* and *cross-sectional.* Each design takes the passage of time into account in a distinctive way. The researcher who uses the **longitudinal design** collects information about a group of children as they grow older over an extended span of time. The researcher who uses the **cross-sectional design** collects information about children of various ages at one time. These designs can be used in conjunction with each other and with any of the techniques of data collection just discussed. Each design has its own advantages and disadvantages.

Longitudinal Designs

Researchers who choose a longitudinal design select a representative sample of the population they want to study and gather data from each person at two or more ages. For example, Jerome Kagan (1994), has led a research team at Harvard University that has traced the behavior of a group of children from shortly after birth into early adolescence. This study provided the evidence, mentioned earlier, that children who are shy and uncertain at 21 months are likely to be timid and cautious at 12 to 14 years. Without longitudinal measurements, it would be impossible to discover if there is continuity in behavior patterns or if the processes change as children grow older. Other influential longitudinal studies have focused on such varied topics as personality (Friedman et al., 1995), mental health (Werner & Smith, 1992), temperament and intelligence (DeFries et al., 1994), language development (Fenson et al., 1994), and social adjustment (Cairns & Cairns, 1994).

longitudinal design A research design in which data are gathered from the same group of children as they grow older over an extended period of time.

cross-sectional design A research design in which children of various ages are studied at the same time.

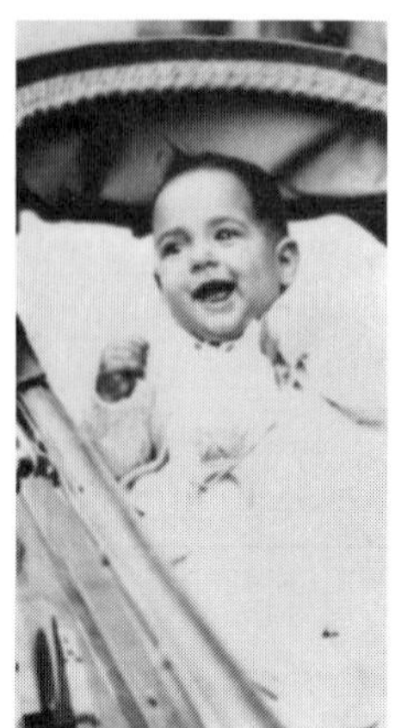

Longitudinal designs follow the same persons through the years as they age.

Longitudinal designs would seem to be an ideal way to study development because they fit the requirement that development be studied over time. Unfortunately, longitudinal research designs have some practical and methodological drawbacks that have restricted their use. To begin with, they are expensive to carry out, particularly if they are to be conducted over several years. They require the long-term commitment of a researcher to an uncertain venture. In addition, some parents refuse to allow their children to participate in a lengthy study. If such refusals are more frequent in one social, economic, or ethnic group than in others, they may make the sample unrepresentative of the study population as a whole. It is also common for some of the children who begin such a study to drop out, further changing the sample in ways that weaken the conclusions that can be drawn.

Another difficulty with longitudinal designs is that the people in the sample may become used to the various testing and interviewing procedures. In other words, they may learn how to respond as expected. As a consequence, it is difficult to know whether changes in a person's responses over time represent normal development or simply the effect of practice in taking the tests and responding to interviews.

Finally, longitudinal designs sometimes confound (mix together) the influence of age-related changes and the influence of factors related specifically to the sample group's cohort. A **cohort** is a population of persons born about the same time, and people of a given cohort may share experiences that differ from those of people born earlier or later. In longitudinal research, differences that appear to be related to differences in age may actually arise because of differences in cohort. Consider, for example, a longitudinal study of the development of children's fears from birth onward that began in London in 1932. In their early years, the children in this study would have been living through the Great Depression. At the age of 9 or 10, many of these children would have lost one or both parents in World War II, and many others would have been sent away from their parents to the countryside in an effort to keep them safe from nightly bombings of the city. If the results of such a study indicated that the children's fears centered on hunger in their first years and that later, around the age of 9, they began to fear that they would lose their parents, it would not be possible to determine whether the observed age trends reflected general laws of development, true at any time and any place, or whether they were the result of growing up in a particular time and place, or both (Elder, 1998).

Resources permitting, researchers can use various means to overcome these shortcomings. Some have used a **cohort sequential design,** in which the longitudinal method is replicated with several cohorts, each of which is studied longitudinally. This modification of the longitudinal design allows age-related factors in developmental change to be separated from cohort-related factors.

cohort A group of persons born about the same time who are therefore likely to share certain experiences.

cohort sequential design An experimental design in which the longitudinal method is replicated with several cohorts.

Cross-Sectional Designs

The most widely used developmental research design is called the *cross-sectional design* because groups representing a cross section of ages are studied at a single time. To study the development of memory, for example, one might first test samples of 4-year-olds, 10-year-olds, 20-year-olds, and 60-year-olds to see how well they remember a list of familiar words. By comparing how people in the four age groups go about the task and what the results of their efforts are, one could then form hypotheses about developmental changes in memory processes. (Figure 1.8 compares longitudinal and cross-sectional research designs.) In fact, researchers have carried out a great many cross-sectional studies of memory development that have demonstrated both quantitative and qualitative developmental changes that we will examine in later chapters (Schneider & Bjorklund, 1998).

The advantages of the cross-sectional design are readily apparent. Because it samples several age levels at once, this design is less time-consuming and less expensive than a longitudinal approach. The short time commitment required of the participants also makes it more likely that a representative sample will be recruited and that few participants will drop out of the study.

Despite these attractive features, cross-sectional designs also have drawbacks. In order to be properly conducted, such studies need to ensure that all relevant factors other than age are kept constant. That is, the makeup of all the age groups should be the same in terms of sex, ethnicity, amount of education, socioeconomic status, and so on. However, like longitudinal designs, cross-sectional designs can confound age-related changes and characteristics particular to a specific cohort. Consider the possibilities for a hypothetical study of memory development. Suppose that the study was conducted in 2000. Suppose further that the study showed that the 70-year-olds performed significantly more poorly than the 20-year-olds. These results might reflect a universal tendency for memory to decline with age. But the difference might also be caused by differences in childhood nutrition, which has been shown

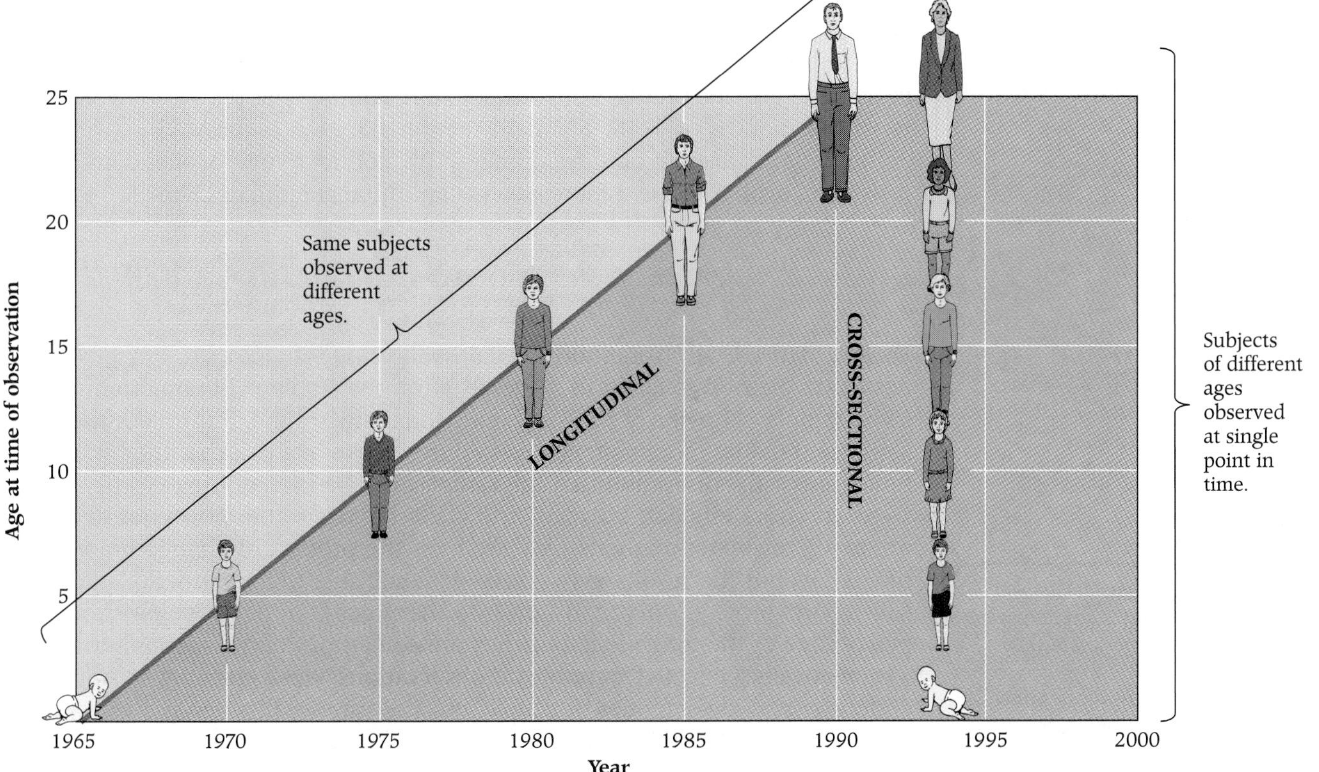

FIGURE 1.8
The difference between longitudinal and cross-sectional research designs.

to affect intellectual development (Pollitt, 1994); nutrition was generally not as good in the 1930s, when the 70-year-olds were children, as it was in the 1980s, when the 20-year-olds were children. The 70-year-olds are also likely to have received less education than the 20-year-olds. A college education was much more common in the 1990s than it was in the 1950s, and education has been shown to increase performance on memory tests (Cole, 1996). In addition, because memory performance is maintained by the constant practice provided by schooling, it is possible that the 70-year-olds performed less well because they had been out of school a long time. The possible presence of such confounding cohort effects means that great care must be taken when interpreting cross-sectional studies.

A second difficulty with cross-sectional designs is that, by sampling the behavior of different-aged people at one time, they inappropriately slice up the ongoing process of development into a series of disconnected snapshots. While such a design may be used to contrast the general ways in which 4- and 10-year-olds remember a list of words, for example, it cannot take into account the developmental process by which memory abilities and strategies change over time because it doesn't follow the same children over time. Thus when theorists formulate hypotheses about development on the basis of cross-sectional designs, they must engage in a good deal of extrapolation and guesswork about processes of change.

Microgenetic Methods

A common concern with both longitudinal and cross-sectional methods is that they do not provide direct evidence about the *process* of developmental change. To try to get closer to observing change processes, developmentalists sometimes use special procedures called **microgenetic methods,** in which they study children's development intensively over relatively short periods of time, sometimes only a few hours or a few days (Miller & Coyle, 1999; Siegler, 1998; Vygotsky, 1978). As a rule, microgenetic methods are used with children who are thought to be on the threshold of a significant developmental change so that, if they are provided dense experience with figuring out the right way to deal with a complex developmental challenge, it will be possible to see them develop more sophisticated forms of behavior right before the observer's eyes.

Robert Siegler (1996) offers a useful analogy for understanding how microgenetic methods differ from studies that sample children's behavior at intervals of months or years. Standard methods, he writes, provide us with discontinuous *snapshots* of development. By contrast, microgenetic methods provide us with a *movie,* a more or less continuous record of change.

RESEARCH DESIGNS AND DATA-COLLECTION METHODS IN PERSPECTIVE

Each design and each method for data collection has its uses, but no single design or method is likely to serve all purposes (Table 1.1). Longitudinal designs sample behavior of the same individuals over time, but unless they are supplemented by more complex procedures, there is a risk that they will confound age with cohort and that the samples will be biased. Cross-sectional designs are more efficient but may artificially break up the process of development. Microgenetic methods may lay bare the process of change on a small time scale, but the results may not be generalizable to longer periods of time. Self-reports provide unique insight into the process of development from the perspective of the individual, but they are sometimes of questionable validity. Systematically collected naturalistic observations yield essential information about the real-life activities of people, but they are weak when it comes to establishing causal relationships. Experiments can isolate causal factors in specific settings, but the results obtained may not be generalizable beyond the

microgenetic method A research method in which children's development is studied intensively over a relatively short period of time.

theory A broad framework or set of principles that can be used to guide the collection and interpretation of a set of facts.

TABLE 1.1 RESEARCH TECHNIQUES AND DESIGNS

	Advantages	Disadvantages
Technique		
Self-report	Provides access to unique information	Unreliable and of uncertain validity
Naturalistic observation	Reveals full complexity of behavior and its ecology	Difficult to establish causal relations
Experiment	Best method of testing causal hypotheses	Sometimes impossible for ethical reasons Artificial procedures may distort validity of results
Clinical interview	Focuses on dynamics of individual development	Difficult to generalize beyond unique case or to establish causal relations
Design		
Longitudinal	Traces development as a process occurring over time	Repeat testing may invalidate results Costly and difficult to use Results may be confounded with historical time
Microgenetic	Observes process of change over short periods of time	Care must be taken when generalizing to longer time periods
Cross-sectional	Takes relatively little time to administer	Loses sense of continuity in development
	Reveals age trends	Findings are vulnerable to confounding with variables other than age

artificial boundaries of the experimental situation. Clinical interview methods can reveal the dynamics of individual thought and feelings, but they are difficult to generalize beyond the individual case. In the chapters that follow, the advantages and problems of the various research methods will be noted time and again as they apply to specific aspects of development.

THE ROLE OF THEORY

Contrary to widely held belief, facts do not "speak for themselves." The facts that developmental psychologists collect help us to understand development only when they are brought together and interpreted in terms of a **theory**, a framework of ideas or body of principles that can be used to guide the collection and interpretation of a set of facts. Like heredity and environment, facts and theories go together. Neither comes "first"; they arise and exist together.

To draw upon an example to which we return in Chapter 11 (p. 455), people from two cultures may agree that a child is behaving wildly and irreverently in a preschool classroom but interpret the same facts in very different ways. Developmental psychologists (as well as parents) from Japan and the United States hold different *theories* of what causes children to misbehave. These theories get them to notice and emphasize different aspects of the same behavior. Where an American investigator is likely to see uncontrolled aggression, a Japanese investigator is likely to see an expression of dependency disorder. Their different theories and the data they focus on to evaluate those theories lead, in turn, to different prescriptions about how to deal with this worrisome behavior.

Today's developmentalists use physiological measures in addition to behavioral observations to understand the complex factors in development. Here a University of California scientist uses electrodes to monitor an 8-week-old infant's brain activity in response to changing color patterns and the ringing of a bell.

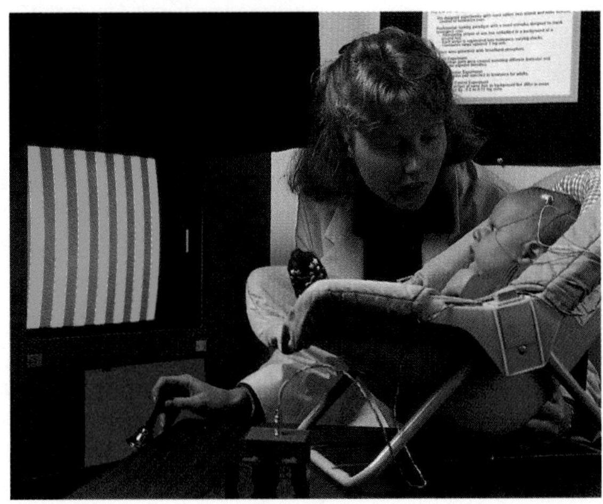

Albert Einstein pointed out that theory is silently present even when we think that we are "objectively observing the world." Observation of the world may be useful, he said,

> but on principle, it is quite wrong to try founding a theory on observable magnitudes alone. In reality the very opposite occurs. It is the theory which decides what we can observe. (Quoted in Sameroff, 1983, p. 243)

Einstein's point applies to psychologists' attempts to understand the human world just as forcefully as it applies to investigations of the physical world. A deeper understanding of human development will not automatically come from the continuous accumulation of facts. Rather, it will come through new attempts to make sense of the accumulating evidence on development in the light of a relevant theory.

At the present time, there is no single broad theoretical perspective that unifies the entire body of relevant scientific knowledge on human development. Instead, the field is approached from several theoretical perspectives. These perspectives can be grouped into four frameworks, according to the ba-

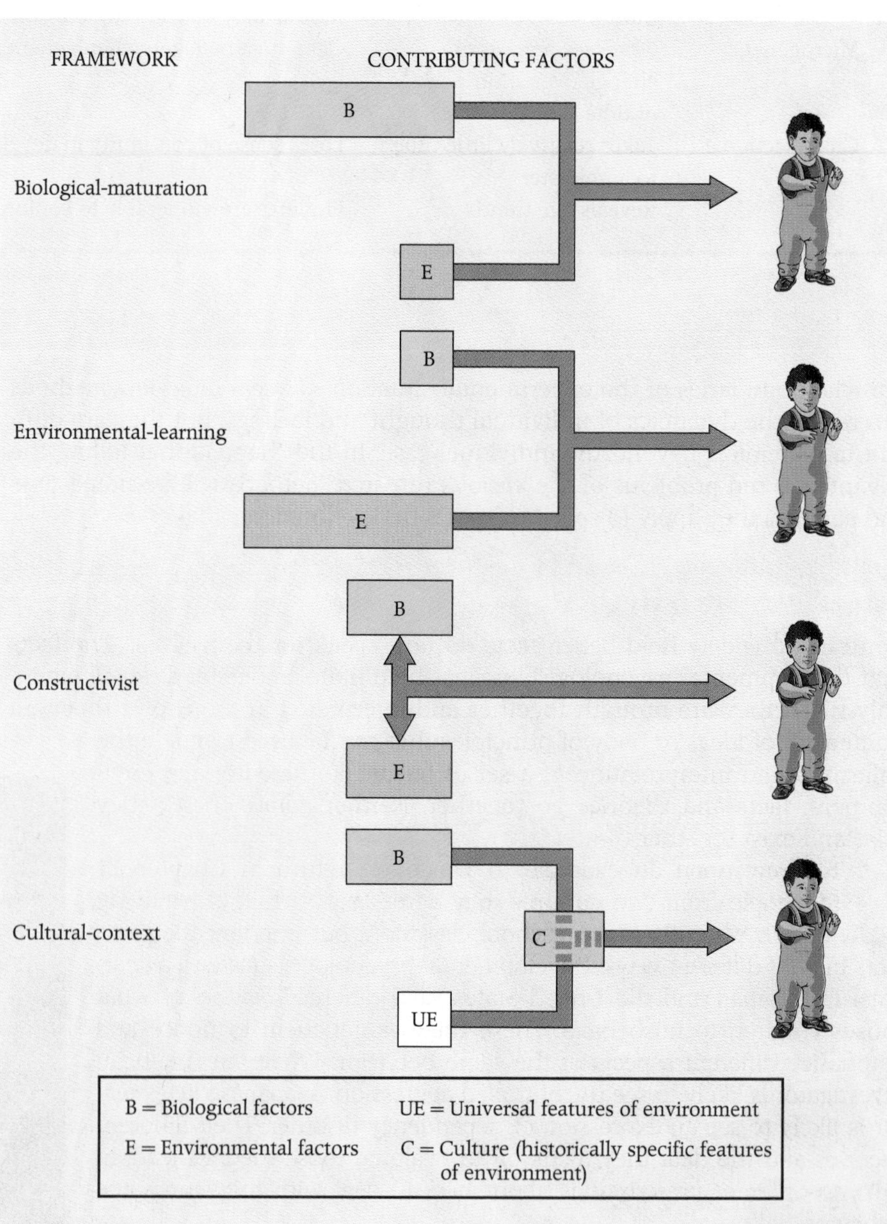

FIGURE 1.9

Four frameworks for interpreting the influence of nature and nurture. In the first three frameworks, biological and environmental factors directly interact with each other to shape the individual. In the fourth, the cultural-context framework, biological inheritance and universal features of the environment act indirectly through the medium of culture.

sic answers they give to the three central questions of development cited earlier: (1) What are the relative contributions of nature and nurture to development? (2) Is the process of developmental change continuous or discontinuous? (3) What accounts for individual differences? Throughout this book we refer to these four broad frameworks as the *biological-maturation,* the *environmental-learning,* the *constructivist,* and the *cultural-context* frameworks (see Figure 1.9).

The difficulty with any simplified categorization of the study of human development is that it leaves out important cases. In our use of four broad frameworks, for example, we have omitted the psychodynamic approach, associated with the names of Sigmund Freud and Erik Erikson, two foundational figures in developmental psychology. Although their work remains influential, it is controversial because both Freud and Erikson derived most of their data by clinically interviewing adults about their childhoods and because, being primarily clinicians, both often viewed normal development through the prism of mental illness.

Each of the broad frameworks encompasses many specific theories that focus on particular aspects of human development. In later chapters we will encounter theories about such topics as the origins of concepts in early postnatal development, the appearance of a distinctive sense of self at the end of infancy, the emergence of new forms of play in middle childhood, and the development of the ability to reason hypothetically in adolescence. The broad frameworks we have identified provide distinctive, valuable ways of looking at the overall process of development. What follows here is only a brief overview of the four frameworks. In subsequent chapters we will return to them to explore what they can tell us about particular aspects of developmental change.

The Biological-Maturation Framework

All the theories within the biological-maturation framework share a central view that the source of changes that characterize human development is

Arnold Gesell testing a child in the observation room at the Yale Child Study Center.

endogenous The term applied to causes of development that arise as a consequence of the organism's biological heritage.

maturation A sequence of changes that are strongly influenced by genetic inheritance and that occur as individuals grow older.

exogenous The term applied to causes of development that come from the environment, particularly from the adults who shape children's behavior and beliefs.

learning The process by which an organism's behavior is modified as a result of experience.

endogenous; that is, change comes from inside the organism as a consequence of the genes the organism inherits. The major cause of development from this viewpoint is **maturation,** a sequence of genetically determined changes that occur as individuals age from their immature starting point at conception to full adulthood.

Psychologists whose theories fall into the biological-maturation framework are likely to see psychological development as a progression of stagelike changes that accompany (and are caused by) stagelike changes in the biological structure of the organism. In their view, the role of the environment is secondary in shaping the basic course of development. This view was clearly expressed by Arnold Gesell (1880–1961), one of the most influential developmental psychologists of the early twentieth century:

> Environment . . . determines the occasion, the intensity, and the correlation of many aspects of behavior, but it does not engender the basic progressions of behavior development. These are determined by inherent, maturational mechanisms. (1940, p. 13)

As we noted earlier, the ideas of Sigmund Freud (1856–1939) have exerted a tremendous influence on modern concepts of human nature. Among theorists of development, Freud was the first to emphasize the centrality of emotional life to the formation and function of human personality. Freud's well-known belief that the gratification of basic biological urges is the primary motive of human behavior places him among the biological-maturation theorists. When he considered the process of individual development, however, Freud, like Gesell, accorded some role to the environment. "The constitutional factor," he wrote, "must await experiences before it can make itself felt" (Freud, 1905/1953a, p. 239). In other words, the basic human drives are biologically determined, but the social environment directs the way these drives will be satisfied, thereby shaping individual personalities.

The biological-maturation perspective on human development was out of favor in the middle of the twentieth century, but in recent decades it has enjoyed renewed attention. Modern studies of language acquisition are a prominent example. The ability to use language is inherited by all human beings and appears to mature at a fixed pace, suggesting to some researchers that the environment plays only a triggering role in the realization of linguistic potential (Pinker, 1994). In addition, researchers have shown that some aspects of personality and intelligence have a strong genetic basis (Plomin et al., 1997). It is also claimed that several basic intellectual competencies are present in rudimentary form at or near birth, so it seems that their origin does not depend on interactions with the postnatal environment (Baillargeon, 1998; Spelke, 1996).

The Environmental-Learning Framework

Theories that fall into the environmental-learning perspective do not deny that biological factors provide a basic foundation for development, but they argue that the major causes of developmental change are **exogenous;** that is, they come from the environment, particularly from the adults who shape children's behavior and beliefs by the way they reward and punish children's actions. According to theories in this framework, **learning,** defined as the process by which an organism's behavior is modified by experience, is the major mechanism of development. John B. Watson (1878–1958), an early learning theorist, was so certain of the prime role of learning in human development that he boasted:

> Give me a dozen healthy infants, well-formed, and my own specified world to bring them up in and I'll guarantee to take any one at random and train him to become any type of specialist I might select—doctor, lawyer, artist, merchant-

> chief, and, yes, even beggar-man and thief, regardless of his talents, penchants, tendencies, abilities, vocations, and race of his ancestors. (1930, p. 104)

Although modern environmental-learning theories no longer share Watson's extreme view, they do assert that the environment, acting through learning mechanisms, is overwhelmingly important in shaping development (Gewirtz & Pelaez-Nogueras, 1992). Perhaps the most compelling evidence in support of such theories comes from studies done on children who have lived in near isolation owing to some quirk of circumstances or who have been brought up in orphanages with little intellectual stimulation. This research shows that enriching the social and cognitive experiences of such children dramatically improves their later social and cognitive development (Clarke & Clarke, 1986). Research has also shown that learning plays a significant role in such "biological" processes as gender development and aggressiveness (Maccoby, 1998; Patterson et al., 1998).

Their focus on the environment as the primary influence on development leads many environmental-learning theorists to emphasize the gradual and continuous nature of developmental change. This intuition is captured nicely by B. F. Skinner's metaphorical description of how the environment

> shapes behavior as a sculptor shapes a lump of clay. Although at some point the sculptor seems to have produced an entirely novel object, we can always follow the process back to the original undifferentiated lump, and we can make the successive stages by which we return to this condition as small as we wish. At no point does anything emerge which is very different from what preceded it. The final product seems to have a special unity or integrity of design, but we cannot find a point at which this suddenly appears. (1953, p. 91)

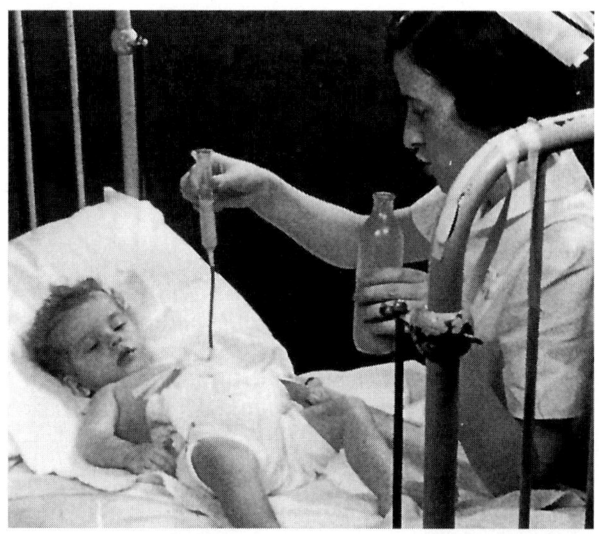

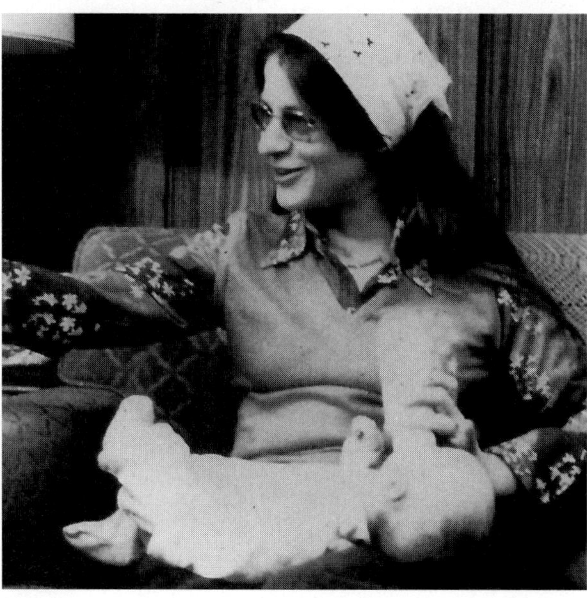

Because of a birth defect requiring her to be fed through a tube directly into the stomach, Monica was never fed orally or held in arms while she was fed as a baby. When she was older, she fed her dolls and later, bottlefed her daughter, who had no such defect, in the same position as she had been fed. The persistence of her unique behavior reflects the enduring importance of children's earliest learning experience.

The Constructivist Framework

In contrast to the biological-maturation and environmental-learning theorists, psychologists whose theories fall into the constructivist view find it inappropriate to attribute more importance to either nature or nurture. They assert that nature and nurture are *equally* necessary for development. A leading adherent of this view was the Swiss developmental psychologist Jean Piaget (1896–1980). Piaget began his scientific career as a biologist and continued to be concerned with biological development, much like a biological-maturation theorist. At the same time, he, like supporters of the environmental-learning framework, believed that the environment's role in development goes well beyond triggering the child's innate potential:

> The human being is immersed right from birth in a social environment which affects him just as much as his physical environment. Society, even more, in a sense, than the physical environment, changes the very structure of the individual. . . . Every relation between individuals (from two onwards) literally modifies them. . . . (Piaget, 1973, p. 156)

What especially distinguishes constructivist theories from the biological-maturation and environmental-learning frameworks is the importance constructivists attach to children's active role in shaping their own development. Piaget argued that "knowledge is not a copy of reality" (1964, p. 8), emphasizing the fact that the knowledge we acquire results from the way we modify and transform the world. According to the constructivist way of thinking, children *construct* successively higher levels of knowledge by

Jean Piaget, whose work has had a profound influence on developmental psychology, observing children at play.

actively striving to master their environments. They are *biosocial* beings because both maturational *and* environmental circumstances are reciprocally involved in the process of developmental change.

Piaget and his followers also maintain that the environment does not influence children in the same way at all ages. Instead, the influences of the environment depend on the child's current stage of development. The size, gender mix, and influence of the peer group, for example, depend very much on whether it is a peer group of 4-year-olds or 14-year-olds.

On the basis of data from other cultures, Piaget (1966) also believed that development can be speeded up or slowed down by variations in the environment (such as the presence or absence of formal schooling) but that all children go through the same basic sequence of changes. In this important sense, a constructivist approach assumes that the processes of developmental change are the same in all human groups: They are universal in the species.

As we will see in later chapters, contemporary psychologists who follow in the tradition established by Piaget have refined or amended a number of his ideas. Nevertheless, these investigators agree with Piaget's emphasis on the central role of children's active engagement of the world and with his insistence that biology and the environment play reciprocal roles in developmental change.

The Cultural-Context Framework

Psychologists whose work falls within the three theoretical frameworks just described assume that development arises from the interaction of two factors: children's biological heritage and their environment. The frameworks diverge in the relative weight they give to each of these two sources of influence on development and also in the way they see them interacting to produce development.

Psychologists who work within the cultural-context framework also concur that biological and experiential factors have reciprocal roles to play in development and, like the constructivists, believe that children construct their own development through active engagement with the world. But they differ from the other theorists by asserting that a "third force"—culture—is part of the mixture. As indicated at the bottom of Figure 1.9, according to the cultural-context view, nature and nurture do not interact *directly.* Rather, they interact indirectly through *culture,* the designs for living that are based on the accumulated knowledge of a people, encoded in their language, and embodied in the physical artifacts, beliefs, values, customs, and activities that have been passed down from one generation to the next (Bruner, 1996; Greenfield, 1997; Valsiner, 1998; Vygotsky, 1978).

One way culture influences development can be seen in children's acquisition of mathematical understanding. The kinds of mathematical thinking children develop do not depend only on their ability to deal with abstractions and on adults' efforts to arrange for them to learn mathematical concepts. They also depend on the adults' own knowledge of mathematics, which in turn depends on their cultural heritage. Children growing up among the Oksapmin, a group living in the jungles of New Guinea, appear to have the same universal ability to grasp basic number concepts as children growing up in Paris or Pittsburgh, but instead of learning to use a number system to count, they learn to count by using the parts of their body. This system would be unwieldy for children who must solve arithmetic problems in school and later in the money economy of Western culture, but it is perfectly adequate for dealing with the tasks of everyday life in traditional Oksapmin culture (Saxe, 1994). The development of mathematical knowledge is also influenced by the contexts in which the knowledge is used. In Brazil, for example, child street vendors develop remarkable mathematical skills in the course of everyday buying and selling. But while these children can handle mathematical problems in the marketplace with ease, they have difficulties with the same problems when they are presented to them in a school-like format (Nuñes et al., 1993). In each of these cases, culture has contributed to the course of development by arranging the conditions under which biological and environmental factors interact.

Lev Vygotsky, a prominent theorist of the role of culture in development, and his daughter.

The cultural-context and constructivist points of view are similar in several respects. Both hold that the individual undergoes qualitative changes in the course of development, and both emphasize that development is impossible without the individual's active participation. They differ, however, in three important respects. First, the cultural-context framework assumes that both children *and* their caretakers are active agents in the process of development. Development is, in this sense, "*co*constructed." Second, the cultural-context framework does not look for stagelike consistency in abilities and behavior. It anticipates wide variability in a given individual's performance as the person moves from one kind of activity to another. Third, the cultural-context framework is more open to the idea that the sequence of developmental changes a child experiences—and, indeed, even the existence or nonexistence of a particular stage of development—may depend on the child's cultural-historical circumstances (Rogoff, 1998).

None of the theories we have outlined is sufficiently comprehensive to provide a full picture of all the complexities of human development. Indeed, these theories might best be thought of as filters, with each theory highlighting certain features of the overall process of development. The "full" picture, if one were to be achieved, would be a perfect coordination of the pictures seen through all the different filters.

THIS BOOK AND THE FIELD OF DEVELOPMENTAL PSYCHOLOGY

Given the lack of a comprehensive and widely accepted developmental theory that unifies the field, this book adopts an integrative approach that makes it possible to present and evaluate different theorists' claims in a systematic way. And since development is a process that emerges over time, this book also adopts a chronological approach as the best way to understand the processes involved.

Telling the story of development chronologically presents two major difficulties, however. The first is how to segment the story of development into specific periods and how much significance to attribute to each of these periods. The second is how to keep track of the many aspects of development that are occurring simultaneously, how to depict the ways they combine and recombine to constitute a whole, living person.

Our solution to these difficulties has been to adopt a perspective that provides a principled way of looking at the periods of childhood and at the same time emphasizes the simultaneous action of many factors. This perspective, put forth by Robert Emde and his colleagues (Emde et al., 1976), emphasizes key stagelike changes that Emde and his colleagues refer to as *"bio-behavioral shifts"*—points in development at which the interaction of biological maturation and behavioral changes result in a reorganization of the child's functioning. The prototype for such a shift is the transition that occurs when, at 2½ to 3 months of age, infants first make concentrated eye contact and smile in response to the smile of another person. This first "reciprocal smile" creates a new quality of emotional contact between infant and parents and is recognized in several societies as an indicator of a new stage of development. There is no one "cause" for reciprocal smiling. It emerges

bio-social-behavioral shift A transition point in development during which a convergence of biological, social, and behavioral changes converge to cause distinctively new forms of behavior.

from changes occurring in the neural fibers connecting the eye to the brain, increased density of cells in the retina of the eye, the presence of adults ready to smile at the child, and the special emotional response that this new form of connectedness evokes. Emde and his colleagues refer to this kind of transition as a bio-behavioral shift because the resulting reorganization in the child's functioning emerges from the interaction of biological and behavioral factors.

In adopting the idea of a bio-behavioral shift, we add the social dimension of development because, as Emde and his colleagues themselves note, every bio-behavioral shift involves a change in the relationship between children and their social worlds. As the onset of social smiling indicates, not only do children experience the social environment in new ways as a result of the changes in their behavior and biological makeup; they also are treated differently by other people. We therefore use the term **bio-social-behavioral shift** to refer to major transition points in development during which a convergence of biological, social, and behavioral changes gives rise to distinctively new forms of behavior. (Table 1.2 outlines the bio-social-behavioral shifts that appear to be prominent in the development of the child from conception to adulthood. Although not all of the shift points have been equally well established, they nevertheless provide a fruitful means of organizing discussions of development because they require us to consider both the sources of change and the evidence concerning developmental continuity and discontinuity in a systematic way.)

Cultural-context approaches pay special attention to variations in children's development arising from differences in the human-made parts of the environment.

In the Lesser Sudas of Indonesia, a girl works side by side with her mother and grandmother processing cotton for spinning.

In addition, we take into account how the cultural context of children's development enters into the timing and organization not only of bio-social-behavioral shifts but of developmental processes at all ages. From the earliest hours of life, cultural conceptions of what children are and what the future holds for them influence the way parents interpret their children's behavior and shape their experience. For example, parents who believe that men have to be aggressive and tough to survive in the world are more likely to treat their baby boys differently than do those parents who believe that male aggression is a problem. And as we mentioned earlier, in some cases the timing, the essential character, and even the existence of a developmental period may be strongly influenced by cultural factors (Rogoff, 1998; Whiting, Burbank, & Ratner, 1986).

The notion of bio-social-behavioral shifts fits reasonably well with a traditional convention that divides the time between conception and the start of adulthood into five broad periods: the *prenatal period, infancy, early childhood, middle childhood,* and *adolescence.* Each period is accorded a major section of this text. Within this chronological framework, our aim is to make clear how the fundamental biological, social, behavioral, and cultural aspects of development are woven together in the process of change from one period to the next. The text subdivides infancy, a period in which change is particularly rapid, into three subperiods marked by important transitions where distinctively new and significant forms of behavior emerge.

In Mexico young children play close by as their female relatives work.

These children are playing by themselves in front of their apartment building in New York City.

TABLE 1.2 PROMINENT BIO-SOCIAL-BEHAVIORAL SHIFTS IN DEVELOPMENT

Shift Point	New Developmental Period
Conception: genetic material of parents combines to form unique individual	
	Prenatal period: formation of basic organs
Birth: transition to life outside the womb	
	Early infancy: becoming coordinated with the environment
2½ months: cortical-subcortical brain connections form; social smiling; new quality of maternal feeling	
	Middle infancy: increased memory and sensorimotor abilities
7–9 months: wariness of novelty; fear of strangers; attachment	
	Late infancy: symbolic thought; distinct sense of self
End of infancy (24–30 months): grammatical language	
	Early childhood (2½–6 years): strikingly uneven levels of performance; sex-role identity; sociodramatic play
5–7 years: assigned responsibility for tasks outside of adult supervision; deliberate instruction	
	Middle childhood: peer-group activity; rule-based games; systemic instruction
11–12 years: sexual maturation	
	Adolescence: sex-oriented social activity; identity integration: formal reasoning
19–21 years: shift toward primary responsibility for self and raising of next generation	
	Adulthood (19+)

Our adoption of a bio-social-behavioral framework for the study of development does not imply a commitment to a strict stage theory. Rather, it provides a systematic way to keep in mind the intricate play of forces that combine to produce development. Nor does it imply a uniform "direction of causality" from biological characteristics of the individual to social and cultural factors or the other way around. Rather, it emphasizes the emergent nature of developmental change and the unceasing interplay between the biological, social, individual, and cultural sources of development.

Throughout the chapters that follow, the large questions of development that captivated Itard and his contemporaries are constantly recurring themes: What makes us human? Can our natures be remolded by experience, or are the characteristics inscribed in our genes at conception relatively fixed? Can we use our knowledge of development to help us plan our futures and guide the growth of our children? These questions are not likely to be satisfactorily answered until and unless a unified theory of development emerges. Because the issues are so complex and the field's knowledge is still limited, we have tried to design each chapter to set forth basic facts, methods, and theories in a manner that will help the reader think usefully about the fundamental questions of the field.

SUMMARY

- The study of child development is the study of the changes that children undergo starting from the moment of conception until they are adults.

EARLY BEGINNINGS

- One of the earliest efforts in the study of child development involved Jean Marc Itard's work with the Wild Boy of Aveyron. This unusual case posed fundamental questions about human nature:
    1. What distinguishes humans from other animals?
    2. What would we be like if we grew up isolated from society?
    3. To what degree are we the product of our upbringing and experience, and to what degree is our character the product of inborn traits?
- Both Itard's faith in the promise of scientific methods to resolve enduring questions about human nature and many of his specific techniques served as models for the scientific study of human development.
- The early rise of the discipline of developmental psychology is closely linked to social changes wrought by the Industrial Revolution, which fundamentally altered the nature of family life, education, and work.
- Darwin's thesis that human beings evolved from previously existing species furthered the scientific interest in children, inspiring scientists to study children for evidence of evolution.

MODERN DEVELOPMENTAL PSYCHOLOGY

- Modern developmental psychologists study the origins of human behavior and the sequence of physical, cognitive, and psychosocial changes that children undergo as they grow older.
- An important task for developmental psychologists is to apply the knowledge they acquire to the promotion of healthy development.

THE CENTRAL QUESTIONS OF DEVELOPMENTAL PSYCHOLOGY

- Many scientific and social questions about development revolve around three fundamental concerns:
    1. Is the process of development gradual and continuous, or is it marked by abrupt, stagelike discontinuities?
    2. How do nature and nurture interact to produce development?
    3. How do people come to have stable characteristics that differentiate them from one another?
- Questions about continuity branch into more specific questions:
    1. How alike and how different are we from our near neighbors in the animal kingdom?
    2. Does development involve the gradual accumulation of small quantitative changes, or are there qualitatively distinct stages of development?
    3. Are there critical periods in development?
- Questions about sources of development have given rise to competing views about the contributions of biology (nature) and the environment (nurture) to the process of development.

- The issue of individual differences focuses on two questions:
  1. What makes individuals different from one another?
  2. To what extent are individual characteristics stable over time?

THE DISCIPLINE OF DEVELOPMENTAL PSYCHOLOGY

- Developmental psychologists use several data-collection methods in their efforts to connect abstract theories to the concrete realities of people's everyday experience. These methods are designed to ensure that the data used to explain development are objective, reliable, valid, and replicable.
- Prominent among the methods of data collection used by developmental psychologists are (a) self-reports, (b) naturalistic observation, (c) experimentation, and (d) clinical interview methods.
- Research designs that include systematic comparisons among children of different ages enable researchers to establish relationships among developmental phenomena. Some basic research designs are:
  1. Longitudinal designs—the same children are studied repeatedly over a period of time.
  2. Cross-sectional designs—different children of different ages are studied at a single time.
  3. Cohort-sequential designs—the longitudinal method is repeated with several cohorts, each of which is studied longitudinally.
  4. Microgenetic designs—the same children are studied repeatedly over a short span of time during a period of rapid change.
- No one method or research design can supply the answers to all the questions that developmental psychologists seek to resolve. The choice of research design depends on the specific issue being addressed.
- Theory plays an important role in developmental psychology by providing a broad conceptual framework within which methods and research designs are organized and facts can be interpreted.
- Four major theoretical frameworks organize a large proportion of research in children's development:
  1. According to the biological-maturation framework, the sources of development are primarily endogenous, arising from the organism's biological heritage.
  2. According to the environmental-learning framework, developmental change is caused primarily by exogenous factors arising in the environment.
  3. According to the constructivist framework, development arises from the active adaptation of the organism to the environment. The roles of environmental and biological factors are of equal magnitude.
  4. Like the constructivist framework, the cultural-context framework accords importance to both biological and environmental factors in development, but it also emphasizes that the interactions out of which development emerges are crucially shaped by the designs for living that make up the culture of any given group.

THIS BOOK AND THE FIELD OF DEVELOPMENTAL PSYCHOLOGY

- The concept of the bio-social-behavioral shift highlights the ways in which biological, social, and behavioral factors interact in a cultural context to produce developmental change. Keeping these factors in mind helps us maintain a picture of the whole developing child.

KEY TERMS

baby biography, p. 17
bio-social-behavioral shift, p. 38
child development, p. 5
clinical method, p. 24
cohort, p. 28
cohort sequential design, p. 28
control group, p. 22
correlation, p. 21
critical period, p. 11
cross-sectional design, p. 27
culture, p. 8
developmental niche, p. 18
developmental stage, p. 9
ecology, p. 18
endogenous, p. 34
ethnographers, p. 18
ethology, p. 18
exogenous, p. 34
experiment, p. 21
experimental group, p. 22
learning, p. 34
longitudinal design, p. 27
maturation, p. 34
microgenetic method, p. 30
naturalistic observation, p. 17
nature, p. 13
nurture, p. 13
objectivity, p. 16
ontogeny, p. 9
phylogeny, p. 8
reliability, p. 16
replicability, p. 16
representative sample, p. 16
scientific hypothesis, p. 21
self-report, p. 17
sensitive period, p. 11
theory, p. 31
validity, p. 16

THOUGHT QUESTIONS

1. Using arguments from the four theoretical perspectives described in this chapter, give four possible explanations for the appearance and behavior of the Wild Boy of Aveyron.
2. On the basis of your own experience, give an example of how the scientific study of child development has affected the way the current-generation children in your neighborhood are being raised.
3. What is one question you have about the development of children? How do you think scientists might go about finding the answer?
4. List three ways in which the person you were at the age of 5 differed from the person you were at the age of 15. Label those differences as either qualitative or quantitative.
5. List two major ways in which you are like your best friend and two major ways in which the two of you are different. What causal factors do you think are primarily responsible for each of these similarities and differences?

PART I

In the Beginning

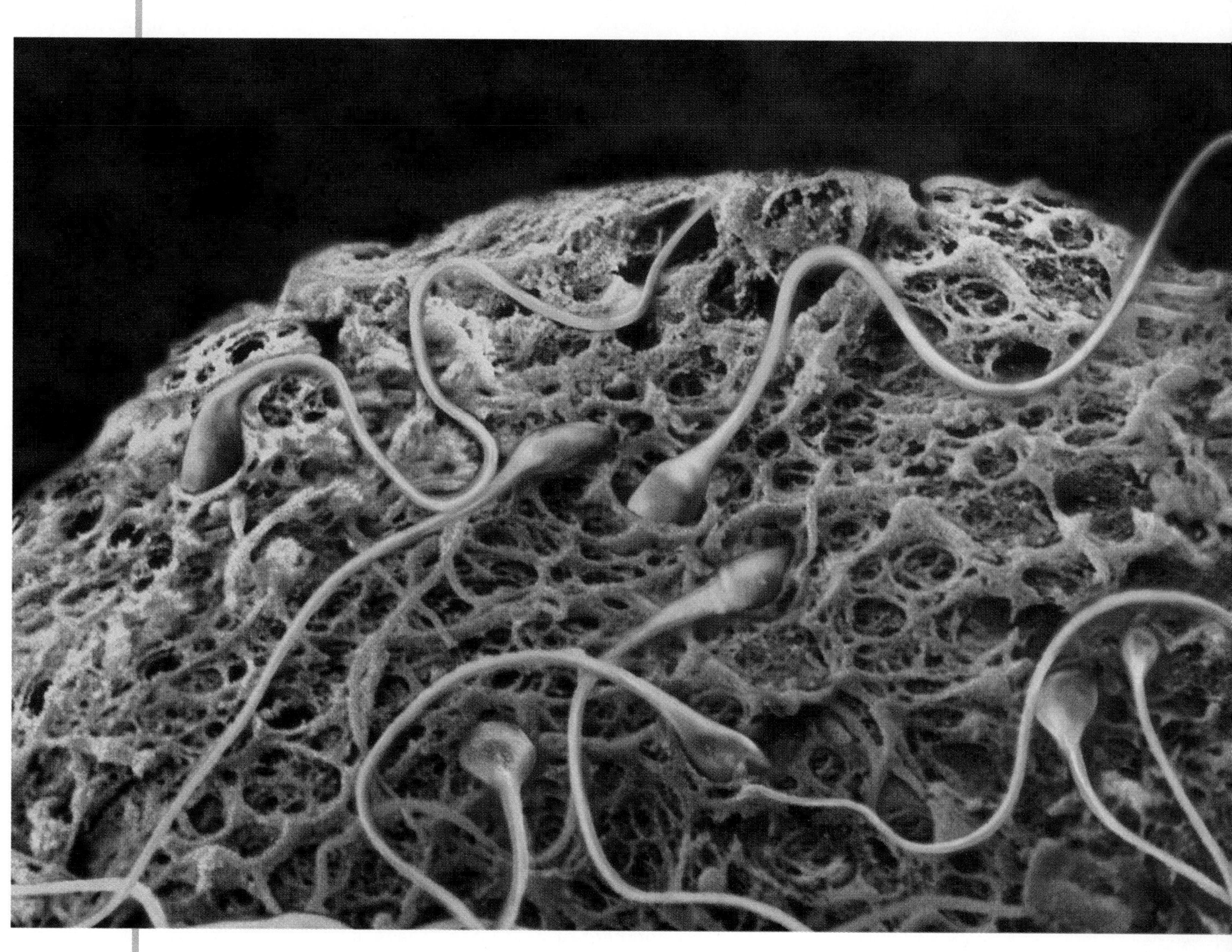

The development of every human being starts with the formation of a single cell at the time of conception. However, each individual human life is but a tiny drop in the vast stream of life that reaches back through thousands of generations and unimaginable millennia of evolutionary time. As such, it is a product of the evolutionary past of our species. Moreover, the environment each baby will experience is a product of the earth's history and the development of culture and society.

Science views the life process as a constant interplay of forces that create order and pattern, on the one hand, and of forces that create variation and disorder, on the other. In the modern scientific view, the interaction of these competing forces is the engine of developmental change.

What are the forces that create order and diversity in human development? In Chapter 2 we will see that the beginning of an explanation can be found in our biological inheritance. Order, the ways in which all human beings are alike, initially arises from the finiteness of our species' pool of genetic possibilities. Variation initially arises through sexual reproduction, which in virtually every instance ensures that each individual will inherit a unique combination of genes from the common pool.

Chapter 2 describes the basic mechanisms of genetic transmission, the processes of gene–environment interaction, and some of the diseases that result from genetic abnormalities. It also discusses the contribution to our development of cultural evolution, a distinctly human mode of inheritance.

Chapter 3, which discusses prenatal development and birth, traces the changes that transform the single cell created at conception into a newborn infant with millions of cells of many kinds.

The process of prenatal development illustrates many principles that will recur in later chapters. For example, the changes in form and activity that distinguish the organism at 5 days from the organism at 5 weeks or 5 months after conception are excellent examples of qualitative changes, changes that distinguish one stage of development from another, as opposed to quantitative changes, which for the most part are merely increases in the developing organism's size. We will also see some important examples of critical periods of development, in particular, the specific time during prenatal growth when the embryo is highly sensitive to hormonal secretions, which trigger the development of new body organs, and to such external agents as drugs that can disrupt organ development.

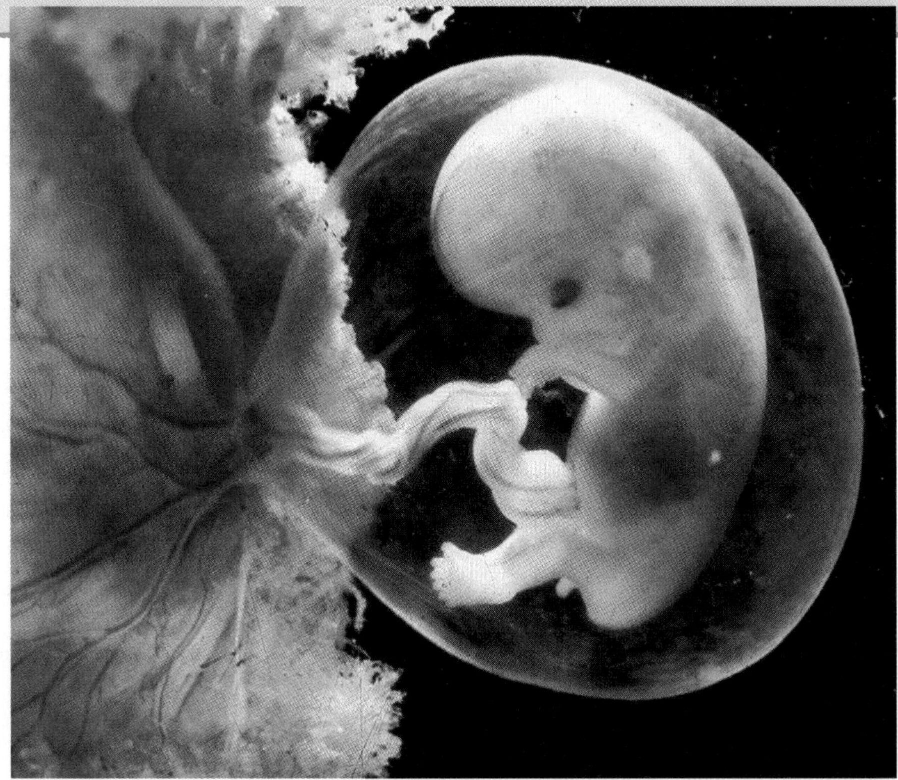

After 9 months of growth and nurturing within the mother's body, chemical changes initiate the birth process. Birth constitutes the first major bio-social-behavioral shift in development. The baby is no longer able to obtain life-giving oxygen and nutrients automatically from the mother's body. Instead, the newborn must use the biological capacities that it developed during the prenatal period to breathe and eat. Other behavioral changes that occur at birth are no less remarkable, as babies gain direct access to the sights, sounds, and smells around them and begin to provide some sights, sounds, and smells of their own! Still, the newborn is completely dependent on others. Without the support of parents who structure their baby's interactions with the environment according to culturally prescribed patterns, the baby would not survive. Parents must feed, clothe, and protect their offspring for many years before they are able to take care of themselves.

Thus begins the lifelong process in which the biological forces that created the new organism at conception interact with the forces of the culturally organized environment that greets the child at birth. Barring unforeseen calamities, in about 20 years the process will begin again with a new generation.

CHAPTER 2

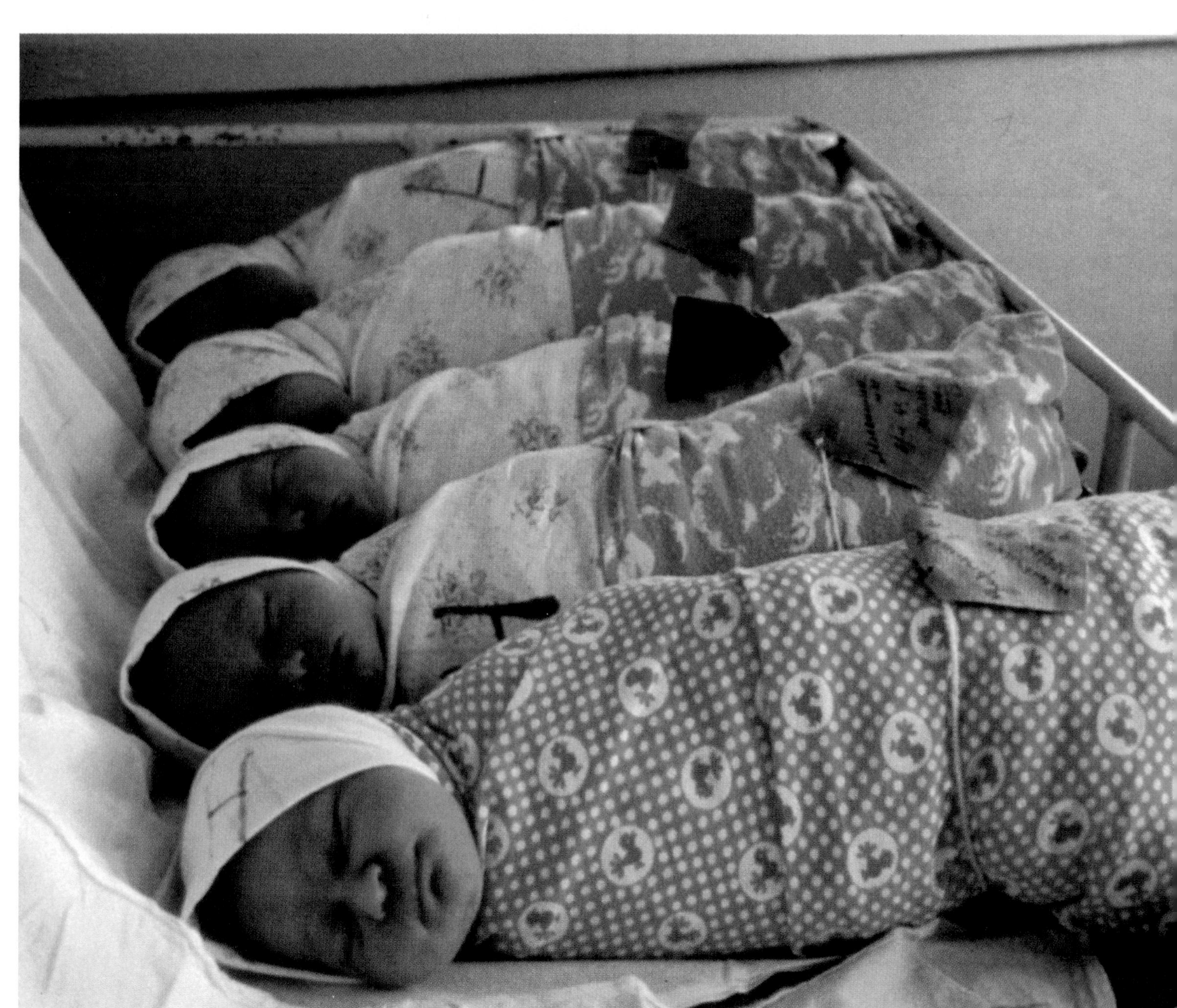

The Human Heritage: Genes and Environment

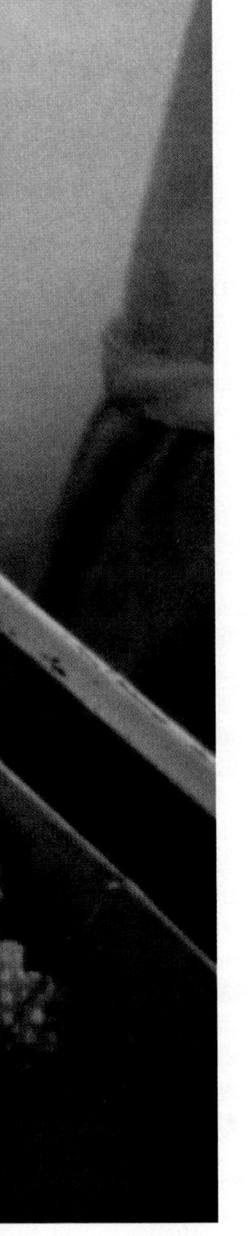

Every child conceived by a given couple is the result of a genetic lottery. He is merely one out of a large crowd of possible children, any one of whom might have been conceived on the same occasion if another of the millions of sperm cells emitted by the father had happened to fertilize the egg cell of the mother—an egg cell which is itself one among many. . . . If we go to all the trouble it takes to mix our genes with those of somebody else, it is in order to make sure that our child will be different from ourselves and from all our other children.

François Jacob, *The Possible and the Actual*

A maternity-ward nursery provides an interesting setting for thinking about the origins and development of human beings. In some racially homogeneous communities, the babies may look and behave so much alike that it is difficult for an observer to tell one from another. In other communities, some babies may be easily distinguished by their skin color. Beyond this, newborns' features and actions give few clues about how each child will look and behave later. Nevertheless, when these infants are mature adults, the differences among them will have increased so much that it will be quite easy to tell them apart. Some will be men, and some will be women; some will be tall, some short; some will have curly hair, some no hair at all. They may speak different languages, engage in different types of work, and enjoy different kinds of food. Some will often be morose, whereas others will usually be cheerful; some will be impulsive, others reflective; some will be gifted at mathematics, others at growing rice or selling stocks. Despite this great variation, none will be mistaken for a member of any other species; all will clearly belong to *Homo sapiens.* Such observations raise a fundamental question about the sources of developmental change: What causes us to be so different from each other but, at the same time, more like each other than like members of any other species?

Both the similarities and the differences among people come ultimately from the interaction between environmental and genetic influences. The similarities that mark us as members of a single species arise both because we inherit our genes from other human beings and because, over the course of human evolution, those genes have interacted within the global environment of the planet Earth. The differences among us come from the same two sources. Due to the process of sexual reproduction, each of us inherits a combination of genes that is, with rare exceptions, unique. The specific environments with which these genes interact also contribute to variations among people by promoting the development of certain characteristics and discouraging that of others. For example, children born into families living deep in the forests of the Amazon basin, where people still live by hunting and gathering, must develop physical endurance and become close observers of nature. Conversely, children born into families living in a North American suburb must develop the ability to sit still for long hours in school in order to acquire the knowledge and skills they will need for economic success as adults. In addition to being shaped by the historical and cultural circumstances in which they live, children are also shaped by their more immediate environments. Within a particular family, for example, each child lives through a unique set of experiences that further influences the characteristics he or she develops (Dunn & McGuire, 1994).

We begin this chapter by discussing sexual reproduction, the mechanism for what this chapter's opening quote calls the "genetic lottery"—the chances

chromosome A threadlike structure made up of genes. In humans, there are 46 chromosomes in every cell, except sperm and ova.

deoxyribonucleic acid (DNA) A long double-stranded molecule that makes up chromosomes.

genes The segments on a DNA molecule that act as hereditary blueprints for the organism's development.

zygote The single cell formed at conception from the union of the sperm and the ovum.

of any given individual's being conceived. We will also consider the basic laws of genetic inheritance to which that "lottery" is subject. Next we will discuss genetic influences and the lifelong process of interaction between genes and environment that shapes development. To illustrate the crucial importance of an individual's genetic constitution and the principles of gene–environment interaction, we will then discuss the origins and effects of genetic abnormalities. Lastly, we will take a look at the way biology and culture interact in the process of human development.

SEXUAL REPRODUCTION AND GENETIC TRANSMISSION

At his climax during sexual intercourse, a man ejaculates about 350 million sperm into a woman's vagina. The head of each tadpole-shaped sperm contains 23 **chromosomes.** Each chromosome is a single molecule of **deoxyribonucleic acid (DNA)**—a long double-stranded molecule in which the two strands twist about each other. Each chromosome, in turn, contains thousands of segments called **genes,** which are the basic unit of heredity. Genes code for sequences of amino acids that form the thousands of proteins from which the body's cells are created, as well as the enzymes that regulate the cells' functioning (see Figure 2.1). The 23 chromosomes carried by the sperm provide half of the genetic information necessary for the development of a new individual. The other half is provided by the woman's ovum (egg), which also has 23 chromosomes and genes that correspond with those carried by the sperm.

Following ejaculation, the sperm attempt to swim up the woman's uterus and into the fallopian tubes. This perilous journey, which represents the final step of the genetic lottery, is completed by only a few hundred of the millions of sperm that began it. Should one of those surviving sperm encounter an ovum and penetrate its membranes, the result is conception: the ovum and sperm fuse to form a **zygote,** a single cell containing 46 chromosomes—23 from the father and 23 from the mother—which are arranged in pairs. All the cells that the child will have at birth come from this single cell with its 23 pairs of chromosomes.

(a)

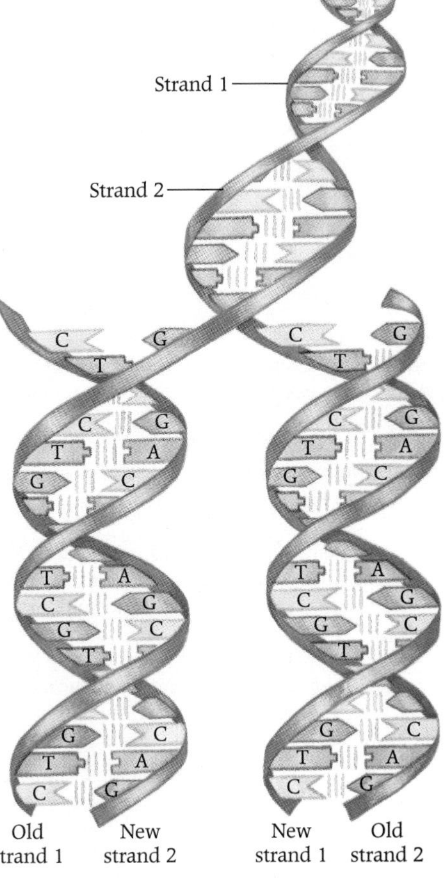

(b)

FIGURE 2.1
(a) A computer-generated, color-coded model of DNA allows researchers to rotate the image and study it from various angles.
(b) A strand of DNA (top) replicates by splitting down the middle of the rungs of its ladder-like structure. Each free base (center) picks up a new complementary partner: cytosine (C) pairs with guanine (G), and adenine (A) pairs with thymine (T).

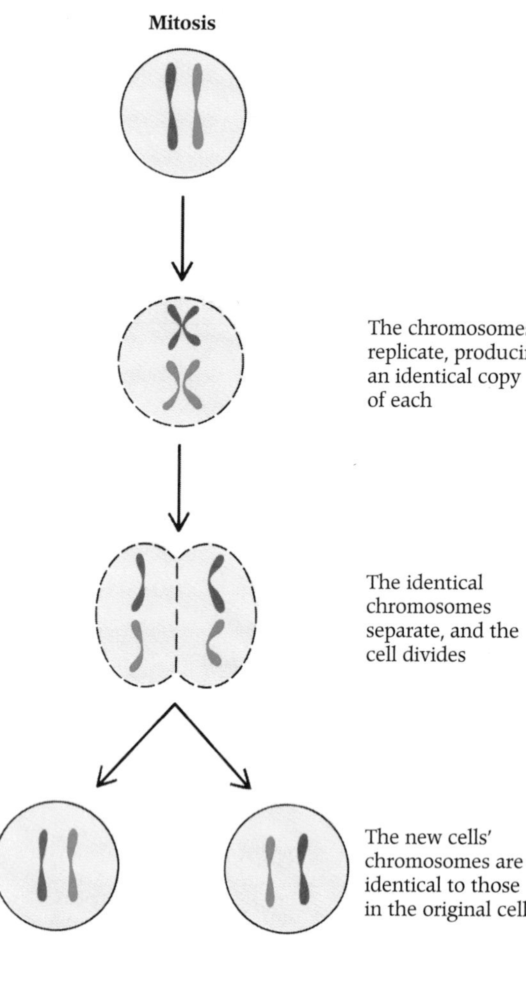

FIGURE 2.2
Mitosis is the process of cell division that generates all the cells of the body except the germ cells. During mitosis each chromosome in the cell replicates, producing a new chromosome identical to the first. The cell then splits, the chromosomes separating so that one of them goes to each new cell. Mitosis ensures that identical genetic information is maintained in the body cells over the life of the organism.

MITOSIS: A PROCESS OF CELL REPLICATION

The zygote creates new cells through **mitosis,** the process of cell duplication and division that generates all the individual's cells except sperm and ova. Mitosis begins within a few hours of conception. The 46 chromosomes move to the middle of the zygote, where they produce exact copies of themselves—a process known as *replication* (see Figure 2.2). These chromosomes separate into two identical sets, which migrate to opposite sides of the cell. The cell then divides in the middle to form two daughter cells, each of which contains 23 pairs of chromosomes (46 chromosomes in all) identical to those inherited at conception. These two daughter cells go through the same process to create two new cells each, which themselves divide as the process repeats itself again and again.

Mitosis continues throughout the life of an individual, creating new **somatic (body) cells** and replacing old ones. Each new somatic cell contains copies of the original 46 chromosomes inherited at conception. Under the ordinary conditions of life, the genetic material carried by our chromosomes is not altered by the passage of time or by the experiences that shape our minds and bodies but is faithfully copied in each instance of mitosis. (Genes can be altered by direct exposure to radiation and to certain chemicals, however. As we will see later in this chapter, the consequences of such changes can be disastrous.)

MEIOSIS: A SOURCE OF VARIABILITY

Although mitosis is responsible for the replication of somatic (body) cells, it is not involved in the replication of **germ cells**—the sperm and ova. If mitosis did govern the production of sperm and ova, the total number of chromosomes inherited by the offspring would double in each succeeding generation. Instead, the germ cells are formed by a cell-division process called **meiosis,** which ensures that the normal zygote contains only 46 chromosomes.

Meiosis represents the initial stage of the genetic lottery. In the first phase of this process, the 23 pairs of chromosomes in the cells that produce sperm or ova duplicate themselves, just as in mitosis. But then the cell divides not once, as in mitosis, but twice, creating *four* daughter cells (see Figure 2.3). Each of these daughter cells contains only 23 unpaired chromosomes—half the original set from the parent cell. Thus when the ova and sperm fuse at conception, the zygote receives a full complement of 46 chromosomes (23 pairs).

Because half of the zygote's chromosomes come from each parent, each newly conceived individual is genetically different from both the father and the mother. This reproductive process creates genetic diversity across generations, enhancing the species' chances for survival. Genetic diversity is further increased by a processes called **crossing over,** in which genetic material is exchanged between a pair of chromosomes during the first phase of meiosis.

mitosis The process of cell duplication and division that generates all the individual's cells except sperm and ova.

somatic (body) cells All the cells in the body except for the germ cells (ova and sperm).

germ cells The sperm and ova, which are specialized for sexual reproduction and have half the number of chromosomes normal for a species.

meiosis The process that produces sperm and ova, each of which contains only half of the parent cell's original complement of 46 chromosomes.

crossing over The process in which genetic material is exchanged between chromosomes containing genes for the same characteristic.

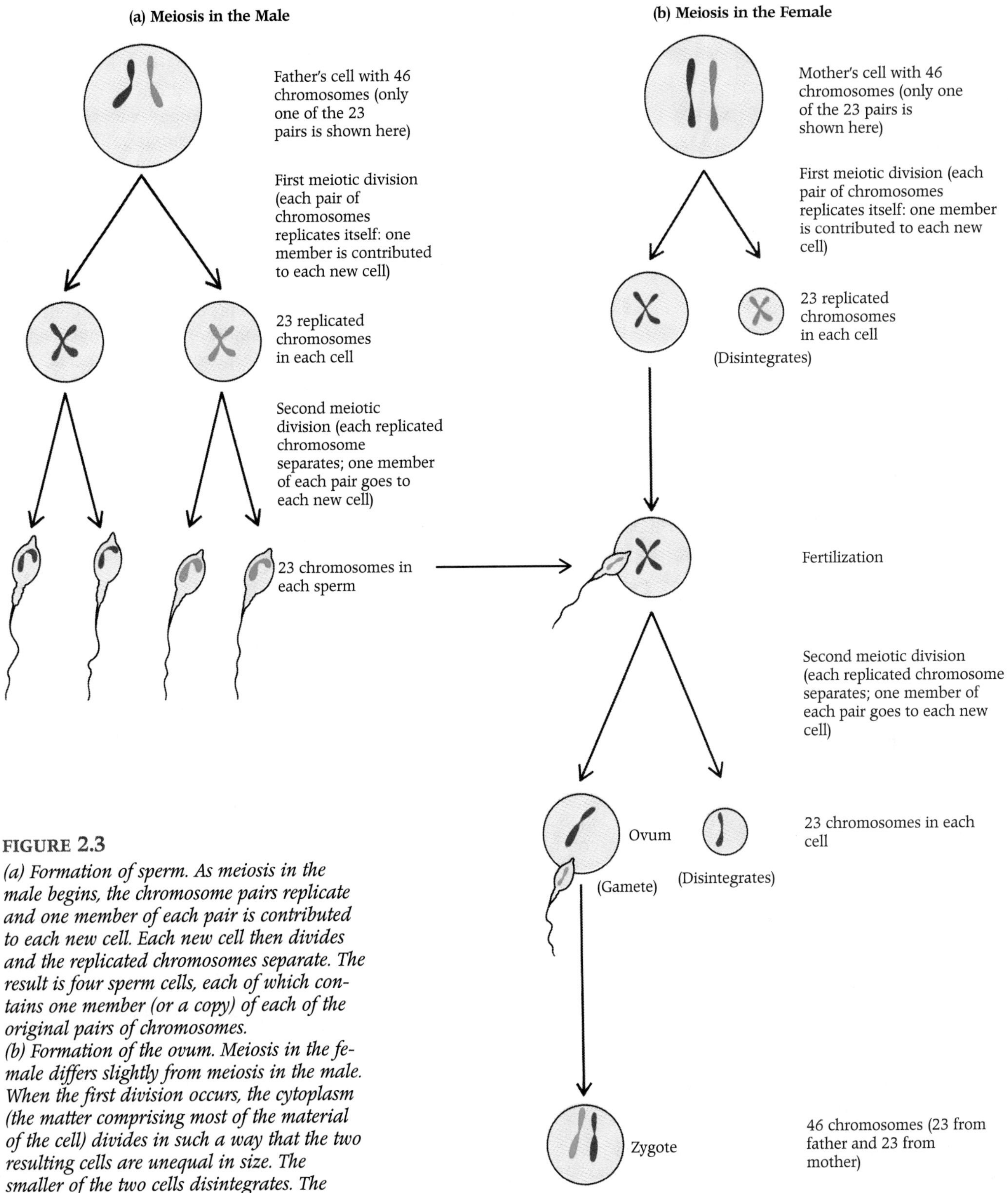

(a) Meiosis in the Male

Father's cell with 46 chromosomes (only one of the 23 pairs is shown here)

First meiotic division (each pair of chromosomes replicates itself: one member is contributed to each new cell)

23 replicated chromosomes in each cell

Second meiotic division (each replicated chromosome separates; one member of each pair goes to each new cell)

23 chromosomes in each sperm

(b) Meiosis in the Female

Mother's cell with 46 chromosomes (only one of the 23 pairs is shown here)

First meiotic division (each pair of chromosomes replicates itself: one member is contributed to each new cell)

23 replicated chromosomes in each cell

(Disintegrates)

Fertilization

Second meiotic division (each replicated chromosome separates; one member of each pair goes to each new cell)

Ovum

(Gamete)

(Disintegrates)

23 chromosomes in each cell

Zygote

46 chromosomes (23 from father and 23 from mother)

FIGURE 2.3

(a) Formation of sperm. As meiosis in the male begins, the chromosome pairs replicate and one member of each pair is contributed to each new cell. Each new cell then divides and the replicated chromosomes separate. The result is four sperm cells, each of which contains one member (or a copy) of each of the original pairs of chromosomes.

(b) Formation of the ovum. Meiosis in the female differs slightly from meiosis in the male. When the first division occurs, the cytoplasm (the matter comprising most of the material of the cell) divides in such a way that the two resulting cells are unequal in size. The smaller of the two cells disintegrates. The large cell, the ovum, does not divide again unless it is fertilized. If fertilization occurs, the replicated chromosomes in the ovum separate into two new cells. Again the cytoplasm divides unequally, and the smaller of the resulting cells disintegrates. The 23 chromosomes of the larger cell fuse with the 23 chromosomes of the sperm to form the zygote with its 46 chromosomes.

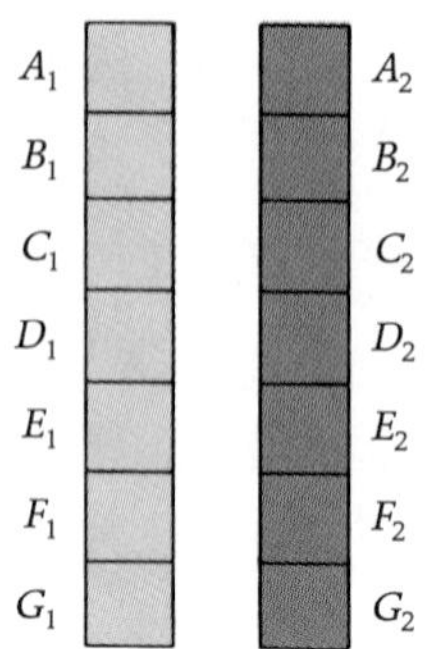

STEP 1
Each chromosome pair aligns before segregation into separate germ cells (letters designate different genes)

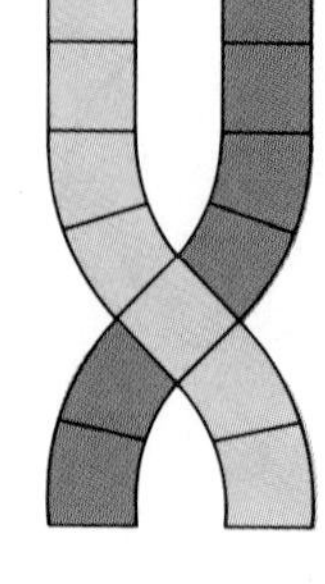

STEP 2
The chromosomes cross

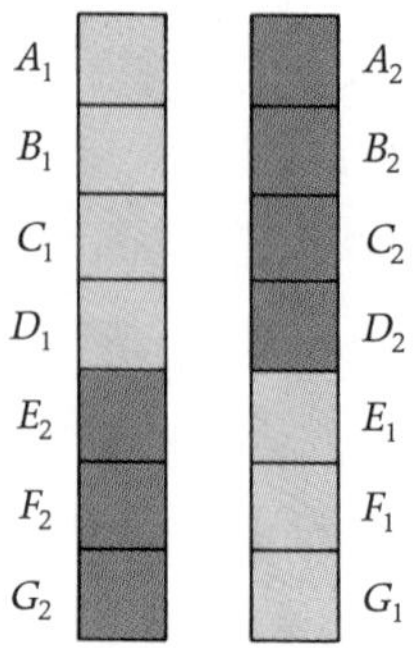

STEP 3
Chromosomes break at the point of crossing, exchange genetic material, and segregate into separate germ cells

FIGURE 2.4

The crossing-over process. (From Shaffer, 1985.)

While the pair of chromosomes, each containing genes that influence the same particular characteristics, lie side by side, a section of one of the chromosomes may change places with the corresponding section of the other chromosome (see Figure 2.4). This exchange alters the genetic composition of each of the two chromosomes; genes originally carried on one chromosome are now carried on the other.

We can now better appreciate the extreme improbability that genes of any two children, even siblings, will be exactly alike, except in the special case of monozygotic twins (see Box 2.1). Although we receive 23 chromosomes from each of our parents, it is a matter of chance which member of any pair of chromosomes ends up in a given germ cell during meiosis. According to the laws of probability, there are 2^{23}, or about 8 million, possible genetic combinations for each sperm and ovum, so there is at best 1 chance in 64 trillion that a particular genetic combination will be repeated (Scheinfeld, 1972).

SEXUAL DETERMINATION: A CASE OF VARIABILITY

In 22 of the 23 pairs of chromosomes found in a human cell, the two chromosomes are similar in type; that is, they are of the same size and shape and carry corresponding genes. Chromosomes of the twenty-third pair may differ, however. This pair of chromosomes determines a person's genetic sex, a crucial source of variety in our species. In normal females, both members of the twenty-third pair of chromosomes are of the same type and are called **X chromosomes.** The normal male, however, has just one X chromosome paired with a different, much smaller chromosome called a **Y chromosome** (see Figure 2.5). Since a female is always XX, each of her eggs contains an X chromosome. In contrast, half of a man's sperm carry an X chromosome and half

X and Y chromosomes The two chromosomes that determine the sex of the individual. Normal females have two X chromosomes, while normal males have one Y chromosome inherited from their fathers and one X chromosome inherited from their mothers.

FIGURE 2.5

Human X (above) and Y (below) chromosomes. Note how much larger the X chromosome is. Males have both an X and a Y chromosome but females have two X chromosomes.

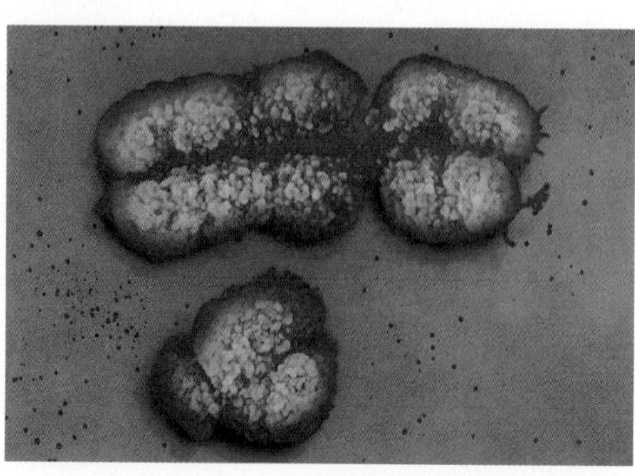

TABLE 2.1 APPROXIMATE SEX RATIOS FOR THE U.S. WHITE POPULATION

Age	Male : Female
Conception	120 : 100
Birth	106 : 100
18 Years	100 : 100
50 Years	95 : 100
67 Years	70 : 100
87 Years	50 : 100
100 Years	21 : 100

Note: Are females really the majority? In the adult population, yes. The facts that more male babies are conceived than born, and that the ratio of males to females declines over the life span, appears to reflect the greater vulnerability of males to genetic diseases and other life-threatening conditions (McKusick, 1975). The ratio of males to females at birth can also be influenced by cultural factors, as recently developed methods of identifying the sex of the fetus lead to selective abortion in societies where males are more highly valued than females (Hsi & Adinolfi, 1997). Source of statistics: Lerner & Libby (1976).

carry a Y chromosome. If a sperm containing an X chromosome fertilizes the egg, the resulting child will be XX, a female. If the sperm contains a Y chromosome, the child will be XY, a male. Given this fact, it might seem that each conception has a 50–50 chance of resulting in a boy or a girl. As Table 2.1 indicates, however, many more male than female zygotes are conceived, and slightly more boys than girls are actually born (Motulsky, 1986).

monozygotic twins Twins that come from one zygote and therefore have identical genotypes.

dizygotic twins Twins that come from two zygotes.

BOX 2.1

TWINNING

During the first few mitotic divisions after the zygote is formed, the daughter cells occasionally separate completely and develop into separate individuals. When such a division results in two individuals, they are called **monozygotic twins,** because they are twins that have come from one zygote. Having originated from the same zygote, monozygotic twins inherit identical genetic information. Thus they potentially have the same physical and psychological makeup, susceptibility to disease, and life expectancy. Monozygotic twins occur about once in every 250 conceptions. The reason for the separation of cells after the first few mitotic divisions is not known.

Most twins originate not from a single zygote but rather from two zygotes formed by the fertilization of two separate ova. Because these twins—referred to as **dizygotic twins**—come from different zygotes, they are no more alike at birth than are any other children of the same parents. Unlike the case with monozygotic twins, dizygotic twinning is known to be influenced by a number of factors, including race, heredity, the mother's age, the number of prior pregnancies, and the use of fertility drugs. African American women, mothers who are themselves dizygotic twins, women between 35 and 40 years of age, women who have had four or more children, and those who have taken fertility drugs are all more likely to give birth to dizygotic twins.

As discussed in the text, twins are of special interest to psychologists because a knowledge of their similarities and differences can help answer questions about the influences of nature and nurture.

These dizygotic twins illustrate the great potential for variety in two individuals conceived by parents at the same time.

Monozygotic twins not only look alike naturally, they can sometimes be dressed alike and treated similarly by others so that their similarity is accentuated.

Gregor Mendel, discoverer of the basic principles of genetics.

GENOTYPE AND PHENOTYPE

The ways in which genes influence development must be understood at two levels. One level is the **genotype**, the individual's genetic endowment or, in other words, the particular gene forms that the individual has inherited. The genotype is constant over the lifetime of the individual. The second level is the **phenotype**, the observable characteristics of the individual—his or her physical and psychological traits, health, and behavior. The phenotype develops through interactions between the genotype and the **environment**—the totality of conditions and circumstances that surround the organism. We will turn our attention first to the mechanisms of genetic inheritance and to the laws that govern them; then we will consider the ways in which genetic inheritance expresses itself through interaction with the environment.

THE LAWS OF GENETIC INHERITANCE

Scientific understanding of the mechanisms by which parents transmit their genetic material to the next generation dates from pioneering studies by Gregor Mendel (1822–1884). Through experiments in which he cross-bred varieties of garden peas, Mendel deduced that parents transmit certain traits to their offspring, and he proposed that they do so through discrete physical entities that he referred to as "characters." It was not until many years later that Mendel's hypothetical "characters" were shown to operate in humans and to correspond to actual physical structures—gene-carrying chromosomes in the nucleus of the cell.

In the simplest form of hereditary transmission, a single pair of genes, one from each parent, contributes to a particular inherited characteristic. Genes that influence a specific trait (for example, the presence or absence of a cleft in the chin) can have the same or different forms, called **alleles.** When the corresponding genes inherited from the two parents are of the same allelic form (both "cleft" or both "noncleft"), the person is said to be **homozygous** for the trait. When the alleles are different (one "cleft" and one "noncleft"), the person is said to be **heterozygous** for the trait. The distinction between homozygous and heterozygous allele pairing is essential for understanding how different combinations of genes produce different characteristics.

When a child is homozygous for a trait with particular characteristics that is affected by a single pair of alleles, only one outcome is possible: the child will display the particular characteristics associated with that allele. When a child is heterozygous for such a trait, one of three outcomes is possible:

1. The child will display the particular characteristics that are associated with only one of the two alleles. The allele whose characteristics are expressed is referred to as a **dominant allele,** and the allele whose characteristics are not expressed is called a **recessive allele.**
2. The child will be affected by both alleles and will display characteristics that are intermediate between those "called for" by the two alleles.
3. The child will display characteristics that are affected by both alleles, but rather than being intermediate, the characteristics will be distinctively different from those linked to either contributing allele. This outcome is **codominance.**

The inheritance of blood type illustrates the homozygous outcome and two of the heterozygous outcomes. There are *three* alleles for blood type—A, B, and O—and four basic blood types—A, B, AB, and O. If children receive two type A, two type B, or two type O alleles, they are homozygous for the trait and will have type A, type B, or type O blood, respectively. But if they inherit either the type A or the type B allele from one parent and the type O allele

---

genotype The genetic endowment of an individual.

phenotype The organism's observable characteristics that result from the interaction of the genotype with the environment.

environment The totality of conditions and circumstances that surround the organism.

allele An alternate form of a gene coded for a particular trait.

homozygous Having inherited two genes of the same allelic form for a trait.

heterozygous Having inherited two genes of different allelic form for a trait.

dominant allele The allele that is expressed when an individual possesses two different alleles for the same trait.

recessive allele The allele that is not expressed when an individual possesses two different alleles for the same trait.

codominance A trait that is determined by two alleles but is different from the trait produced by either of the contributing alleles alone.

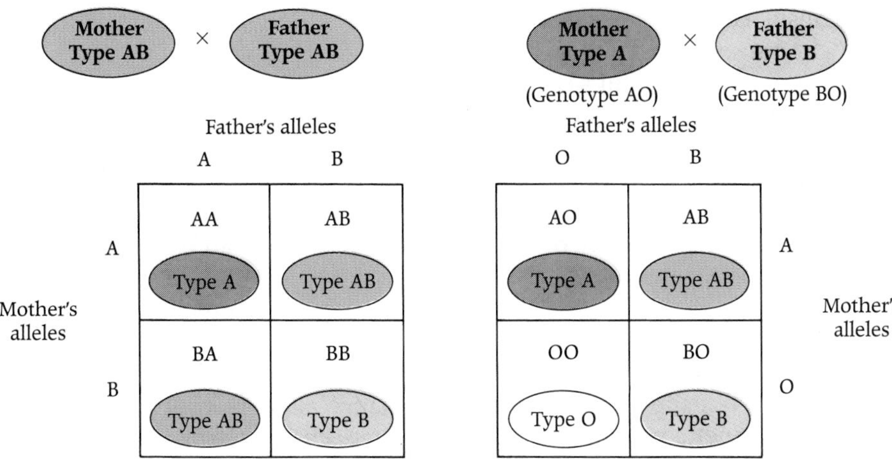

FIGURE 2.6
Inheritance of alleles for blood type. The alternative forms of a gene for blood type, inherited in various combinations from the parents, produce different blood phenotypes. The combination of one allele from each parent is the genotype, and the resulting blood type of the child is the phenotype.

from the other, they will have type A or type B blood, even though their genetic code for blood type is AO or BO. The O allele is recessive, so it does not affect the exhibited blood type. Finally, if children inherit one type A allele and one type B allele, they will exhibit a codominant outcome—type AB blood, which is qualitatively different from either type A or type B blood. Figure 2.6 shows some of the outcomes of various combinations of the three alleles for blood type.

The case of blood types provides a good way to illustrate the study of the laws of genetic inheritance because it involves a well-known and simple set of relationships, but it also greatly oversimplifies the picture of human genetic inheritance. This is true, in part, because most traits are *polygenic.* A **polygenic trait** involves not two or three genes but several—perhaps even hundreds in the case of complex behavioral traits.

Sex-Linked Genetic Effects

Some inherited human characteristics are affected by genes found on only the X or the Y chromosome and are thus called **sex-linked characteristics.** Most of these inherited sex-linked characteristics are carried on the X chromosome (as we have seen, it is much larger than the Y chromosome). Because females receive two X chromosomes, they get two sets of corresponding X-chromosome sex-linked genes, one from each of their parents, as with the genes on any of the other chromosomes. But because normal males receive only one X chromosome, they have only one of each gene that is on the X chromosome, which always comes from their mothers.

This asymmetry in genetic material makes males susceptible to genetic defects that ordinarily do not affect females. If a daughter has a harmful recessive gene on one X chromosome, she will usually have a normal dominant gene on the other X chromosome to override it. Thus the recessive gene is not expressed at the phenotypic level. However, a son who inherits a harmful recessive gene on his X chromosome has no such complementary allele to override the recessive gene's harmful effects. Or, if a gene is missing from the X chromosome, males will not have another copy to code for the trait in question. Red-green color blindness is an example of such a sex-linked recessive trait. It is caused by the absence of genetic material that codes for color-absorbing pigments in the retina of the eye. For a daughter to exhibit this trait, she must be homozygous for it; that is, she must have a father who is red-green color blind and a mother who is either color blind or heterozygous for the trait. By contrast, if a son receives the gene for red-green color blindness on the X chromosome he inherits from his mother, he will be unable to

polygenic trait A genetic trait that is determined by the interaction of several genes.

sex-linked characteristics Traits determined by genes that are found on only the X or the Y chromosome.

behavioral geneticist A researcher who studies how genetic and environmental factors combine to produce individual differences in behavior.

distinguish red from green light because there is no corresponding gene on the Y chromosome that will enable him to see red and green light.

Other, more harmful sex-linked traits that primarily affect males include hemophilia (a defect that delays the clotting of the blood), certain types of night blindness, atrophy of the optic nerve, hypogammaglobulin (the inability of the body to produce the antibodies necessary to fight bacterial infections), vitamin D resistance (which causes rickets), Duchenne's muscular dystrophy (a progressive wasting away of the muscles that leads to an early death), and some forms of diabetes (Motulsky, 1986).

GENES, THE ORGANISM, AND THE ENVIRONMENT

Knowledge about the laws of genetic inheritance alone is insufficient for understanding genetic influences on an individual's characteristics. We must also take into account the effects of the environment in all its myriad forms. *Genes do not exist in isolation; they exist only within an environment. It is only through the interactions of their genes with their environments—from the intracellular to the ecological and cultural levels—that organisms are able to develop.*

Studying Gene–Environment Interactions

The relation of genes to their environments is complex and multileveled. As we mentioned at the beginning of the chapter, genes are merely chemical codes that specify the sequences of amino acids in the proteins produced by cells. Cells, in turn, provide the immediate environment in which the genes exist. Thus the genes and the cell material are in constant interaction. The system of cells as a whole—the organism—is also in constant interaction with its environment. The interactions of the organism with its larger environment determine the conditions of the individual cells and hence the immediate environment of the genes (Futuyma, 1998).

Behavioral geneticists, developmentalists who seek to understand how genetic and environmental factors combine to produce individual differences in behavior, have identified several principles that apply to these interactions (Rutter et al., 1997). One principle is that interactions between organisms and their environments need to be studied in a broad, ecological framework because variations in the environment at any level can have profound effects on the development of the phenotype. Albert Winchester (1972) vividly demonstrated this principle in a set of experiments with Himalayan rabbits. The Himalayan rabbit normally has a white body and black ears, nose, feet, and tail. The rabbit's extremities are normally colder than the rest of its body, and this uneven distribution of temperatures causes the typical variations in its coat. If a patch of the white fur on a rabbit's back is removed and an ice pack is kept placed over the area until new fur grows in, the new fur will be black (see Figure 2.7). This result shows that the phenotype for fur color depends on the temperature at the specific site where hair grows. In other words, while the

(a)

(b)

(c)

FIGURE 2.7
The effect of environment on the expression of a gene for fur color in the Himalayan rabbit. Under normal conditions (a) only the rabbit's feet, tail, ears, and nose are black. If fur is removed from a patch on the rabbit's back and an ice pack is placed there, creating a cold local environment, (b) the new fur that grows in is black (c). (Adapted from Winchester, 1972.)

The kinds of gene–environment interactions that enable a child to manipulate a stick depend greatly on the cultural context that specifies how the stick is to be used. Note the differences associated with cultural context among three Pacific Island nations: Japan, Indonesia, and Tonga.

gene for black color is expressed at the phenotypic level only at low temperatures, it is not sufficient simply to specify the temperature of the rabbit's general environment to predict the color of its fur; the temperatures at *specific sites* on the rabbit are the relevant environments for predicting the expression of the gene for black fur.

A second principle of gene–environment interaction, is that this *inter*action is indeed a *two-way* process. For example, certain people are genetically predisposed to become depressed when they have stressful experiences. But, at the same time, the occurrence of depression increases the likelihood of stressful experiences. Songbirds inherit genes that may result in their acquiring the phenotypic sounds of "their" song, but only if they are exposed to the songs of their species (Mello et al., 1992). Rats inherit genes that may support using their whiskers to explore the environment, but these genes are not expressed in the rat's sensory cortex until the rats' whiskers have been stimulated (Mack & Mack, 1992). Both directions of influence, organism → environment and environment → organism, must be taken into account.

A third principle of gene–environment interaction is that genetic factors often play a role in determining what environments individuals inhabit and how they shape and select their own experiences (Scarr & McCartney, 1983). Children who, partly for genetic reasons, respond positively to high levels of stimulation may like to listen to music that is loud and raucous, and this in turn can influence their choice of peers with whom to spend time, as well as which peers choose to spend time with them.

These principles make it clear that developmentalists must keep a multitude of factors in mind as they seek to understand the dynamic process by which genes and the environment interact over the course of development.

Range of Reaction

In order to encompass the full variety of interactions that can occur between genes and the environment, developmentalists seek to investigate as many combinations of gene–environment interactions as possible. When conducting research on gene–environment interactions in such organisms as plants, fruit

range of reaction All the possible phenotypes for a single genotype that are compatible with the continued life of the organism.

canalization The process that makes some traits relatively invulnerable to environmental events.

flies, and mice, geneticists use two approaches to meet this goal. In one they attempt to keep the environment constant so that any variation in phenotype can be attributed to variations in the genes. In the other they keep the genotype constant while they vary the environment so that variations in the phenotype can be attributed to variations in the environment. The first procedure highlights genetic influences on development; the second highlights the influences of the environment. Either approach by itself would give us only a partial picture of gene–environment interaction, but by combining the two approaches, the double-sided nature of gene–environment interactions can be revealed.

By charting the changes that occur in the phenotype as the environment of a particular genotype is varied, researchers can discover the **range of reaction** for that genotype. Ideally, this range represents all the possible gene–environment relationships that are compatible with the continued life of the organism, so that it includes all the possible developmental outcomes. In the case of the Himalayan rabbit, the range of reaction for fur color would be bounded at one end by the temperature at which the rabbit would freeze to death and at the other end by the temperature that would be too high to permit it to live. As the temperature approaches the lower boundary, we would expect the rabbit's fur to be predominantly black. As the temperature approaches the higher boundary, even the extremities might remain white. The variations in the phenotypic expression of fur color as the temperature is varied from one extreme to the other is the range of reaction for the Himalayan rabbit's genotype for fur color.

Canalization

The concept of the range of reaction focuses attention on the wide array of possible phenotypes that can result from the combination of a given genotype and the range of environments that can sustain the life of the organism. The developmental geneticist Conrad Waddington (1947) introduced the notion of **canalization** to highlight another aspect of gene–environment interactions: the fact that certain characteristics typical of a species may be restricted to a narrow range despite wide variations in environmental conditions. Just as a canal channels the flow of water into a narrow range, the genes affecting canalized traits channel the development of those traits so that they vary little in response to environmental events. The capacity of developing children to acquire language is often cited as an example of a canalized developmental process in humans. As we shall see in Chapter 8, children in all societies not only acquire language without needing deliberate instruction, they even acquire language when they suffer from mental retardation or when input from the environment is greatly reduced by loss of hearing. Only the most severe and prolonged deprivation of language input seems capable of deflecting language development from its species-typical developmental path.

Canalized processes also exhibit a strong tendency to self-correct after the organism is exposed to deviant experiences. Physical growth is an example of this principle. During an illness or a period of starvation, children's physical growth slows down, but when they recover or begin eating again, they grow at a faster rate than usual until they catch up with their original growth curves. When development is not highly canalized, variability in the environment produces more frequent and more marked differences between individuals, and self-correction is less likely to occur in the wake of any unusual experiences.

Waddington thought that canalization is the product of genetic mechanisms, but Gilbert Gottlieb (1997) has argued that canalization can also result from early developmental experiences. He demonstrated that if mallard ducklings are not exposed early in life to the species-specific sounds of their mother's assembly call, they may instead respond to the call of a female of some other species and adhere to that species' call for the rest of their lives.

The Study of Genetic Influences on Human Behavior

The task of applying the principles of genetics to human beings is a difficult matter, both ethically and scientifically. Ethically, the study of human behavioral genetics is restricted by the impossibility of carrying out the experiments needed to establish a range of reaction. Such experiments would fit the logical needs of science, but they would also require totalitarian control over the lives of research subjects and would expose children to dangerous environments purely for the purpose of scientific interest. Obviously, such experiments would be immoral and should not be carried out.

Scientifically, the impossibility of using experimental control to measure the ranges of reaction for human behavioral characteristics deprives behavioral geneticists of strict causal analysis. As a consequence, their conclusions about the role of genes with respect to behavioral characteristics such as mental retardation, language delay, temperament, and so on, are likely to use the phrase "genetically *influenced*" or "*heritable*" rather than "genetically *caused*." There are additional good reasons for this care in the use of words.

First, behavioral geneticists know that, with rare exceptions, they cannot specify exactly which genes are associated with the behavior in question, nor can they provide a detailed description of the environments within which genes find their specific expression. Second, any behavior that shows a large range of individual differences—shyness, say—is almost certainly influenced by multiple genes in interaction with the environment. Consequently, when a behavioral geneticist says that a characteristic such as shyness is "genetically influenced," this does not mean that a gene or set of genes that corresponds to shyness has been discovered. Nor does it mean that the environment plays no role in producing shyness. Rather, it means that there is a statistical correlation between a behavioral characteristic called shyness and the genetic variation in the population being studied (see Box 2.2). To determine such a correlation, behavioral geneticists rely on kinship studies.

Estimating Genetic Influence through Kinship Studies

Behavioral geneticists make use of the naturally occurring conditions provided by kinship relationships to estimate the genetic and environmental contributions to a particular phenotype (Plomin et al., 1997). That is, they determine the degree to which relatives of varying degrees of genetic closeness are similar on a given trait. Parents and their children share 50 percent of their genes; siblings also share 50 percent of their genes—except for identical twins, who share 100 percent of their genes; half siblings share 25 percent of their genes; and so on. If the degree of similarity on the trait correlates with the degree of genetic closeness, it can be inferred that the trait is heritable. Behavioral geneticists examine the similarity among relatives using three types of kinship designs: family, twin, and adoption.

In the typical **family study**, relatives who live together in a household—parents, offspring, half offspring—are compared with one another to determine how similar they are on a given trait. The shortcoming of family studies for estimating the *degree* of genetic influence is the obvious fact that parents and siblings not only share genes but also participate in the same family environment. Thus whatever similarities are found among them could be attributed to environmental influences as well as to hereditary ones.

In order to obtain more precise estimates of genetic and environmental contributions to individual differences, behavioral geneticists capitalize on two related strategies. One is the **twin study**, in which groups of monozygotic (identical) twins and dizygotic (fraternal) twins of the same sex are compared with each other and to other types of kin relationships for similarity on a given trait. Since monozygotic twins have 100 percent of their genes in common, whereas dizygotic twins (and other siblings) share 50 percent of their

heritability A measure of the degree to which a variation in a particular trait among individuals in a specific population is related to genetic differences among those individuals.

eugenics A policy of attempting to rid the gene pool of genes considered undesirable by preventing individuals who have the genes from reproducing, thereby ensuring that these genes are not passed on to the next generation.

family study A study that compares members of the same family to determine how similar they are on a given trait.

twin study A study in which groups of monozygotic (identical) and dizygotic (fraternal) twins of the same sex are compared with each other and to other family members for similarity on a given trait.

BOX 2.2 THE CONCEPT OF HERITABILITY AND MYTHS ABOUT GENETIC INFLUENCES

In their research on genetic influences, behavioral geneticists study relatively large samples of families, sometimes several thousand (McGue et al., 1993). These large numbers allow them to apply the techniques of mathematical statistics to arrive at a quantitative estimate of heritability.

Heritability refers to the degree to which variation in a particular characteristic among individuals in a specific population (such as shyness) is related to genetic differences among those individuals. Heritability is often represented by a statistical measure called a *heritability coefficient,* referred to as h^2. In mathematical terms, h^2 is defined as the proportion of variation in a behavior or trait, within a population, that can be attributed to genetic variation. As a formula, it is written

$$h^2 = \frac{\text{Variance due to genes}}{\text{Total variance}}$$

The denominator (total variance) can be calculated directly from the measurements of the trait in question obtained from all the individuals in the sample. The numerator (variance due to genes) cannot be directly calculated. It must be estimated by comparing individuals who differ in their degree of genetic relationship to each other (Plomin et al., 1997).

Using this formulation, behavioral geneticists have calculated h^2 for a number of human characteristics, ranging from height, which for North Americans is about 90 percent, to personality traits such as conscientiousness, which is estimated at around 38 percent. Again, bear in mind that heritability is a population statistic. It does not apply to individual cases. To say that height is 90 percent heritable does not mean that in someone who is 72 inches tall, $64\frac{1}{2}$ of those inches are attributable to genes and the rest to the environment. Rather, it means that for the population as a whole, 90 percent of the variation from the average height is the result of genetic factors. The reason for the high heritability of height in the United States is the relative lack of environmental diversity; that is, nutritional levels are much the same throughout the population. This fact highlights another important principle of heritability: Heritability decreases as environmental diversity increases; and heritability increases as genetic diversity increases and environmental diversity decreases.

The increasing use of quantitative measures of heritability in the study of human development, and the potential confusion surrounding their use, have led Michael Rutter and Robert Plomin to warn against a number of widespread misconceptions about the nature of genetic influences on behavior (Rutter & Plomin, 1997). Their major points are summarized below.

Myth 1: Heritability estimates have a "true" fixed value for each trait.

Finding significant heritability for a trait does not mean that the trait has some "true" level of heritability that holds true for all times, places, and populations. As Rutter and Plomin (1997) explain, "Estimates of heritability apply only to the population studied at that particular time, and under the environmental conditions that prevail at that point" (p. 209). For example, in studies conducted in the United States, estimates of the heritability of intelligence (as measured by IQ scores) increase between the ages of 16 and 20 presumably because there are significant increases in the range of environments inhabited by young people during this period of their lives (McGue, 1995).

Myth 2: High heritability means that environmental interventions will be ineffective.

Many people have argued that a trait that is highly heritable is relatively immune to environmental influences. This is simply not true. The most prominent example of a highly heritable trait associated with strikingly different phenotypes is height. The heritability for height in North America at present is 90 percent, but there has been a large increase in height in many nations during the twentieth century owing to improved nutrition (Tizard, 1975).

Myth 3: High heritability within populations means that differences between populations are also genetically determined.

It cannot be too heavily emphasized that h^2 is derived from variations among people *within* a given population. There are also, of course, average differences in the manifestation of various traits *between* populations. A common mistake is to assume that high heritability on a given trait within groups means that differences *between* two groups on that trait are genetically based. This mistake is often made in discussions of IQ (which we deal with at length in Chapter 13). The h^2 for IQ test performance during childhood is approximately 0.50 and there are significant differences between various population groups in their average IQ test performances (Japanese as a group, for example, score higher than North Americans, and white Americans as a group score higher than African Americans). Knowing the h^2 of individual differences *within* the groups tells you nothing about the cause of the average differences *between* these groups because they are likely to differ in their environmental circumstances.

adoption study A study in which genetically related individuals who are raised in different family environments are compared to determine the extent to which heredity or environment controls a given trait.

genes, monozygotic twins raised together should show greater similarity than dizygotic twins or siblings, insofar as genetic differences contribute to the trait being compared. By the same logic, dizygotic twins and siblings should be more similar than half sisters and half brothers.

The second strategy is the **adoption study,** which compares children reared apart from their biological parents. Some adoption studies compare

Myth 4: Genetic effects are determinative.

Many people incorrectly assume that there is a one-to-one correspondence between a gene and a disorder associated with it. They assume that if you inherit the gene, you inherit the disorder. There are examples of this kind of correspondence, such as Huntington's disease, but such cases are rare. Even if only a few genes are associated with a disorder and the environment is held constant, the effects from person to person are likely to vary at the level of the phenotype. In addition, most disorders are determined by *many* genes acting in concert with an ensemble of environmental influences; this is the case for common medical conditions such as diabetes, hypertension, and asthma, as well as for such mental illnesses as depression.

Myth 5: Genes associated with a disease must be bad.

It seems natural to suppose that genes associated with a disease are bad for development. That myth is incorrect in two ways. First, some genes associated with a disease actually operate protectively. For example, about half the people in China and Japan possess an allele that blocks the metabolism of alcohol if the person is homozygous for it. If a person carrying this form of the gene drinks alcohol, the disruption of alcohol metabolism results in unpleasant symptoms such as flushing and nausea (McGue, 1993). It is believed that this genetic variant is responsible for the relatively low rates of alcoholism in Asian populations (Hodgkinson et al., 1991).

Second, the same genetic influence may be a risk factor for certain behavioral outcomes but a protective factor for others. This is true of shyness, which is a risk factor for anxiety disorder but a protective factor against antisocial behavior (Biederman et al., 1995).

Myth 6: "Bad" genes justify both eugenic programs and termination of pregnancy.

Eugenics is the policy of attempting to rid the gene pool of genes considered undesirable by preventing individuals who have the genes from mating or by aborting fetuses known to carry particular genes, thereby ensuring that these genes are not passed on to the next generation. Eugenics is a bad idea based on a basic misunderstanding of the nature of heritability. First, many genetically related diseases arise from genetic anomalies and mutations that *are not inherited* (for example, Down syndrome). Second, as we have seen, genes are only probabilistically related to phenotypes and are only one of many risk factors for any disease. That eugenics is an ill-conceived notion is highlighted by the fact that we all carry some "risk" genes that make us more susceptible to harmful phenotypes. We usually do not realize we carry such risk genes because they have not led to a particular disease—either because we do not have the other required risk genes or we have not encountered the specific environment that would lead to their expression.

Myth 7: Gene therapy will be widely applicable.

It is often assumed that once the genetic basis of many diseases has been determined, it will be possible to modify the involved genes early in development. There is the possibility that in the very near future defective genes can be replaced with normal genes through gene therapy (Birnstiel, 1996; Crystal, 1995). In some circumstances this technique may be useful. It is doubtful, however, that gene therapy will have any significant place in the treatment of most disorders that are caused by the interaction of many genes and the environment.

"The good news is that you will have a healthy baby girl. The bad news is that she is a congenital liar."

Drawing by Handelsmann; ©1996. The New Yorker Magazine, Inc.

twins or siblings who have been adopted into different families. Other adoption studies compare biologically unrelated parents and children living in the same family. The basic purpose of this strategy is to determine if adopted children are more similar to their biological parents and siblings, who share their genes, or to their adoptive parents and siblings, with whom they share a common family environment.

TABLE 2.2 FAMILY AND ADOPTION RESULTS FOR EXTROVERSION

Type of Relative	Actual Correlation	Percentage of Shared Genes
MZ twins raised together	.51	100
DZ twins raised together	.18	50
MZ twins raised apart	.38	100
DZ twins raised apart	.05	50
Parents/children living together	.16	50
Adoptive parents and children	.01	00
Siblings raised together	.20	50
Siblings raised apart	−.07	50

Source: Loehlin, 1992.

Many studies using family, twin, and adoption strategies have shown that the degree of similarity among kin decreases as the degree of genetic similarity decreases. This pattern has been obtained for such varied characteristics as personality (Bouchard, 1994), intelligence (as measured by IQ scores) (Plomin & DeFries, 1983; Scarr & Weinberg, 1983), the perception of self-worth (McGuire et al., 1994), and susceptibility to schizophrenia (Gottesman, 1991).

The typical results of these studies are reflected in Table 2.2, which presents results from a massive study of the correlations between the personalities of family members who differ in their degree of genetic relatedness (Loehlin, 1992). The personality trait under investigation was called "extroversion," which includes general sociability, impulsiveness, and liveliness.

Both genetic and environmental influences are evident in the table. If we focus first on genetic influences, we see that the correlations for monozygotic (MZ) twins are markedly greater than those for dizygotic (DZ) twins or siblings, whether they are raised together in a single family or apart in different families. We also see that the degree of correlation between personality scores decreases consistently with decreasing degrees of family relationship. Turning our attention to environmental influences, we can see that they are just as clearly in evidence. The correlation between test scores for the monozygotic twins is well below 1.0, although these twins share 100 percent of their genes. Finally, the correlation between biological relatives who are raised together is higher than that for biological relatives raised apart.

Despite their usefulness, kinship studies, even those that permit comparison between monozygotic and dizygotic twins and include children who are adopted, are not without problems. It is possible, for example, that monozygotic twins may be treated more similarly than dizygotic twins or other siblings, and to the extent that they are, monozygotic twins may be more alike than dizygotic twins for environmental rather than genetic reasons (Plomin et al., 1997). Even when siblings are adopted by different families and raised apart, the rearing environments may be similar because adoption agencies are likely to make every attempt to place children in secure, loving homes, often with people whose social and cultural backgrounds match those of the biological parents (Scarr, 1981). Thus the extent to which adopted children are similar to their biological families cannot be attributed entirely to the similarity of their genes; it may also be due to the similarity of the environments in which the families live.

At the same time, it cannot be assumed that children in a given family necessarily share the same environment. Some researchers have drawn attention to the fact that the family environment is *not* identical for all family members and that differences in the family-linked experiences of children living in the same home create differences between them (Dunn & Plomin, 1990; Hetherington et al., 1994). These researchers point to a variety of factors that contribute to differences in the environments of siblings raised in the same family. For example, not only do parents treat each of their children differently, but siblings offer different environments for each other, and they are likely to have different teachers at school and different friends (see Box 2.3).

The fact that the distinctive environments experienced by different children in the same family can lead to differences in their development in no way minimizes the importance of genetic factors. Rather, it affirms the principle that genes and the environment are two aspects of a single process of development. In later chapters, when we begin to examine the effects of the environment on development, it will be important to keep in mind the fact that

BOX 2.3

SIBLINGS: SO MUCH IN COMMON, BUT SO DIVERSE

Judy Dunn and Robert Plomin provide intriguing examples of how different two siblings can be, despite the fact that they share 50 percent of their genes. The first example is from the American writer Mark Twain:

> My mother had a good deal of trouble with me but I think she enjoyed it. She had none at all with my brother Henry, who was two years younger than I, and I think that the unbroken monotony of his goodness and truthfulness and obedience would have been a burden to her but for the relief and variety which I furnished in the other direction. I never knew Henry to do a vicious thing toward me or toward anyone else but he frequently did righteous ones that cost me as heavily. It was his duty to report me, when I needed reporting and neglected to do so myself, and he was very faithful in discharging that duty. He is Sid in Tom Sawyer. But Sid was not Henry. Henry was a very much finer and better boy than Sid ever was. (Quoted in Dunn & Plomin, 1990, p. 1)

The second example, involving the poet Alfred (A. E.) Housman and his brother Laurence, who was a writer, is described by the editor of Alfred's letters, Henry Maas:

> Alfred resembled Laurence only in the ability to write. Otherwise he was a complete contrast. Where Laurence was diffuse, impulsive, and warm-hearted, Alfred was precise, disciplined and reserved. Laurence lavished his gifts on too many books, Alfred constricted his poems within the bounds of a tiny oeuvre [body of work]. Laurence was always getting into trouble, Alfred carefully kept out of it. Laurence was a visionary and idealist, to whom his elder brother must at times have seemed a reactionary pedant. (Quoted in Dunn & Plomin, 1990, p. 3).

Over the last two decades, researchers in the fields of child development, family relations, and behavioral genetics have documented that siblings in the same family are often as different from each other as the siblings in these examples (for example, Boer, 1991; Dunn & Plomin, 1990; Hetherington et al., 1994; McHale & Pawletko, 1992). The key to understanding how such marked difference between genetically related children comes about is that siblings do not share the same environment even inside the family. One reason for this is that parents treat their children differently because the siblings have different personalities. Judith Harris (1998) provides a clear example of how a mother might treat her two children differently because they react differently to the same event:

> Not long ago I was in my front yard with my dog. A mother and her two children—a girl of about five and a boy of about seven—walked by in the street. My dog, who is trained not to go into the street, ran to the curb and started barking at them. The two children reacted in very different ways. The girl veered straight toward the dog, asking, "Can I pet him?" despite the fact that the dog was acting in an unfriendly manner. Her mother said quickly, "No, Audrey, I don't think the dog wants you to pet him." Meanwhile, the boy had retreated to the other side of the street and was standing there looking scared, unwilling to walk past the barking dog even though the width of the street was between them. "Come on, Mark," his mother said, "the dog won't hurt you." (p. 25)

Such differential treatment in which the mother inhibits the fearless behavior of her daughter while encouraging her son to be less fearful can affect the relationship between the siblings. For example, children who receive more parental discipline and less parental warmth relative to their siblings manifest higher levels of behavior problems and greater hostility in sibling relationships during childhood and adolescence (for example, Brody et al., 1992; Conger & Conger, 1994; McGuire et al., 1995).

In addition, of course, siblings often have very different experiences outside the family when they are with peers and attending school, and these experiences contribute to differences between them (Harris, 1998). These considerations have led behavioral geneticists to focus more closely on the environment of development in their search for a better understanding of heritability.

mutation An error in the process of gene replication that results in a change in the molecular structure of the DNA.

each of us experiences the world in a distinctive way that depends not only on the unique combination of genes we inherit from our parents but also on the unique environment each of us inhabits.

MUTATIONS AND GENETIC ABNORMALITIES

Despite its fantastic power to produce diversity in human beings, sexual reproduction is restricted to recombining genes that are already present in the human gene pool. The gene pool can change, however, through **mutation,** an error in the process of gene replication that results in a change in the molecular structure of the DNA. A mutation can cause a change in a particular gene or a change in the sequence of genes on a chromosome. A mutation also results when only part of a chromosome is duplicated or when a part is lost. Mutations change the overall set of genetic possibilities that sexual reproduction then rearranges.

Mutations sometimes occur in the somatic (body) cells—in cells of the skin, liver, brain, or bones, for example. The somatic cells that carry these mutations pass on the changed genetic instructions to the cells that descend from them by mitosis. These changes affect only the person in whom they occur; they are not passed on to following generations. Mutations can also occur in a parent's sperm or ovum, in which case the changed genetic information may be passed on to the next generation. Geneticists assume that spontaneous mutations have been occurring in germ cells constantly and randomly since life on Earth began, introducing new genes into the gene pool of every species. Indeed, mutation is part of the evolutionary processes by which new subspecies and species are formed. The fact that mutations are a natural and fundamental part of life does not, however, mean that they usually benefit the individual organisms in which they occur. Each living organism is an intricate whole in which the functioning of the separate parts is interdependent. It is little wonder, then, that the introduction of even a small change in the genes can have serious repercussions for the individual (Figure 2.8).

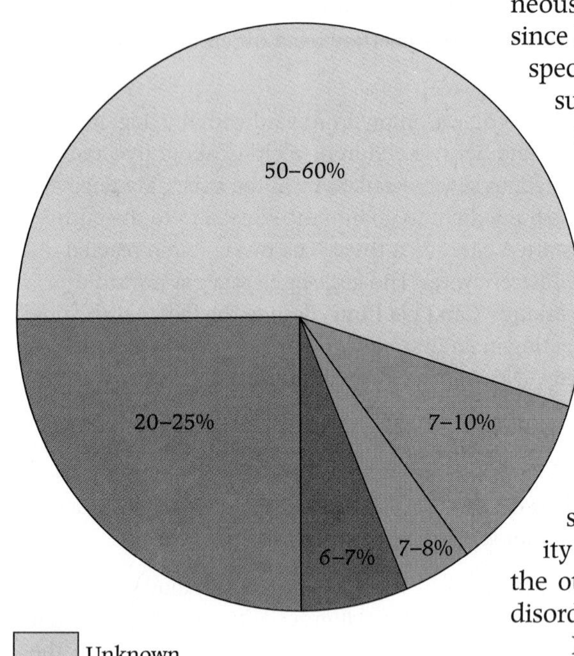

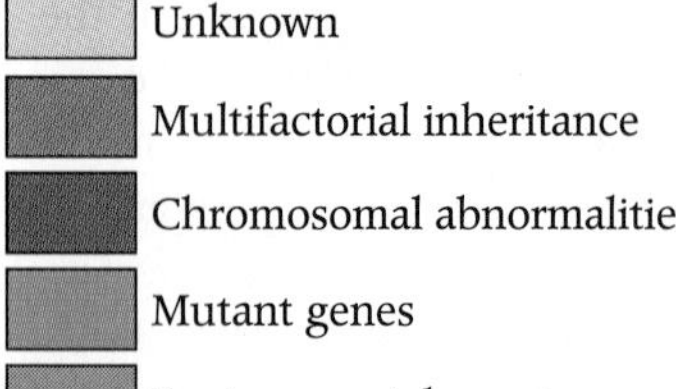

FIGURE 2.8
The leading causes of congenital abnormalities. Note that the causes for most anomalies are unknown, and that 20 to 25 percent are caused by a combination of genetic and environmental factors. (Moore et al., 1994.)

It is estimated that as many as half of all human conceptions have some sort of genetic or chromosomal abnormality. The majority of these mutations and abnormalities are lethal and result in early miscarriage (Connor & Ferguson-Smith, 1991). Still, about 3.5 percent of all babies are born with some kind of genotypic aberration (Ward, 1994). Many of the more serious genetic abnormalities tend to be recessive, and an individual who receives a gene associated with an abnormality from one parent usually receives a normal gene or chromosome from the other parent that counteracts it. Some of the more commonly occurring disorders related to genetic abnormalities are listed in Table 2.3.

Developmental psychologists are interested in studying mutations and genetic abnormalities for several reasons:

1. Because mutations disturb the well-integrated mechanisms of development, an understanding of mutations can help reveal the intricate ways in which heredity and the environment interact.
2. If the existence of genetic abnormalities can be detected at a very early stage of development, ways may be found to prevent or ameliorate the birth defects that would normally result.
3. When children are born with genetic abnormalities, developmentalists are often responsible for finding ways to reduce the impact of the abnormalities on the children and their families.

These concerns are reflected in the current research being conducted on sickle-cell anemia, Down syndrome, certain sex-linked chromosomal abnormalities, and phenylketonuria.

TABLE 2.3 COMMON GENETIC DISEASES AND CONDITIONS

Disease or Condition	Description	Mode of Transmission	Incidence	Prognosis	Prenatal/Carrier Detection Possible?
Cystic fibrosis	Lack of an enzyme causes mucous obstruction, especially in lungs and digestive tract	Recessive gene	1 in 3000 Caucasian births in U.S.; 1 in 17,000 African American births	Few victims survive to adulthood	Yes/Yes
Down syndrome	See text				
Hemophilia (bleeding disease)	Blood does not clot readily	X-linked gene; also occurs by spontaneous mutation	1 in 10,000 live births of males	Possible crippling and death from internal bleeding; transfusions ameliorate effects	Yes/Yes
Klinefelter syndrome	Males fail to develop secondary sex characteristics	Extra X chromosome	1 in 1000 U.S. white males	? Treatable?	Yes/No
Muscular dystrophy (Duchenne's type)	Weakening and wasting away of muscles	X-linked gene	1 in 3500 males under age 20	Crippling; often fatal by age 20	Yes/Yes
Neuro-fibromatosis	Highly variable; includes café au lait spots, benign tumors on peripheral nerves, optic nerve tumors, learning disabilities	Dominant gene; 50% of cases are new mutations	1 in 3000 births	Variable depending on severity of disease; treated by surgery	No in case of spontaneous mutations/ No
Phenylketonuria (PKU)	Lack of an enzyme causes buildup of substances in bloodstream that inhibit brain development	Recessive gene	1 in 15,000 U.S. white infants	Severe retardation; treatable by restricted diet	No/Yes
Sickle-cell anemia	Abnormal blood cells cause circulatory problems and severe anemia	Recessive gene (victims are homozygous, but heterozygous subjects are mildly affected)	8–9% of U.S. blacks	Crippling; treatable with medication	Yes/Yes
Tay-Sachs disease	Lack of an enzyme causes buildup of waste in brain	Recessive gene	1 in 3600 among Ashkenazi Jews in U.S.	Neurological degeneration leading to death before age 4	Yes/Yes
Thalassemia (Cooley's anemia)	Abnormal red blood cells	Recessive gene	1 in 500 births in populations from subtropical areas of Europe, Africa, Asia	Listlessness, enlarged liver and spleen, occasionally death; treatable by blood transfusions	Yes/Yes
Turner syndrome	Females fail to develop secondary sex characteristics	Lack of an X chromosome	1 in 5000 females	? Treatable?	Yes/No

Sources: Jorde et al., 1999; Rimoin et al., 1997; Simpson & Globus, 1993.

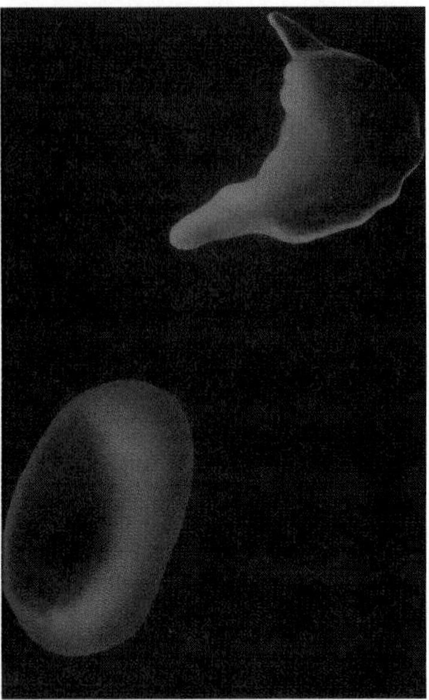

FIGURE 2.9
A normal, round, red blood cell (bottom) and a sickle-shaped red blood cell (top) from a person with sickle-cell anemia.

SICKLE-CELL ANEMIA: AN EXAMPLE OF GENE–ENVIRONMENT INTERACTION

The mutation that gives rise to the sickle-cell trait provides a good illustration of the interaction of heredity and environment. People who inherit the recessive gene for the sickle-cell trait from both of their parents, and thus are homozygous for it, suffer from *sickle-cell anemia,* a serious abnormality of the red blood cells. Normal red blood cells are round. In people with sickle-cell anemia, however, these cells take on a curved, sickle shape when the supply of oxygen to the blood is reduced, as it may be at high altitudes, after heavy physical exertion, or while under anesthesia (see Figure 2.9). These abnormal blood cells tend to clump together and clog the body's smaller blood vessels. Because sickle-cell anemia impairs circulation, people who suffer from the disease experience severe pains in the abdomen, back, head, and limbs. The disease causes the heart to enlarge and deprives the brain of blood. The deformed blood cells rupture easily, and the rupturing may lead to severe anemia and even to early death. In contrast, people who are heterozygous for the sickle-cell gene usually do not suffer the severe symptoms associated with sickle-cell anemia. They may encounter some circulatory problems (40 percent of their red blood cells may assume the sickle shape when the supply of oxygen to the blood is reduced), but they are not at risk of death from the trait, as are those who are homozygous for it.

The gene–environment interaction involved in sickle-cell anemia is reflected in the varying rates of incidence. Sickle-cell anemia is found largely among people of African descent. In the United States, the incidence of the sickle-cell trait among African Americans is about 8 to 9 percent (Connor & Ferguson-Smith, 1991). But in West Africa, the area from which the ancestors of most African Americans were brought to this continent, the incidence of the sickle-cell trait is greater than 20 percent. This difference is explained by the fact that heterozygous carriers of the sickle-cell trait are highly resistant to the parasite that causes malaria. Thus, in malaria-infested areas, such as the West African coast, people who carry the gene are at a selective advantage because they are less likely to suffer from malaria, which can be deadly, and are more likely to survive to reproduce. Because of this selective advantage, the frequency of the sickle-cell gene has been maintained in the West African population despite the losses caused by the death of homozygous carriers. In the United States, where the sickle-cell trait confers no advantage, it is gradually being eliminated from the gene pool.

DOWN SYNDROME: A CHROMOSOMAL ERROR

Down syndrome was the first human disease to be linked with a specific chromosomal disorder. More than 95 percent of the children born with Down syndrome have 47 chromosomes, one more than normal. Instead of two copies of chromosome 21, they have three. (For this reason, the disorder is sometimes called *trisomy 21*). Most children with Down syndrome are mentally and physically retarded and have several distinctive physical characteristics: slanting eyes; a fold on the eyelids; a rather flat facial profile; ears lower than normal; a short neck; a protruding tongue; dental irregularities; short, broad hands; a crease running all the way across the palm; small curved fingers; and abnormally wide spaced toes (see Figure 2.10). On the average, children with this disorder are more likely than other children to suffer from heart, ear, and eye problems, and they are more susceptible to leukemia and to respiratory infections. As a result, they are more likely to die young (Frid et al., 1999).

Over 10 percent of the people in institutions for the retarded suffer from Down syndrome (Plomin et al., 1997), but how effectively Down-syndrome children function as they grow up depends not only on the severity of their

FIGURE 2.10
Individuals with Down Syndrome can benefit from education and supportive activities tailored to their needs, such as the Special Olympics.

disorder but also on the environment in which they are raised. Supportive intervention that includes special education by concerned adults can markedly improve the intellectual functioning of some of these children. Thus this genotype apparently has a wide range of reaction.

Down syndrome occurs in about 1 of every 1000 births in the United States (Pueschel, 1992). A strong relationship has been found between the incidence of Down syndrome and the age of the parents, particularly the mother's. Up to the age of 30 a woman's risk of giving birth to a live Down syndrome infant is less than 1 in 800. The risk increases to 1 in 100 by age 40, to 1 in 32 by age 45, and to 1 in 12 by age 49 (Chan et al., 1998; Hook, 1982). The risk is thought to increase because at birth the human female carries all the potential egg cells that she will ever produce. Thus the older a woman is, the more time she has had to be exposed to such environmental agents as viruses, radiation, and certain chemicals that can damage the chromosomes or interfere with the process of meiosis. This view is supported by the fact that the risk of other chromosomal anomalies, such as Klinefelter syndrome, also increases with the mother's age.

SEX-LINKED CHROMOSOMAL ABNORMALITIES

Half of all chromosomal abnormalities in newborns involve the twenty-third pair of chromosomes—the X and Y chromosomes that determine the baby's sex. Occasionally a boy is born with an extra X or Y chromosome and has either an XXY or XYY genotype. Girls are sometimes born with only one X chromosome (XO) or three X chromosomes (XXX). Additionally, the X chromosome, which carries many genes, may be brittle and break into two or more pieces. Each of these chromosomal abnormalities has different implications for cognitive behavior.

The most common sex-linked chromosomal abnormality is *Klinefelter syndrome,* the condition in which males are born with an extra X chromosome (XXY). It is estimated that this abnormality occurs in about 1 of every 900 males born in the United States (Smith & Bremner, 1998). Males who are XXY appear to develop normally until adolescence, when they fail to show the typical signs of maturity: their sex organs do not mature, they do not acquire facial hair, their voices do not change, they have low levels of the male hormone testosterone, and they are sterile. Most have speech and language problems and, as a result, have problems in school (Mandoki et al., 1991).

gene pool The total genetic information possessed by a sexually reproducing population.

Another sex-linked disorder, *fragile X syndrome,* causes mental retardation. In this disease, an abnormal repetition of a sequence of DNA occurs in a particular location on the X chromosome and damages the corresponding gene. The syndrome is twice as likely to occur in boys as in girls. Only half the girls with fragile X are affected by this condition because one of the X chromosomes in girls is inactive. In most cases, those affected by fragile X syndrome are either moderately or mildly retarded. A majority of these children show physical deformities, language difficulties, very slow speech, poor eye contact, impulsivity, and hyperactivity (Plomin et al., 1997).

The most common sex-linked abnormality in females is *Turner syndrome.* About 1 out of every 5000 females is born with only one X chromosome (the genotype designated as XO) (Connor & Ferguson-Smith, 1991). At puberty, girls with Turner syndrome fail to produce the female hormone, estrogen. As a result, they do not develop breasts or pubic hair, rarely menstruate, and are sterile. As a group, such girls have been found to be about average in verbal ability, although they frequently score below average on tests of spatial ability and have difficulty with such tasks as following a road map and copying a geometric design (Downet et al., 1991).

The frequency of sex-linked abnormalities varies greatly depending on the particular trait in question and the population in which it occurs. For example, one form of genetically caused anemia, a condition in which the blood is deficient in red blood cells, occurs in 60 percent of male Kurdish Jews living in Israel, whereas only 0.5 percent of male European Jews have this condition (Lerner & Libby, 1976). The difference in the incidence of the disease reflects the different frequencies of the allele that causes it in the two gene pools. A **gene pool** is the total genetic information possessed by a sexually reproducing population.

PHENYLKETONURIA: A TREATABLE GENETIC DISEASE

The modern history of *phenylketonuria (PKU),* an inherited metabolic disorder that leads to severe mental retardation if it is not treated, shows dramatically how the effects of a genetic defect can be ameliorated by changing the environment in which a child develops. It is estimated that 1 in every 10,000 infants born each year in the United States has PKU and that 1 in 100 people of European descent is a carrier of the recessive mutant gene (Güttler, 1988). The incidence of PKU is lower among blacks than among whites (Connor & Ferguson-Smith, 1991).

PKU was discovered in 1934 in Norway after Dr. Ashborn Følling found that two mentally retarded children who had been brought to him had abnormal amounts of phenylpyruvic acid in their urine. Spurred by this discovery, Dr. Følling tested other retarded children in institutions and found that some of them also had this symptom. We now know that PKU is caused by a defective recessive gene that reduces the body's ability to convert one amino acid (phenylalanine) into another (tyrosine). As a result, PKU children produce too much phenylalanine in their bloodstreams, which retards development of brain cells in the prefrontal cortex (Diamond et al., 1997).

Knowledge of the abnormal biochemistry of the condition led researchers to hypothesize that if the accumulation of phenylalanine and phenylpyruvic acid could be prevented, infants with PKU might develop normally. Physicians have tested this hypothesis by feeding PKU infants a diet low in phenylalanine. (Phenylalanine is highly concentrated in such basic foods as milk, eggs, bread, and fish.) Such treatment reduces the severity of mental retardation significantly below that characteristic of untreated children with PKU, although current treatments are not sufficient to entirely eradicate PKU's effects (Diamond et al., 1997). The timing of the intervention is crucial. If phenylalanine intake is not restricted by the time a PKU infant is 1 to 3 months of age, the brain will already have suffered irreversible damage.

Most states require that newborns be given a blood test for PKU. This PKU screening is not infallible, however, and some PKU babies are not identified in time. PKU can be detected prenatally (Nightingale & Meister, 1987), and genetic testing can identify people who carry the recessive PKU gene, allowing carriers of the gene to decide whether they want to risk having a child with the disease. (Box 2.4 discusses prenatal detection methods and genetic counseling.)

BIOLOGY AND CULTURE

Today we know that mutations are the source of biological variation among species, but at the time Darwin wrote *The Origin of Species* (1859), the genetic basis of hereditary transmission was unknown. Ignorance of genetics and a limited knowledge of the fossil record helped create a basic confusion about precisely how hereditary transmission works. In attempting to account for the differences observed among species and among peoples past and present, many scientists argued that the mechanisms that produced historical change and cultural differences were the same as those that produced biological change (see Figure 2.11). Further examination of this confusion can give us a broader perspective on the relation between our genetic and environmental heritages and on why any attempts to separate the influences of nature and nurture are so problematic.

ACQUIRED CHARACTERISTICS

In the absence of knowledge about genetics, many prominent biologists in the nineteenth and early-twentieth centuries hypothesized that characteristics acquired by individuals during their lifetimes are transmitted biologically to the next generation. This belief raised concerns that parents who engaged in criminal activity, for example, would pass on a tendency to criminality to their children in the same way that they passed on the genes that determined the colors of their eyes and hair (Gould, 1977b).

The erroneous idea that characteristics acquired through environmental experience can be biologically inherited is referred to as *Lamarckism,* after the

FIGURE 2.11
The coevolution of toolmaking abilities and Homo sapiens. *Rudimentary forms of culture were already present during early phases of human evolution.*

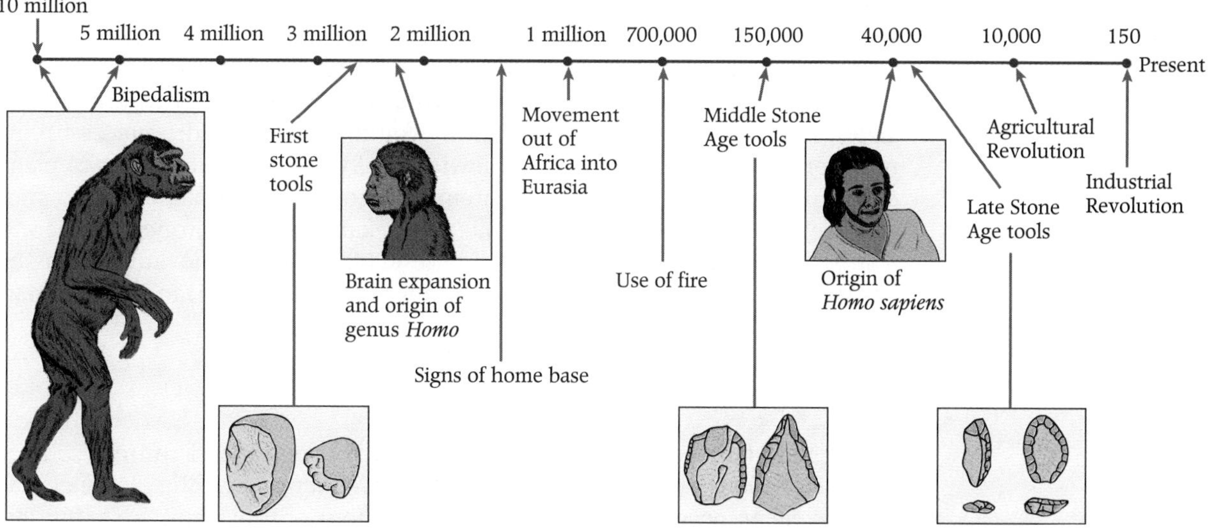

BOX 2.4 GENETIC COUNSELING

Thanks to recent advances in the field of genetics, many potential genetic problems can be avoided through genetic testing and counseling. The main responsibilities of genetic counselors are to test potential at-risk parents to learn whether they are carriers of a genetic disease and to determine the probability that a particular couple will bear a child with that disease.

Genetic counselors are often called on by couples who have already had one child with a genetic defect and who want to know the likelihood that a second child will have the same abnormality. Genetic counseling is also recommended for potential parents who have relatives with a genetic disease, who have physical anomalies they suspect are genetic, who have had several pregnancies that have ended in spontaneous abortion, or who are over the age of 35. Several inherited disorders are especially likely to be found in specific groups of people. For example, the recessive allele for Tay-Sachs disease, in which a missing enzyme inevitably leads to death before the age of 4, is carried by 1 in 30 Ashkenazi Jews in the United States. The recessive allele for thalassemia, a blood disease, is carried by 1 in 10 Americans of Greek or Italian descent (Omenn, 1978). Potential parents with genetic links to those groups can also benefit from genetic counseling.

Detecting the carriers of the gene for some genetic disorders is relatively simple. The alleles for Tay-Sachs disease and sickle-cell anemia can be detected through blood tests. Female carriers of Lesch-Nyhan syndrome (a metabolic disorder affecting male children that leads to the overproduction of uric acid) can be identified through an analysis of their hair follicles. Carriers of chromosomal abnormalities, such as the translocation of chromosome 21, which causes Down syndrome, can be identified through the analysis of a cell from the body. The carriers of certain chromosomal disorders are sometimes signaled by specific patterns in the prints of their fingers and palms and the soles of their feet.

On the basis of test results and family histories, the genetic counselor tries to determine whether there is a potential problem and what the odds are that a child of the couple will be affected by it. Such predictions can now be made for diseases and traits that are caused by a single recessive or dominant gene or that are sex-linked, and in some cases for those caused by several genes acting together. They cannot be made for defects caused by spontaneous mutations.

It must be kept in mind that genetic theory generates statistical probabilities that apply to whole populations. Thus a genetic counselor may not be able to say for certain in advance of conception that a particular couple will have a child who will suffer from a genetic abnormality. Once potential parents have been informed of the risks, they must make their own decision about whether to attempt pregnancy.

After conception, the principal techniques used to determine whether a given fetus suffers from a genetic defect are alpha-fetoprotein assay, sonograms, amniocentesis, sampling of the chorionic villi, and fetoscopy. The *alpha-fetoprotein assay* is a blood test that is used mainly to detect the presence of defects in the fetus's neural tube, which forms the

French biologist Jean-Baptiste Lamarck (1744–1829), whose ideas were extremely influential among early evolutionary theorists. Although the inheritance of acquired characteristics has been discredited as a mechanism of *biological* evolution, the idea behind it is not irrelevant to the study of development: *cultural* evolution does operate in a Lamarckian way. Consider how the habit of making marks on objects has gradually evolved into symbol systems for writing and numerical calculation. Today the millions of children who are learning to read and do arithmetic in schools all over the world are mastering symbol systems that are vastly more complex than those used by any humans as recently as 10,000 years ago. This increased sophistication is not a consequence of biological evolutionary change through the action of genes. Rather, it is the result of cultural evolution, in which the successful innovations of earlier generations—knowledge of when to hunt deer or to plant a field, of the alphabet, of the theorems of geometry—are passed on to succeeding generations through language, by example, and through deliberate instruction (Donald, 1991). There is little evidence that innovative forms of behavior are passed on from one generation to the next in most nonhuman species (Tomasello, 1999).

COEVOLUTION

For a great many years it was believed that the biological and cultural characteristics of *Homo sapiens* developed in a strict sequence: first the biological capacities we associate with humanity evolved to a critical point, and then an spinal column and brain. Incomplete closure of the neural tube is the most common birth defect in the United States, occurring in 1 of every 1000 live births. When a fetus has a neural-tube defect, large amounts of alpha-fetoprotein pour out of the open spine or skull into the amniotic fluid. From there it enters the mother's bloodstream, where it can be detected. The results of this blood test are only suggestive, however. Women whose alpha-fetoprotein levels are abnormally high are usually offered sonograms and amniocentesis to verify or disconfirm the problem.

The *sonogram,* or ultrasound, uses high-frequency sound waves to produce a visible image of the fetus. Sonograms are used to diagnose such malformations as an abnormally small head. They can also be used to diagnose multiple births, to estimate the fetus's age, to determine the rate of its growth, and to locate the placenta.

In *amniocentesis* a small amount of amniotic fluid—which contains cells and other substances from the fetus—is tested for signs of chromosomal abnormalities or certain genetic disorders. To perform an amniocentesis, the doctor first determines the position of the fetus by means of a sonogram. The doctor then inserts a long hollow needle into the mother's abdomen and extracts some of the amniotic fluid from the sac surrounding the fetus. Amniocentesis cannot be performed until midpregnancy, and 2 weeks are needed to determine the results.

Another way to detect chromosomal disorders is to sample cells taken from the villi (hairlike projections) on the chorion, a tissue that forms the placenta. One advantage of such *chorionic villi sampling* is that it can be performed as early as the ninth week of pregnancy and its results are available within a few days. Thus, if the fetus has a condition that causes the parents to decide to terminate the pregnancy, an abortion can be performed early, when it is safest. Some controversy still surrounds the procedure with regard to both its safety and the accuracy of the findings (Smidt-Jensen, 1998).

A physician performs a *fetoscopy* by piercing the uterus with a long, narrow tube through which a fetoscope is inserted. The physician then can observe the fetus and the placenta directly through the fetoscope. This procedure is most often used when a malformation is suspected. It can also be used to take blood or tissue samples from the fetus for diagnostic purposes.

When a genetic disorder is detected by any of these tests, parents usually have only two alternatives: the woman can carry the pregnancy to term and give birth to a child who is genetically defective in some way, or she can terminate the pregnancy. This is not an easy choice, especially since the diagnosis often fails to predict the degree of disability the affected child will suffer or the quality of life that can be expected. The severity of a neural-tube defect, for example, can vary greatly, and many people who suffer from such defects have lived productive lives. In some cases, fetal surgery and other kinds of prenatal and postnatal interventions, such as a special diet or blood transfusions, can ameliorate the effects of a defect.

additional biological change occurred that allowed *Homo sapiens* to use language and generate culture. Now, however, the situation is believed to have been far more complicated. Contemporary studies of human origins have found evidence that rudimentary forms of culture were already present during early phases of human evolution. *Australopithecus* (one of our primitive ancestors, who lived some 3 million years ago) domesticated fire, built shelters, engaged in organized hunting, and used tools—flint knives, cooking utensils, and notation systems (Casper, 1997).

Such findings indicate that the biological evolution of our species did not end with the appearance of culture. The brain of a modern person is about three times larger than the brain of *Australopithecus.* Most of this increase has occurred in the frontal lobes, those areas that govern complex, specifically human capacities (Donald, 1991). Insofar as the capacity to engage in cultural activities and to reason through the use of cultural tools—such as calendars, which permit people to know at what time of year their hunting, fishing, or planting is most likely to be successful—confers a selective reproductive advantage, it is probable that the more effective users of culture have been more successful in passing on their genes to succeeding generations. In short, culture has influenced biology, and the two forms of evolution, biological and cultural, have interacted with each other in a process called **coevolution** (Futuyma, 1986).

coevolution The combined process that emerges from the interaction of biological evolution and cultural evolution.

As a consequence of the coevolution of human physical and cultural characteristics, attempts to separate the influences of nature and nurture on the development of group differences between contemporary children are

A standardized track and stopwatch provide an excellent mechanism for measuring running performance, but the ability to run may develop in any of many possible environments. There is no general formula for determining the relative contributions of culture and genes in shaping such abilities.

even more problematic than our earlier discussion of heritability suggests. The physical demands placed on people vary dramatically in different parts of the world. Furthermore, the cultural histories, as well as the gene pools, of people living in different locales have differed greatly for tens of thousands of years. These differences in environment and culture have clearly contributed to the physical differences among people, but whether they have also resulted in mental differences is by no means certain. When Japanese children excel at mathematics, for example, their performance might be attributed to a combination of genetically transmitted characteristics that have been shaped by Japanese culture (Gardner, 1983). The same can be said of the extraordinary navigational abilities of Micronesian sailors, who can cross thousands of miles of ocean from one tiny island to another in small canoes without the aid of a compass (Hutchins, 1983). There are no general formulas for determining the relative contributions of culture and genes in shaping group differences in human abilities.

The complex interactions between genetic heritage and the environment begin when genes in the zygote start to express themselves and guide the creation of new cells. Each new human being is a variant within the overall range of possibilities that defines *Homo sapiens.* Chapter 3 follows the course of gene–environment interaction from the moment the genetic material of the mother and father come together. In later chapters, as we follow the general patterns of the development of children, we will repeatedly see instances of gene–environment interaction, with culture always playing a mediating role.

SUMMARY

SEXUAL REPRODUCTION AND GENETIC TRANSMISSION

- The particular set of genes each human being inherits comes from his or her parents. Sexual reproduction rearranges the genetic combination in each new individual. With the exception of monozygotic twins, every person inherits a unique combination of genes, so great diversity among people is guaranteed.

- Throughout the life cycle new body cells are created by mitosis, a copying process that replicates the genetic material inherited at birth.
- The germ cells (sperm and ova) that unite at conception are formed by meiosis, a process of cell division that maintains a constant total of 46 chromosomes in each new individual.
- The sexes differ genetically in the composition of one pair of chromosomes. In females, the two chromosomes that make up the twenty-third pair are both X chromosomes (XX). Males have one X and one Y chromosome (XY).

GENOTYPE AND PHENOTYPE

- The influence of genes on development must be studied at two levels—the individual's genetic constitution (genotype) and the individual's visible characteristics (phenotype)—because some genes are dominant and others are recessive and because a genotype can result in a wide variety of phenotypes, depending on the environment in which it develops.
- Genes associated with a particular characteristic can take different forms. If the corresponding genes inherited from two parents have the same form, the child will develop that form's associated characteristics. If the genes have two different forms, one may dominate the other, there may be an intermediate outcome, or an entirely new characteristic may emerge.
- The genes carried by the twenty-third pair of chromosomes give rise to sex-linked characteristics. Because females receive two X chromosomes, they get two doses of X-linked genes, one from each parent. Normal males receive only one X chromosome, and therefore only one dose of genes on the X chromosome, which always comes from the mother. Thus men are susceptible to genetic defects that usually do not affect females.
- In the study of gene–environment interactions several principles are widely used: (1) Many levels of the environment, from the local to the global, must be taken into account. (2) The notion of gene–environment *inter*action means that influences work in both directions. (3) Children actively shape the environments that influence their development.
- The overall relationship between genotype and phenotype can be established only by exposure of the genotype to a variety of environments. By charting the changes that occur in the phenotype as the environment is varied, geneticists can establish a range of reaction. Ideally, such a range specifies all possible phenotypes that are compatible with life for a single genotype.
- The range of reaction of most human characteristics has not been established because moral precepts and ethical standards make it impossible to carry out investigations that would expose people to all the environments that are compatible with human life.
- Some characteristics, such as language development in human beings, appear to be canalized; that is, they are restricted to a narrow range of variation and show a strong tendency to self-correction after the organism is exposed to deviant experiences.
- As a substitute for experimental studies to establish the ranges of reaction of human traits, behavioral geneticists rely on the study of various kinship relations to estimate the relative influences of the genotype and the environment on the phenotype.

- ➢ Three types of kinship methods are widely used by behavioral geneticists: (1) In family studies, relatives who live together in a household are compared. (2) In twin studies, monozygotic and dizygotic twins are compared. (3) In adoption studies, children living apart from their biological parents are studied.
- ➢ Results of large-scale studies using family, twin, and adoption methods demonstrate the heritability of a wide range of traits, as well as the influence of the environment on development, but methods for estimating "how much" genetic and environmental factors contribute to the phenotype remain controversial.

MUTATIONS AND GENETIC ABNORMALITIES

- ➢ Mutation is a major source of variability in living organisms. Some mutations are compatible with normal life. Often, however, the changes brought about by mutation result in death or disorders.
- ➢ Studies of mutations and genetic abnormalities are of interest to developmentalists both for what they reveal about the process of gene–environment interaction in development and because of the need to devise preventive techniques and methods of therapy.

BIOLOGY AND CULTURE

- ➢ Culture provides human beings with a mode of adaptation that other species do not have. Cultural evolution occurs when adaptations that arise in one generation are learned and modified by the next.
- ➢ Cultural evolution and biological evolution of human beings have interacted with each other in a process called coevolution, which greatly complicates attempts to separate the influences of nature and nurture in development.

KEY TERMS

adoption study, p. 62
allele, p. 56
behavioral geneticist, p. 58
canalization, p. 60
chromosome, p. 50
codominance, p. 56
coevolution, p. 73
crossing over, p. 52
deoxyribonucleic acid (DNA), p. 50
dizygotic twins, p. 55
dominant allele, p. 56
environment, p. 56
eugenics, p. 61
family study, p. 61
gene pool, p. 70
genes, p. 50
genotype, p. 56
germ cells, p. 52
heritability, p. 61
heterozygous, p. 56
homozygous, p. 56
meiosis, p. 52
mitosis, p. 52
monozygotic twins, p. 55
mutation, p. 66
phenotype, p. 56
polygenic trait, p. 57
range of reaction, p. 60
recessive allele, p. 56
sex-linked characteristics, p. 57
somatic (body) cells, p. 52
twin study, p. 61
X chromosome, p. 54
Y chromosome, p. 54
zygote, p. 50

THOUGHT QUESTIONS

1. Can you think of a way in which the cultural values and preferences of your own ancestors may have influenced your genetic makeup?
2. Describe the complementary roles of mitosis and meiosis in the process of reproduction.
3. Name a behavioral tendency that you believe you have inherited. In what ways do you think this trait has been affected by your environment? Has it affected the way you have experienced your environment?
4. Reread the description of girls born with Turner syndrome. Why might the symptoms of this disorder be of interest to researchers studying child development?

CHAPTER 3

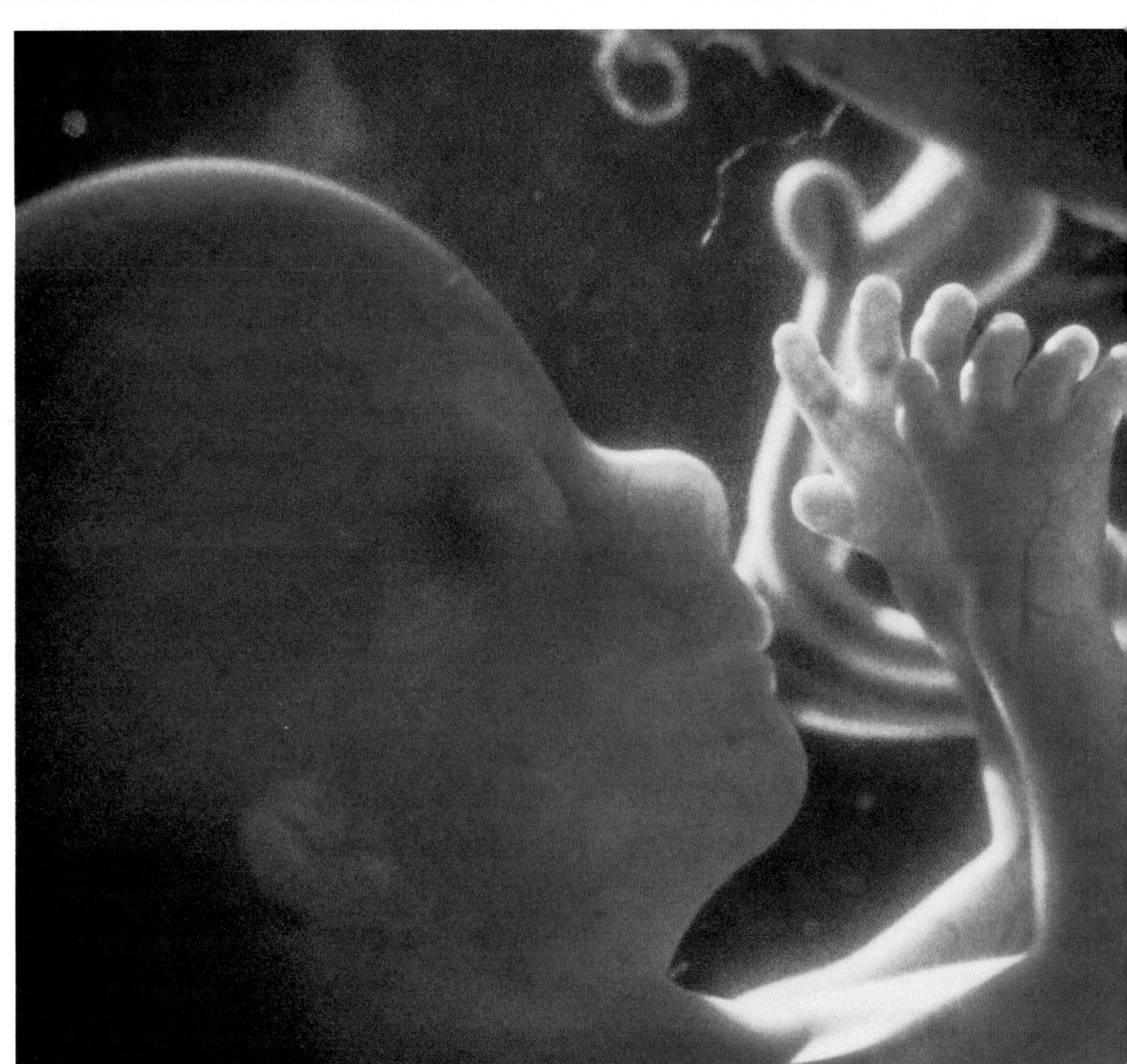

Prenatal Development and Birth

Every man is some months older than he bethinks him, for we live, move, have being, and are subject to the actions of the elements and the malice of disease, in that other world, the truest Microcosm, the womb of our mother.

Sir Thomas Browne, *Religio Medici,* 1642

Of all our existence, the 9 months we live inside our mother's womb are the most eventful for our growth and development. We begin as a zygote, a single cell the size of a period on this page, weighing approximately fifteen-millionths of a gram. At birth we consist of some 2 billion cells and weigh, on the average, 7 pounds. The changes that occur in our form are no less remarkable than the increase in our size (see Figure 3.1). The first few cells to develop from the zygote are all identical, but in a few weeks there will be many different kinds of cells arranged in intricately structured, interdependent organs.

A basic task in the study of prenatal development is to explain how these changes in form and size take place. Understanding prenatal development is important for both theoretical and practical reasons. Many theorists look upon development during the prenatal period as a model for development during all subsequent periods, from birth to death. Indeed, a number of the principles of development are first seen in action during the prenatal pe-

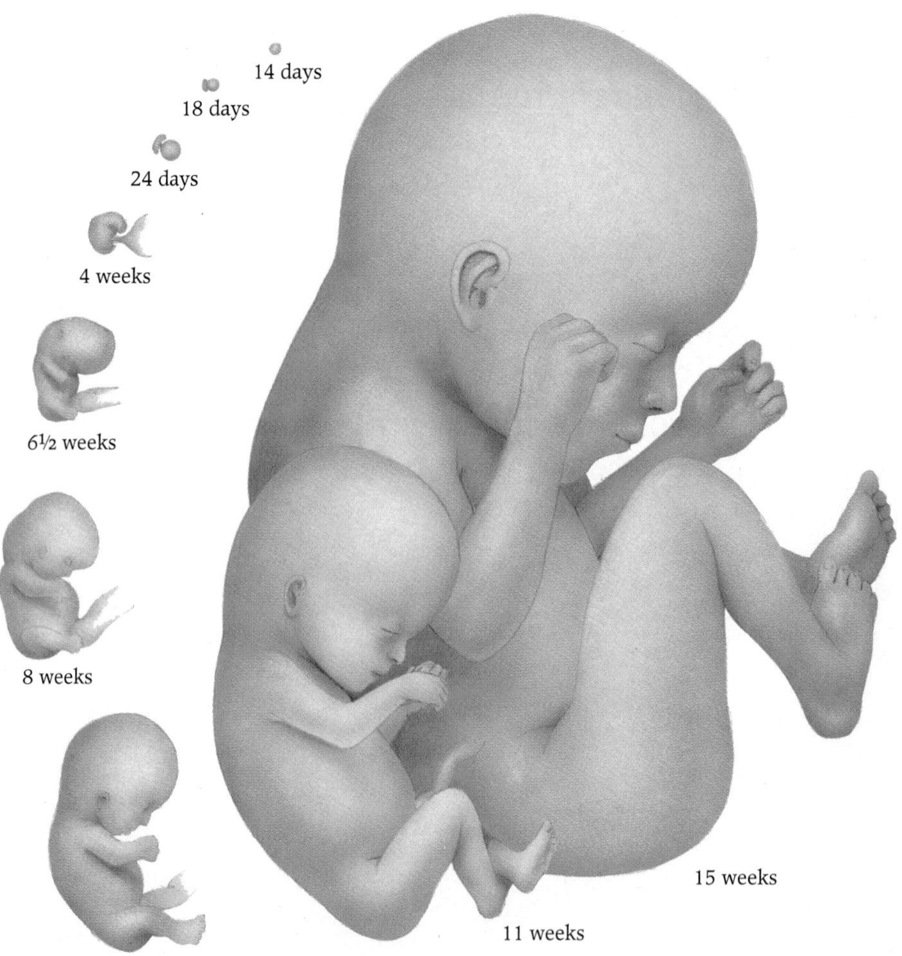

FIGURE 3.1
Changes in the size and form of the human body from 14 days to 15 weeks after conception. (Adapted from Arey, 1974.)

riod. For example, stagelike changes occur in which the organism acquires qualitatively distinct new physical forms that follow each other in a regular sequence. Each new stage is associated with distinct kinds of interaction between the developing organism and its environment.

On the practical side, understanding the prenatal period is important because the developing organism can be positively or adversely affected by the mother-to-be's nutritional status, health, and habits, including whether or not she uses drugs or alcohol. Considerable research has been devoted to learning how to promote healthy prenatal development and prevent damage to the growing organism during this foundational period.

In order to understand the relation of prenatal development in the womb to later development in the world, we first must trace the changes that take place as the organism progresses from zygote to newborn and examine the environmental factors that support or threaten development. Then we can consider the circumstances surrounding the newborn's entrance into the world.

THE PERIODS OF PRENATAL DEVELOPMENT

The transformations that occur during prenatal development are nothing short of amazing. Through a microscope, the fertilized ovum appears to be made up of small particles inside larger ones. The chromosomes bearing the genes are contained within the nucleus at the center of the cell. Surrounding the nucleus is the cell matter, which serves as the raw material for the first few cell divisions. The entire zygote is contained within the **zona pellucida,** a delicate envelope only a few molecules thick. Within the first few weeks after conception, this single cell subdivides many times to form many kinds of cells with vastly different destinies. In approximately 266 days these cells will have been transformed into a wriggling, crying infant.

As a first step toward understanding these transformations, scientists often divide prenatal development into three broad periods, each characterized by distinctive patterns of growth and interaction between the organism and its environment:

1. The **germinal period** begins when the mother's and father's germ cells are joined at conception and lasts until the developing organism becomes attached to the wall of the uterus, about 8 to 10 days later.
2. The **period of the embryo** extends from the time the organism becomes attached to the uterus until the end of the eighth week, when all the major organs have taken primitive shape.
3. The **period of the fetus** begins the ninth week after conception, with the first signs of the hardening of the bones, and continues until birth. During this period, the primitive organ systems develop to the point where the baby can exist outside the mother without medical support.

At any step in these prenatal periods, the process of development may stop. One study estimates that approximately 25 percent of all pregnancies end before the woman even recognizes that she is pregnant (Wilcox et al., 1999). If all goes well, however, the creation of a new human being is under way.

THE GERMINAL PERIOD

During the first 8 to 10 days after conception, the fertilized ovum moves slowly through the fallopian tube and into the uterus (see Figure 3.2). The timing of this journey is crucial. If the new organism enters the uterus too soon or too late, the uterine environment will not be hormonally prepared and the organism will be destroyed.

zona pellucida The thin envelope that surrounds the zygote and later the morula.

germinal period The period from fertilization until implantation of the developing organism in the wall of the uterus.

period of the embryo The period that begins when the organism becomes attached to the uterus and lasts until the end of the eighth week, when the major organs have taken shape.

period of the fetus The period from 9 weeks after conception until birth.

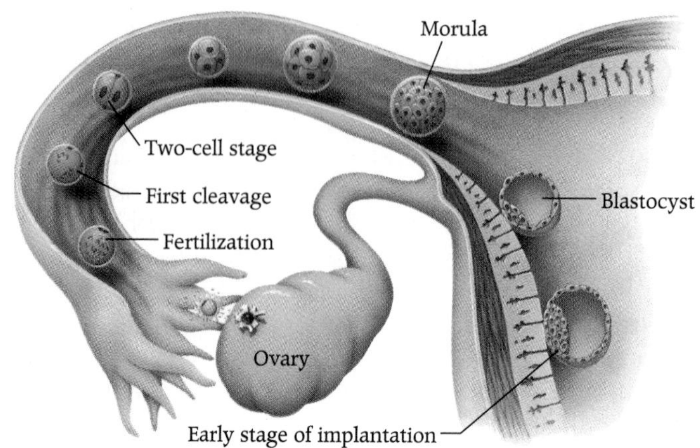

FIGURE 3.2
Development of the human embryo in the mother's reproductive tract from fertilization to implantation. (Adapted from Tuchmann-Duplessis, David, & Haegel, 1971.)

cleavage The mitotic division of the cells in the zygote.

heterochrony Variability in the rates of development of different parts of the organism.

heterogeneity Variability in the levels of development of different parts of the organism at a given time.

morula The cluster of cells inside the zona pellucida.

The First Cells of Life

As explained in Chapter 2 (p. 51), all body cells reproduce through the process of duplication and division known as mitosis. **Cleavage,** the mitotic division of the zygote into several cells, begins about 24 hours after conception as the fertilized ovum travels down the fallopian tube. The single-cell zygote divides to produce two daughter cells, each of which then divides to produce two more daughter cells, and so on (see Figure 3.3). Thanks to this periodic doubling, the developing organism will already consist of hundreds of cells by the time it reaches the uterus.

An important characteristic of cleavage is that the cells existing at any given moment do not all divide at the same time. Instead of proceeding in an orderly fashion from a two-cell stage to a four-cell stage and so on, the cells divide at different rates (Gilbert & Raunio, 1997). This is the first instance of developmental **heterochrony,** whereby different parts of the organism develop at different rates. Heterochrony literally means "variability in time." Because different parts of the organism develop at different rates, the organism's behavior will be more or less mature depending on which of the organism's parts are involved in the given behavior in question. The unevenness of development rates gives rise to another prominent feature of development—variability in the *levels* of development of different parts of the organism at a given time. This type of variability is referred to as **heterogeneity.** Both kinds of variability play an important role in the process of development throughout the life of the child.

FIGURE 3.3
A zygote after two cleavages, resulting in four cells of equal size and appearance.

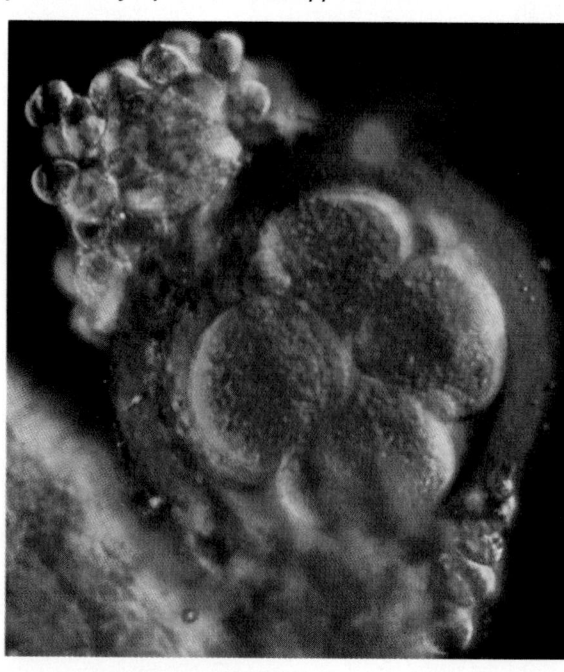

The Emergence of New Forms

As the first several cleavages occur, a cluster of cells called the **morula** takes shape inside the zona pellucida. For the first 4 or 5 days after conception, the cells in the morula become smaller and smaller with each cleavage until they are all approximately the size of the average body cell. Apart from being smaller, they look identical to their parent cells and resemble a large number of Ping-Pong balls crowded into a balloon.

As the cells in the morula reach the size of average body cells, the morula passes into the uterus. In the uterus, fluid passes into the morula and collects between the cells. The first noticeable changes in the organism's internal form emerge simultaneously with this interaction. As the fluid increases in the morula, the cells of the morula separate into two parts—an outer cell mass and a group of centrally located cells (see Figure 3.4). The morula has now become the

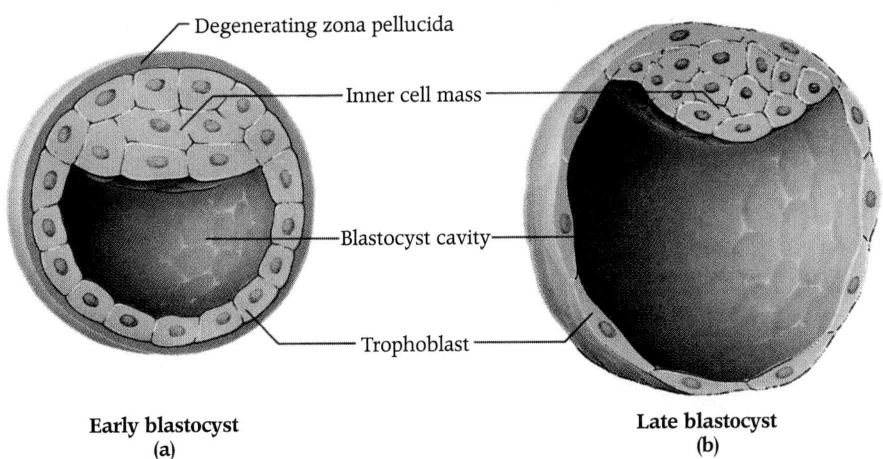

FIGURE 3.4
Two stages in the development of the blastocyst: (a) the formation of the inner cell mass in the early blastocyst stage, and (b) the differentiation of the trophoblast cells in the late blastocyst stage. By the late blastocyst stage, the zona pellucida has disappeared. (Adapted from Moore & Persaud, 1993.)

blastocyst. This transformation of the morula is the earliest instance of a repeating pattern in which development is manifested as a process of differentiation and reintegration. In this case, the identical cells of the morula are differentiated into two kinds of cells that are then reintegrated into the more mature form of the organism that is the blastocyst.

The two kinds of cells in the blastocyst play different roles in development. The knot of small cells clustered along one side of the central cavity of the blastocyst is called the **inner cell mass.** These cells give rise to the organism itself. Around the inner cell mass and the cavity, a double layer of large, flat cells called the **trophoblast** forms a protective barrier between the inner cell mass and the environment. Later the trophoblast will develop into the membranes that will protect the developing organism and transmit nutrients to it. (Appropriately, "trophoblast" is derived from the Greek *trophe,* "nourishment.") As the cells of the blastocyst differentiate, the zona pellucida surrounding it disintegrates. The trophoblast layer now serves as a kind of pump, filling the inner cavity with life-giving fluid from the uterus, which enables the cells to continue to divide and the organism to grow.

Although it is easy enough to describe the transformations of the undifferentiated cells of the zygote, first into the two kinds of cells in the blastocyst and eventually into the multitudes of kinds of cells present at birth, the mechanisms by which these changes occur remain a central puzzle of development. What makes the different groups of cells take on different forms?

Current explanations emphasize the idea that each new form emerges as a result of the interactions that take place between the preceding form and its environment, a process called **epigenesis** (from a Greek expression meaning "at the time of generation") (Gottlieb, 1997). In the case of the morula, the "environment" varies according to the location of the cells in question. The cells at the center of the morula are surrounded by other morula cells. Those on the outside have some contact with other morula cells, but on one side they are also in contact with the zona pellucida, which in turn is in contact with the mother's reproductive tract and its fluids. When the morula begins to take in nutrients, those nutrients must pass through the cells on the outside to reach the cells on the inside. As a result, the outside cells are subject to different environmental influences than are those on the inside. According to the epigenetic explanation of embryonic development, cell division under such different environmental conditions is what leads to the creation of different kinds of cells and new forms of interaction between the organism and the environment (Gilbert & Raunio, 1997). This pattern is repeated again and again in the course of the organism's development.

blastocyst The hollow sphere of cells that results from the differentiation of the morula into the trophoblast and the inner cell mass.

inner cell mass The collection of cells inside the blastocyst that eventually becomes the embryo.

trophoblast The outer layer of cells of the blastocyst that develop into the membranes that protect and support the embryo.

epigenesis The process by which new forms emerge through the interactions of the preceding form and its current environment.

implantation The process by which the blastocyst becomes attached to the uterus.

amnion A thin, tough, transparent membrane that holds the amniotic fluid.

chorion One of the membranes that develops out of the trophoblast. It forms the fetal component of the placenta.

placenta An organ made up of tissue from both the mother and the fetus that serves as a barrier and filter between their bloodstreams.

umbilical cord A soft tube containing blood vessels that connects the developing organism to the placenta.

ectoderm Cells of the inner cell mass that develop into the outer surface of the skin, the nails, part of the teeth, the lens of the eye, the inner ear, and the central nervous system.

Implantation

As the blastocyst moves farther into the uterus, the trophoblast cells put out tiny branches that burrow into the spongy wall of the uterus until they come in contact with the mother's blood vessels. Thus begins **implantation,** the process by which the blastocyst becomes attached to the uterus. Implantation marks the transition between the germinal and embryonic periods. Like many of life's transitions (birth being an especially dramatic example), implantation is hazardous for the organism and pregnancy loss is common during this process. Intriguingly, one hazard that might be expected seldom arises: If any other bit of alien tissue were introduced into a woman's uterus, it would be attacked by the mother's immune system and expelled. However, for reasons that are still not well understood, rejection of the blastocyst does not usually occur (Jones, 1997).

THE EMBRYONIC PERIOD

If the blastocyst is successfully implanted, the developing organism enters the period of the embryo, which lasts for about 6 weeks. During the embryonic period, all the basic organs of the body take shape, and the organism begins to respond to direct stimulation. The organism's rapid growth during this period is facilitated by the efficient way the mother now supplies it with nutrition and protects it from harmful environmental influences.

Sources of Nutrition and Protection

Early in the embryonic period, membranes emerge from the trophoblast to provide the developing organism with the nutrients and protection it will need to survive (see Figure 3.5). The **amnion,** a thin, tough, transparent membrane that holds the amniotic fluid ("bag of waters"), surrounds the embryo. The amniotic fluid cushions the organism as the mother moves about, provides liquid support for its weak muscles and soft bones, and gives it a medium in which it can move and change position.

The human embryo at 3 and 5 weeks after conception.

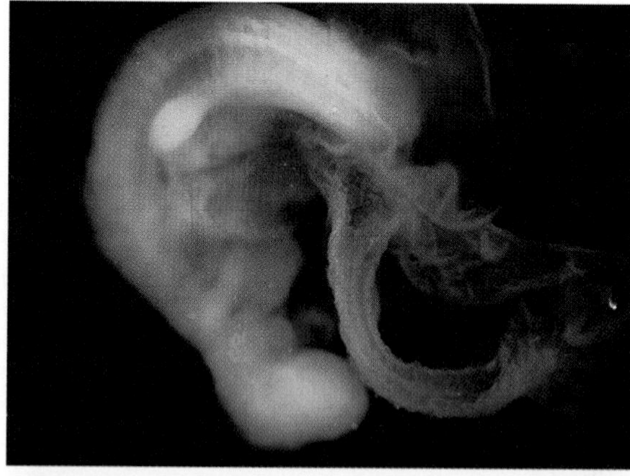

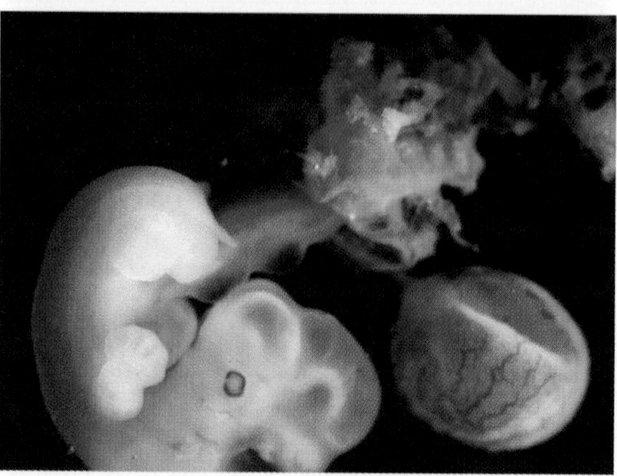

Surrounding the amnion is another membrane, the **chorion,** which becomes the fetal component of the **placenta,** a complex organ made up of tissue from both the mother and the embryo. The placenta and the embryo are linked by the **umbilical cord.** Until birth, the placenta acts simultaneously as a barrier that prevents the bloodstreams of the mother and the infant from coming into direct contact and as a filter that allows nutrients and oxygen to be exchanged. It converts nutrients carried by the mother's blood into food for the embryo. It also enables the embryo's waste products to be absorbed by the mother's bloodstream, from which they are eventually extracted by her kidneys. Thus the mother literally eats, breathes, and urinates for two.

The Growth of the Embryo

While the trophoblast is forming the placenta and the other membranes that will supply and protect the embryo, the growing number of cells in the inner cell mass begin to differentiate into the various kinds of cells that eventually will become all the organs of the body. The first step in this process is the separation of the inner cell mass into two layers. The **ectoderm,** the outer layer, gives rise to the outer surface of the skin, the nails, part of the teeth, the lens of the eye, the inner ear, and the nervous system (the brain, the spinal cord, and the nerves). The **endoderm,** the inner layer, develops into the digestive system and the lungs. Shortly after these two layers form, there appears a middle layer, the **mesoderm,** which will eventually become the muscles, the bones, the circulatory system, and the inner layers of the skin (Gilbert & Raunio, 1997).

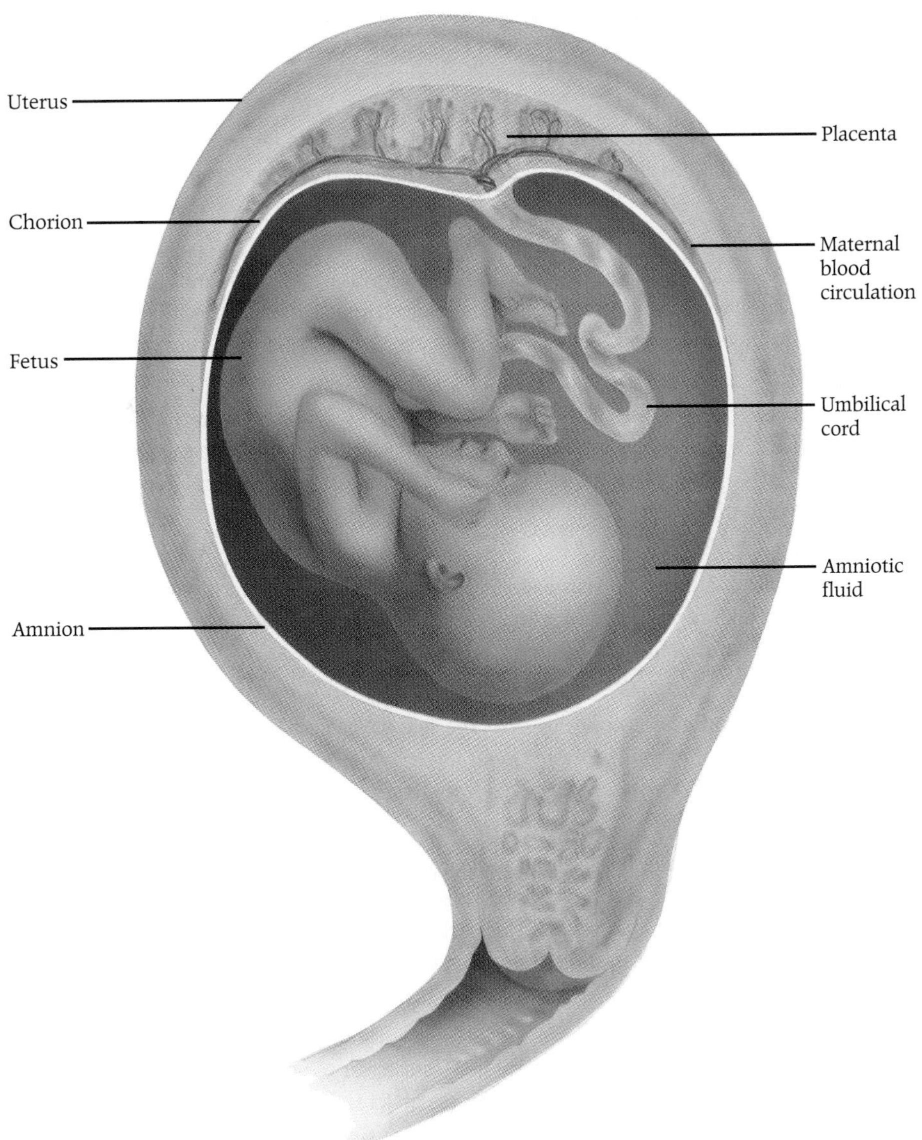

FIGURE 3.5
The fetus in its protective environment. (Adapted from Curtis, 1979.)

As Table 3.1 makes clear, the embryo develops at a breathtaking pace. The table also reflects two patterns of body development that are maintained until the organism reaches adolescence. In the first, the **cephalocaudal pattern**, development proceeds from the head down. The arm buds, for instance, appear before the leg buds. In the second, the **proximodistal pattern**, development proceeds from the middle of the organism out to the periphery. Thus, the spinal cord develops before the arm buds; the upper arm develops before the forearm; and so on. In general, the process of organ formation is the same for all human embryos, but in one major respect—sexual differentiation—it varies. This aspect of development is discussed in Box 3.1.

endoderm Cells of the inner cell mass that develop into the digestive system and the lungs.

mesoderm The cells of the inner cell mass that give rise to the muscles, the bones, and the circulatory system.

cephalocaudal pattern The pattern of development that proceeds from the head down.

proximodistal pattern The pattern of development from the middle of the organism out to the periphery.

The Emergence of Embryonic Movement

When the essential organ systems and the nerve cells of the spine have formed, the embryo becomes capable of its first organized responses to the environment. Studies of spontaneously aborted embryos indicate that the 8-week-old embryo will turn its head and neck in response to a light touch to the area around the mouth. Its arms will quiver, the upper body will flex, and in many cases its mouth will open (de Vries, 1992; Hooker, 1952). Within the

TABLE 3.1 GROWTH AND DEVELOPMENT OF THE EMBRYO

Days 10–13

Cells separate into ectoderm, endoderm, and mesoderm layers. The neural plate, which eventually will become the brain and the spinal cord, forms out of the ectoderm.

Third Week

The three major divisions of the brain—the hindbrain, the midbrain, and the forebrain—begin to differentiate by the end of the third week. Primitive blood cells and blood vessels are present. The heart comes into being, and by the end of the week it is beating.

Fourth Week

Limb buds are visible. Eyes, ears, and a digestive system begin to take form. The major veins and arteries are completed. Vertebrae are present, and nerves begin to take primitive form.

Fifth Week

The umbilical cord takes shape. Bronchial buds, which eventually will become the lungs, take form. Premuscle masses are present in the head, trunk, and limbs. The hand plates are formed.

Sixth Week

The head becomes dominant in size. The halves of the lower jawbone meet and fuse, and the components of the upper jaw are present. The external ear makes its appearance. The three main parts of the brain are distinct.

Seventh Week

The face and neck are beginning to take form. Eyelids take shape. The stomach is taking its final shape and position. Muscles are rapidly differentiating throughout the body and are assuming their final shapes and relationships. The brain is developing thousands of nerve cells per minute.

Eighth Week

The growth of the gut makes the body evenly round. The head is elevated and the neck is distinct. The external, middle, and inner ears assume their final forms. By the end of this week the fetus is capable of some movement and responds to stimulation around the mouth.

womb, such movements are not detected by the mother because the embryo is still exceedingly small.

THE FETAL PERIOD

The fetal period begins once all the basic tissues and organs exist in rudimentary form and the tissue that will become the skeleton begins to harden, or ossify (Gilbert, 1991). During the fetal period, which lasts from the eighth or ninth week of pregnancy until birth, the fetus increases in length from approximately 1¼ inches to 20 inches and in weight from 8 grams to 3250 grams (see Figure 3.6).

Over the course of the fetal period, each of the organ systems increases in complexity. By the tenth week after conception, the intestines have assumed their characteristic position in the body. Two weeks later, the fetus's external sexual characteristics are visible, and its neck is well defined. By the end of the 16 weeks, the head is erect, the lower limbs are well developed, and the ears, which began to take form in the fourth week, migrate from the neck to the sides of the head. By the end of the fifth month, the fetus has almost as

BOX 3.1 The Development of Sexual Differentiation

Sexual differentiation provides a striking example of the pattern of differentiation and reintegration that characterizes an organism's development. At each stage of prenatal sexual development we find a new configuration of the parts that were present during the preceding stage, and new mechanisms appear that will regulate sexual development in the next stage (Jones, 1997).

The genes that influence sexual determination are located on the X and Y chromosomes inherited at conception. Zygotes with one X and one Y chromosome are genetically male, whereas zygotes with two X chromosomes are genetically female. For the first 6 weeks after conception, however, there is no structural difference between genetically male and genetically female embryos. Both males and females have two ridges of tissue, called *gonadal ridges,* in the urogenital region from which the sex organs will develop. These ridges give no clue to the sex of the embryo.

If the embryo is genetically male (XY), the process of sexual differentiation begins during the seventh week of life, when the gonadal ridges begin to form testes. If the embryo is genetically female (XX), no changes are apparent in the gonadal ridges until several weeks later, when ovaries begin to form. Thus the genes inherited at the moment of conception determine whether the sex glands that develop from the gonadal ridges will be male testes or female ovaries.

At the end of the seventh week after conception, genetically male and genetically female embryos have the same urogenital membrane and primitive phallus, the future penis or clitoris. From this point on, though, it is not the presence of the Y chromosome itself but rather the presence or absence of male gonads that determines whether the embryo will develop male or female genital ducts. The male hormones produced by the male gonads, called *androgens,* determine maleness. Chief among the androgens is testosterone. If testosterone is present, the membranes are transformed into the male penis and scrotum. If testosterone is not present, female external genitalia are formed. This pattern of changes shows that femaleness depends on the absence of testosterone, *not* on the secretion of hormones by the ovaries. The influence of androgens is not limited to the gonads and the genital tract. During the last 6 months of prenatal development, the presence of testosterone suppresses the natural rhythmic activity of the pituitary gland, located in the brain. If testosterone is absent, the pituitary gland establishes the cyclical pattern of hormone secretion that is characteristic of the female and eventually comes to control her menstrual cycle (Wilson et al., 1981).

Embryologists are still uncertain about how the presence of androgens creates differences in brain activity, but data from animal research suggest that androgens may shape the development of certain neural pathways in the brain (Toran-Allerand, 1984). These studies show that a dose of testosterone given to a rat at a critical period in the prenatal development of its brain will cause it to be responsive to male hormones and insensitive to female hormones from then on, no matter what its genetic sex. If the brain does not receive testosterone at this critical period, it will be responsive to female hormones.

Because the embryo has the potential to develop into either a male or a female, errors in sex development sometimes result in a baby's having sex organs that show characteristics of both sexes. A baby with this condition is called a *hermaphrodite.* Hermaphroditism is caused by either excessive androgen action in an embryo that is chromosomally female (XX) or inadequate androgen action in an embryo that is chromosomally male (XY).

There are three types of hermaphrodites. *True hermaphrodites,* who are the rarest type, are usually chromosomally female and always have a uterus, but they have both ovarian and testicular tissue and their genitalia can be all-female, all-male, or exhibit features of both sexes. *Female pseudohermaphrodites* are chromosomally female and have normal internal sex organs, but their genitalia are masculinized (usually including an enlarged clitoris) or exhibit characteristics of both sexes. *Male pseudohermaphrodites* are chromosomally male, but their testes remain undescended, they often have a uterus and fallopian tubes, and their genitalia are either female or ambiguous.

many nerve cells as it will ever have as a person. By the end of the seventh month, the lungs are capable of breathing air, and the eyes, which have been closed, open and can respond to light. By the end of the eighth month, many folds of the brain are present, and during the ninth month, the brain becomes considerably more convoluted. In the final weeks before birth, the fetus doubles in weight.

Fetal Activity

The increasing complexity of the organism during the fetal period is accompanied by the appearance of new behaviors and changes in the level of its activity. Within 8 weeks, the fetus begins to make generalized movements. Over the next few weeks, body movements become increasingly varied and coordinated

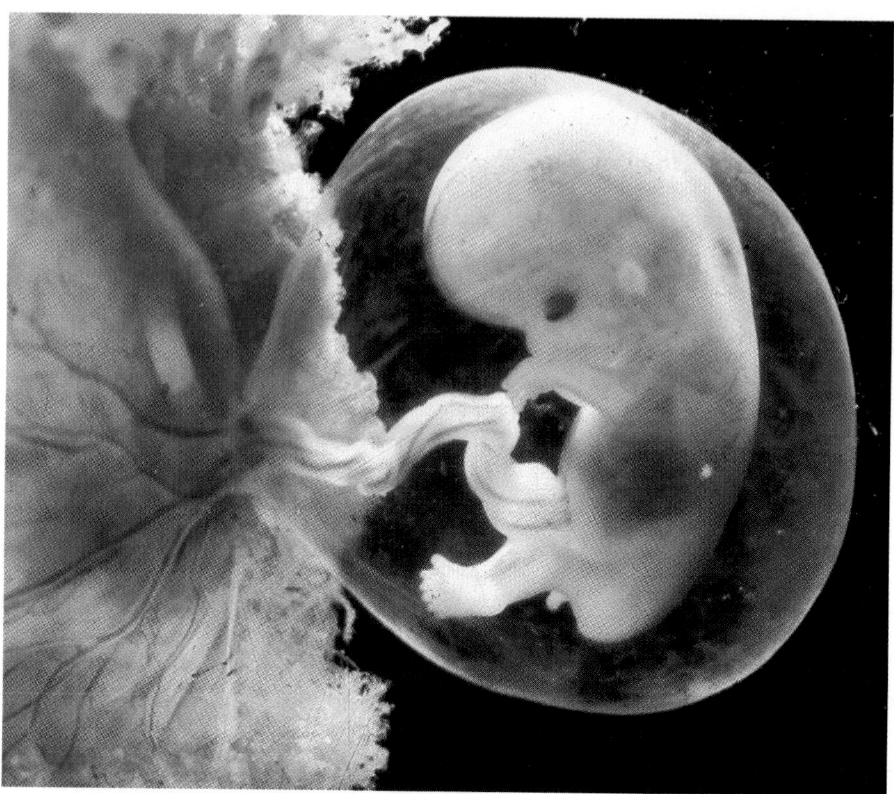

FIGURE 3.6
The fetus at the beginning of the fetal period (approximately 9 weeks). The way the umbilical cord is attached to the placenta is clearly visible.

(see Table 3.2). At 15 weeks of age, the fetus is capable of all the movements observable in newborn infants (James et al., 1995). Toward the end of the fourth month, the fetus is big enough for the mother to feel its movements.

From 24 to 32 weeks after conception, the relatively high rate of fetal activity begins to be interrupted by quiet periods, and there is a gradual decrease in the fetus's movements (Kisilevsky & Low, 1998). At the same time, certain kinds of activity, such as "breathing" movements of the lungs and chest, increase (Natali et al., 1988). The periods during which general activity levels are reduced are believed to reflect the development of neural pathways

TABLE 3.2 Appearance of Fetal Movements in Early Pregnancy

Movement	Gestational Age (weeks)
Any movement	7
Startle	8
Generalized movements	8
Hiccups	8
Isolated arm movements	9
Head retroflexion	9
Hand–face contact	10
Breathing	10
Jaw opening	10
Stretching	10
Head anteflexion	10
Yawn	11
Suck and swallow	12

Source: De Vries et al., 1982. Adapted by permission.

that inhibit movement. The appearance of these inhibitory pathways is related to maturation in the higher regions of the brain (see Figure 3.7).

Functions of Fetal Activity

Evidence indicates that spontaneous fetal activity is important to development (Smotherman & Robinson, 1996). Experiments with chick embryos, for example, suggest that prenatal activity is crucial to normal limb development. Under normal circumstances, the spinal cord sends out neurons, or nerve cells, to connect the limbs to the brain—many more neurons than the animal will need when it is fully coordinated. Many of these neurons die off, while the remainder are connected to muscles in an efficient way. If chick

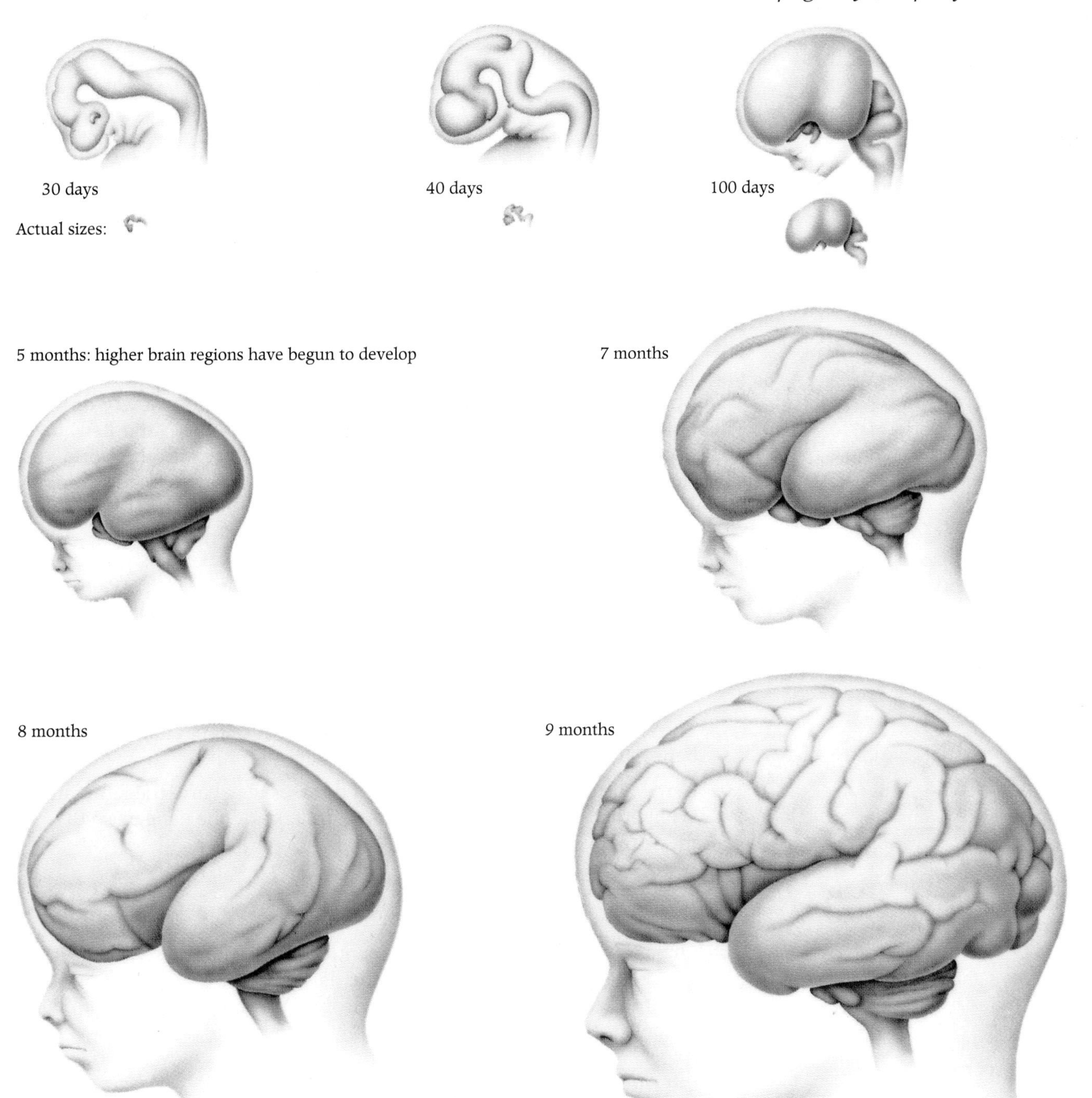

FIGURE 3.7
The prenatal development of the brain. The primitive parts of the brain are present very early. The cerebral hemispheres, with their characteristic convolutions, do not make their appearance until the middle of pregnancy. (Adapted from Cowan, 1979.)

The idea that a baby is growing inside the mother becomes much less abstract when you listen to its heartbeat.

embryos are treated with drugs that prevent them from moving, the elimination of excess neurons that ordinarily accompanies neuromuscular development fails to occur. The results are disastrous. In as little as 1 or 2 days, the failure to prune away all but the neurons compatible with coordinated movement causes the joints of the chick embryos to become fixed into rigid structures, a result showing that movement is necessary for normal limb development (Pittman & Oppenheim, 1979). Fetal movements are believed to play a similar role in establishing basic neuronal connections in humans.

Breathing movements are another good example of the importance of prenatal activity to the human fetus. The fetus does not breathe in utero. It obtains oxygen through the placenta. Yet if the fetus does not make "breathing" movements with its chest and lungs, the muscles necessary for respiration after birth would be insufficiently developed.

THE DEVELOPING ORGANISM IN THE PRENATAL ENVIRONMENT

The marvelous ways in which the mother's body provides a protective and supportive environment for prenatal growth can blind us to the realization that even in the womb the fetus is not independent of the larger world. Modern research makes it clear that the organism is affected not only by its immediate environment but by the world outside the womb as well.

The fetus is influenced by its uterine environment in a variety of ways. The mother's digestive system and heart are sources of noise, and her movements provide motion stimuli. The fetus comes in contact with the world outside the mother through the wall of her abdomen and, less directly, through the placenta and umbilical cord. Nutrients, oxygen, some viruses, and some potentially harmful chemicals all cross the placenta to the fetus. Through these biologically mediated routes, a mother's experiences, illnesses, diet, and social circumstances can affect the child before it is born (Nijhuis, 1992).

Understanding the effect of the larger environment on the developing fetus is important for several reasons:

- Substances and stimulation coming from the environment may have a significant impact on fetal development.
- The fetus's responses to the environment provide clues about the behavioral capacities that the child will have at birth.
- Certain drugs, pollutants, and several diseases may harm the fetus, and it is important for prospective parents to understand the dangers so that they can take preventive action.

THE FETUS'S SENSORY CAPACITIES

Using modern techniques of measurement and recording, researchers have begun to produce a detailed picture of the development of sensory capacities before birth (Lecanuet & Schaal, 1996). This information is essential for determining how the fetus is influenced by its environment.

Sensing Motion

The vestibular system of the middle ear, which controls the sense of balance, begins to function in the human fetus about 5 months after conception and is fully mature at birth (Lecanuet & Schaal, 1996). This early maturity means that the fetus is capable of sensing changes in the mother's posture and orienting itself as it floats inside the fluid-filled amniotic sac.

Vision

Little is known for certain about the extent of the fetus's visual experience. At 26 weeks following conception, fetuses respond to light; it causes their heart rates to change and it causes them to move (Abrams et al., 1995). Aidan Macfarlane (1977) suggests that toward the end of pregnancy, the fetus may be able to see light that has penetrated the mother's stretched stomach wall. He likens the fetus's visual experience to the glow seen when the palm of the hand covers the lens of a flashlight.

Sound

The fetus is able to respond to sound at 5 to 6 months after conception (Shahidullah & Hepper, 1993). Studies in which tiny microphones have been inserted into the uterus adjacent to the fetus's head reveal that the average sound level inside the womb is approximately 75 decibels, about the level at which we hear the outside world when we ride in a car with the windows up. This background noise is punctuated by the sound of air passing through the mother's stomach and, every second or so, by the more intense sound of the mother's heartbeat (Krasnegor & Lecanuet, 1995). For many years it was believed that these sounds were so loud they would mask most noise coming from outside the mother's body. More recently, however, it has been found that fetuses hear sounds coming from outside the mother's body and can discriminate among them. Their hearing improves steadily during fetal life (Hepper & Shahidullah, 1994).

Of all such sounds, the mother's voice is heard best because it is also transmitted as vibrations through her body. When the mother speaks brief sentences aloud, it is possible to detect changes in the fetus's heart rate (Lecanuet & Schaal, 1996).

Because external sounds must pass through the mother's abdomen and the amniotic fluid before the fetus can hear them, things sound different in the womb than they do outside it. In experiments using recordings of the mother's natural voice and her voice when it has been filtered to resemble how it sounded to the fetus while in the womb, newborns prefer the latter (Fifer & Moon, 1995).

FETAL LEARNING

The folklore of many societies includes the belief that the fetus can learn while in the womb (Verny & Kelly, 1981). Although such beliefs have met with considerable skepticism, there is evidence that the fetus learns from at least some events both inside and outside the mother (Hepper, 1996; Lecanuet et al., 1995).

One line of evidence for fetal learning comes from an unusual experiment by Lee Salk (1973). Working in a hospital where mothers and their newborn infants were customarily separated a good deal of the time, Salk arranged for three groups of infants to experience three different experimental conditions. One group was exposed to the sound of a normal heartbeat of 80 pulses per minute, the rate they would have heard while in the womb; another group heard a heart beating 120 times per minute; and a third group heard no special sounds at all. The infants who heard the accelerated heartbeat became so upset that Salk terminated their part in the experiment. The babies who heard the normal heartbeat, however, gained more weight and cried less over the 4 days that the experiment continued than did the group that heard no special sounds. The specific influence of the sound of the

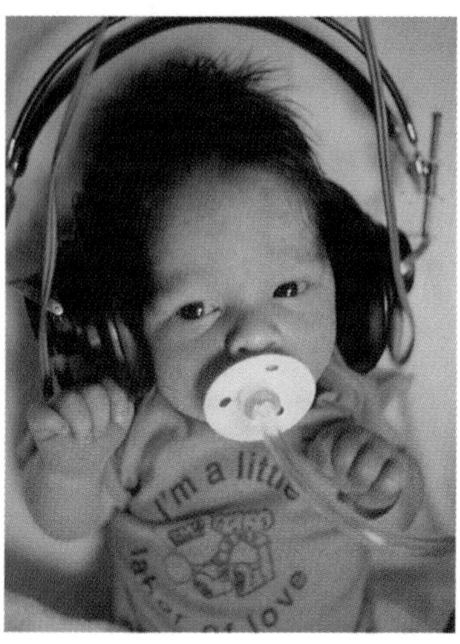

FIGURE 3.8
This baby is listening to a recording of its mother telling a story. The apparatus records changes in sucking to determine how newborns react to stories read to them while they were in the womb.

normal heartbeat suggests that the infants' experience in the womb had made this sound familiar and therefore reassuring.

Salk's experiment suggests that fetuses learn from experiences that originate inside the mother. Evidence of similar learning from stimuli originating outside the mother comes from several sources (DeCasper & Spence, 1986; Hepper, 1996; Sandman et al., 1997). Anthony DeCasper and Melanie Spence (1986), for example, asked 16 pregnant women to read aloud a particular passage from *The Cat in the Hat,* a well-known rhyming children's story by Dr. Seuss, twice a day for the last month and a half before their babies were due. By the time the babies were born, the passage had been read to them for a total of about 3½ hours.

Two or three days after the babies were born, DeCasper and Spence tested them with a special pacifier that had been wired to record sucking rates (see Figure 3.8). First the babies were allowed to suck for 2 minutes to establish a baseline sucking rate. Afterward, changes in the rate of sucking turned on or off a tape recording of their mothers reading a story. For half of the babies, increasing their sucking rates turned on the passage from *The Cat in the Hat* that their mothers had previously read aloud, while decreasing their sucking rate turned on a story their mothers had not read. For the other half, increased sucking turned on the new story, while decreased sucking produced *The Cat in the Hat.* The key finding was that the infants modified their rates of sucking in the direction that produced *The Cat in the Hat.* The investigators concluded that the babies had indeed heard the stories being read to them by their mothers and that their learning in the womb influenced the sounds they found rewarding after birth.

DeCasper and his colleagues (1994) confirmed this conclusion by testing 17 pregnant women living in Paris. First they asked the women to read aloud a French children's rhyme called *La Poulette* ("The Chicken") three times a day for a month beginning 6 weeks before their babies were due. Four weeks later the researchers brought the women to their laboratory and played tape recordings of *La Poulette* and an unfamiliar story over a speaker just above the women's stomachs. The researchers found that the fetuses' heart rates decreased when *La Poulette* was presented (a sign of attention in infants) but that the new story produced no change in heartbeat.

MATERNAL CONDITIONS AND PRENATAL DEVELOPMENT

In addition to being affected by stimuli that impinge directly on its senses, the fetus is affected by the mother's physical, social, and psychological conditions. These influences reach the fetus through changes in the mother that are then transmitted to the fetus through the placenta. Her body chemistry may be altered by factors as diverse as her attitude toward having the baby, her emotional state, the food she eats, and her general health.

The Effects of Maternal Attitudes and Psychological Stress

Many physicians who care for pregnant women and newborn infants suspect that a woman's feelings of well-being and her attitude toward her pregnancy affect the well-being of the fetus and of the child after its birth. This suspicion is supported by evidence that the presence of a sympathetic mate and other supportive family members, adequate housing, and steady employment—factors that give a woman a basic sense of security—appear to enhance the prospects for a healthy baby (Pritchard & MacDonald, 1980; Thompson, 1990).

The clearest evidence that a mother-to-be's negative attitudes can affect her baby's development comes from an extensive investigation conducted in Czechoslovakia in the 1960s and 1970s. Henry David (1981) studied the lives of 220 children whose mothers indicated strong negative attitudes toward having them by twice asking for an abortion. The refusal of the abortion was an indication that medical authorities believed these women to be capable of carrying through the pregnancy and raising the child.

The unwanted children were compared with a carefully matched control group of children whose mothers either had planned for or had accepted their pregnancies. The mothers in the two groups were matched for socioeconomic status and age; the children were matched for sex, birth order, number of siblings, and date of birth. At birth, the unwanted children weighed less and needed more medical help than the children in the control group, even though their mothers had ready access to medical care and were judged to be in good health themselves.

Even when a child is wanted, and a pregnant woman has a supportive family, a moderate amount of stress can be expected during pregnancy. The mother-to-be has to adjust her life to accommodate new responsibilities. One who decides to quit her job may have to cope with a reduced income. Another may be working so hard that she feels she does not have enough time to take care of herself, let alone her expected child. And if the pregnancy was unplanned, as many are, the stress that normally accompanies pregnancy may be magnified.

Studies have shown that a mother who is under stress or becomes emotionally upset secretes hormones, such as adrenaline and cortisone, that pass through the placenta and have a measurable effect on the fetus's motor activity (Van Den Bergh, 1992). Although the evidence is still sketchy, several studies have found an association between psychological stress and pregnancy complications. The most frequent findings are that stress during pregnancy is associated with premature delivery and low birth weight (Hedegaard et al., 1993; Lou et al., 1994). In the relatively favored circumstances of middle-class life in industrialized countries, many women may experience little stress during pregnancy; but most of the world's women are poor, live in difficult circumstances, and must worry about how to provide for their children before and after birth. Even with a sympathetic mate or relatives to ease the burden, stress seems unavoidable under such conditions and is part of a pattern of environmental circumstances that puts many women and their unborn children at risk.

Nutritional Influences on Prenatal Development

Fetuses are totally dependent on their mothers for the nutrients that keep them alive and allow them to develop. Research indicates that a pregnant woman needs to consume between 2000 and 2800 calories daily in a well-balanced diet that includes all the essential vitamins and minerals (National Academy of Sciences, 1989). In addition, pregnant women are advised to increase their intake of folic acid (a member of the vitamin B complex group commonly found in green vegetables and fruit), calcium, and iron (Rosso, 1990).

The foods believed to be good for pregnant women are determined by cultural beliefs and practices (Rosso, 1990). In the United States, for example, the increased consumption of foods rich in calcium is widely believed to prevent the loss of "one tooth per pregnancy" (Adair, 1987). Milk is a good source of calcium, and in the United States, physicians recommend that pregnant women drink several glasses a day.

Extreme Malnutrition

Poor maternal nutrition can have detrimental effects on prenatal development. In cases of extreme malnutrition, the effects can be profound. The clearest evidence of this effect comes from studies of sudden periods of famine. In the fall and winter of 1944–1945, for example, famine struck the large cities of western Holland when the Nazi occupation forces embargoed all food shipments because Dutch railway workers had gone on strike to aid the advancing

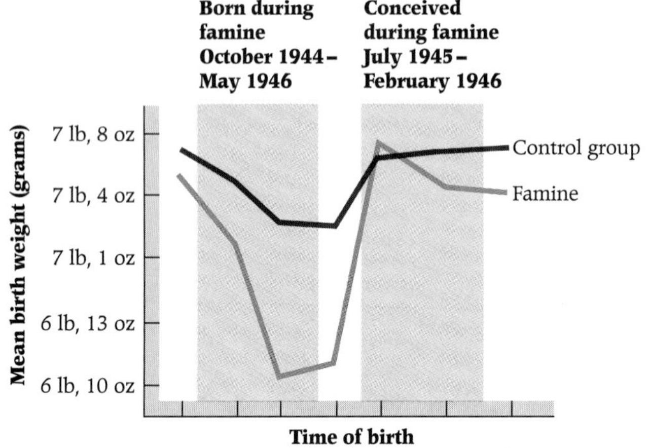

FIGURE 3.9

The average birth weights of children born and children conceived in Rotterdam, Holland (famine group) during a period of severe famine following World War II and the average birth weights of children from other parts of Holland (control group) where conditions were less severe. Note that the Rotterdam children born during the famine are significantly lighter than the control group children, who received better nutrition during gestation. (Adapted from Stein et al., 1975.)

Allied armies. During and after the famine, spontaneous abortions, stillbirths, malformations, and deaths at birth increased markedly. Many of those babies who were born alive weighed significantly less than normal, as Figure 3.9 indicates (Stein et al., 1975).

A more severe wartime famine occurred in the Soviet Union. In September 1941 Leningrad (now St. Petersburg) was encircled by the German army, and no supplies reached the city until February 1942. The standard daily food ration in late November 1941 was 250 grams of bread (four slices) for factory workers, 125 grams (two slices) for everybody else. The bread was 25 percent sawdust. The number of infants born in the first half of 1942 was much lower than normal, and stillbirths doubled. Very few infants were born in the second half of 1942, all of them to couples who had better access to food than did the rest of the population. These babies were, on the average, more than a pound lighter than babies born before the siege, and they were much more likely to be premature. They were also in very poor condition at birth; they had little vitality and were unable to maintain body temperature adequately (Antonov, 1947).

The sudden famine in Leningrad produced nutritional variations so extreme that normal environmental influences on prenatal development were dwarfed by comparison. Consequently, the specific effects of maternal malnutrition on the developing fetus during particular segments of the prenatal period could be isolated with a high degree of certainty. Severe nutritional deprivation during the first 3 months of pregnancy was most likely to result in abnormalities of the central nervous system, premature birth, and death. Deprivation during the last 3 months of pregnancy was more likely to retard fetal growth and result in low birth weight.

Undernourishment and Associated Factors

Studies of the relation between maternal nutrition, prenatal development, and neonatal health suggest that lesser degrees of malnourishment also increase risks to the fetus. Undernourishment can lead to low birth weight and even miscarriage (Jones, 1997). There is also some evidence that undernourished fetuses are at greater risk for heart disease, strokes, and other illnesses in later life (Barker, 1995; Godfrey, 1998). This association is thought to result from the fetus's adaptation to an inadequate supply of nutrients during a sensitive period in early prenatal life which leads to permanent changes in physiology and metabolism.

However, it is often difficult to isolate the effects of poor nutrition, because malnourished mothers frequently live in impoverished environments where housing, sanitation, education, and medical care, including prenatal care, are also inadequate. (Table 3.3 shows just how important prenatal care can be for low-income mothers and their children.) Expectant mothers with low incomes are more likely to suffer from diseases or simply to be in a weakened state than are women who live in better material circumstances. Their babies are more likely to suffer from a wide variety of birth defects and illnesses and to be born prematurely (Luke et al., 1993). According to a variety of studies conducted in many parts of the world, including the United States, low-income mothers are also more likely to have babies who die at birth or soon after birth (United Nations Children's Fund, 1999).

The possibility of preventing or reducing the damaging effects of malnutrition and an impoverished environment has been demonstrated by several studies. In the basic design of this type of research, some expectant mothers and their offspring receive supplemental food and medical attention and are compared with those who do not. One of the largest intervention programs

TABLE 3.3 RELATIONSHIP BETWEEN BIRTH COMPLICATIONS AND PRENATAL MEDICAL CARE

	Number of Complications per 100 Births	
Complication	**Without Prenatal Care**	**With Prenatal Care**
Premature rupture of membranes	13	2
Ominous fetal heart rate	10	5
Prematurity	13	2
Low birth weight (less than 2500 grams)	21	6
Low Apgar score (a measure of immediate risk)	8	2
Hospital stay of more than 3 days	24	12
Prenatal death	4	1

Note: The data are for low-income women in San Diego, California.
Source: Moore et al., 1986.

designed to assess the effects of a massive supplemental food program for women, infants, and children—dubbed *WIC*—was initiated by the U.S. government in 1972. Low-income women in the program are given vouchers for such staples as milk, eggs, fruit juices, and dried beans. Women who have participated in the WIC program have been found to have fewer babies who die during infancy than do comparable women who have not participated in the program (Moss & Carver, 1998).

Food supplements during pregnancy have also been found to be important to the baby's postnatal intellectual development. In a study carried out in Louisiana, children whose mothers had participated in the WIC program were evaluated on a variety of intellectual measures when they were 6 or 7 years old and were already enrolled in school. Those children whose mothers had received food supplements during the last 3 months of their pregnancies—the period in which the fetal brain undergoes especially rapid development—outperformed the children of mothers who did not receive food supplements until after their children were born (Hicks et al., 1982). Similar results were obtained in a study of a food supplement program in rural Guatemala (Pollitt, 1994).

These conclusions concerning maternal and fetal malnutrition must be considered with some caution because they are not always based on carefully controlled studies. However, the overall evidence strongly suggests that millions of children throughout the world are damaged by undernourishment both before and after birth. Most of these children do not receive food supplements, and even fewer receive high-quality educational help. Quite the opposite: they experience a cascade of risk factors, of which malnutrition is only one (see Figure 3.10). Together such conditions lead to high rates of infant mortality and shorter life expectancies (Pollitt et al., 1993).

TERATOGENS: ENVIRONMENTAL SOURCES OF BIRTH DEFECTS

Other threats to the prenatal organism come from **teratogens**—environmental agents that can cause deviations in normal development and can lead to serious abnormalities or death (see Figure 3.11). (The term comes from the Greek

teratogens Environmental agents that cause deviations from normal development and lead to abnormalities or death.

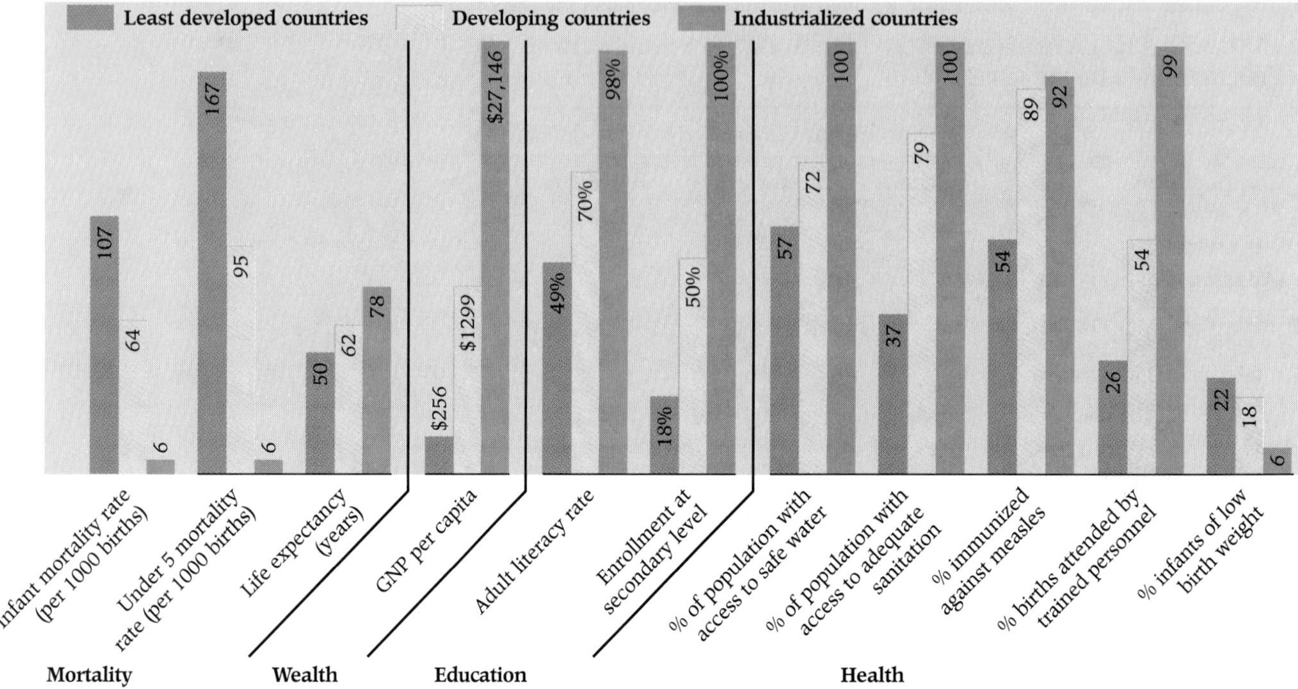

FIGURE 3.10

In many countries of the world, poor economic conditions create a set of risk factors. For example, poor health conditions and parents' lack of education negatively influence child health and welfare. (Adapted from United Nations Children's Fund [UNICEF], 1999.)

teras, "monster.") Commonly encountered teratogens include certain drugs and infections, radiation, and pollution.

Drugs

Most pregnant women in the United States take some medication during pregnancy, primarily over-the-counter analgesics, antinauseants, or sleep medications. Fortunately, most of these drugs do not appear to harm the fetus, but there are some that do. It is also estimated that a sizable minority of women use nonmedical drugs during pregnancy, ranging from caffeine, alcohol, and the chemical substances in cigarette smoke to "hard" drugs such as cocaine and heroin. Most of these drugs are harmful to prenatal development (Cunningham et al., 1997).

FIGURE 3.11

This young woman demonstrates some of the devastating effects of agent orange, an environmental pollutant used during the Vietnam War.

Prescription and Nonprescription Drugs The potential teratogenic effects of prescription drugs first came to light in the case of thalidomide. From 1956 until 1961, thalidomide was used in Europe as a sedative and to control nausea in the early stages of pregnancy. The women who took the drug were unharmed by it, and many of the children they bore suffered no ill effects. Some children, however, were born without arms and legs; their hands and feet were attached directly to their torsos like flippers. Some had defects of sight and hearing as well. About 8000 deformed children were born before their problems were traced to the drug and it was removed from the market (Persaud, 1977).

Since the disastrous effects of thalidomide were discovered, other prescription drugs have been found to cause abnormalities in the developing organism, including the antibiotics streptomycin and tetracycline, anticoagulants, anticonvulsants, most artificial hormones, Thorazine (used in the treatment of schizophrenia), Valium (a tranquilizer), and Accutane (used to treat difficult cases of acne). In large doses, aspirin can also cause abnormalities. Indeed, all drugs are capable of entering the bloodstream of the developing organism, and only a few have been studied well enough to determine whether they are "safe" for expectant mothers. Therefore, pregnant women are advised to check with their physicians before taking any nonprescription drug, and physicians are advised to prescribe only the most necessary therapeutic drugs for their pregnant patients.

Caffeine Caffeine, which is found in coffee, tea, and cola, is the most common drug used by pregnant women. There is no evidence that caffeine causes malformations in the fetus. However, some studies have found that caffeine in large doses is associated with an increased rate of spontaneous abortion and with low birth weight (Dlugosz & Bracken, 1992; Heller, 1987). On this basis, women are advised to limit their caffeine intake during pregnancy.

Tobacco Smoking tobacco is not known to produce birth defects, but it has been found to harm the fetus in a variety of ways. Smoking is related to an increase in the rate of spontaneous abortion, stillbirth, and neonatal death (Roquer et al., 1995). Nicotine, the addictive substance in tobacco, causes abnormal growth of the placenta, resulting in a reduction in the transfer of nutrients to the fetus. It also reduces the oxygen and increases the carbon monoxide in the bloodstreams of both mother and fetus. As a result, mothers who smoke usually have babies whose birth weights are lower than those of infants born to women who do not smoke (see Figure 3.12). The effects of cigarette smoke seem to be dose-related: mothers who smoke more have babies who weigh less (Roquer et al., 1995). Recent findings suggest that even if a mother does not smoke herself, the birth weight of her baby can be significantly affected by the cigarette smoke of others (Roquer et al., 1995). There is also some evidence that maternal smoking during pregnancy and smoking after pregnancy may increase the risk of sudden infant death, a syndrome in which a baby stops breathing and dies silently without apparent cause (Niebyl, 1994).

Alcohol After smoking, alcohol is the most commonly abused drug. About 4 percent of all U.S. women of childbearing age suffer from alcoholism (Stratton

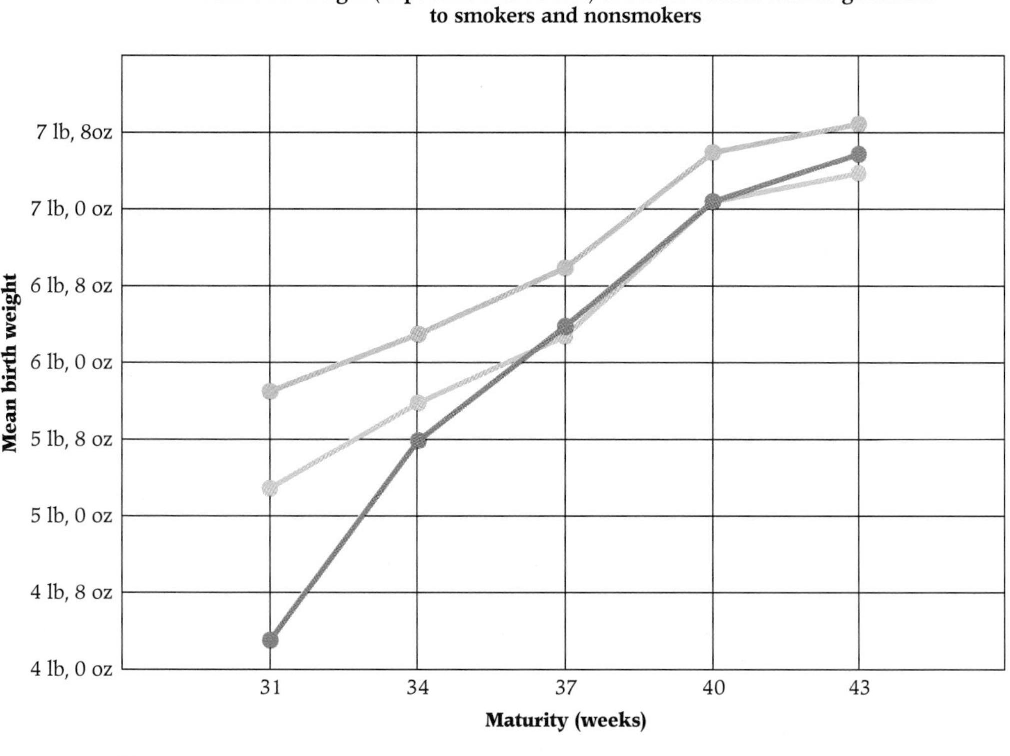

FIGURE 3.12
Mean birth weight of babies born at various gestations (weeks of maturity) to smokers (both heavy and light smokers) and nonsmokers. Note that the infants born to heavy smokers can be more than a pound lighter than those born to nonsmokers. (Naeye, 1978.)

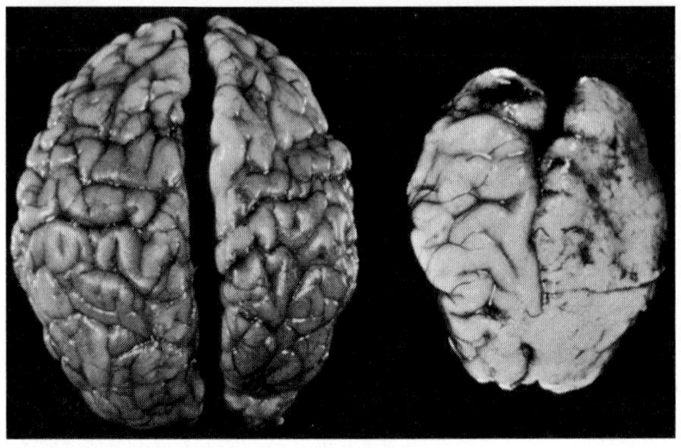

FIGURE 3.13

Children who suffer from fetal alcohol syndrome do not merely look abnormal (upper photo); their brains are underdeveloped and many are severely retarded. The brain of a child who suffered from fetal alcohol syndrome (lower right) lacks the convolutions characteristic of the brain of a normal child (lower left).

et al., 1996). Women who drink substantial amounts of alcohol while they are pregnant are in danger of having a baby with serious birth defects. One study found that 71 percent of the infants born to mothers who were heavy drinkers during pregnancy—that is, who drank 3 ounces or more of 100-proof liquor a day—were abnormal in some way (Niebyl, 1994). Many of these babies suffered from **fetal alcohol syndrome**, a set of symptoms that includes an abnormally small head and underdeveloped brain, eye abnormalities, congenital heart disease, joint anomalies, and malformations of the face (see Figure 3.13). The physical growth and mental development of children with this syndrome are likely to be retarded (Jacobson et al., 1993; Niebyl, 1994). Women who drank heavily during the first trimester of pregnancy and then reduced their consumption of alcohol during the second and third trimesters do not reduce the risk of having children with this affliction (Vorhees & Mollnow, 1987). Binge drinking—that is, the periodic consumption of 5 or more drinks on a single occasion—early in pregnancy has been found to be associated with a subtle impairment of learning and behavior in adolescence (Olson et al., 1997).

The effects of lower levels of alcohol consumption on development are currently in dispute. Research has found that in some cases the equivalent of one or two glasses of wine, either occasionally or daily, causes no discernible harm to the fetus. In other cases, such drinking results in "fetal alcohol effects," which include subtle but measurable deficits in cognitive and motor functioning. These effects will vary with both the amount of prenatal exposure to alcohol and the timing of the exposure.

Given the uncertainty of the risks of moderate drinking during pregnancy, it is generally recommended that pregnant women abstain from drinking entirely. In addition, some of the most serious damage from alcohol can be caused in the first weeks of pregnancy, so women who are trying to become pregnant are also advised to abstain (Cunningham et al., 1997).

Marijuana A national survey of 4 million women in the United States who gave birth in 1992 found that 2.9 percent had used marijuana at some time during their pregnancies (Lee, 1998). Marijuana has not been definitely found to cause birth defects, but its use is associated with low birth weight. Some researchers have also found an increase in premature delivery among women who use marijuana more than once a week. However, it is uncertain whether these effects can be solely attributed to the use of marijuana. Women in the United States who use marijuana during pregnancy tend to be poorer, less educated, younger, single, and more likely to use other illegal drugs than mothers who do not use marijuana. They also receive less prenatal care and gain less weight.

In the United States and Canada, babies whose mothers used marijuana when they were pregnant have been found to startle more readily, have tremors, and experience problems with their sleep cycles. However, in a study carried out in Jamaica, where the use of the drug is commonly accepted and is not associated with the use of other drugs or the consumption of alcohol, it was found that on tests of physiological and social responses, 1-month-olds who had been exposed to marijuana in utero performed as well as or slightly better than babies whose mothers did not use the drug when they were pregnant (Dreher et al., 1994). Such findings illustrate the importance of the cultural and social context within which a drug is used. They do not detract from the fact that the drug has the potential to be a risk factor in the unborn child's development.

fetal alcohol syndrome A syndrome found in babies whose mothers were heavy consumers of alcohol while pregnant. Symptoms include an abnormally small head and underdeveloped brain, eye abnormalities, congenital heart disease, joint anomalies, and malformations of the face.

Cocaine Cocaine is a stimulant that rapidly produces addiction in the user. It may result in numerous medical complications for the mother-to-be, including heart attacks, strokes, rupture of the aorta, and seizures (Cunningham et al., 1997). Babies born to cocaine-addicted mothers have a variety of problems, most of which can be attributed to a decreased fetal, uterine, and placental blood flow caused by the drug. These babies are more likely to be stillborn or premature, to have low birth weights, to have strokes, and to have birth defects (Niebyl, 1994). Babies born to cocaine-addicted mothers are described as being irritable, liable to react excessively to stimulation, uncoordinated, and slow learners (Alessandri et al., 1993; Benderky & Lewis, 1998).

Residual effects of cocaine exposure during the prenatal period may last for several years. For example, preschool-age children who were exposed to cocaine prenatally are likely to experience difficulty regulating their attention and emotional arousal when presented with novel tasks (Mayes et al., 1998).

Despite the justified concern about the effects of prenatal exposure to cocaine, some researchers have been critical of claims that cocaine itself is the cause of these problems (Coles, 1993). These critics note that many mothers who use cocaine also drink alcohol and use other drugs. In addition, many of them are poor and live in stressful circumstances. All these factors are known to contribute to symptoms such as those attributed to prenatal cocaine exposure (Lester & Tronick, 1994).

Methadone and Heroin Babies of mothers who are addicted to either heroin or methadone are born addicted themselves and must be given heroin or methadone shortly after birth if they are not to undergo the often life-threatening ordeal of withdrawal. These babies are more likely to be premature, underweight, and vulnerable to respiratory illnesses (Kaltenbach et al., 1998).

While these babies are being weaned from the drugs to which they were born addicted, they are irritable and have tremors, their cries are abnormal, their sleep is disturbed, and their motor control is diminished. The effects of the addiction are still apparent in their motor control 4 months later. Even after a year, their ability to pay attention is impaired (Jones & Lopez, 1990).

Several studies have reported long-term developmental problems in children exposed in utero to heroin, methadone, or opiate derivatives, but, as with cocaine, whether these problems can be entirely attributed to the mother's drug use is still open to question (Wagner et al., 1998).

Infections and Other Conditions

A variety of infection-causing microorganisms can endanger the embryo, the fetus, and the newborn. Most infections spread from the mother to the unborn child across the placental barrier. In a few instances, however, the baby may become infected during the passage through the birth canal. Some of the more common infections and other maternal conditions that may affect the developing human organism are summarized below; Table 3.4 summarizes others.

Rubella In 1941 Dr. N. M. Gregg, an Australian, noticed a sudden increase in the number of infants who were born blind. He interviewed their mothers and found that many of them recalled having had a mild rash, swollen lymph glands, and a low fever—all symptoms of rubella, or German measles—early in their pregnancies. Gregg (1941) wrote an article suggesting that there might be some connection between a rubella epidemic in the summer of 1940 and the subsequent increase in the number of babies who were born blind; it alerted the medical community to this danger for the first time. Since then, researchers have found that rubella causes a syndrome of congenital heart disease, cataracts, deafness, and mental retardation in 54 percent of all babies born to mothers who suffer from the disease during the first 12 weeks of

TABLE 3.4 SOME MATERNAL DISEASES AND CONDITIONS THAT MAY AFFECT PRENATAL DEVELOPMENT

Sexually Transmitted Diseases	
Gonorrhea	The gonococcus organism may attack the eyes while the baby is passing through the infected birth canal. Silver nitrate or erythromycin eyedrops are administered immediately after birth to prevent blindness.
Genital herpes	Infection usually occurs at birth as the baby comes in contact with herpes lesions on the mother's genitals, although the virus may also cross the placental barrier to infect the fetus. Infection can lead to blindness and serious brain damage. There is no cure for the disease. Mothers with active genital herpes often have a cesarean delivery to avoid infecting their babies.
Syphilis	The effects of syphilis on the fetus can be devastating. An estimated 25 percent of infected fetuses are born dead. Those who survive may be deaf, mentally retarded, or deformed. Syphilis can be diagnosed by a blood test and can be cured before the fetus is affected, since the syphilis spirochete cannot penetrate the placental membrane before the twenty-first week of gestation.
Other Diseases and Maternal Conditions	
Chicken pox	Chicken pox may lead to spontaneous abortion or premature delivery, but it does not appear to cause malformations.
Cytomegalovirus	The most common source of prenatal infection, cytomegalovirus produces no symptoms in adults, but it may be fatal to the embryo. Infection later in intrauterine life has been related to brain damage, deafness, blindness, and cerebral palsy (a defect of motor coordination caused by brain damage).
Diabetes	Diabetic mothers face a greater risk of having a stillborn child or one who dies shortly after birth. Babies of diabetics are often very large because of the accumulation of fat during the third trimester. Diabetic mothers require special care to prevent these problems.
Hepatitis	Mothers who have hepatitis are likely to pass it on to their infants during birth.
Hypertension	Hypertension (chronic high blood pressure) increases the probability of miscarriage and infant death.
Influenza	The more virulent forms of influenza may lead to spontaneous abortion or may cause abnormalities during the early stages of pregnancy.
Mumps	Mumps is suspected of causing spontaneous abortion in the first trimester of pregnancy.
Toxemia	About 5 percent of pregnant women in the United States are affected during the third trimester by this disorder of unknown origin. Most common during first pregnancies, the condition mainly affects the mother. Symptoms are water retention, high blood pressure, rapid weight gain, and protein in the urine. If untreated, toxemia may cause convulsions, coma, and even death for the mother. Death of the fetus is not uncommon.
Toxoplasmosis	A mild disease in adults with symptoms similar to those of the common cold, toxoplasmosis is caused by a parasite that is present in raw meat and cat feces. It may cause spontaneous abortion or death. Babies who survive may have serious eye or brain damage.

Sources: Moore, 1982; Stevenson, 1977.

pregnancy (Boué, 1995). (Thereafter, rubella infections are less likely to cause congenital malformations.) A rubella epidemic in the United States during the winter of 1964–1965 resulted in 30,000 stillbirths and 20,000 infants who suffered congenital defects (Lavigne, 1982).

The development of a vaccine for rubella in 1969 has greatly reduced the incidence of the disease, but it has not been eradicated. Women are advised to avoid becoming pregnant for at least 6 months after they receive the vaccine. A few states offer a test for immunity to rubella as part of the blood test given before a marriage license is issued.

Acquired Immunodeficiency Syndrome (AIDS) In the United States, over 7000 pregnancies a year are complicated by HIV, the virus that causes AIDS (Franscino, 1995). Approximately 30 percent of the babies born to mothers who test positive for the AIDS virus acquire this disease (Cunningham et al., 1997). The virus may be transmitted from the mother to her baby either by the virus's passing through the placental barrier or by the baby's exposure to the mother's infected blood during delivery (Wiesenfeld & Sweet, 1994). The risk of transmission increases with the length of time the mother has been infected (Boué, 1995). There is no known cure for AIDS, and AIDS is now the seventh leading cause of death in children under the age of 4. However, if HIV-positive women are administered the drug zidovudine (AZT) during pregnancy and at the time of delivery, the chances of their passing the virus on to their children are reduced by 50 percent (Morris, 1998).

Rh Incompatibility Rh is a complex substance on the surface of the red blood cells. One of its components is determined by a dominant gene, and people who have this component are said to be Rh-positive. Fewer than one in ten people inherit the two recessive genes that make them Rh negative (de Vrijer et al., 1999).

When an Rh-negative woman conceives a child with an Rh-positive man, the child is likely to be Rh-positive. During the birth of the baby, some of its blood cells usually pass into the mother's bloodstream while the placenta is separating from the uterine wall. The mother's immune system creates antibodies to fight this foreign substance, and the antibodies remain in her bloodstream after the birth. If the mother again becomes pregnant with an Rh-positive child, the antibodies produced during the birth of her first child will pass into the new baby's bloodstream, where they will attack and destroy its red blood cells. The resultant Rh disease can lead to serious birth defects and even death. Since it takes time for the mother's system to produce Rh antibodies, firstborn children are rarely affected, but the danger increases with each successive child. Fortunately, physicians can prevent Rh disease by giving the Rh-negative mother an injection of anti-Rh serum within 72 hours of the delivery of an Rh-positive child. The serum kills any Rh-positive blood cells in the mother's bloodstream so that she will not develop antibodies to attack them. Children who are born with Rh disease can be treated with periodic blood transfusions (Fanaroff & Martin, 1997).

Radiation Massive doses of radiation often lead to serious malformations of the developing organism and in many cases cause prenatal death or spontaneous abortion (Moore & Persaud, 1993). Somewhat lower doses may spare the life of the organism, but they may have a profound effect on its development. These dangers became tragically evident after the atomic blasts at Hiroshima and Nagasaki in 1945. Many of the pregnant women who were within 1500 meters of the blasts survived, but they later lost their babies. Of the babies who appeared to be normal at birth, 64 percent were later diagnosed as mentally retarded. The effects of radiation on the fetus's developing central nervous system were found to be greatest during the eighth through the fifteenth week of the prenatal period, a time of rapid proliferation of the cortical nerve cells (Vorhees & Mollnow, 1987).

The effects of low doses of radiation on human beings have not been firmly established. Because X rays may cause malformations in the embryo, women who are pregnant, or who have been trying to become pregnant, should inform their doctors of this when there is a need for them to be X-rayed.

Pollution Most of the thousands of chemicals that are used in industrial production and in the preparation of foods and cosmetics have never been tested to see if they are harmful to prenatal development, although some of these substances reach the embryo or fetus through the placenta (Jones, 1997). Some herbicides and pesticides have been shown to be harmful or even fatal to unborn rats, mice, rabbits, and chicks. Several pollutants sometimes found in the atmosphere and drinking water also appear to be teratogenic. Moreover, some of the effects are cumulative, as concentrations of the chemicals build up in the body.

In 1953 it was discovered that the consumption of large quantities of fish from Minimata Bay in Japan was associated with a series of symptoms that have come to be known as *Minimata disease.* The symptoms include cerebral palsy (a disorder of the central nervous system), deformation of the skull, and sometimes an abnormally small head. The bay was polluted by mercury from waste discharged into the Minimata River from nearby industrial plants. The mercury passed in increasingly concentrated amounts through the food chain from the organisms eaten by fish to humans who ate the fish. Pregnant women who ate the contaminated fish then passed the mercury on to their unborn babies. "Minimata disease" has since become synonymous with mercury poisoning (Tuchmann-Duplessis, 1975).

The incidence of birth defects is also known to be abnormally high in areas of heavy atmospheric pollution. In the Brazilian industrial city of Cubatão, for instance, the air pollution from petrochemical and steel plants alone exceeds that generated by all the combined industries in the Los Angeles basin of California. During the 1970s, 65 of every 1000 babies born in Cubatão died shortly after birth because their brains had failed to develop—double the rate of this defect in neighboring communities that were not so heavily polluted (Freed, 1983). Fortunately, strong environmental safety efforts have greatly reduced the pollution in Cubatão, and the death rate of infants there has declined remarkably (Brooke, 1991).

Atmospheric pollution in U.S. cities is not so high as it used to be in Cubatão, but it is high enough in many of them to cause concern about its effects on prenatal development. There is also a good deal of concern about the risk to pregnant women and their unborn children who live near chemical dumps. Unfortunately, much more research is required before it is known what actual risks these environmental hazards pose for prenatal development.

Principles of Teratogenic Effects

Although the effects of teratogens on the developing organism vary with the teratogen, several general principles apply to all of them (Hogge, 1990; Moore & Persaud, 1993):

- *The susceptibility of a developing organism to a teratogenic agent varies with the developmental stage of the organism at the time of exposure.* Overall, the gravest danger to life comes during the first 2 weeks, before the cells of the organism have undergone extensive differentiation and before most women are even aware that they are pregnant (see Figure

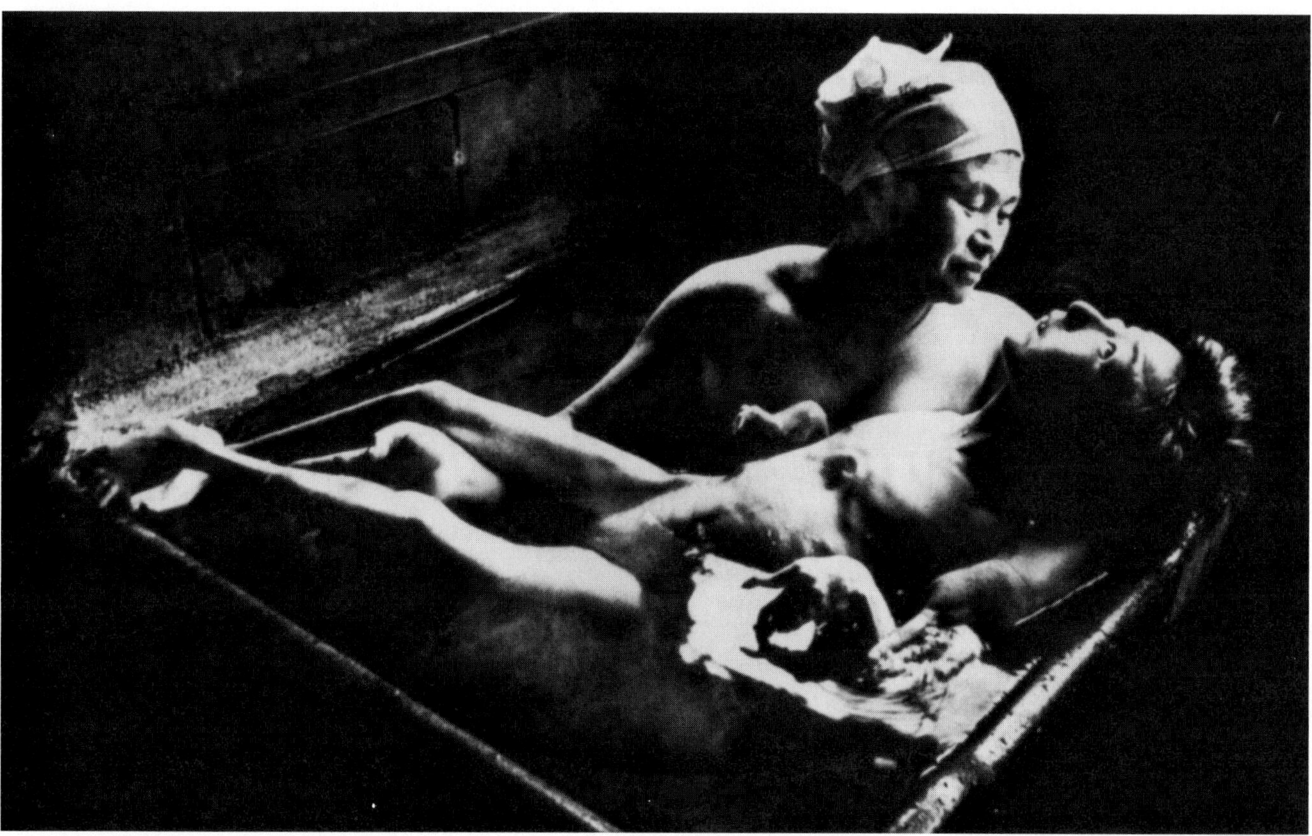

The tragic consequences of prenatal mercury poisoning, or Minimata disease. This disease first came to the world's attention in the 1950s because of the pollution in Minimata Bay, Japan.

3.14). During this critical period, a teratogenic agent may completely destroy the organism. Once the various body systems have begun to form, each is most vulnerable at the time of its initial growth spurt. As Figure 3.14 indicates, the most vulnerable period for the central nervous system is from 15 to 36 days after conception, whereas the upper and lower limbs are most vulnerable from 24 to 49 days after conception.

- *Each teratogenic agent acts in a specific way on specific developing tissue and therefore causes a particular pattern of abnormal development.* Thalidomide, for example, causes deformation of the legs and arms, and mercury compounds cause brain damage that is manifested as cerebral palsy.
- *Not all organisms are affected in the same way by exposure to a given amount of a particular teratogen.* The way a developing organism responds to teratogenic agents depends to some degree on its genetic vulnerability to these agents. Fewer than one-quarter of the pregnant women who used thalidomide during the period when the embryo's limbs were forming gave birth to malformed babies.
- *Susceptibility to teratogenic agents depends on the physiological state of the mother.* The mother's age, nutrition, uterine condition, and hormonal balance all affect the action of teratogens on the developing organism. The risk of malformation is highest when the mother is younger than 20 or older than 40. The precise reason is not known. Nutritional deficiency in the mother intensifies the adverse effects of some teratogens. The impact of teratogens also appears to increase if the mother suffers from diabetes, toxemia, a metabolic imbalance, or liver dysfunction, among other disorders.

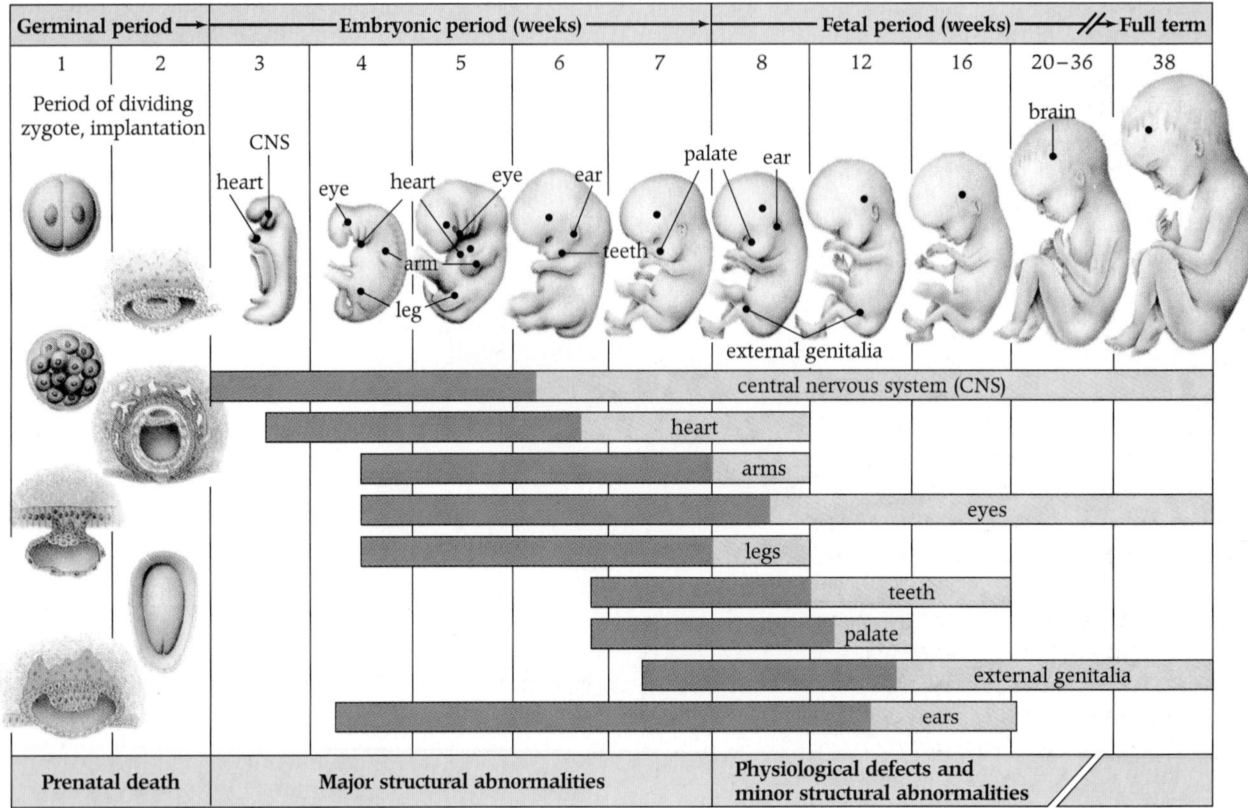

FIGURE 3.14

The critical periods in human prenatal development occur when the organs and other body parts are forming and therefore are most vulnerable to teratogens. Before implantation, teratogens either damage all or most of the cells of the organism, causing its death, or damage only a few cells, allowing the organism to recover without developing defects. In the figure, orange portions of the bars represent periods of highest risk of major structural abnormalities; the yellow portions represent periods of reduced sensitivity to teratogens. (Adapted from Moore & Persaud, 1993.)

- *In general, the greater the concentration of teratogenic agents to which the organism has been exposed, the greater the risk of abnormal development.*
- *Some diseases (such as rubella) that have little or only a temporary effect on the mother can lead to serious abnormalities in the developing organism.*

PRENATAL DEVELOPMENT RECONSIDERED

As we noted earlier, many developmental psychologists view the prenatal period as a model for all subsequent development because many of the principles that apply to prenatal development also explain development after birth. Before we move on to birth and life outside the uterus, it is worthwhile to review these explanatory principles as they apply to the prenatal period. They are ideas we will return to throughout our study of child development.

- *Sequence is fundamental.* One cell must exist before there can be two. Muscles and bones must be present before nerves can coordinate movement. Gonads must secrete testosterone before further sexual differentiation can occur.

- *Timing is important.* If the ovum moves too rapidly or too slowly down the fallopian tube, pregnancy is terminated. If exposure to a particular teratogen occurs during a particular stage of development, the impact on the organism may be destructive. If the exposure occurs before or after this particular stage, there may be little or no impact. The importance of timing implies the existence of sensitive periods for the formation of basic organ systems.
- *Development consists of differentiation and integration.* The single cell of the zygote becomes the many, apparently identical, cells of the morula. These cells then differentiate into two distinct kinds of cells, which later are integrated into a new configuration of cells called the blastocyst. Similarly, arm buds will later differentiate to form fingers, which will differ from each other in ways that make possible the finely articulate movements of the human hand.
- *Development is characterized by stagelike changes.* Changes in the form of the organism and in the ways it interacts with its environment suggest a series of stagelike transformations. The embryo not only looks altogether different from the blastocyst but also interacts with its environment in a different way.
- *Development proceeds unevenly.* From the earliest steps of cleavage, the various subsystems that make up the organism develop at their own rates. An important special case of such unevenness is physical development, which follows a cephalocaudal (from the head down) and proximodistal (from the center to the periphery) sequence.
- *The course of development seems to be punctuated by periods of apparent regression.* Although development generally appears to progress through time, there are also periods of apparent regression. Regressions appear to reflect a process of reorganization, as when fetal activity decreases as higher regions of the brain are beginning to become active.
- *Development is still a mystery.* The process by which the human organism develops from a single cell into a squalling newborn baby continues to mystify investigators. In one sense, the results of development are present at the beginning, coded in the genetic materials of the zygote, which constrain the kinds of forms that can emerge out of the interactions between the organism and its environment. But new forms are constantly emerging out of the organism–environment interactions that sustain and propel development. In this sense, development is epigenetic.

BIRTH: THE FIRST BIO-SOCIAL-BEHAVIORAL SHIFT

Among all of life's transitions, birth is the most radical. Before birth, the amniotic fluid provides a wet, warm environment, and the fetus receives continuous oxygen and nourishment through the umbilical cord. At birth, the lungs inflate to take in oxygen and exhale carbon dioxide for the first time. The first breath of oxygen acts to shut off the bypass that shunts blood away from the lungs to the placenta. It also causes the umbilical arteries to close down, cutting off fetal circulation to the placenta. Now the baby must obtain oxygen through the lungs, must work for nourishment by sucking, and no longer has the placenta to provide protection against disease-causing organisms.

The social and behavioral changes that occur at birth are no less pronounced than the biological ones, marking birth as the first major bio-social-behavioral shift in human development. The newborn encounters other

FIRST STAGE OF LABOR

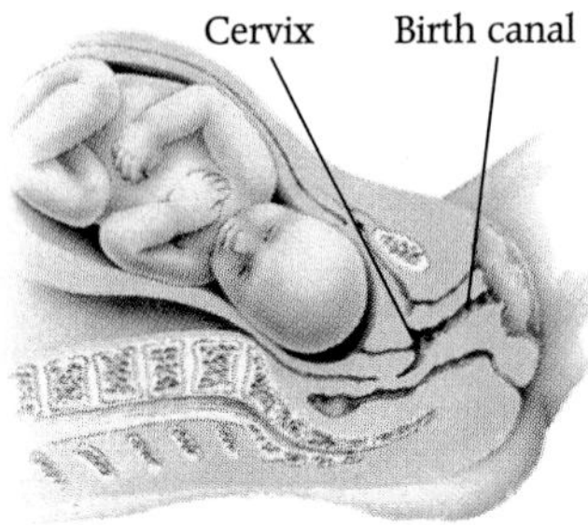

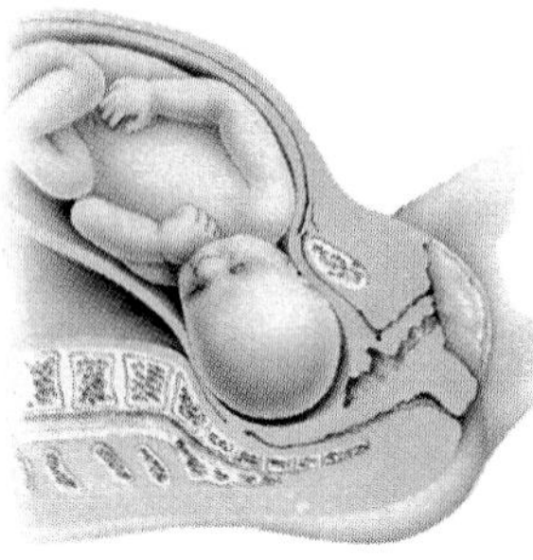

START OF SECOND STAGE
(Transition)

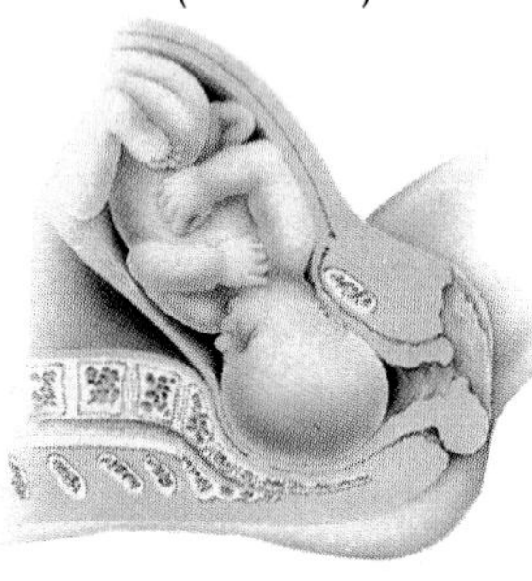

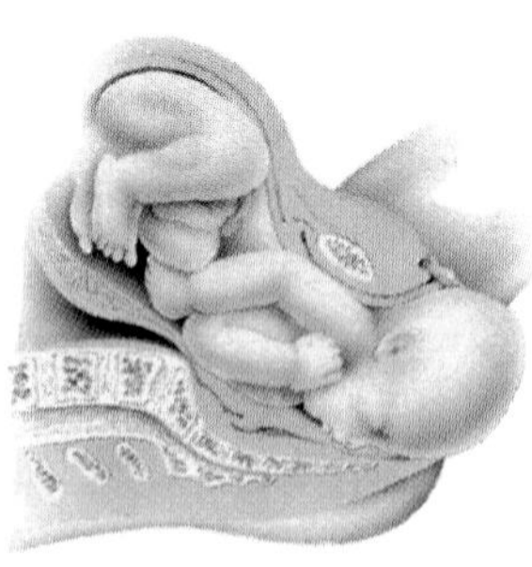

human beings directly for the first time, and the parents get their first glimpse of their child. From the moment of birth, neonates and parents begin to construct a social relationship.

THE STAGES OF LABOR

The biological process of birth begins with a series of changes in the mother's body that forces the fetus through the birth canal. It ends when the mother expels the placenta after the baby has emerged. Labor normally begins approximately 280 days after the first day of a woman's last menstrual period, or 266 days after conception. It is customarily divided into three overlapping stages (see Figure 3.15).

The *first stage of labor* begins when uterine contractions of sufficient frequency, intensity, and duration begin to cause the cervix to dilate. It continues until the opening of the uterus into the vagina is fully dilated and the connections between the bones of the mother's pelvis become more flexible (Cunningham et al., 1997). The length of this stage varies from woman to woman and from pregnancy to pregnancy: it may last anywhere from less than an hour to several days. The norm for first births is about 14 hours (Niswander & Evans, 1996). At the beginning of labor, contractions come 15 to 20 minutes apart and last anywhere from 15 to 60 seconds. As labor proceeds, the contractions become more frequent and more intense and are longer in duration.

The *second stage of labor* begins as the baby is pushed headfirst through the fully dilated cervix into the vagina. (This passage is facilitated by the fact that the baby's head is flexible because the bones of the skull have not yet fused.) The contractions now usually come no more than a minute apart and last about a minute. The pressure of the baby in the birth canal and the powerful contractions of the uterus typically cause the mother to bear down and push the baby out. Usually the top of the baby's head and the brow are the first to emerge. Occasionally babies emerge in other positions, the most common being the breech position, with the feet or buttocks emerging first. In cases where babies are born in a breech position, which occurs in 3 to 4 percent of single births, both mother and fetus are at considerably increased risk (Kunzel, 1994).

The *third stage of labor,* the final one, occurs as the baby emerges from the vagina and the uterus contracts around its diminished contents. The placenta buckles and separates from the uterine wall, pulling the other fetal

FIGURE 3.15

During the first stage of labor, which usually lasts several hours, the cervix dilates, often to 9 or 10 centimeters in diameter. During the second stage, the birth canal widens, permitting the baby to emerge. The final stage (not shown) occurs when the placenta is delivered. (Adapted from Clarke-Stewart & Koch, 1983.)

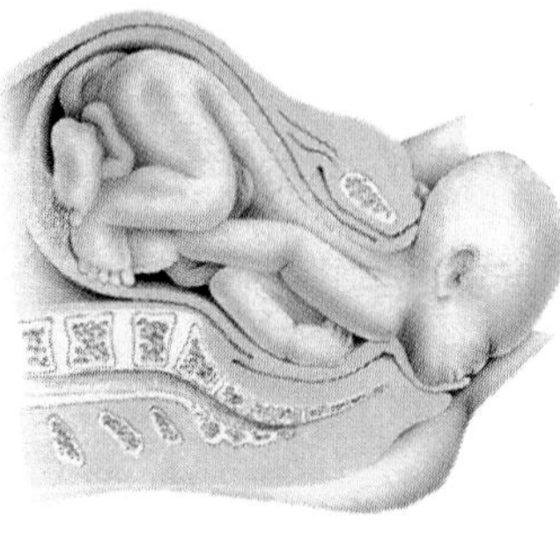

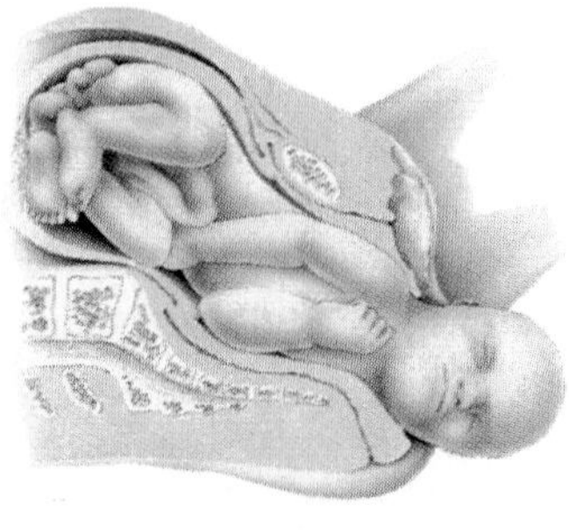

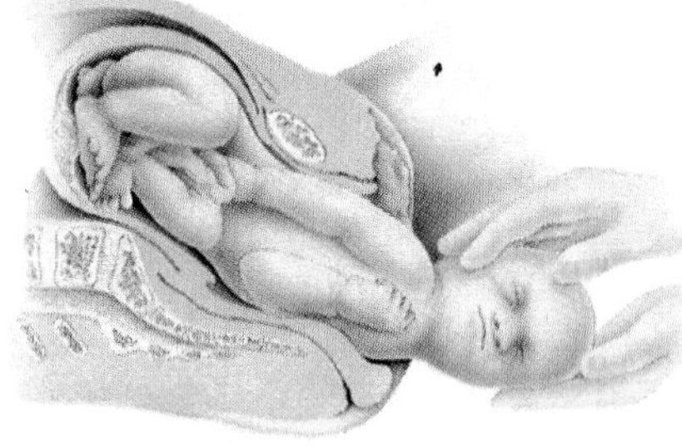

membranes with it. Contractions quickly expel them, and they are delivered as the *afterbirth.*

CULTURAL VARIATIONS IN CHILDBIRTH

As a biological process, labor occurs in roughly the same way everywhere. The experience of giving birth, however, varies with the traditions of the culture. These traditions provide the mother and the community with a prescribed set of procedures to follow during birthing and a set of expectations about how they are going to feel (Jordan, 1983; Kaye, 1982).

In a few societies, giving birth is treated as an unremarkable process, a routine part of a woman's life. Consider the following description of birth among the !Kung, a hunting-and-gathering society in Africa's Kalahari Desert:

> Mother's stomach grew very large. The first labor pains came at night and stayed with her until dawn. That morning, everyone went gathering. Mother and I stayed behind. We sat together for a while, then I went and played with the other children. Later, I came back and ate the nuts she had cracked for me. She got up and started to get ready. I said, "Mommy, let's go to the water well, I'm thirsty." She said, "Uhn, uhn, I'm going to gather some mongongo nuts." I told the children that I was going and we left; there were no other adults around. We walked a short way, then she sat down by the base of a large nehn tree, leaned back against it, and little Kumsa was born. (Shostak, 1981, pp. 53–54)

Such unassisted and unheralded birthing is relatively rare. It is far more common to find several people attending the mother during labor and delivery. In some traditional societies, there is a special house built outside the village that is reserved for childbearing. In most societies, special practices, such as having the mother sit or lie in a particular posture during the birth or giving her anesthesia or herbal infusions to drink, are used to help her and her baby through the dangerous transition.

Who actually gets to play a role in the childbirth process also varies across cultures. Among the Ngoni of East Africa, for example, men are totally excluded from the process. The women even conceal the fact that they are pregnant from their husbands as long as they can. "Men are little children. They are not able to hear those things which belong to pregnancy," the women claim (Read, 1960/1968, p. 20). When a woman learns that her daughter-in-law's labor has begun, she and other female kin move into the woman's hut, banish the husband, and take charge of the preparations. They remove everything that belongs to the husband—clothes, tools, and weapons—and all household articles except old mats and pots to be used during labor. Men are not allowed back into the hut until after the baby is born.

CHILDBIRTH IN THE UNITED STATES

Over the first half of the twentieth century, a marked shift occurred in childbirth practices in the United States. In 1900, most births took place at home, attended only by a midwife, a woman recognized for her experience in assisting childbirth. By the end of the century, 99 percent of all babies were born in hospitals, and 92 percent were delivered by a physician (Centers for Disease Control and Prevention, 2000). Underlying this shift from home to hospital were two developments. First, many drugs were developed to relieve the pain of childbirth, and by law they could be administered only by physicians. Second, hospitals became better equipped to provide both antiseptic surroundings and specialized help to deal with any complications that might arise during labor and delivery.

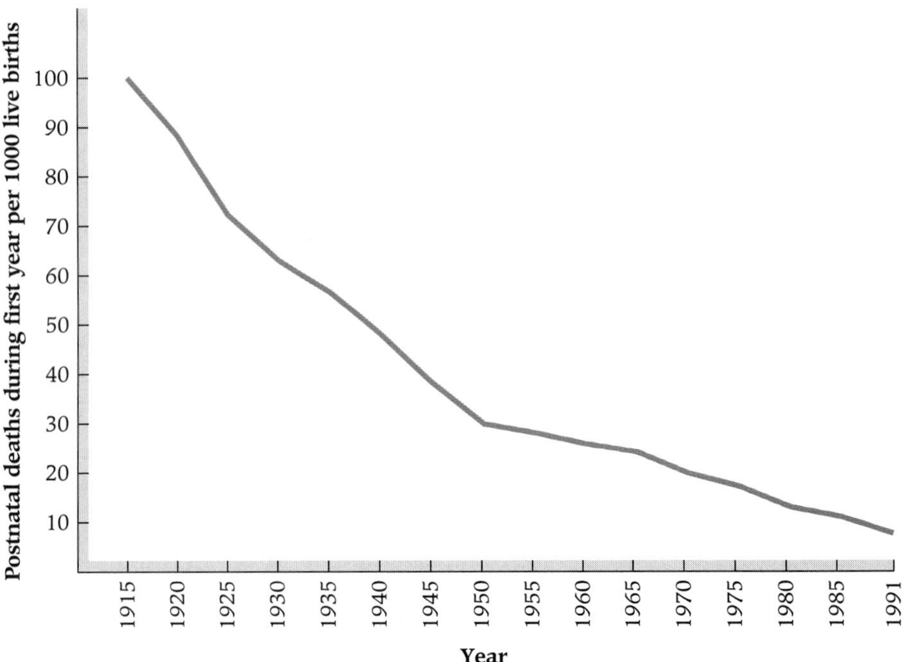

FIGURE 3.16
Over the course of the twentieth century, the death rate among children in the United States under 1 year of age dropped dramatically.

The lives of thousands of babies and mothers are saved each year by the intervention of doctors using modern drugs and special medical procedures (Figure 3.16). In 1915 approximately 100 of every 1000 babies died in their first year, and almost 7 of 1000 mothers died giving birth. By 1997 (the last year for which data are available), infant deaths had been reduced to 7.2 of every 1000 babies born (Centers for Disease Control and Prevention, 1999a). In the same year, only 7.7 women of every 100,000 who gave birth in the United States died of causes related to pregnancy, childbirth, or postnatal complications (Centers for Disease Control and Prevention, 1999b).

Unfortunately, the reduction in death rates has not been evenly spread through all segments of the population. While the mortality rate has declined significantly for both African American and white infants, African American infants are still almost twice as likely to die during the first year of life as other infants. Moreover, African American mothers are three times as likely to die in childbirth as other mothers (Centers for Disease Control and Prevention, 1999).

Despite the reductions in maternal and infant mortality, health-care professionals and parents alike have pointed to problems arising from medical intervention during normal, uncomplicated births (Martin, 1998; U.S. Dept. of Health and Human Services, Public Health Service, 1991). These concerns center on two questions: (1) What is the safest method for dealing with pain during childbirth? (2) What precautions are necessary to ensure the health of the mother and the baby?

Childbirth Pain and Its Medication

In developed nations, a variety of drugs are used to lessen the pain of labor and delivery. They include anesthetics (which dull overall feeling), analgesics (which reduce the perception of pain), and sedatives (which reduce anxiety). Current evidence indicates that the drugs administered to the mother to control the pain of labor can affect the baby directly by passing through the placental barrier and entering the fetus's bloodstream (Troyer & Parisi, 1994). They also affect the baby indirectly by reducing the mother's oxygen intake. This causes her blood pressure to drop, a condition that reduces the supply of oxygen to the fetus and may cause the baby to have difficulty breathing after birth. Obstetric medications seldom threaten the lives of healthy, full-term babies, but they have been found to affect the neonate's condition. The newborns of mothers who receive one or another of a variety of drugs during labor and delivery are less attentive and more irritable, have poorer muscle tone and less vigorous sucking responses, and are weaker than those whose mothers receive no medication (Jones, 1997).

Because of their concern about the possible adverse effects of drugs on the neonate, many women are turning to alternative methods of controlling the pain of labor. Typically these methods include educational classes that give the mother-to-be an idea of what to expect during labor and delivery and teach her relaxation and breathing exercises to help counteract pain. Often they also involve having someone—the husband, a sympathetic friend, or a midwife—be constantly at the woman's side during labor to provide comfort and emotional support.

Childbirth education has become a traditional part of preparing for pregnancy for many American couples expecting a new baby.

Medical Interventions during Childbirth

In addition to administering drugs to ease the pain of labor, doctors may use medical procedures to safeguard the lives of mother and child. When the baby is significantly overdue or when the mother is confronted with some life-threatening situation, physicians commonly induce labor, either by rupturing the membranes of the amniotic sac or by giving the mother some form of the hormone oxytocin, which initiates contractions.

Another commonly used procedure is the *cesarean section,* or surgical removal of the baby from the mother's uterus. This procedure has typically been used in cases of difficult labor, when the baby is in distress during delivery, or when the baby is not in the headfirst position.

Although modern medical techniques have made childbirth a great deal safer than it was in the past, some medical personnel claim that many of these technologies are used more often than they should be (Martin, 1998; U.S. Dept. of Health and Human Services, Public Health Service, 1991). The use of cesarean deliveries is one prominent example. The number of cesarean sections performed in the United States began to increase significantly during the 1970s. By 1997, 21 out of every 100 births in the United States were by cesarean section (Centers for Disease Control and Prevention, 1999). Critics argue that many of the cesarean operations performed in the United States not only are unnecessary but raise the cost of childbirth, expose the mother to the risk of postoperative infection, and cause mothers to be separated from their infants while they heal from surgery. They may also be detrimental to the babies' well-being (see Box 3.2). Concerns about unnecessary medical intervention also extend to other procedures, such as induced labor, which has doubled during the past decade, and electronic monitoring of the vital signs of the fetus during labor, which has been associated with the increase in cesarean sections (Jones, 1997; Martin, 1998).

In part because of such concerns, there has been increased interest in the use of certified nurse-midwives and doctors of osteopathy in cases of low-risk childbirth. A study carried out in Washington State found that in low-risk pregnancies, certified nurse-midwives were less likely to use fetal monitoring and had lower rates of induced labor than physicians. Their patients also were less likely to have a spinal injection of anesthesia and cesarean sections than the patients of both family physicians and obstetricians (Rosenblatt et al., 1997).

THE NEWBORN'S CONDITION

The vast majority of babies born in developed nations are full-term and robust. However, to first-time parents, especially those who imagine that new-

BOX 3.2

The Baby's Experience of Birth

What is birth like for the baby? For several hours the fetus is squeezed through the birth canal, where it is subjected to considerable pressure and occasionally is deprived of oxygen. Finally the newborn infant is delivered from the warm, dark shelter of the womb into a cold, bright hospital room. A popular psychological theory maintained that this experience must represent a trauma for the baby (Rank, 1929).

However, modern research on the experience of birth, which has focused on the biological mechanisms that equip the baby to cope with the stress involved, presents a different picture. Hugo Lagercrantz and Theodore Slotkin (1986) have suggested that as the birth process begins, a surge in the fetus's production of adrenaline and other "stress" hormones protects it from the adverse conditions—the pressure on the head and the deprivation of oxygen—it experiences. They go on to suggest that the events that cause the production of stress hormones are of vital importance because these hormones prepare the infant to survive outside the womb.

In support of their hypothesis, Lagercrantz and Slotkin point out that infants delivered by cesarean section often have difficulty breathing. They believe that the procedure deprives babies of the experiences that produce high levels of adrenaline and other hormones in the hours before birth, hormones that facilitate the absorption of liquid from the lungs and the production of surfactin, which allow the lungs to function well. In addition, the hormones appear to produce an increase in the newborn's metabolic rate, which mobilizes readily usable fuel to nourish cells.

Lagercrantz and Slotkin also believe that the stress hormones are instrumental in increasing blood flow to such vital organs as the heart, lungs, and brain and thus increase the chances of survival of a baby who is experiencing breathing difficulties. Furthermore, these researchers speculate that the hormonal surge during the birth process puts the newborn in a state of alertness. Immediately following birth, most normal newborns have a prolonged period of quiet alertness, lasting as long as 40 minutes, during which their eyes are open in a wide-eyed gaze (Klaus et al., 1993).

borns look like the infants pictured on jars of baby food, the real neonate's appearance may cause alarm and disappointment. The baby's head is overly large in proportion to the rest of the body, and the limbs are relatively small and tightly flexed. Unless the baby has been delivered by cesarean section, the head may look misshapen after its tight squeeze through the birth canal. (The head usually regains its symmetry by the end of the first week after birth.) The baby's skin may be covered with *vernix caseosa,* a white, cheesy substance that protects it against bacterial infections, and it may be spotted with blood.

In the United States, neonates weigh an average of 7 to 7½ pounds, although babies weighing anywhere from 5½ to 10 pounds are within the normal range. During their first days of life, most babies lose about 7 percent of their initial weight, primarily because of loss of fluid. They usually gain the weight back by the time they are 10 days old.

The average neonate is 20 inches long. To a large extent, the length of the newborn is determined by the size of the mother's uterus. It does not reflect the baby's genetic inheritance, because the genes that control height do not begin to express themselves until shortly after birth (Tanner, 1990).

ASSESSING THE BABY'S VIABILITY

In medically assisted births, medical personnel check the neonate for indications of danger so that immediate action can be taken if something is wrong. They take note of the baby's size, check vital signs, and look for evidence of normal capacities. A variety of scales and tests are used to assess the neonate's physical state and behavioral condition.

Physical Condition

In the 1950s Virginia Apgar (1953), an anesthesiologist who worked in the delivery room of a large metropolitan hospital, developed a quick and simple method of determining if a baby requires emergency care. The **Apgar Scale,** which is now widely employed throughout the United States, is used to rate babies 1 minute after birth and again 5 minutes later using five vital signs: heart rate, respiratory effort, muscle tone, reflex responsivity, and color. Table 3.5 shows the criteria for scoring each of the signs. The individual scores are totaled to give a measure of the baby's overall physical condition. A baby with a score of less than 4 is considered to be in poor condition and to require immediate medical attention.

Apgar Scale A quick, simple test used to diagnose the physical state of newborn infants.

Brazelton Neonatal Assessment Scale A scale used to assess the newborn's neurological condition.

Behavioral Condition

During the past half century, many scales have been constructed to assess the more subtle behavioral aspects of the newborn's condition (Brazelton, 1984; McCollam et al., 1997). One of the most widely used is the **Brazelton Neonatal Assessment Scale,** developed by the pediatrician T. Berry Brazelton and his colleagues. A major purpose of this scale is to assess the neurological condition of newborns who are suspected to be at risk for developmental difficulties. It is also used to assess the developmental progress of infants, to compare the functioning of newborns of different cultures, and to evaluate the effectiveness of interventions designed to alleviate developmental difficulties (Beeghly et al., 1995; Brazelton et al., 1987).

The Brazelton scale includes tests of infants' reflexes, motor capacities, muscle tone, capacity for responding to objects and people, and capacity to control their own behavior (such as turning away when overstimulated) and attention. When scoring a newborn on such tests, the examiner must take note of the degree of the infant's alertness and, if necessary, repeat the tests when the baby is wide awake and calm. Here are some typical items on the Brazelton scale:

> *Orientation to animate objects—visual and auditory.* The examiner calls the baby's name repeatedly in a high-pitched voice while moving his head up and down and from side to side in front of the baby. Does the baby focus on the examiner? Does she follow the examiner with her eyes smoothly?
>
> *Pull-to-sit.* The examiner puts a forefinger in each of the infant's palms and pulls him to a sitting position. Does the baby try to right his head when he is in a seated position? How well is he able to do so?
>
> *Cuddliness.* The examiner holds the baby against her chest or up against her shoulder. How does the baby respond? Does she resist being held? Is she passive, or does she cuddle up to the examiner?
>
> *Defensive movements.* The examiner places a cloth over the baby's face and holds it there. Does the baby try to remove the cloth from his face either by turning his head away or by swiping at it?

TABLE 3.5 THE APGAR SCORING SYSTEM

	Rating		
Vital Sign	**0**	**1**	**2**
Heart rate	Absent	Slow (below 100)	Over 100
Respiratory effort	Absent	Slow, irregular	Good, crying
Muscle tone	Flaccid	Some flexion of extremities	Active motion
Reflex responsivity	No response	Grimace	Vigorous cry
Color	Blue, pale	Body pink, extremities blue	Completely pink

Source: Apgar, 1953.

gestational age The time that has passed between conception and birth. The normal gestational age is between 37 and 43 weeks.

preterm The term for babies born before the 37th week of pregnancy.

Self-quieting activity. The examiner notes what the baby does to quiet herself when she is fussy. Does she suck her thumb, look around?

In addition to their primary goal of screening for infants at risk, neonatal assessment scales are also used to predict aspects of newborns' future development such as their temperaments or typical learning rates. Research over the past decade shows that these scales are, in fact, satisfactory guides for determining when medical intervention is necessary and that they are also fairly good at characterizing whether the baby is developing normally in the period following birth (Hart et al., 1999; Schuler et al., 1999). They are not so useful when it comes to predicting later intelligence or personality, however.

PROBLEMS AND COMPLICATIONS

Though most babies are born without any serious problems, some are in such poor physical condition that they soon die. Others are at risk for later developmental problems. Newborns are considered to be at risk if they suffer from any of a variety of problems, including asphyxiation or head injury during delivery (either of which may result in brain damage), acute difficulty breathing after birth, or difficulty digesting food owing to an immature digestive system (Korner, 1987). These are the kinds of problems that are likely to result in low scores on the Apgar Scale. Most of the newborns who are at risk are premature, abnormally underweight, or both (Witter & Keith, 1993).

Prematurity

Prematurity is measured in terms of **gestational age,** the time that has passed between conception and birth. The normal gestational age is 37 to 43 weeks. Babies born before the thirty-seventh week are considered to be **preterm,** or premature. In the United States, approximately 10 percent of all births are preterm (Cunningham, 1997). Disorders related to premature birth are the fourth leading cause of infant mortality. With the expert care and technology now available in modern hospitals (see Figure 3.17), mortality rates for premature infants are declining in the United States.

The leading cause of death among preterm infants is immaturity of the lungs (Arias-Camison et al., 1999). The other main obstacle to the survival of

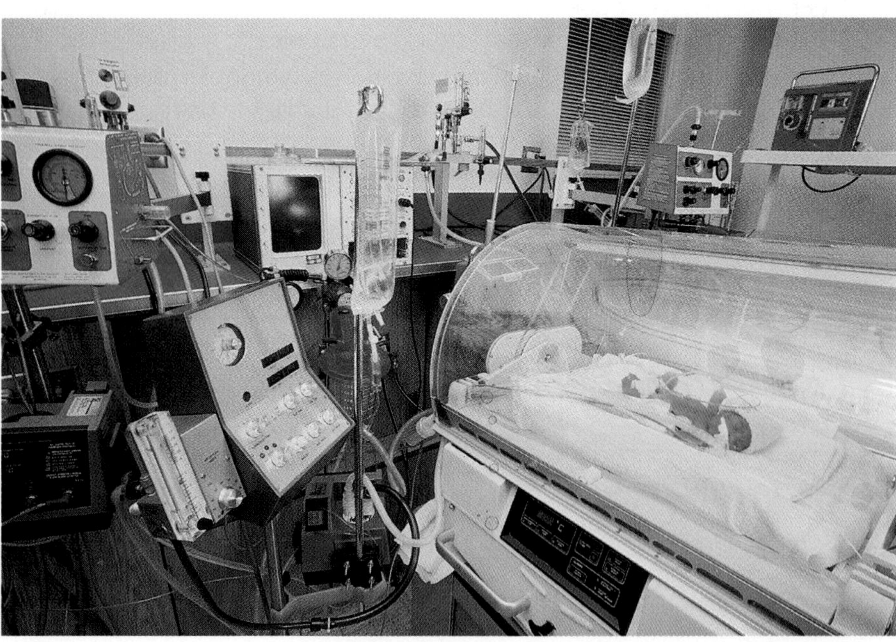

FIGURE 3.17
Technological improvements in recent years have greatly increased the chances for survival for the 10 percent of U.S. babies who are born premature.

FIGURE 3.18
Evidence that premature infants experience difficulty breathing led Evelyn Thoman and her colleagues to create a "breathing teddy bear" attached to an air pump outside the crib. The rhythmic stimulation provided by the bear helps establish a regular breathing pattern in the infant, as well as improving the infant's quality of sleep and reducing crying and other expressions of negative emotions. (Ingersoll & Thoman, 1994.)

preterm infants is immaturity of their digestive and immune systems. Even babies of normal gestational age sometimes have difficulty coordinating sucking, swallowing, and breathing in the first few days after birth. These difficulties are likely to be more serious for preterm infants (see Figure 3.18). Their coordination may be so poor that they cannot be fed directly from breast or bottle, so special equipment must be used to feed them. Moreover, their immature digestive systems often cannot handle normal baby formulas, so they must be fed special formulas.

There are many potential contributors to prematurity, some of them known. Twins are likely to be born about 3 weeks early, triplets and quadruplets even earlier. Very young women whose reproductive systems are immature and women who have had many pregnancies close together are more likely to have premature babies. So are women who smoke, who are in poor health, or who have intrauterine infections. The chances of giving birth to a premature infant also vary with socioeconomic status (Witter & Keith, 1993). Poor women are twice as likely to give birth to small or preterm infants as are more affluent women. This disparity can be explained by the fact that poor women are more likely to be undernourished or chronically ill, to have inadequate health care before and during pregnancy, to suffer from infections, and to experience complications during pregnancy. Cultural factors such as the use of fertility drugs and fasting can also play a role (see Figure 3.19, which shows the increased risk of giving birth prematurely owing to fasting.)

Many other causes of prematurity are still not well understood. At least half of all premature births are not associated with any of the identified risk factors and occur after otherwise normal pregnancies to healthy women who are in their prime childbearing years and have had good medical care.

Low Birth Weight

Babies are considered to have a **low birth weight** if they weigh 2500 grams or less, whether or not they are premature. (Premature babies tend to be small, but not all small babies are premature.) Newborns whose birth weights are especially low for their gestational age are said to suffer from **fetal growth retardation;** in other words, they have not grown at the normal rate. Multiple

low birth weight The term for babies weighing 2500 grams or less at birth whether or not they are premature.

fetal growth retardation The term for newborns who are especially small for their gestational age.

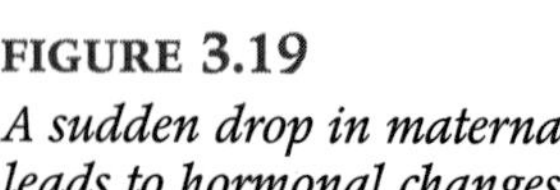

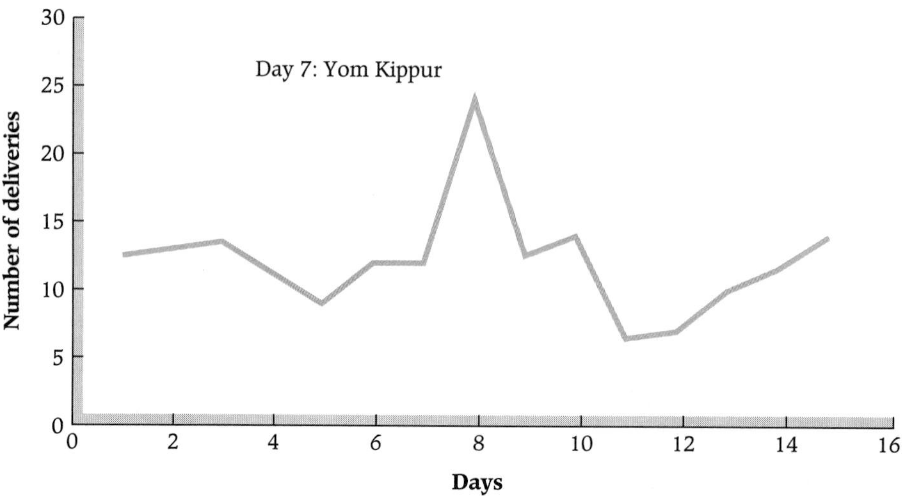

FIGURE 3.19
A sudden drop in maternal food intake leads to hormonal changes that cause some women to go into labor prematurely. This graph shows a doubling of the birthrate among Jewish women on the day following the 24-hour total food and water fast of Yom Kippur. (Adapted from Kaplan et al., 1983.)

births, intrauterine infections, chromosomal abnormalities, maternal smoking or use of narcotics, maternal malnutrition, and abnormalities of the placenta or umbilical cord have all been identified as probable causes of fetal growth retardation (Spellacy, 1994).

Developmental Consequences

Intensive research has been conducted on the developmental consequences of prematurity and low birth weight. Babies who fall into either category are at risk for later developmental problems, but they differ in the probable course of their development (Cunningham et al., 1997).

Low-birth-weight infants are at increased risk for developmental difficulty whether they are premature or full-term. Two-thirds of the deaths that occur in the period immediately following birth are among low-birth-weight infants. In addition, low-birth-weight infants are three times more likely to have neurologically based developmental handicaps than are other babies, and the smaller the baby, the greater the risk (Tsang et al., 1993).

One common outcome for low-birth-weight babies is a decrease in intellectual capacities (Taylor et al., 1998). A study that compared 11- and 12-year-olds who were born prematurely at a weight of less than 1500 grams with full-term children born at a normal weight found that the premature children performed more poorly on tests of intelligence, verbal ability, and memory (Rose & Feldman, 1996).

Several factors appear to be important in determining the long-term outcome of prematurity. For example, premature babies who are of normal size for their gestational age stand a good chance of catching up with full-term babies (Brooks-Gunn et al., 1993). However, there is some evidence that even in the absence of any clinically detectable disability, when compared to full-term children, children born prematurely have problems with maintaining attention and with visual–motor coordination when they are school-age (Foreman et al., 1997). Those babies who are both premature and low in birth weight and have medical complications are more likely to have future developmental difficulties. Among premature babies who are particularly light for their gestational age, those who have very small heads at birth and whose heads grow slowly during the first 6 weeks of postnatal life are especially likely to suffer long-term developmental problems (Eckerman et al., 1985).

The importance of a supportive environment in overcoming the potential risks of prematurity is underscored by research on the social ecology of the families of premature and low-birth-weight infants. Babies who are raised in comfortable socioeconomic circumstances with an intact family and a mother who has had a good education are less likely to suffer negative effects from their condition at birth than are children who are raised without these benefits (Liaw & Brooks-Gunn, 1993).

BEGINNING THE PARENT–CHILD RELATIONSHIP

Because human infants are dependent on the active support and protection of their caretakers for their very survival, the development of a close relationship between infants and their parents is crucial to infants' well-being. However, love and caring between parent and child is neither inevitable nor automatic. The large numbers of infants who are neglected, abused, abandoned, or murdered the world over each year should convince even the most sentimental and optimistic observer of this harsh fact. How, then, is the bond between parent and child formed? And when no strong attachment develops, what has gone wrong? These are broad questions that we will encounter again and again in subsequent chapters, because a close parent–child relationship is not formed in an instant; it develops over many years (see Box 3.3). Here we will examine the factors that come into play immediately after birth and that many people believe set the stage for the future: the initial reactions of the parents to their baby's appearance, and the expectations parents have for their babies.

THE BABY'S APPEARANCE

In their search for the sources of attachment between mother and infant, some developmentalists have turned to *ethology*—the study of animal behavior and its evolutionary bases. These developmentalists believe that examination of what causes nonhuman mothers to protect or reject their young can shed light on the factors that influence human mothers. One important factor that seems to influence animals' responses to their young is their offsprings' appearance. Konrad Lorenz (1943), a German ethologist, noted that the newborns of many animal species have physical characteristics that distinguish them from the mature animal: a head that is large in relation to the body, a prominent forehead, large eyes that are positioned below the horizontal midline of the face, and round, full cheeks (see Figure 3.20). This combination of features, which Lorenz called babyness, seems to appeal to adults and, more significantly, to evoke caregiving behaviors in them.

FIGURE 3.20
Side-by-side sketches of the heads of infants and adults of four species make clear the distinguishing features of "babyness." (From Lorenz, 1943.)

Evidence in support of the idea that "babyness" evokes positive adult responses comes from a study by William Fullard and Ann Reiling (1976). These researchers asked people ranging in age from 7 years to young adulthood which of matched pairs of pictures—one depicting an adult and the other depicting an infant—they preferred. Some of the pictures were of human beings; others were of animals. They found that adults, especially women, were most likely to choose the pictures of infants. Children between the ages of 7 and 12 preferred the pictures of adults. Between the ages of 12 and 14, the preference of girls shifted quite markedly from adults to children. A similar shift was found among boys when they were between 14 and 16. These shifts in preference coincide with the average ages at which girls and boys undergo the physiological changes that make them capable of reproducing.

Adult responses to the appearance of infants may explain why mothers find it difficult to care for malformed offspring (Weiss, 1997). Mothers of dogs, cats, guinea pigs, and some other species will kill malformed offspring. Though human parents usually do not

BOX 3.3

The Bonding Myth

It is popularly believed that the initial contacts between human newborns and their parents, particularly their mothers, produce a special bond that has a profound effect on their future relationship with their parents. [Stories urging parents to "discover the magic and mystery of bonding with your baby" are common fare at local supermarket magazine stands (Baker, 1993)]. Despite its popularity, this belief is not sustained by contemporary scientific evidence.

The origins of the bonding myth can be found in research with nonhuman animals several decades ago. For example, if a baby goat is removed from its mother immediately after birth and returned, say, 2 hours later, the mother will attack it. But if the baby goat is allowed to stay with its mother for as little as 5 minutes after its birth before it is removed for a few hours, the mother will welcome its return (Klopfer et al., 1964). Peter Klopfer and his colleagues interpreted this phenomenon as evidence of a sensitive period during which the mother and baby become imprinted on each other.

Not long after Klopfer and his colleagues reported these results, Marshall Klaus, John Kennell, and their co-workers began research on mothers whose premature babies where being kept in incubators. Until the babies were mature enough to be held, the mothers had little contact with them. Some of these mothers appeared to lose interest in their babies, and the researchers thought that these infants might be especially at risk of being abused once they left the hospital. They speculated (Klaus et al., 1970) that the early sensitive period for mother–infant bonding among goats had its parallel in a similar sensitive period for the bonding of human mothers and their babies.

Next, in a widely publicized study, the same researchers divided 28 first-time mothers into an experimental and a control group. The mothers in the control group had the amount of contact with their newborn infants that was traditional in many hospitals in the late 1960s: a glimpse of the baby shortly after its birth, brief contact with the baby between 6 and 12 hours later, and then 20- to 30-minute visits for bottle feedings every 4 hours. In between these periods, the baby remained in the nursery. The mothers in the experimental group, however, were given their babies to hold for 1 hour within the first 3 hours after delivery. The babies were undressed so that their mothers could have skin-to-skin contact with them. In addition, the mother and child spent 5 hours together each afternoon for the 3 days after delivery. Many of the mothers reported that, although they were already excited by being able to fondle their infants immediately after birth, their excitement rose higher when they succeeded in achieving eye contact with them.

When the mothers and babies in both groups returned to the hospital 1 month later, the mothers in the experimental group were more reluctant to leave their infants with other caretakers. They also seemed more interested in the examination of their infants, were better at soothing them, and seemed to gaze at and fondle their babies more than did the mothers in the control group. Eleven months later, the extended-contact mothers still seemed more attentive to their babies and more responsive to their cries than were the mothers in the control group (Kennell et al., 1974).

Drawing an analogy with animal behavior, Klaus and Kennell (1976) suggested that if a mother and child are allowed to be in close physical contact immediately after birth, "complex interactions between mother and infant help to lock them together" (p. 51). The researchers speculated that hormones generated by the mother's body during the birth process may make her more ready to form an emotional bond with her baby. If these hormones dissipate before the mother has any extended contact with her newborn, presumably she will be less responsive to it (Kennell et al., 1979).

The publication of these findings coincided with a broad popular movement to reform hospital childbirth practices to allow mothers and fathers to have prolonged contact with their newborn babies. Pediatricians, nurses, and parents who supported these reforms found in Klaus and Kennell's work a strong rationale for the changes they wanted to make. However, the research also provoked a lot of criticism (Eyer, 1992). First, it was pointed out that the experimental and control groups in Klaus and Kennell's study were quite small and unrepresentative of the population at large (there were only 14 women in each group, all low-SES African Americans). Furthermore, the mothers in the experimental group were probably aware of the special treatment they received, creating the suspicion that this awareness, rather than the extended contact with their babies, was the source of their behavior. In the years since the study was conducted, other researchers have generally failed to discover any long-lasting, significant differences between the mother–child relationships of experimental and control groups (Eyer, 1992).

Most researchers today agree that while immediate contact between mother and newborn is helpful for getting the process of development off to a good start, it is not essential for the establishment of a long-term, positive emotional relationship. Most mothers who are anesthetized during delivery or suffer complications, and who therefore do not see their babies for several hours or even days after their birth, do not reject them; nor do mothers whose babies must be kept in incubators or fathers who are not present for their children's birth. In short, the great majority of mothers and fathers form attachments to their babies over time, as well as under all sorts of circumstances.

kill their malformed babies, they do interact less frequently and less lovingly with infants they consider unattractive than with those they consider attractive (Langlois, 1986). They also attribute less competence to unattractive babies (Stephan & Langlois, 1984). This pattern is particularly noticeable for baby girls. While still in the hospital with their newborn girls, mothers of less attractive babies directed their attention to people other than their babies more often than did mothers of attractive babies (Langlois et al., 1995).

SOCIAL EXPECTATIONS

During pregnancy, most parents-to-be develop specific expectations about what their babies will be like, and no sooner does a baby emerge from the womb than the parents begin to examine the neonate's looks and behaviors for hints of his or her future. Will she have her grandmother's high, round forehead? Does his lusty cry mean that he will have his father's quick temper?

Naturally, the baby will differ in some respects from the one the parents have been imagining. Usually, though, the parents begin to accommodate themselves to the reality of their child at the moment of its birth. One of the adjustments parents frequently have to make is to the actual sex of the child when the other sex was wanted. The initial stages of such an adjustment can be seen in Box 3.4.

Whether the baby is a boy or a girl, the parents' beliefs and expectations begin to shape their responses to the baby even before the child displays any truly distinctive features. One study found that parents who saw an ultrasound picture of their baby-to-be while it was still in the womb rated female fetuses as softer, littler, cuddlier, calmer, weaker, more delicate, and more beautiful than male fetuses (Sweeney & Bradbard, 1988). In another study, first-time mothers and fathers were asked to choose words that described their newborn babies within 24 hours after their birth (Rubin et al., 1974). The male and female babies did not differ in length or weight or in their scores on the Apgar Scale. Nevertheless, the parents described their daughters as "little," "beautiful," "pretty," or "cute" and as resembling their mothers, whereas they described their sons as "big" and as resembling their fathers. Fathers, the researchers found, were more likely than mothers to sex-type their babies.

There is every reason for their baby's sex to be important to the parents. Children's sex determines what they are named, how they are dressed, how they are treated, and what will be expected of them in later life. There is a disconcerting side to this process, however. We like to think of ourselves as individuals, and we want to be treated with an awareness of who we are, not of what others expect us to be. It therefore comes as something of a shock to realize that so many important aspects of our future may be shaped at the outset by our parents' expectations.

Unless parental expectations are held so rigidly that they become destructive, they do not represent a failing on the parents' part. Rather, parents' responses to their newborns reflect the fact that human infants are not just biological organisms but cultural entities as well. For their parents and for other members of the community, infants have special meanings that are shaped by the culture's ideas about people and about the events that infants are likely to encounter as they grow to adulthood. These meanings in turn shape the ways adults construct the environmental contexts within which children develop. When differences are found in the ways boys and girls are treated, they occur not just because parents think that infant boys and girls are different to begin with but, perhaps more significantly, because they believe that men and women have different roles to play (Fagot, 1995).

This orientation to the future is expressed in clear symbolic form by the Zincantecos of south-central Mexico (Greenfield et al., 1989). When a son is born, he is given a digging stick, an ax, and a strip of palm used in weaving mats, in expectation of his adult role. Such future orientation is not only

BOX 3.4

THE PARENTS' RESPONSE TO THE BABY'S ARRIVAL

Aidan Macfarlane, an English pediatrician, recorded the following conversation in a delivery room as Mrs. B., age 27, gave birth to her first child. The concern it reveals about the baby's physical soundness is all but universal, and so is the power of the culture's belief system to shape the parents' initial responses to their newborn child.

Doctor: Come on, junior. Only a lady could cause so much trouble. Come on, little one.

(A baby is delivered)

Mother: A girl.
D: Well, it's got the right plumbing.
M: Oh, I'm sorry, darling.
Father: (laughs)
D: What are you sorry about?
M: He wanted a boy.
D: Well, you'll have to try again next week, won't you!
M: (laughs)
D: She looks great. Want to see her? Bloody and messy, but that's not from her.
M: Oh, she's gorgeous.
F: Looks like you.

(Mother kisses father)

M: Is she all right?
D: Why don't you ask her? She's quite capable of letting you know how she feels about the situation.
M: She's noisy, isn't she?
D: Yes, just like the modern generation.
F: Yes.
M: Well, Dr. Murphy, I was right. I had a sneaky feeling it was a girl, just because I wanted a boy.
F: Well, it will suit your mum, won't it?
M: (laughs)
D: Often tactically best to have a girl first—she can help with the washing up.

(Baby given to mother)

M: Hello, darling. Meet your dad. You're just like your dad. *(Baby yells)*
F: I'm going home!
M: Oh you've gone quiet. *(laughs)* Oh darling, she's just like you—she's got your little tiny nose.
F: It'll grow like yours.
M: She's big, isn't she? What do you reckon?
D: She's quite good-looking, despite forceps marks on her head—but don't worry about that. She'll have little bruises around her ears—well, they usually have. I don't know if she does.
M: There's one—there. . . . Oh look, she's got hair. It's a girl—you're supposed to be all little.
D: What do you think she weighs, Richard? I think about seven and a half.
M: Oh, she's gorgeous, she's lovely. She's got blue eyes. You hold her. Come on.

present in ritual; it is coded in a Zincantecan saying: "For in the newborn baby is the future of our world."

Organization of the present in terms of the future is a fundamental cultural source of developmental change and a powerful environmental source of developmental continuity. As the anthropologist Leslie White (1949) wrote, only among humans does the world of ideas come "to have a continuity and permanence that the external world of the senses can never have. It is not made up of the present only, but of a past and a future as well" (p. 372).

Just as infants arrive at childbirth with a set of genetically built-in capacities to learn about and to act upon the world, parents arrive at this moment with their own tendencies to respond in certain ways that have developed through their experience as members of their culture. The relationship between child and parents that begins at birth is an essential part of the foundation on which later development builds.

SUMMARY

THE PERIODS OF PRENATAL DEVELOPMENT

- Many developmental theorists look upon the prenatal period as a model for all periods of development from conception to death.

F: No.
M: Why not? *(laughs)* You're all of a tremble, aren't you?
D: I dropped the first one I held.
F: Charming!
M: Oh look, oh mine. Hello, darling. Good lungs, hasn't she? She's got a dimple—where'd she get that from?
D: That's probably from the forceps. Actually, have you got dimples?
M: Oh no, neither of us have. Oh, you're lovely. Look . . . she's lovely. I thought she'd be all mauve and crinkly.
D: Oh, she's in great nick.
M: Yes. I was expecting her to be all mauve and shriveled, but she's not, is she?
D: Not at all. In front of the cameras she's a real lady.
M: Oh dear. Having your photo taken, darling? Oh.
D: Ma'am, can I ask you to drop your ankles apart?
M: She doesn't go much on this.

(Nurse attaches name-tag to baby)

F: Like British Rail, labeling her like a parcel.
M: Oh look, darling, look at the size of her feet. She's got no toenails.
D: What do you mean, she hasn't got any toenails?
M: She hasn't got any toenails. They're soft.
D: I don't think you'd like it scratching around inside you.
M: Look—fabulous. Aren't you pleased with her.
F: Yes, of course.
D: I'm not putting her back.
M: You said that if it was a girl it could go back.
D: Back to the manufacturers, yes.
M: Well, it came from him in the first place.
D: It's his spermatozoa that decides the sex.
M: Quite. *(kisses the baby and laughs)*
F: I shall be worried to death when she's eighteen.
M: You'll imagine her going out with all sorts of blokes like you were. *(laughs)* In a sort of odd way I was after his money really.
D: Yes?
M: All two quid. Go, go to dad.

(Macfarlane, 1977, pp. 61–67)

Mr. and Mrs. B. are not the only parents who find they must quickly change their plans and make a virtue out of having a daughter instead of a son. In the United States, it is a fairly common occurrence in spite of the changing attitudes about sex roles. Polls conducted in the United States indicate that most people want their first child to be a son, and if they are to have only one child, they prefer that the child be a boy (Frankiel, 1993). Despite their initial hopes and expectations, most parents eventually accept the sex of their newborns.

- ≻ Prenatal development is often divided into three broad periods:
  1. The germinal period, in which the zygote enters the uterus and becomes implanted there.
  2. The period of the embryo, which begins with implantation and ends with the first signs of ossification at the end of the eighth week. During this period the basic organs are formed.
  3. The period of the fetus, during which the brain grows extensively and the separate organ systems become integrated.
- ≻ As the organism grows from a single cell to a full-term newborn child, new forms constantly emerge. According to the epigenetic hypothesis, interactions between the cells and their environment generate the new forms.
- ≻ At implantation, the organism becomes directly dependent on the mother's body for sustenance.
- ≻ The embryo becomes active with the first pulses of a primitive heart, beginning about 1 month after conception.

THE DEVELOPING ORGANISM IN THE PRENATAL ENVIRONMENT

- ≻ The fetus is subject to environmental influences originating from outside as well as inside the mother. The fetus sometimes experiences outside influences directly through its own sensory mechanisms, but often such influences work indirectly, through their effects on the mother.

- Babies' reactions to events they first experienced in the womb seem to indicate that fetuses are capable of learning.
- The mother's reactions to her environment—her feelings and attitudes—are associated with the fetus's well-being. Children born to mothers who do not want them or who are under stress are subject to developmental risk.
- The nutritional status of the mother is an important factor in fetal development. Extreme malnutrition in the mother has a devastating effect on her ability to produce a normal child. Lesser degrees of malnourishment associated with other forms of environmental deprivation also increase the risks to fetal and postnatal development.
- Teratogens (environmental agents that can cause deviations from normal fetal development) take many forms. Drugs, infections, radiation, and pollution all pose threats to the developing organism. Several basic principles apply to the effects of teratogens:
    1. The susceptibility of the organism depends on the stage of its development.
    2. A teratogen's effects are likely to be specific to a particular organ.
    3. Individual organisms vary in their susceptibility to teratogens.
    4. The physiological state of the mother influences the impact of a teratogen.
    5. The greater the concentration of a teratogenic agent, the greater the risk.
    6. Teratogens that adversely affect the developing organism may affect the mother little or not at all.

PRENATAL DEVELOPMENT RECONSIDERED

- Several basic principles of development are seen in the prenatal period:
    1. Sequence is fundamental.
    2. Timing is important.
    3. Development consists of differentiation and integration.
    4. Development is characterized by stagelike changes.
    5. Development proceeds unevenly.
    6. The course of development seems to be punctuated by periods of regression.

BIRTH: THE FIRST BIO-SOCIAL-BEHAVIORAL SHIFT

- Birth is the first bio-social-behavioral shift in human development.
- The process of birth begins approximately 266 days after conception, when changes in the mother's body force the fetus through the birth canal.
- Labor proceeds through three stages. It begins with the first regular, intense contractions of the uterus, and it ends when the baby is born, the umbilical cord is severed, and the afterbirth is delivered. Although the biological process of labor is roughly the same everywhere, there are marked cultural variations in the organization of childbearing.

- Drugs given to the mother to reduce pain may have negative effects on the neonate.

THE NEWBORN'S CONDITION

- The infant's physical state at birth is usually assessed by the Apgar Scale, which rates the infant's heart rate, respiratory effort, reflex responsivity, muscle tone, and color. Babies with low Apgar scores require immediate medical attention if they are to survive.
- Scales have been developed to assess the neonate's behavioral capacities. These scales are satisfactory for identifying neonates who require medical intervention; they appear to be modestly useful, at best, for predicting later patterns of development.
- Many premature babies who are of normal size for their gestational age can catch up with full-term infants if they are well cared for. Those who have low birth weights and small heads are especially at risk for long-term developmental problems.

BEGINNING THE PARENT–CHILD RELATIONSHIP

- A newborn's appearance plays a significant role in the parents' responses to it.
- The parents' expectations, patterned by the culture's belief system, influence the child's environment in ways that shape the child's development and promote the continuation of cultural traits from one generation to another.

KEY TERMS

amnion, p. 84
Apgar Scale, p. 111
blastocyst, p. 83
Brazelton Neonatal Assessment Scale, p. 111
cephalocaudal pattern, p. 85
chorion, p. 84
cleavage, p. 82
ectoderm, p. 84
endoderm, p. 84
epigenesis, p. 83
fetal alcohol syndrome, p. 98
fetal growth retardation, p. 113
germinal period, p. 81
gestational age, p. 112
heterochrony, p. 82
heterogeneity, p. 82
implantation, p. 84
inner cell mass, p. 83
low birth weight, p. 113
mesoderm, p. 84
morula, p. 82
period of the embryo, p. 81
period of the fetus, p. 81
placenta, p. 84
preterm, p. 112
proximodistal pattern, p. 85
teratogens, p. 95
trophoblast, p. 83
umbilical cord, p. 84
zona pellucida, p. 81

THOUGHT QUESTIONS

1. Give examples of quantitative and qualitative changes that take place during prenatal development. What are the important differences between the two kinds of changes?
2. What makes transitions from one stage of prenatal development to the next risky for the organism?

3. What is the role of activity in fetal development?
4. Skim back through the chapter to list as many examples as you can of instances where the environment plays a significant role in prenatal development. Do you think that the role of the environment changes after birth? How?
5. Parents have well-formed expectations about the future behaviors of their newborn babies. How might these expectations shape the child's development?

PART II

Infancy

All cultures recognize infancy as a distinct period of life. Its starting point is clear; it begins when the umbilical cord is severed and the child starts to breathe. The end of infancy is not so easily defined. According to the ancient Romans, an infant is "one who does not speak," and the ability to speak a language is still considered an important indicator that infancy has come to an end. It is not a sufficient marker by itself, however. Modern developmentalists look for converging changes in several spheres of children's functioning to determine when one stage has ended and another has begun. These changes include not only infants' acquisition of language but changes in their physical capacities, modes of thought, and social relations as well. It is this ensemble of changes that marks the transformation of babies from helpless infants into young children who, though still dependent upon adults, are on their way to independence.

The chapters in Part II are organized to highlight the important sequences of changes in each sphere and the interactions among them. Chapter 4 begins with a description of infants' earliest capacities for perceiving and acting on the world. It then traces events in infant development from birth to the age of about 2½ months. The most obvious requirement of this earliest postnatal period is that infants and their caretakers become sufficiently coordinated in their interactions that adults are able to provide infants with enough nourishment to support their continued growth. This requirement is met through a wide variety of cultural systems of infant care that call upon infants' basic capacities to learn from experience.

If all goes well, by the end of this period, the development of crucial brain structures will have enhanced infants' abilities to experience the world, resulting in a reordering of the social and emotional interactions between infants and their caretakers. This ensemble of changes is the first postnatal bio-social-behavioral shift.

Between 2½ and 12 months of age, the period covered in Chapter 5, the infant's capacities in all spheres of development progress markedly. Increases in size and strength are accompanied by increases in coordination and mobility: the ability to sit independently appears at about 5 or 6 months; crawling at about 7 or 8 months; and walking at about 1 year. Both memory and problem-solving abilities improve, providing infants with a finer sense of their environment and how to act upon it.

Sometime between 7 and 9 months, infants' increased physical ability and intellectual power bring about additional changes in their emotions and social relations. They are likely to become wary of strangers; they become upset when left alone; and they begin to express strong emotional attachments to their caretakers. They also begin to make their first speechlike sounds. These changes mark what appears to be a second bio-social-behavioral shift during infancy.

Chapter 6 describes the changes that occur between 12 months and 2½ years, culminating in the bio-social-behavioral shift that signals the end of infancy. Rapid growth in the baby's ability to use language is accompanied by the emergence of pretend play and more sophisticated forms of problem solving. Toward the end of infancy, children begin to show a concern for adult standards, and they attempt to meet those standards. Caretakers, for their part, view these changes as a sign that children are no longer "babies." They begin to reason with their children, to explain things to them, and to make demands upon them.

The coverage of infancy ends with Chapter 7, which takes up an enduring question: Does the pattern of development that is established during infancy persist into later years, fixed and unchangeable, or can it be significantly altered by the maturational changes and experiences that will occur during childhood and adolescence? This scientific question has a practical counterpart: Should society intervene in the lives of at-risk infants to prevent later problems, or should it wait until there are actual problems? As we shall see, opinions about these matters are sharply divided. Nevertheless, the efforts of developmentalists to study them underscore how important it is to consider the whole child in the context of both family and community if we are to gain a scientific understanding of development and make informed decisions about social policies that affect children.

CHAPTER 4

Early Infancy: Initial Capacities and the Process of Change

Babies control and bring up their families as much as they are controlled by them; in fact, we may say that the family brings up a baby by being brought up by him. Whatever reaction patterns are given biologically and whatever schedule is predetermined developmentally must be considered to be a series of potentialities for changing patterns of mutual regulation.

Erik Erikson, *Childhood and Society*

As the evidence concerning prenatal development clearly showed, babies arrive in the world with at least elementary abilities to see and hear their environment, move, learn, and remember. But compared with many animals that are able to negotiate their environments at birth almost as well as their parents, human beings are born in a state of marked immaturity. At birth, the capacities developed during the prenatal period are not adequate in themselves to ensure the baby's survival. The ability to suck, for example, is of no help in obtaining food unless the infant's mouth is in touch with a source of milk, and newborns cannot yet bring the nipple to their mouths by themselves. They must be physically aided to accomplish even such an elementary function as feeding.

The relative helplessness of human babies at birth has two obvious consequences. First, for many years, human offspring must depend on their parents and other adults for their survival. Second, in order to survive on their own and eventually reproduce, humans must acquire a vast repertoire of knowledge and skills that they do not possess at birth.

This chapter describes the capacities of the child at birth and the processes of developmental change that occur in the initial period of infancy, a period beginning immediately after birth and ending some 2½ months later. During this time, significant changes take place in several important biological, behavioral, and social processes. These changes converge about 2½ months after birth to make new kinds of behavior possible, allowing a qualitatively different social and emotional relationship to develop between infants and their caregivers. This convergence of changes in different domains is the kind of qualitative reorganization in the child's functioning that we have designated a bio-social-behavioral shift.

DEVELOPMENT OF THE BRAIN

We begin by examining changes in the brain that are central to all the developments we present in this chapter. As we saw in Chapter 3 (pp. 88–92), well before full-term babies are born, their brains and central nervous systems support elementary sensory and motor functions: fetuses respond to distinct sounds, for example, and they move spontaneously. These basic capacities are sufficient for them to learn to recognize the sound of their mothers' voices and the language spoken around them and form the basis for newborns' earliest adaptations to their new environment.

In a still authoritative study, Cowan (1979) found that during the period of maximum prenatal brain development, which occurs between 10 and 26 weeks after conception, the brain grows at a rate of as many as 250,000 brain cells per minute. It is estimated that the cerebral cortex, the area of the brain which most distinctively distinguishes human beings from other animals, contains more than 10 *billion* nerve cells. Each of these nerve cells makes multiple connections with other nerve cells.

At birth the brain contains the vast majority of all the cells it will ever have, yet it will become four times larger by the time the baby reaches adulthood. To understand how such growth comes about, we need to look more closely at the basic operative unit of brain activity—the nerve cell referred to as the **neuron**—and the brain structures into which neurons are organized.

neuron A nerve cell.

axon The main protruding branch of a neuron that carries messages to other cells in the form of electrical impulses.

dendrite The protruding part of a neuron that receives messages from the axons of other cells.

synapse The tiny gap between axons and dendrites.

neurotransmitter A chemical secreted by the cell sending a message that carries the impulse across the synaptic gap to the receiving cell.

myelin A sheath of fatty cells that insulates axons and speeds transmission of nerve impulses from one neuron to the next.

NEURONS AND NETWORKS OF NEURONS

The function of neurons is to transmit information to other neurons or to muscle or gland cells. This function causes neurons to differ from other body cells in several respects. Most body cells look smooth and regular, more or less in the shape of a sphere or a disk. By contrast, neurons have highly irregular shapes, with many spiky areas sticking up from their surfaces (see Figure 4.1). Every neuron has one main protruding branch, called an **axon,** along which it sends information to other cells in the form of small electrical impulses. If a neuron needs to communicate with more than one other nerve cell, its axon forms branches at its tip to make the necessary connections. The other parts of the neuron that protrude from its surface are called **dendrites.** The dendrites, as well as other parts of the cell body, are the receiving zones for messages coming from the axons of other cells.

The actual site at which one neuron is linked to another is a tiny gap between axons and dendrites called the **synapse.** When an impulse from the axon arrives at the synapse, the sending cell secretes a chemical, called a **neurotransmitter,** that carries the impulse across the synaptic gap, setting off a reaction in the receiving cell.

The combination of a sending and a receiving neuron creates an elementary neuronal circuit. As a rule, neurons are connected to only a few, specific, receiving neurons and, in turn, receive impulses from only a few neurons. However, in some cases, one axon branches to come in contact with many diverging neuronal networks; in other cases, many axons converge on a receptor neuron. The results of such multiple forms of connectivity, combined with the fact that there are billions of neurons, make possible a virtually infinite variety of patterns of brain activity and behavior.

The basic architecture of neurons and neuronal circuits suggests two reasons for the fourfold growth in brain size that occurs by adulthood. First, there is an increase in the size and complexity of the dendrites that protrude from every neuron. Second, there is an increase in the number of branches that axons form as they create connections to multiple receiving neurons. These two sources of growth combine to increase the number of synapses and to form more complex neural circuits (see Figure 4.2).

A third source of increased brain size and complexity of brain functions is *myelination,* the process by which axons become covered by **myelin,** a

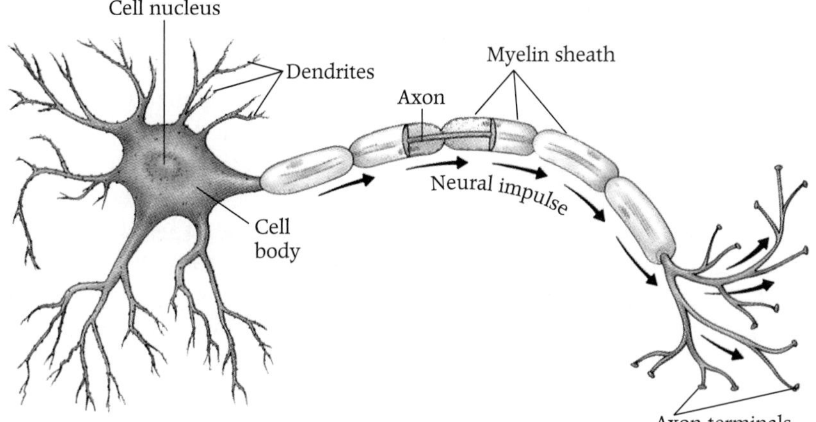

FIGURE 4.1
The neuron receives information from other neurons through its dendrites and feeds that information to other neurons through its axon.

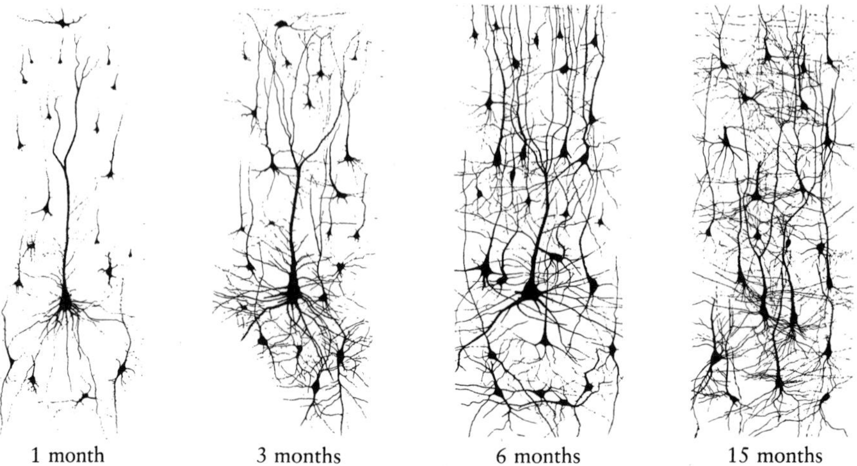

FIGURE 4.2
These drawings from photomicrographs of infant brain tissue show the marked increases in the size and number of cerebral neurons during the first 15 months of postnatal life. (From Conel, 1939/1963.)

sheath of fatty cells that insulates them and speeds transmission of nerve impulses from one neuron to the next. Myelinated axons transmit signals anywhere from 10 to 100 times faster than unmyelinated axons, making possible more effective interconnections between parts of the brain and more complicated forms of thought and action.

THE CENTRAL NERVOUS SYSTEM AND THE BRAIN

The central nervous system is conventionally divided into three major sections—the spinal cord, the brain stem, and the cerebral cortex.

The **spinal cord** extends from the waist to the base of the brain. The nerves that lie within the spinal cord carry messages back and forth from the brain to the spinal nerves along the spinal tract. The spinal nerves that branch out from the spinal cord communicate with specific areas of the body. Some of these neurons carry messages to the brain from the skin and other body parts and organs; others carry messages from the brain to the various body parts to initiate actions such as muscle movement.

The brain itself grows out of the top of the spinal cord (see Figure 4.3). At its base is the **brain stem,** which controls such elementary reactions as blinking and sucking, as well as such vital functions as breathing and sleeping. All these capacities can be found in at least rudimentary form during the latter stages of prenatal development, and at birth the brain stem is one of the most highly developed areas of the central nervous system.

The neurons of the brain stem do not respond to specific forms of sensory input in a precise, one-to-one manner, with different sensory inputs arriving at the brain as isolated signals. Instead, the brain stem contains neural pathways that mix various sources of sensory inputs with impulses from other regions of the brain and the body. Stimulation that reaches the brain stem from the sensory receptors is modulated and reorganized within these pathways, increasing the complexity of behaviors that it can support.

Structures in the brain stem connect to the **cerebral cortex,** the brain's outermost layer. The cerebral cortex is divided into two hemispheres, each of which is divided into four sections or *lobes,* separated by deep grooves. Under ordinary conditions of development, the *occipital lobes* are specialized for vision; the *temporal lobes,* for hearing and speech; the *parietal lobes,* for spatial perception; and the *frontal lobes,* for motor control and coordination of the functions of other cortical areas.

It has been estimated that an average cerebral cortex is capable of a million billion connections, creating a biological organ of incredible complexity

spinal cord The part of the central nervous system that extends from the waist to the base of the brain.

brain stem The base of the brain, which controls such elementary reactions as blinking and sucking, as well as such vital functions as breathing and sleeping.

cerebral cortex The brain's outermost layer. The networks of neurons in the cerebral cortex integrate information from several sensory sources with memories of past experiences, processing them in a way that results in human forms of thought and action.

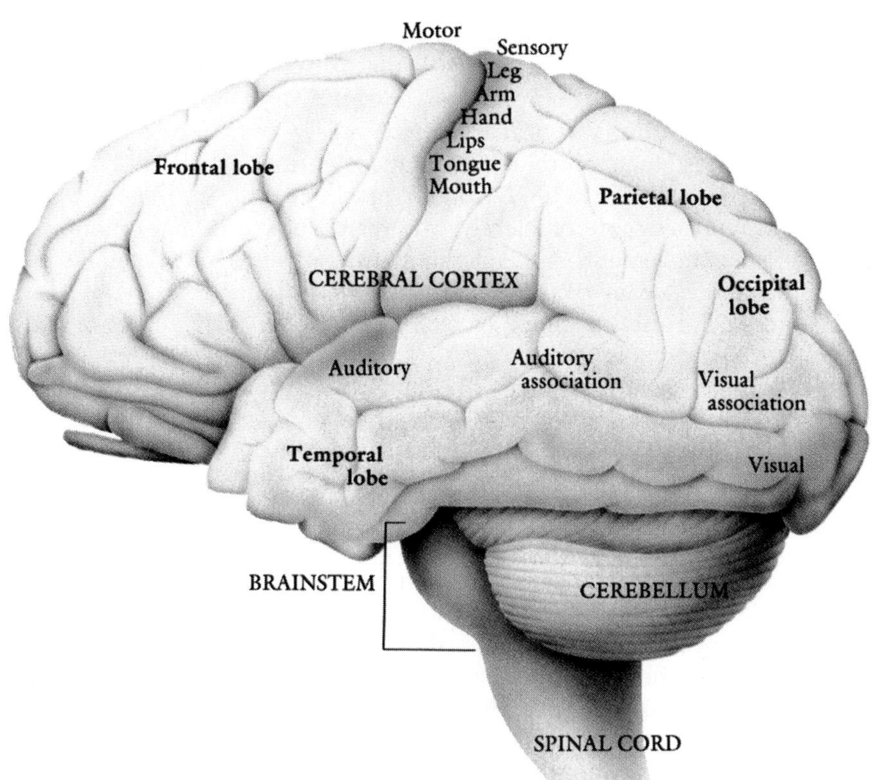

FIGURE 4.3
A schematic view of the brain, showing the major lobes or divisions of the cerebral cortex (including the areas where some functions are localized), the brain stem, the cerebellum, and the spinal cord. (Adapted from Tanner, 1978.)

(Edelman, 1984). Once stimulation from the environment reaches the cerebral cortex, it travels through networks of interacting neurons so complex that scientists have thus far found it impossible to trace completely the fate of a single stimulus event, such as a touch on the cheek. The networks of neurons in the cerebral cortex integrate information from several sensory sources with memories of past experiences, processing them in a way that results in distinctively human forms of thought and action.

Although various areas of the brain are named according to the functions that they will later carry out, for many functions there is considerable interplay among areas. In addition, the human cortex, unlike that of other animals, has large areas that are not "prewired" to respond directly to external stimulation in any discernible way (see Figure 4.4). These "uncommitted" areas provide infants with the capacity to develop brain circuits that fit the needs of the experiences they will encounter later in life.

In general, the lower-lying areas of the central nervous system, the spinal cord and the brain stem, mature (that is, grow more dendritic trees, have more myelin, increase the complexity of their neural circuitry) ahead of the cerebral cortex. At birth the circuitry of the cerebral cortex is both relatively immature and poorly connected to the lower-lying parts of the nervous system that receive stimulation from the environment. Because of their relative maturity, the spinal cord and brain stem enable movements and visual responses without cortical involvement (Woodruff-Pak et al., 1990). As the nerve fibers connecting the cortex with the brain stem and spinal cord become myelinated, the infant's abilities expand.

Different parts of the cerebral cortex continue to develop at different times throughout infancy and well into childhood and adolescence (Thatcher, 1994). Using criteria such as the size and complexity of neurons, their degree of myelination, and the complexity of their

FIGURE 4.4
In these six mammalian species the proportions of the brain mass that are devoted to different functions vary widely. The areas designated "uncommitted cortex" are not dedicated to any particular sensory or motor functions and are available for integrating information of many kinds. (Adapted from Fishbein, 1976.)

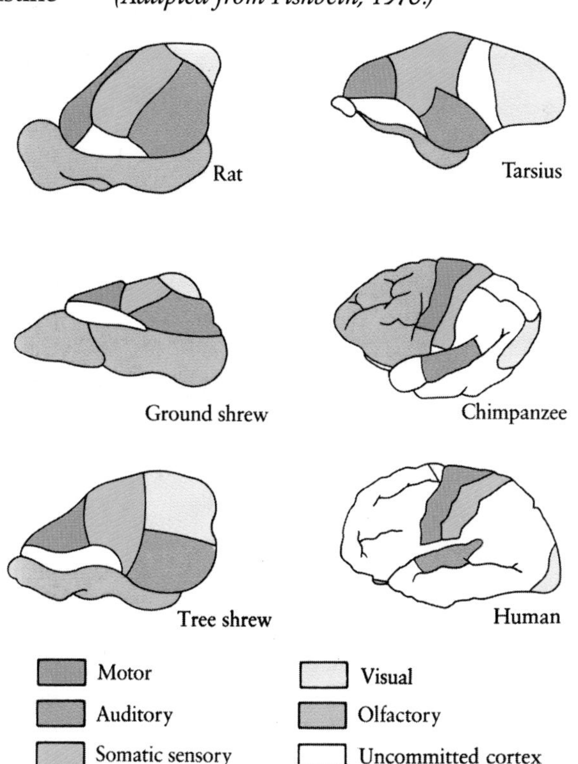

primary motor area The area of the brain responsible for nonreflexive, or voluntary, movement.

primary sensory areas The areas of the cerebral cortex responsible for the initial analysis of sensory information.

connections, scientists estimate that the first area of the cerebral cortex to undergo important developmental change is the **primary motor area,** which is the area responsible for nonreflexive, or voluntary, movement (Kolb & Whishaw, 1996). Within the primary motor area, the first cells to become functional are those that control the arms and the trunk. By about 1 month of age, the neurons in this area are becoming myelinated, so they can now conduct neural impulses more efficiently. The region of the primary motor area that governs leg movements is the last to mature; it is not fully developed until sometime in the second year (Kolb & Whishaw, 1996).

As a result of this sequence of biological changes, the development of voluntary movement in the arms and legs follows the cephalocaudal (from-the-head-down) pattern, introduced in Chapter 3 (p. 85). At the end of the first month, many infants can raise their heads while lying on their stomachs. At 3 months of age, they have more voluntary control of the muscles that move the upper trunk, shoulders, arms, and forearms. A few months later, they begin to gain voluntary control of leg movements.

The **primary sensory areas** of the cortex—those areas that are responsible for the initial analysis of sensory information—also mature in the months after birth. The nerve fibers responsible for touch are the first to mature, followed by those in the primary visual area and then those in the primary auditory area (Huttenlocher, 1990). By 3 months of age, all the primary sensory areas are relatively mature (Tanner, 1990).

The frontal cortex, which is essential in a wide variety of voluntary behaviors, including behaviors that require planning, begins to function in infancy but continues to develop throughout childhood (Fischer & Rose, 1995; Johnson, 1998).

EARLIEST CAPACITIES

Scholars interested in development have always had a special fascination with the question of neonates' initial capacities to perceive, to act upon, and perhaps even to think about the world into which they are born. A century ago there was broad agreement with William James's belief that infants' perceptual world is a "buzzing, blooming confusion." By the 1990s, scientific opinion had swung strongly in the opposite direction, to the belief that children are born with greater capacities for perceiving and acting in the world than their normally observed behavior reveals, a belief summed up in the idea of "the precocious infant" (Haith & Benson, 1998).

This difference of opinion about the "starting points" of development strongly influences the kind of theory needed to explain the process of developmental change. The idea of the precocious infant points to biology and processes of maturation as the essential driving force of development, while the idea of an infant initially confronting total confusion suggests that development depends heavily upon information from the environment.

Despite the importance of understanding infants' initial capacities, developmentalists have yet to agree on what they are. You don't have to spend much time with a newborn infant to understand the difficulties of arriving at a definitive conclusion. First of all, the baby sleeps a lot and when in an alert state often seems to be simply "taking in the scene." From time to time it appears that something catches the baby's attention, but such moments are fleeting.

The constant fluctuations in the state of the newborn make it difficult in some cases for developmentalists to repeat each other's experiments and provide reliable and replicable evidence on the state of some capacities. And, as we shall see, the resulting disagreements about data go together with different theories about the process of later change.

SENSORY PROCESSES

Organisms receive information from the environment through their sensory systems. Normal full-term newborns enter the world with all sensory systems functioning, but not all of these systems have developed to the same level. This unevenness illustrates the general rule of development *(heterochrony)* that we remarked on with respect to the fetal period: The various organ systems develop at different rates throughout the child's development.

The basic method scientists use to evaluate infants' sensory capacities is to present them with a sensory stimulus and observe how their overt behaviors or physiological processes are affected by it. An investigator might sound a tone or flash a light, for example, and watch for an indication that the newborn has sensed it—a turn of the head, a variation in brain waves, a change in the rate at which the baby sucks on a nipple. Sometimes the researcher presents two stimuli at once to determine if the baby will attend to one longer than to the other. If so, the baby must be able to tell the stimuli apart, and perhaps even prefers the one that it attends to longer.

Another widely used technique for assessing sensory capacities is to present a stimulus to which the infant clearly attends and then to continue presenting it until the infant gets bored and stops paying attention. The process in which attention to novelty decreases with exposure is called **habituation.** The next step is to make a change in some aspect of the stimulus: the frequency of a musical tone or the arrangement of elements within a visual array, for example. If the infant's interest is renewed after the change in the stimulus, the infant is said to exhibit **dishabituation** and the investigator can conclude that the infant perceived the change.

Hearing

Make a loud noise and infants only minutes old will startle and may even cry. They will also turn their heads toward the source of the noise, an indication that they perceive sound as roughly localized in space (Morrongiello et al., 1994). Yet newborns' hearing is not so acute for some parts of the sound spectrum as it will be when they are older (Werner & Vanden Boss, 1993). Sensitivity to sound improves dramatically in infancy and then more slowly until the age of 10, when it reaches adult levels.

Even in their first hours, newborns are especially attuned to the sounds of speech. Infants can distinguish the sound of the human voice from other kinds of sounds, and they seem to prefer it. They are particularly interested in speech directed to them that is spoken with the high pitch and slow, exaggerated pronunciation known as "baby talk" (Werker & Tees, 1999). There is even evidence that by the time they are 2 days old, some babies would rather hear the language that has been spoken around them than a foreign language (Moon et al., 1993).

One of the most striking discoveries about the hearing of very young infants is that they are also particularly sensitive to the smallest sound categories in human speech that distinguish meanings. These basic language sounds are called **phonemes.** (Linguists denote phonemes and other language sounds by enclosing them in slashes, as we do here.)

Phonemes vary from language to language. In Spanish, for example, /r/ and /rr/ are two phonemes; "pero" and "perro" sound different ("perro" has a rolling "r") and have different meanings. In English, however, there is no such distinction. Similarly, /r/ and /l/ are different phonemes in English but not in Japanese.

Peter Eimas and his colleagues demonstrated that even 2-month-olds can distinguish among a variety of phonemes. They began by having the infants suck on a nipple attached to a recording device in a special apparatus

habituation The process in which attention to novelty decreases with repeated exposure.

dishabituation The term used to describe the situation in which an infant's interest is renewed after a change in the stimulus.

phonemes The smallest sound categories in human speech that distinguish meanings. Phonemes vary from language to language.

FIGURE 4.5

Apparatus for presenting artificially manipulated speech sounds to young infants. The baby sucks on a pacifier connected to recording instruments as speechlike sounds are presented from a loudspeaker just above the Raggedy Ann doll.

(see Figure 4.5) (Eimas, 1985). After establishing a baseline rate of sucking for each baby, the researchers presented the speech sound /pa/ to the babies each time they sucked. At first the babies' rate of sucking increased as if they were excited by each presentation of the sound, but after a while they settled back to their baseline rates of sucking. When the infants had become thoroughly habituated to the sound of /pa/, some of them heard a new sound, /ba/, which differed from the original sound only in its initial phoneme—/b/ versus /p/. Others heard a sound that differed an equal amount from the original sound but was within the /pa/ phoneme category. The babies began sucking rapidly again only when they heard a phoneme of a different category, an indication that they were especially sensitive to the difference between the /b/ and /p/ sounds (see Figure 4.6).

Other studies have shown that very young infants are able to perceive all the categorical sound distinctions used in all the world's various languages. Japanese babies, for example, can perceive the difference between /r/ and /l/, even though adult speakers of Japanese cannot. The ability to make phonemic distinctions apparently begins to narrow to just those distinctions that are present in one's native language at about 6 to 8 months of age, the same age at which the baby's first halting articulations of languagelike sounds are likely to begin (Kuhl et al., 1992) (see Figure 4.7).

These data make it tempting to conclude that human infants are born with special perceptual skills that are pretuned to the properties of human speech, but studies have long indicated that other species can make similar distinctions (Aslin et al., 1998; Kuhl & Miller, 1978). The difference is that humans use this ability as a stepping-stone to the mastery of language, an achievement that is beyond the capacities of other animals.

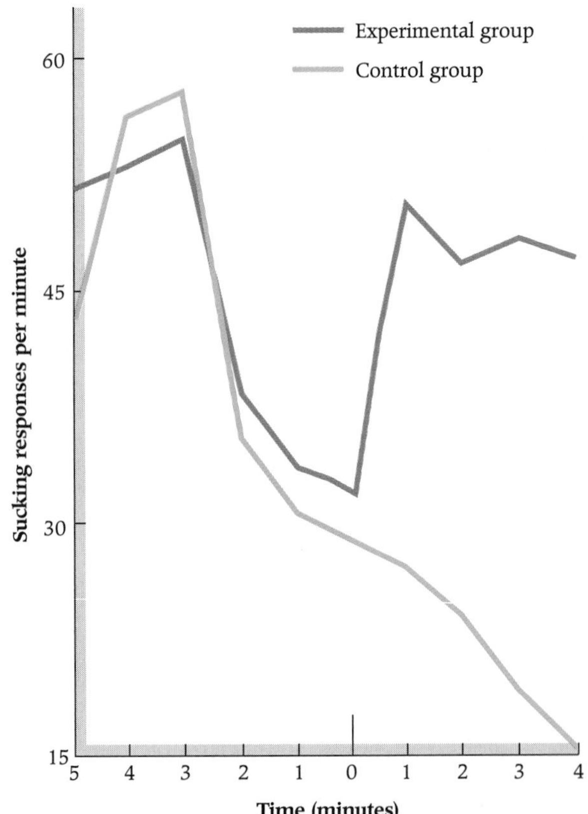

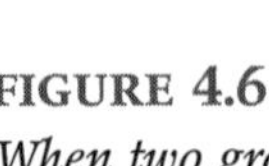

FIGURE 4.6

When two groups of infants were repeatedly presented with a single consonant over a 5-minute period, their rates of sucking decreased to just over 30 sucks per minute. For half of the infants (the experimental group) the consonant was changed at the time marked 0. Note that their rate of sucking increased sharply. For the remaining infants (the control group), who continued to hear the same consonant, the rate of sucking continued to decrease. (Adapted from Eimas, 1985.)

Vision

The basic anatomical elements of the visual system are present at birth, but they are not fully developed and they are not well coordinated. The lens of the eye and the cells of the retina are somewhat immature. In addition, the movements of the baby's eyes are not coordinated well enough to make the images on the two retinas sufficiently complementary to form a clear composite image. The result is that the baby's vision is blurry. The immaturity of some of the neural pathways that relay information from the retina to the brain further limits the newborn's visual capacities (Atkinson, 1998; Martin, 1998).

Color Perception Newborns seem to possess all, or nearly all, of the physiological prerequisites for seeing color in a rudimentary form. When two colors are equally bright, however, they do not discriminate the difference between them. By 2 months of age, their ability to perceive different colors appears to approach adult levels (Kellman, 1998; Teller, 1997).

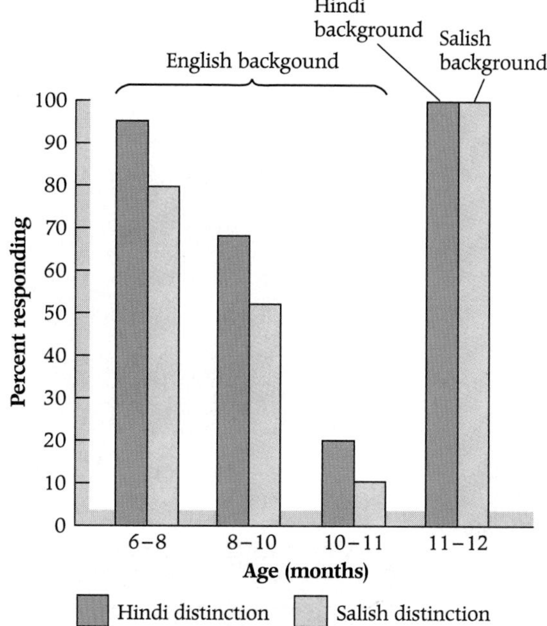

FIGURE 4.7

Infants can distinguish among language sounds that do not occur in their native language, but this capacity diminishes during the first year of life. Note the decrease in the proportion of infants from an English-speaking background who respond to consonants in Hindi and Salish (a North American Indian language). In contrast, at 1 year Hindi and Salish infants retain the capacity to distinguish sounds in their native langauges. (Adapted from Eimas, 1985.)

Visual Acuity A basic question about infants' vision is how nearsighted they are. To determine newborns' visual acuity, Robert Fantz and his colleagues (Fantz et al., 1962) developed a test based on the fact that when a striped visual field moves in front of the eyes, the eyes start to move in the same direction as the pattern. If the gaps between the stripes are so small that they cannot be perceived, the eyes do not move. By varying the width of the gaps and comparing the results obtained from newborns with those obtained from adults, these researchers were able to estimate that neonates have 20/300 vision—that is, they can see at 20 feet what an adult with normal vision can see at 300 feet. The exact estimate of newborn acuity differs somewhat according to the particular measures used, but all suggest that the newborn is very nearsighted (Martin, 1998). (See Figure 4.8, which shows what infants can see at different ages.)

Poor visual acuity is probably less troublesome to newborns than to older children and adults. After all, newborns are unable to move around unless someone carries them, and they cannot hold their heads erect without support. Still, their visual system is tuned well enough to allow them to see objects about a foot away—roughly the distance of the mother's face when they are nursing. This level of acuity allows them to make eye contact, which is important in establishing the social relationship between mother and child (Stern, 1985). Between 2 and 3 months of age, infants can coordinate the vision of both their eyes (Atkinson, 1998). By 7 or 8 months of age, when infants are able to crawl, their visual acuity is close to the adult level.

Visual Scanning Despite their nearsightedness and their difficulty in focusing, newborns actively scan their surroundings from the earliest days of life (Bronson, 1997; Haith, 1980). Marshall Haith and his colleagues developed recording techniques that allowed them to determine precisely where infants were looking and to monitor their eye movements in both light and dark rooms. They discovered that neonates scan with short eye movements even in a completely darkened room. Since no light is entering their eyes, this kind of scanning cannot be caused by the visual environment. It must therefore be *endogenous,* originating in the neural activity of the central nervous system. Endogenous eye movements seem to be an initial, primitive basis for looking behavior.

Haith's studies also revealed that neonates exhibit an early form of *exogenous* looking, that is, looking that is stimulated by the external environment. When the lights are turned on after infants have been in the dark, they

FIGURE 4.8
Infants' visual capacity increases dramatically over the first few months of life. By the age of four months, a baby can see nearly as distinctly as an adult, as seen in this artist's conception of the appearance of a visual scene for infants of different ages.

pause in their scanning when their gaze encounters an object or some change of brightness in the visual field. This very early sensitivity to changes in illumination, which is usually associated with the edges and angles of objects, appears to be an important component of the baby's developing ability to perceive visual forms (Haith, 1980).

Perception of Patterns What do babies see when their eyes encounter an object? Are they able to see objects much as adults do?

Until the early 1960s it was widely believed that neonates perceived only a formless play of light. Robert Fantz (1961, 1963) dealt a severe blow to this assumption by demonstrating that babies less than 2 days old can distinguish among visual forms. The technique he used was very simple. Babies were placed on their backs in a specially designed "looking chamber" (see Figure 4.9) and shown various forms. An observer looked down through the top of the chamber and recorded how long the infants looked at each form. Because the infants spent more time looking at some forms than at others, presumably they could tell the forms apart and preferred the ones they looked at the longest. Fantz found that neonates would rather look at patterned figures, such as faces and concentric circles, than at plain ones (see Figure 4.10).

Fantz's findings set off a search to determine the extent of newborns' capacity to perceive form and the reasons they prefer some forms over others.

That research has confirmed that infants visually perceive the world as more than random confusion, but it has also provided evidence that infants do not enter the world prepared to see it in the same way adults do. Gordon Bronson (1991, 1994, 1997), for example, studied the way 2-week-old and 12-week-old babies scan outline drawings of simple figures, such as a cross or a "v," on a lighted visual field. When adults are shown such figures, they scan the entire boundary, but Bronson found that babies 2 weeks of age appear to focus only on areas of high contrast, such as lines and angles (see Figure 4.11). This kind of looking behavior is clearly not random, but it does not constitute evidence that children are born with the ability to perceive basic patterns. At 12 weeks of age, as Figure 4.11 indicates, infants scan more of the figure, although their scanning movements are sometimes off the mark and may still be arrested by areas of high contrast. In a follow-up study, Bronson (1994) found that 13-week-old infants scanned more rapidly and extensively than infants 10 weeks and under. The developmental change was so marked that "by 3 months of age [the] infants appear[ed] to be quite different organisms, at least with respect to their scanning characteristics" (p. 1260). Bronson suggests that as the nervous system matures, it becomes more sophisticated and can begin to control visual scanning.

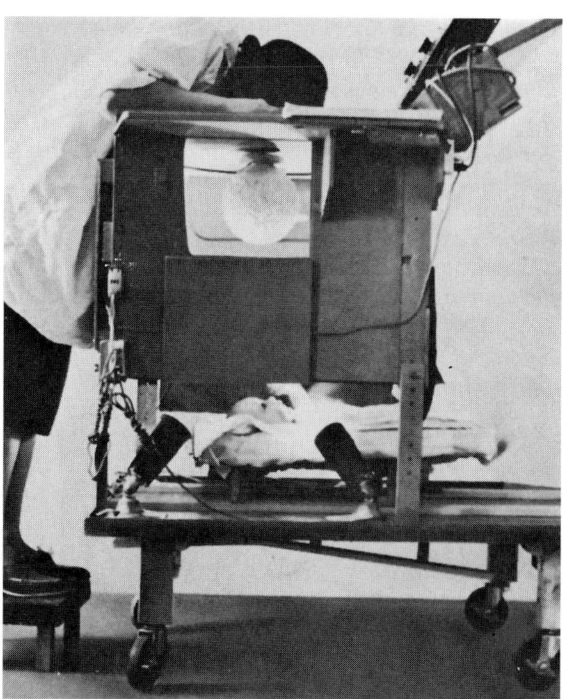

FIGURE 4.9
The "looking chamber" that Robert Fantz used to test newborns' visual interests. The infant lies in a crib in the chamber, looking up at the stimuli attached to the ceiling. The observer, watching through a peephole, determines how long the infant looks at each stimulus.

Perception of Faces In Fantz's early studies, one of the complex forms presented to the babies was a schematic human face. When Fantz (1961, 1963) presented newborn infants with a schematic face and a form in which facial elements had been scrambled, he found that the infants apparently could distinguish the schematic face from the jumbled face (see Figure 4.12). Although the preference for the schematic face over the scrambled face was small, the finding that newborns have an unlearned preference for a biologically significant form naturally attracted great interest. In the years since Fantz conducted his studies, solid evidence has been amassed that newborns are especially attracted to faces (Bushnell, 1998; Simion et al., 1998).

A key finding of this later research has been that motion critically influences newborns' preference for facelike stimuli. In Fantz's studies and later replications, researchers used only stationary schematic representations of faces. Several studies have shown that babies as young as 9 *minutes* old will turn their heads to gaze at a schematic face if it moves in front of them and will look at it longer than at a moving scrambled face (Mondock et al., 1999; Morton & Johnson, 1991).

FIGURE 4.10
Infants tested during the first weeks of life show a preference for patterned stimuli over plain stimuli. The length of each bar indicates the relative amount of time the babies spent looking at the corresponding stimulus. (Adapted from Fantz, 1961.)

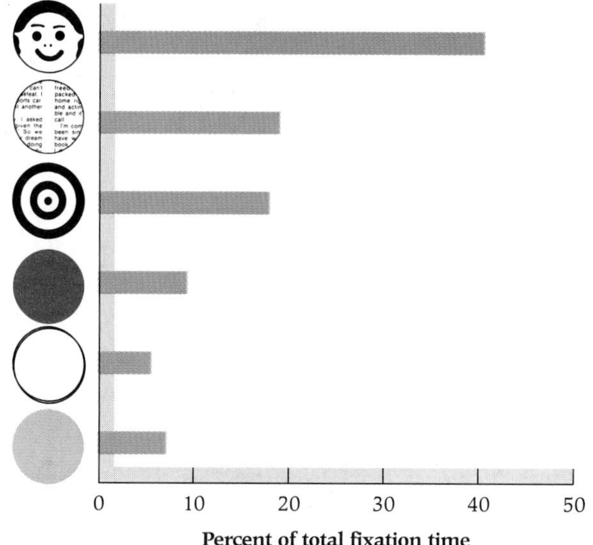

In real life, people move both their heads and the features of their faces. Under these naturalistic conditions, newborns only 2 days old demonstrate an ability to recognize the face they have seen most often, usually the mother's (Bushnell et al., 1989; Simion et al., 1998). This recognition depends on their ability to detect differences in hairline contours (Bushnell, 1989; Pascalis et al., 1995).

Taste and Smell

Neonates have a well-developed sense of both taste and smell (Crook, 1987). Trygg Engen and his colleagues demonstrated newborn abilities to smell by placing 2-day-old infants on a "stabilometer," an apparatus that measures physical activity (Engen et al., 1963). The experimenters held either an odorless cotton swab or a swab soaked in one of various aromatic solutions under the newborns' noses. Babies were judged to react to an odor if their activity increased over the level it had reached in response to the odorless cotton swab. The infants reacted strongly to some odors, such as garlic and vinegar, and less strongly to others, such as licorice and

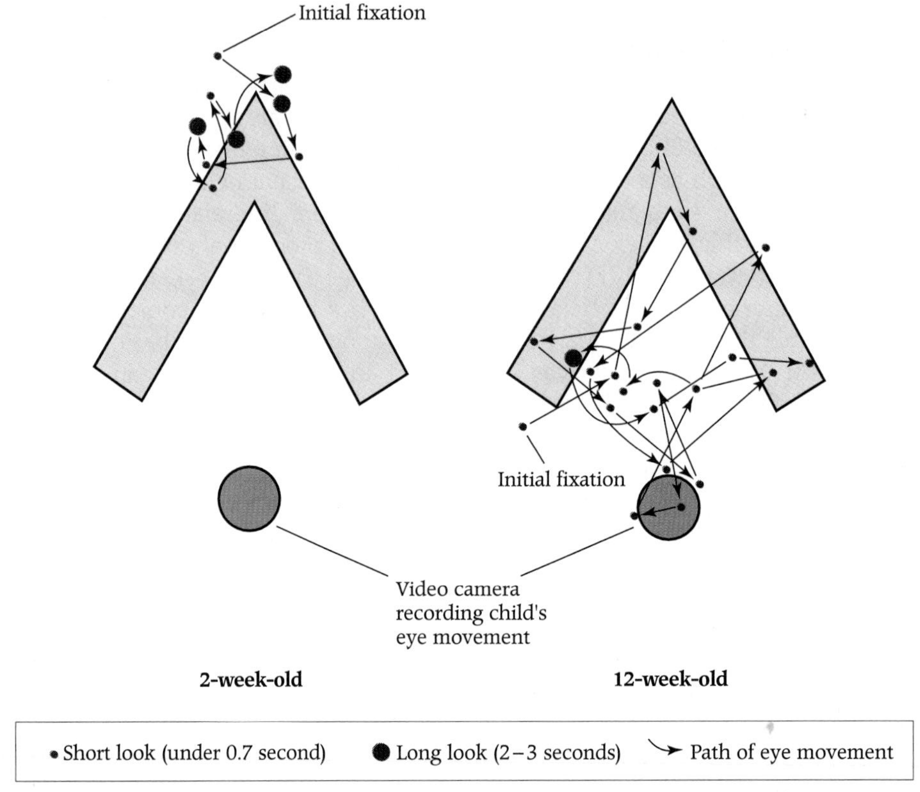

FIGURE 4.11
Visual scanning of a triangle by young infants. The triangle was mounted on a wall. A video camera was mounted just beneath it, positioned to record the eye movements of an infant as it gazed at the triangle. Note that the 2-week-olds concentrated their gaze on only one part of the figure, whereas the 12-week-olds visually explored the figure more fully. Large dots indicate long fixation times; small dots represent short ones. (Adapted from Bronson, 1991.)

FIGURE 4.12
Visual preferences of infants for (a) a schematic face, (b) a scrambled schematic face, and (c) a nonfacelike figure, all having equal amounts of light and dark area. The infants preferred both facelike forms over the nonfacelike form, and they accorded the "real" face slightly more attention than the scrambled face. (Adapted from Fantz, 1961.)

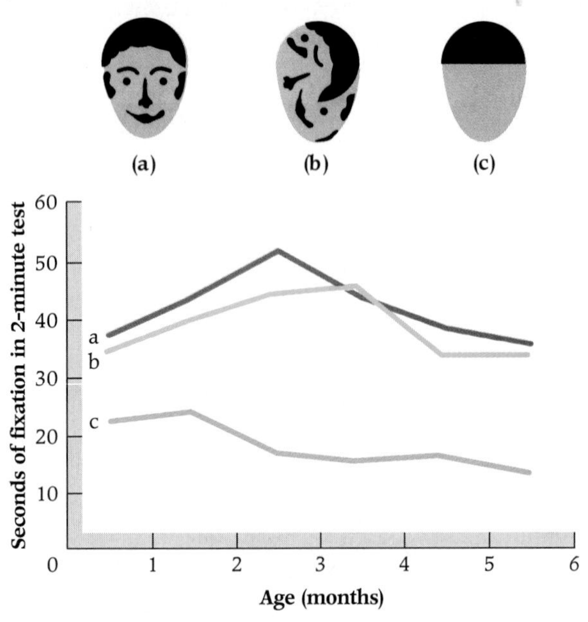

alcohol. Their responses indicated not only that they were sensitive to odors but also that they could tell one odor from another. This early sensitivity to odors has been confirmed in a more naturalistic way by Aidan Macfarlane (1975), who showed that by 5 days of age newborns will turn toward a pad soaked with breast milk, and by 8 to 10 days they will show a preference for the smell of their mothers' milk over the milk of another woman.

Newborns' sense of taste, like their sense of smell, is acute (Crook, 1987). They prefer sweet to sour tastes, and they will suck longer and more continuously on a bottle containing sweet substances than on one containing plain water. The characteristic facial expressions they make in response to various tastes look remarkably like those adults make when they encounter the same tastes, evidence that these expressions are innate (Rosenstein & Oster, 1988) (see Figure 4.13).

Touch, Temperature, and Position

The abilities to detect a touch to the skin, changes in temperature, and changes in physical position develop very early in the prenatal period. Although these sensory capacities have not received as much attention as vision and hearing, they are no less important to the baby's survival.

Newborns show that they sense they have been touched by making a distinctive movement, such as withdrawing the part touched or turning toward the touch. According to Tiffany Field (1990), newborns can feel the touch of a slight puff of air that is barely perceived by adults. Sensitivity to touch increases over the first several days of life (Haith, 1986).

Neonates indicate that they are sensitive to changes in temperature by becoming more active if there is a sudden lowering of the temperature (Pratt, 1954). They also respond to abrupt changes in their physical position, such as being spun around, with distinctive,

TABLE 4.1 EARLY SENSORY CAPACITIES

Sense	Capacity
Hearing	Ability to distinguish phonemes
	Preference for native language
Vision	Slightly blurred, slightly double vision at birth
	Color vision by 2 months of age
	Ability to distinguish patterned stimuli from plain
	Preference for moving, facelike stimuli
Smell	Ability to differentiate odors well at birth
Taste	Ability to differentiate tastes well at birth
Touch	Response to touch at birth
Temperature	Sensitivity to changes in temperature at birth
Position	Sensitivity to changes in position at birth

reflex A specific, well-integrated, automatic (involuntary) response to a specific type of stimulation.

reflexlike eye movements. Such responses indicate that the mechanism for detecting changes in position, which is located in the middle ear, is operating.

Overall, there is extensive evidence that babies come into the world with sensory capacities in good working order and far more structured than were once thought. (Infants' sensory capacities are summarized in Table 4.1.) The question then arises: What capacities do infants have for acting on the world? By combining the ability of infants to take in information from the environment with their abilities to act on it, it becomes possible to begin to characterize the starting point of postnatal psychological development.

FIGURE 4.13
Facial expressions evoked by various tastes in an infant and an adult: (a) a neutral expression follows the presentation of distilled water; (b) a hint of a smile follows the presentation of a sweet stimulus; (c) the pucker comes in response to a sour stimulus; (d) a bitter stimulus evokes a distinctive grimace. (Adapted from Steiner, 1979.)

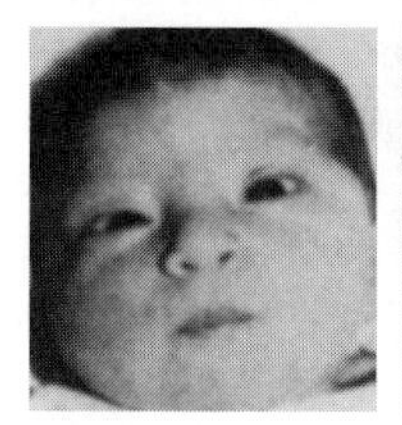

(a)

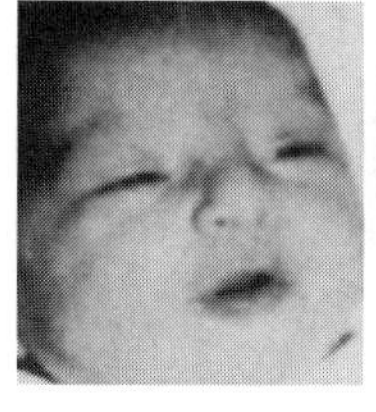

(b)

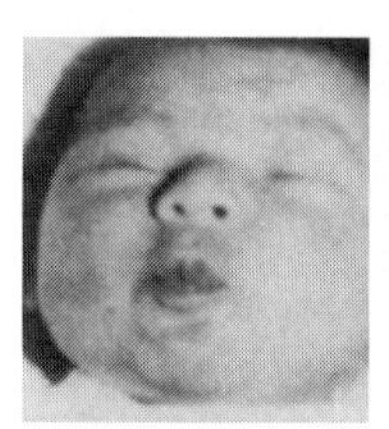

(c)

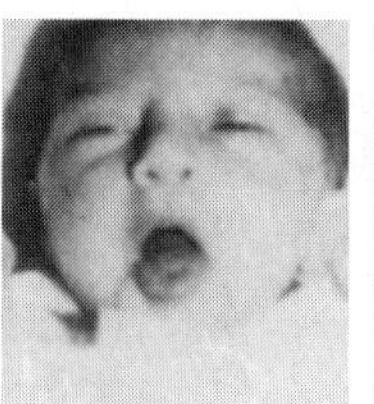
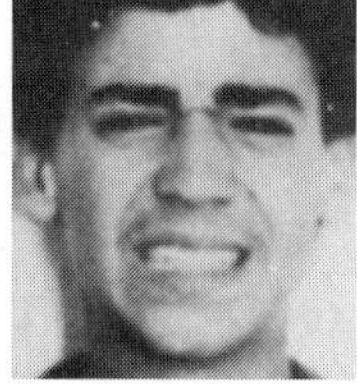

(d)

RESPONSE PROCESSES

As the previous examples indicate, infants are born with a variety of ways of acting on, and responding to, the world they perceive themselves to be in. Here we will examine infants' initial capacities as displayed in three fundamental categories of responsiveness: reflexes, emotions, and temperament.

Reflexes

Newborn babies come equipped with a variety of **reflexes**—specific, well-integrated, automatic (involuntary) responses to specific types of stimulation. Some of the reflexes with which infants are born are described in Table 4.2. Virtually all developmentalists agree that reflexes are important building blocks out of which various complex behavioral capacities of later life are constructed. They disagree, however, about the nature of the initial reflexes and how they contribute to the development of more complex capacities.

Some reflexes are clearly part of the baby's elementary survival kit. The *eyeblink reflex,* for example, has a clear function: it protects the eye from overly bright lights and foreign objects that might damage it. The *sucking* and *swallowing reflexes* are essential to feeding. The purpose of some other reflexes, such as the *grasping reflex* (closing fingers around an object that is pressed against the palm) (see Figure 4.14) or the *Moro reflex* (grasping with the arms when hearing a loud noise or suddenly experiencing a feeling of being dropped), is not as clear. Some developmentalists believe that these reflexes currently serve no purpose but were functional during earlier evolutionary stages, allowing infants to cling to their mothers in threatening situations, as do infants of most primate species (Jolly, 1999). Others believe that such presumably useless reflexes may still be functional because they promote a close relationship between mother and infant (Bowlby, 1973; Prechtl, 1973).

TABLE 4.2 REFLEXES PRESENT AT BIRTH

Reflex	Description	Developmental Course	Significance
Babinski	When the bottom of the baby's foot is stroked, the toes fan out and then curl	Disappears in 8 to 12 months	Presence at birth and normal course of decline are a basic index of normal neurological condition
Crawling	When the baby is placed on his stomach and pressure is applied to the soles of his feet, his arms and legs more rhythmically	Disappears after 3 to 4 months; possible reappearance at 6 to 7 months as a component of voluntary crawling	Uncertain
Eyeblink	Rapid closing of eyes	Permanent	Protection against aversive stimuli such as bright lights and foreign objects
Grasping	When a finger or some other object is pressed against the baby's palm, her fingers close around it	Disappears in 3 to 4 months; replaced by voluntary grasping	Presence at birth and later disappearance is a basic sign of normal neurological development
Moro	If the baby is allowed to drop unexpectedly while being held or if there is a loud noise, she will throw her arms outward while arching her back and then bring her arms together as if grasping something	Disappears in 6 to 7 months (although startle to loud noises is permanent)	Disputed; its presence at birth and later disappearance are a basic sign of normal neurological development
Rooting	The baby turns his head and opens his mouth when he is touched on the cheek	Disappears between 3 and 6 months	Component of nursing
Stepping	When the baby is held upright over a flat surface, he makes rhythmic leg movements	Disappears in first 2 months but can be reinstated in special contexts	Disputed; it may be only a kicking motion, or it may be a component of later voluntary walking
Sucking	The baby sucks when something is put into her mouth	Disappears and is replaced by voluntary sucking	Fundamental component of nursing

Within a few months after birth, several of the reflexes infants are born with disappear, never to return. Others disappear for a while and then reappear as part of a more mature behavior. Still others are transformed into more complex behaviors without first disappearing. Many researchers see these changes in the structure of early reflexes as important evidence about the way the maturation of higher brain centers changes behavior (Fox & Bell, 1990; Oppenheim, 1981).

The Moro reflex is an example of a reflex that disappears in the months after birth. It is seen again only in the event of injury to the central nervous system. Another behavior that disappears is commonly referred to as the "stepping reflex." When newborn babies are held in an upright position with their feet touching a flat surface, they make rhythmic leg movements as if they were walking (see Figure 4.15), but they stop doing so at around 3 months of age. At about 1 year of age, babies use similar motions as a component of walking, a voluntary activity that is acquired with practice.

There are competing explanations for the developmental changes in these rhythmic leg movements. According to Philip Zelazo (1983), the newborn's movements are a genuine reflex, and their disappearance is an instance of the suppression of a lower reflex by the maturation of higher cortical functions. He maintains that the old reflex reappears in a new form as a component of voluntary walking after a period of brain reorganization.

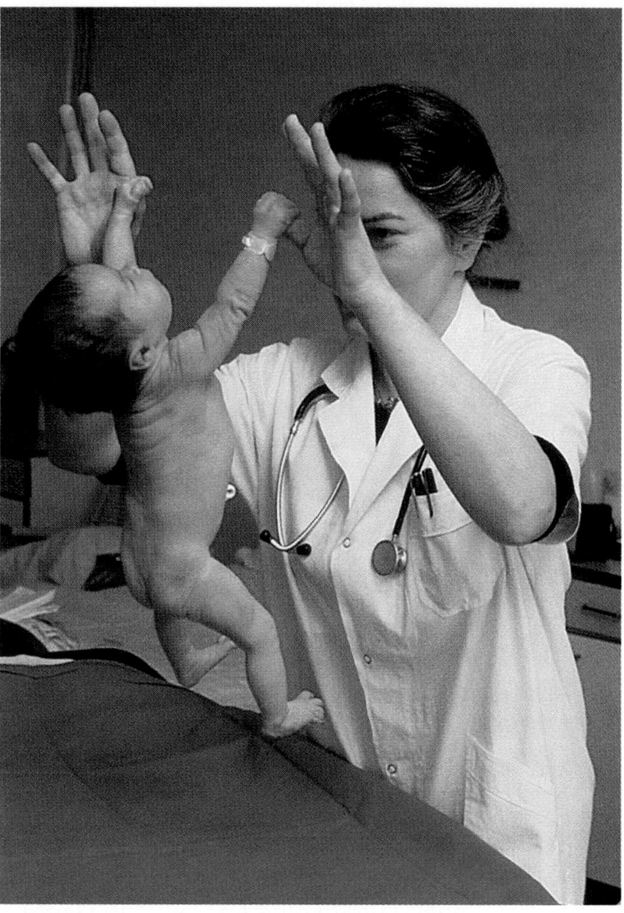

FIGURE 4.14 *The grasping reflex is an important component of normal neurological development in newborns. This baby can almost support its own weight.*

Esther Thelen and her colleagues reject this explanation: they believe that the stepping reflex is really a form of kicking (Thelen 1995; Thelen et al., 1989). According to these researchers, early upright kicking behavior disappears because of changes in the baby's muscle mass and weight that make kicking difficult, not because of changes in the cortex.

In support of their view, Thelen and her colleagues hypothesized that if infants were partially submerged in water and supported to stand, the behavior described as the stepping reflex would reappear. They reasoned that the buoyancy of the water would counterbalance the infant's increased weight and relative lack of leg strength. They were correct: when they held infants who had stopped exhibiting the stepping reflex upright in water up to their waists, the kicking behavior reappeared.

Emotions

When we talk about emotions in everyday conversation, we are usually referring to the feelings aroused by an experience. If we unexpectedly win a prize, we feel happy and excited. When we say good-bye to a loved one whom we will not see for some time, we feel sad. If someone prevents us from achieving a goal, we become angry.

Emotions as Complex Systems Developmentalists believe that the feelings aroused by such experiences are only one aspect of emotions. In addition to feelings, emotions include the following features (Saarni et al., 1998):

- *A physiological aspect.* Emotions are accompanied by identifiable physiological reactions such as changes in heart rate, breathing, and hormonal functioning.

emotion A feeling state produced by the distinctive physiological responses and cognitive evaluations that motivate action.

- *A communicative function.* Emotions communicate our internal feeling states to others through facial expressions and distinctive forms of behavior.
- *A cognitive aspect.* The emotions we feel depend upon how we appraise what is happening to us.
- *An action aspect.* How we act depends jointly on how we evaluate experiences, the physiological states that are produced, and the feelings that result. When something causes us to be suddenly joyful, for example, we laugh or cry or do both at once. Sometimes we jump up and hug the nearest person.

Technically speaking, then, **emotion** can be defined as a feeling state produced by the distinctive physiological responses and cognitive evaluations that motivate action. The intimate ties between feelings and thought are clearly revealed by our habit of equating the two in everyday speech, as when we routinely use "I think you are wrong" and "I feel you are wrong" as substitutes for each other. Emotions simultaneously communicate *to* others and regulate interactions *with* others. They are complex processes that emerge from many elements.

The Origins of Emotion Developmentalists have long been divided on the question of which emotions are present at birth. Some favor the view that emotions develop out of two primitive states, contentment and distress. Others believe that all humans are born with a core set of primary emotions.

Developmentalists who believe that a set of core, primary emotions is present at birth have relied heavily on the assumption that facial expressions are reliable indicators of one's emotional state (Ekman, 1997). Specifically, they believe that certain facial expressions universally communicate a basic set of emotional states to others and that the facial expressions of very young infants signal the presence in them of the corresponding basic emotion. On the basis of their babies' facial expressions and vocalizations, for example, the mothers interviewed in one study reported that their infants were expressing several emotions by the age of 1 month, including joy, fear, anger, surprise, sadness, and interest (Johnson et al., 1982).

FIGURE 4.15
Babies held upright with their feet touching a flat surface move their legs in a fashion that resembles walking. Experts have debated the origins and developmental history of this form of behavior, called the stepping reflex.

Mothers' reports about their babies are notorious for being biased, as we noted in Chapter 1 (p. 18). Recognizing this problem, Carroll Izard and his colleagues videotaped infants' responses to a variety of emotion-arousing events such as having an inoculation or the approach of a smiling mother (Izard, 1994; Izard et al., 1980). He showed the videotapes, or stills from them, to college students and nurses, who agreed fairly consistently about which facial expressions communicated interest, joy, surprise, and sadness (see Figure 4.16). To a somewhat lesser extent, they also agreed on which expressions showed anger, disgust, and contempt.

Additional support for the idea that there is a universal set of basic emotions and corresponding facial expressions comes from the cross-cultural research of Paul Ekman and his associates (Ekman, 1994, 1997). These researchers asked people in various literate and nonliterate cultures to pose expressions appropriate to such events as the death of a loved one or being reunited with a close friend. Both literate and nonliterate adults configured their faces in the same way to express each emotion. When shown photographs of actors posing the different expressions, the literate and nonliterate adults also agreed on the photographs that represented happiness, sadness, anger, and disgust.

Yet facial expressions, no matter how universal their meanings among adults, may not be valid indicators of the same emotional states

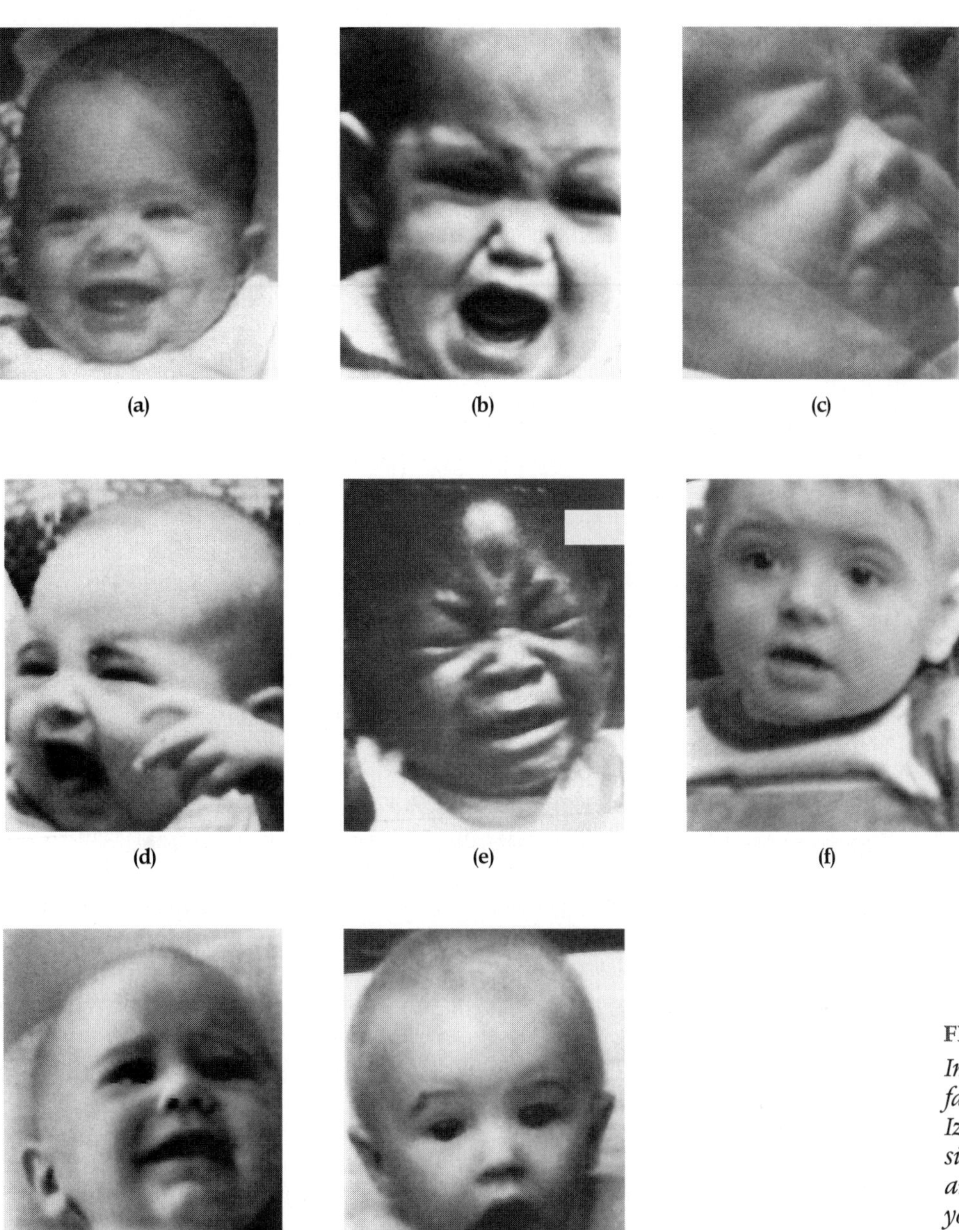

FIGURE 4.16
Images from a videotaped recording of infants' facial expressions used by Carroll Izard and his colleagues to assess the possible universal relation between emotion and facial expression. What emotion do you think each facial expression represents. The responses most of Izard's adult subjects gave are printed upside down below. (Izard et al., 1980.)

among newborns. Newborns may cry because they are hungry. In this case, their facial expressions and associated emotion are responses to their immediate physical discomfort. Adults may cry, however, because they feel guilty, ashamed, sad, or chagrined. Their tears are the result of complex evaluations of their actions and circumstances and depend upon the development of cognitive abilities that involve interaction among the higher brain centers. None of these aspects of emotion are developed at birth. Consequently, some of the key processes that link facial expressions of newborns to emotions may differ from those reflected by the same facial expressions in older infants, children, and adults.

It is this type of uncertainty that motivates the research of developmentalists who believe that, initially, newborns experience only two general kinds of emotion, one positive (contentment), the other negative (distress). According to this view, additional emotions arise by splitting off, or *differentiating*

(a) joy; (b) anger; (c) sadness; (d) disgust; (e) distress/pain; (f) interest; (g) fear; (h) surprise.

temperament The term for the individual modes of responding to the environment that appear to be consistent across situations and stable over time. Typically included under the rubric of temperament are such characteristics as children's activity level, their intensity of reaction, the ease with which they become upset, their characteristic responses to novelty, and their sociability.

themselves, from these original two states as the baby develops: joy becomes differentiated from contentment at about 3 months; anger and fear differentiate from discontent at about 4 months and 6 months, respectively (Lewis, 1993).

Whatever their views about the initial repertoire of emotions present at birth, developmentalists agree that the feeling states associated with emotions and modes of emotional expression develop throughout the course of childhood. As infants grow older, their initial repertoire of emotions (whether two, or four, or a few more) becomes entwined with their developing intellectual capacities and the new kinds of social relations into which they enter. New emotions, such as pride, shame, and guilt, emerge as infants act, think, communicate, and relate to others in new ways. Thus, in the chapters ahead, we will frequently find ourselves considering the development of emotions in connection with the development of the intellectual, social, and physical aspects of development.

Temperament

A commonly held intuition about human nature is that people are born differing from one another in their characteristic predispositions to respond to the world. Our daughter, for example, has a tendency to approach life with boundless energy and an optimistic demeanor. Confronted with barriers, she rarely gives up, but finds some way to surmount them or to go around them. Her brother, by contrast, is a dreamier person. He is more likely to intellectualize a problem and more likely to vent his frustration. **Temperament** is the name given to these individual modes of responding to the environment that appear to be consistent across situations and stable over time (Allport, 1937; Rothbart & Bates, 1998).

A wide variety of characteristics seen in babies have been interpreted as evidence of infants' temperamental qualities. They include the newborns' activity level, the ease with which they become upset, the intensity of their reactions, their characteristic reaction when something unusual happens, and their sociability (Allport, 1937; Rothbart & Bates, 1998). Such temperamental characteristics are believed to be core elements in the formation of a child's personality.

Pioneering studies of temperament and its role in development were conducted by Alexander Thomas, Stella Chess, and their colleagues. Their work has had great influence over the years, both because the techniques they used to assess temperament have come to be widely used and because they assessed the stability of temperament by following children's development into early adulthood. They began their research in the late 1950s with a group of 141 middle- and upper-class children in the United States. Later they broadened their longitudinal study to include 95 working-class Puerto Rican children and several groups of children suffering from diseases, neurological impairments, and mental retardation (Thomas & Chess, 1977, 1984; Thomas et al., 1963). The researchers asked parents to fill out questionnaires periodically, beginning shortly after the birth of their child. Included were questions about such matters as how the child reacted to the first bath, to wet diapers, and to the first taste of solid food. As the children grew older, the questionnaires were supplemented by interviews with teachers and by tests of the children.

When Chess and Thomas analyzed their data, they found they could identify nine behavioral traits: activity level, rhythmicity (the regularity or irregularity of the child's basic biological functions), approach–withdrawal (the baby's response to novelty), adaptability, threshold of responsiveness, intensity of reaction, quality of mood (negative or positive), distractibility, and attention span or persistence. Taken together, these traits provided an overall description of a child's temperament (see Table 4.3). After scoring the children on

TABLE 4.3 Basic Indicators of Temperament According to Chess and Thomas

Trait	Definition	Example
Activity level	The level of movement typical of a given child's actions and the relative amount of time spent in action and inaction	Even in the uterus some babies kick and move around a lot, while others are relatively still; similar differences are seen in the level and frequency of arm waving and kicking in early infancy and in the tendency of some young children to spend most of their waking hours in rapid motion
Rhythmicity	The degree of regularity and predictability of basic biological functions	Beginning shortly after birth, marked individual differences can be seen in the ease with which babies adapt to regular feeding and sleeping schedules and to bodily functions such as defecation
Approach–withdrawal	The nature of the baby's initial response to something new	Novel experiences such as the first substitution of a bottle for the breast, meeting a strange person, or the sudden appearance of a jack-in-the-box cause some children to be fearful and withdraw, while others actively explore and seek further stimulation
Adaptability	The ease with which a baby's initial responses to a situation are modified	Whether they initially withdraw from or take to a new experience, babies differ in how rapidly the novelty wears off and how esily they adjust to new circumstances, such as being given solid food in place of milk or being left with a baby-sitter
Threshold of responsiveness	The intensity level required in order for a stimulus to evoke a response	It takes very little noise to make some babies awaken from a nap or very little moisture in their diapers to make them cry, whereas others appear to react only when the stimulation becomes relatively intense
Intensity of reaction	The energy level of a response	It seems that whatever the circumstances, whether pleasant or unpleasant, some babies remain relatively placid in their responses, cooing when pleased and frowning when upset, whereas others laugh heartily and cry vigorously
Quality of mood	The amount of joyful, pleasant, and friendly behaviors in comparison to unpleasant and unfriendly behaviors	Some babies laugh frequently and tend to smile at the world, whereas others seem to be unhappy an unusual amount of the time
Distractibility	The extent to which novel stimuli disrupt or alter ongoing behaviors	Parents often seek to distract a crying baby by offering a pacifier or teddy bear, but such tactics work best with distractible babies
Attention span/persistence	The extent to which an activity, once undertaken, is maintained	Some babies will stare at a mobile or play happily with a favorite toy for a long time, whereas others quickly lose interest and move frequently from one activity to another

Source: Chess & Thomas, 1982.

each of these nine traits, they found that most of the children could be classified in one of three broad temperament categories from the time they were infants:

- *Easy babies* are playful, are regular in their biological functions, and adapt readily to new circumstances.
- *Difficult babies* are irregular in their biological functions, are irritable, and often respond intensely and negatively to new situations or try to withdraw from them.

- *Slow-to-warm-up babies* are low in activity level, and their responses are typically mild. They tend to withdraw from new situations, but in a mild way, and require more time than easy babies to adapt to change.

Although these three categories of temperament are widely used by developmentalists, a number of efforts have been made to refine Chess and Thomas's approach. For example, analyzing data from a large study of New Zealand children whose health and development were studied systematically over many years, Denise Newman and her colleagues distinguished five different clusters of temperamental characteristics: well adjusted, undercontrolled, reserved, confident, and inhibited (Newman et al., 1997). In another approach, Mary Rothbart and her colleagues in the United States created a "child behavior questionnaire" that provided scores on 195 questions divided into 15 different scales. Parents were asked to decide how well each item applied to their child in the past half year. Statistical analysis of the results suggested three dimensions of temperamental variation, providing a unique "profile" of children's temperamental proclivities:

- *Reactivity*—the characteristic level of arousal, or activeness
- *Affect*—the dominant emotional tone, gloomy or cheerful
- *Self-regulation*—control over what one attends to and reacts to

The fact that different researchers come up with different basic dimensions of temperament suggests that the items used in the different questionnaires are not strictly comparable. However, statistical analysis shows that there is a large degree of overlap among the different scales currently in use. Consequently, the specific choice of scale is not essential to the general conclusions that are drawn from a particular study, allowing results from studies using slightly different scales to be combined (Goldsmith et al., 1991; Rothbart & Bates, 1998).

Temperament scales have been used to assess ethnic and national differences in the basic dimensions of temperament. Comparing large groups of children from the People's Republic of China and the United States, Mary Rothbart and her colleagues found that their three basic dimensions emerged from the data within *both* countries, suggesting that dimensions of temperament are found in all cultures (Ahadi et al., 1993). When they made between-country comparisons, they also found differences. For example, they found that the Chinese children were less active than the American children, a fact they attributed to Chinese child-rearing practices. Chinese parents place a high value on interdependence, and this leads them to discourage high levels of activity and impulsiveness.

Although the last finding suggests that there can be an environmental, cultural component to temperament, there is widespread agreement that genetic factors provide the foundation for temperamental differences as measured by a variety of scales (Plomin et al., 1997; Rothbart et al., 1994). The strongest evidence for the heritability of temperamental traits comes from twin studies. For example, Arnold Buss and Robert Plomin (1984) found that identical twins (who have identical genes) received strikingly similar parental ratings for emotionality, activity level, and sociability but that fraternal twins (who inherit different mixes of genes from their parents) did not. H. H. Goldsmith and Irving Gottesman (1981) obtained similar findings in respect to individual differences in activity level.

The possibility that temperamental traits are stable "biases" in the way individuals respond to their environment implies that if the right measurements are taken in early infancy, it should be possible to predict the characteristic style with which individuals will behave at later stages of development. Evidence for the stability of temperamental characteristics comes from an Australian study by Robert Pedlow and his colleagues. They based their conclusion on data from temperament questionnaires filled out by parents beginning when their children were between 4 and 8 months old and continuing yearly until the children were 8 years old (Pedlow et al., 1993). The questionnaires tapped such traits as irritability, persistence, and flexibility. The researchers reported significant temperamental stability over the 8 years they studied the children. Similar results have been reported by Robert Plomin and his colleagues (Plomin et al., 1993; Saradeno et al., 1999).

It needs to be emphasized that even when statistical evidence indicates that temperamental traits remain somewhat the same from one time to the next, most studies find that the degree of stability is modest. The limited stability of temperamental traits over time arises both because of differences in the rate of development of the biological systems that are responsible for temperament and because of changes in the environments that children inhabit as they develop (Rothbart & Bates, 1998; Slabach et al., 1991).

BECOMING COORDINATED WITH THE SOCIAL WORLD

The basic behavioral capacities with which babies are born are sufficient for their survival only if they are coordinated with the activities of their caregivers. But caregivers cannot always be hovering over their baby, anticipating every need before it is expressed. They must find a way to meet their infant's needs within the confines of their own rhythms of life and work. Whether parents work the land and must be up with the sun or work in an office where they are expected to appear at 9 A.M. sharp, they need to sleep at night. This need is often in direct conflict with their infant's sleep and hunger patterns, a conflict that for many caregivers means getting up several times a night. Such circumstances cause parents to attempt to modify their babies' patterns of eating and sleeping so that they will fit into the life patterns of the household and the community.

In the United States such attempts to modify an infant's initial pattern of sleeping and eating behavior are often referred to as "getting the baby on a schedule." Getting the baby on a schedule is more than a convenience. Through the coordination of activities that results, babies and parents create a system of mutual expectations that serves as the foundation for later developmental change.

Parents' efforts to achieve a common schedule with their baby focus on the infant's sleeping and eating. Crying is the baby's earliest means of signaling when these efforts fall short.

This newborn is smiling during REM sleep.

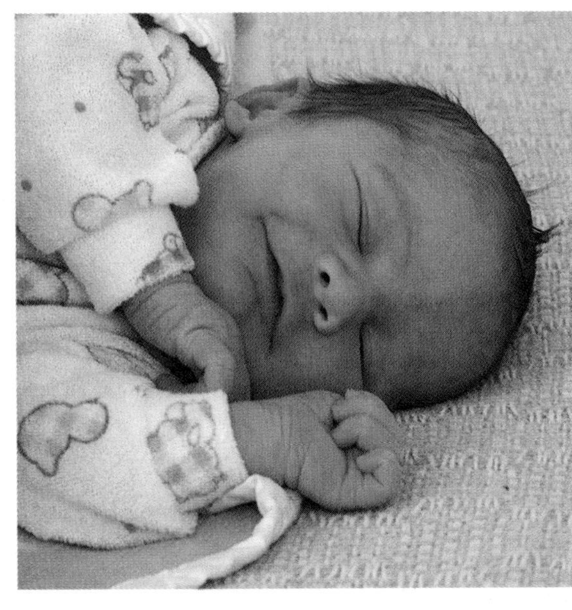

SLEEPING

As with adults, the extent of newborns' arousal varies from complete rest to frantic activity. The patterns of their rest and activity are quite different from those of adults, however, particularly in the first weeks after birth. To find out about newborns' arousal patterns, Peter Wolff (1966) studied babies during their first weeks after birth. On the basis of such observable behaviors as muscle activity and eye movement, Wolff was able to distinguish seven states of arousal. (They are described in Table 4.4.) Additional research has shown that a distinctive pattern of brain activity is associated with each state of arousal (Berg & Berg, 1987; Emde et al., 1976). In this kind of research, a device called an *electroencephalograph (EEG)* is used to record the tiny electrical currents generated by the brain's cells; the currents are detected by electrodes placed on the scalp.

EEG recordings of infants' brain waves shortly after birth distinguish two kinds of sleep that are the precursors of adult sleeping pat-

TABLE 4.4 STATES OF AROUSAL IN INFANTS

State	Characteristics
Non-rapid-eye-movement (NREM) sleep	Full rest; low muscle tone and motor activity; eyelids closed and eyes still; regular breathing (about 36 times per minute)
Rapid-eye-movement (REM) sleep	Increased muscle tone and motor activity; facial grimaces and smiles; occasional eye movements; irregular breathing (about 48 times per minute)
Periodic sleep	Intermediate between REM and NREM sleep—bursts of deep, slow breathing alternating with bouts of rapid, shallow breathing
Drowsiness	More active than NREM sleep but less active than REM or periodic sleep; eyes open and close; eyes glazed when open; breathing variable but more rapid than in NREM sleep
Alert inactivity	Slight activity; face relaxed; eyes open and bright; breathing regular and more rapid than in NREM sleep
Active alert	Frequent diffuse motor activity; vocalizations; skin flushed; irregular breathing
Distress	Vigorous diffuse motor activity; facial grimaces; red skin; crying

Source: Wolff, 1966.

terns: (1) an active pattern, called *rapid-eye-movement (REM) sleep,* which is characterized by uneven breathing, rapid but low-level brain-wave activity, and a good deal of eye and limb movement; and (2) a quiet pattern, called *non-rapid-eye-movement (NREM) sleep,* in which breathing is regular, brain waves are larger and slower, and the baby barely moves (see Figure 4.17). During the first 2 to 3 months of life, infants begin their sleep with active (REM) sleep and only gradually fall into quiet (NREM) sleep (Emde et al., 1976). After the first 2 or 3 months, the sequence reverses, and NREM sleep precedes REM sleep. Although this reversal is of little significance to parents, who are most concerned with the child's overall pattern of sleeping and waking, it is an important sign of developmental change because it shows a shift toward the adult pattern.

Neonates spend most of their time asleep, though the amount of sleep they need gradually decreases. This trend is clearly evident in a study in which mothers were asked to keep a record of their babies' sleep time for sev-

FIGURE 4.17

The contrast between quiet and active sleep patterns in newborns is seen in the patterns of respiration, eye movements, and brain activity (EEG). Active sleep is characterized by irregular breathing, frequent eye movements, and continuous low-voltage brain activity. (Adapted from Parmelee et al., 1968.)

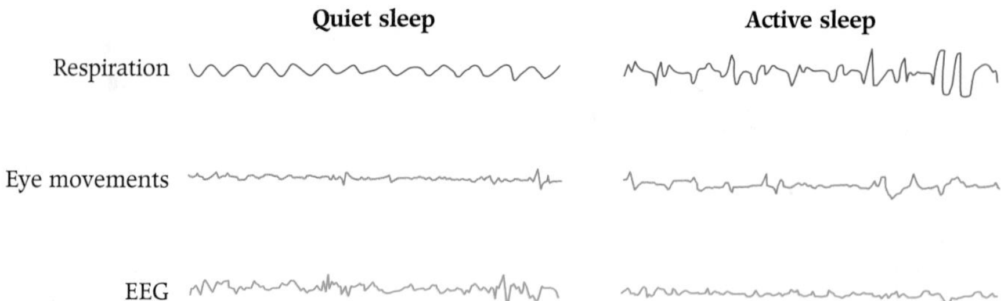

eral weeks after birth (Emde et al., 1976; Thoman & Whitney, 1989). The results showed that babies sleep about 16½ hours a day during the first week of life. By the end of 4 weeks, they sleep a little more than 15 hours a day; and by the end of 4 months, they sleep a little less than 14 hours a day.

If babies sleep most of the time, why do parents lose so much sleep? The reason is that newborns tend to sleep in snatches that last anywhere from a few minutes to a few hours. Thus they may be awake at any time of the day or night. As babies grow older, their sleeping and waking periods lengthen and coincide more and more with the night/day schedule common among adults (see Figure 4.18).

A marked shift toward the adult night/day cycle occurs in the first weeks after birth among many American babies: by the end of the second week, their combined periods of sleep average 8½ hours between 7 P.M. and 7 A.M. (Kleitman, 1963). But their sleep pattern still results in some loss of sleep for their parents because the longest sleep period may be only 3 or 4 hours.

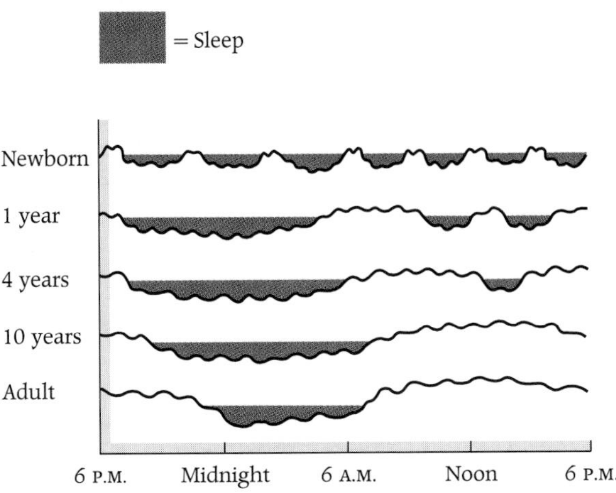

FIGURE 4.18
The pattern of sleep/wake cycles among babies in the United States changes rapidly during infancy. A long period of sleep comes to replace many brief periods of alternating sleep and wakefulness. (From Kleitman, 1963.)

Although babies' adoption of the night/day sleep cycle seems natural to people who live in industrialized countries and urban settings, studies of infants raised in other cultures suggest that it is at least partly a function of cultural influences on the infant. The role of social pressure in rearranging the newborn's sleep is clear when we contrast the development of the sleep/wake behavior of U.S. infants with that of Kipsigis babies in rural Kenya. In the United States, parents typically put their infants to bed at certain hours—often in a separate room—and they try not to pick them up when they wake up crying at night, lest they "get the idea" that someone will come running whenever they make a fuss. In rural Kenya, infants are almost always with their mothers. During the day they sleep when they can, often while being carried on their mothers' backs as the mothers go about their daily round of farming, household chores, and social activities. During the night they sleep with their mothers and are permitted to nurse whenever they wake up (see Box 4.1). Among Kipsigis infants, the longest period of sleep reported at 1 month is only about 3 hours; many shorter periods of sleep are sprinkled throughout the day and night. Eventually Kipsigis infants begin to sleep through the night, but not until many months after American infants have done so. Even as adults, the Kipsigis are more flexible than Americans in their sleeping hours (Super & Harkness, 1972).

In the United States, the length of the longest sleep period is often used as an index of the infant's maturation. Charles Super and Sara Harkness (1972) suggest that parents' efforts to get babies to sleep for long periods of time during the early weeks of life may be pushing the boundaries of what young infants can adapt to. They believe that the many changes that occur in a newborn's state of arousal in every 24-hour period reflect the immaturity of the infant's brain, which sets a limit on how quickly the child can conform to an adult routine. This may be the explanation for the failure of some infants in industrialized countries to adopt a night/day pattern of sleeping and waking as quickly and easily as their parents would like them to.

FEEDING

Besides attempting to regulate their babies' sleeping patterns, parents encourage their infants to adjust to a regular pattern of feeding. Pediatricians' recommendations as to when babies should be fed have changed significantly over the years. Today, pediatricians often tell parents to feed their newborn babies as often as every 2 to 3 hours. But from the early 1920s through the 1940s, mothers were advised to feed their babies only every 4 hours, even if the babies showed signs of hunger long before the prescribed time had elapsed. As one pediatrician expressed the wisdom of the time:

> Feed him at exactly the same hours every day.
> Do not feed him just because he cries.
> Let him wait until the right time.
> If you make him wait, his stomach will learn to wait.
> (Weill, 1930)

For a very small infant, 4 hours can be a long time to go without food, as was demonstrated by a study of mothers and infants in Cambridge, England. The mothers were asked to keep records of their babies' behaviors and their own caregiving activities, including when they fed their babies and the time their babies spent crying. All the mothers were advised to feed their babies on

BOX 4.1

Sleeping Arrangements

One of the benefits of comparisons across cultures is that they make us aware of practices that are so common in our own culture that we assume they are the only way things can possibly be done. The ability of cross-cultural research to teach us about ourselves is nicely illustrated by studies to determine where and with whom young infants sleep.

In a study of 120 societies around the world, 64 percent of the mothers surveyed reported that their infants sleep in the same bed with them (a practice referred to as *co-sleeping*). Societies where co-sleeping is widely practiced include highly technological countries, such as Japan and Italy, as well as rural communities in many countries. The United States was the only country surveyed where it is common to have young babies sleep in their own beds in their own rooms and where they are expected to sleep through the night at an early age (Wolf et al., 1996). The practice of having infants sleep separately is particularly common among college-educated, middle-class American families and is less widely practiced by other social groups in the United States and in certain regions of the country. Among a group of newborns in eastern Kentucky, for example, 36 percent shared their parents' beds and 48 percent shared their parents' rooms. Space did not seem to be the issue (Abbott, 1992). African American babies are more likely than Caucasian children to have a caregiver present when they fall asleep, to sleep in their parents' rooms, and to spend at least part of the night in their parents' beds (Wolf et al., 1996).

Sleeping practices are related to broad cultural themes regarding the organization of interpersonal relations and the moral ideals of the community (Bell et al., 1999). Whereas American mothers emphasize the values of independence and self-reliance, mothers in societies where co-sleeping is the norm emphasize the need for babies to learn to be interdependent and to be able to get along with and be sensitive to the needs of others (Caudill & Plath, 1966; Shweder et al., 1998). These underlying values are reflected in a study by Gilda Morelli and her colleagues, who interviewed rural Mayan peasants in Guatemala and middle-class American mothers about their infants' sleeping arrangements (Morelli et al., 1992). None of the American parents in the study allowed their infants to sleep with them. Many parents kept the sleeping child in a nearby crib for the first few months but soon moved the baby to a separate room. They gave such reasons for their arrangements as "I think he would be more dependent . . . if he was constantly with us like that," and "I think it would have made any separation harder if he wasn't even separated from us at night."

In contrast, the Mayan mothers always had each new child sleep in the same bed with them until the next baby was born. They insisted that this was the only right thing to do. When they were told about the typical U.S. practice, they expressed shock and disapproval at the parents' behavior and pity for the children. They seemed to think the American mothers were neglecting their children. Similar sentiments have been voiced by mothers from other societies where co-sleeping is a common practice.

An emphasis on independence versus interdependence is not the only cultural value reflected in sleeping arrangements. For example, Richard Shweder and his colleagues found that in Orrisa, India, such moral values as female chastity, respect for hierarchy, and protection of the vulnerable exerted strong influences on specific choices of who slept with whom (Shweder et al., 1995). The people of Orrisa are more likely than Americans to arrange for the father and mother to sleep apart, and to avoid having children of very different ages sleeping in the same room.

The object of such comparisons is not to show that one arrangement is better or worse for infants. Whether the infant sleeps in a bed alone or with its mother does not seem to make a great deal of difference at the time. All cultural systems are relatively successful in seeing that infants get enough sleep.

The major point in describing cultural differences in family sleeping arrangements is to highlight the fact that they are all organized with a view to the ways in which children will be expected to act at a later time. This is another case, like the parents' discussion about their baby's future as the child emerges from the womb (Chapter 3, p. 118), where cultural beliefs organize the current environment to accord with people's expectations for the future.

a strict 4-hour schedule, but not all followed the advice. The less experienced mothers tended to stick to the schedule, but the more experienced mothers sometimes fed their babies as soon as 1 hour after a scheduled feeding. Not surprisingly, the reports of the less experienced mothers showed that their babies cried the most (Bernal, 1972).

What happens if babies are fed "on demand"? In one study, the majority of newborn babies allowed to feed on demand preferred a 3-hour schedule (Aldrich & Hewitt, 1947). The interval gradually increased as the babies grew older. At 2½ months, most of the infants were feeding on a 4-hour schedule. By 7 or 8 months, the majority had come to approximate the normal adult schedule and were choosing to feed about four times a day. (Some parents reported the four feedings as "three meals and a snack.") It should be noted, however, that the figures given here are averages; at every age studied, about 40 percent of the babies did not fit the norm.

CRYING

One of the most difficult problems parents face in establishing a pattern of care for their babies is how to interpret their infants' needs. Infants obviously cannot articulate their needs or how they are feeling, but they do have one important way of signaling that something is wrong—they can cry.

Crying increases from birth to approximately 6 weeks of age and then begins to decrease. This pattern of change occurs in infants around the world, including preterm infants (once adjustment is made for gestational age). Such regularity leads to the conclusion that the pattern reflects universal processes of maturation (St. James-Roberts et al., 1995).

Crying is a complex behavior that involves the coordination of breathing and movements of the vocal tract. Initially it is coordinated by structures in the brain stem, but within a few months the cerebral cortex becomes involved, enabling babies to cry voluntarily. This change in the neural organization of crying is accompanied by physical changes in the vocal tract that lower the pitch of infants' cries. At this point, parents in the United States begin to report that their infants are "crying on purpose," either to get attention or because they are bored (Lester et al., 1992).

Babies' cries have a powerful effect on those who hear them. Experienced parents and childless adults alike respond to infants' cries with increases in heart rate and blood pressure, both of which are physiological signs of anxiety (Bleichfeld & Moely, 1984). New parents react even more strongly to infants' cries than childless adults or experienced parents do (Boukydis & Burges, 1982). When nursing mothers hear babies' cries, even on recordings, their milk may start to flow (Newton & Newton, 1972).

This infant's cries are likely to be taken as a peremptory command for someone to do something quickly.

Presumably newborns cry because something is causing them discomfort. The problem for the anxious parent is to figure out what that something might be. Both parents and those who are not regularly in contact with newborn babies can distinguish among infants' cries (Zeskind et al., 1992). According to Phillip Zeskind and his colleagues, the higher-pitched the cries and the shorter the pauses between them, the more urgent and unpleasant adults perceive them to be. In addition, listeners in a variety of cultures can distinguish the higher-pitched cries of normal infants from the cries of low-birth-weight babies and babies who have been exposed prenatally to alcohol or the chemicals from cigarette smoke (Worchel & Allen, 1997; Zeskind et al., 1996).

In spite of their ability to distinguish between types of crying, even experienced parents often cannot tell precisely why their baby is distressed from the cry sounds alone. One reason is that prolonged crying of all kinds eventually slips into the rhythmic pattern of the hunger cry. In many instances, then, only the intensity of the distress is evident. Hunger is, of course, a common

BOX 4.2

Comforting the Fussy Baby

All infants occasionally cry or seem to be mildly distressed for no readily identifiable reason, especially during the first 2½ months of life. Generally referred to as fussiness, or colic, this distress often peaks in the evenings for reasons not yet understood (St. James-Roberts et al., 1996). Infants also cry for perfectly understandable reasons—when they are given an immunization shot, for example (Lewis & Ramsay, 1999). But no matter why the baby is crying, the person who is taking care of the baby is likely to intervene to reduce the baby's distress.

Sometimes fussy babies can be soothed by nursing. If they have just been fed and still cry, their caretakers often assume that their diapers are wet or that they are cold. And, indeed, changing babies' diapers and wrapping them up warmly does tend to quiet them. However, research has shown that what calms infants is being picked up, not getting dry diapers.

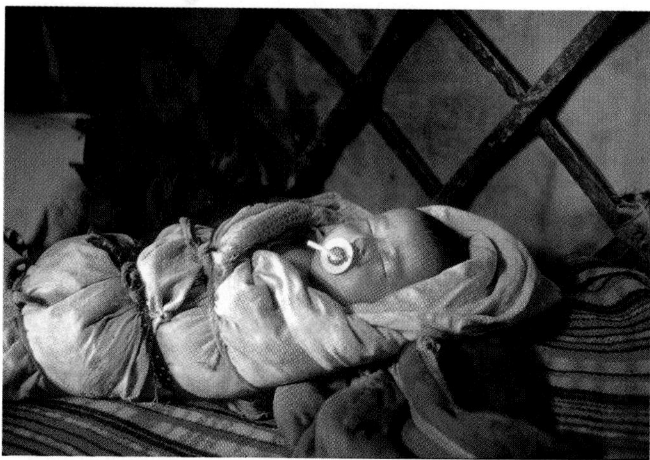

This Mongolian baby is being comforted in two popular ways—by being swaddled in traditional blankets and by sucking on a pacifier.

If babies are picked up and their wet diapers are put back on them, they stop crying as frequently as they do if they are given dry diapers (Wolff, 1969).

Annaliese Korner and her associates found that holding babies to the shoulder is an effective way to make them stop crying (Korner & Thoman, 1970). An added benefit when babies are held to the shoulder is that they are more likely to become attentive to their surroundings.

Other methods mothers use to calm crying infants include rocking, patting, cuddling, and swaddling them. *Swaddling,* or wrapping babies tightly in a blanket so that they cannot move their arms and legs, often appears effective (Fearon et al., 1997). The blanket provides infants with constant touch stimulation and, by restricting their movements, reduces the amount of stimulation they receive from those movements.

The usefulness of giving the baby a bottle depends upon what is in it. Elliott Blass and his colleagues report that giving a bottle with sweetened water or baby formula quiets newborns while one with plain water does not (Blass, 1997; Blass & Smith, 1992). Even giving the baby a bottle with liquid that is sour can reduce crying. A common mechanism that appears to underlie successful techniques used by caregivers to reduce the infant's overt signs of distress is that they all disrupt the rhythm of the infant's crying.

There is some uncertainty about the degree to which disruption of crying and fussing relieves the underlying distress itself, however (Lewis & Ramsay, 1999). Even when babies stopped crying to suck on a bottle with formula in it, their blood continued to show a high level of cortisol (a stress-related steroid) for an extended period of time.

Between 2 and 4 months of age, there is a sharp decline in the length of time it takes infants to recover from bouts of distress, such as that caused by an injection (Barr, 1990). This shift is thought to indicate the beginning of infants' ability to regulate their own emotions.

reason for a newborn baby to cry. Studies of crying before and after feedings have confirmed that babies cry less after they are fed (Wolff, 1969).

It is widely believed that some children suffer from a medical condition called *colic,* which causes them to cry excessively. However, while there are marked individual differences in the amounts that infants cry, the cries of babies thought to suffer from colic are not distinguishable from others who cry frequently. Such results have led Ian St. James-Roberts and his colleagues to conclude that the auditory features of crying may be less important in parental reactions than "its unpredictable, prolonged, hard to soothe, and unexplained nature" (St. James-Roberts et al., 1996, p. 375).

These uncertainties make it difficult for parents to know what to do when their baby cries, especially when the cry does not signal acute pain. One natural response is to seek to comfort the infant (see Box 4.2). When parents are under stress or the crying is persistent, however, the uncertainty about how to comfort the child and the negative emotions that crying evokes in adults are sometimes too much to bear, and some parents respond by physically abusing their infants (Frodi, 1985).

Caregivers' efforts to get babies on a schedule and to comfort them when they are distressed continue as the months go by. These parenting activities are so commonplace that it is easy to overlook their significance, but they are crucially important for establishing the background for the more obviously dramatic changes of the first months of life.

MECHANISMS OF DEVELOPMENTAL CHANGE

Almost immediately after birth, the behavioral repertoire of neonates begins to expand, enabling them to interact ever more effectively with the world around them. The changes in behavior that occur during the first months of life are partly a matter of perfecting capacities that already exist. As infants become able to suck more effectively, for example, they obtain more food, so they can go longer between feedings without distress. The perfecting of existing behaviors does not, however, explain how new behaviors arise. By the age of 2½ months, infants raise their heads to look around, smile in response to the smiles of others, and shake rattles put into their hands. A major goal of the developmental sciences is to explain how these new forms of behavior arise. We will address this issue by first focusing on a crucial new behavior that emerges in early infancy—nursing. Then we will consider the various explanations that the four major theoretical perspectives offer for the development of this new behavior.

FROM SUCKING TO NURSING

One new behavior that appears in early infancy is nursing. When we compare the way newborn infants feed with the nursing behavior of 6-week-old infants, a striking contrast is evident. As noted earlier, newborns possess several reflexes that are relevant to feeding: rooting (turning the head in the direction of a touch on the cheek), sucking, swallowing, and breathing. These component behaviors are not well integrated, however, so babies' early feeding experiences are likely to be discoordinated affairs. When newborns are first held to the breast, a touch to the cheek will make them turn their heads and open their mouths, but they root around in a disorganized way. When they do find the nipple, they may lose it again almost immediately, or the act of sucking may cause the upper lip to fold back and block the nostrils, eliciting a sharp head-withdrawal reflex (see Figure 4.19). Furthermore, breathing and sucking are not well coordinated at first, so newborns are likely to have to stop sucking to come up for air.

By the time infants are 6 weeks old, a qualitative change is evident in their feeding behavior, a change that is more than just a perfection of the sucking reflex. For one thing, infants anticipate being fed when they are picked up and can prepare themselves to feed. More significant, they have worked out the coordination of all the component behaviors of feeding—sucking, swallowing, and breathing—so they can perform them in a smooth, integrated sequence (Bruner, 1968). In short, feeding has become nursing. In fact, babies become so efficient at nursing that they can accomplish in less than 10 minutes what originally took them as long as an hour.

Nursing is clearly not a reflex. It is a new form of behavior that develops through the reorganization of the various reflexes with which infants are born. Although the acquisition of nursing is commonplace, it raises in clear form the question of how developmental change comes about. Each of the four broad theoretical frameworks—the biological-maturation perspective, the environmental-learning perspective, the constructivist perspective,

FIGURE 4.19
In this sequence the infant's nostrils are blocked while he is attempting to nurse. The consequent blockage of his breathing elicits a head-withdrawal reflex that interferes with nursing.

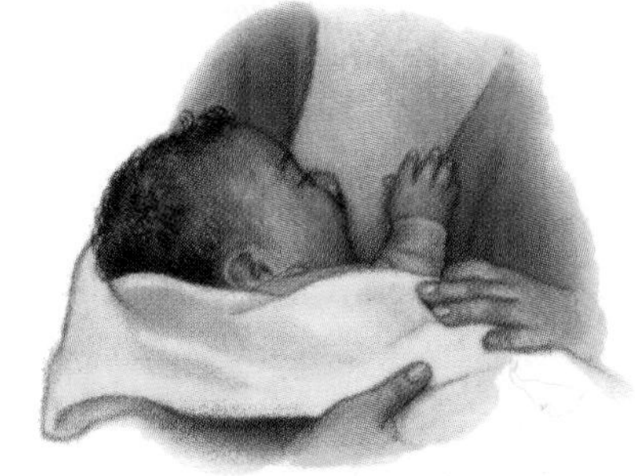

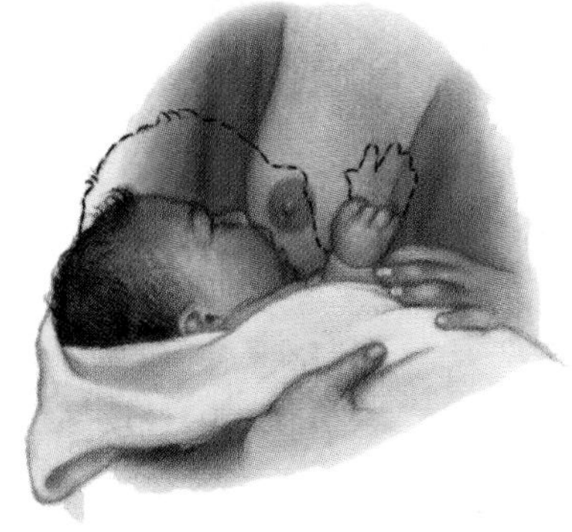

and the cultural-context perspective—emphasizes different factors in its efforts to explain development (see Chapter 1, pp. 33–37). By examining the seemingly simple behavior of nursing from each perspective and understanding the way theorists working within each of them explain the development of this behavior, we can gain a sense of how each perspective contributes to our understanding of the development of other behaviors during infancy and beyond.

THE BIOLOGICAL-MATURATION PERSPECTIVE

To explain the development of nursing and other new behaviors after birth, biologically oriented developmental theorists invoke precisely the same mechanism that they use to explain all aspects of prenatal development—maturation. New behaviors, they say, arise from old behaviors as a result of distinct maturational changes in the physical structures and physiological processes of the organism. In their view, the role of the organism's genetic inheritance is considered to be of paramount importance, and the role of the environment in development is considered to be minimal, just as during the prenatal period.

Reflexes and the Brain

According to the biological-maturation perspective, the baby becomes able to interact with the environment in more complicated and refined ways because of brain maturation. In this view, the infant's increasing success at nursing, like the gradual lengthening of the intervals between feedings and between periods of sleep, appears to depend at least in part on the maturation of underlying brain structures.

One compelling piece of evidence for this view comes from studies of a rare abnormality in which infants are born with an intact brain stem but little or no cerebral cortex. Such babies may have normal reflexes at birth—sucking, yawning, stretching, and crying (see Figure 4.20). They also exhibit habituation (see Figure 4.21). Such responses suggest that newborns' initial reflexes are controlled by the brain stem and do not require input from the cerebral cortex (Gamper 1926/1959; Graham et al., 1978; Kolb & Whishaw, 1996).

Babies born without a cerebral cortex seldom live long, however. Those that do live more than a few days fail to develop the complex, well-coordinated behaviors, including nursing, seen in normal babies. In contrast, if a baby's brain and central nervous system are developing normally, both the number and the efficiency of connections between the brain stem and the cerebral cortex begin to increase dramatically following birth.

FIGURE 4.20
Even babies like this one, born with little or no cerebral cortex, display basic reflexes such as sucking.

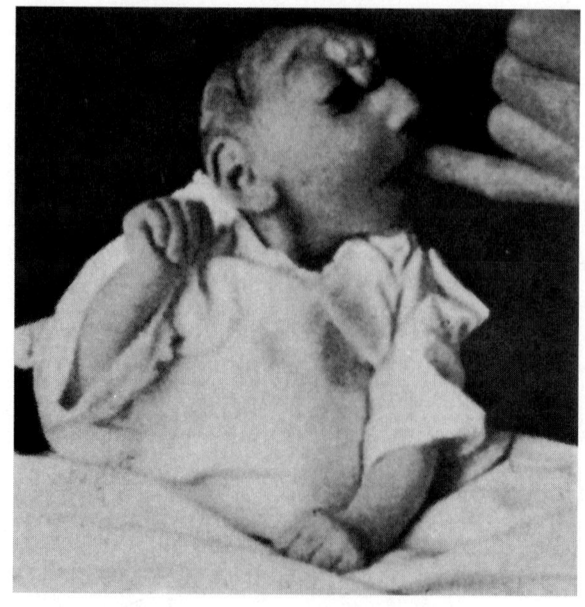

Additional evidence that maturation of the cerebral cortex plays a role in the development of nursing is suggested by the developmental pattern of other reflexes that become transformed in the first months of life. One such reflex is *prereaching*, or *visually initiated reaching*. With this reflex, newborns reach toward an object that catches their attention and simultaneously make grasping movements (Von Hofsten, 1984, 1997). However, they often fail to grasp an object even after repeated attempts, because their reaching and grasping reflexes are not coordinated with each other (Von Hofsten & Siddiqui, 1993).

At about 3 months of age, and coincidental with maturational changes in the visual and motor areas of the cerebral cortex, the visually initiated reaching reflex is transformed into a voluntary behavior. Now, once infants locate an object by either seeing or hearing it, they can use feedback from their own movements to adjust the trajectory of their reach and get their hands close to the object (Clifton et al., 1993). A short time thereafter, infants begin to open their hands as soon as they start to reach for an object and begin to close their

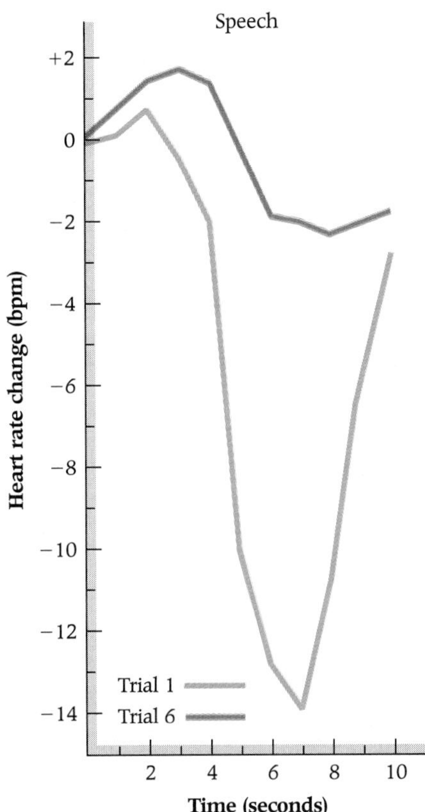

FIGURE 4.21
Evidence of habituation in a 1-month-old baby born with no cerebral cortex. On the first exposure to the sound of human speech, there is a marked decrease in heart rate, indicating attention. After five additional presentations of the sound, the infant's heart rate no longer changes dramatically, indicating habituation. (Adapted from Graham et al., 1978.)

hands a brief interval before they touch it, clear evidence that they have begun to coordinate reaching and grasping (Von Hofsten & Rönnqvist, 1988).

Although no one has yet identified the cortical areas responsible for such new behaviors as nursing and visually guided reaching, it seems safe to say that the maturation of the baby's cortical structures (along with development of the baby's muscles) must be an important factor in the development of these behaviors. At the same time, it is not clear that all the brain connections associated with coordinated reaching and nursing develop before the baby begins to reach and nurse, or that they develop independent of environmental influence, as some biological maturationists seem to imply. Rather, some of these brain developments appear to grow out of infants' interactions with their environment (see Box 4.3).

THE ENVIRONMENTAL-LEARNING PERSPECTIVE

Whatever biology may contribute to an infant's development of nursing behavior, some form of adaptation to the environment is also clearly necessary. Otherwise, a mother would have to continue to present her breast in precisely the position required to elicit the sucking reflex throughout her child's infancy. In fact, babies quickly become accustomed to nursing in any number of positions, adjusting to each for maximum comfort and efficiency.

How do a baby's innate reflexes become coordinated with one another and with appropriate stimuli in the environment to transform reflex sucking into nursing? Environmental-learning theorists argue that such coordinations require **learning,** a relatively permanent change in behavior brought about by the experience of events in the environment. Several types of learning are believed to operate throughout development, including habituation (described on p. 133), classical conditioning, operant conditioning, and perhaps imitation (see Box 4.4).

learning A relatively permanent change in behavior brought about by experience of events in the environment.

BOX 4.3

Experience and Development of the Brain

The principle that development emerges from the interaction of the organism and the environment applies no less to the development of the brain than to the development of behavior (Gottlieb, 1998). Early demonstrations of how experience influences the brain were provided by studies in which Austin Riesen (1950) raised normal chimpanzees in darkness for the first 16 months of their lives. When the chimpanzees were then placed in a normally lighted environment, they were unable to learn simple pattern and color discriminations and their visual acuity was severely impaired. Eye examinations revealed that their retinas had failed to develop normally. Subsequently, anatomical and biochemical analyses have shown that animals deprived of visual experience suffer disturbances of protein synthesis in the visual cortex; as a result, the neurons of the visual cortex have fewer and shorter branches and up to 70 percent fewer synapses than normal (Blakemore & Mitchell, 1973). Significantly, the degree and duration of these effects depend on the age at which the animal is deprived of light. If the deprivation ends early enough, recovery is possible. This finding is consistent with the idea of critical periods.

Additional animal research has shown other ways in which visual experience shapes the neural connections between the eyes and the visual cortex. Certain cells in a cat's brain, for example, normally respond best to horizontal lines, whereas other cells respond best to vertical lines. Both kinds of cells are present in large numbers in kittens that have not yet opened their eyes (Hubel & Wiesel, 1979). When kittens are raised in an environment that allows them to see only horizontal lines for several months, the nerve cells that respond to vertical lines are less developed than those of normal kittens, so their ability to detect vertical lines does not develop normally (Hirsch & Spinelli, 1971).

The visual cortex is not the only part of the brain to be affected by experience. In pioneering studies by Mark Rosenzweig and his colleagues (Rosenzweig, 1984), groups of young male laboratory rats from the same litter were raised in three different environments. The first group was housed individually in standard laboratory cages. Members of the second group were housed together in standard laboratory cages. The third group was provided with enriched conditions. Its members were housed in a large cage that was furnished with a variety of objects they could play with. A new set of playthings, drawn from a pool of 25 objects, was placed in the cage every day. Often the animals in this group were given formal training in running a maze or were exposed to a toy-filled open field.

At the end of the experimental period, which lasted anywhere from a few weeks to several months, behavioral tests and examinations of the animals' brains revealed differences that favored the animals raised in enriched conditions. These rats demonstrated

- increased rates of learning in standard laboratory tasks, such as learning a maze;
- increased overall weight of the cerebral cortex;
- increased amounts of acetylcholinesterase, a brain enzyme that enhances learning;

Classical Conditioning

Classical conditioning is learning in which previously existing behaviors come to be elicited by new stimuli. The existence of this very basic learning mechanism was demonstrated at the turn of the century by the Russian physiologist Ivan Pavlov (1849–1936). Pavlov (1927) showed that after several experiences of hearing a tone just before food was placed in its mouth, a dog would begin to salivate in response to the tone before it received any food. In everyday language, the dog began to expect food when it heard the tone, and its mouth watered as a result.

In the terminology of environmental-learning theories, Pavlov paired a **conditional stimulus (CS)**—a tone—with an **unconditional stimulus (UCS)**—food in the mouth. The food is called an unconditional stimulus because it "unconditionally" causes salivation, salivation being a reflex response to food in the mouth. Salivation, in turn, is called an **unconditional response (UCR)** because it is automatically and invariantly (that is, unconditionally) elicited by food in the mouth. The tone is called a conditional stimulus because the behavior it elicits depends on (is conditional on) the way it has been paired with the unconditional stimulus. When the unconditional response (salivation in response to food in the mouth) occurs in response to the CS (the tone), it is called a **conditional response (CR)** because it depends on the pairing of the CS (the tone) and the UCS (the food). The key indicator that learning has occurred is that the CS (tone) elicits the CR (salivation) before the presentation of the UCS (food) (see Figure 4.22).

classical conditioning Learning in which previously existing behaviors come to be elicited by new stimuli.

conditional stimulus (CS) In classical conditioning, a stimulus that elicits a behavior that is dependent on the way it is paired with the unconditional stimulus.

unconditional stimulus (UCS) In classical conditioning, the stimulus, such as food in the mouth, that invariably causes the unconditional response (UCR).

unconditional response (UCR) In classical conditioning, the response, such as salivation, that is invariantly elicited by the unconditional stimulus (UCS).

conditional response (CR) In classical conditioning, a response to the conditional stimulus (CS).

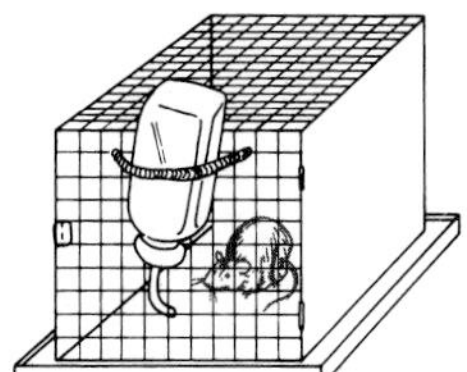

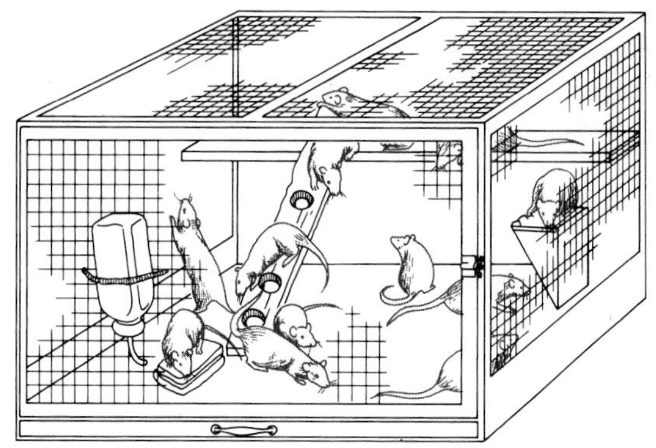

The standard laboratory cage in which laboratory rats are typically housed (left) provides little opportunity for complex interactions with the environment in comparison with a cage that provides for an enriched environment (right). (Adapted from Rosenzweig et al., 1972.)

- larger neuronal cell bodies and glial (supportive) cells; and
- more synaptic connections.

These findings have been replicated and extended numerous times in recent decades (Nelson & Bloom, 1997; Rosenzweig & Bennett, 1996).

Active interaction with the environment is a crucial factor in the production of these changes. In one study, rats were raised within an enriched environment but were housed singly in small cages so that they could do no more than observe what was going on around them. The learning capacity of these rats differed in no way from that of the animals that were housed in individual cages away from the enriched environment (Forgays & Forgays, 1952).

Although these results were obtained with nonhuman animal species, they are consistent with what is known about the importance of active involvement with the environment for human development. They show that behavioral changes should not be thought of as secondary consequences of changes that occur in the brain. Behavioral changes induced by culturally organized environmental stimulation can themselves lead to changes in the brain that then support more complex forms of behavior.

A number of developmentalists seized on Pavlov's demonstrations as a possible model for the way infants learn about their environments. One of Pavlov's co-workers demonstrated conditioned feeding responses in a 14-month-old infant (Krasnogorski, 1907/1967). The baby opened his mouth and made sucking motions (CRs) at the sight of a glass of milk (CS). When a bell (a new CS) was sounded on several occasions just before the glass of milk was presented, the baby began to open his mouth and suck at the sound of the bell, an indication that classical conditioning built expectations in the infant by a process of association. The crucial point to these observations is that there is no *biological* connection between the sight of a glass of milk or the sound of a bell and the mouth-opening and sucking responses they elicited. Rather, the fact that the new stimuli elicited these responses shows that learning has occurred.

Pavlov's ideas soon won a large following in the United States, and several studies were conducted with the intention of demonstrating the importance of classical conditioning as a mechanism of infant learning. Dorothy Marquis (1931), in one of the early studies of classical conditioning in newborn infants, showed that sucking motions could be conditioned to the sound of a buzzer if the buzzer sounded just before the baby was given a bottle.

More recently, intensive research has demonstrated that classical conditioning can occur within hours of birth if infants are presented with stimuli that are biologically significant to them and if they are alert at the time the experiments are performed. Elliott Blass and his associates, for example, condi-

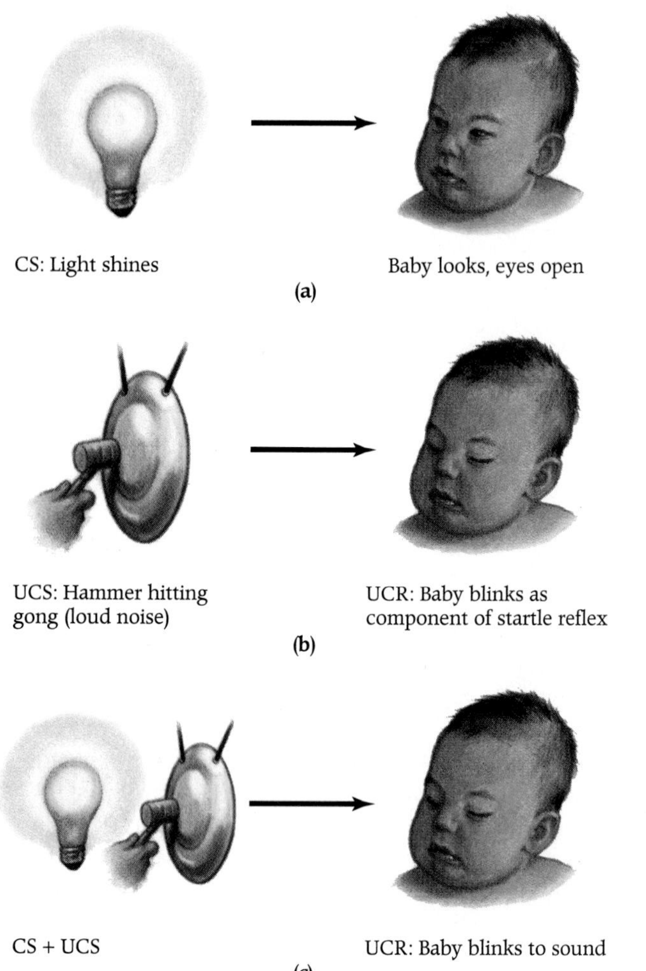

FIGURE 4.22

Classical conditioning. In the top panel (a) the sight of a light (CS) elicits no particular response. In (b) the loud sound of a gong (UCS) causes the baby to blink (UCR). In (c) the sight of the light (CS) is paired with the sound of the gong (UCS), which evokes an eyeblink (UCR). Finally (d), the sight of the light (CS) is sufficient to cause the baby to blink (CR), demonstrating that learning has occurred.

tioned infants to suck whenever their foreheads were stroked (Blass et al., 1984). These researchers assumed that such tactile stimulation occurs naturally during feeding but that it does not ordinarily produce sucking. The infants were only a few hours old when the experimenters began to stroke their foreheads and then feed them a small dose of sugar water (sucrose) through a pipette. Infants in a control group were also stroked and given sugar water, but the researchers performed the two acts independently and at variable intervals to preclude the possibility that the infants would form an association between them. After several repetitions of this procedure, the infants in the experimental group began to suck and pucker their faces—a response pattern the researchers dubbed a "pucker-suck"—when they were stroked on the forehead. The infants in the control group did not. One of the most convincing bits of evidence that classical conditioning had occurred was the way the infants reacted when the investigators later stroked their foreheads but did not give them sugar water. The first or second time this happened, the infants in the experimental group responded by frowning or making an angry face and then crying or whimpering. In contrast, when the researchers stopped giving sugar water to the infants in the control group after stroking their foreheads, the infants in this group did not make a face or cry. Carolyn Rovee-Collier (1987), a researcher who has been influential in promoting the study of classical conditioning in infants, commented that this finding "suggests that infants in the experimental group had learned the predictive relation between stroking and sucrose delivery and cried because their expectancy was violated" (p. 113).

Classical conditioning in young infants has also been demonstrated by Lewis Lipsitt and his colleagues, who succeeded in showing that neonates will form a conditioned reflex to a noxious stimulus—a puff of air to the eye. Infants 10, 20, and 30 days of age learned to shut their eyes in anticipation of an air puff that came 1½ seconds after a tone sounded. The youngest infants did not seem to retain what they had learned, but those 20 and 30 days old showed indications of remembering the experience 10 days later (Lipsitt et al., 1990).

Operant Conditioning

Classical conditioning explains how infants begin to build up expectations about the connections between events in their environment, but it does little to explain how even the simplest changes take place in infants' behavioral repertoires. The kind of conditioning that gives rise to new and more complex behaviors is called **operant conditioning**, in which changes in behavior are shaped by the consequences of that behavior. In other words, the basic idea of operant conditioning is that organisms will tend to repeat behaviors that lead to rewards and will tend to give up behaviors that fail to produce rewards or that lead to punishment (Skinner, 1938; Thorndike, 1911). A consequence (such as receiving a reward) that increases the likelihood that a behavior will be repeated is called a **reinforcement.** According to an operant explanation of the development of nursing, such behaviors as turning the head away from the bottle or burying the nose in the mother's breast will become less frequent because they do not lead to milk—a result the infant would find unsatisfying. At the same time, such behaviors as well-coordinated breathing, sucking, and swallowing will become more frequent because they are likely to be rewarded with milk.

Operant conditioning in young infants has been experimentally demonstrated with a variety of reinforcers, such as milk, sweet substances, an inter-

operant conditioning Learning in which changes in behavior are shaped by the consequences of that behavior, thereby giving rise to new and more comples behaviors.

reinforcement A consequence such as a reward that increases the likelihood that a behavior will be repeated.

esting visual display, a pacifier, and the sound of a heartbeat or the mother's voice (De Casper & Fifer, 1980; De Casper & Sigafoos, 1983; Moon & Fifer, 1990; Rovee-Collier, 1987). Einar Siqueland (1968), for example, demonstrated that neonates can learn to turn their heads in order to suck on a pacifier. The key requirement of operant learning is that a behavior has to occur before it can be reinforced. Head turning is ideal in this respect because it is something even the youngest neonates do. While the babies lay in laboratory cribs, Siqueland placed a band around their heads that was connected to a device for recording the degree their heads moved to either side (see Figure 4.23). Siqueland first recorded how often the babies naturally turned their heads. Once this baseline rate was established, he set his apparatus to signal when the babies had turned their heads at least 10 degrees to either side. As soon as they did, they were given a pacifier to suck on. After only 25 occasions on which the head turning was reinforced with the pacifier, most of the babies had tripled the rate at which they turned their heads.

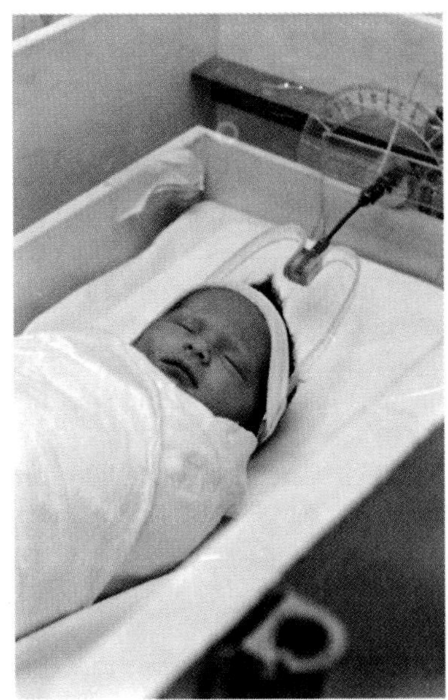

FIGURE 4.23
A newborn with a specially designed head-piece that records head turning. In Siqueland's operant-conditioning experiment, head turns of more than 10 degrees were reinforced by the opportunity to suck on a pacifier.

To make certain that the increase in babies' head turning was not due to the excitement of being placed in the crib, Siqueland included another group of infants in his experiment who were rewarded with a pacifier for holding their heads still. These infants learned to move their heads less during the course of the experiment.

Sidney Bijou and Donald Baer (1966), two prominent environmental-learning theorists, summarize how a behavior such as nursing, as well as changes in the form and complexity of a wide variety of infant behaviors, could arise from operant conditioning. In their view, the changes brought about by operant conditioning can be described as the stringing together of a collection of operants in a chain: "An infant may be capable of a variety of arm motions. These may be linked in slightly different order to produce behavior described as a wave or a pat, making patti-cake, beating a drum, grabbing a cookie, fending off, sweeping away, etc." (Bijou & Baer, 1966, p. 83). This same line of explanation is used to suggest the modification of behavior involved in the change from sucking to nursing.

Support for the argument that learning is an important contributor to behavioral development comes from studies that show that even very young infants are capable of remembering what they have learned from one testing session to the next (Rovee-Collier & Boller, 1995; Swain et al., 1993). These studies also suggest that memory for newly learned behaviors improves markedly during the first several months of life, a finding to which we will return at the end of this chapter and again in Chapter 5 (pp. 203–205).

The environmental-learning theorists' emphasis on the power of the environment to shape behavior provides an important counterweight to the biological-maturation theorists' emphasis on the primacy of genetic influences in determining the course of development. In addition to focusing on the role of learning in development, the environmental-learning approach differs from the biological-maturation perspective by emphasizing continuity in developmental processes as children grow older. However, whether attempting to explain the transformation of the sucking reflex into nursing or to explain any other aspect of developmental change, the environmental-learning approach has difficulty accounting for individual differences in behavior. According to this perspective, such differences can be accounted for only by differences in the experiences of individuals; the effects of genetic variation are discounted. Contemporary research on individual differences has made this extreme view difficult to justify.

THE CONSTRUCTIVIST PERSPECTIVE: PIAGET

Jean Piaget, the most prominent champion of the constructivist perspective, sought to understand how children come to know the world and to act effectively within it. He objected to both the biological-maturation and

BOX 4.4

Imitation in the Newborn?

Imitation is widely considered an important way to learn during childhood and later life. Despite newborns' limited visual capacities and uncoordinated movements, several studies show that babies are capable of rudimentary forms of imitation from birth (Maratos, 1998; Meltzoff & Moore, 1998). These studies have generated intense interest among developmentalists because it had long been believed that imitation does not become possible until several months after birth (Abravanel et al., 1976; Piaget, 1962).

In research conducted by Andrew Meltzoff and Keith Moore (1977, 1989, 1994), an adult stood over alert newborn babies and made distinctive facial expressions, such as opening his mouth very wide and sticking out his tongue. Meltzoff and Moore reported that the infants often imitated the facial expression of the adult. Aware that their claims were going to be viewed skeptically, the researchers took special precautions to ensure that their results could not be attributed to procedural errors. As a check of their findings, they photographed the infants and the adult model independently. They then asked judges who had not been present during the experimental sessions to look at the photographs of the infants and, on the basis of the baby's expression, guess what sort of face the adult had made. The judges guessed correctly more often than they could have done by chance, indicating that the infants were indeed imitating the distinctive adult facial expressions they saw.

Yet the results were not so clear-cut as the report of the findings suggests. On the 97 trials when the researcher stuck out his tongue, for example, the babies "most often" stuck out their tongues in return. But the "most often" means that they stuck out their tongues on 30 trials. On 20 trials, they opened their mouths, and on the remaining trials, they puckered their lips or moved their fingers. The imitative response won out, but just barely.

Meltzoff and Moore's research has generated many follow-up studies. Tiffany Field and her colleagues found support for Meltzoff and Moore's conclusions when they used somewhat different procedures and responses (Field et al., 1982). They arranged for an adult to model three facial expressions—happy, sad, and surprised—for babies who were an average of 36 hours old. The babies showed that they could distinguish among the model's facial expressions by the fact that they habituated to the repeated presentation of a single expression but then began to pay close attention again when the model presented them with a different facial expression. Most important, the babies appeared to imitate these new expressions. An observer who could not see the model and who did not know what expressions were being presented to the babies was able, on a statistically reliable basis, to determine the facial expression of the model from the facial movements of the babies. These results are difficult to explain without assuming that the infants somehow matched what they did with what they saw the model doing. Precisely how infants accomplished this matching remains uncertain.

The fact that imitation occurred only part of the time and was restricted to elementary movements of the face led some researchers to doubt if the babies were actually imitating what they saw. These researchers suggest that either there was some peculiarity in Meltzoff and Moore's procedures or the be-

the environmental-learning theories of his day. He criticized biological explanations for their failure to spell out how the environment of human infants interacts with their biological capacities to produce developmental change (Piaget & Inhelder, 1969). At the same time, he was critical of environ-mental-learning explanations because they assumed that the environment is the originator of developmental change, they gave too little emphasis to the role of children's actions in producing development, and they denied the existence of qualitative, stagelike changes during development.

Piaget's Theory of Developmental Change

In Piaget's view, infants' knowledge is acquired (in his words, "constructed") through action. Consequently, to understand development, one must begin at the beginning with the most elementary potentials for action present at birth, reflexes.

To Piaget, a reflex is a primitive *schema,* the basic unit of psychological functioning in his theory. A **schema** is a mental structure that provides an organism with a model for action in similar or analogous circumstances (Piaget & Inhelder, 1969).

During the first month of life, the "reflex schemas" babies are born with provide them with a kind of skeleton for action that is gradually fleshed out by experience. Eventually these initial schemas are either strengthened or

schema In Piagetian terms, a mental structure that provides an organism with a model for action in similar or analogous circumstances.

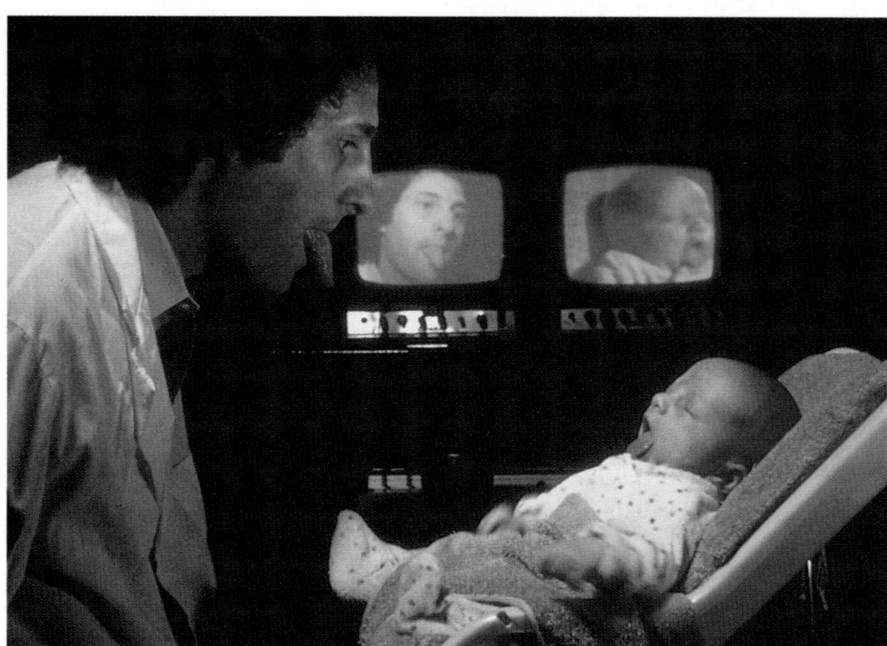

Demonstration from one of Andrew Meltzoff and Keith Moore's studies that some newborns can imitate adult facial expressions.

havior they observed is a very special form of imitation (Abravanel & Sigafoos, 1984; Kaitz et al., 1988). Evidence indicating that newborn imitation is a special form unto itself comes from studies that trace changes in imitation over the first year of life (Maratos, 1998; Meltzoff & Moore, 1998). First, newborns' imitations are restricted to movements of the face and head, whereas older babies imitate sounds and a variety of movements. Second, newborn imitation is slow and inconsistent, while the imitation of a 9-month-old is rapid and consistent, suggesting that a different mechanism is at work. Hence, while it is clear that imitation is a mechanism of learning by 6 months of age, it may be less important as a mechanism of learning in the newborn.

transformed into new schemas through **adaptation,** a twofold process involving what Piaget termed *assimilation* and *accommodation.*

During **assimilation,** various experiences are mentally taken in by the organism and incorporated into existing schemas, strengthening those schemas and making them work more efficiently. Take the primitive schema of reflex sucking, for example. Initially it is so closely tied to a small group of eliciting stimuli, such as a nipple placed in the mouth, that in Piaget's view the newborn is unable to distinguish between sucking and the object sucked upon. But sucking does not remain strictly bound to particular eliciting objects for long. Soon babies are likely to find, say, a pacifier instead of a nipple touching their lips and start sucking on it. Since a pacifier is designed to be similar to a nipple, the infants can suck on it in pretty much the same way they suck on the nipple. In other words, they *assimilate* the pacifier, a new object, into their existing sucking schema.

Not every object babies encounter can be assimilated into an existing schema. If they encounter a blanket, for instance, they may try to suck on it. However, because the qualities of the blanket—the satin binding, perhaps, or the cloth of the blanket itself—are so unlike the qualities of a nipple or a pacifier, they are unable to assimilate the blanket as an object to suck on. They will therefore make some **accommodation;** that is, they will modify the way they suck, perhaps by choosing a corner of the blanket and sucking

adaptation Piaget's term for the twofold process involving assimilation and accommodation.

assimilation Piaget's term for the process by which various experiences are mentally taken in by the organism and incorporated into existing schemas.

accommodation In Piagetian terms, a modification of a previous schema so that it can be applied to both old and new experiences.

equilibration The Piagetian term for the back-and-forth process of the child's seeking a fit between existing schemas and new environmental experiences.

sensorimotor stage Piaget's term for the stage of infancy during which the process of adaptation consists largely of coordinating sensory perceptions and simple motor behaviors to acquire knowledge of the world.

on that, using approximately but not exactly the same schema as they had used to suck on a nipple. In its modified form, the sucking schema can now be applied to new environmental experiences. If a baby encounters a toy truck and tries to suck on it, accommodation is unlikely to occur because the toy is so difficult to suck on; in this case, the baby's sucking schema will be unmodified.

One way to summarize Piaget's theory is to view development as a constant tug-of-war between assimilation and accommodation as the infant acts on the world. Piaget referred to this back-and-forth process of the child's seeking a fit between existing schemas and new environmental experiences as **equilibration.** This process of achieving a balance, or equilibrium, between the individual's present understanding of the world and new experiences of it creates a more inclusive, more complicated form of knowledge, bringing the child to a new level of development. But during childhood the balance does not last for long because the process of biological maturation and the accumulation of experience/knowledge leads to new imbalances, initiating a new tug-of-war between assimilation and accommodation in the search for a new equilibrium and a still higher, more inclusive, level of adaptation.

Piaget believed that periods of equilibrium created by the cycles of assimilation and accommodation form a sequence of qualitative transformations, or stages, in the overall structure and functioning of the child. He believed that there are four major developmental stages between birth and adulthood, corresponding to infancy, early childhood, middle childhood, and adolescence.

Table 4.5 provides a summary of the four stages of development described by Piaget. The *sensorimotor stage,* which occurs during infancy, is discussed below and in Chapters 5 and 6. We will examine the *preoperational, concrete operational,* and *formal operational* stages in Chapters 9, 12, and 16, respectively.

The Sensorimotor Period and Its Substages

Piaget (1952b) referred to infancy as the **sensorimotor stage** because during this period the process of adaptation consists largely of coordinating *sensory perceptions* and simple *motor* behaviors to acquire knowledge of the world—the infant progresses from, say, reflexively grasping at an object such as a spoon, to firmly grasping the spoon, to banging it to make an interesting noise or dropping it to see where it falls, and then to using it to get food to the mouth. This stage lasts from birth to about the age of 2 years. Within the sensorimotor period Piaget identified six substages, each of which builds on the accomplishments of the one before. We will discuss the first two substages of the sensorimotor period here because they correspond to the early months of postnatal life.

Substage 1 lasts from birth to approximately 1 to 1½ months. It is the stage during which infants *learn to control and coordinate their reflexes.* Piaget believed that the reflexes present at birth provide the initial connection between infants and their environments. However, these initial reflexes add nothing new to development because they undergo very little accommodation. In this sense, they reflect the "preestablished boundaries of the hereditary apparatus" (Piaget & Inhelder, 1969).

Nevertheless, according to Piaget, the initial reflexes do provide the conditions for new development, because they *produce* stimulation at the same time that they are responses to stimuli. When infants suck, for example, they experience tactile pressure on the roof of the mouth, which stimulates further sucking, which produces more tactile pressure, and so on. This stimulus-producing aspect of basic reflexes is the key to the development of the second sensorimotor substage because it results in the earliest extensions of the reflexes babies are born with.

TABLE 4.5 Piaget's Stages of Cognitive Development and the Sensorimotor Substages

Age (years)	Stage	Description	Characteristics of Sensorimotor Substage
Birth to 2	**Sensorimotor**	Infants' achievements consist largely of coordinating their sensory perceptions and simple motor behaviors. As they move through the six substages of this period, infants come to recognize the existence of a world outside themselves and begin to interact with it in deliberate ways.	**Substage 1 (0–1½ months)** *Reflex schemas exercised:* involuntary rooting, sucking, grasping, looking **Substage 2 (1½–4 months)** *Primary circular reactions:* repetition of actions that are pleasurable in themselves **Substage 3 (4–8 months)** *Secondary circular reactions:* dawning awareness of the effects of one's own actions on the environment; extended actions that produce interesting change in the environment **Substage 4 (8–12 months)** *Coordination of secondary circular reactions:* combining schemas to achieve a desired effect; earliest form of problem solving **Substage 5 (12–18 months)** *Tertiary circular reactions:* deliberate variation of problem-solving means; experimentation to see what the consequences will be **Substage 6 (18–24 months)** *Beginnings of symbolic representation:* images and words come to stand for familiar objects; invention of new means of problem solving through symbolic combinations
2 to 6	Preoperational	Young children can represent reality to themselves through the use of symbols, including mental images, words, and gestures. Still, children often fail to distinguish their point of view from that of others, become easily captured by surface appearances, and are often confused about causal relations.	
6 to 12	Concrete Operational	As they enter middle childhood, children become capable of mental operations, internalized actions that fit into a logical system. Operational thinking allows children mentally to combine, separate, order, and transform objects and actions. Such operations are considered concrete because they are carried out in the presence of the objects and events being thought about.	
12 to 19	Formal Operational	In adolescence the developing person acquires the ability to think systematically about all logical relations within a problem. Adolescents display keen interest in abstract ideas and in the process of thinking itself.	

Substage 2 lasts from about 1 month to about 4 months. The first hints of new forms of behavior are found in the way ***existing reflexes are extended in time*** (as when infants suck between feedings) or ***are extended to new objects*** (as when infants suck their thumbs). Piaget noted that babies may suck their thumbs accidentally as early as the first day of life. (We now know they may do so even before birth; see Chapter 3, p. 88.) He believed, however, that the thumb-sucking seen during substage 2 (from about 2 to 4 months of age) reflects a qualitatively new form of behavior.

In substage 1, infants suck their thumbs, but only when they accidentally touch their mouths with their hands. During substage 2, in contrast, if a baby's thumb falls from her mouth, the baby is likely to bring the thumb back to her mouth so she can suck it some more. In other words, infants in this substage repeat pleasurable actions for their own sake. Piaget used the term

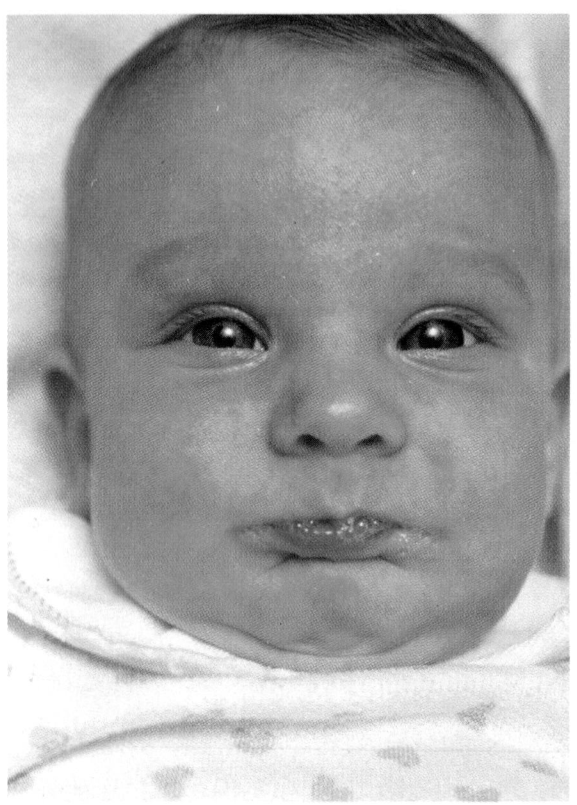

Blowing bubbles is an early instance of a primary circular reaction in which an accidental aspect of sucking is prolonged for the pleasure of continuing the sensation.

primary circular reaction to characterize such behavior, which he viewed as the prime characteristic of substage 2. Actions of this kind are called *primary* because the objects at which they are directed are parts of the baby's own body; they are called *circular* because they lead only back to themselves. (Table 4.5 lists all of Piaget's sensorimotor substages and the behaviors characteristic of each.)

Piaget's evidence for many of his ideas about the earliest substages of the sensorimotor period can be seen in the notes he kept about his own children's behavior. The following observations illustrate the kind of behaviors he referred to as primary circular reactions. In the examples, note how new behaviors arise in the process of attempting to repeat something just for the pleasure of it:

> After having learned to suck his thumb, Laurent continues to play with his tongue and to suck, but intermittently. On the other hand, his skill increases. Thus at 1 month, 20 days I notice he grimaces while placing his tongue between gums and lips and in bulging his lips, as well as making a clapping sound when quickly closing the mouth after these exercises.
>
> From 2 months, 18 days, Laurent plays with his saliva, letting it accumulate within his half-open lips and then abruptly swallowing it. About the same period he makes sucking-like movements, without putting out his tongue. (Piaget, 1952b, p. 65)

Piaget believed that such primary circular reactions are important because they offer the first evidence of cognitive development. "The basic law of dawning psychological activity," he wrote, "could be said to be the search for the maintenance or repetition of interesting states of consciousness" (Piaget, 1977, p. 202).

Over the first few months of life, these circular reactions undergo both *differentiation*—infants learn to use different grasps for different objects and learn not to suck on toy trucks—and *integration*—infants can grasp their mothers' arms with one hand while sucking on a bottle in a newly coordinated way. All the while, infants' experiences are providing more nourishment for their existing schemas and are forcing them to modify those schemas, permitting them to master more of the world.

In contrast to the infants portrayed by biological-maturation and environmental-learning approaches, Piagetian infants are active, problem-solving beings who are busy acting on the environment in the process of adapting to it right from birth. All three perspectives discussed thus far designate inborn reflexes as the starting point for development, but they view the significance of these reflexes in different ways. Because Piaget saw reflexes as schemas for action, he downplayed the role of the environment in evoking or reinforcing particular behaviors or maturational processes in the brain and instead emphasized the role of infants' constructive activity in shaping the way the environment will exert its effects.

Piaget's Theory and the Social Environment

Piaget acknowledged that the social environment is an important influence on early development, yet discussions of social context are virtually absent from his writing about early development. Nevertheless, a close look at the acquisition of new forms of behavior during the first 2½ months of life reveals that changes in a baby's behavior are intimately related to changes in the mother's behavior. The changes in maternal behaviors appear to be just as essential to the infant's development as are the changes that occur in the infant's relations to objects or brain functioning.

Nursing clearly demonstrates how the mother's behavior contributes to the infant's development. In the beginning, the mother's nursing behavior may not be much more coordinated than her baby's. She must learn how to

primary circular reaction The term Piaget used to describe the infant's tendency to repeat pleasurable bodily actions for their own sake.

hold the baby and adjust herself so that the nipple is placed at exactly the right spot against the baby's mouth to elicit the sucking reflex. She must also learn not to press the baby so tightly to her breast that the infant's breathing is disrupted, triggering the head-withdrawal reflex.

When the mother breast-feeds, the baby's (reflex) sucking initiates reflex responses in her that combine with her voluntary efforts to maximize the amount of milk the baby receives. This system of mutually facilitating reflexes in infant and mother changes the consequences of reflex sucking, as shown in Figure 4.24. The infant's sucking not only transports milk from nipple to mouth but also stimulates the production of more milk, thereby increasing the adaptive value of the sucking reflex.

A different type of mutual facilitation arises from the physical movements mothers make while they are feeding their infants by either breast or bottle. Kenneth Kaye (1982) and his colleagues found that even during the very first feeding, mothers occasionally jiggle the baby or the bottle. These jiggles come not at random intervals but during the pauses between the infant's bursts of sucking. The jiggles increase the probability of sucking and prolong the feeding session, thereby increasing the amount of milk the neonate receives.

Sucking in response to jiggling is not a reflex in the sense that rooting is a reflex. Rooting is an automatic, involuntary response to being touched on the side of the mouth. There are no known neural connections that make sucking an inevitable response to the mother's jiggle. Yet sucking in response to jiggling happens, is to some extent automatic, and has clear adaptive value. Scholars do not know for sure where such adaptive patterns come from. Kaye calls them "preadapted responses," implying that they may have arisen in the course of human evolution.

Kaye speculates that the mother's jiggle between her infant's bursts of sucking is her way of intuitively "conversing" with her baby by filling in her "turn" during the pauses in the baby's rhythmic sucking. Mothers' reports support Kaye's view. Although they are not aware that they are jiggling their babies in a systematic way, mothers report that they actively try to help their babies nurse. They notice and disapprove of the pauses between bursts of

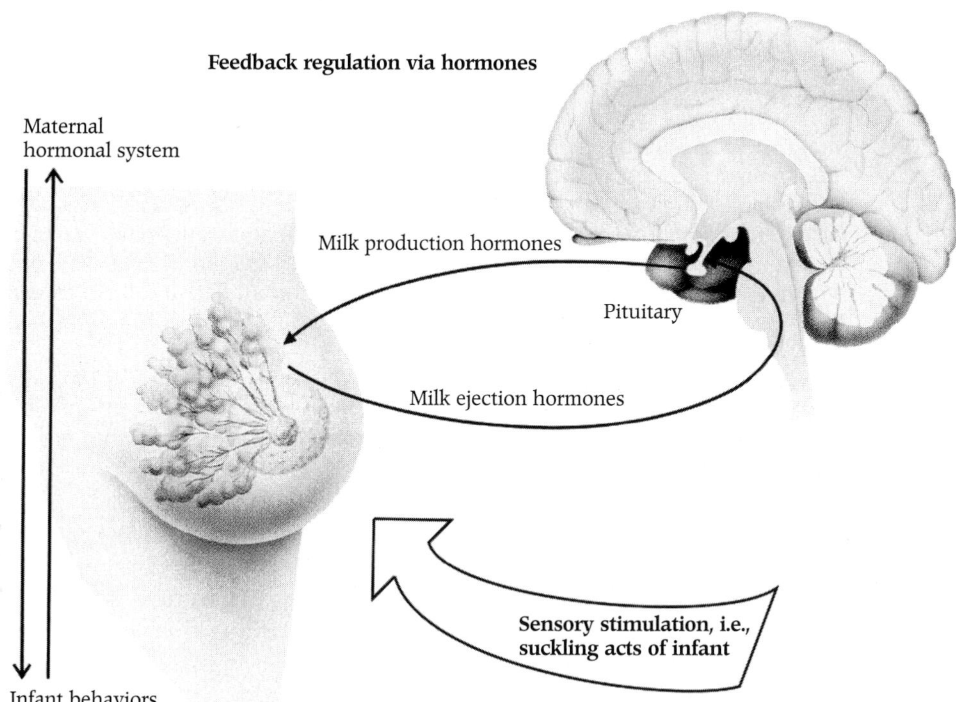

FIGURE 4.24

The reflexes that establish a reciprocal relationship between the infant being fed and the mother. The infant's sucking stimulates the release of hormones that increase milk production and help trigger the ejection of milk from the mammary glands. (Adapted from Cairns, 1979.)

sucking. When mothers are asked about their jiggling behavior, a typical response is that the baby "gets lazy, or dozes off, so I jiggle her to get her going again."

Jiggling during feeding is just one of the myriad ways in which mothers actively structure their children's experience, and just one small example of how development is influenced by the interaction between the child and the child's environment. The fact that Piaget did not give much attention to the active role of the child's environment is considered by many a major weakness in his theory. It is a weakness that is particularly apparent from the cultural-context perspective.

THE CULTURAL-CONTEXT PERSPECTIVE

As we indicated in Chapter 1 (p. 37), the cultural-context perspective shares Piaget's beliefs that (1) development occurs as individuals act on their environment and (2) biology and experience play equal and reciprocal roles in the development of a human being. However, cultural-context theorists also consider two additional sources of developmental change: (1) the active contribution of other people in the child's community and (2) the cultural "designs for living" accumulated over the history of the larger social group. Such designs for living are present in all human societies, and in this sense they are universal. But their particular shape varies from one society to the next, giving rise to culturally specific modes of interaction. These culture-specific variations encourage development along certain lines while discouraging it along others, thereby producing distinctive patterns of change (Greenfield, 1997). Let us look once again at the process through which sucking develops into organized feeding, this time to see how the universal facts of maturation, learning, and maternal support vary culturally in ways that shape infants' behavior in the present and give hints of further changes to come.

In their discussion of culture and development, Margaret Mead and Frances Macgregor (1951) noted that cultures "differ from each other in the way in which the growth process is interwoven with learning" (p. 26). This principle, they went on to explain, first operates in the various ways adults of different cultures respond to such basic neonatal capacities as the sucking reflex and to the fact that the mother's milk does not begin to flow until a day or two after she has given birth:

> The existence of the sucking reflex at birth . . . will be taken advantage of in some cultures by putting the baby at once to the mother's breast, so that the infant's sucking is used to stimulate the flow of the mother's milk while the infant itself remains hungry, or the infant may be put at the breast of a wet nurse with a well-established flow of milk, in which case the infant's sucking behavior is reinforced but the mother is left without the stimulation that it would have provided. As another alternative, the infant may be starved until the mother has milk, and as still another, the infant may be given a bottle with a different kind of nipple. (p. 26)

Despite such differences, the infant feeding practices of all cultures are equivalent in that they are all ways in which parents arrange for infants' innate sucking reflexes to become part of nursing. In this respect, nursing is universal (Figure 4.25).

According to the cultural-context perspective, however, cultural variations in the way nursing is handled may have a direct effect on the infant's early experience and an indirect effect on later experiences. To continue with the example provided by Mead and Macgregor, if a baby is bottle-fed until the mother's milk begins to flow, changes in the baby's sucking that are adaptive to bottle-feeding may interfere with subsequent breast-feeding. If the interference is great, breast-feeding may be given up altogether. This outcome will alter both the kind of milk that the infant receives and the forms of social interaction between infant and mother that are a part of feeding.

Because specific cultural practices such as breast-feeding, bottle-feeding, or the use of a wetnurse are linked to larger patterns of social life that will shape the child's future experiences, the child's later development is likely to be affected by which method of feeding is decided upon. For example, if a mother who stays at home gives her baby a bottle because she believes that bottled milk is more nutritious than her own, the use of a bottle rather than breast-feeding may have no differential impact on the development of social relations between the mother and child. However, if an employed mother leaves her baby at a day-care center because her workplace has no on-site child care, the relationship between the mother and her baby is less than exclusive. For this baby, bottle-feeding is likely to become part of patterns of social interaction that include peers and a succession of caregivers.

An important implication of the cultural-context perspective that is not captured by the example of nursing is that cultures provide people with a framework for interpreting their experiences that includes their view of their own babies. The way newborn babies are treated depends very much on what a society defines babies to be. In the United States today, for example, well-educated, middle-class adults tend to have a higher opinion of the psychological capacities of young infants than do adults of many other cultures or various subcultures within the United States (Harkness & Super, 1996).

When the behavioral consequences of this cultural belief are viewed in isolation from usual child-care contexts, they can be quite striking. The pediatrician T. Berry Brazelton and his colleagues placed 1-week-old infants in infant seats in the laboratory and asked their mothers to spend several minutes interacting with them. Here's how the scene unfolded:

> Our mothers were faced with the problem of communicating with infants who, if they were not crying or thrashing, were often hanging limply in the infant seat with closed or semiclosed eyes or, just as frequently, were "frozen" motionless in some strange and uninterpretable posture—staring at nothing. . . . Perhaps the most interesting response to the challenge of facing an unresponsive infant is this. The mother takes on facial expressions, motions, and postures indicative of emotion, as though the infant were behaving intentionally or as though she and he were communicating. Frequently, in response to a motionless infant, she suddenly acquires an expression of great admiration, moving back and forth in front

FIGURE 4.25
Although babies are nursed in all cultures, there are wide variations in the way babies' nursing behavior is organized.

> of him with great enthusiasm; or again in response to an unmoving infant, she takes on an expression of great surprise, moving backward in mock astonishment; or in the most exaggerated manner, she greets the infant and, furthermore, carries on an animated extended greeting interchange, bobbing and nodding enthusiastically exactly as though her greeting were currently being reciprocated. (Brazelton et al., 1974, pp. 67–68)

In sum, these mothers were unwilling or unable to deal with neonatal behaviors as if they were meaningless or unintentional. Instead, they endowed the smallest movements with highly personal meaning and reacted to them emotionally. They insisted on joining in and enlarging on even the least possibly interactive behaviors, acting as if highly significant interaction had taken place. In contrast, an observer from a different culture might have concluded that there was no possibility of interaction at all. The Kaluli, for example, who live in the rain forests of Papua New Guinea, have a far different set of beliefs about babies, and they treat their babies quite differently as a result. As Eleanor Ochs and Bambi Schieffelin (1984) report, the Kaluli see their babies as helpless creatures who have "no understanding." Although they may greet their infants by name, they do not talk to them in the way middle-class American adults do. Nor do Kaluli mothers engage in extended eye contact with their babies, because the Kaluli believe that it is impolite to gaze at the person to whom you are talking. Kaluli mothers hold their infants facing outward so that they can see and be seen by others, and they take their infants' part in interactions with other members of the social group. Reflecting their belief in their infants' helplessness, Kaluli mothers speak *for* their infants. As Ochs and Schieffelin point out, "In taking this role the mother does for the infant what the infant cannot do for itself, that is appear to act in a controlled and competent manner, using language" (p. 290).

Notice that the words Ochs and Schieffelin use to describe the intent of the Kaluli mothers could also be applied to the U.S. mothers, even though the specific actions involved are quite different. In both cultures, beliefs about what babies are, what they can do, and what they will need to do in the fu-

Every culture works out its own way of transporting babies that is consistent with its beliefs about what babies are, what their needs are, and the kind of individuals they will grow up to be.

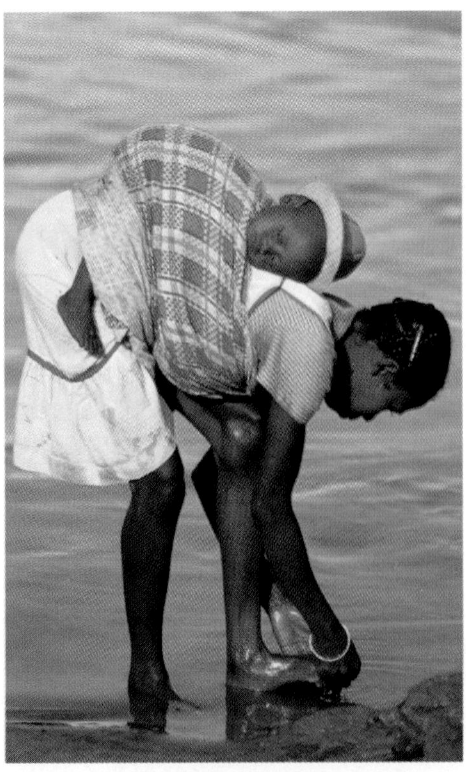

ture all affect the way babies are treated by those around them and thus the way they experience the environment. In short, different cultural patterns lead to different child-rearing practices, which have different effects on further development, as we will see in later chapters. For this reason it is essential to keep cultural factors in mind when we consider the mechanisms of developmental change (Greenfield, 1997).

INTEGRATING THE SEPARATE THREADS OF DEVELOPMENT

The complexities involved in accounting for the way nursing develops during the first months of life provide some hint of the enormous difficulties involved in attempting to account for human development as a whole. Even for a behavior as seemingly simple as nursing, the contributions of biological and environmental factors, including cultural influences and the specific circumstances in which infants find themselves, must all be considered. And the difficulties do not end there. A child's various behaviors develop not in isolation but as parts of an integrated system of developing behaviors. Thus developmentalists must also study the parts of the system in relation to one another. Nursing, for instance, must be understood as but one element in a system of developing behaviors that includes increasingly longer sleeping and waking periods and the buildup of elementary expectations about the environment.

For meeting the requirement that developing behaviors be considered individually and as parts of a larger whole, we have found the analytical strategy developed by Robert Emde and his associates to be especially useful (Emde et al., 1976). As we mentioned in Chapter 1 (pp. 38–41), this strategy involves tracing developments in the biological, behavioral, and social domains *as they relate to one another.* It allows the identification of bio-social-behavioral shifts, those periods when changes in the separate domains converge to create the kind of qualitative reorganization in the overall pattern of behaviors that signals the onset of a new stage of development. We can see the usefulness of this approach by examining the first postnatal bio-social-behavioral shift after birth, which occurs when a full-term baby is about 2½ months old.

THE FIRST POSTNATAL BIO-SOCIAL-BEHAVIORAL SHIFT

Emde and his co-workers agree that during the first 2 months of postnatal life infants learn by acting on their environments and by interacting with their caregivers. During the third month, however, the "modes and mechanisms" of their behavior undergo a rather abrupt shift (Emde et al., 1976). This shift arises from the convergence of developmental changes that previously had proceeded in relative isolation. Table 4.6 lists in capsule form the changes in the separate domains that converge to create the first postnatal bio-social-behavioral shift. To appreciate the far-reaching significance of this and subsequent bio-social-behavioral shifts, we must visualize what it means for all the changes listed in Table 4.6 to occur at about the same time. Following the lead of Emde and his colleagues, we will illustrate the meaning of a bio-social-behavioral shift by tracing how changes in infants' smiling are related to other aspects of their development.

THE EMERGENCE OF SOCIAL SMILING

During the first week of life, the corners of a baby's mouth often curl up in a facial expression that looks for all the world like a smile. Most experienced

TABLE 4.6 ELEMENTS OF THE FIRST POSTNATAL BIO-SOCIAL-BEHAVIORAL SHIFT (2½ MONTHS)

BIOLOGICAL DOMAIN	Central nervous system: Myelination of cortical and subcortical neural pathways Myelination of primary neural pathways in some sensory systems Increased cortical control of subcortical activity Increases in the number and diversity of brain cells Psychophysiology: Increases in amount of wakefulness Decreases in active (REM) sleep as a proportion of total sleep time Shift in pattern of sleep; quiet (NREM) sleep begins to come first
BEHAVIORAL DOMAIN	Learning is retained better between episodes Increases in visual acuity More complete visual scanning of objects Onset of social smiling Decreases in generalized fussiness and crying Visually initiated reaching becomes visually guided reaching
SOCIAL DOMAIN	New quality of coordination and emotional contact between infants and caretakers Beginning of "crying on purpose"

mothers do not pay much attention to such smiles, however, because they are most likely to come when the infant is asleep or very drowsy. During the second week, smiles begin to appear when the infants are awake, but they do not correlate with any particular events in the environment. Between the ages of 1 month and 2½ months, infants begin to smile indiscriminately at almost any form of external stimulation. Thus this earliest form of smiling is not really social, even when it is stimulated from the outside.

To become truly social, babies' smiles must be reciprocally related to the smiles of others; that is, the baby must both smile in response to the smiles of other people and elicit others' smiles. This is precisely what begins to happen for the first time around the age of 2½ to 3 months.

The changes in infants' behavior that accompany the social smile are not lost on their parents. Quite the opposite; the parents report a new emotional quality in their relationship with their child. The following remarks made by a mother concerning her feelings about her baby before the shift and the description of a mother's interactions with her baby after the shift provide an idea of the social and emotional implications of the new kind of smiling:

> BEFORE THE SHIFT
> I don't think there is interaction. . . . They are like in a little cage surrounded by glass and you are acting all around them but there is no real interaction. . . . I realized I was doing things for him he couldn't do for himself but I always felt that anyone else could do them and he wouldn't know the difference. (Robson & Moss, 1970, pp. 979–980)
>
> AFTER THE SHIFT
> His eyes locked on to hers, and together they held motionless. . . . This silent and almost motionless instant continued to hang until the mother suddenly

> shattered it by saying "Hey!" and simultaneously opening her eyes wider, raising her eyebrows further, and throwing her head up and toward the infant. Almost simultaneously the baby's eyes widened. His head tilted up . . . , his smile broadened. . . . Now she said, "Well hello! . . . hello . . . heeelloooo!," so that her pitch rose and the "hellos" became longer and more stressed on each successive repetition. With each phrase the baby expressed more pleasure, and his body resonated almost like a balloon being pumped up. (Stern, 1977, p. 3)

After the shift the baby displays a new emotion, joy—expressed in his smile and his whole body—which helps account for the mother's feeling that the relationship is more connected.

The significance of the emergence of the social smile as a marker of a new level of development is clearly reflected in a special ritual traditionally practiced by the Navaho:

> When visitors come to the hogan it is polite to inquire: "Has the baby laughed yet?" When it does so, this is an occasion for rejoicing and for a little ceremony. The baby's hands are held out straight by the mother, and some member of the family (usually a brother or a sister) puts a pinch of salt with bread and meat upon them. . . . The person who sees the baby smile first should give a present (with salt) to all members of the family. The father or mother will kill a sheep and distribute this among relatives along with a bit of salt for each piece. (Leighton & Kluckhohn, 1947/1969, p. 29)

BIOLOGICAL CONTRIBUTIONS TO SOCIAL SMILING

Several lines of evidence point to important biological changes as part of the emergence of social smiling. In their pioneering studies, Emde and his colleagues recorded the brain waves of babies when they were and were not smiling. They found that in the early days after birth babies' smiles came primarily during REM sleep and were accompanied by bursts of brain-wave activity originating in the brain stem. Emde and Jean Robinson (1979) call these endogenous smiles *REM smiles.* They found that even when the infants were awake, their smiles were accompanied by the pattern of brain waves characteristic of drowsiness and REM sleep. The frequency of REM smiles decreased rapidly during the next several weeks, to be replaced at about 2½ months by smiles that were no longer associated with brain waves characteristic of REM sleep.

Subsequent research has shown that the visual system, including parts of the cerebral cortex that underpin vision, also undergoes important maturational changes between 2½ and 3 months (Chugani & Phelps, 1986). Some of these changes were mentioned in earlier sections of this chapter, such as the increased visual acuity associated with maturation of the eye. In addition, research has shown that during the same period there is a marked increase in the activity of the occipital and parietal lobes of the brain, both of which are involved in processing visual information. The improved visual capacity resulting from these biological changes permits babies to focus their eyes, and thus their smiles, on people, allowing earlier forms of smiling stimulated by the environment to become truly reciprocal, *social* smiling.

This father and son from Kaokoland, Namibia, are sharing an important sense of connectedness.

THE SOCIAL SMILE AND SOCIAL FEEDBACK

The importance of social feedback and reciprocity to the achievement of bio-social-behavioral shifts is dramatically demonstrated in research conducted on the development of congenitally blind infants. Like sighted infants, blind babies exhibit REM smiles. But unlike sighted infants, they may not exhibit the same shift to social smiling at 2½ months. Since, under normal conditions of growth, the social smile depends on increased visual capacity and on visual feedback from people who smile back, it would seem that blind infants lack the feedback loop they need in order to develop social smiling. The frequent

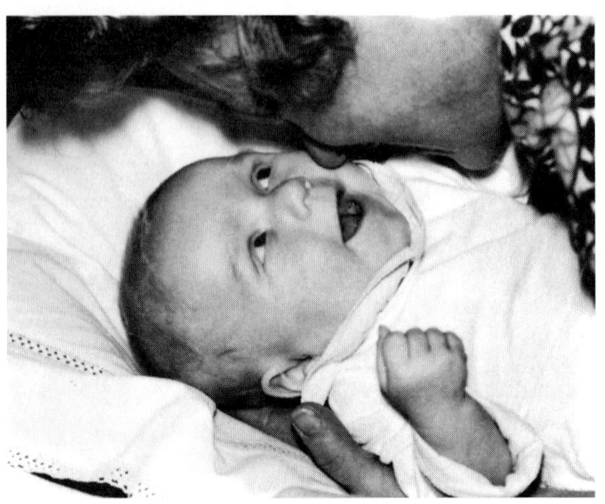

This 2½-month-old blind infant smiled and turned her face toward her mother upon hearing her mother's voice.

failure of blind infants to make the expected shift toward social smiling also means that their sighted parents cannot use their baby's facial expressions to gauge how their infants respond to them.

However, all this does not mean that blind infants receive no social feedback or that they cannot acquire social smiling. After all, their brains are maturing like those of sighted children. The problem is that they cannot express their increased capacities in visually related ways. In the absence of this major channel for social feedback, parents must find alternative ways to interact with their blind children.

The intuitive solution that some parents of blind children work out is to establish communication through touch. In her work with blind children, Selma Fraiberg (1974) noticed that many of these parents bounce, nudge, and tickle their children far more than the parents of sighted children. At first all this manipulation struck Fraiberg as socially abnormal, but then she noticed that the touching made the children smile and realized that tactile stimulation was a good substitute for the smiling face that elicits the smiles of sighted babies. Through touch the parents had found a way to get the feedback they needed from their infants—and to provide feedback the infants needed from them. Fraiberg used this observation to design a training program to help blind infants and their parents. Parents were taught to attend carefully to the way their children used their hands to signal their intentions and reactions. They were also taught to play with their babies' fingers and to provide rattles and other toys that would allow them and their babies to play together. Once the parents were able to provide the babies with appropriate feedback, the babies began to smile socially.

The success of Fraiberg's training program indicates that social smiling does not arise simply from the fact that an infant's brain has matured to the point where social smiling is possible. For social smiling to emerge, appropriate interaction with others is necessary; when this new behavior does emerge, a new emotional quality is able to develop between infants and their parents. As we will see in other periods of a child's life, development results from a complex interaction of biological, social, and behavioral changes. The notion of bio-social-behavioral shifts helps us to keep this important principle in mind.

SUMMING UP THE FIRST 2½ MONTHS

Looking back over the first 2½ months or so of postnatal life, we can see a remarkable set of changes in infants' behaviors. Babies are born with a rudimentary ability to interact with their new environment. They have reflexes that enable them to take in oxygen and nutrients and expel waste products. They are able to perceive objects, including people, although they tend to focus on only a part of the entire stimulus. They are sensitive to the sounds of human language, and they quickly develop a preference for the sound of their mothers' voices. Although they sleep most of the time, they are occasionally quite alert.

From the moment of birth, infants interact with and are supported by their parents or other caregivers, who come equipped with the biological and cultural resources necessary to see that their babies receive food and protection. Despite these resources, the first interactions of babies and their caregivers are tentative and somewhat uncoordinated. Within a matter of days, however, a process of mutual adjustment has begun that will provide an essential framework for later development.

The developmental changes that characterize the first 10 to 12 weeks have clear origins in biology and in both the physical and social environments. In the domain of biology, there is rapid maturation of the central nervous system, particularly in the connections between the brain stem and the cerebral cortex. As a consequence of frequent feeding, the baby grows bigger and stronger. As a consequence of practice at feeding, the elementary reflex of sucking becomes efficient nursing, an accomplishment that owes a good deal to the complementary efforts of the baby's caregivers, primarily the mother.

Between the ages of 2½ and 3 months, several lines of development that have been proceeding more or less independently now converge. The consequences are qualitatively different forms of behavior and a new type of social relationship between babies and their caregivers. The story of the development of the seemingly simple behavior of social smiling illustrates the intricate way in which these different lines of development must relate to one another for a transition to a qualitatively new level of development to occur:

1. Maturation of the visual system enables a new level of visual acuity and a new ability to analyze the visual field.
2. As a consequence, smiling, a seemingly unrelated behavior, may be transformed.
3. With the advent of social smiling, parents report that they experience a new sense of connectedness with their babies, and babies begin to express a new emotion, joy.

This transformation will take place only if the infant's caregivers provide proper feedback. Without appropriate feedback, as in the case of some blind children, social smiling does not develop. And if social smiling does not develop, the development of social interactions may be disrupted.

In later chapters we will see versions of this pattern repeated again and again. For a stretch of time the child's overall level of development remains stable while various systems undergo changes in relative isolation. Then there is a brief period during which these separate lines of development converge, resulting in a new level of organization with regard to the child's behaviors, the social reciprocity between child and caregiver, and the range of emotions that the child expresses. Later in life, it will not always be possible to identify the specific biological, social, and behavioral factors that contribute to the emergence of new stages of development with equal certainty and rigor. But as a means of keeping the whole child in mind, it is useful to always consider the various domains that enter into the process of developmental change.

The moment parents and their babies make eye contact is pleasurable for both parties.

SUMMARY

DEVELOPMENT OF THE BRAIN

- At birth the brain contains most of the cells (neurons) it will ever have, but it will become four times larger by adulthood.
- Increased size results primarily from an increase in the connections among neurons and increased myelination, which insulates axons and speeds transmission of impulses.
- Different parts of the brain develop at different rates throughout childhood. The brain stem, which initially controls most reflexes, is relatively mature at birth. Areas of the cortex that mature most rapidly following birth are the primary motor and sensory areas.

EARLIEST CAPACITIES

- Infants are born with remarkable sensory and behavioral capacities with which to experience and respond to their postnatal circumstances.
    1. Neonates are not able to hear sounds in the range of frequencies that are audible to older children and adults, but they display a special sensitivity to the basic sound categories of human language.
    2. Although infants are nearsighted, they systematically scan their surroundings and are sensitive to areas of high contrast between light and dark. They will track moving facelike forms at birth, and within a few days they seem to be able to distinguish their mothers' faces from others'.
    3. Neonates can distinguish various tastes and smells. They prefer sweet tastes, and their sense of smell is sufficiently acute that they can distinguish the smell of their mothers' milk from that of another woman's.
    4. The senses of touch, temperature, and position are relatively mature at birth.
- A variety of reflexes, or automatic responses to specific environmental events, are present at birth.
- At birth infants display at least two primary emotional states: contentment and distress. Many developmentalists believe that they also experience several basic emotions—joy, fear, anger, surprise, sadness, and interest—though there is some doubt about whether or not such emotions have the same quality as do those experienced by older children and adults.
- Individual variations in temperament—in style of response and dominant mood—are present at birth. Temperamental characteristics include activity level, irritability, intensity of reaction, response to novelty, and sociability. Individual differences in certain aspects of temperament may be relatively stable and thus may constitute an important source of developmental continuity.

BECOMING COORDINATED WITH THE SOCIAL WORLD

- The basic behavioral capacities with which infants are born are sufficient for their survival only if they are coordinated with adult caregiving activities.
- "Getting the baby on a schedule" is more than a convenience. By coordinating schedules, babies and their parents create a system of mutual expectations that supports further development.

- Newborn babies sleep approximately two-thirds of the time, but their periods of sleep are relatively brief and are distributed across all 24 hours of the day. When babies finally begin to sleep through the night depends in part on the sleep patterns of the adults who care for them, and those patterns vary from culture to culture.
- Newborn babies tend to eat about every 3 hours if they are given constant access to food. Babies fed only every 4 hours may have trouble adjusting to such a schedule, although most infants adopt a 4-hour schedule spontaneously by the time they reach 2½ months of age.
- Infants' crying is a primitive means of communication that evokes a strong emotional response in adults and alerts them that something may be wrong. Certain distinctive patterns of early cries may indicate difficulties.

MECHANISMS OF DEVELOPMENTAL CHANGE

- In the beginning, feeding is based on primitive reflex mechanisms that are not well coordinated. Within several weeks, this form of behavior is reorganized and becomes voluntary; the various constituent reflexes become integrated with one another, and the baby becomes well coordinated with the mother.
- The four basic perspectives on development can all be applied to the earliest forms of infant development; each emphasizes a different way in which biological and environmental factors contribute to early developmental change.
- According to the biological-maturation perspective, postnatal development follows the same principles as prenatal development. New structures are said to arise from endogenous (inherited) capabilities that unfold as the baby matures. Changes in nursing as well as in other behaviors, according to this view, result from such factors as the increased myelination of neurons and the growth of muscles.
- The maturation of brain structures contributes to the reorganization of early reflexes. Some of these early reflexes disappear completely within a few months of birth. Others may disappear and then reappear later as an element in a new form of activity. Still others remain and are transformed into voluntary behaviors under the control of the cerebral cortex.
- Environmental-learning theories assign the environment a leading role in the creation of new forms of behavior through the mechanism of learning.
- Infants' ability to learn from experience is present from the earliest days of life. Classical conditioning permits infants to form expectations about the connections between events in their environment. Operant conditioning provides a mechanism for the emergence of new behaviors as a consequence of the positive or negative events they produce. Some evidence indicates that young infants can exhibit some kinds of imitation, but it seems unlikely that imitation is an important mechanism of learning in the first months of life.
- Constructivist theories assign equal weight to biological and environmental factors in development. Reflexes, in this view, are coordinated patterns of action (schemas) that have differentiated from the more primitive state of global activity characteristic of the prenatal period.
- In the view of Jean Piaget, the leading constructivist of the twentieth century, developmental change is constructed through the interplay of

assimilation (modification of the input to fit existing schemas) and accommodation (modification of existing schemas to fit the input). The interplay of assimilation and accommodation continues until a new form of equilibrium between the two processes is reached. New forms of equilibrium constitute qualitatively new forms of behavior; they are new stages of development.

- According to Piaget, infancy is characterized by sensorimotor ways of knowing. He divides the sensorimotor period into six substages, the first two of which occur during the first 10 to 12 weeks of postnatal life:
  1. Substage 1 is characterized by the exercise of basic reflexes.
  2. Substage 2 is characterized by the beginning of accommodation and the prolongation of pleasant sensations arising from reflex actions.
- Careful observations of interactions between mothers and infants reveal that some part of the work that Piaget attributed to infants is in fact contributed by the people with whom they interact.
- Cultural-context theories of development emphasize the active roles of both the child and the people around the child, as well as the historically accumulated "designs for living," as contributors to the process of developmental change.
- Significant and pervasive cultural variations in parents' everyday activities and their interactions with their newborn children influence both short-term and long-term development.

INTEGRATING THE SEPARATE THREADS OF DEVELOPMENT

- In order to explain development, it is necessary to understand how different parts of the process change with respect to each other, as parts of an integrated bio-social-behavioral system in its cultural context.

THE FIRST POSTNATAL BIO-SOCIAL-BEHAVIORAL SHIFT

- At approximately 2½ months of age a bio-social-behavioral shift occurs in the overall organization of infants' behavior. Changes in brain function owing to maturation are accompanied by increased visual acuity and the ability to perceive the forms of objects and people, increased wakefulness, and social smiling. Caregivers respond with new feelings of connectedness to the infant.

KEY TERMS

accommodation, p. 161
adaptation, p. 161
assimilation, p. 161
axon, p. 129
brain stem, p. 130
cerebral cortex, p. 130
classical conditioning, p. 156
conditional response (CR), p. 156
conditional stimulus (CS), p. 156
dendrite, p. 129
dishabituation, p. 133
emotion, p. 142
equilibration, p. 162
habituation, p. 133
learning, p. 155
myelin, p. 129
neuron, p. 129
neurotransmitter, p. 129
operant conditioning, p. 158
phonemes, p. 133
primary circular reactions, p. 164
primary motor area, p. 132
primary sensory areas, p. 132
reflex, p. 139
reinforcement, p. 158
schema, p. 160
sensorimotor stage, p. 162
spinal cord, p. 130
synapse, p. 129
temperament, p. 144
unconditional response (UCR), p. 156
unconditional stimulus (UCS), p. 156

THOUGHT QUESTIONS

1. In the quote at the chapter's opening, Erik Erikson writes, "Babies control and bring up their families as much as they are controlled by them." Explain this statement.
2. Many years ago William James characterized infants' perceptual world as a "buzzing, blooming confusion." How does this description fare in light of recent research on the perceptual world of the young infant?
3. What is the developmental significance of "getting on a schedule"?
4. List the ways in which neonatal development is continuous with development before birth. List the ways in which it is discontinuous.
5. Explain the development of social smiling at 2½ to 3 months of age. Why is this development a good example of a bio-social-behavioral shift?

CHAPTER 5

The Achievements of the First Year

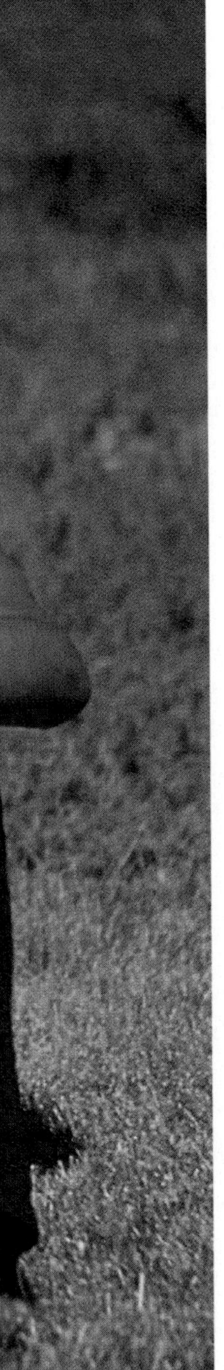

BIOLOGICAL CHANGES
- Size and Shape
- Muscle and Bone
- The Brain

PERCEPTUAL-MOTOR DEVELOPMENT
- Reaching and Grasping
- Locomotion

COGNITIVE CHANGES
- Piaget's Constructivist Explanation
- Are Infants Precocious? Challenges to Piaget's Theory
- Assessing the Evidence for Infant Precocity
- Categorizing: Knowledge about Kinds of Things
- The Growth of Memory
- Recall and Wariness: Evidence for a Developmental Discontinuity?

A NEW RELATIONSHIP WITH THE SOCIAL WORLD
- The Role of Uncertainty in Wariness
- A New Form of Emotional Relationship
- The Changing Nature of Communication

A NEW BIO-SOCIAL-BEHAVIORAL SHIFT

The question . . . is not where or when mind begins. Mind in some . . . form is there from the start, wherever "there" may be.

Jerome Bruner, *In Search of Mind*

Two neighbors—Jake, who is about to celebrate his first birthday, and his mother, Barbara—have been out for a walk and have stopped by our house. Sheila is in the kitchen preparing dinner. Jake is sitting on his mother's lap at the kitchen table, drinking apple juice from a plastic cup while the two women chat.

Jake finishes his juice, some of which has dribbled onto his shirt, and puts the cup down on the table with a satisfied bang. He squirms around in his mother's lap so that he is facing her. He tries to get her attention by pulling at her face. When Barbara ignores him, Jake wriggles out of her lap to the floor, where he notices the dog.

"Wuff wuff," he says excitedly, pointing at the dog.

"Doggie," Barbara says. "What does the doggie say, Jake?"

"Wuff wuff," Jake repeats, still staring at the dog.

Following his pointing finger, Jake toddles toward the dog. His walk has a drunken, side-to-side quality, and he has a hard time bringing himself to a stop. Barbara grabs hold of Jake's extended hand, redirecting it from the dog's eyes.

"Pat the doggie, Jake."

Jake pats the dog's head.

The dog does not like the attention and escapes into the living room. Jake toddles after her like a pull toy on an invisible string. The dog leads him back into the kitchen, where Jake bumps into Sheila's legs and falls to a sitting position.

"Well, hello, Jake," Sheila says, as she bends over and picks him up. "Did you fall down? Go boom?"

Jake, who until now hasn't taken his eyes off the dog, turns, looks at Sheila with a smile, and points at the dog. "Wuff wuff," he repeats.

Then Jake's body suddenly stiffens. He stares searchingly at Sheila's face for an instant, then turns his head away and holds his arms out to his mother.

Sheila hands Jake to Barbara, who says, "Did you get scared? It's only Sheila."

But Jake eyes Sheila warily and hides in his mother's arms for several minutes.

At almost 1 year of age, Jake behaves far differently than a baby of 2½ months. At that early age, Jake's main activities were eating, sleeping, and gazing around the room. He could hold his head up and turn it from side to side, but he could not readily reach out and grasp objects or move around on his own. He took an interest in mobiles and other objects when they were immediately in front of him, but he quickly lost interest in them when they were removed from his view. Although he seemed most comfortable with his mother, he did not seem particularly unhappy when he was cared for by someone else. His communications were restricted to cries, frowns, and smiles.

The contrast between Jake's behavior then and his behavior at 1 year gives us a picture of some of the amazing changes that occur in the first year of infancy and that present a challenge to the developmentalists who seek to explain them. Perhaps most obvious are the outwardly visible biological changes (see Figure 5.1). Infants are markedly larger and stronger at 12 months than at 2½ months. Invisible but essential maturation has also taken place in the nervous system, particularly the cerebral cortex and other parts of the brain.

Largely as a result of these changes, infants exhibit notable increases in mobility and coordination. At 3 months infants are just beginning to be able to roll over. Their parents know that they will remain more or less wherever they are put down. At about 7 to 8 months they begin to crawl, and at about 1 year they begin to walk. All during this period, infants also become much more adept at reaching for objects and grasping them. They prod, bang, squeeze, push, and pull almost anything they can get their hands on, and they often put objects into their mouths to learn about them. This combination of increasing mobility and curiosity means that parents must be constantly on guard lest infants harm themselves or destroy things.

FIGURE 5.1
The differences in size, strength, shape, and motor control between small infants and babies in their second year are evident in the contrast between the infant supported in this mother's arms and the older infant beginning to use a mortar and pestle.

As infants near their first birthdays, they also exhibit important changes in their cognitive abilities. They learn more rapidly and remember what they have learned for longer periods of time. They have expanded the rudimentary categories they use to interpret their experience and guide their actions to an astonishing degree. They anticipate the course of simple, familiar behavioral routines, and they act surprised if their expectations are violated. This new understanding of events makes it possible for them to play simple games such as peekaboo.

Finally, the social and emotional relationship between infants and their caregivers undergoes distinctive changes toward the end of the first year. Infants become upset when they are separated from their caregivers, and sometimes they are wary of strangers, as Jake was when he noticed Sheila. They also begin to check their caregivers' facial expressions for indications of how to behave in uncertain situations. These changes are accompanied by the ability to comprehend a few words, extending the ways in which they can maintain contact with their caregivers.

As we shall see, these changes in biological makeup, motor behavior, cognitive capacities, range of emotions, and forms of social relationship converge to produce another bio-social-behavioral shift in development as babies approach their first birthdays. The new qualities that emerge from this reorganization of developmental processes provide the context for further changes that will bring children to the end of infancy.

BIOLOGICAL CHANGES

The extensive changes that occur in babies' motor behavior and cognitive abilities between the ages of 2½ months and 1 year depend on changes in their body proportions, muscles, bones, and brains.

SIZE AND SHAPE

During their first year, most healthy babies triple in weight and grow approximately 10 inches, with the typical 1-year-old in the United States weighing about 20 pounds and standing 28 to 30 inches tall. As Figure 5.2 shows, the rate of physical growth is greatest in the first months after birth; it then

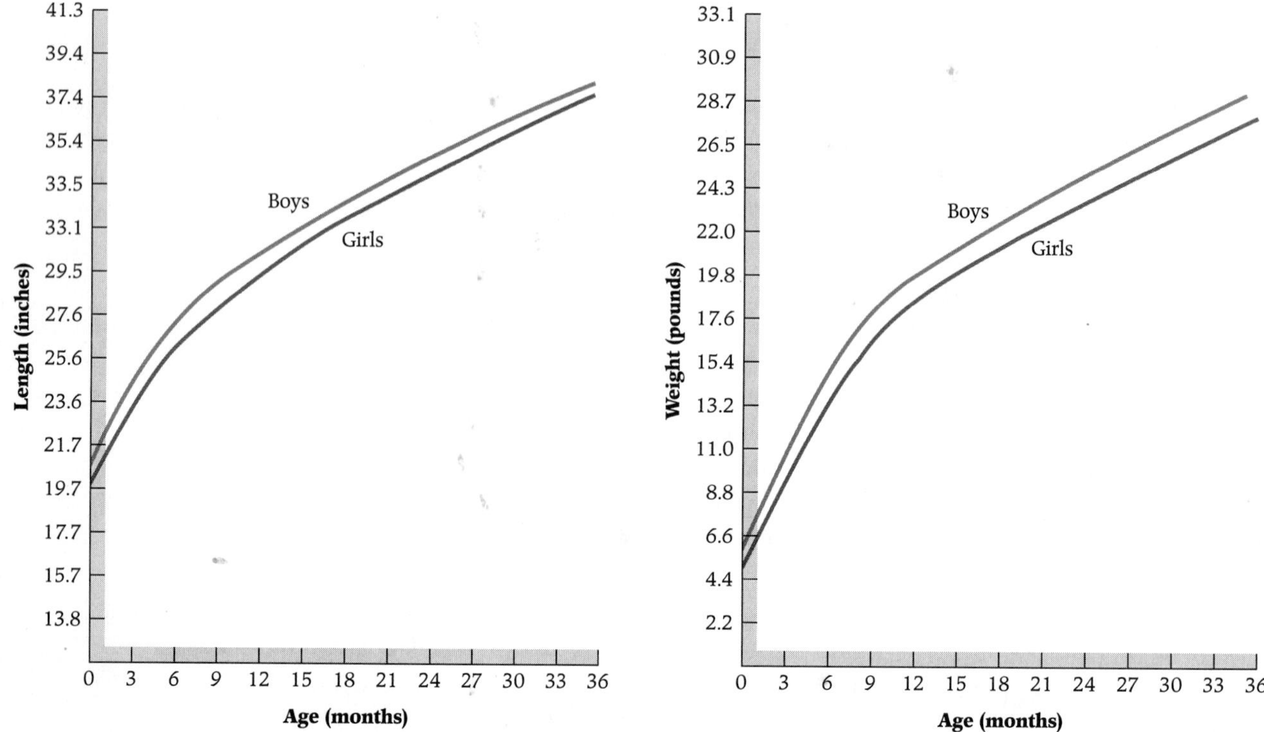

FIGURE 5.2

Babies' lengths roughly double and their weights increase by five or six times during the first 3 years of life. (From the U.S. Department of Health, Education, and Welfare, National Center for Health Statistics, 1976.)

gradually tapers off through the rest of infancy and childhood until adolescence, when there is another growth spurt.

The rates at which individual children normally grow vary widely (Tanner, 1990). Many factors contribute to the variations in size and shape, ranging from children's diet, genetic constitution, and socioeconomic status to their exposure to sunlight (which is necessary for the production of vitamin D) (Johnson et al., 1973).

Increases in babies' height and weight are accompanied by changes in their body proportions (see Figure 5.3). At birth the baby's head is 70 percent of its adult size and accounts for about 25 percent of the baby's total length. At 1 year of age the head will account for 20 percent of body length, and by adulthood, 12 percent. Infants' legs at birth are not much longer than their heads. By adulthood the legs account for about half of a person's total height. One key effect of these changes in body proportions is a lower center of gravity by about 12 months of age, making it easier for the child to balance on two legs and begin to walk (Thelen, 1995).

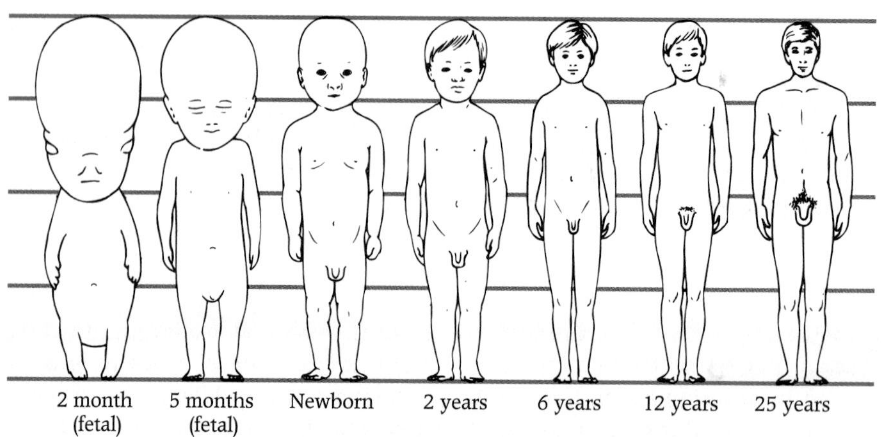

FIGURE 5.3

The proportions of body length accounted for by the head, trunk, and legs at different stages of development. During the fetal period, the head accounts for as much as 50 percent of body length. The head decreases from 25 percent of body length at birth to 12 percent in adulthood. (From Robbins et al., 1929.)

MUSCLE AND BONE

As babies grow, the bones and muscles needed to support their increasing bulk and mobility undergo corresponding growth. Most of a newborn's bones are relatively soft, and they harden only gradually as minerals are deposited in them in the months after birth. The bones in the hand and wrist are among the first to ossify (Tanner, 1990). They harden by the end of the first year, making it easier for a baby to grasp objects, pick them up, and play with them.

At the same time, infants' muscles increase in length and thickness, a process that will continue throughout childhood and into late adolescence. In infancy, increases in muscle mass are closely associated with the development of the baby's ability to stand alone and walk.

Sex Differences in Rate of Growth

Research supports the common wisdom that girls mature faster than boys. In fact, sex differences in growth rate are apparent even before birth. Halfway through the prenatal period, the skeletons of female fetuses are some 3 weeks more advanced in development than those of male fetuses. At birth, X rays of the growth centers (*epiphyses*) at the ends of bones show that the female's skeleton is 4 to 6 weeks more mature than the male's, and by puberty it is 2 years more advanced. Girls are more advanced in the development of other organ systems as well. Girls get their permanent teeth, go through puberty, and reach their full body size earlier than boys (Tanner, 1990). The earlier maturation of females is a characteristic human beings share with many other mammals.

THE BRAIN

The entire nervous system continues to grow in size and complexity between the ages of 3 and 12 months. Especially noteworthy is an increase in the number of synapses, which reach a level of density roughly double what it will be by early adolescence. This growth in synaptic density is so rapid and extensive that it has been given a special name, **exuberant synaptogenesis** (Huttenlocher & Dabholkar, 1997). Developmentalists believe that the brain massively overproduces synapses and that, over time, these synapses are either selectively reinforced or eliminated, depending on the individual's experience. This idea fits closely with the Darwinian idea that evolution proceeds by a process of random reproduction and subsequent natural selection. As a result of the early overproduction of synapses, infants are prepared to establish neural connections for virtually any kind of experience they may have. Over time, the environment makes its contribution: synapses that are regularly used flourish and are strengthened, while those that go unused are gradually "pruned away"—that is, they atrophy and die off.

The rate of brain development differs according to the region of the brain in question (Huttenlocher & Dabholkar, 1997; Johnson, 1998). At 2½ to 4 months of age, the visual cortex undergoes an explosive surge in the creation of new synapses. This proliferation of new synapses appears crucial to the changes associated with the first bio-social-behavioral shift at 2½ to 3 months of age (see Chapter 4, p. 170). Similar changes occur in the other areas of the brain, but more slowly. In the motor cortex a spurt in the formation of new synapses at approximately the age of 6 months accompanies changes in coordinated reaching and leg movements. A variety of evidence indicates that roughly between 7 and 9 months of age there is a spurt in frontal cortex development that is reflected by increases in various measures of brain-wave activity. The prefrontal area of the cortex plays a particularly important role in the development of voluntary behavior. When this area begins to function in

exuberant synaptogenesis The rapid growth in synaptic density that occurs between 3 and 12 months of age.

a new way sometime between 7 and 9 months, infants' ability to regulate themselves increases and they can, for example, stop themselves from grabbing the first attractive thing they see. With the emerging ability to inhibit action, they can also better control what they attend to (Harman & Fox, 1997). In effect, they begin to be able to stop and think (Diamond et al., 1994).

PERCEPTUAL-MOTOR DEVELOPMENT

One of the most dramatic developments of the first year of life is the enormous increase in infants' ability to explore their environment by looking at it, moving around in it, listening to it, and manipulating it. Perceiving and acting are intimately connected. It would be nearly impossible for babies to move from one place to another, for example, if their coordinated motor actions were not constantly modulated by perceptual information about the layout of the environment and their spatial orientation. Infants, no less than adults, perceive in order to obtain information about how to act and then act in order to obtain more information (Gibson, 1997).

FIGURE 5.4
(Top) In the first months after birth, eye–hand coordination takes effort. (Bottom) Only after a few months of attention and practice can infants perform such complex actions as eating with a spoon.

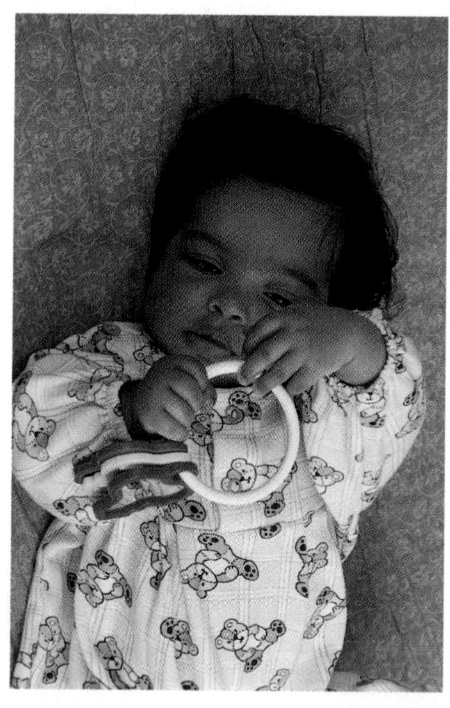

REACHING AND GRASPING

In Chapter 4 (pp. 154–155) we saw evidence that shortly after birth, perception and action are linked—when infants perceive an object moving in front of them, they reach for it. At first the perceptions and actions involved in reaching and grasping are not yet coordinated. Infants may reach for an object but fail to close their hands around it, usually because they close their hands too soon. Then, as a part of the bio-social-behavioral shift at about 2½ months, babies begin to gain voluntary control over their movements when they reach for an object. At the same time, reaching and grasping begin to become coordinated in the proper sequence. At first, the coordination necessary for reaching and grasping successfully requires concentration, and babies are likely to glance back and forth between the objects they wish to grasp and their hands. With practice, their perceptual-motor coordination gradually improves, although there are marked individual differences in the rapidity and vigor of their reaching movements (Thelen et al., 1993; Von Hofsten, 1992) (see Figure 5.4). At about 5 months of age, infants can gauge when an object is beyond their reach, and they no longer attempt to reach for it (Yonas & Hartman, 1993). By the time they are 9 months old, most babies can guide their movements with a single glance, and the movements they use to reach for and grasp objects look as well integrated and automatic as a reflex (Mathew & Cook, 1990). This is the time when caretakers need to "babyproof" their homes by putting dangerous or fragile objects out of the infant's reach. They also have to watch out for the sudden appearance of unexpected items in the grocery cart if the baby is along for the ride.

In the period between 7 and 12 months of age, fine motor movements of the hands and fingers become notably more subtle and better coordinated. As Figure 5.5 indicates, 7-month-olds are still unable to use their thumbs in opposition to their fingers to pick up objects, but by 12 months they are able to move their thumbs and other fingers into positions appropriate to the size of the object they are trying to grasp. As their reaching and grasping become better coordinated and more precise, their explorations of objects become more refined. In addition, they become increasingly able to perform more complicated action sequences, such as drinking from a cup, eating with a spoon, and picking raisins out of a box (Connolly & Dalgleish, 1989).

Rachel Karniol (1989) found that there is an invariable sequence in the way babies manipulate objects as their fine motor skills increase during the first 9 months of life. They begin by simply rotating an object, then progress to moving it, shaking it, and holding it with one and then two hands, until they can use it as part of a sequence of actions to achieve a goal such as placing a block into a hole in a box. Such sequences provide classic cases for theories that view development as a sequence of qualitative changes in the organization of the biology and behavior of the child.

With respect to the exploratory behaviors themselves, Eleanor Gibson (1988) points out that as babies gain control over their hands, different objects invite them to explore in different ways: "Things can be displaced, banged, shaken, squeezed, and thrown—actions that have informative consequences about an object's properties" (p. 20). In Gibson's view, the environment "affords" different ways for babies to use the perceptual and action systems that are a part of their species heritage in the service of their own development. Babies appear to perceive that different objects offer different **affordances,** that is, properties that support, or "lend themselves" to, particular ways of interacting with them. Consider the affordances of two objects often given to infants, rattles and soft dolls. Rattles lend themselves to making noises, while soft dolls lend themselves to pleasurable touching. It is no surprise, then, that an infant is more likely to imitate its mother when she shakes a rattle or rubs a cloth doll against her cheek than when she shakes the doll and rubs the rattle against her cheek (Von Hofsten & Siddiqui, 1993).

Studies of the development of reaching and grasping leave little doubt that the importance of babies' increasing skills goes beyond the capacity to grab hold of things. Perceptual-motor exploration is an all-important way to find out about the environment and to gain control over it.

28 weeks

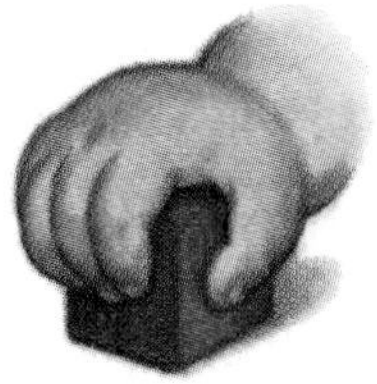

36 weeks

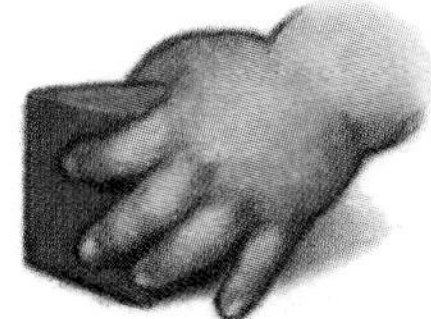

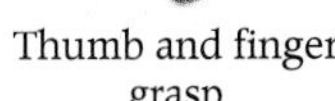

Thumb and finger grasp

Scissors grasp

52 weeks

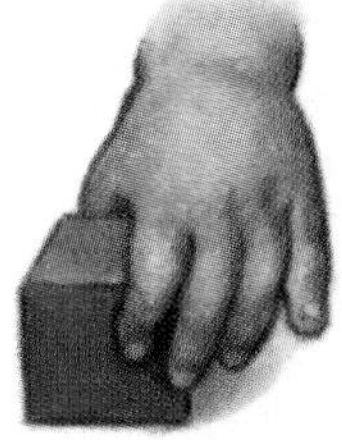

FIGURE 5.5

Babies find ways to grasp objects from an early age, but good coordination of the thumb and forefinger requires at least a year to achieve. (Adapted from Halverson, 1931.)

LOCOMOTION

Progress in **locomotion,** the ability to move around on one's own, is central to the pattern of developmental changes that occur toward the end of the first year of postnatal life. The ability to get around on their own separates infants from their caregivers in a distinctive way that changes the basic conditions for their further development. It also provides them with a wider field for exploration of the objects in their environment, which they can now approach or crawl away from, touch and push away.

Before infants can move around the environment effectively, however, they must be able to integrate the movements of many parts of their bodies. Crawling, babies' first effective way of getting around, takes a few months to develop and progresses through phases (see Figure 5.6). During the first month of life, when movements appear to be controlled primarily by subcortical reflexes, infants may occasionally creep short distances, propelled by the rhythmic pushing movements of their toes or knees. At about 2 months of age this reflexive pushing disappears, but it will be another 5 or 6 months before babies can crawl about on their hands and knees (Adolph et al., 1998; Gesell & Ames, 1940).

Although they can hold up their heads from about 2 months of age, young infants still have difficulty moving their arms in a coordinated way. Karniol (1989) places this milestone at about the end of the third month. Once they have managed to coordinate their arm movements, babies can wiggle along. Slightly later they can get on their hands and knees, but having reached such heights, all that some can do is rock back and forth because their arms and legs are not yet working in a coordinated way. A little later they may be

affordances Properties of an object that support, or lend themselves, to particular ways of interacting with that object.

locomotion The ability to move around on one's own.

FIGURE 5.6
Phases in the development of creeping and crawling. (a) Newborns creep by making pushing movements with their knees and toes. (b) The head can be held up, but leg movements diminish. (c) Control over movement of head and shoulders has increased. (d) Ability to support the upper body with the arms improves. (e) Babies have difficulty coordinating shoulders and midsection; when the midsection is raised, the head lowers. (f) Babies can keep the midsection raised, but they are unable to coordinate arm and leg movements, so they tend to rock back and forth. (g) Coordinated arm and leg movements enable the baby to crawl. (From McGraw, 1975.)

able to actually move, but they are as likely to move backward as forward. Most infants can crawl on regular surfaces with some skill by the time they are 8 to 9 months of age. Some achieve this milestone without first belly crawling, but if they do not go through this intermediate experience, it takes them longer to gain coordination (Adolph et al., 1998). By whatever route, when the various components of crawling are knitted into the well-coordinated action of

TABLE 5.1 AGE (IN MONTHS) AT WHICH INFANTS REACH MILESTONES IN MOTOR DEVELOPMENT

	Percentage That Have Reached Milestone			
Motor Milestone	**25%**	**50%**	**75%**	**90%**
Lifts head up	1.3	2.2	2.6	3.2
Rolls over	2.3	2.8	3.8	4.7
Sits without support	4.8	5.5	6.5	7.8
Pulls self to stand	6.0	7.6	9.5	10.0
Walks holding on to furniture	7.3	9.2	10.2	12.7
Walks well	11.3	12.1	13.3	14.3
Walks up steps	14.0	17.0	21.0	22.0
Kicks ball forward	15.0	20.0	22.3	24.0

Source: Frankenburg et al., 1992.

cognitive processes Psychological processes through which children acquire, store, and use knowledge about the world.

the whole body, infants explore their environment in a new way, acquiring new information about the world and how to get along in it.

Babies usually do not master walking until several months after they begin to crawl. As we will see in Chapter 6, the transition from crawling to walking requires a reorganization of component skills that is even more complex than the one involved in the transformation from creeping to crawling.

The ages at which U.S. children achieve various other milestones in motor development are shown in Table 5.1 (Frankenburg & Dodds, 1967). Note the wide variations in the ages at which normal children are able to perform the various behaviors. Although 50 percent of the babies studied could walk by the time they were just over 1 year old, for example, some 10 percent were still not walking 2 months later (Box 5.1).

Babies who are just beginning to stand up find other people and furniture to be handy aids. (top) The Filipino baby who lives in a house on stilts is being trained at an early age in the essential skill of climbing a ladder. (bottom) Here a Balinese child is holding on to the anthropologist Margaret Mead.

COGNITIVE CHANGES

Just as most psychologists once believed that newborns experience the world as a confusing jumble of sensations, so they believed that children's **cognitive processes**—psychological processes through which children acquire, store, and use knowledge about the world—are built up slowly over the course of infancy and early childhood. Certainly there is pervasive evidence that between 3 and 12 months of age infants are acquiring a greater ability to manipulate objects in their environments, to think systematically about their surroundings, and to remember their experiences. However, developmental psychologists are currently deeply divided in their views about the ages at which infants acquire various cognitive milestones. Their disagreements reflect uncertainty both about the best methods to assess cognitive changes and about the sources and nature of cognitive development itself.

PIAGET'S CONSTRUCTIVIST EXPLANATION

As we saw in Chapter 4, Piaget held that children come to know the world by acting on it. In his terms, children actively seek to *assimilate* their experiences to fit their existing action schemas (the forms in which their knowledge is currently structured). To the extent that their experiences do not fit existing schemas, they must *accommodate* those schemas by modifying them to accord with the environmental realities they encounter. According to Piaget, through the interplay between assimilation and accommodation children actively construct higher levels of cognitive development.

Sensorimotor Development

Recall that in Piaget's constructivist framework there are four major stages of cognitive development. Piaget referred to infancy as the stage of *sensorimotor development,* the stage in which, he believed, children acquire knowledge exclusively through sensorimotor actions. He combined the terms "sensory" and "motor" to emphasize the intimate relationship between sensing the world and acting upon it. Each influences the other: what we perceive depends on what we are doing, and what we do depends on what we perceive (Piaget, 1973).

In order to understand Piaget's depiction of sensorimotor development, it is important to keep in mind his central idea that the endpoint of all cognitive stages is a qualitatively new way of knowing about the world. The endpoint of sensorimotor development is the ability to picture the world mentally and think about it without having to act upon

BOX 5.1

The Role of Practice in Motor Development

Studies of motor development were among psychologists' earliest strategies for discovering the relative roles of nature and nurture in development. During the 1930s and 1940s, it was commonly believed that learning and experience played little or no role in the development of such motor milestones as sitting and walking. One of the studies widely cited to bolster this view was conducted by Wayne and Margaret Dennis (1940) among Hopi families in the southwestern United States. In traditional Hopi families, babies were wrapped up tightly and strapped to a flat cradle board for the first several months of life. They were unwrapped only once or twice a day so that they could be washed and their clothes changed. The wrapping permitted very little movement of the arms and legs and no practice in such complex movements as rolling over. When the Dennises compared the motor development of traditionally raised Hopi babies with that of babies of less traditional parents who did not use cradle boards, they found that the two groups of babies did not differ in the age at which they began to walk by themselves. This finding was consistent with the notion that basic motor skills do not depend on practice for their development.

Observations of babies from other cultural settings, however, provide some evidence that practice can have an effect on the age at which babies reach universal motor milestones. Charles Super (1976) reports that among the Kipsigis people of rural Kenya, parents begin to teach their babies to sit up, stand, and walk shortly after birth. In teaching their children to sit up,

At the age of 7 months, 29 days, Parks Bonifay is water-skiing. Although early practice can speed up motor development in infancy, it does not seem to affect basic motor skills in the long term.

it first. He called this new way of knowing *representation*. Piaget believed that representation begins to emerge at about 8 months of age but does not become fully developed until 18 to 24 months of age. As we shall see, the question of when and how representation arises is a major point of contention among competing theories of cognitive development during infancy and beyond.

In Chapter 4 (p. 162) we described the first two sensorimotor substages. During substages 1 and 2 infants progress from diffuse movement and simple reflex activity to the ability to prolong actions they find pleasurable (*primary* circular reactions). In the first substage, self and world are still undifferentiated; that is, infants have no awareness of the world as separate from themselves. Even at the end of the second substage, infants appear to have little or no understanding that their actions are separate from the environment. Piaget believed that it is between the ages of 4 or 5 months and 12 months that infants start to form an idea of an external reality, and this idea enables them to relate to the objects and people in their world in a new way. This cognitive growth occurs as they complete substages 3 and 4 of sensorimotor development (see Table 5.2). (Substages 5 and 6 will be taken up in Chapter 6.)

Substage 3: Secondary Circular Reactions (4 to 8 months) In substage 3, infants are no longer restricted to the maintenance and modification of reflex or body-centered actions. Now they direct their attention to the external world—to objects and outcomes. This interest in things external gives rise to characteristic activity observed in infants during substage 3—the repetition of actions that produce interesting changes in the environment. Piaget termed for example, Kipsigis parents seat their babies in shallow holes in the ground that they have dug to support the infants' backs, or they nestle blankets around them to hold them upright. They repeat such procedures daily until the babies can sit up quite well by themselves. Training in walking begins in the eighth week. The babies are held under the arms with their feet touching the ground and are gradually propelled forward. Kipsigis babies reach the developmental milestones of sitting 5 weeks earlier and walking 3 weeks earlier, on the average, than babies in the United States. At the same time, they are not advanced in skills they have not been taught or have not practiced. They learn to roll over or crawl no faster than American children, and they lag behind American children in their ability to negotiate stairs. Similar results have been reported among West Indian children, whose caregivers put them through a culturally prescribed sequence of motor exercises during the early months of infancy (Hopkins & Westen, 1988).

Further evidence for the impact that practice—or the lack of it—can have on early motor development comes from the Ache, a nomadic people living in the rain forest of eastern Paraguay. Hilliard Kaplan and Heather Dove (1987) report that Ache children under 3 years of age spend 80 to 100 percent of their time in direct physical contact with their caregivers and are almost never seen more than 3 feet away from them. A major reason is that Ache, who move around in small hunter-gatherer groups, do not create clearings in the forest when they stop to make camp. Rather, they remove just enough ground cover to make room to sit down, leaving roots, trees, and bushes more or less where they found them. For safety's sake, caregivers either carry their infants or keep them within arm's reach. As a result of these restrictions on their movement, Ache infants are markedly slower to acquire gross motor skills such as walking than are North American infants. They begin walking, for example, at about 23 months of age, almost a full year later than children in the United States.

At about the age of 5, however, when Ache children are deemed old enough to be allowed to move around on their own, they begin to spend many hours in complex play activities that serve to increase their motor skills. Within a few years they are skilled at scaling tall trees and at cutting vines and branches while they balance high above the ground in a manner that bespeaks normal, perhaps even exceptional, perceptual-motor skills.

Although special early practice does not appear to have any long-term advantages in the development of basic motor skills, as anyone knows who has tried some unfamiliar sport, or tried to play the violin, specialized motor skills are not acquired without extensive practice and in some cases years of instruction as well. In recognition of this fact, specialized training in highly valued skills, such as playing a musical instrument or dancing, is begun quite early in many cultures, producing high levels of proficiency.

these new actions **secondary circular reactions** because the focus of action is on objects external to the infant. He noted that such reactions depend on the kind of coordination of seeing, reaching, and grasping discussed earlier in this chapter (p. 184). When babies in this substage accidentally discover that a particular action, like squeezing a rubber toy, produces an interesting effect, like squeaking, they will repeat the action again and again to produce the effect. Similarly, when babies vocalize by cooing or gurgling and a caregiver responds, they will repeat the sound they made. In each case, the reaction is not only secondary but circular—it produces its own feedback. This circularity remains a central feature of all interactions between children and their environments from this stage on.

The change from primary circular reactions to secondary circular reactions indicated to Piaget that infants are beginning to realize that objects are more than extensions of their own actions. In this substage, however, babies still have only rudimentary notions of objects and space, and their discoveries about the world seem to have an accidental quality.

Substage 4: Coordination of Secondary Circular Reactions (8 to 12 months) The hallmark of the fourth sensorimotor substage is the emergence of the ability to engage in behaviors directed toward achieving a goal, which Piaget referred to as **intentionality.** Rather than being limited to the accidental object-oriented actions characteristic of the prior substage, infants in substage 4 can coordinate elementary schemas in order to achieve something they want. Piaget believed that this ability to coordinate two schemas with each other in the service of achieving a goal is the earliest form of true problem solving.

secondary circular reactions The behavior characteristic of the third substage of Piaget's sensorimotor stage in which babies repeat actions to produce interesting changes in their environment.

intentionality The ability to engage in behaviors directed toward achieving a goal.

TABLE 5.2 PIAGET'S STAGES OF COGNITIVE DEVELOPMENT AND THE SENSORIMOTOR SUBSTAGES

Age (years)	Stage	Description	Characteristics of Sensorimotor Substage
Birth to 2	**SENSORIMOTOR**	Infants' achievements consist largely of coordinating their sensory perceptions and simple motor behaviors. As they move through the six substages of this period, infants come to recognize the existence of a world outside themselves and begin to interact with it in deliberate ways.	**Substage 1 (0–1½ months)** *Reflex schemas exercised:* involuntary rooting, sucking, grasping, looking **Substage 2 (1½–4 months)** *Primary circular reactions:* repetition of actions that are pleasurable in themselves **Substage 3 (4–8 months)** *Secondary circular reactions:* dawning awareness of the effects of one's own actions on the environment; extended actions that produce interesting change in the environment **Substage 4 (8–12 months)** *Coordination of secondary circular reactions:* combining schemas to achieve a desired effect; earliest form of problem solving **Substage 5 (12–18 months)** *Tertiary circular reactions:* deliberate variation of problem-solving means; experimentation to see what the consequences will be **Substage 6 (18–24 months)** *Beginnings of symbolic representation:* images and words come to stand for familiar objects; invention of new means of problem solving through symbolic combinations
2 to 6	PREOPERATIONAL	Young children can represent reality to themselves through the use of symbols, including mental images, words, and gestures. Still, children often fail to distinguish their point of view from that of others, become easily captured by surface appearances, and are often confused about causal relations.	
6 to 12	CONCRETE OPERATIONAL	As they enter middle childhood, children become capable of mental operations, internalized actions that fit into a logical system. Operational thinking allows children mentally to combine, separate, order, and transform objects and actions. Such operations are considered concrete because they are carried out in the presence of the objects and events being thought about.	
12 to 19	FORMAL OPERATIONAL	In adolescence the developing person acquires the ability to think systematically about all logical relations within a problem. Adolescents display keen interest in abstract ideas and in the process of thinking itself.	

Piaget's son Laurent provided a demonstration of intentionality when he was 10 months old. Piaget had given him a small tin container, which Laurent dropped and picked up repeatedly (a secondary circular reaction characteristic of behavior in substage 3). Piaget then placed a washbasin a short distance from Laurent and struck it with the tin box, producing an interesting sound. From earlier observations, Piaget knew that Laurent would repeatedly bang on the basin to make the interesting sound occur (another typical secondary circular reaction). This time Piaget wanted to see if Laurent would combine the newly acquired "dropping the tin box" schema with the previously acquired "make an interesting sound" schema. Here is his report of Laurent's behavior:

> Now, at once, Laurent takes possession of the tin, holds out his arm and drops it over the basin. I moved the latter as a check. He nevertheless succeeded, several times in succession, in making the object fall on the basin. Hence this is a fine ex-

ample of the coordination of two schemas of which the first serves as a "means" whereas the second assigns an end to the action. (Piaget, 1952b, p. 255)

As a result of traversing substages 3 and 4 of sensorimotor intelligence, infants have become capable of intentional action directed at objects and people around them.

object permanence The understanding that objects have substance, maintain their identities when they change location, and ordinarily continue to exist when out of sight.

Object Permanence: The Growth of Representation

As noted earlier, the endpoint of sensorimotor development is representational thought, the ability to picture the world and act on it mentally. According to Piaget, representation begins to emerge in substage 4, in the form of **object permanence.** To adults, object permanence is the understanding that objects have substance, maintain their identities when they change location, and ordinarily continue to exist when they are out of sight. Piaget maintained that until substage 4 of sensorimotor development, infants lack object permanence entirely and therefore cannot keep absent objects in mind. Consequently, they experience the world of objects as a flow of discontinuous "pictures" that are constantly being "annihilated and resurrected." It is a world in which objects come and go from the infant's line of sight, each as "a mere image which reenters the void as soon as it vanishes, and emerges from it for no apparent reason" (Piaget, 1954, p. 11). If we interpret him literally, Piaget believed that until babies understand that an object exists when they are not perceiving it, out of sight is literally out of mind.

Evidence that children cannot keep absent objects in mind comes from observations of 5- and 6-month-old babies, as the following cases illustrate:

- *Observation 1.* A baby seated at a table is offered a soft toy. He grasps it. While he is still engrossed in the toy, the experimenter takes it from him and places it on the table behind a screen. The baby may begin to reach for the toy, but as soon as it disappears from sight he stops short, stares for a moment, and then looks away without attempting to move the screen (see Figure 5.7) (Piaget, 1954).
- *Observation 2.* A baby is placed in an infant seat in a bare laboratory room. Her mother, who has been playing with her, disappears for a moment. When the mother reappears, the baby sees three of her, an illusion the experimenter has created through the use of carefully arranged mirrors. The baby displays no surprise as she babbles happily to her multiple mother (Bower, 1982).

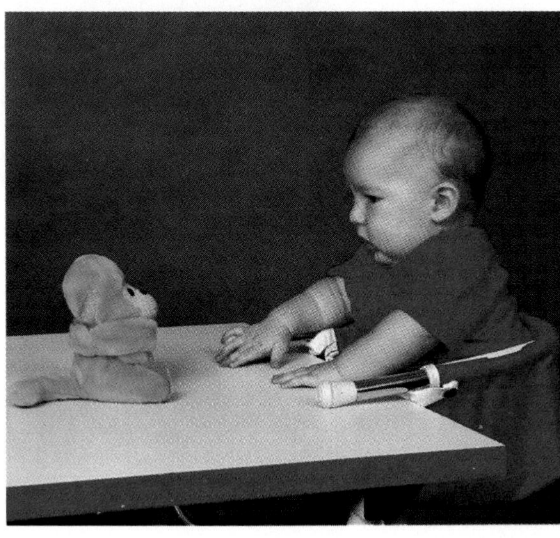

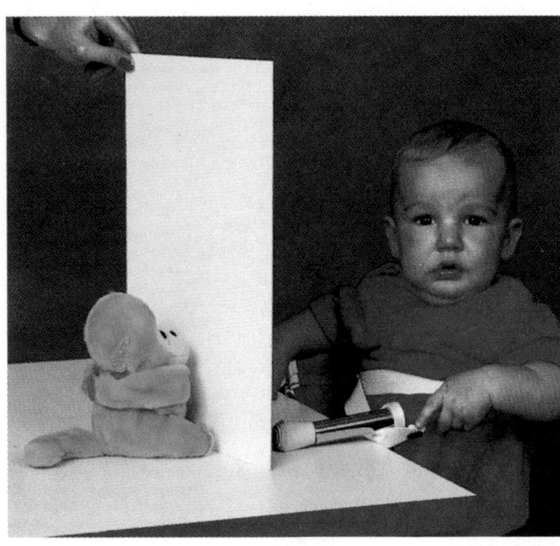

FIGURE 5.7 *Instead of searching behind the screen when his toy disappears, this infant looks dumbfounded. This kind of behavior led Piaget to conclude that objects no longer in view cease to exist for infants younger than 8 months of age.*

- *Observation 3.* From the comfort of his mother's lap, a baby follows a toy train with his eyes as it chugs along a track (see Figure 5.8). When the train disappears into a tunnel, the child's eyes remain fixed on the tunnel's entrance rather than following the train's expected progress through the tunnel. When the train reappears at the other end of the tunnel, it takes the child a few seconds to catch up with it visually and the child shows no surprise when the train that comes out of the tunnel is a different color or shape (Bower, 1982).

Piaget maintained that infants respond in this manner because they cannot represent the object to themselves when it is out of sight. To Piaget, the ability to understand that objects continue to exist when they are out of sight is demonstrated only after infants begin to search for the absent object actively, as when—in a classic Piagetian test—they uncover a toy they have just seen the experimenter hide under a cloth or behind a barrier. According to Piaget, this ability first appears at around 8 months of age.

Initially, however, infants' grasp of object permanence is incomplete. In searching for missing objects, babies between 8 and 12 months tend to make a characteristic mistake: if, after they have successfully searched for an object hidden in one location, the object is then hidden in a new location right before their eyes, they will still search for the object where they previously found it. Suppose, for example, an object is hidden under cover A and the baby is allowed to retrieve it. Then, in full view of the baby, the object is placed under cover B. When allowed to retrieve the object a second time, the

FIGURE 5.8
Infants who have yet to gain a firm understanding of object permanence, according to Piaget's criteria, fail to track the motion of a toy train when it enters a tunnel. (From Bower, 1979.)

Infant watches train approach tunnel.

Infant watches train enter tunnel.

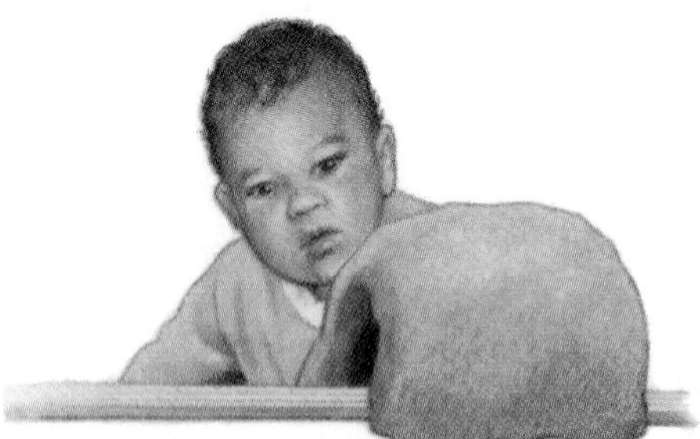

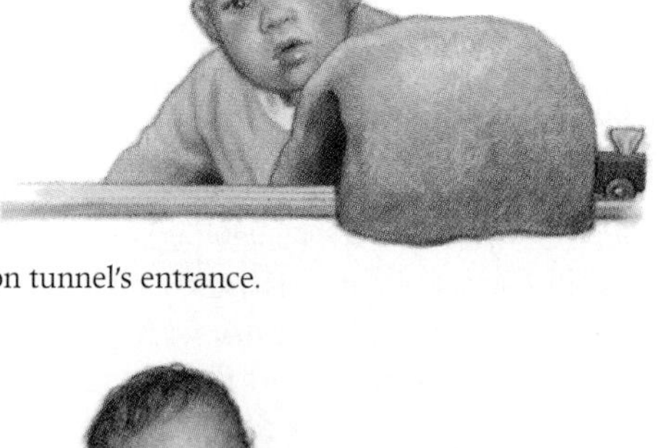

Infant's eyes remain fixed on tunnel's entrance.

Infant notices train moving away from tunnel.

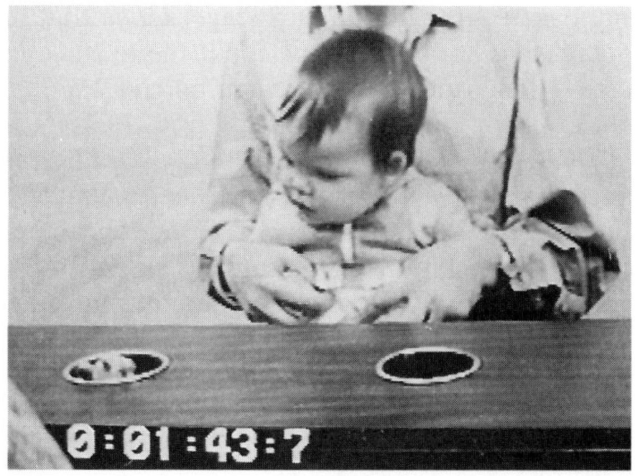

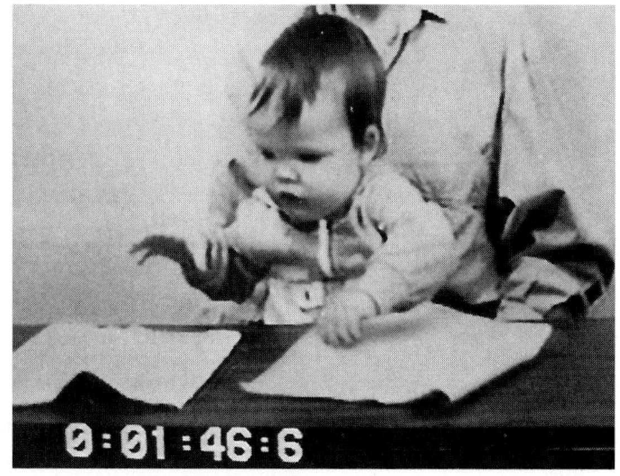

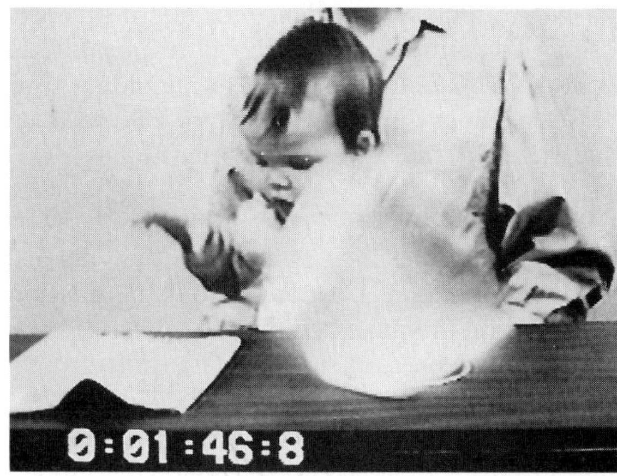

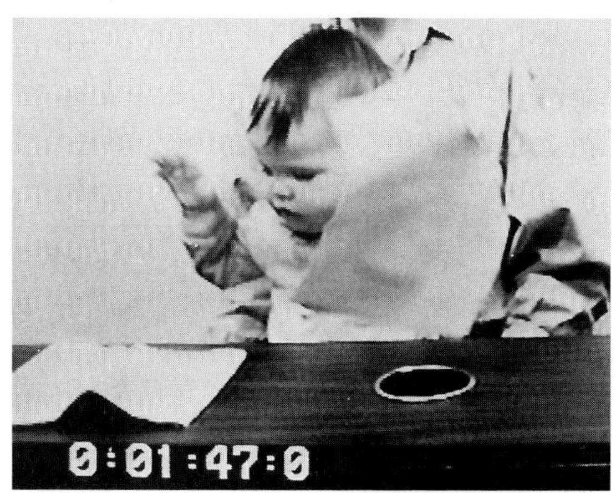

FIGURE 5.9
In this movie sequence, an object is placed in the circle on the left (position B), and then both circles (positions A and B) are covered with a cloth while the baby watches. In a previous trial, the object had been placed in the right-hand circle (position A), and the baby had correctly retrieved it. This time, while remaining oriented toward the hidden object at position B, the baby nonetheless picks up the cloth at position A, where the object was hidden before. (Courtesy of A. Diamond.)

baby will typically look under cover A, where the object was found before, rather than under cover B, where the baby has just seen it placed (Piaget, 1954) (see Figure 5.9). Piaget interpreted this pattern of responding as evidence that the child remembered the existence of the object but could not reason systematically about it. He believed that true representation, the ability both to keep in mind the existence of an absent object *and* to reason about that absent object, does not appear until the last months of the second year, after further developments in sensorimotor ways of knowing.

ARE INFANTS PRECOCIOUS? CHALLENGES TO PIAGET'S THEORY

There is little disagreement about Piaget's descriptions of how young infants actually behave at various ages. The sequence of changes in children's progress through sensorimotor stages and their developing understanding of object permanence have been widely replicated, not only in Europe and the United States but in traditional societies as well. For example, Baoulé infants living in rural areas of the West African country of Ivory Coast have been found to proceed through the same sequence of sensorimotor stages on almost exactly the same timetable as European children, despite vast differences in their cultural environments (Dasen, 1973). In fact, the sequence and timing of sensorimotor stages occurs so reliably that Piaget's procedures were long ago standardized for assessing the development of children who are at risk because of disease, physical impairment, or extreme environmental deprivation (Décarie, 1969; Uzgiris & Hunt, 1975).

However, there is growing controversy both about Piaget's idea that infants need to *construct* their increasing knowledge and about his reliance on infants' overt actions to measure their understanding. During the 1980s, a number of researchers began to suggest that certain forms of early knowledge do *not* have to be constructed. Some offered evidence suggesting that infants are born with at least a rudimentary understanding of many basic concepts, such as number and physical cause and effect, or at least have an inborn predisposition to acquire these concepts quickly. Other researchers provided evidence that infants at or near birth are predisposed to combine knowledge from different senses (see Box 5.2).

If very young infants could be shown to possess innate knowledge, this would support biological-maturational theories of the processes of change, casting doubt not only on Piaget's idea that such knowledge must be constructed but also on explanations of environmental- and cultural-context theories, which do not attribute much influence to innate knowledge. It should come as no surprise, then, that before long, the evidence for infant precocity was also challenged. In addressing this controversy, which will reappear in different guises in the following chapters, we begin by providing three examples of research supporting the "precocious infant" idea and then turn to recent challenges to this currently popular notion.

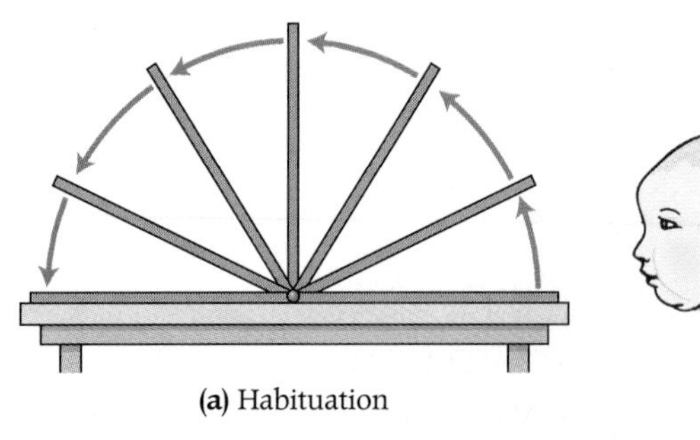

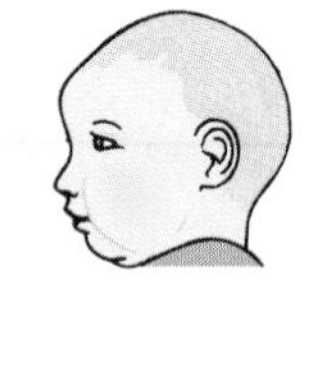

(a) Habituation

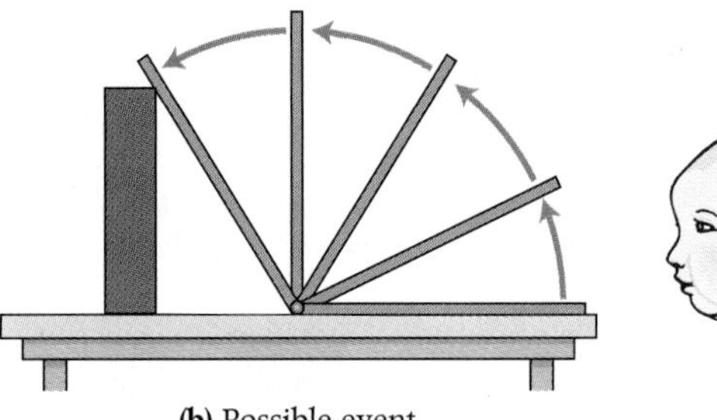

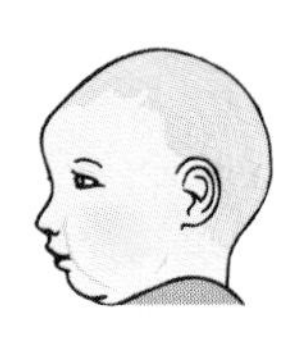

(b) Possible event

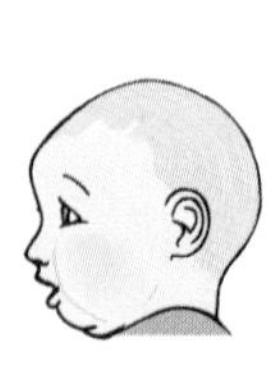

FIGURE 5.10

The habituation and test events arranged for babies by Renée Baillargeon and her colleagues. In the habituation event (a), the screen is unimpeded and rotates 180 degrees. In the possible event (b), a box stands in the way of the screen and stops it from rotating the full distance. In the impossible event (c), a box stands in the way of the rotating screen but the screen appears to pass right through it. (From Baillargeon, 1987.)

Reasoning about Nonvisible Objects

In a widely cited series of studies, Renée Baillargeon and her colleagues tested infants for signs of object permanence using methods that did not require that the infants take action. First, they arranged for young infants to watch a screen as it slowly rotated forward and backward through a 180-degree arc on a hinge attached to the floor of the viewing surface (Baillargeon, 1987; Baillargeon et al., 1985). The screen could rotate toward the babies until it was lying flat and away from them until it was again lying flat. In its upright position, the screen was like a fence behind which an object might be hidden from view (see Figure 5.10a).

When 3½- and 6-month-old infants were first shown the rotating screen, they stared at it for almost a full minute, but after several trials they seemed to lose interest and looked at the display for only about 10 seconds. Once the infants were habituated to the rotating screen, the experimenters placed a box behind the screen so that the infant could see it when the screen lay flat but not when the screen moved into its perpendicular position. Next, they arranged for the screen to move in one of two ways. For half of the infants at each age, they rotated the screen until it reached the point where it should bump up against the box (see Figure 5.10b) and then returned it to its flat starting position. For the other half of each group, they secretly lowered the box through the floor of the apparatus as soon as the screen had hidden it from view and rotated the screen through its full 180-degree arc, as if it were moving right through the "hidden" box (see Figure 5.10c).

The researchers reasoned that if the infants thought the box still existed even when it was hidden by the screen, they would stare longer (dishabituate) when the screen moved through the space where the box was supposed to be than they would when the screen seemed to bump into the box before returning to its starting point. On the other hand, if the infants failed to represent the box when their view of it became blocked by the screen, they should stare longer when the screen stopped after it had rotated part of the way before returning to its starting position. In fact, the infants showed no special interest when the screen rotated only partway and seemed to bump into the box, but even the 3½-month-olds dishabituated when the

BOX 5.2 CROSS-MODAL PERCEPTION

Developmental psychologists long assumed that newborn babies respond to the sight, sound, and other sense impressions of an object as if they were completely disconnected from one another. According to this view, shared by Piaget as well as environmental-learning theorists, infants must acquire a certain amount of experience with an object before they become able to associate the object's various sensory aspects with each other. They would need to learn, for example, that the voice coming from the other room and the face they see a few moments later are two aspects of the same person or that the gold color of the stuff on the spoon goes with its awful taste.

The understanding that certain features of an object perceived in one sensory mode go together with features perceived in a different sensory mode is known as intermodal perception, or **cross-modal perception** (Gibson & Walker, 1984; Rose & Ruff, 1987). Several ingenious studies have shown that elementary forms of cross-modal perception either do not have to be learned or are learned rapidly and quite early in infancy.

Elizabeth Spelke (1976, 1984) presented pairs of filmstrips to 4-month-old babies to see if they knew what sort of sound should accompany the event depicted in each film. To assess knowledge of sight–sound correspondences, she showed two films simultaneously, side by side. One depicted percussion instruments being played, and the other showed a game of peekaboo. A loudspeaker located between the two screens would sometimes play sounds appropriate to the percussion instruments, while at other times it played sounds appropriate to the game of peekaboo. The infants looked most often at whatever film corresponded to the loudspeaker's sounds, indicating they associated sounds with the appropriate sights.

In a later study, Arlette Streri and Elizabeth Spelke (1988) sought to determine if sight and touch are also closely linked in 4-month-olds' perceptions of objects. In this case the researchers arranged for the infants to hold two rings, one in each hand, under a cloth that prevented them from seeing the rings or their own bodies (see figure). For some infants the rings were connected by a rigid bar and therefore moved together. For others the rings were connected by a flexible cord and therefore moved independently. All the infants were allowed to hold and feel just one or the other type of rings until they had largely lost interest (habituated). They were then shown both types of rings. The babies looked longer at the rings that were different from those they had been exploring with their hands. That is, babies who had been handling the independently moving rings looked longer at the rigid ones, while babies who had been holding the rigidly connected rings looked longer at the flexibly connected ones. These and other data on cross-modal perception (Rochat, 2000; Spelke, 1990; Spelke & Van de Walle, 1993) strongly suggest that infants perceive the sights, sounds, feel, and other basic properties of objects as being related aspects of the same object; they do not have to acquire this information through an extended process of learning.

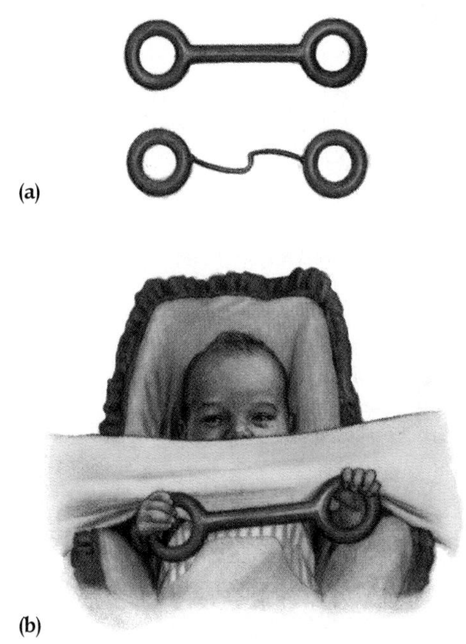

Objects (a) and apparatus (b) for experiments on the way infants use information gained in one sensory modality to recognize the same object in another. (a) Rings connected by rigid bar or flexible cord, one of which is presented until baby habituates. (b) This infant is feeling the rigid rings hidden from sight and later will be able to distinguish them by sight from the flexible ones. (From Streri & Spelke, 1988.)

screen appeared to pass right through the place where the box had been located. Their seeming lack of interest when the screen bumped into the hidden object and their increased interest when the screen continued to rotate "through the hidden object," even *though this was the habitual pattern of events,* is, according to Baillargeon, difficult to explain unless it is assumed that the infants believed (1) that the object continued to exist behind the screen and (2) that it is impossible for screens to move through solid objects. In Baillargeon's terms, they stared longer at an "impossible event" than at a possible one. These results led Baillargeon (1993) to conclude that "contrary to what

cross-modal perception The understanding that certain features of an object perceived in one sensory mode go together with features perceived in a different sensory mode.

Piaget claimed, infants as young as 3.5 months of age represent the existence of occluded [hidden] objects" (p. 272).

Infant Arithmetic

A particularly striking phenomenon supporting the idea of the precocious infant comes from studies in which young infants appear to carry out simple arithmetic operations on small arrays of objects that are hidden behind a screen (Wynn, 1992, 1996). Karen Wynn (1992) showed 4-month-old infants the events depicted in Figure 5.11. First, a mouse doll was placed on an empty stage while the baby watched. Then a screen was raised to hide the doll from the baby's view. Next, a hand holding an identical doll went behind the screen and then withdrew without the doll. The screen was then lowered. In half the cases there were two dolls behind the screen (the expected outcome); in the other half there was only one doll (the unexpected outcome). The infants looked longer at the display when there was only one doll, a result suggesting that they had mentally calculated the number of dolls that ought to be behind the screen. Similarly, when the experiment began with two dolls on stage and the infants observed the hand remove one doll from behind the screen, their looking patterns showed surprise on trials in which the screen was lowered to reveal two dolls. Such experiments appear to demonstrate that infants are capable not only of numerosity but also of at least rudimentary representation well ahead of Piaget's timetable.

Early Understanding of Causality

Piaget believed that while young infants had a dim awareness that their own actions could be the cause of an effect—at 10 months of age his daughter took his hand and pressed his fingers in order to make him squeeze a doll to make it sing—it is not until stage 5 of sensorimotor intelligence, when infants begin to invent new means to achieve their goals through active experimentation, that they begin to appreciate causal relations external to themselves. As noted in Table 5.2, this milestone is typically reached after 12 months of age.

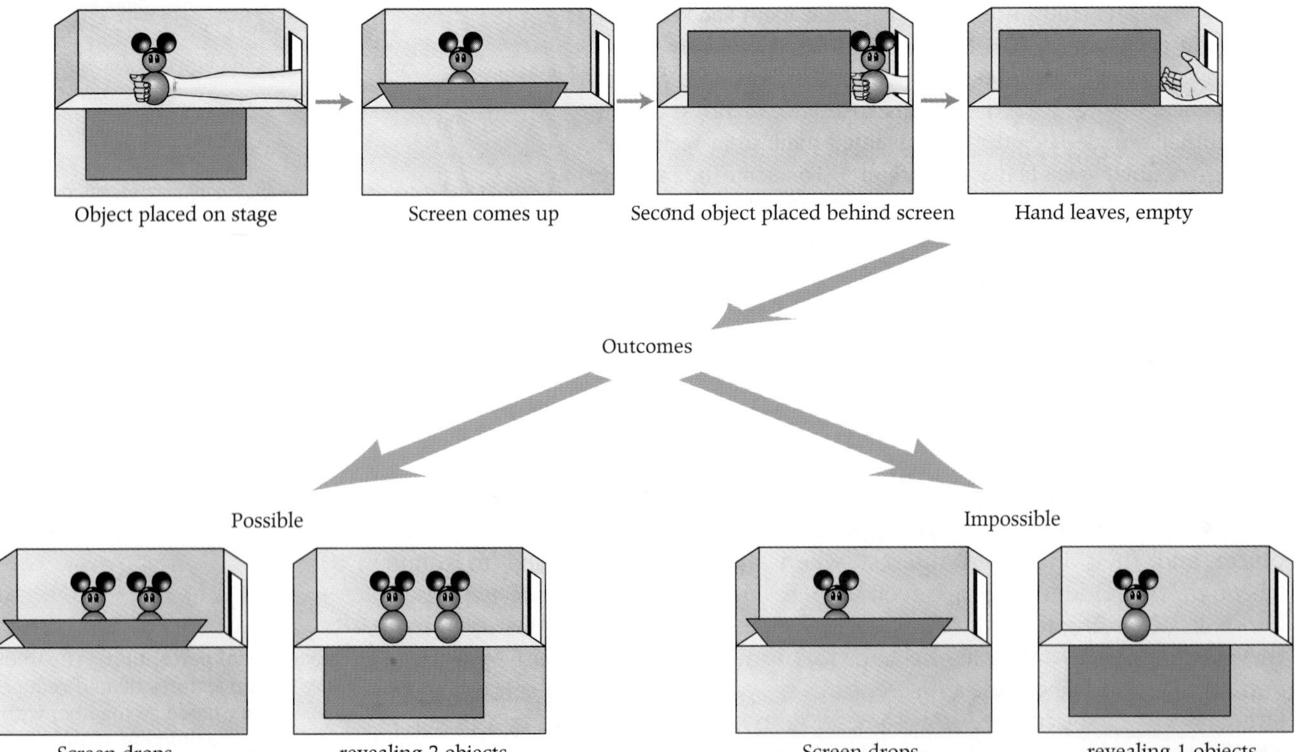

FIGURE 5.11
After 4-month-olds observe the sequence of events at the top of the figure, they show surprise when the screen is removed and only one mouse remains. Apparently the babies not only remember the presence of the first mouse hidden behind the screen but mentally add the second mouse and expect to see it. (After Wynn, 1992.)

However, Alan Leslie and his colleagues have argued that Piaget seriously misconstrued the nature of causal thinking. In Leslie's view, primitive knowledge about physical causality is innate—it does not require prior experience of the world to develop (Leslie, 1994; Leslie & Keeble, 1987). These researchers presented 6-month-old children (the youngest they could test reliably) with a computer display in which one dot appeared to bump into a second and the second dot moved. In one case, the second dot moved immediately, suggesting causation. In the other case, there was a delay in the movement of the second dot, suggesting an absence of causation. The researchers showed the infants the causal event several times in a row and then showed them either a different causal event or the "noncausal" event. The infants stared longer at the noncausal event, thus supporting Leslie's contention that they were sensitive to causality as it is manifested in these simplified circumstances, even though the events they witnessed were not connected in any way to their own actions.

ASSESSING THE EVIDENCE FOR INFANT PRECOCITY

The wide range of studies that used habituation or differential-looking procedures to make claims about young infants' precocious conceptual capabilities shifted opinion among developmental psychologists strongly in the direction of biological-maturation theories of development (Gelman & Williams, 1998; Spelke & Newport, 1998; Wellman & Gelman, 1998). This belief became sufficiently widespread in the past decade to attract considerable attention from the popular press.

But the shift to a belief in infant precocity and the biological-maturation theory of development that it suggested was by no means complete. A number of psychologists began to argue that the results of the differential-looking studies do *not* provide evidence that infants possess innate knowledge. Instead, according to these researchers, those who believe in innate knowledge about objects and events have been misled by their theoretical expectations into attributing too much knowledge to small infants when simpler mechanisms can explain the infants' looking behaviors. To bolster their argument, they began attempting to replicate the key experiments of those who believed in infant precocity and to test alternative explanations for the pattern of results described above.

For example, Cara Cashon and Leslie Cohen (2000) repeated Baillargeon's "impossible event" experiment with 8-month-old infants. As in Baillargeon's procedures, infants were habituated to a screen that rotated 180 degrees. They were then shown the possible event (in which the screen stopped moving when it bumped into a block placed behind the screen) and an impossible event (in which the screen rotated the full 180 degrees "through the block"). Like Baillargeon, they found that the infants stared longer at the screen that rotated 180 degrees, the so-called impossible event. However, they suspected that something other than the belief that an event is impossible might be responsible for the infants' responses, so they also tested other patterns of screen movement with and without the block that had not been previously investigated. For example, they included a procedure in which the infants were habituated to the *impossible* event (the screen moving 180 degrees "through" the block) and then were tested on a *possible* event in which there was no block and the screen continued to rotate 180 degrees. Although the latter event was perfectly possible, and although the babies had been habituated to a screen that moved 180 degrees, they now stared more than twice as long at this *possible* event as they had at the impossible event to which they had been habituated! When Cohen and Cashon combined the results from all the trials using different combinations of degrees of screen rotation and presence or absence of a block, they obtained the results depicted in Figure 5.12. As the figure indicates, the critical variable accounting for how long the

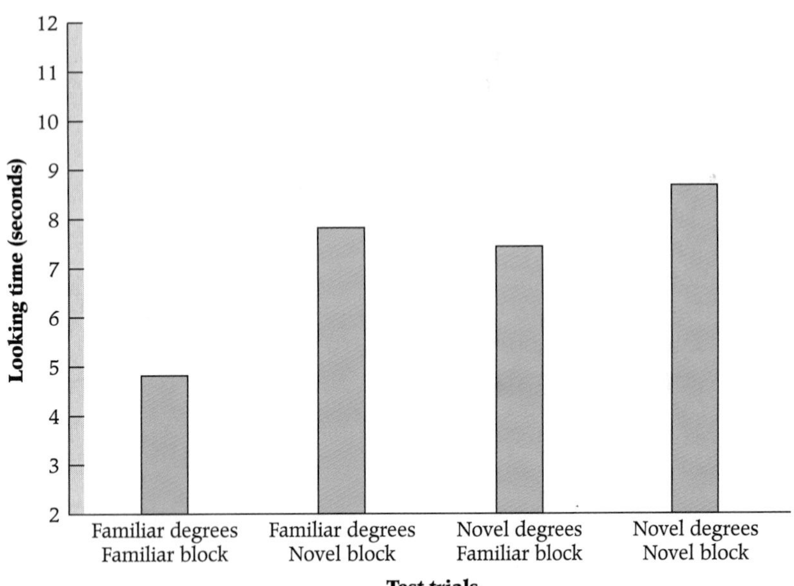

FIGURE 5.12
When 8-month-old infants were habituated to "possible" and "impossible" movements of a screen and subsequently shown either familiar or novel events, they looked longer at the novel events, whether possible or impossible. (From Cashon & Cohen, 2000.)

infants looked was *the similarity of the testing conditions to the habituation conditions:* when screens moved farther in the testing conditions than in the habituation conditions, or some novel object was introduced into the testing conditions, the babies' attention was unaffected by whether the events were possible or impossible.

Similar counterdemonstrations to claims for infant precocity have recently been reported in tests of a variety of the tasks involving "impossible events," including Wynn's evidence for precocious number abilities and Leslie's evidence for precocious understanding of physical causation. In some of these counterdemonstrations, the researchers were unable to produce evidence of differential attention to impossible events (indicating that the infants did not have some concept of the possible). In others, through experimental manipulations like those in the counterdemonstration for the Baillargeon experiment, they concluded that the original findings actually resulted from primitive responses to novelty and not from precocious understanding (Bogartz et al., 1997; Cohen, 1998; Cohen et al., 1998; Haith, 1998; Rivera et al., 1999).

At present there is no consensus on how much innate knowledge to attribute to small infants. Those who adhere to a Piagetian position are inclined to see the counterdemonstration data as undermining the idea of infant precocity and as justification for his constructivist theory (Rivera et al., 1999). From this perspective, it is through repeated cycles of assimilation and accommodation in which infants act on the world that cognitive processes develop (see Box 5.3).

Biological-maturation theorists grant the weakness in some of the experimental evidence for innate knowledge but argue that many of their experiments have not been undermined and that they need not give up their basic conclusion that infants are born with a good deal more knowledge than Piaget gave them credit for. From this perspective, there is no need for babies to go through the long process of construction he claims they do (Baillargeon, 1998; Spelke, 1998).

Environmental-learning theorists view the recent demonstrations that infants are not born precocious knowers as favoring their view that the only innate knowledge young infants possess is restricted to very general processes for attending to primitive perceptual features of the environment such as novelty and intensity. Knowledge of physical principles such as causality or object permanence, they believe, is acquired through learning, both from simply observing the world and through acting on it (Cohen, 1998).

Between these well-established positions, there is also a "middle ground" that sees the initial, "innate" knowledge as merely "skeletal," needing experience to "flesh it out" (Gelman & Williams, 1998). We will return to examine this position in more detail in Chapter 9.

CATEGORIZING: KNOWLEDGE ABOUT KINDS OF THINGS

categorizing The process of responding to different things as equivalent because of a similarity between them.

Categorizing is the process of responding to different objects as equivalent because of a similarity between them. The ability to categorize is essential to the process of human cognitive development. Categorizing allows infants to treat specific objects, animals, and events they have never seen before as if

BOX 5.3

ACTION AND UNDERSTANDING

Piaget's hypothesis that children's own activities are the driving force of their development has led many psychologists to study the developmental consequences of restricted or enhanced movement early in life. A basic intuition guiding such research is the idea that locomotion not only allows babies to learn how to move their bodies in space but also provides them with a new understanding of the objects, including other people and themselves, that fill space. As Selma Fraiberg (1959) has noted:

> Travel changes one's perspective. A chair, for example, is an object of one dimension when viewed by a six-month-old baby propped up on the sofa, or by an eight-month-old baby doing push-ups on a rug. It's even very likely that the child of this age confronted at various times with different perspectives of the same chair would see not one chair, but several chairs, corresponding to each perspective. It's when you start to get around under your own steam that you discover what a chair really is. (p. 52)

A classic study demonstrating a close link between locomotor experience and the understanding of spatial relations was carried out by Richard Held and Alan Hein (1963) with kittens who were raised from birth in total darkness. When the kittens were old enough to walk, they were placed two at a time in an apparatus called a "kitten carousel." One kitten, harnessed to pull the carousel, controlled the movements of the carousel, so what it saw depended upon how it moved. The other kitten was carried in the gondola of the carousel and except for head movements, its movements did not control what it saw. Instead, the visual experiences of the passive kitten were controlled largely by the actions of the kitten pulling the carousel. Each pair of kittens was given 3 hours of visual experience in the carousel every day for 42 days. Between these sessions, they were returned to the dark. Thus the only visual experience the kittens had, and hence the only opportunity they had to learn to coordinate vision and movement, was the time they spent in the carousel.

The influence of active versus passive movement on the kittens' responses to their environment became strikingly apparent when Held and Hein lowered them onto the surface of a visual cliff similar to the one shown in Figure 1.6 of Chapter 1 (p. 21). This apparatus had stripes painted on it like the stripes around the sides of the kitten carousel, except that they were painted to look as if one side of the apparatus were far below the other. The kittens that had been active in the carousel shied away from the deep side of the visual cliff and appropriately stretched out their legs to land on it. The passive kittens did not try to avoid the deep side of the cliff, nor did they make appropriate adjustments in the positions of their legs in anticipation of landing on it.

This finding fits well with the results of the experiment by Joseph Campos and his co-workers described in Chapter 1 (p. 21) that confirmed the importance of movement in human cognitive development (Bertenthal et al., 1984). In that study, 5-month-old babies who had not yet begun to crawl did not seem to be afraid of a visual cliff when they first saw it. They began to be afraid of heights only after they had begun to move around on their own or after they had gained experience in locomoting in baby walkers.

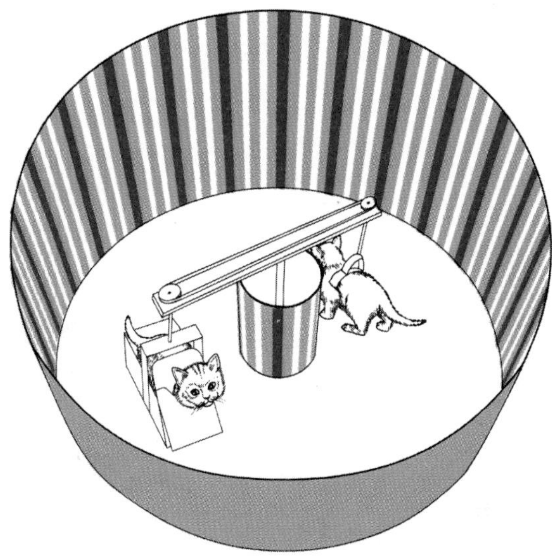

The kitten carousel used in Held and Hein's classic experiment demonstrating the importance of active experience to development. (From Held, 1965.)

Campos and his co-workers have also shown that locomotion enhances the development of infants' understanding of object permanence. Babies who had extensive experience in moving around in baby walkers before they could move about on their own were more adept at locating hidden objects in standard object permanence tests than were children of the same age who had no such experience (Campos et al., 1986, 2000). Martha Ann Bell and Nathan Fox (1997) report that the onset of locomotion is accompanied by changes in the activity of the frontal lobes, which, in turn, are associated with more successful performance on object permanence tasks. (Parents of infants should take note, however, that some children have been injured as a result of using walkers; this raises the question of whether the benefits of using a walker outweigh the risks [Atkinson, 1997]).

A very different kind of evidence for the close connection between locomotion and development at the level of behavior is provided by a study of the development of infants who suffered from a neural-tube defect that impeded locomotion (Telzrow et al., 1987). Such children were found to be delayed 5 to 6 months in the development of object permanence. They began to search for hidden objects correctly only after they had begun to move voluntarily.

The results of these experiments suggest that active engagement with the world does make a fundamental contribution to development at every level: biological changes in the brain and body; psychological changes in problem solving, classification, and memory; and interpersonal changes in emotional attachment and interpersonal understandings.

they are somehow similar to, or "the same as," previous experiences, so it is not necessary to learn about them all over again. For example, infants who have encountered a cat and learned that it meows and has soft fur that is nice to pet do not have to learn this information about cats again whenever they see a new cat.

Categories vary from specific to global. Cats are different from dogs, but they are both kinds of animals. Cats and dogs differ from cars and airplanes both at a specific category level (cats versus cars, for example) and at the more global level (animals versus vehicles).

Researchers have used a variety of techniques to study the development of categorizing abilities during early infancy. From evidence presented in Chapter 4 (p. 134) it is clear that some forms of categorizing ability—such as the ability to respond to the sounds of human language as distinct from other sounds—are present at birth. During the first year, infants acquire the ability to categorize a vast array of objects and experiences, including the gender of voice sounds, geometric patterns made of dots and lines, and a great variety of other objects, such as different kinds of animals, furniture, vehicles, and the like (Haith & Benson, 1998; Mandler, 1998).

To demonstrate early forms of infant categorizing, Peter Eimas and Paul Quinn have used the kind of differential-looking procedure described earlier. Eimas and Quinn demonstrated that 3-month-old infants respond to a variety of animals as members of distinct categories (Eimas & Quinn, 1994; Quinn & Eimas, 1996). They showed infants a series of pictures of horses, two at a time. The horses in each pair were different, so the babies never saw the same horse twice. After the babies had seen pictures of six pairs of horses, they were shown three new pictures of horses, but this time the horses were paired with pictures of a cat, a zebra, and a giraffe. In all three test cases, the infants looked longer at the pictures of the other animals than they did at the pictures of the horses even though the two pictures on each test were similar in overall appearance. This preferential looking indicated that the infants had formed a category for horses compared with other animals. When the investigators ran the same procedure using cats paired first with other cats and then with dogs and lions, they found that 3- and 4-month-olds formed a category of cats that excluded dogs and lions (see Figure 5.13) (Quinn et al., 1993).

Young infants also respond to more inclusive categories. In one demonstration of this ability, 3- to 4-month-olds were familiarized with pictures of eight different kinds of mammals (cats, dogs, tigers, and so on). Then they were shown one of three new pictures: a mammal they had not been shown before; an animal that is not a mammal (for example, a bird or a fish); or a piece of furniture, such as a table or chair. The infants looked longer at nonmammals and furniture than at the new mammal, a result indicating that they had formed a category for mammals (Behl-Chadha et al., 1995).

The ability of young infants to respond to a variety of categories has also been shown using an operant conditioning procedure that demands more active responding on the infants' part than does differential looking. In one of many such studies, 3-month-old infants were shown trinkets embossed with the letter "A" dangling from a mobile. If they kicked their legs, which were attached to the mobile by a ribbon, the mobile would move (see Figure 5.14) (Hayne et al., 1987). In second and third sessions, the color of the A-embossed trinkets was changed (from blue to green to red, say). At the end of all three of these sessions, infants kicked at a consistently high rate to make the mobile with its A-embossed trinkets move. Lastly, the infants were shown test mobiles on which the trinkets either were embossed with letters of the same form but yet another color (a black A, say) or were different in both form and color (say, a black B). The infants kicked at high rates in response to the test mobile with the same form and a novel color but not to the mobile with the new form. Ap-

Trial 1

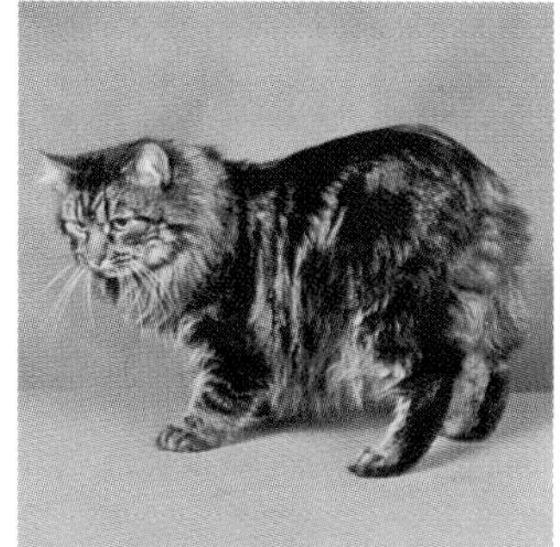

Trial 2

Trial 3

Test trial

FIGURE 5.13 *Three-month-old babies shown a sequence of pictures of cats are surprised when they see a picture of a dog, indicating that they are sensitive to the category of cats.*

parently they were categorizing the mobiles on the basis of the specific shape of the forms embossed on the trinkets, so when the shape of the letter changed, they no longer responded to it.

Although the ability of young infants to form categories is well established, developmentalists are sharply divided on how the process of categorization changes during the first year of postnatal life. It is generally assumed that categories formed in the experiments we have just described are based on *perceptual* similarity. (In the examples we have given, the similarity involves the way the objects look: "A's" look different from "B's"; cats are furry and have differently shaped heads than dogs, shorter legs than horses, and so on). Given

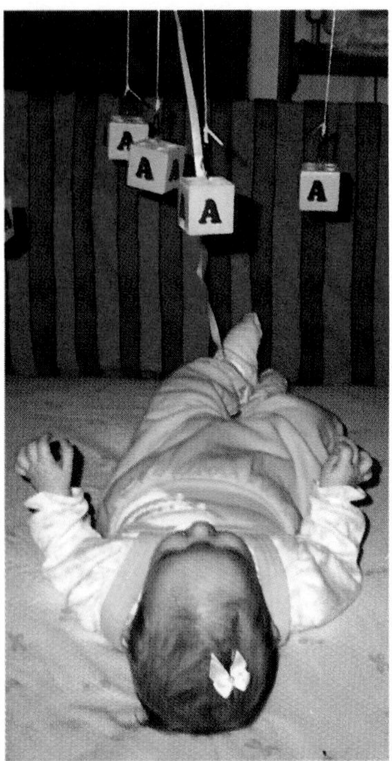

FIGURE 5.14

A 3-month-old baby viewing a mobile with blocks inscribed with an A that moves when the baby kicks. After three 15-minute sessions, each with a different-color A, the baby will kick a mobile with yet a fourth color. But if a new shape is inscribed on the blocks used in the fourth session (for example, a B), the baby will not kick.

3- and 4-month-old babies' limited experience of objects and events, as well as their limited ability to grasp things with their hands and to move around, it is not surprising that perceptual features would provide the dominant basis for forming categories. According to some developmental psychologists, categorization continues to be based on perceptual principles throughout development.

However, some researchers believe that as infants approach their first birthdays, they undergo a change in the nature of category formation. These researchers believe that in addition to engaging in **perceptual categorization** based on how things look, feel, and taste, infants become capable of **conceptual categorization,** that is, categorization based on such features as what things do and how they come to be the way they are. For example, cats are placed in the same category not only because they have fur, a distinctive body shape, and four legs but also because they purr when you pet them and scratch if you are rough with them.

To demonstrate the existence of an early shift in categorizing ability, Jean Mandler and Laraine McDonough (1993) showed that 7-month-old babies responded to toy birds and toy airplanes as if they were members of the same category. By contrast, 9- to 11-month-olds treated toy airplanes and birds as members of different categories even though they looked very much alike: the toy birds all had outstretched wings and looked like the airplanes (see Figure 5.15). They concluded that before the end of the first year of life, infants are capable of making genuine *conceptual* categories in addition to perceptual categories.

What makes these results puzzling is that the apparent shift from perceptual categorizing to conceptual categorizing could not result from actual experience with the objects involved. Infants between 9 and 11 months have little or no direct experience with birds, let alone airplanes. So what brings about change in the way they categorize them? Mandler (1998) suggests that beginning at 3 to 4 months of age, infants are capable of a process she calls "perceptual analysis." She believes perceptual analysis transforms incoming perceptual information into primitive conceptual categories, without the need for infants to act directly on what they see. In addition, she believes that perceptual categorizing is a more primitive process because it occurs automatically, while conceptual categorizing requires a conscious process in which infants begin to think about the contents of their categories.

Those who believe that the development of categorization follows a sin-

FIGURE 5.15

Seven-month-old babies treat plastic toy birds or airplanes, which are perceptually similar, as if they are members of the same category. Babies 9 to 11 months old treat them as members of different categories, despite their perceptual similarity.

gle set of principles during early development provide an alternative explanation for the behavior of the infants in Mandler and McDonough's study. They argue that although the 9- to 11-month-old babies appeared to be making a conceptual distinction between birds and airplanes, they were actually displaying a greater ability to make finer perceptual distinctions. In this case, for example, the babies could have noticed that the tails of the birds and those of the airplanes were slightly dissimilar and categorized them on the basis of that perceptual difference. According to this view, the development of categorization comes about because infants gradually obtain more information about objects in their world until at some point, perceptual patterns are integrated with knowledge about functions to form more complex categories (DeLoache et al., 1998; Quinn & Eimas, 1996).

perceptual categorization Categorization based on how things look, feel, sound, and taste.

conceptual categorization Categorization based on such features as what things do and how they become the way they are.

Taking a somewhat different approach, Carolyn Rovee-Collier and her colleagues have argued that if young infants are provided with a way to obtain the relevant experiences, they are capable from an early age of forming categories that go beyond perceptual features of objects (Hayne & Rovee-Collier, 1995). In their view, category formation can occur at all ages as the result of both perceptual and functional features of the environment. They used the kicking-to-move-a-mobile method mentioned earlier to demonstrate the ability of 3- to 4-month-olds to form a conceptual category based on function. First the babies learned to kick to make a mobile move. Then they were shown a mobile made of unfamiliar figures. Ordinarily they would not kick because the mobile *looked* different. But in this case, the experimenter made the new mobile move while the infants watched it (the infants were not attached to the mobile, so their actions did not affect its movement). Even though they had never before seen the novel mobile, they began kicking as if they had. According to Rovee-Collier and her colleagues, the new mobile had entered the category of "familiar mobiles" not because of how it *looked* but because of how it *functioned.*

THE GROWTH OF MEMORY

We have seen ample evidence that infants steadily acquire skills and knowledge over the course of the first year of postnatal life. But we have not yet examined the question of how they retain this skill and knowledge over time—how they remember. Memory, like other cognitive functions, undergoes developmental changes in early infancy.

Studies of the development of memory for past events have repeatedly found that young animals of many species, including human beings, forget rapidly (Spear, 1978). However, Carolyn Rovee-Collier and her colleagues have demonstrated that remembering in humans increases rapidly during the first year of life (Hartshorn et al., 1998). Adapting the procedure in which babies make a mobile move by kicking, the researchers removed babies of various ages from the test setting when they had learned to kick vigorously as soon as one of their legs was attached to the mobile. They brought the babies back after different waiting periods to assess what they remembered from their earlier experience. These researchers found that 2-month-olds started kicking immediately following a 24-hour delay, a finding indicating that the infants remembered the initial experience. But after 3 days, 2-month-olds seemed to forget their training; they took just as long to start kicking as they had taken when they were first trained to do so. Three-month-olds could remember their training for 8 days but not for 13. Six-month-olds showed almost perfect recall for 14 days but none at 21 days. A recent extension of this research in which infants up to 18 months of age learned to press a lever to make a train move showed a steady increase in the number of days that infants could remember their prior training (Hartshorn et al., 1998). (See Figure 5.16.)

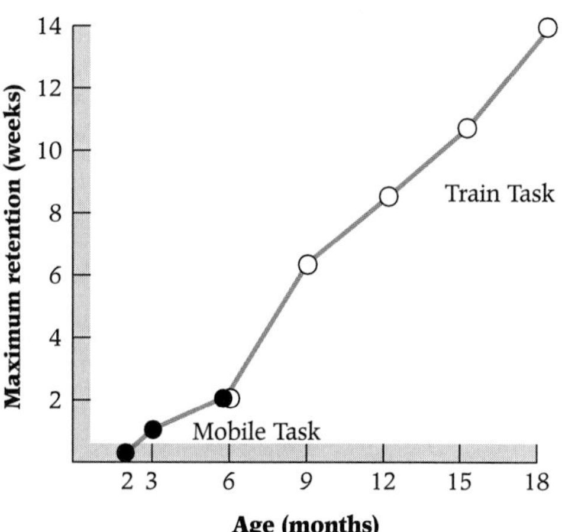

FIGURE 5.16
Results of memory retention studies on babies aged 2 months to 18 months. Note that 6-month-olds were tested in both the mobile and train tasks. [Data for mobile task are from Vander Linde et al., 1985 (2-month-olds); Greco et al., 1986 (3-month-olds); and Hill et al., 1988 (6-month-olds). Data for train task are from Hartshorn & Rovee-Collier, 1997.]

Additional studies have shown that if infants are given a brief visual reminder, they can remember their earlier training much longer (Rovee-Collier, 1998). In one such study, Rovee-Collier and her colleagues again trained a group of 3-month-old babies to activate a mobile by kicking. They then let an entire month elapse before putting the babies into the experimental situation again. They knew that this was more than enough time for the babies to forget their training. However, 1 day before being retested, the 3-month-olds were shown the mobile as a reminder (without allowing them to kick). The next day, these infants started kicking as soon as the ribbon was tied to one of their legs (Rovee-Collier et al., 1980). The mere sight of the mobile a day earlier seemed to remind the babies of what they had learned to do *1 month* earlier.

RECALL AND WARINESS: EVIDENCE FOR A DEVELOPMENTAL DISCONTINUITY?

In the previous sections we have discussed the development of categorization and the development of memory as if they are separate phenomena. In fact, however, there are important links between the two classes of cognitive phenomena. How infants remember experiences depends, at least in part, on how those experiences have been categorized. And how they categorize current experiences depends, in part, on how they categorized, and thus remember, prior experiences.

Changes in Memory and Classification

On the basis of their work showing that babies begin to remember at a very early age and that their memory continues to improve steadily during the first year of life, Rovee-Collier and her colleagues have concluded that the improvement in memory over the course of the first year of life is a continuous process that does not involve any new principles of learning or remembering (Hayne & Rovee-Collier, 1995; Rovee-Collier, 1997). This conclusion parallels the view that the development of categorization is also a gradual process of change that does not involve the appearance of qualitatively new abilities (Quinn & Eimas, 1998; Rovee-Collier, 1998).

However, just as there are developmentalists who believe that categorization shifts from perceptual to conceptual categories sometime between 6 and 9 months of age, there are those who believe that a qualitative shift in memory occurs at the same time. According to the latter view, young infants move from being able to *recognize* what they have experienced before to being able to *recall* ("call to mind") absent objects and events without any clear reminder (Kagan et al., 1978; Mandler, 1998). Recall memory is considered an especially important cognitive achievement because it seems to require the conscious generation of a mental representation for something that is not present to the senses—the same criterion that is used by those who believe that conceptual categorization begins to supplement perceptual categorization during the same period. As was true when trying to make a firm distinction between perceptual and conceptual categories in young infants, the task of distinguishing between recognizing and recalling is a tricky one.

One technique that is used by those who study the early origin of recall memory is to test children's ability to engage in delayed or **deferred imitation,** that is, imitation of a new behavior the infant witnessed at a previous time. In one such test, Andrew Meltzoff (1988b) demonstrated three simple actions to 9-month-old infants seated on their parents' laps. First he took a small board attached in an upright position to a base by a hinge and pushed it until it lay flat on its base; then he pushed a black button that sounded a beeper; and then he rattled an orange plastic egg with nuts and bolts in it. After watching him do these things, the babies were taken home. The next day they were brought back to the laboratory and allowed to play with a few small toys. Then the

deferred imitation The ability to imitate an action observed in the past.

board, the buzzer, and the plastic egg were brought out. Although the babies had never themselves done such things, most of them imitated one or more of the actions they had seen Meltzoff perform with these objects the day before (see Figure 5.17). According to Meltzoff, they had *recognized* the items, and they had *recalled* his use of them. In similar studies, McDonough and Mandler (1994) showed that 11-month-olds who observed a number of unusual events could imitate them after a delay of an entire year! These data clearly demonstrate that by their first birthdays, infants are capable of remembering past events for considerable periods of time.

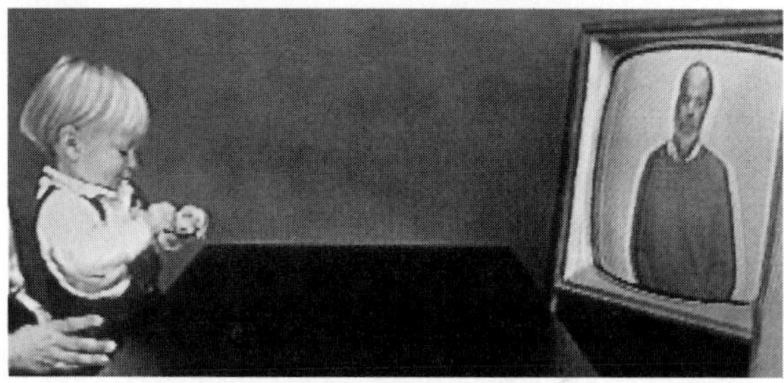

FIGURE 5.17
Studies by Andrew Meltzoff (1988a) have shown that young infants imitate live models and will also imitate actions they have seen on television. This child observes a televised adult model manipulate blocks, and then immediately the child imitates the adult's actions. Meltzoff also demonstrated that infants who watch a televised model on one day will reproduce the model's behavior 24 hours later. (Courtesy of A. Meltzoff.)

Memory, Categorization, and the Onset of Wariness

The question of how changes in remembering are related to changes in categorization takes on added importance because at some time between the ages of 6 and 9 months, babies begin to be overtly wary and even afraid whenever something out of the ordinary happens (see Figure 5.18) (Rothbart, 1988). Some researchers believe that such wariness would not be possible if infants had not first developed the ability to recall earlier events. To demonstrate the onset of wariness, Rudolph Schaffer (1974) repeatedly presented babies between the ages of 4 and 9 months of age with a strange object until they became habituated to it. He then presented them with a new strange object, a plastic model of an ice cream sundae. Most 4-month-olds strained toward the sundae immediately, without any hesitation. Most 6-month-olds hesitated for a second or two, showing that they noticed the change, and then reached for the sundae impulsively, often bringing it to their mouths. Nine-month-olds tended to hesitate longer, and some of them even turned away or started to cry.

Some researchers believe that the 9-month-olds' wariness is caused by a newly acquired ability to compare current events with remembered past events in a systematic way that definitely fits the definition of recall (Fox et al., 1979; Mandler, 1988). Thus 9-month-olds not only note that strange new objects (like ice cream sundaes) are unfamiliar but search their memories to determine if such an object corresponds to any category of things they have seen before, and they become upset because it does not.

FIGURE 5.18
Infants who are exposed to something new—even a spoonful of cereal from a stranger—display the wariness characteristic of the bio-social-behavioral shift that occurs at 6 to 9 months.

The question of when recall memory first appears and how it is related to changes in categorization is by no means settled. On the basis of their experiments in eliciting infants' imitation of facial expressions (Box 4-4, pp. 160–161), Andrew Meltzoff and Keith Moore (1994) argue that recall memory may appear as early as 6 weeks! They found that 6-week-old infants not only imitate a person who sticks out his tongue as soon as they see him do it but also they repeat that movement when they see the same person 24 hours later, even though he or she does not make any funny faces this time. Meltzoff and Moore suggest that perhaps what is special about memory late in the first year of life is that it can operate on objects as well as people. Other investigators believe that early forms of imitation such as tongue protrusion are specialized, restricted responses that newborns are unconscious of making; these researchers want to credit infants with recall only when they must deliberately bring prior information to mind (Mandler, 1998). Whether the form of remembering in these experiments reflects recall or recognition may be difficult to decide. But what is clear is that developments in remembering, categorization, and infant responses to strange events become intertwined toward the end of the first year of life.

A NEW RELATIONSHIP WITH THE SOCIAL WORLD

Jake's wariness of Sheila at 12 months, described at the start of this chapter, belongs to a new pattern of social behaviors that first appears around 7 months of age. When Jake was 2 months old, he did not show any overt sign of distress when Sheila cared for him. This does not necessarily mean that he did not notice the difference between Sheila and his mother. Keiko Mizukami and her colleagues have shown that when 2- to 4-month-olds see their mothers leave the room and a stranger appears over their cribs, their skin temperature drops—a physiological indicator that they are concerned. But such early indicators are not yet apparent in behavior (Mizukami et al., 1990). At 1 year of age, however, Jake was not only surprised when he looked up and saw Sheila where he expected his mother to be; he was also distressed, and he showed it by turning away and reaching for his mother.

Many developmental psychologists agree that in the second half of the first year, babies' fear of an unfamiliar adult and their distress when their primary caregiver disappears are closely connected to their increasing ability to move around, to categorize, and to remember (Bertenthal et al., 1984; Campos et al., 1997).

THE ROLE OF UNCERTAINTY IN WARINESS

When we try to discover why the combination of infants' beginning to locomote, increased understanding of the nature of objects, and improved memory should be associated with overt wariness and fear, we have to remember the predicament babies are in. They are constantly encountering new situations and new objects, but they have little experience to guide their responses and little physical strength or coordination to respond with. They cannot eat, dress, or take off an uncomfortable diaper by themselves. What is more, they have no reliable system of communication. Therefore, to get through each day reasonably well fed and comfortable, they must depend on adults and older siblings to know what needs to be done and how to do it, as the following case illustrates:

Amy, almost 4 months old, sat in her father's lap in a booth at the coffee shop. He was talking to a friend. Amy was teething on a hard rubber ring he had brought along for her. Her father supported Amy's back with his left arm, keeping his hand free. Twice he used that hand to catch the ring when it fell to her lap or his own lap. When Amy dropped the ring for the third time, he interrupted his conversation, said "Klutz," picked it up, and put it on the table. She leaned toward it, awkwardly reached out and touched it, but was not able to grasp it well enough to pick it up. Her father had returned to his conversation, and this time without interrupting it (though he was glancing back and forth between Amy's hand and his friend) he tilted the ring upward toward Amy so that she could get her thumb under it. She grasped the ring and pulled it away from him. Absorbed in chewing on the toy, Amy did not look at him. He went on talking and drinking his coffee, paying no further attention to her until he felt the toy drop into his lap once again. (Kaye, 1982, pp. 1–2)

zone of proximal development The gap between what children can accomplish independently and what they can accomplish when they are interacting with others who are more competent.

Here we see a few of the ways in which adults who care for babies act for them and with them so that the babies can function effectively despite their relative ineptness. The adult's actions must be finely coordinated with the baby's abilities and needs, or else the baby will experience some form of difficulty.

The kind of finely tuned adult support that assists children in accomplishing actions that they will later come to accomplish independently creates what Lev Vygotsky (1978) called a **zone of proximal development.** Vygotsky attributed great significance to such child–adult interactions throughout development. The zone he referred to is the gap between what children can accomplish independently and what they can accomplish when they are interacting with others who are more competent. The term "proximal" (nearby) indicates that the assistance provided goes just slightly beyond the child's current competence, complementing and building on the child's existing abilities instead of directly teaching the child new behaviors. Notice, for example, that Amy's father did not put the teething ring in Amy's hand, nor did he hold it up to her mouth for her to teethe on. Instead, he tilted it upward so that she could grasp it herself, and he did so almost automatically while doing something else. To coordinate behaviors in this way, the adult must know what the child is trying to do and be sensitive to the child's abilities and signals.

By the time infants are 6 or 7 months old, they begin to play a more active role in getting adults to help them. Christine Mosier and Barbara Rogoff (1994) studied the development of help-seeking behavior in 6- to 13-month-old babies. They arranged for mothers to play out brief scripted events in which the infants would be likely to want their mothers' help. A toy was placed out of reach on a shelf or the floor, for example. In about 40 percent of the trials with 6-month-olds, the infants glanced back and forth between the toy and their mothers and made sounds like "ugh" to get their mothers to give them the toy. The infants who were a year old sought their mothers' help in 75 percent of the episodes. Significantly, only a few 6-month-olds ever pointed or uttered a recognizable sound to communicate their goal. As a consequence, the 6-month-olds had to depend almost exclusively on their mothers' understanding of what they wanted. One-year-olds also remained dependent on their mothers' special knowledge and goodwill to achieve their goals, but they were markedly more adept in signaling their needs through conventional sounds and words.

These findings provide an important clue to the sources of infants' wariness of strangers. The adults young infants interact with every day provide a predictable and supportive environment for them at a time when their communicative abilities are restricted, and there are only a few people young infants can count on to arrange the environment appropriately in accordance with their expectations. Before babies reach the age of 7 months, their capacity to classify people as "those who can be trusted to help" versus "unpredictable strangers," and to remember the likely implications each category of person has for them, is

attachment An enduring emotional bond between babies and specific people.

at best limited. Once infants can firmly form such categories, however, and use them to compare a current situation with past ones, there is a qualitative change in the way they respond to strangers. Babies realize that strangers do not have routines for interacting with them and cannot be depended upon to notice and understand their signals or to do what they need them to do.

A NEW FORM OF EMOTIONAL RELATIONSHIP

All the developments we have discussed in this chapter converge late in the first year of life with a change in the emotional relationships between parents and their infants. According to Joseph Campos and his colleagues, locomotion is the critical factor in these changes. As a way of getting empirical evidence about the role of locomotion in orchestrating psychological change between 6 and 9 months, Campos and his colleagues interviewed parents of 8-month-old infants, some of whom had begun to crawl and some of whom had not. Parents of children who had begun to crawl had more intense positive and negative feelings about their infants than did parents whose infants had not yet begun to crawl. The parents of children who were crawling said that they now gave their children tighter hugs, roughhoused with them more, and talked to them more affectionately. They also reported that they became angry at their babies and increased their attempts to control them with angry remarks.

Infants' expressions of emotion also seemed to change in conjunction with locomotion. The parents of babies who had begun to crawl reported that their babies now became angry more frequently and more intensely when their efforts to achieve a goal were frustrated. The babies who crawled also seemed to become more upset when their parents left their sides. One mother reported:

> If I leave [the room] she gets upset unless she's busy and doesn't see it. But as soon as she notices, she starts hollering. I don't think it mattered the first four months. When she started doing more, sitting up, crawling, that's when she'd get upset when I would leave. (Campos et al., 1992, p. 33)

Many developmental psychologists believe that these new forms of emotional expression signal a new, emotionally charged bond, which they call **attachment.** Eleanor Maccoby (1980) lists four signs of attachment in babies and young children:

1. They seek to be near their primary caregivers. Before the age of 7 to 8 months, few babies plan and make organized attempts to achieve contact with their caregivers; after this age, babies often follow their caregivers closely, for example.
2. They show distress if separated from their caregivers. Before attachment begins, infants show little disturbance when their caregivers walk out of the room.
3. They are happy when they are reunited with the person they are attached to.
4. They orient their actions to the caregiver, even when he or she is absent. Babies listen for the caregiver's voice and watch the caregiver while they play.

The special relationship with their primary caregivers that babies begin to display between 7 and 9 months of age undergoes significant change during the remainder of infancy and beyond. We will take up these later changes in attachment in Chapter 6. At this point, we need to pause to take into account all the different processes that become coordinated in the bio-social-behavioral shift.

THE CHANGING NATURE OF COMMUNICATION

The pleasure this baby and mother take in their face-to-face interaction is an example of the kind of emotional sharing referred to as primary intersubjectivity.

As we saw in Chapter 4 (p. 171), by 3 months of age infants and their caregivers are jointly experiencing pleasure in simple face-to-face interactions (recall Daniel Stern's (1977) description of the baby whose "body resonated [with pleasure] almost like a balloon being pumped up" during one such episode [p. 3]). The coordinated turn-taking that accompanies the onset of social smiling is accompanied by strong, positive, emotional feeling. Colwyn Trevarthen (1993, 1998) refers to the emotional sharing that occurs between very young infants and their caregivers at such moments as **primary intersubjectivity.** This early form of communication is restricted to direct face-to-face interactions and still depends for most of its support on the efforts of the adult participant.

Between 6 and 9 months of age, babies begin to interact with others in a new and more complex way that Trevarthen calls **secondary intersubjectivity.** The hallmark of secondary intersubjectivity is that infants and caregivers share understandings and emotions that refer beyond themselves to objects and other people. If a mother and her 5-month-old baby are looking at each other and the mother suddenly looks to one side, the infant will not follow the mother's gaze. If the mother points at something across the room, the infant will stare at her finger. In contrast, at 6 months of age, babies look in the direction their caregivers are looking and will focus on objects and events that their caregivers call to their attention (Butterworth, 1998; Butterworth & Jarrett, 1991).

Social Referencing

A phenomenon known as *social referencing* provides a striking example of secondary intersubjectivity, and reflects both the new emotional relationship between infants and their caregivers and the infants' increasingly complex communicative skills (Campos et al., 1997). **Social referencing** refers to babies' tendency to look at their caregivers for some indication of how they should feel and act when they encounter something unfamiliar. It becomes a common means of communication as soon as babies begin to move about on their own (Campos & Stenberg, 1981). When babies notice that the caregiver is looking at the same unfamiliar thing they are looking at and appears to be concerned, they hesitate and become wary. If instead the caregiver smiles and looks pleased, they relax (Walden & Baxter, 1989). Babies will even check back to see how the caregiver responds to an object after they have made their own appraisal of it (Rosen et al., 1992).

Researchers in the United States have found a difference in the ways baby boys and baby girls respond to their caregivers' worried looks. Baby girls are more likely than baby boys to move away from an object their caregivers have looked at with fear. Perhaps as a result, caregivers find it necessary to use more intensely fearful facial expressions when communicating worried concern to their sons (Rosen et al., 1992).

Smiles and other facial expressions are only rudimentary means of communication. As babies become more mobile and more likely to wander out of their caregivers' sight and reach, facial expressions become less available as a source of information. A new means of interaction, one that will allow babies and caregivers to communicate at a distance, now becomes an urgent necessity. We refer, of course, to language.

primary intersubjectivity The emotional sharing that occurs between very young infants and their caregivers. It is restricted to face-to-face communication.

secondary intersubjectivity The sharing between infants and their caregivers of understandings and emotions that refer beyond themselves to objects and other people.

social referencing Babies' tendency to look at their caregivers for some indication of how they should feel and act when they encounter something unfamiliar.

The Beginnings of Language Comprehension and Speech

Infants are able to recognize their own names and distinguish them from names with similar stress patterns, such as "Amy" versus "Suzie," as early as 4 months of age (Jusczyk, 1997). By 6 months of age they begin to show the first

This newcomer to the world of upright posture is looking back to see what his mother thinks of his exploits. His inquiring gaze is an example of social referencing.

signs of comprehending words for highly familiar objects such as "mommy" or "daddy," and by the time they are 8 to 9 months of age they begin to identify phrases as they listen to streams of speech (Jusczyk, 1997; Tincoff & Juszyk, 1999). These abilities function as "perceptual scaffolding" on which language-learning capacities can be built (Hirsh-Pasek et al., 1987, p. 282).

At about 9 months of age, children begin to understand some common expressions such as "Do you want your bottle?" "Wave bye-bye," and "Cookie?" when they are used in highly specific, often routine, situations. One little girl observed by Elizabeth Bates and her colleagues touched her head when asked, "Where are your little thoughts?" Another would bring her favorite doll when she was asked to "bring a dolly," but she did not understand the word "doll" to refer to any doll but her own (Bates et al., 1979).

The ability to produce language, which appears at or about the same time as do pointing and social referencing, can be traced back to the cooing and gurgling noises babies begin to make at 10 to 12 weeks of age (Butterworth & Morisette, 1996; Harris et al., 1995). Soon thereafter, babies with normal hearing not only initiate cooing sounds but also begin to respond with gurgles and coos to the voices of others. When their cooing is imitated, they will answer with more coos, thereby engaging in a "conversation" in which turns are taken at vocalizing. They are most likely to vocalize with their caregivers and other familiar people.

Babbling, a form of vocalizing that combines a consonant and vowel sound, such as "dadadadadadada" or "babababababa," begins around 7 months of age (Adamson, 1995). At first babbling amounts to no more than vocal play, as babies discover the wealth of sounds they can make with tongue, teeth, palate, and vocal cords. They practice making these sound combinations endlessly, much as they practice grasping objects or rolling over. Early babbling is the same the world over, no matter what language the baby's family speaks, and babies even produce syllables they have never heard before and will not use when they learn to speak (Blake & de Boysson-Bardies, 1992). At about 9 months of age, however, babies begin to narrow their babbling to the sounds produced in the language that they hear every day. Since babies often babble when they play alone, early babbling does not seem to be an attempt to communicate. It is almost as if children are singing to themselves using repeatable parts of their language.

Toward the end of the first year, babies begin to babble with the intonation and stress of actual utterances in the language they will eventually speak. Such vocalizations are called **jargoning.** At this point, as Lauren Adamson (1995) describes it, "a stream of babbling often flows like speech, following its distinctive intonational patterns of declarations, commands, and questions" (p. 163). At about the same time, babies start to repeat particular short utterances in particular situations, as if their utterances have some meaning. When Jake was about 10 months old, for example, if he wanted the juice bottle in the bag hanging on the back of his stroller, he would turn around in his seat, say, "Dah, dah," and reach toward the bag while looking up at his mother in appeal. She immediately knew what he wanted and gave it to him.

By about 12 months of age, infants are able to comprehend about a dozen common phrases, such as "Give me a hug," "Stop it!" and "Let's go bye-bye." During the same period, the first distinguishable words make their appearance, although their use is restricted to only a few contexts or objects (Fenson et al., 1994).

The course of vocalizing by deaf children provides an instructive contrast to that of hearing children. It used to be thought that deaf children be-

babbling A form of vocalizing by babies that includes consonant and vowel sounds like those in speech.

jargoning Babbling with the stress and intonation of actual utterances in the language that the baby will eventually speak.

gan to babble at the same age as hearing children (Lenneberg et al., 1965). Work by D. Kimbrough Oller and Rebecca Eilers (1988), however, has shown that the vocalizations of deaf and hearing infants differ markedly in ways that indicate that only deaf children with residual hearing actually babble. By 1 year of age or so, totally deaf children rarely vocalize. However, if their caregivers communicate with each other in sign language, these infants "babble" with their hands, making the movements that will become the elements of sign language (Pettito & Marentette, 1991).

These budding linguistic abilities, which we discuss in more detail in Chapters 6 and 8, are part and parcel of the reorganization of babies' perceptual-motor, cognitive, and social capacities that signals the advent of a new bio-social-behavioral shift.

A NEW BIO-SOCIAL-BEHAVIORAL SHIFT

Table 5.3 summarizes prominent changes that converge to create a bio-social-behavioral shift in infants' development between 7 and 9 months of age (Brazelton, 1990; Emde et al., 1976; Fischer & Rose, 1994). Whereas the crucial biological events at the 2½-month bio-social-behavioral shift involved changes in the connections between the sensory cortex of the brain and the brain stem, the shift that occurs at 7 to 9 months involves changes in the frontal lobes of the cerebral cortex, which are essential for planning and executing deliberate action. Equally significant are increases in the strength of muscles and bones, which are necessary to support locomotion.

As we noted earlier, locomotion appears to orchestrate the reorganization of many other functions that have been developing in parallel with it during infancy. For one thing, the acquisition of new motor skills leads infants to discover many properties of objects in their immediate environment. They become capable of reaching for objects efficiently and picking them up, feeling them, tasting them, moving around them, and using them for various

TABLE 5.3 ELEMENTS OF THE BIO-SOCIAL-BEHAVIORAL SHIFT AT 7 TO 9 MONTHS

Biological Domain	Growth of muscles and hardening of bones
	Myelination of motor neurons to lower trunk, legs, and hands
	Myelination of cerebellum, hippocampus, and frontal lobes
	New forms of EEG activity in cortex
Behavioral Domain	Onset of crawling
	Fear of heights
	Coordinated reaching and grasping
	Action sequences coordinated to achieve goals
	Object permanence displayed in actions
	Recall memory
	Wariness in response to novelty
	Babbling
Social Domain	Wariness of strangers
	New emotional response to caregiver (attachment)
	Social referencing

purposes of their own. As babies learn that some of the "objects" out there move and respond in coordination with them, their interactions with people take on a whole new dimension. They begin to recognize that sympathetic adults buffer them against discomfort and danger. These adults can be counted on to understand their signals, to complete their actions for them, and to arrange things so that they can act more effectively for themselves.

These experiences would not amount to much, however, if memories of them did not accumulate adequately in infants' minds. Once babies are able to move away from the immediate presence of watchful adults, they can no longer rely on the adults' assistance and protection as they did before. It is not enough to recognize that one has seen an object before or to respond with curiosity if it is new. Babies must be able to recall ("bring to mind") their earlier experiences with objects, including people, so that they can anticipate how to behave effectively.

Both the baby and the caregiver must accommodate themselves to the uncertainties of their increasing separation as babies begin to move about on their own. Babies begin to exhibit emotions, such as anger when their efforts to reach a goal are frustrated, fear when confronted by strangers, and wariness when encountering something unexpected, as well as strong feelings of attachment for their caregivers. Caregivers arrange the environment so that the baby is likely to come to no harm, and they keep a watchful eye (or ear) open for anything amiss. Babies, for their part, keep an eye on the caregiver's face and listen to the tone of the adult's voice, which communicates his or her evaluation of the situation.

As their first birthdays approach, many babies have progressed from crawling to walking upright. Walking increases both their independence and the importance of using all their accumulating cognitive and communicative abilities to coordinate their actions with those of their caregivers.

Sophisticated as 1-year-olds may be in comparison with babies of 2½ months, the pattern of adaptation that they have achieved is destined to change. The factor that seems to play a pivotal role during the next period of development will be a new level of symbolic capacity, that is, an enhanced capacity to represent the world to oneself and to use tools and symbols.

SUMMARY

BIOLOGICAL CHANGES

- Although there is great individual variation, most healthy babies triple in weight during the first year of life. Changes in size are accompanied by changes in overall body proportions that are important for the eventual achievement of balanced walking.
- Hardening of the bones and increases in muscle mass contribute to the development of crawling, walking, and coordinated movements of the arms and hands.
- There is massive overproduction of synapses between the ages of 3 and 12 months that are then reduced in number as a result of experience.
- Development in the prefrontal cortex makes possible the voluntary control and planning that begin to emerge between 3 and 12 months of age.

PERCEPTUAL-MOTOR DEVELOPMENT

- The initial stage of poorly coordinated reaching and grasping, controlled primarily by subcortical brain centers, is followed by a stage of visually guided reaching and grasping, which gives way to swift and accurate voluntary movements after several months of practice.

- Increasing skill in grasping objects with the hands makes possible the discovery of many new properties of objects.
- Locomotion, which begins during the second half of the first year of life, brings about a fundamental change in infants' relationships with their environments. Motor control of the body begins at the head and neck and proceeds gradually to the trunk and legs. At 7 to 8 months, infants begin to crawl or creep, using a combination of leg and arm movements. Walking is achieved a few months later, around the first birthday.
- Motor development can be speeded up by extensive practice, but early practice has little influence on the eventual level of proficiency of basic motor skills.

COGNITIVE CHANGES

- According to Piaget, infants progress through two additional sensorimotor substages before the end of the first year. Between 4 and 8 months they pay increased attention to external objects and prolong actions that produce interesting changes in their environment (substage 3). Between 8 and 12 months of age, they acquire the ability to coordinate separate actions in order to achieve a goal (substage 4).
- Important changes occur in infants' ability to keep in mind and act upon objects that are out of sight:
  1. For the first 3 months of life, infants appear to forget objects not present to their senses.
  2. There is uncertainty about what infants between 4 and 8 months old understand about objects that are out of sight. Some experiments indicate that infants understand that objects exist even when they cannot see them but they are incapable of acting on this knowledge. Other experiments indicate that infants this young fail to understand the continuing existence of objects that are out of sight.
  3. At about 8 months of age, infants begin to search for hidden objects but quickly become confused or forget their location.
  4. Memory for the location of objects continues to improve into the second year of life, as does the ability to search for hidden objects.
- The belief that infants are born with rudimentary knowledge of such concepts as object permanence, number, and physical causality has led to the idea of the "precocious infant." The existence of such precocious knowledge is hotly contested, but it is fairly certain that by 3 to 4 months of age, infants are able to perceive the correspondence between such varied properties of objects as the way they look and how they feel. It is not known how early such understandings develop or what aspects of them are present at birth.
- The ability to perceive a variety of objects as members of a single category appears as early as 3 months of age. There is uncertainty about the course of early categorization abilities. Some believe that early categories are based on similarity of perceptual features and that categories based on conceptual features do not begin to appear until the

end of the first year. Others believe that conceptual categories are present as early as they can be tested for.

- Between the ages of 2½ and 12 months, memory increases steadily. When provided with a specific reminder of training received a month earlier, infants as young as 3 months of age remember how to make a mobile move.
- About the same time that babies begin to crawl, they show signs of being able to recall objects and people that are not present and activities they have not practiced.
- The development of memory and categorizing abilities combine to make infants wary when they encounter unfamiliar events.

A NEW RELATIONSHIP WITH THE SOCIAL WORLD

- Changes in social and emotional behavior accompany changes in motor skills and cognition. Infants become wary of strangers and upset when they are separated from their primary caregivers, with whom they have formed an emotional bond called attachment.
- Increased locomotion is accompanied by a new form of communicative activity. Babies begin to monitor the expression on the caregiver's face to determine the caregiver's reaction to an object or event they are both attending to. Such social referencing helps babies to evaluate their environment.
- Infants begin to comprehend and produce aspects of the language in their environment.

A NEW BIO-SOCIAL-BEHAVIORAL SHIFT

- Events in the major developmental domains converge between the ages of 7 and 9 months in a bio-social-behavioral shift that ushers in a qualitatively new stage of development.

KEY TERMS

affordances, p. 185
attachment, p. 208
babbling, p. 210
categorizing, p. 198
cognitive processes, p. 187
conceptual categorization, p. 202
cross-modal perception, p. 195
deferred imitation, p. 204
exuberant synaptogenesis, p. 183
intentionality, p. 189
jargoning, p. 210
locomotion, p. 185
object permanence, p. 191
perceptual categorization, p. 202
primary intersubjectivity, p. 209
secondary circular reactions, p. 189
secondary intersubjectivity, p. 209
social referencing, p. 209
zone of proximal development, p. 207

THOUGHT QUESTIONS

1. List some of the physical and intellectual abilities a baby needs in order to eat a cookie without help from anyone else.
2. Why is it so difficult to determine how precocious infants really are? In other words, why is it so difficult to determine what knowledge is innate and what knowledge is acquired as a result of experience, on the basis of evidence from this chapter?

3. How does the way infants search for hidden objects cast light on their mental abilities for thinking about the world?
4. What sorts of links are believed to connect wariness of strangers to changes in memory and categorizing ability late in the first year of life?
5. What are the major elements of the bio-social-behavioral shift that occurs between 7 and 9 months of age?

CHAPTER 6

The End of Infancy

The self and its boundaries are at the heart of philosophical speculation on human nature, and the sense of self and its counterpart, the sense of other, are universal phenomena that profoundly influence all our social experiences.

Daniel Stern, *The Interpersonal World of the Infant*

Just before Jake's second birthday, his mother, Barbara, and his father and sisters went to Switzerland for a few weeks, leaving Jake in the care of his Aunt Retta. Before the trip, Jake's mother arranged to spend a week at her sister's with Jake so that he would have a chance to become familiar with the household.

At first Jake ignored everyone at his aunt's house except his mother and his 4-year-old cousin, Linda. The first afternoon in the sandbox with Linda, he sat and watched with fascination as she conducted a tea party for her teddy bear and bunny rabbit. After a while he placed several small containers in a row on the edge of the sandbox, filled a large container with sand, and then poured its contents into the smaller ones in perfect imitation of his cousin. Then Linda caught his eye. Calling, "Beep-beep! Get out of my way!" she took a toy truck and ran it along the edge of the sandbox, knocking over the teacups and stuffed animals. In an instant Jake was yelling, "Beep-beep!" and knocking over his containers with a toy car. Linda laughed wildly. Jake laughed too and chased her truck around the edge of the sandbox with his car.

From then on Jake followed Linda around the house. If she asked her mother for something to eat or drink, he was right behind her, waiting for his share. Jake did not talk to his aunt directly, and he would not permit her to change his diaper or help him. A lot of the time he refused help from anyone, but if he really couldn't manage, he said, "Mommy do it." Jake knew that Barbara was leaving. "You goin', Mommy?" he asked her several times during that week.

At the airport Jake held Linda's hand and watched bravely as his mother disappeared into the plane. But that afternoon he cried. Linda tried to distract him, but he would not join her in play. Finally she brought him his favorite pillow, which he carried around for the next few days. Then he seemed to adjust to his mother's absence so well that he began to call his aunt "Mommy."

When Jake's family returned 20 days later, there was much excitement at the airport. No one paid any attention when Jake sat on his aunt's lap on the ride back to her house.

That afternoon Jake fell and scraped his knee while he was kicking a ball. He ran crying to his father. His father, who was busy at that moment, suggested that he ask his mother to put a Band-Aid on his scrape. Jake ran into the kitchen where his aunt and his mother were sitting. "Mommy fix it," he said, showing his injured knee to his aunt and ignoring his mother. When Barbara offered to help, Jake refused.

Later, in the swimming pool, Jake was showing his father all the new things he had learned to do. "Show Mommy," his father said, suspecting something. His suspicions were confirmed when Jake turned and tried to get his aunt's attention.

Jake had called his uncle "Daddy" throughout his stay, but as soon as his father was on the scene again, his uncle became "Uncle Len" and his father became "Daddy." No such switch occurred for "Mommy." For the 3 days that Jake's family remained at his aunt and uncle's house, Jake ignored Barbara and refused to allow her to do anything for him. When they were preparing to return to their own home, however, Jake looked up at his aunt and said, "Bye, Auntie Retta." Then, turning to Barbara, he addressed her directly for the first time since she had returned. "Let's go, Mom," he said, raising his arms as a signal for her to pick him up.

The changes that have occurred in Jake's behavior since his first birthday reveal a lot about the developmental phenomena that mark the second year of life. On his first birthday, Jake was just beginning to walk; approaching his second, he runs and climbs with ease. He is also far more skilled in manipulating small objects. At 12 months of age his vocabulary consisted primarily of single words and a few set phrases—"juice," "woof," "Mommy," "All gone"; now Jake's language skills enable him to communicate more effectively and to participate in imaginative play with another child. Jake is still wary of strange people and places, and he is still so strongly attached to his parents that it was difficult for him to adapt to being left at his aunt's home. Cognitively, he is sufficiently sophisticated to "punish" his mother for her absence by treating his aunt as his mother right up to the moment of getting in the car to go home.

Jake's behavior provides excellent examples of the kinds of changes that infants undergo as they complete the period of infancy. As a result of changes in brain, body, and experience, children's reasoning about, and interactions with, the world of objects and people become increasingly sophisticated. In their second year, children acquire the ability to, among other things, imitate complex sequences of actions, engage in pretend play, communicate using language, experience new kinds of emotions, and participate in social relationships with other children and their caregivers in a new way. Each of these facets of development is interesting in its own right, a single thread in a tapestry. What is most important, however, is the way in which these separate aspects of development converge to create a new bio-social-behavioral shift marking the end of infancy and the beginning of a new, broad stage of development.

BIOLOGICAL MATURATION

During the second year of life, children's bodies continue to grow rapidly, but the rate of their growth is much slower than it was in the first year (Tanner, 1990). Among children raised in the United States today, average height increases from 29 to 38 inches and weight increases from 20 to 33 pounds, although there is considerable variation from one child to the next.

There are several changes in brain structures during the second year that many developmentalists believe are linked to the emergence of new psychological capacities (Diamond, 1990a; Huttenlocher & Dabholkar, 1997). For example, the second year brings accelerated myelination both within the cerebral cortex and between the brain stem and the cerebral cortex (see Figure 4.2, p. 130). This development improves the functioning of the neurons that link the prefrontal cortex and frontal lobes to the brain stem, where emotional responses are partially generated, and to cortical centers, where visual and auditory input is analyzed. These centers now begin to work in greater synchrony (Thatcher, 1997). This increase in synchronized brain activity appears vital to the emergence of psychological functions that define late infancy, including a new and more complex form of self-awareness, more systematic problem solving, the voluntary control of behavior, and the acquisition of language.

There is also evidence that toward the end of infancy the length and the degree of branching of the neurons in the cerebral cortex approach adult magnitudes: each neuron now has multiple connections with others, usually numbering in the thousands. At this time, the various areas of the brain, which have been maturing at very different rates, reach similar levels of development. For the first time, the overall pattern of development among the various brain systems begins to approximate that of adults (Chugani, 1998; Raybaud & Gerard, 1998). The brain will undergo additional bursts of growth in later years, but after infancy the brain generally develops at a more modest pace, and it appears that a great deal of the brain structure that eventually will support adult behavior is present by the end of the second year.

PERCEPTUAL–MOTOR COORDINATION

As a result of the biological maturation that occurs during the second year, children gain increased control of arm, hand, bladder, bowel, and leg muscles, as well as improved coordination of perceiving and acting.

LOCOMOTION

As infants approach their first birthday, they become able to stand up and walk, which allows them to cover more distance and frees their hands for exploring and manipulating objects. At first they need assistance of some kind in order to walk. This assistance can come in several forms. Many babies pull themselves into a standing position by grasping a chair leg or reaching up to hold on to the seat of a couch. Seeing such attempts, caretakers often help by holding both the baby's arms to support the initial hesitant steps.

This child's first steps display the posture and uncertainty characteristic of toddlers just learning to walk.

In a series of studies, Esther Thelen and her colleagues traced how a number of separately developing skills converge to enable the child to walk (Thelen & Ulrich, 1991; Thelen et al., 1989). One crucial element in this process is the ability to coordinate leg movements with shifts of body weight from one foot to the other as each foot steps forward in its turn. The researchers found, for example, that if infants are placed on a treadmill and given the needed support, they execute the pattern of leg movements needed for walking as early as 7 months of age. They also begin to make walking movements when placed in water deep enough to support their bodies (see Chapter 4, p. 141). But babies this age cannot yet walk on a stationary surface without support that enables them to shift their weight, keep their balance, and coordinate their arm and leg movements.

No one factor can be considered the key to walking; rather, walking becomes possible only when all the component skills (upright posture, leg alternation, weight shifting, sense of balance) have been developed and when the child has been able to practice combining them (Thelen, 1995).

The onset of walking requires not only the coordination of new sets of muscles, but also increased sensitivity to perceptual input from the environment. Walking ability, and the ability to perceive the conditions of the environment, develop together. Karen Adolph and her colleagues demonstrated the confluence of these developments by arranging for infants to move up and down ramps of varying steepness (Adolph, 1997; Adolph et al., 1993). The children were studied from before they were able to crawl until after they had been walking for a few months (for this group of children, crawling began on average at about 8½ months while walking began between

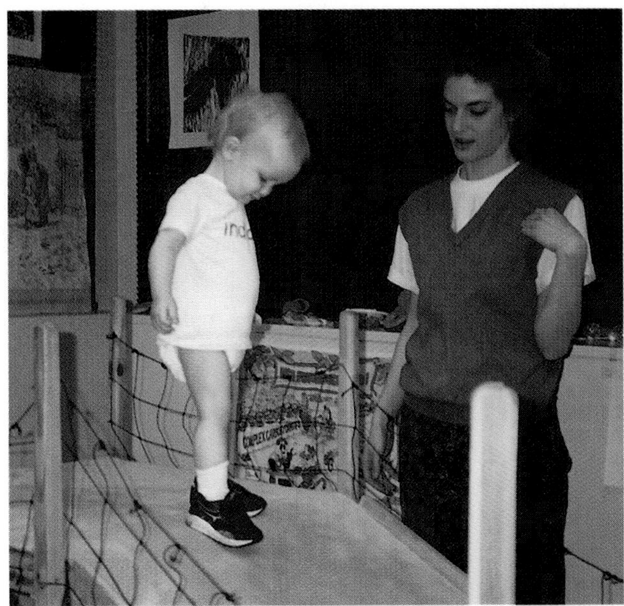

FIGURE 6.1
Between the ages of 8 and 14 months, the transition from crawling to walking changes the way these two babies approach the task of going down a ramp. (left) *The 8½-month-old sees that there is a slope but plunges down it just the same.* (right) *The toddler hesitates and feels the incline of the ramp with his foot before attempting to descend it.*

12 and 13 months). The researchers wanted to know if all the infants would perceive the degree of slope and adjust their movements accordingly so as not to fall, and whether the ability to crawl up and down slopes carried over to walking (see Figure 6.1).

When these children first began to crawl, they demonstrated that they perceived how steep the ramp was—they spent more time exploring the surface of the steeper ramps and exhibited increased caution. But when they did try to crawl down a steep ramp, they had difficulty adjusting their movements appropriately. Many tumbled down the ramps into their mother's waiting arms. With experience crawling, infants worked out efficient ways to crawl down the slope, such as inching down backward, and they learned not to attempt ramps that were too steep for them.

Experience crawling up and down slopes did not seem to carry over to walking. Infants who were just beginning to walk had to learn all over again how to gauge a ramp's slope relative to their abilities from an upright position. Beginning walkers experienced great difficulty with even a gently sloping ramp. By contrast, when more experienced walkers encountered a gentle slope, they climbed it without hesitation. But when it was steeper, especially if they had to descend it, they hesitated and tried various alternative methods of getting down. Often they would sit and slide down the slope or revert to crawling, backing down slowly on their hands and knees. The work of Adolph and her colleagues provides a good illustration of how maturational factors and experience combine to create a flexible new system of behaviors.

When they take their first steps on their own, babies become "toddlers," so named for the characteristic way they spread their legs and toddle from side to side. Most 1-year-olds are unbalanced and fall often, but falling does not stop them. The fall is a short one after all, and walking is too exciting to give up on, so they simply get up and rush ahead to the next tumble. Within a few months of their first steps, infants are usually walking in a coordinated fashion (Clark & Phillips, 1993) (see Figure 6.2).

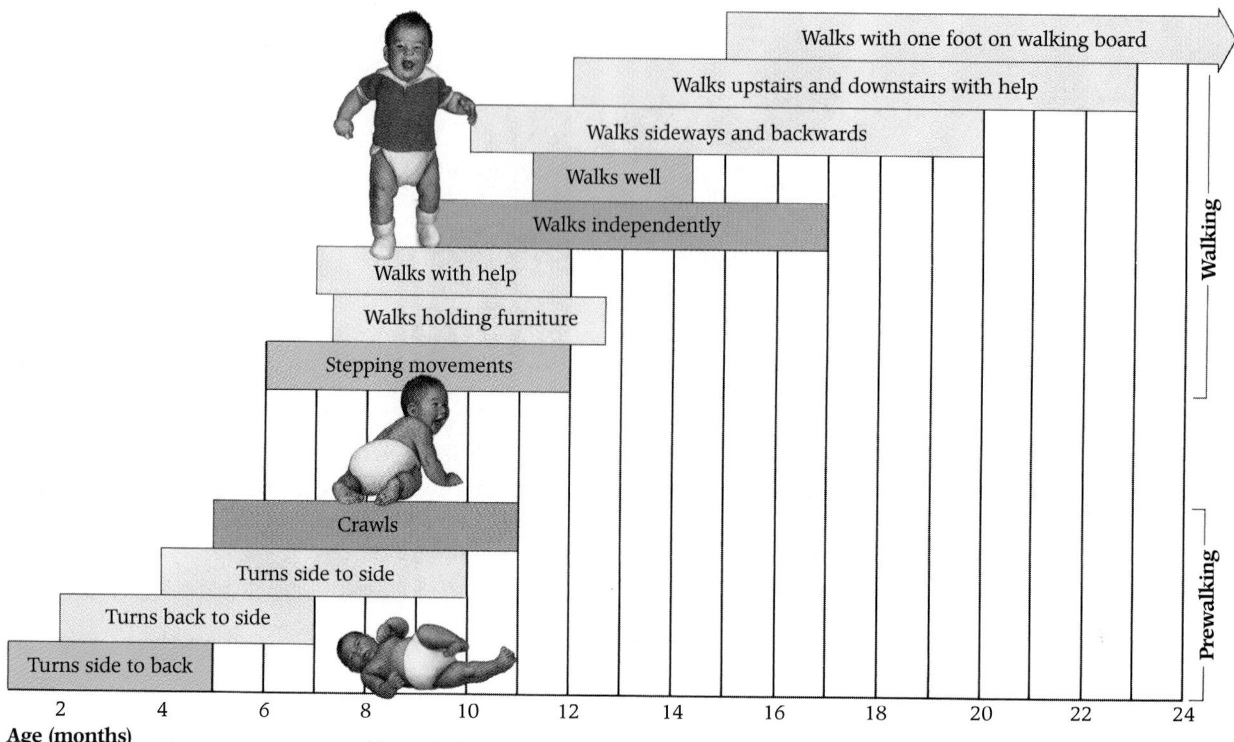

FIGURE 6.2

The progression from creeping to crawling to walking follows a classic developmental sequence. Each new stage in locomotion allows children to move more rapidly and involves a qualitative change in the pattern of their behavior.

Walking brings even more changes to babies' lives than crawling did. As Selma Fraiberg (1959) so eloquently put it, walking represents "a cutting of the moorings to the mother's body. . . . To the child who takes his first steps and finds himself walking alone, this moment must bring the first sharp sense of uniqueness and separateness of his body and his person, the discovery of the solitary self" (p. 61).

MANUAL DEXTERITY

Coordination of fine hand movements increases significantly between 12 and 30 months. Infants 1 year old can only roll a ball or fling it awkwardly; by the time they are 2½, they can throw it. They can also turn the pages of a book without tearing or creasing them, snip paper with scissors, string beads with a needle and thread, build a tower six blocks high with considerable ease, hold a cup of milk or a spoon of applesauce without spilling it, and dress themselves (as long as there are no buttons or shoelaces) (Gesell, 1929). Each of these accomplishments may seem minor in itself, but each skill requires a good deal of practice to master, and each increases infants' overall competence.

Even an act as elementary as using a spoon requires incredibly precise coordination (Connolly & Dalgleish, 1989). Figure 6.3 depicts the variety of ways in which infants between 10 and 23 months of age attempt to hold a spoon. After the spoon is dipped into the food, it must be held level so that nothing spills while it is raised to the lips. Then its contents must be emptied into the mouth. At 10 to 12 months of age, babies can do only simple things with a spoon, such as banging it on the table or dipping it repeatedly into the bowl. Slightly older children can coordinate the actions of opening their mouth and bringing the spoon to it, but as often as not, the spoon is empty when it arrives. This problem is the next one to be solved, as infants learn to get food onto the spoon, carry it to the mouth without spilling it, and put the food in the mouth. Once this elementary sequence of actions is achieved, it is then adjusted until it is smooth and automatic. With all these coordinated

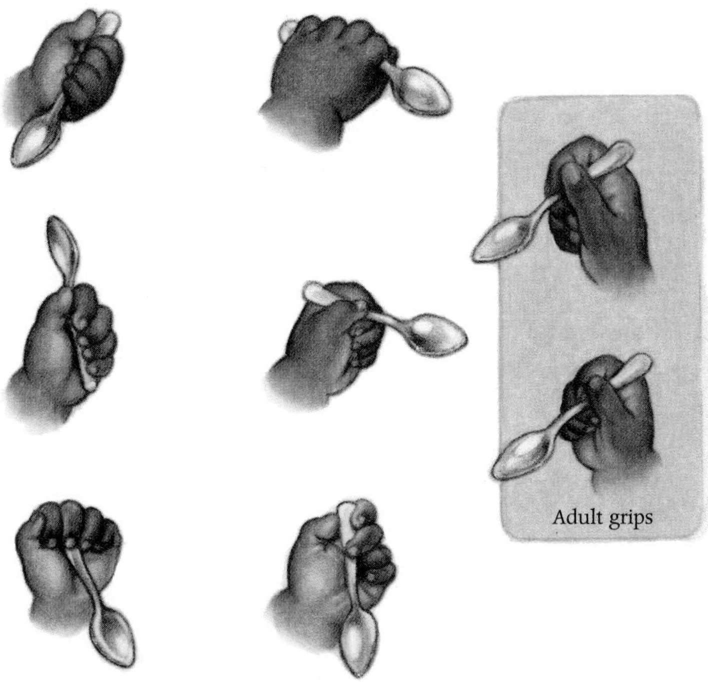

FIGURE 6.3
Grip patterns. Babies initially grip a spoon in many different ways. As they accumulate experience and gain motor control, they eventually adopt an adult grip.

One of the ways toddlers express independence is by taking their clothes off. And as their manual dexterity increases during the second year, they can even put their clothes on by themselves.

actions to be assembled, no wonder it isn't until age 2 or older that you can leave a child with a spoon and a bowl of cereal and expect much of the cereal to get into the child's mouth!

CONTROL OF ELIMINATION

Another important element in the growing ability of children to act on their own is the acquisition of voluntary control over the muscles that govern elimination. In the early months of life, elimination is an involuntary act. When the baby's bladder or bowels are full, they stimulate the appropriate sphincter muscles, which open automatically, causing elimination. Before a baby can control these muscles voluntarily, the sensory pathways from the bladder and bowels must be mature enough to transmit signals to the cortex of the brain. Children must then learn to associate these signals with the need to eliminate. They must also learn to tighten their sphincters to prevent elimination and to loosen them to permit it.

Until the 1950s, toilet training in many countries was begun as early as possible, not only for convenience in an era before there were washing machines and disposable diapers but also because it was believed that early training would ensure bowel regularity, which was considered important for good health. (The first edition of *Infant Care,* a magazine for parents published by the U.S. Children's Bureau in 1914, advised mothers to begin bowel training by the third month or even earlier [Wolfenstein, 1953]). Then, with the advent of the aforementioned conveniences, parental practices began to change. For example, Remo Largo and his colleagues found that in the 1950s, Swiss parents strongly believed that early toilet training was desirable: 96 percent of Swiss parents began toilet training before their infants were 12 months old. By the mid-1970s parental beliefs and practices had changed radically, with the vast majority of Swiss parents not beginning toilet training until 36 months of

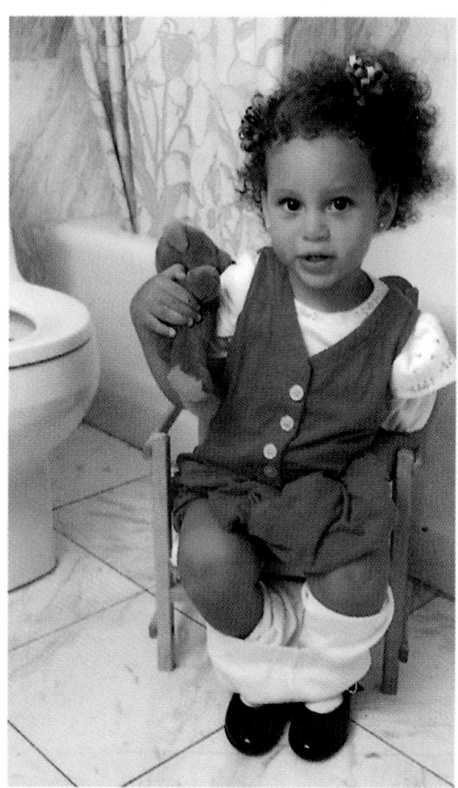

This little girl has brought along her teddy bear as she practices using a potty.

age. The toilet training of the earlier generation succeeded in the limited sense that young infants learned to eliminate *when placed on the potty.* But there was no change at all in the ages at which children gained sufficient control over their bladder and bowel functions to stay dry at night (Largo et al., 1996). These results provide strong evidence that the processes of gaining voluntary control over bowel and bladder are under maturational control.

By the time they are 2 years old, some children are able to remain dry during the day, owing in large measure to the watchfulness of adults who place them on the potty when they show signs of needing it. Many children in the United States and Europe today, however, do not achieve this milestone until sometime later, and most do not manage to stay dry while they are asleep until they are 4 years old (Berk & Friman, 1990; Largo et al., 1996).

A NEW MODE OF THOUGHT

During the second year of life, as toddlers are perfecting their ability to get around on their own two legs, to eat with utensils, and to control their body functions, they also begin to display more sophisticated ways of thinking.

COMPLETING THE SENSORIMOTOR SUBSTAGES

As we saw in Chapters 4 and 5, Piaget believed that all of an infant's actions in the first four substages of sensorimotor development are very much tied to the here and now—to what the infant is currently experiencing—and that before age 1, infants' ability to think about absent objects is severely limited (see Table 6.1).

However, around the age of 2 to 2½ years, according to Piaget, children's thinking undergoes a qualitative transformation, which he attributed to the emergence of **symbolic thought**, or **representation**—that is, the ability to mentally have one thing stand for, or *represent,* another. Even developmentalists who disagree with much of Piaget's theory agree that around the end of the second year, children begin to think in a new way (Case, 1998; Fischer & Bidell, 1998; Kagan, 1982; Vygotsky, 1934/1987).

In Piaget's view, the pathway to symbolic thought leads through substage 5, which is traversed between 12 and 18 months of age, and substage 6, which is completed by about the age of 2.

Substage 5: Tertiary Circular Reactions (12–18 Months)

As you will recall, in substage 4, infants develop the ability to combine simple actions to achieve a simple goal. The fifth substage of the sensorimotor period is characterized by an ability to vary the simple instrumental actions of substage 4 systematically and flexibly. Piaget referred to this as the substage of **tertiary circular reactions.** Whereas primary circular reactions are centered on the child's body and secondary circular reactions are focused on objects, tertiary circular reactions are focused on the relationship between the two. Now, in addition to making interesting events last by using already established secondary circular reactions, infants become capable of deliberately varying their action sequences, thereby making their explorations of the world more complex. Piaget referred to tertiary circular reactions as "experiments in order to see," because children seem to be experimenting in order to find out about the nature of objects (1952b, p. 272). Piaget observed this kind of behavior in his son Laurent, then aged 10 months and 11 days. Laurent is lying in his crib:

> He grasps in succession a celluloid swan, a box, etc., stretches out his arm and lets them fall. He distinctly varies the positions of the fall. . . . Sometimes he stretches out his arm vertically, sometimes he holds it obliquely, in front of or be-

symbolic thought (representation) The mental ability to have one thing represent, or stand for, another.

tertiary circular reactions The fifth stage of sensorimotor period, which is characterized by the deliberate variation of action sequences to solve problems and explore the world.

TABLE 6.1 SENSORIMOTOR SUBSTAGES AND STAGES OF OBJECT PERMANENCE

Substage	Age Range (months)	Characteristics of Sensorimotor Substage	Developments in Object Permanence
1	0–1½	*Reflex schemas exercised:* involuntary rooting, sucking, grasping, looking	Infant does not search for objects that have been removed from sight.
2	1½–4	*Primary circular reactions*: repetition of actions that are pleasurable in themselves	Infant orients to place where objects have been removed from sight.
3	4–8	*Secondary circular reactions:* dawning awareness of relation of own actions to environment; extension of actions that produce interesting changes in the environment	Infant will reach for a partially hidden object but stops if it disappears.
4	8–12	*Coordination of secondary circular reactions:* combining schemas to achieve a desired effect; earliest form of problem solving	Infant will search for a completely hidden object; keeps searching the original location of the object even if it is moved to another location in full view of the infant.
5	**12–18**	*Tertiary circular reactions:* deliberate variation of problem-solving means; experiments to see what the consequences will be	Infant will search for an object after seeing it moved but not if it is moved in secret.
6	**18–24**	*Beginnings of symbolic representation:* images and words come to stand for familiar objects; invention of new means of problem solving through symbolic combinations	Infant will search for a hidden object, certain that it exists somewhere.

> hind his eyes, etc. When the object falls in a new position (for example, on his pillow), he lets it fall two or three times more on the same place, as though to study the spatial relations; then he modifies the situation. (p. 269)

This kind of trial-and-error exploration distinguishes tertiary circular reactions from secondary circular reactions, which involve only previously acquired schemas. But according to Piaget's observations, although infants in substage 5 can manipulate objects in their immediate physical environment in various ways, they still do not seem able to picture actions and their probable consequences mentally prior to actually enacting them.

Substage 6: Representation (18–24 Months)

According to Piaget, the hallmark of substage 6, the final stage of the sensorimotor period, is that babies begin to base their actions on internal, mental symbols, or *representations,* of prior experiences. Before substage 6, children can act only on a "present" world. When they can re-present the world to themselves—that is, when they can present it to themselves over again, mentally—they can be said to be engaging in true mental actions.

Piaget cited several new behaviors as evidence of the emergence of symbolic representational thought. Chief among them are

- the ability to imagine objects that are not present (shown by systematic search for hidden objects);
- the appearance of systematic problem solving;
- the emergence of pretend play; and
- the ability to imitate events well after they have occurred.

MASTERY OF OBJECT PERMANENCE

Changes in sensorimotor modes of knowing are reflected in changes in the way that infants search for hidden objects. As you will recall from Chapter 5, when substage 4 infants find an object hidden in one location and then observe it being hidden in a second location, they will search for the object in its original hiding place. In substage 5, infants are markedly less likely to become confused by the switching of hiding places while they are watching and will now search for the object in its new location. However, substage 5 babies are still likely to become confused and stop searching if an object's location is changed without their seeing it moved. For example, if you pretend to hide an object in your hand while you really hide it behind your back, a substage 5 baby will continue to search for it in your hand, failing to reason that it must be somewhere else nearby. A version of this procedure that is used in many studies is shown in Figure 6.4.

(a) Infant sees apple

(b) Researcher hides apple as infant watches

(c) Researcher distracts infant and moves apple

(d) Infant is confused

(e) Infant searches for apple under wrong cloth

FIGURE 6.4
Children in stage 5 of the development of object permanence cannot maintain a firm idea of the permanence of an object when its location is changed without their knowledge. (From Bower, 1982.)

Piaget (1952b) believed that infants' mastery of object permanence comes between the ages of 18 and 24 months as a result of the new representational abilities of substage 6. That is, because they are able to hold a representation of the hidden object in mind, substage 6 infants continue to search for it even if the object has been moved without their knowledge. They appear to be able to reason, "Well, the toy wasn't where I expected, but it must be here somewhere," so they systematically check other possible locations.

Once they have mastered object permanence, infants are able to anticipate the trajectory of a moving object that has disappeared behind a barrier and predict the location of its reemergence. When a ball rolls under a couch, for example, a 2-year-old will go around to the other side of the couch to look for it instead of looking under the couch.

PROBLEM SOLVING

The ability to reason about the locations of unseen objects is only one manifestation of infants' increased ability to solve a variety of problems through the manipulation of mental representations. Piaget's observations of his daughters nicely illustrate how this ability permits older infants to solve problems systematically instead of by trial and error. Both girls were confronted by the same problem—how to pull a stick through the bars of their playpen (see Figure 6.5)—but they solved the problem in significantly different ways because one, Jacqueline, was in substage 5 and the other, Lucienne, was in substage 6. Jacqueline, age 15 months, is seated in her playpen.

> Outside is a stick 20 centimeters long, the distance of about three spaces between the bars. At first Jacqueline tries to pull the stick into her playpen horizontally, but it will not go through the bars. The second time, she accidentally tilts the stick a little in raising it. She perceives this and reaches through the bars and tilts the stick until it is sufficiently vertical to pass through the bars. But several subsequent attempts make it clear that this is an accidental success; she does not yet understand the principle involved. On the next several tries she grasps the stick by the middle and pulls it horizontally, against the bars. Unable to get it in that way, she then tilts it up. It is not until the seventeenth try that she tilts the stick up before it touches the bars, and not until the twentieth that she does so systematically. (Adapted from Piaget, 1952b, p. 305)

FIGURE 6.5
This child in substage 5 of the sensorimotor period carries out deliberate problem solving but still relies on trial and error.

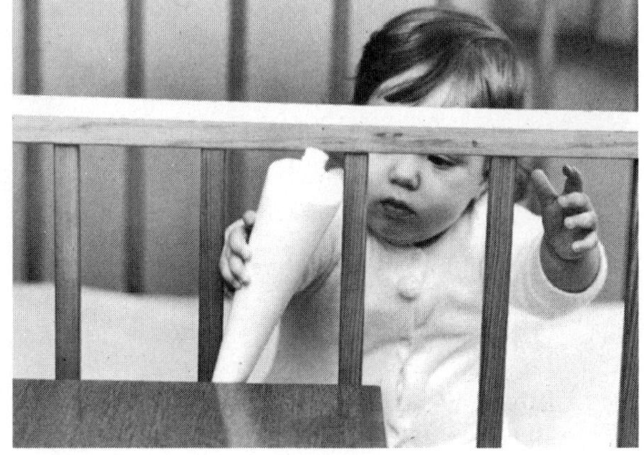

Jacqueline seemed to have a clear goal in mind because she was certainly persistent. She continued to work at the problem until it was solved. But her efforts were rather hit-or-miss. When she succeeded, she did not understand why. She grasped the solution only after many trials and many errors. This experience is typical of substage 5 of the sensorimotor period.

Although she was 2 months younger than Jacqueline was when she was presented with this problem, Lucienne's problem solving was more sophisticated, a reminder that age norms associated with Piagetian stages, like other developmental norms, are only approximate.

> Lucienne grasps the stick in the middle and pulls it horizontally. Noticing her failure, she withdraws the stick, tilts it up, and brings it through easily. When the stick is again placed on the floor, she grasps it by the middle and tilts it up before she pulls it through, or she grasps it by one end and brings it through easily. She does this with longer sticks and on successive days. Unlike her sister Jacqueline, who had to grope her way toward a solution, Lucienne profits from her failure at once. (Adapted from Piaget, 1952b, p. 336)

symbolic play (pretend, fantasy play) Play in which one object stands for, or represents, another.

In Lucienne's actions we see the essence of substage 6 sensorimotor behavior; she seems to be using information that is not immediately available to her senses to solve the problem. Instead of going through the slow process of trial and error, as her sister did, Lucienne seems to have pictured a series of events in her mind before she acted. She imagined what would happen if she pulled the stick horizontally. She then inferred that if she turned the stick so that it was vertical and parallel to the bars, it would fit between them. Piaget singled out Lucienne's ability to solve the problem through inference alone as the key evidence for the existence of a new form of thought in substage 6.

PLAY

Many developmentalists see in children's play clear parallels to their current stage of cognitive development. The early origins of play can be seen in sensorimotor behavior, as when infants kick their feet while being bathed for the sheer pleasure of the feel and sight of splashing water (a primary circular reaction). Later sensorimotor play goes beyond the baby's own body to incorporate objects and relations between objects (secondary and tertiary circular reactions) and to involve other people, as in peekaboo.

During the period from 12 to 30 months of age, new forms of play arise that appear to reflect new mental abilities (Bretherton & Bates, 1985; Piaget, 1962; Zukow, 1986). At 12 to 13 months, babies use objects in play much as adults would use them in earnest; that is, they put spoons in their mouths and bang with hammers. However, at about 18 months babies begin to treat one thing as if it were another. They stir their "coffee" with a twig and comb the doll's hair with a toy rake or, as Jake and his cousin did, act as if the edge of a sandbox were a roadway. This kind of behavior is called **symbolic play** (also **pretend** or **fantasy play**): it is play in which one object stands for—that is, represents—another, as the rake stands for a comb.

This child, who is "giving Godzilla a drink," is engaging in the kind of complicated symbolic play that appears to emerge between the ages of 18 and 24 months.

Studies have shown that symbolic play becomes increasingly complex after it makes its appearance during the second year (Howes et al., 1989; Hughes, 1995; Watson & Fischer, 1980). In the simplest case, children direct their play actions at themselves (for example, an infant pretends to feed herself with a spoon). In the most complicated cases, which are not usually seen until about 30 months of age, children can make a toy (in developmental parlance, an "agent") perform actions fitting a social role (for example, the infant makes a mother doll feed her baby doll) (see Table 6.2).

Many developmentalists believe that children's play is not only an index of their cognitive development but also serves important functions for cognitive and social growth. Piaget believed that play during infancy consolidates newly acquired sensorimotor schemas (Piaget, 1962). Cultural context theorists speculate that early forms of play provide opportunities to acquire abilities that will become important later, just as the seemingly aimless movements of the embryo are a vital part of the process of fetal development (Göncü, 1999; Nicolopoulou, 1993; Packer, 1994). As we will discuss in more detail in Chapter 9 (p. 362), according to this interpretation, the "as if" nature of pretend play allows children to perform actions that are developmentally more advanced than those they can perform on their own. Thus a child can "pour tea" in a make-believe game in which the demands for precision are far more lenient than they would be if the child were to try to pour a glass of milk at the breakfast table.

TABLE 6.2 FOUR STEPS IN THE DEVELOPMENT OF AGENT USE IN PRETENDING

Type of Agent Use	Example
Self as agent	The infant puts his or her head on a pillow to pretend to go to sleep
Passive other agent	The infant puts a doll on a pillow to pretend that it goes to sleep
Passive substitute agent	The infant puts a block on a pillow to pretend that it goes to sleep
Active other agent	The infant has a doll place a block on the pillow to go to sleep, as if the doll were actually "putting the block to bed"

Source: Adapted from Watson & Fischer; 1980.

Also, as the cultural context approach would predict, the level of sophistication of infants' social play depends on the social context in which it occurs. Barbara Fiese (1990) found that children's play lasted longer and was more sophisticated when children played with their mothers than when they played by themselves. Other researchers found that mothers modeled possible pretend play topics—pretending, for example, to talk on a toy phone and then offering the toy phone to the child to "continue" the conversation. They also adjusted the level of their play to that of their children, maximizing its attractiveness (Tamis-Le Monda & Bornstein, 1994). Interestingly, toddlers' play is often more advanced when they play frequently with older siblings than it is when they play with their mothers, probably because the siblings are better able to enter into the fantasy than the adults (Farver & Wimbarti, 1995; Zukow-Goldring, 1995).

Despite the popularity of the belief that play facilitates general development, studies explicitly designed to demonstrate beneficial effects of play among infants are generally lacking. Peter Smith, who has been active in this field of research, cautions that the belief that play is "good for babies" goes beyond the existing evidence (Smith, 1988). His doubts are supported by cross-cultural work indicating that Central American Mayan infants engage in less play in the first 2 years of life than North American infants but equal them in performance on standardized tests of development (Gaskins, 1990, 1999).

IMITATION

Within Piaget's theoretical framework, the ability to imitate an action observed in the past *(deferred imitation)* provides one of the key lines of evidence that children have acquired the capacity to represent experience mentally. The following example, taken from Piaget's work (1962), illustrates both deferred imitation and the importance that Piaget attributed to deferred imitation as evidence that children are beginning to think in a new, more representational way. Jacqueline, now 16 months old, was astonished by the temper tantrum of an 18-month-old boy.

> He screamed as he tried to get out of his playpen and pushed it backwards, stamping his feet. J. stood watching him in amazement, never having witnessed such a scene before. The next day, she herself screamed in her playpen and tried to move it, stamping her foot lightly several times in succession. The imitation of the whole scene was most striking. Had it been immediate, [the imitation] would naturally not have involved representation, but coming as it did after an interval of more than twelve hours, it must have involved some representative or pre-representative element. (p. 63)

Piaget's example of deferred imitation does, indeed, offer a clear instance of representation. However, as we saw in our discussion of the development of memory in Chapter 5 (p. 205), deferred imitation of actions directed toward objects makes its first appearance as part of the bio-social-behavioral shift that occurs between 6 and 9 months of age (Barr et al., 1996), well before infants enter substage 6. Recall, for example, Andrew Meltzoff's demonstration that infants this age would imitate actions they had seen him perform 24 hours earlier such as rotating a board, pushing a button to make a noise, and rattling bolts in a plastic cup (Chapter 5, p. 205).

Meltzoff and Elizabeth Hanna used a somewhat different imitation task to show that by the age of 14 months, children can learn from one another by imitation (Hanna & Meltzoff, 1993). To demonstrate this kind of learning, the researchers selected outgoing and sociable infants at a day-care center to model several novel actions, such as poking a finger into a small black box to make a buzzer sound, pulling a triangular block across a table by a string, and picking up a string of pink beads and putting them into a cup. The infants modeled these actions at the table where all the children ordinarily engaged in group activities. Two days later an adult observer brought the objects used in the demonstration to the homes of the children who had watched it and presented them one at a time to the children. Even after a 2-day delay and a marked change in context, the children imitated approximately three of the actions they had seen at the day-care center.

Thus, Piaget underestimated infant capacities to engage in deferred imitation (and by implication, their ability to represent prior experiences to themselves). Nevertheless, an intriguing experiment by Meltzoff indicates that a new ability to represent nonvisible actions does arise at about 18 months, as Piaget assumed. At this age, infants "imitate" actions that people *intend* but do not actually complete (Meltzoff, 1995). To demonstrate this ability, Meltzoff arranged for 18-month-old infants to observe an adult repeatedly trying to pull the ends off a wooden dumbbell or trying to hang a bead necklace over a wooden cylinder. With half the children, the adult succeeded in those tasks; with the other half, the adult did not complete the actions. The adult then gave the objects to the infants to see if they would imitate the actions they had just observed. The babies who had seen the adult try repeatedly, but fail, to complete the action nevertheless "imitated" and completed the action just as frequently as those babies who had observed the actions being completed. Since the first group had not seen the complete action they themselves produced, Meltzoff reasoned that they must have understood, and imitated, the adult's intentions.

To see if children attribute intentions exclusively to people, Meltzoff conducted a second study in which he substituted a mechanical device for the human model (see Figure 6.6). Of the infants who observed the mechanical device as it either "tried and failed" or succeeded in removing the two end blocks from a wooden dumbbell, only one in ten imitated the machine. Meltzoff argues that such behavior is evidence that babies attribute intentions to other

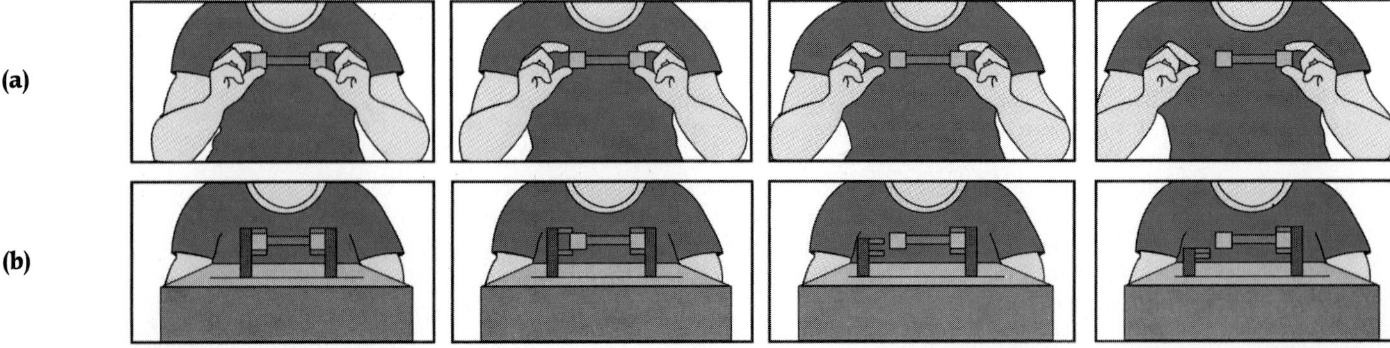

FIGURE 6.6
Procedure used by Andrew Meltzoff to determine if infants imitate intended actions, even if they are not completed. (a) An adult tries to pull the ends off the dumbbell. (b) The analogous actions being modeled by a mechanical device.

human beings, but not to machines, indicating that they have acquired the ability to represent the mental states of other people, which, of course, are not visible.

THE GROWTH OF THE ABILITY TO CATEGORIZE

As we saw in Chapter 5 (p. 200), even very young infants display an ability to recognize categories. For example, they respond differently to what they experience depending on whether it appears to be animate and intentional or inanimate without intentions. They distinguish events in which they can cause a difference in the environment from cases where they cannot. Note, however, that these are all, so to speak, "natural" categories. They are categories that in some sense come from the natural world in which we live. They involve, in Gelman's (1999) terms, "core" principles toward which infants are innately predisposed—principles that organize the acquisition of knowledge in core domains such as rudimentary biology, physics, and psychology.

FIGURE 6.7

How many ways can you see to organize these objects? The ability to categorize boats of one color and dolls of another and to subcategorize them according to color and form emerges during late infancy. (From Sugarman, 1983.)

However, a lot of the categorizing that we do does not involve such species-wide, easily acquired, core principles. Rather, it involves artifacts, things produced by people, which are part of the *cultural environment.* The world of objects made by human beings is often categorized in a bewildering variety of ways in different cultures (Gelman, 1999; Mantovani, 1999). According to Gelman, in contrast with learning that involves core principles and can therefore build on the skeletal knowledge that is present in early infancy, learning that involves artificial categories has to be "learned from scratch." One illustration of the development of this capacity that arises during infancy is the ability to categorize what appears to be a jumble of artificial objects according to multiple features.

This ability was clearly demonstrated by Susan Sugarman (1983). She presented 12- to 30-month-old babies with a haphazard array of eight objects that could be classified according to such features as shape and color. (Figure 6.7 shows one such set of objects, composed of blue and red boats and blue and red dolls.) To determine what kinds of groupings they would create, the toddlers, who were sitting on their mother's lap, were urged to "fix up" the random array of objects. If this suggestion failed to produce results, Sugarman showed them ways to group the objects and then urged them to continue grouping the objects themselves. She noted four stages in the progression of categorizing behavior:

1. One-year-olds would pick up one of the toys, look it over, and then touch it to the other toys one at a time. The only indication that they noticed the similarities between individual objects was that they were most likely to touch the toy they picked up to other toys that had the same shape.
2. The 18-month-olds would create a little work space in front of them and put two or three objects of the same kind in it.
3. The 24-month-old toddlers divided the objects into two distinct categories, working on one category at a time. For example, they would select all the boats first and then all the dolls. If Sugarman offered a boat to children who were collecting dolls, they immediately set the boat aside and kept working on the dolls.
4. The 30-month-old children simultaneously coordinated their work on the two major categories and created subcategories in which the objects were grouped according to color as well. They began by making a work space in front of them and then created two categories within it. They filled the categories by picking up whatever toy was nearest at hand and adding it to the appropriate group. If these children were handed a doll right after they had placed a boat in its group, they put it with the other dolls.

It appears, then, that one of the key cognitive changes associated with the end of infancy is the ability to go beyond *recognition* of conceptual relationships to make *active use* of these relationships. Children can now construct categories according to conceptual differences and correspondences in a more flexible and systematic way.

THE ABILITY TO PERCEIVE PICTURES AS REPRESENTATIONS

Another indication of a fundamental shift in children's thought processes at the end of infancy is the ability to understand that pictures are representations of objects, not the objects themselves, and to use this information effectively. This form of ability to engage in representational thought has been highlighted in research by Judy De Loache and her colleagues (summarized in De Loache et al., 1998). One series of studies focused on children's ability to use pictures as a source of information to find objects. In the first of these studies, 9- and 20-month-olds were shown realistic photos of various objects. The 9-month-olds explored the pictures with their fingers and even tried to grasp the objects in them, indicating that the babies were confusing the pictures with the objects they represented. This kind of confusion was rarely observed in the 20-month-olds.

However, even 2-year-olds are still not adept at using the information in pictures to draw inferences, for example, about the location of a hidden object. To test this ability, the researchers showed children pictures of rooms and indicated where a toy was hidden in the picture. Then they took the children to the actual room shown in the picture and asked them to find the toy. Two-year-olds rarely could make use of the pictorial information. However, by the time they were 2½, these children were usually successful in finding the hidden toy (De Loache & Burns, 1994).

A second series of studies focused on infants' ability to use models to guide their actions (De Loache, 1987, 1995). In the first of these studies De Loache asked 2½- and 3-year-olds to watch while she hid an attractive toy within a scale model of the room they were in. Then the children were asked to find an analogous toy that had been hidden in the corresponding place in the room itself. The 2½-year-olds could not use the model as a guide and were confused by the task but the 3-year-olds completed it rather easily (Figure 6.8).

De Loache suspected that the younger children found this task difficult because they could not think of the scale model both as a symbol and as the thing itself. In a follow-up study, she and her colleagues arranged to convince half of a group of 2½-year-olds that it is possible (with a special machine) to shrink an actual tent into a small model replica or to expand the model into the real tent (De Loache, 1995). When the children believed that the model and tent were the same thing made large or small by the machine, they successfully used the model to find objects in the tent. But the children who were told that the model was a toy version of the tent could not use information about an object's location in one to help them locate a corresponding object in the other. De Loache believes that the key difficulty facing the 2½-year-olds is that they cannot keep in mind the dual nature of the model: it is both an interesting object in and of itself and it stands for the thing it models. When they interpret the model as a shrunken version of the original, it does not function for them psychologically as a symbol, so the complicating aspect of the task has been removed. Three-year-olds are able to see the model as both a symbol and an object, so they effectively use the model to find objects in the normal-size space and do not have to have the problem simplified for them.

(a)

(b)

(c)

FIGURE 6.8 *The ability to guide one's behavior using a model emerges at the end of infancy. (a) The experimenter (Judy De Loache) hides a small toy troll in a scale model as a 3-year-old watches. (b) The child retrieves a larger toy troll that was hidden in the corresponding place in the room. (c) The child retrieves the small toy that she originally observed being hidden in the model.*

THE CHANGING RELATIONS BETWEEN WORDS, THOUGHTS, AND ACTIONS

Longitudinal studies indicate that during the second year of life there is a steady increase in the number of words and phrases that infants can understand and use properly (Fenson et al., 1994). Infants as young as 14 to 16 months understand an average of approximately 150 words such as "doggie," "head," "drink," and "stop," as well as a number of common phrases such as "more milk" or "Mommy is going bye-bye." By 21 months of age, toddlers are able to follow relatively complex verbal instructions. When told to "put the block under the doll's chair," for example, they can place the block correctly. Their ability to create multiword sentences also increases, making possible the expression of more complex ideas.

The use of words that stand for people, objects, and events is sufficient by itself to show that children have begun to engage in mental representation. But what especially intrigues developmentalists are the connections between children's use of representational words and the development of the other forms of mental representation such as symbolic play, searching for hidden objects, deferred imitation, and the ability to form categories (Bloom et al., 1985; Bretherton & Bates, 1985; Gopnik & Meltzoff, 1997).

The link between deferred imitation and word acquisition is perhaps the most obvious, since to a great extent, children's early use of words is closely tied to words they have heard adults speak. "More," for example, was one of the first words used by our daughter Jenny. Earlier, whenever she finished drinking a cup of milk or juice, Jenny would bang the empty cup on the tray of her highchair. We would then ask her, "Do you want some more?" Shortly before her first birthday, she began to hold up her cup and say "More" before anyone asked her if that was what she wanted.

Likewise, there is a clear association between language and symbolic play, both of which involve the representation of absent persons, objects, or actions. In symbolic play, arbitrary objects are used to stand for other objects—a banana is treated as a telephone, for example, or a sandbox railing becomes a highway. In language, sounds are the substitutes for objects and events. Initially, children's fantasy play is restricted to single actions and their utterances are restricted to single words. But at about 18 months of age, when children begin to combine two actions in play they also begin to create two-word sentences (Bretherton & Bates, 1985; McCune-Nicolich & Bruskin, 1982). So, for example, about the same time that children begin to say "All-gone milk," they also begin to pretend that they are pouring water into a cup and helping a baby drink it.

Karen Lifter and Lois Bloom demonstrated close relationships between the early acquisition of vocabulary and the sophistication with which infants search for hidden objects and play with objects (Lifter & Bloom, 1989). They found that children began to speak their first words at about the same time that they first began to search for hidden objects, and that they underwent a spurt in the rate of acquiring new words at approximately the same time that they began to exhibit logical search patterns. The same sort of linkages appeared when Lifter and Bloom looked at the sophistication of play: children who had not begun to talk moved toys around but did not combine their actions with them, as they do when they use a toy teapot to pour pretend water into a cup and then pretend to drink it. Such combinatory play appeared with children's first words, and more complex constructions appeared in conjunction with a spurt in vocabulary. Alison Gopnik and Andrew Meltzoff also found that a spurt in vocabulary occurs at approximately the same time as do several cognitive shifts, including the ability to classify objects into two groups, sophisticated behaviors in searching for objects, and insightful problem solving (Gopnik & Meltzoff, 1997).

Infants' acquisition of new words is often related to their interest in the events they experience. For example, Gopnik and Meltzoff report that between 12 and 24 months, when infants show an intense interest in the appearance and disappearance of objects, they are also likely to say "gone" every time something disappears. In fact, research in several cultures has shown that a term equivalent to "gone" or "all gone" is one of the most frequent words in children's vocabularies at 18 months (Fenson et al., 1994; Gopnik & Choi, 1990). Gopnik describes one 18-month-old who liked to hide a ring under a pillow. On one occasion the child hid the ring 13 times in a row, each time saying "gone" as he did so.

THE DEVELOPMENT OF CHILD–CAREGIVER RELATIONS

During the second year of life, children find novelty and excitement everywhere. A walk to the corner drugstore with a 1½-year-old can take forever. Each step presents new and interesting sights to explore: a bottle cap lying by the edge of the sidewalk requires close examination; a pigeon waddling across a neighbor's lawn invites a detour; even the cracks in the sidewalk may prompt sitting down to take a closer look.

As we saw in Chapter 5, however, things that attract babies may also cause them to be wary. Whizzing cars, strange people, and novel objects are often frightening to toddlers as well as fascinating. There needs to be balance between interest and fear as infants continue to explore and learn about the world. They cannot spend their entire lives in close proximity to their parents, but they cannot survive for long if they wander off on their own too soon.

Research with both monkey and human mothers and babies is starting to show us how the balance between exploration and safety is created and maintained in ways that allow development to continue. A key element in this process is the emotional bond called *attachment* that develops between children and their caregivers sometime between the ages of 7 and 9 months, which we briefly described at the end of Chapter 5 (p. 208). Explaining how this attachment comes about and how it influences later development has proved to be a major challenge to developmentalists.

Many small children become strongly attached to a teddy bear, a blanket, or some other object. The British psychiatrist D. W. Winnicott (1971) has called such objects "transitional objects." They support children in their attempts to understand and deal with the reality that exists beyond their own bodies. The strong attachment this little girl feels for her teddy bear is written all over her smiling embrace.

EXPLANATIONS OF ATTACHMENT

The fact that 7- to 9-month-old children everywhere begin to become upset when they are separated from their primary caregivers suggests that attachment is a universal feature of development (Thompson, 1998). This possibility has led to a lively debate about the evolutionary reasons for attachment, the causes of changes in attachment as children grow older, and the influence of the quality of attachment on children's later development. Three major explanations of the basis of attachment have dominated this debate: Sigmund Freud's suggestion that infants become attached to the people who satisfy their need for food; Erik Erikson's idea that infants become attached to those they can trust to help them; and John Bowlby's somewhat similar hypothesis that infants become attached to those who provide them with a firm foundation for exploring the world.

Sigmund Freud's Drive-Reduction Explanation

The process of attachment plays an important role in Sigmund Freud's theory of development. Freud held that the early interactions between children and their social environment, particularly the people who care for them, set the pattern for later personality and social development. He believed that human beings, like other organisms, are motivated in large part by **biological drives**—states of arousal, such as hunger or thirst, that urge the organism to obtain the basic prerequisites for its survival. When a drive is aroused, the organism seeks to satisfy the need that gives rise to it. Pleasure is felt when the need is satisfied, reducing the drive, and the organism returns to a more comfortable biological equilibrium. In this sense pleasure-seeking is a basic principle of existence.

In Freud's view, "love has its origin in attachment to the satisfied need for nourishment" (Freud, 1940/1964:188). Thus, the first person infants become attached to is expected to be the mother, who is the one most likely to nourish them. Freud believed that attachment to the mother is central to the formation of children's personalities as they progress through later stages of development. In adulthood, the relationship with the mother becomes "the prototype for all . . . love relations for both sexes" (p. 188).

Freud's theory of early human attachment continues to accord with the common sense of many parents, but it has not fared well among contemporary developmentalists. The major problem is that research has not substantiated his notion that attachment is caused by the reduction of the hunger drive.

Erik Erikson's Psychosocial Explanation

A more promising explanation of attachment than Freud's was proposed by Erik Erikson, one of Freud's most influential students (Erikson, 1963). Erikson, whose theory of development will figure in many discussions throughout the remainder of this book, believed that there are eight stages in the human life cycle, each characterized by a distinctive conflict that the individual must resolve. (These stages are laid out in full in Box 10.3, p. 399).

biological drives States of arousal, such as hunger or thirst, that urge the organism to obtain the basic prerequisites for its survival.

The conflicts characteristic of the first two stages that Erikson proposes provide an explanation for the increase in children's anxiety when they are separated from their mothers late in the first year of life and its decline during the second year. According to Erikson's scheme, during the first stage of development, which lasts from birth to roughly 1 year of age, the issue that infants deal with is *trust.* Babies either learn to trust others who care for them or they learn to mistrust them. In Erikson's view, children become attached to the people who reliably minister to their needs and who otherwise foster a sense of trust. Once babies gain faith in their caregivers, usually during the second year, they cease to be distressed during brief separations because they trust their caregiver to come back. This understanding prepares them for the second stage of development, which lasts until about the age of 3. During this stage of development, infants must deal with the issue of being able to do things for themselves. They must learn to exert their will and to control themselves or they begin to doubt that they can do things by themselves and are ashamed.

John Bowlby's Ethological Explanation

John Bowlby's theory of attachment arose from his study of the mental health problems of British children who had been separated from their families during World War II and were cared for in institutions (Bowlby, 1969, 1973, 1980). Bowlby reviewed observations of children in hospitals, nurseries, and orphanages who had either lost their parents or been separated from them for long periods of time. He also looked at reports of clinical interviews with psychologically troubled or delinquent adolescents and adults. He found a similar sequence of behaviors described in these various sources. When children are first separated from their mothers, they become frantic with fear. They cry, throw tantrums, and try to escape their surroundings. Then they go through a stage of despair and depression. If the separation continues and no new stable relationship is formed, these children seem to become indifferent to other people. Bowlby called this state of indifference **disattachment.**

In his attempt to explain the distress of young children when they are separated from their parents, Bowlby was particularly influenced by the work of the ethologists who emphasize a broad, evolutionary approach to understanding human behavior (see Chapter 1, p. 18). Ethological studies of monkeys and apes revealed that infants of these species spend their initial weeks and months of postnatal life in almost continuous, direct, physical contact with their biological mothers. Bowlby noted that these primate infants consistently display several apparently instinctual responses that are essential to human attachment: clinging, sucking, crying, and following. After a few weeks or months (depending on the species of primate), infants begin to venture away from the mother to explore their immediate physical and social environments, but they scurry back to their mother at the first signs of something unusual and potentially dangerous (Suomi, 1995). These primate behaviors, Bowlby hypothesized, are the phylogenetic basis for the development of attachment in human babies as well.

Bowlby conceived of the process of attachment formation by analogy to a thermostat. Just as a thermostat switches a furnace on or off when the temperature falls or rises past a set point, attachment functions to provide a balance between infants' need for safety and their need for varied learning experiences. Bowlby (1969) believed that attachment normally develops through four broad phases during the first two years of life, eventually producing a "dynamic equilibrium between the mother–child pair" (p. 236).

1. *The preattachment phase* (birth to 6 weeks). In the first few weeks of life, while infants and caregivers are working out the initial systems of

disattachment The state of indifference to others that children manifest when there is a continuing separation from their caregiver.

coordination (see Chapter 4, pp. 147–152), infants remain in close contact with their caregivers, from whom they receive food and comfort. They do not seem to get upset when left alone with an unfamiliar caregiver (indeed, they may not even seem to realize the difference).

2. *The "attachment-in-the-making" phase* (6 weeks to 6–8 months). Infants begin to respond differently to familiar and unfamiliar people, and by the time they are 6 or 7 months old they start to show signs of wariness when confronted with unfamiliar objects and people (as discussed in Chapter 5, pp. 205–207).
3. *The "clear-cut attachment" phase* (6–8 months to 18–24 months). During this period children display full-blown **separation anxiety,** becoming visibly upset when their mother or other caregiver leaves the room. Once this phase of attachment is reached, it regulates the physical and emotional relationship between children and the objects of attachment. Whenever the distance between attachment figures and the child becomes too great, one or the other is likely to become upset and act to reduce that distance: just as babies become upset if their mothers leave them, mothers become upset if their babies wander out of sight. Attachment provides the child with a feeling of security. The mother becomes a **secure base** from which babies can make exploratory excursions and to which they come back every so often to renew contact before returning to their explorations. During the early months of the attachment phase, the mother bears the greater responsibility for maintaining the equilibrium of the attachment system, because the infant's capacities to act and interact are quite restricted.
4. *The phase of reciprocal relationships* (18–24 months and later). As the child becomes more mobile and spends increasing time away from the mother, the pair enter a reciprocal state in which they share responsibility for maintaining the equilibrium of the system. Every so often, either the mother or the child will interrupt what they were doing to renew contact with one another. Among humans, this transitional phase lasts several years.

Once achieved, a firm, reciprocal emotional relationship between infants and caregivers helps children to retain feelings of security during the increasingly frequent and lengthy periods of separation from their caregivers. It is noteworthy that this phase develops at the same time that symbolic representation is becoming a dominant element in children's thought processes. Bowlby believed that as a consequence of infants' growing symbolic capacities, parent–child attachment begins to serve as an **internal working model** that children use as a mental standard to guide their interactions not only with caregivers but with other people as well.

separation anxiety The distress that babies show when the person to whom they are attached leaves.

secure base Bowlby's term for the people whose presence provides the child with the security that allows him or her to make exploratory excursions.

internal working model A mental model that children construct as a result of their experiences with their caregivers that they use to guide their interactions with their caregivers and others.

Evidence from Animal Experiments

Ethical considerations make it difficult, if not impossible, to conduct experiments to determine the sources of human attachment. When Harry Harlow and his co-workers wished to test ideas about attachment, they carried out a series of experiments with rhesus monkeys. They began by testing the drive-reduction theory of attachment (Harlow, 1959). In one of these studies, the researchers separated eight baby monkeys from their mothers a few hours after birth and placed them in individual cages with two inanimate substitute mothers—one made of wire, the other of terry cloth (see Figure 6.9). Four of the infant monkeys received milk from the wire mothers, four from the terry cloth mothers. The two types of substitute mothers were equally effective as sources of nutrition: all eight babies drank the same amount and gained weight at the same rate. Only the feel of bodily contact with the substitute mothers differed.

FIGURE 6.9
This baby monkey spent most of its time clinging to the terry cloth substitute mother even when its nursing bottle was attached to a wire substitute mother nearby. This preference indicates that bodily contact and the comfort it gives are important in the formation of the infant's attachment to its mother.

FIGURE 6.10
(Top) This baby monkey clings to its terry cloth substitute mother and hides its eyes when it is frightened by the approach of a mechanical teddy bear. (Bottom) After gaining reassurance, the baby monkey looks at the strange intruder. The terry cloth mother, which does not provide nourishment, acts as a secure base, whereas the wire mother, which does provide nourishment, does not. This contradicts drive-reduction theories of attachment.

Over the 165-day period that they lived with the substitute mothers, the baby monkeys showed a distinct preference for the cloth mothers. Even if they obtained all of their food from a wire mother, the babies would go to it only to feed and would then go back to cling to the terry cloth mother. From the perspective of drive-reduction theory, it made no sense at all for the four infant monkeys who received their food from a wire mother to prefer to spend their time with a terry cloth mother that might feel good but satisfied no apparent biological drive, such as hunger or thirst. Harlow concluded, "These results attest to the importance—possibly the overwhelming importance—of bodily contact and the immediate comfort it supplies in forming the infant's attachment for its mother" (Harlow, 1959:70).

In later investigations, Harlow and his colleagues sought to determine whether attachment to their substitute mothers had any effect on the infants' explorations, a crucial test of Bowlby's evolutionary theory (Harlow & Harlow, 1969). Knowing that normal human and monkey babies run to their mothers for comfort when faced with a strange situation, the researchers created such a situation for the monkeys who had received milk from the wire substitute mothers. They placed a mechanical teddy bear that marched forward while beating a drum in their cages. The terrified babies fled to the terry cloth mothers, not to the wire ones (see Figure 6.10). Once the babies had overcome their fear by rubbing their bodies against the cloth mother, however, they turned to look at the bear with curiosity. Some even left the protection of the terry cloth mother to approach the object that had so terrified them only moments before.

The infant monkeys demonstrated their attachment to the terry cloth mothers after separations of up to a year. The researchers would place the monkeys in an apparatus in which, by pressing on one of three levers, they could choose to look at the terry cloth mother, the wire mother, or an empty box. The monkeys who had been raised with a wire mother that provided milk and a milkless terry cloth mother spent more time pressing the lever that gave them a glimpse of the terry cloth mother than the lever that allowed them to see the wire mother. They were no more interested in the wire mother than in the empty box. Even monkeys who had been raised with only a wire mother showed no signs of attachment when they were given a chance to view it (Harlow & Zimmerman, 1959).

Harlow concluded that soothing tactile sensations provide the baby with a sense of security that is more important to the formation of attachment than food. This finding undermines the drive-reduction hypothesis that infants become attached to the people who feed them. At first glance it may also seem to undermine Bowlby's idea of the reciprocal nature of attachment, since the terry cloth mothers did nothing for the infant monkeys except provide soothing physical contact. However, as Harlow's team discovered, although soothing tactile sensations appear to be necessary for healthy development, they are not sufficient. As these monkeys grew older, they showed signs of impaired development: they were either indifferent or abusive to other monkeys and none of them could copulate normally. The researchers concluded that

> the nourishment and contact comfort provided by the nursing cloth covered mother in infancy does not produce a normal adolescent or adult. The [substitute] cannot cradle the baby or communicate monkey sounds and gestures. It cannot punish for misbehavior or attempt to break the infant's bodily attachment before it becomes a fixation. (Harlow & Harlow, 1962:142)

The later social behavior of these monkeys supports Bowlby's belief that attachment is a highly evolved system of regulation between the mother and the infant. Such regulation is a two-sided process that requires social interaction for healthy emotional development. The infant monkeys clearly turned to the terry cloth mothers for security, but in the absence of a live mother, all the adjusting was left to the baby, and a proper regulatory system did not form.

strange situation A procedure designed to assess children's attachment on the basis of their responses to a stranger when they are with their mothers, when they are left alone, and when they are reunited with their mothers.

PATTERNS OF ATTACHMENT

The maladaptive social behavior of monkeys raised with inanimate substitute mothers poses a pointed question: What kinds of interactions between mother and child provide the most effective basis for the development of healthy human social relations?

Because no two mother–infant pairs are alike and because the environmental conditions into which human babies are born vary enormously, we should not expect to find "one right pattern" of attachment that meets the basic requirements for social development in all cultures (Hinde, 1982). Many investigators believe, however, that it is possible to identify general patterns of mother–child interaction that are most conducive to development.

Research on such patterns of mother–child interaction has been greatly influenced by the work of Mary Ainsworth. On the basis of observations of mother–infant pairs in Africa and the United States, she concluded that there are consistent, qualitatively distinct patterns in the ways mothers and infants relate to each other during the second and third years of infancy (Ainsworth, 1967, 1982). Most of the mother–infant pairs she observed seemed to have worked out a comfortable, secure relationship by the third year, but some of the relationships were characterized by persistent tension and difficulties in regulating joint activities.

To test the security of the mother–child relationship, Ainsworth designed a procedure called the **strange situation.** The basic purpose of this procedure is to observe how babies respond to a stranger in three sequential conditions: when they are with their mother, when their mother has just departed the room, and when they are reunited with their mother a few minutes later. Different patterns of reactions, she reasoned, would reflect different kinds of relationships. The following case study, summarized from research reported by Mary Ainsworth and Barbara Wittig, illustrates the strange-situation procedure and how a typical 12-month-old middle-class North American child behaved in it (Ainsworth & Wittig, 1969:116–118).

[An observer shows a mother and her baby into an experimental room that has toys scattered on the floor.] *Brian had one arm hooked over his mother's shoulder as they came into the room. . . . He looked around soberly, but with interest, at the toys and at the observer.*

[The observer leaves the room.] *After being put down, Brian immediately crept towards the toys and began to explore them [Figure 6.11a]. He was very active. . . . Although his attention was fixed on the playthings, he glanced up at his mother six times.*

[After three minutes the stranger enters, greets the mother, and sits down quietly in a chair.] *Brian "turned to look at the stranger . . . with a pleasant expression on his face. He played with the tube again, vocalized, smiled, and turned to glance at his mother. . . . When the stranger and his mother began to converse, he continued to explore actively. . . . When the stranger began her approach by leaning forward to offer him a toy, he smiled, crept towards her, and reached for it [Figure 6.11b].*

[The mother leaves the room, leaving her purse on the chair, while the stranger distracts Brian's attention.] *He did not notice his mother leave. He*

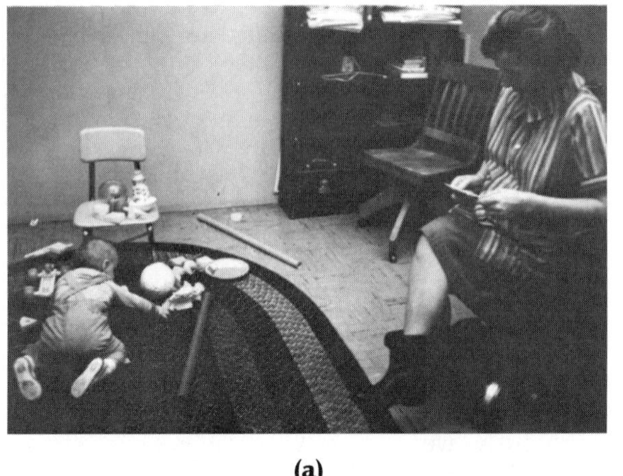

(a)

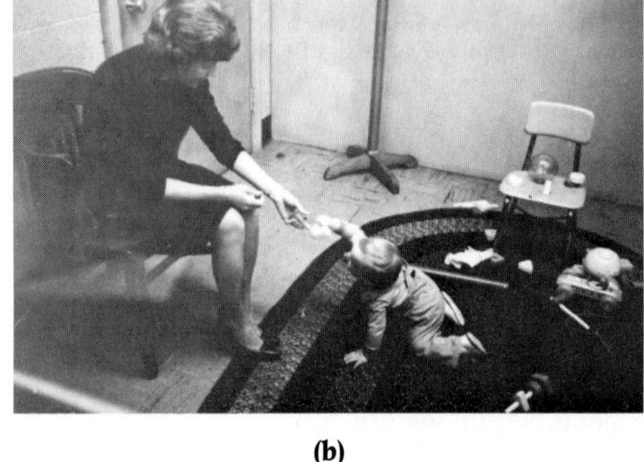

(b)

(c)

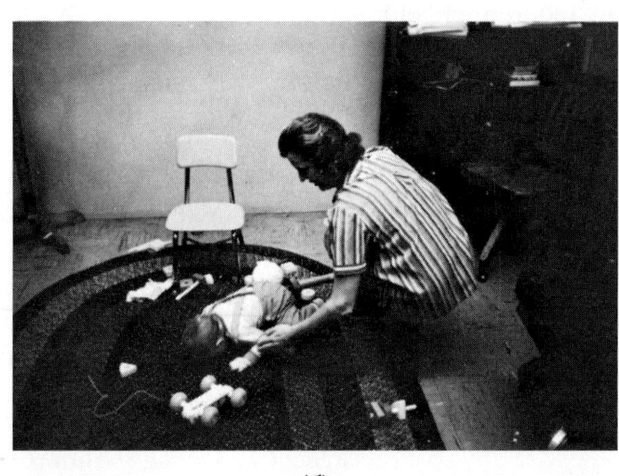

(d)

(e)

FIGURE 6.11

Brian in the strange situation. (a) Brian explores the toys. (b) Brian responds to the stranger. (c) Brian hugs his mother when she returns to the room after a brief absence. (d) Brian throws himself on the floor when his mother puts him down. (e) Brian cries and rocks back and forth when he is left alone again.

continued to watch the stranger and the toys. . . . Suddenly, he crept to his mother's chair, pulled himself up into a standing position, and looked at the stranger. She tried to distract him with a pull-toy . . . but he glanced again at his mother's empty chair. He was less active than he had been when alone with his mother, and after two minutes his activity ceased. He sat chewing the string of the pull-toy and glancing from the stranger to his mother's chair. He made an unhappy noise, then a cry-face, and then he cried. The stranger tried to distract him by offering him a block; he took it but then threw it away.

[Brian's mother returns to the room.] *Brian looked at her immediately and vocalized loudly . . . then* he *crept to her quickly [emphasis added], and pulled himself up, with her help, to hold on to her knees. Then she picked him up, and he immediately put his arms around her neck, his face against her shoulder, and hugged her hard [Figure 6.11c]. . . . He resisted being put down; he tried to cling to her and protested loudly. Once on the floor, he threw himself down, hid his face in the rug, and cried angrily [Figure 6.11d]. His mother knelt beside him and tried to interest him in the toys again. He stopped crying and watched. After a moment she disengaged herself and got up to sit on her chair. He immediately threw himself down and cried again.*

[Brian's mother gets up and leaves the room again.] *As she said "bye-bye" and waved, Brian looked up with a little smile, but he shifted into a cry before she had quite closed the door. He sat crying, rocking himself back and forth [Figure 6.11e].*

[The stranger, who had earlier left the room, reenters.] *Brian lulled slightly when he saw the stranger enter, but he continued to cry. She first tried to distract him, then offered her arms to him. Brian responded by raising his arms; she picked him up, and he stopped crying immediately. . . . Occasionally he gave a little sob, but for the most part he did not cry. But when she put him down, he screamed. She picked him up again, and he lulled.*

At the moment that his mother returned Brian was crying listlessly. He did not notice his mother. The stranger half-turned and pointed her out. Brian looked towards her, still crying, and then turned away. But he soon "did a double take." He looked back and vocalized a little protest. His mother offered her arms to him. He reached towards her, smiling, and leaned way out of the stranger's arms and his mother took him.

secure attachment A pattern of attachment in which children play comfortably and react positively to a stranger as long as their mothers are present. They become upset when their mothers leave and are unlikely to be consoled by a stranger, but they calm down as soon as their mothers reappear.

anxious/avoidant attachment The attachment pattern in which infants are indifferent to where their mothers are sitting, may or may not cry when their mother leaves, are as likely to be comforted by strangers as by their mothers, and are indifferent when their mother returns to the room.

anxious/resistant attachment The attachment pattern in which infants stay close to their mothers and appear anxious even when their mothers are near. They become very upset when their mothers leave but are not comforted by their return. They simultaneously seek renewed contact with their mothers and resist their efforts to comfort them.

To permit systematic comparisons between children, Ainsworth and her colleagues worked out a method of categorizing infants' responses in the "strange situation" (Ainsworth et al., 1971; Ainsworth et al., 1978). The categories are based on the child's behaviors when the child and mother are alone in the playroom together, when the mother leaves the room, when a strange woman offers comfort, and when the mother returns. The researchers found that the way the child reacts to the return of the mother is the key element and that the responses fall into three categories: *secure attachment* and two types of *insecure* attachment, *anxious/avoidant* and *anxious/resistant.*

Secure attachment. Brian is a classic example of secure attachment. As long as the mother is present, securely attached children play comfortably with the toys in the playroom and react positively to the stranger. These children become visibly and vocally upset when their mothers leave, and they are unlikely to be consoled by a stranger. When the mother reappears and they can climb into her arms, however, they quickly calm down and soon resume playing. This pattern of attachment is shown by about 65 percent of U.S. middle-class children.

Anxious/avoidant attachment. During the time the mother and child are left alone together in the playroom, anxious/avoidant infants are more or less indifferent to where their mothers are sitting. They may or may not cry when their mothers leave the room. If they do become distressed, strangers are likely to be as effective at comforting them as their mothers. When the mother returns, these children may turn or look away from her instead of going to her to seek closeness and comfort. About 23 percent of U.S. middle-class children show this pattern of attachment.

Anxious/resistant attachment. Anxious/resistant children have trouble from the start in the strange situation. They stay close to their mothers

Attachment between mother and child can be observed in the emotions they express when reunited after a period of separation.

BOX 6.1

Attachment to Fathers and Others

Discussions of infant attachment have tended to focus almost entirely on the role of mothers to the exclusion of fathers, siblings, and other caretakers. There are several reasons for this one-sided treatment of babies' social relationships.

Perhaps the most legitimate reason for focusing on the mother's role is that in most of the world's societies the mother spends far more time with her infant than any other adult (Parke, 1995). In the United States, for example, Michael Lamb and his colleagues reported that in two-parent families in which the mother does not work outside the home, fathers spend only 25 to 30 percent as much time in one-to-one interaction with their infants as mothers do. Perhaps more significant, even when these fathers are with their children, they assume little or no responsibility for their day-to-day care or rearing (Lamb et al., 1987). Similar patterns of interaction are found in societies as diverse as India and China (Roopnarine & Carter, 1992).

The imbalance in childcare roles is not the result of fathers' parental indifference or lack of caregiving ability. When fathers in the United States have been observed feeding their infants, for example, they respond as sensitively to their babies' feeding rhythms and engage their babies in social episodes just as often as mothers (Parke & Tinsley, 1981). Moreover, the infants of fathers who are judged to be sensitive caregivers are likely to be as securely attached to them as they are to their mothers (Cox et al., 1992).

Fathers may spend less time caring for their children, but they are far more likely than mothers to play with their infants while they are interacting with them (Munroe & Munroe, 1994). Across a broad range of societies, the vast majority of exchanges between fathers and their babies are brief play episodes that come at a specific period of the day (Lamb, 1987; Roopnarine & Carter, 1992).

Among the Aka of the Ituri forests, men play a major role in the care of their young children, promoting close emotional bonds.

Given the differences in both the quantity and nature of fathers' interactions with their infants, developmentalists have naturally been interested to learn what factors may enhance father–infant attachments. In general, they have found that the more time the father spends with his infant and the more playful and physically affectionate he is with the child, the more secure the father–child attachment (Cox et al., 1992; Kotelcuck, 1976). Research also suggests that there are no intrinsic differ-

and appear anxious even when they are near. They become very upset when the mother leaves, but they are not comforted by her return. Instead, they simultaneously seek renewed contact with the mother and resist her efforts to comfort them. They may cry angrily to be picked up with their arms outstretched, but then arch away and struggle to climb down once the mother starts to pick them up. These children do not readily resume playing after the mother returns. Instead, they keep a wary eye on her. About 12 percent of U.S. middle-class children show this pattern of attachment.

As experience using the strange situation accumulated, researchers noted that some children were difficult to classify in terms of one of the three main categories. After reviewing videotapes of over 200 cases that seemed not to fit easily in the established categories, Mary Main and her colleagues suggested a fourth category, which they labeled *disorganized* (Main & Solomon, 1990). Children who fit this category seemed to lack any coherent, organized method for dealing with the stress they experienced. This disorganization expressed itself in a variety of ways. Some children cried loudly while trying to climb on to their mother's lap; others approached her while refusing to look at her; still others stood at the door and screamed while she was gone but moved away from her silently when she returned. In some extreme cases, the ences in infants' attachment to their mother and father but that there can be differences related to contextual factors. In a series of studies in the United States, Michael Lamb observed infants in their homes to determine if they showed a preference for one or the other parent by staying near, approaching, touching, and asking to be held by one parent more than the other. He found that in traditional families infants displayed no *general* preference for one parent over the other, but when they became distressed, they were more likely to turn to their mother for comfort (Lamb, 1979). However, in nontraditional families in which fathers have the role of primary caregiver, babies turn to their fathers for comfort when they are under stress (Geiger, 1996).

A case that reinforces the conclusion that contextual factors rather than the sex of the parent account for differences in infants' attachment behaviors with their mothers and fathers is provided by the Aka pygmies, a hunter-gatherer group who live in Central Africa. According to Barry Hewlett, the Aka place a high value on egalitarianism. Men, women, and children generally hunt together, and Aka adult couples spend more time together than do couples in any other documented social group (Hewlett, 1992; Morell et al., 1999). Hewlett reports that "Aka fathers are within an arms reach of their infants 47% of the day and are more likely than mothers to hug or soothe their infants while holding them than are mothers" (p. 238). In contrast with families in the United States, India, and many other countries, Aka fathers are more likely than their wives to pick up infants who crawl over to them and request to be held. Hewlett concludes on the basis of his findings that when cultural patterns lead fathers to be closely involved in their children's upbringing, attachment to the two parents occurs in the same way.

Several researchers point out that the quality of father–child attachment is influenced by the personal characteristics that both fathers and babies bring to the relationship. Baby boys were found to be more likely to be securely attached to their fathers if their fathers had extroverted and agreeable personalities and if they had positive attitudes toward the baby and their parenting role (Belsky, 1996; Goodnow & Collins, 1990). For their part, fathers in many societies tend to treat their infants differently depending on their attractiveness, their temperaments, and their sex. They stimulate attractive infants more than they do unattractive infants and they are more affectionate with them (Parke, 1979). They are also more likely to persist in their interactions with a baby who is difficult if that baby happens to be a boy (Parke, 1995).

Other evidence suggests that the quality of the marital relationship plays an important role in parents' attachment relationships with their baby, but this seems to be particularly true for fathers (Belsky et al., 1984). Given this fact, it is no surprise that fathers in supportive, satisfying marriages are more likely to have secure relationships with their infants than fathers in marriages that are unsatisfying (Cox et al., 1989).

Of course, parents are not the only people with whom infants form attachments. Babies also form attachments with peers and siblings (Stewart & Marvin, 1984; Tronick et al., 1985). In some societies, such as that of the !Kung of the Kalahari Desert, babies are cared for in groups of children beginning around the age of 1 year so that their mothers can resume their work as the society's food gatherers (Konner, 1977). Under such circumstances, babies form strong attachments to many older children in the group in addition to adults. Babies may also form attachments with older children, especially siblings who are not primary caregivers.

children seemed to be in a dazed state and refused to move while in their mother's presence.

Over the past three decades, developmentalists have conducted a good deal of research trying to understand the causes of these basic patterns of attachment behavior (Ainsworth, 1993; Isabella, 1995; Thompson, 1998). Most of this research has focused on the mother–infant relationship, although other attachments that are important in children's lives have also been studied (see Box 6.1).

Two major questions have dominated the study of attachment patterns. First, what are the causes of variations in the patterns of attachment? Second, do these variations have important consequences for later development? We will concentrate on the first question here. We address the consequences of different patterns of attachment for later development in Chapter 7.

The Causes of Variations in Patterns of Attachment

Research on what leads to variations in patterns of attachment has focused on several likely factors: the behavior of the caretaker toward the child, the capacities and temperamental disposition of the child, stresses within the family, and the child-rearing patterns of the cultural group to which the mother and child belong.

Parental Behaviors In an early study of the antecedents of attachment, Mary Ainsworth and Silvia Bell (1969) hypothesized that different patterns of attachment were the result of differences in mothers' sensitivity to their infants' signals of need. They found that 3-month-olds whose mothers responded quickly and appropriately to their cries and who were sensitive to their needs during feeding were likely to be evaluated as securely attached at 12 months.

Over the past several decades many additional studies have been conducted on the relationship of parental behaviors to measures of attachment. Although Ainsworth and Bell's basic findings have often been confirmed, some researchers have failed to find the expected relationship between sensitivity and attachment, and even when present, the strength of the relationship has been relatively small (De Wolff & van Ijzendoorn, 1997). In cases where parental behaviors do predict infant attachment, parents of securely attached infants have been found to be more involved with their infants, more in synchrony, and more appropriate in their responsiveness (Lamb et al., 1998). As might be expected, children raised by extremely insensitive or abusive caregivers are especially likely to be rated as insecurely attached or disorganized (Thompson, 1998).

Characteristics of the Child Close observation of the interactions between parents and their children reveals that interactional synchrony is a joint accomplishment: just as infants need responsive parents to develop secure attachments, parents need a responsive infant in order to achieve their full potential as caregivers. To test the idea that infant behaviors contribute to attachment relations, Michael Lewis and Candice Feiring observed 174 infant–mother pairs at home when the infants were 3 months old, noting in particular the relative rates at which the infants engaged in object play or interacted with their mothers (Lewis & Feiring, 1989). They then evaluated the infants' reactions in a version of the strange situation 9 months later. They found that infants who had been observed to spend more time playing with objects than interacting sociably with their mothers during the home observations were more likely to display signs of insecure attachment later on.

Such observations have led a number of researchers to focus on the role of the infant's temperament in the development of attachment. It seems intuitively reasonable, for example, that mothers would find it more difficult to establish interactional synchrony with infants who are fearful or who easily become upset than with infants who are temperamentally easy. However, studies that compare attachment behaviors of children displaying different temperamental characteristics have, like those that focused on the relationship of sensitivity to attachment, yielded small effects. Some studies, for example, have found that infants judged to have difficult temperaments are more likely to be evaluated as insecurely attached at 1 year of age (Seifer et al., 1996). Others have found no relationship between temperament and attachment (Bates et al., 1985; Bohlin et al., 1989; Vaughn et al., 1989). On the basis of these mixed results, Ross Thompson, a leading attachment researcher, concludes that there is a real, but modest, role of infant temperament in shaping attachment relations (Thompson, 1998). At present, psychologists are seeking more adequate measures of both temperament and attachment in the hope of being able to clarify how individual differences in temperament interact with qualities of caregiving to shape attachment relationships.

Family Influences A variety of factors that contribute to stress on parents have been found to reduce the probability that infants will display secure attachment. One of the most important such factors is low socioeconomic status: children living in poverty are less likely than economically more secure children to exhibit secure attachment behaviors (Shaw & Vondra,

1993; Vaughn et al., 1984). Another factor is marital discord: couples who are experiencing problems in their marriage are more likely to have insecure children (Belsky & Isabella, 1988). Researchers believe that these stressors are related to insecure attachment in two ways. First, difficult conditions within the family are likely to lower parental sensitivity, which in turn decreases the likelihood of a secure attachment relationship forming. Second, witnessing angry or violent interactions between adult caretakers or experiencing unpredictable changes in caregiving arrangements is likely to make children feel that the adults involved are not reliable sources of comfort and safety.

Cultural Influences The pattern of attachment between children and their caregivers may also be influenced by the child-rearing practices of their society. Children who grow up on some Israeli kibbutzim (collective farms), for example, are raised communally from an early age. Although they see their parents daily, the adults who look after them are usually not family members. When, at the age of 11 to 14 months, such communally raised children were placed in the strange situation with either a parent or a caregiver, many of them became very upset; half were classified as anxious/resistant, and only 37 percent appeared to be securely attached (Sagi et al., 1985).

Abraham Sagi and his colleagues suspected that the high rate of insecure attachment among these children was caused by the fact that the communal caregivers could not respond promptly to the individual children in their care, and by staffing rotations that did not allow the adults to provide the children in their care with individualized attention. To test this hypothesis, these researchers compared the attachment behaviors of children raised in traditional kibbutzim, where children slept in a communal dormitory at night, with those of children from kibbutzim where children returned to sleep in their parents' home at night (Sagi et al., 1994). Once again they found a low level of secure attachments among the children who slept in communal dormitories. Those who slept at home displayed a significantly higher level of secure attachments, supporting the idea that cultural differences in the opportunities for sensitive caregiving accounted for cultural differences in attachment quality.

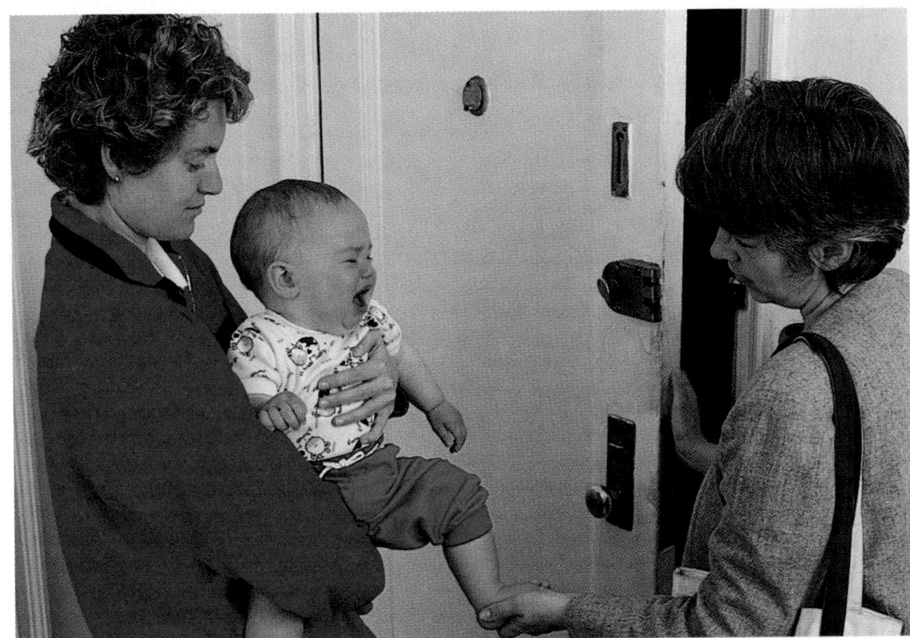

In resisting his mother's attempt to leave him in someone else's arms, this little boy is showing the distress that babies experience at being separated from their mothers.

A low percentage of securely attached babies has also been observed among northern German children. Researchers in one study found that 49 percent of the 1-year-olds tested were anxious/avoidant and only 33 percent were securely attached (Grossmann et al., 1985). Having made extensive observations of northern German home life, these researchers were able to reject the possibility that a large proportion of northern German parents are insensitive or indifferent to their children. Rather, they contend, these parents adhere to a cultural value that calls for the maintenance of a relatively large interpersonal distance and to a cultural belief that babies should be weaned from parental bodily contact as soon as they become mobile. The researchers suggest that among northern German mothers, "the ideal is an independent, nonclinging infant who does not make demands on the parents but rather unquestioningly obeys their commands" (p. 253).

Intriguingly, researchers have found a large proportion of anxious/resistant infants among traditional Japanese families, but no anxious/avoidant infants at all (Miyake et al., 1985). Kazuo Miyake and his colleagues explain this pattern by pointing out that traditional Japanese mothers rarely leave their children in the care of anyone else, and they behave toward them in ways that foster a strong sense of dependence. Consequently, the experience of being left alone with a stranger is unusual and upsetting to these children. This interpretation is supported by a study of nontraditional Japanese families in which the mothers were pursuing careers requiring them to leave their children in the care of others (Durrett et al., 1984). Among the children of these mothers, the distribution of the basic patterns of attachment was similar to that seen in the United States.

There is still no agreement about the significance of the different distributions of attachment patterns displayed in the strange situation in different cultures. Some researchers believe that they indicate basic and important differences in psychological makeup (Grossmann & Grossmann, 1990, 1997). Others believe that cultural differences in the meaning attached to the strange situation make it difficult to use this procedure as a measure of the true nature of the emotional bonds between the parents and their children and lead to false conclusions when patterns discovered in one culture are used to reason about patterns in a different culture (Takahashi, 1990a, 1990b). Consequently, while current research clearly demonstrates major cultural differences in the ways infants and their caregivers interact in the strange situation, the psychological significance of these differences remains uncertain.

The Developmental Course of Attachment

No single factor seems to account for the various patterns of attachment. The complicated interrelationships among the caregivers' behaviors, the temperamental characteristics of the children, stresses on the family, and the cultural context, as well as many other aspects of children's life circumstances, create many developmental paths. This point is made quite forcefully by Robert Hinde, an eminent British ethologist, in his summary of research on human attachment (Hinde, 1982).

> We must accept that individuals differ and society is complex, and that mothers and babies will be programmed not simply to form one sort of relationship but a range of possible relationships according to circumstances. So we must be concerned not with normal mothers and deviant mothers but with a range of styles and a capacity to select appropriately between them.
>
> At one level of approximation, there are general properties of mothering necessary whatever the circumstances. At a more precise level, the optimal mothering behavior will differ according to the sex of the infant, its ordinal position in the family, the mother's social status, caregiving contributions from other family

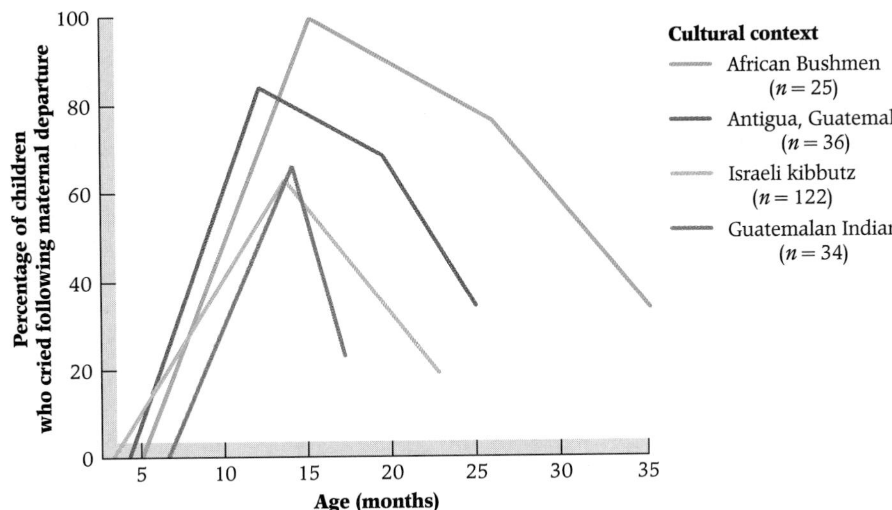

FIGURE 6.12
Curves depicting the increases in crying among children of various ages from four cultures after their mothers' departure from the room in the strange situation. Note the overall similarities among the curves, suggesting that this pattern of crying is universal. (From Kagan et al., 1978.)

members, the state of physical resources, and so on. *Natural selection must surely have operated to produce conditional maternal strategies, not stereotypy.* (p. 71; italics in original)

Much the same sort of complexity characterizes the long-term consequences of attachment. We will see when we discuss this hotly debated topic in Chapter 7 that there is conflicting evidence about the significance of the various patterns of attachment for later development. Some developmentalists suggest that early attachment patterns set the pattern for the child's later relationships; others argue that the long-term influence of early attachment patterns depends crucially on the stability of the environments in which the early patterns formed.

As we noted, there are marked individual and cultural differences in the precise patterns of behavior that infants display in the strange situation. Interpretations of those differences are equally varied and a matter of debate among developmental psychologists. The bottom line, however, is that infants all over the world, in every cultural setting, appear to show great consistency in the age at which they first express distress on being separated from their mothers. As Figure 6.12 indicates, 5-month-old babies do not appear to be distressed when their mothers leave. It is not until they are about 7 months old that babies begin to show distress. After that age, the proportion of children who are upset when the mother leaves the room increases up to about 15 months and then begins to wane. This changing pattern of distress indicates that the developmental course of attachment is a general characteristic of human infants and that, as time passes, the attachment relations established earlier in life become integrated into a new psychological system.

A NEW SENSE OF SELF

By the time they are 6 months old, infants have acquired a great deal of experience interacting with objects and other people and have developed an intuitive sense of themselves as a result (Rochat, 1997, 2000). The ability to locomote provides them with still further experience of their separateness from their caregivers and promotes new forms of social relations. Infants at that age begin to learn that they can share experiences and compare reactions, especially through their emerging use of language (Trevarthen, 1998). As infancy comes to an end, at around 2½ to 3 years of age, the process of developing a distinctive sense of self undergoes yet another transformation, one that is recognized by parents the world over.

On the South Pacific island of Fiji, parents say that children gain *vakayalo*—sense—around their second birthday; they can be held responsible for their actions because they are supposed to be able to tell right from wrong. Similarly, the Utku of the Hudson Bay area say that the 2-year-old has gained *ihuma,* or reason. Parents in the United States acknowledge the end of infancy from a different perspective: they tend to focus on their infants' newly acquired independence and the dwindling of their own control over them, labeling the change as the onset of the "terrible twos."

However parents describe it, the distinctive pattern of infants' behavior at around the age of 2 signals to adults that a new stage of development has been entered. This new stage seems to comprise several interconnected elements: children's increasing self-awareness, including the ability to recognize themselves in a mirror; their growing sensitivity to adults' standards of what is good and bad; their new awareness of their own ability to live up to those standards; an ability to create plans of their own that they then judge against adult standards; and a strong desire to see that their plans are not thwarted by adults (Harter, 1998; Kagan, 1981; Stern, 1985). As a result of all of these elements taken together, children begin to experience new emotions appropriate to their more active and complicated participation in the events of everyday life (Lewis, 1993). Their increasing competence provides the basis for the growing sense of autonomy that Erikson says normally characterizes this time of life (Erikson, 1963).

SELF-RECOGNITION

Consciousness of self is among the major characteristics said to distinguish human beings from other species and 2-year-olds from younger children. This is an interesting idea, but finding a way to demonstrate it convincingly has been a problem.

Several decades ago, Gordon Gallup reported an ingenious series of experiments using mirrors with chimpanzees that has since been repeated with children (Gallup, 1970). Gallup showed adolescent wild-born chimpanzees

Children's ability to recognize themselves in a mirror attests to the emergence of a new sense of self at the end of infancy.

their images in a full-length mirror. At first the chimps acted as if another animal were in the room: they threatened, vocalized, and made conciliatory gestures to the "intruder." After a few days, however, they began to use the mirror to explore themselves; for example, they picked bits of food from their faces, which they could see only in the mirror.

To make certain of the meaning of these reactions, Gallup anesthetized several chimps and painted a bright, odorless dye above one eye and on the ear on the opposite side of the head. When they woke up and looked in the mirror, the chimps immediately began to explore the marked spots with their hands. Gallup concluded that they had learned to recognize themselves in the mirror.

This kind of self-recognition is by no means universal among monkey species. Gallup gave a wild-born macaque monkey over 2400 hours of exposure to a mirror over more than 5 months, but it never showed any sign of self-recognition. The problem was not simply dealing with the mirror image, because the monkey quickly learned to find food that it could see only in the mirror. The monkey simply could not recognize itself.

Gallup's procedure has been replicated with chimpanzees and, in modified form, used with human infants between the ages of 3 and 24 months (Povenelli, 1995). The results fit nicely with the evidence that there are several stages in learning to recognize oneself in a mirror (Bertenthal & Fischer, 1978; Lewis & Brooks-Gunn, 1979). Before the age of 3 months, children held up to a mirror show little interest in their own images or in the image of anyone else. At about 4 months, if a toy or another person is reflected in the mirror, babies will reach out and touch the mirror image. At this stage, they clearly don't understand that they are seeing a reflection. Ten-month-olds will reach behind them if a toy is slowly lowered behind their back while they are looking in the mirror, but they will not try to rub off a red spot that has been surreptitiously applied to their nose. Not until children are 18 months old will they reach for their own nose when they see the red spot. Some try to rub the spot off; others ask, "What's that?" Within a few months, whenever someone points to the child's mirror image and asks, "Who's that?" the child will be able to answer unhesitatingly, "Me."

THE SELF AS ACTOR

When speech first emerges, most of children's one-word utterances name objects they are looking at. Children point at or pick up an object and say its name. These first descriptions include no explicit reference to the self. Between the ages of 18 and 24 months, about the same time that children begin to use two-word utterances, they also begin to describe their own actions. A child completing a jigsaw puzzle exclaims, "Did it!" or "Becky finished." When a tower of blocks falls down, a child exclaims, "Uh-oh. I fix." In these utterances we see not only children's ability to refer to themselves explicitly but also their ability to represent in words their recognition of adult standards of behavior and their desire to meet them.

A SENSE OF STANDARDS

As we have seen repeatedly, infants are sensitive to perceptual events that violate their expectations. Around the age of 2 years, children also become emotionally sensitive to events that violate the way things are "supposed to be." Children at this age become upset if the plastic eye of their teddy bear is missing or if there is mud on the hem of a new dress. When 14-month-olds are brought to a playroom where some of the toys are damaged, they seem to be unaware of the flaws and play as if nothing were wrong. But 19-month-olds say disdainfully, "Yucky" or "Fix it" (Kagan, 1981:47). Apparently their emerging ability to classify objects extends to an ability to classify events as proper and improper according to adult standards.

Children also express sensitivity to adult standards when they feel that they are supposed to imitate an adult. In several studies, Jerome Kagan had an adult perform various activities in front of children in a play setting (Kagan, 1981). The adult might make one toy monkey hug another monkey, or build a stack of blocks, or enact a small drama using toy blocks as animals. Many of the acts were too complex for 2-year-olds to imitate. Starting around 18 months of age, the children in Kagan's study seemed to feel that they were expected to do what the adult had done even when they couldn't. As a result, many of them started to fret, stopped playing, and clung to their mothers. Kagan concluded that their distress signaled a new ability to recognize adult standards and an associated sense of responsibility to live up to them.

Further evidence that toddlers develop a sense of standards comes from situations in which children set themselves a goal or adults set goals for children. It is not at all unusual, for example, to encounter 2½-year-olds struggling to achieve the self-imposed goal of using all the available blocks to build a tower or to fit every available doll into a single toy baby carriage so that all the babies can go on a trip.

In a study designed to trace children's ability to adhere to task standards set by adults, Merry Bullock and Paul Lütkenhaus showed infants how to carry out such tasks as building a tower of blocks, dressing a doll, and washing a blackboard and then asked the infants to perform these tasks (Bullock and Lütkenhaus, 1989). At 17 months, the children performed the activity that was requested, but few of them could keep the desired goal in mind and frequently needed to be reminded. At 20 months, they started out to do the tasks according to adult standards but got caught up by the materials and ended up playing according to their own whims. It was only at 26 months that they first showed that they could stick to the task until they met adult standards. However, it was not until they approached their third birthday that this kind of self-control became the rule rather than the exception. These findings led the researchers to conclude that children's problem solving is easily sidetracked until they are able to think of themselves in relation to a future goal.

Once children can set goals for themselves and realize that there are standards of performance that they must meet, they begin to interact with their parents in a new way: they actively seek their parents' help in reaching the goals and meeting the standards—though not always directly. When confronted with a task that appeared too difficult, one child is reported to have said, while clinging to his mother, "It's Mommy's turn to play" (Kagan, 1981:49). More routinely, children around 20 months of age begin to recruit adult help to achieve a difficult goal.

THE EMERGENCE OF SECONDARY EMOTIONS

Whether they believe emotions are present at birth or develop in the months after birth, developmentalists agree that babies experience and communicate six primary emotions by the time they reach their first birthdays—joy, fear, anger, surprise, sadness, and disgust (see Chapter 4, p. 143). They also agree that sometime between the ages of 18 and 24 months, babies begin to experience new emotions, including embarrassment, pride, shame, guilt, and envy. These new emotions are referred to as **secondary emotions** because they depend on babies' newly acquired abilities to recognize, talk about, and think

secondary emotions Emotions such as embarrassment, pride, shame, guilt, and envy that depend on children's ability to recognize, talk about, and think about themselves in relation to others.

about themselves in relation to other people. Primary emotions bear a simple and direct relation to the events that elicit them. Distress, for example, is a direct response to pain; disgust is a direct response to something that tastes or smells terrible; fear is a direct response to a visible threat. Secondary emotions, by contrast, are reflective and indirect. They do not appear until children are able to think about and evaluate themselves in terms of some social standard, rule, or desired goal. In this sense, secondary emotions can be considered social emotions (Barrett, 1995). Because they involve either injury to, or enhancement of, the child's sense of self, Michael Lewis refers to secondary emotions as "self-conscious" emotions (Lewis, 1993).

Take pride, for example. To feel pride, toddlers must be able to judge their own behavior as proper and admirable in the eyes of other people. Until they are about 18 months old, babies have no basis for feeling pride because they are incapable of thinking about other people's standards and their own behavior at the same time (Tomasello, 1999). But 2-year-olds can measure their behavior against the expectations of others. Pride can be observed in a toddler's self-satisfied smile when placing the last block on a still-standing stack or when putting on socks without assistance. Shame or embarrassment can be seen when toddlers lower their eyes, hang their heads, cover their faces with their hands, or hide after doing something they know is "bad."

Adults and other members of the child's community play an important role in the development of secondary emotions. They provide the standards of behavior against which toddlers learn to measure themselves. By observing and learning from others, toddlers discover when it is appropriate to feel guilt, shame, pride, and other secondary emotions.

The secondary emotions play an important role in children's social development. Pride and shame, for example, enter into children's feelings about others as well as about themselves. Guilt functions to motivate children to make amends. Interpreted in this way, the development of secondary emotions can be seen as part of a larger ensemble of changes that mark the beginning of a new stage in the process of growing up.

THE END OF INFANCY

The changes in children's autonomy and self-concept between the ages of 18 and 30 months—including the decline in the level of distress they show when they are separated from their caregivers and their increased ability to engage in symbolic play, to adhere to adult standards, to form more complex categories, to engage in more complex problem solving, and to express themselves in elementary words and phrases—combine to produce a stagelike transition in overall behavior that we have identified as a bio-social-behavioral shift. Table 6.3 summarizes the changes that occur in the months surrounding a child's second birthday. It provides a reminder that the social and cognitive changes that have figured so prominently in this chapter are part and parcel of other, seemingly more mundane behavioral changes, such as coordinated walking and bladder control, that depend on the physical development of the body.

The new configuration of characteristics that emerges early in the third year does not, of course, permit children to survive on their own. Far from it. But it does set the stage for a new form of interdependence and a new system of interaction between children and their environments. If all goes well, the individual aspects of development will undergo further modification over time, and this new, distinctive stage of development will give way to the next.

TABLE 6.3 THE BIO-SOCIAL-BEHAVIORAL SHIFT AT THE END OF INFANCY

Biological Domain	Myelination of connections among brain areas
	Leveling off of brain growth
	Maturation of brain areas in roughly equal degrees
Behavioral Domain	Walking becomes well coordinated
	Manual dexterity becomes adequate to pick up small objects
	Control over bladder and bowels
	Planful problem solving
	Symbolic play
	Conceptual representations
	Elementary vocabulary and beginning of word combinations
	Smile accompanying mastery
Social Domain	Decline of distress at separation
	Distinctive sense of self
	Acceptance of adult standards
	Emergence of secondary emotions

SUMMARY

- Sometime between their second and third birthdays, children complete the period of development called infancy. The end of infancy is marked by changes in biological processes, by expanding physical and mental abilities, and by the appearance of a new relationship with oneself and the social world.

BIOLOGICAL MATURATION

- Important connections in the cerebral cortex and between the cortex and the brain stem become myelinated and the cortical centers work in greater synchrony. Neurons in the brain begin to achieve adult length and density, the pattern of development of the various brain systems begins to approximate that of adults, and the rate of overall brain growth slows.
- Children gain increasing control over several muscle systems, which makes it possible for them to walk upright and, several months later, to run and jump.
- Increased manual dexterity makes it possible for infants to execute such movements as eating with a spoon and picking up small objects.
- Voluntary control over elimination becomes possible, although total control is not achieved for some time.

A NEW MODE OF THOUGHT

- A new configuration of cognitive abilities is manifested in many domains: problem solving, play, categorization of objects, and communication.
- According to Piaget's theory, toddlers' completion of the sensorimotor stage of development is marked by several achievements:
  1. Systematic problem solving to achieve goals makes its appearance.

2. Children search systematically for hidden objects.
3. Solutions to problems are achieved without extensive overt trial and error.

- Play evolves from consisting primarily of variations in patterns of movements to the pretend use of objects in imaginary situations.
- Pretend play itself evolves. Children 1 to 1½ years old can use themselves as agents to carry out a single pretend act at a time. By the time they are 2 years old, children can carry out a sequence of pretend actions in which objects such as dolls are used as the agents.
- Piaget believed that infants become capable of deferred imitation toward the end of the second year of life as a result of the ability to represent absent objects. Current evidence indicates that deferred imitation can occur several months earlier.
- Coincident with the onset of pretend play is the appearance of a new form of categorizing. Presented with a collection of objects to group, toddlers create a separate work space and categorize objects in accordance with adult criteria.
- Toddlers' vocabularies grow rapidly at the same time that they begin to solve problems insightfully and to search logically for hidden objects.
- The ability to combine words to make elementary two-word sentences coincides with the ability to combine objects in pretend play.

THE DEVELOPMENT OF CHILD–CAREGIVER RELATIONS

- Developmentalists interpret infants' distress when they are separated from their mothers as an indicator of feelings of attachment. This distress increases steadily until sometime in the second year and then declines.
- A variety of theories offer competing explanations for the onset of attachment.
  1. Freud believed that attachment has its roots in the reduction of biological drives such as hunger.
  2. Erikson explained attachment as the establishment of a trusting relationship between parent and child.
  3. Bowlby hypothesized that attachment serves to reduce fear by establishing a secure base of support from which children can explore their environments.
- Research with monkeys has disproved the drive-reduction theory by showing that infant monkeys can become attached to inanimate substitute mothers that provide soothing tactile sensations but no food.
- The social incapacity of monkeys raised with inanimate substitute mothers has focused research on the role of maternal responsiveness in the development of normal social interactions.
- The "strange situation" has been widely used to assess distinctive patterns of infants' attachment to their primary caregiver. Research has focused on the causes and consequences of three broad patterns of attachment: secure, anxious/avoidant, and anxious/resistant.
- Patterns of attachment can be affected by a variety of factors.
  1. The best predictor of secure attachment is attentive, sensitive caregiving. Abusive, neglectful, or inconsistent caregiving is likely to lead to insecure attachment.

2. Children's own characteristics may contribute to the quality of their attachments. Children who are easily upset or who display less interest in people than in objects may be more difficult for adults to coordinate with, impeding the development of a secure attachment.
3. Attachment status can be affected by the presence or absence of such family stressors as low socioeconomic status and marital discord.
4. There appear to be marked cultural variations in patterns of response in the strange situation. Traditions both of exclusive mothering and of communal upbringing can result in manifestations of anxiety in the strange situation. The psychological significance of these findings is uncertain.

A NEW SENSE OF SELF

➤ A new sense of self appears around the time of a child's second birthday. It is manifested in:

1. Immediate recognition of one's image in the mirror and the emergence of self-reference in language
2. A growing sensitivity to adult standards, a concern about living up to those standards, and a new ability to set one's own goals and standards
3. The appearance of secondary emotions as the child assesses the self and others in relation to a set of social standards

THE END OF INFANCY

➤ The convergence of biological, perceptual-motor, cognitive, and social changes in the months surrounding a child's second birthday produces a new bio-social-behavioral shift and the beginning of a new stage of development.

KEY TERMS

anxious/avoidant attachment, p. 241
anxious/resistant attachment, p. 241
biological drives, p. 235
disattachment, p. 236
internal working model, p. 237
secondary emotions, p. 250
secure attachment, p. 241
secure base, p. 237
separation anxiety, p. 237
strange situation, p. 239
symbolic play (pretend, fantasy play), p. 228
symbolic thought (representation), p. 224
tertiary circular reactions, p. 224

THOUGHT QUESTIONS

1. How do changes associated with the development of upright walking illustrate the close connection between changes in perceptual and motor abilities?
2. What common new ability appears to underlie the cognitive changes associated with the end of infancy?

3. What are some of the strengths and weaknesses of the "strange situation" as a way to investigate changing social and emotional relationships between infants and their caretakers in the second year of life?
4. Argue for and against the view that play promotes cognitive development.
5. What kinds of cognitive changes appear to be linked to the appearance of secondary emotions?

CHAPTER 7

Early Experience and Later Life

Two roads diverged in a yellow wood,
And sorry I could not travel both
And be one traveler, long I stood
And looked down one as far as I could
To where it bent in the undergrowth;
Then took the other, as just as fair,
And having perhaps the better claim,
Because it was grassy and wanted wear;
Though as for that the passing there
Had worn them really about the same,
And both that morning equally lay
In leaves no step had trodden black.
Oh, I kept the first for another day!
Yet knowing how way leads on to way,
I doubted if I should ever come back.
I shall be telling this with a sigh
Somewhere ages and ages hence:
Two roads diverged in a wood, and I—
I took the one less traveled by,
And that has made all the difference.

Robert Frost, "The Road Not Taken"

One of the most fundamental processes in development consists in the closing of doors, . . . in the progressive restriction of possible fates.

Joseph Needham, *Order and Life*

The poet and the scientist agree. Paths taken early in our lives launch us on a course that, once set, may be difficult to change. Insofar as children's fates are shaped by their experiences in the world, it seems reasonable to conclude that their earliest experiences, the paths they first travel down, will be the most significant for their later development. This idea is called **primacy.** We can find the concept in our proverbs—"As the twig is bent, so grows the tree"—and in our heritage from the Greeks. Plato (428–348 B.C.) expressed this view when he wrote:

> And the beginning, as you know, is always the most important part, especially in dealing with anything young and tender. That is the time when the character is being molded and easily takes any impress one may wish to stamp on it. (1945, p. 68)

During the twentieth century, primacy has come to be associated with the idea that children's experiences during infancy determine their future development. This line of thought was greatly influenced by Freud's claim that psychological illness in adulthood can be traced back to unresolved conflicts in the first years of life (Freud, 1940/1964). It is by no means restricted to Freudian theorists, however. In summarizing his research on intellectual development, the psychologist Burton White argued that "*to begin to look at a child's educational development when he is two years of age is already much too late,* particularly in the area of social skills and attitudes" (White, 1975, p. 4;

primacy The idea that children's earliest experiences determine their later development.

italics added). Similarly, Alan Sroufe and his colleagues maintain that the nature of children's first attachments greatly influences the way they form subsequent relationships (Sroufe et al., 1999).

In this chapter we focus on the question of whether, and, if so, to what extent, the experiences of infancy exert more influence than later experiences on the course of development. The answers to these questions are central to such issues as how society and parents can best provide for infants to ensure their optimal development and what can be done to improve the lives of children who have suffered deprivation early in life. As we will see, there is no doubt that infants' experiences *can* have a significant effect on their later development. But whether they *will* have long-lasting effects depends heavily on the extent to which subsequent experiences act to reinforce or counteract the patterns set up in infancy. Consequently, while focusing on infancy, our discussion will examine the lives of older children as well. Consideration of later experience is essential to understanding the extent to which early experiences are or are not especially important.

A few words of caution are in order about the nature of the research featured in this chapter. In many of the studies we discuss, the data involve children who have suffered some kind of unusual deprivation that is not under the investigators' control: they have been raised in an orphanage, or in poverty, or by parents who are mentally unstable. In such studies, the basic principle of a true psychological experiment is violated; the subjects are not assigned at random to experimental and control conditions. As a consequence, it is not possible to conclude with certainty that any differences between these and other groups of children in later life are caused by the particular form of deprivation that the children experienced during infancy and early childhood; it is possible that some covarying factor is the real cause of the observed differences. (Review the discussion of correlation and causation in Box 1.2, p. 22.) For example, any differences found between children growing up in orphanages and in homes might actually reflect the fact that children in orphanages generally come from poorer families or were born in a time of war, where multiple physical and psychosocial risk factors are more frequently encountered.

OPTIMAL CONDITIONS FOR INFANT DEVELOPMENT

The widespread belief that the experiences of infancy have a major impact on the characteristics that infants will have as adults has led many researchers to try to identify the conditions that will best foster babies' initial growth and development. Such information could be very useful to parents who want to do all they can to ensure a happy and healthy life for their children, and to policy makers who must pass laws that affect the welfare of children. Ideas about the nature of optimal development depend, of course, on cultural values, but in Western societies it is commonly held that the ideal conditions are those that provide for a rich variety of educational experiences and that allow as many doors as possible to remain open for a child's future.

In such societies, it is often suggested that development is best fostered when the mother, or whoever else cares for the baby, is sensitive and responsive to the baby's signals and states (Thompson, 1998). We encountered this idea in Chapter 6 (p. 244) in research on the conditions that promote secure attachment. A particularly powerful vision of the sensitive mother is provided by the nineteenth-century Danish philosopher Søren Kierkegaard:

> The loving mother teaches her child to walk alone. She is far enough from him so that she cannot actually support him, but she holds out her arms to him. She imitates his movements, and if he totters, she swiftly bends as if to seize him, so that

In many parts of the world, large numbers of children do not survive to celebrate their fifth birthdays. Many such deaths could be prevented with better sanitary conditions, nutrition, and health care. The plight of these Rwandan refugee children is further complicated by political and ethnic strife.

the child might believe that he is not walking alone. . . . And yet, she does more. Her face beckons like a reward, an encouragement. Thus, the child walks alone with eyes fixed on his mother's face, not on the difficulties in his way. He supports himself by arms that do not hold him and constantly strives towards the refuge in his mother's embrace, little suspecting that in the very same moment he is emphasizing his need for her, he is proving that he can do without her, because he is walking alone. (Quoted in Sroufe, 1979, p. 462)

Kierkegaard's "loving mother" is so finely tuned to her child's needs that she creates the illusion of physical support where none exists. This illusion provides the child with a sense of capability and self-confidence that encourages maximum effort and courage. These character traits are widely admired in western European and North American cultures. Consequently, the child-rearing behaviors that foster them are often considered the optimal conditions for development.

Although Kierkegaard's maternal ideal is unattainable as a general condition of development in any society, his idea of a mother who is maximally supportive of her children is approximated by what Burton White and Jean Carew Watts call *A mothers* (White & Carew, 1973). These researchers found that A mothers, more than *C mothers,* who were less supportive overall, enjoyed being with their toddlers and took pleasure in teaching them and providing them with intellectually stimulating experiences. While C mothers were observed, on average, to spend 5 percent of an observation period on such intellectual activities as reading a book or working on a puzzle, A mothers devoted 15 percent of their time to such activities. Unlike the C mothers, they placed more importance on their children's exploration and learning than on the appearance of their homes, which were organized to be safe and interesting for toddlers. They allowed their children to take minor risks, but they set reasonable limits for them. They might allow their 1½-year-olds to negotiate stairs while holding on to the banister, for instance, but not to climb up on the edge of the bathtub. Their close attention to their children was complemented by their prevailing mood: they were busy and happy rather than unoccupied and depressed. Compared with the children of C mothers, the children of A mothers were judged, on the basis of their performance on a battery of tests and the researchers' observations, to be more competent than their peers when they were in preschool. (Table 7.1 lists some of the characteristics of competent 3-year-olds.)

The A mothers did not spend all day attending to their toddlers. In fact, they spent less than 10 percent of their time actually caring for them. Some had part-time jobs, and some had several other children. When they were at

TABLE 7.1 CHARACTERISTICS OF COMPETENT 3-YEAR-OLDS

Social Abilities

- Getting and holding an adult's attention in socially acceptable ways
- Using adults as resources after concluding that they cannot handle the task themselves
- Expressing affection and mild hostility
- Engaging in role play

General Intellectual Skills

- Understanding and communicating effectively
- Engaging in complex problem solving, including finding materials and using them to make a product
- Self-control in the absence of external constraints
- Ability to plan for and prepare for an activity
- Ability to explore novel objects and situations systematically

Source: White & Watts, 1973.

home, however, they were nearly always available to answer questions, set up a new activity, or give encouragement. The researchers concluded that neither a lot of money nor a lot of education was necessary to be an A mother, although poverty did make a mother's work more difficult. Some of the A mothers were on welfare, and some of them had not graduated from high school.

White and Watts's description of "effective" maternal behaviors tells us something about the caregiving environments that foster successful early adaptation to a society in which behaving oneself and performing well in school are basic demands. But it does not help answer many important questions that parents and other caregivers must face: What is the "right" kind of responsiveness? How much support is too much, and how much is not enough? Will the same kind of responsiveness that prepares children to succeed in school also prepare them as adults to cope with frustration, inadequate housing, discrimination, or extended periods of unemployment?

As we indicated earlier, answers to questions about what constitutes adequate preparation for later life depend on the historical and cultural circumstances into which a child is born. Japanese mothers, for example, like mothers in the United States, aspire for their children to develop into effective adults. But when viewed through an American cultural lens, Japanese mothers seem excessively responsive to their children, to the point of encouraging considerable emotional dependence (Miyaki et al., 1986). Japanese mothers' high level of responsiveness, however, does not mean that they provide inappropriate environments for their children's development. In contrast to American society, which values self-determination and independence, Japanese society values interdependence and cooperation. Accordingly, Japanese mothers strive to foster a different overall pattern of adult characteristics in their children than American mothers do (Lebra, 1994). It makes sense that their strategies for achieving their "optimal" pattern should differ as well.

A quite different set of circumstances prevails in the poverty-stricken areas of northeastern Brazil (Scheper-Hughes, 1992). The environment into which babies are born there is extremely hostile to survival: the drinking water is contaminated, there is little food to eat, there are no sanitary facilities, and there is little medical care. Almost 50 percent of the children born in these communities die before the age of 5 years. For those who survive, success in later life is rarely influenced by academic ability, since little schooling

Famine conditions, like those that have ravaged Ethiopia, have a devastating impact on the development of those children who survive.

is available. Most of these children can look forward to labor as unskilled farm workers, which affords no hope of economic advancement or even of a comfortable living.

In response to these conditions, according to Nancy Scheper-Hughes (1992), the mothers of this region have developed beliefs and behaviors about child rearing that seem harsh and uncaring by the standards of middle-class families in either the United States or Japan. They are fatalistic about their infants' well-being. They view children who are developmentally delayed or who have a passive, quiet temperament as inherently weak and unlikely to survive. Consequently, they may neglect these children or simply leave them to die if they become sick. In such circumstances, where weakness means death and resources are few, the favored children are those who are precocious, active, and demanding, because they are judged to be the ones who will survive. Further, mothers expect children who have lived to the age of 5 or 6 years to start contributing to the family's livelihood. The boys are allowed to roam the streets, searching for food and stealing if necessary. The girls are required to pick sugar cane or do housework.

From the perspective of financially secure families in the United States, the form of mothering observed among impoverished Brazilian families may appear abusive. But as the report by Scheper-Hughes makes evident, these mothers are doing the best they can to prepare their children to survive in an environment where weakness almost certainly leads to death. Cross-cultural research of this kind shows us that judgments about the optimal conditions for development must take into account the actual conditions in which children and their families live.

EFFECTS OF PARENT–CHILD SEPARATION

A variety of circumstances can separate parents from their children for a time, and during those periods it is impossible for the parents to fine-tune their children's upbringing. The need to earn a living often separates parents from their young children for many hours several days a week. A family upheaval such as divorce, the death of a parent, or prolonged illness requiring hospitalization also separates children from their parents. A major disaster—war, flood, famine—can dislocate a whole population.

Given their belief in the importance of sensitive parenting, developmentalists have long been interested in finding out how separation from their parents affects children's development, in both the near and the long term (Ruttenberg, 1997; Rutter & Hersov, 1985; Theut & Mrazek, 1997). This knowledge is essential both to help them understand the actual dynamics of development and to guide the search for effective therapies for children who have been adversely affected by such separations. In the following discussion, we will consider babies who have experienced one or another of a wide range of separations, including enrollment in day care, hospitalization of themselves or their mothers, and residence in a foster home or orphanage.

TEMPORARY SEPARATION FROM PARENTS

Babies who spend part of each weekday being cared for by a nonfamily member while their parents work undergo a relatively mild form of separation. Many researchers are convinced that the degree of separation involved in high-quality day care has no lasting negative impact on infants' later development (NICHD Early Child Care Research Network, 1996, 1998a, 1998b, 1998c). Some, however, claim that no matter what its quality, extensive day care for babies under the age of 1 year does have lasting negative effects (Chase-Lansdale, 1994). This controversy is examined in Box 7.1. (We will return to the subject of day care in Chapter 11, where we discuss its impact on slightly older children.)

Another form of separation occurs when young children must spend time in a hospital. Several studies have evaluated the consequences of hospitalization on later emotional development. Michael Rutter (1976), for example, studied 400 10-year-olds to see if early hospitalization had influenced their later psychological adjustment. He found that a single hospital stay that lasted a week or less before the age of 5 produced no emotional or behavioral disturbances that could be detected at the age of 10. Repeated hospitalization, however, was found to be associated with behavior problems and delinquency in later childhood.

As we noted earlier, caution is in order when we interpret the results of studies in which differences in experience arise naturally rather than as a result of the experimenter's manipulation. Therefore, Rutter was careful to consider other possible explanations for his findings. For example, the later psychological problems seemingly associated with hospitalization may have resulted from the stress of continued ill health or the parents' response to the ill health rather than from the children's separation from their parents. Another possibility suggested by subsequent research is that children who have been hospitalized repeatedly are more likely than children who have not been hospitalized to come from socially and economically disadvantaged families (Quinton & Rutter, 1976). The negative effect of repeated hospitalization may be less a reflection of disturbed social relations (owing to separation) than a reflection of chronically difficult home circumstances or ill health. There are many factors that influence the adjustment of children who experience illness besides separation from their parents. Consequently, it is difficult to make a clearcut determination of the causes of developmental problems (Berison, 1998).

A more traumatic form of family separation often occurs in time of war (Apfel & Bennett, 1996). When the German air force carried out an intensive bombing campaign against the civilian population of London and other English cities in the early 1940s, large numbers of English children were sent to live in the safer countryside while their parents remained behind. Dorothy Burlingham and Anna Freud (1942) studied the reactions of a group of such children ranging in age from a few months to 4 years who were sent to live in a group home. They found that many of the children were greatly distressed at being separated from their parents. When first left at the orphanage, many would cry incessantly, turn their face to the wall when someone approached them, and refuse to respond when spoken to. The severe states of depression manifested by the children were of great concern to their caregivers, who worried about the long-term consequences of their traumatic experiences. When these children were examined 20 years later, however, the researchers found no instances of severe mental illness among them; their behavior as young adults fell within normal limits (Maas, 1963).

Every day, large numbers of children are orphaned as a result of war, famine, and disease. This child's father was killed during fighting between Croatians and Serbs after the breakup of Yugoslavia in 1992.

EXTENDED SEPARATION FROM PARENTS

An extreme form of separation is experienced by children who spend their early lives in orphanages because their parents are dead or are unable to care for them. Because many orphanages keep good records of the children they care for, studies of orphanage-raised children provide some of the most systematic data on how separation from parents influences children's development. Among orphaned children, the risk is highest for those whose separation is coupled with residence in a facility with multiple caregivers and a suboptimal range of experiences.

Children of the Crèche

A classic long-range study of orphanage-raised children was carried out by Wayne Dennis (1973) and his colleagues in a crèche (orphanage) in Lebanon.

BOX 7.1

Out-of-Home Care in the First Year of Life

Questions about the primacy of infancy reach beyond scientific research into the lives of individuals and the arena of public policy. The increasingly common practice in the United States of placing infants in some form of out-of-home care during the first year of life has been the subject of controversy among developmentalists for several decades (Lamb, 1998). According to some widely read and influential childcare experts, very early day-care experience puts children at risk for long-term social and emotional difficulties (Fraiberg, 1977; Leach, 1994). According to others, little or no risk is associated with early high-quality childcare (NICHD Early Child Care Research Network, 1997, 1998a, b, c).

The issue of out-of-home care for infants potentially affects the lives of many people because of two trends in North American society: (1) the growing number of single-parent households and (2) the increasing economic need for both parents to work full-time. At present, women constitute the fastest-growing segment of the workforce, and a majority of women who work and become mothers return to their jobs before their infants are 1 year old. More than half of all infants and toddlers in the United States spend some time in the care of people other than their parents during the first year of life (Casper, 1996).

Prominent among those who questioned the effect of out-of-home care during the first year of life was Jay Belsky (Belsky, 1986, 1990; Belsky et al., 1996). His concern was aroused by evidence that children who had experienced extensive nonmaternal care (more than 20 hours a week) during the first year of life were more likely to exhibit insecure patterns of attachment in the "strange situation," were less compliant in meeting adults' demands, and were more aggressive in interactions with peers.

Belsky's concerns were supported by studies that found that firstborn children who had been placed in day-care arrangements before their first birthday were significantly more likely to display insecure forms of attachment when they were 12 to 13 months old than were children who stayed at home with their mothers (Bargelow et al., 1987).

These questions about the effects of day care were taken seriously by the U.S government, which initiated a massive study to determine the influence that various kinds of day care

With the majority of U.S. mothers returning to work within a year of the birth of their children, more and more babies are being cared for outside their homes. Developmentalists are studying and debating the effects of such care on the children's social and emotional development.

The children were brought to the crèche shortly after birth. Once there, they received little attention; there was only one caregiver for every ten children. These caregivers had themselves been brought up in the crèche until the age of 6, when they were transferred to another institution. According to Dennis, the caregivers showed little regard for the children's individual needs or temperaments. They rarely talked to the children, did not respond to their infrequent vocalizations, and seldom played with them while bathing, dressing, changing, or feeding them. Instead, they left the babies to lie on their backs in their cribs all day and the toddlers to sit in small playpens with only a ball to play with.

INDICATORS OF DAY-CARE QUALITY

Qualitative Ratings	Definition
Sensitivity/responsiveness to nondistressed communication	Caregiver responds to infant's social gestures and is attuned to infant's needs and moods
Detachment/disengagement	Caregiver is emotionally uninvolved, disengaged, and unaware of infant's needs
Intrusiveness	Caregiver is highly controlling and adult-centered in interactions with infant
Stimulation of cognitive development	Caregiver engages in activities that can facilitate infant's learning, such as talking to infant or demonstrating a toy
Positive regard	Caregiver expresses positive feelings in interaction with infant
Sensitivity/responsiveness to infant distress	Caregiver responds to the infant's distress signals consistently, promptly, and appropriately

Source: NICHD Early Child Care Research Network, 1996.

during infancy and early childhood have on children's later development. The study was carried out by a network of leading researchers from centers in ten different geographical locales (NICHD Early Child Care Research Network, 1996, 1998a, b, c). Data were collected on characteristics of the children's families, including their educational and income levels, ethnicity, and size. The quality of the care provided was judged using both measures of the general setting such as the ratio of adults to children, group sizes, quality of facilities, and the quality of caregiving the children received (see table). To assess the effects of the care on the children, data were collected on the children's emotional attachment, self-control, compliance with adult demands, mental development, and language development. The results of these studies, which have now been extended to include children who are 3 and 4 years of age, indicate that children who spend 30 or more hours in day care are not distinguishable from those children who spend less than 10 hours in comparable circumstances.

However, such findings depend on the quality of the day care. When care was judged to be poor—that is, when each caregiver had a large number of children to care for, the caregivers were inadequately trained, or there was a high turnover of caregivers—the outcomes for the children were, as anyone might suspect, not good. This result is of genuine concern because almost half of the centers studied were found to offer poor-quality day care.

The main finding, however, was that poor-quality day care became an especially significant risk factor for cognitive and social difficulties when it was combined with other risk factors, including insensitive mothering or difficult economic circumstances (Cost, Quality & Child Outcomes Study Team, 1995; Galinsky et al., 1994; NICHD Early Child Care Research Network, 1998a, b, c). In addition, research that has looked at families who are experiencing significant internal conflict indicates that children who received 20 or more hours of nonmaternal care during the second year of life experienced increased developmental difficulties (Belsky et al., 1996).

The stakes in assessing the effects of day care are very high. On the one hand, everyone is aware that it is in the interests not only of the children in question but of society as a whole to ensure that children grow up to be emotionally stable and socially competent adults. If they do not, society will incur a huge toll in later social service costs and economic productivity. On the other hand, economic and social pressures are bringing many mothers into the workforce and keeping fathers there. The problem is how best to deal with these conflicting realities to maximize children's life chances. Belsky suggests that this goal could best be achieved if parents received a subsidy for staying home with their infants during their first year of life. Others argue that what is called for instead is better and more available day care.

The harmful effects of this low level of stimulation and human contact were evident within a year. Although the children were normal at 2 months, as measured by an infant scale, Dennis found that they had developed intellectually at only half the normal rate when he tested them at the end of the first year.

The later developmental fates of these children depended on their subsequent care. Those who were adopted into families made a remarkable recovery. The children who were adopted before they were 2 years old were functioning normally when they were tested 2 to 3 years after their adoption, and those who were adopted between 2 and 6 years of age were only slightly retarded in their intellectual functioning.

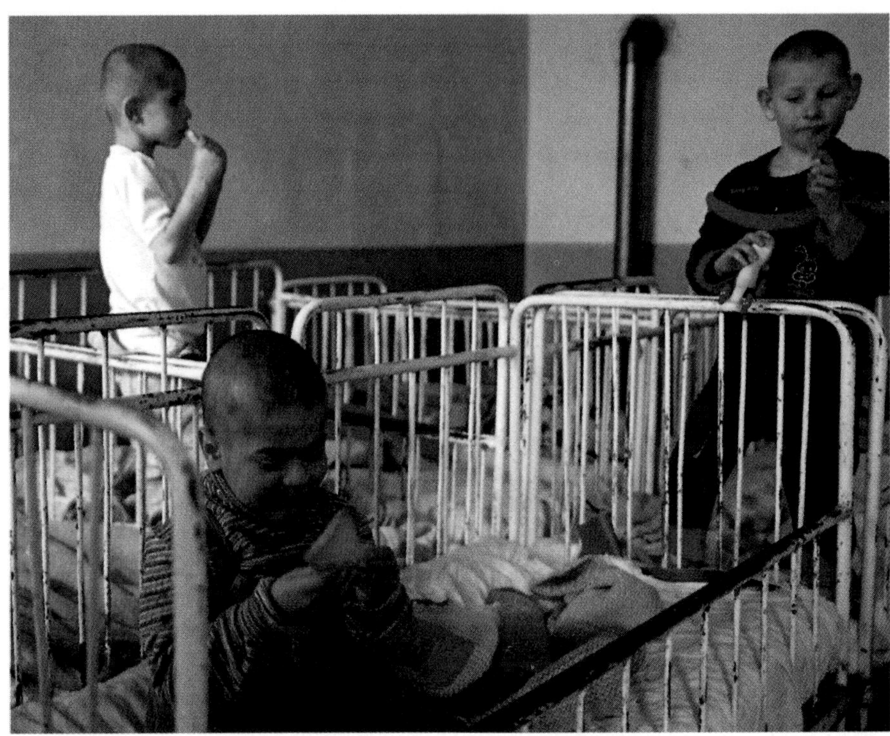

The conditions in orphanages such as this one in Romania provide insufficient stimulation for normal mental development.

The children who remained institutionalized fared less well. At the age of 6, the girls were sent to one institution and the boys to another. The girls' institution, like the crèche, provided few stimulating experiences and virtually no personal attention. When these girls were tested at 12 to 16 years of age, they were found to be so retarded intellectually that they would be unable to function in modern society. They could barely read, they could not tell time, and they were not able to dial a seven-digit telephone number or count out change in a store.

The outcome for the boys was quite different. The institution to which they were transferred provided far more intellectual stimulation and more varied experiences than did the crèche. What is more, the boys had frequent contact with the workers at the institution, who came from the surrounding communities. As a result, when the boys were tested at 10 to 14 years of age, they showed a substantial recovery from their initial intellectual lag. Although their performance on standardized tests was below the norm and below the performance of the children who had been adopted, it was within the range that would allow them to function in society.

More recently, Kim Chisholm (1998) followed up the development of a group of infants and young children who were adopted into Canadian homes from orphanages in Romania, where they had lived in conditions similar to those described by Dennis. Chisholm found that those Romanian children who were adopted before they were 4 months of age were indistinguishable from native-born Canadian children who lived in the homes of their biological parents. However, children who had spent 8 months or more in an orphanage showed residual effects of their earlier experiences. Although a special attachment interview indicated that they all had formed emotional attachments to their adoptive parents, they tended to display more evidence of insecure attachment in the strange situation than the children adopted before the age of 4 months. They also tended to be overly friendly to strangers, which seems to indicate that they were hungry for attention.

Chisholm is cautious in attempting to account for the residual effects of their early experiences on these later-adopted children. They had spent, on average, more than a year in the orphanage, while the children who had been adopted before they were 4 months old had spent an average of only a month in institutional care. Perhaps the differences in the age at which they were adopted or the length of time they spent in institutional care was a critical factor. Chisholm also noted that children who displayed evidence of insecure attachment were most likely to have been placed with economically less well off Canadian families, and he suggested that perhaps the extra burden these families experienced with children who came to them in a state of medical and psychological distress made it difficult for them to create optimal conditions for helping the children recover.

Children Reared in Well-Staffed Orphanages

The grim picture painted by research on children from poorly run orphanages has provoked further studies of orphanage-raised children in an effort to determine if the negative consequences they point to were the result of the particularly poor forms of orphanage care involved. Barbara Tizard and Jill Hodges studied 65 English children of working-class backgrounds who were raised in residential nurseries from just after birth until they were at least 2 years old (Hodges & Tizard, 1989a, 1989b; Tizard & Hodges, 1978; Tizard & Rees, 1975). The nurseries were judged to be of high quality. The children were fed well, the staff was trained, and toys and books were plentiful. The turnover and scheduling of staff members, however, discouraged the formation of close personal relationships between adults and children. Tizard and Hodges estimated that some 24 nurses had cared for each child by the time the children were 2 years old. By the age of 4½, each child had been cared for by as many as 50 nurses. This situation certainly appears to preclude the kind of intimate knowledge and caring that presumably underlie sensitive caregiving.

Tizard and her colleagues evaluated the developmental status of the children when they were 4½ years old and 8 years old, and again when they were 16 years old. They grouped the children into three categories:

1. Children who had returned to their families after the age of 2
2. Children who were adopted between the ages of 2 and 8 years
3. Children who remained in the institutions

The researchers also evaluated a control group consisting of children with a similar working-class background who had always lived at home.

They found that leaving institutional care had a positive effect on the children, as the studies we have described would lead us to expect. But how much difference it made depended on what kind of environment they entered and what aspect of psychological functioning was looked at. One of the surprising findings was that the children who were restored to their biological families did not fare as well as the children who were adopted. The adopted children scored higher on standardized tests of intellectual achievement, and they were able to read at a more advanced level. In addition, almost all the children who were adopted formed mutual attachments with their adoptive parents, no matter how old they were when they were adopted. This was not the case for the children who returned to their biological parents. The older they were when they left the nurseries, the less likely it was that mutual attachment developed.

One reason the adoptive homes may have produced better outcomes than the biological homes was that many of the families who took back their children were not altogether happy to have them. Many of the mothers expressed misgivings, but they accepted the responsibility because the children were their own. Often the children returned to homes in which there were other children who required their mother's attention or a step-

Being adopted by loving older parents provides a child with a greater likelihood of successful development than does remaining in an orphanage or foster care.

father who was not interested in them. Most of the adoptive parents, by contrast, were older, childless couples who wanted the children and gave them a good deal of attention. Also, most of the adoptive families were financially better off than the children's biological families had been (Tizard & Hodges, 1978).

One area in which most of the institutionalized children were reported to suffer was their social relations at school. In comparison with the control group who had always lived at home, the institutionalized children, like the Romanian children described earlier, were seen to be "overly friendly." They had "an almost insatiable desire for adult attention, and a difficulty in forming good relationships with their peer group" (Tizard & Hodges, 1978:114). Why these children experienced difficulties in social relations at school but not at home is not clear. Perhaps their early experiences in institutions gave them few clues about how to form peer relationships. Alternatively, they may have learned styles of interaction that were adaptive in the institutions but maladaptive outside them (Rutter & Garmezy, 1983).

When Hodges and Tizard (1989a, 1989b) contacted the children at the age of 16, they found that the pattern had persisted. Children who had returned to their parents showed a high rate of antisocial behavior. Those adopted into new families did not, but even adopted children who developed normal attachment relations with their adoptive parents experienced difficulties dealing with their peers and society at large as teenagers.

The improvements seen in most children who leave institutional care speak against the theory that children can form emotional attachments only during a critical period in early infancy. Although the environment in orphanages usually prevents children from forming emotional attachments with their caregivers, most children who were adopted into new families formed attachments with their adoptive parents, even the children who were past their second birthday when they left the orphanage. At the same time, the research by Tizard and her colleagues confirms the idea that characteristics of children's environments during later periods of their life are influential in determining whether or not the lack of early attachments will prove to be an enduring problem.

ISOLATED CHILDREN

The most extreme cases of neglect on record are those of children who have been separated from human contact altogether. During the past 200 years several of these so-called feral children have been discovered, the most famous being the Wild Child, Victor, discussed in Chapter 1. Such children never fail to excite public interest because the idea of little children fending for themselves in nature is so dramatic. But the circumstances leading to such children's isolation and their condition before they became isolated are usually unknown. As a result, it is rarely possible to draw firm conclusions about the effects of their experiences during their isolation.

There are, however, a few well-documented modern cases of children who have been isolated early in life by sociopathic parents. Because public officials now keep good birth records and other health records, enough is known about the early lives of these children to permit more solidly based conclusions about the developmental impact of their bizarre circumstances (Skuse, 1984b). Studies of isolated children leave little doubt that severe isolation can profoundly disrupt normal development, but they also show that early deprivation of caregiving and of normal interaction with the environment is not necessarily devastating to later development (Skuse, 1984a).

Jarmila Koluchova (1972, 1976) studied one of these cases, which involved identical twin boys born in Czechoslovakia in 1960 to a mother of normal intelligence. The mother died shortly after the twins' birth and, when the boys were about 1½ years old, their father married a woman who took an active dislike to the babies. At her insistence, the twins were forced to live in a small, bare closet without adequate food, exercise, or sunshine. They were not allowed to enter the parts of the house where other family members lived, and they were rarely visited.

The boys came to the attention of the authorities when they were 6 years old. They were abnormally small and suffered from rickets, a disease caused by a vitamin deficiency that leaves bones soft and bent. They could barely talk, they did not recognize common objects in photographs, and they were terrified of the new sights and sounds around them. The twins were taken to a children's home where they were well cared for and housed with children younger than themselves in a nonthreatening environment.

In these new circumstances, the twins soon began to gain weight, take an active interest in their surroundings, and learn to speak. When they were first tested at the age of 8 years, the boys' intelligence measured well below normal. But year by year their performance improved until, at the age of 14, both of them manifested perfectly normal intelligence (see Figure 7.1).

FIGURE 7.1

After the twins studied by Koluchova were released from isolation, their intellectual abilities showed gradual recovery and eventually became normal. (Adapted from Koluchova, 1976.)

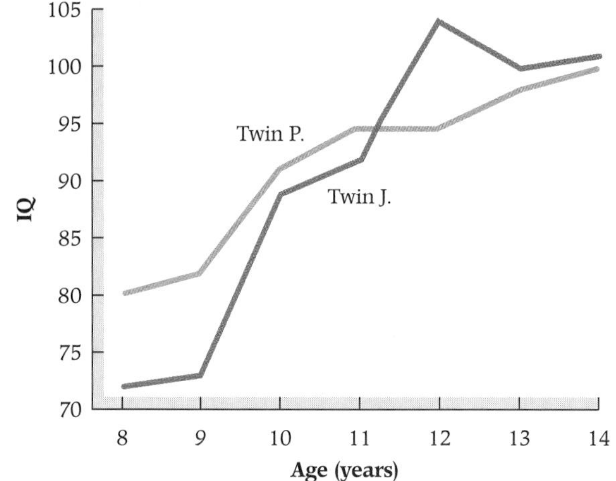

An even more severely neglected child was Genie, who was kept locked in a room by herself, beginning sometime before her second birthday (Curtiss, 1977). For more than 11 years, Genie spent her days chained to a potty and her nights tied up in a sleeping bag. No one spoke to her. When her father came to tie her in for the night or to bring her food, he growled at her like a beast and scratched her with his fingernails.

Genie was a pitiful creature when she was liberated from these horrible circumstances. Although she was 13 years old, she weighed only 59 pounds and was only 4 feet, 6 inches tall. She did not make intelligible sounds and was not toilet-trained. She could not walk normally; instead, she shuffled her feet and swayed from side to side. Remarkably, a battery of psychological tests revealed that Genie had an amazing ability to perceive and think about spatial relationships even though she had little to look at in her room.

Genie learned to control her bowels and to walk normally, but she never developed normal language. When first found, she showed no emotion at all when people left her; eventually, though, she became attached to other people who lived in her hospital rehabilitation unit. She developed ways to make her visitors stay longer and became upset when they finally did leave. However, her social behavior never improved to the point where she could live without special care.

Fortunately, such cases are extremely rare. However, because they are, it is still not known how long and how severe a child's isolation has to be before the damage it causes is irreversible. The infrequency of such cases also makes it difficult to assess the impact of isolation on individual aspects of development. Emotional, intellectual, and physical development may all be affected by isolation, but probably not all are affected in the same way (Clarke & Clarke, 1986).

An important question raised, but not answered, by the studies of extreme isolation is, How do environmental conditions during and following isolation interact with each other? Is it important, for example, that the twins described by Koluchova had each other for company when they were isolated? Was Genie's aptitude for spatial thinking a special intellectual ability that would have shown up regardless of her isolation, or did it develop as a consequence of her immobility and her social isolation? The answers to such questions would contribute to an understanding of both the developmental risks faced by children raised in less extreme but still adverse circumstances and the factors that might enable them to recover despite these circumstances.

VULNERABILITY AND RESILIENCE

Even in times of relative peace and prosperity many poor and working-class families find life a struggle. In trying to satisfy their own pressing needs, they create environments that are less than optimal for their children. Precisely because these situations are not extreme, they may persist for years and become permanent features of the family environment that shapes the development of the children. They may eventually contribute to delinquent behavior, failure in school, and mental health problems.

Developmentalists use the term **risk factor** to refer to personal characteristics or environmental circumstances that increase the probability of negative outcomes for children. Risk is a statistic that applies to groups, not individuals. One can say, for example, that children who have depressed parents are more likely than the general population to become depressed themselves. But one cannot say that a particular child whose father or mother is depressed will *inevitably* become depressed. Most risk factors are not the direct cause of the developmental problems or disorders with which they are associated. For example, having a poorly educated mother is a risk factor for school failure, but a mother's lack of education does not *cause* her children to fail in school. However, because of her lack of education and familiarity with the demands of school, her children may have more difficulty succeeding academically than children whose parents are educated.

In a series of studies of 150 English families in urban London and the isolated Isle of Wight, Michael Rutter and his colleagues found four risk factors that, taken together, were strongly associated with childhood behavior problems and psychiatric disorders (Rutter et al., 1975):

1. Family discord
2. Parental social deviance of either a criminal or a psychiatric nature
3. Social disadvantage, including low income, inadequate housing, and a large number of children close in age
4. A poor school environment, including high rates of turnover and absence among staff and pupils and a large proportion of pupils from economically depressed homes

risk factors Personal characteristics or environmental circumstances that increase the probability of negative outcomes for children. Risk is a statistic that applies to groups, not individuals.

None of these risk factors by themselves were strongly associated with psychiatric disorders in childhood. But if as few as two of them were present at the same time—for example, if one parent had a personality disorder and the family had a low income—the risk that the child would suffer from a psychiatric disorder increased significantly.

The emphasis Rutter and his colleagues placed on the cumulative nature of risk factors is substantiated by a growing body of research (Cicchetti & Toth, 1998; Shaw et al., 1998). Many studies have demonstrated that a combination of biological, social, and environmental risk factors, interacting over a considerable period of time, is associated with most serious developmental problems (Garmezy & Rutter, 1988; Kopp & McIntosh, 1997; Sameroff et al., 1998) (see Figure 7.2). At the same time, all these studies find marked individual differences in outcome among children who live in highly stressful circumstances. Some of these children seemed to be **resilient**—they had the ability to recover quickly from the adverse effects of early experience or to persevere in the face of stress with no apparent negative psychological consequences. Such observations have led psychologists to search for the sources of children's resilience in the face of hardship. These sources of resilience are referred to as **protective factors.**

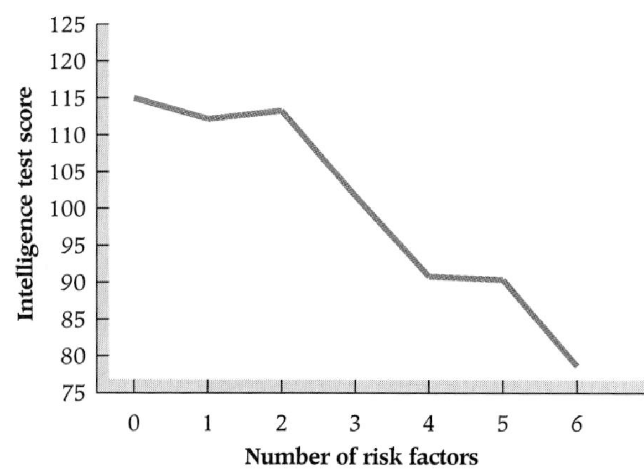

FIGURE 7.2
The average IQ scores for 13-year-olds decrease markedly when their development is affected by more than two risk factors. (From Sameroff et al., 1993.)

Three sources of risk and protective factors have been extensively studied: characteristics of the family, characteristics of the community, and characteristics of the child (Bradley & Whiteside-Mansell, 1998; Cicchetti & Toth, 1998).

CHARACTERISTICS OF THE FAMILY

The family is the main support system for the child. We would expect, then, that variations in the kinds of support that families provide for children should be associated with children's ability to withstand threats to their development. This idea is borne out by a variety of research (Bradley & Whiteside-Mansell, 1998). Many of the ways in which family characteristics influence risk factors and resilience can be seen in the results of an ambitious longitudinal study of a multiracial group of 689 children born on the Hawaiian island of Kauai in 1955 (Werner & Smith, 1982). Of these children, 201 were considered especially likely to suffer developmental problems because they experienced four or more risk factors by the time they were 2 years old. The risk factors included being a member of a low-income family, being born premature or suffering from stress during the birth process, having a mother whose educational level was low, and having a parent who had some form of psychopathology. Box 7.2 discusses another family factor that may put children at risk. The researchers found that the following family circumstances gave these children some protection against developmental difficulties:

- The family had no more than four children.
- More than 2 years separated the child studied and the next younger or older sibling.
- Alternative caregivers were available to the mother within the household (father, grandparents, or older siblings).
- The work load of the mother, even when she was employed outside the home, was not excessive.
- The child had a substantial amount of attention by caregivers during infancy.
- A sibling was available as a caregiver or confidant during childhood.

resilience The ability to recover quickly from the adverse effects of early experience or persevere in the face of stress with no apparent special negative psychological consequences.

protective factors Environmental and personal factors that are the source of children's resilience in the face of hardship.

- ➢ The family provided structure and rules during the child's adolescence.
- ➢ The family was cohesive.
- ➢ The child had an informal, multigenerational network of kin and friends during adolescence.
- ➢ The cumulative number of chronic stressful life events experienced during childhood and adolescence was not great.

BOX 7.2

Maternal Depression as a Risk Factor

Extensive research over the past decade has shown that chronic maternal depression (depression that lasts for 6 months or more) is a risk factor in children's development (Campbell et al., 1995). Such prolonged depression, which extends well beyond the "baby blues" that many mothers experience following the birth of a child, interferes with mothers' daily functioning and is related to a variety of negative developmental outcomes for their babies.

As we have seen in a variety of examples presented in earlier chapters, normal social interchanges between mothers and their infants are jointly regulated. The baby smiles and the mother smiles back at her baby in response; the baby vocalizes and the mother answers with a vocalization. This kind of responsive turn-taking is what developmentalists are talking about when they refer to sensitive mothering that facilitates the infant's goal of communicating and acting on the world.

In cases of chronic maternal depression, by contrast, mothers are less responsive and sensitive to their babies' signals and they have difficulty providing an adequate level of social stimulation for their babies (Weinberg & Tronick, 1997). Depressed mothers don't touch their babies as often as other mothers do and they engage them in fewer activities and games. Compared with nondepressed mothers, depressed mothers speak to their babies less often and are less sensitive to their babies' vocalizations. Instead of responding to their babies' smiles with answering smiles, depressed mothers are more likely to look sad and anxious when interacting with their infants.

Correspondingly, the babies of depressed mothers tend to have lower activity levels, smile less, and frown more than babies of nondepressed mothers. They do not vocalize or play as much as other babies, and they tend to be more fussy and tense. They are also less likely to be securely attached to their mothers (Teti et al., 1995). The negative style of these babies' interactions with their mothers even carries over to their interactions with strangers who are not suffering from depression (Field, 1995).

Psychologists and psychiatrists who work with the children of depressed mothers are well aware of these facts but cannot be certain how to interpret them. The depressed behavior of some of these babies is similar enough to that of their mothers to suggest that they became depressed either in imitation of their mothers' negative style of responsiveness or in reaction to their mothers' depressed behavior. There is some evidence, however, that at least some babies who behave this way are depressive from birth, suggesting that genetic or prenatal factors may cause their depression (Field, 1994; Murray & Cooper, 1997). For example, Tiffany Field and her colleagues studied a group of women who were diagnosed as suffering from depression while they were still pregnant. When their babies were assessed shortly after birth, they were found to be more irritable, to have less developed motor tone and depressed activity levels, and to show limited responses to social stimulation (Abrams et al.,1995).

The effects of early infant depression, whether the result of the mother's behavior or inherited factors, continue if the mother's depression continues. Older children of mothers who were depressed when they were infants and remain depressed over time are not only at risk for depression but also have been found to perform more poorly than other children on measures of cognitive, linguistic, and social functioning at 3 years of age (NICHD Early Child Care Research Network, 1999). School-aged children of chronically depressed mothers have been found to get in trouble in school because their attention wanders, they fidget in class, and they fight with other children on the playground (Dodge, 1990; Hammen,1991).

However, if the mother recovers from her depression, it is possible for the child to begin to function more normally. It is cases where the mother's depression is persistent, or comes and goes in cycles, that make children especially at risk for long-term developmental problems. In these cases, the presence of supportive adults other than the depressed mother is very important (Carro et al., 1993).

To help prevent depression in infants of depressed mothers, developmentalists have been creating therapeutic techniques geared to modifying the mother's behavior (Field, 1997). Some of the most effective interventions include teaching the depressed mother to imitate her baby's positive social behaviors, to communicate clearly when she talks to her baby, and to play games with her baby that are appropriate to the baby's developmental level. Babies whose mothers are given this kind of "interaction coaching" show increased eye contact and fewer expressions of distress (Field, 1997), creating more favorable conditions for their future development.

This boy is clearly upset by his parent's remarriage, but the eventual outcome of this change in his life will depend on the relationships that develop over the coming months and years.

CHARACTERISTICS OF THE COMMUNITY

The characteristics of the communities in which children live also seem to affect the likelihood that children will develop problems. In general, children in poor communities are more likely to suffer from developmental difficulties than are children in affluent communities (McLoyd, 1998). In addition, those who live in poor inner-city neighborhoods have a significantly higher risk of developing a psychological disorder than do those who live in poor small towns or rural areas (Richters & Martinez, 1993).

One factor found to protect children against the impact of negative community characteristics is the strength of the social support networks provided by kin, neighbors, and social service agencies (Cochran & Niego, 1995). For example, Patricia Hashima and Paul Amato found that poor parents who had friends and neighbors they could turn to for advice and call on in an emergency were significantly less likely to yell at their children or hit them than were poor parents who lacked such support (Hashima & Amato, 1994). Similarly, Susan Crockenberg (1987) found that teenaged mothers in England who received the community-based social support services for parents provided by the National Health Service showed significant increases in the amount and quality of their interactions with their infants.

Another factor outside the home that helps to buffer children from stressful and depriving life circumstances is the school. Children in disadvantaged and discordant homes are less likely to develop psychological problems if they attend schools that have attentive personnel and good academic programs (Rutter, 1987).

CHARACTERISTICS OF THE CHILD

Research on how characteristics of the child relate to developmental risk suggest that different temperamental characteristics are likely to put children at risk, but somewhat differently, depending on the child's age (Carey & McDevitt, 1995). In infancy and early childhood, U.S. and British children who are difficult—that is, who display irregularity of biological functions, negative responses to new situations and people, and frequent negative mood—and who have a high activity level are at greater risk than placid, easy children. In middle child-

Children growing up in war-torn parts of the world such as Bosnia face substantial obstacles to normal development.

hood, children who are easily distracted, who have a short attention span, and who have a hard time adjusting to new circumstances are at greater risk.

It should be noted that whether or not a particular temperament represents a risk factor can depend on cultural circumstances. Research by Marten De Vries provides dramatic evidence that temperamental traits considered "difficult" in the United States can be crucial to development in another cultural setting (De Vries, 1994). In one study, De Vries developed a temperament questionnaire based on Chess and Thomas's classifications and administered it to mothers of 48 4- to 5-month-old Masai children in East Africa (De Vries, 1987). At the time this research was conducted, a severe drought was plaguing Masai country and many people were moving out of their villages in search of food. When De Vries returned several months later to conduct follow-up tests with the 10 most difficult and 10 least difficult infants identified by the earlier questionnaires, he could locate only 13 families, 7 from the "easy child" group and 6 from the "difficult child" group. To his distress, De Vries found that 5 of the 7 "easy" children had died; 5 of the 6 "difficult" children remained alive. Coupled with the work of Scheper-Hughes in Brazil (p. 261), this study suggests that in chronically deprived circumstances, being demanding (which children with difficult temperaments tend to be) may actually help the child to survive.

Emmie Werner and Ruth Smith (1992) offer additional evidence that personal characteristics can help the child to survive difficult circumstances. On the basis of records provided by health, mental health, and social service agencies and educational institutions, as well as personal interviews and personality tests, they report that the children who were able to cope best with their life circumstances during their first two decades were those whom their mothers described as "very active" and "socially responsive" when they were infants. The mothers' reports were verified by independent observers, who noted that these children displayed "pronounced autonomy" and a "positive social orientation." When they were examined during their second year of life, these children scored especially well on a variety of tests, including measures of motor and language development.

Table 7.2 summarizes the risk and protective factors associated with early childhood behavior problems, which are grouped according to the levels of the environment depicted in the ecological system model of development discussed in Chapter 1 (p. 19).

TABLE 7.2 EXAMPLES OF RISK AND PROTECTIVE FACTORS ASSOCIATED WITH CHILDHOOD PROBLEMS

RISK FACTORS	PROTECTIVE FACTORS
Child Characteristics	
Difficult infant temperament	Easy infant temperament
Physiological dysregulation	Adaptive physiological regulation
Dysregulated affect	Adaptive affect regulation
Limited cognitive abilities	High intelligence
Insecure attachments	Secure attachments
Low self-esteem	High self-esteem
Poor peer relations	Positive peer relations
School difficulties	Positive adaptation to school
Psychopathology	Good mental health
Physical illness	Pride over personal accomplishment
Transient stressors	Positive relationship with current teacher
Task failures	
Microsystem	
Domestic violence	Good marital relations
Financial hardship	Consistent employment
Chronic unemployment	Positive family relations
Chronic stress conditions	Good parental mental health
Hostile family environment	Positive child-rearing skills
Intergenerational abuse	Getting a job
Parental psychopathology	Finding adequate housing
Maladaptive child-rearing skills	Accessing child care
Job loss	
Divorce	
Daily hassles	
Exosystem	
Community violence	Supportive social network
Crime in neighborhood	Good community resources
Social isolation	Supportive church
Impoverished community	Gaining community resources
Losing community resources	Accessing social support networks
Lack of community services	
Macrosystem	
Violent culture	National support for education
Parenting customs	Beliefs in children's rights
Racism	National commitment to rehabilitating substance abusers
Social acceptance of violence	Lower unemployment rate
Recession	Elected officials committed to improving plight of disadvantaged
	Reducing availability of illegal drugs

Source: Adapted from Cicchetti et al., 2000.

The Impact of Later Circumstances

We have seen that studies of developmental risk predict a greater likelihood of long-term developmental damage when several factors are present. It is important to remember that the effects of these factors do not occur in isolation; they interact and influence each other. It is also important to recognize that the impact of these factors can be moderated by later circumstances. This fact is highlighted by **transactional models** that suggest how risk factors enter into the general process of development (Clarke & Clarke, 1986; Sameroff,

transactional models Models of development that trace the ways in which the characteristics of the child and the characteristics of the child's environment interact across time ("transact") to determine developmental outcomes.

1995). Transactional models trace the ways in which the characteristics of the child and the characteristics of the child's environment interact across time ("transact") to determine developmental outcomes.

Thomas and Chess (1984) used a transactional model to show how later circumstances and parents' changing interpretations of the child's personality and behavior can interact with a child's temperamental traits to influence the child's mental health. The girl they describe, starting in her preschool years, exhibited a difficult, demanding, and volatile personality.

> [Her] father responded with rigid demands for quick, positive adaptation and hostile criticisms and punishment when the girl could not meet his expectations. The mother was intimidated by both her husband and daughter and was vacillating and anxious in her handling of the child. With this extremely negative parent–child interaction, the girl's symptoms grew worse. Psychotherapy was instituted, with only modest improvement. But when she was 9–10 years of age, the girl blossomed forth with musical and dramatic talent, which brought her favorable attention and praise from teachers and other parents. This talent also ranked high in her parents' own hierarchy of desirable attributes. Her father now began to see his daughter's intense and explosive personality not as a sign of a "rotten kid," his previous label for her, but as evidence of a budding artist. He began to make allowances for her "artistic temperament," and with this the mother was able to relax and relate positively to her daughter. The girl was allowed to adapt at her own pace, and by adolescence all evidence of her neurotic symptoms and functioning had disappeared. (p. 7)

As this description suggests, transactional histories are characterized by complex interactions between a changing environmental context and the particular characteristics of the child that are highlighted in each new situation.

Transactional analysis is applied to groups of people as well as to individuals. Michael Rutter and his colleagues used a transactional model to explain the later life adjustments of young Londoners who had spent significant parts of their infancy and childhood in childcare facilities (Quinton & Rutter, 1985; Rutter et al., 1990). These children had been placed in institutions not because of any behavioral problems but because their parents could not cope with child rearing. Many of them remained in institutions throughout their infancy and early childhood. At 21 to 27 years old, they were compared with another group of the same age from the same part of London who had been raised by their parents without interruption.

Focusing first on "ex-care" (formerly institutionalized) women, Rutter and his colleagues found that these young adults had experienced difficulties that the women in the comparison group had not. To begin with, 42 percent had become pregnant before the age of 19, and 39 percent of them were no longer living with the fathers of their children. One-third had experienced a relatively serious breakdown in caring for their children. By contrast, only 5 percent of the women in the comparison group had become pregnant by the age of 19, all were living with the fathers of their children, and none had experienced a serious breakdown in the care of their children. When the women's current parenting practices were studied, the "ex-care" women were far more likely to receive poor ratings than were the women in the comparison group (see Table 7.3).

At first these findings may appear to be straightforward evidence of the long-term effects of early misfortune. But when they are viewed from the perspective of a transactional model, it becomes clear that the early misfortune set in motion a series of events that tended to perpetuate the difficulty. Institutional care led first to a lack of strong attachments during infancy and childhood and difficulties in forming good relationships with peers. These problems increased the likelihood of teenage pregnancy. The early pregnancy reduced the likelihood of further education or job training. The ensuing economic pressures created a disadvantaged environment, which in turn created the stresses that were the immediate cause of poor parenting.

TABLE 7.3 CHILD-CARE BEHAVIORS IN TWO GROUPS OF MOTHERS

Childcare Difficulty	Mothers Raised in Institutions ($n = 40$)	Comparison Group ($n = 43$)
Lack of expression of warmth to children	45%	19%
Insensitivity	65%	28%
Lack of play with children	33%	16%
At least two of the above	59%	23%

Source: Quinton & Rutter; 1985.

Early institutionalization did not *necessarily* lead to continual misfortune, however. Those women raised in institutions who had supportive husbands were found to be just as effective at parenting as the women in the comparison group. These positive results led the researchers to conclude that institutionalization during infancy and childhood and the lack of strong personal attachments that goes with it do not necessarily doom women to become poor mothers. If the usual chain of consequences can be broken and favorable transactions established, normal behavior is likely to follow.

The profiles of the young men who had spent time in childcare institutions showed that positive later-life experiences decreased their risk of long-term difficulties as well. One particularly interesting gender difference was that men were more likely than women to find a supportive spouse and to raise their children in an intact family, thus blocking the transmission of their own negative early experiences to the next generation (Rutter et al., 1990).

RECOVERY FROM DEPRIVATION

The mounting evidence that the long-term consequences of misfortune depend to a significant degree on later circumstances has spurred a search for principles of successful intervention. A key element in any effort to repair developmental damage is removal from the damaging environment, but such a change alone is not sufficient for recovery. When the Lebanese children were moved from the crèche to other institutions, they did not reach normal levels of development, nor did Genie ever show sufficient recovery to become normal for her age. Could the Lebanese children or Genie have fared better? (See Box 7.3.) What conditions are necessary to foster more complete recovery from early deprivation? Is it possible that some as yet undiscovered environmental conditions might have allowed them to regain normal functioning? Or did their deprivation start too early and last too long to permit them ever to recover completely?

Such questions are impossible to answer in full because human babies cannot deliberately be assigned to live in potentially damaging circumstances to satisfy the quest for scientific knowledge. Research with monkeys, however, combined with scattered studies of human subjects, suggests what some of the aids to recovery might be.

HARLOW'S MONKEYS REVISITED

In Chapter 6 we examined Harry Harlow's studies of infant monkeys raised in isolation with inanimate substitute mothers. One of Harlow's important findings was that infant monkeys had difficulty developing normal social relations after they were introduced into cages with their peers. This was the case even with the monkeys who had become attached to substitute terry cloth

BOX 7.3

Genie and the Question of Ethics Revisited

Research done with Genie, the girl who was kept locked up for over 11 years by her abusive father, strikingly demonstrates how scientific and ethical issues can conflict, even when everyone involved in a research program has good intentions. The ethical controversy surrounding Genie focuses on whether the scientists who studied her development after she escaped from her confinement did all they could to ensure her recovery, or whether their desire to solve a scientific puzzle led them to subordinate Genie's well-being to the goal of scientific progress.

Russ Rymer (1993), who wrote a book about the case, argues that Genie's well-being was indeed sacrificed in the name of scientific inquiry. The scientists in charge of Genie's care deny any wrongdoing; they contend that Genie was treated as well as possible given the very unusual and difficult circumstances of her history and condition.

When Genie was first liberated, she was placed in Los Angeles Children's Hospital. Because her case was one of the most severe cases of child isolation on record it quickly drew scientific interest. According to David Rigler, then chief psychiatrist at the hospital and the man who eventually became Genie's principal investigator, human values and science alike called for a systematic study of Genie's development:

> Theories of child development hold that there are essential experiences for achievement of normal psychological and physical growth. If this child can be assisted to develop in cognitive, linguistic and social, and other areas, this provides useful information regarding the critical role of early experience which is of potential benefit to other deprived children. The research interest inherently rests upon successful achievement of rehabilitative efforts. The research goals thus coincide with (Genie's) own welfare and happiness. (Rymer, 1993:58)

Unfortunately for Genie, this is not how things worked out. For the first several months after her liberation, Genie lived at Children's Hospital. David Rigler obtained a research grant to bring consultants together to decide what approach to take with Genie. Some saw Genie as a scientific opportunity to answer questions about the development of language and thought. Inspired in part by the questions left unanswered by the case of Victor, the Wild Boy of Aveyron, they wanted to use Genie to test the hypothesis that there is a critical period—up until puberty—after which language cannot be acquired. They proposed a program of intensive training to see if she could still develop language.

Others argued that therapy for Genie should come first and that everything else should be a secondary consideration. The psychologist David Elkind, one of the consultants, wrote, "Too much emphasis on language could be detrimental if the child came to feel that love, attention, and acceptance were primarily dependent upon her speech" (Rymer, 1993:59).

Those pushing for a scientific investigation prevailed, and the researchers obtained a grant that focused on Genie's acquisition of language—not so much teaching Genie language as watching how she learned it. Shortly after this decision was made, Genie was taken into the home of Jean Butler, her teacher at Children's Hospital. In the next 2 months, Genie made enormous strides in acquiring vocabulary. But Jean Butler strongly objected to the intrusiveness of the scientists who were studying Genie. She said that their training procedures were disrupting the girl's life and impeding her recovery. A battle for Genie's custody ensued. Butler applied to the Department of Public Social Services to become Genie's foster parent, but her request was denied in favor of Rigler and his wife.

Genie lived in the Rigler household for 4 years. During that time she was treated as much as possible like a member of the family. She was taught how to chew solid food, to behave properly at the table, to express her emotions and indicate her desires appropriately, and to stop masturbating, which she had been doing whenever and wherever she felt the urge to. But she was also being constantly observed and tested by linguists and psychologists.

Within a short time after her move to the Riglers' home, Genie's progress in language learning slowed to a standstill. Her speech resembled the language used in telegrams. She never learned to ask a real question or to form a proper negative sentence. Nor did she learn to behave normally in social situations. Scientists at the National Institutes of Mental Health, which sponsored the research on Genie, became dissatisfied with the project. Largely because it was a single case study based on anecdotal evidence and no controls were possible, they denied further funding for her study.

When the project ended, Genie was returned to her mother's custody. Her mother could not cope with Genie's disabilities and placed her in foster care. She is now residing in a home for mentally retarded adults in southern California. Overall, her behavior has significantly regressed. She is stooped and rarely makes eye contact. She cannot talk normally and continues to engage in inappropriate social behaviors.

Rigler and his colleagues chose to focus on Genie's language deprivation rather than on any of the other major domains of development. What if they had instead followed the lead of research on recovery from severe isolation? Would Genie have recovered more fully if they had provided her with social therapy emphasizing attachment and loving relations with others? There is no way to know. Russ Rymer titled his book *Genie: A Scientific Tragedy.* It tells the unfortunate sequel to the personal tragedy of a parent's inhuman treatment of a helpless child.

mothers, although the severity of the behavioral disruption varied with the length of the isolation and the age of the monkey when the isolation began (Suomi & Harlow, 1972). Monkeys who were totally isolated for only the first 3 months of life, for example, did not seem to be permanently affected by the experience. When they were moved to a group cage, they were overwhelmed by the more complex environment at first, but within a month they had become accepted members of the social group.

Monkeys who were totally isolated for their first 6 months of life, in contrast, rocked, bit, or scratched themselves compulsively when they were placed in a cage with other monkeys. Monkeys who had been isolated during the second 6 months of life (but not the first) became aggressive and fearful when they were put back with other monkeys.

The long-term behavior of these groups of monkeys also differed. Those whose isolation began after 6 months of social interaction in the colony recovered quickly and were able to mate normally when they came of age. But those whose 6-month isolation started at birth recovered only partially. At 3 years of age, when they should have been able to mate, they proved to be incapable of normal sexual behavior.

Total isolation for the entire first year of life produced full-fledged social misfits who showed no propensities for social play or social interchange with monkeys the same age (Harlow & Novak, 1973). When they were placed in a group cage, these monkeys were often the targets of their peers' aggression. As time passed, they showed no signs of spontaneous recovery.

RECOVERY FROM THE EFFECTS OF ISOLATION

After their initial experiments, Harlow and his associates thought that the period from birth to 6 months of age might be critical for social development in these monkeys. If this were the case, recovery would be impossible for monkeys isolated throughout the 6-month period, regardless of any subsequent changes in their environment. The researchers tried various ways of aiding the adaptation of such monkeys to their new social world. One technique they used was to punish the monkeys for inappropriate behaviors by administering a mildly painful shock. Another approach was to introduce them to the new environment slowly, on the assumption that an abrupt change from total isolation to the busy activity of the group cage induced an "emergence trauma" that blocked recovery. The ineffectiveness of all these efforts seemed to support the idea that there was a critical period for social development. As it turned out, such was not the case at all.

The first hint that there might be an effective therapy for these monkeys came from observations of the maternal behaviors of the females, who had been artificially inseminated (Suomi et al., 1972). Many of them beat their newborns and sat on them, and few of the babies survived. If a baby did live, however, the mother began to recover. As the researchers watched these babies with their mothers, they began to suspect how this change came about. If the baby monkeys could manage to cling to their mother's chest, as newborn infant monkeys normally do, they survived. While clinging, they not only had access to life-sustaining milk but also could usually escape their mothers' attempts to harm them. The longer they held on and the stronger they grew, the more time their mothers spent behaving in ways that were approximately normal, if not loving. By the end of the usual period of nursing, the mothers were no longer abusive and interacted more or less normally with their babies. Even more striking was the caregiving behavior of these mothers when they had a second baby. It was indistinguishable from that of their nondeprived peers. They had recovered normal social functioning.

This mature female monkey, who was isolated for the first 6 months of life, finds it difficult to react to the baby monkey. But if the baby is sufficiently persistent in its attempts to interact with her, the older monkey may eventually learn to interact more or less normally with it.

This baby monkey is "providing therapy" to an older monkey raised in isolation.

The recovery of these mothers led Harlow and his colleagues to speculate that it might be possible to reverse the social pathologies of previously isolated monkeys by introducing them into a mother–infant type of relationship with a younger monkey (Harlow & Novak, 1973; Suomi & Harlow, 1972). The researchers introduced normal 2- to 3-month-old monkeys, who were strong enough to survive the abuse they were likely to receive, into a cage with monkeys who had been isolated for 12 months. The playful, love-seeking babies provided an environment that allowed the older monkeys to learn appropriate social behaviors. Over a period of 18 weeks, the former isolates gradually stopped rocking and clasping themselves and they stopped abusing the baby monkeys. They began to move around more, to explore their environments, and to engage in social play. In the end, all of the former isolates became so well adjusted that even experienced researchers could seldom tell them from monkeys who had been raised normally.

IMPLICATIONS FOR HUMAN RECOVERY

Harlow's research with monkeys suggests that placing previously isolated children in an environment in which they can interact with younger children may be therapeutic. This idea seems to be supported by the limited information available about the recovery of human children from extreme social deprivation. When the twins Koluchova (1972, 1976) studied were removed from their isolation, for example, they were at first placed in a special environment in which they lived with younger children. The twins recovered normal functioning despite their years of isolation.

A more formal test of the therapeutic potential of having socially isolated children interact with younger children was conducted by Wyndol Furman, Donald Rahe, and Willard Hartup (1979). Through observations in day-care centers, the researchers identified 24 children between the ages of 2½ and 5 years who interacted so little with their peers that they were judged to be "socially isolated." These children were randomly assigned to three groups of eight children each. The children in the first group participated in one-on-one play sessions with a child 1 to 1½ years younger than they were. The children in the second group participated in one-on-one play sessions with a child their own age. The final group served as a control and received no special treatment. Each child in the first two groups had 10 of these play sessions of 20 minutes each over a 6-week period. During each session, the two children were placed together in a room in which there were blocks, puppets, clothes to dress up in, and other toys that might promote positive social interaction. An observer sitting in the corner of the room took notes but otherwise tried not to interfere with the children.

After the last play session, the social interactions of all the children in the day-care classrooms were rated by observers who did not know which children had participated in the study. Their reports showed that the rate of peer interaction had almost doubled for the socially isolated children who had played with a younger child. Right from the start they provided help to, and shared with, the younger child. The children who had played with an agemate showed some improvement, but they did not differ statistically from the control group. These results show that interactions with younger children, even for a relatively brief period, can reduce the effects of social isolation. Furman and his colleagues suggested that the key benefit for the "socially isolated" children in having younger and less capable playmates was that it gave them the opportunity to initiate and direct social activity.

Such evidence of successful therapeutic intervention suggests the intriguing possibility that a given child's failure to recover from isolation or other forms of social deprivation may actually result from a failure to arrange the proper therapeutic environment, not to some irreversible damage done to the child. Obviously, the best environment for a formerly deprived or isolated child is not necessarily one that is common or easy to create. Practitioners ordinarily have limited time to spend with children, and they may not instinctively provide the special forms of attention and playfulness that will help deprived children to reorganize their patterns of social interaction. Nevertheless, cases of significant recovery both in young animals and in children who have experienced extreme isolation or deprivation show that practitioners should not write such children off; rather, a concerted effort should be made to give them as therapeutic an environment as possible.

THE PRIMACY OF INFANCY RECONSIDERED

When children must live through extremely undesirable life circumstances beginning in infancy, especially circumstances that are abnormal for the society in which they live, it should be expected that their negative experiences will have detectable effects on their later development. Even the children described earlier as making remarkable recoveries showed some residual signs of their past deprivation. The children in Dennis's study who were adopted after infancy continued to exhibit somewhat depressed levels of intellectual ability, and the Romanian children who had spent 8 or more months in an orphanage, like the British children studied by Tizard and Hodges, continued to have problems in social adjustment several years later.

In attempting to arrive at an overall conclusion about the primacy of infancy, it is helpful to return to the proverb "As the twig is bent, so grows the tree." If forces in the environment bend a sapling long enough, the tree may finally grow so low to the ground that its leaves cannot get the light they must have if the plant is to flower and hence to reproduce. But if the forces bending the tree are relieved in time, or if a gardener provides secure stakes to hold the tree upright, the only lasting effect may be a slight bend in the trunk. The tree will go on to flower and reproduce.

Three factors appear to be able to modify the impact of early experiences on the later development of human lives. The first is the one we have been focusing on: changes in the environment. Whether these changes are positive (such as a supportive school environment or a community-based social support network) or negative (such as the outbreak of war or the death of a parent), they may create discontinuities in children's experiences that will set them on a new path into the future.

The second factor that may act to modify the long-term effects of experience is the bio-social-behavioral shifts that reorganize physical and psychological functions into qualitatively new patterns. Such factors as the acquisition of language, new cognitive capacities, and a new relationship with the social world that emerge at the end of infancy, for example, result in a new way of experiencing and dealing with the world. A 12-month-old who is easily frustrated when she cannot get her own way may become a placid preschooler once she has learned to speak and can better coordinate with her surroundings on her own terms. Alternatively, a placid baby who seems to take little interest in the world around him may suddenly display enormous curiosity and energy once he begins to walk. Such observations have led Jerome Kagan to argue that "each life phase makes special demands, and so each phase is accompanied by a special set of qualities" (Kagan, 1984:91). Kagan believes that discontinuities between succeeding life phases are so marked that some of one's past history is actually "inhibited or discarded." This strong view of developmental discontinuities implies that early developmental problems do not inevitably lead to later developmental problems; in effect, each new stage presents its own opportunities.

The third factor is the change in the way children experience their environments as a result of their increased capacities. The separation anxiety shown by 1-year-olds when their caregivers are not present, for example, may be a realistic response for a helpless, relatively immobile infant because of the loss of crucial support that such separation entails. But 3-year-olds, who have a greater sense of autonomy because they can talk, walk, and run, are less dependent on their caregivers. Consequently, an experience that has a big effect on a 1-year-old may not affect a 3-year-old in the same way.

Given the complicated interplay of the child's developing capacities, the changes these capacities bring about in the way the child experiences the environment, and changes in the environment itself, developmentalists who study the possible long-term effects of experience in infancy point to three factors that require further understanding:

1. The sources and extent of discontinuity between infancy and later periods
2. The significant threads of continuity between infancy and later life
3. The mechanisms by which characteristics evident in early life are transformed or preserved in the transition from infancy to early childhood

Two psychological domains that have been studied intensively with respect to these issues are attachment and cognition.

ATTACHMENT

In research on the long-term consequences of the various patterns of attachment, the basic strategy is to assess children's attachment just before their first birthday and then again several years later to determine in what ways, if any, their behavior corresponds with their attachment status (Bretherton & Waters, 1985). The evidence concerning later developmental outcomes of particular attachment patterns is mixed (see Chapter 6, pp. 243–246).

Alan Sroufe and his colleagues have reported that when children who are judged to be securely attached at 12 months of age are assessed at 3½, they are more curious, play more effectively with their agemates, and have better rela-

The distress this French child exhibits as his mother drops him off at day care bespeaks the continued importance of attachment relations beyond infancy.

tionships with their teachers than do children who were insecurely attached as infants (Erikson et al., 1985; Frankel & Bates, 1990; Sroufe & Fleeson, 1986).

In follow-up observations with these children, Sroufe and his colleagues found that their attachment classification during infancy predicted the quality of their interactions into middle childhood and adolescence. When the children were 10, the researchers arranged for them to attend a summer camp where their interactions with peers and camp counselors could be observed. Children who had been assessed as securely attached in infancy were more skillful socially, formed more friendships, displayed more self-confidence, and were less dependent than other campers, according to both their counselors' reports and the researchers' observations. Five years later the researchers arranged a camp reunion for these children. The children they initially assessed as securely attached were more open in expressing their feelings and in forming close relationships with other teenagers. (For a recent summary, see Sroufe et al., 1999.)

Researchers who see patterns of attachment as tending to remain consistent throughout development emphasize that such consistency depends on one key fact. In their view, children's attachment to their primary caregiver serves as the model for all later relationships. Drawing on a formulation by John Bowlby (1969), Inge Bretherton proposed that on the basis of their interactions with their primary caregiver, infants build up an *internal working model* of the way to behave toward other people and then use the model to figure out what to do each time they enter a new situation (Bretherton, 1985). As long as their working model allows them to function effectively with the people they interact with, children can be expected to continue to use it in all of their relationships. But if their application of the working model leads to difficulties, they may change or replace it. In short, continuity and discontinuity depend on the cumulative outcomes of everyday transactions between children and their environments.

To see how children's transactions influence developmental continuity, consider the finding that anxious/resistant children tend to cling to their mothers (Chapter 6, p. 241). Suppose that we observe such a child in a preschool setting. If she is using her internal working model, which is based on her prior interactions to guide her behavior, this little girl can be expected to try to stay close to the teacher. The consequences of her use of this internal working model at school will depend on how it is interpreted. If the teacher sees such behavior as politeness, cooperation, and eagerness to learn, the child will be likely to find this internal working model effective. Thus the same pattern of interaction will probably continue and may even be reinforced by the teacher. But suppose the teacher interprets the little girl's behavior as overly dependent. She may arrange for the girl to help younger, shyer children, thereby providing her with the experience of a new form of social interaction. As a result, the child's internal working model may change and her subsequent interactions with others may diverge from the earlier pattern.

Here we see, on the one hand, how internal working models of relationships can produce continuity in social interactions over time and, on the other hand, why it may be difficult to predict whether infants' patterns of interaction will be maintained in later life. The degree of continuity will depend on the nature of the initial internal working model and the extent to which it proves to be adaptive in children's transactions in the many contexts they encounter later in life.

Application of a transactional approach to understanding attachment relationships helps to account for cases in which infant attachment status fails to predict later attachment behaviors (Thompson, 1998). For example, in a longitudinal study of 100 children, Michael Lewis assessed the children's attachment to their mother when they were 1 year old and then interviewed the children when they were 18 years old to assess their current attachment to their parents and their memory of social and emotional relationships when they were children (Lewis, 1997). He also asked the 18-year-olds and their teachers to fill out a questionnaire that was designed to measure their emotional development.

Lewis's findings cast doubt on the idea that attachment relationships in infancy set the pattern for later socioemotional relationships. First, he found that the "young adults' current attachments bore absolutely no relation to what they actually were like at one year of age, neither for the entire group of children nor even for those children who were insecurely attached earlier" (p. 62). Second, the 18-year-olds' current mental health status, whether based on what the teenagers or their teachers reported, bore no relationship to their attachment status in infancy.

According to Lewis, these data support the view that attachment relations early in life do *not* provide a working model, or template, that lasts into adulthood and causes a particular pattern of attachment relations to persist. Instead, he contends, prior models always are interpreted through the filter of current understandings.

At present it appears that, under some circumstances, there can be measurable long-term consequences of early attachment status, but there are many exceptions to this generalization. Research that would resolve these disagreements remains to be done.

COGNITIVE DEVELOPMENT

For many decades researchers believed that individual differences in infants' intellectual development did not predict later achievement. In their view, there was little continuity in cognitive processes from infancy to later life. After reviewing many studies that attempted to correlate scores on infant developmental scales with later intelligence test scores, Claire Kopp and Robert McCall (1982) unequivocally concluded that "tests given during the first 18 months of life do not predict childhood IQ to any useful or interesting degree" (p. 35). Although the correlations between the test scores was better when the first test was administered after the children had reached the age of 24 months, even tests given at 3, 4, and 5 years of age were not sufficiently predictive of children's subsequent IQ to be useful unless the initial scores deviated a great deal from the norm, signaling possible problems or giftedness (McCall, 1981; Sameroff, 1978).

In recent years, developmental psychologists have been somewhat more successful in demonstrating that individual cognitive characteristics measured in infancy do predict later intellectual abilities. The key difference between the earlier studies and more recent ones is that the earlier studies did not tap the same psychological processes both times the children were tested; the earlier standardized tests of infants' abilities focused heavily on the sensorimotor sphere, whereas tests of older children's intellectual ability focused on the conceptual sphere.

To overcome this problem, Susan Rose and Judith Feldman (1997) chose to study recognition, a memory function known to exist early in infancy (see Chapter 5, p. 204). They used a preferential-looking technique with 7-month-old babies and a test of recognition memory using the drawing of patterns with 11-year-olds. They report a significant correlation between the performance of the children when they were babies and their performance when they were 11 years old.

Even in successful cases, however, the degree of association between early and later cognitive performances, though statistically significant, is low enough to make it clear that such continuity is characteristic of only some children some of the time. Too little is known about the critical experiences that enhance, disrupt, or transform cognitive processes to enable us to specify the transactional mechanisms that work to sustain or change those processes.

COMING TO TERMS WITH LIMITED PREDICTABILITY

Although recent research into continuity in various psychological spheres points to significant continuities between infancy and later developmental periods, it falls well short of implying that any trait is always continuous and predictable. As noted, the correlations between behaviors in infancy and later behaviors are generally very modest. Consequently, data showing marked recovery from early traumatic conditions (which suggest that psychological functioning can change markedly after infancy) and data showing a moderate correlation in individual behavioral traits over time (which imply continuity of functioning) should not be seen as contradictory. Together they provide evidence that a child's development is *simultaneously continuous and discontinuous.*

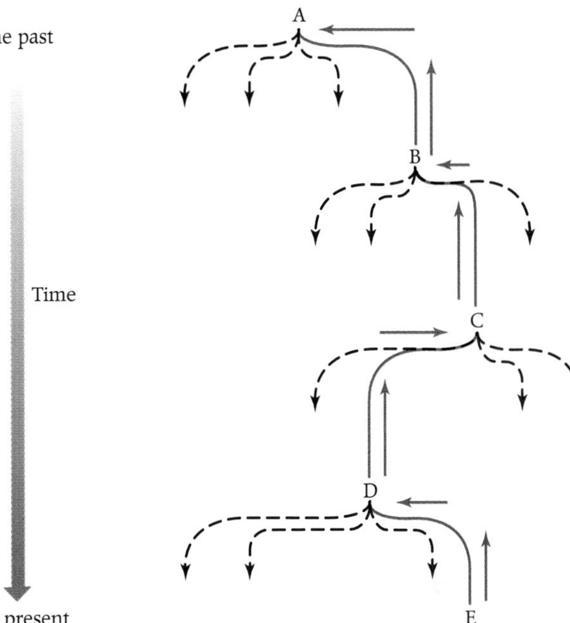

FIGURE 7.3
It is relatively easy to trace development backward to its origins (red arrows). But the many decision points with uncertain outcomes (A, B, C, D) that confront the individual during the life span defeat efforts to predict his or her future. (Adapted from Emde et al., 1976.)

Many years ago Freud (1920/1924) pointed out that whether development seems continuous and predictable or discontinuous and uncertain depends to a certain extent on one's vantage point:

> So long as we trace the development [of a psychological process] from its final stage backwards, the connection appears continuous, and we feel we have gained an insight which is completely satisfactory or even exhaustive. But if we proceed the reverse way, if we start from the premises inferred from the analysis and try to follow these up to the final result, then we no longer get the impression of an inevitable sequence of events which could not be otherwise determined. We notice at once that there might have been another result. (p. 226)

Figure 7.3 is a schematic representation of Freud's insight regarding retrospective analysis. If we start at some point in later life, E, and trace a person's history back to its beginnings, A, we can build a convincing case for why that precise life history proceeded as it did; the developmental state at time E resulted from events at time D, which resulted from events at time C, and so on. At each decision point, we believe we can distinguish the various contributing factors and discern which had the most influence. Only one route leads into the past at each point. But standing at the beginning, A, and looking ahead to the future, we cannot foresee the choices that will be made at points B, C, and D. To borrow Robert Frost's metaphor (p. 258), the bends in the diverging roads are hidden in the undergrowth.

For parents, the unpredictability of the outcome of their caregiving efforts is a natural source of anxiety. Research on primacy, however, shows us that this uncertainty has its good side. A perfectly predictable future holds no possibility of choice. Without the uncertainties that arise from changes in the environment and the changes in the child that accompany development, parents could not dream about influencing the course of their baby's future. It would be immutable. With these uncertainties come the possibility and the challenge of taking advantage of those changes to promote the child's welfare.

SUMMARY

- Many people believe that experiences in infancy are the most significant forces in the shaping of later behavior.

OPTIMAL CONDITIONS FOR INFANT DEVELOPMENT

- To foster optimal development, the caregiver must be sensitive and responsive to the infant's needs and signals. The kinds of sensitivity and responsiveness that are considered optimal in child rearing, and the way they are expressed, depend on the historical and cultural circumstances into which the child is born.

EFFECTS OF PARENT–CHILD SEPARATION

- Separation from parents is upsetting to babies. However, such separations have long-term negative consequences only when they are of long duration or are repeated.
- Experts dispute the consequences of short daily separations resulting from out-of-home care during the first year of life.
- Extended residence in a poorly staffed orphanage retards both mental and social development. Residence in a well-staffed orphanage produces less pronounced developmental difficulties. The degree to which children recover from such experiences depends on their subsequent environments and the age at which they leave the institution.
- Total isolation leads to severe mental and social retardation. If children are moved to a supportive environment before they are 6 or 7 years old, recovery is sometimes possible. If their circumstances are not changed until adolescence, full recovery appears to be impossible.

VULNERABILITY AND RESILIENCE

- Personal characteristics or environmental circumstances that increase the probability of negative outcomes for children are called risk factors. Risk factors are cumulative in nature.
- Protective factors buffer children against risk.
- Children's vulnerability to stressful circumstances depends on several factors, including:
  1. Family factors, such as the number of siblings, the mother's work load, and the presence of a network of kin and friends
  2. Community characteristics, such as whether the neighborhood is in an urban slum or a rural area and the quality of the local school
  3. Individual characteristics, such as variations in temperament
- The processes that lead to various developmental outcomes can be thought of as transactions between child and environment over an extended period of time.

RECOVERY FROM DEPRIVATION

- Studies of monkeys suggest that recovery from early isolation can be achieved later than was once thought possible if an adequate therapeutic environment can be arranged.
- Research has shown that similar principles can be applied to socially isolated children.

THE PRIMACY OF INFANCY RECONSIDERED

- Three factors limit the degree to which the psychological characteristics of infants can predict later development.
  1. Changes in the child's environment

2. The bio-social-behavioral shifts that qualitatively reorganize the child's physical and psychological characteristics
3. An increase in the child's capacity to cope with the environment

KEY TERMS

primacy, p. 258
protective factor, p. 271
resilience, p. 271
risk factors, p. 270
transactional models, p. 275

THOUGHT QUESTIONS

1. Think of a time in your life when two pathways lay before you and consider what might have happened if you had taken a different path. What makes it possible to imagine the alternative? What makes it hard to imagine?
2. Imagine that you are the director of an orphanage. In view of the information provided in Chapters 4 through 7, what are some of the practices you would promote to provide the best possible development for the children in your institution?
3. Imagine that you are the director of a community program to improve the early experiences of children living in a poor community. What sorts of programs would you try to promote? Give a research-based rationale for your suggestions.
4. How does a transactional approach to developmental change relate to the adage, "As the twig is bent, so grows the tree"?
5. Why are retrospective explanations of development problematic?

PART III

Early Childhood

By the age of 2½ or 3, children are clearly infants no longer. As they enter early childhood—the period between ages 2½ and 6—they lose their baby fat, their legs grow longer and thinner, and they move around the world with a great deal more confidence than they did only 6 months earlier. Within a short time, they can usually ride a tricycle, control their bowels, and put on their own clothes. They can get out of bed quietly on Sunday morning and turn on the TV to amuse themselves while their parents still sleep. They can help their mothers bake cookies and take the role of flower girl or ring bearer at an aunt's wedding. Most 3-year-olds can talk an adult's ears off, even if their train of thought is difficult to follow, and they provide an avid audience for an interesting story. They can be bribed with promises of a later treat, but they won't necessarily accept the terms that are offered, and they may try to negotiate for a treat now as well as later. They develop theories about everything from where babies come from to why the moon disappears from the sky, and they constantly test their theories against the realities around them.

Despite their developing independence, 3-year-olds need assistance from adults and older siblings in many areas. They cannot hold a pencil properly, cross a busy road safely by themselves, or tie their shoes. They do not yet have the ability to concentrate for long without a great deal of guidance. As a result, they often go off on tangents in their games, drawings, and conversations. One minute a 3-year-old may be Mommy in a game of house, the next minute Cinderella, and the next a little girl in a hurry to go to the toilet.

In early childhood, children still understand relatively little about the world in which they live and have little control over it. Thus they are prey to fears of monsters, the dark, dogs, and other apparent threats. They combat their awareness of being small and powerless by wishful, magical thinking that turns a little boy afraid of dogs into a big, brave, cowboy who dominates the block.

Although developmentalists have studied early childhood for decades, considerable uncertainty remains about how best to characterize this period of life. In some respects, it appears to be a distinctive stage with its own special modes of thinking, feeling, and acting. In other respects, it appears to be simply the beginning of a long period of gradual change that extends into adolescence and adulthood. In recent years the picture of early childhood has become even more complicated by research suggesting that 3- and 4-year-olds appear to be capable of doing some things that it was once believed only children of 7 or 8 could do.

Our discussion of early childhood development covers four chapters. Chapter 8 examines the nature of language and its development. Once children begin to acquire language, they can experience the world in an entirely new way. Language is the medium through which they learn about their roles in the world, acceptable behavior, and their culture's assumptions about how the world works. Simultaneously, language enables children to ask questions, to explain their thoughts and desires, and to make more effective demands on the people around them.

Chapter 9 examines thinking during early childhood. Leading theories are compared for their ability to explain how young children can behave with logical self-possession at one moment only to become fanciful and dependent the next. The chapter considers whether their apparently illogical behavior is the result of their lack of experience or is governed by its own special logic.

Chapter 10 considers young children's social development and personality formation, their ideas about themselves, the ways they think about rules of proper behavior, and their relations with the people around them. The chapter focuses on the acquisition of sex roles and on children's changing ability to get along with each other, particularly as they learn to balance their own desires with the demands of their social group.

With these general characteristics of early childhood as background, Chapter 11 addresses the influence of various contexts on preschoolers' development: first, the family, where children come to learn about who they are and what adults expect of them; then, day-care centers, preschools, and the media, all of which have important socializing effects on young children.

CHAPTER 8

guage Acquisition

Girl (on toy telephone): David!
Boy (not picking up second phone): I'm not home.
Girl: When you'll be back?
Boy: I'm not here already.
Girl: But when will you be back?
Boy: Don't you know if I'm gone already, I went before so I can't talk to you!

George Miller, *Language and Speech*

So here I am, in the middle way, having had twenty years –
Twenty years largely wasted, the years of l'entre deux guerres –
Trying to learn to use words, and every attempt
Is a wholly new start, and a different kind of failure
Because one has only learnt to get the better of words
For the thing one no longer has to say, or the way in which
One is no longer disposed to say it.

T. S. Eliot, "East Coker"

In the period between 2 and 6 years of age, children's mental and social lives are totally transformed by an explosive growth in the ability to comprehend and use language. Children are estimated to learn several words a day during this period, and by the time they are 6 years old, their vocabularies have grown to anywhere between 8,000 and 14,000 words (Anglin, 1993; Templin, 1957). They can understand verbal instructions ("Go wash your face—and don't come back until it's clean"), chatter excitedly about the tiger they saw at the zoo, and insult their sisters and brothers. Although they will continue to acquire linguistic nuances and a more extensive vocabulary, 6-year-old children are competent language users. Without this achievement, they could not carry out the new cognitive tasks and social responsibilities that their society will now assign them.

We begin this chapter by reviewing and elaborating on the early foundations of linguistic communication that we discussed in earlier chapters. Next we trace the course of children's mastery of the four basic subsystems that constitute language: the sound system, the words, the grammar, and the uses to which language is put. With the facts of language development in hand, we turn to competing theories about the processes that underlie this unique and fundamental human capacity. Then we examine what is known about the necessary prerequisites for acquiring human language and how language affects thought.

PRELINGUISTIC COMMUNICATION

The evidence presented in previous chapters leaves little doubt that children are born into the world predisposed to attend to language and to communicate with the people around them. At birth they show a preference for language over other kinds of sounds and are capable of differentiating the basic sound categories, or phonemes, characteristic of the world's languages. Within a few days after birth they can distinguish the sounds of their native language from those of a foreign language. Well before they are able to speak intelligibly, the range of sound distinctions they recognize becomes narrowed to the sound categories of the languages they hear around them (p. 210).

Newborns' abilities to communicate are initially limited to a small set of facial expressions and crying. Though variations in cry patterns are not particularly informative, they do provide caregivers with rudimentary information about the causes of distress. At about 2½ months, babies' communicative ability is enhanced by social smiles. Their sound repertoire expands to include cooing, which in turn is supplanted by *babbling* and then *jargoning* (see Chapter 5, p. 210); each change brings the baby closer to producing recognizable words.

At the same time that babies' capacity to distinguish and produce linguistic signals increases, they are also becoming more adept at interacting with the people and objects around them. At birth their weak muscles and restricted vision make it difficult for them to carry out the most elementary functions, such as nursing and examining an object in a coordinated way. Within a few weeks, with a good deal of support from their parents, these functions become part of a daily routine that gives structure to babies' limited experiences. *Primary intersubjectivity,* the ability to match one's behavior to that of another person and to share experiences in direct face-to-face interaction, emerges at about 3 months of age (Chapter 5, p. 209). This ability is evident in the rounds of greeting noises and smiling in which mothers and babies engage, to their mutual delight.

Between 9 months and a year, babies acquire *secondary intersubjectivity,* the ability to share mental states with another person when the joint focus of attention is a third person, an activity, or an object (Chapter 5, p. 209). The close link between secondary intersubjectivity and communication is seen clearly in the form of behavior called *social referencing,* through which babies check their caregiver's reactions to an uncertain event or an unfamiliar person to guide their behavior. Secondary intersubjectivity is a crucial precursor to language acquisition: when babies and their caregivers signal to one another, they are sharing knowledge about the objects and events that are the focus of their joint attention (Tomasello, 1999).

Secondary intersubjectivity is also apparent when babies begin to point at objects (Bruner, 1983a; Franco & Butterworth, 1991). Pointing is clearly a communicative act intended to create a joint focus of attention, but it is a primitive one. When 12-month-olds see a remote-controlled car roll past them, first they point at it and then they look to see how their caregivers react to it (social referencing). At 18 months of age, the function of pointing becomes communicative in a more complex way. Now children are more likely first to look at their caregivers to see if they are looking at the car and then to point to it. If babies this age are alone in the room when the electric car appears, they do not point until the caretaker walks back into the room, clearly demonstrating that their pointing has a purpose and is meant to communicate to another person (Butterworth, 1998).

As we will see, during the second year of life, children's repertoire of words grows considerably, slowly to begin with and then at an increasing rate. As this is happening, children's ability to produce and understand the patterned sequences of words that make up sentences increases.

In sum, when we look at development from birth to the start of the third year of life, we can see that the capacity for communication has already developed to a remarkable degree well before the child can actually hold a conversation. The question that intrigues developmental scientists is how this capacity arises.

THE PUZZLE OF LANGUAGE DEVELOPMENT

Although language is one of the most distinctive characteristics of our species, its development in the individual is still very poorly understood. Linguists, who specialize in the study of language, can tell us a great deal about the structure of adult language, the history and meanings of words, and the physical apparatus that transmits utterances from one person to another. But it has been difficult for generations of linguists and developmentalists to answer such basic questions as how children acquire language and how either children or adults compose and comprehend it. Two basic questions have proved especially difficult to answer. The first involves the problem of reference: How do children discover what words mean? The second involves the problem of grammar: How do children learn to arrange words and parts of words in a way that has meaning to others?

THE PROBLEM OF REFERENCE

Perhaps the most basic intuition that we have about language is that each word refers to something: words name real or imagined objects and relationships in the world. This idea seems so commonsensical that it is difficult to grasp the mystery it conceals, a mystery that no philosopher, linguist, or psychologist has ever adequately explained: How, among all the many things or relations to which any word or phrase may refer, do we ever learn to pick out its intended referent—the object to which it refers?

In Figure 8.1 we see the difficulty of determining what a word refers to. Imagine that you are the child in the picture, and try to decide what the Russian father is saying. It's a puzzle, isn't it?

Some people may argue that the example is unfair because the utterance is in a foreign language. A little more reflection reveals that the example may be fair after all: in the beginning, all languages are foreign to newborn children, who must somehow figure out that the sounds they hear are in fact meant to refer to something in the ongoing flow of experience—to indicate an actual object, event, or feeling.

To make the difficulty clearer, suppose you know all the words that the father says except one: "Look, son, there sits a *ptitsa*." Even this additional information does not tell you which of the objects in the scene is a *ptitsa*. The

FIGURE 8.1
For children just beginning to acquire language, the problem of learning what words refer to is particularly acute. What is this father referring to?

FIGURE 8.2
An adult can point to the animal in this picture or to many parts of the animal and apply the same kind of declaratory statement: "That's a ________." How do children know what is being referred to? (From Miller, 1991.)

cat sitting on the wall? The helicopter sitting on the roof? Or the bird sitting in the tree? If you know Russian, you know that the father is pointing at the bird. But the language-learning child, even the Russian language–learning child, is not born knowing the meaning of the sound package *ptitsa.* Somehow the child must learn that when the father says *ptitsa* he is talking about the winged creature in the tree and not about any of the other objects.

The problem of how children come to know what words refer to is complicated by the fact that a single object or event has many parts and features, which can be referred to in a great many ways. George Miller (1991) illustrates this problem with the example in Figure 8.2. If an adult points to the object in Figure 8.2 and refers to it in the various ways indicated, how is the child to avoid the conclusion that "rabbit," "ear," "white," and "Harvey" are synonyms? Yet somehow, despite all the apparently confusing ways in which objects and actions are referred to, children learn the meanings associated with all of the different kinds of references.

THE PROBLEM OF GRAMMAR

For words to be combined into a comprehensible sentence, they must be related not only to objects and events but to one another. That is, they must be governed by **grammar,** the rules of a given language for the sequencing of words in a sentence and the ordering of parts of words.

Recent evidence using the habituation technique discussed in Chapter 4 (p. 133) indicates that by the time they are 7 months old, infants are not only sensitive to the ordering of words in simple sentences presented to them but can extract abstract patterns of word usage from such sentences (Marcus et al., 1999). This ability comes into play several months later as children begin to create their own multiword utterances and is instrumental in their subsequent acquisition of grammatical rules.

One indicator that children who are beginning to produce multiword utterances have some grasp of grammar comes from the errors they make when they string words together. When we hear a child make such statements as "My doggy runned away" or "Mommy, Johnny camed late," we know immediately that the child has confused one grammatical form with another. Such errors are so common that it is easy to overlook their significance. Children cannot have been taught to say such things, nor could they have learned them

grammar The rules of a given language for the sequencing of words in a sentence and the ordering of parts of words.

recursion The embedding of sentences within each other.

by simple imitation, because they virtually never hear such incorrect sentences uttered. Where could these sentences come from?

No less puzzling is the appearance in children's language of **recursion,** the embedding of sentences within each other. Recursion is one of the central properties of human language. It provides language with great economy and flexibility of expression. For example, the three sentences "The boy went to the beach," "He saw some fish," and "The boy got sunburned" can easily be combined to create "The boy who went to the beach saw some fish and got a sunburn": three sentences for the price of one. There is no evidence that recursion is ever consciously taught to young children. How, then, do they develop it?

The problems of reference and grammar illustrate the central puzzle of language acquisition. On the one hand, almost all children, even many who have severe cognitive impairments, acquire the ability to communicate with words, so language appears to be a fundamental capacity that is easy for humans to acquire, like learning to walk. On the other hand, the complexities and subtleties of language are so great that it is difficult to understand how word meanings or grammatical rules could ever be acquired.

Somehow, in the space of a very few years, children accomplish something denied all other species. What is it they do, and how do they manage to do it?

FOUR SUBSYSTEMS OF LANGUAGE

Language, according to Webster's Tenth New Collegiate Dictionary, is "the words, their pronunciation, and the methods of combining them used and understood by a community." This definition identifies four central aspects of language: sounds, words, methods of combining words, and the communal uses that language serves. We will describe the development of each of these aspects separately, but it is important to keep in mind that language is a system: each of its aspects is connected to all of the others, and each aspect is itself a distinctive subsystem of elements. Unless some pathology interferes with normal development, these separate subsystems of language form a unified, organic whole.

SOUNDS

In the change from babbling to pronouncing words that occurs late in the first year, children give up their indiscriminate freedom to play with sounds and begin to vocalize the particular sounds and sound sequences that make up the words in the particular language of their community (Kuhl et al., 1992).

Learning to make language sounds properly takes time and practice.

It takes children several years to master the pronunciation of the separate words of their native language. Their first efforts may be no more than crude stabs at the right sound pattern that frequently leave out parts of words (resulting in "ca" instead of "cat," for example). Multisyllable words are often turned into a repeating pattern. For example, a child may use the sound pattern "bubba" to say "button," "butter," "bubble," and "baby." A long word, such as "motorcycle," can come out sounding like almost anything: "momo," "motokaka," or even "lomacity" (Preisser et al., 1988).

Children's command of the sound system of their native language develops unevenly. Sometimes a child will find a particular sound especially difficult to master, even after he or she understands many words that employ that sound. At the age of 2½, for example, Alexander could not say /l/ sounds at the beginning of words, so he could not pronounce the name of his friend's dog, Lucky. Instead, he consistently pronounced the name "Yucky," much to the amusement of his family. This error didn't concern Alex at all; he knew what other people were talking about when they referred to Lucky, and Lucky didn't seem to notice. When Alex called him, he came.

Neil Smith (1971) showed that such substitutions do not arise because children are incapable of pronouncing certain sounds. When he asked one young child to say the word "puddle," the child responded with "puzzle," and when he asked for "puzzle," the response was "puggle"! Another child would always say "fick" instead of "thick," but he had no difficulty in saying "thick" when he meant to say "sick." Both examples suggest that the basic sounds of a language are learned as parts of the overall sound patterns of the language, rather than as isolated sounds.

Evidence presented earlier shows that even newborn children can perceive the differences between the basic sounds of their language (p. 134). This does not mean, however, that the ability to hear and produce phonemes (sound categories) is "just there" at birth. When, for example, a child learns to employ the English phoneme /l/, more is involved than learning to reproduce a particular sound wave by creating a particular mouth shape. In reality, /l/ is a phoneme of English because in our language it contrasts with other phonemes, such as /y/, as part of meaningful words. We hear /l/ and /y/ as different sounds only because they can create different meanings: English speakers must learn that "lap" and "yap" or "lard" and "yard" are not simply variations in the pronunciation of a single word, as they could be in another language. Children's attention to the differences between sounds is not simply a mechanical skill but develops along with their growing understanding of the meanings of words.

The close connection between phonemes and meanings becomes clear when one is attempting to learn a foreign language. Some native speakers of Spanish, for whom /b/ and /v/ sound much the same, find it difficult to produce or to hear any difference between them. To native English speakers "boat" and "vote" sound quite different; to Spanish speakers, these two words sound much the same and thus may be spoken interchangeably. Likewise, the English speaker frequently has difficulty hearing and producing the difference between the French *u* and *ou,* because that difference does not exist in English.

Although it is often convenient to think of words as the basic units of meaning in language, many words contain more than one meaning-bearing part, or **morpheme.** A morpheme may be a whole word or only a part of one. The word "transplanted," for example, is made up of three morphemes. The root of the word is *plant,* which means "to fix in place." The morpheme *trans* means "across, over, beyond," and the morpheme *ed* is a marker of past tense. We do not stop to ponder all of these relations when we say a sentence with the word "transplanted" in it. In fact, until the rules are pointed out, we rarely stop to think about the parts of words or the way we compose them. Yet every child must acquire the ability to decipher and reproduce just such intricate interweavings of sound and meaning. By the time they are 8 or 9 years old, children can use knowledge about morphemes to figure out the meanings of new words such as "treelet" (Anglin, 1993).

WORDS

Precisely when a given child utters his or her first real words is often difficult to determine. Parents may be so eager to claim their child's ability to speak that they discover "words" in early cooing and babbling. Genuine words, however, appear only late in the first year, after children have been babbling for

morpheme The smallest unit of meaning in the words of a language.

some time and after the contours of their sounds—or of their hand movements, if they are learning American sign language—have gradually become more speechlike (as we saw in Chapter 5, p. 210).

It is useful to think of the process of word formation as a peculiar sort of joint effort, or collusion. Neither the adult nor the child really knows what the other is saying. Each tries to gather in a little meaning by supposing that the other's utterance fits a particular sound pattern that corresponds to a particular meaning. This joint effort may eventually result in something common, a word that both can understand. This process may also fail. As the following examples make clear, the process can proceed in a variety of ways, depending on how the parent interprets the relation between the child's sounds and actions.

At 8 months of age, Pablo began to say "dahdee." Although this "first" word sounds like "daddy," Pablo used "dahdee" for commands and requests when his father was nowhere to be seen, so it must have had some other meaning for him. Adults interpreted "dahdee" to mean either "Take it from me" (when Pablo said it while he offered something to someone) or "Give it to me"; they ignored the fact that Pablo's first word sounded like "daddy." At about the age of 12 months, "dahdee" disappeared from Pablo's vocabulary (Shopen, 1980).

A different fate befell Brenan's first word, "whey." Around 1 year of age, Brenan began to say "whey" after one of his parents had spoken. In this case, "whey" not only sounded something like "why" but also came at a position in normal conversational turn-taking where "why" would be a possible (if not always appropriate) thing to say. Brenan's parents therefore responded to "whey" as if Brenan had asked a question and rephrased what they had said in order to "answer his question," expanding on their original utterance. Over time, Brenan pronounced and used "whey" more and more like a true "why" until it became a genuine "why" in the English language (Griffin, 1983).

Yet another route to the formation of the first word is taken by Samoans, who believe that once children begin to walk, they become cheeky and willful. In accordance with this belief, the only word that Samoan parents acknowledge as a child's first word is *tae,* which is a Samoan curse word meaning "shit." They explain this remarkable singularity of initial speech as confirmation of Samoan common knowledge—that young children are defiant and angry. In fact, young Samoan children may make a number of sounds that might be interpreted as words, but Samoan adults choose to hear and acknowledge only *tae* (Ochs, 1982).

Each of these instances differs from the others in significant ways, but all are variations of a single process in which adults collude with each other and their children to create word meanings.

Words as Mediators

From birth onward, infants' cries and coos express their emotional states. At some point, usually around 11 to 12 months of age, babies discover that the sound sequences they make can recruit adults' attention and help. What began as a process of making sounds that merely expressed emotion becomes a process of producing sounds that also anticipate, guide, and stimulate their own and others' action and feeling. With the emergence of the capacity to use words, children acquire the ability to express themselves and organize their activity in a new way.

This additional feature of language is illustrated in observations that Elizabeth Bates (1976) made of a 13-month-old girl:

> C. is seated in a corridor in front of the kitchen door. She looks toward her mother and calls with an acute sound *ha.* Mother comes over to her, and C. looks toward the kitchen, twisting her shoulders and upper body to do so. Mother carries her to the kitchen, and C. points toward the sink. Mother gives her a glass of water, and C. drinks it eagerly. (p. 55)

In this interaction we also see two key features of the process of early word use. First, it is an excellent example of secondary intersubjectivity in verbal communication; initially the linguistic object, *ha,* and then its referent, the glass of water, are jointly attended to by mother and child. Second, the episode illustrates clearly that it is the relation of the sound to action (C.'s looking toward the kitchen, and then pointing to the sink), and not just some property of the sound itself, that gives the sound its meaning. Of course, in this case *ha,* the "word" in question, functions in a very small community, that is, the mother and child. Nonetheless, the child's use of "ha" displays an important new ability. Instead of trying to act *directly* on the object (by, for example, attempting to toddle over to the sink), the child operates *indirectly* through an idiosyncratic sound that evokes the desired action from another person.

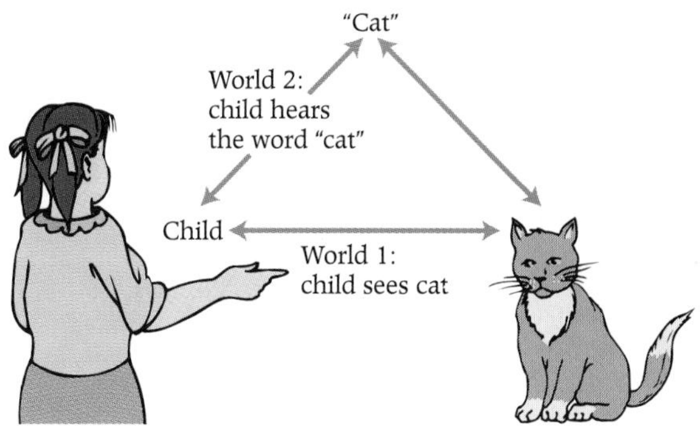

FIGURE 8.3
Children experience the world in two distinctive ways once they acquire language: directly through their sensory contact with the physical environment (World 1) and indirectly (symbolically) through language (World 2). This double relation illustrates the mediated nature of language-based action.

In this and the remaining chapters of this book, we will refer to the property of language illustrated in Bates's example as the mediated character of linguistic behavior. Until children acquire the ability to use and understand words, they are restricted to immediate, or direct, actions. But with the advent of language, they can also deliberately act indirectly, using words to mediate their actions. They can make something happen without doing the thing themselves. The same principle applies to the way children can be influenced by others; once they start to understand words, children can be influenced by others both directly, via nonverbal actions, and indirectly, through the mediating power of words and the culturally organized knowledge that words embody (see Figure 8.3).

Alexander Luria (1981) beautifully summarized the new intellectual power that human beings obtain when their behavior begins to be mediated by words:

> In the absence of words, humans would have to deal only with those things which they could perceive and manipulate directly. With the help of language, they can deal with things which they have not perceived even indirectly and with things which were part of the experience of earlier generations. Thus, the word adds another dimension to the world of humans. . . . Animals have only one world, the world of objects and situations which can be perceived by the senses. Humans have a double world. (p. 35)

The Earliest Vocabulary

Developmental linguists have gathered much of their evidence concerning children's earliest words by having parents keep records of their children's vocabulary development or by making recordings of children's speech in their homes or in organized play facilities (Bloom, 1993; Clark, 1995; Tardif et al., 1997). A number of studies have shown that although there are wide individual differences among children, infants, on average, acquire the ability to use approximately 10 words by 13 to 14 months of age, 50 words by the time they are 17 to 18 months old, and from 200 to 300 words by the time they reach their second birthday. However, there is a great deal of variation in the ages at which children reach particular levels of language production (see Figure 8.4). Their receptive vocabulary—that is, the vocabulary they understand—is considerably larger. For example, when they can produce 10 words, they can understand over 100 (Fenson et al., 1994).

For infants, pointing is a precursor to liguistic communication.

One of the most common findings in research among children in the United States is that nouns referring to objects make up a large proportion of the early vocabularies of young children (Bloom et al., 1993). For example, in a study in which

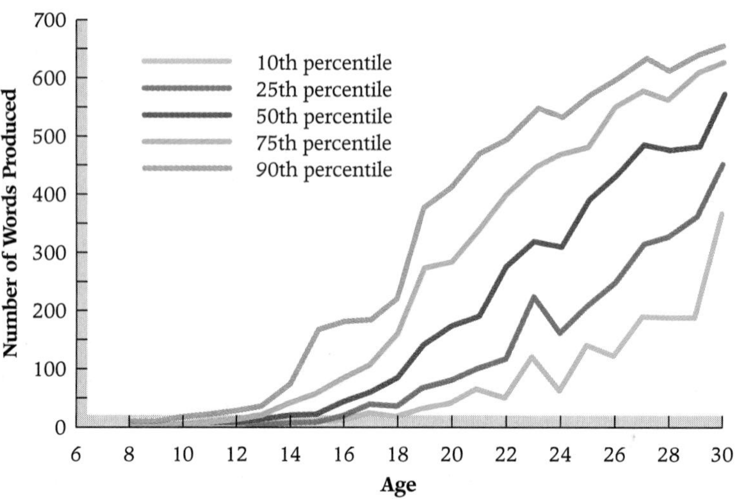

FIGURE 8.4

There are wide individual differences in the rate at which children acquire vocabulary. These data from the work of Elizabeth Bates and her colleagues are grouped to show acquisition rates for the top and bottom 10% of a large sample of U.S. children as well as children who fall at various levels between the two extremes (from Bates, 1999).

18 families kept track of everything their children said during the months they were acquiring their first words, Katherine Nelson (1973) found that most early words (65 percent) labeled things and classes of things at the same time, such as "doggie," "juice," and "ball," or particular things, such as "Mommy," "Daddy," and pet names. Nelson (1976) points out that the first words children acquire are often closely linked to actions that they can accomplish with the things named. "Hat" and "sock" are common in the initial vocabularies of American children, but "sweater" and "diapers" are not, perhaps because little children can put on and take off hats and socks more or less effectively, but cannot do the same with sweaters and diapers. In addition, objects that can change and move and thus capture children's attention (such as cars and animals) are likely to be named, whereas large, immobile objects such as trees and houses are "just there" and are not likely to be named.

Although nouns used to label objects dominate the first 100 or so words that English-speaking children learn, as their vocabularies grow, more verbs and adjectives appear; by the time they are 2 years old, nouns usually account for less than half of their vocabularies (Bloom, 1993). Moreover, in some languages, such as Mandarin Chinese and Korean, verbs may outnumber nouns in children's early vocabularies (Choi & Gopnik, 1995; Tardif et al., 1999).

Toddlers' growing vocabularies also include a variety of relational words that are used to communicate about changes in the state or location of an object (Gopnick & Meltzoff, 1986). "Gone" may be said when an object disappears, and "here" may announce its appearance. One of the most useful relational words in children's early vocabularies is "no," which can fulfill such important communicative functions as rejection, protest, and denial. "No" can also be used to comment on unfulfilled expectations and on an object's absence. Given these multiple functions, it is little wonder that "no" is among the earliest and most frequently used words in a child's early vocabulary (Bloom, 1973).

Allison Gopnick and Andrew Meltzoff (1997) identify an additional class of words that children begin using around the age of 2 years to comment on their successes ("There!" "Hooray!") and failures ("Uh-oh"). The appearance of these words seems to support the idea that children this age become sensitive to social expectations and begin to set standards for themselves (see Chapter 6, p. 250).

Problems of Referential Ambiguity

As they learn their first words, children confront a number of ambiguities that complicate their task. One major problem is that words do not have unique or fixed meanings. "Table," for example, can refer to an article of furniture, or an arrangement of data in rows and columns, or the action of putting off a topic for discussion (as in "let's table the motion"). Nonetheless, the illusion that there is one word for each real-world referent remains strong.

The ambiguity inherent in words can never be completely eradicated. But as children gain familiarity with the ways people around them use words, their own uses come to conform more and more closely to the general uses in their cultural group. They achieve this feat by narrowing the range of objects and events to which they apply a particular label, by broadening the range of application of other labels, and by learning to use words at an appropriate level of abstraction (Anglin, 1993).

overextension A term for the error of applying verbal labels too broadly.

underextension A term used for applying verbal labels in a narrower way than adults do.

Overextensions It is common for young children to use a single label in circumstances in which adults use many. Adults are amused, for example, when a 2-year-old wanders into a room full of adults and proceeds to call each of the men there "daddy." This form of mislabeling, in which many members of a category are referred to by a single term that is conventionally used to label only one of them, is called an **overextension** (Naigles & Gelman, 1995).

Children's early overextensions appear to be strongly influenced by perceptual features of the items named as well as by the way children perceive the functioning of the named items (Naigles & Gelman, 1995). A word such as "kitty" may be extended to cover a wide variety of small four-legged animals because of their common shape, or it may cover a variety of soft, furry objects because of their similar texture, or it may even refer to other small animals such as rabbits that people keep as pets. (See Table 8.1.)

Underextensions Children also commit the error of **underextension**, using words in a narrower way than adults do (Barrett, 1995). It is common, in fact, for children's early words to have a unique reference that is closely associated with a particular context (Golinkoff et al., 1994). For example, 1½-year-old Emmy used "bottle" only for the plastic bottle she drank from, not other kinds of bottles. Young children may hotly deny that a lizard, a fish, or a mommy is

TABLE 8.1 TYPICAL OVEREXTENSIONS IN THE SPEECH OF YOUNG CHILDREN

Child's Word	First Referent	Extensions	Possible Common Property
Bird	Sparrows	Cows, dogs, cats, any moving animal	Movement
Mooi	Moon	Cakes, round marks on window, round shapes in books, tooling on leather book covers, postmarks, letter O	Shape
Fly	Fly	Specks of dirt, dust, all small insects, his own toes, crumbs, small toad	Size
Koko	Cock crowing	Tunes played on a violin, piano, accordion, phonograph, all music, merry-go-round	Sound
Wau-wau	Dogs	All animals, toy dog, soft slippers, picture of old man in furs	Texture

Source: De Villiers & De Villiers, 1979.

an animal. They may also believe that "cat" applies only to their family's cat, not to cats in the neighborhood or on television.

Levels of Abstraction In choosing how to refer to something, children must learn to deal with the fact that several words can be used to refer to the same object. In speaking of someone she sees at the supermarket, a child may point and say, "Mommy, look at Sally," or "Mommy, look at that girl," or "Mommy, look at her," or "Mommy, look at that person." All these forms of referring to the girl are equally accurate, but they are not equally appropriate in all circumstances. If the girl being talked about is well known to the mother and daughter, it would be inappropriate to refer to her as "that person" or "that girl." It might be appropriate under some circumstances to refer to the girl as "her" instead of "Sally," but to do so would change the meaning of the utterance. It requires time and experience for children to choose words that are at the appropriate level of abstraction.

An interesting characteristic of the level of abstraction of the early words that children say is that they tend to refer to objects at a *basic level* of abstraction (Golinkoff et al., 1995; Rosch & Mervis, 1981). Words at the basic level refer to objects that look alike, provide similar kinds of interactions, and have many component parts in common (Poulin-Dubois, 1995). Young children say "car," for example, rather than "vehicle," which has a more general meaning, or "Chevy," which has a more specific meaning. Only later do children acquire words that are more general or more specific. These early words seem to classify the world in categories that are neither too big nor too small.

To illustrate young children's use of basic category labels, Jeremy Anglin (1977) showed children posters that contained four pictures of objects that could be related at some level of abstraction and asked them for a label that applied to the whole set (see Figure 8.5). One poster might have four pictures of roses, which could be labeled by the relatively specific category "roses"; another might have a rose, a daisy, a carnation, and a pansy, which could be labeled at the basic level of abstraction as "flowers"; a third might have an elm, a rose, a rubber plant, and a cactus, which could be labeled at a higher level of abstraction as "plants." Anglin found that adults were able to vary the level of generality of their labels appropriately, whereas children between the ages of

FIGURE 8.5

Young children fail to differentiate levels of abstractness in the way they label sets of objects, using an intermediate level more frequently than adults do. (Adapted from Anglin, 1977.)

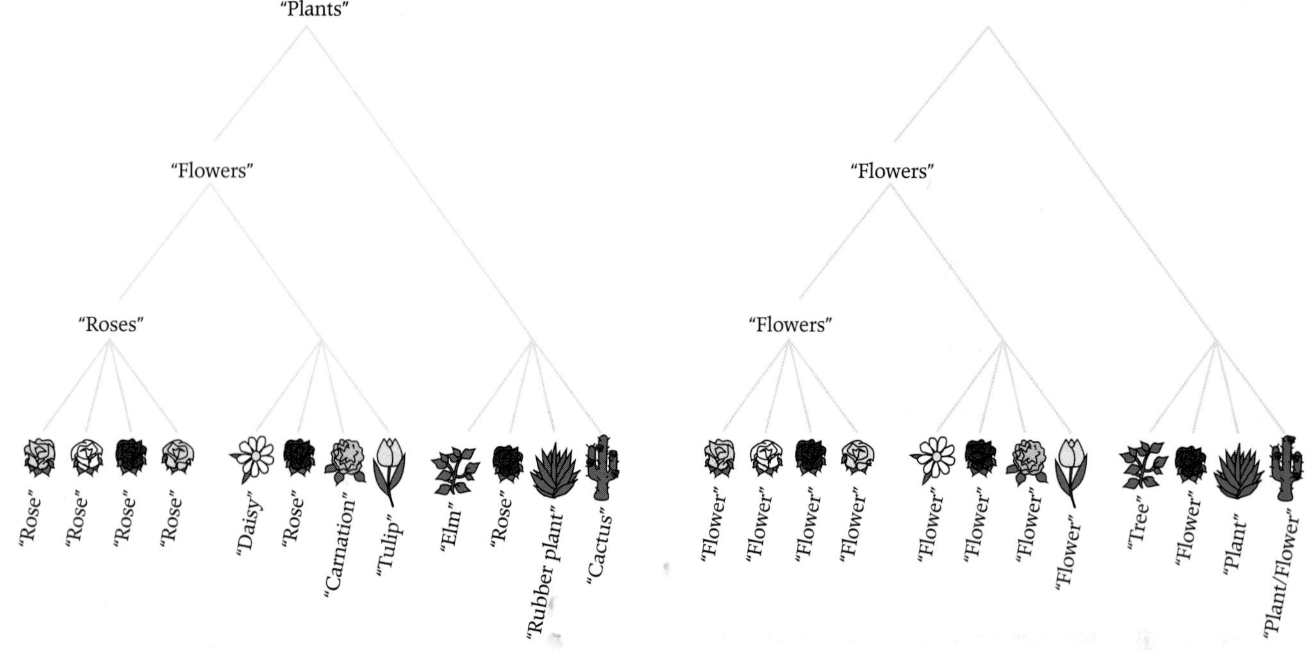

2 and 4 tended to label all the sets at the same intermediate level of generality. They not only called the set containing the daisy, rose, carnation, and pansy "flowers," but also called all four roses "flowers," and were unable to provide a single label for the four plants. Most 4- and 5-year-olds were able both to name specific flowers and to use the general term "plants," but they too tended to use the basic-level term "flowers" far more than the adults did. These same results were obtained with many other category hierarchies, such as "animals, dogs, collies."

Children's limitations in labeling specific objects and general categories do not indicate that they fail to understand differences between objects. Even children who labeled all pictures of dogs and cats as "cat" could still pick out the picture of the proper animal when they were asked to do so (Fremgen & Fay, 1980; Naigles & Gelman, 1995). Moreover, Jean Mandler and Patricia Bauer (1988) have demonstrated that, even though they tend to stick to the basic level in their initial verbal labels, children under 2 years of age have some knowledge of higher-level categories (vehicles) as well as basic-level categories (truck, train, airplane) through the way they explore sets of objects.

The Changing Structure of Children's Vocabularies

Clearly, the growth of children's vocabularies involves more than a simple increase in the number of individual words they know and more than a simple improvement in the accuracy with which they apply labels to objects. Vocabulary growth is accompanied by fundamental changes in the ways children relate words to one another and to the contexts in which they use them, ultimately creating qualitatively new systems of meaning (Carey, 1985; Clark, 1995).

We can see the changing structure of word meanings by tracing the developmental course of children's use of a word such as "dog." The first words and phrases children use are likely to represent the specific circumstances of the first time they associate the sound and its referent, with their feelings playing as important a role as their thoughts. "Dog" may mean something terrible if the child has just been bitten; the same word may mean something wonderful if the dog lies on the rug and allows the child to burrow in its fur.

As children gain experience with dogs, the word "dog" begins to evoke a range of situations in which "dog" is only one element. The structure of the vocabulary at this stage is dominated by the pattern shown in Figure 8.6*a*. There "dog" is a unifying element in several situations: dog growls, dog barks, dog is petted, dog runs away, dog fights. Each situation is connected to "dog" in a specific way as part of a specific kind of action.

Further experience reveals that dogs are not the only creatures that bite. Cats bite too, and so do babies. At the same time, it becomes clear that cats do not bark (seals do) and they rarely take walks (but mommies do). Some of the things you can say about dogs you can just as easily say about cats (or seals or mommies), but some you cannot. When children are familiar with a large number of concrete situations in which the same word is used, words begin to acquire conceptual meanings that do not depend on any one context, or even on a real-world context. This aspect of language development is depicted in Figure 8.6*b*.

Once a word's meaning is influenced by the logical categories of the language, the word "dog" evokes more than the single emotion of fear or the single concrete image of Fido begging at the table. It has become part of an abstract system of word meanings independent of any particular situation. "Dog" becomes an instance of the category "do-

FIGURE 8.6
(a) For a young child, word meanings are dominated by the contexts of action in which the words have played a role. (b) As children acquire the formal conceptual categories of their language, the structure of word meanings changes accordingly. (Adapted from Luria, 1981.)

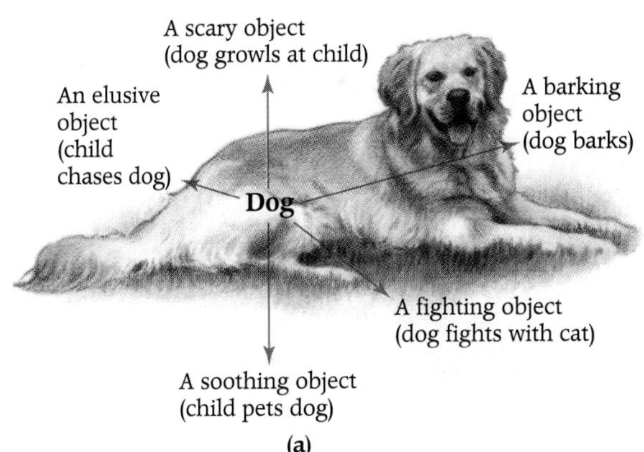

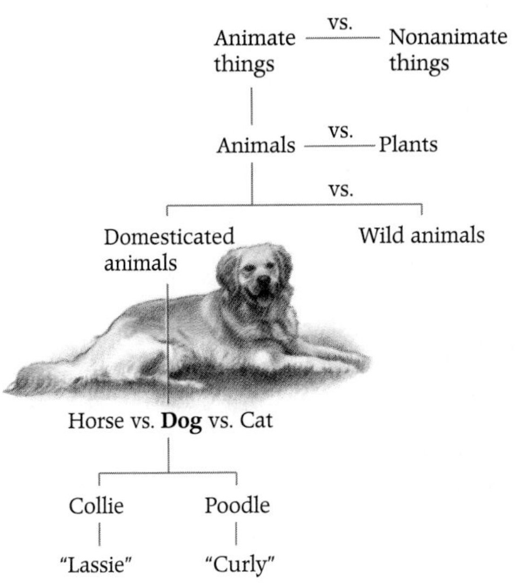

holophrase A term for babies' simple-word utterances that some believe stand for entire phrases or sentences.

mestic animal," or the more general category "animal," or the still more general category "living thing."

One of the simplest ways to assess the changing structure of children's vocabularies is to ask children of different ages to say the first word that comes to mind in response to a set of words. Early in their language development, children respond to "dog" with a word related to specific actions they associate with dogs, such as "bites" or "barks"; later they respond to "dog" with a general category word, such as "cat" or "animal" (Nelson, 1977). Very similar results are obtained when children are asked, "Tell me all you can about ________s" or "What kind of a thing is a ________?" (Anglin, 1985).

Although new forms of word meaning reshape the child's vocabulary, old forms do not disappear. Adults, no less than children, respond with fear, love, or some other emotion to "dog." And much of adults' use of language depends on a fine-tuned appreciation of the way words relate to each other in particular contexts. What distinguishes the adult's vocabulary from the child's, other than its greater size, is the presence of several alternative forms of meaning for each word, which provide a richer arsenal of linguistic tools for reasoning about dogs, cats, and everything else, and for talking about these things with other people.

Do Early Words Stand for Sentences?

Investigators believe that even when children can utter only single words, they are still communicating whole ideas and even sentences. Some argue that these single-word sentences, called **holophrases,** like "up" or "bottle," represent whole sentences to the child (McNeill, 1970). But Patricia Greenfield and Joshua Smith (1976) offer a different interpretation—paying more attention to the nonverbal elements of the child's speech. They believe that the verbal, single-word utterance stands for one element of the situation the child wants to talk about, not the whole idea. Greenfield and Smith point out that children's single words are almost always accompanied by nonverbal elements, such as gestures and distinctive facial expressions. The single word *in conjunction with the gestures and facial expressions* is the equivalent of the whole sentence. By this account, the single word is not a holophrase, but one element in a complex of communication that includes nonverbal actions.

This child is making clear the close connection between words and gestures.

It is difficult to decide between competing theories of children's linguistic understanding at the stage of single-word utterances because too little information is available. Certainly, adults respond *as if* the child's single-word utterances are meaningful. A child says "shoe," for example, and the father responds by saying, "Oh, you want Daddy to tie your shoelace." But it is impossible to say how much of this meaning is the child's and how much of it is the adult's interpretation of the utterance based on information gleaned from the context in which the child speaks. Although this problem of interpretation never completely disappears, it becomes less vexing when the child begins to string words together.

SENTENCES

As we saw in Chapter 6, a watershed of language development is reached toward the end of infancy, when children begin to produce utterances consisting of two or more words. Although they seldom form grammatical sentences, even two-word utterances carry more than twice as much information about the child's meaning as a single word alone, because of the meaning conveyed by the relationship between the two words. With as few as two words children can indicate possession ("Daddy chair"), nonexistence ("All-gone cookie"), and a variety of other meanings. They can vary the order of the words to create different meanings ("Chase Daddy" and "Daddy chase"). This new potential for creating meaning by varying the arrangement of linguistic elements marks the birth of grammar. (See Table 8.2 for a sample of two-word utterances that mark the beginning of grammar.)

TABLE 8.2 Sample Two-Word Utterances

See boy	Mail come
See sock	Mama come
Night night office	Bunny do
Night night boat	Want do
More care	Boat off
More sing	Water off

Source: Braine, 1963.

However, sentences restricted to two words often remain ambiguous. This shortcoming of two-word utterances is illustrated in an amusing way by a series of incidents in *Higglety, Pigglety, Pop,* Maurice Sendak's tale of an adventurous dog who accepts a job as nanny for Baby, a child caught in the grip of the terrible twos. At first the dog attempts to get the baby to eat, and the baby says, "No eat!" When the dog decides to eat the food himself, the baby again says, "No eat!" Finally the baby and dog find themselves confronted by a lion, and the baby says for the third time, "No eat!"

Aware of the context surrounding each utterance, we have no difficulty understanding what the child means. Devoid of context, these two-word utterances provide no clue in themselves to the meaning intended. Similarly, the ambiguity of many young children's two-word utterances is likely to restrict effective communication to occasions when listeners can reliably interpret the context in which the child is operating.

Increasing Complexity

At the same time that children begin to string more and more words together to form complete sentences, they increase the complexity and the variety of words and grammatical devices they use. These changes are illustrated by the following prodigious sentence spoken by an excited 2-year-old girl: "You can't pick up a big kitty 'cos a big kitty might bite!" (De Villiers & De Villiers, 1978, p. 59).

grammatical morphemes Words and parts of words that create meaning by showing the relations between other elements within the sentence.

This sentence is by no means typical of 2-year-olds, but it provides a good opportunity to assess how utterances that are more complex communicate more explicitly. The sentence communicates not only that the little girl doesn't want to pick up a big cat but also that no one should pick up a big cat; it also conveys her understanding that big cats sometimes bite but do not invariably do so. Such complex sentences communicate shades of meaning that help adults to respond sensitively to children's experiences.

As Figure 8.7 indicates, the length of 2-year-olds' utterances grows explosively, along with their vocabularies and grammatical abilities (Brown, 1973; Fenson et al., 1994). Note that the growth in the length of utterances is indicated by the average number of *morphemes* per utterance (or the "mean length of utterance" [MLU]), rather than by the average number of words. The phrase "That big bad boy plays ball," for example, contains six words and seven morphemes, whereas the phrase "Boys aren't playing" contains only three words but six morphemes *(boy, s, are, [not], play, ing)*. Assessing linguistic complexity by counting morphemes rather than words provides an index of a child's total potential for making meaning in a particular utterance.

FIGURE 8.7
This graph shows the rapid increase in the mean length of utterances made by three children during the first four years of life. (From Brown, 1973.)

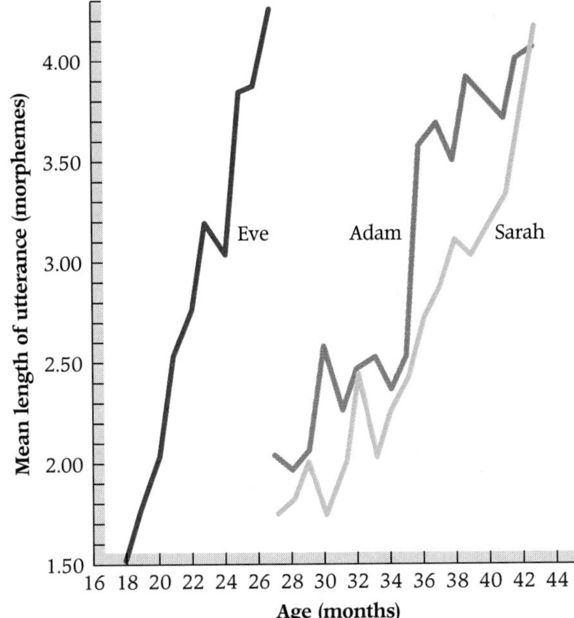

Grammatical Morphemes The complexity of the little girl's long sentence about picking up cats is attributable in large measure to just those little words and word parts that are systematically absent in two-word utterances. The article "a" ("a big kitty") indicates that it is big cats in general, not just this particular big cat, that are worrisome. The word "'cos" connects two propositions and indicates the causal relationship between them. The contraction "can't" specifies a particular relationship of negation. These elements are called **grammatical morphemes** because they are units that create meaning by showing the relations between other elements within the

TABLE 8.3 Usual Order of Acquiring Grammatical Morphemes

Morpheme	Meaning	Example
Present progressive	Temporary duration	I walk*ing*
In	Containment	*In* basket
On	Support	*On* floor
Plural	Number	Two ball*s*
Past irregular	Prior occurrence	It *broke*
Possessive inflection	Possession	Adam'*s* ball
To be without contraction	Number; prior occurrence	There it *is*
Articles	Specific/nonspecific	That *a* book That *the* dog
Past regular	Prior occurrence	Adam walk*ed*
Third person regular	Number; prior occurrence	He walk*s*
Third person irregular	Number; prior occurrence	He do*es* She *has*
Uncontractible progressive auxiliary	Temporary duration; number; prior occurrence	This *is going*
Contraction of *to be*	Number; prior occurrence	That'*s* book
Contractible progressive auxiliary	Temporary duration; prior occurrence	I'*m* walking

Source: Brown, 1973.

sentence. Whether the rate of language acquisition is fast or slow, grammatical morphemes appear in roughly the same sequence in the speech of all children (at least those who acquire English as a first language).

As Table 8.3 indicates, the grammatical morpheme likely to appear first in children's language production is *ing,* indicating the present progressive verb tense. This verb form allows children to describe their ongoing activity. Morphemes indicating location, number, and possession make their appearance next. Morphemes that mark complex relations, such as *am* in "I'm going" (which codes a relation between the subject of the action and the time of the action), are generally slower to emerge.

The appearance of grammatical morphemes is a strong indicator that children are implicitly beginning to distinguish nouns and verbs, because their speech conforms to adult rules that specify which morphemes should be attached to which words in a sentence. Children demonstrate their intuitive grasp of the rules for using grammatical morphemes by the fact that they do not apply a past-tense morpheme to a noun ("girled"); nor do they place articles before verbs ("a walked").

Evidence collected by a number of language-development researchers shows that although children begin to produce grammatical morphemes relatively late in the language acquisition process, they are sensitive to the existence of grammatical morphemes in the language they hear at least by the time they are starting to produce their first multiword utterances (Golinkoff et al., 1999). It remains unclear how this ability first arises, but the fact that children comprehend grammatical morphemes early in the process of acquiring the ability to create grammatical sentences provides additional evidence that they are sensitive to the structure of language at a very early age.

Complex Constructions Between the ages of 2 and 6, children begin to use a great many grammatical devices, the "grammatical rules" that bedevil students in language classes throughout their schooldays. Some of these grammatical constructions obey rules of such subtlety that, although we follow them intuitively in our speech, we can't say why we use them as we do.

Consider a common grammatical form known as the tag question (Dennis et al., 1982)—words added to the end of a declarative sentence to turn it into a question. "They won the prize, didn't they?" and "You will come, won't you?" are typical tag questions. It's no easy matter to provide a rule specifying how such questions are formed, is it?

A somewhat more complicated demonstration of the gap between our ability to use language and our ability to understand the principles that underlie our talk is provided by the following sentences:

1. John is easy to please.
2. John is willing to please.

Both sentences seem to follow the same ordering principle. But these sentences, despite their surface similarity, differ grammatically. We can clarify the difference by adding a single word to the end of each sentence while still preserving the order of elements. Compare the two new sentences:

3. John is willing to please Bill.
4. John is easy to please Bill.

Sentence 3 is just as acceptable in the English language as sentences 1 and 2, but even though the surface ordering principles are unchanged, sentence 4 is not grammatically acceptable, and we cannot interpret it.

Such examples suggest that acquiring the grammar of a language involves mastery of highly abstract rules that even adult speakers of a language cannot explain (unless they are linguists!). Yet such rules appear to be acquired by all normal children, regardless of the language they speak.

Children's difficulties in mastering the subtle grammatical constructions demanded by adult language have been studied by Carol Chomsky (1969). She tells of Lisa, 6½ years old, who was seated at a table on which there was a doll with a blindfold over its eyes.

> *Adult:* Is this doll easy to see or hard to see?
> *Lisa:* Hard to see.
> *Adult:* Will you make her easy to see?
> *Lisa:* If I can get this [blindfold] untied.
> *Adult:* Will you explain why she was hard to see?
> *Lisa:* [to doll] Because you had a blindfold over your eyes.
> *Adult:* And what did you do?
> *Lisa:* I took it off.

Before this interchange, Chomsky had made certain that Lisa knew the meaning of "easy." Lisa knew that it is easy to sit in a chair but hard to climb a tree. What, then, was her difficulty in the case of the blindfolded doll? Chomsky argues that children still assume that the person mentioned at the beginning of a sentence is the one who carries out the action (in this case, that it is the doll who does the seeing). This assumption is often correct, but it is not correct in the case of "easy to see."

THE USES OF LANGUAGE

In order to communicate effectively, children must master more than the grammatical rules of their language and the meanings of its words. Such knowledge would be of little use if they did not simultaneously master the **pragmatic uses of language**—that is, the ability to select words and word orderings that are appropriate to their actions in particular contexts.

pragmatic uses of language The ability to select words and word orderings that are appropriate to their actions in particular contexts.

conversational acts Actions that achieve goals through language.

Conversational Acts

One way of describing how language is used for pragmatic purposes is to think of utterances as **conversational acts,** actions that achieve goals through language. According to Elizabeth Bates and her colleagues (Bates et al., 1975), children's earliest conversational acts fall into two categories, protoimperatives and protodeclaratives. *Protoimperatives* are early ways of engaging another person to achieve a desired object. When our daughter, Jenny, first began holding up her cup and saying "More," she was using a protoimperative.

Protodeclaratives are early ways of referring that are important because they allow young children both to initiate and maintain dialogues with adults. Perhaps the earliest form of a protodeclarative is the act of pointing. This form of referring is soon accompanied by words, as when a baby points to a dog and says "Dog-gie." Another early form of protodeclarative conversation is giving. As babies master this form, they may be seen bringing all their toys, one after another, to lay at a visitor's feet if each gift is acknowledged by a smile or a comment (Bates et al., 1987).

In the process of acquiring the pragmatic aspects of language, children also come to understand that a single sequence of words may accomplish several alternative goals. For example, the sentence "Is the door shut?" has the grammatical form of a request for information. But it may also be a request for action or a criticism, being pragmatically equivalent to "Please shut the door" or "You have forgotten to shut the door again."

As children's vocabularies grow and their command of grammar improves, the range of actions they can be verbally induced to perform expands. Marilyn Shatz (1974, 1978) found that children as young as 2 years old responded correctly to their mother's indirect commands, such as "Is the door shut?" Instead of responding to the surface grammatical form and answering "Yes" or "No," Shatz's toddlers went to shut the door. At the same time, children's ability to control others verbally increases. A 3-year-old observed by John Dore (1979) used three different grammatical forms to achieve a single goal: "Get off the blocks!" "Why don't you stay away from my blocks?" and "You're standing on my blocks."

In the hope of getting a proper overall picture of language development, a number of scholars have attempted to catalog the full set of language functions that children have to master (Dore et al., 1979). This task has proved to

Young children take great delight in their ability to communicate by using their rapidly developing linguistic skills.

be formidable because there is so much variety in the uses of speech, even by 3-year-olds. The 3- and 4-year-olds these researchers studied have come a long way from mere pointing or the use of idiosyncratic "words" such as "ha." They can solicit information ("What happened?") or action ("Put the toy down!"). They can assert facts and rules ("We have a boat"), utter warnings ("Watch out!"), and clarify earlier statements.

cooperative principle The conversational principle to make your contributions to conversation at the required time and for the accepted purpose of the talk exchange.

Conversational Conventions

As part of the task of learning how to achieve their goals through talking, children must come to appreciate basic rules that apply in any conversation. Their failure to understand such rules is a common source of misunderstanding when they are talking to adults.

The master rule of ordinary conversation, according to the philosopher H. P. Grice (1975, p. 45), is the **cooperative principle:** make your contributions to conversation at the required time and for the accepted purpose of the talk exchange. Grice lists four maxims that must be honored if the cooperative principle is to operate effectively:

1. *The maxim of quantity:* Speak neither more nor less than is required.
2. *The maxim of quality:* Speak the truth and avoid falsehood.
3. *The maxim of relevance:* Speak in a relevant and informative way.
4. *The maxim of clarity:* Speak so as to avoid obscurity and ambiguity.

In conversation among adults, everyone understands that these rules are often violated to make deliberately nonconventional statements. The act of encouraging a child, for example, may evoke an exaggerated statement such as "You can do it, Suzie. You're a big girl now, and you know that big girls try hard. They don't give up. I'm sure you can do it." This kind of talk might violate the maxim of quantity (the speaker is saying more than is required) except for the fact that it is acceptable for the special task of providing encouragement.

Some figurative uses of language (such as irony, in which someone means the opposite of what he or she says) depend on deliberate violation of a conversational maxim (see Box 8.1). Learning the circumstances in which the basic speech-act conventions do not apply requires years of additional experience (Winner, 1988).

Children must also acquire knowledge of the social conventions that regulate what is to be said and how to say it (Ninio & Snow, 1999). These conventions may vary markedly from one culture to another. In the United States, children are expected to say "please" when they request something and "thank you" when they are given something. But in a Colombian mestizo community such verbal formulas are frowned upon in the belief that "please" and "thank you" signal the speaker's inferiority; obedience, not formulaic politeness, is what these adults expect of their children (Reichel-Dolmatoff & Reichel-Dolmatoff, 1961).

Taking Account of the Listener

The core meaning of the word "communicate" is "to place in common." Language is said to communicate when speakers and listeners come to share a common interpretation of what is said. Yet a major limitation of the language of young children, as we have seen, is that it leaves so much of the interpretive work to the listener. In this sense, children's language is not fully communicative. Children's increasing knowledge of word meanings and mastery of grammatical rules reduce this problem but by no means eliminate it.

One of the skills that children must master in order to make their language communicative is saying things in such a way that the meaning will be clear

BOX 8.1

METAPHOR

A 2½-year-old points at his yellow plastic baseball bat and says with delight, "Corn, corn!" A 1½-year-old moves a toy car along his mother's arm in a twisting fashion and exclaims, "Nake!" (snake). At first glance these children may appear to be overextending the meanings of their words. But a variety of evidence suggests that not long after children begin to name objects, they begin to use metaphors. A *metaphor* is a figure of speech containing an implied comparison in which a word or a phrase ordinarily used to name one thing is used for another ("All the world's a stage," "Fresh as a daisy").

The use of metaphors provides evidence that language production is a creative process, not a simple imitative one. In order to generate a metaphor, children must recognize a similarity between two things and express that similarity in a way that they have never heard before (Dent-Read, 1997; Winner, 1988).

Significantly, the beginnings of metaphorical language coincide with the onset of symbolic play. In both forms of behavior, the 2-year-old child treats objects and events nonliterally; the properties of one object are attributed to another—a yellow plastic bat is seen in terms of an ear of corn.

Winner and her coworkers identify two distinct routes for the development of nonliteral, metaphoric speech (Winner, 1988; Winner et al., 1979). Some metaphors are closely tied to action: a 2-year-old rubs a fur teddy bear against a wooden armchair, then holds up the teddy bear and says, "Zucchini." Then he points to the arm of the chair and calls it "grater." A teddy bear does not look at all like a zucchini, and most wooden chair arms do not look like vegetable graters; the resemblance that makes these words metaphorically meaningful is the way the objects are used in the action sequence. Perceptual metaphors, by contrast, take on meaning from the physical similarities of the objects being compared. When a little child exclaims, "Corn, Corn," while looking at a yellow bat or "Oh, Mommy, how balloony your legs look!" she is using perceptual metaphors (Chukovsky, 1968).

Although children between the ages of 2 and 6 years use many metaphors, they often fail to understand the figurative meaning of adult speech that does not refer to simple actions or to an object's perceptual characteristics. Kornei Chukovsky, a Russian linguist, translator, and children's poet, collected examples like the following one that are difficult to improve upon:

> Four-year-old Olya, who came with her mother to visit a Moscow aunt, looked closely at this aunt and her husband as they were all having tea, and soon remarked with obvious disappointment: "Mama! You said that Uncle always sits on Aunt Aniuta's neck [a Russian expression for being bossy and controlling] but he has been sitting on a chair all the time that we've been here." (Chukovsky, 1968, pp. 12–13)

The ability to understand and use metaphors develops throughout childhood. During middle childhood, children have difficulty understanding metaphors that link physical terms to people. Such metaphors ("That kid is a bulldozer") require the child to compare human personality traits to perceptual characteristics of the object world. This kind of comparison appears difficult because young children still lack knowledge about personality traits, so they find it difficult to understand what aspect of similarity underlies the metaphor. As they enter adolescence, children gain sufficient knowledge of the domains that are used in common metaphors to be able to make metaphors based on many kinds of similarity. In the eyes of many developmentalists, metaphors are essential tools of human thought (Ortony, 1993).

from the listener's point of view. This skill develops slowly in the years from 2½ to 8—though even after it is firmly established, children, as well as adults, sometimes fail to take their listener's knowledge and perspective into account.

Children as young as 2½ years of age show that they are able to take the listener into account by modifying what they say to include information important to the listener (Wellman & Lempers, 1977). By the time they are 3½ years old they are sufficiently mindful of what another person needs to know that, when they try to communicate their choice of a toy from an array laid out in front of the person, they provide more information to someone who is blindfolded than to someone who is not (Maratsos, 1973). They also use simpler language when they talk to younger children than when they talk to adults, an indication that in some way they know the younger child's language ability is more primitive than their own (Tomasello & Mannle, 1985). Similarly, when playing with 2-year-olds, 4-year-olds shorten their sentences, speak more slowly, and simplify both their vocabulary and their grammar to make it easier for the younger children to understand (Shatz & Gelman, 1973).

This ability to modify speech so that younger children can easily understand it does not depend on experience in talking to younger children. Only children are just as likely to simplify their speech as children with little brothers and sisters. Interestingly, small children make the same kinds of simplifications in their speech when they play with a baby doll, but not when they play with a grown-up doll (Sachs & Devin, 1973).

Even 4-year-olds adapt their language when they speak to younger children.

EXPLANATIONS OF LANGUAGE ACQUISITION

During much of the twentieth century, two widely divergent theories have organized a great deal of the research on language acquisition. These theories correspond roughly to the polar positions on the sources of human development—nature versus nurture. The *learning-theory approach* attributes language to nurture; it accords the leading role in language acquisition to children's environments, especially to the language environment and teaching activities provided by adults. The *nativist approach* attributes language acquisition largely to nature; it assumes that children are born ready to learn language and that as they mature, their language-using capacity appears naturally, with only minimum input from the environment and without any need for special training.

In recent decades a variety of *interactionist approaches* to language acquisition have gained prominence. Interactionists acknowledge that language is an innate propensity of human beings but deny that it is a separate capacity that develops according to its own rules. Instead, interactionists believe that the development of children's language is closely tied to their overall mental development and place in society. Table 8.4 summarizes the basic concepts of the major competing approaches to the development of language.

THE LEARNING-THEORY EXPLANATION

The basic assumption of the learning-theory view is that the development of language is just like the development of other behaviors and conforms to the same laws of learning. According to this point of view, language acquisition depends on learning by association, through the mechanisms of classical and operant conditioning, and on imitation (Miller & Dollard, 1941; Skinner, 1957; Staats, 1968).

Perhaps the first statement of this view was provided by the early Christian philosopher St. Augustine (A.D. 354–430). Recalling his childhood, he wrote:

> When they named any thing, and as they spoke turned towards it, I saw and remembered that they called what one would point out by the name they uttered. . . . And thus by constantly hearing words, as they occurred in various sentences, I collected gradually for what they stood; and having broken in my mouth to these signs, I thereby gave utterance to my will. (Augustine, 1961, p. 4)

TABLE 8.4 MAJOR APPROACHES TO LANGUAGE ACQUISITION

Theory	Major Causal Factor	Mechanism	Major Phenomenon Explained
Learning	Environment	Imitation, conditioning	Word meaning
Nativist	Heredity	Triggering	Syntax
Interactionist (cognitive hypothesis)	Interaction of social and biological factors	Assimilation-accommodation	Correlation of cognitive and linguistic developments
Interactionist (cultural-context approach)	Cultural mediation of social-biological interaction	Coordination in cultural scripts	Language-thought relationships

Classical and Operant Conditioning

The process of associating objects and words described by St. Augustine is similar to the process that learning theorists refer to as classical conditioning (see Chapter 4, p. 156). According to learning theorists, the meaning of a word such as "candy" is the sum of all the associations that the word evokes after it has been paired with a wide variety of experiences (Mowrer, 1950).

Learning theorists use the classical conditioning model to account for the way children learn to understand language, but this mechanism does not account for a child's ability to produce language. To explain this aspect of language acquisition, learning theorists point to the mechanism of operant conditioning.

The operant conditioning explanation begins with the observation, described in Chapter 4 (p. 159), that children emit a rich repertoire of sounds more or less at random during the early phases of babbling. These sounds represent the initial elements of spoken language, which, according to the learning theorists, are gradually shaped through reinforcement and refined through the child's practice. The sound "da," for example, might be shaped into "dog," or "mo" into "more," by a parent's enthusiastic attention to the child's successively closer approximations to the correct sound of the word.

The process of language acquisition proposed by learning theorists applies to all societies at all times, but the particulars will vary from one language environment to another. An American child growing up in Boston will acquire a different way of pronouncing "Boston" ("Baaston") than a New Yorker ("Bawstin"). A Kpelle child growing up in Liberia, West Africa, will learn to be sensitive to the sound contours of words because they affect meaning (for example, the word *kali* pronounced with a rising tone on "a" means "hoe," and with a falling tone means "leopard"). An American child, whose history of reinforcement has rendered rising and falling tones insignificant to meaning, may not even hear the difference.

Imitation

It seems obvious that imitation is involved in language acquisition if only because children acquire the languages they hear around them, rather than inventing totally new languages that adults cannot understand. Moreover, modern research has shown that young children often learn to name things by hearing someone else name them and then repeating what they hear (Leonard et al., 1983).

Simple imitation, however, does not appear to explain how children acquire the ability to compose complex grammatical patterns or the tendency to use grammatical forms they have never heard to express new ideas. Children often use a grammatical morpheme correctly the first several times they say it and then go through a period of incorrect usage before returning to the correct form. After months of using the correct plural form for "hand," for instance, children may go through a period in which they say "handses" before returning to "hands." They certainly never heard anyone say "handses," so although they may have learned to say "hands" by imitation, imitation cannot explain the development of their use of this deviant grammatical form.

These and similar complexities have led researchers to a more refined description of how imitation functions in language learning. With respect to "handses," for example, Gisela Speidel and Keith Nelson (1989) suggest that children selectively use imitation with different attributes of the referent. Initially the child may attend to and imitate the whole word "hands." Then, as the child becomes sensitive to grammatical morphemes, the plural ending "es" becomes a target of imitation, and the child applies it to "hand" and many other words. Eventually the child learns to form some plurals with "s," others with "es," and still others in even more irregular ways (mouse/mice, goose/geese, and so on).

Pondering the mechanisms by which imitation is involved in language acquisition, Albert Bandura (1977, 1986), a leading learning theorist, described a kind of imitation called *abstract modeling*. Bandura called this kind of modeling abstract because, in his view, even when children imitate specific utterances, they abstract from them the general linguistic principles that underlie them. Thus a child repeating "Juana walked home" abstracts the grammatical principle of adding "ed" to show past tense and can then go on to say "Juana fixed the toy" without having to hear those exact words first.

THE NATIVIST EXPLANATION

The nativist view of language acquisition has been dominated by the work of the linguist Noam Chomsky (1975, 1986). According to Chomsky, the fact that children produce a vast array of sentences that they have never before heard makes it impossible to claim that language could be acquired primarily through learning mechanisms such as classical and operant conditioning or by imitation of the kind Bandura proposed. This does not mean that experience has *nothing* to contribute to language acquisition; Chomsky acknowledges that "children acquire a good deal of their verbal and non-verbal behavior by casual observation and imitation of adults and other children" (1959, p. 49). But such factors, he argued, cannot fully account for language acquisition.

Chomsky believes that the capacity to comprehend and generate language is innate, and that the principles by which it develops are not the same as those underlying other human behaviors. His view is echoed by Steven Pinker (1994) in a book pointedly titled *The Language Instinct*. In Pinker's words, language is a "distinct piece of the biological makeup of our brains . . . distinct from more general abilities to process information or behave intelligently" (p. 18).

Chomsky's strategy for discovering the nature of language and the conditions for its acquisition is to determine the grammatical rules that are common to a variety of sentences despite variability from one utterance to the next. He refers to the actual sentences that people produce as the **surface structure** of the language. At the level of surface structure, there is great variability in the grammatical rules of different languages. However, according to Chomsky, there exists a basic set of rules shared by all languages. This basic set of rules from which the surface structures of different languages can be derived is called the **deep structure** of the linguistic system.

Chomsky suggested that the ability to use language arises from a mechanism he dubbed the **language acquisition device (LAD).** The LAD is like a genetic code for the acquisition of language, programmed to recognize the universal rules for the deep structures that underlie any particular language that a child might hear. At birth the child's language acquisition device is presumed to be still in an embryonic state. Chomsky theorizes that as the child matures and interacts with the environment, maturation of the LAD enables the child to fit increasingly complex language forms into the preexisting structure of the LAD. The eventual result of this process is the adult capacity to use language.

Those who, like Chomsky, believe that language development is a maturational process argue that the language children hear around them and the feedback they get on their early utterances provide insufficient information for them to induce the rules of grammar. Hence, innatist theorists conclude, there must be some preexisting linguistic structure that functions to guide children's language learning (Chomsky, 1980; Meisel, 1995; Pinker, 1994). Attempts to evaluate this argument have focused on documenting how much feedback children actually receive about their use of language. In an influential study of this kind, Roger Brown and Camille Hanlon (1970) found, in fact, that when children say something like "Why the dog don't eat?" most parents

surface structure In Chomskian terms, the actual sentences that people produce.

deep structure In Chomskian terms, the basic set of rules of a language from which the actual sentences that people produce are derived.

language acquisition device (LAD) Chomsky's term for an innate language-processing capacity that is programmed to recognize the universal rules that underlie any particular language that a child might hear.

"No, Timmy, not 'I sawed the chair.' It's 'I saw the chair' or 'I have seen the chair.'"

Drawing by Glenn Bernhardt.

do not explicitly correct such errors. Furthermore, even when parents do attempt to correct erroneous grammar, the effort is likely to fail, as shown in the following exchange reported by David McNeill (1966, pp. 106–107):

> *Child:* Nobody don't like me.
> *Mother:* No, say "nobody likes me."
> *Child:* Nobody don't like me.
>
> *[This interchange is repeated several times. Then:]*
>
> *Mother:* No, now listen carefully; say "nobody likes me."
> *Child:* Oh! Nobody don't likes me.

Extreme resistance to such corrections, even when the child is obviously trying to cooperate, seriously undermines the idea that specific teaching is important to language acquisition and bolsters the nativist position that language acquisition depends only minimally on the environment.

In summary, nativists contend that the essential structures that make language acquisition possible—the universals of grammar—operate on different principles than other psychological processes and are determined far more by the evolutionary history of our species than by the experiential history of particular children. Experience does of course determine which of the many possible human languages a child actually acquires. Children who never hear Chinese spoken will not grow up speaking Chinese, even though they are genetically capable of learning that language. The experience of hearing a particular language, however, does not modify the LAD; it only triggers the innate mechanisms designed for language acquisition.

INTERACTIONIST EXPLANATIONS

Surveying alternative explanations of language acquisition in the 1970s, George Miller, a leading researcher on the psychology of language, remarked wryly that psychologists are faced with two unsatisfactory explanations of language development. One of them, the idea that language arises entirely from conditioning, is impossible. The other explanation, the nativist view, is miraculous. Interactionist approaches to language acquisition may be viewed as attempts to create a bridge between the impossible and the miraculous explanations of language development (Bates, 1999; Bloom, 1998; Bruner, 1982; Hirsh-Pasek & Golinkoff, 1996). Within this overall position, scholars differ significantly about what those bridging mechanisms are and how they work.

Interactionist theories concur with nativist theories that innate features of the human nervous system play an important role in the acquisition of language. They deny, however, that language is a system unto itself. Instead, they attempt to link language development either to the development of general cognitive processes such as remembering, categorizing, and attending, on the one hand, or to social organization of the environment, on the other (Elman et al., 1996; Meltzoff & Gopnik, 1997; Rogoff, 1999; Tomasello, 1999). Those who take the first approach sometimes draw upon ideas associated with Piaget's constructivism, which emphasizes the way cognitive development sets the stage for and constructs language development. Those who take the second approach, which is associated with the cultural-context perspective, emphasize the way the sociocultural environment enters into partnership with the child. Adherents of this approach to thinking about language development focus on the ways that children participate in a broad range of cultural practices that allow them to be achieving language, culture, and individual development simultaneously.

A great deal of language learning takes place in casual interactions among family members. In this Asian American family, foreign words are likely to be mixed with the children's English vocabulary.

Emphasizing Cognition

Alison Gopnik and Andrew Meltzoff suggest that changes in the way children use words at around 18 months arise as a consequence of the kind of cognitive changes described by Piaget (Gopnik & Meltzoff, 1997). As we have seen, 18 months is the age at which infants begin to reason systematically about displacements of hidden objects and to deliberately vary the way they combine actions to achieve a goal (see Table 4.5, p. 163). Correspondingly, before 18 months of age, children are restricted to "social words" such as "Bye-bye" and "Hereyare" in connection with the events they are experiencing at the moment (a mother leaving for work or discovering a searched-for toy). After the age of 18 months, however, they begin to acquire words such as "gone" for talking about absent objects. This is also the time when they begin to use such expressions as "Uh-oh" to mark their failure in trying to do something, indicating that they know they have failed to achieve a desired standard.

An important challenge to interactional theories of language acquisition is to explain the acquisition of grammar, because grammatical structures appear to be well beyond the ability of young children (or many adults) to understand. One approach to this challenge has been proposed by Elizabeth Bates and her colleagues, who have been central to implementing an interactionist approach to language development. In their view, the mastery of grammatical structures is a by-product of the growth of vocabulary and of children's attempts to express increasingly complex thoughts (Elman et al., 1996).

To illustrate how complex grammatical structures may arise from verbal interactions that do not explicitly have the construction of those grammatical structures as their goal, Bates (1999) points to the way a complex beehive is formed as a by-product of the process by which bees collect and store honey. To make a structure to store the honey, bees secrete wax from their abdomen and, with their heads, push their load up against the wax deposited by other bees. This process creates a honeycomb labyrinth made up of hexagonal cells. Certainly, bees inherit genes that influence the development of their round heads, but it is implausible to conclude that bees inherit a gene to make hexagons. Instead, as Bates points out, hexagons are inevitably created whenever circles or spheres are packed together in as small a space as possible. Bates applies this same logic to linguistic structures. She argues that grammars emerge from packing words together as "solutions to the problem of mapping a rich set of meanings onto a limited speech channel, heavily constrained by the limits of memory, perception, and motor planning" (p. 3).

Evidence for this view comes from research demonstrating an intimate link between the size of children's vocabularies and the degree of complexity of the grammatical utterances they can make (Bates & Goodman, 1999). As we saw earlier (Figure 8.4, p. 302), individual children vary greatly in the rates at which they acquire vocabulary. The same is true for their acquisition of grammar (Fenson et al., 1994). However, when grammatical complexity is related directly to the number of words that children know, there is an almost perfect relationship between vocabulary size and grammatical complexity, *regardless of how old the children are.* Bates and her colleagues argue that such data show directly how grammar develops to deal with a growing vocabulary (see Figure 8.8).

Emphasizing Social Interaction

Interactionists who emphasize the role of cultural context in the development of language focus on a different way in which language is not a process unto itself—the fact that the acquisition of language is necessarily a social process. Cultural-context theorists emphasize that the social environment is highly organized to incorporate the child as a member of an already existing language-using group and must do so for its own survival (Bruner, 1983a; Harkness, 1990; Nelson, 1988; Ochs & Schieffelin, 1995; Tomasello, 1999). According to Jerome Bruner (1982), the earliest social structures for language development involve what he calls **formats**—recurrent socially patterned activities in which

format Recurrent socially patterned activities in which adult and child do things together.

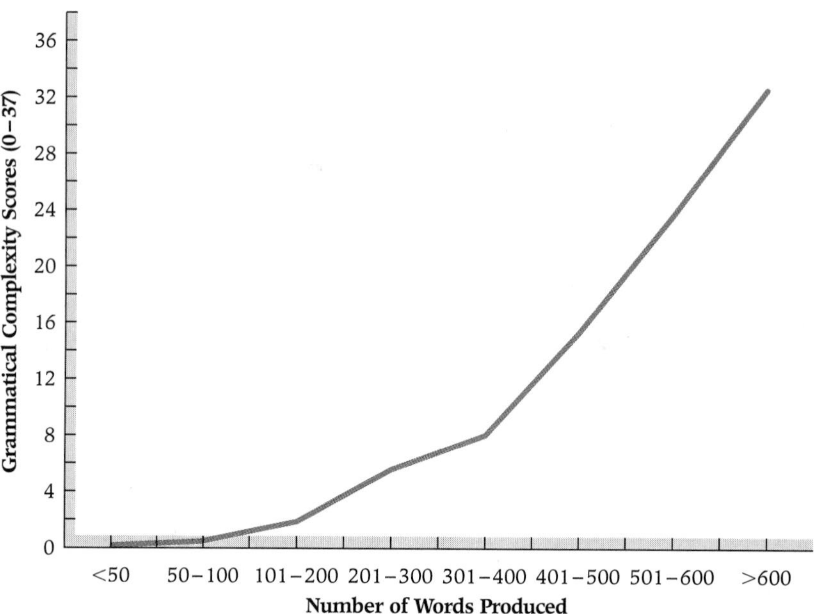

FIGURE 8.8
When the size of children's vocabulary is plotted against the degree of grammatical complexity of their utterance, there is a clear, positive relationship. These data are used by Elizabeth Bates and her colleagues to argue that grammar emerges from the need to use many words to convey complex messages. Note that there is an acceleration of grammatical complexity that begins when children's vocabularies reach approximately 400 words (from Bates, 1999).

adult and child do things together. Simple formatted activities include such games as peekaboo and the routines surrounding bathing, bedtime, and meals, which provide a structure for communicative interaction between babies and caregivers even before babies have learned any language. In this way, formats serve as "crucial vehicles in the passage from communication to language" (p. 8).

Bruner (1982) nicely captured the cultural context view of language development:

> Language acquisition cannot be reduced to either the virtuoso cracking of a linguistic code, or the spinoff of ordinary cognitive development, or the gradual takeover of adults' speech by the child through some impossible inductive *tour de force.* It is, rather, a subtle process by which adults artificially arrange the world so that the child can succeed culturally by doing what comes naturally, and with others similarly inclined. (p. 15)

Bruner argues that, as an ensemble, the formatted events within which children acquire language constitute a **language acquisition support system (LASS),** which is the environmental complement to the innate, biologically constituted LAD emphasized by nativists.

Whether they point inward toward the development of general cognitive capacities that enable the acquisition of language, or outward at the way in which the culturally organized environment structures children's experience of language, interactionists deny that language is simply triggered by children's exposure to it. Rather, it emerges from the many different contributing factors we have identified in the preceding pages of this chapter.

ESSENTIAL INGREDIENTS OF LANGUAGE ACQUISITION

language acquisition support system (LASS) Bruner's term for the parental behaviors and formatted events within which children acquire language. It is the environmental complement to the innate, biologically constituted LAD.

Regardless of theoretical preferences, developmentalists agree that the ability to use language is especially highly developed, if not unique to our species, and in this sense innate. They also agree that actual participation in a language-using community is essential for its development. Alternative approaches help to explain one or more of the many elements of the overall phenomenon. But none of the theories so far advanced provides a complete explanation of all the processes at work in the development of language. To shed further light on the issues we have been considering thus far, we can pose three questions:

1. What biological properties must an organism have to be able to acquire human language?
2. What aspects of the environment are crucial to the development of language among human beings, and how do they operate?
3. How does the acquisition of language influence other aspects of development, particularly the development of thought?

This chimp is using a specially designed keyboard composed of lexical symbols to communicate.

THE BIOLOGICAL PREREQUISITES FOR LANGUAGE

The question of biological contributions to language acquisition has been addressed in two fundamentally different ways. The first is to inquire whether other species are capable of producing and comprehending language. If they are not, then membership in the human species is a biological prerequisite for language development. The second is to investigate children with marked biological deficits to see if and how those deficits affect their acquisition of language.

Is Language Uniquely Human?

For most of human history it has seemed obvious that the basic requirement for acquiring language is that the learner be a human being. Many other species make a variety of communicative sounds and gestures, but none has evolved a system of communication as powerful and flexible as human language (Lieberman, 1991). At this very basic level of analysis, virtually all developmentalists agree with Chomsky that the process of language development has a significant genetic basis.

However, current research with chimpanzees is challenging the assumption that only human beings can acquire language. One strategy in this research has been to raise chimpanzees in the home as though they were human children, hoping that these near phylogenetic neighbors would acquire oral language if they were treated just like human beings. Early research with chimpanzees raised at home demonstrated that chimpanzees can, in fact, learn to comprehend dozens of spoken words and phrases (Hayes & Hayes, 1951; Kellogg & Kellogg, 1933). But the chimps never themselves produced language. Subsequent research that relied on manual signs instead of spoken words produced clear evidence that chimps can learn to use words to request and to refer to things. However, the evidence that they have syntax (flexible, rule-bound variation in the ordering of their words to produce meaningful phrases) is still being disputed (Savage-Rumbaugh et al., 1998; Tomasello, 1999).

Current enthusiasm for the idea that chimpanzees have the capacity to understand and produce language has been inspired by the work of Sue Savage-Rumbaugh and Duane Rumbaugh (Rumbaugh et al., 1994; Savage-Rumbaugh & Rumbaugh, 1993). The Rumbaughs combined several strategies that had been developed by others and added some of their own. They provided their chimpanzees with a "lexical keyboard" whose keys bore symbols that stood for words and they used standard operant-learning reinforcement techniques to teach the chimpanzees the basic vocabulary symbols ("banana," "give," and so on). In addition, the people who worked with the chimpanzees used natural language in everyday, routine activities such as feeding.

The Rumbaughs' most successful student has been Kanzi, a pygmy chimpanzee who initially learned to use the lexical keyboard by being present when his mother was being trained to use it. Kanzi is able to use the keyboard to ask for things and to comment on activities he is engaged in, and he can comprehend the meanings of lexigrams created by others. He has also learned to understand spoken English words and phrases (Savage-Rumbaugh et al., 1998; Savage-Rumbaugh & Rumbaugh, 1993).

Kanzi's comprehension of a wide variety of unusual sentences is roughly comparable to that of a 2-year-old child. For example, Kanzi correctly acted out the spoken request to "feed your ball some tomato" (he picked up a tomato and placed it in the mouth of a soft sponge ball with a face embedded in it). He also responded correctly when asked to "give the shot [syringe] to Liz" and then to "give Liz a shot": in the first instance, he handed the syringe to the girl, and in the second, he touched the syringe to the girl's arm.

Kanzi's ability to produce language is not so impressive as his comprehension, however. Most of his "utterances" on the lexical keyboard are single words that are closely linked to his current actions. Most of them are requests. He also uses two-word utterances in a wide variety of combinations, however, and occasionally makes observations. For example, he produced the request "car trailer" on one occasion when he was in the car and wanted (or so his caretakers believed) to be taken to the trailer rather than to walk there. He has created such requests as "play yard Austin" when he wanted to visit a chimpanzee named Austin in the play yard. When a researcher put oil on him while he was eating a potato, he commented, "potato oil."

Despite these achievements, there remain important differences between the communicative behavior of chimpanzees and human language. After years of hard work, chimpanzees can learn several dozen signs; but children with no special training learn thousands of words. Chimpanzees also learn to construct sequences of signs analogous to babies' multiword utterances, but the internal complexity of these constructions remains rudimentary. Consequently, even scholars who are enthusiastic about the language-learning abilities of primates are likely to refer to their communicative behavior as "proto-language," emphasizing its underdeveloped status (Greenfield & Savage-Rumbaugh, 1990).

Children with Severe Biological Handicaps

Among human children, some degree of language competence can be developed even in the face of intellectual impairment. In Chapter 2 (p. 69) we briefly described Down syndrome, a genetic disease that is associated with moderate to severe mental retardation. Although children with Down syndrome are able to hold a conversation, their vocabulary is relatively restricted and their talk is grammatically simple. When tested for the ability to produce and comprehend complex linguistic constructions, they fail. Such results suggest that normal language development requires normal cognitive functioning (Chapman, 1995).

This conclusion is brought into question, however, by research on children who suffer from a rare genetic disorder called Williams syndrome. Children afflicted with Williams syndrome are also mentally retarded, yet many of them show nearly normal ability to produce sentences that are grammatical, clearly pronounced, and understandable. They are also able to tell stories that are meaningful and display considerable subtlety in their portrayal of human feelings (Bellugi et al., 1999; Clahsen & Almazan, 1998).

Data such as these suggest that at least some aspects of language develop independently of general cognitive functioning. However, coordinated development of the phonetic, grammatical, semantic, and pragmatic aspects of language, all of which are essential to normal linguistic functioning, is clearly dependent on some minimum level of biological maturation and inherited capacity.

THE ENVIRONMENT OF LANGUAGE DEVELOPMENT

Evidence from studies of nonhuman primates' abilities to communicate suggests one absolute biological precondition for full language acquisition: one must be a human being. Evidence discussed below, as well as evidence from cases such as that of Genie, the girl who grew up in total isolation from normal human interaction and language (described in Chapter 7), suggests the corresponding precondition on the environmental side: one must grow up among humans who provide a language-acquisition support system. Beyond the specification of these two minimum requirements, however, important questions remain: Which aspects of the environment are necessary to trigger language? How are they arranged? What is the optimal support system for ensuring that the language capacity will be fully developed?

A variety of evidence shows that in order to acquire language, children must be included in normal human activities with others who have already acquired a language. The crucial role of active participation in human activity mediated by language is demonstrated by research on children who grow up in an environment without direct exposure to language but with normal human interaction in a language-mediated environment. One such situation occurs in the case of deaf children whose hearing parents do not know sign language and discourage its use (Feldman et al., 1978; Goldin-Meadow, 1985, 1997). We know that the biological condition of deafness need not be an impediment to normal language acquisition: deaf children born to deaf parents who communicate in sign language acquire language at least as rapidly and fully as hearing children born into hearing households (Padden & Humphries, 1989). Thus, any delays or difficulties in deaf children's language development must result from the way the environment is organized.

In studies of deaf children conducted by Susan Goldin-Meadow and her colleagues, the parents of the children did not know sign language and refused to use it because they believed that their children could and should learn to read lips and to vocalize sounds. As a consequence, at an age when other children are hearing (or seeing) language, these children received extremely restricted language input in their home surroundings. However, they did participate in everyday, formatted, routine activities coordinated through the language and cultural system of the adults.

Earlier studies had shown that deaf children raised under these circumstances will spontaneously begin to gesture in "home sign," a kind of communication through pantomime (Fant, 1972). Goldin-Meadow and her colleagues wanted to find out if the home-sign systems developed by the deaf children displayed the characteristic features of language acquisition. They discovered that, indeed, the gestures these children developed exhibited certain characteristics of language, even though the children had no one to show them the signs.

Home sign begins as pointing. The children gesture one sign at a time—at the same age when hearing children develop single-word utterances. Home-sign gestures seem to refer to the same kinds of objects, and to fulfill the same functions, as the early words of hearing children or of deaf children with signing parents. Remarkably, home-signing children go on to make patterns of two, and sometimes three or more, signs around their second birthday, about the same time that hearing children utter multiword sentences.

Analysis of these multipart signs reveals ordering principles much like those seen at the two-word stage in hearing children. In addition, Goldin-Meadow reports that these deaf children were embedding sign sentences within each other ("You/Susan give me/Abe cookie that is round"). This is the property of recursion, which, as we pointed out at the beginning of this chapter, is characteristic of all

This little girl is signing the word "sleep." (Copyright Ursula Bellugi, The Salk Institute for Biological Studies; reprinted with permission.)

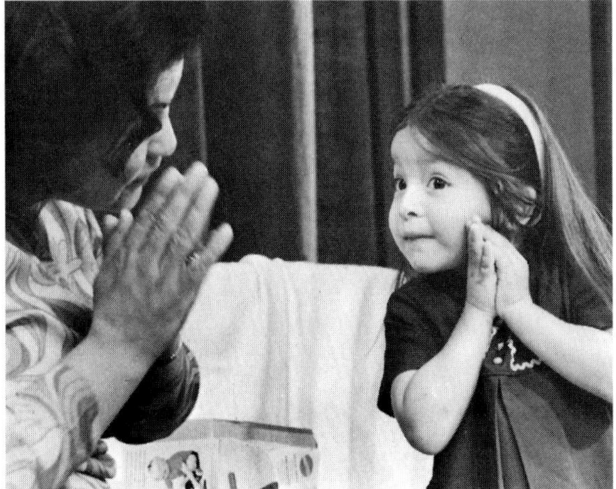

human languages and absent from the communicative system of chimpanzees or other creatures even after long training. Goldin-Meadow and Susan Mylander observed home sign among the deaf children of Mandarin-speaking parents living in Taiwan, where child-rearing practices and the use of gesture to accompany speech are quite different from those in the United States (Goldin-Meadow & Mylander, 1998). They observed the same patterns of spontaneous home-sign production, despite difference in the cultural environments of the children, suggesting that universal processes of language creation are at work.

However, once these children are able to make two- to three-word "utterances" in their home sign and begin to embed sign sentences within each other, their language development appears to come to an end. They fail to acquire grammatical morphemes or to master complex grammatical distinctions. Thus it seems that the mere fact of being raised in an environment where the actions of all the other participants are organized by human language and culture is sufficient to allow the child to acquire the rudiments of linguistic structure, but that without access to the additional information provided by the sights (or sounds) of language in the environment, the child has no opportunity to discover its more subtle features. Confirmation of this conclusion comes from the case of a hearing child raised by deaf parents (Sachs et al., 1981). This child's parents exposed him to neither conventional oral nor conventional manual language input. He heard English only on TV and during a brief time spent in nursery school. The course of development for this child was precisely the same as for the deaf children of hearing parents: he developed the basic features of grammar but not the more complex ones. Once he was introduced to normal American sign language, at the age of 3 years and 9 months, he quickly acquired normal language ability.

Taken together, such studies narrow the search for the critical environmental ingredients of language development. The beginnings of language may appear during the second year of life even in the absence of direct experience of language, as long as children participate in the everyday life of their family. However, the kind of language that appears under such linguistically impoverished conditions resembles the language behavior of children at the two-word phase. Apparently, participation in culturally organized activity, while necessary, is not always sufficient to enable the child to realize the full potential of language (Schaller, 1991).

How Interaction Contributes to Language Acquisition

On the basis of the evidence just presented, it seems clear that in order for children to acquire more than the rudiments of language, they must not only participate in family or community activity but must also hear (or see) language as they mature. When children are included in the everyday activities of the language-speaking members of their community, they acquire words quickly and with little apparent effort. What makes this rapid acquisition possible?

Fast Mapping Elsa Bartlett and Susan Carey's study of vocabulary development (mentioned in Chapter 1, p. 24) is one of many current attempts to understand how new words are acquired. These researchers made use of the normal routine of a preschool to find out what happens when a totally new word is introduced into conversation with children. They chose to study the acquisition of color terms. None of the 14 children in the classroom knew the name of the color that adults call olive; some children called it brown, others called it green, and some didn't refer to the color by name at all. Bartlett and Carey decided to give it an implausible name, chromium, just in case some children had partial knowledge of the real name that they had not revealed.

After the children had been tested to determine that they did not know the name of the color olive, one cup and one tray in the classroom were painted "chromium" (olive). While preparing for snack time, the teacher found an opportunity to ask each child, "Please bring me the chromium cup; not the red one, the chromium one" or "Bring me the chromium tray; not the blue one, the chromium one."

This procedure worked. All of the children succeeded in picking the correct cup or tray, although they were likely to ask for confirmation ("You mean this one?"). Some of the children could be seen repeating the unfamiliar word to themselves.

One week after this single experience with the new word, the children were given a color-naming test with color chips. Two-thirds of the children showed that they had learned something about this odd term and its referents; when asked for chromium, they chose either the olive chip or a green one. Six weeks later many of the children still showed the influence of this single experience.

Bartlett and Carey's findings have been confirmed by a variety of procedures, including exposure of children to new words in a television program (Rice, 1990). Such findings contradict both the idea that children acquire language because adults explicitly reward their efforts and the idea that children learn by the simple process of imitation. Rather, when children hear an unfamiliar word in a familiar, structured, and meaningful social interaction, they seem to form a quick, "first-pass" idea of the word's meaning. Psychologists refer to this form of rapid word acquisition as **fast mapping.** Fast mapping has been observed in children as young as 15 months of age in controlled experiments (Schafer & Plunkett, 1996). The challenge is to explain how participation in normal activities makes fast mapping possible.

fast mapping The way in which children quickly form an idea of the meaning of an unfamiliar word they hear in a familiar and highly structured social interaction.

The Child's Contribution Developmentalists have proposed several cognitive principles that young children could be using to quickly narrow their guesses about what words mean, making fast mapping possible (Golinkoff et al., 1994; Woodward & Markman, 1998):

- *The whole-object principle.* When children hear a new word in connection with some object, they assume that the word applies to the whole object. Young children appear to assume, for example, that when the word "cup" is used in conjunction with the thing that holds their juice, the new word applies to the entire object, not just the handle.
- *The categorizing principle.* Children appear to assume that object labels extend to classes of similar objects. For example, toddlers use the word "dog" to refer not only to the family dog but to other dogs as well (Waxman & Hall, 1993).
- *The mutual-exclusivity principle.* Children assume that an object can have only one name. As a consequence, if they already know a label for dog, they will think that a new label they hear while they are looking at a group of animals that includes dogs, such as "giraffe," does not apply to dogs.

A study by Sandra Waxman and Rochel Gelman shows how very young children use the categorizing principle to help them figure out word meanings (Waxman & Gelman, 1986). These researchers asked 3-year-olds to interact with three "very picky" puppets, each of which liked only one of three kinds of things—animals, clothing, or food. Children were offered a set of objects to give to the puppets in one of three ways. One third of the children were instructed that "this puppet likes animals" (for example) and were asked to give the puppet several objects from an array that contained all three kinds of objects. A second group was shown several instances from a category (for example, animals) and told that "this puppet likes dogs, horses, and ducks" without mentioning the word "animal." The children were then asked to give the puppet several objects from the same array. A third group of children was also shown three examples of what the puppet liked and in addition encouraged to consider the objects as a group by such comments as "Look, those make a really good group. They really go together well, don't they?" But again, the word "animal" was not mentioned.

The researchers found that unless the 3-year-olds were directly introduced to a group label such as "animal," they ignored the categories and gave the "picky puppets" objects from all three categories. Showing examples, even with broad hints to consider them as a category, was not effective.

In a follow-up study, the researchers substituted an unfamiliar (Japanese) word for the correct label. Even though the children could not know what the word actually referred to, the mere fact that the adults applied a verbal label to a group of objects was enough to induce the 3-year-olds to use the category information effectively.

Although the various principles offered to explain fast mapping differ in their details, they all suggest that the process of acquiring new words involves the child's making certain simplifying assumptions (new words apply to whole objects and categories) and comparing his or her existing knowledge of word meanings with new words. These strategies permit new meanings to be incorporated into the child's preexisting system of meanings. Over time, this set of meanings provides a richer and richer foundation for rapidly acquiring still more vocabulary.

Language is acquired in the context of ongoing activity. This mother is talking and playing with her baby as a routine part of getting him dressed.

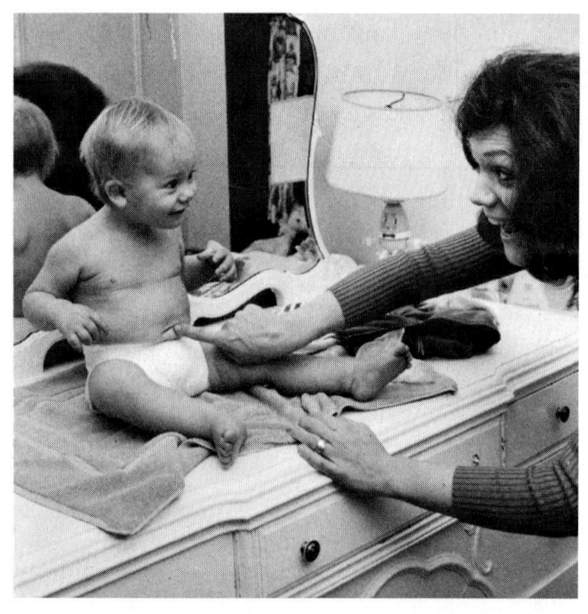

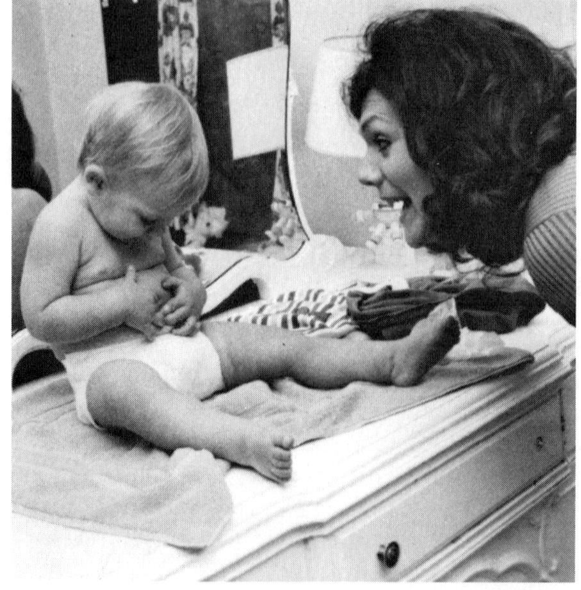

Contributions from the Social Context Another source of support for language acquisition is the child's social context. As demonstrated by the study in which children were asked to fetch a "chromium" tray, fast mapping occurs when social interaction introduces new words into the normal flow of events at precisely the right moment so that everything but the new word is treated routinely.

The crucial role of finely tuned and well-timed interaction in supporting word learning is seen in a series of studies by Michael Tomasello and his colleagues (summarized in Tomasello, 1999). These researchers videotaped mothers interacting with their young children in order to identify the precise moment at which the mothers referred to objects in the immediate environment. They found that the mothers talked mostly about objects that were already a part of the child's current actions and the focus of the child's and mother's joint attention, thus greatly reducing the child's problem in figuring out the referents of the mother's words. In a related study, these investigators deliberately taught new words to the children in one of two ways: with half the children, an experimenter named an object that was not the focus of the child's attention in an effort to direct the child's attention to it; with the other half, the experimenter named an object after the child had focused on it. The strategy of naming an object after the child was already attending to it proved more effective than trying to get the child to attend to a new object and a new word at the same time.

The social conditions that enable rapid acquisition of vocabulary clearly correspond well to the kinds of adult-guided constructive processes emphasized by cultural-context theorists (Ochs & Schieffelin, 1995; Rogoff, 1998). As cultural-context theorists see it, explicit rewards for learning language are unnecessary. The reinforcement comes from children's increased success at communicating and their enhanced participation with others in valued activities.

Is There a Role for Deliberate Instruction?

As we have described it thus far, language acquisition appears to require several elements, each of which is emphasized by one of the major theories:

1. A biologically programmed sensitivity to language present at birth, which develops as the child matures (the nativist view)
2. The ability to learn from and imitate the language behavior of others (the environmental-learning view)
3. The acquisition of basic cognitive capacities, including schemas for actions with objects, the ability to represent the world mentally, and the presence of lexical principles (the constructivist version of an interactionist view)
4. The inclusion of children in familiar routines in which language is one of many forms of interaction (the cultural-context version of an interactionist view)

Missing from this list is the role of deliberate instruction ("This is an apple," "This is a truck") or the use of explicit rewards for learning emphasized in some environmental-learning explanations of language acquisition. Are deliberate efforts to foster language development by teaching about language at all effective?

Adults in many cultures certainly seem to think so, and believe that it is important to actively teach their children how to talk (Ochs & Schieffelin, 1995). The Kaluli of New Guinea, for example, believe that children must be explicitly taught language just as they must be taught other culturally valued forms of behavior. The Kaluli make no effort to start teaching language until they believe the child is ready, which they judge to be as soon as the child's first words are spoken. Then the parents begin to engage their babies in a form of speech activity called *elema:* the mother provides the utterance she wants the child to repeat followed by the command *"Elema"* ("Say like this"). Eleanor Ochs (1982) described similar practices among Samoans, and Peggy Miller (1982) reported that working-class mothers in Baltimore, Maryland, follow a similar strategy with respect to teaching vocabulary.

Even in societies where adults do not engage in deliberate teaching strategies, many investigators have noted that when speaking to young children, adults are likely to use a special speech register dubbed *child-directed speech,* or more popularly, **motherese.** This speech is characterized by a special high-pitched voice, an emphasis on the boundaries between idea-bearing clauses, and a simplified vocabulary (Fernald, 1991; Snow, 1995). Such modifications to normal speech are believed to provide a variety of clues that children can use in segmenting the flow of speech to identify words (Hirsh-Pasek & Golinkoff, 1996).

motherese Speech directed to young children that is characterized by a special high-pitched voice, an emphasis on the boundaries between idea-bearing clauses, and a simplified vocabulary.

As Table 8.5 indicates, middle-class parents in the United States simplify virtually every aspect of their language when they speak to their children. Several studies have shown that the complexity of adults' speech to children is graded to the level of the complexity of the child's speech (Bohannon & Warren-Leubecker, 1988; Snow, 1995).

Catherine Snow (1972) shows how such tailoring processes can work in the case of a mother directing a child to put away toys: "Put the red truck in the box now. . . . The red truck. . . . No, the red truck . . . in the box. . . . The red truck in the box." Note the sequence of the mother's directions. Snow argues that this kind of grading of language, in which statements are gradually simplified and their meaning highlighted, isolates constituent phrases at the same time that it models the whole correct grammatical structure.

In their efforts to aid children's comprehension (and perhaps their discovery of how to use language), American adults not only simplify what they say to children; they also enlarge on what children say. This phenomenon was pointed out by Roger Brown and Ursula Bellugi (1964), who called this

TABLE 8.5 SIMPLIFICATIONS USED BY MIDDLE-CLASS U.S. ADULTS SPEAKING TO SMALL CHILDREN

Phonological Simplifications
- Higher pitch and exaggerated intonation
- Clear pronunciation
- Slower speech
- Distinct pauses between utterances

Syntactic Differences
- Shorter and less varied utterance length
- Almost all sentences well formed
- Many partial or complete repetitions of child's utterances, sometimes with expansion
- Fewer broken sentences
- Less grammatical complexity

Semantic Differences
- More limited vocabulary
- Many special words and diminutives
- Reference to concrete circumstances of here and now
- Middle level of generality in naming objects

Pragmatic Differences
- More directives, imperatives, and questions
- More utterances designed to draw attention to aspects of objects

Source: De Villiers & De Villiers, 1978.

kind of adult speech *expansion* because it seems to expand the child's utterance into a grammatically correct adult version. A mother whose child says "Mommy wash," for example, might respond with "Yes, Mommy is washing her face"; and to the declaration "Daddy sleep," she might respond "Yes, Daddy is sleeping. Don't wake him up."

Despite widespread belief that adult teaching, simplifying, and highlighting behaviors help children to master language, the necessity of such practices has been the subject of longstanding disagreement among scholars who study language acquisition. When Courtney Cazden (1965) attempted to "force-feed" children with a heavy diet of feedback by expanding and correcting their incorrect sentences, she found no special effect on language development. Subsequent studies have sometimes found effects of parental expansions or corrections (Farrar, 1992; Saxton, 1997), but failures to find such effects are at least as numerous (Gleitman et al., 1984). Consequently, no firm conclusions about the influence of deliberate parental feedback are yet possible.

Nevertheless, the sheer amount of language that children hear does have a strong influence on the development of vocabulary (Hart & Risely, 1995). Betty Hart and Todd Risely recorded the language spoken in the homes of welfare families, working-class families, and professional families. The differences were quite marked: the 1- to 3-year-old children in welfare homes heard only 33 percent as much language as the children in working-class families, and only 20 percent as much language as children from professional families. The rate at which children acquired vocabulary closely tracked the amount of language they heard.

Perhaps the most important conclusion to come out of several decades of work on the relation between special adult behaviors and children's acquisition of language, over and above the sheer amount of talk children hear, is that the differences in the everyday, intuitive practices of adults throughout the world make relatively little difference in the rate at which children acquire language: all normally developing children become competent language users. All cultural groups take into account the fact that small children do not understand language and make some provision for seeing that they have the opportunity to acquire it. However, it has not been possible to prove that a particular practice that might be called "teaching the child to speak" has an important impact on language acquisition or that one method of structuring children's language experience is universally essential.

LANGUAGE AND THOUGHT

The research reviewed in this chapter makes it clear that language is complexly related to activity and the surrounding world. Children learn early to use this relationship to influence their interactions with the world. And all the time that their language capacities are growing, children are acquiring more knowledge. How are the development of language and the development of thought processes related?

THE ENVIRONMENTAL-LEARNING PERSPECTIVE

According to learning theorists, children begin to grasp what different language forms signify by relating what they hear to what they understand to be going on around them (Bandura, 1986; Skinner, 1957). Eventually a great deal of their thought comes to be based on language and, as a result, thought develops in new, more complex ways:

> By manipulating symbols that convey relevant information, one can gain understanding of causal relationships, expand one's knowledge, solve problems, and deduce consequences of actions without actually performing them. The functional value of thought rests on the close correspondence between the symbolic system [in this case, language] and external events, so that the former can be substituted for the latter. (Bandura, 1986, p. 462)

Language, according to this view, is more than a means of communication with others. Words deepen a child's understanding of certain aspects of objects and of the subtle relations among various events. Associations among words provide a kind of mental map of the world, which shapes the way a child thinks. This view suggests that thinking should change markedly when children begin to acquire language.

THE PIAGETIAN INTERACTIONIST PERSPECTIVE

In contrast, Piaget believed that language is a verbal reflection of the individual's conceptual understanding (Piaget, 1926, 1983). As we have seen, at the end of infancy, and of the sensorimotor period, children become able to think symbolically. According to Piaget, the acquisition of language symbols speeds up thinking because a sequence of thoughts can usually be carried out more quickly than a sequence of actions. But since language reflects thought, language developments cannot *cause* cognitive development. Rather, cognition determines language.

According to Piaget, the influence of cognition on language can be seen in children's early language efforts. At the end of the sensorimotor period, children have developed a basic understanding that they are a part of a world that exists apart from them, but, as we will see in Chapter 9, they still have difficulty adopting other people's points of view. They still do not understand, for example, that someone might not have the same knowledge they do or that someone looking at an object from a vantage point different from their own would not see the object the same way they do. If language is

collective monologue Exchanges between preschoolers in which their remarks actually focus on what they are doing by themselves, with no real regard for their partner and with no apparent intent to communicate.

mental module A highly specific mental faculty that is tuned to particular kinds of environmental input.

determined by thought, it follows that early speech, like early thought, must be egocentric and fail to take into account others' points of view.

Piaget supported his hypothesis with data collected from preschool children's conversations. What struck him about these exchanges was that while preschoolers appear to be playing and conversing together, their remarks actually focus on what they are doing by themselves, with no real regard for their partner and with no apparent intention of actually communicating. Piaget (1926) called this type of language a **collective monologue.** He believed that collective monologues mirror a profoundly egocentric mode of thought. The following conversation between two American preschoolers illustrates his point:

> *Jenny:* They wiggle sideways when they kiss.
> *Chris:* *(vaguely)* What?
> *Jenny:* My bunny slippers. They are brown and red and sort of yellow and white. And they have eyes and ears and these noses that wiggle sideways when they kiss.
> *Chris:* I have a piece of sugar in a red piece of paper. I'm gonna eat it but maybe it's for a horse.
> *Jenny:* We bought them. My mommy did. We couldn't find the old ones. These are like the old ones. They were not in the trunk.
> *Chris:* Can't eat the piece of sugar, not unless you take the paper off.
> *Jenny:* And we found Mother Lamb. Oh, she was in Poughkeepsie in the trunk in the house in the woods where Mrs. Tiddywinkle lives.
> *Chris:* Do I like sugar? I do, and so do horses.
> *Jenny:* I play with my bunnies. They are real. We play in the woods. They have eyes. We all go in the woods. My teddy bear and the bunnies and the duck, to visit Mrs. Tiddywinkle. We play and play.
> *Chris:* I guess I'll eat my sugar at lunch time. I can get more for the horses. Besides, I don't have no horses now. (Stone & Church, 1957, pp. 146–147)

Piaget believed that as children grow older, their ability to adopt others' points of view increases and collective monologues give way to genuine dialogues.

Piaget's idea that language depends on thought but that thought is not influenced by language was tested by Hermione Sinclair de Zwart (1967), who taught French-speaking preschoolers the correct meanings of the terms for "more" and "less," then tested their ability to solve problems involving the relationships of more and less. She found that the children who had learned to use the words appropriately in the training situation showed no advantage over untrained children when these relationships were actually needed to solve a problem. This failure of language training to influence problem solving seems to confirm Piaget's theory that language does not affect thought.

THE NATIVIST PERSPECTIVE

Nativist theorists such as Noam Chomsky explicitly deny that it is possible for language to grow out of sensorimotor schemas, declaring that there are no known similarities between the principles of language and the principles of sensorimotor intelligence (Chomsky, 1980). Rather, as we explained earlier, Chomsky believes that language acquisition is made possible by a specifically human language acquisition device (LAD).

To indicate the self-contained nature of the capacity to acquire and use language, Chomsky refers to the LAD as a mental module. A **mental module** is a highly specific mental faculty that is tuned to particular kinds of environmental input. In claiming that language forms a distinctive mental module, Chomsky seems to be declaring that language and thought do not depend on each other. In support of this position, nativists note that some severely retarded children have relatively advanced linguistic abilities even though their other intellectual abilities are extremely limited (see p. 320). However,

Chomsky does not go so far as to say that there is no connection between these two domains of mind. When Piaget's colleague Barbel Inhelder challenged Chomsky on this issue, he replied:

> I take it for granted that thinking is a domain that is quite different from language, even though language is used for the expression of thought, and for a good deal of thinking we really need the mediation of language. (Chomsky, 1980, p. 174)

A CULTURAL-CONTEXT PERSPECTIVE

The most prominent cultural theory of language and thought was developed by Lev Vygotsky (1934/1987, 1978). Pointing out that children's development always occurs in a context organized and watched over by adults, Vygotsky insisted that children's experience of language is social from the outset.

In accord with evidence we presented earlier, Vygotsky (1934/1987) argued that even children's initial words are communicative acts, mediating their interactions with the people around them. More generally, he believed that every new psychological function in children first appears during children's interactions with others who can support and nurture their efforts. These shared efforts are gradually taken over by the child and transformed into individual abilities. Applied to the area of language, this sequence suggests a progression from social and communicative speech to internal dialogue, or inner speech, in which thought and language are intimately interconnected. This is just the opposite of the way language, cognition, and the social world are related in Piaget's framework, and, as might be expected, Vygotsky's interpretation of collective monologues (or "egocentric speech") also differs from Piaget's.

Vygotsky and his colleagues conducted a series of studies to test Piaget's idea that egocentric speech serves no cognitive or communicative function (Vygotsky, 1934/1987). In one such study, they demonstrated that egocentric speech fulfills important cognitive functions: when children were faced with a difficulty in solving a problem, they raised the level of their overt self-regulatory speech. For example, a young child experiencing difficulty walking down a flight of stairs might tell herself, "Hold on, hold the railing, go slow." (This finding was replicated by Kohlberg, Yaeger, and Hjertholm [1968].) In a second study, they demonstrated that egocentric speech serves a communicative function as well. In this case, preschoolers were placed among deaf-mute children. Vygotsky reasoned that if egocentric speech was really not intended to communicate, the preschools' production of it would not be affected by their realization that their present playmates could not hear them. Instead, the preschoolers' rate of egocentric speech decreased markedly from its level in the presence of hearing children (described in Wertsch, 1985).

Vygotsky believed that the relationship between language and thought changes over the course of development. According to Vygotsky, during the first two years of life, language and thought develop more or less independently. Beginning around 2 years of age, however, thought and language begin to intermingle. This intermingling, wrote Vygotsky (1934/1987), fundamentally changes the nature of both thinking and language, providing the growing child with a uniquely human form of behavior in which language becomes intellectual and thinking becomes verbal (see Figure 8.9).

In Vygotsky's framework, language allows thought to be individual and social at the same time. It is the medium through which individual thought is communicated to others, while at the same time it allows social reality to be converted into the idiosyncratic thought of the individual. This conversion of language from the social to the individual is never complete, however—even in the

FIGURE 8.9

A schematic representation of Vygotsky's idea that as children acquire language, both thinking and speech undergo transformations: language becomes an intellectual function while thinking becomes verbal.

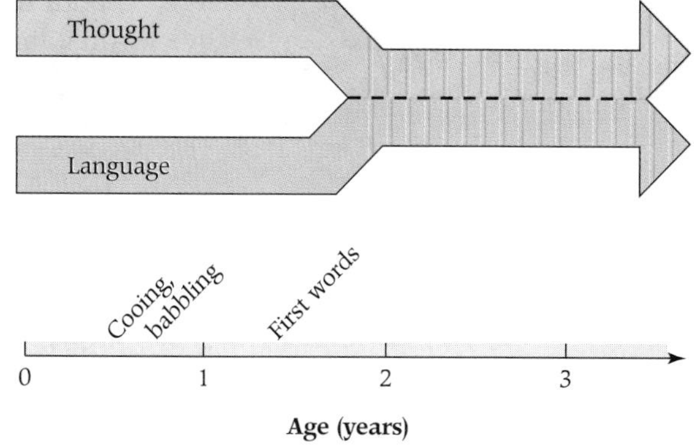

adult—because individual thought processes are continually shaped by the conventional meanings present in the lexicon, the speech habits of the culture, and the precise social circumstances.

There appears to be reasonable agreement among developmentalists that language and thought are separable psychological functions; neither can be reduced to the other. There is also agreement that the two functions intermingle in normal development. The field is still far from being in agreement, however, on the extent to which development in one domain influences development in the other and on their combined roles in the development of the child as a whole.

THE BASIC PUZZLES OF LANGUAGE ACQUISITION RECONSIDERED

At the beginning of this chapter we introduced two basic questions about the way children acquire language: How do they come to understand what words mean and how do they acquire the ability to arrange words in acceptable sequences to express and understand the complex meanings needed to interact successfully with other people?

The information we have presented in this chapter does not definitively answer these questions, because neither language nor the way children acquire it is fully understood. But research discussed in this chapter has at least narrowed the scope of the quest.

Consider the problem posed in Figure 8.1, in which the father and son are gazing out of a window and the father tells the boy to look at the *ptitsa* (bird). What this picture leaves out is a history of interaction between parent and child, in the course of which they have developed many routines for understanding each other. It also leaves out any indication of what they were in the midst of doing when the father said, "Look, son, there sits a *ptitsa*." Perhaps they had been playing naming games, or perhaps they had been feeding their pet bird. A full account would also include the other words the child already knew, because, as we learned from the data on fast mapping (pp. 322–323), children use the words they already know to help them figure out what new words mean. Knowing these things would certainly reduce the mystery of how the child might come to understand the father but would not eliminate it entirely.

The puzzle of grammar remains even more mysterious. Perhaps, as nativist theorists claim, linguistic competence is achieved through an innate language acquisition device. Or perhaps, as Elizabeth Bates and her colleagues argue, grammar emerges as a byproduct of vocabulary growth. But it is still unclear what minimal environmental conditions are needed to permit this device to function properly. Goldin-Meadow's work with deaf children in hearing households suggests that participation in normal cultural routines can be sufficient for the rudiments of language to appear. And evidence collected in both the United States and other societies indicates that children acquire normal linguistic competence without special instruction if they can have access to language (either oral or sign) and if they participate in routine, culturally organized activity, which serves as a language-acquisition support system. As Jerome Bruner whimsically suggested, language is born from the union of the LAD and the LASS.

Although children 2½ to 3 years of age can properly be considered language-using human beings, their language development is obviously incomplete (see Table 8.6). All aspects of language continue to develop during childhood, and in some cases into adulthood. Moreover, as children begin to acquire the specialized skills they will need to cope with adult life in their culture, deliberate teaching may begin to play a conspicuous role in language de-

TABLE 8.6 THE PROGRESS OF LANGUAGE DEVELOPMENT

Approximate Age	Typical Behavior
Birth	Phoneme perception
	Discrimination of language from nonlanguage sounds
	Crying
3 months	Cooing
6 months	Babbling
	Loss of ability to discriminate between nonnative phonemes
9 months	First words
	Holophrases
12 months	Use of words to attract adults' attention
18 months	Vocabulary spurt
	First two-word sentences (telegraphic speech)
24 months	Correct responses to indirect requests ("Is the door shut?")
30 months	Creation of indirect requests ("You're standing on my blocks!")
	Modification of speech to take listener into account
	Early awareness of grammatical categories
Early childhood	Rapid increase in grammatical complexity
	Overgeneralization of grammatical rules
Middle childhood	Understanding of passive forms ("The balls were taken by the boys")
	Acquisition of written language
Adolescence	Acquisition of specialized language functions

velopment. Such specialized activities as reciting nursery rhymes, acting in a play, and writing an essay are all forms of language activity that require practice and instruction. We shall return to examine some of the more specialized language developments associated with middle childhood in Chapter 13.

SUMMARY

PRELINGUISTIC COMMUNICATION

- Linguistic communication builds on an extensive foundation of prelinguistic communicative achievements, including babbling, turn-taking, and the ability to focus one's attention on objects and activities in concert with other people.

THE PUZZLE OF LANGUAGE DEVELOPMENT

- Despite intensive investigation, scientists' understanding of language acquisition remains incomplete. No theory is able to explain satisfactorily how children come to understand either the meanings of words or the rules that govern their arrangement (grammar).

FOUR SUBSYSTEMS OF LANGUAGE

- In the transition from babbling to talking, children begin to conform to the restricted set of sounds of the language their parents speak. The basic sounds of a language (phonemes) are those that distinguish one word from another.
- Early words for objects are associated with actions and with changes in an object's state or location.

- Early words indicate children's emerging ability to operate on the world indirectly (in a mediated way) as well as directly.
- Early word meanings often correspond to an intermediate level of abstraction. As a consequence, words may be used too broadly (overextension) or too narrowly (underextension) to conform to adult definitions.
- As children's vocabularies expand, their understanding of word meanings changes fundamentally; meanings embedded in particular contexts of action are supplemented by meanings dominated by logical categories.
- Children's first words are often nonconventional; interpretation depends to a great extent on the listener's knowledge of the context in which they are used.
- Two-word utterances allow children to take advantage of the relationships of words within utterances to convey meaning, marking the birth of grammar. As the length of utterances increases, so does the complexity of the grammatical rules governing the arrangement of words within sentences and of elements (morphemes) within words.
- The growth of children's vocabularies and their increased ability to use complex grammatical constructions are accompanied by a corresponding growth in their ability to engage in conversational acts that achieve a variety of goals.
- Central to the successful use of language is the ability to say things in a way that is understandable to one's partner in conversation. Children reveal at an early age their ability to tailor their language to their listeners' needs.

EXPLANATIONS OF LANGUAGE ACQUISITION

- Three theories dominate current explanations of language acquisition.
    1. Learning theories claim that words and patterns of words are learned through imitation and through classical and operant conditioning.
    2. Nativist theories claim that children are born with a language acquisition device (LAD) that is automatically activated by the environment when the child has matured sufficiently.
    3. Interactionist theories emphasize the cognitive preconditions for language acquisition and the role of the social environment in providing a language acquisition support system (LASS).

ESSENTIAL INGREDIENTS OF LANGUAGE ACQUISITION

- Language is a particularly human communicative ability, but aspects of languagelike communication can be found among chimpanzees and other primates.
- Children acquire the basic elements of language with no special assistance from adults if they are raised in normal speaking or signing homes where communication is appropriate to the hearing ability of the child. Development of the full range of language abilities, however, requires both participation in human activity and exposure to language as part of that activity.

LANGUAGE AND THOUGHT

- Each of the various theories of language acquisition has its own view of the relationship between language and thought.
  1. According to environmental-learning theorists, language and thought are two aspects of a single process; hence, the acquisition of language has a great impact on thinking, and vice versa.
  2. According to nativist theorists such as Chomsky, language and thought develop independently of each other, but thought is often mediated by language.
  3. According to Piagetian interactionist theorists, developments in thought are the preconditions for language development.
  4. According to cultural-context theorists such as Vygotsky, language and thought arise independently but fuse in early childhood to create specifically human modes of thinking and communication.

KEY TERMS

collective monologue, p. 328
conversational acts, p. 310
cooperative principle, p. 311
deep structure, p. 315
fast mapping, p. 323
format, p. 317
grammar, p. 297
grammatical morphemes, p. 307
holophrase, p. 306
language acquisition device (LAD), p. 315
language acquisition support system (LASS), p. 318
mental module, p. 328
morpheme, p. 299
motherese, p. 325
overextension, p. 303
pragmatic uses of language, p. 309
recursion, p. 298
surface structure, p. 315
underextension, p. 303

THOUGHT QUESTIONS

1. George Miller said that both the environmental-learning and nativist approaches to the acquisition of language were unsatisfactory, the first because it was impossible and the other because it was miraculous. What did he mean? Was this a fair statement of the problem?
2. Jerome Bruner characterized language acquisition as "a subtle process by which adults artificially arrange the world so that the child can succeed culturally by doing what comes naturally." What sorts of subtle arranging appear necessary for language acquisition to occur?
3. Once children move beyond the single-word stage of language development, how does their ability to combine two words to form a sentence affect their ability to create meaning?
4. What makes the cartoon on p. 316 both humorous and relevant to theories of language acquisition?
5. Some developmental psycholinguists now claim that nonhuman primates can be trained to acquire a protolanguage that makes their communicative ability equivalent to that of a 2- to 2½ year-old child. How do the communicative capacities of such animals help us to gain a better understanding of the development of human language?

CHAPTER 9

Early Childhood Thought: Islands of Competence

In every sentence, . . . in every childish act [of the 2- to 5-year-old] is revealed complete ignorance of the simplest things. Of course, I cite these expressions not to scorn childish absurdities. On the contrary, they inspire me with respect because they are evidence of the gigantic work that goes on in the child's mind which, by the age of 7, results in the conquest of this mental chaos.

Kornei Chukovsky, *From Two to Five*

A group of 5-year-old children have been listening to "Stone Soup," a folktale retold by Marcia Brown. "Stone Soup" is about three hungry soldiers who trick some peasants into feeding them by pretending to make soup out of stones. "Do stones melt?" asks Rose, one of the children. Master Teacher Vivian Paley reports the conversation that followed this question:

"Do you think they melt, Rose?"

"Yes."

"Does anyone agree with Rose?"

"They will melt if you cook them," said Lisa.

"If you boil them," Eddie added.

No one doubted that the stones in the story had melted and that ours, too, would melt.

"We can cook them and find out," I said. "How will we be able to tell if they've melted?"

"They'll be smaller," said Deana.

The stones are placed in boiling water for an hour and then put on the table for inspection.

Ellen: *They're much smaller.*
Fred: *Much, much. Almost melted.*
Rose: *I can't eat melted stones.*
Teacher: *Don't worry, Rose. You won't. But I'm not convinced they've melted. Can we prove it?*

Ms. Paley suggests weighing the stones to see if they will lose weight as they boil. The children find that they weigh two pounds at the start. After they have been boiled again, the following conversation ensues:

Eddie: *Still two [pounds]. But they are smaller.*
Wally: *Much smaller.*
Teacher: *They weigh the same. Two pounds before and two pounds now. That means they didn't lose weight.*
Eddie: *They only got a little bit smaller.*
Wally: *The scale can't see the stones. Hey, once in Michigan there were three stones in a fire and they melted away. They were gone. We saw it.*
Deana: *Maybe the stones in the story are magic.*
Wally: *But not these.*

(Adapted from Paley, 1981, pp. 16–18)

We can see that when Ms. Paley entices the children into reconciling the world of the story and the world of their senses, the children exhibit a pattern of thinking that is typical during the preschool years—a mixture of sound logic and magical thinking. The children correctly believe that when things are "cooked down," they grow smaller, and that small stones should be lighter than big ones. At the same time, they are willing to believe that there really are such things as magical stones that melt, and so they miss the point of "Stone Soup." Their way of thinking appears to wobble back and forth between logic and magic, insight and ignorance, the reasoned and the unreasonable.

A similar patchwork of competence and incompetence can be found in preschoolers' ability to remember. It is quite common for young children to recall the names and descriptions of their favorite dinosaurs, details of trips to the doctor's office, or the location of their favorite toy with an accuracy that can astound their parents (Baker-Ward et al., 1993; De Loache et al., 1985). At the same time, they have difficulty recalling a set of words or toy objects immediately after they are asked to remember them, a task that would be easy for older children and adults (Schneider & Bjorklund, 1998).

The patchworklike quality of young children's intellectual performances raises in a new way the basic questions of development. Should early childhood be considered a distinct stage of development? But if it is a stage, how are we to account for the unevenness of young children's thinking? Are young children simply inconsistent? Or do their thought processes vary from one task to the next because they are more familiar with some tasks than with others? Or might it be that their abilities vary because the parts of their brain that govern these abilities mature at different rates? In attempting to answer such questions, developmentalists must be sensitive to the possibility that preschoolers may sometimes appear to be illogical or unable to remember things only because their still-fragile language skills prevent them from fully understanding what is said to them or from adequately communicating their thoughts to others.

We begin our discussion of these issues by outlining Piaget's account of cognitive development in early childhood, an account that dominated the study of mental development in the latter half of the twentieth century. As in the case of infancy, Piaget's empirical observations about children's cognitive growth have been widely replicated even when his theoretical explanations of its causes have been challenged. His influence has been so great that many specialists who disagree with Piaget's theories use his work as the starting point for their own.

Next we summarize research that questions Piaget's interpretations of the data he collected and points toward different explanations of cognitive development during early childhood. Again, as in the case of infancy, current

Reading to young children instills the idea that reading is a pleasurable activity; it also serves to convey a wealth of widely held cultural knowledge.

research suggests that young children are more competent than Piaget believed, but sharp disagreements remain about the nature of children's cognitive abilities and the processes of cognitive change that characterize early childhood.

PIAGET'S ACCOUNT OF MENTAL DEVELOPMENT IN EARLY CHILDHOOD

In Piaget's theoretical framework, early childhood is a time of transition between the thinking of infancy, which is based on overtly physical acts (sensorimotor schemas) like grasping and sucking objects, and the thinking of middle childhood, which involves the manipulation of symbols, or internalized (mental) actions (Piaget & Inhelder, 1969). When children have completed the final sensorimotor substage (described in Chapter 6), they have acquired the rudiments of symbolic, or representational, thought. Forever after, they are able to think symbolically, using one thing to stand for another. This is the fundamental capacity on which their newfound ability to use language is based.

Around the age of 7 or 8, Piaget believed, children become capable of **mental operations,** mental "actions" in which they combine, separate, and transform information in a logical manner, as they do when they arrange their stamp collection according to country of origin and estimated value, for example, or assemble a complex new toy right out of the box. They are better able to formulate explicit strategies because they can think through alternative actions and modify them mentally before they actually act. Until children are able to engage in mental operations, their thinking is subject to limitations of the kind that was evident when Ms. Paley's class tried to answer her questions about "Stone Soup."

Piaget's belief that young children are often led into error and confusion because they are still unable to engage in true mental operations is captured in the name that he gave to his second stage of development, the **preoperational stage.** In Piaget's view, the thinking of 3-, 4-, and 5-year-olds is not yet fully operational, and cognitive development during early childhood can thus be seen as a process of overcoming the limitations that stand in the way of true operational thought.

The limitation that Piaget believed to be the key feature of thinking during early childhood is its "one-sidedness." Children of preschool age focus their attention (or "center," as Piaget called it) on no more than one salient aspect of whatever they are trying to think about. Only after overcoming this limitation, Piaget believed, do children make the transition to the stage of operational thinking, in which they are able to coordinate two perspectives simultaneously. Two classic examples of centering from Piaget's work have greatly influenced all subsequent research on cognitive development in early childhood; each is said to illustrate how centering on a single aspect of a problem to the exclusion of all others limits the young child's ability to reason.

The first example is perhaps Piaget's most famous demonstration of the difference between preoperational thinking and the concrete operational thinking of middle childhood, in which children can mentally combine and manipulate information about concrete objects and events. The child is presented with two identical beakers, each filled with exactly the same amount of water. While the child watches, the water in one of the beakers is poured into a third, narrower and taller beaker, with the result that the level of the water in the new beaker is higher than that of the water in the original beaker. Witnessing this event, 3- and 4-year-olds ordinarily conclude that the amount of water in the new beaker has somehow increased.

Piaget maintained that young children make this error because they center on only a single dimension of the problem—in this case, the height of

mental operations In Piaget's theory, the mental process of combining, separating, or transforming information in a logical manner.

preoperational stage According to Piaget, the stage of thinking between infancy and middle childhood in which children are unable to decenter their thinking or to think through the consequences of an action.

the water in the beakers. They are unable to consider the height and width of the beakers simultaneously. Once they are capable of mental operations, however, children firmly deny that the amount of water has changed, presumably because they can consider several aspects of the problem at once. This ability allows them to mentally coordinate the relative effects of changes in width and height. It also allows them to imagine the reversal of the process they have witnessed and thus to think through what would happen if the water were poured back into its original beaker. (We will return to research based on these examples in Chapter 12 because it also plays a central role in disputes about the nature of mental development in middle childhood.)

egocentrism In Piaget's terms, to "center on oneself," to consider the world entirely in terms of one's own point of view.

In the second classic example of the inability to coordinate two perspectives, young children are shown a set of wooden beads, most of which are brown and the remainder white. When they are asked, "Which are there more of, brown beads or wooden beads?" they claim that there are more *brown* beads. According to Piaget, preschoolers make this mistake because they center on only one level of categorization at a time. That is, they can think about the beads as divided into two subclasses (brown versus white), and they can think about the united common class (wooden beads), but they cannot think about both levels simultaneously. In middle childhood, according to Piaget, children can keep the two levels of categorization in mind and thus are not led into this kind of error.

Piaget considered young children's inability to keep two aspects of a problem in mind to be at the heart of what he saw as the three salient characteristics of thinking during early childhood: (1) egocentrism, (2) the confusion of appearance and reality, and (3) nonlogical reasoning.

EGOCENTRISM

Egocentrism has a narrower meaning in Piaget's theory than in everyday speech. It does not mean selfish or arrogant. Rather, **egocentrism** refers to the tendency to "center on oneself," to consider the world entirely in terms of one's own point of view. According to Piaget, preschoolers cannot "decenter"; they are trapped in their own point of view, unable to see things from someone else's perspective.

The cognitive limitations that correspond to egocentrism were documented by Piaget and many later researchers who have been inspired by his work. The particular limitations one sees depend on the specific task at hand. We will examine three such tasks: perspective taking, conversing with playmates, and thinking about other peoples' thought processes.

Lack of Spatial Perspective Taking

One way in which the egocentric nature of young children's thought shows itself is in the difficulty they have imagining what things look like from another person's visual perspective. The classic example of this form of egocentrism is the three-mountain problem. Piaget and Inhelder (1956) confronted young children with a large diorama containing models of three mountains that were distinctively different in size, shape, and landmarks (see Figure 9.1). First, the children were asked to walk around the diorama and become familiar with the landscape from all sides. Once the children had done this, they were seated on one side of the diorama. Next, a doll was placed on the opposite side of the diorama so that it had a "different view" of the landscape. The children were then shown pictures of the diorama from several perspectives and were asked to identify the picture that corresponded to the doll's point of view. Even

FIGURE 9.1
Preschool children shown this diorama of three mountains with a distinctive landmark on each mountain were unable to say how the scene might look from perspectives other than the one they had at the moment. (From Piaget & Inhelder, 1956.)

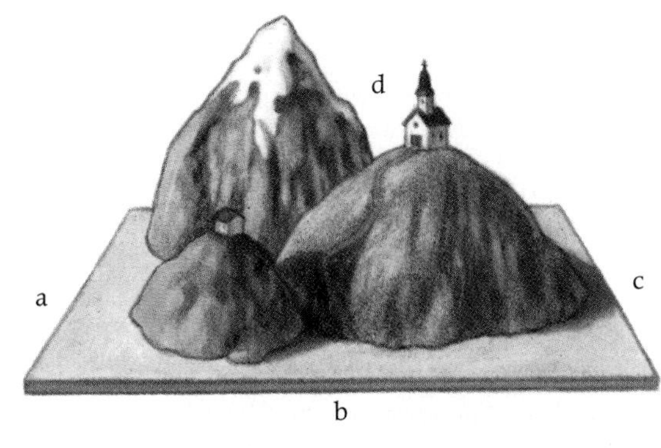

though they had seen the diorama from the location the doll was in, the children almost always chose the picture corresponding to their own point of view, not the doll's.

Egocentric Speech

The egocentric quality of children's thought also appears in their speech. Recall from Chapter 8, for example, the tendency of young children to engage in "collective monologues" rather than true dialogues when they play together (p. 328). Such behavior suggested to Piaget that young children, owing to their inability to decenter, are not yet even trying to communicate. This same quality becomes evident in experiments in which two youngsters are seated at a table and asked to communicate with each other about identical sets of objects arrayed before them. In experiments of this kind, a small screen is placed between the children so that they cannot see each other. One child is designated the speaker; the other is the listener. The speaker must describe the objects on her side of the screen one at a time, and the listener must choose the corresponding object from his own array. A typical experimental arrangement is shown in Figure 9.2. (Yule [1997] reviews the literature on this topic.)

Most 4- and 5-year-old children in the role of speaker provide too little information for the listener to be able to choose the correct object. If the objects are toy dogs, cats, and elephants, for example, the speaker might say only, "This one is a dog," or even "Take this one," failing to realize that the listener doesn't have enough information to know exactly which object is being referred to. Young listeners also have difficulty with this task: when given the chance to ask for more information, they are unlikely to do so. These communication problems persist to the end of early childhood, as evidenced by studies conducted in England and Italy, which found that 6-year-old children had the same difficulties. By the age of 9 years, children were as good about seeking additional information as adults when the message they were receiving was ambiguous (Lloyd et al., 1995).

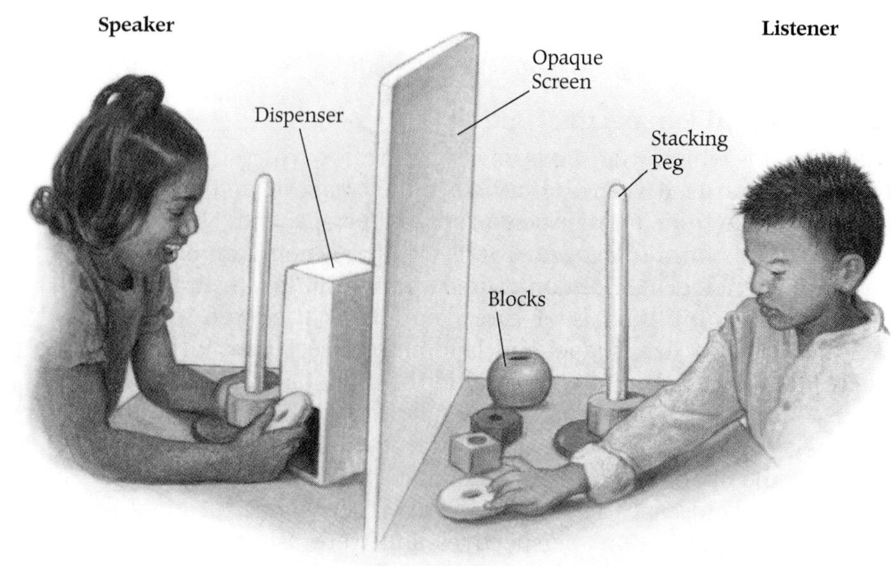

FIGURE 9.2
Preschoolers often experience difficulty with the task of keeping in mind what someone else needs to be told in order for effective communication to occur. The girl on the left must describe the blocks on her side of the screen, being careful to mention their distinguishing features, so that the boy on the right will stack them in the same order she does. (From Krauss & Glucksberg, 1969.)

Failure to Understand Other Minds

A related form of egocentrism in early childhood is the failure to realize that others can have thoughts different from one's own (Astington, 1993; Flavell & Miller, 1998). One of the major methods currently being used to study the development of children's thinking about other people's thought processes focuses on children's ability to understand that another person may hold a false belief. Two examples indicate the kinds of methods developmentalists use to determine young children's ability to understand the possibility of false beliefs.

mental perspective taking The ability to think about what goes on in another person's mind and to take their perspective.

theory of mind The ability to think about other people's mental states and form theories of how they think.

In the first method, children are presented with a brief scenario and then asked to predict how one of the characters in the scenario will behave. The scenario and prediction question are designed to reveal the child's ability to engage in **mental perspective taking**—to think about what goes on in another person's mind. Here is a typical scenario and follow-up question:

> SCENARIO: Once there was a little boy who liked candy. One day he put a chocolate bar in a box on the table and went away for a while. While he was gone, his mother came. She took the candy out of the box and put it in the top drawer of the bureau where he kept his socks. The little boy came back. He was hungry and went to get his candy.
>
> QUESTION: Where do you think the little boy will look?

When 3-year-olds are asked this question, they respond as if the boy who left the room had the same information that they do; they say that the boy will look in the top drawer of the bureau. Five-year-olds are far more likely to say that the little boy will look in the box on the table; presumably they understand that the child who left the room has a false belief about the location of the candy.

In the second method, children are directly involved in a task in which they themselves experience a false belief (Gopnik & Astington, 1988; Perner et al., 1987). In this task, children are shown a box covered with pictures of candy, such as M&Ms, and are asked what they think is in the box. All, of course, answer, "Candy." Then they are shown that they are wrong—the box actually contains something else, such as a pencil. Next the children are asked what a friend who has not yet seen inside the box would think it contains. Even though they have just gone through the process of being deceived themselves, most 3-year-olds say that the friend will think the box contains a pencil.

A variety of evidence based on data from such tasks indicates that the ability to think about other people's mental states, often referred to as a **theory of mind,** does not make its appearance until children are 4 or 5 years old (Astington, 1993; Flavell & Miller, 1998).

Taken together, the evidence that young children have difficulty with spatial perspective taking of the sort required by the three-mountain problem, fail to provide adequate information to others in conversation, and fail to appreciate that someone may have a false belief provides support for Piaget's theory of the egocentric nature of children's thinking.

FIGURE 9.3

A phenomenon that requires the viewer to distinguish between appearance and reality is the bending of light that occurs when a straight stick is partially submerged in water: the stick looks broken, but we know that this appearance is not reality; it is an illusion. Young children, however, may believe the stick has actually changed.

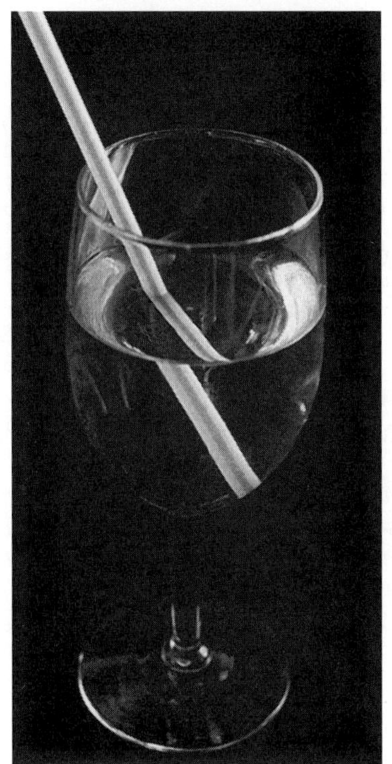

CONFUSING APPEARANCE AND REALITY

As we noted above, an important manifestation of the limitations of early childhood thought is children's tendency to focus exclusively on the most striking aspects of an object—that is, on its surface appearance (Figure 9.3). Piaget believed that this perceptual tendency makes it difficult for the young child to distinguish between the way things *seem* to be and the way they *are.* Because they have difficulty with the appearance–reality distinction,

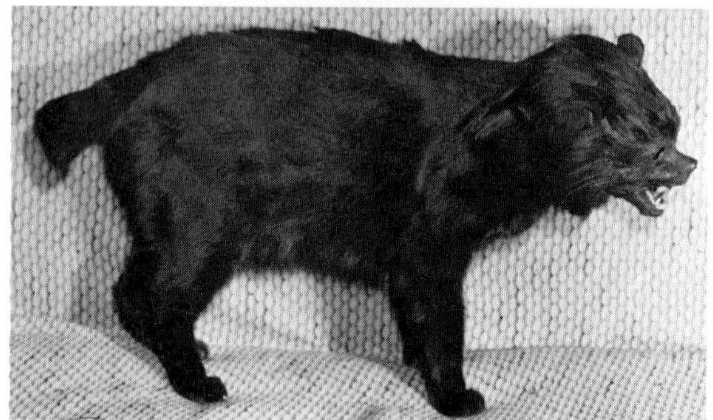

(a)

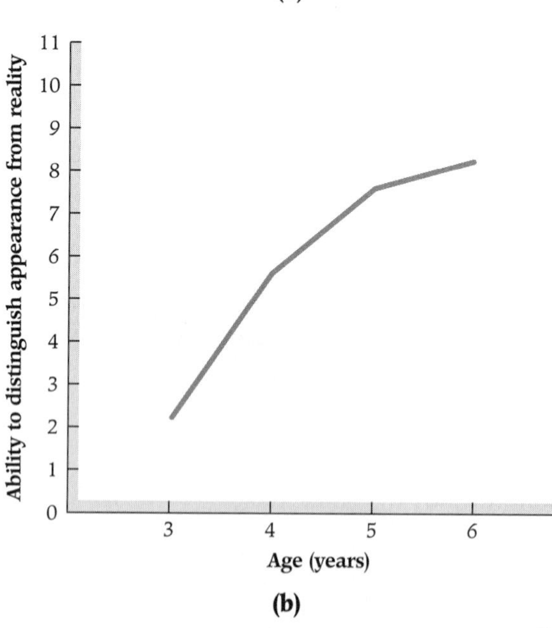

(b)

FIGURE 9.4

(a) Maynard the cat, without and with a dog mask. (b) A chart plotting the age-related increase of children's ability to understand that Maynard remains a cat even when his appearance is changed so that he looks like a dog. (Adapted from De Vries, 1969.)

2½-year-olds may become frightened when an older child puts on a mask at Halloween, as if the mask had actually changed the wearer into a witch or a dragon (Flavell et al., 1993).

Rheta De Vries (1969) studied the development of the appearance-reality distinction with the help of Maynard, an unusually well behaved black cat. At the start of the experiment all the children said that Maynard was a cat. After they played with Maynard for a short while, De Vries hid Maynard's front half behind a screen while she strapped a realistic mask of a ferocious dog onto his head (see Figure 9.4*a*). As she removed the screen, De Vries asked a set of questions to assess the children's ability to distinguish between the animal's real identity and its appearance: "What kind of animal is it now?" "Is it really a dog?" "Can it bark?" The strength of children's ability to distinguish appearance and reality was measured on an 11-point scale. Children who said that the cat had turned into a dog were given a score of 1, while children who said that the cat only appeared to turn into a dog but could never really become one were given a score of 11.

By and large, the 3-year-olds focused almost entirely on Maynard's appearance (see Figure 9.4*b*). They said he had actually become a ferocious dog, and some of them were afraid he would bite them. Most of the 6-year-olds scoffed at this idea, understanding that the cat only looked like a dog. The 4- and 5-year-olds showed considerable confusion. They didn't believe that a cat could become a dog, but they did not always answer De Vries's questions correctly.

Similar confusions between appearance and reality have been reported by John Flavell and his colleagues, who showed young children various objects that appeared to be one thing but were really another: a sponge that appeared to be a rock; a stone that appeared to be an egg; and a small piece of white paper placed behind a transparent piece of pink plastic so that the paper appeared to be pink. The children were shown the objects and asked, "What does that look like?" (the appearance question) and "What is it really?" (the reality question) (Flavell et al., 1986; Melot & Houde, 1998).

Consistent with Piaget's claims about the difficulties that young children experience in distinguishing reality from appearance, Flavell and other researchers have found that 3-year-olds are likely to answer appearance–reality questions incorrectly. For example, it is to be expected that the children would initially think that the sponge "rock" was a rock because it was realistic enough to "fool the most discerning" observer. But once they discover by touching it that the "rock" really is a sponge, they begin to insist that it not only *feels* like a sponge but also *looks* like a sponge! Four-year-olds seem to be in a transition state; they sometimes answer correctly, sometimes incorrectly. Five-year-olds have a much firmer grip on the appearance–reality distinction in these circumstances and usually answer the experimenters' questions correctly.

Flavell (1990, pp. 14–15) offers three lines of evidence to argue that young children's difficulties with the appearance–reality distinction are "nontrivial, deep-seated, [and] genuinely intellectual ones":

1. Chinese, Japanese, and British 3-year-olds experience similar difficulties (Flavell et al., 1983; Harris & Gross, 1988).
2. Various attempts to simplify the task do not help young children over their difficulties (Flavell et al., 1987).
3. Attempts to train young children to make the appropriate distinctions have failed (Melot & Houde, 1998; Taylor & Hort, 1990).

PRECAUSAL REASONING

precausal thinking Piaget's description of the reasoning of young children that does not follow the procedures of either deductive or inductive reasoning.

Nothing is more characteristic of preschoolers than their love for asking questions. "Why is the sky blue?" "What makes clouds?" "Where do babies come from?" Clearly, children are interested in the causes of things.

Despite this interest, Piaget believed that because young children are not yet capable of true mental operations, they cannot engage in cause-and-effect reasoning like older children and adults. He claimed that instead of reasoning from general premises to particular cases (deduction) or from specific cases to general ones (induction), young children think *transductively,* from one particular to another. As an example, he described how his young daughter missed her customary nap one afternoon and remarked, "I haven't had a nap, so it isn't afternoon." As a consequence of such reasoning, young children are likely to confuse cause and effect. Because he believed that transductive reasoning precedes true causal reasoning, Piaget referred to this aspect of young children's thinking as **precausal thinking** (Piaget, 1930).

Our own daughter gave a splendid demonstration of how transductive reasoning can lead a young child to confuse cause and effect. At the age of 3½, Jenny happened to walk with us through an old graveyard. Listening to us read the inscriptions on the gravestones, she realized that somehow the old moss-covered stones represented people. "Where is she now?" she asked when we finished reading the inscription on one stone.

"She's dead," we told her.

"But where is she?"

We tried to explain that when people die, they are buried in the ground, in cemeteries. After that, Jenny steadfastly refused to go into cemeteries with us and would become upset when we were near one. At bedtime every evening, she repeatedly asked us about death, burial, and graveyards. We answered her questions as best we could, yet she kept repeating the same questions and she was obviously upset by the topic. The reason for her fear became clear when we were moving to New York City. "Are there any graveyards in New York City?" she asked anxiously. We were exhausted by her insistent questions, and our belief that we should be candid and honest was crumbling.

"No," we lied. "There are no graveyards in New York City." At this response, Jenny visibly relaxed.

"Then people don't die in New York," she added a couple of minutes later.

Jenny had reasoned that since graveyards are places where dead people are found, graveyards must be the cause of death. This reasoning led her to the comforting but incorrect conclusion that if you can stay away from graveyards, you are not in danger of dying.

THE STUDY OF YOUNG CHILDREN'S THINKING AFTER PIAGET

The examples we have provided thus far (summarized in Table 9.1) are only a sample of the phenomena supporting the idea that there is a distinctive mode of thought associated with early childhood. But they are sufficient to give the flavor of the sorts of evidence collected by Piaget and others to argue for the idea of a preoperational stage. At this age, children's thinking is dominated by the inability to "decenter," preventing them from taking account of others' points of view and beliefs, keeping appearance and reality separate, and reasoning logically.

In recent decades, however, evidence collected using a variety of new methods has inspired a broad reexamination of the idea that preoperational thinking is generally characteristic of early childhood thinking (Case, 1998; Fischer & Biddel, 1998; Gelman & Williams, 1998; Wellman & Gelman, 1998).

TABLE 9.1 PIAGET'S STAGES OF COGNITIVE DEVELOPMENT: PREOPERATIONAL

Age (years)	Stage	Description	Characteristics and Examples
Birth to 2	Sensorimotor	Infants' achievements consist largely of coordinating their sensory perceptions and simple motor behaviors. As they move through the 6 substages of this period, infants come to recognize the existence of a world outside of themselves and begin to interact with it in deliberate ways.	
2 to 6	**Preoperational**	Young children can represent reality to themselves through the use of symbols, including mental images, words, and gestures. Objects and events no longer have to be present to be thought about, but children often fail to distinguish their point of view from that of others, become easily captured by surface appearances; and are often confused about causal relations.	Centration, the tendency to focus (center) on the most salient aspect of whatever one is trying to think about. A major manifestation of this is egocentrism, or considering the world entirely in terms of one's own point of view. • Children engage in collective monologues, rather than dialogues, in each other's company. • Children have difficulty taking a listener's knowledge into account in order to communicate effectively. • Children fail to consider both the height and width of containers in order to compare their volumes. • Children confuse classes with subclasses. They cannot reliably say whether there are more wooden beads or more brown beads in a set of all wooden beads. Confusion of appearance and reality. • Children act as if a Halloween mask actually changes the identity of the person wearing it. • Children may believe that a straight stick partially submerged in water actually does become bent. Precausal reasoning, characterized by illogical thinking and an indifference to cause-and-effect relations. • A child may think a graveyard is a cause of death because dead people are buried there. A form of moral reasoning that sees morality as being imposed from the outside and that does not take intentions into account.
6 to 12	Concrete Operational	As they enter middle childhood, children become capable of mental operations, internalized actions that fit into a logical system. Operational thinking allows children mentally to combine, separate, order, and transform objects and actions. Such operations are considered concrete because they are carried out in the presence of the objects and events being thought about.	
12 to 19	Formal Operational	In adolescence the developing person acquires the ability to think systematically about all logical relations within a problem. Adolescents display keen interest in abstract ideals and in the process of thinking itself.	

THE PROBLEM OF UNEVEN LEVELS OF PERFORMANCE

Much of the new evidence regarding Piaget's theory indicates that cognitive development is a good deal more uneven than Piaget's depiction of it would seem to suggest and that, under some circumstances, children show signs of having certain cognitive abilities earlier than Piaget realized. Piaget himself was well aware that a child's performance could vary somewhat from one version of a problem to another, even though the problems seemed to require the same logical operations. He referred to such cases as instances of **horizontal décalage** (literally, horizontal misalignment). He believed that subtle differences in the logical requirements of the different versions of a task are an important source of variations in children's performance in what appear to be logically identical cognitive tasks. He was also aware that the interview technique, from which much of his data derived, might itself obscure the thought process being studied, producing an apparent unevenness in performance, especially in young children who were still novices in the use of language (Piaget, 1929/1979). However, his own work convinced him that he had overcome the problems of interviewing young children and that his research accurately demonstrated that preoperational children consistently fail to distinguish their point of view from that of someone else, become easily captured by surface appearances, and are often confused about causal relations.

horizontal décalage Variations in performance from one version of a problem to another, even though the problems seem to require the same logical operations.

Nevertheless, a variety of studies have seemed to show that Piaget misjudged the special difficulties caused by his reliance on verbal interviews and contrived tasks as his key source of data. Although uncertainties remain, there is now a body of evidence that, depending on the test methods used, children's cognitive performance can vary more than Piaget realized and that more sensitive methods of assessment reveal greater cognitive competence in young children than he was able to uncover. (Flavell et al. [1993], Gellman & Williams [1998], and Wellman & Gelman [1998] review the evidence.)

Nonegocentric Reasoning about Spatial Perspectives

In one often-cited test of Piaget's ideas about spatial egocentrism, Helen Borke (1975) replicated Piaget and Inhelder's three-mountain experiment (Figure 9.1) with children between the ages of 3 and 4 years. She then presented the children with an alternative form of the problem, a farm scene that included such landmarks as a small lake with a boat on it, a horse and a cow, ducks, people, trees, and a building (Figure 9.5). In this alternative version, Grover, a character from *Sesame Street,* drives around the landscape in a car. From time to time he stops and takes a look at the view. The child's task is to indicate what that view looks like from Grover's perspective.

Children as young as 3 years old performed well on this perspective-taking problem, whereas their performance on the three-mountain version of the problem had been poor, just as Piaget and Inhelder's work would have predicted. These contrasting levels of performance led Borke to conclude that when perspective-taking tasks involve familiar, easily differentiated objects and when care is taken to make it easy for young children to express their understanding, young children demonstrate that they are able to take spatial perspectives other than their own.

Understanding Other Minds

We have seen that young children do not usually perform well on experimental tasks involving an understanding of others' false beliefs. Nevertheless, researchers have amassed ample evidence that in some circumstances children can appreciate the mental states of others at much younger ages than Piaget thought they could.

By changing the child's role in false-belief tasks from that of the deceived to that of the deceiver, Kate Sullivan and Ellen Winner found that even 3-year-olds exhibit some appreciation of other people's thought processes (Sullivan & Winner, 1993). Using a variation of the pencil-in-the-candy-box task, Sullivan and Winner arranged for the child to be accompanied by an adult, who was actually an accomplice in the experiment. In this version, the experimenter first pulls the standard candy-box trick (p. 341) on the child and the adult and then leaves the room. Next the adult companion suggests that she and the child play a trick on the experimenter just like the trick that

FIGURE 9.5

Borke's modification of Piaget's three-mountain perspective-taking task. When a diorama contains familiar objects, preschoolers are more likely to be able to say how it looks from a point of view other than their own.

the experimenter has played on them. Making a great display of being a co-conspirator in the plot to fool the experimenter, the adult takes a crayon box out of her purse and helps the child remove the crayons and replace them with something unexpected. Finally, while the experimenter is still out of the room, the adult, in a hushed conspiratorial tone, asks the child what the experimenter will think is in the crayon box when she returns. In this gamelike situation, 75 percent of 3-year-olds predicted that the experimenter would mistakenly expect crayons, indicating that the children were, in at least these circumstances, able to think about the thought processes of others. By comparison, only 25 percent were correct in the standard false-belief task, a rate that was in line with the typically reported results. The researchers suggest that their version of the task engaged the children in the scripted activity of fooling someone else, which primed the children to think about other people's mental states.

Distinguishing Appearance from Reality

According to the data we presented earlier (pp. 341–342), children do not begin to distinguish between appearance and reality consistently until somewhere between the ages of 4 and 6 years. However, additional research suggests that the difficulties experienced by the youngest children in making the distinction depend in part on the special features of the experimental procedures being used.

Catherine Rice and her colleagues (1997) repeated and extended the studies of 3- to 4-year-olds' ability to judge the reality of sponge "rocks" and other such misleading objects by using a procedure that engaged the children in a scripted deception activity. The experimenter began by enlisting the children in an effort to try to fool another adult with a fake object such as the sponge rock. While the second adult was conveniently out of the room, the experimenter and child placed the trick object on the table. While waiting for the second adult to return, the experimenter asked the child several questions: what the object is, really; what it looks like; and what the absent adult would think it was. In this conspiratorial, playlike context, the children were able to say that the object was a sponge but that it looked like a rock—and that the adult would think it was a rock. Thus, they were clearly able to distinguish reality from appearance. The researchers suggest that contrary to Flavell's results described earlier (p. 342), children have a conceptual grasp of the distinction between reality and appearance, but to be able to use this knowledge, they have to be primed by making the knowledge part of an ongoing activity that the child understands. These findings illustrate just how careful experimenters must be to create appropriate versions of their tasks so that they are meaningful for young children.

FIGURE 9.6

These drawings show how children of different ages and mental abilities perceive the way a bicycle works. (a) The child who is 5 years, 3 months old has no clear idea how the different parts of the bicycle fit together. (b) A retarded 9-year-old has captured part of the mechanism in the illustration but fails to link the pedal to the cogwheel and chain. (c) A normal 8-year, 3-month-old child can represent all of the essential mechanisms. (After Piaget, 1930.)

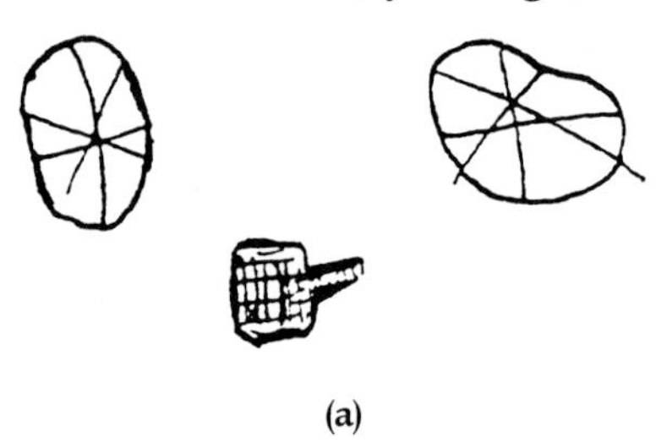

(a)

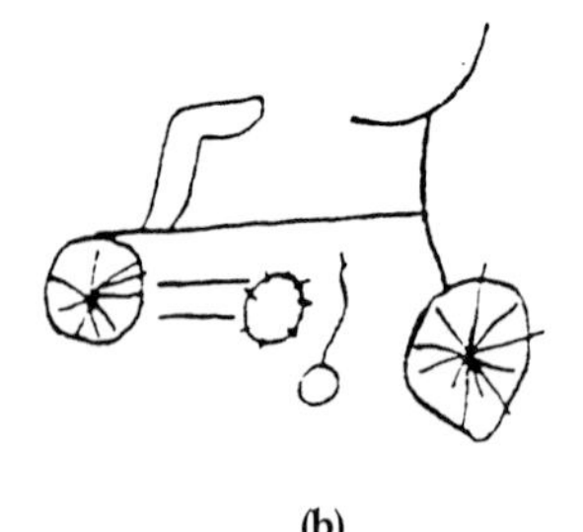

(b)

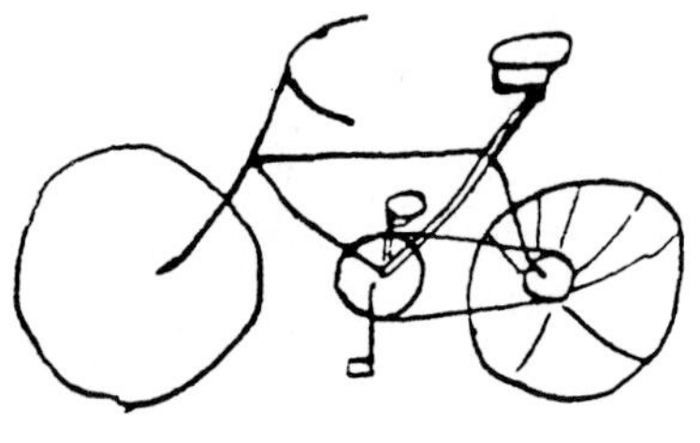

(c)

Effective Causal Reasoning

One of Piaget's best-known examples of precausal reasoning came from his interviews with children about how bicycles work. In the course of the interview, he also asked the children to draw a picture illustrating their explanations (see Figure 9.6). During the interview a bicycle was propped against a chair in front of the child. An interview with Grim, aged 5½, provides the kind of evidence that led Piaget to conclude that the reasoning of young children is precausal (Piaget, 1930, p. 206):

> *Piaget:* How does the bicycle move along?
> *Grim:* With the brakes on top of the bike.
> *Piaget:* What is the brake for?
> *Grim:* To make it go because you push.
> *Piaget:* What do you push with?
> *Grim:* With your feet.
> *Piaget:* What does that do?

Grim: It makes it go.
Piaget: How?
Grim: With the brakes.

In the late 1920s Piaget visited the Malting House School in Cambridge, England, where Susan Isaacs was also conducting research on young children. Isaacs was skeptical about Piaget's ideas on preoperational thought. When she spotted one of her preschoolers riding by on a tricycle, she put her visitor's theory to an impromptu test:

> At that moment, Dan [aged 5 years, 9 months] happened to be sitting on a tricycle in the garden, back-pedaling. I went to him and said, "The tricycle is not moving forward, is it?" "Of course not, when I'm back-pedaling," he said. "Well," I asked, "how does it go forward when it does?" "Oh, well," he replied, "your feet press the pedals, that turns the crank round, and the cranks turn that round" (pointing to the cog-wheel), "and that makes the chain go round, and the chain turns the hub round, and then the wheels go round—and there you are!" (Isaacs, 1966, p. 44)

Isaacs offered this anecdote as evidence against Piaget's theory that young children are incapable of causal reasoning. Before accepting either conclusion, most developmentalists would require more information about both boys, their experience with tricycles and bicycles, and the way the interviews were conducted. Is Dan simply an especially advanced preschooler? Is the difference in their performances the result of differences in the way the problems were posed to them? Systematic answers to such questions require experiments that deliberately vary the way the problems are presented.

Merry Bullock and Rochel Gelman, for example, tested the ability of 3- to 5-year-olds to understand the basic principle that causes come before effects, using the apparatus shown in Figure 9.7 (Bullock, 1984; Bullock & Gelman, 1979). Children observed two sequences of events. In the first, a steel marble was dropped into one of two slots in a box, both of which were visible through the side of the box. Two seconds after the marble disappeared at the bottom of the slot, a Snoopy doll popped out of the hole in the apparatus's middle. At that moment, a second ball was dropped into the other slot. It too disappeared, with no further result. The children were then asked to say which of the balls had made Snoopy jump up and to provide an explanation.

FIGURE 9.7
The apparatus used by Bullock and Gelman to test preschoolers' understanding that cause precedes effect. (a) A marble was dropped into one of the slots. (b) Two seconds after the marble disappeared, a Snoopy doll popped out of the hole in the middle of the apparatus. At the same moment, a second marble was dropped into the other slot, where it disappeared, with no further result. Preschoolers are generally able to indicate which marble caused Snoopy to jump up. (Based on Bullock & Gelman, 1979.)

Even children as young as 3 usually said that the first ball had caused Snoopy to jump up. The 5-year-olds had no difficulty with the task at all. However, there was a marked difference between the age groups in their ability to explain what had happened. Many of the 3-year-olds could give no explanation or said something completely irrelevant ("It's got big teeth"). Almost all the 5-year-olds could provide at least a partial explanation of the principle that causes precede effects. This finding suggests one reason why Piaget may have underestimated the cognitive competence of young children: his research techniques relied heavily on verbally presented problems and verbal justifications of reasoning, both of which put young children at a disadvantage (see Box 9.1).

Overall, the weight of the evidence for significant unevenness in young children's cognitive development is now widely regarded as too important to ignore. Accordingly, a number of researchers are currently using theories and research methods from both Piagetian and other perspectives to understand the phenomenon of islands of competence.

BOX 9.1

Young Children as Witnesses

The nature of young children's thought processes becomes an important social issue when they are called upon to give testimony in a court of law, either as witnesses to a crime or as possible victims of a crime. Adults have long been reluctant to believe the word of a young child. Psychologists have traditionally viewed children as suggestible (Stern, 1910); unable to distinguish fantasy from reality (Piaget, 1926, 1928; Werner, 1948); and prone to fantasize sexual events (Freud, 1905/1953a). Judges, lawyers, and prosecutors have also expressed reservations about children's reliability as witnesses (Goodman et al., 1998). Legal rulings on the admissibility of children's testimony continue to reflect these longstanding doubts. In many states, for example, the judge determines whether a child below a certain age (which varies from state to state) is competent to testify.

Owing to a growing concern about the prevalence of sexual and physical abuse of children in recent years, the legal community has reexamined the reliability of children's testimony. At the same time, psychologists are trying to determine when and under what conditions young children can testify reliably about past events (Ceci & Bruck, 1998; Wright & Loftus, 1998). At the heart of the current discussion of child testimony are two questions: How good are children's memories at various ages? How susceptible are young children to suggestions that might change their memories?

Reason for concern is provided by children's behavior both in actual criminal trials and in experimental studies conducted by psychologists. When researchers ask young children about events that have personal significance for them, such as whether or not they were given an injection when they went to the doctor's office, they are likely to provide correct answers (Goodman et al., 1990). However, a series of studies in which children ranging in age from 3 to 7 were interviewed immediately after a visit to the doctor and then again at intervals from 1 to 12 weeks later found that, as time passed, the youngest children were increasingly likely to become inaccurate in their answers (Ornstein et al., 1997). This finding is important for legal proceedings in which children are likely to be interviewed about the same event repeatedly over a period of several months, if not years.

An additional problem highlighted in these studies is that the youngest children often provided little information in response to the open-ended question "Can you tell me what happened when you went to the doctor?" (Ornstein et al, 1997). In their attempts to probe their memory and susceptibility to giving erroneous information more fully, the interviewers then asked all the children several strange and silly questions, such as, "Did the doctor cut off your hair?" or "Did the nurse lick your knee?" The youngest children were much more likely than the older children to say that these things happened even though they didn't.

Stephen Ceci and Maggie Bruck (1998) suggest that one reason the older children are more consistent in their responses to strange questions than the younger ones is that they have better knowledge of the scripts for doctor's visits and do not need to check their memories before they answer. They know already that "things like that" don't happen at the doctor's office.

In actual criminal proceedings, children are often asked to tell and retell their stories to several people, who question them and sometimes, in an attempt to probe their recall of events more deeply and build a case, ask suggestive questions based on erroneous assumptions. There are several ways in which such questioning procedures can lead the young child to make false statements. First, when an interviewer, probing a child's testimony, makes an erroneous suggestion about what happened, the suggestion tends to become blended with the child's original memory to produce a new, hybrid "memory." This hybrid memory can block the original memory, preventing the child from accurately recall-

POST-PIAGETIAN EXPLANATIONS OF DEVELOPMENT IN EARLY CHILDHOOD

In recent decades several schools of thought have developed to deal with the perceived shortcomings of Piaget's account of cognitive development. Many developmentalists continue to argue that Piaget's theory remains correct in its overall picture of development and that apparently contradictory evidence results from either faulty experimentation or a failure to understand Piaget's theory. Orlando Lourenço and Armando Machado, for example, argue that young children may be more competent than Piaget believed, but most of the studies that have challenged his results are based on "methodological errors and conceptual confusions" (Lourenço & Machado, 1996, p. 146).

Other psychologists think that the problems with Piaget's theory are more serious. A characteristic shared by many of these critics is their belief that cognition begins as a process that is specific to domains of knowledge such as music, space, and number and changes differently in each domain.

ing the actual events. It is also possible that the child remembers both what the adult suggested happened and what really happened but can no longer tell which version is authentic (Ceci & Bruck, 1993).

The following transcript from an actual interview in the case of Kelly Michaels, a New Jersey nursery school teacher who was convicted and jailed for sexually abusing children in her school, provides an example of how such suggestions might be made:

> *Interviewer:* Well, what about the cat game?
> *Child:* Cat game?
> *Interviewer:* Where everybody went like this, "Meow, Meow."
> *Child:* I don't think I was there that day.

Despite the fact the child denied knowing about a cat game when she was interviewed, later, at the trial, she described a cat game in which all the children were naked and licking each other (from Ceci & Bruck, 1998).

Although we do not know why this child testified the way she did after telling the interviewer she didn't think she was present at the game, we can speculate that she may have genuinely come to recall such a cat game after being told of one by the interviewer. Her answer may also have reflected the fact that young children are likely to believe that adults know more than they do. When they are being questioned in a legal proceeding, as this child was, they may incorporate the adult's suggestions in their answers to please the adult, even when they know the adult's suggestions are wrong. Asked the same questions more than once, they change their answers because they assume that something was wrong with their first answer (Siegal, 1991).

Children are by no means the only ones whose memories are vulnerable to the suggestions of the people who question them. Adults, too, can be led astray in such situations (Loftus, 1996; Massoni et al., 1999). Young children are considered to be especially susceptible, however, because of their limited ability to remember, their lack of experience with legal proceedings, and their tendency to try to please adults.

Three-year-old Amanda Conklin looks out at a crowded Van Nuys, California, courtroom as the judge questions her during the trial of her father for the murder of her mother.

These scholars differ, however, in how they conceive of domains and the extent to which they believe that there are developmental changes in general cognitive processes, such as memory and attention, that operate across domains (Case, 1998; Goswami, 1999).

NEO-PIAGETIAN THEORIES OF COGNITIVE DEVELOPMENT

The term *neo-Piagetian* refers to developmentalists who agree with major features of Piaget's approach but seek to modify certain aspects of his theory in response to modern criticisms. Neo-Piagetians retain the idea that the acquisition of knowledge goes through stagelike changes, but they believe that individuals' passage through the stages occurs at different rates in different domains. A child may be a demon chess player or a precocious musician, yet solve typical Piagetian tasks no better than her age-mates (Feldman, 1999).

However, at the same time that they emphasize domain-specific development, neo-Piagetians emphasize that there are also general age-related limits on children's cognitive capacities, particularly memory limitations, that apply to all forms of thinking. The problem neo-Piagetians face, then, is to reconcile domain-specific and general developmental transformations. To do this, Robbie Case and his colleagues focus on what Case has termed *central conceptual structures* (Case, 1992; Case & Okamoto, 1996). A **central conceptual structure** is a network of concepts and conceptual relations that permits children to think in the same way about a broad range of problems within a given domain such as checkers, map following, and drawing—all examples of tasks in the spatial domain. According to Case, when researchers make certain that different tasks from the same domain are familiar, involve equally demanding content, and have the same memory demands, children will proceed through the same developmental changes on each task at approximately the same age, reflecting a coordinated change within central conceptual structures.

In one demonstration of the possibility of identifying coordinated development in two different tasks that are a part of the same central conceptual structure, Case and his colleagues constructed two sets of number problems that differed in their specific content but shared identical logical structures. The first required children to judge the "juiciness" of a drink made of different mixtures of orange juice and water. Would a mixture of five parts juice and three parts water, for example, taste as juicy as a mixture made of four parts juice and one part water? The second, logically equivalent problem concerned two boys, each of whom was having a birthday party and each of whom wanted polished stones for his birthday (in the school where the investigators were conducting their research, polished stones were highly prized). The children were shown how many stones each boy wanted and how many he actually received. Then they were asked, "Which child would be happier?"

The researchers questioned children of different ages and found that their levels of performance go through a series of stagelike changes for each of the two kinds of problems, thus confirming the notion of stagelike change. In addition, for 89 percent of the children tested, the level of cognitive development was either the same for both kinds of problems or only slightly different (Case et al., 1986). The fact that the children reached virtually the same levels of reasoning on two tasks that belong to the domain of number but that had different contents supports the neo-Piagetian idea that the timing of changes for different problems within a domain can be the same. But unevenness will be the rule across different domains unless care is taken to ensure that the tasks are equivalent in all respects, including the central conceptual structure upon which they draw. Case leaves open the possibility that there may be general forms of conceptual understanding that apply to all the domains that children experience, as Piaget suggested, but to date, he writes, he has been unable to identify any (Case & Okamoto, 1996, p. 288).

central conceptual structure The mental equivalent of knowledge common to a broad range of examples within a domain.

INFORMATION-PROCESSING APPROACHES

During the 1960s, when Piaget's ideas were becoming popular among developmentalists, a different view of cognitive functioning was also gaining attention: the **information-processing approach.** According to information-processing theorists, thinking can best be understood by analogy with the workings of a digital computer. Investigators who employ the metaphor of child-as-information-processor generally conceive of cognitive development as the result of changes both in children's neural "hardware," such as increased myelination of a particular brain region, and in children's "software," such as the acquisition of a new strategy for remembering (Siegler, 1996).

The main components of this view of the mind are illustrated in Figure 9.8. At the left side is the presumed starting point of any problem-solving process, the **sensory register,** which stores incoming information for a fraction of a second before it is selectively processed. Stimulation from the environment ("input," in the language of computer programming) is detected by the sensory organs and is passed on to the sensory register. If the input is not attended to, it will disappear almost immediately. If it is attended to, it may be "read into" **short-term (working) memory,** where it can be retained for several seconds. Working memory is the part of the information-processing system where active thinking takes place. Working memory functions by combining incoming information from the sensory register with memory of past experiences, or **long-term memory,** changing the information into new forms. If the information in working memory is not combined with information in long-term memory, it is easily forgotten.

information-processing approach A strategy for explaining cognitive development based on an analogy with the workings of a digital computer.

sensory register That part of the information-processing system that stores incoming information for a fraction of a second before it is selectively processed.

short-term (working) memory That part of the information-processing system that holds incoming sensory information until it is taken up into long-term memory or forgotten.

long-term memory Memory that is retained over a long period of time.

FIGURE 9.8
The major components of an information-processing model of mental actions. (Adapted from Atkinson & Shiffrin, 1980.)

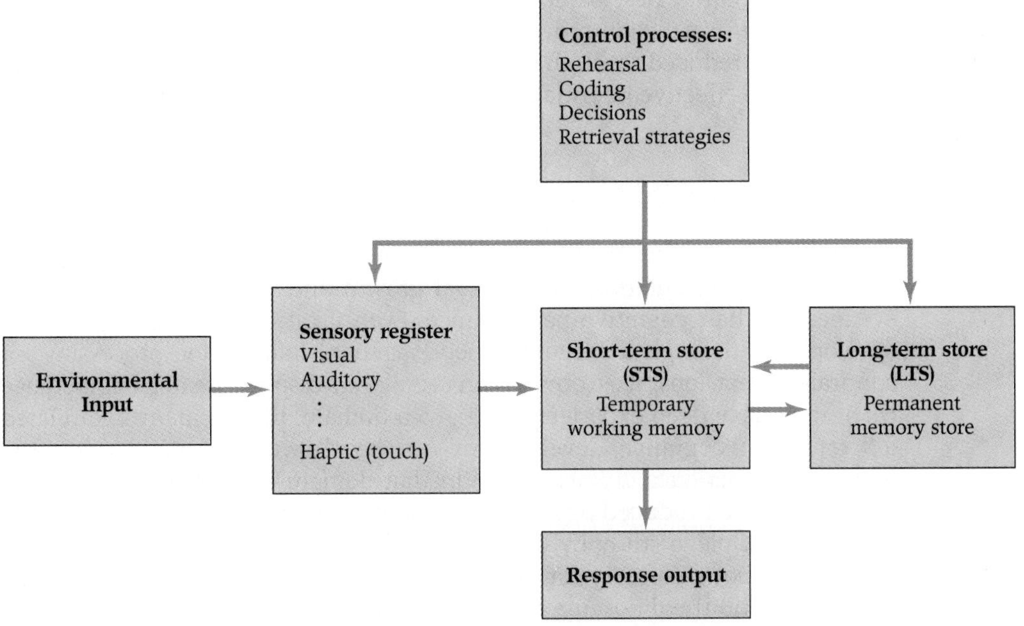

Figure 9.8 also shows the way in which the flow of information between sensory register, working memory, and long-term memory is coordinated by *control processes,* which determine how the information temporarily held in working memory is to be applied to the problem at hand. Important control processes include attention, rehearsal, and decision making. "Software" that is a crucial part of the control processes determines the particular information that must be attended to, whether long-term memory must be searched more thoroughly to make an adequate response, or whether a particular problem-solving strategy should be used. Control processes also determine whether a piece of information in short-term memory needs to be retained or can be forgotten.

We can give an overall idea of the information-processing approach by considering what occurs when a mother tries to teach her 4-year-old daughter to remember the family phone number. The mother sits with the child at the phone and shows her the sequence of buttons to push, say, 543-1234. The child watches what the mother does and hears what her mother is saying. First the set of numbers enters the child's sensory register as a sequence of sounds and is transferred to short-term memory. Next, meanings corresponding to those sounds are retrieved from long-term memory and matched with the sounds in short-term, working, memory. The child recognizes each number and applies control processes in order to "try to remember," perhaps by repeating each item to herself. Remembering occurs when the information concerning the numerical sequence enters long-term memory.

The young child in our example may experience difficulty at any one of the phases of this process. She may pay insufficient attention to what her mother is saying, in which case the information will not enter her sensory register. Being young, she has a small (immature) working-memory capacity and may not be able to hold all the numbers in mind as she tries to remember them. The speed with which she can transfer information from the sensory register to working memory to long-term memory may be relatively slow, causing her to forget some of the numbers before they can be stored in long-term memory. Lastly, she may have little experience with intentional memorization and hence no repertoire of strategies for holding information in working memory for an extended period or for manipulating numbers in working memory.

In sum, from an information-processing perspective, young children's cognitive difficulties are caused by limitations in knowledge, memory, attentional control, and the speed with which they can process information, as well as by limited strategies for acquiring and using information (Siegler, 1996). Children's performance improves as they grow older because these limitations are gradually reduced through maturation of the "hardware" and the development of more effective information-processing routines ("software").

AN ENVIRONMENTAL-LEARNING ACCOUNT: AMOUNT OF EXPERIENCE

The environmental-learning perspective also provides important insights into sources of young children's intellectual growth and the reasons for the unevenness of their cognitive performance. Even if one is looking at cognitive development through a Piagetian, neo-Piagetian, information-processing, or cultural-context lens, it is obvious that children display greater competence when they have deep experience in a given domain. In fact, many age-related differences in cognitive development can be shown to depend upon the amount of experience children have in that domain and the richness of the knowledge base produced by a lot of experience.

For example, a study by Michelline Chi and Randi Koeske focused on a 4½-year-old boy's memory for dinosaurs. Chi and Koeske (1983) first elicited the names of all the dinosaurs the child knew (46 in all for this unusually well versed child!) by questioning him on various occasions. Next they drew up two lists consisting of the 20 dinosaurs he mentioned most frequently and the 20 he mentioned least frequently. In order to study how the child's comparative knowledge influenced his memory and reasoning about each group, Chi and Koeske then read the two lists of dinosaurs to the child three times each and at each reading asked him to memorize as much of the list as he could. He recalled twice as many items from the list of dinosaurs he knew more about than from the list with which he was less familiar (an average of 9.7 dinosaurs versus 5.0 dinosaurs). The researchers concluded that the more one knows about a topic, the easier it is to recall items that pertain to it.

Subsequent research showed that extensive domain knowledge also affects reasoning: the more you know, the more powerful your ability to reason will be. Chi and her colleagues (1989) showed that young dinosaur "experts" organize their knowledge about dinosaurs in more integrated and coherent ways than novices do. For example, they mentally group dinosaurs according to common behaviors ("meat eaters" versus "plant eaters") and the common attributes that go with these classes ("has sharp teeth" versus "has a duckbill"), whereas those who know less about dinosaurs mentally group them according to less significant features, such as size. The shift from novice to expert is often slow and appears to be continuous. But if they do develop a sufficiently rich knowledge base, children become experts and appear to engage the task in qualitatively new ways. Insofar as the novice-to-expert change represents a change in the child's stage of development for the domain in question, the environmental-learning explanation appears capable of accounting for stage-like changes. These new "stages" will, of course, be only islands of expertise.

BIOLOGICAL ACCOUNTS OF MENTAL DEVELOPMENT IN EARLY CHILDHOOD

So far our discussion of the unevenness that young children display in tests of their cognitive abilities has focused on the content of tests, the social situation in which they are presented, the demands that the tasks place on children's memory and logical abilities, and the domain-specific knowledge that the tasks tap. It is also possible, however, that the unevenness of young children's cognitive abilities is the result of innate brain processes that develop on a species-wide timetable.

The Growth of the Brain

At the start of early childhood, the brain has attained about 50 percent of its adult weight. By the time children are 6, it has grown to 90 percent of its full weight (Huttenlocher, 1994; LeCours, 1982). Much of this overall enlargement results from the continuing process of myelination, which speeds the transmission of neural impulses within and among different areas of the brain. Consistent with the evidence on the rate of myelination, studies of changes in the brain's electrical activity show a rapid increase during early childhood in the overall frequency and size of brain waves when children are engaging in cognitive tasks (Fischer & Rose, 1996; Thatcher, 1997). (Figure 4.2, p. 131, provides an overview of major brain areas.)

It is not difficult to see how the relative immaturity of the brain can explain general limitations on children's problem solving. For example, low levels of myelination in the hippocampus, which supports short-term, working memory, may account for the restricted working memories of young children, and hence their difficulties in tasks that require them to keep several things in mind at once. Similarly, immaturity of the frontal cortex, or of connections between the frontal cortex and other areas, could explain failures to consider someone else's point of view or to think through the consequences of one's actions. Because these general biological limitations have different psychologi-

modularity theory The belief that many cognitive processes consist of separate systems, each with their own properties, that are present at birth and do not need special tutoring in order to develop.

cal consequences, depending upon the particular cognitive demands of the tasks that young children are asked to confront, they provide one way of understanding the unevenness of development during this age period.

An additional source of unevenness in cognitive development is that such processes as dendrite formation and myelination do *not* occur at an even rate throughout the nervous system. When one part of the brain develops more rapidly than others, or when the neural pathways connecting a particular combination of cortical areas undergo a spurt in myelination, the psychological processes supported by those brain systems can be expected to undergo rapid change as well. High levels of performance are expected to occur when a given task calls upon brain systems that are highly developed, and, correspondingly, low levels of performance are expected to occur when a given task calls upon brain systems that are not yet mature.

Mental Modules

The clearly important role that preprogrammed brain development and functioning have in cognitive growth has led some theorists to conceive of cognitive development in terms of *mental modules,* highly specific mental faculties that respond to environmental inputs related to particular domains (Atran, 1998; Fodor, 1983). The term mental module comes from the work of Noam Chomsky and his followers (see Chapter 8, p. 328), who argued that many cognitive processes are like language in that they "consist of separate systems with their own properties" (Chomsky, 1988, p. 161). They do not need special tutoring in order to develop. They are present "at the beginning" in the normal human genome. This line of thinking is known as **modularity theory.**

According to modularity theory, owing to the overall organization of the brain, there are "hard-wired" systems of brain processes that receive inputs from particular classes of objects in the environment and produce as output corresponding domain-specific information about the world. Recognition of faces, the perception of music, and elementary perception of causality provide popular examples of mental modules (Hirschfeld & Gelman, 1994; Wellman & Gelman, 1998). The way in which modularity theory carries Chomsky's ideas into cognitive development more generally is revealed by the key assumptions that cognitive modularity theory shares with Chomsky's concept of the language faculty.

1. Psychological operations are presumed to be domain-specific. For each domain, they apply to different objects, follow different principles, and organize human experience in a distinctive way. The mental operations required to perceive and create music are different from those required to recognize a face; and the operations of both processes differ from those required to describe someone's face when that person is listening to a particular piece of music.
2. The psychological principles that organize the operation of each mental module are assumed to be innately specified; that is, they are coded in the genes and need no special instruction to develop. They depend upon a fixed neural structure, they operate automatically, and they need only be "triggered" by the environment.
3. It is assumed that different modules do not interact directly; each represents a separate mental domain, only loosely connected to the rest through a "central processor" that assembles the information from the separate modules.

According to modularity theorists, evidence for the modular origins of cognitive development is already observable in infancy. They point to data, reviewed in Chapters 4 and 5, showing that within a few months of birth young infants display rudimentary knowledge of persons and of many physical principles, including physical causality and a sensitivity to the number and frequency of events. And, of course, modularity theorists draw upon Chomsky's proposals about the modularity of language as discussed in Chapter 8 (p. 328).

A second line of evidence supporting the modularity position comes from prodigies—children whose overall level of development is normal, but who demonstrate islands of brilliance. Wolfgang Amadeus Mozart, for example, was an accomplished composer and musician when he was a young child, but in other ways he was not markedly different from other children his age. The extraordinary accomplishments of Mozart and other prodigies appear to fit the idea of mental modules. Each of their accomplishments falls within a domain that has its own distinctive structure—music, language, arithmetic, and so forth (Feldman, 1994).

Core Domains and Skeletal Principles

The evidence that several mental capacities display the properties of domain specificity proposed by modularity theorists lends credence to the idea that knowledge acquisition is domain-specific and linked to the long-term evolutionary processes that control maturation. However, like all theories that propose innate mechanisms, modularity theories do little to specify precisely what kinds of interactions with the environment are required for development to occur. Using language as an example, the evidence in Chapter 8 makes it clear that language cannot occur without language input and normal interactions with other human beings. And an environment that is organized by language to which children do not have access (as in the example of deaf children of hearing parents) is not sufficient to produce mature forms of language. But a modularity theory of language like Chomsky's has nothing to say about the specific environmental inputs required for the presumed module to operate effectively.

The same shortcoming applies to other examples of cognitive functioning said to be modular in origin and functioning. For example, the fact that children respond to a ball's moving after another ball hits it as a distinctive event (taken by some as evidence for a "physical-causality module") does not mean that they have achieved the level of understanding of physical causality characteristic of the children and adults around them. A great deal of learning is involved to get from the highly limited achievements of the newborn to the understandings of adults.

Skeletal Principles These considerations have led other developmentalists sympathetic to the modular position to formulate alternative ways to conceive of domain-specific development that provide a more explicit role for environmental experience (Carey & Wellman, 1998; Gelman & Williams, 1998). Rochel Gelman and Earl Williams (1998) argue that instead of modules that provide children with "ready-made" cognitive processes, it is more appropriate to think of domain-specific support for development as the result of **skeletal principles,** innate basic cognitive principles that direct mental processes, such as attention and remembering, toward relevant aspects of the problem at hand. The skeletal principles get a cognitive process started and provide some initial direction, but subsequent experience is needed in order to realize the potential in the principles to support sophisticated cognitive processes.

We have already seen evidence that something like basic cognitive principles have been found in early forms during infancy when children respond to stimuli involving the operations of different physical movements, correspondences between number of sounds and number of object movements, and the imitation of human intentions, to name a few. A wide variety of evidence has been collected in recent years to illustrate that children 4 to 5 years old, and sometimes even 3-year-olds, reveal rich knowledge when the content of the tasks presented to them involves questions about core cognitive

skeletal principles Domain-specific principles that get particular cognitive processes started and provide some initial direction, but require subsequent experience in order to realize their potential.

domains for which there are innate skeletal principles. Living creatures provide an example of a core domain about which there has been a good deal of research.

The Domain of Living Creatures Children's ability to think about the difference between living and nonliving entities is a striking example of how skeletal principles underpinning a core domain can guide the acquisition of knowledge. By the time they are 1 year old, infants respond differently to movements of objects in their environment that are self-generated than to movements that are externally caused (Gergely et al., 1995). The distinction between self-generated movement and externally caused movement provides a skeletal principle for acquiring information about living creatures that is essential to reasoning about the world.

For example, Christine Massey and Rochel Gelman (1988) demonstrated the generalizations that 3- to 4-year-olds make on the basis of a distinction between self-initiated and externally initiated movements by showing them photographs of unfamiliar objects and asking if each of the objects could walk uphill "all by itself." The photographs included unfamiliar animate creatures (for example, marmoset, tarantula) and artifacts (statues of animals, objects with wheels like a golf caddy, and complex, rigid objects like a camera).

Most of the 3-year-olds and almost all of the 4-year-olds knew that only the animate objects could move uphill on their own. Even though the animals were not seen in motion and their feet were generally not pictured, the children's comments often focused on feet and legs. For example, in a case where the animal's feet were not visible, the conversation went like this (Gelman, 1990, p. 93):

Child: It can move very slowly . . . it has these little legs.
Adult: Where's the legs?
Child: Underneath.

The animacy-versus-inanimacy distinction that grows out of different forms of movement is accompanied by other knowledge relevant to the domains of living and nonliving things such as the difference between "inside" and "outside." When researchers have asked 3- to 4-year-olds about the insides and outsides of various combinations of animate and inanimate objects, the children attributed different kinds of insides to the animals. They said that animals have bones and blood and "soft stuff," while artifacts such as a camera or natural objects such as a rock have "hard stuff" on the inside, just like they have "hard stuff" on the outside.

Young children also know that animate objects grow and change their appearance, in contrast with artifacts, which may get scuffed up or broken but do not grow. And they know that artifacts do not ingest food. In their study of early concepts of biology, Giyoo Hatano and Keiko Inagaki found that most 5- to 6-year-olds argue that it would be impossible to keep a baby rabbit small. One child exclaimed, "No we cannot keep the baby the same size forever, because he takes food. If he eats, he will become bigger and bigger and be an adult" (Inagaki & Hatano, 1987, p. 1015).

Yet another aspect of animacy understood by preschoolers is that living things have offspring and that the offspring inherit characteristics from their parents; artifacts do not reproduce themselves and cannot transmit their properties. Gelman and Wellman (1991) demonstrated this understanding among 4-year-olds by telling the children about baby animals that were raised by members of another species—for example, kangaroos that were raised by goats. They showed the children a picture of a blob they called a "baby kangaroo" and a picture of a goat farm and asked them what characteristics a baby kangaroo that grew up in such a place would have. Almost all the children were sure that the baby "blob" would grow up with a pouch and be good at hopping like a kangaroo.

To be sure, young children have little detailed knowledge about biological creatures and artifacts—for example, about the real insides of animals or automobiles and how they function. But they certainly have a collection of "working theories" about living and nonliving things that they use to confront experience whether in a zoo or a local toy store. Subsequent cognitive development in the domain of living creatures involves the continual testing of current theories in everyday practice, from which may come the development of a still more powerful theory.

The same story can be told, as we have seen, for a core theory of physics, of persons, and so on. When the content of the problems children are presented with involves core domains, an island of competence is likely to appear. However, as we noted in Chapter 6, when children have to deal with the cultural domain, they have a lot of learning yet to do.

scripts Event schemas that specify who participates in an event, what social roles they play, what objects they are to use during the event, and the sequence of actions that make up the event.

CULTURE AND MENTAL DEVELOPMENT IN EARLY CHILDHOOD

There are several obvious ways in which the cultural-context approach contributes to the discussion of the unevenness of cognitive development during early childhood. As we noted in Chapter 1 (p. 37), the cultural-context approach focuses on the ways that biological, social, and physical-ecological influences on development are brought together and shaped by the particular cultural contexts of human activity. The cultural contexts that children inhabit can be thought of as developmental niches, places where the physical and social context in which children live, the child-rearing and educational experience that are organized for the children, and the culturally organized beliefs and practices of adults interact with the child's genetic endowment, producing specific opportunities for, and limitations on, the child's development (Super & Harkness, 1986).

In terms of mental development, developmental niches are the contexts in which society makes available essential cultural resources for the development of thought and action. Among the most important of those cultural resources is language.

The Mental Representation of Contexts

A major task of all theories of cognitive development is to explain how children convert the world into mental structures during the course of their development. As we have seen, Piaget held that in the course of their activity, children construct schemas, organized patterns of individual knowledge that represent objects and their interrelationships. These schemas are conceived of as internal mental structures that determine the way the child understands and acts; they develop in a logical progression.

Schemas are also important in cultural-context explanations of development, but here they are conceived of somewhat differently. Katherine Nelson (1981, 1996) suggests that as a result of their participation in routine, culturally organized events, children acquire generalized event representations, or **scripts.** Scripts are schemas that specify who participates in an event, what social roles they play, what objects they are to use during the event, and the sequence of actions that make up the event. Scripts exist both as external, cultural artifacts—the words, the customary procedures, the customs and routines that punctuate daily experience—and as internal representations of those artifacts. Scripts are, in both their internal and external aspects, tools of thought.

Initially, scripts are a good deal more external than internal. Anyone who has made the attempt knows that "taking a bath" is something an adult does *to* a 2-month-old infant. An adult fills a sink or appropriate basin with warm water, lays out a towel, a clean diaper, and clothing, then slips the infant into the water, while holding the infant tightly to keep its head above water. The

"Taking a bath" as done to an infant.

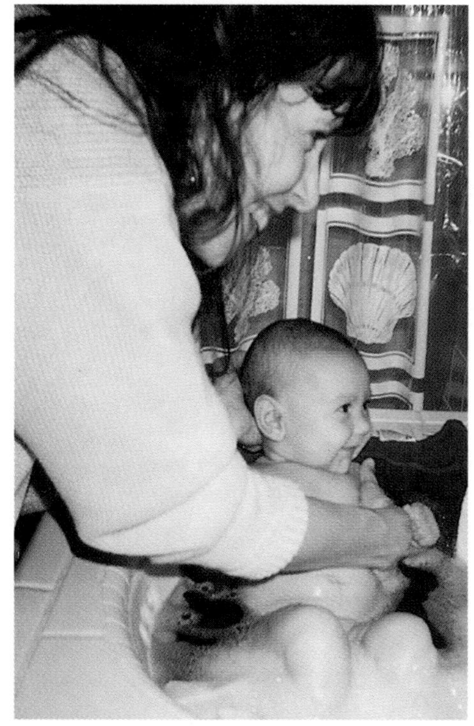

infant's contribution consists of squirming around. Gradually, however, as they become stronger and more familiar with the script of bath taking (and their caregivers perfect their role as bath givers), babies acquire more competence in parts of the activity and assume a greater role in the process.

By the age of 2 years, most children have "taken" many baths. Each time, roughly the same sequence is followed, the same kinds of objects are used, the same cast of characters participates, and the same kinds of talk accompany the necessary actions. Water is poured into a tub, clothes are taken off, the child gets into the water, soap is applied and rinsed off, the child gets out of the water, dries off, and dresses. There may be variations—a visiting friend may take a bath with the child or the child may be allowed to play with her water toys after washing—but the basic sequence has a clear pattern to it.

During the preschool period, adults still play the important role of "bath giver" in the scripted activity called "taking a bath." Adults initiate children's baths, scrub their ears, wash their hair, or help them dry off. Not until adulthood will the child be responsible for the entire event, including scouring the tub and worrying about clean towels, hot water, and the money to pay for them.

Nelson points out that, as in the "taking a bath" script, children grow up inside other people's scripts. As a consequence, human beings rarely, if ever, experience the natural environment "raw." Rather, they experience the world, including such simple activities as taking a bath and eating a meal, in a way that has been prepared (cooked up!) according to the scripts prescribed by their culture.

Nelson and her colleagues have studied the growth of scripted knowledge by interviewing children and by recording the conversations of children playing together. When Nelson asked children to tell her about "going to a restaurant," for example, she obtained reports like the following:

> *Boy aged 3 years, 1 month:* "Well, you eat and then go somewhere."
> *Girl aged 4 years, 10 months:* "Okay. Now, first we go to restaurants at nighttime and we, um, we, and we go and wait for a while, and then the waiter comes and gives us the little stuff with the dinners on it, and then we wait for a little bit, a half an hour or a few minutes or something, and, um, then our pizza comes or anything, and um, [interruption]. . . . [The adult says, "So then the food comes."] Then we eat it, and um, then when we're finished eating the salad that we order we get to eat our pizza when it's done, because we get the salad before the pizza's ready. So then when we're finished with all the pizza and all our salad, we just leave." (Nelson, 1981, p. 103)

Participation in scripted activities, such as Caterina's birthday party in Tuscany, Italy, provide a context within which children can develop more complex understandings of their culture's basic concepts and ways of doing things.

Even these simple reports demonstrate that scripts represent generalized knowledge. For one thing, the children are describing general content: they are clearly referring to more than a single, unique meal. The 3-year-old uses the generalized form "You eat" rather than a specific reference to a particular time when he ate. The little girl's introduction ("First we go to restaurants at nighttime") indicates that she, too, is speaking of restaurant visits in general.

Besides containing general content, the scripts are organized into a general structure, similar to that of adult scripts. Even very young children know that the events involved in "eating at a restaurant" do not take place haphazardly. Instead they describe a sequence: "First we do this, then we do that." Children evidently abstract the content of a script and its structure from many events and then use that knowledge to organize their behavior.

The Functions of Scripts

Scripts are guides to action. They are mental representations that children and adults use to figure out what is likely to happen next in familiar circumstances. Until children have acquired a large repertoire of scripted knowledge, they must use a lot of mental effort to construct scripts as they participate in unfamiliar events. When they lack scripted knowledge, they must pay attention to the details of each new activity. As a consequence, they may be less likely to distinguish between the essential and the superficial features of a novel context. The little girl interviewed by Nelson, for example, seemed to think that eating pizza is a basic part of the "going to a restaurant" script, whereas paying for the meal was entirely absent. However, because the little girl has grasped a small part of the restaurant script, she will be free to attend to new aspects of the setting the next time she encounters it. Over time, she will gain a deeper understanding of the events she participates in and the contexts of which they are a part.

A second function of scripts is to allow people within a given social group to coordinate their actions. This function of scripts becomes possible because, according to the cultural-contextualist perspective, script knowledge is knowledge generally held in common, including its embodiment in a common language. "Without shared scripts," Nelson says, "every social act would need to be negotiated afresh." In this sense, "the acquisition of scripts is central to the acquisition of culture" (Nelson, 1981, pp. 109, 110). When children go to the average restaurant in the United States, they learn that first you ask the host or hostess for a table and are assigned a seat. A somewhat different script applies to fast-food restaurants. Discoordination can result if the script is violated (for example, if the child were to enter a restaurant and to sit down at a table where an elderly stranger was midway through a meal).

A third function of scripts is to provide a means by which abstract concepts that apply to many kinds of events can be acquired and organized. When, for example, children acquire scripts for playing with blocks, playing in the sandbox, and playing house, they are accumulating specific examples of play that they can then subsume in a general category (Lucariello & Rifkin, 1986). (See Box 9.2.)

Cultural Context and the Unevenness of Development

Once children leave the confines of their cribs and their caregivers' arms, they begin all at once to experience a great variety of contexts that compel them to acquire a variety of new scripts, even as they refine their knowledge of the scripts with which they are already familiar. Thus it is natural, according to the cultural-context approach, that development during early childhood should appear to be so uneven. The content and structure of the new events in which young children participate will depend crucially on the contexts provided by their culture and on the roles they are expected to play within those contexts. In familiar contexts, where they know the expected sequence of actions and can properly interpret the requirements of the situation, young children are most likely to behave in a logical way and adhere to adult stan-

The meaning of an activity such as weaving and the development of the skills needed to do it vary markedly from one culture to another.

dards of thought. But when the contexts are unfamiliar, they may apply inappropriate scripts and resort to magical or illogical thinking.

Overall, cultures influence the unevenness of children's development in several basic ways (Laboratory of Comparative Human Cognition, 1983; Rogoff, 1998, 2000; Super & Harkness, 1997):

1. *By arranging the occurrence and nonoccurrence of specific activities:* One cannot learn about something without observing or hearing about it. A 4-year-old growing up among the !Kung of the Kalahari Desert is unlikely to learn about taking baths in bathtubs or pouring water from one glass to another. Children growing up in Seattle or Singapore are unlikely to be skilled at tracking animals or finding water-bearing roots in a desert.
2. *By determining the frequency of basic activities:* Dancing is an activity found in all societies, but all societies do not focus equally on dancing. Owing to the importance placed on traditional dancing in Balinese culture, many children growing up in Bali become skilled dancers by the age of 4 (McPhee, 1970), while Norwegian children are more likely to become good skiers and skaters. Likewise, children growing up in a Mexican village famous for its pottery may become skilled potters, whereas children living in a nearby town known for its weaving are more likely to become skilled weavers who have little exposure to pottery making (Price-Williams et al., 1969). Insofar as practice makes perfect, the greater the frequency of practice, the higher the level of performance.
3. *By how they relate different activities:* If molding clay is associated with making pottery, it is experienced in the company of a whole host of related activities: digging from a quarry, firing clay, glazing clay, selling the products. Molding clay as part of a nursery school curriculum will be associated with an entirely different pattern of experience and knowledge.
4. *By regulating the child's role in the activity:* Children enter most activities as novices who bear little responsibility for the outcome. They depend on others as guides to what is important to master.

The social and cultural environment also provides general source of support for children by selecting and shaping their activities. Barbara Rogoff

(1990, 2000), a prominent cultural-context theorist, calls the overall process by which adults select and shape young children's actions in everyday activities **guided participation.** Through guided participation, children receive help in adapting their understanding to new situations, in structuring their problem-solving attempts, and eventually in achieving mastery. One form of such collaborative interaction occurs when an adult or more competent peer provides support for a child's participation, offering suggestions on how to manage the task or taking over parts of the task when necessary, allowing the child to stretch his or her abilities beyond what they would be if the child were performing the task alone. This kind of interaction is an example of what Vygotsky referred to as a zone of proximal development (see Chapter 5, p. 207).

guided participation The ways that adults and children collaborate in routine problem-solving activities so that children receive help in adapting their understanding to new situations, in structuring their problem-solving attempts, and eventually in achieving mastery.

sociodramatic play Make-believe play in which two or more participants enact a variety of social roles.

Sometimes the form of guidance represented by a zone of proximal development is deliberate, but often such supportive interactions are carried out implicitly and without a deliberate effort to instruct. Typically, the process of guided discovery and creation, or zones of proximal development, are deeply embedded in the casual interactions that are part of everyday activities. An interaction between Rogoff and her 3½-year-old daughter illustrates the implicit and two-sided nature of the process of guided participation.

> I was getting ready to leave the house, and I noticed that a run had started in the foot of my stocking. My daughter volunteered to help sew the run, but I was in a hurry and tried to avoid her involvement by explaining that I did not want the needle to jab my foot. I began to sew, but could hardly see where I was sewing because my daughter's head was in the way, peering at the sewing. Soon she suggested that I could put the needle into the stocking and she would pull it through, thus avoiding sticking my foot. I agreed, and we followed this division of labor for a number of stitches. (Rogoff, 1990, p. 109)

Another common form of casual interaction that provides the guidance and support of a zone of proximal development is (see Box 9.2) **sociodramatic play,** make-believe play in which two or more participants enact a variety of social roles.

It is a general expectation of cultural-context approaches that interactions which have this kind of supportive structure will be especially productive of developmental change and high levels of performance.

Assessing the Cultural-Context Explanation

In the Piagetian view of development, cognitive structures undergo generalized transformations as children mature and gain experience. In the cultural-context view, by contrast, children's developing abilities are seen as tied to the content and structure of the activities in which they participate. The extent to which new and more sophisticated ways of thinking and acting become general across contexts depends crucially on the extent to which those psychological processes are useful in other settings as well (Laboratory of Comparative Human Cognition, 1983). In fact, according to cultural-context theorists, magical thinking, failure to take another's perspective, and confusion of appearance and reality don't actually disappear following early childhood; they are also seen in older children and adults (Subbotski, 1991). But older children and adults display these traits more rarely, in specialized contexts that are outside the experiences they have accumulated in everyday reality.

While not discounting the possibility of specific, module-like brain processes, a cultural-context view of development is more compatible with the idea that children inherit skeletal principles in broadly defined domains that are "fleshed out" through interactions in cultural contexts to produce more developed cognitive abilities. Just as Bruner proposed that a LASS must accompany Chomsky's LAD in order to produce language, so cultural-context theories propose that domain-specific skeletal principles require appropriate, culturally organized environments in order for them to emerge and develop.

BOX 9.2

SOCIODRAMATIC PLAY

Play occupies a conspicuous role in young children's cognitive development, as well as their physical and social development. At the age of 2, children are able to pretend that a matchbox is a car that can zoom around the sandbox, or that a block is an iron. Such play, however, is largely solitary in the sense that even when several young children are in a room together, their play is unlikely to be interconnected (Bretherton, 1984). In early childhood, pretend play becomes more social and more complex (Göncü & Kessel, 1988). Instead of solitary pretending, children begin to engage in *sociodramatic play*—make-believe play in which two or more participants enact a variety of related social roles. Sociodramatic play requires a shared understanding of what the play situation involves, which often must be negotiated as part of the play.

In the United States and many European countries, early childhood can be considered the "high season of imaginative play" (Singer & Singer, 1990). Children are provided with a wide variety of toys, and symbolic play is encouraged as an important contributor to development. This kind of play is illustrated by the following scene involving several children in preschool. As we enter the scene, the girls in the group have agreed upon the roles they will play: mother, sister, baby, and maid.

> *Karen:* I'm hungry. Wa-a-ah!
> *Charlotte:* Lie down, baby.
> *Karen:* I'm a baby that sits up.
> *Charlotte:* First you lie down and sister covers you and then I make your cereal and then you sit up.
> *Karen:* Okay.
> *Karen: (to Teddy, who has been observing)* You can be the father.
> *Charlotte:* Are you the father?
> *Teddy:* Yes.
> *Charlotte:* Put on a red tie.
> *Janie: (in the "maid's" falsetto voice)* I'll get it for you, honey. Now don't that baby look pretty? This is your daddy, baby.
>
> (Adapted from Paley, 1984, p. 1)

This transcript illustrates several features of young American children's sociodramatic play. The children are enacting social roles and using scripts that they have encountered numerous times in their daily lives, on television, or in stories. Babies make stereotypic baby noises, maids get things for people, and fathers wear ties. At the same time that they are playing their roles in the pretend world, the children are also outside it, giving stage directions to one another and commenting on the action. The "baby" who sits up has to be talked into lying down, and the boy is told what role he can play.

Although children draw upon familiar scenes in their sociodramatic play, the scripts and social phenomena they act out are far from precise imitations. As Catherine Garvey notes, when a boy engaged in sociodramatic play walks into the house and announces, "Okay, I'm all through with work, honey. I brought home a thousand dollars," he has probably never heard that said before. Rather, he has abstracted certain behaviors characteristic of husbands in his society and embellished them with fantasy (Garvey, 1990).

For many decades developmentalists have sought to determine if sociodramatic play is of any special significance to later cognitive development (Sutton-Smith, 1997). Jean Piaget and Lev Vygotsky have been especially influential in these investigations. Piaget minimized the significance of play for cognitive development. In his view, the special quality of play during the preoperational period derives directly from the characteristics of egocentrism. As he phrased it, "For egocentric thought, the supreme law is play" (Piaget, 1928, p. 401). He believed that children may consolidate schemas for action they have already acquired, but the egocentric nature of play prevents new levels of development from occurring. Rather, the nature of play depends on the nature of the child's thought processes. He argued that once they achieve the stage of concrete operations and their egocentrism abates, sociodramatic play decreases as children become interested in games with rules and try to distance themselves from that "little kids' stuff."

Unlike Piaget, Lev Vygotsky (1978) believed that pretend play provides children with a *zone of proximal development* that allows them to think and act in more complex ways than is likely if they act on their own outside of a play context. In real life, children depend on adults to help them by providing the rules and by filling in for them in little ways. Vygotsky believed that the freedom to negotiate reality that is essential to games of "let's pretend" provides children with analogous support. As a consequence, wrote Vygotsky, "In play a child is always above his average age, above his daily behavior; in play it is as though he were a head taller than himself" (p. 102).

M. G. Dias and Paul Harris (1988, 1990) provided interesting support for Vygotsky's idea that play creates a zone of proximal development in a study of the way pretending influences young children's ability to reason deductively. Dias and Harris presented 4- to 6-year-old children with a series of logical problems in which they had to reason from two premises to reach a conclusion. Most children do not solve this kind of problem until they are considerably older. In fact, Piaget believed that such reasoning does not emerge until adolescence.

The problems presented by Dias and Harris were of the following kind:

> All fishes live in trees.
>
> Tot is a fish.
>
> Does Tot live in the water?

These problems were presented to half of the children in a matter-of-fact tone of voice. With the other half of the children the experimenter started off by saying, "Let's pretend that I am from another planet," and went on to present the problem in the sort of dramatic voice that is ordinarily used in storytelling.

Sociodramatic play—"let's pretend"—is a leading activity for children from the ages of $2\frac{1}{2}$ to 6.

The children's ability to solve these reasoning problems varied greatly from one presentation condition to the other. The children who were instructed in a matter-of-fact tone had difficulty reasoning according to the premise of the problem. They said, for example, that Tot the fish lives in the water and justified their answers by asserting their knowledge of where fish live. In comparison, the children who participated in the "let's pretend" version of the problem were much more successful, and the way they justified their answers provided clear evidence that they had entered into the hypothetical nature of the tasks. Typical justifications for their correct answers were such statements as "I said Tot lives in a tree because we're pretending that fishes live in trees."

Although pretend play can be found in every society, there are wide cultural variations in when, where, and how often such play occurs, who the participants are, and the role that adults attribute to their children's play activities (Göncü, 1999). In some societies, adults arrange for children to engage in a great deal of pretend play with others about their own age (play occupies a major role in many European preschools, for example). In other societies, play occupies a much less conspicuous role in young children's everyday activities because by the age of 3 to 4, young children are expected to make economic contributions to the family (Gaskins, 1999). Even in industrial societies where young children attend preschools as preparation for formal schooling, the content of play, play partners, and the role of adults in organizing play varies widely (Farver, 1999; Göncü et al., 1999; Roopnarine et al., 1998).

Joanne Farver observed a number of differences in the play of two groups of preschool children in Los Angeles, one of European background, the other made up of Korean-American children whose parents had emigrated to the United States in recent years (Farver, 1999). The European-American children engaged in significantly more play involving fantastic characters and themes of danger. The Korean-American children's sociodramatic play focused primarily on family roles and everyday activities. Farver traced these differences to a number of sources, one of which was adult beliefs. The Korean-American adults attributed less value to pretend play than did European-American adults. The preschools they organized were much more school-like, with children sitting at desks and practicing academic skills they would need later. Another factor shaping the level of pretend play was the nature of the play opportunities the children were provided. Differences in the play of Korean-American and European-American children were most prominent in an unstructured play setting. However, when the children were given a complex toy to play with (a toy castle with toy kings, princesses, horses, and other play objects that could be used in a game), differences between the two groups disappeared.

Whatever society they live in, as children grow older, sociodramatic play occupies less and less of their time. However, this does not mean that pretending disappears with age. Rather, its forms change. Dorothy and Jerome Singer (1990) believe that once middle childhood is reached, pretend play "goes underground" because other forms of play are considered socially more acceptable. Douglas Hofstader argues that pretend play never disappears because throughout their lives people constantly create mental variants on the situations they face:

> [The manufacture of "as-if" worlds] happens so casually, so naturally, that we hardly notice what we are doing. We select from our fantasy a world which is close, in some internal mental sense, to the real world. We compare what is real with what we perceive as almost real. In so doing what we gain is some intangible kind of perspective on reality. (1979, p. 643)

At present there are no firm reasons for claiming that sociodramatic play is essential to normal development. Whether they grow up in a society that devalues pretend play and emphasizes children's work responsibilities or one that goes to great lengths to provide young children with the opportunity to engage in pretend play, children generally grow up to be competent members of their societies.

THE DEVELOPMENT OF DRAWING: APPLYING THE THEORETICAL PERSPECTIVES

Each of the current theories of early childhood cognition provides a distinctive perspective from which to view development. The relative strengths and weaknesses of alternative views can best be viewed when the various approaches attempt to explain the same phenomenon. Picture drawing—an activity with many cognitive components—is a case in point, and every theoretical viewpoint has something to say about it. In accord with Piaget's constructivist approach, children's drawing seems to go through a regular series of stages. In accord with an information-processing approach, changes in drawing can in some cases be tied closely to the ability to hold several aspects of an object in mind at one time. In accord with the modularity approach, children whose linguistic, mental, or social development is severely retarded may nonetheless draw at a high level of competence. And in accord with the cultural-context approach, the development of drawing ability depends on the opportunities the child is given to engage in that activity and the ways such opportunities are structured by adults.

FIGURE 9.9
Drawing of the human figure develops through a sequence of steps. At first a child draws a big circle that stands for a whole person. The child's global representation of a person soon evolves into a circle or an ellipse with the face in the upper part and two protruding lines underneath (a "tadpole figure"). Gradually the circle comes to represent only the head, and the body descends between the two vertical lines. Some months later; the child adds a second circle to represent the body, with another pair of lines extending from it as arms. (From Goodnow, 1977.)

CONSTRUCTING THE STAGES OF DRAWING

In every culture where children are given an opportunity to draw from an early age, their drawings appear to pass through the same sequence of stages (Gardner, 1980; Golomb, 1974; Lange-Küttner & Thomas, 1995). In the beginning they scribble. Children are not "making pictures" when they scribble. What seems to matter to them is not the look of the product but the joy of moving their hands and the trail of their movements to which the scribbling bears witness.

Children take a giant step beyond scribbling around the age of 3, when they begin to recognize that the marks and lines they make can represent things in the world. This realization is reflected early on when children begin to draw circles and ellipses that are cleared of the whorls and lines that filled their scribbles earlier. The circular line encloses an inside area that seems more solid to them than the field it is on, indicating that the drawing is clearly representing something. These initial drawings develop along two dimensions: they begin to include more details in the objects they depict and they include spatial relationships—both relationships between the depicted objects and between those objects and the child who is doing the drawing.

More detailed children's drawings are likely to involve the inclusion of more and more stereotyped elements. A house is a pentagon; the sun is a circle with lines extending from its surface; a flower is a circle surrounded by ellipses; humans and animals appear as tadpole figures (see Figure 9.9).

Three- and four-year-old children appear to represent what they *know* about the objects in their pictures and not what they see with their own eyes. If shown a cup at eye level so that its handle cannot be seen, children will nevertheless draw the cup with a handle, placing it somewhere to the side, because they know that cups have handles (see Figure 9.10). Between the ages of 6 and 11 to 12 years of age, children increasingly draw what they actually see of an object. At the same time, their drawings begin to represent the perspective from which the object is seen. Eventually children begin to combine representations of people and things to make scenes depicting a variety of experiences (see Figure 9.11).

FIGURE 9.10
A 6-year-old's drawing of a cup. Note that the handle is included although the child was shown the cup from a perspective where the handle was not visible.

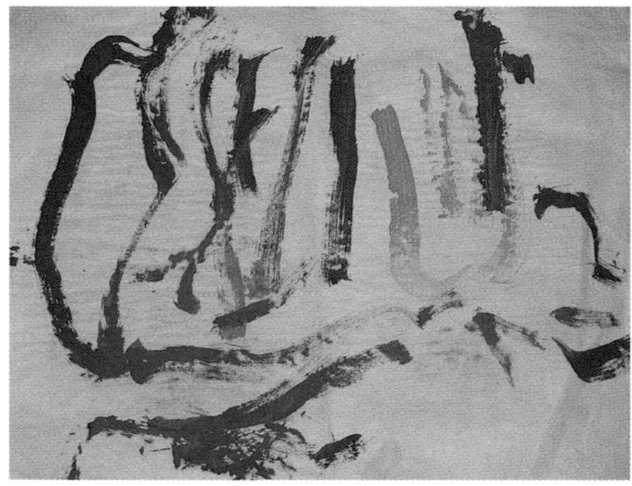

(a)

(b)

(c)

(d)

(e)

FIGURE 9.11
A sequence of drawings by an American child. (a) At 2½ years, Carrie was drawing lines of different colors; (b) at 3½ years, she began to draw global representations of a person; (c) at 5 years, she added a body and legs to the creatures she drew, and she set her main figure in a scene. (d) Motion, rhythm, and greater realism are evident in the drawings she produced at 7½ years. (e) At 12 years, she was able to draw a cartoon of a realistic scene. (Courtesy of Carrie Hogan.)

Many of these stages, observed in the drawings of North American and European children, can be found in all societies in which drawing is a cultural practice. The universals in the development of artistic representation are the kind of phenomena that are central to Piaget's theory of cognitive development.

AN INFORMATION-PROCESSING ACCOUNT OF DRAWING

From an information-processing perspective, the increasing sophistication of children's drawings arises from a combination of improved fine motor skills, increased knowledge of the rules and conventions of drawing, and increased ability to keep in mind several aspects of the drawing task (Willats, 1995). Figure 9.12 shows the developmental sequence that children go through in learning to draw a schematic house in three dimensions. The youngest children collapse three dimensions into two. Then the third dimension is partially added, but it is partially collapsed into one of the other two, creating drawings that appear somehow illogical. Finally, children acquire ways to represent the third dimension (Willats, 1987). From an information-processing perspective, this sequence follows directly from children's growing knowledge of drawing rules and their ability to remember the need to represent all three spatial coordinates in their drawings.

DRAWING AS A MENTAL MODULE

Although the development of children's ability to draw normally passes through the series of stages we have just described, some important exceptions suggest that drawing is a distinctive cognitive domain and that drawing ability may be modular in some conditions. A compelling example is provided by Nadia, a child suffering from autism, a condition that interferes with normal social and cognitive development (Selfe, 1983). At first Nadia seemed to develop normally, but by the age of 3 she had forgotten the few words she had learned, her behavior was lethargic, and she did not engage in pretend play. At the age of 3½, Nadia began to display unusual artistic ability. Without any apparent practice, she began to incorporate perspective and other artistic techniques when she copied pictures, an ability that usually is acquired only after years of experience in drawing (Figure 9.13). Nadia's dexterity when she was drawing was quite remarkable, yet in everyday activities her hand movements were ordinarily uncoordinated. Extensive testing showed that Nadia had an extraordinary ability to form and remember visual images. She would often study a drawing for weeks before producing a version from memory. It seemed as if she was building up a mental image so that at some later time her "mind's eye" could guide her hand in re-creating the image on paper. Howard Gardner (1980), who has conducted research on the cognitive basis of art, uses terms reminiscent of Chomsky's and of Fodor's idea of mental modules in his discussion of Nadia's case:

> Nadia may have been operating with a high-powered mental computational device—one seldom, if ever, exploited by others but perhaps available to at least a sample of the human species. (pp. 186–187)

Nadia's unusual development is not unique. Researchers have identified a number of children whose language ability and general mental functioning are quite low but whose ability to create graphic images is exceptionally high (Sacks, 1995). These cases fit nicely with the idea that mental modules, such as language and perception, can develop in relative isolation from one another.

Evidence from less extreme cases also suggests that passing through the ordinary sequence of stages is not necessary to mastery. Gardner (1980) re-

FIGURE 9.12

The developmental sequence for drawing of an object in three dimensions. Drawing (a) leaves out the third dimension. Drawings (b) and (c) introduce the third dimension in partially correct ways. Drawings (d) and (e) represent the full three dimensions according to two conventions. (Adapted from Willats, 1987.)

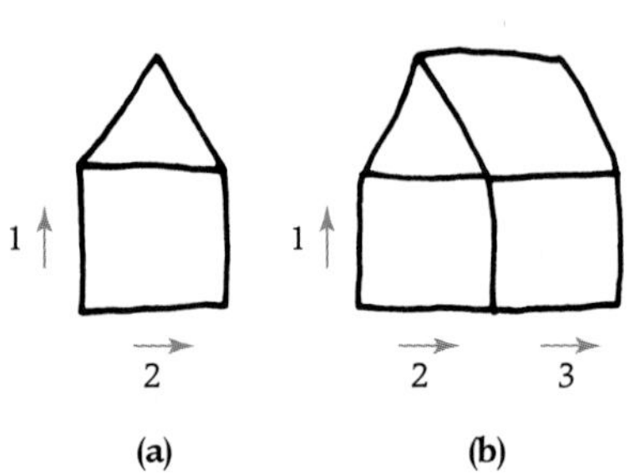

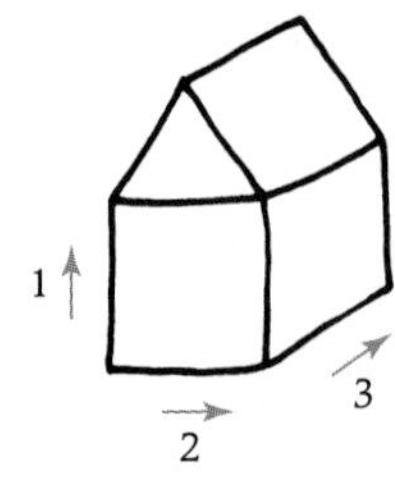

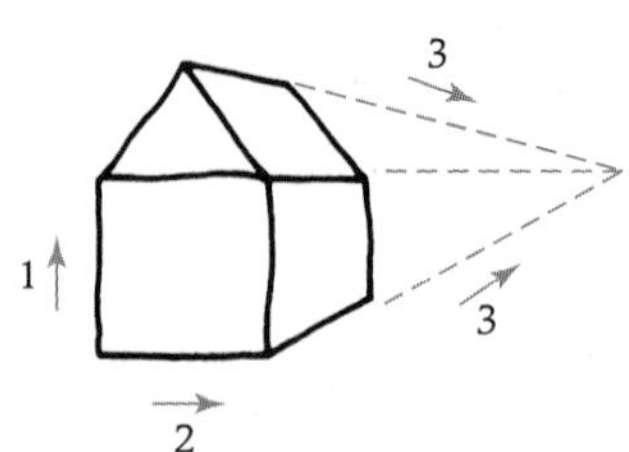

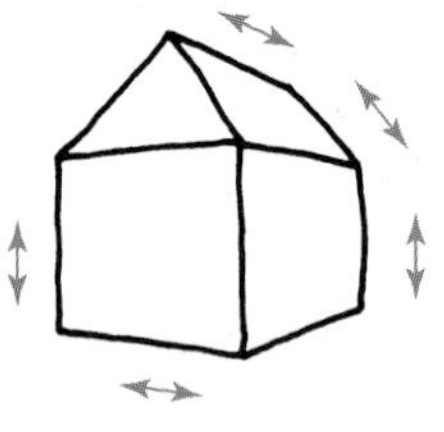

ports that children deprived of the opportunity to draw during early childhood may skip the initial stages of drawing altogether when they finally do get an opportunity to draw. If true, this finding would run counter to the Piagetian position that stages follow each other in an invariant sequence.

A CULTURAL-CONTEXT ACCOUNT OF THE DEVELOPMENT OF DRAWING

A cultural-context view of the development of drawing focuses on the culturally organized nature of the processes that transform children's potential for drawing into the actual execution of specific kinds of meaningful representations.

An important indicator of the culturally organized nature of children's drawing is found in the ways adults talk to children about what they are doing. For example, when an adult asks a young child, "What are you drawing?" the very form of the question assumes that there is something to be drawn and that the child is attempting to represent it. In response to the question, children often go along with the way the adult scripted the interaction by making up after-the-fact stories about what they have drawn, stories that are not tied to anything that an adult can perceive on the paper. After children have gained some experience, however, their explanations of their drawings become connected to the discovery that the marks they have made resemble an actual object in the world—but this discovery is made only after the drawing is completed (Golomb, 1974).

The following dialogue between 3-year-olds Roslyn and Don, recorded in a U.S. preschool, illustrates the rudimentary nature of young children's understanding of drawing, as well as some of the ways those understandings change (adapted from Gearhart & Newman, 1980, p. 172):

> *Roslyn:* I got brown. *(Holds up her crayon)*
> *Don:* I got another color. *(Draws short lines back and forth)*
> *Roslyn:* I made a brown circle. *(Illustrates with counterclockwise gesture, holding crayon over the paper)*
> *Don:* I got another color.
> *Roslyn:* I, I, I made a big brown circ-er square. *(Repeats the illustrative gesture)*
> *Don: (Makes a counterclockwise form on his paper)* Look what I'm making, Roslyn.
> *Roslyn:* Huh! Ehh! *(Looks)*
> *Don:* I, I went round like this. *(Illustrates with larger counterclockwise movements)*
> *Roslyn:* Well. . . . Now watch what I am making, I'm making mountains. *(Immediately draws a series of short vertical lines)*

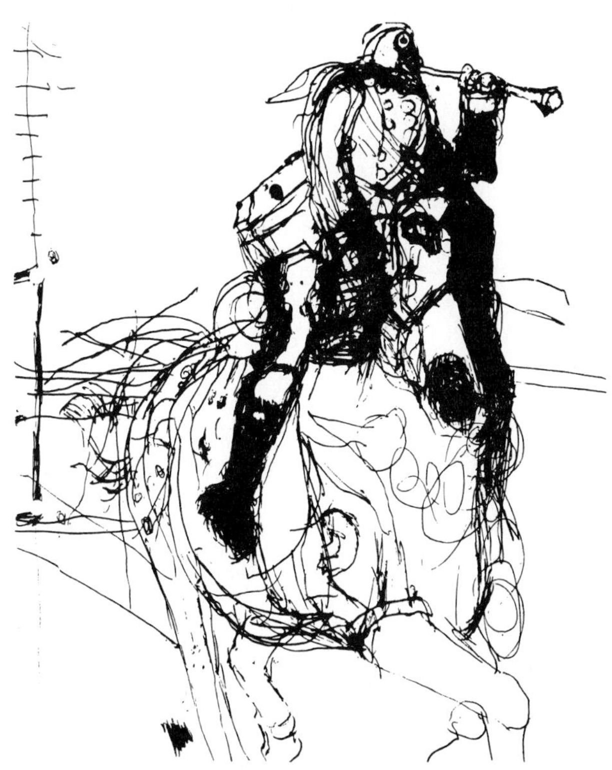

FIGURE 9.13
Nadia, an autistic preschooler with only minimal exposure to models, displayed an uncanny ability to capture form and movement in her drawings. This drawing is her copy of a picture of a horse.

These children's words and actions clearly indicate that neither child has a fixed, individual drawing in mind. All their talk refers either to something they have just done ("I made a brown circle") or to something they are doing ("I'm making"). There is little talk about plans for their pictures. Each child imitates elements introduced by the other, with no overall plan of how that element might fit into the whole.

Even these children's drawings have progressed beyond scribbling, however. As they show each other crayons and figures, swapping comments and ideas, they are talking as if the drawings represented things (circles, squares, mountains) even if the correspondence is by no means clear to outsiders.

The way the teacher arranged for a picture to be called "finished" was also important in helping the children to discover what it means to draw a

Young children learn to represent reality in their drawings and paintings in part because of the way adults interpret their pictures after they have been completed.

picture. Before writing the child's name on the picture and pinning it up on the board, she asked open-ended questions about what the child had been drawing, again behaving as if the child had been drawing a particular thing.

> *Teacher:* Jeff? [Come] tell me about your picture. *(Jeffrey comes and looks at his drawing)*
> *Jeffrey:* Uh, it has two mountains on orange, two orange circles.
> *Teacher:* Two orange circles *(as she writes his name on the drawing).*
>
> (Adapted from Gearhart & Newman, 1980, p. 182)

In this dialogue the teacher selectively accepts the part of the child's account (two orange circles) that accords with her notion of "thingness." The scribbled "mountains" are ignored. As a consequence, Jeffrey learns something about which sort of marks count as a drawing of mountains or circles in the eyes of adults and which do not.

The existence of scripted activities for drawing does not contradict the possibility that there is a mental module for drawing or the idea that drawing goes through stages of increasing complexity. Rather, it suggests that the ways in which adults organize instruction provide essential opportunities for modular potential to be triggered and stages constructed. Over the course of a year or two, the teacher's assumptions become second nature to the children. They learn not only the possibility of drawing pictures of "things" but a good many techniques for making those things take shape on the paper. Most important, they come to understand and share the teacher's concept of what "drawing a picture" means. This common understanding then becomes the basis for further instruction.

RECONCILING ALTERNATIVE PERSPECTIVES

Scholarly explanations of the phenomena of young children's thought are reminiscent of the parable of the blind men feeling an elephant: the man who feels the trunk believes that the creature is a snake; the man who feels the leg believes that the creature is a tree; and the man who feels the tail is

The development of drawing depends on the traditions of the culture into which the child is born. This drawing was done by a 7-year-old Chilean child.

certain that he has hold of a rope. Lacking a coordinated understanding, each man mistakes his part for the whole, which is distinctively different from the parts. It seems that the uneveness of young children's thinking is matched by the uneveness with which their thought is explained by developmentalists!

Nevertheless, the past decade has witnessed a number of efforts to arrive at a synthesis that incorporates the major concerns of each of the competing theoretical positions. An increasing number of developmentalists, it seems, believe that these competing approaches are most usefully viewed as complementary to each other. We have seen several partial moves in the direction of synthesis in this chapter. Information-processing approaches are combined with Piagetian stage theory. Domain specificity is widely accepted as a real phenomenon, although arguments persist about just how the domains should be identified and whether their source is in biology (as modules or skeletal constraints) or in culture (as activities and cultural contexts). At present there are even a number of promising efforts to provide a comprehensive explanatory framework in which all of the competing approaches are brought into a single, overarching framework (Case & Okamoto, 1995; Feldman, 1994; Fischer & Biddel, 1998; Gelman & Williams, 1998; Greenfield, 1997; Siegler, 1996). However, agreement on precisely how the various factors interact with each other to produce cognitive development remains as elusive for mature scientists as agreement among preschoolers on precisely what effect boiling has on the size and weight of stones!

We also need to keep in mind that a child's total psychological development encompasses far more than the restricted abilities described here. Still to be explored are the ways young children's thought processes influence how they think about themselves and behave as members of their social worlds and the ways they are influenced by the activity settings and cultural contexts they inhabit. With that infomation in hand, we will be in a better position to think about early childhood as a whole and the kinds of changes that await the onset of middle childhood.

SUMMARY

Young children's thought processes are characterized by great unevenness; islands of competence exist in a sea of uncertainty and naiveté.

PIAGET'S ACCOUNT OF MENTAL DEVELOPMENT IN EARLY CHILDHOOD

- Piaget's explanation of thought during early childhood stresses its one-sided nature: the inability to think simultaneously about two aspects of a problem in relation to each other causes children to "center" on the most salient feature of the problem.
- Cognitive limitations that Piaget associated with egocentric thought include the inability to take the perspective of another person, to understand other people's thought processes, to distinguish appearance from reality, and to reason about cause and effect.

THE STUDY OF YOUNG CHILDREN'S THINKING AFTER PIAGET

- Many believe that the unevenness of children's thought is greater than Piaget realized, calling into question his explanation of the preoperational stage. Some developmental psychologists want to refine his theory, while others have suggested alternatives.
- Neo-Piagetian explanations of young children's thought retain Piaget's theory of stages but account for uneven development by
    1. Criticizing evidence used to characterize the extreme unevenness of development
    2. Proposing that stages occur within specific domains of knowledge, each with its own conceptual structure, rather than generally
- According to the information-processing view, cognitive development is a process of expanding the young child's limited attentional, memory, and problem-solving capacities. The unevenness of young children's thought is explained by differences in children's familiarity with specific task settings and in the demands made by the various settings.
- Biologically oriented theories emphasize the innate organization of the brain in the development of young children's thought. According to some, the brain is organized into mental modules that are domain-specific, innately structured, and relatively isolated from one another. The mental capacities of prodigies (children who excel in a single domain at an early age) and of some autistic children support this hypothesis. According to others, innate organization of the brain is restricted to skeletal principles that must be fleshed out by experience. From this perspective, both differential development of different brain structures and differential experience account for the uneveness of young children's cognitive developement.
- In the cultural-context view, contexts give coherence to otherwise isolated sources of development in everyday interactions with other people.
- Contexts are represented mentally in the form of scripts—conceptual structures that are guides to action, a means of coordination between people, and a framework in which abstract concepts applicable across contexts are formed.
- Culture mediates society's influence on mental development by arranging for the occurrence and frequency of specific contexts and associated

scripts children participate in, by organizing how different activities relate to each other, and by regulating the child's role in the activity.

THE DEVELOPMENT OF DRAWING: APPLYING THE THEORETICAL PERSPECTIVES

- Normally a child's ability to draw passes through a series of stages.
- In many cases, these stages are domain-specific in ways that fit with neo-Piagetian and modularity theories.
- As one stage follows another, the child's drawings represent more and more aspects of the objects drawn, in line with an information-processing approach.
- Learning to draw is culturally organized in ways that fit with cultural-context theories. The ways adults interpret the children's effort is central to this process.

RECONCILING ALTERNATIVE PERSPECTIVES

- The various theories of early childhood development are best treated as complementary perspectives, rather than as competing explanations.

KEY TERMS

central conceptual structure, p. 350
egocentrism, p. 339
guided participation, p. 361
horizontal décalage, p. 345
information-processing approach, p. 351
long-term memory, p. 351
mental operations, p. 338
mental perspective taking, p. 341
modularity theory, p. 354
precausal thinking, p. 343
preoperational stage, p. 338
scripts, p. 357
sensory register, p. 351
short-term memory, p. 351
skeletal principles, p. 355
sociodramatic play, p. 361
theory of mind, p. 341

THOUGHT QUESTIONS

1. Young children appear to become confused about the relationship between a general class of objects and its subclasses. How does this difficulty relate to features of linguistic development discussed in Chapter 8?
2. Suppose you were Piaget and you were confronted with evidence that even young infants appear to be surprised when the events they observe contradict laws of physical location. How might you interpret the data to fit your theory that young children are precausal thinkers?
3. In what ways is the biologically inspired concept of a mental module similar to the constructivist concept of a skeletal principle? In what ways do the two approaches differ?
4. Write out your own going-to-a-restaurant script. In what ways does it differ from the scripts quoted on pages 357–359? What might be some of the reasons for those differences?
5. Using different theories of learning how to draw as a foundation, how would you design an instructional program to teach drawing?

CHAPTER 10

Social Development in Early Childhood

ACQUIRING A SOCIAL AND PERSONAL IDENTITY
- Sex-Role Identity
- Ethnic and Racial Identity
- Personal Identity

DEVELOPING THE ABILITY TO REGULATE ONESELF
- Learning about Good and Bad
- Self-Control
- Internalization

AGGRESSION AND PROSOCIAL BEHAVIOR
- The Development of Aggression
- What Causes Aggression?
- Individual Differences in Aggressive Behavior
- Controlling Human Aggression
- The Development of Prosocial Behavior

THE DEVELOPMENT AND REGULATION OF EMOTIONS
- Understanding the Emotions of Others
- Regulating One's Own Emotions
- Learning to Display Emotions Appropriately
- Regulation of Emotions and Social Competence

TAKING ONE'S PLACE IN THE SOCIAL GROUP AS A DISTINCT INDIVIDUAL

The incorporation of the individual as a member of a community, or his adaptation to it, seems like an almost unavoidable condition which has to be filled before he can attain the objective of happiness. . . . Individual development seems to us a product of the interplay of two trends, the striving for happiness, generally called "egoistic," and the impulse towards merging with others in the community, which we call "altruistic."

Sigmund Freud, *Civilization and Its Discontents*

In the quotation above, Sigmund Freud is describing **social development,** a two-sided process in which children simultaneously become integrated into the larger social community and differentiated as distinctive individuals. One side of social development is **socialization,** the process by which children acquire the standards, values, and knowledge of their society. The other side of social development is personality formation, the process through which children develop their own unique patterns of feeling, thinking, and behaving in a wide variety of circumstances.

As we shall see in this and later chapters, societies around the world differ markedly in the ways that their members conceive of the relationship between individuals and their communities. Of special interest has been the extent to which the dominant values of a society place greater emphasis on the independence of individuals or on their interdependence with other members of their social group (Geenfield & Cocking, 1994; Kagitçabasi, 1997). Since the very meaning of the term "social development" depends on the relationship between the individual and the community, it should be no surprise that cultural variations in social development are an especially active area of contemporary research (Rubin et al., 1998; Turiel, 1998).

The process of socialization begins as soon as a child is born and her mother says, for example, "She's never going to be a rugby player," or her father remarks, "I shall be worried to death when she's eighteen" (see Chapter 3, p. 118). Such predictions are not just idle talk. The beliefs that give rise to such statements lead parents to shape their child's experience in ways they deem appropriate. Socialization continues as an aspect of every encounter children have with other members of their society as they learn to eat and sleep on a schedule, to prefer clothes appropriate to their gender, to be polite to their elders, to take their vitamins, and to love their brother.

Both adults and children play active roles in social development. Adults communicate to children how they should behave, display pleasure or disapproval with the way they do behave, and reward, ignore, or punish them accordingly. Adults also select the neighborhoods their children live in, the day-care centers or preschools they attend, and other contexts in which they become conversant with their culture's funds of knowledge and rules of behavior. But children do not automatically or passively absorb the lessons adults intend. They have goals of their own. As a consequence, conflict is as much a part of socialization as nurturing and caring.

What children learn also depends on how they interpret their experiences and what they select from the many messages they receive. For example, if 4-year-old Mark admires his older cousin Eric and wants to be like him, will he imitate Eric's socially appropriate style of dress, his socially inappropriate use of slang, or both?

In order to acquire an understanding of the social categories that apply to them, children must somehow figure out what people mean when they say

social development A two-sided process in which children simultaneously become integrated into the larger social community and differentiated as distinctive individuals.

socialization The process by which children acquire the standards, values, and knowledge of their society.

such things as "You are my son" and "Act like a lady." These terms stand for **social roles** that reflect adult expectations about the child's rights, duties, and obligations, as well as appropriate forms of behavior. It is not sufficient for children simply to learn what adults mean by words such as "son" and "lady"; it is also necessary for them to learn to fill these social roles in ways that correspond to adults' expectations and values. It is not surprising that adults take the necessity of socializing their children for granted. What is remarkable is that most children come to accept the socially prescribed roles and rules as reasonable and even necessary.

social roles The social categories such as son, daughter, and student that specify a person's relations to the social group and the person's rights, duties, and obligations in that role.

personality The unique pattern of temperament, emotions, interests, and intellectual abilities that a child develops as the child's innate propensities and capacities are shaped by his or her social interactions with kin and community.

self-concept The way in which children come to conceive of themselves in relation to other people.

The second side of social development, **personality,** is the unique pattern of temperament, emotions, interests, and intellectual abilities that a child develops as the child's innate propensities and capacities are shaped by his or her social interactions with kin and community. Since no two people have precisely the same experiences, no two people ever have precisely the same personality, not even identical twins.

The early origins of personality are no less visible at birth than the presence of socializing influences. As we saw in Chapter 4 (p. 144), neonates display individual differences in characteristic levels of activity, responses to frustration, and readiness to engage in novel experiences. We referred to these patterns of responsivity and associated emotional states as *temperamental traits* and noted that temperament is moderately stable over time: children who draw back from novel experiences in infancy, for example, are more likely to behave shyly when they first enter a nursery school.

Although temperamental traits provide a foundation for personality, by the time children reach the age of 3 or 4, there is more to their personalities than temperament (Caspi, 1998; Thomas & Chess, 1989). We cannot say that a child is honest or compulsive at birth, because there is no temperamental characteristic corresponding to honesty or compulsiveness, or to a host of other personality characteristics, such as stinginess, compliance, or a desire to please other people. Those characteristics are gradually acquired as children's initial temperamental styles of interacting with their environments are integrated with their developing cognitive understanding, emotional responses, and habits.

An important aspect of personality is the way children come to conceive of themselves in relation to other people—their **self-concept.** Self-concept provides a double-sided link between personality and social development that was described at the turn of the century by one of the founders of developmental psychology, James Mark Baldwin (1902):

> The development of the child's personality could not go on at all without the constant modification of his sense of himself by suggestions from others. So he himself, at every stage, is really in part someone else, even in his own thought of himself. (p. 23)

These little flower girls are simultaneously fulfilling a traditional role in a wedding and learning about many important aspects of the social roles and behaviors expected of them when they grow up.

Personality formation and socialization are in constant tension as children discover the dilemma Freud wrote about—the fact that their individual desires and ideas often conflict with their culture's norms and the desires of others. A 5-year-old boy who sucks his thumb may be discouraged from doing so by his parents and teased by his peers. A child who is jealous of the attention her baby brother receives must learn that she can't get what she wants by pinching him and that she must find some socially acceptable way to gain her mother's attention and to deal with her socially unacceptable feelings.

During early childhood, children learn a great deal about the roles they are expected to play, how to behave in accordance with social standards, how to control aggressive feelings, and how to respect the rights of others. But these are difficult lessons and not every child is able to, or cares to, comply with adult expectations. With increasing age, children learn not only how to be "good" but

identification A psychological process in which children try to look, act, feel, and be like significant people in their social environment.

also how to manipulate situations in order to upset those around them (Turiel, 1998).

As they gain experience interacting with a variety of people, young children develop a more explicit sense of themselves, their abilities, and the ways in which they can use the rules and tools that society is attempting to press upon them to their own advantage. The resulting changes in social development do not, of course, occur independently of the biological and cognitive changes discussed in Chapter 9. Socialization, personality formation, biological maturation, and cognitive development occur simultaneously.

ACQUIRING A SOCIAL AND PERSONAL IDENTITY

Developmentalists agree that one factor essential to the process of socialization is **identification,** a psychological process in which children try to look, act, feel, and be like significant people in their social environment. They disagree, however, about the mechanisms by which identification is achieved.

The development of identification can be studied with respect to almost any social category—a family, a religious group, a neighborhood clique, or a nationality. The overwhelming majority of studies on identification in early childhood, however, focus on the acquisition of sex roles. Consequently, we will devote the lion's share of our attention to this social category before turning to ethnic identity, which is an especially important social category in today's world that has been the object of increased research by developmentalists.

SEX-ROLE IDENTITY

Because sex-role identity is so central to adult experience, the question of how children acquire a personal sense of their sex-role identity and how they interpret that sex role* is of great interest to developmental psychologists. Central issues in acquiring a sex-role identity during early childhood are seen in the following conversations:

> "When I grow up," says [4-year-old] Jimmy at the dinner table, "I'm gonna marry Mama."
>
> "Jimmy's nuts," says the sensible voice of 8-year-old Jane. "You can't marry Mama and anyway, what would happen to Daddy?" . . .
>
> "He'll be old," says [Jimmy], through a mouthful of string-beans. "And he'll be dead."
>
> Then, awed by the enormity of his words, [Jimmy] adds hastily, "But he might not be dead, and maybe I'll marry Marcia instead." (Fraiberg, 1959, pp. 202–203)

The next conversation took place when our daughter, Jenny, was 4 years old. She was lying on her mother's side of her parents' bed, watching her mother comb her hair:

> *Jenny:* You know, Mommy, when you die I am going to marry Daddy.
> *Sheila:* I don't think so.
> *Jenny:* *(nodding her head gravely)* I am, too.
> *Sheila:* You can't. It's against the laws of God and man.
> *Jenny:* *(close to tears)* But I want to.

* Some psychologists recommend the use of the word "gender" instead of "sex" when this topic is discussed because they believe that the term "sex" implies that all sex-typed behavior is ultimately determined by biology. Others argue against the term "gender," which they think implies that sex-linked behavior is ultimately determined by the environment (Gentile, 1993; Unger & Crawford, 1993). We will use both "sex" and "gender" in contexts where they appear most appropriate, without implying either that sex/gender roles are basically biological or that they are basically environmental.

These preschool girls are participating in a beauty contest. This kind of experience gives them an idea of what the adults in their community expect of girls.

Sheila: (going to comfort her) You'll have your own husband when you grow up.
Jenny: No, I won't! I want Daddy. I don't like you, Mommy.

The 4-year-olds' thinking in these conversations is easy to understand. Both children have had several years to observe the family life around them. Jimmy knows that he is a boy, and Jenny knows that she is a girl. Although neither has a deep understanding of what these labels imply, they know that they want the things that big boys and big girls have. The "big girl" in Jenny's household has a special relationship with Daddy. The "big boy" in Jimmy's household has a special relationship with Mommy. At this early stage of sex-role identification, the best way children can think of to get what they want is literally to take the place of the person they want to be like, to "stand in the person's shoes" (or sleep on that person's side of the bed).

Boys and girls in early childhood tend to choose same-sex parents as models to identify with. Yet the developmental paths that bring the two sexes to their respective identities differ in at least one respect. Although family configurations vary widely both within and among societies, the person who usually looms largest in the lives of both boys and girls during the first 2 years of life is the mother. She is likely to be the single greatest source of physical comfort, food, and attention for the very young child, whether a boy or a girl. She is, in Freud's terms, the "first love object." But while little girls soon begin to identify with their mothers, little boys generally do not.

As children enter their third year, their demonstrations of strong and obvious attachment to their mothers diminish (see Chapter 6, p. 247). During this period of early childhood, the feeling of "wanting to be near" that is dominant in infancy is supplanted by "wanting to be like." (See Figure 10.1.)

For boys, becoming like their father requires that they become different from the person with whom they have had the closest relationship: their mother. Girls, on the other hand, seek to become like the person with whom they have had the closest relationship.

FIGURE 10.1
In addition to wanting to be near parents, children want to do what their parents do. This small girl may not be able to shovel much snow, but she is accomplishing an important identify formation task by helping her father.

BOX 10.1

SIGMUND FREUD

Trained as a neurologist, Sigmund Freud (1856–1939) sought throughout his career to create a theory of human personality that would enable him to cure the patients who came to him with such symptoms as extreme fear, emotional trauma, and an inability to cope with everyday life. Although many of these symptoms appeared similar to neurological disorders, Freud found that he could best understand his patients' problems by tracing their symptoms back to traumatic, unresolved experiences in early childhood.

On the basis of his clinical data, Freud constructed a general theory of development that gave primacy to the manner in which children satisfy their basic drives—the drives that act to guarantee their survival. Survival of the individual child, however, is not sufficient for survival of the species. Influenced by Charles Darwin's theory of evolution, Freud reasoned that whatever their significance for individual adaptation, all biological drives have but a single goal: the survival and propagation of the species. Since reproduction, the necessary condition for the continuation of the species, is accomplished through sexual intercourse, it followed for Freud that, starting from the earliest days of life, all biological drives must ultimately serve the fundamental sex drive, on which the future of the species rests.

Although Freud believed that gratification remains sexual in nature throughout life, the forms of that gratification change. Sexual gratification passes through an orderly series of stages defined in terms of the parts of the body that people use to satisfy their drives. Human beings strive to satisfy the drives that dominate the stage they are in at the moment.

The first year of life is the *oral stage,* in which the mouth is the primary source of pleasure. The mother's gratification of the baby's need to suck and gain nourishment is critically important. In the second and third years of life, the *anal stage,* the child is preoccupied with gaining control of the smooth muscles involved in defecation.

Freud believed that during the fourth year children begin to focus their pleasure-seeking on the genital area. During this *phallic stage,* development for boys and girls diverges. Boys become aware that they have a penis. They develop sexual feelings toward their mothers and become jealous of their fathers. Girls become aware that they do not have a penis and begin to resent their mothers for sending them out into the world "ill equipped." Freud believed that resolution of these conflicts produces the most basic form of sexual identification.

Between the ages of 6 and 7 years, the child enters the *latency stage,* which lasts until the beginning of puberty, 5 or 6 years later. During the latency stage, sexual desires are suppressed and no new areas of bodily excitation emerge. Instead, sexual energy is channeled into the acquisition of skills that will be needed in adulthood for earning a living.

The physiological changes of puberty, the onset of sexual maturity, cause the repressed sexual urges to reappear in full force, marking the beginning of the *genital stage.* Now sexual urges are no longer directed toward the parents or repressed. This is the onset of adult sexuality, directed toward peers of the opposite sex for the ultimate purpose of reproduction.

Freud (1920/1955) held that the way children experience the conflicts they encounter in each of the early stages of development determines their later personality. He also believed that from early childhood onward the personality is made up of three mental structures. The **id,** which is present at birth, is the main source of psychological energy. It is unconscious and pleasure-seeking and demands that bodily drives be satisfied immediately (Freud, 1933/1964). The **ego** is the intermediary between the demands of the id and those of the social world. The ego develops out of the id as the infant is forced by reality to cope with the fact that its desires are often at odds with the

---

Disagreements about the implications of this sex-linked difference in developmental goals has sparked intense debate about the process by which children acquire the sex-role identification they will have as adults.

The Psychodynamic View: Identification through Differentiation and Affiliation

By far, the best-known account of identity formation is Sigmund Freud's (1921/1949, 1933/1964). Although many of Freud's specific hypotheses about development have not been substantiated, he remains an influential theorist. He proposed that boys and girls go through two, quite different, processes of identity formation.

Identification through Differentiation Freud believed that early in life, perhaps late in the first year, infants recognize that some objects in the external world are like themselves. He called this primitive recognition **primary identification.** The tendency of young infants to imitate other people, but not mechanical devices, which was described in Chapter 6 (p. 230) is one example of primary identification (Meltzoff, 1995). **Secondary identification,** which Freud

id In Freudian theory, the mental structure present at birth that is main source of psychological energy. It is unconscious and pleasure-seeking and demands that bodily drives be satisfied.

ego In Freudian theory, this is the mental structure that develops out of the id as the infant is forced by reality to cope with the social world. The ego's primary task is self-preservation, which it accomplishes through voluntary movement, perception, logical thought, adaptation, and problem solving.

primary identification In Freud's terms, the recognition by infants that some objects in the external world are like themselves.

requirements of the social world. The ego's primary task is self-preservation, which it accomplishes through voluntary movement, perception, logical thought, adaptation, and problem solving. It performs its tasks by bringing the instinctual demands of the id under control and deciding where, when, and how they are to be satisfied.

The **superego,** which is equivalent to a conscience, begins to form during early childhood and becomes a major force in the personality during middle childhood. It represents the authority of the social group, embodied in the image of the father. In effect, the superego sits in stern judgment of the ego's efforts to hold the id in check.

Sigmund Freud.

The three structures that make up human personality are rarely, if ever, in perfect equilibrium. Instead, dominance shifts as the superego and the id battle for control of the ego. This constant battle is the engine of developmental change, which Freud spoke of as ego development. The patterns of individual behavior that arise in this process constitute the personality.

Summarized in this brief fashion, Freud's theory may appear to be fanciful. His theory of infantile sexuality provoked outrage when he proposed it, and it has remained controversial to this day. Freud's psychoanalytic method has been criticized as ineffective and unscientific. It must also be noted that all of Freud's claims about infancy and early childhood are based on his observations of disturbed adults. Freud is certainly vulnerable to criticism on both methodological and theoretical grounds, yet he remains one of the most influential forces in contemporary developmental theorizing.

Robert Emde (1992) points to several of Freud's enduring contributions to developmental psychology. First, Freud was among the most influential champions of the view that understanding adult personality must rely on a developmental analysis. Thus he made a developmental approach the center of any theory of personality. Second, he emphasized the need to arrive at scientific generalization through intensive study of individual human beings. Third, he was among the first psychologists to point out and study the complex dynamics between unconscious motives and conscious understanding, between fantasy and reality. Finally, he insisted that a human being is a complex, dynamic creature who can be understood only by study of the person as a whole.

(1921/1949) defined as "the endeavor to mold a person's own ego after the fashion of one that has been taken as a model" (p. 63), emerges during the third year of life. In other words, having noticed that a particular adult, or perhaps an older child, is somehow similar to themselves, children strive to take on his or her qualities. They "identify with" that person.

By Freud's account, when Jimmy says that he wants to "marry Mama," he is playing out the universal male predicament of boys around the age of 3 or 4, the dilemma of the **phallic stage** of development, which follows the oral and anal stages in his theory of development (see Chapter 6 and Box 10.1). It is in this period, the time of secondary identification, that children begin to regard their own genitals as a major source of pleasure. Here's how Freud (1940/1964) saw the conflict that this new pleasure and new kind of identification evoke:

> In a word, his early awakened masculinity seeks to take his father's place with [his mother]; his father has hitherto in any case been an envied model to the boy, owing to the physical strength he perceives in him and the authority with which he finds him clothed. His father now becomes a rival who stands in his way and whom he would like to get rid of. (p. 189)

superego In Freudian terms, the conscience. It represents the authority of the social group and sits in stern judgment of the ego's efforts to hold the id in check. It becomes a major force in the personality in middle childhood.

secondary identification In Freudian terms, the effort of a child to take on the qualities and copy the behavior of a person with whom he or she identifies.

phallic stage In Freudian theory, the period around the fourth year when children begin to regard their own genitals as a major source of pleasure.

Oedipus complex In Freudian theory, the fear, guilt, and conflict evoked by a little boy's desire to get rid of his father and take the father's place in his mother's affections.

latency stage In Freudian theory, the period of middle childhood when children's sexual desires are suppressed as a defense against the dangerous feelings they evoke and children display a great interest in learning the skills possessed by adults.

These feelings cause Jimmy a lot of mental anguish. He is old enough to know that feelings like wanting your father to die are bad, and he is young enough to believe that his parents, who are powerful figures in his life, are always aware of what he is thinking. So he lives in fear of being punished and feels guilty about his bad thoughts.

Freud called this predicament the **Oedipus complex,** referring to the ancient Greek tragedy in which Oedipus, king of Thebes, unknowingly kills his father and marries his mother. Little boys do not, of course, literally repeat this tragedy. Rather, according to Freud, as they leave infancy and enter childhood, boys must mentally reorder their emotional attachments by distancing themselves from their mothers and becoming closer to their fathers. In other words, they must *differentiate* themselves from their mothers and *affiliate* with their fathers. This process is driven by complex social emotions such as guilt and envy.

According to Freud, male children achieve this differentiation in the transition between early childhood and middle childhood. He called the next stage of personality development the **latency stage** because it is a time when children's sexual desires are suppressed as a defense against the dangerous feelings they evoke and a time when children display a great interest in learning the skills possessed by adults.

Identification through Affiliation According to Freud (1933/1964), the key event in the development of a girl's sex-role identity is her discovery that she does not have a penis: the girl is "mortified by the comparison with boys' far superior equipment" (p. 126). She blames her mother for this "deficiency" and transfers her love to her father. Then she competes with her mother for her father's affection.

As is the case with boys, the wish to replace the same-sex parent results in guilt. The girl is afraid that her mother knows what she is thinking and that she will be punished by loss of her mother's love. She overcomes her fear and guilt by repressing her feelings for her father and intensifying her identification with her mother. As a result of this sequence, Freud said, a woman's psychological makeup never becomes as independent of its emotional wellsprings as does a man's, because the object of her primary identification and the object of her secondary identification are the same person—her mother. Freud believed that this pattern of identity formation, in which women affiliate with their mothers, renders women "underdeveloped" versions of men because their attempts to differentiate themselves from their mothers were short-circuited. He concluded that women show less sense of justice than men, that they are less ready to submit to the great challenges of life, and that their judgments are more often colored by their emotions (Freud, 1925/1961, pp. 257–258).

Not surprisingly, Freud's argument has been strongly attacked. Even people who support his general line of interpretation point out that his views depended heavily on the historical era in which he lived and were unduly influenced by its rigid sexual mores (Dufresne, 1997). In particular, Freud has been criticized for claiming that the lack of a penis makes girls feel inferior to boys, for assuming that a girl's sexual identification occurs only as a defense mechanism, and for concluding that women's path to identity renders them inferior to men.

Nancy Chodorow (1974), for example, acknowledged the difference in the two sexes' experience of early social interaction and their differing biological roles, but her conclusion differs from Freud's. Chodorow considered identification a two-way process involving both the parent and the child. She argued that just as daughters identify with mothers, so mothers experience their daughters as like themselves. In contrast, "mothers experience their sons as a male opposite" (pp. 166–167). In defining themselves as masculine, boys reinforce their mothers' reactions to them and thereby facilitate the differentiation process. In defining themselves as feminine, daughters evoke further feelings of similarity in their mothers, fusing the process of attachment with the experience of sex-role identity. Because daughters do not have to go through the alienating experience of differentiating themselves from their mothers, they "emerge from this period with a basis for empathy built into their primary definition of self in a way that boys do not" (p. 167). Put differently, because girls' identity is based on affiliation with their mothers, girls have a built-in basis for understanding the needs of others.

In many respects Chodorow's formulation is similar to Freud's, but as Carol Gilligan (1982) points out, the difference in its emphasis is important. Freud assumed that because girls experience less differentiation from their mothers, they are less developed than boys the same age who have gone through the separation and reorientation to the father. Chodorow does not equate differentiation with development. By her account, the two paths to sex-role identity result in two complementary developmental endpoints, each with its own strengths and weaknesses. Males achieve identity through separation; as a result, males see themselves as threatened by intimacy. Females, on the other hand, achieve identity through attachment. They see themselves as threatened by separation.

Whereas Chodorow reinterprets Freud's description of sex-role development, other developmental psychologists, even many who are generally supportive of Freud's ideas, dispute his basic description of how sex roles are acquired (Emde, 1992). First, critics reject Freud's belief that female development is somehow secondary to male development. If any priority is to be given to one sex or the other, it is more likely to be given to the female. As we saw in Chapter 3 (p. 83), the sex organs and the brain of all human embryos initially follow a female path of development; these organs become male only if they are modified through the action of male hormones. Second, modern research indicates that there is more to children's achievement of sex-role identities than resolving the Oedipus complex, because aspects of identity formation can be discerned well before the age at which Freud assumed it to occur (Ruble & Martin, 1998). Third, researchers now consider adults in the child's family, not the child, to be the primary carriers of sexual fantasies. Disturbances in identity formation currently are thought to result from psychological traumas caused by parents who are sexually abusive or seductive and not from children's inability to resolve infantile sexual desires (Coates & Wolf, 1997).

Freud's ideas, however, continue to influence both popular and scholarly thinking about the acquisition of sex roles. The challenge facing those who dispute his theories is to provide a better account of the processes at work.

Many young boys are fascinated by their father's act of shaving, just as many young girls are fascinated by their mother's act of applying makeup. Seldom, however, do children become fascinated with the cosmetic rituals of the other-sex parent. Why this is the case would be explained differently by each of the major theoretical perspectives.

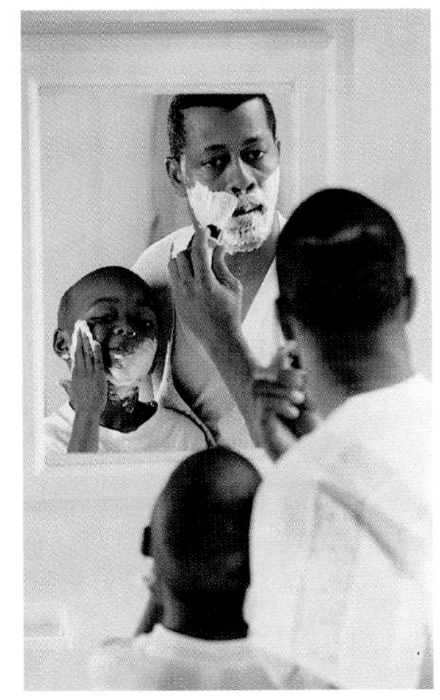

A Social-Learning View: Identification through Observation and Imitation

Freudian theories of identification assume that young children are caught in hidden conflicts between their fears and their desires. Identification is their way of resolving those conflicts.

Social-learning theorists have a very different perspective on how children adopt adult sex roles. They assume that the process of identification is not driven by inner conflict but is simply a matter of observation and imitation of a model. For example, as a 4-year-old, our son loved to run down the hallway and slide feet-first into a pillow. He was not driven by desire for his mother, who strongly disapproved of his hallway play, fearing that it bothered the downstairs neighbors and would wear holes in his pants. Nor was his father's disapproval enough to stop him. Sasha was modeling his behavior on that of a highly publicized baseball star. He desired to be like that person, to be "in his shoes."

Social-learning theorists believe that behavior like Sasha's is acquired through direct observation and reinforcement (Bandura, 1969, 1986; Mischel,

1966). According to this view, children observe that male behavior and female behavior differ. From this observation, they develop hypotheses about appropriate male and female behaviors. Further, children learn that adults reward boys and girls for different kinds of behavior, so they choose to engage in sex-appropriate behaviors that will lead to rewards (Perry & Bussey, 1984).

Bandura (1969, 1986) believes that the ability to learn from observation depends on several factors:

1. *Availability.* The behavior to be learned must be available in the child's environment, either directly or through a medium such as a book or television program.
2. *Attention.* Children cannot learn from observation unless they pay attention to the model (the mother, the father, a celebrity, or a fictional character) and perceive the significant features of the behavior in question. Children usually choose to imitate the actions of people whom they admire or whom they see as like them in some way. Sometimes they also need to see the behavior in question more than once in order to determine its significant features. A little boy who watches his father drive the family car, for example, may have to watch his father several times before he understands that there is more to driving than having your hands on the steering wheel.
3. *Memory.* Observation will have no lasting effect if children immediately forget what they observe. Bandura believes that when children have a name for modeled events, their observation becomes especially effective and memorable. Significantly, early childhood is the time when children are acquiring both language and knowledge of basic social categories—and their memory capacities are also increasing.
4. *Motor reproduction.* In order for a child to imitate and learn an observed behavior, the behavior must be within, or almost within, the child's physical ability. If a behavior is too complex (such as doing a backward flip off a diving board), the child will usually not try to perform it.
5. *Motivation.* For imitation and subsequent learning to occur, the observer must perceive some payoff to the observed behavior. If little Ben wants to be thought well of by grown-ups and he hears Daddy praise his sister Lisa for taking her glass to the sink when she finishes her apple juice, he may be motivated to take his next empty glass to the sink as well. If Daddy's good opinion means little to him, he probably will not be motivated to learn from this observation.

There is abundant evidence that parents not only provide models for children to imitate but also reward what they consider sex-appropriate behavior and punish cross-sex behavior. For example, in a series of studies in which she observed children and their parents in their homes, Beverly Fagot found that many parents rewarded their daughters with smiles, attention, and praise for dressing up, dancing, playing with dolls, or simply following them around the house. By contrast, parents rewarded boys more than girls for playing with blocks and toy vehicles. The same parents who criticized their girls for manipulating objects, running, jumping, and climbing criticized their boys for playing with dolls, asking for help, or volunteering to be helpful (Fagot, 1978a, 1978b). Such findings have been replicated often and support social-learning theorists' basic assumption that sex-appropriate behaviors are shaped by the distribution of rewards and punishments (Maccoby, 1998; Ruble & Martin, 1998).

Despite many attractive features, social-learning theory has a serious problem in defining one of its central concepts: reward. To some degree, rewards, like beauty, are in the eye of the beholder. A 2-year-old boy and a 2-year-old girl may both be pleased when their grandparents give them a doll for good behavior. But 2 years later, while the girl may find another doll rewarding, the boy may turn away in disgust at "those girl things." Such incidents make it appear that children's conceptions about what is proper behavior for boys and girls shape their ideas of sex-appropriate rewards. In short, the environment does not act *directly* on the child, it acts *indirectly. Environmental effects are mediated through the child's prior understandings of the situation.* Where do these prior conceptions come from?

A Cognitive View: Identity Formation as Conceptual Development

The belief that a child's own conceptions are central to the formation of sex-role identity is the cornerstone of the cognitive-developmental approach to sex-role acquisition proposed by Lawrence Kohlberg (1966). In contrast to the social-learning theorists, Kohlberg argues that "the child's sex-role concepts are the result of the child's active structuring of his own experience; they are not passive products of social training" (p. 85). In contrast to Freud, Kohlberg claimed that the "process of forming a constant sexual identity depends less on guilt and fear than on the general process of conceptual development" (p. 85).

Kohlberg believed that sex-role development goes through three stages:

1. Basic sex-role *identity.* By the time children are 3 years old, they are able to label themselves as boys or girls.
2. Sex-role *stability.* During early childhood, children begin to understand that sex roles are stable over time—boys grow up to be men and girls grow up to be women.
3. Sex-role *constancy.* Young children may believe that their sex may be changed by changing their outward appearance in some way. Their sex-role development is completed when they understand that their sex remains the same no matter what the situation. They know that even if they dress up as a member of the opposite sex for Halloween, they won't turn into a member of the opposite sex.

Whereas the social-learning theorists assume that the thought sequence of male children is "I want rewards, I am rewarded for doing boy things, therefore I want to be a boy," Kohlberg (1966) proposed the following sequence: "I am a boy; therefore I want to do boy things; therefore the opportunity to do boy things (and to gain approval for doing them) is rewarding" (p. 89).

There is a good deal of evidence that the development of sex-role identity goes through the general sequence proposed by Kohlberg (Slaby & Frey, 1975; Szkrybalo & Ruble, 1999). However, psychologists remain divided about the processes that produce the sequence. Kohlberg himself believed that sex-role identity begins to guide thoughts and actions only after children attain sex-role constancy, because only then are they "categorically certain" that their sex is unchangeable (Kohlberg, 1966, p. 95). Current data, however, do not support Kohlberg's strict idea of sex-role constancy as the critical turning point in the development of sex-role identity. For example, well before they attain sex-role constancy as defined by Kohlberg's criteria, children prefer the same toys as other members of their sex and imitate the behavior predominantly of same-sex models (Figure 10.2) (Bussey & Bandura, 1992; Maccoby, 1998).

A Combined Approach: Gender Schema Theory

To many psychologists it appears that an adequate explanation of how children's sex-role identity develops must include features of both social-learning and cognitive-developmental theories. One such approach is *gender schema theory.*

Gender schema theory is similar in some respects to Kohlberg's cognitive-developmental theory. Adherents of both approaches believe that the environment affects the child's understanding indirectly, through a *schema,* or

FIGURE 10.2
Girls are often rewarded for traditionally feminine role behavior, such as dressing up or taking dancing lessons.

cognitive structure. Once formed, this schema guides the way the child selects and remembers information from the environment. It also provides a model for action. A **gender schema,** then, can be considered a mental model containing information about males and females that is used to process gender-relevant information.

Gary Levy and Robin Fivush (1993) point out that children form gender schemas not only for objects and people but for familiar events as well. Accordingly, at the same time that they are discovering how to classify people and objects in terms of their gender, gender information is becoming a part of the scripts that boys and girls are expected to draw upon and apply in different circumstances (a barbecuing script or a grocery shopping script, for example) (see Figure 10.3).

Gender schema theory departs from Kohlberg's cognitive-developmental theory in two ways:

1. Gender schema theorists believe that even in the earliest stages of gender development, children's developing schematic knowledge motivates and guides their gender-linked interests and behavior.
2. Gender schema theorists often use an information-processing approach to describe how the cognitive and learning elements of the system work together.

Carol Martin and Charles Halverson (1987) conceive gender schema theory in terms of the diagram in Figure 10.4. A little girl who can say that she is a girl and that her brother is a boy is presented with four objects to play with. Two of the objects are gender-neutral—an orange and an artichoke—and two are stereotypically male or female—a truck and a doll. When the girl is presented with the doll, she must first decide if it is specifically relevant to her. She decides that "dolls are for girls" and that "I am a girl," so "dolls are relevant for me." As a result of this decision, write Martin and Halverson (1981), "she will approach the doll, explore it, ask questions about it, and play with it to obtain further information about it" (p. 1121). This sequence is depicted by the thick green line in the diagram.

When the little girl is presented with a truck, by contrast, she will think, "Trucks are for boys" and "I am a girl." This reasoning will lead her to decide that "trucks are not relevant for me." As a result, she will avoid the truck and not be interested in knowing anything else about it. Asked about

gender schema A mental model containing information about males and females that is used to process gender-relevant information.

these toys later on, she will remember more about the doll than about the truck.

In their efforts to evaluate the merits of gender schema theory and its rivals, psychologists have tried to determine the precise relationships between children's increasingly complex sex-role understandings and their sex-role behaviors.

Sex-Role Knowledge and Sex-Role Behavior

It is clear that long before they have any conceptual knowledge of sex roles, boys and girls behave differently. Male infants are more active than females (Eaton & Yu, 1989). This heightened activity level may explain the fact that little boys engage in significantly more rough-and-tumble play than girls (Humphreys & Smith, 1987). Carol Jacklin and Eleanor Maccoby (1978) found that when infant boys play together and get into a tug-of-war over a toy, for example, the tug-of-war is likely to become part of the game. But when a girl and boy get into the same kind of tug-of-war, the girl is likely to retreat and simply observe the boy playing. The same pattern is seen in early childhood, as illustrated by an observational study of 5- to 7-year-old Irish children riding wheeled vehicles in the playground: the boys played "ramming games," delighting in running into each other on purpose, whereas the girls rode around cautiously, seeking to avoid collisions (Dunn & Morgan, 1987).

FIGURE 10.3
Parental encouragement is one reason boys assume traditional masculine roles, such as that of cowboy.

These differences in preferred play styles appear to underlie repeated observations that even in early childhood boys and girls tend to self-segregate when they are not closely supervised by adults. Boys spend more time playing with boys; girls, with girls (Maccoby, 1998). The early connection between play styles and preferences for same-sex interactions has been confirmed in several cultures (Leaper, 1994; Whiting & Edwards, 1988). These findings led Eleanor Maccoby (1998) to conclude that "genetic predispositions are probably involved, to some degree, in childhood gender segregation" (p. 292).

Not only do boys and girls play differently from an early age; they also often prefer to play with different things. When children age 1 to 3 years were observed in their own homes, researchers found that boys were more likely to play with trucks and cars while girls chose dolls and soft toys (Caldera, et al., 1989; O'Brien & Huston, 1985a, b). The children spent more time playing with toys that fitted their culture's sex-role stereotypes than with equally available toys that were not sex-typed. This finding indicates that the children had already developed sex-typed *preferences* well before they had developed a firm sex-role identity.

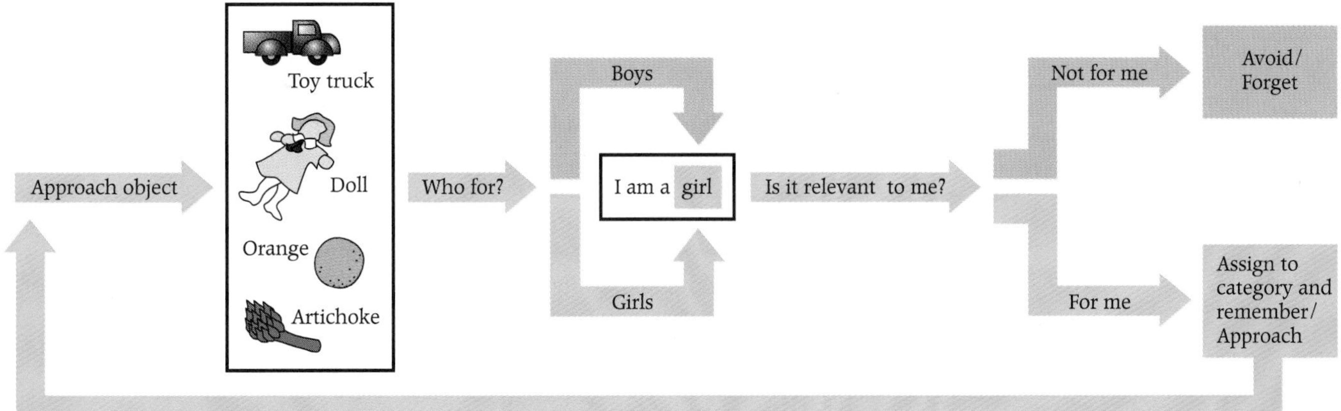

FIGURE 10.4
An example of an information-processing sequence associated with gender schema formation. In this case, the child is a girl who has been offered four objects to play with. (Adapted from Martin & Halverson, 1981.)

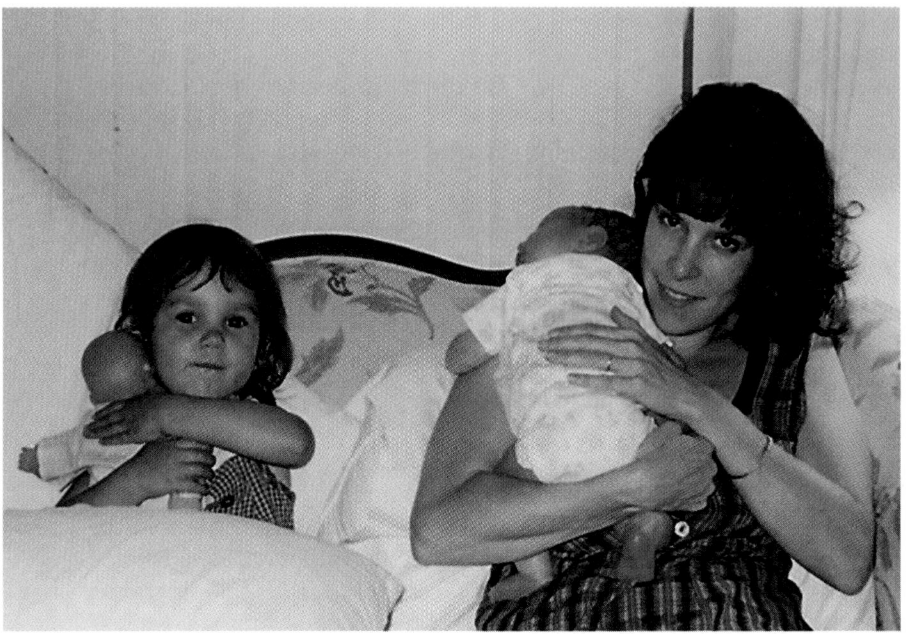

Caring for others is an important component of socialization. Here a little girl willingly learns about infant care by imitating her mommy.

Between 2½ and 3 years of age, about the same time that children enter the earliest stage of gender schema formation, their talk shows the beginnings of a conceptual grasp of the more obvious attributes of sex roles in their culture. Judy Dunn, who observed young children in their homes, recorded the following conversation involving a 36-month-old girl, her older brother, and their mother. The children are arguing over who can play with a toy vacuum cleaner that belongs to the girl but has just been repaired by her brother. As the boy plays with it, his sister tries to get it back:

> *Boy: (to mother)* I wanted to do it because I fixed it up. And made it work.
> *Mother: (to boy)* Well, you'll have to wait your turn.
> *Mother: (to girl)* Are you going to let David have a turn?
> *Girl:* I have to do it. Ladies do it.
>
> (Dunn, 1988, p. 57)

Even though young children can say that ladies do certain things and men do others, their notions about sex roles are still fragmentary, as the following dialogue between two 3-year-olds in Vivian Paley's classroom reveals:

> *Mollie:* Are you a sister, Margaret?
> *Margaret:* I'm a brother's sister.
> *Mollie:* They call a brother they sometimes call a boy.
> *Margaret:* Brothers are boys, girls are girls.
> *Mollie:* You're a girl, Margaret.
> *Margaret:* So are you, Mollie. L-M-N-O. That spells "girl."
>
> (Paley, 1986, p. 35)

As children's gender-identity schemas begin to take shape, there are corresponding changes in their behavior (Fagot et al., 1986). Beverly Fagot and her colleagues demonstrated this by asking children to look at photographs of children and adults and identify their sex. They found that children under 26 months of age were unlikely to label the pictures correctly, whereas those 36 months and older generally succeeded. Most important, once children of any age could correctly label the people in the photographs by sex, they were more likely to select children of their own sex to play with. This selectivity is evidence that their emerging gender schema is beginning to affect their behavior. Gender schema theory is also supported by the fact that girls who correctly labeled the

BOX 10.2

How to Tell a Girl from a Boy

Sandra Bem (1989, p. 662) reports the kinds of difficulties that young children can encounter when their knowledge about the basis of sex-role categories is more (or less) sophisticated than that of their friends. Her young son, Jeremy, decided one day to wear barrettes to his nursery school. Another boy insisted repeatedly that Jeremy had to be a girl because "only girls wear barrettes." Although Jeremy argued that he was a boy because he had a penis and testicles, the other boy persisted in calling him a girl. Exasperated, Jeremy pulled down his pants to prove his sexual identity. The other boy was not impressed: "Everybody has a penis: only girls wear barrettes."

photographs (and hence, have acquired the corresponding gender schema) displayed less overt aggression than those who did not.

Such findings do not mean that the 3-year-olds had a deep understanding of the basis for the difference between boys and girls (see Box 10.2). Very few of the 2- and 3-year-old children who were able to label pictures of boys and girls correctly could also correctly identify which kinds of objects are usually associated with girls (such as flowers and butterflies) and which are usually associated with boys (such as fire engines and automobiles). Moreover, the children who were able to label pictures correctly according to gender category did not always choose sex-stereotyped toys when they were allowed to play freely on their own (Fagot et al., 1986).

Once basic gender identity is achieved, however, the variety of ways that children use sex-role knowledge to interpret, categorize, and remember the world, as well as their tendency to engage the world in sex-role-appropriate ways increase. One factor that promotes this development is children's increasing interest in the objects and activities that fit their gender-identity schema. To demonstrate this increasing interest, Mary Bradbard and her colleagues (Bradbard et al., 1986) invited a group of children to explore several sets of objects, none clearly stereotyped according to gender: a burglar alarm, a shoe stretcher, and a number puzzle, for example. Although the objects were gender-neutral, the experimenters labeled one set of objects "things for girls," another set "things for boys and girls," and a third set "things for boys." The children were given some information about each object and told to try to remember it, because they would be asked to recall it a week later. As gender schema theory would predict, the boys explored "boy things" more than "girl things" and the girls spent more time looking at "girl things." The results for the neutral "boy and girl" things fell between the two extremes. When the children were asked to remember all they could about each of the objects a week later, the same pattern held: their recall was better for the objects that fitted their own gender identity. More recently, Melissa Welch-Ross and Constance Schmidt (1996) found that 4- to 6-year-olds' recall of story elements was better when the elements fit in with stereotypical gendered behavior.

At this time no single theory appears to be able to encompass all the data concerning children's acquisition of sex-role identity (see Table 10.1). Recent cognitive approaches have confirmed the importance of such signposts as the ability to label one's own sex and the realization that one's sex remains constant over time and in different contexts. Cognitive theory does not, however, explain the fact that young children's toy preferences and behaviors become gender-appropriate even before they can label their own sex. It seems plausible that this intuitive knowledge comes from the fact that everyone around them is treating them either as little boys or little girls and is praising or criticizing them according to their sex-role categorization. That is, social learning is a part of the process from the very beginning. Biological factors, such as sex differences in levels of activity and play style, are also important. The continuing challenge facing researchers who study gender and personal-

TABLE 10.1 PATHS TO SEX-ROLE IDENTITY

Process	Influential Theorists	Hypotheses/Variations
Differentiation and integration	Freud	Boys differentiate from their mothers and identify with their fathers through resolution of the Oedipus complex; girls identify with their mothers after resolving their anger over the lack of a penis.
	Chodorow	A girl's path to identity formation is through affiliation, thus providing a basis for development of intimacy. A boy's path is through differentiation; as a consequence, boys tend to reject intimacy.
Observation and imitation	Bandura	Boys observe and imitate male behavior because they are rewarded for doing so, while girls are rewarded for female behavior. This ultimately produces observed gender differences.
Cognition	Kohlberg	Children first form a permanent schema of their gender and then define what is rewarding in terms of that schema.
Combined mechanisms	Gender schema theory (Martin & Halverson)	Sexual identity emerges from a combination of observation, imitation, and schema formation. The development of gender knowledge *both* depends on *and* is changed by the development of more sophisticated gender schemas.

ity formation is to document the complex interplay between developing cognitive understandings and behavior in the overall process of social development.

A shortcoming shared by all these approaches is that they do not account for the role of such emotions as guilt, fear, and envy in shaping sex-role identity formation. As a consequence, many of the emotional phenomena that inspired the explanations of Freud and his followers remain to be incorporated into a comprehensive account of how sex-role identities are formed.

How Modifiable Is the Process of Forming a Sex-Role Identity?

Uncertainties about the process of sex-role identity make it difficult to know the extent to which adults can shape the final outcome of a child's sex-role development.

For somewhat different reasons, both Freudian and cognitive-developmental theorists believe that the child's sex-role identification and subsequent sex-role behavior are unlikely to be affected by any but the most drastic changes in environmental circumstances. According to Freud's famous dictum that "biology is destiny," males and females are biologically different forms of *Homo sapiens* that no cultural conditioning can change. In Kohlberg's version of the cognitive-developmental view, sex-role identity grows out of universal forms of experience and laws of cognitive development, with cultural influence playing a minor role. Gender schema theorists accord more importance to environmental factors but still place great emphasis on universal mechanisms of information processing and schema formation. Finally, the social-learning view implies a greater role for culture in the shaping of sex-role identification and behavior, thus suggesting that changes in the culture can produce significant changes in sex-role behavior. From this perspective, the essential requirement for changing behavior is a change in the models and rewards.

A variety of studies show that individual adults may exert some influence on children's developing concepts of sex roles and associated behavior. Beverly Fagot and her colleagues (Fagot et al., 1986) studied children at their university-based laboratory. They found that children who learn early to label the people in pictures by sex were more likely to have mothers who initiated play with their children by giving them a toy that fitted the stereotype for their sex. These mothers also expressed more traditional beliefs about sex roles. Evidence that gender-typed behaviors are influenced by parental attitudes and behavior was also obtained in a large study of 4-year-olds in England and Hungary (Turner & Gervai, 1995).

However, such influence often seems to be limited. Thomas Weisner and Jane Wilson-Mitchell (1990) conducted a study to determine if families that sought to promote sex egalitarianism in their children were successful in modifying their children's sex-role stereotypes and behaviors. When they compared the sex-typed preferences for friends, toys, and modes of dress of children raised in such families with those of children whose families adhered to existing cultural norms, they found only scattered differences. A similar conclusion is suggested by Vivian Paley (1986), who devoted one school year to minimizing the development of sex-stereotyped play patterns among her preschoolers. Although she found that she could bring about changes as long as she remained directly in control of the children's actions, the children "reverted to type" as soon as she relaxed her controls.

Such results do not mean that sex-role acquisition is unaffected by social pressure. Comparisons of different cultural groups have shown that many attributes, including types of gestures, speech patterns, dress, activities, interests, and occupations, that are considered masculine in one society may be considered feminine in another (Rosaldo & Lamphere, 1974). Clearly such behaviors are learned from experience. In various countries and at various times in history, men have worn robes as everyday attire; in the United States, this form of dress would be considered decidedly feminine. Such contrasts reveal that whatever the contribution of biology to the shaping of sex roles, at least part of our conception of sex roles and our attitudes toward them is culturally based. In fact, the conclusion reached by Weisner and Wilson-Mitchell and by Paley is that the prevailing culture provides so many lessons in how to behave according to its sex-typed scripts that the family and preschool are not sufficiently powerful to make much of a difference.

ETHNIC AND RACIAL IDENTITY

In a society populated by many ethnic groups and races, children's developing sense of their own ethnic or racial identity is an important social issue. As a consequence, researchers have studied how children acquire the racial and ethnic categories prevalent in their community, identify their own race or ethnic group, and form stable attitudes toward their own and other groups (Cross & Phagen-Smith, 1996; Jackson et al., 1997).

Jean Phinney (1996) defines *ethnic identity* as "an enduring, fundamental aspect of the self that includes a sense of membership in an ethnic group and the attitudes and feelings associated with that membership" (p. 922). Perhaps the most famous research on the development of ethnic and racial identity was carried out by Kenneth and Mamie Clark (1939, 1950), who asked African American children and European American children to make preferential choices between pairs of dolls. The children, who were 3 years old and older, were presented with pairs of dolls representing the two racial groups and were asked to choose "which boy [doll] you would like to play with" or "which girl you don't like." The Clarks reported that most of the youngest children could distinguish between the categories of dolls and, more important, that African American children of all ages seemed to prefer the white dolls. On the basis of this research, many psychologists concluded that African American children define themselves entirely in terms of the majority group, thereby denying the importance of their own families and communities in shaping their identities (Jackson et al., 1997). Plaintiffs in the case of *Brown* v. *Board of Education of Topeka* (1954) used the Clarks' evidence in their argument that racial segregation in the schools leads to a negative sense of self among African American children. On the basis of this and other evidence, the U.S. Supreme Court ruled that racial segregation in the public schools is unconstitutional.

Studies conducted since the 1950s have confirmed the Clarks' findings (McAdoo, 1985; Spencer & Markstom-Adams, 1990) and extended them to other groups, including Native Americans (Annis & Corenblum, 1987) and Bantu children in South Africa (Gregor & McPherson, 1966). However, these studies have also cast doubt on the notion that minority-group children acquire a generalized negative ethnic or racial self-concept. Margaret Spencer (1988), for example, showed that while many of the 4- to 6-year-old African American children she interviewed said that they would prefer to play with a white doll, 80 percent of these children displayed positive self-esteem. Ann Beuf (1977) reported incident after incident in which Native American children who chose white dolls made evident their understanding of the economic and social circumstances that make their lives difficult in contrast to the lives of white people. In one study, 5-year-old Dom was given several dolls representing Caucasians and Native Americans (whose skins were depicted as brown) to put into a toy classroom:

> *Dom: (holding up a white doll)* The children's all here and now the teacher's coming in.
> *Interviewer:* Is that the teacher?
> *Dom:* Yeah.
> *Interviewer: (holding up a brown doll)* Can she be the teacher?
> *Dom:* No *way!* Her's just an *aide.*
>
> (Beuf, 1977, p. 80)

In Beuf's view, the children's choices are less a reflection of their sense of personal self-worth than of their desire for the power and wealth of the white people with whom they had come in contact. Her views are echoed by James Jackson and his colleagues, whose review of existing data provided little support for the idea that minority-group children's recognition that they are members of a relatively powerless group translates into a negative personal sense of themselves (Jackson et al., 1997).

Other studies have shown that young children's expressed ethnic or racial preferences vary with the circumstances. Focusing on the interview situation itself, one study reported that Native American children show a greater preference for dolls representing their own group when they are tested in their native language (Annis & Corenblum, 1987). Harriette McAdoo (1985) reports that African American preschoolers' professed preference for white dolls has declined since the 1950s. She does not speculate on the reasons for this trend, but the end of racial segregation and several decades of political and cultural activism in the African American community are likely candidates. This conclusion is supported by Beuf's (1977) finding that young children of parents who were active in promoting Native American cultural awareness and social rights more often chose dolls representing Native Americans than did children whose parents took little interest in Native American affairs.

In sum, the results of these studies on ethnic and racial identity indicate that children are aware of group ethnic and racial differences by the time they are 4 years old. At the same time, or soon thereafter, they also become aware of their own ethnicity and form judgments about it. Their attitudes toward their own and other people's ethnicity depend on both the attitudes of their adult caregivers and their perceptions of the power and wealth of their own group in relation to others.

PERSONAL IDENTITY

autobiographical memory A personal narrative that helps children acquire an enduring sense of themselves.

Developing a sex role and ethnic identity are just two aspects of children's increasingly complex sense of self that develops during early childhood. Traditionally psychologists like James Mark Baldwin (quoted on p. 375) view the self as double-sided (Baldwin, 1902; James, 1890). One side, the subjective side, or the "I," is the person looking out at the world. This side includes the sense of oneself as a person who exists over time and who acts and experiences the world in a particular way. The other side of the self is the objective side, the side looking from the outside, or the "me." This side includes the characteristics that others see, such as our physical appearance, abilities, and personality traits. The "I" and the "me" are two sides of the same coin; they are shaped by and shape each other continuously over the course of development. We saw this double-sided process at work with the emergence of the distinctive sense of self and the advent of conversational uses of language at the end of infancy (p. 250)—children who exhibit a need to live up to adult standards are likely to say "I want to do it myself" when confronted with a new and challenging task.

The continuing process of developing both the "I" and the "me" senses of oneself is greatly influenced in early childhood by children's increasingly sophisticated use of language. Recall from Chapter 8 (p. 317) that language is acquired in routine, scripted activities in which young children interact with their caregivers. The same routine activities in family settings are crucial contexts for further development of the self. Not only do caregivers tell children that they are good or bad, boys or girls, black or white, Japanese or Jewish, but they also help them acquire an enduring sense of themselves by helping them to create a personal narrative about themselves. This personal narrative is referred to as **autobiographical memory.**

Autobiographical memory is usually created in situations in which adults help children recall and interpret events in which they have participated (Fivush, 1998; Fivush et al., 1996). A father might ask his little boy, "Do you remember when we stopped at the light and the man in the ape suit waved?" The child nods his head silently, or says, "I was scared." Initially, the father carries the burden of remembering and structuring the conversation. Gradually, with increasing age and growing facility with language, the child assumes a more active role, as our daughter Jenny did when she was about 2½ years old. "Tell me what Jenny did?" she would ask us every night at bedtime, and we would oblige her by recounting the events of the day in a schematic way that highlighted events that were particularly interesting or worrisome to her. These conversations would go like this: "Do you remember this morning, when we went to pick up Michael, and Mandy (the dog) came running out?" and Jenny would say, "Doggie go *wuff, wuff, wuff.*" "And what did Mandy do?" we would prompt. "Wagged her tail," Jenny would respond. "And what else did Mandy do?" we would ask, and she would laugh remembering, "She kissed me!" Although we continued to guide the narrative, as she grew older, she increasingly corrected us and added details of her own until she stopped asking us to tell her what happened and started telling us the events of her day (or refusing to tell us, as she often did).

Like all parents in such interactions, we were not simply mirrors reflecting Jenny's experiences. As participants in creating the stories that became part of her autobiographical memory, we strongly influenced what events she remembered and how she remembered them, and in doing this, we were influenced by the larger culture and by our personal histories, values, and interests. What is more, in telling Jenny these stories about herself, we did not try to be objective. Rather, we liked to embellish and exaggerate to heighten the stories and make them more exciting. We tended to play down Jenny's incompetence and some of her fears and exaggerate her capabilities and bravery.

Other parents might stay closer to the objective facts in recounting the events in their children's lives, or they might structure the stories of prior events so that they teach moral lessons. There are great variations among individuals in what events they remember and how such personal narratives are structured (Bretherton, 1993; Nelson, 1993, 1996). Despite this variation, by the time most children are 4 years old, they have internalized the narrative structures appropriate to their culture and can recount their personal experiences by themselves.

Once children are old enough, developmentalists often assess their self-knowledge by asking them to describe themselves, either in face-to-face interviews or through questionnaires. This research has found a predictable pattern of development in how children describe themselves. In early childhood, children's self-description focuses on their physical characteristics ("I am a girl and I have brown hair"), what they can do ("I can run real fast," or "I know the ABCs"), their possessions ("I have a cat"), social relations ("I am a big sister"), and preferences ("My favorite color is red"). Children tend to focus on specific, concrete characteristics rather than combining them into generalized traits such as "being smart" or "being a good athlete." This makes their descriptions somewhat disjointed. Although young children can tell you that they are unhappy or that they are scared, most are incapable of appreciating that they can be both sad and happy or curious and afraid at the same time.

Young children's self-evaluations tend to be unrealistically positive because they have difficulty distinguishing between what they want to do and what they can do. For example, a child will say, "I can say all my letters," or "I can swim the whole way across the pool," when he or she can do neither of these things. By the time children are 4 or 5 years old, they are able to group some of their attributes into categories. A child might say, for example, "I am good at running, jumping, and climbing." While children know that "good" is the opposite of "bad," their cognitive limitations typically prevent them from acknowledging their negative characteristics. As a result they continue to describe themselves only in positive terms (Harter, 1999).

DEVELOPING THE ABILITY TO REGULATE ONESELF

In the process of learning about basic social roles, their niche in society, and their sense of identity, children are also learning which behaviors society considers good and bad. Their parents expect them not only to learn the rules of behavior appropriate to their roles but to follow those rules willingly, without constant supervision. In short, children are expected to adopt the standards of proper conduct in their culture and to accept them so thoroughly that they "behave themselves."

LEARNING ABOUT GOOD AND BAD

Children develop their first, primitive ideas of what is good and bad from the ways in which the significant people in their lives respond to their behavior. The following discussion with several 5-year-olds clearly shows that adult evaluations about right and wrong are more than an external fact; they are the basis for children's self-evaluations:

Eddie: Sometimes I hate myself.
Teacher: When?
Eddie: When I'm naughty.
Teacher: What do you do that's naughty?
Eddie: You know, naughty words. Like "shit." That one.
Teacher: That makes you hate yourself?

Eddie: Yeah, when my dad washes my mouth with soap.
Teacher: What if he doesn't hear you?
Eddie: Then I get away with it. Then I don't hate myself.
Wally: If I'm bad, like take the food when it's not time to eat yet and my mom makes me leave the kitchen, then I hate myself because I want to stay with her in the kitchen.
Eddie: And here's another reason when I don't like myself. This is a good reason. Sometimes I try to get the cookies on top of the refrigerator.
Teacher: What's the reason you don't like yourself?
Eddie: Because my mom counts to ten fast and I get a spanking and my grandma gets mad at her.
Deana: Here's when I like myself: when I'm coloring and my mommy says, "Stop coloring. We have to go out." And I tell her I'm coloring and she says, "Okay, I'll give you ten more minutes."
Teacher: What if you have to stop what you're doing?
Deana: When she's in a big hurry. That's when she yells at me. Then I don't like myself.

(Paley, 1981, pp. 54–55)

heteronomous morality A kind of morality that is based on externally imposed controls.

autonomous morality Morality that is based on an understanding of rules as arbitrary agreements that can be changed if everyone agrees.

As Vivian Paley (1981) comments, "Bad and good depended on the adult response. . . . An angry parent denoted a naughty child. To the adult, the cause of the punishment was obvious, but the child only saw the stick and judged himself accordingly" (p. 55).

Paley is echoing the opinion of Jean Piaget (1932/1965), who called this pattern of thinking the "morality of constraint," or **heteronomous morality** (morality subject to externally imposed controls). Piaget proposed that children's beliefs grow out of their experience of the restrictions placed on them by powerful elders. It has always been the child's experience that older people announce the rules, compel conformity, and decide what is right and wrong.

According to Piaget, as children enter middle childhood and begin increasingly to interact with their peers outside of situations directly controlled by adults, heteronomous morality gives way to a more **autonomous morality.** This new form of moral thinking is based on an understanding of rules as arbitrary agreements that can be challenged and even changed if the people who are governed by them agree. (This idea will be discussed further in Chapter 14.)

Contemporary studies of young children's moral development emphasize that the various rules they must learn are not all of the same kind. Three major categories of social rules can be distinguished from one another according to the seriousness of the consequences if the rule is broken and how broadly the rule applies (Nucci, 1996; Turiel, 1998) (see Table 10.2). At the most general level are *moral rules,* social regulations based on principles of justice and the welfare of others. Moral rules are often believed to derive from a divine source; they are obligations that cannot be transgressed. Such rules are found in some form in all societies.

At the next level of generality are *social conventions*—rules that are important for social coordination in a given society. Social conventions are important aspects of the cultural scripts that young children are acquiring. They include prescriptions about the kinds of behavior that are appropriate for males and females or the kind of clothes people should wear in public, as well as rules about who has authority over other people, how authority is exercised, and how it is acknowledged. Social conventions vary tremendously, not only among societies but also among various subcultural groups within a society. Consequently, it may be difficult, at least from the child's perspective, to tell when one has broken a moral rule or a social convention. Among Samoans, when a young child says "shit," the act is treated as a violation of a social convention; but when Eddie says "shit" and his mouth is washed out with soap, he might well believe that he has broken a moral rule!

TABLE 10.2 EVENTS AND INFRACTIONS OF MORAL RULES, SOCIAL CONVENTIONS, AND PERSONAL RULES

Sample Event Types	Sample Infractions
Moral Rules	
Physical harm	Hitting, pushing
Psychological harm	Hurting feelings, ridiculing
Fairness and rights	Refusing to take turns
Prosocial behaviors	Laughing when another child is crying
Social Conventions	
School rules	Chewing gum in class, talking back to the teacher
Forms of address	Calling a physician "Mr." when he is working
Attire and appearance	Wearing pajamas to school
Sex Roles	Boy wears barrette to keep hair out of eyes while playing football
Etiquette	Swearing, making loud noises while eating
Personal Rules	
Hygiene	Not brushing teeth
Social	Forgetting to thank someone for a gift, forgetting best friend's birthday

Source: After Turiel et al., 1987.

At the most specific level are the rules that govern the *personal sphere,* in which children can make decisions on the basis of their personal preferences. They are allowed to choose which game they want to play after dinner and whom, among the children they know, they want to be friends with. Rules in the personal sphere govern particular events, such as "I sleep with the light on because I am afraid of the dark" or "I always eat the cake part first and save the icing for last." It is in the personal sphere that children are able to develop what is unique about the way they deal with the world (Nucci, 1996; Turiel et al., 1987).

Several studies have found that children as young as 3 or 4 years from a variety of cultures can distinguish among moral, social, and personal rules. For example, they respond quite differently to *moral* rule violations, such as hurting another child or taking another's favorite toy, than they do to violations of a *social convention,* as occurred when Jeremy wore a barrette to school (see Box 10.2) (Turiel, 1998).

Just as there are cultural variations in the boundaries between the moral and social conventional spheres, so there are differences within a culture on what is considered conventional behavior and what is a matter of personal choice. Parents, for example, may treat wearing a bathing suit at the beach as a matter of social convention; it is something everybody does. Their little children, however, may treat wearing a bathing suit as a matter of personal choice, so they take it off to play naked in the water. The borders between the three levels of rules are not easy to keep straight. It takes children many years to acquire their culture's normative separations, and even then, deciding which rules should be applied in which situations requires a good deal of negotiation (Nucci, 1996; Smetana, 1997).

self-control The capacity of children to act in accordance with the expectations of their caregivers, even when they do not want to and are not being directly monitored.

SELF-CONTROL

Obviously, knowing the kinds of behaviors that are expected of them does not mean that children automatically behave according to their society's standards. In addition to learning what they should and should not do, children must acquire the capacity to act in accordance with the expectations of their caregivers, even when they do not want to and are not being directly monitored. This kind of compliance is called **self-control** (Kopp & Wyer, 1994).

At the core of the development of all forms of self-control is the ability to inhibit one's initial impulses; in other words, to stop and think before acting. Eleanor Maccoby (1980) identifies four kinds of inhibition that children must eventually master to gain self- control:

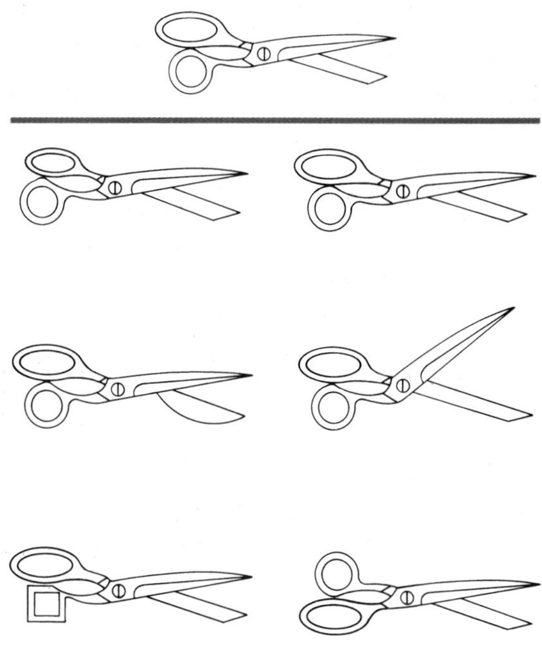

FIGURE 10.5
An item from the Children's Matching Familiar Figures Test. Which of the six pairs of scissors at the bottom of the figure matches the model at the top? (Courtesy of Jerome Kagan.)

1. *Inhibition of movement.* It has long been known that it is easier for small children to start an action than to stop one they are already engaged in (Luria, 1981). A child who does not know when or how to stop is likely to step on someone else's toes, both literally and figuratively. The same problem applies to verbal commands. In a follow-the-leader game such as "Simon says," for example, the leader's commands are supposed to be obeyed only when they are preceded by the words "Simon says." Young children find it very difficult to keep from responding when they hear a command such as "Touch your tummy" or "Raise your arms" that is not preceded by "Simon says" (Kochanska et al., 1996).
2. *Inhibition of emotions.* During early childhood, children begin to gain control over the intensity of their emotions. Maccoby (1980) recounts an incident in which a mother found her 4-year-old with a cut on his hand that ordinarily would have led to tears. When she said to him, "Why, honey, you've hurt yourself! I didn't hear you crying," the youngster replied, "I didn't know you were home."
3. *Inhibition of conclusions.* When presented with a difficult problem, children younger than 6 years old tend to respond quickly, failing to recognize the difficulty of the task. A popular way to assess the ability to inhibit the impulse to jump to conclusions is to ask children to match a familiar figure with its mate in a set of confusing alternatives (Figure 10.5). Young children respond almost immediately to this task and consequently perform poorly. As they grow older, children take time to reflect on the problem and their performance improves (Figure 10.6) (Kochanska et al., 1996; Messer, 1976).
4. *Inhibition of choice.* An important element of adult self-control is the ability to pass up short-term gratification for a larger long-term goal. It is an ability children seem to take a number of years to acquire. For example, given a choice between receiving a small candy bar immediately and a large candy bar the next day, kindergartners overwhelmingly take the small candy bar; not until they are about 12 years old do children choose to wait for the better offering (Mischel, 1968).

Several researchers have studied the early development of children's self-control by focusing on how they comply with adult norms (Gralinski & Kopp, 1993; Kochanska & Aksan, 1995). Grazyna Kochanska and Nazan Aksan videotaped and analyzed the behavior of more than 100 children between the ages of 2 and 5 years of age. The children were studied while they interacted with their mothers in two situations. In the first, the mother and child were given a large number of attractive toys to play with in their own home. After the children played with the toys for a while, their mothers asked them to put them away.

Kochanska and Aksan noted three patterns in the children's responses to the request to put away the toys. These patterns varied

FIGURE 10.6
Between the ages of 5 and 10, children become increasingly cautious in responding to the task of matching familiar figures. Children older than 10 respond more rapidly because the problems are relatively easy for them. (Adapted from Salkind & Nelson, 1980.)

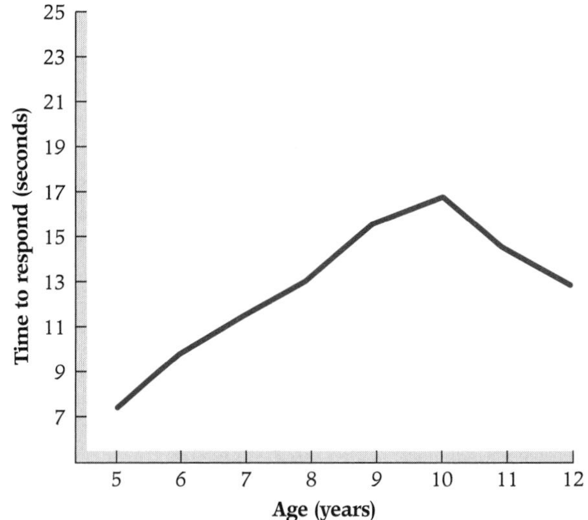

from "committed compliance" (the children wholeheartedly embraced their mothers' agenda) to "outright defiance" (the children threw a tantrum). Between these extremes was "situational compliance" (the children had to be continually prompted by their mothers to do as they were told). The children overtly disobeyed their mothers only 10 percent of the time. Older children were generally more compliant than younger children, and girls were more compliant than boys. However, most of this compliance was of the situational kind. The children clearly found it difficult to put away the attractive toys with which they were still playing.

The second session took place in a laboratory arranged like a living room, where the children were also given toys to play with. The mothers were instructed to tell their children not to touch a set of especially attractive toys on a shelf. After the children had been playing for a while, the researchers asked each mother to come to an adjoining room to see if her child would continue to obey her even when she was not watching. At the end of the session, the mother returned and asked her child to put away the toys.

The injunction not to touch the forbidden toys turned out to be easier to obey than the command to put the toys away. At the end of the "put away the toys" session, approximately 75 percent of the children complied with their mothers' request to put away the toys. And as was true when this situation occurred at home, most of the children's compliance was of the situational kind—again, the mothers had to continually remind the children to complete the cleanup.

By contrast, in the "don't touch" situation, not only did a somewhat larger proportion of the children continue to comply with their mothers' request not to touch the toys on the shelf, but most of them seemed to do so wholeheartedly. Some of the children were heard to talk to themselves, saying such things as "We don't touch these." Their use of the word "we" in such circumstances is a clear sign that they identified with their mothers. When children begin to control themselves in this manner, which corresponds to the idea of "committed compliance," psychologists speak of the associated rules and forms of behavior as "internalized."

INTERNALIZATION

Internalization is the process by which external culturally organized experience becomes transformed into internal psychological processes that, in turn, organize how people behave. Internalization appears to be essential if socialization is to be successful (that is, for the child to grow into an accepted member of the community). Children must have both the ability and the desire to behave in ways that others find acceptable. If they do not, they will be perceived as bad and treated accordingly.

According to Freud (1940/1964), by about age 5, children's internalization of adult standards, rules, and admonitions results in the formation of a new mental agency. This mental agency "continues to carry on the functions which have hitherto been performed by the [parents]: it observes the ego, gives it orders, judges it and threatens it with punishments, exactly like the parents whose place it has [partially] taken. We call this agency the superego and are aware of it in its judicial functions as our conscience" (Freud, 1940/1964, p. 205).

Conscience, then, can be defined as the facet of the personality that emerges once children have developed generalizable, internalized standards for the way they behave (Kochanska & Thompson, 1997). One sign that children are acquiring a conscience can be seen in their expressions of guilt that occur when they put off going to the toilet because they are playing and then wet their pants or when they climb up on the counter to help themselves to the cookies and knock over a dish. The emergence of a conscience in early

internalization The process by which external, culturally organized experience becomes transformed into internal psychological processes that, in turn, organize how people behave.

conscience The facet of the personality that emerges once children have developed generalizable, internalized standards for how to behave.

childhood fits with the views of Erik Erikson (see Box 10.3), who believed that early childhood is the time when children experience, and must try to resolve, the conflict between the need to achieve certain goals of their own and the negative feelings that arise when their initiative leads to disapproval: "Conscience . . . forever divides the child within himself by establishing an inner voice of self-observation, self-guidance, and self-punishment" (Erikson, 1968b, p. 289).

Overall, research on self-control indicates that a host of important changes occur between 2½ and 6 years of age. As children develop greater cognitive sophistication, including the ability to plan and to reason more systematically, they also acquire a greater appreciation of social rules and a desire to act in accordance with those rules. One major result of this process is a more distinctive sense of both themselves and their social worlds. Another is an increasing ability to comply with parental requests and cultural norms in the absence of overt control.

AGGRESSION AND PROSOCIAL BEHAVIOR

Our discussion of internalization and compliance makes it clear that the development of conscience and self-control is more than an individual matter. These personal qualities take shape in culturally organized social contexts. Thus far, however, the discussion has focused on situations in which young children are interacting with authority figures, usually their parents. An equally important aspect of social development is the emerging ability of young children to behave themselves when they are interacting with other children their own age. In order to be accepted as members of their social group, young children must learn to regulate their anger when their goals are thwarted and to subordinate their personal desires to the good of the group when the situation demands. Learning to control aggression and learning to help others are two of the most basic tasks of young children's social development.

As we saw in Chapter 4 (pp. 142–143), children begin to display the rudiments of both aggression and prosocial behavior shortly after birth. The earliest precursors of aggression are the angry cries and thrashing around of newborns whose rhythmic sucking has been interrupted or who are restrained against their will (Stenberg & Campos, 1990). The first signs of prosocial behavior are manifested just as early, when newborns react to the cries of other babies by starting to cry themselves (Dondi et al., 1999). It is widely believed that this "contagious crying" is the precursor of **empathy**, the sharing of another's feelings, which is the basis for helping and for a variety of other behaviors through which individual members contribute to the overall good of the group (Eisenberg & Fabes, 1998; Radke-Yarrow et al., 1983).

THE DEVELOPMENT OF AGGRESSION

Aggression is difficult to define. At the core of its meaning is the idea of a person committing an act intended to hurt another (Coie & Dodge, 1998; Parke & Slaby, 1983). According to this definition, aggression can begin only after children understand that they can be the cause of another person's distress. This understanding seems to take shape very early, especially within the family.

As children mature, two forms of aggression enter their behavioral repertoire (Hartup, 1974). **Instrumental aggression** is directed at obtaining something—for example, threatening or hitting another child to obtain a toy. **Hostile aggression**, ordinarily referred to as "bullying," is more specifically aimed at hurting another person as a way of establishing dominance, which may gain the aggressor advantages in the long run.

empathy The sharing of another's emotions and feelings. Empathy is widely believed to provide the essential foundations for prosocial behavior.

aggression The committing of an act intended to hurt another.

instrumental aggression Aggression that is directed at obtaining something.

hostile aggression Aggression that is aimed at hurting another person as a way of establishing dominance, which may gain the aggressor advantages in the long run.

BOX 10.3

Erik Erikson

Erik Erikson (1902–1994), a student of Freud, combined a background in art, teaching, psychoanalysis, and anthropology in his approach to the process of development throughout the individual life span. Erikson is best known for adding an important social and cross-cultural dimension to Freud's biological determinism.

Erikson built on many of Freud's basic ideas about development, including the importance of early childhood in the formation of personality, the existence of the three basic psychological structures (id, ego, and superego), and the existence of unconscious drives. He held that the main theme of life is the quest for identity, which he conceived of as the stable core of personality. *Identity* in Erikson's terms can be thought of as a relatively stable mental picture of the relation between the self and the social world in the various contexts of socialization. But unlike Freud, Erikson saw identity formation as a lifelong process that goes through many stages. Each stage builds on, reconfigures, and elaborates on the stage from which it emerges. Throughout their lives people ask themselves "Who am I?" and at each stage of life they arrive at a different answer (Erikson, 1963, 1968b).

Erik Erikson.

Whereas Freud's stages of development end in adolescence, Erikson proposed that human development passes through eight stages and continues throughout life. Freud's and Erikson's stages of development are outlined in the table on the facing page.

Each stage, Erikson believed, embodies a particular "main task" that the individual must accomplish in order to move on to the next stage of development. Erikson referred to these tasks as "crises" because they are the sources of conflict within the person experiencing them. Each person's sense of identity is formed in the resolution of these crises, which are periods of great vulnerability but also of heightened potential. Thus, whether 2-year-olds are successful in acquiring control over their desires and bodies will determine whether they feel proud of themselves and autonomous or ashamed and doubtful of their ability to control themselves. At each stage, maturation opens up both new possibilities and increased social demands. A young girl's pleasure at being able to play the role of flower girl at an aunt's wedding, for example, is matched by the psychosocial demands from those around her that she stand still and follow directions without too much prompting.

Erikson believed that each crisis provides the individual with a "succession of potentialities," new ways of experiencing and interacting with the world. At the same time these potentialities are continuously being shaped by other individuals, who in turn are shaped by their culture and social institutions. The "widening circle" of significant individuals who interact with the developing person includes parents, siblings, peers, grandparents, aunts, uncles, teachers, teammates, mentors, colleagues, employers, employees, and grandchildren. The personality undergoes changes appropriate to the person's widening contacts with social institutions and cultural practices.

According to Erikson, each individual's life cycle unfolds in the context of a specific culture. While physical maturation writes the general timetable according to which a particular component of personality matures, culture provides the interpretive tools and the shape of social situations in which the crises and resolutions must be worked out.

Judy Dunn (1988), who observed young English children and their siblings in their homes, found that children between the ages of 1 and 2 showed a rapid increase in instrumental aggression toward their siblings (see Figure 10.7). Perhaps her most interesting finding is that until the age of about 18 months, teasing and physical aggression occur with equal frequency. But as

FREUD'S PSYCHOSEXUAL STAGES AND ERIKSON'S PSYCHOSOCIAL STAGES COMPARED

Approximate Age	Freud (Psychosexual)	Erikson (Psychosocial)
First year	*Oral stage* The mouth is the focus of pleasurable sensations as the baby sucks and bites.	*Trust versus mistrust* Infants learn to trust others to care for their basic needs or to mistrust them.
Second year	*Anal stage* The anus is the focus of pleasurable sensations as the baby learns to control elimination.	*Autonomy versus shame and doubt* Children learn to exercise their will and to control themselves or they become uncertain and doubt that they can do things by themselves.
Third to sixth year	*Phallic stage* Children develop sexual curiosity and obtain gratification when they masturbate. They have sexual fantasies about the parent of the opposite sex and feel guilt about their fantasies.	*Initiative versus guilt* Children learn to initiate their own activities, enjoy their accomplishments, and become purposeful. If they are not allowed to follow their own initiative, they feel guilty for their attempts to become independent.
Seventh year through puberty	*Latency* Sexual urges are submerged. Children focus on mastery of skills valued by adults.	*Industry versus inferiority* Children learn to be competent and effective at activities valued by adults and peers or they feel inferior.
Adolescence	*Genital stage* Adolescents have adult sexual desires, and they seek to satisfy them.	*Identity versus role confusion* Adolescents establish a sense of personal identity as part of their social group or they become confused about who they are and what they want to do in life.
Early adulthood		*Intimacy versus isolation* Young adults find an intimate life companion or they risk loneliness and isolation.
Middle age		*Generativity versus stagnation* Adults must be productive in their work and willing to raise a next generation or they risk stagnation.
Old age		*Integrity versus despair* People try to make sense of their prior experience and to assure themselves that their lives have been meaningful or they despair over their unachieved goals and ill-spent lives.

children approach their second birthdays, they are much more likely to tease their siblings than to hurt them physically. Teasing is a subtle form of aggression requiring the ability to understand the specific characteristics of another child. Dunn reports, for example, that 16- to 18-month-olds already know so well what will upset their siblings that they may break off a fight with a

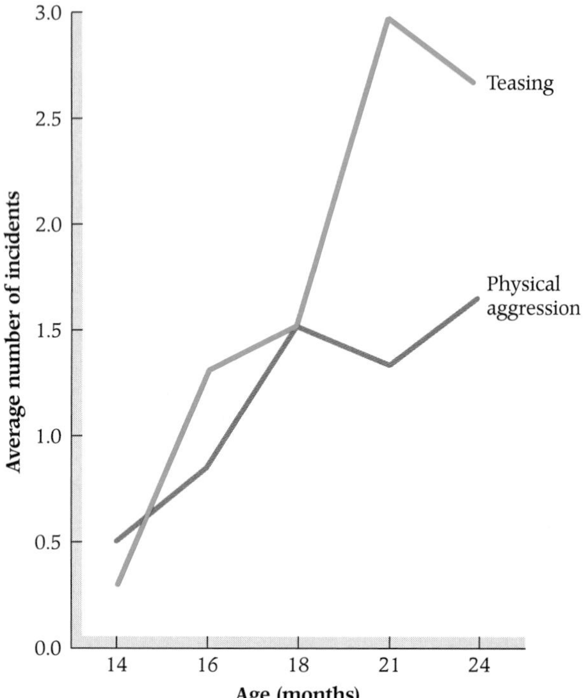

FIGURE 10.7

Early in the second year of life, siblings are as likely to hurt each other physically as to tease each other; but as they approach their second birthdays, teasing becomes much more frequent than physical aggression. (Adapted from Dunn, 1988.)

brother or sister in order to do something to "get" the child indirectly, like destroying his or her favorite toy.

One of the causes of increased instrumental aggressiveness is that as children approach the age of 2 (just when a new and distinctive sense of self seems to emerge, as we saw in Chapter 6, p. 249), they begin to worry about "ownership rights." At this point, having one's toys commandeered becomes a serious affair.

To trace the early development of aggressive behavior, Wanda Bronson (1975) invited several 2-year-olds to a playroom as a group. She gave them toys to play with, and she permitted their mothers to be present to give them a sense of security. As the children explored and played, Bronson watched for occasions when two children wanted the same toy. She noted that often the 2-year-olds struggled over a toy that neither child had shown any interest in before and that neither cared about once the conflict ended. The fact of possession itself, as well as the possibility of "winning out," were new elements in their interactions.

When Wanda Bronson observed older children, she identified changes between the ages of 3 and 6 that appeared to be interrelated. First, physical tussles over possessions decrease, while the amount of verbal aggression—threats, teasing, insults—continues to increase. Second, bullying, or hostile aggression, makes its appearance—one child attempts to hurt another even though no possessions are at stake.

Many studies of childhood aggression from around the world have reported that boys are more aggressive than girls in a wide variety of circumstances (Segall et al., 1997). Boys are more likely than girls to hit, push, hurl insults, and threaten to beat up other children (Coie & Dodge, 1998; Loeber & Hay, 1993). This difference seems to emerge during the second and third years of life (Fagot & Leinbach, 1989; Legault & Strayer, 1990). As we see in Figure 10.8, which plots the frequency of overtly aggressive acts among young children, overt aggression by girls drops markedly as they approach their second birthdays, while boys become slightly more likely to exhibit overt aggression at this time.

relational aggression A form of aggression in which harm is done to another child's friendships or a child is excluded from the group.

This does not mean that girls are not aggressive at all. Qualitative analysis of boys' and girls' social interactions has shown that both sexes engage in aggressive behavior but the forms of their aggression differ (Crick et al., 1997; Hennington et al., 1998). Girls are more likely to harm another child's friendships or exclude that child from the group. This form of aggression, called **relational aggression,** can be heard in such statements as "We don't want to play with you," "I won't be your friend if you play with her," and "Emily says she doesn't like you anymore." As anyone who has been on the receiving end of such statements knows, they can hurt as much as a punch on the arm or a kick to the shin.

FIGURE 10.8

As children in a nursery school approach their second birthdays, acts of aggression decline significantly among girls but increase slightly among boys. (After Legault & Strayer, 1990.)

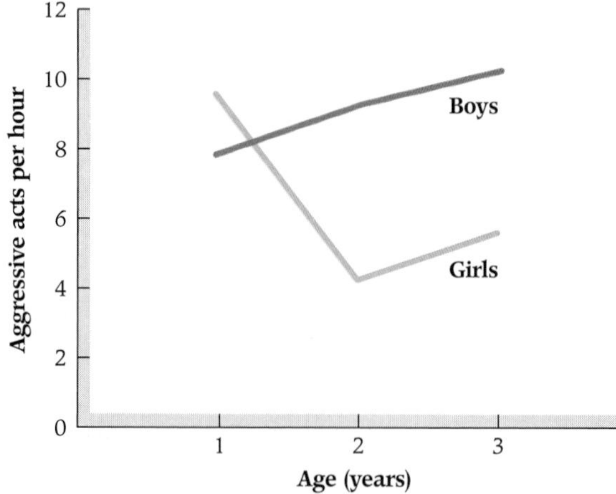

WHAT CAUSES AGGRESSION?

More people have died in wars during the twentieth century than in all earlier centuries combined. Every day our newspapers carry stories of people killing other people for money, to avenge a perceived wrong, or for no apparent reason at all. Among all the questions that can be asked about human social relations, none are more fraught with concern and uncertainty than questions about the causes of aggression and the means of controlling it (see Box 10.4).

Explanations for the development of aggressive behavior focus on three contributing factors: (1) the presence of aggression in the evolutionary precursors of our species, (2) the ways societies reward

BOX 10.4

Parental Beliefs about Causes of Aggression

The following anecdote comes from Ann McGillicuddy-DeLisi

My 4-year-old was practicing "pumping" himself on the swing and didn't want me distracting him, so I sat on a swing myself and watched the Frisbee game that two fathers were having around their 3-year-old sons. One of the little boys was getting all excited. He yelled "hi-yahh!" and kicked karate-like at the other boy, who ran away laughing. One father threw the Frisbee to the karate kid, who spun around until he was dizzy and then released it. The fathers then went back to their Frisbee game and the two little boys ran around, making contact occasionally, falling and laughing, and then separating again.

The little kicker was getting more excited and more physical and aggressive with each interlude, however. I thought, "That's the difference between mothers and fathers. A mother would see that this behavior is escalating and someone is bound to get hurt. She'd intervene now." I was wondering why mothers and fathers seem to react so differently to the same behavior from a child. The father called to the boy who had just connected a kick to his playmate's leg and threw the Frisbee again. The kid missed the Frisbee, ran to it and then ran off with it. The father caught him, wrestled playfully with him, took it away and resumed the steady back-and-forth toss with the other father.

Suddenly there were screams. The karate kid was sitting on his friend, swinging his little fists, pummeling his friend, and laughing while the other boy screamed. The father ran over, pulled the aggressor off the other child, and spanked him hard, three times. He shouted, "I told you never to hit! Now say you are sorry!" I was thinking, "Boy, this guy never heard of Bandura." I was about to go into a daydream concerning the beliefs parents hold about their children, and how this might affect their child-rearing strategies, when a neighbor on the swing next to me said, "It's really amazing, isn't it? I knew that kid was going to go wild." Aha . . . a kindred spirit who knew that this man behaved the way he did because he believed in negative feedback as a means of conveying messages regarding appropriate behavior, . . . giving little importance to the role of imitation, identification, and so forth in children's personal-social development. I said (in my best distancing voice), "Why do you think he did that?" looking for my neighbor's rationale for the father's behavior. My neighbor answered, "Boys are just so aggressive and physical. They can't help it."

She [the neighbor] watched exactly the same interactions as I did, and yet her construction of the event was different. I saw the child's activity level and physical aggressiveness as a learned behavior that continued to escalate as a result of the intermittent reinforcement of his father's attention following aggressive acts, as well as through imitation of the father's own physical aggressiveness with the boy. The neighbor saw the same behavior as an expression of an inborn trait that is characteristic of boys. She and I would have reacted to the child's behavior differently because we differed in our beliefs about the source to which the behavior was attributed. (1992, pp. 115–116)

aggressive behaviors, and (3) the tendency of children to imitate the behavior of older role models.

Teeth are a favorite weapon when preschoolers engage in peer-oriented aggression.

The Evolutionary Argument

Noting that no group in the animal kingdom is free of aggression, many students of animal behavior have proposed that aggression is an important force in animal evolution (Lorenz, 1966). According to Darwin (1859/1958), a species gradually comes to assume the characteristics of its most successful individuals. Darwin defined as "successful" those individuals who manage to pass on their genetic characteristics to the next generation. Because each individual is, in some sense, competing with every other individual for the resources necessary for survival and reproduction, evolution would seem to favor competitive and selfish behaviors. Such animal behaviors as defense of a territory, which ensures that a mating pair will have access to food, have been interpreted as survival-oriented competition (Wilson, 1975). According to this interpretation of evolution, aggression is natural and necessary; its appearance automatically accompanies the biological maturation of the young.

Rewarding Aggression

A second explanation, generally associated with the social-learning view, is that people learn to behave aggressively because they are often rewarded when they do so (Patterson et al., 1992; Segall et al., 1997). For example, G. R. Patterson and his colleagues (Patterson et al., 1967) spent many hours watching the aggressive behavior of nursery school children. Whenever they observed an incident of aggression, they noted who the aggressor was, who the victim was, and what the consequences were. They found that aggressive actions occurred several times an hour and that well over three-quarters of the aggressive acts they observed were followed by positive consequences for the aggressor: the victim either gave in or retreated. Each victory increased the probability that the aggressor would repeat the attack.

These researchers also found that parents of aggressive children often reinforce their children's aggressive behaviors (Patterson et al., 1992). In some cases, they provide positive reinforcement by paying more attention, laughing, or signaling approval when their children are aggressive. In other cases, children are reinforced for their aggression by the fact that it gets their parents to stop coercing them. Patterson and his colleagues suggest that in coercive households aggressive behavior in a child is functional because it makes it possible for the child to survive in punishing social circumstances.

Modeling

Social-learning theorists believe that in the act of punishing their children, parents may inadvertently teach them how to behave aggressively. One line of evidence for this mechanism comes from a famous series of experiments conducted by Albert Bandura and his co-workers (Bandura, 1965, 1973; Bandura et al., 1963). They arranged for several groups of preschool children to watch as an adult yelled at a large, inflatable "Bobo" doll, hit it on the head with a mallet, threw it across the room, punched it, and otherwise abused it (see Figure 10.9). In some cases the children watched a normally dressed adult attacking the doll; in others, they saw a filmed version of the same events; in still another case, the model was costumed as a cartoon cat.

After the children watched the episodes of aggressive behavior, the experimenters arranged for them to engage in other activities for a while. Then they brought the children to a playroom containing a Bobo doll and invited them to play, in order to see if they would imitate the adult they had ob-

FIGURE 10.9
In the top row of photos, an adult behaves aggressively toward a Bobo doll. In the two lower rows, youngsters imitate her aggressive behavior.

served. As social-learning theory would predict, the aggressive behavior of children who had observed adult aggression was substantially higher than that of children in a control group who had watched nonaggressive interactions. Not only did the children who had been exposed to an aggressive model imitate specific forms of aggression; they also made up forms of their own, such as pretending to shoot the doll or spanking it. It made little difference whether the adult models were live or filmed, but the children were somewhat less likely to imitate the aggression of the cartoon character. The conclusion from this research seems inescapable: Once children are old enough to understand that they can get their way by harming others, they learn from adults both specific types of aggression and the general idea that acting aggressively may be acceptable (Figure 10.10).

FIGURE 10.10
Among the Dani of New Guinea, boys are socialized to be aggressive and warlike from an early age through organized practice sessions and many opportunities to observe admired older males in battle. These boys are watching men from their village fight against men from another village.

A second line of evidence that children learn to behave aggressively by observing adults comes from cross-cultural research (Segall et al., 1997). This work shows that societies differ markedly in the levels of interpersonal violence they consider normal. For example, Douglas Fry (1988) compared the levels of aggression of young children in two Zapotec Indian towns in central Mexico. On the basis of anthropological reports, Fry chose one town that was notable for the degree to which violence was controlled and a second town that was notable for the fact that people often fought at public gatherings, husbands beat their wives, and adults punished children by beating them with sticks.

Fry and his wife established residences in both towns so that they could get to know the people and develop enough rapport to be able to make their observations unobtrusively. They then collected several hours of observations of 12 children in each town as they played in their houses and around the neighborhood. When the researchers compared the aggressive acts of the children in the two towns, they found that those in the town with a reputation for violent behavior performed twice as many violent acts as the children in the other town.

Because these data were collected in naturally occurring interactions, it is not possible to assert that observational learning was the only factor in the levels of aggression displayed by the children. Fry reports, for example, that adults in the more violence-prone town sometimes directly encouraged their sons and daughters to be aggressive and did not always break up fights between their children. The differences he observed, however, could not plausibly be explained by reference to biological dispositions, so the results fit most comfortably within an environmental-learning or cultural-context approach. At the same time, it should not be overlooked that even in the town that discouraged aggression, the children sometimes acted aggressively, a fact that is difficult to explain purely in terms of social learning mechanisms.

INDIVIDUAL DIFFERENCES IN AGGRESSIVE BEHAVIOR

Some children seem to be more aggressive than others and to have more problems with antisocial behavior. There is substantial evidence that 3-year-old children who behave defiantly and disobediently with adults, are aggressive toward their peers, and are impulsive and hyperactive are likely to still have these problems during middle childhood and adolescence (Coie & Dodge, 1998). A number of longitudinal studies have found that, for boys in particular, the earlier the age at which children begin to exhibit such problem behaviors, the greater the likelihood that they will continue to behave in those ways later in life (Patterson et al., 1998).

Studies of both twins and children who have been adopted indicate that genes play a role in individual differences in aggressive behavior (Eley et al., 1999). This does not mean that there are genes for aggressive behavior that some individuals have more of than others. Rather, genetic influences on aggression come about indirectly through their effects on physiologically based characteristics, which in turn influence behavior.

One such physiologically based characteristic that has often been cited as an explanation for the difference in the levels of aggression between boys and girls is the hormone testosterone. There is a correlation between circulating testosterone levels and aggression in both boys and girls during childhood (Dobbs, 1992). However, this correlation does not mean that testosterone directly *causes* aggressive behavior. Studies with both animals and humans have found that increased levels of testosterone can be the *result* of dominance over others or success in conflict. In other words, testosterone both influences and is influenced by dominance (Mazur & Booth, 1998).

Researchers currently believe that testosterone affects behavior indirectly by affecting a child's activity level. As we have seen, in general, boys have higher activity levels than girls, which, in turn, lead them to exhibit play preferences different from those of girls. Boys are often involved in more physical games than girls typically engage in, and they tend to play in larger groups than girls do. These differences might make physical aggression more functional for boys than for girls (Boulton, 1996; Coie & Dodge, 1998). The sex differences in levels of aggression interact with individual differences in children's temperaments to determine whether particular children are more likely than their peers to behave aggressively.

Other physiological processes that seem indirectly to make one child more aggressive than another include differences in levels of neurotransmitters (decreased serotonin functioning has been associated with aggressive behavior) and differences in nervous-system activity. Difficult temperaments and organically damaged attention processes have also been linked to aggression (Coie & Dodge, 1998).

Ecological factors and social stressors also contribute to individual differences in aggressive behavior. Kerry Bolger and her colleagues found that even temporary poverty increases the likelihood that children will behave aggressively. The longer and more pervasive the poverty, the stronger the effects (Bolger et al., 1995; Patterson, 1995). As we shall see in Chapter 11 (p. 436), parents living in poverty are psychologically stressed and have relatively little control over their lives. In responding to their children while under stress, they are more likely to use harsh and inconsistent discipline. As we have just seen (p. 437), such parental behavior can be expected to increase children's aggressive behavior.

The likelihood of a child's acting aggressively can also be affected by his or her mental abilities. How accurately one can take another's perspective, for example, determines how one understands social interactions. Aggressive children often misinterpret social interactions in negative ways that evoke aggressive responses in inappropriate contexts (Coie & Dodge, 1998).

Needless to say, all these sources of development come together in a unique manner for every individual child. The result is the tremendous range of ways in which children experience and use aggression in their everyday lives. Taken as a whole, the evidence concerning the possible causes of aggression cautions us not to pit environmental and biological explanations of aggressive behavior against each other in a simplistic way. Such either/or thinking is not sufficient to explain a form of behavior as complex as aggression, which grows out of the interactions between deep-seated biological characteristics and culturally organized environmental influences. Nor can we understand aggression without looking at the various mechanisms that counteract it, since aggression is just one among several factors that regulate social behavior.

CONTROLLING HUMAN AGGRESSION

The same theories that attempt to explain aggression also point to mechanisms that are likely to be effective in controlling it. Three such mechanisms that have been extensively studied are (1) the *evolution of hierarchical systems of control,* (2) *the use of reward and punishment, and* (3) *cognitive training.*

Evolutionary Theories

While aggression is widespread among animal species, so are mechanisms that limit it. The aggressive behavior in litters of puppies, for example, changes in accordance with a maturational timetable (James, 1951). At about 3 weeks, puppies begin to engage in rough-and-tumble play, mouthing and nipping one another. A week later the play has become rougher; the puppies growl and snarl when they bite, and the victims may yelp in pain. A few weeks later, if littermates are left together, their attacks become serious. Often the larger puppies concentrate their attacks on the runts of the litter, and among some breeds the smallest animals will be killed if they are not removed. Once injurious attacks become really serious, however, a hierarchical social structure emerges, with some animals dominant and others subordinate. After such a **dominance hierarchy** is formed, the dominant puppy needs only to threaten in order to get its way; it has no need to attack. At this point, the frequency of fighting diminishes (Cairns, 1979). Throughout the animal kingdom one finds such hierarchies, which regulate interactions among members of the same species (see Figure 10.11).

FIGURE 10.11
Many species of animals have innate mechanisms for signaling defeat to allow the establishment of a social dominance hierarchy without bloodshed.

The developmental history of aggression and its control among puppies is similar in some interesting ways to development in human children. F. F. Strayer (1980, 1991) and his colleagues observed a close connection between aggression and the formation of dominance hierarchies among 3- and 4-year-olds in a nursery school. They identified a specific pattern of hostile interactions among children: when one child would aggress, the other child would almost always submit by crying, running away, flinching, or seeking help from an adult. These dominance encounters led to an orderly pattern of social relationships within the group. One child who dominated another also dominated all children below that child in the dominance hierarchy of the group.

As dominance hierarchies in the nursery school take shape, they influence who fights with whom and under what circumstances. Once children know their position in such a hierarchy, they challenge only those whom it is safe for them to challenge. They leave others alone, thereby reducing the amount of aggression within the group.

The existence of similarities across species in these patterns of aggression and its control should not blind us to important differences. The young of other species often must rely entirely on the dominance hierarchy, whereas human offspring are watched over by their parents and older siblings, who set limits to small children's initial expressions of aggression to keep them from harming others. These older members of the group also invoke rules about proper behavior, which the children begin to internalize, thus helping to pave the way for self-control.

Frustration and Catharsis

One of the most popular and persistent beliefs about aggression is that providing people with harmless ways to be aggressive will reduce their aggressive and hostile tendencies. This belief is based on the assumption that unless aggressive urges are "vented" in a safe way, they build up until they explode violently. Psychologists refer to this process of "blowing off steam" as **catharsis,** a general term for the release of fear, tension, or other intense negative emotions. According to this theory, the way to control aggression is to arrange for it to be vented before trouble erupts (Bemak & Young, 1998).

dominance hierarchy A hierarchical social structure in which some members have dominant status and others have subordinate status.

catharsis A general term for the release of fear, tension, or other intense negative emotions.

Despite the popularity of this hypothesis in folk belief and clinical practice, there is little convincing evidence to support catharsis as a means of controlling aggression. In a rare experimental study of the efficacy of catharsis, Shahbaz Mallick and Boyd McCandless (1966) asked two groups of third-grade boys to build a house of blocks within a limited amount of time in order to win a cash prize. One group had its building efforts interfered with by a "clumsy" boy—who was actually a confederate of the experimenters—and became angry because they lost the opportunity to win the prize. The other group was allowed to work uninterrupted. Some of the boys were then given the opportunity to shoot a play gun at animated targets of people and animals or at a bull's-eye target. Others were asked to solve arithmetic problems. Next, the boys were asked to administer uncomfortable shocks to the boy who had interrupted their building task (actually, no shocks were delivered to the boy). The number of "shocks" they gave was used as the measure of their aggression.

The experimenters found that frustration did appear to increase the children's aggression. The boys who had been interrupted administered more "shocks" than the other children. Contrary to the catharsis hypothesis, however, the opportunity to blow off steam did not reduce the boys' aggressive behavior: the boys who shot at targets delivered just as many "shocks" as the children who had solved arithmetic problems.

Although experimental confirmation is lacking, the idea that catharsis releases negative emotions is widely applied in psychotherapy with young, troubled children (Ginsberg, 1993). Catharsis-based therapies are most likely to take place through play in which children's actions are believed to communicate to the psychologist their otherwise-hidden fears and emotions (Jones, 1992).

Punishment

Another common belief about aggressive behavior is that it can be eliminated if it is punished whenever it occurs. This tactic suppresses aggressive behavior under some circumstances, but often it does not. If punishment is used as a means of socialization, it is most likely to suppress aggressive behavior when the child identifies strongly with the person who does the punishing (Eron et al., 1971) and when it is employed consistently. Used inconsistently, punishment is likely to provoke children to further aggression (Block et al., 1981; Parke & Slaby, 1983).

When a family adopts coercive child-rearing behaviors, the levels of violence may escalate to create patterns of serious abuse. Evidence suggests that such patterns may perpetuate themselves in the next generation when young parents who were abused as children abuse their own children.

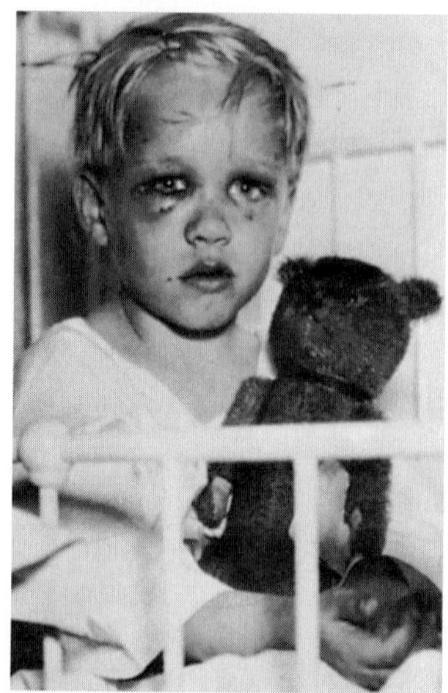

Several studies have found that attempts to control children's behavior by means of physical punishment, or by threats to apply raw power, actually increase the children's aggressiveness (Coie & Dodge, 1998; Patterson, 1995). Gerald Patterson and his colleagues have observed how this effect is produced under natural conditions. They observed two groups of boys age 3 to 13½ along with parents in their homes. The boys in the first group had been referred to the researchers by schools and clinics because of their excessively aggressive behavior. The second group of boys had not been referred for help. The investigators found that punitive child-rearing tactics were more frequent in the homes of the referred boys. These tactics were often associated with a higher level of aggression in the family as a whole (Patterson, 1976, 1979, 1982).

Patterson's findings involve correlational data and do not isolate causal factors, but his observations suggest that punitive child-rearing tactics may facilitate the learning of aggression. Say, for example, that a younger brother hits his older sister in order to obtain a toy. His sister hits him back. He shouts at her and, while pulling on the toy, hits her again. She resists. The mother comes running to see what is the matter. She shouts at the children to stop, but they do not listen. Exasperated, she lashes out and slaps her son and roughly shoves her daughter. The boy withdraws, breaking the cycle for the moment. If matters stopped here, this would just be a case of corporal punishment. But now the mother's behavior has been modified. Since her aggressive intervention successfully stopped the children's fighting, she is more likely to be aggressive in future incidents. Observing the success of the aggression she models, her children may also learn to interact in an aggressive way.

Kenneth Dodge and his colleagues have conducted extensive research on the mechanisms that link parental punishment to later aggression by their children (Dodge, 1994; Strassberg et al., 1994; Weiss et al., 1992). In one study they contacted 584 boys and girls at the time of their preregistration for kindergarten. In the spring before the children entered kindergarten, a researcher went to each child's home to interview the parents about how they handled their child's misbehavior, asking specifically about whether they had ever slapped, spanked, hit, or beaten their child and whether their child had ever been physically harmed by such punishment to the point of being bruised or needing medical attention. The researchers found that 12 percent of the children had been so harmed.

In a separate interview, the children were shown short videos in which child actors carried out negative social actions, such as knocking over another child's building blocks or excluding another child from a play group. In some cases, the videos made it clear that these negative social acts were intentional. In other cases, the negative acts were either clearly accidental or ambiguous. Immediately after seeing each video, the children were asked to recall what had happened and then to tell how they might have behaved if the same negative things had happened to them, why they thought the children in the video behaved the way they did, and what they thought the probable outcome of the situation would be.

Six months later, after the children had entered kindergarten, each child was observed for twelve 5-minute periods in the playground and in the classroom by trained observers who did not know the child's punishment history. In addition, the child's teacher and peers were asked to rate the child's aggression.

In accord with the belief that physical punishment begets aggression, the children who had been physically harmed when they were disciplined were rated as more aggressive by both their peers and their teachers than were the children who had not been harmed. The ratings were confirmed by the direct observations of the children in their classroom and in the playground. Children who had been severely punished were three times more likely than other children to react to either real or imagined harm by lashing out against the other child with a shove, punch, or kick.

An interesting finding was that the children's aggression did not seem to be the *direct* result of learning to be aggressive, as learning theory suggests. Rather, the aggression seemed to be an *indirect* result of the way the children interpreted the events that provoked them. Children who had been severely punished appeared to misread the social events depicted in the videos they were shown at the beginning of the study. They were more likely than the other children to believe that accidental and ambiguous provocations were intentionally hostile, justifying an aggressive response.

Dodge and his colleagues believe that these results support the idea that children who are frequently and severely punished acquire chronic patterns of processing social information that incline them to interpret unpleasant interactions as hostile and directed at them. This pattern of interpretation tends to perpetuate itself, because the children's aggressive reactions evoke hostility in their targets, falsely "confirming" their original interpretation of hostile intent. The result is the development of chronic aggression.

Rewarding Nonaggressive Behaviors

Since young children sometimes become aggressive in order to gain attention, a recommended strategy for reducing aggression has been to ignore it and to pay attention to children only when they are engaged in cooperative behavior. One way for adults to employ this strategy is to step in between the children involved in an altercation and to pay attention only to the victim, ignoring the aggressor (Allen et al., 1970). The adult may comfort the injured child, give the child something interesting to do, or suggest nonaggressive ways in which the victim might handle future attacks. Children are taught to say, for example, "No hitting" or "I'm playing with this now." When teachers are trained to use this selective-attention technique, aggression in their classroom declines significantly (Brown & Elliot, 1965).

Such selective-attention procedures may work to reduce aggression in several ways. First and foremost, the aggressor is rewarded neither by the adult's attention nor by the victim's submission. In addition, because the victim is taught how to deal with such attacks without becoming an aggressor, the aggression is kept from escalating. Moreover, other children who may have observed the scene are shown that it is appropriate to be sympathetic to the victim of aggression and that nonviolent assertion in the face of aggression can be effective.

Cognitive Training

Another way to control aggression is to use reason. Though it is sometimes difficult to hold a rational discussion with a 4-year-old who has just grabbed a toy away from a playmate, such discussions have been found to reduce aggression even at this early age. In one demonstration of this, Shoshana Zahavi and Steven Asher (1978) arranged for the teacher in a preschool program to take the most aggressive boys aside, one by one, and engage them in a 10-minute conversation aimed at teaching them (1) that aggression hurts another person and makes that person unhappy; (2) that aggression does not solve problems and only causes resentment in the other child; and (3) that children can often resolve conflicts by sharing, taking turns, and playing together. The teacher taught each concept by asking the child leading questions and encouraging the desired response. After these conversations, the boys' aggressive behavior decreased dramatically and their positive behavior increased.

An important component of this technique was that the children were made aware of the feelings of those they aggressed against. Indeed, all the successful techniques for teaching children to control their aggression go beyond the mere suppression of aggressive impulses. Instead, aggression is controlled by encouraging children to stop their direct attacks and to consider another way to behave.

THE DEVELOPMENT OF PROSOCIAL BEHAVIOR

When Charles Darwin published *The Origin of Species,* the public's understanding of evolution was dominated by such famous phrases as Herbert Spencer's "survival of the fittest" and Tennyson's "Nature, red in tooth and claw." Even Darwin (1859/1958) said that Spencer's expression was "more accurate" than his own "natural selection" (Chap. 3). Yet we recognize now that Spencer's characterization presents an inaccurate, one-sided picture of evolution, for it takes no account of behaviors that offer no direct reward to the benefactor but do benefit the group. Such prosocial behaviors—altruism, cooperation, and helping—are common. When a preschooler offers her teddy bear to a friend who is crying because she scraped her knee or brings candy to share with friends, she is engaging in prosocial behavior. Why do such behaviors occur and how do they develop?

Evolutionary Explanations

Prosocial behavior, like aggression, is not an exclusively human trait. Many animals, among them social insects, hunting dogs, and chimpanzees, exhibit behaviors that at least appear to reflect altruism. The challenge to theories of biological evolution is to show how these behaviors have evolved and how they apply to human beings. Edward O. Wilson (1975), a sociobiologist, has posed the problem and its solution as follows:

> How can altruism, which by definition reduces personal fitness, possibly evolve by natural selection? The answer is kinship: if the genes causing the altruism are shared by two organisms because of common descent, and if the altruistic act by one organism increases the joint contribution of these genes to the next generation, the propensity to altruism will spread through the gene pool. This occurs even though the altruist makes less of a solitary contribution to the gene pool as the price of its altruistic act. (pp. 3–4)

Wilson reasoned that if natural selection "looked for" altruism among lower animals, there must also be a direct genetic basis for altruism among human beings.

Wilson's argument set off a controversy that is still in progress (de Vos & Zeggelink, 1997; Tooby & Cosmides, 1997). Among the animals Wilson studied, a biological explanation of altruism seems applicable because altruism is restricted to kin, individuals with genes very similar to one's own. But human beings extend altruism well beyond kin to total strangers. While it is possible to argue that altruism toward strangers may increase one's chance for survival because it may eventually be reciprocated (a modern version of the notion of casting one's bread upon the waters), to many investigators, the likelihood that such altruism will give one a selective advantage seems remote (Kitcher, 1985).

When we consider this aspect of social development, it is important to keep in mind that both antisocial and prosocial behaviors develop within a single integrated social system. Empathetic impulses develop in the context of social interactions, just as aggressive ones do; both are essential parts of a child's personality, and both are subject to the process of socialization.

Empathy

The psychological state that corresponds to prosocial behavior in the way that anger corresponds to aggression is *empathy,* the sharing of another person's emotions and feelings. Empathy is widely believed to provide the essential foundations for prosocial behavior (Eisenberg, 1992; Hoffman, 1975, 1991). According to Martin Hoffman, a child can feel empathy for another person at any age. As children develop, however, their ability to empathize broadens and they become better able to interpret and respond appropriately to the distress of others.

This child's empathy for his pet is so strong that one might think it was he, not the dog, that was being inoculated.

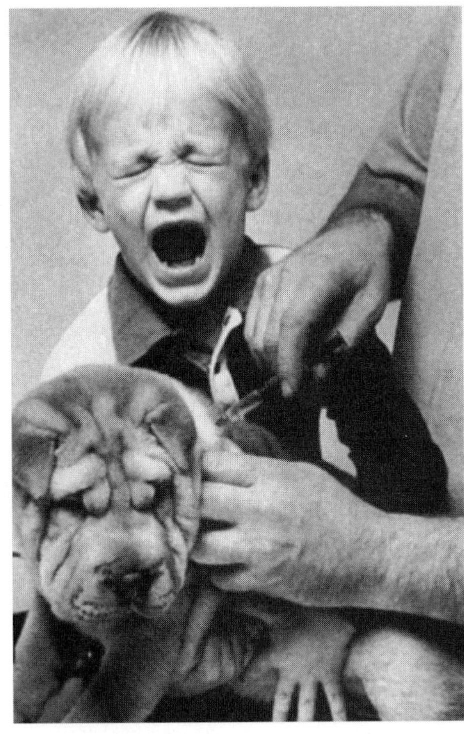

Hoffman has proposed four stages in the development of empathy. The first stage occurs during the first year of life. As we noted earlier, babies as young as 2 days become stressed and cry at the sound of another infant's cries (Dondi et al., 1999). Nancy Eisenberg (1992) calls this phenomenon "emotional contagion." These early "sympathy cries" are akin to innate reflexes, since babies obviously can have no understanding of the feelings of others. Yet they respond as if they were having those feelings themselves.

During the second year of life, as children develop a sense of themselves as distinct individuals, their responses to others' distress change. Now when babies are confronted by someone who is distressed, they are capable of understanding that it is the other person who is upset, not they. This realization allows children to turn their attention from concern for their own comfort to comforting others. Since they have difficulty keeping other people's points of view in mind, however, some of their attempts to help may be inappropriate, such as giving a security blanket to a daddy who looks upset.

The third stage in the development of empathy, corresponding roughly to early childhood, is brought on by the child's increasing command of language and other symbols. Language allows children to empathize with people who are expressing their feelings verbally, without visible emotions, as well as with people who are not present. Information gained indirectly through

prosocial behaviors Behaviors such as sharing, helping, caregiving, and showing compassion.

stories, pictures, or television permits children to empathize with people whom they have never met.

The fourth stage in the development of empathy occurs sometime between the ages of 6 and 9. Children now appreciate not only that other people have feelings of their own but that these feelings occur within a larger set of experiences. Children at this stage begin to be concerned about the general conditions of others, their poverty, oppression, illness, or vulnerability, not just their momentary emotions. Since children in this age range are aware that there are classes of individuals, they are capable of empathizing with groups of people and thus can take a budding interest in political and social issues.

Note that Hoffman's theory of empathy is linked to Piaget's theory of cognitive development. Each new stage of empathy corresponds to a new stage of cognitive ability that allows children to understand themselves better in relation to others.

Perhaps because it is linked so closely to what children understand, Hoffman's explanation of the development of empathy tends to leave out how they feel. It is tacitly assumed that the more children understand, the more intensely they adopt the feelings of the person in distress. The catch, as Judy Dunn (1988) points out, is that children may understand perfectly well why another child is in distress and feel glad as a result.

Evidence on the Development of Prosocial Behaviors

Several studies document the development of such **prosocial behaviors** as sharing, helping, caregiving, and showing compassion as early as the second year of life (see Figure 10.12). Carolyn Zahn-Waxler and Marion Radke-Yarrow (1982) studied the development of prosocial action over a 9-month period among three groups of children, who were 10, 15, and 20 months of age at the start of the observations. Their findings were based on mothers' reports of occasions when their children expressed sympathy for others.

In accord with Hoffman's theorizing, when confronted with someone else's distress, the youngest children responded by crying themselves. As the children grew older, crying decreased and was replaced by worried attention. In the period between 12 and 18 months of age, most children had progressed from diffuse emotional responses to active caregiving and comforting behavior in response to another's distress. The comforting behavior of $1\frac{1}{2}$- and 2-year-olds was sometimes quite elaborate. Children this age did such things as try to put a Band-Aid on someone's cut or cover a resting mother with a blanket. They also began to express their concern verbally and to give suggestions about how to deal with the problem.

FIGURE 10.12
One twin brother shows his sympathy for the other as he tries to comfort him.

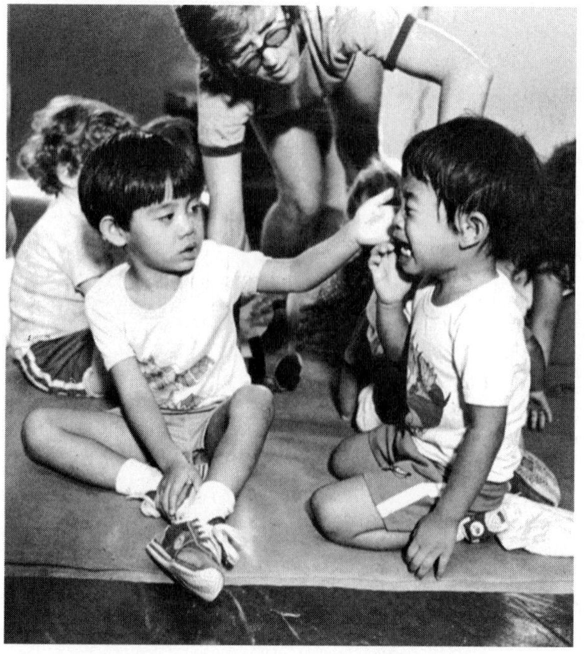

In another study, mothers reported that their young children's helping, sharing, and comforting behaviors in response to another person's distress increased in frequency and variety during the second year of life (Zahn-Waxler et al., 1992). The children expressed concern, attempted to comprehend the situation, and tried to alleviate the other person's distress. These expressions of concern for others emerge about the same time that children are able to recognize themselves in a mirror and begin to refer to themselves (see Chapter 6, p. 249). Zahn-Waxler and her colleagues speculate that these social cognitive capacities, as well as the emerging capacity to imagine and pretend, may help children to connect another's experience with their own and therefore understand it better.

Dunn (1988) reports that the tendency of young children to comfort a sibling in distress increased between 15 and 36 months, as we would expect on the basis of the observations reported by Zahn-Waxler and her colleagues. But she found that such comforting occurred only when the child did not cause the sibling's distress in the first place. Moreover, children of all ages were sometimes observed

Children as young as three or four display empathy and concern for the happiness of their peers.

responding to a sibling's distress by laughing or seeking to make matters worse.

Such observations in the home make it clear that the way children respond to their siblings' distress depends to some degree on the nature of their prior relationship. Not surprisingly, the same can be said for their responses to their peers. In nursery school, 3- and 4-year-old children are more likely to respond prosocially to the distress of children with whom they have ongoing friendly relations than to others (Farver & Branstetter, 1994).

Other evidence about the development of prosocial behavior comes from observations of young children as they follow their parents through their daily rounds of activities, often trying to help them. Harriet Rheingold (1982) invited parents and their 18-, 24-, and 30-month-old children into a laboratory setting that simulated a home. The setting included several undone chores—a table to be set, scraps to be swept up, dusting to be done, a bed to be made, and laundry to be folded. The parents and other adults were instructed to do these chores without asking the children for help. Yet in a 25-minute session, all the 2-year-olds helped their mothers, and 18 of the 20 helped an unfamiliar woman. While they were helping, the children said things that indicated that they knew the goals of the tasks and were aware of themselves as working with others to achieve those goals. They worked spontaneously and eagerly and went well beyond imitation in their helpfulness.

Promoting Prosocial Behavior

Adults are of course eager to encourage children's prosocial behavior. One common strategy that adults use in this endeavor is to reward children for prosocial behaviors. However, when Joan Grusec (1991) observed children in their homes, she found that rewards were not effective in increasing 4-year-olds' prosocial behavior. The 4-year-olds who were most inclined to act prosocially were those who received no recognition for their prosocial acts. These results contrast markedly with the effects of socially rewarding aggression.

As a consequence of such findings, developmentalists suggest two less direct means of promoting prosocial behavior. One such method is **explicit modeling,** in which adults behave in ways they desire the child to imitate. The other method is **induction,** in which adults give explanations of what needs to be done or why children should behave in a prosocial manner that appeal to their pride, their desire to be grown-up, and their concern for others (Eisenberg & Fabes, 1998).

explicit modeling The kind of modeling in which adults behave in ways they desire the child to imitate.

induction A means of promoting children's prosocial behavior in which adults give explanations of what needs to be done and why children should behave in a prosocial manner.

Most studies of explicit modeling contrast the behavior of two groups of schoolchildren. In the "modeling" group, teachers are told to stage periodic training sessions in which they demonstrate sharing and helping behaviors: they share candies among the children with explicit fairness, read stories about helping a child who is feeling sad or who is being teased, and so on. In the "nonmodeling" group, no special arrangements are made for teachers to model prosocial behaviors such as helping and sharing. These studies clearly show that the modeling techniques used do, in fact, increase prosocial behavior among children (Fukushima & Kato, 1976; Toranzo, 1996; Yarrow et al., 1973). Marion Yarrow and her colleagues also found that when the training was carried out in a nurturant, loving way, children showed the effects of the training as long as 2 weeks later—evidence that the effects of prosocial modeling can last for some time.

Since induction strategies involve explanation and reasoning, studies of their efficacy have usually been carried out with older children. For example, Julia Krevans and John Gibbs (1996) found that when parents used inductive discipline strategies, their 12- to 14-year-old children displayed higher levels of empathy and prosocial behavior. A study of early prosocial behaviors in the home found that younger children, too, performed more prosocial acts when their mothers attempted to induce prosocial behavior (Zahn-Waxler et al., 1979). Reason by itself, however, was not the crucial factor; the most effective mothers combined reason with loving concern and high expectations for prosocial behavior.

It is worth remembering that in real life, outside of research settings, the strategies to increase prosocial behavior do not occur in isolation from efforts to decrease aggressive behavior. Rather, a great variety of techniques are likely to be brought into play, interacting with and reinforcing one another to create overall patterns of socialization. (This patterning of socialization is discussed further in Chapter 11.)

THE DEVELOPMENT AND REGULATION OF EMOTIONS

As we noted in Chapter 6 (p. 250), the development of qualitatively new, *secondary* emotions is one of the key changes associated with the transition from infancy to early childhood. Pride, shame, and embarrassment—the self-conscious, social emotions—now join with anger, joy, and the other primary emotions to enable participation in new and more complex social relationships. In discussing forms of behavioral self-control earlier in this chapter, we emphasized that self-control requires the use of cognitive skills. At the same time, self-control in all its forms involves emotions that children must also learn to control.

To control their emotions effectively, children must learn to modify them in light of a cognitive appraisal of what is transpiring. Overall, to become socially competent members of their social group, young children must learn to interpret the emotional states of those around them, acquire methods for modifying their own emotions, and learn how to mask their true emotions when the situation calls for it.

UNDERSTANDING THE EMOTIONS OF OTHERS

To behave properly in the many new social situations they encounter in early childhood, children must expand their understanding of other people's emotions. Recall that by the time they are 6 or 7 months old, babies can "read" their mothers' faces as a guide to how they are expected to feel about a situation. By the time they are 2 years old, they know that other people feel bad when you hit them and that giving them something nice makes them feel good. At this early age, such statements as "Katie had tears. I pushed Katie out of the chair. I'm sorry" and "Daddy angry, I cry in crib" show that young children have some understanding of how others feel (Bretherton et al., 1986).

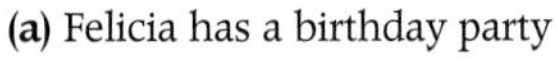

(a) Felicia has a birthday party

(b) Felicia s mother has pink hair

(c) Felicia s dog runs away

(d) Felicia s food tastes awful

(e) Her sister knocks over Felicia s tower of blocks

(f) Felicia gets lost in the supermarket

FIGURE 10.13
As children's understanding of social events increases, so does their ability to predict Felicia's feelings in these scenes. (From Michalson & Lewis, 1985.)

To track the development of children's ability to assess other people's emotions and the causes of those emotions, Richard Fabes and his colleagues (1991) observed a large number of 3- to 6-year-old children in a day-care center as they interacted over the course of the day. When the observers noted overt signs of emotion and its probable cause (Jennifer laughed because Suzy was tickling her), they approached one of the nearby children and asked, "How does Jennifer feel?" and "Why does Jennifer feel that way?" Even 3-year-olds could usually interpret other children's emotions correctly, and the 5- to 6-year-olds agreed with the adults' assessment of other children's emotional states and the events likely to have caused them more than 80 percent of the time.

A similar developmental pattern in the ability to assess others' emotions has been found in interview studies in which children are asked to interpret how other children would feel in hypothetical circumstances (Saarni, 1999). For example, Linda Michalson and Michael Lewis (1985) presented the pictures shown in Figure 10.13 to children between the ages of 2 and 5. Each picture was accompanied by a story about a little girl called Felicia. In Figure 10.13*a*, for example, Felicia is having a birthday party, and the children were asked to say how Felicia feels. At 2 years of age the children could say that Felicia was happy about the birthday party. But they could not say that Felicia was afraid when she was lost in the supermarket (Figure 10.13*f*) or sad when her dog ran away (Figure 10.13*c*). The older children were much better at assessing the negative emotions. Here again we can see a clear tie to cognitive changes that we discussed in Chapter 9. The younger children are less knowledgeable about emotional-display rules and more prone to egocentric interpretations of events. They "bias" their interpretation of pictured events to fit the way they wish things were. The older children were better at assessing the emotions in general, and particularly better at providing interpretations of the more negative situations.

REGULATING ONE'S OWN EMOTIONS

Even very young babies are capable of modulating their emotions to some extent. They quiet themselves by sucking on their fingers, a pacifier, or the edge of a blanket and by rocking themselves.

In the years from 2 to 6, children continue to use these strategies and develop others to help them keep their emotions under control (Grolnick et al., 1996; Saarni, 1999; Thompson, 1998). They avoid or reduce emotionally charged information by closing their eyes, turning away, and putting their hands over their ears. They use their budding language and cognitive skills to help them reinterpret events to create a more acceptable version of what is occurring ("I didn't want to play with her anyway; she's mean"), to reassure themselves ("Mommy said she'll be right back"), and to encourage themselves ("I'm a big girl; big girls can do it"). At the age of 3 our daughter Jenny displayed a useful strategy for regulating her fright when hearing Maurice Sendak's story *Where the Wild Things Are:* she hid the book so we couldn't read it to her.

Another source of evidence about the development of children's ability to regulate their emotions, and their actions as well, is situations in which they must resist temptation. Lisa Bridges and Wendy Grolnick (1999) arranged for 3½- to 4½-year-olds to visit a room in which they were shown an attractive toy but were told not to play with it. One of the strategies the children used to control their interest in the forbidden toy was to reorient their attention to other toys and play with them in a focused way. This strategy, which the researchers called *active engagement,* was rarely used by children before they were 2 years old. Between the ages of 2½ and 5, however, children become better able to distract themselves from temptation by using active engagement to control themselves.

LEARNING TO DISPLAY EMOTIONS APPROPRIATELY

The ability to display emotions in a socially appropriate way requires that children regulate the expression of their emotions. Young infants display no such ability. They communicate their emotions directly, regardless of the circumstances. A 2-month-old who becomes upset during a wedding because he is hungry is not going to stop crying until he is fed. It takes several years for children to learn to control the emotions they display. In the United States, for example, it is considered socially inappropriate to act disappointed when someone gives you a present. You are expected to thank the present giver and to say something nice about the present, whether or not you like it. Several researchers have studied the ability of children to understand the need to mask their real emotions and their ability to do so (Cole, 1986). In some studies, children were asked to interpret stories about a child who expects an exciting present and gets something undesirable instead. In other studies, the children themselves are put in situations where they expect a desirable object and experience disappointment (as when, for example, they are led to expect a toy car as a prize for playing a game but get a picture book instead).

Several general results come from this type of research (summaries are provided in Saarni, 1999, and Thompson, 1998). First, during early childhood, children around the world appear to gain the ability to recognize when someone is masking his or her feelings. Second, girls are generally able to recognize, and display, masked emotion better than boys are. Third, there are wide cultural variations in the age at which children learn about masking emotion and the conditions under which it is expected. For example, one study found that young English children acquired display rules for masking negative emotions earlier than young Italian children did (Manstead, 1995), while 4-year-old girls from Bombay were more sensitive to the need to conceal negative emotions than were their English counterparts (Joshi & MacLean, 1994).

socioemotional competence The ability to behave appropriately in social situations that evoke strong emotions.

REGULATION OF EMOTIONS AND SOCIAL COMPETENCE

Children's increasing ability to read the emotions of others and to control their own emotional expression is measured in terms of **socioemotional competence,** the ability to behave appropriately in social situations that evoke strong emotions. Carolyn Saarni (1999) proposed a set of eight component skills that contribute to socioemotional competence, most of which are acquired in early childhood:

1. An awareness of one's own emotional state.
2. An ability to discern other people's emotions.
3. An ability to talk about emotion in the vocabulary typical for one's culture.
4. A capacity for empathetic and sympathetic involvement in others' emotions.
5. The realization that an inner emotional state may not correspond to outward expression and that there are times and places when it is appropriate to display or to hide certain emotions.
6. A capacity to adapt to strong, unpleasant emotions with self-regulatory strategies.
7. An awareness of the important role that emotions play in social relationships and how they are affected by differences in power and status.
8. Overall feelings of emotional self-efficacy—the feeling that one is comfortable with one's feelings

It should come as no surprise that preschool children who display the characteristics of socioemotional competence are better liked by both their peers and their teachers (Eisenberg et al., 1993; Saarni, 1999). One reason may be that socially competent children are easier to get along with. During free play in a day-care center, for example, socially competent 4½-year-olds were observed to respond to anger-inducing provocations by effectively regulating their emotions and not retaliating. These children would try to get away from the provocateur or to verbally express their emotions without taking action. In this way they were able to minimize the potential damage to their social relationships (Fabes & Eisenberg, 1992).

In recent years psychologists have developed methods for categorizing and comparing children in terms of their level of socioemotional competence and for investigating the factors that promote it. These methods have led to the creation of experimental social programs for improving the competence of children who are having difficulty learning to behave in a socially acceptable manner. In these programs, children are explicitly taught methods for responding to aggression in acceptable ways, for empathizing with others, and for maintaining positive group interaction (Beelman et al., 1994).

TAKING ONE'S PLACE IN THE SOCIAL GROUP AS A DISTINCT INDIVIDUAL

The kindergartners in Vivian Paley's classroom are discussing the story of Tico, a wingless bird who is cared for by his black-winged friends. Their discussion reveals considerable sophistication about the dilemma described by Freud at the beginning of this chapter: How can a person achieve happiness as an individual and at the same time win acceptance as a member of the group?

In the story, the wishingbird visits Tico one night and grants him a wish. Tico wishes for golden wings. When his friends see his golden wings in the morning, they are angry. They abandon him because he wants to be better than they. Tico is upset by his friends' rejection and wants to gain readmission to the group. He discovers that he can exchange his golden feathers for black ones by performing good deeds. When at last he has replaced all the golden feathers with black ones, he is granted readmission by the flock, who comment, "Now you are just like us" (Leoni, 1964).

> *Teacher:* I don't think it's fair that Tico has to give up his golden wings.
> *Lisa:* It is fair. See, he was nicer when he didn't have any wings. They didn't like him when he had gold.
> *Wally:* He thinks he's better if he has golden wings.
> *Eddie:* He is better.
> *Jill:* But he's not supposed to be better. The wishingbird was wrong to give him those wings.
> *Deana:* She has to give him his wish. He's the one who shouldn't have asked for golden wings.
> *Wally:* He could put black wings on top of the golden wings and try to trick them.
> *Deana:* They'd sneak up and see the gold. He should just give every bird one golden feather and keep one for himself.
> *Teacher:* Why can't he decide for himself what kind of wings he wants?
> *Wally:* He has to decide to have black wings.
>
> (Paley, 1981, pp. 25–26)

This conversation shows that the children understand that by wishing for golden wings, Tico has wished himself a vision of perfection. Each child has done the same thing countless times: "I'm the beautiful princess"; "I'm Superman; I'll save the world." For the blissful, magic moments when the world of play holds sway, perfection is attainable, even by a lowly bird or a preschool child. Wally and his friends also appreciate the dilemmas of perfection. In their eyes, Tico not only thinks he is better but is better—yet he is not supposed to be. Try as they may to conceive of a way for Tico to retain his prized possessions, the children realize that conformity is unavoidable. Wally's summary is difficult to improve upon: Tico has to choose to conform.

The children's discussion of Tico and his community of birds reveals more than an appreciation of the heavy hand of society as it is experienced by children everywhere. It also shows the children's awareness that individuals have a responsibility for regulating social relations. They understand that it is the wishingbird's job to grant wishes, so it is not the wishingbird's fault that Tico wished himself to be better than the others. Tico should have been able to control himself and make a reasonable wish.

This story returns us to the theme with which this chapter began—that social development and personality development are two aspects of a single process. When children engage in acts of sharing and comforting, they reveal their ability to know another person's mental state. At the same time, they are displaying their own ways of thinking and feeling—in other words, their personalities. As part of the process of personality formation within the social group, individual strengths and weaknesses, interests, and opportunities will lead to increasing differentiation between the self and others.

As they approach their sixth birthdays, children have by no means completed the socialization process; but they have come a long way from infancy, when their sense of themselves and the social world was general and undifferentiated (Eder, 1989).

Before we turn in Part IV to the wide range of new roles and rules that children encounter in middle childhood and the corresponding changes that take place in their sense of themselves, we need to round out the discussion of early childhood by investigating the range of contexts and social influences that make up the world of the young child. As we shall see in Chapter 11, even young children are exposed to a great variety of social influences and cultural prescriptions. It is in the course of dealing with the variety of concrete circumstances that structure their everyday experiences that children create the synthesis of cognition and emotion called personality and acquire their social identities.

SUMMARY

ACQUIRING A SOCIAL AND PERSONAL IDENTITY

- Social development is the two-sided process in which children become integrated into their community while differentiating themselves as distinct individuals.
- One side of social development is socialization, the process by which children acquire the standards, values, and knowledge of their society.
- The other side of social development is personality formation, the process by which children come to have distinctive and consistent ways of feeling and behaving in a wide variety of situations.
- Identification, the process of molding one's behavior to that of a person one admires, contributes to children's distinctive sense of themselves at the same time that it places each of them in a salient social category, such as male or female.
- Competing theories of identification emphasize four mechanisms:
    1. Identification as a process of differentiating oneself from others.
    2. Identification as a process of affiliation—empathy with and attachment to others.
    3. Identification resulting from observation and imitation of powerful others and from the rewards gained by appropriate behavior.
    4. Identification resulting from the cognitive capacity to recognize oneself as a member of a social category and the desire to be like other members of that category.
- Sex-role identity goes through a sequence of cognitive milestones that begin with the early ability to identify oneself as a boy or girl, followed by the understanding that one's sex does not change over time, and finally a full understanding that one's sex is a permanent characteristic.
- Current evidence indicates that both conceptual change and learning of appropriate behaviors contribute to the development of sex-role identity, but the precise relationship between these processes is not well understood.
- Children acquire a sense of ethnic identity around the age of 4. Their attitudes toward their race or ethnicity are heavily influenced by how their social group is perceived in the society as a whole.
- By the age of 4, children have acquired a sense of personal identity which includes a narrative about their own lives. However, their self-evaluation remains unrealistically positive.

DEVELOPING THE ABILITY TO REGULATE ONESELF

- Children's initial ideas about good and bad behavior come from the social standards displayed by adult models with whom they identify.

- Toward the end of early childhood, heteronomous morality based on external controls gives way to a more autonomous morality based on an understanding of rules as agreements that can be challenged and changed.
- Young children distinguish three categories of social rules: moral rules, social conventions, and rules in the personal sphere, and adults react differently to children's infractions in each of these domains.
- Self-control requires persistence and inhibition of action. Children develop four kinds of inhibition:
    1. Inhibition of motion.
    2. Inhibition of emotion.
    3. Inhibition of conclusions.
    4. Inhibition of choice.
- Internalization of social roles and standards of behavior provides children with cognitive resources for controlling their own impulses.
- Early forms of self-control are situational. They require adult supervision. As children internalize adult standards, situational compliance is augmented by committed compliance.
- Conscience is the new quality of personality that emerges once children have internalized adult standards.

AGGRESSION AND PROSOCIAL BEHAVIOR

- Children display the rudiments of both aggression and altruism shortly after birth.
- Aggression, which is the committing of an act that is intended to hurt others, does not appear until the second year of life.
- Instrumental aggression is directed at obtaining desirable resources. Hostile aggression may also gain resources, but it is more directly aimed at causing pain to another person.
- Boys' and girls' aggressive behaviors often differ. Whereas boys tend to use instrumental aggression to cause physical pain, girls more often use relational aggression to create psychological pain.
- There are two major contributors to human aggression:
    1. Aggression is a result of our evolutionary past. Aggression is observed among animals of many species. From an evolutionary perspective, aggression is seen as a natural consequence of competition for resources.
    2. Aggressive behavior is learned. It may increase among children because they are directly rewarded for it or because they imitate the aggressive behavior of others. The influence of learning on aggression may be seen in wide cultural variations in the amount of aggression.
- There are large and stable individual differences in the levels of aggression among individuals arising from the interweaving of biological, social, and cultural factors.
- Several mechanisms have been suggested as means of controlling aggression:
    1. The development of aggression is accompanied by the development of social dominance hierarchies, which control aggression.
    2. Among humans, additional effective means for controlling aggression are rewards for nonaggressive behaviors and cognitive training that induces children to consider the negative consequences of aggressive behaviors.

- Physical punishment, which is widely used to deal with aggression, is generally ineffective because it often engenders more aggression.
- Our species is characterized as much by prosocial behavior as by aggression. Empathy—the ability to feel what another person is feeling—may be the basis for the development of prosocial behavior.
- The development of the ability to hurt other people is paralleled by and interacts with the ability to help others. Helping, sharing, and other prosocial behaviors can be observed as early as the first 3 years of life.

THE DEVELOPMENT AND REGULATION OF EMOTIONS

- Emotional development in early childhood requires that children understand their own and other people's emotions, regulate their own emotions, and control the way they display emotions.
- Children who quickly master these aspects of emotional regulation are more likely to get along well with others and to be considered socially competent.
- In acquiring a distinctive way of interacting with other people, both prosocially and antisocially, children acquire a sense of themselves and their own personalities.

KEY TERMS

aggression, p. 397
autobiographical memory, p. 391
autonomous morality, p. 393
catharsis, p. 405
conscience, p. 396
dominance hierarchy, p. 405
ego, p. 378
empathy, p. 397
explicit modeling, p. 411
gender schema, p. 384
heteronomous morality, p. 393
hostile aggression, p. 397
id, p. 378
identification, p. 376
induction, p. 411
instrumental aggression, p. 397
internalization, p. 396
latency stage, p. 380
Oedipus complex, p. 380
personality, p. 375
phallic stage, p. 379
primary identification, p. 378
prosocial behaviors, p. 410
relational aggression, p. 400
secondary identification, p. 378
self-concept, p. 375
self-control, p. 395
social development, p. 374
social roles, p. 375
socialization, p. 374
socioemotional competence, p. 415
superego, p. 379

THOUGHT QUESTIONS

1. James Mark Baldwin said that as children develop, they are "really in part someone else," even in their own thoughts of themselves. What does this characteristic of mental life imply for the development of personality?
2. In Kochanska and Aksan's study of compliance (p. 396), the children found it easier to adhere to the "don't touch" instructions than to the "clean up" instructions. Propose an explanation for this finding, and design a study to test your ideas.
3. What basic cognitive abilities must children acquire before they will be able to tease a sibling?
4. Give examples of how 5-year-olds might demonstrate each of the components of socioemotional competence proposed by Saarni (p. 415).
5. Reread the children's discussion of Tico on page 416. How does it relate to Freud's statement about the process of individual development at the opening of the chapter?

CHAPTER 11

The Contexts of Early Childhood Development

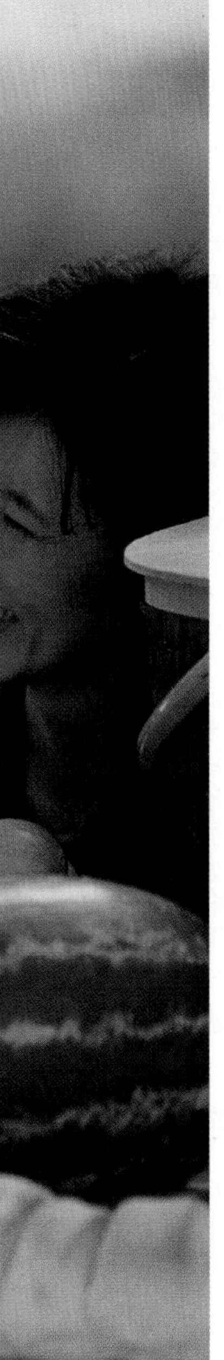

A new level of organization is in fact nothing more than a new relevant context.

C. H. Waddington, *Organizers and Genes*

Thus far we have treated the settings that children inhabit during early childhood primarily as a background to our discussions of children's cognitive, physical, and social development. In this chapter we alter our focus to highlight the ways in which the contexts of children's lives and the activities children engage in are part and parcel of their development.

As we shift our attention to the contexts of early childhood, it is helpful to refer once again to Urie Bronfenbrenner's idea that the environments of development should be thought of as the nested arrangement of ecosystems that are represented in Figure 1.5 (p. 19). The innermost system in this diagram, the microsystem, includes such contexts as the home, the church, the local park, the preschool, and so on. Also important are the contexts of the exosystem, such as the parents' workplaces, government agencies, and the mass media, which influence children either directly, as television does, or indirectly, through their impact on parents and other family members.

Each level of context in Bronfenbrenner's ecological model is reciprocally related to the other levels. Children are directly influenced by what occurs in their homes, but what occurs in their homes indirectly influences their experience at school, on the playground, and in other settings. The parents' behavior at home is influenced by the experiences they have at work and in their communities, while the society of which the community is a part both shapes and is shaped by its members.

The context that most directly influences young children's development is the family. Parents influence their children's development in two complementary ways. First, they shape their children's cognitive skills and personalities by the tasks they pose for them, the ways they respond to their particular behaviors, the values they promote, both explicitly and implicitly, and the patterns of behavior they model. But that is only part of the story. Parents also influence their children's development by selecting many of the other contexts to which children are exposed, including the places they visit, the means by which they entertain themselves, and the other children with whom they play.

From the very beginning, of course, the shaping influence of parent–child interaction goes both ways, for children also shape their parents' behavior. Each child's distinctive interests, temperament, appearance, verbal ability, and other characteristics all play their roles in the process of social development by influencing how the parents interact with the child (Bugental & Goodnow, 1998; Park & Buriel, 1998).

We begin our discussion of the early contexts of development by summarizing some of the universal features of families. Then we compare family configurations and personality development in two markedly different societies. This cross-national comparison is followed by an examination of the major varieties of family configuration and child-rearing patterns in North America. Next, we examine the influence of books and television, two communications media that link the family to the larger society. Finally, we discuss the socializing effects of two social institutions designed specifically to serve young children and their families in modern industrialized societies: day care, which substitutes for parental care at home; and preschools, which go beyond minding children to fostering their cognitive and social development.

THE FAMILY AS A CONTEXT FOR DEVELOPMENT

nuclear family A family consisting of a husband, a wife, and their children.

On the basis of his study of child-rearing practices in diverse cultures, the anthropologist Robert Le Vine (1988) has proposed that three major goals are shared by parents the world over:

1. *The survival goal:* to ensure that their children survive by providing for their health and safety.
2. *The economic goal:* to ensure that their children acquire the skills and other resources needed to be economically productive adults.
3. *The cultural goal:* to ensure that their children acquire the basic cultural values of the group.

These goals form a hierarchy. The most urgent goal for parents is their children's physical survival. It is not until the safety and health of their children appear secure that parents can focus on the other two goals, passing on the economically important skills and cultural values the children will need as adults to ensure the continued existence of their family and community.

To achieve these two goals, families seek to establish stable daily routines. Routines provide predictable, scripted sets of activities that ensure a workable fit between the family's resources and its local ecology. Although basic parenting goals are universal and all families seek to create routine activities to ensure that they are achieved, the manner in which parents go about achieving them vary dramatically, depending on local economic, social, and cultural circumstances; in fact, even the nature of the social unit called a "family" varies considerably from one society to another around the world. The conventional image of a family in North America, for example, is a household with a husband, a wife, and two or three children (see Box 11.1). Anthropologists refer to this social unit as a **nuclear family** (Murdock, 1949). Although such families can be found in most North American communities, they are by no means representative of the full range of family configurations in North America. In many North American households, children are raised by a single parent (usually the mother) or by several adults in an extended family. When we consider variations in family configuration on a world scale, the North American ideal of a nuclear family is actually unusual. *Polygyny,* in which one man is married simultaneously to more than one woman, is the preferred pattern among 75 percent of the world's societies, although even in societies where polygyny is preferred, it coexists with other

In their efforts to ensure that their children acquire the values of the larger group, parents cannot directly control how successfully their children perform or the enthusiasm with which they enter new forms of activity.

BOX 11.1

SIBLINGS AND SOCIALIZATION

Most theories of socialization concentrate on relations between one child and two parents when they address such questions as the development of sex-role identity, aggression, and prosocial behavior. But actual families and actual socialization are more complex. Single-child families are a distinct minority the world over. In North America, most families include at least two children.

Studies show that although parents are of primary importance in children's socialization, siblings also play significant roles in it (Parke & Buriel, 1998). The roles of siblings are most obvious in agricultural societies, like the Gusii discussed in this chapter, where much of the child care is performed by older siblings or by the mother's younger sisters. It is through these child caretakers, who are sometimes no more than 4 years older than their charges, that many of the behaviors and beliefs of the social group are passed on (Zukow-Goldring, 1995). In industrialized societies, where families tend to have fewer children and those children attend school from the age of 5, boys and girls have less responsibility for their younger siblings. Nevertheless, siblings still influence one another's socialization in important ways.

There is ample evidence that younger children learn a lot from their older siblings. Margarita Azmitia and Joanne Hesser (1993) arranged for young children to play with building blocks while their older sibling and an older friend (who were approximately 9 years old) were block building too. The younger children spent more time imitating and consulting with their sibling than with the friend. Their older sibling, in turn, offered more spontaneous help than did the friend. When the two older children were asked to help a younger child build a copy of a model out of blocks, the sibling again provided more explanations and encouragement.

Older siblings may not always play the role of tutor, however. Other research has shown that until about the age of 7 or 8, older siblings may simply take over and do such tasks for their younger brothers or sisters rather than explaining or helping them to do it themselves (Perez-Granados & Callanan, 1997).

On the basis of research conducted in England and Japan, Joseph Perner and his colleagues report that having an older sibling appears to enhance children's social perspective-taking skills (Perner et al., 1994; Ruffman et al., 1998). In their studies, each child was administered the "false belief" task described in Chapter 9 (p. 341): a story in which someone returns to a room where an object last seen in one place has been moved to another place, and the child is asked to say where the person in the story will look for it. The researchers found that the more older siblings a child has, the more likely he or she is to understand that people may hold false beliefs. Having younger siblings did not influence the children's performance. In Perner's words, older siblings provide a "rich database" for understanding the mental processes of other people.

Further evidence of links between the experience of sibling relationships and cognitive development comes from studies in which mothers and two siblings participated in a modified version of the "strange situation" described in Chapter 6 (p. 239) (Garner et al., 1994; Howe, 1991). The mother and two children spent some time in a room where the children could play. Then the mother left, asking the older child to look after the younger one for a few minutes. Children who scored higher on tests of the ability to take another person's perspective were also better able to comfort and distract their younger siblings during the mother's absence.

Younger siblings are not only charges to be taken care of; they are also someone to play with. It is while they are playing together that older siblings exert their greatest influence on their younger brothers and sisters. When they are still very young, a lot of the play is imitative. During the first year, it is the firstborn who imitates the new baby; then the tables are turned and it is the little sibling who becomes the imitator (Abramovitch et al., 1982). As they approach the age of 4, younger siblings take an increasingly active role in their relationships with their older siblings and intervene more and more effectively in the interactions between their mothers and older siblings (Dunn & Shatz, 1989). They also become more interesting as conversation partners for their older siblings (Brown & Dunn, 1991). Even so, the older sibling continues to dominate the relationship and is the one who is most likely to initiate play as well as altruistic and aggressive interactions (Abramovitch et al., 1986).

Sibling relationships are often ambivalent, impossible to characterize as either consistently friendly or consistently hos-

patterns (Saxon, 1993). The ways that families are organized, the economic activities they engage in, and the particular arrangements of their everyday lives, as well as how adults think about and treat their children, all contribute to children's development.

A CROSS-CULTURAL STUDY OF FAMILY ORGANIZATION AND SOCIAL DEVELOPMENT

A classic study by Beatrice and John Whiting (1975) nicely illustrates how differences in family life shape the development of children. The Whitings organized teams of anthropologists to observe child rearing in six communities in

Sibling relationships are often marked by ambivalence, loving and protective one minute, hostile and aggressive the next. These brothers' studied inattention to their sister's distress suggests that they may have just done something to "get" her.

tile. The obvious explanation for the ambivalence is that siblings compete for their parents' love and attention. The birth of a second baby is often upsetting to firstborns, especially if they are less than 4 years old. Since the firstborn had no competition until the second child arrived on the scene, these feelings are understandable. The firstborn may respond to the mother's inattentiveness by being demanding and showing more negative behavior, by becoming more independent, by taking a larger role in initiating conversations and play, or by becoming detached from the mother (Dunn, 1984).

Another factor in sibling relationships is the issue of individual differences in personality and temperament (Stocker et al., 1989). Children who have "difficult" temperaments, who are hostile, active, or intense, are more likely than children who have "easy" temperaments to have conflictual relationships with their siblings (Munn & Dunn, 1988). One might expect that the sexual composition of the sibling pair would affect the nature of the relationship, but the findings here are weak and inconsistent. Some studies show that same-sex sibling pairs get along better than mixed-sex pairs (Dunn & Kendrick, 1979), and some show the opposite (Abramovitch et al., 1986).

One factor that reliably affects the siblings' relationship is the emotional climate of their family (Brody, 1998; Erel et al., 1998). Siblings are more likely to fight when their parents are not getting along well together, when their parents divorce, and when a stepfather enters the family, especially if one or both of the siblings are boys (Hetherington, 1988).

Also certain to affect sibling relationships is the equitability of parental treatment. Parents usually do not treat their children in an identical fashion. They make accommodations for each child's age, personality, behavior, and sex. Many children understand the reasons why their parents treat them differently than their siblings and think such treatment is fair (Kowal & Kramer, 1997). However, when children interpret their parents' differential behavior as an indication that one child is being favored over another, they often feel antagonistic toward the sibling (Boer, 1990; Brody, 1998; Brody et al., 1992).

Faced with conflicts between their children, parents frequently intervene to try to settle their disputes. But several studies have found that the more often parents intervene in their children's disputes, the more disputes there are. What is not clear is what is cause and what is effect. Parental intervention may increase fighting between siblings because the children quarrel in order to get their parents' attention and because parental intervention deprives them of the opportunity to learn how to resolve their conflicts. But it may also be that parents intervene in their children's quarrels when they become intense; in this case, the proper conclusion would be that children who have intense quarrels also have frequent ones regardless of what their parents do (Dunn & McGuire, 1992).

the United States, India, Kenya, and Mexico that differed in social complexity, dominant economic activities, cultural belief systems, and domestic living arrangements. A comparison of two of the groups studied by these teams, the Gusii of Nyansongo, Kenya, and Americans in a small New England town, illustrates how differences in life circumstances produce variations in basic economic activities and family life that influence the way parents treat their children and the effect of their socialization practices on the children's personality and social development.

At the time of the Whitings' work in the 1950s, the Gusii, who at one time were herders, were agriculturalists living in the fertile highlands of western Kenya. Women, who did most of the farmwork, usually lived with their children in separate houses within the family compound, apart from their husbands. Men, no longer active as cattle herders, sometimes took wage-earning jobs but also spent a lot of time in local politics. Family groups were generally polygynous, with several wives living in a single compound that contained one house for the husband. The community had no specialized occupations, few specialized buildings, and almost no differences in social rank or wealth among its inhabitants.

Because they spent most of their daytime hours working on the family farm, Gusii mothers often left their infants and toddlers in the care of older siblings and elderly family members. As is typical of agrarian societies, children's labor was valued for the production of food and the care of younger children. Beginning at the age of 3 or 4, Gusii children were expected to start helping their mothers with simple household tasks. By the age of 7, their economic contributions to the family were indispensable.

New England's "Orchard Town" represented the opposite extreme in family organization and social complexity. Most of the men of Orchard Town were wage earners who lived with their wives and children in single-family dwellings, each with its own yard. A few of the mothers had part-time jobs, but most spent their time caring for their children, their husbands, and their homes. The town had many specialized buildings (see Figure 11.1), and townspeople engaged in a wide variety of specialized occupations—physician, firefighter, auto mechanic, teacher, librarian, merchant, and many more.

Children in Orchard Town were observed to spend more time in the company of adults than did the children of Nyansongo. At home, Orchard Town children played in the house or in the yard within earshot of their mothers. At school they were constantly supervised by their teachers. In contrast to the Gusii children, Orchard Town children were rarely asked to do chores. Instead of contributing to their families economically, they represented a drain on their families' incomes. (Raising children continues to be a costly affair in most technologically complex societies. It has been estimated that the cost of raising a child in a middle-income family in the United States from birth to the age of 17 is approximately $157,000 [Lino, 1999].)

FIGURE 11.1

The village of Orchard Town in New England in the 1950s. Each husband and wife lived with their children in their own house. (From Whiting & Whiting, 1975.)

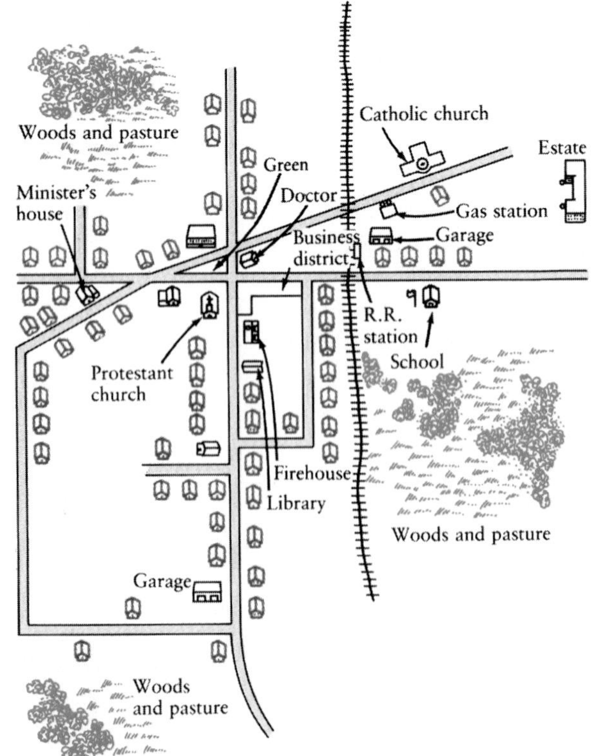

When the Whitings examined the children's behavior patterns in these cultures, they found notable overall differences (see Table 11.1). The Gusii children, for example, were more likely to engage in what the Whitings called "nurturant-responsible" behaviors, offering help and support and making responsible suggestions to others. At the same time, Gusii children also reprimanded and assaulted other children, behavior that the Whitings characterized as "authoritarian-aggressive." Orchard Town children, on the other hand, were more often observed seeking help and attention or trying to control other children. The Whitings called this a "dependent-dominant" pattern of behavior. And in contrast to the authoritarian-aggressive pattern of the Gusii, the Orchard Town children were more often observed engaging in sociable horseplay, touching others, and joining groups in an amiable way. This pattern was referred to as "sociable-intimate."

To explain the social behavior of children in the two societies, the different patterns observed by the Whitings need to be related to the conditions of family life in the two societies. The Whitings believed that the Gusii children were more nurturant and responsible because of the child-tending role their parents' work required them to assume. This conclusion has considerable support: many other researchers report that in societies where children are expected to contribute to the economic well-being of the family and community, adults encourage them to develop a sense of self based on social interdependence (Greenfield & Cocking, 1994; Le Vine et al., 1994).

TABLE 11.1 PATTERNS OF SOCIAL BEHAVIOR DISTINGUISHING GUSII AND U.S. CHILDREN

Category of Behavior	Specific Kinds of Behavior	Cultural Group
Nurturant-responsible	Offers help Offers support Makes responsible suggestions	Gusii
Dependent-dominant	Seeks help Seeks dominance Seeks attention	U.S.
Sociable-intimate	Acts sociably Engages in horseplay Touches	U.S.
Authoritarian-aggressive	Reprimands Assaults Insults	Gusii

Source: Whiting & Whiting, 1975.

The authoritarian-aggressive aspect of Gusii children's behavior was also shaped by their family's circumstances, as well as their role within family life. Infant mortality was high among the Gusii, so in order to meet the primary goal of child survival, parents exerted a good deal of direct authority over their children. Correspondingly, when the older Gusii children were assigned child-minding duties, they had legitimate authority over their younger siblings. They were given this authority not to dominate their young charges but to control them, both for safety's sake and to teach them to adhere to cultural norms (including respect for one's elders). Evidence from a variety of agricultural societies with child-rearing customs similar to those of the Gusii shows that while older siblings might hit or tease the children they are put in charge of, they will be punished by their elders if they do so excessively (Zukow-Goldring, 1995).

According to the Whitings, children of industrialized societies, such as those in Orchard Town, are less nurturant and responsible because their chores are less clearly related to their families' economic welfare and may even seem arbitrary. Also, Orchard Town children spent most days in school, where, instead of helping other children, they were expected to compete with them for good grades and were encouraged to think of themselves as individuals rather than as members of a group. Like children in other complex, technological societies, they were encouraged to develop a more autonomous and individualistic sense of self (Kagitçibasi, 1997).

The same set of factors helps to explain why the Orchard Town children were more sociable-intimate than the children of Nyansongo. Orchard Town children lived in nuclear households. The father ate at the same table with his wife and children, slept with his wife, was likely to have been present when the children were born, and helped to care for them. These conditions, made possible and even necessary by the economic demands and cultural traditions of New England, helped create intimacy within the family. Gusii fathers, on the other hand, typically had more than one wife. In addition, the Gusii lived in extended families headed by a grandfather. Property was owned by the family as a group. Children belonged to their father's clan. A Gusii man lived in the village where he grew up, surrounded by his parents, brothers, and other kin, while his wives left their home communities when they married. As Figure 11.2 indicates,

FIGURE 11.2
A plan of a typical residential compound in the village of Nyansongo, Kenya. Each wife lived in her own house. Older children also lived in separate houses. A husband might have slept in the house of one of his wives but did not share his bed with her. (From Whiting & Whiting, 1975.)

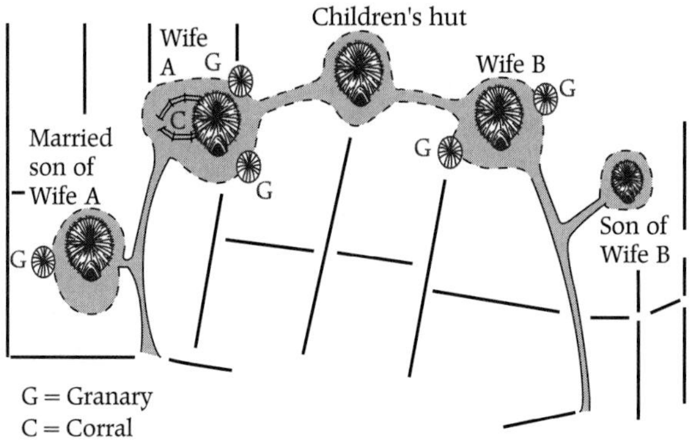

In many non-Western cultures, young children are responsible for daily care of infant siblings. These children live in Mozambique.

each wife had her own house. Her husband may have slept in the same house with her periodically, but not in the same bed, and the preferred pattern was for him to sleep and eat in a separate house. By American standards, there was little intimacy between husbands and wives or between fathers and children, but there was a strong cultural value placed on group membership.

From a middle-class North American point of view, these arrangements may appear strange, even unpleasant. Most Americans believe it is immoral for a man to have more than one wife, and they are unlikely to approve of children's behavior that they consider authoritarian and aggressive. But the child-rearing customs of Gusii fit Gusii expectations and the Gusii way of life, so to the Gusii these arrangements seem both proper and desirable. In fact, when told about American child-rearing practices, such as allowing young children to cry without offering some form of nurturance, Gusii parents were shocked (Le Vine et al., 1994).

FAMILY CONFIGURATIONS AND SOCIALIZATION PRACTICES IN NORTH AMERICA

Research in the United States has shown that while child-rearing practices vary widely, the dimensions along which they vary, such as how demanding the parents are or how warm they are toward their children, are fairly restricted. Precisely how many dimensions are identified and how they are best defined differ somewhat from one researcher to another. On the basis of an extensive review of many studies of parental behavior, Eleanor Maccoby and John Martin (1983) proposed a scheme that characterizes parenting practices along two dimensions. The first corresponds to the degree to which parents try to control the way their children behave—that is, whether they are strictly controlling or allow a good deal of autonomy. The second dimension is the amount of affection that parents display toward their children—that is, whether they are accepting and responsive or unresponsive and rejecting. These two dimensions give rise to four possible parenting patterns, as shown in Table 11.2.

Many studies of family socialization have sought to determine the importance of patterns of parenting, such as those in Table 11.2, for children's development. This research addresses two key questions: What mix of control, autonomy, and expression of affection contributes most to healthy develop-

TABLE 11.2 A Two-Dimensional Classification of Parenting Patterns

	Responsive: Parent is accepting and child-centered.	**Unresponsive:** Parent is rejecting and parent-centered.
Demanding: Parent expects much of child.	*Authoritative parenting.* Relationship is reciprocal, high in bidirectional communication.	*Authoritarian parenting.* Relationship is controlling, power-assertive, high in unidirectional communication.
Undemanding: Parent expects little of child.	*Indulgent parenting.* Relationship is permissive, low in control attempts.	*Neglectful parenting.* Relationship is indifferent, uninvolved.

ment? How are family socialization patterns influenced by social class and ethnicity? We begin our examination of these questions with research on the middle-class nuclear family. We then examine the socialization practices of other family types frequently encountered in North America at the end of the twentieth century.

Parenting Styles in the Middle-Class North American Nuclear Family

In one of the best-known research programs on the developmental consequences of parenting styles, Diana Baumrind (1971, 1980) arranged for trained observers to record children's behavior during routine activities in a

TABLE 11.3 Sample Items from the Baumrind Rating Scale for Preschool Behavior*

Hostile–friendly	Selfish Understands other children's position in interaction
Resistive–cooperative	Impetuous and impulsive Can be trusted
Domineering–tractable	Manipulates other children to enhance own position Timid with other children
Dominant–submissive	Peer leader Suggestible
Purposive–aimless	Confident Spectator
Achievement-oriented–not achievement-oriented	Gives best to play and work Does not persevere when encounters frustration
Independent–suggestive	Individualistic Stereotyped in thinking

*Items grouped into statistically related clusters.
Source: Baumrind, 1971.

authoritarian parenting pattern A parenting pattern in which the parents try to shape, control, and evaluate the behavior and attitudes of their children according to a set standard. They stress the importance of obedience to authority and favor punitive measures to bring about their children's compliance.

authoritative parenting pattern A parenting pattern in which the parents take it for granted that children also have rights. They attempt to control their children by explaining their rules or decisions and by reasoning with the children. They are willing to consider the child's point of view, even if they do not always accept it. They set high standards for their children's behavior.

preschool. The observers rated the children's behavior on a 72-item scale and correlated these ratings to obtain seven clusters of scores, representing seven dimensions of preschool behavior (such as hostile vs. friendly, resistive vs. cooperative, domineering vs. tractable) (Table 11.3). The children's behavior could then be correlated with their parents' styles of parenting, as measured by observations and interviews.

The researchers interviewed each child's parents, both separately and together, about their child-rearing beliefs and practices. Then they visited the children's homes twice to observe family interactions from just before dinner until after the child went to bed (Table 11.4). When the interviews and observations were scored and analyzed, Baumrind and her colleagues found that parenting behaviors in 77 percent of their families fit one of three patterns:

- **Authoritarian parenting pattern:** Parents who follow an authoritarian parenting pattern try to shape, control, and evaluate the behavior and attitudes of their children according to a set traditional standard. They stress the importance of obedience to authority and discourage verbal give-and-take between themselves and their children. They favor punitive measures to curb their children's willfulness—whenever their children's behavior conflicts with what they believe to be correct.
- **Authoritative parenting pattern:** Parents who demonstrate an authoritative pattern take it for granted that although they have more knowledge and skill, control more resources, and have more physical power than their children, the children also have rights. Authoritative parents are less likely than authoritarian parents to use physical punishment and less likely to stress obedience to authority as a virtue in

TABLE 11.4 SAMPLE ITEMS IN BAUMRIND'S SCALE OF PARENTAL BEHAVIORS*

Set regular tasks
Demand child put toys away
Provide intellectually stimulating environment
Set standards of excellence
Many restrictions on TV watching
Fixed bedtime hour
Mother has independent life
Encourage contact with other adults
Demand mature table behavior
Clear ideals for child
Stable, firm views
Cannot be coerced by child
Use negative sanctions when defied
Force confrontation when child disobeys
Parents' needs take precedence
Regard themselves as competent people
Encourage independent action
Solicit child's opinions
Give reasons with directives
Encourage verbal give-and-take
Inhibit annoyance or impatience when child dawdles or is annoying
Become inaccessible when displeased
Lack empathetic understanding

*Items observed in home interactions.
Source: Baumrind, 1971.

itself. Instead, these parents attempt to control their children by explaining their rules or decisions and by reasoning with them. They are willing to consider the child's point of view, even if they do not always accept it. Authoritative parents set high standards for their children's behavior and encourage the children to be independent.

- **Permissive parenting pattern:** Parents who exhibit a permissive pattern exercise less explicit control over their children's behavior than do both authoritarian and authoritative parents, either because they believe children must learn how to behave through their own experience or because they do not take the trouble to provide discipline. They give their children a lot of leeway to determine their own schedules and activities, and they often consult them about family policies. They do not demand the same levels of achievement and mature behavior that authoritative and authoritarian parents do.

permissive parenting pattern A parenting pattern in which the parents exercise less explicit control over their children's behavior. They give their children a lot of leeway to determine their own schedules and activities, and they often consult them about family policies. They do not demand the same levels of achievement and mature behavior that authoritative and authoritarian parents do.

Baumrind found that, on the average, each style of parenting was associated with a different pattern of children's behavior in the preschool:

- Children of *authoritarian parents* tended to lack social competence in dealing with other children. They frequently withdrew from social contact and rarely took initiative. In situations of moral conflict, they tended to look to outside authority to decide what was right. These children were often characterized as lacking spontaneity and intellectual curiosity.
- Children of *authoritative parents* appeared more self-reliant, self-controlled, and willing to explore, as well as more content than those raised by permissive or authoritarian parents. Baumrind believes that this difference is a result of the fact that while authoritative parents set high standards for their children, they explain to them why they are being rewarded and punished. Such explanations improve children's understanding and acceptance of the social rules.
- Children of *permissive parents* tended to be relatively immature; they had difficulty controlling their impulses, accepting responsibility for social actions, and acting independently.

Baumrind also reported differences in the way girls and boys responded to the major parenting patterns. The sons of authoritarian parents, for example, seemed to show more pronounced difficulties with social relations than the daughters did. They were also more likely than other boys to show anger and defiance toward people in authority. The daughters of authoritative parents were more likely to be independent than their brothers, while the boys were more likely to be socially responsible than the girls.

Research conducted in the years since Baumrind's initial publications has generally supported her observations and extended them to older children (Bornstein et al., 1996). For example, Sanford Dornbusch and his colleagues found that authoritative parenting is associated with better school performance and better social adjustment than authoritarian parenting among high school students, just as it is among preschoolers (Dornbusch et al., 1987; Herman et al., 1997).

Despite the consistency of these findings, the conclusion that authoritative parenting is most conducive to intellectual and social competence must be qualified in two important ways. First, it is important to remember that the basic strategy for relating parental behaviors to child behaviors used in this line of research relies on correlational data. Consequently, there can be no certainty that differences in parenting styles caused the differences in children's behavior (we discussed this problem in Chapter 1, pp. 22–23). Avshalom Caspi (1998) has summarized a variety of research suggesting that it is just as likely that parenting style is influenced by the child's characteristics as it is that the child is shaped by a particular style of parenting. A particularly active

Verbal discipline coupled with explanation is characteristic of the authorative pattern of parenting.

and easily frustrated child, for example, may elicit authoritarian parenting whereas, from the same parents, an easygoing or timid child might elicit an authoritative style.

In support of this view, research on the personalities of biologically unrelated children in the same household has shown the children to be quite different from one another, even though they were being raised by the same parents (Plomin & Bergeman, 1991). Such findings imply one of two things: patterns of caregiving do not have much effect on a child's behavior, or parents' patterns of caregiving vary from one child to the next. Either conclusion undermines the idea that parental styles of socialization are the causes of variations in children's development (Harris, 1998).

Baumrind is well aware of these difficulties. She agrees that children's temperaments influence parenting styles, but she is convinced that her evidence shows clearly that parenting styles have a significant impact on children's personalities and later school achievement (Baumrind, 1991a). Researchers are currently using a variety of strategies to isolate the effects of parenting styles on patterns of child development (Collins et al., 2000).

The second reason to qualify conclusions from Baumrind's research program is that her families were not representative of North American families as a whole: they were, in general, suburban, white, largely middle-class, two-parent families. If we are to get a broad understanding of the family as a context of development, we have to consider how various family configurations, in combination with educational experience, economic circumstances, ethnic background, and cultural heritage, influence socialization.

Baumrind herself was the first to raise this concern. She reported that the expected relationship between authoritarian parenting and personality development was not found among a group of 16 African American children and their families in her sample. She noted that the African American daughters of authoritarian parents she observed took initiative and behaved assertively on the playground yet could be self-controlled, polite, and quiet at a church meeting. More recent research has found that African American teenagers whose parents adopted an authoritarian style were more likely to succeed in school than were students whose parents adopted an authoritative style (Lamborn et al., 1996).

Other replications of Baumrind's work raise the same issue. Like Baumrind, Sanford Dornbusch and his colleagues found that authoritative parenting was associated with better school performance among European American children (Dornbush et al., 1987). However, Dornbusch and his colleagues also found that Asian American students, whose parents were reported to have the highest scores for authoritarian parenting practices, were the group that did best in school. The level of authoritarian parenting practices did not predict the school performance of these students as it did for white and Latino students.

In a follow-up study comparing Chinese American and European American families and their children, researchers encountered a major obstacle when they attempted to apply such categories as "authoritarian" and "authoritative" to two groups with different languages and cultural backgrounds: these words do not have the same meanings for both groups (Chao, 1994). In describing this study, Ruth Chao wrote that the English word "authoritarian" carries with it many negative connotations—such as hostility, aggressiveness, mistrust, dominance—that are not applicable to the core methods of socialization in the Chinese family. While it is true that Chinese place high value on obedience and parental control, the preferred Chinese pattern of socialization is closer to the American notion of "training." Chao maintains that Chinese parents exercise control over their children and demand their obedience "in the context of a supportive, highly involved, and physically close mother–child relationship" (p. 112).

Chao (1996) tested her idea that Baumrind's parenting categories do not apply well to Chinese parenting patterns by administering a questionnaire to 50 Chinese American and 50 European American mothers. The questionnaire included standard items such as those used by Baumrind (Table 11.4) plus a set of questions that related specifically to Chinese notions of training young children for life (the mothers were asked, for example, to indicate their level of agreement with the statement "Mothers must train their children to work very hard and to be disciplined"). As others had done before her, Chao found that the Chinese American mothers scored higher on the standard measures of control and authoritarianism. But even after she controlled for their scores on control and authoritarianism, the Chinese American mothers were distinguished from the European American mothers on the measure of training, indicating a culturally distinctive pattern of parenting was at work.

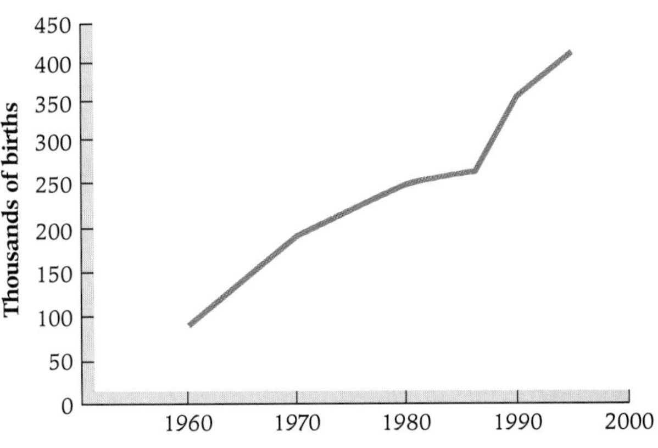

FIGURE 11.3
The number of children born to unmarried teenage mothers in the United States, 1960–1995. (U.S. Bureau of the Census, 1995 and U.S. Department of Health and Human Services, 1998.)

If we think back to the cross-cultural comparison between the Gusii in Nyansongo and the Americans in Orchard Town, Chao's findings should come as no surprise. After all, the Whitings demonstrated many years ago that the use of a term such as "authoritarian" to describe parenting practices has to be considered in the light of local categories and cultural practices. What the more recent work on parenting styles and personality development in the United States has shown is that this lesson is equally applicable to the study of different ethnic groups in a heterogeneous society (Parke & Buriel, 1998).

Patterns of Socialization in Single-Parent Families

In 1998, approximately 28 percent of U.S. children were living in single-parent households, almost always with their mothers (U.S. Bureau of the Census, 1998). Among African American families, the percentage was more than 60 percent. What are the consequences of growing up with only one parent, especially when that parent is both young and unmarried?

Young Unmarried Mothers and Their Children Many single women who are raising children are still teenagers. As Figure 11.3 indicates, the number of births among unmarried teenagers grew rapidly during the 1970s and 1980s. Despite a decline in births to unmarried teenagers in the 1990s, the number of single teenage mothers in the United States remains high. This situation is of great concern because research has shown that children of unmarried teenage mothers are at a developmental disadvantage. Preschool children of single teenage mothers have been found to be more aggressive, less self-controlled, and less cognitively advanced than the children of older, married mothers (Coley & Chase-Lansdale, 1998; Dunn et al., 1998).

Frank Furstenberg and his colleagues (1992) believe that three factors contribute to the negative developmental effect of being raised by a young unmarried mother:

1. Young mothers are often less prepared to bring up children and have little interest in doing so. As a consequence, they tend to vocalize less with their babies than older mothers do. A lack of verbal communication seems to lead in turn to lowered cognitive ability in preschool and elementary school.
2. Young mothers, especially those without husbands, are likely to have very limited financial resources. As a consequence, they are likely to be poorly educated, to live in disadvantaged neighborhoods, to obtain poor health services for themselves and their children, and to be socially isolated. It has proved difficult to specify how much each of these factors contributes to the developmental problems of children raised by young unmarried mothers because the factors are so closely intertwined (Duncan & Brooks-Gunn, 1997). We will return to the topic of young unmarried single mothers when we explore how poverty and racial prejudice shape family configurations and socialization practices (pp. 436–437).

The Consequences of Divorce Approximately half of all marriages in the United States end in divorce, and it has been estimated that about 30 percent of all children born to married couples will see their parents divorce sometime before they are 18 years old (Furstenberg & Cherlin, 1991). While the divorce rate in the United States is by far the highest in the world, the rate of divorce in Canada and Europe is rising rapidly.

Children whose parents have divorced are twice as likely as children whose parents are still together to have problems in school, to act out, to be depressed and unhappy, to have less self-esteem, and to be less socially responsible and competent (Amato & Keith, 1991; Hetherington et al., 1998). Eventually, most children whose parents divorce make some adjustment to the situation and develop into competent individuals who function normally (Emery & Forehand, 1994). In the short run, however, the breakup of a family is dislocating for everyone involved. Often, immediately following a divorce there is a deterioration in parenting. Mavis Hetherington and her colleagues found that after a divorce, mothers tend to make few demands on their children and to communicate with them less effectively than do other parents. Their discipline becomes erratic, and they are harsh. They are also less likely to explain their actions or to reason with their children (Hetherington et al., 1982).

Divorce leads to several other changes in children's life experiences that might be expected to harm their development. Many of the problems associated with divorce are of the same kind as those faced by unmarried single women. First, the average income of single-parent families created by divorce or separation falls by 37 percent within 4 months of the breakup, according to a study by the U.S. Bureau of the Census (1991). Only 73 percent of the custodial parents who are due child support receive any money at all from their former spouses, and most receive only a portion of what is owed to them (U.S. Bureau of the Census, 1999). As a consequence, about 30 percent of all custodial parents find themselves living below the poverty threshold. (In 1999 the Census Bureau defined a family of four as poor if its annual income fell below $15,150.) These changes in economic status often mean that after their parents divorce, children have to move away from their friends and neighbors to poorer neighborhoods with different schools and poorer day care. These changes are difficult for children to deal with. According to Mavis Hetherington and her colleagues, even when economic status is not changed by divorce, negative consequences of divorce often remain (Hetherington et al., 1998).

Second, parents raising children alone are trying to accomplish by themselves what is usually a demanding job for two adults. Both fathers and mothers who have sole custody of their children complain that they are overburdened by the necessity of juggling child care and household and financial responsibilities by themselves (Hetherington & Stanley-Hagen, 1987). Divorce, separation, and widowhood force many mothers to enter the workforce at the same time that they and their children are adapting to a new family configuration. Seventy-eight percent of divorced mothers are in the labor force; most of them work full-time (U.S. Bureau of the Census, 1995). Because of the many demands on their mothers' time, children of divorce not only receive less guidance and assistance but tend to lose out on important kinds of social and intellectual stimulation (Hetherington, 1999).

Third, the custodial parents are often socially isolated and lonely (Hetherington et al., 1982). They have no one to support them when the children question their authority and no one to act as a buffer between them and their children when they are not functioning well as a parent. The task of parenting is even more difficult for a custodial mother when the father sees his children only occasionally and is indulgent and permissive on these occasions.

Although it makes intuitive sense that the losses associated with the breakup of a family are the causes of the various behavioral and social problems experienced by children of divorce, a number of studies that collected data about children before their parents divorced have cast doubt on this idea. Noting that divorce is a consequence of disharmony in the family, several researchers have suggested that it is conflict between the child's parents, and not divorce itself, that poses the greatest risk for children (Block et al., 1986).

This conclusion is confirmed by two large longitudinal surveys of children living in intact families in Great Britain and the United States (Cherlin et al., 1991). All the parents were interviewed about their children's behavior when the children were 7 years old and again when they were 11 years old. Children whose parents divorced or separated between the two interviews were compared with children whose families remained intact. In line with earlier research, both studies found that children whose parents had divorced between the two interviews had more behavior problems than children whose families had remained intact. However, when the researchers looked back at the reports on the same children when they were 7 years old and their families were still intact, they found that many of the children whose parents later split up were already exhibiting many behavior problems, including tantrums, bad dreams, resistance to going to school, disobedience at home, and fighting with other children. These are the kinds of behaviors that tend to accompany parental conflict and may also contribute to it (Grych & Fincham, 1997).

Since family harmony and stability are fundamental to children's sense of security and well-being, it should come as no surprise that parental conflict should be threatening and upsetting to most children. Still, there is great diversity in the ways children respond to conflict between their parents and to the subsequent divorce, although some general patterns have emerged.

Boys, who tend to be more active, more assertive, and less compliant than girls to begin with, often react to the turmoil and stress of divorce by becoming unruly and angry. They show a higher rate of behavior disorders and problems in their social relations than do girls whose families have gone through a divorce or children who live with both parents. Sometimes girls react to their parents' divorce with self-criticism, withdrawal, and crying, but it is more common for girls to become demanding and to seek attention (Hetherington et al., 1998).

Temperamentally difficult children are at special risk when their parents are in conflict or divorce. They are more likely to become targets of their parents' anger and criticism than are children who are more easygoing, and they have a harder time coping when that happens.

The findings about the effects of age on children's ability to cope with divorce are contradictory. While some studies have found that young, preschool-age children are at a greater risk for long-term problems in social and emotional development following the breakup of their parents' marriage than older children, other studies have failed to find such effects (Amato & Keith, 1991; Zill, 1994). By 2 or 3 years after the divorce, most children and their parents have made adaptations to the new situation. Some problems remain, however. Often divorced mothers and their sons continue to have coercive exchanges and conflicts over control.

The single most important factor in a child's adjustment after a divorce is how well the custodial parent deals with the stress of the divorce, shields the child from family conflicts, and provides the child with supportive parenting. Children seem to do best when their parents put aside their disagreements and support each other in their parenting roles. Caring grandparents, aunts, uncles, and friends can ease the pain of the marital breakup and reduce children's stress.

In many families today, however, the equilibrium established after a divorce does not last long. Approximately two-thirds of divorced parents remarry within 5 years, requiring their children to cope with yet another major change in their family life, school, and peer group. Several studies have found that the early stages of remarriage are stressful for everyone, parents included, as the members of the blended family make the accommodations and adjustments necessary for them to live in the same house (Forgatch & Paterson, 1998). Some members of the family, especially younger boys in households headed by mothers, seem to benefit from the presence of a stepfather in the home. Others, especially adolescent girls, are more likely to suffer in the new family configuration, seeing their stepfathers as interlopers who threaten their close relationship with their mothers. They often react to their mother's remarriage by ignoring their stepfather and being sulky, resistant, and critical (Hetherington, 1989; Hetherington & Clingempeel, 1992).

Children's long-term adjustment to the new family configurations seems to be determined by several factors, including their sex, their age when the parent remarries, and the duration of the new marriage (Chase-Lansdale & Hetherington, 1990). Authoritative parenting that combines parental warmth, support, involvement with the children, and monitoring of their activities seems to be the key to children's adjustment in the new families created by their parent's remarriage (Hetherington & Clingempeel, 1992).

The Impact of Poverty on Child Rearing

Poverty touches all aspects of family life: the quality of housing and health care, access to education and recreational facilities, and even one's safety as one walks along the street (Duncan & Brooks-Gunn, 1997; McLoyd, 1998a, 1998b). Poverty also appears to affect parents' approach to child rearing. Studies in many parts of the world have found that in families living close to the subsistence level, parents are likely to adopt child-rearing practices that are controlling in a manner akin to the authoritarian pattern described by Baumrind. According to Robert Le Vine (1974), parents who know what it means to eke out a living "see obedience as the means by which their children will be able to make their way in the world and establish themselves economically in young adulthood when the basis must be laid for the economic security of their nascent families" (p. 63).

An emphasis on obedience is also frequently encountered in poor families in the United States, in part for the economically based reason cited by Le Vine. In addition, some researchers have suggested that poor minority mothers in the United States demand unquestioning obedience and discourage their children's curiosity because the dangerous circumstances of their daily

Chronic poverty such as that experienced by Irish tinkers creates multiple risk factors for children's development.

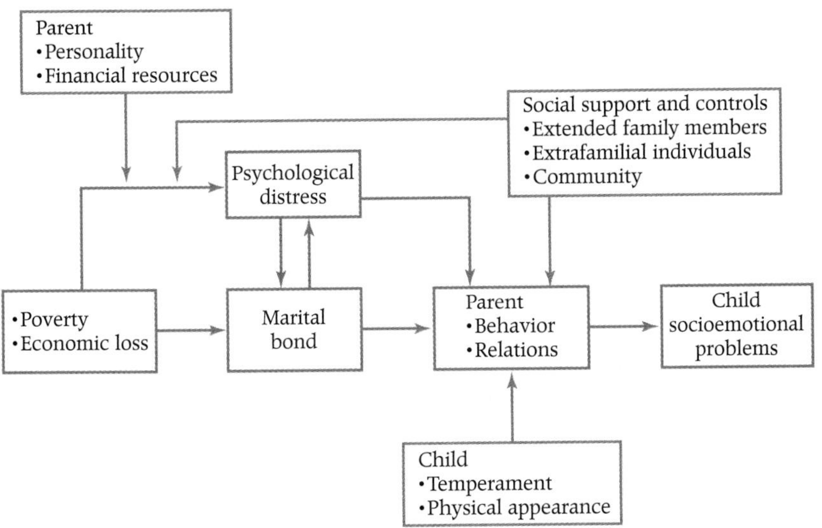

FIGURE 11.4
An analytic model of how poverty and economic loss affect African American children. In this model, poverty increasees psychological distress and weakens the marital bond. These factors also have an adverse effect on parents' social relations with their children, and this may lead to socioemotional problems in the children (blue boxes). Special characteristics of the parents and the child and social support systems modify the way these effects play themselves out in individual cases (red boxes). (After McLoyd, 1990.)

life make independence on the part of their children too risky (McLoyd, 1998b).

Another important way in which poverty influences parenting is by raising the level of parents' stress. Parents who are under stress are less nurturant, more likely to resort to physical punishment, and less consistent when they interact with their children (see Figure 11.4 and the discussion of child abuse in Box 11.2). This relationship between stress and authoritarian parenting was observed by Forgatch and Wieder (summarized in Patterson, 1982), who studied interactions between mothers and children at home over the course of several days. The researchers obtained daily reports from the mothers about such stressful events as unexpectedly large bills, illness in the family, and quarrels with their husbands. A mother's irritability usually increased when things outside her relationship with her children were going badly, and at those times she was more likely to hit or scold her children and more likely to refuse their requests.

The kinds of stress documented by Forgatch and Wieder are by no means restricted to families living in poverty, but poverty makes these universal sources of stress more serious because it increases the likelihood that the family is simultaneously under pressure from several of these sources (Sameroff et al., 1998). Poverty also decreases the likelihood that the family will have the means to deal with multiple stresses.

Although multiple stresses and scant resources offer one explanation for obedience-oriented parenting styles, they are not the only factors. Several studies have shown that the parents' type of work is directly related to their style of interaction with their children at home (Crouter, 1994; Greenberger et al., 1994; Kohn, 1977). Middle-class occupations require the ability to work without close supervision. The content of such work is often complex, and the flow of work is irregular; therefore, workers must be self-directed. In the new forms of cooperative teamwork that are becoming widespread in American industry, work must be not only self-directed but also socially cooperative and democratic. Traditional working-class occupations, by contrast, demand obedience and punctuality. The flow of work is often so routinized that a robot can—and increasingly does—carry out the job just as efficiently as a human being (assembly-line jobs are a classic example). The high incidence of authoritarian parenting styles among the economically disadvantaged is perfectly understandable in light of the combined facts that working-class occupations require obedience in the face of routine work and that poverty creates stressful family circumstances. At the same time, the effects of traditional working-class occupations on family socialization create an additional obstacle—a lack of initiative and independence—which poor children have to overcome if they are to

BOX 11.2

Child Maltreatment in the United States

In recent decades the public has become increasingly aware that many children in the United States are mistreated by their parents, other relatives, or family acquaintances. Scarcely a day goes by without a story in the media about a child who has been neglected, maltreated, or even murdered by a parent or other relative. Between 1990 and 1993 the rate of maltreatment increased from 13.4 to 15.3 per 1000 children but has dropped in recent years to approximately the 1990 rate (National Child Abuse and Neglect Data System, 1999). Despite this recent improvement, it is clear that child maltreatment in the United States is a serious problem.

Media stories might lead one to believe that adult violence against children is a new problem. Yet infanticide was routinely practiced in ancient Greece, Rome, Arabia, and China. In the early part of the twentieth century, children were routinely beaten in schools, and many were forced to work long hours at backbreaking tasks under the worst possible conditions (Zigler & Hall, 1989). Although various movements to protect childrens' rights were initiated in the 1910s and 1920s, it was not until the late 1960s that all 50 states had laws mandating the reporting of suspected child maltreatment. In 1974, faced with public concern and the need to provide uniform standards for legal purposes, Congress passed the Child Abuse Prevention Act, which defines child maltreatment as

> physical or mental injury, sexual abuse, negligent treatment, or maltreatment of any child under the age of eighteen by a person responsible for the child's welfare under circumstances which indicate the child's health or welfare is harmed or threatened thereby. (Public Law 93024, section 2)

More than half of all the reported cases of child abuse are for *neglect* of the physical well-being of the child, which includes inadequate provision of food and clothing, as well as a lack of supervision. *Physical abuse,* such as beating, burning, kicking, or hitting a child with an object, accounts for about a quarter of the reported cases, while *sexual abuse* accounts for 13 percent of the cases. *Emotional maltreatment* was reported in 5 percent of the cases, and *medical neglect* (failing to take a child who is ill or injured to a doctor) was reported in 3 percent of the cases (NCCAN, 1997). Often children who are exposed to one kind of abuse are also exposed to others (Barth, 1998).

With the exception of extreme maltreatment and sexual abuse, judgments about the applicability of these categories are likely to be difficult, because what is deemed appropriate and inappropriate treatment of children, including the frequency and severity of physical punishment, varies dramatically from one family and community to the next (Holden & Zambarano, 1992). According to a variety of surveys, for example, over 90 percent of all parents in the United States have spanked their children. In some families and some communities, spanking is considered appropriate, even expected, when a child misbehaves. In other families and communities, spanking is regarded as abuse no matter what the provocation. Clearly the borders between *culturally acceptable* physical punishment and physical punishment that is defined as *maltreatment* depend very much on parents' beliefs about children and the modes of interaction sanctioned in the children's families and communities.

No matter how broadly or narrowly child maltreatment is defined, many cases of neglect, brutality, and sexual abuse are never reported and go undetected by people outside the family. Many experts consider the officially reported cases of abuse and neglect to be just the tip of the iceberg. The only certainty is that each year large numbers of children are abused or neglected (Finkelhor & Dziuba-Leatherman, 1994).

Who Is at Risk for Being Maltreated?

Any child may be neglected or abused, but some children seem to be at greater risk than others. Age is one factor: children 7 years old and younger represent half the cases of child maltreatment. Of the children who died as a result of abuse in the United States in 1995, 77 percent were under 3 years of age, and almost half were under the age of 1. Gender is a second factor: boys are far more likely than girls to be the target of *physical* abuse, while girls are twice as likely as boys to be the victims of *sexual* abuse. Race is a third factor: in 55 percent of the cases of child maltreatment reported in 1997, the children were white; in 27 percent, they were African American; in 10 percent, Hispanic; and in 2 percent, Native American (NCCAN, 1999). Socioeconomic class is a fourth factor: children living in poverty are more likely than middle-class children to be abused (Barnett et al., 1993; Barth, 1998; Wilson & Saft, 1993).

Who Does the Abusing?

The risk of physically abusing children is inherent for all parents in part because there are times when parents feel that they have to coerce their children into complying with their wishes. Nevertheless, most parents do not abuse their children. Factors found to reduce the likelihood of child maltreatment include the adult's ability to control his or her anger, community sanctions against abuse, and the availability of outside support for the family.

It is generally believed that parents who were physically abused by their parents are more likely to abuse their own children than are parents who were not themselves abused (Belsky, 1993; Kempe et al., 1962). However, only 30 percent of those who were abused become child abusers themselves; 70 percent do not (Kaufman & Zigler, 1989). Hence, a history of abuse may be considered a risk factor in later abuse but cannot be considered a simple cause.

It is also widely believed that children are most likely to be sexually abused by strangers. This is *not* true. Sexual abuse is committed most often by adults, mostly men, who know the children they are abusing. Often they are relatives (Finkelhor, 1994).

What Precipitates Child Maltreatment?

It should be clear from the discussion so far that no single risk factor represents the catalyst for child abuse and neglect. Rather, a complex interplay of multiple risk factors seems to set the stage for maltreatment (Barnett et al., 1997). There is a good deal of evidence that one risk factor is stress on the family. The stresses can be of many kinds, and each one present compounds the others: chronic poverty, recent job loss, marital discord, and social isolation have all been linked to increases in the incidence of child abuse (Goodman et al., 1998). The likelihood of abuse is also higher when the mother is very young, is poorly educated, abuses drugs or alcohol, or receives little financial support from the father (Goodman et al., 1998; Pianta et al., 1989; Sternberg, 1993).

Many scholars who have studied the physical abuse of children in the United States see it as a social disease that accompanies the acceptance of violence in families, local communities, and society at large. Two kinds of evidence support this position: (1) Most child abuse occurs when parents set out to discipline their children by punishing them physically and then end up hurting them (Zigler & Hall, 1989); (2) countries in which the physical punishment of children is frowned upon, such as Sweden and Japan, have very low rates of physical abuse of children (Belsky, 1993; Cicchetti & Toth, 1993).

Sexual abuse of children is frequently seen in situations where the custodial parent divorces and remarries frequently or introduces a series of new partners into the home. But sexual abuse also occurs in relatively stable households (Gomes-Schwartz et al., 1990). Unlike neglect and physical abuse, sexual abuse is committed by adults of every income and educational level.

Effects of Being Abused

Studies that compare the intellectual, social, and emotional consequences of child abuse attest to its negative effects (Cicchetti & Toth, 1998). In infancy, many maltreated infants are sad, fearful, and frequently angry. They rarely initiate social contact, and their attachment behavior in the strange situation is likely to be classified as insecure or avoidant (Toth & Cicchetti, 1993). In preschool, physically abused children find it difficult to get along with other children and are less well liked than their peers (Haskett & Kistner, 1991). Their popularity remains low in middle childhood, because their peers and teachers see them as more aggressive and less cooperative than other children (Salzinger et al., 1993). They are reported to be more afraid than other children of angry interactions between adults (Hennessy et al., 1994). A review of school and social service records found that maltreated children had poorer grades than their peers, performed poorly on standardized tests, and were more likely to have to repeat a grade (Eckenrode et al., 1993).

Like children who have been abused in other ways, children who have been sexually abused tend to be anxious, depressed, withdrawn, and aggressive; these traits get them into trouble at school. They often show a precocious interest in sex and behave seductively (Kendall-Tackett et al., 1993).

Some children, however, seem to emerge from the experience of sexual abuse without any symptoms (Kendall-Tackett et al., 1993). Taken as a whole, the psychological effects of sexual abuse can be seen to depend on the age of the child, the child's relationship with the abuser, the severity and duration of the abuse, and the reactions of other people if the abuse becomes known (Kendall-Tackett et al., 1993).

What Can Be Done?

Shocking as it may seem, because of lack of staff, many of the reports of maltreatment are never investigated, and in many of the cases that are investigated and confirmed, the children involved receive no social services (Barth, 1998). When child protection agencies are able to get involved, they currently use two kinds of interventions to shield children from further abuse: intensive in-home services for the family or placement in foster care. Intensive in-home services include specially trained nurse home visitors to provide emotional support as well as health and parenting education; hotlines for parents to call if they feel themselves getting too upset; and special organizations such as Parents Anonymous, which provides parent education courses, support groups, and a crisis intervention hotline for parents who feel tempted to abuse their children. However, since many interventions last only a month, they can help the family address only its most recent crisis. One study found that while in-home interventions are well received by parents, they do not reduce the likelihood of continued maltreatment (Rzepnicki et al., 1994).

Because there have been cases in which children whose families are receiving in-home care die as a result of being maltreated, some professionals concerned with child welfare are currently advocating that abused children be immediately placed in foster care and kept there until the abusing parents have been rehabilitated (Barth, 1998). This proposal sounds sensible, but it would be difficult to carry out on a large scale for two reasons: Foster care is very expensive, and there are not enough foster homes for children who have experienced abuse.

The long history of child abuse cautions us not to expect meaningful results from piecemeal efforts and mere expressions of community concern. A systematic campaign that attacks several risk factors simultaneously would appear to offer the best hope of reducing the problem in the long run.

extended family A family in which not only parents and their children but other kin—grandparents, cousins, nephews, or more distant family relations—share a household.

improve their socioeconomic situation. Robert Halpern (1990) pinpoints the problem when he remarks that the kind of child-rearing approach that middle-class psychologists recommend, which involves discussion and reasoning with children, may not be appropriate to the real-life circumstances of poor people.

The Extended Family and Social Networks

Many scholars have found that one source of problem-solving and stress-reducing resources for poor, young, minority children is the extended family (Manns, 1997; Wilson, 1995). An **extended family** is one in which not only parents and their children but other kin—grandparents, cousins, nephews, or more distant family relations—share a household. In some cases, an extended family involves children who have been sent for a time to trusted friends or business partners or godparents.

It is uncertain just how widespread the phenomenon of extended families has become in recent decades. Melvin Wilson (1986) estimates that perhaps 10 percent of African American children live in extended families, and there are indications that the figure may be much higher when the mothers are young and single (Sandven & Resnick, 1990). Extended families are also common among Hispanic, Asian Pacific, and Native American households in the United States (Harrison et al., 1990).

Scholars identify two major sources for the formation of an extended family: cultural traditions and economic hardship. Extended family arrangements of various kinds were the norm among the African peoples brought to the Americas and sold into slavery. Strong family affiliations persisted during slavery, despite attempts to destroy them (Genovese, 1976). Richard Griswold del Castillo (1984) offers a similar explanation of the high incidence of extended families among Hispanic Americans. He traces the contemporary Hispanic American family back to the period before the Spanish conquest. Extended kin relations were a central feature of the cultures of these people's Amerindian ancestors.

Many scholars see the extended family as a natural strategy for dealing with the combined handicaps of low income and low social standing (Harrison et al., 1990; Manns, 1997; McLoyd, 1998a). Extended families appear to play an especially important role in providing support for children born to young, single mothers (Chase-Lansdale et al., 1994; Wilson, 1989). They provide income, child care, and help in maintaining the household as well as less tangible assistance, such as emotional support and counseling. In some circumstances, grandmothers provide care that is more responsive and less punitive than that of their teenage daughters (Chase-Lansdale et al., 1994). Furthermore, the presence of other adults in the house makes it possible for the children's mothers to obtain additional education, which in turn improves the family's economic circumstances.

The evidence that extended family relations help to buffer children against the harmful effects of poverty has led psychologists to emphasize the importance of social networks in shaping parental behaviors toward their children (Manns, 1997; Salzinger, 1990). When poor families are isolated from their communities, and especially when single young women attempt to raise their children without a social support system, the children are particularly at risk. By contrast, young mothers who belong to a social network that allows them to interact regularly with friends and neighbors, and to engage in such activities as attending church and participating in community events, raise their children in a more nurturant and sensitive way (Hashima & Amato, 1994; McLoyd, 1998a, 1998b).

MEDIA LINKING COMMUNITY AND HOME

Parents are by no means the only ones in the home who shape children's behavior. Children are affected by their brothers and sisters and sometimes by their grandparents, aunts, uncles, and cousins, as well as by people whom

One of the most effective ways of giving children both a love of books and basic reading skills is to read with them, as this German family is doing.

they encounter in their neighborhoods or who come into their home to provide services or bring news of the world outside. The outside world also enters the home through letters, books, magazines, newspapers, radio, television, videotape, CDs, the Internet, and so on.

The sheer magnitude of children's immersion in modern communications media makes it important to understand the role that experience with these media play in their development. Yet the issue has long been, and remains, a contentious one.

THE LESSONS OF HISTORY

Given the current social approval of reading as "good for children," it might come as a surprise that when literacy was first introduced into Greek society around the fourth century B.C. as a means of gaining information about the world, it was met with suspicion by the philosopher Plato. During Plato's time a significant part of the population knew how to read and write, and written texts and dramas were beginning to replace oral literature as a major means of propagating core cultural knowledge from one generation to the next. In one of his famous dialogues, *The Phaedrus,* Plato argued that contrary to popular opinion, learning to read and write would lead to a weakening of memory, eroding the basis for obtaining wisdom. The true path to knowledge, he believed, was face-to-face dialogue that followed the rules of logic.

The echoes of Plato's arguments can be found in discussions of media effects today, but now literacy is an "old" medium and, despite some concerns, is thought to enhance development. It is the new media of our times that raise the most severe doubts.

Two questions dominate modern research on the developmental impact of various media: (1) How does the physical *form* of the medium contribute to its effects on development? and (2) what role does the *content* of the medium play in shaping any observed effects? In Chapter 13 we consider these issues in the context of schooling. Here we consider them as they influence young children who are in the earliest stages of being enculturated into a literate culture.

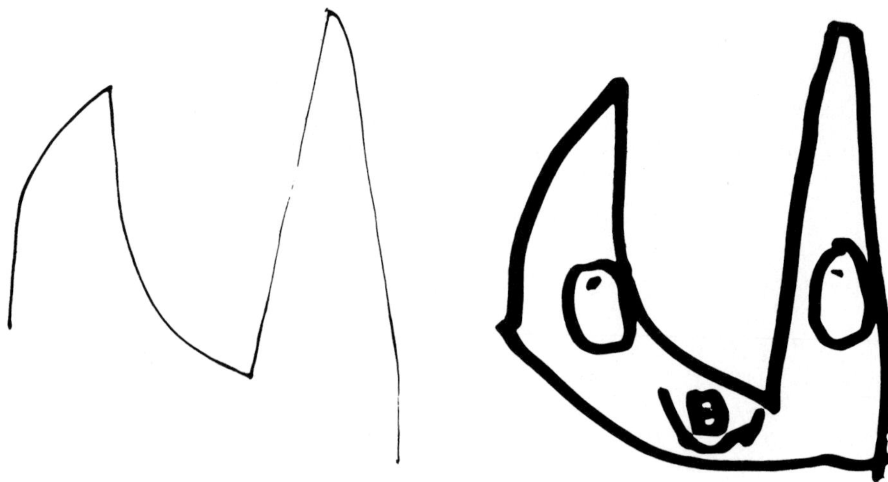

FIGURE 11.5
Left: *"An M . . . What does that spell? It spells* M *for Molly."* Right: *"And it could be a rabbit. See, it's got big ears." Here 3½-year-old Molly uses the letter* M *in two different ways as she begins to get the idea of writing. For Molly, the letter and the drawing are only fragilely differentiated. (From Gardner et al., 1982.)*

BOOKS

In the United States, young children of every social class are exposed to print in some form almost every day, even if only for a few minutes (Purcell-Gates, 1996). Such experiences teach them that the letter symbols on billboards, in picture books, and on the milk cartons at the breakfast table somehow convey information. This form of knowledge about reading and writing is referred to as "emergent literacy" (Whitehurst & Lonigan, 1998) (see Figure 11.5).

The Form of Early Literacy Experiences

An important class of experiences that contributes to emergent literacy is being read to. Evidence indicates that young children who are often read to at home acquire an appreciation of the use of print to make meaning, and that this appreciation helps them when they start school (Reese & Cox, 1999).

Often a child's introduction to print begins with the reader's directing the child's attention to the illustrations that accompany a story. Anat Ninio and Jerome Bruner's (1978) study of parents reading to their 1- to 2-year-old children suggests how such experiences might help children's later reading. In the following example, Richard, who is seated on his mother's lap, is engaged by his mother in a stylized, cyclical form of dialogue focused on the picture in a book. With few exceptions, each cycle in their conversation goes something like this:

> *Mother: (pointing to a picture)* Look at this!
> *Richard: (touches picture or gives some other indication of attention)*
> *Mother:* What is it?
> *Richard:* A doggy.
> *Mother:* Right! *(turns page and initiates a new round)*

When children are very young, adults are likely to fill in the labels for objects and accept any sort of contribution from the child as an adequate turn. As the child's knowledge increases, adults supply less help in keeping the game going. Instead, they raise the stakes by introducing books with words in addition to pictures and by asking more complicated questions about old favorites (Reese & Cox, 1999). This kind of tailored support keeps changing to fit children's growing competence in a manner that creates a "zone of proximal development" (Vygotsky's concept introduced in Chapter 5, p. 207). Zones of proximal development allow children to participate in a full activity (in this case, reading a book) before they are fully competent. Thus children can participate in the adventures of Max as he confronts the "Wild

Things," or say goodnight to the moon even though, if left to their own, they might hold the book upside down and quickly lose interest.

In a study of three groups in a North Carolina mill town, Shirley Brice Heath (1983) found that the way adults structure reading activities differs according to the social class and cultural background of the family. In some families in the study, being read to was primarily an occasion for meaning-making of the kind illustrated in the Ninio and Bruner example. In others, it was an occasion for learning to sit still and be obedient. In still others, it was an occasion for launching into a story of one's own. Such differences are important because when children get to school, reading for meaning that stays close to the text will be the norm. Children who come to school after being inducted into different forms of emergent literacy may have trouble learning to read once they begin school, even if they sit very quietly and behave themselves in class or are able to tell great stories.

Learning to read involves understanding how to hold a book and turn pages, and what to look for on the page.

To prepare children for the kind of reading expected in school, Grover Whitehurst and his colleagues have developed a special form of joint reading that they call **dialogic reading,** which is based on the idea of the zone of proximal development (Lonigan & Whitehurst, 1998; Whitehurst et al., 1994). In dialogic reading, the adult listens actively, asking questions, adding information of interest, and prompting the children to increase the complexity of their contributions until they are retelling the story in their own way. Whitehurst and his colleagures report that after 30 reading sessions spread over 6 weeks, young children spoke more grammatically, expressed their ideas better, and identified the component sounds of words more accurately than children in a control group. Since these achievements are known to be important in learning to read, and since the program has been effective across a wide range of family backgrounds, Whitehurst and his colleagues urge that dialogic reading be taught to parents as a means of promoting children's reading readiness.

Appropriate Content for Young Children

Despite the generally positive orientation that adults have toward books and reading, books that have traditionally been read to children sometimes come under fire. Most fairy tales and myths were created in the centuries before childhood was considered a special "innocent" period of life and before any literature had been specifically devised for children (Sale, 1978). Adults have occasionally argued that fairy tales should not be read to children because they are cruel, brutal, and frightening (Snow White is given a poisoned apple by her stepmother; Hansel and Gretel are shoved into the oven by a witch; and the prince is turned into a frog). Even when benign, fairy tales are sometimes criticized because they are not realistic portrayals of the world. For example, Kornei Chukovsky, a famous Russian author of poems for children, received complaints accusing him of damaging children by writing fantasy. One irate reader condemned him as follows:

> [You are] filling the heads of our children with all kinds of nonsense, such as that trees grow shoes. I have read with indignation in one of your books such fantastic lines as:
>
> Frogs fly in the sky,
> Fish sit in fishermen's laps,
> Mice catch cats
> And lock them up in
> Mousetraps.
>
> Why do you distort realistic facts? Children need socially useful information and not fantastic stories about white bears who cry cock-a-doodle-doo. (Chukovsky, 1968, p. 11)

But the presence of fantastic, and even violent, content in fairy tales has its defenders, such as the psychoanalyst Bruno Bettelheim (1977), who insisted that children *need* fairy tales: "Like all great art, fairy tales both delight and

dialogic reading Reading in which the adult listens actively, asking questions, adding information of interest, and prompting children to increase the complexity of their contributions until they are retelling the story in their own way.

instruct; their special genius is that they do so in terms which speak directly to children" (p. 56). Bettelheim believed that the very unreality of such stories allows children to use them to find solutions to their own inner conflicts; it is certainly less threatening to think about Cinderella's evil stepmother than to think consciously about real negative feelings toward one's own mother or father.

Another frequent complaint about the content of many children's books is that it ignores or misrepresents certain ethnic and racial groups, women, and working-class and poor people. These concerns are well grounded in surveys of the contents of children's books (Pescosolido et al., 1997; Turner-Bowker, 1996).

When we turn from books and reading to television viewing, concerns about the content and form of children's experiences are similar in some respects but different in others. Generally, television's role in development is viewed with concern.

TELEVISION: BENIGN BABY-SITTER OR HARMFUL INTRUDER?

It is estimated that a TV set is on for 6 or more hours each day in the average American home and that young children are in front of it for 2 or more of those hours (Huston & Wright, 1999). Television viewing during childhood is so pervasive that Dorothy and Jerome Singer argue that "no other extraparental influence has penetrated the lives of children as television has" (Singer & Singer, 1990, p. 177).

The evidence that the behavior of young children and even infants can be influenced when they watch TV is irrefutable. In Chapter 5 (p. 205) we saw that 14-month-olds imitate actions they see on a TV screen (Meltzoff, 1988a). Infants and young children also imitate the language they hear on TV. Dafna Lemish and Mabel Rice (1986) report that one 2-year-old they observed at home approached her father, pointed at the bottle of beer in his hand, and declared, "Diet Pepsi, one less calorie." Further, young children identify with superheroes and mythical creatures they see on television. The pervasive influence of such identification can be seen in everything from their fantasy play and the toys they play with to the cereals they insist on having—clear evidence that what children learn from television influences their everyday behavior (Dyson, 1997; Seiter, 1993).

What Is Real?

A special concern about television viewing is that young children easily confuse TV make-believe and reality. Research summarized in Chapter 9 (pp. 341–342) indicated that young children sometimes have trouble distinguishing reality and appearance. It seems reasonable to assume that their confusion is compounded when they watch television entertainment programs in which believable people are shown engaging in behavior and events that could actually be happening. A child in a TV program who runs away from home is a real child filmed on a set that looks like a real home. The question for researchers has been at what age children watching such programs would know whether they are looking at a window on reality or a fantasy on film?

Research concerning the appearance–reality distinction shows that at the end of infancy children have little understanding of the boundary between what they see on television and the rest of their perceptual environment. They are likely to think that a bowl of popcorn shown on TV would spill if the TV set were turned upside down (Flavell et al., 1990). Even 4- and 5-year-olds may display such difficulty, believing, for example, that Sesame Street is a real place or that television characters can see and hear the people who are watching them on TV (Nikken & Peters, 1988).

By the time they are approaching the age of 6, children in the United States have a good feel for the various categories of programming they watch, such as news programs, dramas, educational programming, and cartoons, and they understand that news programs are more likely to be about real events than cartoons or entertainment programs. They generally understand that the objects seen on the screen are not literally inside the TV set, and they can identify a wide variety of fanciful events as "not real" (Davies, 1997). They are still susceptible to confusion, however. Aimee Dorr (1983) reports that children under the age of 7 may have difficulty understanding that when a bad guy is shot on television, the actor isn't really dead, or that when a husband beats his wife, the actress isn't really hurt. Even 7- and 8-year-olds will claim that actors and actresses who play married couples must be friends, and they do not realize that fictional programs are rehearsed (Wright et al., 1994).

Confusion about the reality of television is not restricted to children. From time to time one reads of an irate adult assaulting an actor who portrays an evil character in a soap opera. But the problem is more acute for young children because they have little independent knowledge of the world with which to compare what they see on television.

The Problem of Television Form

Another set of concerns arises from difficulties that young children have in understanding the codes and conventions of television programs. Programming intended to be educational cannot succeed in educating, for example, if it is produced using techniques that are confusing to young children.

One potential source of confusion arises from the way in which images and accompanying dialogue are typically presented. Aware that the viewer's attention is attracted by movement and change, television directors use quick cuts from one scene or one camera angle to another. The popular children's program *Sesame Street,* for example, was deliberately designed to have a new cut on the average of every 30 seconds as a means of maintaining the attention of young children (Lesser, 1974). Other techniques are used to focus viewers' attention and highlight the central message: close-up shots pick out essential details; camera placement gives hints about point of view; flashbacks fill in earlier parts of the story (Schmitt et al., 1999). These thought-shaping techniques are a great resource for conveying meaning, at least for older viewers, but for young children, they have their negative side as well (Huston & Wright, 1996). Unless the subject matter is familiar, young children have difficulty interpreting sequences of quick scene changes without transitions. Juxtapositions of images intended to convey the relation of one action to another may also give them difficulty (see Figure 11.6).

As a consequence of the limitations in their understanding of the conventions of television forms, young children often fail to comprehend a good deal of what they watch, although they do better when the program has been designed to take their special interpretive needs into account (Lorch, 1994). Comprehension improves markedly during middle childhood, but even 9- and 10-year-olds have difficulty understanding fast-paced programs that do not

FIGURE 11.6
An item from a test that assesses children's ability to re-create an entire setting on the basis of partial glimpses. Each card corresponds to a camera angle used in films and television programs. Children are asked to put the four cards together to make a meaningful scene. (From Greenfield, 1984.)

clearly show the continuity of action from one sequence to the next (Huston & Wright, 1996).

Another effect blamed on the fast pacing of television programming is that it makes it difficult for children to stop and ponder what is being presented. As a consequence, according to some psychologists, children acquire a kind of mental laziness that makes it difficult for them to do the mental work required to learn from written texts (Salomon, 1984). However, research over the past two decades has failed to support the idea that television viewing induces any generalized mental laziness (Huston & Wright, 1996).

The Problem of Television Content

Concerns about the influence of television *content* on children's development echo those that appear in discussions of the content of children's literature but are much more prominent. Two special concerns are the social stereotypes that are found on TV and the prevalence of dramatized violence.

Media Stereotypes Throughout the history of television in North America, the people who populated the television screen have not been representative of the population of viewers. Most of the major characters on commercial television are European American men. Even in children's commercial programming, men significantly outnumber women, and, with some exceptions, the situation is not much better on educational programming directed at children (Comstock & Scharrer, 1999).

Surveys of program content conducted in the 1970s and 1980s routinely reported significant differences in the portrayals of men and women. Men were presented as being in control—in relationships, in the workplace, indeed, everywhere. Women, by contrast, were presented as submissive, passive, physically attractive, and sensual. If the women were shown working at all, they were more likely to be nurses or secretaries than doctors and CEOs (Comstock & Scharrer, 1999). Today there are more "liberated" or nontraditional women on some programs and more women appearing as anchors on local TV shows. However, many of the stereotypes remain, although they are less dominant than they once were.

The misrepresentation of ethnic minorities and foreigners is an equally frequent problem, although, again, there have been some changes for some groups. In the early days of television, African Americans did not appear on the screen often, and when they did appear, they were presented primarily as servants and criminals (Barcus, 1986). Currently, African Americans are likely to be portrayed more positively than European Americans are, including engaging in proportionally less violent or criminal behavior. At the same time, Hispanic Americans are even less visible than they were in the 1950s, and they are disproportionally portrayed in criminal roles (Lichter & Amundson, 1999).

Stereotyping on television is of concern because (1) it may create or maintain negative intergroup attitudes, and (2) it may influence young children's attitudes toward their place in society. Bradley Greenberg and Jeffrey Brand (1994) report that when asked about their favorite programs and favorite characters, children identify with the protagonists who are members of their own ethnic group. Thus, the absence of positive role models for certain groups is another source of concern.

Violence No one living in the contemporary United States can escape the widespread and continuing debate about the potential role of television violence as a contributing factor in the epidemic of killings that have plagued U.S. schools in the 1990s. In fact, the high level of violence on television has been a social concern for many years. In 1972 the surgeon general of the United States issued a report arguing that television violence increases aggres-

When families watch TV together, adults have the opportunity to clarify children's misunderstandings and to discuss events that are frightening or disturbing.

siveness among viewers, an opinion that has been frequently repeated by congressional committees in the intervening decades.

Fully 80 percent of the television programs that young Americans watch include at least one violent event, and many contain more (Lichter & Amundson, 1999). To be sure, a large portion of these images are in the form of cartoons, in which the likes of Roadrunner and the Coyote commit mayhem on each other, only to recover miraculously to fight another day. But there is a great deal of graphic and realistic violence as well.

To the public at large, it seems obvious that a constant diet of violent behavior on television, even cartoon violence, fosters the attitude that violence is an acceptable way to settle disputes. To the frustration of many, psychological research assessing the relationship between televised violence and aggressive behavior remains shrouded in controversy. Experimental studies, which in principle should be able to show causal relations between televised violence and aggressive behavior do, in fact, show that after children watch a violent program, they act more aggressively in a laboratory playroom than children who have watched more benign programs. (Such work was described in the discussion of imitation in Chapter 10, p. 402). However, critics have claimed that the artificial circumstances of these studies are so different from the way children view television at home that it is impossible to generalize the results to real-life circumstances.

Many studies that attempt to relate children's levels of viewing violence on television to aggressive behavior also find that more aggressive children watch more violent programming (Comstock & Scharrer, 1999; Huston & Wright, 1996). However, since all this research is correlational, it cannot confirm whether a higher level of watching TV violence is a cause of greater aggressiveness or the consequence of a greater predisposition to aggression.

Some of the most convincing evidence that watching TV violence increases children's aggressive behavior comes from "natural experiments" in which television is introduced into communities that have not previously been exposed to it and children's subsequent behavior is observed. Tannis Williams (1986) conducted one such study in three small communities in Canada in the 1980s. One community had never had TV before, one had a single channel, and one had several available channels. Williams found that in the previously isolated community, elementary school children's behavior on the playground became more aggressive during the 2 years after the introduction of TV. The level of children's aggressiveness did not change in the two communities that already had television, an indication that the introduction of television was the causal factor underlying the increased aggression in the first case. Similar studies carried out in other countries (reviewed by Huston & Wright, 1996) produce similar findings. However, because these were natural experiments, the possibility remains that some change in the affected communities other than the introduction of television could have caused the increase in the children's aggressive behavior.

Despite the technical difficulties of proving a causal link between viewing violence on television and behaving aggressively, the current consensus among psychologists is that watching violence on television does in fact increase aggressive behavior by creating a cultural climate in which aggression and even violence are seen as an acceptable ways to settle disputes. Even so, scholars who specialize in the study of television and its effects are careful to acknowledge the ambiguities that necessarily accompany correlational data (Comstock & Scharrer, 1999; Huston & Wright, 1998).

Family Influences

Concerns about the possible negative effects of television viewing on children have led to repeated suggestions that parents take an active role in supervising their children's experiences with television (American Academy of Child and Adolescent Psychiatry, 1999). In North America, at least, parents generally do not impose severe restrictions on how much TV children watch. However, they do try to restrict children's access to programs that contain a lot of graphic violence, sexuality, or frightening content. They also encourage their children to watch educational programs or programs that they believe provide appropriate entertainment for children (Huston & Wright, 1996).

Research summarized by Aletha Huston and John Wright (1996) indicates that when parents and children watch television together, the viewing experience can be more worthwhile. Adult explanations of the plots, motivations of characters, and events in dramatic programs increase children's understanding of the content. Such conversations also provide ready-made occasions for parents to discuss questions of social values and moral issues.

Unfortunately, while joint television viewing can have positive developmental effects, current evidence indicates that parents generally spend little time watching and discussing TV with young children. Moreover, when they do watch television with their children, the programs are more likely to be ones that the parents want to watch, not programming directed at children (Van Evra, 1998). It appears that adult entertainment, not children's education, provides the major motive for parents and their children to watch television together.

In light of data indicating the positive benefits of parental involvement in their young children's television watching, and the deep concerns about the way that television enters into so many aspects of the growing child's "ecological niche," some developmentalists have created special interventions to help parents overcome what they see as the harmful effects of the medium

(Thoman, 1999). The goal of these interventions is to maximize the educational potential that television can provide while minimizing the potential harm from viewing violent and frightening events (Cantor, 1998; Jason & Hanaway, 1997).

INTERACTIVE MEDIA

During the past decade there has been an explosion of new media pouring into the lives of children in modern, industrialized societies—the "digital" media, which are bringing together the "old" media of telephone and television and the "new" media of computers and the Internet. We will touch only briefly on these media here and will return to consider them more extensively in our discussions of middle childhood, the period on which most of the research on children and the new media has been centered.

The new media are attractive to many young children, owing both to their form and to their content. In the form of computer games, their capacity for graphic and auditory representation makes it possible to present children with attractive cartoonlike scenarios of the kind seen on Saturday morning television. But, unlike television, the new media allow children to interact with the pictures and stories they see, controlling the movements of characters and participating in the action so that they engage in active problem solving at the same time that they are being entertained. Other programs allow children to create sequences of pictures to develop their own stories and even to program their own games using attractive, easily understood symbols.

Beyond their potential as toys and a new mode of expression, digital media are increasingly being used in preschools as a means for teaching basic literacy and numeracy skills. In these settings, the interactive game playing capacity of computers is combined with such tasks as identifying letters of the alphabet, matching colors and shapes, or making elementary arithmetic calculations. Controlled experiments indicate that young children not only acquire vocabulary and a variety of academic skills in such gamelike activities but also learn to carry out a variety of computer operations that many adults are unsure about (Klein & Starkey, 1999).

There is, as yet, not enough systematic evidence to judge the long-term consequences of young children's use of the new media, but some worry that this form of activity, rather than providing useful experiences for small children, promotes short attention span, the expectation that answers and rewards to challenges come easily, and superficial understanding. These are important concerns, but their merit cannot be determined until much more extensive research is conducted.

THE YOUNG CHILD IN THE COMMUNITY

As long as parents remain at home with their young children, they can retain relatively direct control over outside influences, even the influence of television. But when the parents leave their children in the care of other people for several hours a day, the nature of that control, not to mention the nature of their children's experiences, changes in a decisive way. In the United States and other industrialized countries, one of the most important tasks many parents face is selecting the day care or preschool that will provide the upbringing of their children during those hours.

VARIETIES OF DAY CARE

At present more than 63 percent of U.S. mothers with children younger than 6 are working and have placed their children in some form of supervised care

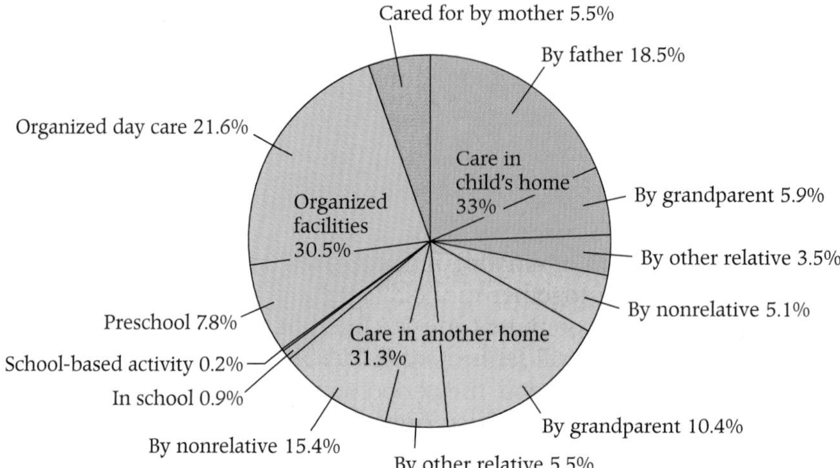

FIGURE 11.7
Primary child-care arrangements used by working mothers for children under 5 years of age in 1995. (From U.S. Bureau of the Census, Current Population Reports, *1998.)*

during their workdays (U.S. Bureau of the Census, 1998). One of the most popular arrangements for children younger than 5 is **home care**–care provided in the children's own homes, primarily by their fathers or grandmothers–while their mothers are at work. **Day-care centers**–organized child-care facilities supervised by licensed professionals–have attracted the most public attention, yet they represent the arrangement least often used. The most commonly used arrangement is **family care**–child care provided in someone else's home, that of either a relative or a stranger (U.S. Bureau of the Census, 1998). The kind of care chosen depends in most cases on availability, cost, the parents' judgments about the quality of care offered, and the age and number of children in need of care (Belsky et al., 1982) (see Figure 11.7).

Home Care

Because child care in the home is private, relatively little is known about it. One study that compared various types of child care confirmed what common sense might lead one to expect. Children cared for at home experience the least change from normal routine: they eat food provided by their parents and take naps in their own beds. They also come in contact with relatively few children their own age (Clarke-Stewart, 1993).

Family Day Care

Family day care often exposes children not only to caretakers from outside the family circle but also to new settings and to children of other families. The children in a family day-care setting may range widely in age, forming a more diverse social group than is likely to exist at home. The routine of activities in family day care, however, is usually very similar to the routine at home (Clarke-Stewart, 1993).

State, county, or local government agencies grant licenses to family day-care homes that meet basic health and safety requirements and maintain acceptable adult–child ratios. A study that examined the quality of care in licensed family child-care homes with respect to the child's safety, the communication between the parent and the day-care provider regarding the child, and the nature of the relationship between the day-care provider and the children found that licensing is no guarantee of high quality. Only 9 percent of the regulated child-care providers were found to offer good care; 56 percent were rated as providing minimal care; and 5 percent were rated as providing inadequate care (Galinsky et al., 1994). Not surprisingly, the children most likely to be in poor-quality family day-care homes are minority children and children whose family incomes are low.

home care Child care provided in the child's own home, primarily by the father or a grandmother–while the mother is at work.

day-care center An organized child-care facility supervised by licensed professionals.

family care Child care provided in someone else's home, that of either a relative or a stranger.

TABLE 11.5 CHARACTERISTICS OF HIGH QUALITY CHILD-CARE CENTERS

1. Children in program are enjoying themselves as they play and learn.
2. There are small groups of children and low ratios of caregivers to children.
3. The activities organized for the children are appropriate to their age levels and abilities.
4. Equal attention and time are devoted to the whole child including cognitive, social, emotional, and physical development.
5. Staff meet regularly to plan and evaluate the program.
6. Parents are welcome to observe, discuss and make suggestions about the program.

Source: National Association for the Education of Young Children, 1999.

Unlicensed day-care homes, which make up the great majority of family day-care homes, tend to provide poorer quality care than licensed homes. In particular, observers have found that unlicensed providers are even less likely than licensed ones to give comfort, verbal stimulation, and guidance to the children in their care (Galinsky et al., 1994; Goelman, 1988).

Day-Care Centers

Licensed day-care centers generally offer a wider variety of formal learning experiences than family or home day care and are likely to employ at least one trained caretaker (see Table 11.5 for six features that are believed to contribute to the quality of day care). Waiting lists for places in day-care centers tend to be long, however, since the demand far exceeds the available openings.

Because licensed day-care centers often receive public financing, they have been more accessible to researchers, who have studied both their characteristics and the way these characteristics affect children's development. Here are some of the findings:

- Day-care centers with populations of more than 60 children place more emphasis on rules than smaller centers do, are relatively inflexible in their scheduling, and offer children fewer opportunities to initiate or control their own activities. Teachers in large centers tend to show less sensitivity to the needs of individual children, perhaps because there are so many children for them to supervise (Clarke-Stewart & Fein, 1983).
- The most important factor for 3- to 5-year-old children, as for younger children (see Chapter 7, p. 265), is the size of the day-care group and the number of children each adult has to care for (Howes et al., 1992). Groups of fewer than 15 to 20 children and groups in which there is at least one adult for every 7 to 9 children allow for more individual contact and verbal interaction between children and adults and for children's active involvement in group activities (Lamb, 1998).
- A committed and stable staff that has some training and an administrator who is experienced increase the quality of a center's care (Cost, Quality, & Child Outcomes Study Team, 1995).

The programs available vary in style and philosophy. Some offer an academic curriculum, emphasize discipline, and have a school-like atmosphere. Others emphasize social development and allow children to exercise more initiative in their activities. In accord with the class differences in modes of parenting discussed earlier in this chapter, most working-class parents have been found to prefer the more school-like day-care centers, while middle-class

These children at a day-care center are obtaining the kind of experience in getting along in groups that is one of the major features of the day-care experience.

parents are likely to choose the less structured centers (NICHD Early Child Care Research Network, 1996).

DEVELOPMENTAL EFFECTS OF DAY CARE

As we saw in Chapter 7 (Box 7.1) the effects of day care during the first 2 years of life depend primarily on the quality of the care provided and not on the mere fact of parent–child separation during the day. Nevertheless, concerns about the effects of day care in later years continue to be raised, primarily regarding children's intellectual and social development.

Intellectual Effects

Evidence from studies of day care in Europe as well as the United States indicates that intellectual development of children in high-quality day-care centers is at least as good as that of children raised at home by their parents (Lamb, 1998) (see Figure 11.8). In some cases experience in high-quality day-care programs lessens or prevents the decline in intellectual performance that sometimes occurs in children of low socioeconomic backgrounds who remain at home with poorly educated parents after the age of 2. Such programs may even lead to marked gains in language and cognitive development among these children (Campbell & Ramey, 1994; Caughy et al., 1994).

FIGURE 11.8

Performance on tests of intellectual development by children cared for in day-care centers and by those cared for at home. The tests were specially constructed to assess children's ability to use language, form concepts, and remember information. (From Clarke-Stewart, 1984.)

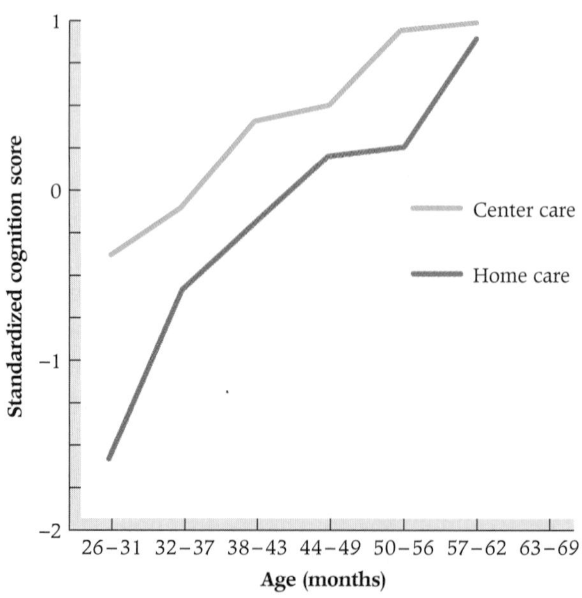

Impact on Social Development

Children who attend day-care centers in the United States tend to be more self-sufficient and more independent of parents and teachers, more helpful and cooperative with peers and mothers, more verbally expressive, more knowledgeable about the social world, and more comfortable in new situations than children who do not attend day-care centers. On the other hand, they also tend to be less polite, less agreeable, less compliant with adults, and more aggressive than children who do not attend day-care centers (see Lamb, 1998, for a review of these data). These effects seem to be related to the number of years a child spends in full-time nonparental care, with more extensive time being associated with more aggressive behavior and a greater likelihood of behavior problems in kindergarten (Bates et al, 1994; Honig & Park, 1993).

It isn't necessary to look far for an explanation of day care's effects on a preschooler's social development. At home the wishes and needs of small children are often anticipated, their social incompetence is usually overlooked, and their failures at communication tend to be filled in by their caregivers. In care supplied outside the home, children are required to get along with caregivers who not only know less about their special likes, dislikes, abilities, and limitations but must also fit several children into a common schedule. In addition, children who receive day care must learn to interact successfully with a variety of other young children, often when the adults present are too busy to negotiate disputes.

These children usually have more opportunities to turn to peers for companionship, affection, amusement, and a sense of identity and belonging. Experience with groups of children their own age helps children to learn about their strengths and weaknesses by comparing themselves with others. The flowering of language at the end of the second year and the beginning of the third adds an important dimension to children's social interactions that influences their experiences in day care. By the time children are 2½ they are able to manage interactions with one another that contain, in fledgling form, the basic features of social interactions among older children and adults—sustained attention, turn-taking, and mutual responsiveness (Rubin et al., 1998). However, they still have a great deal to learn, and day care provides them with a variety of relevant experiences.

Learning to share toys with others is one of the difficult lessons young children have to confront.

Interactions between children at day-care centers and preschools that might influence their social behavior usually occur around a shared activity, such as playing fantasy games or building with blocks. Among 3- and 4-year-olds, the skills necessary to sustain such activities are still quite fragile (Corsaro, 1985). Such group interactions usually last less than 10 minutes and often end abruptly when a playmate leaves the play area without warning. The fragility of such groups requires that children learn how to gain access to another group—or face the prospect of playing alone.

It is experience of group play—gaining access to group activities, learning to become desirable companions, and dealing with rejection—that is the most likely social benefit of day care. On the negative side, some of the behavior children learn in day care may conflict with their parents' standards of appropriate behavior at home and elsewhere.

PRESCHOOL

Day care originated in response to the needs of adults who wanted their children supervised while they worked or went to school. By contrast, the purpose of preschool (which used to be called nursery school) is primarily educational. Preschools came into being early in the twentieth century, initiated by educators' and physicians' concern that the complexities of urban life were overwhelming children and stunting their development. The preschool was conceived as "a protected environment scaled to [children's] developmental level and designed to promote experiences of mastery within a child-sized manageable world" (Prescott & Jones, 1971, p. 54). The basic intuition justifying preschools as environments for development is contained in the botanical metaphor of the child as a budding flower. At the age of 5 many children "graduate" from preschool to kindergarten, a "garden for children" (from the German *Kinder* [children] and *Garten* [garden]). Extending the metaphor,

Entering the play of children of the opposite sex presents special difficulties, but it is by no means impossible, especially if you have control of an attractive plaything.

3- and 4-year-old children are not ready for the rigors of a garden where rain falls, wind blows, and birds forage for seeds. Like the seedlings at a local garden store (a nursery!), they are most likely to develop healthily if they are specially protected until they are ready for transplanting (see Box 11.3).

A typical preschool's layout and schedule reveal prevalent ideas of how best to foster development from the age of 2½ to 6. There are likely to be several kinds of play areas: a sandbox, a water-play table, a doll corner, a block area, a large area with a rug where children can gather to listen to stories or sing songs, a cluster of low tables used for arts-and-crafts projects and for snacks, and an outdoor area with jungle gyms, slides, and swings. Each area provides an environment for developing a different aspect of children's overall potential: their ability to understand physical transformations in play materials; to control their own bodies; to create in language, music, clay, and paint; to adopt various social roles; and to get along with other children.

During the 2½ to 3 hours that children may spend in a preschool, they are guided from one activity area to another. The developmental spirit of preschools is reflected in their lack of pressure on children to perform correctly on preassigned tasks and in their emphasis on exploration.

Preschools and the "War on Poverty"

In the 1960s a variety of scientific and social factors combined to create great interest in preschools' potential to increase the educational chances of the poor. On the scientific side was a growing belief that environmental influence during the first few years of life is crucial to all later abilities, especially intellectual ones (see Chapter 7). This belief coincided with broader historical pressures to improve the status of ethnic and racial minorities and with widespread political concern that social barriers between the rich and the poor and between whites and blacks were creating a dangerous situation in the United States. In his 1963 book, Michael Harrington warned that the United States was creating "an enormous concentration of young people who, if they do not receive immediate help, may well be the source of a kind of hereditary poverty new to American society" (p. 188). Commentators on the lives of poor young children issue the same warning today (Mason et al., 1998).

This combination of social, political, and scientific factors led the U.S. Congress to declare a "war on poverty" in 1964. One of the key programs in this "war" was Project Head Start. Its purpose was to intervene in the cycle of poverty at a crucial time in children's lives by providing them with important learning experiences that they might otherwise miss. Federal support enabled Head Start programs to offer these experiences at no charge to low-income families.

This strategy of social reform through early childhood education rested on three crucial assumptions:

1. The environmental conditions of poverty-level homes are insufficient to prepare children to succeed in school.
2. Schooling is the social mechanism that permits children to succeed in our society.
3. Poor children could succeed in school, and thereby overcome their poverty, if they were given extra assistance in the preschool years.

BOX 11.3

Cultural Variations in Preschool Education

For many children preschool represents their first exposure to formal socialization outside the family context. The practices and values that preschoolers are encouraged to acquire there reflect the core cultural values that they are expected to embrace as adults.

When Joseph Tobin, David Wu, and Dana Davidson (1989) compared preschools in Japan and the United States, they found that even though the preschools were physically similar, the differences in socialization practices were very marked. On the day Tobin and his colleagues were videotaping a group of 4-year-olds at Komatsudani Hoikuen, a Buddhist preschool in Kyoto, Hiroki was acting up. He greeted the visitors by exposing his penis and waving it at them. He initiated fights, disrupted other children's games, and made obscene comments. The group's teacher stood by, doing nothing.

American preschool teachers who later observed the videotape disapproved of Hiroki's behavior, his teacher's handling of it, and many aspects of the Japanese preschool classroom in general. They were shocked to see 30 preschoolers and only one teacher in the classroom. How could this be in a country as affluent as Japan, they asked. They also could not understand why the teacher ignored Hiroki instead of isolating him or giving him "time out" as punishment.

The Japanese teachers viewed the matter quite differently. First, although they acknowledged that it would be very pleasant for them to have a smaller class, they believed it would be bad for the children. Children, they said, "need to have the experience of being in a large group in order to learn to relate to lots of children in lots of kinds of situations" (p. 37). When the Japanese teachers observed a tape of an American preschool with 18 children and two teachers, they worried for the children. "A class that size seems kind of sad and underpopulated," one remarked. Another added, "I wonder how you teach a child to become a member of a group in a class that small."

American and Japanese parents and teachers also had very different interpretations of the probable reasons for Hiroki's outrageous behavior. One American teacher speculated that perhaps Hiroki misbehaved because he was intellectually gifted and became bored easily. The Japanese educators rejected this notion out of hand. To them, "smart" and "intelligent" are almost synonymous with "well behaved" and "praiseworthy," neither of which applied to Hiroki. Hiroki, they believed, had a "dependency disorder." Because his mother was absent from the home, he had not learned how to be properly dependent, so he did not know how to be sensitive and obedient. Isolating Hiroki, they reasoned, would not help. Rather, he needed to learn to get along in his group. To this end his teacher encouraged the other children in the class to take responsibility for helping Hiroki to correct his behavior. Tobin and his colleagues point out that

> Japanese teachers and Japanese society place [great value] on equality and the notion that children's success and failure and their potential to become successful versus failed adults has more to do with effort and character and thus with what can be learned and taught in school than with raw inborn ability. (p. 24)

The difference in social values promoted by the Japanese and American preschools was further highlighted when the Japanese preschool teachers disapproved of the individualism they had observed in the videotape of the American preschool. In their view, "A child's humanity is realized most fully not so much in his ability to be independent from the group as in his ability to cooperate and feel part of the group" (p. 39). In other words, the very qualities the Japanese deplored in the Americans—independence, self-reliance—were the ones the Americans most wished to promote.

At the American preschool, disputes between children were negotiated daily, with the children "playing the roles of plaintiff, defendant, and attorney, and teachers playing the role of judge" (p. 166). This means of resolving classroom disputes struck some of the Japanese as cumbersome and heavy-handed. They believed that children should be left, as much as possible, to devise their own techniques for resolving conflicts. "I was surprised by the way the American teacher got right in the middle of the children's disputes," one Japanese teacher wrote after viewing a fight between two American boys. A Japanese school administrator added:

> For my taste there is something about the American approach [teachers take children who misbehave aside and talk to them] that is a bit too heavy, too adultlike, too severe and controlled for young children. (p. 53)

This comparison of American and Japanese preschools reveals a fundamental fact about the influence of culture on children's development. The pattern of preschool education in each society is shaped by what the adults imagine the future will be for their charges, both in later grades and in later life. The American preschool educators imagine that it is desirable for the children in their classrooms to become self-sufficient and independent adults; the Japanese educators want their young charges to become sensitive adults who have a strong sense of interdependence with their group. Much as parents treat their newborn boys and girls differently, not because they are so very different but because they imagine they will be different as adults, the American and Japanese teachers are helping the children in their classrooms to develop the characteristics they imagine they will need as adults in their society.

Originally conceived as a summer program, Head Start soon began to operate year round, serving approximately 200,000 preschool children at a time (Consortium for Longitudinal Studies, 1983). More than three decades later, Head Start programs have expanded to provide services for more than 750,000 children. Despite its phenomenal growth, the program serves only 38 percent of the children who are eligible to participate (Devaney et al., 1997).

What Difference Does Head Start Make?

Because Head Start preschools have gained considerable social acceptance since the 1960s, it might be assumed that the preschool experience proved to have positive benefits for children. The data are not so clear-cut.

Planners of Project Head Start and other preschool programs with similar goals were sensitive to the need for scientific demonstrations of the usefulness of preschools (Zigler & Finn-Stevenson, 1998). The logical requirements for providing such proof were simple enough: select a large sample of children; give half of them (the experimental group), chosen at random, the experimental preschool experience; and let the other half of the sample (the control group) stay home. But the demand for preschool was so great that every effort was made to provide a place for every child whose parent applied. No parents wanted their children to be part of a control group, so the logic of experimental design was bypassed. As a result, there has been a great deal of controversy over the developmental consequences of Head Start programs.

The first reports were promising. Children who attended a single summer program showed marked gains in standardized test scores. In addition, hundreds of thousands of parents were involved in their children's school lives for the first time, whether as members of Head Start planning boards, as participants in special training programs for parents, or as classroom helpers. For a great many children, Head Start also meant better nutrition and health care.

Doubts about the effectiveness of the program were soon heard, however. In 1969 it was reported that the gains from Head Start slowly disappeared during the first 3 years of elementary school (Grotberg, 1969). A widely publicized evaluation by the Westinghouse Learning Corporation (1969) concluded that although "full-year Head Start appears to be a more effective compensatory education program than summer Head Start, its benefits cannot be described as satisfactory" (p. 11). The report confirmed the doubts

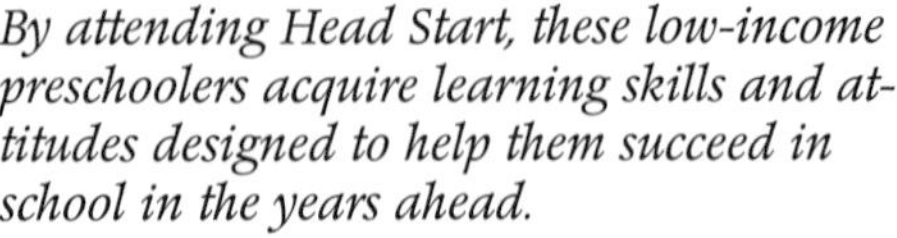
By attending Head Start, these low-income preschoolers acquire learning skills and attitudes designed to help them succeed in school in the years ahead.

The preschool experience is an opportunity to make friends with children one's own age at the same time that children are acquiring culturally valued skills.

of people who had never favored Head Start programs, but it failed to persuade Head Start's supporters. They pointed out that the Westinghouse study lacked any proper control groups and relied on a variety of doubtful statistics instead.

In recent decades a large number of studies have evaluated preschool programs for poor children, including Head Start and a variety of similar efforts (summarized in Lamb, 1998; Zigler & Finn-Stevenson, 1998). Some of the studies have been able to do follow-up evaluations of children as they reached their early twenties and to include broader developmental indicators such as crime rates and earned income in the assessment. These broad evaluations revealed a variety of positive findings, although success has not been uniform. On the positive side, children who attend regular Head Start or special, model programs show meaningful gains in intellectual performance and socioemotional development. Children who attend Head Start are also less likely to be assigned to remedial special-education classes when they attend school. The success of these programs, however, depends upon the quality of the classroom experience, and, unfortunately, while most classrooms have been rated as adequate in quality, very few are considered of high quality.

Nonetheless, the success of well-run programs is now broadly accepted (Lamb, 1998; Zigler & Finn-Stevenson, 1999). In one of the best and most heavily studied cases, the Perry Preschool Program in Ypsilanti, Michigan, it has been possible to follow up the progress of experimental and control children for more than 35 years. The children in the experimental group had higher achievement scores than those in the control group at the ages of 9 and 14. They were more likely to graduate high school, more likely to be employed at the age of 19, less likely to have run afoul of the law by the age of 28, and less likely to have gone on welfare. W. Steven Barnett (1995), who conducted a study of the costs and benefits of the expenditures of the Perry preschool intervention, calculated that for every dollar spent on the program, the public saved $7 from decreased costs for later welfare and incarceration.

The Future of Compensatory Preschool Programs

Head Start and other compensatory preschool programs face an uncertain future in the United States. Two major objections have been raised to the propagation of compensatory preschool programs. First, there is the question of how public money should be spent. Congressional committees that oversee the use of tax dollars have questioned whether even successful programs are successful enough to justify their costs. Recall that the Perry Preschool Project was exemplary but that many federally funded programs do not provide the same quality of experience for children and are not as effective. In his summary of the relationship between the costs and benefits of Head Start programs, Ronald Haskins (1989), a psychologist who worked for the congressional committee overseeing Head Start expenditures, concluded that the savings to taxpayers from Head Start programs are relatively small. This conclusion leads naturally to a search for more effective ways to use the funds. Second, some critics argue that educational programs cannot compensate for the damage caused by poor housing, inadequate nutrition, discrimination, and parental unemployment and that the premise of Project Head Start—giving the children of the poor a "head start" to reduce their poverty—is misguided.

Despite uncertainty about the long-term effects and cost efficiency of the Head Start program, there are reasons to believe that the program may continue to play a role in the government's efforts in support of children. As Haskins (1989) noted, Head Start has become a national symbol of the desire to help poor children advance through self-improvement. Head Start children receive much-needed food, health care, and dental care. They also obtain intellectual stimulation that increases the chances that they will begin their formal schooling with a firmer foundation and greater hopes of long-term success.

ON THE THRESHOLD

This chapter has by no means surveyed all the contexts that significantly influence early childhood development: young children also learn from trips to the beach, outings in the park, attendance at houses of worship, visits to the doctor's office, and trips to the market. Each new context brings with it new social and intellectual challenges as the children gradually piece together a deeper understanding of their world and their place in it.

Recognizing the influence of context on early childhood development helps us make sense of the variable picture each young child presents to the world. In familiar contexts, where children know the appropriate scripts and their own roles in them, they may display mature reasoning and surprising competence. But often they find themselves novices in strange settings where they do not know the appropriate scripts, where they are expected to work out social relationships with strangers, and where they are set new tasks that require them to master new concepts. In these circumstances, their powers of self-expression and self-control are put under great strain, and their thought processes may be inadequate for the heavy demands placed on them.

The problem of being a novice is by no means unique to young children; people face it throughout their lives. But the difficulties are particularly acute at the beginning of early childhood because young children know so little about how their culture works. Consequently, children of this age need almost constant supervision. When they play together, they need some powerful organizing activity, such as pretend play, to support their fragile ability to coordinate with one another.

By the end of early childhood, children's vocabularies and command of grammatical forms have grown immensely. They have greater knowledge about a wide variety of contexts and a more sophisticated sense of themselves; and they are vastly more competent to think about the world, to control themselves, and to deal with other children. In these and many other ways they indicate a readiness to venture into new settings, to take on new social roles, and to accept the additional responsibilities that await them as they enter middle childhood.

SUMMARY

THE FAMILY AS A CONTEXT FOR DEVELOPMENT

- The factors that influence children's lives can be usefully thought of as a nested set of contexts that influence one another.
- The family influences children's development in two ways: by shaping their behavior within the family and by selecting other contexts for them to inhabit.
- Parenting everywhere has three goals: to ensure that the child
  1. Survives into adulthood.
  2. Acquires the skills and resources needed for economic self-sufficiency.
  3. Acquires the cultural values of the group.
- Cross-cultural comparisons of family life reveal that children's social behavior and personalities develop to fit the overall demands of economic activity and community life in their society.
- Family socialization patterns vary within societies, depending on such factors as the family configuration and the values, beliefs, education, income, and personalities of the family members.
- Patterns of socialization can be grouped for purposes of comparison. Child-rearing practices in the United States in most cases follow one of three patterns:
  1. Authoritarian families use set standards and emphasize conformity.
  2. Authoritative families emphasize control through reasoning and discussion.
  3. Permissive families avoid overt control and believe that children should make their own decisions.
- Among white middle-class two-parent families, authoritative child-rearing practices are associated with children who are more self-reliant, self-controlled, and willing to explore than those raised by permissive or authoritarian parents.
- Caution must be used in applying a single set of parenting categories to different cultural groups. Chinese American parenting, for example, is best characterized by an idea of "training" that is not found in European American families.
- A significant number of U.S. children grow up in single-parent families headed by a young unwed mother. These children tend to be more aggressive, less self-controlled, and less cognitively advanced than the children of older, married couples.
- Children whose parents have divorced may display a variety of negative reactions, including sleep disturbances, irritability, and aggressiveness. The severity and duration of the dislocation resulting from divorce depend on a variety of factors, including the family income and the configuration of the new family that results if the custodial parent remarries.
- Poverty affects family life in many ways, increasing the stress on parents at the same time that it reduces their resources for dealing with it. Stress, in turn, is associated with authoritarian parenting styles.
- Extended family arrangements provide one means of coping with poverty. The presence of several adults reduces the stress on the parent or parents and provides resources for dealing with the causes of stress.

MEDIA LINKING COMMUNITY AND HOME

- Influences from the community enter the family through such media as books, newspapers, radio, television, and the Internet. Each medium of communication is assumed to influence children's development in specific ways.
- In evaluating the role of media in the development of children, two basic questions need to be addressed: (1) Are there formal features of the medium that shape the experiences children are a part of? (2) How does the content of media influence development?
- Young children usually encounter books in the form of activity, called "being read to."
- Being read to furnishes young children with an early model of activities that will be important in school.
- Parents have considerable control over both the form and the content of the reading experience of their young children.
- Children learn from television and act upon what they have learned from a very young age.
- Television's potential for realism makes it difficult for children to distinguish reality from fiction in television content, and their understanding of the content is confused by such cinematic techniques as rapid cuts and zoom shots.
- Television content influences people's basic beliefs about the world. Insofar as reality is distorted by television, children who watch television acquire false beliefs about the world.
- A variety of evidence indicates a *correlation* between watching violent programming and engaging in violent behavior. However, there remains uncertainty about whether and how violent programming *causes* aggressiveness in children.
- Parents can influence television's impact on their children by controlling what their children watch and by watching with them and talking about what is happening on the screen.

THE YOUNG CHILD IN THE COMMUNITY

- Once children begin to spend time outside the home, their experience changes in fundamental ways.
- Day-care centers in the United States vary widely in social setting, philosophy, and physical facilities. The size of the group is of special importance to the quality of day care in the United States: the smaller the group, the higher the quality. Other factors that contribute to the quality of care are the stability, commitment, and training of the staff.
- Day care in the United States has more clear-cut effects on children's social behavior than on their cognitive behavior. The major effects are:
    1. Increased self-sufficiency and decreased compliance with adults' wishes.
    2. Increased ability to engage in peer-led group activity.
- Preschools evolved during the twentieth century as a means of promoting the development of children who had to cope with the complexities of urban life.
- Since the early 1960s, preschool education has been promoted as a means of combating school failure among people living in poverty.

ON THE THRESHOLD

- The fact that children begin to spend extended time in unfamiliar contexts is a key feature of development in early childhood.
- Exposure to a variety of new contexts stimulates the social and intellectual development of young children.
- The fact that young children are novices in the new contexts they inhabit is one of the reasons for the unevenness that is characteristic of their thought and action.

KEY WORDS

authoritarian parenting pattern, p. 430
authoritative parenting pattern, p. 430
day-care center, p. 450
dialogic reading, p. 443
extended family, p. 440
family care, p. 450
home care, p. 450
nuclear family, p. 423
permissive parenting pattern, p. 431

THOUGHT QUESTIONS

1. A basic assumption of Bronfenbrenner's cultural-context approach is that contexts are reciprocally related. Give some examples from this chapter in which experiences in one context influence behavior in another.
2. Suggest a research design for isolating the causes and effects of different parenting styles (as a follow-up to Diana Baumrind's research program). What obstacles do you anticipate in carrying out your proposed study?
3. Drawing on the discussion in this chapter and in Chapter 10, how might you explain the psychological difficulties that a young child experiences when his or her mother or father remarries after a divorce?
4. Robert Halpern is quoted on page 440 as saying that the child-rearing practices recommended by mainstream psychologists may not be appropriate for children of low-income families. Why might that be the case?
5. Why is there continuing controversy about the consequences of viewing violence on television?

PART IV

Middle Childhood

Anthropological descriptions of a wide variety of cultures indicate that as children reach the age of 5 to 7 years, they are no longer restricted to the home or to settings where they are carefully watched by adults. Instead, they become responsible for behaving themselves in a variety of new contexts. The new activities they encounter in these contexts vary from one society to the next. Among some of the Mayan people in the highlands of Guatemala, for example, boys go out to gather wood, a solitary activity that takes them well beyond the range of watchful adults, while girls spend more time at home doing domestic work in the company of their mothers and the older women of the village (Rogoff, 2000). In the United States, by contrast, boys and girls alike spend long hours in school, with their peers, receiving formal education.

In spite of such differences, however, the cross-cultural regularities of the changes that occur between the ages of 5 and 7 are so impressive that this period seems to signal the emergence of a new developmental period (Sameroff & Haith, 1996). At first glance, time spent in solitary activity or with peers when no adults are present may appear less important to development than time spent in educational settings. However, solitary activities, such as gathering wood or chasing birds and small animals away from a growing rice crop, and peer interaction, which often consists of little more than playing games, gossiping, or simply "hanging out," are more significant for development than they might initially seem. Being in charge of the family cornfield or a younger sibling or engaging in informal interaction with peers provides children with important opportunities for learning what it means to take responsibility, for exploring social relationships, and for developing moral understanding and personal identity.

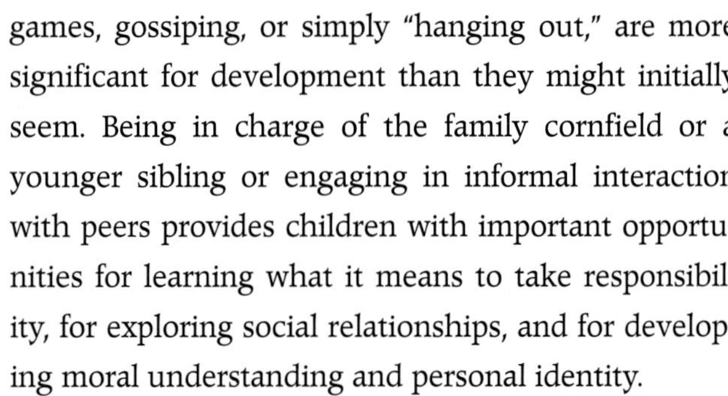

Key to their ability to manage in the new contexts of middle childhood is children's acquisition of the biological and cognitive capacities needed to support their newly granted autonomy and responsibility. As we shall see, evidence from experiments, naturalistic observations, and clinical interviews makes it clear that during middle childhood children develop new abilities to think more deeply and logically, to follow through on a problem once it is undertaken, and to keep track of more than one aspect of a situation at a time.

Our discussion of middle childhood is divided into three chapters. Chapter 12 focuses on the nature of children's biological and cognitive capacities between the ages of 5 and 12. The next two chapters examine children's behavior in two broad categories of social context that are central to development in middle childhood in many countries: school and peer groups. Chapter

13 examines the influence of schooling on development, with particular attention to the organization of school activities and to the intellectual capacities that schooling both demands and fosters. Chapter 14 focuses on the developmental significance of the new social relations that emerge during middle childhood, particularly among peers. The influence of biological, cognitive, and social factors, as they are woven together in different cultural contexts, creates the particular tapestry of middle childhood as it is encountered around the world.

CHAPTER 12

Cognitive and Biological Attainments of Middle Childhood

Walking was my project before reading. The text I read was the town; the book I made up was a map. . . . I pushed at my map's edges. Alone at night I added newly memorized streets and blocks to old streets and blocks, and imagined connecting them on foot. . . . I felt that my life depended on keeping it all straight—remembering where on earth I lived, that is, in relation to where I walked. It was dead reckoning. On darkened evenings I came home exultant, secretive, often from some exotic leafy curb a mile beyond what I had known at lunch, where I had peered up at the street sign, hugging the cold pole, and fixed the intersection in my mind. What joy, what relief, eased me as I pushed open the heavy front door!—joy and relief because, from the very trackless waste, I had located home, family, and the dinner table once again.

An infant watches her hands and feels them move.

Gradually she fixes her own boundaries at the complex incurved rim of skin. Later she touches one palm to another and tries for a game to distinguish each hand's sensations of feeling and being felt. What is a house but a bigger skin, and a neighborhood map but the world's skin ever expanding?

Annie Dillard, *An American Childhood*

In many societies, adults begin to have new expectations when their children approach 6 years of age. Among the Ngoni of Malawi, in central Africa, adults believe that the loss of milk teeth and the emergence of second teeth (which begins around the age of 6) signal that children should begin to act more independently. They are supposed to stop playing childish games and start learning skills that will be essential when they grow up. They are also expected to understand their place and are held accountable for being discourteous. The boys leave the protection and control of women and move into dormitories, where they must adapt to a system of male dominance and male life. Margaret Read (1960/1968) describes the associated stresses for Ngoni boys:

> There was no doubt that this abrupt transition, like the sudden weaning [several years earlier], was a shock for many boys between six-and-a-half and seven-and-a-half. From having been impudent, well fed, self-confident, and spoiled youngsters among the women many of them quickly became skinny, scruffy, subdued, and had a hunted expression. (p. 49)

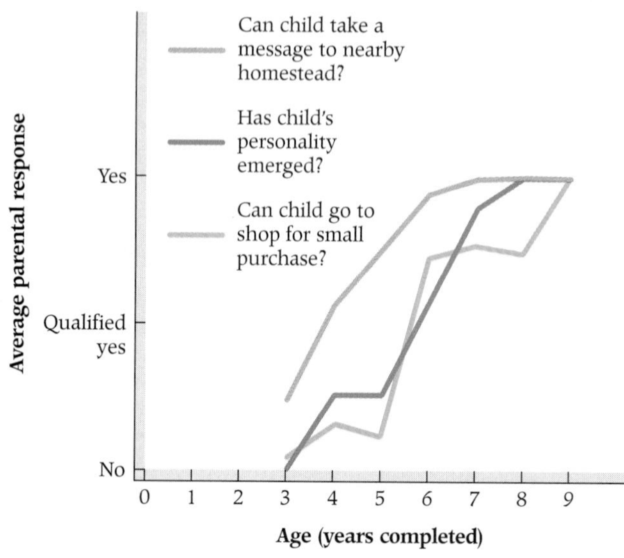

FIGURE 12.1

The ages at which Kipsigis mothers in Kokwet, Kenya, believe their children undergo basic developmental changes. Note the sharp discontinuity in this culture's estimates of personality development and the ability to carry out an errand involving money. But according to this culture, there is continuity in the development of memory needed to convey a message. (From Harkness & Super, 1983.)

Observations of life among the Ifaluk of Micronesia provide a similar picture. The Ifaluk believe that at the age of 6 years, children acquire "social intelligence," which includes the acquisition of important cultural knowledge and skills, as well as the ability to work, to adhere to social norms, and to demonstrate compassion for others—all valued adult behaviors (Lutz, 1987). In Western Europe and the United States, this same transition has long been considered the advent of the "age of reason" (White, 1996).

Adults' expectations that their children will begin to behave more maturely at around the age of 6 or 7 arise from a combination of ecological circumstances, cultural traditions, and their observations of how well their children now cope with new demands (see Figure 12.1) (Sameroff & Haith, 1996). At the age of 6, children are strong and agile enough to catch a runaway

Adults around the world assign children chores in middle childhood that call upon their increased physical strength as well as their ability to control themselves so that they can complete the assigned tasks.

goat or to carry their little sisters on their hips. They know not to let a baby crawl near an open fire. They can wait for the school bus without wandering off. They can, sometimes under duress, sit still for several hours at a time while adults attempt to instruct them, and they are beginning to be able to carry out their chores in an acceptable manner. In short, they can perform tasks independently, formulate goals, and resist the temptation to abandon them.

COPING WITH INCREASED FREEDOM AND RESPONSIBILITY

One of the best ways to gain a sense of how children's lives change as they enter middle childhood is to observe how and where they spend their time. In their research, described in Chapter 1, Roger Barker and Herbert Wright (1951) arranged for observers to follow one child living in "Midwest," a small community in the United States, through every minute of one waking day. The resulting portrait of 7-year-old Raymond Birch, titled *One Boy's Day,* is a classic in the literature of child development. The following account was adapted from it:

Raymond gets up, dresses himself (although his clothes have been laid out for him by his mother), and takes care of his own grooming. He eats breakfast with his mother and father. Then he helps his father to clear the dishes. He negotiates with his mother about the need to wear a jacket to school and grudgingly accepts her judgment that a jacket is in order. He decides on his own not to take his bike to school because it might rain.

After spending a few minutes casting a fishing rod with his father in the backyard (he is the only one who caught fish on their last outing), he accom-

panies his mother to the courthouse where she works. At the courthouse he greets adults politely, and holds the door open for a man who is going out at the same time he is. He plays by himself outside while his mother works. When it is time for him to go to school, he walks the few blocks by himself, crossing the street cautiously. On the playground, he and the other children are unsupervised. A few minutes before 9 A.M. he enters his classroom, which the second-graders share with the first grade. While waiting for school to begin, he draws on the board, looks at a book with a friend, and chats quietly with other children. When the teacher comes into the room promptly at 9 A.M., he turns in his seat (all the seats are arranged in rows, facing front). While the teacher readies the first-graders to go to music, Raymond, who has become worried that he left his coat on the playground, asks permission to search for it. He has forgotten that he has hung it in the cloakroom. When he discovers this, he comes back and makes May baskets out of paper strips with the rest of the second-graders. He goes to music, listens to other children's stories, and goes outside for recess.

In the afternoon he does poorly on the spelling test. When another boy asks, "What did you get on your spelling?" he blushes and looks down at his desk. In a swift hoarse whisper he tells the boy that his grades are his own business. He seems embarrassed when he speaks. Close to dismissal time, the class searches for the money another boy has reported lost. When it turns out to have been in his desk all the time, Raymond smiles companionably at him and leans back to pat his hand. Then the boy pats Raymond's hand. They pat harder and harder, grinning broadly, until the teacher intervenes with a directive for the entire class.

While his mother is preparing dinner after work, Raymond pushes the lawn mower for a minute. He then joins his 11-year-old neighbor Stewart Evarts and Stewart's 3½-year-old nephew Clifford in the vacant lot across the street. Playing with their trucks in a pit that was once the basement of a house, Raymond discovers a dilapidated wooden crate about 5 feet long buried in the weeds. He drags the crate out, and the boys devise several ways to play with it, despite its unwieldy size. They lift it out of the pit and send it crashing back in, get in the crate and pretend it is a cage and that they are monkeys, and hang on with their hands and feet as it rocks and tumbles over and over. At the same time, the older boys are careful that Clifford is not harmed by their games.

FIGURE 12.2
The average number of hours a day that people of various ages in "Midwest" spent in family and community settings. (From Wright, 1956.)

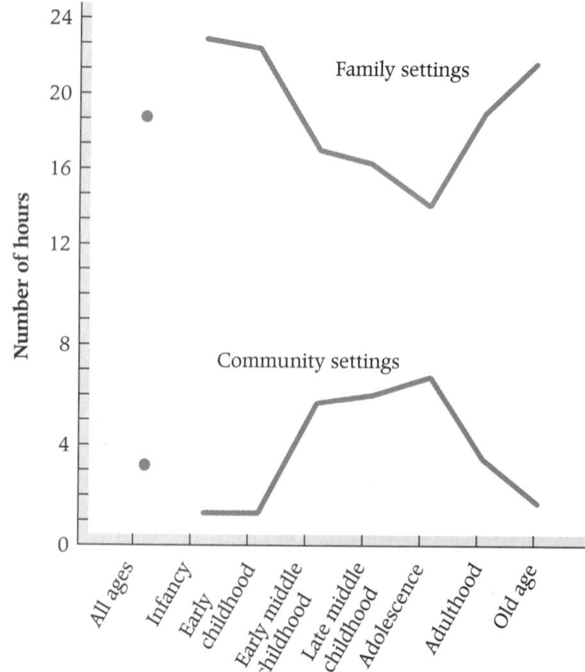

From such observations carried out with many children like Raymond in the early 1950s, Barker and Wright (1955) concluded that the amount of time children spend unsupervised by adults increases markedly during the course of middle childhood (see Figure 12.2). In about one-third of the settings where children Raymond Birch's age spent their time—the streets between home and school and the empty lot across from Raymond's home, for example—they had no adult supervision (see Box 12.1). More recently, similar increases in unsupervised time have been reported among children in urban centers as well as the rural Midwest and among children born in different decades and in quite different societies in several parts of the world (Ellis et al., 1981; Whiting & Edwards, 1988). A major effect of this increase in unsupervised time is that the local neighborhood beyond the family home begins to exert a direct impact on children's development (Brooks-Gunn et al., 1997).

In the years since the observations of Raymond Birch were carried out, American society has undergone many changes that affect

BOX 12.1

WAY-FINDING ON THE HOME RANGE

Middle childhood is a time when children's activities take them farther and farther from home. It is the age at which children typically begin to walk by themselves to school, their friends' houses, the store, the library, the playground, and various other places in their neighborhoods. Finding their way from place to place and returning home safely requires several cognitive skills. Children have to pay attention to where they are going and to such dangers as passing cars. They have to remember important landmarks, and they have to recognize these landmarks from a different perspective when they return.

To trace age-related increases in way-finding ability, Edward Cornell, C. Donald Heth, and Wanda L. Rowat (1992) tested the abilities of 6- and 12-year-old children to find their way back across a university campus and then compared the children's performances with those of 22-year-old college students. First, the children were individually escorted across a corner of the campus of the University of Alberta. As they were walking, their escort instructed some of the children to stop at intervals and look back at where they had been. The idea was to show these children all the vistas that they would see when their direction of travel was reversed. (Anthropologists' observations of hunter-gatherer societies indicate that looking back is a common device used to remember routes. Novices are often instructed to glance back when they have reached an important sight or landmark [Gatty, 1958].) To prevent them from developing alternative strategies for remembering the route, they were not told that they would be asked to lead the way back. A second group of children, who also did not know that they would lead the return trip, were not told to look back. After crossing the campus, both groups were asked to lead their escort all the way back to the place they began, along the same path they had just taken.

As might be expected, given their more limited cognitive abilities and way-finding experience, the 6-year-olds performed less well than the 12- and 22-year-olds, whose performance was virtually the same. This result complements findings that the distance from home that a parent permits a child to venture independently (referred to as the *home range*) expands rapidly during the early elementary school years and remains stable after 10 or 12 years of age (Moore & Young, 1978).

The data that best explain the poor performance of the 6-year-olds are the results for those children who at various points were instructed to stop and look back at where they had been. The 12- and 22-year-olds who were so instructed performed significantly better than those in their age group who were given no special instructions. But the strategy of looking back did not help the 6-year-olds; that is, simple exposure to the memory strategy for that age group did not ensure an improvement in remembering.

Additional experiments by Cornell and his colleagues further pinpointed the 6-year-olds' difficulty. If the 6-year-olds were told to glance back at their path and had memorable landmarks called to their attention, their ability to remember the path they had followed increased significantly (Cornell et al., 1989). On the other hand, if some landmarks, such as garbage cans, signs, or parked bicycles, were surreptitiously changed before the return trip, the 6-year-old children were more apt to lose their way, but the older children's ability to retrace their steps was not diminished because they used more stable and distant landmarks to orient themselves (Heth et al., 1997).

As they begin to navigate away from home on their own, another kind of way-finding becomes even more important for many children than retracing their path: the ability to find their way safely across busy streets. A study of children's ability to find safe ways to cross the road suggests strongly that it would be risky to send 5- to 7-year-olds on an errand if they would have to cross a busy road (Ampofo-Boateng et al., 1993). The researchers arranged to take children individually from their schools to sites close to a fairly busy two-lane road. One site was a crossroads where traffic converged from several directions; at three of the sites visibility was limited by an obstruction or a bend in the road. The children were told to imagine they wanted to cross to the other side of the road and had to select the safest way to get there. They were asked to point out the safest route and explain their choice.

Only 10 percent of the 5-year-olds and 21 percent of the 7-year-olds chose a safe route. Even 11-year-olds chose unsafe routes 25 percent of the time, with boys being more likely than girls to make unsafe choices. The children's performance could be improved, however, by a special safety course that emphasized the importance of visibility and choosing the shortest possible route whenever possible. This research makes it clear that adults should take care to instruct children about environmental risks as the children's home range increases.

the way children spend their time, the amount of freedom they have to explore their communities, and the nature of their responsibilities. It is no longer considered safe, for example, to allow a school-age child to roam the neighborhoods of a big city freely, as Annie Dillard roamed through Pittsburgh when she was a child (see the quotation on p. 468). The Raymond Birches of today are also more likely to spend time after school sitting in front of a television or computer screen or playing interactive video games than making forts over in an empty lot. These differences notwithstanding, middle childhood today, just as it was 50 years ago, is a time when the range of

A challenging game can be a productive way for a child to pass the time on an otherwise tiresome car trip.

contexts children inhabit greatly expands, as does their responsibility to control their own behavior. Their varied activities and the contexts in which they occur provide a wealth of new challenges to children's developing cognitive and social abilities.

In this chapter we focus on changes in children's biological and cognitive functioning that might justify adults' new demands and expectations.

BIOLOGICAL DEVELOPMENTS

An obvious reason that children can do more is that they are bigger, stronger, and more agile than they were when they were younger. Their size and strength increase significantly during middle childhood, although more slowly than in earlier years. Average 4-year-olds in the United States are about 39 inches tall and weigh about 36 pounds; by the time they are 6 years old they are about 45 inches tall and weigh about 45 pounds. At the start of adolescence, 6 or 7 years later, their average height will have increased to almost 5 feet and their weight to approximately 90 pounds.

THE ROLES OF GENES AND ENVIRONMENT IN GROWTH

Like all aspects of development, children's growth depends on the interaction of environmental and genetic factors. Tall parents tend to have tall children. Monozygotic twins reared together are very similar in their patterns of growth, and those reared apart still tend to resemble each other more than do dizygotic twins, who share only 50 percent of their genes. Cases have been reported, however, in which one monozygotic twin is significantly smaller than the other because of the effects of illness or a poor environment (Salvolini et al., 1998).

The genetic contribution to size can also be seen in the variations in the height and rate of growth typical of different populations. When Phyllis Eveleth and J. M. Tanner (1990) compared the heights of well-nourished European, Asian, and African American children from birth to age 18, they found that the Asian boys and girls were distinctly shorter than children of the other two groups. They also reported that African American and Asian children tend to reach their mature height earlier than North American Caucasian children, who in turn reach their full height sooner than European children.

One of the key environmental factors that moderates genetic growth potential is nutrition (see Box 12.2). Lower-class children, who have less access to food and good health care, are usually smaller than children of the same age in well-off families. One study found that during middle childhood, the sons of well-off parents in Nigeria were on average almost 4 inches taller than the boys in less advantaged families (Ashem & Janes, 1978). In many industrialized countries, where the population on the whole is better off than the population as a whole in countries like Nigeria, the gap in size between the children of the poor and those born into well-off families is much smaller. And in some countries, such as Sweden and Norway, where the entire population has access to adequate food and medical care, the difference in height between children whose parents are wealthy and those born to less well-off parents has disappeared altogether (Eveleth & Tanner, 1990).

As indicated, health also plays a role in a child's growth. Growth slows during illnesses, even mild illnesses. When children are adequately nourished, this slowdown is usually followed by a period of rapid "catch-up growth," which quickly restores them to their genetically normative path of growth

(Kang et al., 1998). (The fact that growth processes exhibit a strong tendency to correct themselves after short-term exposure to a deviant environment is an excellent illustration of the canalization process, discussed on p. 60.) When nutritional intake is inadequate, however, the children never do catch up, and their growth is stunted (Greene & Johnston, 1980).

MOTOR DEVELOPMENT

Walking along the beach one day, we saw a girl about 7 years old and her little brother, who was about 4 years old, following their father and older brother, who was 10 or 11 years old. The father and older brother were tossing a ball back and forth as they walked. The girl was hopping along the sand on one foot, while her younger brother scrambled to keep up with her. Suddenly the little girl threw her arms up in the air, leaned over, threw her feet up, and did a cartwheel. She then did another cartwheel. Her younger brother stopped to watch her. Then he tried one. He fell in a heap in the sand, while she continued doing one perfect cartwheel after another. He picked himself up and ran ahead so that he was now between his father and his older brother. His father tossed the ball to him. He missed it, and when he picked it up and tried to throw it back, it flew off to the side. His older brother retrieved it and made a perfect throw.

In such everyday scenes we can see the increases in motor development that occur over the course of middle childhood. Children become stronger and more agile, and their balance improves. They run faster, throw balls farther and are more likely to catch them, and jump farther and higher than they did when they were younger. They also learn to skate, ride bikes, sail boats, dance, swim, and climb trees, as well as acquire a host of other physical skills during this period.

As a general rule, boys and girls differ in their physical skills. By the time they are 5 years old, boys, on average, can jump a little farther, run a bit faster, and throw a ball about 5 feet farther than the average girl. Boys also tend to be better at batting, kicking, dribbling, and catching balls than most girls. Girls, on the other hand, tend to be more agile than boys. Over the course of middle childhood, these sex differences in motor skills become more pronounced (Kalverboer et al., 1993; Malina, 1998). On average, boys tend to be slightly advanced in motor abilities that require power and force, while girls often excel in fine motor skills, such as drawing and writing, or in gross motor skills that combine balance and foot movement, such as skipping and hopping and the skills needed in gymnastics.

Boys tend to have slightly greater muscle mass than most girls and are slightly bigger—until about the age of 10½, when girls spurt ahead in height for a few years—but these sex-related physical differences are not large enough in themselves to account for the superiority of boys in many motor skills during middle childhood. Cultural conceptions of the activities appropriate to boys and to girls also play a large role in shaping these differences in behavior. For example, being able to throw, catch, and hit a baseball is a valued set of skills for boys in American culture. American parents usually encourage their sons, much more than their daughters, to develop these skills by buying them balls and bats, taking them to ball games, talking about baseball with them, playing with them, and enrolling them in Little League. And in all cultures, it is also much truer for boys than for girls that those who are considered to be good athletes are more popular with their peers than those who show no athletic ability. While the participation of girls in such sports as baseball, soccer, and tennis has increased significantly in a number of countries in recent decades, girls are still not given the amount of encouragement and coaching that boys receive in these sports, nor are they rewarded to the extent boys are for having the abilities these sports require.

BOX 12.2

Obesity in Middle Childhood

Despite the high value placed on thinness in the United States, the number of obese children has increased markedly in recent decades (Rossner, 1998; Strauss, 1999). Over recent decades the incidence of childhood obesity has increased more than 50 percent among children between the ages of 6 and 11 years and nearly as much among adolescents age 12 to 17 years. This increase has been greatest for African American and Mexican American children and for children from low-income families (Wolfe et al., 1994).

Many obese children become obese adults. The older children are when they become obese and the more severe their weight problem, the greater their risk of being obese as an adult. A longitudinal study that followed 850 obese children into adulthood found that more than 50 percent of the children who were obese after the age of 6 remained obese as they grew older. Of the obese children who were 10 to 14 years old and who had at least one obese parent, 80 percent remained obese into adulthood. The researchers found no increased risk of adult obesity for children who were obese as infants but who were not obese at later ages. However, they did find that having an obese parent more than doubled the risk of a child's becoming obese at all ages (Whitaker et al., 1997).

There appear to be three critical periods during which there is an increased risk for developing obesity that persists into adulthood (Deitz, 1997; Strauss, 1999). The first is the prenatal period, during which, it is believed, either maternal overnutrition or maternal undernutrition can cause metabolic changes in the fetus that permanently alter the child's appetite regulation. The second critical period is related to what is known as the *adiposity rebound period,* during which children's body fat begins to increase again after a period of decreasing. Normally, the adiposity rebound period occurs at around age 6. Longitudinal studies have found that children whose body fat increases before the age of 5½ are significantly more likely than other children to become and remain obese. One reason for the early weight gain of these children may be that they are maturing early, and early maturation is associated with obesity. Another possible explanation is that children who go through the period of adiposity rebound early may have been exposed to maternal diabetes during the gestational period, which altered their metabolism. The third critical period for the development of persistent obesity is adolescence, when there are changes in the quantity and location of body fat. This period is especially critical for girls. In boys the quantity of body fat normally decreases by about 40 percent, whereas in girls the quantity of body fat increases by about 40 percent, putting girls at elevated risk for becoming and staying obese.

The consequences of becoming obese during childhood and adolescence are severe. Obese children are often rejected by their peers, causing many of them to become withdrawn and suffer from a loss of self-esteem. When these children become adolescents and young adults, they are frequently discriminated against in ways that have serious consequences for their education and their future as wage earners. A study that followed a large group of randomly selected adolescents and young adults for 7 years found that females who were overweight at the beginning of the study completed less school, were less likely to marry, and had lower household incomes—with an almost doubled risk of living in poverty—than those whose weight was normal at the beginning of the study (Gortmaker et al., 1993).

In addition to their social and psychological problems, obese children are more vulnerable to a variety of serious health problems. Obese children have been shown to be at in-

BRAIN DEVELOPMENTS

The years between ages 6 and 8 witness the continued growth of the brain and the development of specific kinds of brain functioning that may underlie changes in cognitive skills:

1. Myelination, particularly in the frontal cortex, continues up to adulthood (Janowsky & Carper, 1996). (Recall from Chapter 4 that myelination provides the axon of cortical neurons with an insulating sheath of tissue that speeds transmission of nerve impulses.)
2. The number of synapses at the ends of neurons increases, creating more connections among neurons; and the output of the chemical neurotransmitters that pass impulses from one neuron to the next also increases (Thatcher, 1991).
3. The activity patterns of the brain as measured by an EEG (electroencephalogram) undergo a dramatic change (see Figure 12.3). Until the age of 5, EEGs recorded when children are awake display more theta activity (characteristic of adult sleep states) than alpha activity (characteristic of engaged attention). Between 5 and 7 years of age, the

creased risk for asthma, heart disease, diabetes, respiratory disease, and orthopedic disorders (Strauss, 1999). In recent years, there has been an alarming increase among obese minority children in the incidence of type II diabetes, a serious condition that can lead to kidney disease, eye disorders, and nervous system problems as well as heart disease and stroke.

The popular belief is that children are fat because they eat a lot. While there is some truth to this observation, not every child who eats large amounts of food is equally at risk for becoming obese. Body weight, like other physical attributes, is determined by an interaction of genetic and environmental factors. A study of 540 Danish adoptees found a strong correlation between the adoptees' weight as adults and the weight of their biological parents, especially their mothers (Stunkard et al., 1986). Twin studies and genetic analysis also point to a strong genetic contribution to obesity (Bouchard, 1997; Stunkard et al., 1986). Still, no one, not even children with a strong genetic propensity to becoming overweight, becomes obese without consuming more calories than his or her body needs. The difference between the caloric intake of a child whose weight is normal and that of a child who becomes obese need not be great. The consumption of as little as 50 extra calories a day can lead to an excess weight gain of 5 pounds over the course of a year (Kolata, 1986).

What is causing the increase in obesity among children? Dietary fat is one of the prime suspects. The diets of obese children have been found to have a higher percentage of calories from fats than the diets of other children. Another suspected culprit is a reduction in activity levels over time. Obese children tend to be less active than children of normal weight. As part of their inactivity, they also tend to watch more television than their normal-weight peers, and television watching in itself has been found to dramatically lower children's metabolic rates—reducing the rate at which children burn calories (Dietz & Gortmaker, 1985; Gortmaker et al., 1996). Decreases in fat intake and increases in physical activity are associated with decreases in children's weight gain, so a combination of these approaches would seem an obvious remedy (Klesges et al., 1995).

Unfortunately, exercising is generally difficult for obese children, and losing weight becomes increasingly difficult once obesity develops because a subsequent loss in weight tends to trigger increased appetite and lowered metabolic rates, driving the person's weight back to its preexisting level (Strauss, 1999). As many as 80 percent of the obese children who do lose weight gain it back (Epstein et al., 1993).

The prevalence of obesity among children and the difficulty of designing therapeutic programs that enable them to attain and retain normal weight have inspired a good deal of research aimed at discovering the most effective forms of therapy. Because children's food preferences and eating habits are influenced by those of their parents, most successful weight-loss programs for children target not only the obese children but also their parents (who are likely to be obese as well) (Epstein et al., 1990; Golan et al., 1998) . The most effective programs also combine clear-cut procedures for identifying high-fat foods with carefully designed exercise programs that specify how many calories are burned up by each form of exercise. In a 5-year follow-up study of one such exemplary therapeutic effort, Leonard Epstein and his colleagues (Epstein et al., 1990) found that the children in the sample had sustained an average weight loss of 12 percent.

amounts of theta and alpha activity are about equal, but thereafter alpha activity (engaged attention) dominates (Corbin & Bickford, 1955).

4. The synchronization of electrical activity in different areas of the brain, called **EEG coherence**, increases significantly, making it possible for different parts of the brain to function more effectively as coordinated systems (see Figure 12.4). Particularly important, according to Robert Thatcher (1994), is evidence of increased coordination between the electrical activity of the frontal lobes and the electrical activity in other parts of the brain.

This pattern of changes in brain structure and function—particularly in the frontal lobes and their connections to other parts of the brain—suggests that maturation of the brain plays an important role in the development of thinking during this period, as in earlier periods (Janowsky & Carper, 1996). The pattern of brain changes between the ages of 5 and 7 permits the frontal lobes to coordinate the activities of other brain centers in a qualitatively more complex way, enabling children to control their attention, to form explicit plans, and to engage in self-reflection, all behaviors that appear to undergo significant development in the transition to middle childhood (see Figure

EEG coherence The synchronization of electrical activity in different areas of the brain.

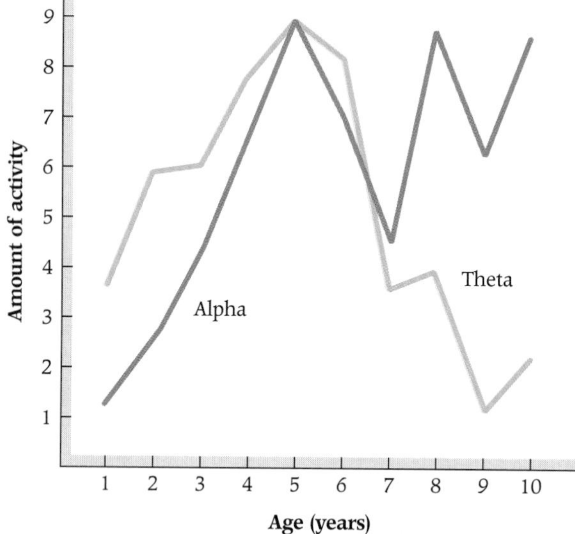

FIGURE 12.3
Changes in the amount of theta (sleeplike) and alpha (alert) EEG activity during development. Note that alpha waves come to predominate over theta waves around the age of 7. (From Corbin & Bickford, 1955.)

12.5). The importance of the frontal lobes in these developments is supported by the fact that when the frontal lobes are damaged in humans and in other animals, behavior deteriorates in specific ways: such individuals are unable to maintain goals; their actions become fragmentary and uncontrolled; and they respond to irrelevant stimuli and are easily thrown off track by interruptions and pauses.

One of the most convincing demonstrations that changes in brain functioning lead to changes in problem-solving processes comes from a study in which the brain activity of 5- to 7-year-old children was recorded as the children were tested on the Piagetian task in which they must judge whether the amount of liquid in a glass increases, decreases, or remains the same when it is poured into a second glass of different dimensions. The children wore caps that contained EEG recording electrodes, allowing the researchers to track the changes in brain activity that accompanied their problem-solving endeavors. Some of the children at each age level succeeded at this task; some did not. Those who did succeed displayed a pattern of brain activity different from the pattern displayed by the children who failed at the task, demonstrating that changes in the brain were associated with the differences in performance (Stauder et al., 1993). The brain patterns of those who failed were similar to those observed among young children (see Chapter 9), a finding supporting the idea that the increasing role of the frontal lobes in overall brain organization is related to the behavioral changes of middle childhood.

Despite this evidence, we must be cautious about inferring direct causal links between particular changes in the brain and specific changes in behavior. The evidence we have cited is correlational: as children grow older, we observe changes in their brains and changes in their behavior, but the direction of causation remains uncertain. As explained in Chapter 5 (Box 5.1, pp. 188–189), the development and strengthening of neural pathways in the brain is affected by the individual's experience. Thus the question becomes, Do children perform in more sophisticated ways because of changes in their brains, or have their brains become larger and more complicated because they have experienced more challenging situations?

FIGURE 12.4
Changes in EEG coherence in the transition from early to middle childhood. (From Thatcher, 1991.)

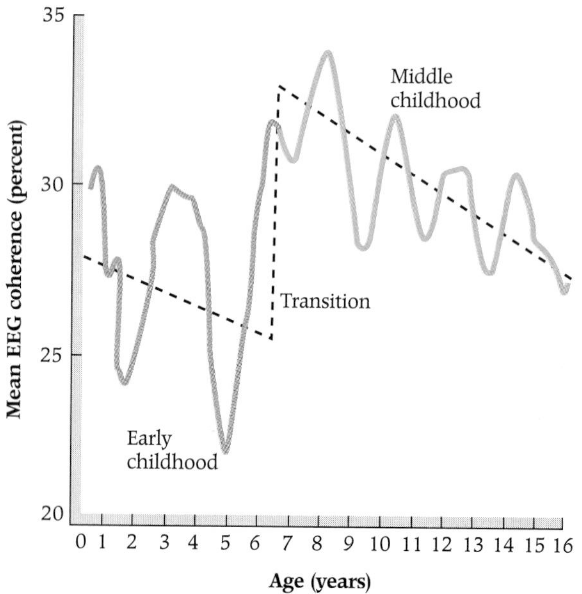

A NEW QUALITY OF MIND?

In early childhood we find islands of competence that become apparent in situations where children can draw upon knowledge from core domains and cultural scripts to guide their thinking (Chapter 9). When we turn to middle childhood, the question naturally arises, What new cognitive developments appear in middle childhood that bridge together those islands of competence to enable children to participate in new and more complex cognitive tasks in a broad variety of contexts? Although the answers proposed by developmentalists differ in their specifics, they all suggest that in middle childhood children's thinking becomes distinctly "two sided"—that is, children can think about objects from more than one perspective, or can hold one characteristic of a situation in mind while comparing it with another. It is children's ability to hold two things in mind simultaneously, in a broad variety of contexts, that permits parents to make new demands on them and to give them greater freedom.

A CHANGE IN THE LOGIC OF ACTION

A vast array of studies show that during middle childhood, children begin more routinely to think through actions and manipulate them

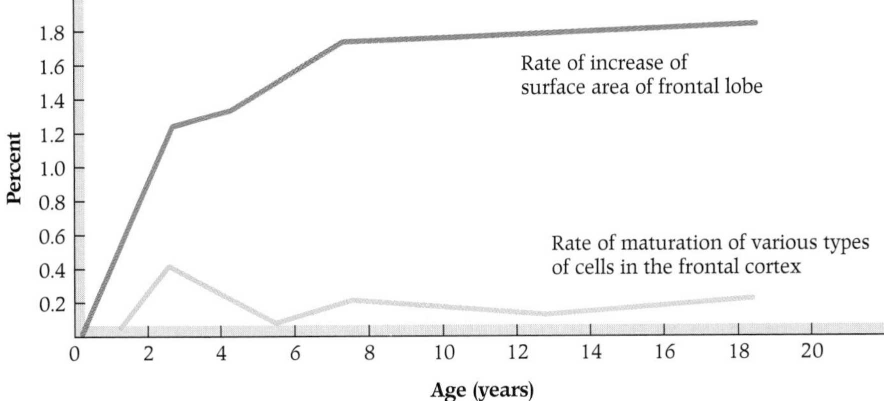

FIGURE 12.5
The rate of increase in the area of the frontal lobes and in the maturation of nerve cells during development. (From Luria, 1973.)

mentally so that they can see them from two sides. Piaget called this form of thought **concrete operations**, coordinated mental actions that fit into a logical system in a way that creates greater unity of thinking. (See Table 12.1 for a summary of concrete operations in relation to other Piagetian stages.) Concrete operations remain concrete in the sense that as mental actions they are directed toward concrete objects in everyday activities. At the same time, concrete operations are distinguished from preoperations by virtue of their double-sidedness.

concrete operations Coordinated mental actions that fit into a logical system in a way that creates greater unity of thinking.

conservation Piaget's term for the understanding that some properties of an object or substance remain the same even when its appearance is altered in some superficial way.

In the transition from early to middle childhood, the advent of concrete operations transforms all aspects of psychological functioning, according to Piaget. The physical world becomes more predictable because children come to understand that certain physical aspects of objects, such as size, density, length, and number, remain the same even when other aspects of the object's appearances have changed. Children's thinking also becomes more organized and flexible. They can think about alternatives and reverse their thinking when they try to solve problems.

Piaget invented a number of problem-solving tasks to enable him to diagnose the presence or absence of concrete-operational thinking. Those involving *conservation of quantity* demonstrate with special clarity why he believed that preoperational and concrete-operational thinking are qualitatively different (Inhelder & Piaget, 1964; Piaget & Inhelder, 1973).

Conservation

Conservation is Piaget's term for the understanding that some properties of an object or substance remain the same even when its appearance is altered in some superficial way. As we saw in Chapter 9, one of the most famous versions of his conservation task involves presenting children with two identical glass beakers containing the same amounts of liquid to see if they understand conservation of quantity (see Figure 12.6). The experimenter begins by pouring the contents of one of the beakers into a third beaker that is taller and narrower. Naturally, the liquid rises higher in the new beaker. The experimenter then asks the child, "Does the new beaker contain more liquid than the old beaker, does it contain the same amount, or does it contain less?"

Ordinarily, 3- to 4-year-old children say that the taller beaker has more. When asked why, they explain, "There's more because it's higher," or "There's more because it's bigger," or even "There's more because you poured it." They appear to focus their attention on a single aspect of the new beaker—its height. (Focusing on a single attribute of an object is the phenomenon of "centering," introduced in Chapter 9, p. 338). Even when the experimenter points out that no liquid was added or subtracted, and even after the liquid is poured back into the original beaker to demonstrate that the amount has not changed, 3- and 4-year-olds still claim that there is more liquid in the taller, narrower beaker.

TABLE 12.1 PIAGET'S STAGES OF COGNITIVE DEVELOPMENT: CONCRETE OPERATIONAL

Age (years)	Stage	Description	Characteristics and Examples
Birth to 2	SENSORIMOTOR	Infants' achievements consist largely of coordinating their sensory perceptions and simple motor behaviors. As they move through the 6 substages of this period, infants come to recognize the existence of a world outside of themselves and begin to interact with it in deliberate ways.	
2 to 6	PREOPERATIONAL	Young children can represent reality to themselves through the use of symbols, including mental images, words, and gestures. Objects and events no longer have to be present to be thought about, but children often fail to distinguish their point of view from that of others, become easily captured by surface appearances; and are often confused about causal relations.	
6 to 12	**CONCRETE OPERATIONAL**	As they enter middle childhood, children become capable of mental operations, internalized actions that fit into a logical system. Operational thinking allows children mentally to combine, separate, order, and transform objects and actions. Such operations are considered concrete because they are carried out in the presence of the objects and events being thought about.	**New features of thinking** • Decentration: Children can notice and consider more than one attribute of an object at a time and form categories according to multiple criteria. • Conservation: Children understand that certain properties of an object will remain the same even when other, superficial ones are altered. They know that when a tall, thin glass is emptied into a short, fat one, the amount of liquid remains the same. • Logical necessity: Children have acquired the conviction that it is logically necessary for certain qualities to be conserved despite changes in appearance. • Identity: Children realize that if nothing has been added or subtracted, the amount must remain the same. • Compensation: Children can mentally compare changes in two aspects of a problem and see how one compensates for the other. • Reversibility: Children realize that certain operations can negate or reverse the effects of others. **Declining egocentrism** • Children can communicate more effectively about objects a listener cannot see. • Children can think about how others perceive them. • Children understand that a person can feel one way and act another. **Changes in social relations** • Children can regulate their interactions with each other through rules and begin to play rule-based games. • Children take intentions into account in judging behavior and believe the punishment must fit the crime.
12 to 19	FORMAL OPERATIONAL	In adolescence the developing person acquires the ability to think systematically about all logical relations within a problem. Adolescents display keen interest in abstract ideals and in the process of thinking itself.	

Piaget found that around the age of 5 or 6 years, children's understanding of conservation goes through a transitional stage. At this point children seem to realize that it is necessary to consider both the height and the circumference of the beakers, but they have difficulty keeping both in mind simultaneously and coordinating the changes so that they can properly compare them.

According to Piaget, children fully master the principle of conservation around the age of 8, when they understand not only that the new beaker is both taller and narrower but that a change in one dimension of the beaker

Step 1: Present two beakers with equal amounts of liquid.

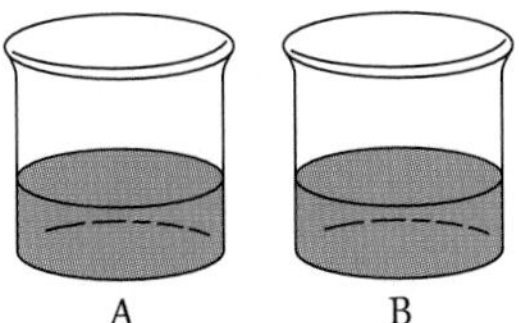

Step 2: Present taller, thinner beaker, and pour contents of B into it.

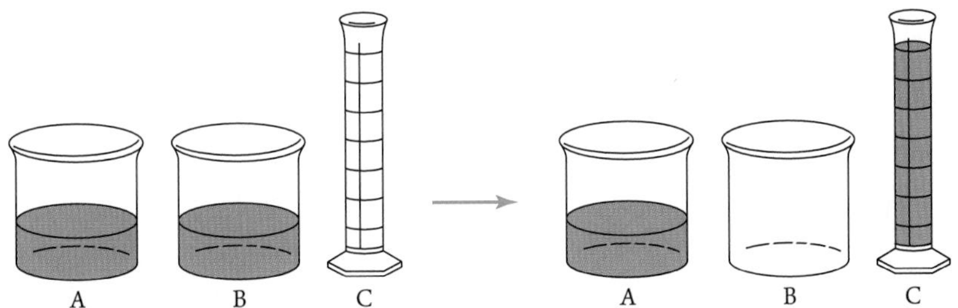

Step 3: Ask: "Which beaker has more liquid, A or C—or do they contain the same amount?'

FIGURE 12.6
The procedure Piaget used to test for the conservation of quantity.

(increasing height) is offset by a change in the other (decreasing circumference). Children who have acquired the concept of conservation of continuous quantity recognize the *logical necessity* that the amount of liquid remain the same despite the change in appearance. When asked the reasons for their judgment, they offer arguments such as the following, showing that they understand the logical relationships involved:

- "They were equal to start with and nothing was added, so they're the same." This mental operation is called **identity;** the child realizes that a change limited to outward appearance does not change the amounts involved.
- "The liquid is higher, but the glass is thinner." This mental operation is called **compensation;** changes in one aspect of a problem are mentally compared with and compensated for by changes in another.
- "If you pour it back, you'll see that it's the same." This mental operation is called *negation* or **reversibility;** the child realizes that one operation can be negated, or reversed, by the effects of another.

Children's developing understanding of conservation of number provides another example of the changes that occur when children acquire concrete operations. By "conservation of number" Piaget meant the ability to recognize the one-to-one correspondence between two sets of objects of equal number, despite a difference in the sizes of the objects or in their spatial positions (Piaget, 1952a).

The basic procedure for testing the ability of children to conserve number is to present them with two rows of objects such as those shown in Figure 12.7*a*. Both the numbers of objects and the lengths of the two lines are equal, and children are asked to affirm that they are. Then one of the rows is either

identity A mental operation in which the child realizes that a change limited to outward appearance does not change the substances involved.

compensation A mental operation in which the child realizes that changes in one aspect of a problem are compared with and compensated for by changes in another.

reversibility A mental operation in which the child realizes that one operation can be negated, or reversed, by the effects of another.

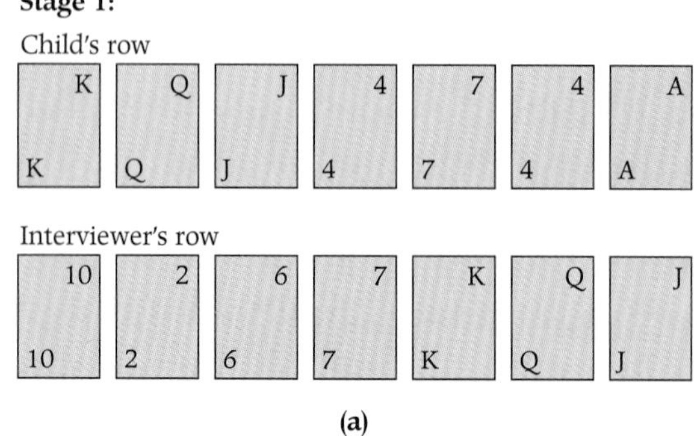

(a)

Stage 2:

Child's row

K Q J 4 7 4 A

Interviewer's row

10 2 6 7 K Q J

(b)

FIGURE 12.7

The procedure used to test for the conservation of number. (a) In stage 1, the child's and the interviewer's seven cards are arrayed at equal intervals. (b) In stage 2, the interviewer spreads out his cards and asks the child if she and the interviewer still have the same number of cards. (From Ginsburg, 1977.)

spread out or compressed (see Figure 12.7*b*), and the children are asked if the numbers of objects in the two rows are still equal. Children below the age of 6 or 7 rarely display conservation of number, saying, for example, that the elongated row has more. In contrast, older children realize that the number must remain the same. Applying concrete operations to the number conservation task, they are able to say to themselves, in effect, "There must be the same number of cards, because if the experimenter moved the cards in his row back to where they were at the beginning, nothing would have changed."

This understanding of logical necessity—that "it *has* to be that way"—is Piaget's key criterion of a stagelike change in thinking.

Is the Acquisition of Conservation Universal?

It was Piaget's (1966) belief that the development of conservation is a universal achievement of human beings, regardless of the cultural circumstances in which they live. The only cultural variation he expected in the acquisition of conservation was that children in some cultures might acquire this form of reasoning earlier than others, because their culture provided them with more extensive relevant experiences.

However, cross-cultural research on the acquisition of conservation has provoked a great deal of controversy regarding its presumed universality. Using Piaget's own conservation tasks, several researchers found not only that children in traditional, nonindustrial societies lag a year or more behind the norms established by Piaget but that in some cases they do not appear to acquire this basic form of reasoning at all, even as adults. Reviewing the evidence available in the early 1970s, Pierre Dasen (1972) wrote, "It can no longer be assumed that adults of all societies reach the concrete operational stage" (p. 31).

This conclusion was immediately challenged because of its wide-reaching implications. For example, Gustav Jahoda (1980), a leading cross-cultural psychologist, rejected outright the possibility that in some cultures people do not eventually achieve the ability to think operationally. As Jahoda points out, it is difficult to see how a society could survive if its members were indifferent to causal relations, incapable of thinking through the implications of their actions, or unable to adopt other people's points of view. He concluded that "no society could function at the preoperational stage, and to suggest that a majority of any people are at that level is nonsense almost by definition" (p. 116).

To resolve this issue, one would have to produce evidence that the findings from the research methods used in these cross-cultural studies somehow misrepresented their subjects' mental capacities, either because the subjects were unfamiliar with the test situation or because the experimenters, working in an unfamiliar culture and language, did not make their intentions clear. (This is the same line of reasoning used to challenge Piaget's views on the thought processes of preschool-age children [see Chapter 9]).

Dasen and his colleagues tackled the problem by training children to solve conservation tasks (Dasen et al., 1979). They reasoned that if the children in traditional cultures did not seem to understand conservation because they were unfamiliar with the procedures, training on similar tasks should be sufficient to overcome their difficulties.

In a series of studies, the researchers demonstrated that by the end of middle childhood, relatively brief training in procedures similar to those used in the standard conservation task was sufficient to change the pattern of performance on the conservation task itself. One such result is shown in Figure 12.8, which compares the performance of rural Australian Aborigine children with the performance of children in the Australian city of Canberra. Without

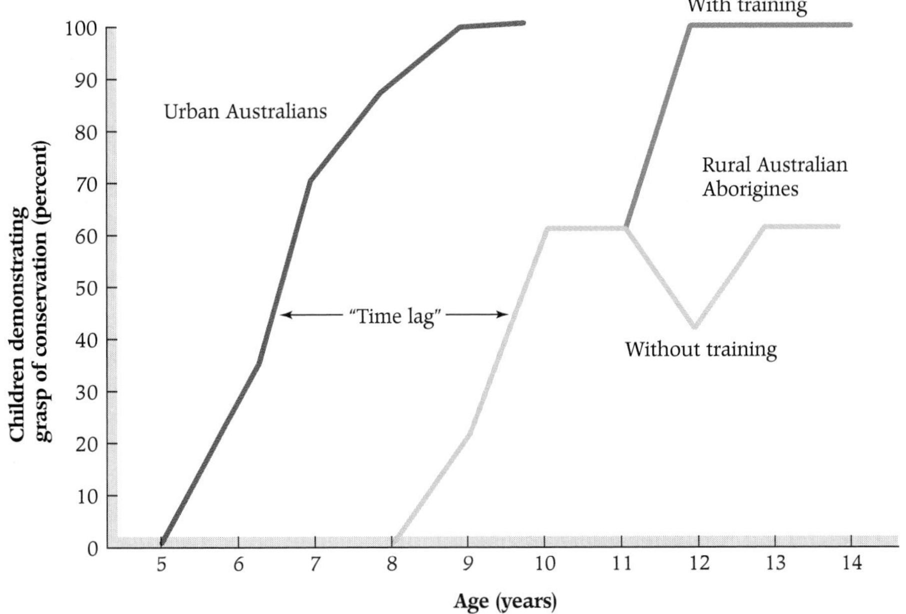

FIGURE 12.8

Curves representing the actual percentages of Australian children who demonstrated a grasp of the concept of conservation. Australian Aborigines lagged behind urban Australian children with European backgrounds. Without training, 50 percent of the Aborigine children as old as 14 years failed to demonstrate an understanding of the concept of conservation. (From Dasen et al., 1979.)

training, half the Aborigine children seemed to fail to acquire the concept of conservation of quantity altogether. But when they were trained, their test results showed that they did understand the basic concept of conservation of quantity. Even with training however, the Aborigine children lagged behind the Canberra children by approximately 3 years, a situation suggesting that their nomadic, hunter-gatherer form of life does not provide the kinds of experiences that accelerate the acquisition of this concept.

A number of developmentalists have suggested that if researchers know the local language and culture well so that subjects will be able to follow the flexible questioning procedures that are the hallmark of Piaget's clinical interviews, their young subjects will demonstrate conservation without any lags. Raphael Nyiti (1982), for example, compared the conservation performances of 10- and 11-year-old children of two cultural groups, both living on Cape Breton, Nova Scotia. Some of the children were of English-speaking European backgrounds, and some were of the Micmac Indian tribe. The Micmac children all spoke Micmac at home, but they had spoken English in school since the first grade. The children of European backgrounds were all interviewed in English by an English speaker of European background. The Micmac children were interviewed once in English and once in Micmac.

Nyiti found that when the children were interviewed on the conservation tasks in their native languages, there was no difference in the performances of the two cultural groups. But when the Micmac children were interviewed in English, only half as many seemed to understand the concept of conservation. Nyiti (1976) obtained similar results in a study of children in his native Tanzania, as did other African researchers in the West African country of Sierra Leone (Kamara & Easley, 1977).

Taken as a whole, these studies, along with others, appear to demonstrate that when Piaget's clinical procedures are applied appropriately, using contents with which people have extensive experience, conservation of liquid quantity (and by extension, concrete operations) is a universal cognitive achievement of middle childhood, just as Piaget assumed it was (Segall et al., 1999). However, the evidence also shows that there are quite dramatic cultural variations in children's familiarity with the contents and procedures used in standard Piagetian tests of conservation and these variations clearly influence children's performances on the tests.

memory span The number of randomly presented items of information that can be repeated immediately after they are presented.

WHAT BRINGS ABOUT DEVELOPMENTAL CHANGES IN REASONING?

Although most theorists acknowledge the general two-sidedness of children's thinking during middle childhood—first emphasized by Piaget—there is considerable disagreement over what brings it about. As we saw in Chapter 4, Piaget believed that all cognitive growth is driven by *assimilation,* the process by which children incorporate new experiences into their existing schemas, and *accommodation,* the process by which they modify existing schemas in light of new experiences.

The idea that children develop cognitively by adapting their present understandings to new experiences seems commonsensical enough, but many theorists feel that it offers little insight into the specifics of cognitive growth. Nearly two decades ago, David Klahr (1982) referred to assimilation and accommodation as "mysterious and shadowy forces . . . the Batman and Robin of developmental processes" (p. 80). "How do they operate?" he asked. "We know no more about them than when they first sprang upon the scene."

Searching for other explanations for the emergence of two-sided thinking in middle childhood, many developmentalists have recently focused on such cognitive phenomena as increased memory capacity, accumulating knowledge, and the development of cognitive strategies, the importance of which has been long stressed by the information-processing perspective.

THE INFLUENCE OF MEMORY ON COGNITION DURING MIDDLE CHILDHOOD

According to many developmentalists, including information-processing theorists and neo-Piagetians, the two-sidedness of thinking is brought about by increased memory abilities that allow children to hold two or more aspects of a problem in mind while they are being processed. For example, a young soccer player racing for the goal can keep in mind the positions of her teammates, the goalie's apparent difficulty with low shots, and the special maneuver her coach taught her in practice. Younger players may have a difficult time simply remembering they are in a soccer game and may run after the ball only when it passes in front of them!

Four factors, taken together, appear to bring about the memory changes characteristic of this period: (1) an increase in the speed of memory processing and memory capacity; (2) an increase in knowledge about the things one is trying to remember; (3) the acquisition of effective strategies for remembering; and (4) the appearance of the ability to think about one's own memory processes (Schneider & Bjorklund, 1998).

FIGURE 12.9

Relationship between memory span and speed of naming. Note that as children grow older in grades kindergarten (K) through 6, their counting span increases accordingly. (From Case et al., 1982.)

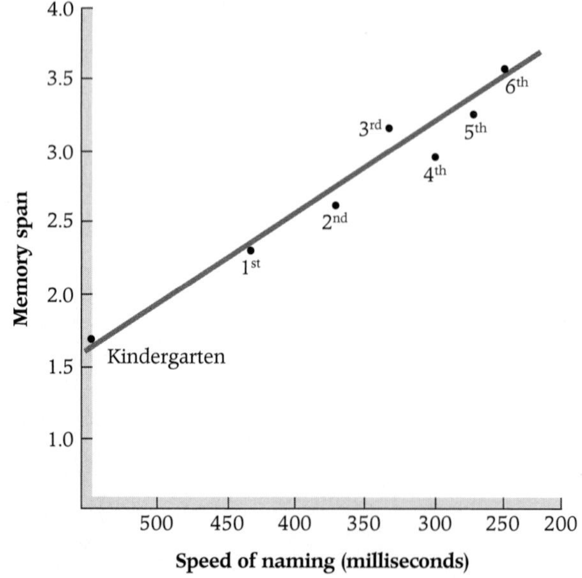

Increases in the Speed and Capacity of Memory Processing

One common method of measuring the changing capacity of working memory is to assess children's **memory span,** the number of randomly presented items of information children can repeat immediately after the items are presented. Most 4- and 5-year-olds can recall four digits presented one after another; most 9- and 10-year-olds can remember about six, most adults can remember about seven (Schneider & Pressley, 1997).

In order to get several numbers presented at random into working memory, children must somehow represent each number to themselves, perhaps by silently repeating "ten, six, eight, two." Young children take longer than older children simply to *repeat* a number such as 10 or 2. Because it takes them longer to say the numbers, memory for the numbers already said is more likely to decay and be lost. Older children name individual numbers quite quickly, reducing the time interval between numbers and thereby increasing the likelihood of retaining the numbers in memory (Figure 12.9) (Case et al., 1982).

Cross-cultural research enriches these conclusions. When Chuansheng Chen and Harold Stevenson (1988) compared the memory spans of U.S. and Chinese children age 4 to 6 years, they found that the Chinese children were able to recall more digits at each of the ages tested. At first, this finding might seem to suggest that the working memory of Chinese children was larger than that of the American children. However, as Chen and Stevenson pointed out, the Chinese words for the digits are shorter than the English words. Thus the task was easier for the Chinese children for the same reason that it was easier for the older North American children: there was a shorter interval between repeated items. This hypothesis was supported by a study in which Stevenson and his colleagues used lists of objects whose names were equal in length in English and Chinese. When these words were presented for remembering, Chinese and American children were found to have equal memory capacities (Stevenson et al., 1985).

Robert Kail and his colleagues have shown that the speed with which children can *retrieve* information already stored in long-term memory also increases from early childhood well into adulthood (Kail, 1991; Kail & Park, 1994). In their studies, 11-year-old American and Korean children retrieved information from long-term memory approximately six times faster than 4- and 5-year-olds. As a consequence of this increase in mental processing speed, older children and adults can be expected to execute more cognitive operations in a given time span than younger children and, therefore, to demonstrate increased intellectual effectiveness.

knowledge base The store of information that children can draw on to deal with a new situation.

strategy A deliberate, controllable cognitive operation performed for the purpose of attaining a particular goal.

Knowledge Base

A second factor that contributes to improved memory during childhood is the greater knowledge that older children are likely to have about any given topic simply because they have accumulated more experience in the world than younger children have. This experience provides older children with a richer **knowledge base,** or store of information, on which to draw in a new situation. As a consequence, when asked to remember new information, they have more prior information to relate it to.

As we saw in Chapter 9 (p. 353), the positive effect that a large knowledge base has on memory development is demonstrated by studies in which younger subjects who have a rich knowledge base in a given area remember more new information related to that area than older subjects whose knowledge base is not as rich. The same is true in middle childhood and throughout life. In one such experiment, Michelene Chi (1978) compared memory for the arrangement of chess pieces among 10-year-old chess buffs with the memory abilities of college-age chess amateurs. The 10-year-olds recalled the chess arrangements that occurred in the course of a game better than the college students, but when the two groups were compared on their ability to recall a random series of numbers, the college students' performances were far superior. A replication of this study by German researchers confirmed the basic results and extended them by showing that when subjects were asked to remember random arrangements of chess pieces, rather than meaningful arrangements that might plausibly occur during a game (thereby removing the importance of knowledge of chess), the advantage of the chess experts was greatly reduced (Schneider et al., 1993).

Skill at cards requires the ability to remember the cards that have been previously dealt and the relative values of different hands, as well as the ability to use strategies to defeat your opponent.

Memory Strategies

A **strategy** is a deliberate, controllable cognitive operation performed for the purpose of attaining a particular goal (Bjorklund & Miller,

1997). All strategies are "two-sided" in the sense that they require children to think simultaneously about a goal and about a way to achieve that goal. When we say that children use memory strategies, we mean that they engage in deliberate actions in order to enhance remembering.

Even children younger than 2 years can be observed to use elementary memory strategies if the tasks involve familiar content and familiar, scripted procedures. For example, Judy De Loache and her colleagues (De Loache et al., 1985) told 1½- to 2-year-old children to remember the location of an attractive stuffed animal that they hid while the children watched. The children were then induced to play with several other attractive toys. After 4 minutes had elapsed, a bell rang and the children were urged to retrieve the stuffed animal. During the time they were playing with the toys, the children often interrupted themselves to look at, point at, peek at, or talk about the hidden stuffed animal. Since they did not engage in such behaviors when the stuffed animal was not hidden, these behaviors were specific to cases in which forgetting was a potential problem. De Loache and her colleagues point out that such behaviors are similar to well-known strategies observed in older children.

A large number of studies have shown that children's spontaneous use of strategies for remembering undergoes a marked increase between early and middle childhood (Schneider & Bjorklund, 1998). Three memory-storage strategies whose development has been intensively studied are rehearsal, organization, and elaboration. **Rehearsal,** which we have touched on previously, is the process of repeating to oneself the material that one is trying to memorize, such as a word list, a song, or a phone number.

It is not an easy task to observe young children rehearsing things that they want to remember, because their repetition is often not visible. In a classic study of the development of rehearsal strategies in children, John Flavell and his colleagues (Keeney et al., 1967) presented 5- and 10-year-olds with seven pictures of objects to remember. The children were asked to wear a "space helmet" with a visor that was pulled down over their eyes during the 15-second interval between the presentation of the pictures and the test for recall. The visor prevented the children from seeing the pictures and allowed the experimenter to watch their lips to see if they repeated to themselves what they had seen. Few of the 5-year-olds were observed to rehearse, but almost all the 10-year-olds did. Within each age group, children who rehearsed the pictures recalled more than children who did not. When those who had not rehearsed were later taught to do so, they did as well on the memory task as those who had rehearsed on their own.

In a more recent study, children who were trying to remember lists of three and five single-digit numbers were videotaped so that the researchers could look for more subtle indicators of rehearsal (McGilly & Siegler, 1989). The researchers found that even kindergarten children are capable of rehearsing the things they want to remember. According to the investigators, this finding suggests that increases that occur in children's short-term memory in middle childhood result from increasingly effective use of strategies and not from the sudden appearance of the ability to use a new strategy.

Marked changes are also found in **memory organization,** a memory strategy in which children mentally group the materials to be remembered in meaningful clusters of closely associated items so that they have to remember only one part of a cluster to gain access to the rest. The use of organizational strategies is often studied by means of a procedure called *free recall.* In a free-recall task, children are shown a large number of objects or read a list of words one at a time and then asked to remember them. This kind of memory is called "free" recall because the children are free to recall the items in any order they choose.

Research has demonstrated that 7- and 8-year-olds are more likely than younger children to group the items they have to remember into easy-to-

rehearsal The process of repeating to oneself the material that one is trying to memorize.

memory organization A memory strategy in which children mentally group the materials to be remembered in meaningful clusters of closely associated items.

remember categories (Schneider & Bjorklund, 1998). The kinds of groupings that children impose on lists of things to be remembered also change with age. Younger children often use sound features, such as rhyme ("cat," "sat"), or situational associations ("cereal," "bowl") to group words they are trying to remember. In middle childhood, children are more likely to link words according to categories such as animals ("cat," "dog," "horse"), foods ("cereal," "milk," "bananas"), or geometric figures ("triangle," "square," "circle"). The consequence of these changes is an enhanced ability to store and retrieve information deliberately and systematically.

Children who do not spontaneously use rehearsal and organizing strategies can be taught to do so (Moely et al., 1995). The effectiveness of this training indicates that there is no unbridgeable gap between the memory performance of 4- to 5-year-olds and that of 7- to 8-year-olds or between children who use strategies spontaneously and those who do not. Over the course of middle childhood, children become increasingly better at using various strategies to help them remember better.

A third kind of strategy, **elaboration,** is a process in which children identify or make up connections between two or more things they have to remember. Elaboration strategies have usually been studied in cases where children are presented with two words and asked to remember the second one when they hear the first. For example, they might be asked to remember the word "street" after hearing the word "tomato." An elaboration strategy for this word pair could be to think of a tomato squashed in the middle of a street.

elaboration A memory strategy in which children identify or make up connections between two or more things they have to remember.

Research with adults shows that elaboration strategies are effective when they are used (Schneider & Bjorklund, 1998). However, it is only during middle childhood that children begin to use elaboration strategies spontaneously, and skill in the use of this kind of strategy continues to increase with age (Miller, 1990).

Cultural Variations in the Use of Memory Strategies Cross-cultural research has revealed striking cultural variations in the use of organizational strategies in free-recall studies, but these results must be interpreted with great caution. For example, Michael Cole and his colleagues studied the development of memory among people living in rural Liberia (Cole & Scribner, 1977; Cole et al., 1971). In one set of studies they presented groups of children of different ages with a set of 20 common objects that were selected to be members of familiar and salient categories, such as food, clothing, and tools. Half the children at each age were attending school, while half were not because there were no schools located in their villages.

The researchers found that children who had never gone to school improved their performance on these tasks very little after the age of 9 or 10. These children remembered approximately 10 items on the first trial, and managed to recall only 2 more items after 15 practice trials on the full set of 20 items. The Liberian children who were attending school, by contrast, learned the materials rapidly, much the way schoolchildren of the same age do in the United States.

Failure to use organizational strategies seemed to be the cause of the poor performance of the children who had not attended school. Schoolchildren in Liberia and the United States used categorical similarities among the items to aid their recall. After the first trial, they clustered their responses, recalling first, say, the items of clothing, then the items of food, and so on. The Liberians who had never attended school did very little clustering, an indication that they were not using the categorical relationships among the items to help them remember.

To track down the source of this difference, the researchers varied aspects of the task. They found that if, instead of presenting a series of objects in random order, they presented the same objects in a meaningful way as part of

Although children from traditional agricultural societies sometimes perform poorly on psychological tests, their cognitive abilities are often manifested in other ways. This Ugandan boy has constructed his toy car out of bits of wire and some wooden wheels.

a story, their nonschooled Liberian subjects recalled them easily, clustering the objects according to the roles they played in the story. When memory for traditional children's stories was tested, cultural differences were also absent (Mandler et al., 1980). Similar results on tests of children's memorization skills have been obtained in research among Mayan people of rural Guatemala (Rogoff & Waddell, 1982).

The implication of these cross-cultural memory studies differs from that of the cross-cultural studies of concrete-operational thinking. The latter studies probed basic mental operations presumed by Piaget and his followers to reflect the logic underlying everyday actions and reasoning in any culture. The ability to remember is also a universal intellectual requirement, but specific strategies for remembering are not universal. Indeed, many of them—the ones most often studied by psychologists—are associated with formal schooling.

As we will see in the next chapter, schooling presents children with specialized information-processing tasks—committing large amounts of information to memory in a short time, learning to manipulate abstract symbols in one's head and on paper, using logic to conduct experiments, and performing many more tasks that have few if any analogies in societies without formal schooling. The free-recall, random-order task that Cole and his colleagues initially used to assess memory among Liberian tribal people has no precise analogy in traditional Liberian cultures, so it is not surprising that subjects who had not attended school failed to show the corresponding way of remembering.

Metamemory

Most 7- and 8-year-olds not only know more about the world in general than preschoolers do but also are likely to know more about memory itself (knowledge referred to as **metamemory**). Even 5-year-olds have *some* understanding of how memory works. In a study that has stimulated a great deal of the subsequent research on memory development, 5-year-olds said they knew that it was easier to remember a short list of words than a long one, to relearn something you once knew than to learn it from scratch, and to remember something that happened yesterday than something that happened last month (Kreutzer et al., 1975).

Nevertheless, most 8-year-olds have a better understanding of the limitations of their own memories than most 5-year-olds do. When shown a set of ten pictures and asked if they could remember them all (something most children at these ages generally cannot do), most of the 5-year-olds—but only a few of the 8-year-olds—claimed that they could. The 5-year-olds also failed to evaluate correctly how much effort they would need to remember the pictures. Given unlimited time to master the set of pictures, the 5-year-olds announced that they were ready right away, even though they succeeded in remembering only a few of the items. The 8-year-olds, by contrast, knew enough to study the materials and to test themselves on their ability to remember (Flavell et al., 1970).

Even when children know that metamemory knowledge can enhance remembering, they often do not use their knowledge, just as they don't always use the rehearsal and organizational strategies they know (Bjorklund et al., 1994). In one memory study, William Fabricius and John Hagen (1984) created a situation in which 6- and 7-year-olds used an organizational strategy on some trials and not on others. When the children used the organizational strategy, they almost always remembered better. The researchers asked the children to tell them what they thought accounted for their better remembering efforts. Some of the children did not notice that the organizing strategy was helpful, even though they had just used it successfully. They attributed their better recall to slowing down and being more careful or to paying more attention to the stimuli. Other children attributed their better recall to the deliberate use of the organizing strategy. When the children were brought back for a second ses-

metamemory The ability to think about one's memory processes.

sion, in which their ability to remember was tested in a slightly different situation, 99 percent of those who had understood the helpfulness of the organizing strategy in the first session used the same strategy the second time around. By contrast, only 32 percent of the children who attributed their better remembering efforts to some other factor used the organizing strategy. These and similar results indicate that children must acquire the ability to use metamemory knowledge in addition to acquiring useful strategies.

COMBINING MEMORY DEVELOPMENT AND LOGICAL STAGES

How do these changes in memory provide a mechanism for changes in logical reasoning? Robbie Case and his colleagues, whose work falls within a neo-Piagetian framework, argue that it is an increase in the capacity of working memory that allows children to think about two or more aspects of a problem at one time (Case, 1998; Okamoto & Case, 1996). These researchers carried out a series of studies designed to probe the ability of 6-, 8-, and 10-year-olds in the domains of number, storytelling, and drawing. The specifics of their procedures naturally differed according to the domain in question, but all the problems they presented to the children required them to mentally manipulate information in working memory in increasingly complex ways.

The researchers' data on the development of children's understanding in the domain of number provides a good example of their overall approach. Case relates the central conceptual structure for the domain of number to the *mental number* line. The problems presented to the children were classified into four categories of difficulty, based on how many number lines the children had to keep in mind and mentally manipulate to come up with the answer:

- *Category 1:* Problems required judgments only about whether specified numbers were more or less than other numbers.
- *Category 2 :* Problems required calculations on a single number line. In typical problems children were asked questions like "What number comes after 7?" or were shown a card with several numbers printed on it (for example, 8, 5, 2, 6) and were asked, "Which number comes first when you are counting?"

The kinds of work that children are assigned afford different kinds of learning opportunities. Young street vendors acquire a variety of arithmetic skills that sometimes surpass those of children of the same age who attend school.

TABLE 12.2 PERCENTAGE OF CORRECT RESPONSES AS A FUNCTION OF AGE AND PROBLEM COMPLEXITY

	6-Year-Olds	8-Year-Olds	10-Year-Olds
Category 1	100	100	100
Category 2	89	97	99
Category 3	28	66	86
Category 4	4	24	49

Source: Okamoto & Case, 1996.

- *Category 3:* Problems required coordinating two number lines to answer the questions. Typical problems were of the following kind: "How many numbers are in between 3 and 9?" To answer this question, the child had to be able to deal with one mental number line to represent the position of the two numbers and a second mental number line to calculate the difference between them.
- *Category 4:* Problems required that children compare the results of two problems like those in category 3 and calculate the difference. A typical problem was of the following kind: "Which difference is bigger, the difference between 6 and 9 or the difference between 8 and 3?"

The study focused on 6-, 8-, and 10-year-olds because prior research had shown that while 4-year-olds can count and can make judgments about whether a given set of objects is "a lot" or "a little," they are unable to integrate these two mental operations into a single system or to answer such questions as "Which is more, 4 or 5?" (Resnick, 1989).

The children were presented with several problems from each category. The scores of each age group of children were averaged together for each category of problems. As shown in Table 12.2, when the problems were simple and required the children only to use one number line to answer such questions as "What number comes after 7?" there was little difference in the performance among the age groups. But the performance of 6-year-olds deteriorated markedly when they had to coordinate two number lines to answer such questions as "How many numbers are in between 2 and 7?" The 8-year-olds had less trouble with such problems, but they ran into serious difficulty when solving category 4 problems that required them to hold in mind two number lines as well as the results of their calculations on each and then compare the two. The 10-year-olds had some difficulty when they were asked to solve category 4 problems, but they were successful half the time.

This pattern of results illustrates the researchers' claims of a close relationship between problem-solving ability and the capacity of working memory, a claim that is a hallmark of the neo-Piagetian approach. Each time the demands on working memory were increased, fewer children at a given age level could manage the task. The same pattern of results has been obtained using a variety of problems for which the number line is the central conceptual structure. Moreover, this kind of analysis has also been applied successfully to other domains, providing additional evidence of a close link between stages of development within a domain and the growth of memory capacity.

COGNITIVE DEVELOPMENT AS THE EVOLUTION OF STRATEGIES

As we have seen, both Piagetian and neo-Piagetian theorists see cognitive development as occurring in stagelike changes. Piagetians see development in

TABLE 12.3 SIX TYPES OF CHANGE THAT CONTRIBUTE TO THE DEVELOPMENT OF STRATEGIC THINKING

1. The acquisition of new strategies.
2. Changes in the frequencies with which existing strategies are used.
3. Changes in the speed of executing strategies.
4. Changes in the accuracy with which strategies are carried out.
5. Changes in the degree to which strategies are used automatically.
6. Changes in the range of situations in which each strategy can be applied.

Source: From Lemaire & Siegler, 1995.

terms of broad, pervasive changes; neo-Piagetians see development in terms of smaller, domain-specific stages. Both views expect to find consistency of thinking within the stages they delineate.

A very different view of the nature of cognitive changes is taken by those influenced by the information-processing perspective. Robert Siegler, for one, has criticized the stage view on the basis of studies of children's discovery and use of strategies to solve intellectual problems (Siegler, 1995, 1996). He has found that at any given age and within any given testing situation, children will use different strategies to solve the same problem. Over time, their use of more effective strategies to solve a particular problem will increase, while their use of less effective ones will become rare or disappear. (See Table 12.3 for a summary of changes that Siegler believes contribute to the development of strategic thinking.) Such evidence has led Siegler to characterize cognitive development in general as a *gradual* shift in the kinds of reasoning strategies that children use. He uses the metaphor of "overlapping waves" to give the overall flavor of his approach. Each wave is made up of a strategy that appears gradually, reaches a peak, and then decreases as it is replaced by another, more sophisticated, strategy.

To illustrate how problem solving develops through strategy development, growth, and selection, Siegler and his colleague, Kevin Crowley, traced strategy development in the game of tic-tac-toe (Crowley & Siegler, 1993). Working with 6-, 7-, and 9-year-olds, they began by describing the strategies that were appropriate to the game (see Figure 12.10). The simplest strategy was to focus entirely on winning by getting three X's or O's in a single row.

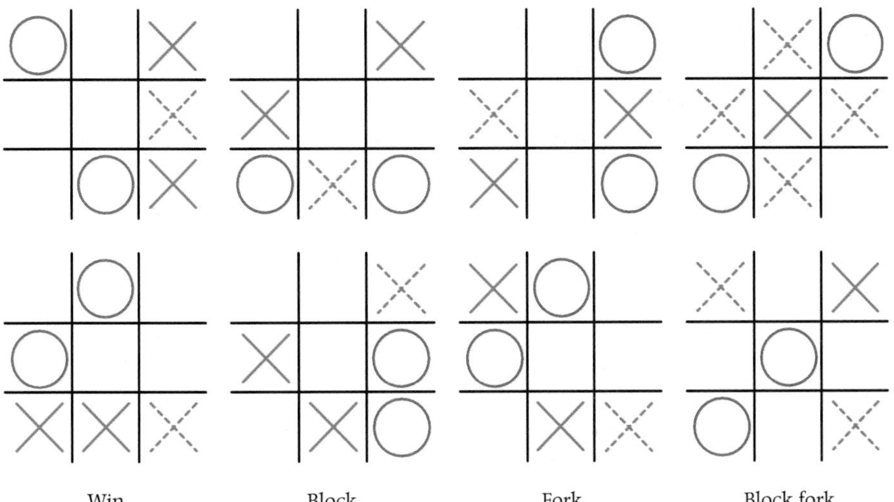

FIGURE 12.10 *Eight game configurations presented to children to see what strategies they would use. The solid X's and O's are already in place. The dashed X's represent the possible correct moves the child could make. (From Crowley & Siegler, 1993.)*

TABLE 12.4 STRATEGY USE BY 6-, 7-, AND 9-YEAR-OLDS

	Type of Game			
	Win	**Block**	**Fork**	**Block Fork**
Kindergartners	95	45	0	0
1st graders	100	80	10	0
3rd graders	100	100	65	0

Numbers give the percentage of subjects of each age who made at least one correct move and provided a consistent explanation for each tic-tac-toe rule
Source: From Crowley & Siegler, 1993.

The next most complex strategy was to block an opponent from winning in order to gain a tie. A still more complicated strategy was to "fork" by choosing a move that made it possible to win along either of *two* rows.

Crowley and Siegler found that children entertained several strategies at once. What changed with age was the mixture of strategies they used to win. Most of the 6-year-olds used a simple win strategy and tried to get three X's or O's in a row. Almost half of the 6-year-old children could also use a second strategy, blocking their opponent when needed. The 7-year-olds all could use the win strategy, almost all used blocking strategies, and a few set up forks. The 9-year-olds used all strategies under the appropriate circumstances, but not the most sophisticated "block-fork" strategy (see Table 12.4).

Siegler (1976, 1996) has applied his strategy-selection approach to a number of Piaget's standard tasks. In one such study, he traced the development of strategies children use to solve balance-beam problems, one of the most influential tasks employed by Piaget to demonstrate developmental changes in problem solving (see Figure 12.11). Complete understanding of the balance-beam problem requires an understanding of the concept of torque, which is the product of weight times distance along the beam. Understanding of torque requires the ability to think simultaneously about two variables (weight and distance) and their interrelationship. It was Piaget's view that a child's developing grasp of this problem would mirror the child's level of cognitive development: over time, the child would attend first to one variable, then to two variables, and then would develop the ability to combine the two variables according to a single rule. Piaget found that the dominant response by children younger than 7 or 8 was to focus only on weight. During middle childhood, he observed, they increasingly took into account both weight and distance. Only adolescents consistently took both weight and distance into account, but few of them achieved full understanding of torque.

To carry out his analysis, Siegler formulated a set of rules, or cognitive strategies, that children might use for predicting the outcome of different arrangements of weights in a manner similar to the way in which he identified the strategies in playing tic-tac-toe:

- *Rule 1:* If the weight on one side is more, that side will go down. If the weights on the two sides are equal, they will balance.
- *Rule 2:* If the weight on one side is more, that side will go down. If the weights are equal, the one farthest from the fulcrum goes down.
- *Rule 3:* Always consider both weight and distance. If both weight and distance are equal, the beam will balance. If the dimensions are in conflict (for example, more weight on one side and greater distance on the other), take a guess, since there is no rule for this case.
- *Rule 4:* Always consider both weight and distance in terms of the concept of torque: downward force equals the distance from the fulcrum times the weight on that side.

A task analysis of the balance-beam problem enabled Siegler to identify various logical arrangements of weights and distances that yielded different specific patterns of errors and correct responses. As Table 12.5 indicates, when both weight and distance are equal, all rules provide correct answers. When weights are unequal but distances are equal, all rules are again correct.

The first problem that distinguishes between children of different ages comes when weights are equal and distances are not. Children who follow rule 1 should make wrong predictions, but those who follow rule 2 and consider distance will be correct. The remaining diagnostic problems are trickier to figure out. In the "conflict-weight" problem, the children who follow rules 1 and 2 get the right answer because neither of those rules is disconfirmed even though it is wrong. The children who follow rule 3 and try to take both weight and distance into account realize the problem is complicated, but they do not know the proper way to combine dimensions, so they must muddle through or guess. The "conflict-distance" and "conflict-balance" problems are set up so that if children are following rule 1 or 2, they will make the wrong response. Only rule 4 solves this problem reliably.

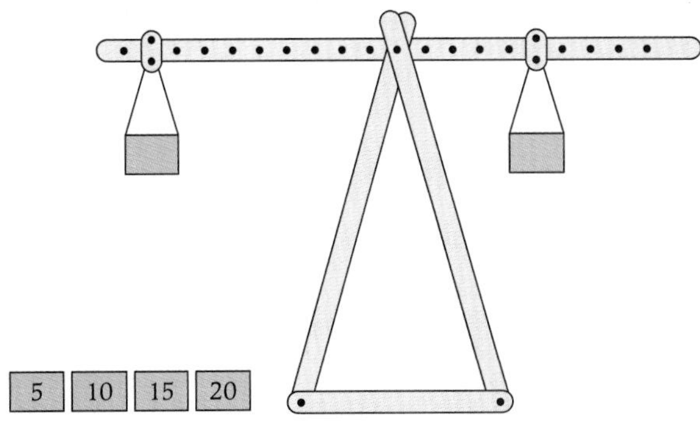

FIGURE 12.11
A balance beam of the kind used by Piaget and Siegler to evaluate the development of logical reasoning.

When Siegler tested children on the balance beam using the kinds of problems illustrated in Table 12.5, he found that he could assign almost all the children's choice patterns to one of the rule categories. Again, children at all ages used more than one rule, and the mixture of rules shifted in a wave-like fashion as they grew older. Most 5-year-olds used rule 1, most 9-year-olds used rule 2 or 3, and the 13- to 17-year-olds used predominantly rule 3. Very few of even the oldest participants used rule 4, an issue to which we will return in Chapter 16.

TABLE 12.5 CORRECT ANSWERS PREDICTED FOR CHILDREN USING DIFFERENT RULES

	Rule			
Problem Type	**1**	**2**	**3**	**4**
Balance	100	100	100	100
Weight	100	100	100	100
Distance	0 (Will say "Sides balance")	100	100	100
Conflict-weight	100	100	33 (Lucky guess)	100
Conflict-distance	0 (Will say "Right side down")	0 (Will say "Right side down")	33 (Lucky guess)	100
Conflict-balance	0 (Will say "Right side down")	0 (Will say "Right side down")	33 (Lucky guess)	100

Source: From Siegler, 1976.

Siegler's analysis of how children at different ages cope with the problems in Table 12.5 demonstrates how the careful task analysis used by information-processing theorists can provide insights into the process of cognitive development. In a Piagetian analysis, all the problems are given equal weight in diagnosing children's underlying thought processes. Siegler's analysis, by contrast, leads to the unusual prediction that for some combinations of distance and weight, younger children, who follow rules 1 and 2 only, should actually outperform children more than twice their age. When he examined the data for the relatively complicated conflict-weight problems, for example, he found that 5-year-olds, who are likely to follow rule 1, are correct 89 percent of the time, because rule 1 guides them to choose the side with the most weight. By contrast, 17-year-olds, most of whom were diagnosed as using rule 3, made the correct response only 51 percent of the time, an indication that they were doing a lot of guessing. This upside-down developmental pattern lends authority to Siegler's analysis.

Siegler offers a radically different view from that of the stage theorists regarding how developmental change occurs, but in one important respect he agrees with those who favor the idea of stagelike changes. The advanced strategies in every case involve the same two-sidedness that other developmentalists have claimed to be characteristic of middle childhood.

ADDITIONAL COGNITIVE BRIDGING PROCESSES

While being able to remember more and to think more logically are important to the activities of middle childhood, they are not sufficient by themselves to explain the increased scope and reliability of children's thinking. To carry out even simple everyday activities—getting along with other children on the playground, doing their schoolwork, running errands for their parents, finding their way to a friend's house and back, or playing soccer or "Mastermind"—children also have to be able to pay attention to the task at hand without being distracted, make plans for handling the task, and know something about their own thinking processes. At the same time, their increasing experience is being coded in language, providing them with a large store of organized, retrievable knowledge with which to meet the demands of daily life. As we will now see, each of these processes provides additional bridges between the islands of competence seen in early childhood.

Attention

From the earliest days of life, children attend to unusual events in their environment that "capture" their interest. In earlier chapters, we saw that infants attend more to some objects or events than others and then gradually stop attending (or habituate) to them as they become used to them. After infancy, there is a steady increase in both the quality of attention and the length of time children pay attention to objects that interest them. Holly Ruff and Katherine Lawson (1990) reported that compared with 3-year-olds, 5-year-olds paid less attention to simply exploring objects and more to trying to construct something with the objects and to problem solving. They believe that this increase in sustained attention reflects both a deeper involvement with the objects and an ability to inhibit attention to extraneous events. A more recent experimental study by Allan Mirsky and his colleagues (Rebok et al., 1997) has shown that the ability to sustain attention grows steadily throughout middle childhood.

The ability to concentrate on what they are doing is not the only aspect of children's attention that develops during early and middle childhood. Children also learn to control their attention to obtain information more efficiently. In a classic study, Elaine Vurpillot (1968) recorded the eye movements of children age 3 to 10 while they examined pairs of line drawings of houses such as those shown in Figure 12.12. On some trials, children were shown identical houses; on others, the houses differed in one or more relatively subtle ways. The children were asked to say whether or not the houses were identical.

Vurpillot found that all the children responded correctly when the houses were identical but that the younger children were more likely to make mistakes when the houses differed, especially if the houses differed in only one particular. Her recordings of eye movements pinpointed the difficulty. Rather than systematically paying attention to each of the houses to see how they differed from one another, the younger children scanned the houses in a haphazard order. By contrast, the older children paid attention to each of the houses in the picture, scanning, and sometimes rescanning, row by row or column by column until they had checked almost all of them. It seems from this that older children have a greater ability to select and execute an effective attentional strategy.

Analogous findings have been reported by Patricia Miller and her colleagues (summarized in Miller, 1990). In this study, 7-, 10-, and 13-year-old children were presented with memory tasks that required them to attend selectively to a cue that told them where to look for information they had to remember. The children watched as pictures of animals and household implements were hidden behind small wooden doors. Half the children had to remember where the picture of each kind of animal was hidden, while the other half had to remember where the pictures of the household items were hidden. As a clue to where the pictures they had to remember were located, the experimenter attached a picture of a cage or of a house to the top of each door. The 7-year-olds did not attend selectively to this information. They tended to simply open all the doors one row at a time. By 10 years of age, however, the children did attend to the relevant information, and their ability to recall the position of the to-be-remembered pictures improved markedly.

FIGURE 12.12
Stimuli used by Vurpillot to assess the development of visual search strategies. It is not until middle childhood that children pay attention to each of the four houses in a systematic way to discover the subtle differences between them. (From Vurpillot, 1968.)

Planning

Being able to develop a plan for achieving goals is a key new aspect of children's thinking during middle childhood. Preschoolers can be heard saying things to one another like, "When you come to my house, we'll play house and have a party," but they have no plans to achieve their goal aside from informing their mothers that they want to play with the other child. During middle childhood, children begin to plan in the sense that they form cognitive representations of the actions needed to achieve a specific goal. To make a plan, they have to keep in mind what is presently happening, what they want to happen in the future, and what they need to do in order to get from the present to the future. They must also have enough self-control to keep their attention on achieving the goal.

Research has demonstrated that increased use of planning in a variety of situations is one of the changes that make children more reliable without direct adult control. Take, for example, the kind of planning that is required in choosing a route to a destination. William Gardner and Barbara Rogoff (1990) asked groups of 4- to 6-year-olds and 7- to 10-year-olds to solve mazes such as the one shown in Figure 12.13. A glance at this maze quickly reveals that a child who simply begins to trace a path from the nearest opening, without first scanning the maze to see what barriers lie ahead, is certain to fail. To see how children's ability to plan a solution to the maze developed, Gardner and Rogoff gave different instructions to half the children in each age group. One subgroup was told that they should plan ahead from the start because it was most

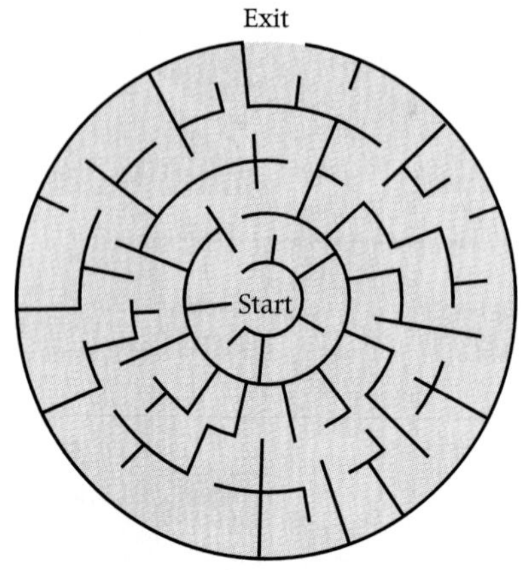

FIGURE 12.13
A maze of the kind used by Gardner and Rogoff (1990) to assess children's ability to plan ahead. Trace the route from start to finish to get a feel for how planning is needed to avoid encountering a dead end.

important to avoid making wrong turns. The other children were told the same thing but were also told that they had to go through the maze as quickly as possible.

When both speed and accuracy mattered, the children in both age groups planned out part of their route ahead of time and then planned only when they came to uncertain choice points. When accuracy in navigating the maze was the only factor that counted, many of the older children realized that a better strategy was to plan their entire set of moves before they began. In contrast, 4- to 6-year-olds did not change their planning when speed didn't matter, either because they did not understand that they would make fewer errors if they planned ahead more systematically or because they could not keep this possibility in mind when they tackled a difficult maze.

A cross-cultural study by Shari Ellis and Bonnie Schneiders (reported in Ellis & Siegler, 1997) enlarges on these findings and shows how differences in cultural values can shape the likelihood that children will plan ahead. Using a schematic drawing of a maze representing a rural scene, Ellis and Schneiders studied the way that Navajo and Euro-American children planned their routes to and from different parts of the maze (see Figure 12.14). They were interested in contrasting these two groups because the two cultures place different values on doing things speedily. The Navajo emphasize doing things thoughtfully rather than quickly (John, 1972). By contrast, speed of mental performance is often treated as an index of intelligence among Americans of European background (Sternberg, 1990). This cultural difference in values was expressed in the children's behavior as they planned their routes through the maze. The Navajo children spent almost ten times as long planning their movements as the Euro-American children did—and as a result, they made significantly fewer errors.

Planning is also important in reasoning tasks. Games that require children to solve logical problems, like checkers or "Mastermind," become popular in middle childhood. To play these games skillfully, children have to analyze both the goals and the means of attaining them. A good example of such a game is the Tower of Hanoi, the goal of which is to move a set of size-graded objects from one location to another. There are two rules: (1) Only one object can be moved at a time; and (2) a larger can must go on top of a smaller one. In an experimental form of this game (Figure 12.15), the child is presented with three cans, the smallest on the bottom, the largest on the top,

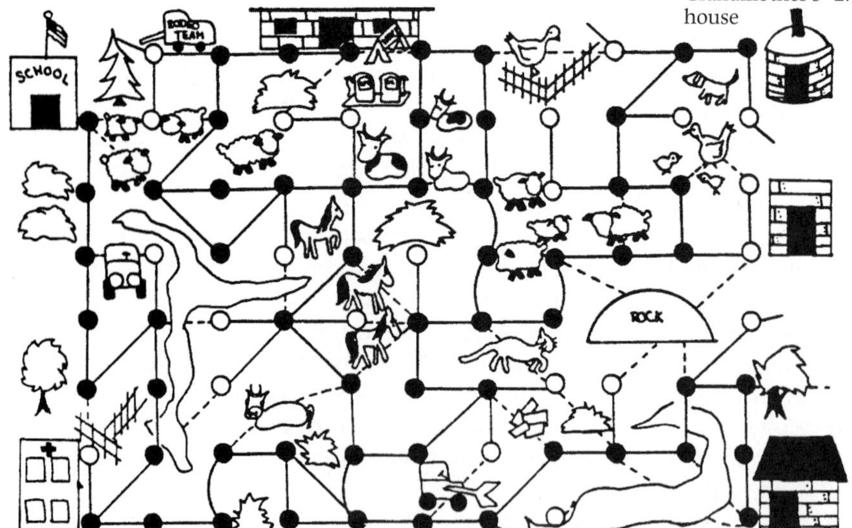

FIGURE 12.14
Schematic drawing of the maze used in Ellis and Schneiders, 1989. Children were asked to find the shortest obstacle-free path from home to Grandmother's house, where they would pick up some money and then go to the store. The dotted lines and open circles on this diagram indicate incorrect routes; solid lines and solid dots are acceptable routes. (From Ellis & Gauvain, 1992. Copyright 1992 by Lawrence Erlbaum Associates.)

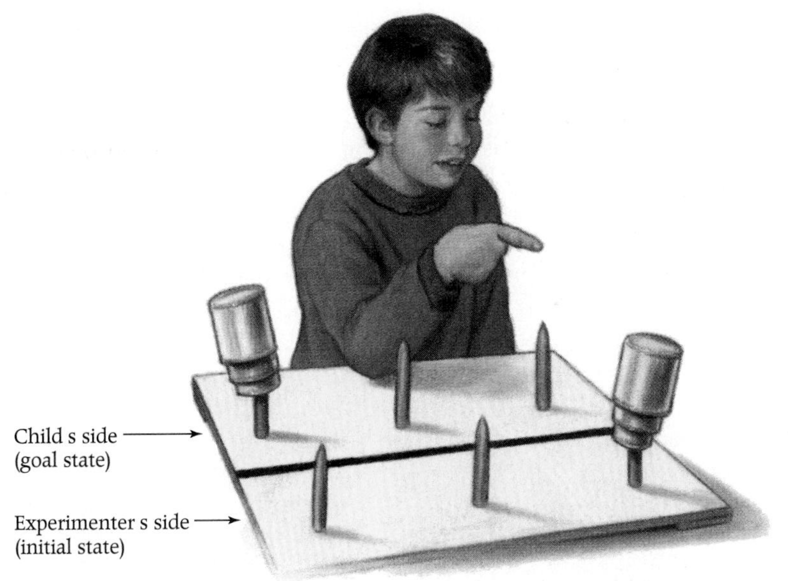

FIGURE 12.15
To solve the Tower of Hanoi problem, the child must move the cans on the pegs before him and recreate the stack on the pegs opposite, on the side of the experimenter. The task requires careful planning, because it is illegal to place a small can on top of a large can as the cans are moved from peg to peg. (After Klahr, 1989.)

and is asked to move the cans to the peg opposite the experimenter's model. The problem depicted in Figure 12.15 requires a logical minimum of seven moves.

A variety of research (summarized in Siegler, 1996) shows that as children grow older, they become better at playing the game (Figure 12.16). This trend is not surprising, since, according to the evidence, older children are increasingly able to keep in mind both their current circumstances and the circumstances they want to create. What makes the pattern of data especially interesting is its similarity to Gardner and Rogoff's findings with respect to negotiating a maze. Three-year-olds could not keep the rules in mind at all. Six-year-olds began to form subgoals that would take them part of the way to a solution, but they could not think the problem all the way through, and they still found it difficult to assemble their subgoals into an overall plan. Even 9- and 10-year-olds fail to plan all the way through problems of this kind if the problems require too many moves (Spitz et al., 1985).

metacognition The ability to think about one's own thought processes.

Metacognition

The ability to think about one's own thoughts, **metacognition,** is widely believed to accompany and promote cognitive development. The term "metacognition" applies to all forms of human cognitive activity (*metamemory* is one kind of metacognitive knowledge). Metacognition allows one to assess how difficult a problem is likely to be and to choose strategies to solve it in a flexible way.

The general pattern of the development of metamemory abilities appears to apply to the development of a wide variety of cognitive processes (Estes, 1998; Flavell et al., 1995). By the age of 4 or 5, children begin to be able to explain what they are doing when they solve such mental puzzles as determining whether a pair of two-dimensional figures are different figures or the same figure in different orientations (Estes, 1998). But in situations where they are not actively engaged in a challenging problem-solving task, they are less likely to realize that they have been thinking about something, even if it is an unusual event.

This difference is illustrated in a series of studies by John Flavell and his colleagues (Flavell et al., 1995). The basic strategy

FIGURE 12.16
The sophistication of the planning strategies that children use in solving the Tower of Hanoi problem shows rapid growth at the start of middle childhood. (From Welsh, 1991.)

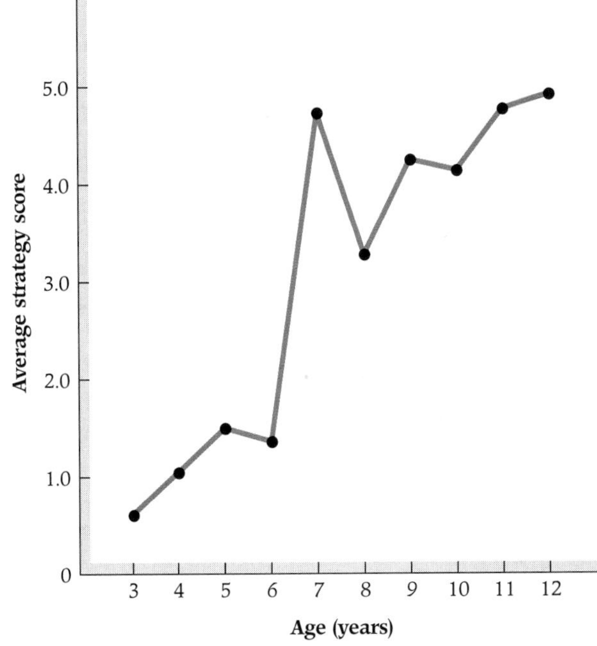

Middle childhood is a time when a combination of physical changes and extended practice enables children to acquire complex, culturally valued skills.

used in these studies was to create a situation that would be expected to cause children to think about something in particular and then to question them to see if they did. For example, in one study, a group of 5-year-olds and a group of 7- to 8-year-olds were shown a magic trick, such as a scarf that changes colors when pulled through the experimenter's hand, or a puzzling object, such as a large pear inside a bottle with a narrow neck. After the children were shown such things, they followed the experimenter to another location nearby. When they arrived at the new location, the experimenter asked them what they had been thinking about on the way. About two out of three 5-year-olds said they weren't thinking about anything at all, and most of the remainder said that they were thinking about something that had nothing to do with the odd event they had just witnessed. About two out of three 7- to 8-year-olds said they *were* thinking about the odd experiences they had just witnessed, thus indicating to the researchers that they had greater awareness of their own thought processes. Nonetheless, the performance of the 7- to 8-year-olds was far from perfect, leaving considerable room for improvement.

The growth of metacognitive skills provides children with important cognitive resources. As metacognitive skills increase, children are better able to keep track of how successfully they are accomplishing their goals, and this allows them to modify their strategies so that they are more successful. Such metacognitive skills are especially important to children when they encounter complex learning tasks in school, as we will see in the next chapter.

The Development of Language and Classification

Essential to the cognitive differences that emerge between early and middle childhood is the continued, rapid development of various language capacities. Changes in the sphere of language take many forms (Garton & Pratt, 1998).

First, the sheer size of children's vocabularies, and hence the range of topics they can understand, increases markedly. Although precise estimates vary, 6- to 7-year-olds understand perhaps 10,000 words. Two years later, the number has doubled, and by the time they are 10 to 11 years old, they possess vocabularies of approximately 40,000 words (Anglin, 1993). Children's expanding vocabulary knowledge, combined with their growing abilities to understand and produce complex sentences, increases the complexity of the events they can think about and communicate about effectively.

As we have seen in earlier chapters, even before they are 7 or 8 years old, children have a large fund of organized conceptual knowledge to draw upon in their thinking about the world, especially in core domains, such as "living things," that apply to the natural world. As their knowledge of the categories to which objects belong is incorporated into their active vocabularies, children can make reasonable inferences about a wide range of events, even ones they have never before seen. Suppose, for example, that a child is invited over to her friend's house to see her new komondor. If the child has never heard the word "komondor" before, she won't know what to expect. But if she asks, "What's a komondor?" and learns that it is a dog breed, she will immediately know that the thing she is going to see is likely to run around, wag its tail, bark, soil the rug until it is trained, and so on.

The dramatic growth in the quantity of real-world knowledge that is organized into categories is accompanied by increasingly complex means of organizing knowledge. One significant change in the organization of knowledge is the ability to understand the hierarchical structure of categories and the logical relation of inclusion that holds between a superordinate class and its subclasses (for example, the subclass of cats is included in the superordinate class of mammals). As we saw in Chapter 9 (p. 339), when 4- to 6-year-old children are shown a set of brown wooden beads and white wooden beads and asked, "Are there more brown beads or more beads?" they are likely to say there are more brown beads than beads. According to Piaget, they answer this way because they cannot attend to the subclass (brown beads) and the superordinate class (beads) at the same time. Instead, they compare one subclass (brown beads) with another subclass (white beads). When concrete operations become routine, subordinate–superordinate relations become more stable.

Another important change in the organization of categorized knowledge is the ability to categorize objects according to multiple criteria. This kind of logical classification can be seen when children begin to collect

Systematic cataloging of a card collection requires the ability to classify according to multiple criteria.

stamps or baseball cards. Stamp collections can be organized according to multiple criteria. Stamps come from different countries. They are issued in different denominations and in different years. There are stamps depicting insects, animals, sports heroes, rock stars, and space exploration. Children who organize their stamps according to type of animal and country of origin (so that, for example, within their collection of stamps from France, all the birds are together, all the rabbits are together, and so on) are creating a multiple classification for their collections. Similarly, the child who groups baseball cards according to league, team, and position creates a multiple classification. The result is a marked increase in the number of relations among objects and events that children can think about and increased flexibility in the particular relations they choose to use under particular circumstances.

Increases in children's linguistically coded knowledge are accompanied by a general increase in a variety of other language-related abilities that have a direct bearing on the increased power and reliability of thought during middle childhood (Warren & McCloskey, 1997). As we saw in earlier chapters (Chapter 8, p. 328, and Chapter 9, p. 340), while young children can sometimes modify what they say to take into account the knowledge or perspective of their conversational partner, their modifications are not always successful and they often fail to recognize when they have strayed from the topic. Older children are better at making sure that they and their conversational partners understand each other and have a greater ability to maintain coherence in a conversation over longer periods of time. The older children's ability to maintain more complex, organized conversations appears to depend upon a mix of factors that include better listening skills, improved memory abilities, and the use of special linguistic markers to signal transitions in topics or to tie what is being said at the moment to something said earlier, such as "Getting back to . . ." or "As I was saying . . ." Older children also provide ongoing feedback to their conversational partners by nodding or saying "Uh hum" to let them know that they are tracking the conversation (Dorval, 1990).

COGNITIVE CHANGES IN MIDDLE CHILDHOOD RECONSIDERED

Taken one at a time, the changes in children's cognitive abilities between early and middle childhood point to specific features of children's thought processes that are becoming more systematic and can be applied across a broader variety of settings. When we consider these changes as part of an ensemble, rather than as isolated achievements, we begin to get a better idea of the reasons why adults can begin to treat children in a different manner during middle childhood.

However, we have not yet taken a direct look at the contexts where experience of the environment exerts its effects. Consequently, we need to withhold judgment on the competing views about the causes of the new behaviors seen in middle childhood. To address the question properly, we first need to reach beyond the relatively narrow range of tasks that have been featured in psychologists' studies of cognitive development and investigate the changes that children display in a variety of social contexts, especially in classrooms and peer groups, where children in middle childhood begin to spend so much of their time. Many developmentalists believe that experiences in both of these contexts are crucial to the cognitive changes associated with middle childhood. Once we have a more well-rounded picture of children's experiences, we can return to examine the central issue of the distinctiveness of middle childhood and the forms of thought that are said to characterize it.

SUMMARY

COPING WITH INCREASED FREEDOM AND RESPONSIBILITY

- The onset of middle childhood is recognized in cultures around the world. When children reach the age of about 6, adults begin to hold them responsible for their own actions and sometimes assign them tasks that take them away from adult supervision. This reorientation in adult behavior implies an increase in children's physical capacities, in their ability to follow instructions, and in their ability to keep track of what they are doing.

BIOLOGICAL DEVELOPMENTS

- Size and strength increase significantly in the years from 6 to 12, but more slowly than during early childhood.
- There is a significant genetic contribution to growth; nutrition and general health factors are two important environmental contributors.
- Agility, balance, and coordination improve markedly during this period. Boys, on average, tend to excel at motor abilities that emphasize power and force, while girls most often excel in fine motor coordination and agility.
- Several significant developments in brain structure and function occur between the ages of 5 and 7:
    1. Myelination continues to increase, particularly in the frontal cortex.
    2. The numbers of synapses and the output of neurotransmitters increase.
    3. Alpha activity comes to dominate theta activity.
    4. The synchronization of electrical activity in different parts of the brain increases significantly, producing marked coordination between the frontal lobes and other areas.

A NEW QUALITY OF MIND?

- There is general agreement that in middle childhood, children's thinking becomes more "two-sided." Disagreements center on what brings about this change.
- Piaget believed that around the age of 7 children become capable of concrete mental operations; they can now combine, separate, reorder, and transform objects mentally. One important manifestation of concrete operations is conservation, the understanding that the appearance of objects may change while their quantity or some other essential feature remains the same.
- Cross-cultural differences on Piagetian conservation problems raise the possibility that people in some cultures fail to achieve concrete operations. However, cultural differences in conservation disappear when the subjects are provided with special training or when the studies are conducted by experimenters who are fluent in the language of the people studied and familiar with their culture.

WHAT BRINGS ABOUT DEVELOPMENTAL CHANGES IN REASONING?

- Dissatisfaction with Piaget's explanation for how cognitive development occurs has led to proposals for alternative mechanisms of change.
- According to many developmentalists, increases in memory account for the ability of children to hold two or more aspects of a problem in mind while they are thinking about it.
- Changes in memory ability are associated with
  1. The capacity to hold several items of information in mind at one time.
  2. Increased knowledge relevant to the information to be remembered.
  3. The use of memory strategies, such as organization and rehearsal.
  4. The ability to think about one's own memory processes.
- Neo-Piagetian scholars have proposed that stagelike changes in the logic of thought are domain-specific. Within-domain change depends upon changes in memory capacity.
- Analyses of children's behavior in a variety of problem-solving tasks reveals the presence of more than one strategy at any given time. From this perspective, development consists of the discovery of new strategies and changes in the frequency, spontaneity, and accuracy with which strategies are used.
- A number of additional processes that help increase cognitive performance during middle childhood have been proposed:
  1. The ability to control attention and not be distracted.
  2. The ability to plan systematically before acting.
  3. The ability to think about and control one's own thought processes.
  4. Increased linguistic abilities and associated classification skills.
- When changes in specific cognitive processes are considered as an ensemble, they help explain why adults can begin to give children greater responsibilities as they move into middle childhood.

KEY TERMS

compensation, p. 479
concrete operations, p. 477
conservation, p. 477
EEG coherence, p. 475
elaboration, p. 485
identity, p. 479
knowledge base, p. 483
memory organization, p. 484
memory span, p. 482
metacognition, p. 495
metamemory, p. 486
rehearsal, p. 484
reversibility, p. 479
strategy, p. 483

THOUGHT QUESTIONS

1. In what significant ways have you observed middle childhood in your community to resemble and to differ from that of Raymond Birch?
2. What is the major evidence to support the view that in middle childhood thought processes are generally more "two-sided" than was true in early childhood?

3. Give specific examples of how various memory strategies might be used to learn the information presented in this chapter.
4. How are biological and cultural factors involved in the behavioral and cognitive changes observed in middle childhood?
5. What are some of your everyday nonacademic tasks that require planning. What role does metacognition play in your planning behaviors?

CHAPTER 13

Schooling and Development in Middle Childhood

I spent that first day picking holes in paper, then went home in a smoldering temper.
"What's the matter, Love? Didn't he like it at school, then?"
"They never gave me the present."
"Present? What present?"
"They said they'd give me a present."
"Well, now, I'm sure they didn't."
"They did! They said: You're Laurie Lee, aren't you? Well you just sit there for the present. I sat there all day but I never got it. I ain't going back there again."

—Laurie Lee, *Cider with Rosie*

In many parts of the modern world, children are required by law to go to school from the ages of about 6 to 16. For nine or more months of the year, 5 or 6 days a week, they spend 5 to 7 hours listening to teachers, answering questions, reading books, writing essays, solving arithmetic problems in workbooks, taking tests, and generally "being educated." Before they take their places as adult workers, most young Americans will have spent more than 15,000 hours in classrooms, and in some countries, the amount of time children spend in school is even greater (Stevenson & Stigler, 1992). It is no surprise, then, that the school context plays a central role in defining children's characteristics in middle childhood and in shaping their later lives.

To determine the specific influences that schooling has on children's development, we need to address a series of questions:

- What is the nature of school as a context for children's development, and under what historical conditions do schools arise?
- How does learning in school differ from learning in other contexts?
- How does schooling influence cognitive development?
- What special abilities does schooling require, and what factors account for success in school?

Answers to these questions have far-reaching significance in modern societies. Children who fail to thrive in school or who drop out may be confined as adults to less interesting, less secure, and lower-paying jobs than children who meet society's expectations by completing high school and higher levels of education (U.S. Bureau of the Census, 1995) (see Figure 13.1). Despite the emphasis society places on education, many millions of young people in the United States do not thrive in school. In the opinion of policy makers, resulting low levels of literacy and mathematical skills jeopardize the country's ability to compete effectively in the international arena (U.S. Department of Education, 1983). These concerns have made the study of learning and development in the schools one of the most active areas of research in developmental psychology.

THE CONTEXTS IN WHICH SKILLS ARE TAUGHT

In Chapter 10 we examined socialization in the family, concentrating on the ways in which young children are raised to acquire the basic knowledge, skills, and beliefs that are essential in their society. Socialization is a universal human process that has always been a part of human experience everywhere. In addition to the socialization that occurs within the family, as we discussed in Chapter 12, sometime around the sixth or seventh year of life, all societies

education A form of socialization in which adults engage in deliberate teaching of the young to ensure that they acquire specialized knowledge and skills.

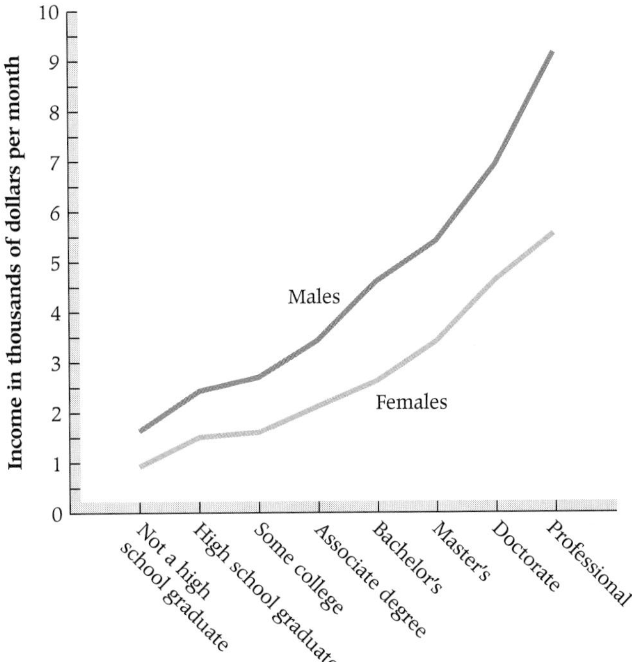

FIGURE 13.1
The relationship between years of schooling and income in the United States. Note that at all levels of schooling, women were paid less than men in 1998. (From U.S. Bureau of the Census, 1999, p. 28.)

begin to socialize children into new tasks that are designed to provide them with the skills necessary for adult life. What is not universal is the specific *content* of the new tasks, or the ways these new activities are socially organized.

One way to arrange for children to acquire adult skills and knowledge is through education. **Education** is a form of socialization in which adults engage in deliberate teaching of the young to ensure their acquisition of specialized knowledge and skills. It is not known if education existed among the hunter-gatherer peoples who roamed the earth hundreds of thousands of years ago, but *deliberate teaching* is not a conspicuous part of socialization in contemporary hunter-gatherer societies (Rogoff, 2000). Among the !Kung of Africa's Kalahari Desert, for example, basic training in the skills expected of adults is embedded in everyday activity, and including children in adult activities is the basic means by which adults ensure that children acquire culturally valued skills and knowledge.

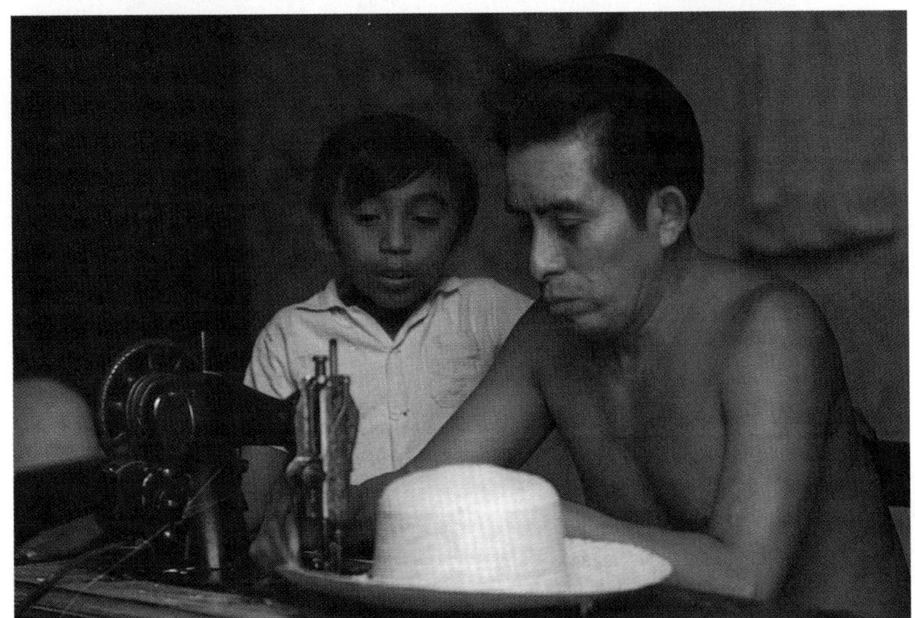

Apprenticeship arrangements in which children learn by observing adults and working alongside them are still an important form of education despite the spread of formal schools.

apprenticeship A form of activity combining instruction and productive labor that is intermediate between the implicit socialization of family and community life and the explicit instruction of formal education.

> There is . . . very little explicit teaching. . . . What the child knows, he learns from direct interaction with the adult community, whether it is learning to tell the age of the spoor left by a poisoned kudu buck, to straighten the shaft of an arrow, to build a fire, or to dig a spring hare out of its burrow. . . . It is all implicit. (Bruner, 1966:59)

When societies achieve a certain degree of complexity and specialization in the roles people play, the tools they use, and the ways they secure food and housing, preparation for some occupations is likely to take the form of **apprenticeship,** a form of activity intermediate between the implicit socialization of family and community life and the explicit instruction of formal education. A young apprentice learns a craft or a skill by spending an extended period of time working for an adult master (Coy, 1989; Lave & Wenger, 1991). The settings in which apprentices learn are not organized primarily for the purpose of teaching. Rather, instruction and productive labor are combined; from the beginning, apprentices contribute to the work process.

Researchers have found that novice apprentices receive relatively little explicit instruction in their craft (Rogoff, 2000). Instead, they are given ample opportunity to observe skilled workers and to practice specific tasks. In many societies, the apprentice's relationship with the master is part of a larger web of family relationships. Often the apprentice lives with the master and does farm or household chores to help pay for his upkeep. In this way the tasks of education and community building are woven together (Goody, 1989).

The earliest forms of formal schooling have been traced back to around 4000 B.C. in the Middle East, when changes in technology made it possible for one sector of a population to grow enough food to support a large number of people besides themselves. This shift made possible a substantial division of labor and the development of city-states. It also created a need for systems of writing and arithmetic (Damerow, 1998; Schmandt-Besserat, 1996). The places where young people were brought together to learn to read and write were the earliest schools (see Figure 13.2).

As it has since developed, schooling differs from informal instruction in the family and from apprenticeship training in four main ways (Lave & Wenger, 1991; Singleton, 1998).

FIGURE 13.2
The earliest writings, which date back to around 4000 B.C., were in the form of clay tablets etched with cuneiform symbols. This type of writing originated from pictograms, basic outline drawings of the objects being referred to. Over time and use, the pictograms became simplified and rendered as wedge-shaped (cuneiform) symbols that could convey sounds and abstract concepts, as well as objects. The tablet shown here, from Tello in ancient southern Mesopotamia, is a tallying of sheep and goats.

1. *Motivation.* Students must work for years to perfect their skills before they can put their knowledge to use in adult work. In the meantime, they are asked to engage in tasks they generally find boring.
2. *Social relations.* Unlike masters of apprentices, schoolteachers are usually assigned a carefully restricted role in their pupils' upbringing that separates education from kinship obligations and economic contributions.
3. *Social organization.* Apprentices are most likely to learn in a work setting among people of diverse ages and skill levels, so they have more than one person to turn to for assistance. At school, children have traditionally found themselves in a large room in the company of other children of about the same age and only one adult. As a rule, they are expected to work individually rather than cooperatively in most classrooms in the Western world.
4. *Medium of instruction.* Apprenticeship instruction is usually conducted orally in the context of production. Speech is also important to formal schooling, but it is often speech of a special kind that requires children to acquire skills and knowledge through the manipulation of written symbols.

Taken together, these differences create **schooling** as a special cultural context, one that can have profound implications for children's development.

schooling A form of education that is characterized by special forms of motivation, social relations, social organization, and communication using written language.

LITERACY AND SCHOOLING IN MODERN TIMES

It was not until the nineteenth century, in response to the Industrial Revolution and the movement of people from their farms into large urban areas, that societies began to institute mandatory schooling and strive for widespread literacy. When mandatory school attendance was in its infancy, there were two kinds of education. *"Mass education,"* was aimed at the great majority of working-class children. It enabled them to recite from a religious text such as the Bible or the Koran, to write for simple purposes, and to calculate small sums. This instruction was obviously not intended to give children a general education as we understand that term today. It stressed "mastery of

Mastery of written symbol systems is the focus of most early education.

"Now you're probably all asking yourselves, 'Why must I learn to read and write?'"

Drawing by Bernard Schoenbaum; © 1994. The New Yorker Magazine, Inc.

the basics" because no one expected the working class to use literacy or numeracy for complex purposes. Teachers in the mass-education system were typically confronted by many students and based their instruction largely on drill and practice combined with group recitation (Gallego & Cole, 2000).

By contrast, children of the political and economic elite and a growing number of children among the rapidly rising professional classes were provided a *"liberal education,"* in which they were taught individually by a tutor or in small groups. These children were expected to go beyond "the basics" to the mastery of more complex subjects, including history, the arts, and the sciences. President Woodrow Wilson articulated the different purposes of the two forms of education in 1910 when he wrote: "We want one class of persons to have a liberal education and we want another class of persons, a very much larger class, to forgo the privilege of a liberal education and fit themselves to perform specific, difficult manual tasks" (quoted in Lucas, 1972:42).

A unique feature of education in most modern nations is that everyone is expected to have the "liberal education" that was once restricted to the upper classes. As a recent report from the National Research Council put it, "To be employable in the modern economy, high school graduates need to be more than merely literate. They must be able to read challenging material, to perform sophisticated calculations, and to solve problems independently" (Snow et al., 1998:20). In short, contemporary life requires *all* children to attain a level of education equal to, or surpassing, the levels once reserved for small elites.

No contemporary society has attained this ideal; many children fail to finish the prescribed number of years of schooling, and many fail to master even the basic skills upon which further learning often depends. School failure is more than a personal problem for children whose development is restricted by poor academic performance. It is also a political and economic problem because of its implications for society as a whole. The first step in remedying this problem is to understand the processes through which children acquire academic skills.

ACQUIRING ACADEMIC SKILLS

From the earliest schools of the ancient Middle East to neighborhood schools throughout the modern world, instruction in school has focused on two basic symbol systems, written language and mathematics, the basic "tools of the intellect" required for all further education. However, given the fact that many children fail to achieve the levels of literacy and numeracy that society holds out as its standard, there has been ongoing controversy about how to design instruction more effectively.

One school of thought begins with the assumption that instruction should proceed from the simple to the complex: start with basic skills, and after these are mastered, move on to teaching how they can be used to solve a variety of more complicated tasks that require higher-order skills. The other school of thought argues that an exclusive focus on the acquisition of basic skills causes children to lose sight of the larger goal—how to use reading, writing, and arithmetic to accomplish interesting and important tasks. The consequence for many children, according to this view, is a loss of motivation and a failure to thrive in school. This fundamental difference of opinion about the appropriate organization of school-based instruction can be clearly seen in the different strategies proposed for teaching reading and numeracy.

Learning to Read

There is broad agreement among psychologists and educators that reading is not a unitary skill; it is a complex system of coordinated skills and knowledge (Snow et al., 1998). A good deal is known about how skilled readers translate marks on a page into meaningful messages. But despite intensive research efforts throughout this century, and especially over the past two decades, the process of learning to read is still not well understood (Bransford et al., 1999).

The specific elements that must be coordinated in order to read depend on the way the orthography of the written language (its graphic symbols) is related to the spoken language. Most countries use an alphabetic system, in which each letter or grapheme corresponds to a significant sound variant (phoneme) in the spoken language. Others use systems that provide a graphic symbol for each syllable (a syllabic system), or even for each idea (an ideographic system). Here we will concentrate on the alphabet (named after the first two characters in the Greek system of writing, alpha and beta) (Olson, 1994).

Prereading The first step that children must take in learning to read is to realize that there is a correspondence between the marks on the printed page and the spoken language. Once they understand that each word is represented by a cluster of graphic signs, they still have to figure out the meaning of the written text. At first, most children believe that there is one symbol for each word. Then they begin to focus on syllables, minimal clusters of spoken language. Eventually they realize that the letters are supposed to correspond to each of a word's phonemes (Tolchinsky & Teberosky, 1998).

In addition to understanding the basic idea that the letters of the alphabet correspond to the sounds that make up words, children must also learn to "see letters." That is, they must recognize which sounds correspond to which letters or combinations of letters. The process of establishing letter-sound correspondences is referred to as **decoding.** Children must also learn to *comprehend* what they read—to use their knowledge of letter-sound correspondences and their knowledge of the spoken language to derive meaning from the text as a whole.

Decoding In order to learn the letter-sound correspondences required to read, children need to be skilled at analyzing sounds (Thompson & Nicholson, 1999). That is, they must learn to "hear phonemes" (for example, to recognize that "balloon" begins with a *b*), a process referred to as **phonemic awareness.** The ability to hear phonemes does not appear to occur without deliberate instruction: nonliterate adults in various parts of the world do not seem to be aware of them (Scholes, 1998).

decoding The process of establishing letter-sound correspondences when reading.

phonemic awareness The ability to "hear phonemes" (for example, to recognize that "balloon" begins with a *b*).

Learning which sounds go with which letters is one of the essential tasks facing beginning readers.

Peter Bryant and his colleagues have conducted a wealth of research demonstrating that children in different countries who find it difficult to break words into their constituent syllables and phonemes in a purely oral task have difficulty linking sounds and letters (Bryant, 1993; Bryant & Nunes, 1998; Ho & Bryant, 1997). This research has spawned special educational programs that provide children with enriched experiences in oral language analysis before they are taught to read or when they experience difficulty in reading. The lessons include practice in rhyming, breaking words down into syllables, and special language games such as pig Latin, in which the first phoneme of each word is moved to the end of the word and then followed by an "ay" (as in "igpay atinlay").

The results of such special instruction can be dramatic (for reviews, see Adams et al., 1998, and Snow et al., 1998). For example, Benita Blachman (1987; 1997) implemented such a program in two inner-city schools during the first and second grades (and in the third grade for children who were still experiencing reading difficulty). Then the children were tested in the fourth grade. Before Blachman's program was introduced, the fourth-grade reading performance in the schools was 7 months behind the national norm. The children in the experimental program, by contrast, scored 7 months above the national norm, and the gains were even greater a year later. Such results not only support the theoretical link between language analysis and reading acquisition but also show that the theory can be usefully applied in practice.

Even after they have acquired the ability to segment the spoken language into phonemes, children who are learning to read and write in English face an additional difficulty: there is no one-to-one relationship between letters of the alphabet and the phonemes that make up English words. Instead, the 26 letters of the English alphabet represent 52 basic phonemes. So, for example, a child acquiring literacy in English must grasp the fact that *t* is pronounced differently in the words "tea" and "both," and such seemingly different letters as *g* and *f* can be used to produce a single sound, as in "muff" and "rough." Similar lessons must be mastered for the entire alphabet.*

* A famous example of the alphabet's complex relation to spoken English is attributed to the British writer George Bernard Shaw (1963). Shaw suggested that the word "fish should be written 'ghoti'; *gh* as in 'cough,' *o* as in 'women,' *ti* as in 'nation.'"

Another difficulty is that the phonemes in a word cannot be correctly sounded out in isolation, as when *c* in "cat" is separated from the *a,* and the *a* from the *t.* Faced with this problem, teachers may resort to a strategy called *blending.* In the case of "cat," they first attempt to pronounce the phoneme that corresponds to each letter ("cuh," "ah," "tuh"). Note that even if children have learned the names of the three letters, "cee," "ay," and "tee," this demonstration may not help much because neither "cuh-ah-tuh" nor "cee-ay-tee" sounds much like "cat." No matter how quickly the children pronounce these letter names in sequence, the result will not blend the sounds to transform *c-a-t* into "cat." This circumstance makes it difficult to teach children who do not spontaneously "get the idea."

Once children catch on to reading, it can become a source of pleasure. This boy's comic book promises him not only the adventures of Tarzan but knowledge of the world of zoology as well.

Bottom-Up Versus Top-Down Processing Thus far we have described the process of learning to read as if children come to read words by first decoding the letters that compose the words "from the bottom up." Proceeding in this way, we could conceive of learning to read as a process in which the child decodes individual letters of a word to get access to its meaning, then puts words together into phrases, then into sentences, then into paragraphs, and so on.

Many teachers adhere to some version of this bottom-up approach. In early grades they emphasize "word-attack skills" and use a variety of workbook assignments to foster the ability to decode automatically (see Figure 13.3). The texts used in this approach are especially designed to give intensive practice in phonemic analysis. While they may be quite successful in this respect, they often do not make for very interesting reading. Aesop's tale of the tortoise and the hare, for example, has been presented in word-attack form like this.

> Rabbit said, "I can run. I can run fast. You can't run fast."
> Turtle said, "Look, Rabbit. See the park. You and I will run. We'll run to the park."
> Rabbit said, "I want to stop. I'll stop here. I can run, but Turtle can't. I can get to the park fast."
> Turtle said, "I can't run fast. But I will not stop. Rabbit can't see me. I'll get to the park." (Quoted in Green, 1984:176)

Although reading instruction is frequently carried out in this way, a good deal of research in recent years has demonstrated that such bottom-up decoding processes represent only half the story of learning to read (Hulme & Joshi, 1998). When adults read for meaning, the information supplied by words and phrases must simultaneously be integrated with the relevant knowledge they already have. Interpretation based on prior knowledge is referred to as "top-down" processing because it begins with general knowledge that becomes increasingly focused as the reader combines it with the bottom-up information obtained from letters and words.

To take the other half of the learning-to-read story into account, a number of alternatives to the bottom-up approach have been proposed. These top-down, or comprehension-first, alternatives are based on the idea that reading is a special case of comprehending the world through symbols, an ability that children acquire when they learn language in the first place. Advocates of a comprehension-first approach argue that reading for comprehension should not be put off until children are fluent decoders. Since children arrive at school eager to "read the world," the main requirement of a good reading curriculum is many rich opportunities to experience written language as a useful tool for exploring and problem solving. Emphasis on correct and automatic decoding is replaced by a belief that children should be encouraged to figure out the overall meaning of what they are reading before they zero in on the details. At first their text interpretation may not be strictly correct according to conventional standards, but that is not a matter for concern. What

FIGURE 13.3
A great deal of reading instruction in the elementary grades is carried out in workbook exercises, such as this one for building decoding skills. Find all the letters with the same last sound.

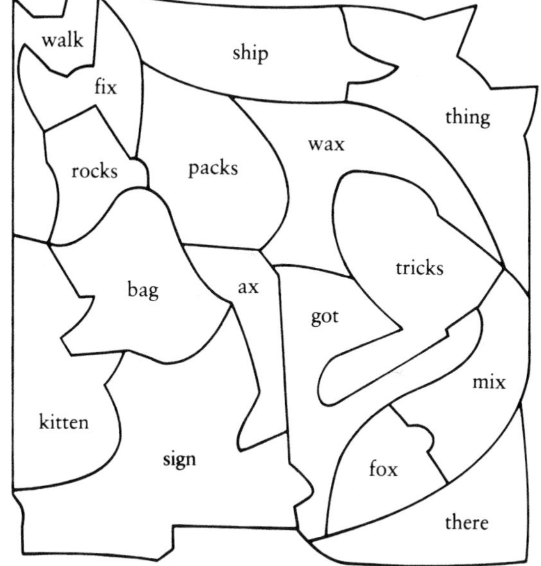

matters is that the children perceive reading as a good way to achieve important goals; gradual mastery of conventional forms will follow.

Kenneth and Yetta Goodman refer to such comprehension-based alternatives as a *whole-language curriculum,* because reading is not taught in isolated lessons. Instead, literacy is made part of the ongoing intellectual life of the classroom; when children begin to experience reading and writing as useful, these theorists argue, they will naturally incorporate it in their repertoire of cognitive skills (K. Goodman, 1996).

The major issue in organizing the process of learning to read is how to balance top-down and bottom-up processes successfully. We will return to discuss research on effective instructional approaches to reading after we consider the other basic skill at the core of schooling, namely, mathematics. As we shall see, the issue of coordinating top-down and bottom-up features arises in math as well as reading, and similar educational strategies are often used in both domains to orchestrate optimal conditions for learning.

Learning Mathematics

Learning mathematics requires children to acquire a distinctive set of concepts and to master a special notation system for dealing with quantity and form.

Kinds of Mathematically Relevant Knowledge Rochel Gelman and her colleagues (Gelman et al., 1986) identify three kinds of knowledge that must be acquired and coordinated for the development of higher-order mathematical skills:

1. **Conceptual knowledge,** the ability to understand the principles that underpin the problem
2. **Procedural knowledge,** the ability to carry out a sequence of actions to solve a problem
3. **Utilization knowledge,** the ability to know when to apply particular procedures

One example of the development of children's conceptual knowledge is provided by Jeffrey Bisanz and Jo-Anne Lefevre's (1990) study of children's understanding of inversion. Inversion is the arithmetic principle that adding and subtracting the same number leaves the original quantity unchanged. Bisanz and Lefevre presented problems of the form $a + b - b$ (for example, 10 + 8 − 8) to subjects ranging in age from 6 years to adulthood. They found that calculating became progressively speedier between 6 and 9 years of age, but that some of the children did not seem to grasp inversion. Instead of creating a shortcut based on the inversion principle, they would dutifully add the second number to the first and then subtract the third number from the sum. The larger the second and third numbers, the longer it took them to get an answer (it required more time to figure out the answer to 4 + 9 − 9, for example, than to solve 4 + 5 − 5). In contrast, most 11-year-olds and virtually all adults responded very rapidly, no matter how large the second and third numbers were, an indication that they had mastered the inversion principle and were using it to cancel out the second and third numbers.

Investigators have also documented the development of children's procedural knowledge in the course of mathematics instruction (Donlan, 1998). Robert Siegler and his colleagues, for example, have applied their theory of "wavelike" strategy development (p. 489) to strategies that are essential to the mastery of procedures for addition, subtraction, and other mathematical operations (Siegler, 1996; Siegler & Stern, 1998). To add a pair of numbers, such as 4 and 3, first- and second-graders may count on their fingers starting with "one" (1-2-3-4 · · · 5-6-7). Eventually they may hit on the strategy of holding up fingers corresponding to the first of the pair and counting up (4 · · · 5-6-

conceptual knowledge The ability to understand the principles that underpin a problem.

procedural knowledge The ability to carry out a sequence of actions to solve a problem.

utilization knowledge The ability to know when to apply particular problem-solving procedures.

7). If asked to add 2 + 9, first-graders may start with 2 and then use their fingers to add 9 more; a year or so later children are more likely to convert 2 + 9 into 9 + 2, a strategy that both simplifies the task and shows their understanding of the principle that order is not important in addition. And, of course, if they think they know the sum "by heart," children will directly recall the answer (or what they believe to be the answer). As children grow older and more knowledgable, direct recall comes to dominate addition of small numbers, and a variety of paper-and-pencil procedures replace fingers as strategic tools under most circumstances.

Counting on fingers is a universal strategy for children just learning arithmetic.

The importance of utilization knowledge—knowing when to use mathematical knowledge according to the context of the problems encountered—was made clear by Terezinha Nunes and her colleagues (1993) who studied mathematical problem solving among Brazilian schoolchildren working as vendors in the streets and marketplaces in the city of Recife. Nunes and her colleagues first posed arithmetic problems to the children "on the job," as part of the process of buying the goods the children were selling. A typical exchange with a 12-year-old child went like this:

> *Interviewer:* How much is one coconut?
> *Child:* 35.
> *Interviewer:* I'd like ten. How much is that?
> *Child: (Pause)* Three will be 105; with three more, that will be 210. *(Pause)* I need four more. That is . . . *(pause)* . . . I think it is 350. (Nunes et al., 1993:18–19)

Under these conditions, the children were correct about 98 percent of the time. The interviewers then gave the children a paper and pencil and asked them to solve identical problems. Again the children were correct 98 percent of the time.

Later, in a follow-up interview, the researchers tested the children on two different sets of math problems, one presented strictly as mathematical operations ("How much is 10 times 35?") and the other presented as real-world word problems. In this interview, the children were correct on the word problems 74 percent of the time but could solve only 37 percent of the problems that required strictly mathematical computation without any real-world connections.

Analysis revealed that in the second, formal interviews, the children failed to use the successful computational strategies they had applied in their selling activity. In the marketplace, for example, one 9-year-old had calculated the price of 12 lemons at 5 cruzeiros each by counting "10, 20, 30, 40, 50, 60" while separating out two lemons at a time. But when she was asked to solve the problem 12 × 5 in the formal interview, she "brought down" first the 2, then the 5, and then the 1 and came up with an answer of 152. She failed to employ a strategy she knew to be effective and produced an answer that, in other circumstances, she would have recognized as ridiculous.

Learning Mathematical Notation Systems Learning to read and write the numbers in mathematical notation systems is one of the basic mathematical skills that is taught in middle childhood. One of the first tasks children face when they encounter mathematics at school is to learn to write the first ten digits. Since it is only a cultural convention that the symbol 9 should stand for the spoken word "nine," the first stage of this process requires memorization.

Once children learn the first ten digits, they must learn the conventions for writing larger quantities and the concept of place value that underpins the decimal notation system. The required correspondences are not intuitively obvious. Some first-graders, for example, have written 23 as 203 (Ginsburg, 1977). This representation, although erroneous, follows the conventions of our

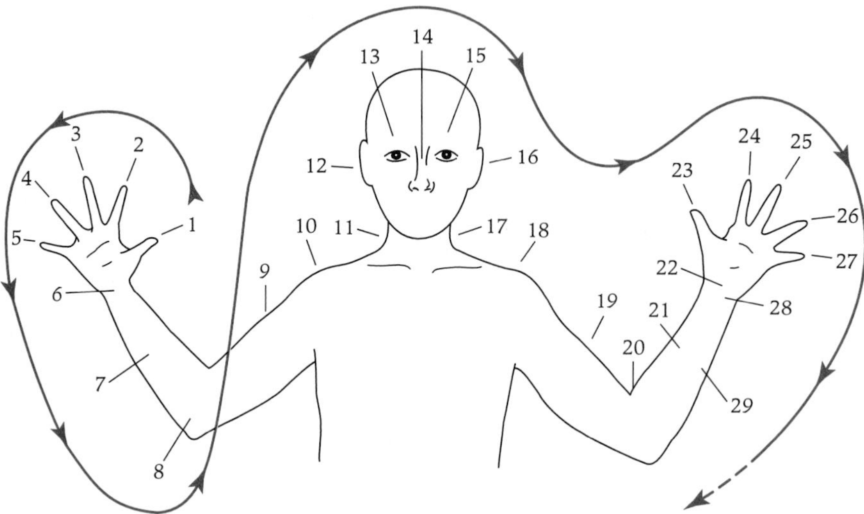

FIGURE 13.4
The Oksapmin of New Guinea do their arithmetic by using a basic set of 29 numbers corresponding to a conventionalized sequence of body parts. (From Saxe, 1981.)

way of speaking (20-3) and our system for representing spoken language in print ("twenty-three"). Unfortunately, from the child's point of view, conventions for representing place value in arithmetic do not follow the conventions of the spoken language. While numbers such as 203 ("two hundred and three") are, so to speak, pronounced from left to right, they are actually constructed right to left from the decimal point, which is ordinarily written only when some fraction of a whole number is to be indicated. So, for example, "Two hundred and three and forty-five-hundredths" is written 203.45. (See Figure 13.4 for a much different type of notation system.)

It takes most children several years to master these complexities, a fact that influences their ability to carry out such basic operations as addition and subtraction on paper. Common mistakes are to add numbers in the order in which they are said—from left to right—and to line up numbers from the left. Misunderstandings of this kind produce such errors as writing 123 + 1 as

$$\begin{array}{l} \ \ 123 \\ \underline{+1} \\ \ \ 223 \end{array}$$

Children who produce such answers are applying previously acquired basic skills inappropriately. Their focus on bottom-up processing produces absurd answers contrary to their own common sense, but they often fail to notice the mistake because they are not attending to the overall meaning of the problem.

Organizing Instruction Recommendations for effective teaching of mathematics cluster at two polar extremes, analogous to the dichotomy between the bottom-up (code-first) and the top-down (meaning-first) approaches to reading instruction. At one end are those who believe that instruction is best carried out through intensive drill and practice on basic building blocks of the overall system. In their view, children need to learn the correct procedures for adding, subtracting, multiplying, and dividing before they can begin to solve the kinds of problems in which they must, for example, calculate where two trains traveling toward each other at different speeds will meet (Stone & Clements, 1998). At the other end are those who believe that learning should begin with problems that draw upon children's real-world experience and that include exposure to mathematical principles necessary for children's continued conceptual growth in the domain of mathematics (Cobb et al., 1997; Davydov, 1999). Again, as in the case of learning to read (p. 511), the agreed-upon solution is to ensure that bottom-up, basic processes and top-down, higher-order processes are properly integrated, but achieving the right balance is a difficult challenge (Sfard, 1999).

THE SOCIAL ORGANIZATION OF CLASSROOM INSTRUCTION

When we turn our focus from the basic processes of reading and writing to inquire about the contexts in which those basic skills are taught, we immediately come up against a constraint faced by all educators. The average public school classroom in more prosperous countries is populated by 25 to 40 children and one adult. This ratio is often much higher in poorer countries. The result is very different from earlier forms of enculturation and apprenticeship in which a few children of various ages and levels of competence participated in a practically important activity that often included several adults.

The Standard Classroom Format

Excavations of classrooms in the ancient world, as well as floor plans of American classrooms during the late twentieth century, bear a striking resemblance to the typical classroom found in schools throughout the world. Far and away the most common arrangement is for the teacher to sit at a desk or stand at a blackboard facing the children who sit in parallel rows, "facing front" (Gallego & Cole, 2000). These physical circumstances, combined with the assumption that the teacher is an authority figure who is there to teach and talk, while the children are there to listen and learn, routinely give rise to **instructional discourse,** a distinctive way of talking and thinking that is typical in school but rarely encountered in everyday interactions in the community or home. The central goals of instructional discourse are to give children information stipulated by the curriculum and feedback on their efforts to learn it, while providing teachers with information about their students' progress (Cazden, 1988; Wells, 1996).

By far the most common form of instructional discourse encountered in classrooms follows what is commonly referred to as a "recitation script" (Mehan, 1998). A distinctive feature of instructional discourse that follows the recitation script is the **initiation-reply-feedback sequence,** demonstrated in Table 13.1. In this pattern, the teacher initiates an exchange, usually by asking a question; a student replies; and then the teacher provides feedback, in this case, an evaluation. The initiation-reply-feedback sequence uses the "known-answer question"—a form of question asking that is rarely encountered in everyday conversation among adults. When the teacher asks Beth, "What does this word say?" the teacher already knows the answer and is actually seeking information about Beth's ability to read, so the question is really a way to evaluate Beth's progress. Learning to respond easily to known-answer questions, in addition to learning the academic content of the curriculum, is an important early lesson of schooling (Mehan, 1997).

The initiation-reply-feedback sequence can be quite flexible. When Ramona hesitates (Table 13.1), the teacher immediately calls on Kim, who provides the answer. This arrangement allows Ramona to learn from Kim's answer and the teacher's response to it at the same time that it allows the teacher to assess Ramona's need for more instruction. On other occasions, the teacher might use the feedback part of the exchange as a means to open up new aspects of the topic at hand or to involve another child in the discussion (Nassaji & Wells, 2000).

Another special facet of instructional discourse is the emphasis placed on the linguistic form of students' replies, shown in the lesson on the use of prepositions in Table 13.2. Note that the teacher gradually builds an understanding of the linguistic form that she considers appropriate by using the

instructional discourse A distinctive way of talking and thinking that is typical in school but rarely encountered in everyday interactions in the community or home.

initiation-reply-feedback sequence An instructional discourse pattern in which the teacher initiates an exchange, usually by asking a question; a student replies; and then the teacher provides feedback.

TABLE 13.1 INITIATION-REPLY-EVALUATION SEQUENCE

Initiation	Reply	Evaluation
T [Teacher]: What does this word say? Beth.	**Beth:** One.	**T:** Very good.
T: What does this word say? Jenny.	**Jenny:** One.	**T:** Okay.
T: Now look up here. What does this word say? Ramona.	**Ramona:** Umm.	
T: Kim.	**Kim:** First.	**T:** Okay.

Source: Mehan, 1979.

turn-taking rules of the recitation script. Second, note that for the purposes of this lesson, the truth of what the children say is less important than the way they say it. Cindy gave her answer in the form the teacher was looking for, but, as Richard noticed, Cindy had named the wrong color! She was correct in school terms, although she clearly violated norms of everyday language use.

In everyday conversations one usually has ample opportunity to check one's interpretations of what is being said against reality. But in the closed world of the classroom, the real-world objects and events that are the content of the conversation are often unavailable to help children interpret what is being said. Consequently, in order to master the specialized knowledge taught in school, children must learn to focus on language itself as the vehicle of information.

Alternative Forms of Classroom Instruction

Although use of the recitation script is widespread in classrooms around the world, many developmentalists argue that it is not the best way of organizing instruction. For example, Marilyn Adams estimated that approximately 25 percent of children taught to read using a "decoding first" strategy are unsuccessful (Adams, 1990). Among other shortcomings, children taught in this manner are placed in the role of passive recipients of predigested information. They gain very little practice formulating problems for themselves. Yet expanding children's knowledge of language functions, including the language of mathematics, is one of the important tasks of schooling (Lampert & Blunk, 1998).

TABLE 13.2 LESSON ON USE OF PREPOSITIONS

Initiation	Reply
T [Teacher]: Make a red flower under the tree. *(pause)* Okay, let's look at the red flower. Can you tell me where the red flower is?	**Children:** Right here, right here.
T: Dora?	**Dora:** Under the tree.
T: Tell me in a sentence.	**Dora:** It's under the tree.
T: What's under the tree, Dora?	**Children:** The flower.
T: Tell me, the flower . . .	**Dora:** The flower is under the tree.
T: Where is the red flower, Richard?	**Richard:** Under the tree.
T: Can you tell me in a sentence?	**Richard:** The flower is under the tree.
T: Cindy, where is the red flower?	**Cindy:** The red flower is under the tree.
Richard: *[noticing that Cindy actually drew the "red" flower with a yellow crayon]* Hey, that's not red.	

Source: Mehan, 1979.

Despite wide variations among them, each of these settings is immediately recognizable as a school.

Alternative means of organizing classroom instruction can be located on a continuum. At one end are whole-group recitation-script lessons combined with seat work in which students practice parts of the lesson. At the other end are project-oriented, activity-based classrooms where teachers spend little time talking to the class as a whole and spend most of the schoolday moving from one small group to another, providing encouragement and intellectual and material resources as they seem needed. The effectiveness of the latter approach is illustrated by two programs—one focused on reading, the other on mathematics.

Reciprocal Teaching **Reciprocal teaching** was designed by Ann Brown and Annemarie Palincsar (1984) as a way to integrate decoding skills and comprehension skills. It was targeted at the many children who have "learned to read" in the sense that they can decode simple texts but have difficulty making sense of what they read.

In the reciprocal-teaching procedure, a teacher and a small group of students read silently through a paragraph of text and then take turns leading a discussion of its meaning. The discussion leader (adult or child) begins by asking a question about the main idea and then summarizes the content in his or her own words. If members of the group disagree with the summary, the group rereads the passage and discusses its contents to clarify what it says. Finally, the leader asks for predictions about what will come in the next paragraph.

Note that each of the key elements in reciprocal teaching—asking questions about content, summarizing, clarifying, and predicting—presupposes

reciprocal teaching A method of teaching reading in which teachers and children take turns reading text in a manner that integrates decoding and comprehension skills.

BOX 13.1

Computers in Schools

Over the past two decades, the growth of computer use in schools has been phenomenal. In 1983 there was approximately 1 computer for every 168 students in U.S. schools. In 1998 there was 1 computer for every 6 students. Moreover, the use of computers in schools is expected to accelerate in the decades to come (Anderson & Ronnkvist, 1999).

This growth in the quantity of computers has been accompanied by falling costs, vastly increased processing speed and memory capacity, and the advent of the Internet and the World Wide Web, which collectively have enabled computers to become a powerful medium of communication. These changes in cost, power, and function have allowed computers to have an impact in classrooms all over the industrialized world.

The actual changes that occur in the classroom environment when computers are introduced depend very much on how many there are, how powerful they are, and how they are used. In many classrooms there is only one computer, which is used to reward well-behaved children with an opportunity to play a computer game. But in some schools, computers have transformed the entire organization of education (Kafai & Resnick, 1996; Littleton & Light, 1999).

Charles Crook (1996) identifies four approaches to the design of computer-based educational activities, each of which uses a distinctive metaphor relating computers to the teaching process.

The Computer-as-Tutor

The earliest use of computers in education was based on the idea that the computer would play the role of a human teacher. The spirit and hopes for this approach were stated early in the computer revolution by Patrick Suppes, a leader in using digital computers in education:

> In a few more years, millions of school children will have access to what Phillip of Macedonia's son Alexander enjoyed as a royal prerogative: the personal services of a tutor as well-informed and responsive as Aristotle. (Suppes, 1966:207)

The prototypic application used in this approach is CAI—computer-aided instruction. It begins by presenting the student with the information to be learned, along with questions that test whether learning has occurred. The computer then records the student's answers and gives appropriate feedback. Basic reading and math skills, as well as a variety of subject matters such as geography and history, have been taught in this way (Ravaglia et al., 1995).

One advantage that CAI has over traditional drill-and-practice workbooks is the capacity to keep track of the individual child's exact performance and to respond accordingly. In a program designed by Patrick Suppes (1988), for example, the computer repeats materials the student had trouble with and even presents scheduled "reminders" of previously learned materials to make sure that the student retains all the information to be learned. Such individualized instruction is impossible in a classroom with 1 teacher and 30 students sitting at their desks—a major argument for the application of computers to education.

With advances in the fields of artificial intelligence and cognitive science, researchers have continued to refine the computer-as-tutor approach. For example, Kenneth Koedenger and John Anderson have created "cognitive tutors" in mathematics (Koedenger & Anderson, 1998). These computerized tutors accumulate a database of users' problem-solving strategies and common errors and then use these data to present specifically relevant problems that are sensitive to the users' cognitive strengths and weaknesses. This and other "intelligent tutoring" programs have been shown to be effective in a variety of circumstances and are always in the process of being modified and improved (van Biljon et al., 1999).

However, to date it has not been possible to create a computerized tutor that rivals the flexibility and subtlety of human teachers. So far, at least, computer programs have been unable to anticipate what children will have trouble with or to find alternative ways to phrase a problem or entice children's curiosity with situationally appropriate hints.

The Computer-as-Pupil

The computer-as-tutor approach allows learners little opportunity to guide the course of their own learning; they can only respond to the problems they are given. Influenced by Piaget's theory that to achieve deep understanding, children must construct their understandings through active exploration of their environments, Seymour Papert and his colleagues at MIT's Media Laboratory developed a simplified computer language called LOGO (Kafai & Resnick, 1996; Papert, 1980).

Using LOGO, children control the movements of a robot turtle that actually moves around the floor of the room follow-

that the purpose of the activity is comprehension: figuring out what the text means. And because these strategies involve talking about (and arguing over) the textual meaning, the children are able to see and hear the teacher and other children model metacognitive behaviors that aid comprehension. For example, the teacher might point to relevant information in a prior paragraph that needs to be taken into account, or relate an idea in the text to ing explicit instructions that the child "teaches it" by programming them into the computer's memory. By learning to "teach the turtle" to carry out their instructions, children acquire ideas and procedures that are fundamental not only to computer programming but to mathematics in general. For example, in order to teach the turtle to run around in a circle or build a house, children acquire basic principles of both algebra and geometry. Papert's colleagues have extended this simple computer language with programmable objects such as Lego blocks, enabling children to build Lego robots and maneuver them through environments that the children create for them (Resnick, 1998).

Research on the effectiveness of treating computers as pupils has shown that Papert's constructionist approach can produce useful educational activities for children (Kafai & Resnick, 1996). However, research also shows that in order to be effective, LOGO applications need to be a central part of classroom life in which teachers are involved along with the children, providing ongoing support and guidance for the children's learning (Pea et al., 1987).

The Computer-as-Resource

The third approach to using computers in school emphasizes the fact that whatever may set it apart from other human technologies, the computer is, at bottom, a tool that can be used to provide a broad range of resources to learners. This idea, which underpins much of the current enthusiasm for the use of computers in the classroom, assumes that if it is possible to provide active learners with abundant information, learning is sure to occur. There is no doubt that computers, with their current multimedia capacities, can provide enormous amounts of information in interesting formats. But as in the case of each of the other uses of computers, there is a tendency of those who champion computers as information resources to lose sight of the fact that these resources are unlikely to be used if the school does not have a social system that encourages and supports children's initiatives.

The Computer-as-Transformer

Several developmentalists argue that one of the greatest potentials of classroom computers is to reorganize the entire fabric of the educational experience by changing children's interactions not only with the materials to be learned but also with the teacher and one another, the school as an institution, and the world at large (Crook, 1996; Koschman, 1998; Papert, 1996; Zech et al., 1998). A few examples give the flavor of this approach.

Researchers associated with the Cognition and Technology Group at Vanderbilt University have taken advantage of the newly emerging combinations of interactive video disks and CD-ROM technology to create a curriculum that begins with a series of televised adventures and mysteries for the children to enter into (Cognition and Technology Group, 1996; Zech et al., 1998). In one such program, called "The River Adventure," learners watch a video about a trip on a houseboat in which the protagonists must take into account such factors as the food and gas they will need, the docking facilities they will require, and so on. The children then determine when and why to use various kinds of data to achieve such goals as docking at a particular marina and returning home quickly under various conditions.

Students who engage in this type of multimedia problem solving acquire many kinds of expertise in using computers and a variety of academic skills as well. Just as important, their interest in school and their self-confidence as students have been shown to increase.

Several research groups have used computer networks to forge relationships between schools in different parts of the world, enabling students to engage in joint learning projects in which, for example, they measure and record levels of acid rain or compare the histories of their cultural groups in relation to each other (Levin et al., 1990; Riel, 1998). The use of computer networks also allows students to participate in projects they find genuinely interesting. For example, they can interact online with scientists engaged in such exciting activities as exploring space, the polar regions, or undersea canyons and be directly involved in analyzing important data and figuring out what it means. These projects naturally promote work in small groups, mastery of many aspects of computer use, and the development of multiple academic skills. Teachers find that they do not need to urge children to attend to such studies; instead, it is common for children to ask permission to keep working on their projects during the lunch break and recess.

Numerous studies have shown that computers can make a positive difference in the classroom when properly used. The challenge now is to realize this potential, making effective uses of the new technology a routine part of every child's education.

some common experience that all the children have had, as a way of making sense of what is being read. As Brown (1997) points out, reciprocal teaching is an application of Vygotsky's notion of a "zone of proximal development" (Chapter 5, p. 207), which allows children to participate in the act of reading for meaning even before they have acquired the full set of abilities that independent reading requires.

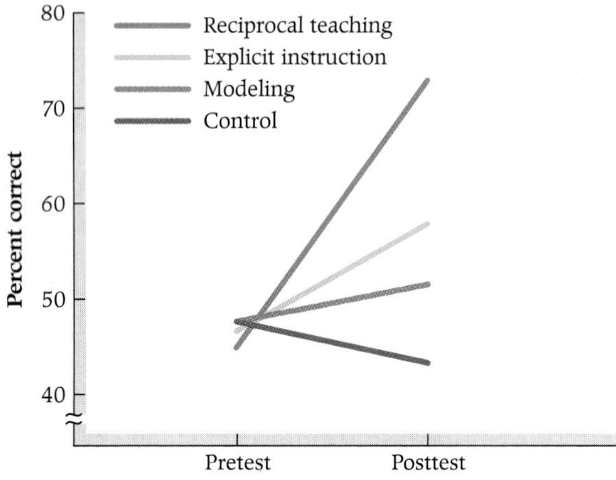

(a) Reading scores

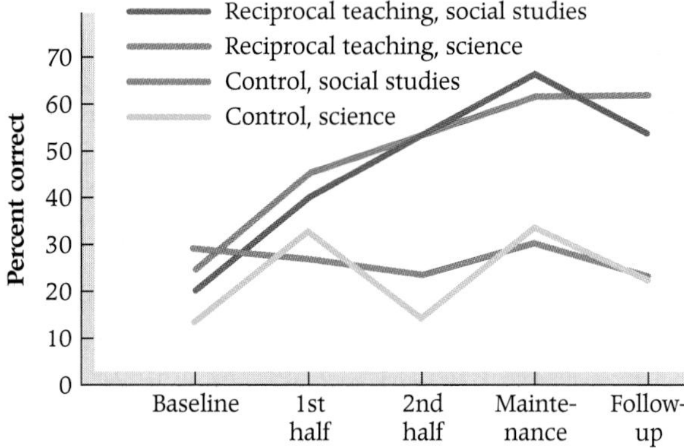

(b) Social studies and science scores

FIGURE 13.5

Reciprocal teaching (a) not only proved to be more effective than either explicit instruction or modeling (b) but also produced marked improvement in children's reading success in social studies and science. Both explicit instruction and reciprocal teaching led to improved reading, but reciprocal teaching was by far the most effective procedure. Students given practice in reciprocal reading showed large and sustained improvements in their social studies and science classes, whereas students who received no special reading instruction did quite poorly. (From Brown et al., 1992.)

A number of studies (summarized in Brown, 1997, and Rosenshine & Meister, 1994) have found that reciprocal teaching can produce rapid and durable increases in children's reading skills. Figure 13.5 shows the findings of a study in which reciprocal teaching was used to improve the reading ability of a group of junior high school students who could decode words adequately but had difficulty reading for meaning. In this case, reciprocal reading was being used in a science class and a social studies class, not as a "reading lesson" but as a way to foster mastery of the course material. Used in this manner, the reciprocal-reading activity goes beyond the teaching of reading for its own sake to reading that increases knowledge of valued subject matter at the same time that it improves reading skills.

Realistic Mathematics Education Recognizing the limitations of recitation scripts and the bottom-up approach, the National Council of Teachers of Mathematics has adopted a set of standards for improving mathematics education that shifts the focus of mathematics instruction from training in basic skills, procedures, and memorization toward conceptual understanding and linkages between mathematics and real-world problems (National Council of Teachers of Mathematics, 1995). An example of a mathematics program that seeks to implement these goals is provided by the work of Paul Cobb and his colleagues, who draw upon a theory of "realistic mathematics education," which is widely used in the Netherlands (Cobb et al., 1997). These researchers offer three basic ideas as the heart of realistic mathematics education:

1. The activities used to introduce mathematical concepts should be meaningful for the students. Thus, for example, a first-grade teacher might introduce counting up to 20 by creating a make-believe situation with a bus conductor on a double-decker bus with 10 seats on each deck who has to keep track of how many people are on the bus. As we have learned from the experimental research on children's problem solving discussed in previous chapters, such pretend stories help to provide a meaningful context for carrying out cognitive operations.
2. Although these introductory activities should connect to children's real-life experience, they should also be chosen to support the development of important mathematical concepts. In the case of the double-decker bus, for example, the teacher wanted children to learn how to group numbers for calculation, to realize that there are 8 people on the bus if there are 4 on top and 4 on the bottom, or 6 on the top and 2 on the bottom, or 2 on the top and 6 on the bottom, etc. Each configuration is a different way of representing a total of 8.
3. As children move through the lessons, they are expected to use models to represent quantities and carry out mathematical actions. Cobb describes a number of studies that use an "arithmetic rack," with two rows containing 10 beads each. For the conductor-on-the-bus context, the arithmetic rack provides a rather precise spatial model with each of its rows corresponding to a deck of the bus. But the beads on the rack can also be used to represent the number of cookies put in or taken out of a cookie jar and a variety of other story contexts that have equivalent mathematical properties.

Over time, children gradually master the conceptual structures that the stories and models initially support, and they can carry out the needed calculations without such aids.

As in the case of reciprocal reading, the creation of classroom norms that support the mixing of bottom-up knowledge with top-down conceptual and utilization knowledge is key. Teachers work to establish a classroom culture in which children are expected to justify their reasoning when they answer a question and to try to understand the reasoning behind other children's answers. In addition, children are expected to be helpful to the group. When working alone, they are encouraged to solicit help from others and to share what they have learned.

"Problem-oriented" approaches that emphasize the processes of reasoning about mathematical problems have been found successful well beyond the elementary school years (Boaler, 1997; Lampert & Blunk, 1998). Jo Boaler observed students in two secondary school classrooms in England. One classroom followed a traditional recitation-script approach to learning mathematics, while the other used a small-group, problem-oriented approach. In the traditional classroom, the teacher began lessons by presenting a standard problem and the standard method for solving it ("Here is how to determine the area of a parallelogram"). The students observed the solution method and then practiced using it on their own. The teacher did not explain why the method worked and did not encourage students to invent their own methods. In the activity-centered classroom, the teacher would begin a lesson by presenting a problem to the whole class designed to intrigue the students. In one case, for example, the students were presented with a problem called "36 pieces of fencing." A fence with 36 planks was depicted and the students were asked to figure out all the different shapes they could make from these materials. After the problem was introduced, the students were encouraged to ask questions as a way of orienting to the task. Then they worked in small groups while the teacher moved around the room providing help when it was requested.

The teachers in both classrooms believed strongly that their approaches were superior, and they passed their enthusiasm on to their students. They also reported that discipline problems were virtually nonexistent, but the researchers noted that the project-oriented classroom was somewhat noisier and that the students more often engaged in "off-task" activities such as chatting with their friends.

When the students were tested at the end of the year on both standard tests and tests that assessed their ability to apply mathematics to new problems, there were striking differences between students in the two classrooms. Students who participated in the traditional instructional format scored better on knowledge of prespecified mathematical procedures, but students in the project-based class were significantly better on conceptual questions and on questions that required them to apply their knowledge to a novel problem, such as designing an apartment.

Overall, the evidence indicates that when properly organized, instructional methods that induce students to be active contributors to classroom discourse can be quite effective. But such methods are more complex to organize and are still encountered in only a minority of classrooms.

THE COGNITIVE CONSEQUENCES OF SCHOOLING

The contrasting success of different modes of instruction should make it clear that what children learn in school depends to some extent on the kind of instruction they receive. However, as we noted earlier, a very high proportion of schools follow whole-class recitation methods, so developmentalists can, as a rough approximation, treat schooling as a uniform kind of experience in seeking to assess how learning about the world through reading and writing in schools affects cognitive development during middle childhood and beyond.

school-cutoff strategy A means of assessing the impact of education while controlling for age by comparing children who are almost the same age but begin schooling a year apart because of school rules that set a specific cutoff date for starting school.

Regardless of instructional approach, schooling expands children's knowledge base, gives them massive experience in deliberate remembering, and trains them in systematic problem solving. Recent decades of research demonstrate that these experiences do affect children, but the effects depend on the particular cognitive processes in question.

There are several ways to assess the cognitive impact of schooling (Christian et al., 2000). One way, which assesses the impact of early schooling, is to compare 6-year-olds who have experienced formal schooling with children of same age who have not yet experienced it. Another way is to conduct research in societies where schooling is not universal, comparing children who have attended school with their age-mates who have not.

USING THE SCHOOL-CUTOFF STRATEGY

In many countries, school boards require that in order to begin attending school, a child be a certain age by a particular date. To enter grade 1 in September of a given year, children in Edmonton, Alberta, Canada, for example, must have passed their sixth birthday by March 1 of that year. Six-year-olds born after that date must attend kindergarten instead, so their formal education is delayed for a year. Such policies allow researchers to assess the impact of early schooling while holding age virtually constant: they simply compare the intellectual performances of children who turn 6 in January or February with those who turn 6 in March or April, testing both groups at the beginning and at the end of the school year. This procedure is known as the **school-cutoff strategy** (Morrison et al., 1995).

Researchers who have used this strategy find that the first year of schooling brings about a marked increase in the sophistication of some cognitive processes but not others. Frederick Morrison and his colleagues (1995), for example, compared the ability of first-graders and kindergartners to recall pictures of nine common objects. The first-graders were, on average, only a month older than the kindergartners, and at the start of the school year the performances of the two groups were virtually identical. At the end of the school year, however, the first-graders could remember twice as many pictures as they did at the beginning of the year, whereas the kindergartners showed no improvement in memory at all. Significantly, the first-graders engaged in active rehearsal during the testing, but the kindergartners did not. Clearly, one year of schooling had brought about marked changes in strategies and performance. The same pattern of results was obtained for standardized reading and mathematics tests (Morrison et al., 1997).

There is an interesting exception to these findings. Jeffrey Bisanz and his colleagues tested children's responses to a standard Piagetian test of number conservation (see Chapter 12, pp. 479–480) and also asked the children to add small numbers (Bisanz et al., 1995). They found that performance in the conservation task improved largely as a consequence of age but that mental arithmetic improved almost exclusively as a consequence of schooling. These findings both confirm the importance of schooling in promoting a variety of relatively specific cognitive abilities and support Piaget's belief that the ability to conserve quantity develops without any special instruction at some time between the ages of 5 and 7.

CROSS-CULTURAL RESEARCH ON THE EFFECTS OF SCHOOLING

Although the school-cutoff strategy provides an excellent way to assess the cognitive consequences of small amounts of schooling, it is, by definition, limited to the first year. For a longer-range picture of the contribution of formal education to cognitive development, researchers have conducted studies in societies where schooling is available to only a part of the population. We will summarize evidence from three cognitive domains that have figured heavily in our discussion of cognitive development: logical thinking, memory, and metacognitive skills.

Logical Thinking

A large number of cross-cultural studies have been conducted to determine if participation in formal schooling enhances performance on Piagetian conservation tasks and other tasks created to reveal concrete operational thinking (Rogoff, 1981; Segall et al., 1999). The results have split more or less evenly between those that find enhanced performance among children who have attended school and those that do not. Consistent with the evidence presented in Chapter 12 (p. 481), when schoolchildren do better than their unschooled peers on the standard Piagetian tests, their greater success appears to have less to do with more rapid achievement of concrete operational thinking than with their greater familiarity with the circumstances of test taking. Such specialized test-taking knowledge includes familiarity with the forms in which questions are asked, a greater ease in speaking to unfamiliar adults, and fluency in the language in which the test is given when the testing is not conducted in the child's native language. When these factors are taken into account, the overall pattern of results indicates that the development of concrete operational thinking increases with age and is relatively unaffected by schooling.

Memory

In Chapter 12 we saw that, unlike North American children, children in some cultures do not show an increase in free-recall memory tasks as they grow older. Research comparing schooled and nonschooled children in other societies, like the comparative data on first-graders and kindergartners presented above, has shown that schooling is the crucial experience underlying these cultural differences. When children in other cultures have had an opportunity to go to school, their memory performance is more similar to that of their North American counterparts in the same grade than it is to that of their agemates in the same village who have not been to school (Cole et al., 1971).

A study by Daniel Wagner (1974) suggests the kind of memory-enhancing information-processing skills that children acquire as a consequence of schooling. Wagner conducted his study among educated and uneducated Mayans in Yucatan, Mexico. He asked 248 people varying in age from 6 years to adulthood to recall the positions of picture cards laid out in a linear array (see Figure 13.6). (To ensure that the items pictured on the cards would be familiar to all the subjects, the items were taken from a local version of bingo called *lotería,* which uses pictures instead of numbers.) On each trial, each of seven cards was displayed for 2 seconds and then turned face-down. As soon as all seven cards had been presented, a duplicate of a picture on one of the cards was shown and the subject was asked to point to its twin. By selecting different duplicate pictures, Wagner in effect manipulated the length of time between the presentation of a picture and the moment its location was to be recalled.

(a) Take a good look and turn the page

FIGURE 13.6
(a) Cards used to test short-term memory. Seven cards are selected and then turned face down. The person being tested is then shown a duplicate of one of the cards (see p. 524) and asked to select the card that corresponds to it from the seven that are face down. (b) Which card has a matching picture? (From Wagner, 1978.)

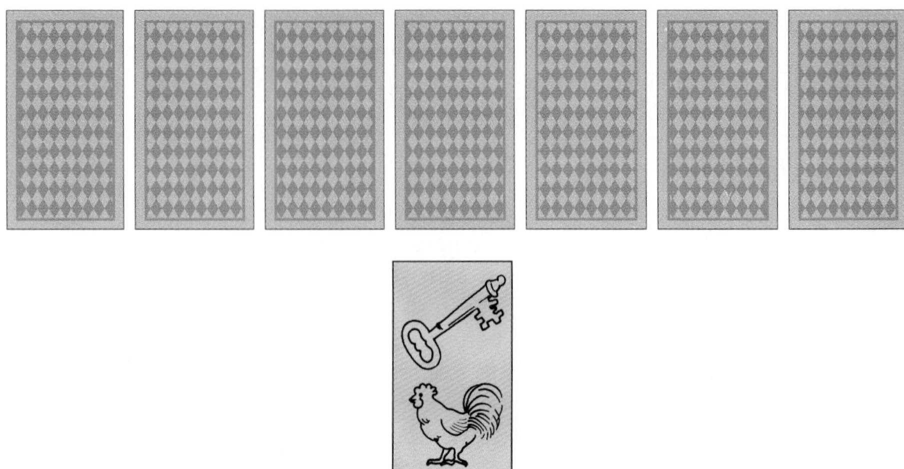

(b) Which card has matching pictures?

As in similar research in the United States (Hagen et al., 1970), Wagner found that the performance of children who were attending school improved markedly with age (see Figure 13.7). However, older children and adults who did not attend school remembered no better than young children, leading Wagner to conclude that it was schooling that made the difference. Additional analyses of the data revealed that the use of rehearsal by those who attended school was responsible for the improvement in their performance.

Evidence such as this does not mean that memory simply fails to develop among children who have not attended school. The difference between educated and uneducated children's performance in cross-cultural memory experiments is most noticeable after several years of schooling and when the materials to be learned are not related to one another according to any everyday script. When the materials to be remembered are part of a meaningful setting, such as the kinds of animals found in a barnyard or the furniture placed in a toy house, the effects of schooling on memory performance disappear (Rogoff & Wadell, 1982). It appears that schooling helps children to develop specialized strategies for remembering and so enhances their ability to commit arbitrary material to memory for purposes of later testing. There is no evidence to support the conclusion that schooling increases memory capacity per se.

FIGURE 13.7

Short-term memory performance as a function of age and number of years of education. In the absence of further education (as among the rural people tested in this study), performance does not improve with age. Thus, schooling appears to be a key factor in one's ability to do well at this task. (Numbers in parentheses represent the average number of years of education for the designated group.) (From Wagner, 1974.)

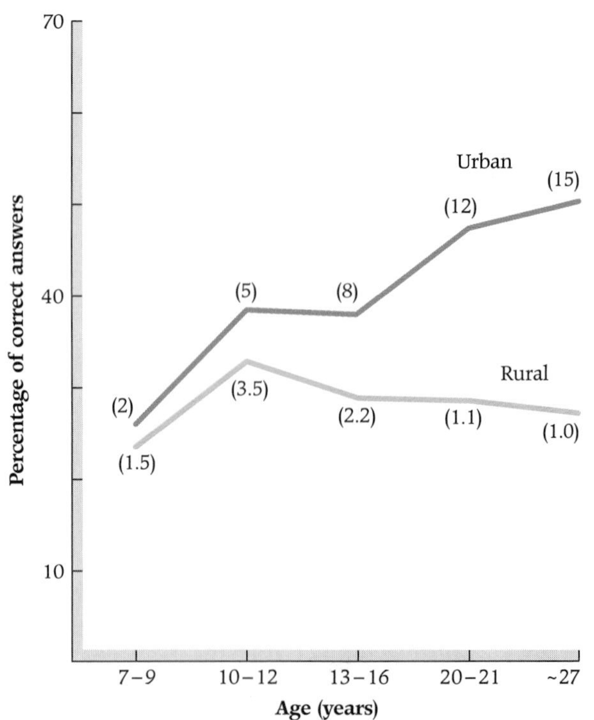

Metacognitive Skills

Schooling appears to influence the ability to reflect on and talk about one's own thought processes (Luria, 1976; Rogoff, 1981; Tulviste, 1991). When children have been asked to explain how they arrived at the answer to a logical problem or what they did to make themselves remember something, those who have not attended school are likely to say something like "I did what my sense told me" or to offer no explanation at all. Schoolchildren, on the other hand, are likely to talk about the mental activities and logic that underlie their responses. The same results apply to metalinguistic knowledge. Sylvia Scribner and Michael Cole (1981) asked educated and uneducated Vai people in Liberia to judge the grammatical correctness of several sentences spoken in Vai. Some of the sentences were grammatical, some not. Education had no effect on the interviewees' ability to identify the ungrammatical sentences; but educated people could generally explain just what it was about a sentence that made it ungrammatical, whereas uneducated people could not.

A Second-Generation Impact of Schooling?

One of the most intriguing lines of evidence for the way in which schooling affects development comes from the research of Robert LeVine and his colleagues, who have studied the impact of schooling on the child-rearing practices of parents who have, or have not, gone to school (LeVine et al., 1996). These researchers found that mothers who had several years of education talked more with their children and used less directive child-rearing methods, a pattern that is similar to that of middle-class parents in North America. Most significantly, their children performed better in school and on standardized tests of cognitive development.

The Evidence in Overview

Overall, extensive research on the cognitive consequences of schooling has produced a mixed picture. On the one hand, there is only minimal support for the idea that schooling is directly responsible for broad changes in the way the mind works "in general." In some ways, as shown by the evidence from children who focus too narrowly on the mathematical procedures taught in school, schooling can actually have a negative impact on the development of mental abilities. When schooling has been found to improve cognitive performance, the effect appears to work in one of three ways: (1) by increasing children's knowledge base, including ways of using language; (2) by teaching specific information-processing strategies that are relevant primarily to school itself; and (3) by changing children's overall life situations and attitudes, which they pass on to their children in the form of new child-rearing practices that promote cognitive development.

Perhaps the most important aspect of schooling for the majority of people is social; schooling is a gateway to economic power and social status. As we noted earlier in this chapter (Figure 13.1), the associations between years of schooling, income, and job status are strong (U.S. Census Bureau, 1995). On the average, the more years of schooling people complete, the higher their incomes are and the more likely they are to obtain white-collar and professional jobs.

Success in school is such an important contributor to children's later economic well-being in literate societies that developmental psychologists and educators are greatly interested in understanding the factors that promote or inhibit it. One commonly held popular belief is that many children who succeed simply have a special "aptitude for schooling" that others lack. But as we shall see, there is more to success in school than academic aptitude. A variety of physical, psychological, and sociocultural factors play an essential role in children's school success.

APTITUDE FOR SCHOOLING

Although people need basic literacy and numeracy skills to function well in many modern societies, many youngsters leave school without having acquired them. It is estimated that as many as 22 percent of adults in the United States read so poorly that they cannot cope adequately with the demands of everyday life (National Center for Educational Statistics, 1993). What gives rise to this high failure rate and what can be done to promote greater success in the kinds of learning that takes place in school? All during this century, answers to such questions have been influenced by the idea that people vary in an aptitude called "intelligence" and that these variations explain the differences in their school performance.

The concept of intelligence is very widely accepted. All languages have terms that describe individual differences in people's ability to solve various kinds of problems (Segall et al., 1999; Serpell, 1993). But the precise meanings of these terms vary among cultures, and it has proven difficult—some people say impossible—to define intelligence so that it can be measured as precisely as weight or height.

For example, Robert Serpell (1993) reports that the nearest equivalent to "intelligence" among the Chewa of Zambia emphasizes cooperation and obedience. Pierre Dasen and his colleagues report that among that Baoulé of the Ivory Coast the concept of *n'glouèlê,* which appears to function like the word "intelligence" in English, includes two dimensions (Dasen et al., 1985). One dimension involves social components (obedience, honesty, responsibility, politeness, reflectiveness, wisdom), while the other involves technological components (observation, fast learning, manual dexterity, memorizing ability). An emphasis on the social dimension of "intelligence" appears quite widespread in more traditional societies (Segall et al., 1999:145ff), but it is the technological dimension that dominates notions of intelligence in Europe and North America.

Despite uncertainties about what intelligence "really is," almost all children growing up today in North America can expect to take an intelligence test at some time before they complete their education. Such tests are used to decide the kind of education they will receive and the kind of work they will do, which in turn will influence the lives they will lead as adults. It is thus important to understand the nature of intelligence embodied in these tests, as well as the nature of intelligence testing itself as a factor in children's development.

THE ORIGINS OF INTELLIGENCE TESTING

Interest in measuring intelligence became widespread at the beginning of the twentieth century, when mass education was becoming the norm in industrialized countries. Though most children seemed to be able to profit from the instruction they were given, some seemed unable to learn in school. Concerned educational officials tried to determine the causes of these difficulties and find remedies for them.

In 1904 the French minister of public instruction named a commission to ensure the benefits of instruction for what he termed "defective" children. The commission asked Alfred Binet, a professor of psychology at the Sorbonne, and Théophile Simon, a physician, to create a means of identifying those children who needed special instruction. Binet and Simon set out to construct a psychological examination to diagnose mental subnormality that would have all the precision and validity of a medical examination. They especially wanted to avoid incorrectly diagnosing children as "mentally subnormal" (Binet & Simon, 1916).

The diagnostic strategy adopted by Binet and Simon was to present children of different ages with a series of problems, the solving of which was considered indicative of intelligence in the culture of their time. The problems were tailored to differentiate between children at each age, so that children who were far behind could be identified and given special instruction. Binet and Simon surmised, for example, that one aspect of intelligence is the ability to follow directions on a task while keeping several components of the task in mind at once. To test for this ability, they presented children aged 4 to 6 with tasks such as the following:

> Do you see this key? You are to put it on the chair over there (pointing to the chair); afterwards shut the door; afterwards you will see near the door a box which is on a chair. You will take that box and bring it to me. (p. 206)

At 4 years of age, few children could carry out all parts of this task without help. At 5 years, about half of the children responded adequately, and at 6 years, almost all children completed the task fully. This age-linked pattern of achievement provided Binet and Simon with the test characteristics they needed. A 4-year-old who passed the test was considered precocious, while a 6-year-old who failed was considered retarded with respect to this ability.

mental age (MA) The measure of intelligence proposed by Binet and Simon to describe the test performance of an average child of a given age.

Other tasks required children to identify the missing parts of a picture, to name colors, to copy geometric figures, to remember strings of random digits, to count backward from 20, to make change for 20 francs, and so on. After extensive pretesting, Binet and Simon tested slightly more than 200 children ranging in age from 3 to 12 years, giving a different set of questions to each age group. As they had hoped, almost precisely 50 percent of these children scored at the expected age level. Of the remainder, 43 percent were within 1 year of expectation and only 7 percent deviated above or below the norm by as much as 2 years.

Binet and Simon concluded that they had succeeded in constructing a scale of intelligence. They called the basic index of intelligence for this scale **mental age (MA).** A child who performed as well on the test as an average 7-year-old was said to have an MA of 7; a child who did as well as an average 9-year-old was said to have an MA of 9; and so on. The MA provided Binet and Simon with a convenient way to characterize mental subnormality. A "dull" 7-year-old child was one who performed like a normal child one or more years younger.

To verify that their scale reflected more than a lucky selection of test items, Binet and Simon tested their findings against teachers' judgments of the children's intelligence. To a high degree, their scale's identification of most and least able children coincided with the teachers' assessments.

Turning their attention to the causes for school failure, Binet and Simon suggested that a child might lack either the "natural intelligence" (the "nature") needed to succeed in school or the cultural background (the "nurture") presupposed by the school.

> A very intelligent child may be deprived of instruction by circumstances foreign to his intelligence. He may have lived far from school; he may have had a long illness . . . or maybe some parents have preferred to keep their children at home, to have them rinse bottles, serve the customers of a shop, care for a sick relative or herd the sheep. In such cases . . . it suffices to pass lightly the results of tests which are of a notably scholastic character, and to attach the greatest importance to those which express the natural intelligence. (pp. 253–254)

This approach may appear intuitively plausible, but in fact it contains a crucial ambiguity: nowhere do Binet and Simon offer a definition of "natural intelligence" that would allow them to separate tests of natural intelligence from tests of a "scholastic character." Instead of defining natural intelligence in a way that distinguishes it from cultural experience (which they refer to as a problem of "fearful complexity"), they contented themselves with pointing out that whatever natural intelligence is, it is not equivalent to success in school. In their view, not only is there more to intelligence than schooling; there is also more to schooling—and to life—than intelligence:

> Our examination of intelligence cannot take account of all these qualities, attention, will, regularity, continuity, docility, and courage which play so important a part in school work, and also in after-life; for life is not so much a conflict of intelligences as a combat of characters. (p. 256)

THE LEGACY OF BINET AND SIMON

Many refinements of Binet and Simon's original tests have been made since the early days of intelligence testing, and a number of new tests have been devised. Some follow Binet and Simon's approach by including many different kinds of items in order to sample a broad range of possible abilities. These tests contain "subscales" that ask test takers to give the meaning of words,

FIGURE 13.8

Simulated items from the Wechsler Intelligence Scale for Children (Copyright © 1948, 1974, 1991 by the Psychological Corporation. Reproduced by permission. All rights reserved.)

Information (30 items)

How many wings does a bird have?

What is steam made of?

Picture Completion (26 items)

What is the missing part of the picture?

Similarities (17 items)

In what way are a lion and a tiger alike?

In what way are an hour and a week alike?

Picture Arrangement (12 items made up of 3 to 5 picture cards each)

(The person is asked to arrange the cards so that the story of the woman weighing herself makes sense.)

Comprehension (17 items)

What should you do if you see someone forget his book when he leaves a restaurant?

What is the advantage of keeping money in a bank?

solve arithmetic word problems, assemble a jigsaw puzzle, complete a series of pictures, indicate which of a series of words doesn't belong with the others, and so on (see Figure 13.8). This broad sampling approach was followed by Lewis Terman, a professor at Stanford University, who modified the original Binet-Simon scales to create the Stanford-Binet Intelligence Scale (Terman, 1925), and David Wechsler, who devised tests for use with both adults and children (Wechsler, 1939). Other tests focus on only a single kind of ability. For example, the Peabody Picture Vocabulary Test seeks to measure vocabulary size by having children name items in pictures, and the Raven's Progressive Matrices are designed to assess reasoning about perceptual patterns (see Figure 13.9).

From Mental Age to IQ

William Stern (1912), a German developmental psychologist, introduced an important refinement in the way intelligence tests were thought about and applied. He suggested that intelligence should be the ratio of children's mental age to their chronological age (CA). Thus was born the unit of measurement that we use today, the **intelligence quotient (IQ):**

$$IQ = (MA/CA)100$$

The stratagem of multiplying the relative magnitude of MA/CA by 100 is simply a convenience. Calculation of IQ in this fashion ensures that when children are performing precisely as expected for their age, the resulting score will be 100; thus 100 is an "average IQ" by definition (see Figure 13.10). A 9-year-old child with a mental age of 10, for example, is assigned an IQ of 111 ($10/9 \times 100 = 111$), while a 10-year-old child with a mental age of 10 is assigned an IQ of 100 ($10/10 \times 100 = 100$).

In recent decades the method of calculating IQ has been refined to take into account the fact that mental development is more rapid early in life than later. Raw IQ scores do not, for example, take into account the fact that the difference between 4- and 5-year-olds' mental functioning is greater than the difference between 14- and 15-year-olds'. To overcome this difficulty, psychologists now use a score referred to as a "deviation IQ" (Wechsler, 1974). Calculation of IQ scores as deviations takes advantage of the statistical fact, illustrated in Figure 13.10, that the raw IQ scores calculated for a large sample form an approximately normal distribution. When psychologists base the IQ scores assigned to children on the differences between their raw scores and the standardized mean of 100, they have a statistical standard that is the same for all children.

Despite various revisions, the logic of the procedures devised by Binet and Simon is still the basis of standardized intelligence tests. The key tasks in the creation of an IQ test are as follows:

1. To select a set of items that produces a range of performances among children at the same age level
2. To arrange the items in the order of difficulty, so that as children grow older, they are more likely to answer each successive item correctly
3. To make certain that the items are so designed that performance on the test corresponds to performance in school

The adoption and refinement of their testing methods represents only part of Binet and Simon's legacy. Equally important have been the questions they brought to the fore, three of which have dominated research on intelligence ever since. The first question focuses on the nature of intelligence itself: How is intelligence to be defined? Is it a general characteristic of a person's entire mental life, or is it a bundle of relatively specific abilities? Second is the nature-nurture question: What causes variations in intelligence test scores?

intelligence quotient (IQ) The ratio of mental age to chronological age, calculated as IQ = (MA/CA)100. Calculation of IQ in this fashion ensures that when children are performing precisely as expected for their age, the resulting score will be 100; thus 100 is an "average IQ" by definition.

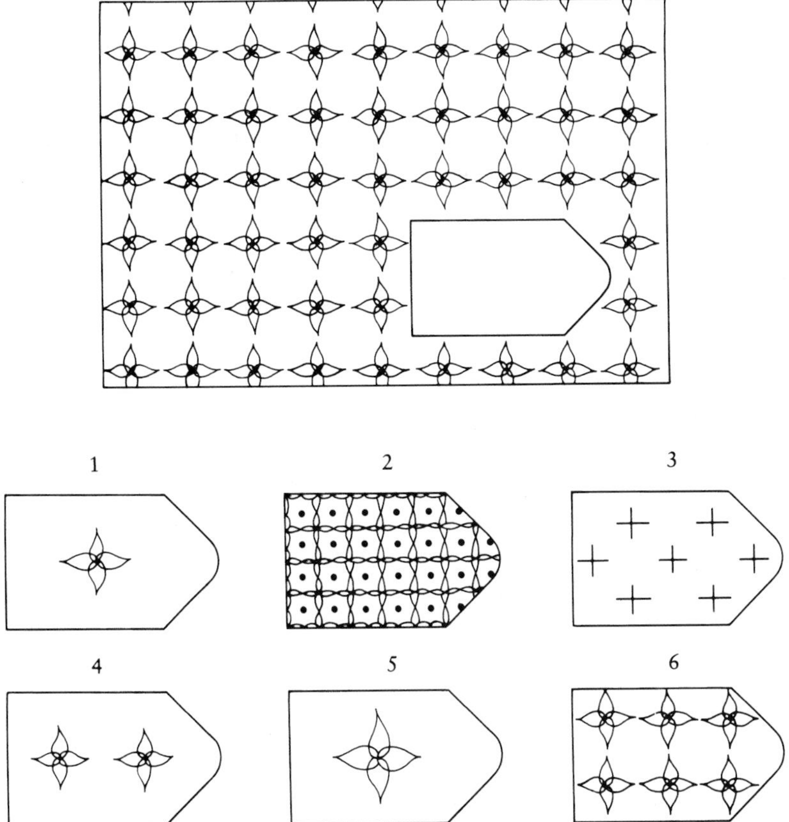

FIGURE 13.9

A sample item from a widely used intelligence test designed to assess the ability to perceive patterns. Note that though these test items do not require elaborate verbal formulation, they assume that the test taker is familiar with two-dimensional representations of figures, a convention that does not exist in many cultures. (From Raven, 1962. Reprinted with permission of J. C. Raven Limited.)

The third focuses on the relationship between test scores and school success: Why do variations in IQ scores predict variations in school performance?

The Nature of Intelligence: General or Specific?

Although Binet and Simon were skeptical about the possibility of defining intelligence, they attempted to specify the quality of mind they were trying to test for with the following characterization:

> It seems to us that in intelligence there is a fundamental faculty, the alteration or lack of which is of the utmost importance for practical life. This faculty is judgment, otherwise called good sense, practical sense, initiative, the faculty of adapting oneself to circumstances. To judge well, to comprehend well, to reason well, these are the essential activities of intelligence. (p. 43)

By referring to intelligence as " a fundamental faculty" Binet and Simon signaled their belief that intelligence is a general characteristic. Many others have followed this approach, although their views of exactly what kind of faculty intelligence is have varied (Mackintosh, 1998). For example, Charles Spearman (1927), an English psychologist, demonstrated a significant correlation among individuals' scores on the different subscales and items used by Binet and Simon and by subsequent IQ tests. He argued that the fact that people who score high (or low) on one task tend to score high (or low) on the others indicated the existence of a general faculty which he called *g*, for "general intelligence." He believed that *g* measures the ability to see relationships among objects, events, and ideas. Arthur Jensen (1998), who reignited interest in intelligence testing in the 1970s, lent support to the idea of *g*, arguing that neural processing speed is the "fundamental faculty" that underpins *g* and results in differences in intelligence.

However, many psychologists reject the idea of general intelligence. Spearman himself noted that although there was a positive

FIGURE 13.10

An idealized bell-shaped curve of the distribution of IQ scores. A bell-shaped curve is a distribution of scores on a graph in which the most frequent value, the mode, is in the center and the less frequent values are distributed symmetrically on either side. By definition, the modal IQ score is 100.

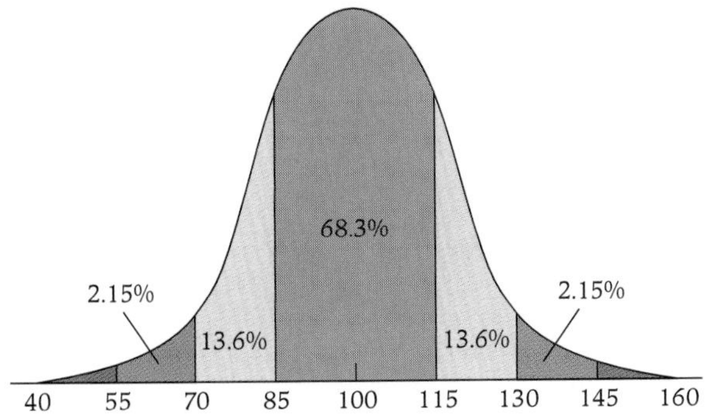

correlation among scores on separate test items, the correlation was far from perfect. He suggested that *g* is supplemented by secondary, specific, abilities. L. L. Thurstone (1938), an American psychologist, subsequently argued that there are seven "primary mental abilities." He created a Primary Mental Abilities Test, which contained subscales for verbal ability, inductive reasoning, perceptual speed, facility with numbers, spatial relations, memory, and verbal fluency. Others have since proposed as many as 120 kinds of specific intelligences (Guilford, 1967).

Currently two approaches that depict intelligence in terms of distinctive capacities have been particularly prominent. Howard Gardner (1983, 1998) has proposed a theory of multiple intelligences, each of which coincides with a different cognitive module and follows its own developmental path (see Table 13.3). For example, musical intelligence often appears at an early age; logical mathematical intelligence seems to peak in late adolescence and early adulthood; and the kind of spatial intelligence on which artists rely may reach its peak much later. Gardner argues that the expression of each kind of intelligence depends upon a combination of three factors: (1) innate biological brain structures; (2) the particular forms of intelligence that a given culture emphasizes; and (3) the extent to which a child is provided deliberate instruction in activities associated with the various forms of intelligence.

Robert Sternberg (1985, 1999) has proposed what he calls a "triarchic" theory of intelligence governed by three distinct principles. According to Sternberg, the three kinds of intelligence are

1. *Analytic,* the abilities we use to analyze, judge, evaluate, compare, and contrast
2. *Creative,* the abilities we use to create, invent, discover, and imagine or suppose
3. *Practical,* the abilities to apply knowledge by putting it into practice

Sternberg reports that an individual's performance level can vary from one kind of intelligence to another and argues that only analytic intelligence is measured by standard IQ tests.

TABLE 13.3 GARDNER'S MULTIPLE INTELLIGENCES

Kind of Intelligence	Characteristics
Linguistic	Special sensitivity to language, which allows one to choose precisely the right word or turn of phrase and to grasp new meanings easily
Musical	Sensitivity to pitch and tone, which allows one to detect and produce musical structure
Logical-mathematical	Ability to engage in abstract reasoning and manipulate symbols
Spatial	Ability to perceive relations among objects, to transform mentally what one sees, and to re-create visual images from memory
Bodily-kinesthetic	Ability to represent ideas in movement; characteristic of great dancers and mimes
Personal	Ability to gain access to one's own feelings and to understand the motivations of others
Social	Ability to understand the motives, feelings, and behaviors of other people

Source: Gardner, 1983.

The distinction between analytic and practical intelligence has been made by a number of psychologists who link analytic intelligence with "academic" intelligence (Ceci & Hembrooke, 1995; Neisser, 1976). Several characteristics seem to distinguish the analytic problems demanded by schools from problems encountered in everyday settings:

- School problems are formulated for the learner by other people, whereas everyday problems require learners themselves to recognize or formulate problems.
- School problems generally have little or no intrinsic interest to the learners, whereas everyday tasks are intrinsically important to them.
- School problems are clearly defined, whereas everyday problems are generally poorly defined.
- School problems usually have a single correct answer that can be reached by a single method, whereas everyday problems have several acceptable solutions that can be reached by a variety of routes.
- School problems come with all the information needed to deal with them, whereas everyday problems require people to seek new information.
- School problems are detached from ordinary experience, whereas everyday problems are embedded in routine experiences.

Population Differences and the Nature–Nurture Controversy

Along with their disagreements about what intelligence means and whether it is specific or general, theorists also disagree about why people's intelligence-test performances vary. The current debate dates back to the beginning of World War I, when Robert Yerkes proposed that all military recruits be given an intelligence test to determine their fitness to serve in military capacities. The testing also generated data about the intelligence of the U.S. male population as a whole (Yerkes, 1921). Approximately 1.75 million men were given IQ tests in groups—written tests for those who could read and write English, a picture-completion test for those who could not (see Figure 13.11). Never before had IQ tests been administered to such large groups of people at one time or to people for whom the language of the tests was not their native language.

Yerkes's research began a controversy that has continued to the present time. Two results appeared to be particularly problematic. First, the average mental age of native-born Anglo Americans was assessed to be 13 years. Since, by the standards of the time, a mental age of 8 to 12 years was considered subnormal for an adult, it appeared that a substantial part of the Anglo population consisted of "morons." Second, there was a substantial difference between the scores obtained by recruits of European American and African American origin. Overall, the average for recruits of European origin was a mental age of 13.7 years, whereas African Americans averaged slightly more than 10 years.

Several of the pioneer testers of intelligence interpreted such differences as the result of innate, immutable differences in natural intelligence ("nature"). According to this **innatist hypothesis of intelligence,** some people are born generally smarter than others, and no amount of training or variation in the environment can alter this fact. The generally lower test scores of members of ethnic minority groups and the poor (who often, but not always, are the same people) were widely interpreted to mean that such groups are innately and irrevocably inferior (Herrnstein & Murray, 1994).

During the 1930s and 1940s the general-intelligence, innatist position was balanced by an **environmentalist hypothesis of intelligence,** which asserted that intelligence is both specific and heavily dependent on experience (Klineberg, 1980). It was demonstrated, for example, that after people had

innatist hypothesis of intelligence The hypothesis that some people are born generally smarter than others and no amount of training or variation in the environment can alter this fact.

environmentalist hypothesis of intelligence The hypothesis that intelligence is both specific and heavily dependent on experience.

FIGURE 13.11
Items from the picture-completion test used by Robert Yerkes and his colleagues to test recruits during World War I. Each picture is incomplete in some way; the task is to identify what is missing. (From Yerkes, 1921.)

moved from rural areas to the city, their intelligence test scores rose (Klineberg, 1935), and that when orphans were removed from very restricted early environments, their intelligence test scores improved markedly (see Chapter 7).

One of the most striking lines of evidence for the environmental hypothesis of intelligence is the fact that worldwide there has been a steady increase in IQ test performance since testing began (Flynn, 1999). Although the amount of improvement differs somewhat according to the kind of test that is used and the particular country in which it is administered, the general result for the 20 countries where such testing has been widely carried out for many decades indicates that IQ scores have been going up an average of 10 to 20 points for every generation. This means, for example, that the average African American adult in 1990 had a higher IQ than the average European American adult in 1940, and that the average English person in 1900 would score at the level currently considered to indicate mental retardation.

There is no clear consensus about what environmental factors are causing IQ scores to go up, but it is certain that the change is environmental in origin, since it cannot be from a rapid change in the genetic constitution of people all over the world. As Flynn (1999) points out, it is almost impossible to determine *how* the environment contributes to the development of intelligence because all the possible causal factors are closely connected with each other, and all lead to changes that are in the same direction. The list of the possible causal factors ranges from improved nutrition and increasing years of education to an increase in the complexity of life, and even to the spread of interactive video games. (For extensive discussions of what environmental factors might be at work in raising IQ scores, see Neisser, 1998).

IQ Performance and the Nature of Testing

At the present time, no responsible scholar believes that the variation in intelligence-test scores from person to person can be attributed entirely to either environmental or genetic factors As we noted in Chapter 2, a number of large-scale studies report significant heritability of IQ test performance. At the same time, even those who believe that genetic variation plays a major role in variations in IQ readily acknowledge a significant role for the environment (Ceci & Hembrooke, 1995; Mackintosh, 1998). Those who claim that genetic heritage makes a large contribution to academic success agree that all behavior, including performance on IQ tests and in school, is an aspect of a person's phenotype (that is, one's observable characteristics) and that the phenotype arises from the joint action of the genotype (the set of genes one inherits) and the environment.

As we pointed out in Chapter 2, the attempt to tease apart the specific gene–environment interactions that shape human beings is especially difficult in relation to traits, like intelligence, that are polygenic—that is, traits that are shaped by several or many genes acting in combination in a given set of environmental conditions. Thus, even when it has been possible to estimate the genetic contribution to a trait, little can be said about precisely which genes are interacting with the environment in what way. Efforts to separate the various influences of nature and nurture on the phenotype are further complicated by the fact that parents contribute both to their children's genetic constitution and to the environment in which their children grow up. And then there is the final knot in the parsing of gene-environment interaction: in response to both genetic and environmental influences, children actively shape their own environments.

Attempts to understand how genetic and environmental factors combine to create the phenotypic behavior called "intelligence" face another, even greater difficulty. As we noted earlier, psychologists disagree profoundly about what, precisely, they are measuring when they administer an intelligence test. All they can say with any confidence is that these tests predict later school performance to a moderate degree. (The typical correlation between test performance and school performance is .50 [Neisser et al., 1996]). We can understand this problem better if we compare the gene–environment interactions that might determine intelligence with those that determine height.

To determine how environmental variation influences height, we might study sets of monozygotic (identical) and heterozygotic (fraternal) twins. Suppose that the twins to be studied were all born in Minnesota. Suppose further that some of the twins were separated, with one member of each pair being sent to live among the !Kung of the Kalahari Desert. The environments of Minnesota and the Kalahari Desert do not represent the most extreme variations compatible with human life, but they are sufficiently different in climate, diet, daily activities, and other relevant factors to represent a plausible test of the relative importance of genetic and environmental contributions to height.

"You can't build a hut, you don't know how to find edible roots and you know nothing about predicting the weather. In other words, you do terribly *on our IQ test."*

If, within this environmental range, genetic factors dominate the expression of the phenotype (measured height), then we would expect two facts to emerge:

- The heights of identical twins should be roughly as much alike when the twins are raised far apart as when they are raised in the same family.
- The similarity between the heights of identical twins should be greater than the similarity between the heights of fraternal twins. In fact, the similarity of the heights of identical twins raised in very different environments might be greater than that of fraternal twins raised in the same environment.

Note that whether the children are in Minnesota or in the Kalahari Desert, we can be pretty confident about our measure of height. Whether we use a yardstick or a metric scale, we have a valid standard for measuring the twins' heights, regardless of the context in which we use it.

At first glance, IQ tests may appear to be standard measures logically similar to a yardstick. But this appearance is an illusion. Precisely because intelligence tests derive their validity from their correlation with academic achievement, they are rooted in the schooled society in which they are developed and bound to the graphic systems of representation that are central to all schooling. But these modes of representation are generally absent in nonliterate societies. To be administered to a !Kung child, every existing intelligence test would thus require some modification—and not just translation from English to !Kung. If, for example, one of the test questions asks how many fingers are on two hands, the testers might assume that the test could be adapted to !Kung with only minimal modification—but that assumption would be wrong. The number system used by the !Kung is not the same as that used by Minnesotans, and it plays a different role in their lives. In !Kung society, the relative importance of knowing the number of fingers on a hand is less important than knowing how to tie knots with those fingers.

When it comes to the tests that require interpretation of pictures or some form of written answer, even more serious difficulties arise. The !Kung have no tradition of either drawing or writing, and research with nonliterate peoples in several parts of the world (Segall et al., 1997) and with young children in the United States (Pick, 1997) shows that people without such experience do not automatically interpret two-dimensional pictures of objects as they would the objects themselves. For them, interpreting the pictures requires additional mental work. As a result, tests that used pictures or required copying figures graphically would be inappropriate, as would any tests that depended on the ability to read. We thus cannot assume that an IQ test is like a yardstick, yielding equivalent measures in all cultural environments.

Various attempts have been made to create "culture-free" tests, but no generally satisfactory solution has yet been found: all tests of intelligence draw on a background of learning that is culture-specific (Cattell, 1949; Davis, 1948). (More recent attempts to deal with the difficulties of comparing intelligence across racial and cultural lines are described in Irvine & Berry, 1987, and Neisser et al., 1996.)

The fact that intelligence cannot be tested independently of the culture that gives rise to the test greatly limits the conclusions that can be drawn from IQ testing in different social and cultural groups. A number of studies have used comparisons of identical and fraternal twins to distinguish genetic from environmental contributions to intelligence, but those studies suffer an important limitation. According to the logic of twin studies, the twins' environments must differ enough for it to be possible to detect their differential contributions with the test. But if the environmental variation is very great, as in the case of a child transported from Minnesota to the Kalahari Desert, both twins' intelligence cannot be validly measured by the same test.

Despite these difficulties, a large literature has grown up around studies of twins' IQ test performance, along with studies of children of interracial marriages and of children adopted across racial and ethnic lines (reviewed in Mackintosh, 1998). Controversy continues to attend this work, but the following conclusions appear to be the most defensible.

1. Some part of individual differences in performance on IQ tests is attributable to inheritance. The degree of heritability is in dispute: some investigators claim that it is very high (Herrnstein & Murray, 1994); some claim that it is very low or indeterminate (Bronfenbrenner & Ceci, 1993). One influential summary estimates that perhaps 50 percent of the variation in test performance within population groups is controlled by genetic factors (Plomin et al., 1997).
2. There are significant differences among ethnic groups in their average IQ scores. Americans of European origin score about 15 points higher than African Americans, while Asian Americans score a few points higher than European Americans. Other ethnic groups in the United States, such as Native Americans and Hispanics, score at some intermediate level between African Americans and European Americans (Herrnstein & Murray, 1994; Mackintosh, 1998).
3. There is no evidence that the average difference in scores among ethnic groups in the United States is the result of inherited differences in intelligence, however defined.

At first glance, the first two facts may appear to conflict with the third: if inheritance is responsible for a part of the differences between individuals in tested intelligence, and if there are differences between groups in tested intelligence, why wouldn't it be reasonable to conclude that the source of the differences among groups is the same as the source of the differences among individuals?

There are two answers to this question, one logical and the other empirical. The logical answer was provided by Richard Lewontin (1976). It can be illustrated by an example from plant genetics (see Figure 13.12). Suppose that a farmer has two fields, one fertile and the other depleted of nutrients. He randomly takes corn seed from a bag containing several genetic varieties and plants them in the two fields. He cares for them equally. When the plants have reached maturity, he will discover that in each field some plants have grown taller than others. Since all the plants within a given field experienced roughly the same environment, their variation can be attributed to genetic factors. But the farmer will also discover variation between the fields: the plants grown in the fertile field will, on average, be taller than the plants grown in the nutrient-poor field. The explanation for this average difference in the heights of the plants lies in their environments, even though the degrees of heritability in the two fields may be equal.

This same argument applies to variations in test performance between ethnic and racial groups. Even though the heritability of intelligence within ethnic or racial groups may be the same, the average difference in performance between groups may still be caused not by their genetic endowment but by differences in the environments in which the children have been raised.

Lewontin's example also illustrates another important point about heritability that applies equally to IQ. As pointed out in Chapter 2, heritability is a population statistic: it applies to groups, not to individuals. If the heritability statistic for height in a field of corn or a set of IQ scores is .50, it does not mean that 50 percent of the height of each corn plant or each IQ score is determined by genetic factors. It means, rather, that 50 percent of the variation in height in the entire field of corn or of the variation in scores in the entire set of IQ scores can be traced to genetic differences. The other 50 percent of the variation must somehow be explained in terms of environmental factors.

FIGURE 13.12
The difference in the heights of the plants in each box reflects genetic variations in the seeds planted in it. The difference between the average heights of the plants in the two boxes is best explained by the quality of the soil, an environmental factor. Differences in IQ test scores of human groups are explained by the same principle. (Adapted from Gleitman, 1963.)

Suggestive evidence concerning environmental factors that account for ethnic, racial, and class differences in tested IQ comes from a study of ethnicity and IQ among a large sample of 5-year-old African American and European American low-birth-weight premature children, most of whom were from relatively poor families (Brooks-Gunn et al., 1996). The researchers studied these children from birth, and in addition to giving the children IQ tests when they were 5 years old, they collected data on neighborhood and family poverty, the social structure of the families, maternal characteristics such as education and IQ, and the degree of cognitive stimulation in the home environment. In line with prior research, the African American children's IQ scores were significantly lower than the scores for the white children (85 versus 103). When adjustments were made for ethnic-group differences in poverty, however, the difference in IQ score was reduced by over half. When the differences in the cognitive stimulation provided in the home environment were also controlled for statistically, the ethnic differential in IQ was reduced by another 28 percent. As the authors note, these results do not imply that heredity has no role in IQ, because they are not based on twin studies that allow estimates of heritability. They do show clearly, however, that when socioeconomic differences in the lives of African American and European American children are taken into account, IQ differences between the groups are all but eliminated.

PERSONAL AND SOCIAL BARRIERS TO SCHOOL SUCCESS

Evidence for strong family and community influences on children's school success confirms Binet and Simon's declaration that there is more to school success than can be captured by an intelligence test. In the following sections, we examine different factors related to the lack of school success among children whose tested intellectual aptitude is in the normal range. Some of these factors appear to be clearly related to the propensities of individual children; others implicate social factors.

Specific Learning Disabilities

Specific learning disabilities is a term used to refer to the academic difficulties of children who fare poorly in school despite normal IQ test performance. The U.S. government defines specific learning disabilities as follows:

> Children with special learning disabilities exhibit a disorder in one or more of the basic psychological processes involved in understanding or in using spoken or written language. These may be manifested in disorders of listening, thinking, talking, reading, writing, spelling, or arithmetic. They include conditions which have been referred to as perceptual handicaps, brain injury, minimal brain dysfunction, dyslexia, developmental aphasia, etc. They do not include learning problems which are due primarily to visual, hearing, or motor handicaps, to mental retardation, emotional disturbance, or to environmental disadvantage (U.S. Office of Education, 1977).

Identifying children with learning disabilities presents special challenges to developmentalists. Unlike physical disabilities such as blindness or deafness, specific learning disabilities are not readily apparent until children enter school. Even then, it is sometimes impossible to identify children with specific learning disabilities until they begin to use graphic symbols as a tool of communication.

Even greater difficulties in identifying learning-disabled children are reflected in the official definition of learning disability. There are so many factors included in the list of identifying criteria! What, for example, distinguishes a child who has a disorder of "listening, thinking, talking, reading, writing, spelling, or arithmetic" from a child who is retarded? How do we know if a specific disorder arises from features of the brain or the conse-

specific learning disabilities A term used to refer to the academic difficulties of children who fare poorly in school despite having normal intelligence.

quences of living in a "disadvantaged environment"? Disputes over how best to isolate the critical criteria for specific learning disabilities have made it difficult to estimate the number of children who suffer from them (Stanovich & Stanovich, 1996; Wong, 1996).

The most widely used method to distinguish children with a specific learning disability from their classmates is to analyze their performance on both an intelligence test and on an academic-achievement test that covers many parts of the curriculum. According to this approach, to qualify as *specifically* learning-disabled (and not retarded), a child should have an overall IQ test score in the normal range but a large discrepancy between different parts of the test (for example, a high score on a subtest that taps verbal ability but low scores on subtests that tap quantitative ability). The profile of the child's academic performance should correspond to the pattern in the IQ test. That is, we would expect a child with low verbal ability and high quantitative ability to be able to learn arithmetic normally but to have difficulty learning to read. This pattern of performance, called *dyslexia,* is the most frequent form of specific learning disability. Other children display a pattern of performance called *dyscalculia,* in which verbal IQ is high and quantitative IQ is low. Correspondingly, their ability to read is normal but they have great difficulty learning arithmetic. Yet another pattern characterizes *dysgraphia,* or special difficulties in learning to write, and so on. We focus our discussion on dyslexia, which is the most frequently encountered specific learning disability and the one about which the most is known.

Children who are considered dyslexic may have difficulty reading for several different reasons (Siegel, 1993, 1998). Among the primary reasons is difficulty in phonological processing. As we saw earlier, phonological awareness—the ability to understand the rules that relate graphic symbols of the writing system (graphemes) to phonemes—is important for learning to read an alphabetic language (p. 510). As might be suspected, severe delays in the development of phonological processing skills is one of the key indicators of dyslexia (Hulme & Joshi, 1998).

The leading test of phonological processing skills employs *pseudowords,* pronounceable combinations of letters that are not real words but can be read by following the rules for converting graphemes into phonemes. "Shum," "laip," and "cigbet" are all pseudowords. Even though they are not real words (and hence their pronunciation could not have been learned before the experiment), these letter combinations can be read by anyone who knows the rules for decoding English words.

To demonstrate the link between deficient phonological processing and dyslexia, Linda Siegel and Ellen Ryan studied the ability to read pseudowords in normal and disabled readers between 7 and 14 years of age (Siegel & Ryan, 1988). By 9 years of age, the normal readers were quite proficient in reading the pseudowords, but 14-year-old disabled readers could perform the pseudoword task no better than normal readers who were 7 years old. Even when disabled readers and normal readers were matched for reading level on a standardized test (and hence the disabled readers were considerably older than the normal readers), the disabled readers performed significantly more poorly when asked to read pseudowords.

The dominant theories about the causes of dyslexia assume that the difficulties arise because of anomalies in brain development, but there is still great uncertainty about how to link specific reading difficulties to specific abnormalities in specific areas of the brain. One promising line of research suggests that the auditory cortex is involved in the problem (Miller & Tallal, 1995; Tallal et al., 1993). Paula Tallal and her colleagues discovered this possibility when they studied children who were experiencing difficulty in acquiring a first language. The children seemed to be unable to process very brief components of auditory information presented to them in rapid succession. Tallal

academic motivation The ability to try hard and persist at school tasks in the face of difficulties.

and her colleagues began one experiment by asking a group of language-impaired children and a group of normal children to judge whether two tones, presented one right after the other, were the same or different. When the interval between the tones was half a second or more, the children in both groups almost always judged correctly; but whenever the interval was less than half a second, the performance of the language-impaired children plummeted.

Next, these researchers demonstrated that the language-impaired children had the same difficulty with the phonemes of spoken language and, in fact, with any rapid sequence of stimuli in any sensory modality. They also reported research from magnetic resonance imaging (MRI) showing that language-impaired children have fewer cells in areas of the brain that support language.

Tallal and her colleagues found that dyslexic children could be divided into two groups—those who showed general delays in the development of oral language and those who did not. It appears very likely that the reason for the reading difficulties of the children with oral-language impairment is an inability to process critical information rapidly enough. The reasons for the difficulties of the dyslexic children who do not have an oral-language impairment remain uncertain.

Remedial programs have been designed both for dyslexic children who have an oral-language deficit and for those who do not. For children whose language development is delayed, Tallal has created computer games that provide rich practice in making accurate discriminations between very brief, rapidly changing sounds. With as few as 16 hours of such therapy, children learned to recognize brief and rapidly changing speech sounds (Merzinich et al., 1996; Tallal et al, 1998). Remedial programs for dyslexic children whose oral language is not delayed generally focus on fostering phonemic awareness by using rhyming and word-game techniques, such as those described on p. 510, which have been shown to promote reading acquisition.

This student seems to be the personification of academic motivation: if she happens to give an incorrect answer this time, she won't give up and will likely work harder to get it right the next time.

Motivation to Learn

As we noted earlier, a distinctive aspect of formal education is that children are expected to pay attention and to try hard even though the material they are asked to learn may be difficult for them to master and hold little interest for them. They must also learn to cope with the fact that they will not always be successful in their schoolwork. In such circumstances, a significant proportion of children lose their **academic motivation**—the ability to try hard and persist at school tasks in the face of difficulties.

Over a period of many years, Carol Dweck and her colleagues have been studying the question of why some children are motivated to try hard in school in the face of difficulties and even failure, while others stop trying as soon as they encounter difficulty (Dweck, 1999; Heyman & Dweck, 1998). Dweck and her co-workers have hypothesized two patterns of motivation that can be observed in early childhood and become especially prominent once children enter school, where their failures and successes are visible to their classmates.

According to this hypothesis, some children develop a motivational pattern that these researchers refer to as a *mastery orientation*. Even if these children have just done poorly or failed at a task, they remain optimistic and tell themselves, "I can do it if I try harder next time." As a result of this kind of thinking, they tend to persist in the face of difficulties and to look for challenges similar to those they are struggling with. Over time, this kind of motivational pattern allows these children to improve their academic performance. By contrast, other children develop a *helpless* motivational pattern. When they fail at a task, they tell themselves, "I can't do that," and they give up trying altogether. When they encounter similar tasks in the future, they tend to avoid them. This helpless orientation toward difficulty and failure lowers children's chances of achieving academic success.

Dweck tested her hypotheses by presenting several jigsaw puzzles to 4- and 5-year-old children. Unknown to the children, only one of the puzzles actually could be completed. Some of the children did not become upset when they failed at the impossible puzzles and took the task as a challenge, showing a mastery motivational pattern; others became upset and gave up, showing the helpless pattern, just as Dweck had predicted. When these same children were invited back to play with the puzzles at a later time, those who did not persist on the impossible puzzles wanted to play only with the puzzle they had successfully completed, while the more mastery-oriented children wanted to try again to solve the puzzles that had stumped them (Dweck, 1991; Smiley & Dweck, 1994).

It might be thought that more able students would be the ones who typically display the mastery-oriented pattern and that less able students would be the ones who readily give up in the face of difficulty and avoid challenges. Yet Dweck and her colleagues found that these two patterns were *not* related to children's IQ scores or their academic achievement. She reports that many able students give up in the face of difficulty and many weaker students show a mastery orientation (Dweck, 1999; Licht & Dweck, 1984).

Around the age of 12, when children make the transition from elementary to middle school, the two motivational patterns begin to relate to school success. Dweck attributes this effect not only to an intensification of the demands that are made on children as they move from elementary school to junior high school but also to the increased complexity in children's thinking about concepts such as intelligence, effort, and success. At about 12 years of age, North American children begin to articulate theories about what it means to "be intelligent." Some children have an *entity* model of intelligence. They see intelligence as a fixed quality that each person has a certain amount of. Other children, by contrast, have an *incremental* model of intelligence. They see intelligence as something that can grow as one learns and has new experiences.

Middle-school children's theories about intelligence also include ideas about how effort is related to outcome. Some children believe that academic success depends primarily on ability, which they believe to be a fixed category; others believe that academic success depends on effort, and that expending effort can lead to increased intelligence.

Dweck has found that children who develop the helpless pattern generally hold an entity view of intelligence. They believe that they fail because they lack ability and that nothing they can do will change this. Because they view intelligence as a fixed entity, they try to avoid situations that put them at risk for failure and feel hopeless when they are confronted with challenging tasks. Children who develop a mastery-orientation pattern adopt precisely the opposite way of interpreting challenging situations because they view intelligence as incremental. They believe that if they apply themselves, and try hard enough, they will succeed and become more intelligent. When these children fail, their response is to try harder the next time. As children encounter the more challenging environment of middle school, their particular ways of interpreting and responding to failure cause notable achievement gaps between students who adopt one or the other of the two motivational patterns.

Findings such as these challenge developmentalists to devise ways to assist children who develop a helpless motivational pattern. One approach has been to train teachers to provide feedback to students in ways that foster a mastery orientation. Another has been to retrain the children themselves so that they attribute their failures to a lack of effort rather than a lack of ability (Dweck, 1999).

The cultural emphasis on interdependence in Japan is reflected and reinforced in Japanese classrooms, which, far more than their U.S. counterparts, stress full group participation and adjust the pace of instruction to accommodate the abilities of the class as a whole. Some researchers believe that, in the United States, children whose home culture is interdependence-oriented may be at a disadvantage in classrooms that promote independence and academic competition.

Mismatches between Home and School Cultures

Each of the factors discussed so far applies to the school achievement of children from all family backgrounds. We now shift our focus away from universal psychological processes "in the child" to cultural and economic circumstances that structure the child's experience of schooling. A number of general cultural factors have been identified, some focusing on broad cultural patterns, some focused on language, and some focused at the junction between language and culture as they intertwine in everyday interactions. (For a broad cross-national look at schooling, see Box 13.2.)

Cultural Styles A number of scholars have proposed that every culture can be described in terms of its own particular world view, a dominant way of thinking about and relating to the world that arises from a people's common historical experience (Greenfield & Cocking, 1994; Kagitçabasi, 1997). One such description places cultures on a continuum in terms of their emphasis on the importance of the individual versus the group. Some cultures, like the dominant culture in the United States, for example, emphasize *independence* and the importance of the individual, while others, like Japanese culture, for example, place more emphasis on *interdependence* and the importance of the individual's relations to others.

Patricia Greenfield and her colleagues have proposed that the cultural practices of standard American classrooms favor children who come from home cultures that emphasize independence, with the goal of socializing children to become autonomous individuals who enter into social relations by personal choice (an individualistic orientation). Correspondingly, they believe that the standard culture of American schools represents a disadvantage to children from cultures that emphasize *interdependence,* with the goal of socializing children to become adults who place a strong value on social networks, especially the family, and who downplay personal achievement (a collectivist orientation). (Table 13.4 summarizes the differences between independent and interdependent cultural models.) According to Greenfield and her colleagues, in the classroom, children from interdependence-oriented homes are not likely to respond well to being singled out for praise or criticism in front of the other children, and they may engage in helping behaviors that teachers interpret as cheating.

Other researchers have found that even if children come from families that adopt an interdependent cultural model that conflicts with the cultural norms of the classroom, the family can play a strong positive role in the success of their children's schooling. One example involves the children of

TABLE 13.4 CULTURAL STYLES: INDEPENDENT (INDIVIDUALIST) VERSUS INTERDEPENDENT (COLLECTIVIST)

Individualist	Collectivist
Emotional detachment from in-group	Self-defined in in-group terms
Personal goals have primacy over in-group goals	Behavior regulated by in-group norms
Behavior regulated by attitudes and cost-benefit analysis	Hierarchy and harmony within in-group
Confrontation is OK	In-group is seen as homogeneous
	Strong in-group–out-group distinctions

Source: Triandis et al., 1990.

refugees who fled to the United States from Vietnam, Cambodia, and Laos during the 1970s and 1980s. These children, whose home cultures are characterized by an interdependent cultural model, have been conspicuously successful in educational pursuits (Caplan et al., 1989). Although they had lost from one to three years of formal education in refugee camps, and most were unable to speak English when they entered school in the United States, eight out of ten students surveyed had a B average or better within 3 to 6 years. Almost half received A's in mathematics. These achievements are all the more noteworthy because they were attained in schools in low-income, inner-city areas traditionally associated with fewer resources and less motivated, more disruptive students.

In trying to account for the spectacular success of these immigrants, Nathan Caplan and his colleagues (1989) found the parents' involvement with their children to be crucial. Almost half of the parents surveyed said that they read to their children, many in their native language. Apparently, the parents' knowledge of English had less effect on their children's school performance than did the emotional associations of being read to and the cultural wisdom they shared as they read the stories. The parents demonstrated their commitment to education not only by owning books and reading to their children but also by requiring their children to do extensive homework. Parents reported that their children devoted an average of almost 3 hours of every weekday evening to homework, twice the average for native-born American children.

The Structures and Purposes of Language Use Even when people speak the same language, or a dialect of the same language, it does not mean that they use their language in the same way. Language is used in schools in rather distinctive ways, as we have seen. Many of the ways children experience oral and written language in the home differ not only from language practices at school but from other homes within the same community.

Shirley Heath (1983) worked in and studied three populations over a period of years in order to gain insight into how oral and written language used in the home differs from that associated with school success. The populations she studied, all from the same geographical locale, included the families of a group of European American schoolteachers, a group of European American textile workers, and a group of African Americans engaged in farming and textile jobs. Conducting observations both in people's homes and in their children's classrooms, Heath found that the families of European American teachers experienced the least mismatch with the school. As we have already seen, "instructional discourse" involving known-answer questions is a prominent feature of classrooms, and Heath found that it also appeared in about half of the conversations she recorded in the teachers' homes. In addition, the teachers involved their children in labeling objects, naming letters, and reading. When reading with their children, they went well beyond the text itself to make clear the relationships between what was in the book and other experiences the child might have had or might have in the future. In a sense, the teachers were being teachers at home as well as at school. As a result, their children did well in school.

The families of European American textile workers, like the teachers, gave their children practice in naming the letters of the alphabet, labeling objects, and learning to answer such questions as "What is that?" They also taught them to listen attentively while a story was being read. But, unlike the teachers, these parents encouraged their children to look for the moral of the stories they were read and they discouraged them from imaginatively linking the stories to life. Children from these working-class European American homes generally did well in the early grades of school when their habits of focusing on the literal meaning of a text fit the task, but in the higher grades,

Research has shown that parents' involvement in their children's education, including reading to them regularly and discussing what is being read, can contribute signifcantly to their schoolchildren's achievement.

BOX 13.2

SCHOOLING IN THREE CULTURES

Typical classrooms and school curricula appear very similar whether they are found in crowded cities such as New York and Tokyo or rural villages in West Africa and Australia. Yet many studies of classroom life and academic performance in different societies reveal that despite surface similarities, both the process and the products of schooling vary markedly from one culture to the next (Serpell & Hatano, 1997).

In the classrooms of rural Liberia, for example, children are taught basic reading, writing, and arithmetic through rote instruction (Cole et al., 1971). A favorite method used by Liberian teachers is to have the entire class recite lessons in unison, with little attention devoted to the meaning of the recitation. When John Gay and Michael Cole (1967) asked a Liberian student questions about arithmetic, he launched into a singsong patter ("La lala lala, la lala lala, la lala lala"). Asked what he was doing, he answered that he was adding numbers, but that so far he had learned only the tune, not the words. Not surprisingly, the academic achievement of the typical Liberian child is low by U.S. standards.

But the achievement of American schoolchildren is itself low in comparison with that of children in many other industrialized societies (TIMSS, 1997). This finding has spurred attempts to identify the factors responsible for variations in children's achievement from one society to the next. A series of studies initiated by Harold Stevenson has provided a good deal of insight into the ways in which cultural differences in elementary school education lead to variations in children's performance (Lee, 1996; Stevenson & Stigler, 1992; Stigler & Perry, 1990). These studies focused on classrooms in three countries: the United States, Japan, and Taiwan.

The accompanying diagrams provide a capsule look at schoolchildren's mathematical performance in the three societies on three tests of mathematical achievement: computational skill, word problems, and conceptual knowledge of mathematics. With the single exception of the test of conceptual understanding in the first grade, American children performed far below the level of both Asian groups. As might be expected, this evidence of marked national differences in the development of mathematical thinking sparked a debate about their causes. Richard Lynn (1982) argued, on the basis of comparative performance on IQ tests, that Japanese children enjoy a genetic superiority in intelligence. Careful evaluations of this hypothesis, however, have shown it to be false. Large comparative studies demonstrating differences in mathematics performance revealed no corresponding differences in intelligence scores (Stevenson et al., 1985).

Looking for other factors to explain the differences between Asian and American math-test scores, Stevenson and his colleagues focused on the process of instruction in the classroom. They found that the two factors in which American and Asian schooling differed the most were the amount of time spent in the teaching and learning of mathematics and the social organization of classroom interactions.

The Asian children in both the first and fifth grades attended school more days each year than did the American children (240 days vs. 180). At the fifth-grade level, Japanese children went to school 44 hours a week, Chinese students, 37 hours a week, and American children, 30 hours a week. On each school day the two Asian groups spent as much time on mathematics as they did on reading and writing, but the American group spent almost three times as much on language arts. As James Stigler and Michelle Perry (1990:336) note, the disparity in the sheer number of hours spent on mathematics lessons was large enough to "go a long way toward explaining the differences in mathematics achievement."

However, the differences in the Asian and American approaches to education are not restricted simply to gross amounts of time spent on mathematics: Asian classrooms are organized quite differently from American classrooms. By and large, classrooms in the two Asian countries are centrally organized, with the teacher instructing the whole class at once. The American classrooms are generally more decentralized; often the teacher devotes attention to one group at a time while the other children work independently at their seats. Two important differences in the quality of teacher–student interactions are correlated with these differences in classroom organization. First, American children spend a good deal of time being instructed by no one. This might not make much difference if the children were absorbed by their workbooks and truly working independently. But here another difference in students' behavior comes into play: American children do not use their independent study time well, spending almost half of it out of their seats or engaged in inappropriate behavior such as gossiping with friends or causing mischief. Asian children spend far more time attending to schoolwork than their American counterparts do.

There are also differences in the content of the lessons. First, the Japanese teachers devote twice as much instruction time to helping children reflect on and analyze mathematics problems as the Chinese and American teachers do. Second, both the Chinese and Japanese teachers are more likely than their American counterparts to have students use concrete manipulable objects in working out math problems and to provide a meaningful context for the mathematics problems they teach. Third, the Asian teachers stress the connections between problems encountered at different points in the lesson, or even between problems in one lesson and another, giving greater coherence to their teaching.

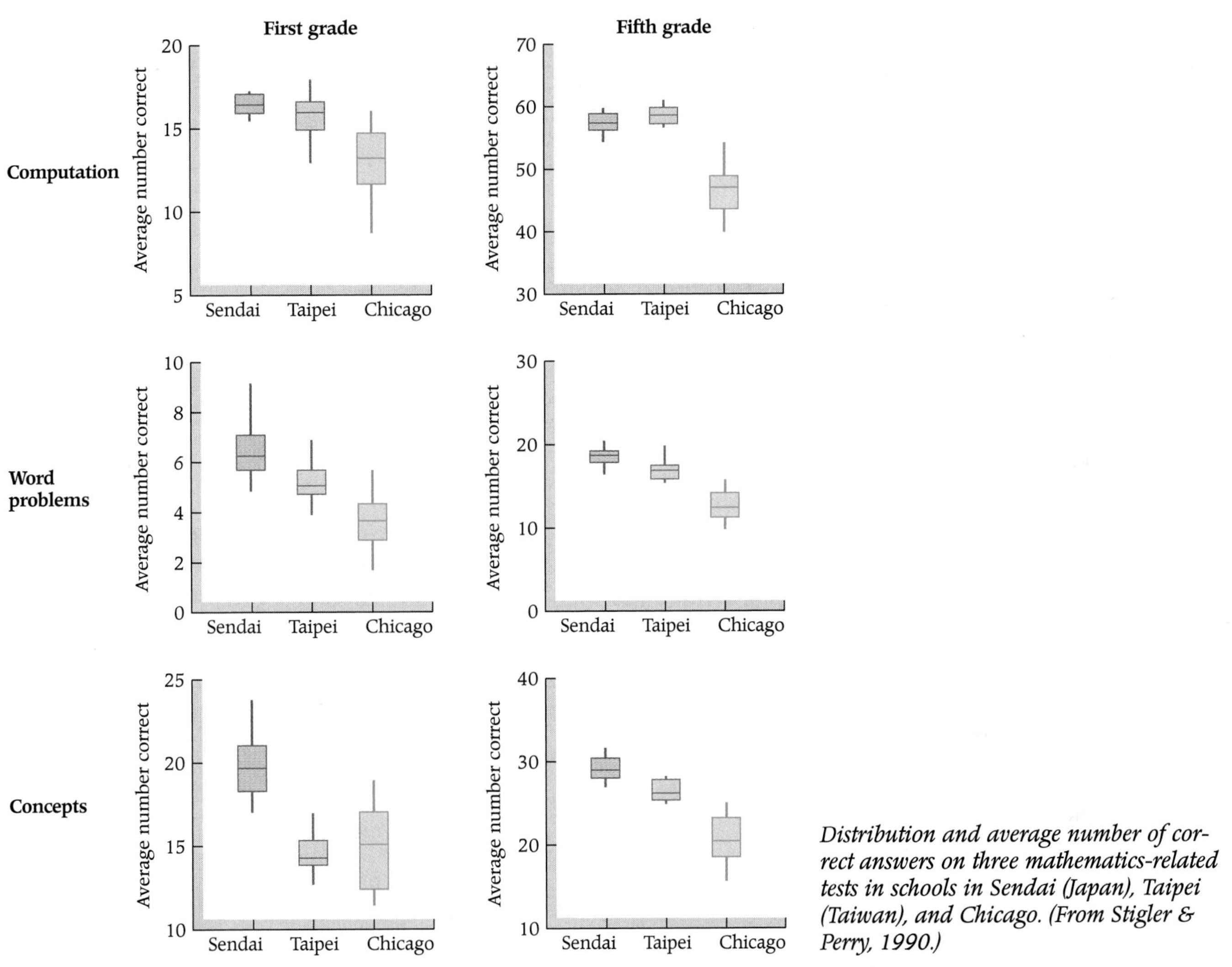

Distribution and average number of correct answers on three mathematics-related tests in schools in Sendai (Japan), Taipei (Taiwan), and Chicago. (From Stigler & Perry, 1990.)

An easy conclusion is that if American educators want children to match the performance of their Asian counterparts, all they need to do is lengthen the school year and copy Asian classroom teaching methods. However, Giyoo Hatano and Keiko Inagaki believe that this "importation" approach is bound to fail because the effectiveness of the Japanese system does not rest on any one method (Hatano & Inagaki, 1996). Rather, the success results from the way in which Japanese classrooms build upon deep traditions in Japanese culture that have become a part of their educational practices over many decades. Instead of attempting to "import" one or another specific teaching method, Hatano and Inagaki argue, "it is necessary to 'translate' [Japanese] technologies and beliefs so that they can be harmonious with indigenous practices" (1996:101–102).

Stigler and Perry (1990) sound a similar note. They point out that although their research suggests that instruction can be organized so that children learn mathematics at a higher level than they are currently doing in American schools, it does not indicate how to draw on American cultural traditions to achieve this result. Quoting the sociologist Merry White (1987), they remind us that cross-cultural research does not provide a blueprint for improving the education of children. Rather, it provides a mirror that sharpens awareness of our own cultural practices and provides some hints about how they might be changed to make teaching and learning more effective.

where it becomes necessary to draw novel inferences from complex texts, their performance fell. Overall, these children did not do well in school.

A third pattern of language use was characteristic in the homes of the African American children. These children were rarely asked known-answer questions about some fact ("What color is your jacket?"). Rather, adults most often asked children questions that encouraged them to think about similarities across situations related to the children's own experience (" Do you think you can get along with your cousin on this visit?"). Such questions often served as the pretext for discussing some interesting event and helped children think about their shifting roles and responsibilities in different situations. Heath also documented many inventive uses of language in teasing and storytelling. But the children never heard language used in the ways expected of them at school, and they, too, generally did not perform well. Similar findings have been reported for Latino children (Vasquez et al., 1994).

These patterns are perfectly understandable in terms of local cultural practices. At the same time, it is the goal of teachers to be successful with all children. So the question becomes one of how to design educational interventions to make it possible for everyone to learn effectively.

Schooling in a Second Language

We noted above that for some parts of the U.S. population, especially recent immigrants, school-going children may have little or no command of the local language of official life, including the language of the school. Unless something is done quickly to solve the problems these children face because they cannot speak English, their life chances are reduced through school failure.

In a landmark decision in 1974, the U.S. Supreme Court recognized the seriousness of this situation by declaring that children who arrive at school unable to speak or understand English must be given special help to deal with the challenges they face. According to the Court's ruling, such special help will be considered adequate only if it prevents children from being foreclosed from meaningful education (*Lau v. Nichols,* p. 26). Since the ruling, local school districts have spent a great deal of money trying to meet its requirements. This effort has been complicated by the fact that the Court did not specify what form the "special help" should take, leaving the matter up to the states and local school districts.

Further complicating efforts to develop English proficiency in non-English-speaking children and promote their scholastic achievement are sharp divisions of opinion regarding how these goals should be achieved (Krashen, 1996; Rossell & Baker, 1996). On one side of the debate are those who believe that children should be immersed in the English language—hearing and speaking English exclusively—so that they can quickly achieve the competence necessary to participate in all aspects of the curriculum. Educators who favor this view believe that time spent communicating in the child's native language only postpones the day when the child will be fluent in English. On the other side are those who believe that providing the children with a firm grounding in basic literacy and numeracy skills in the child's home language promotes later academic achievement in a broad variety of courses taught in English (see Augusta & Hakuta, 1998).

Research on this issue is clouded by the difficulty of conducting experiments in which ideal versions of the competing strategies can be pitted against each other. It is simply not possible to set up a true experiment, since it would require controlling the curricula and language policy of a group of schools and randomly assigning children to those schools. To test their hypotheses researchers have had to make do with "quasi-experiments" that use spontaneously occurring differences in language programs. For example, some school districts have adopted an English-only policy; other districts provide instruction to the children in their home language for 2 or 3 years before moving them to English-based instruction; and still others have made their schools bilingual, with everyone spending half their instruction in their home language—which is often Spanish—and half their instruction in English (Augusta & Hakuta, 1998; Cloud et al., 2000).

Comparisons of performance in these schools represent one way to test competing theories of how to arrange instruction. But conclusions from such tests are still open to doubt because they cannot guarantee that the programs being compared differ *only* in the variable being studied—the use of English-only versus home-language-first instruction, for example. Since the comparisons are often made across different schools in different parts of a town or even another town, the local schools may vary on such relevant characteristics as the social class of the students, the training and enthusiasm of the teachers, and the resources available for teaching. Such variations could be expected to have a significant impact on academic achievement no matter what language approach was being used.

As a result of these difficulties in evaluating competing theories of effective bilingual education, controversy remains. Christine Rossell and Keith Baker, for example, published a review of 72 studies comparing English-only programs against bilingual programs designed to ease children into full English use after 3 or 4 years (Rossell & Baker, 1996). They concluded that there is no evidence that bilingual programs are any better than simple immersion in English. This conclusion was immediately contested by Stephen Krashen (1996), who argued that when one considered only those studies that had adequate bases for comparison and reliable quantitative data, the evidence showed that bilingual programs are more effective than immersion programs. This same conclusion was reached by a panel of the National Research Council (Augusta & Hakuta, 1998).

Krashen (1996) based his conclusion on an extensive review of the literature, which suggested that four features lead to the creation of an effective environment for helping immigrant children to learn English:

1. Easy-to-understand lessons in English, using techniques that have been shown useful in teaching English as a second language
2. Teachers who have command of their subject matter and who can teach in the child's native language when appropriate
3. Literacy development in the child's native language
4. Continued development in the child's native language, for cognitive and economic advantages

As a starting point for effective bilingual education, this approach requires that teachers take seriously the child's cultural context as it is embodied in the language, values, and practices of his or her home.

An important factor not mentioned by Krashen is the need to give the process of acquiring the second language enough time. This point was demonstrated in a study by Lily Wong-Fillmore (1985), who found that although minority-language children generally become reasonably fluent in colloquial English within 2 or 3 years of starting school in the United States, they need as many as 4 to 5 years to master the language skills needed for academic success.

A major obstacle to successfully applying the lessons from the research on bilingual education is that there are far too few qualified bilingual teachers to teach the many languages represented by the school-aged population of the United States. In California, for example, English was a second language for 37 percent of the children (nearly 1.5 million) attending school in 1997, and in the lower grades, the percentage was considerably higher. If the current research is valid, such a situation certainly seems to call for bilingual instruction, but that solution is difficult to implement in some areas, because

BOX 13.3 TEACHERS' EXPECTATIONS AND SCHOOL SUCCESS

Most of you have spent more than a dozen years in classrooms and know from personal experience that teachers' attitudes toward students vary. Teachers expect some students to do better than others in mastering academic material. Research has shown that these attitudes and expectations influence students' performance in a variety of ways.

Perhaps the most famous, and certainly the most controversial, research on the effect of teachers' expectations was initiated in the 1960s by Robert Rosenthal and his colleagues (Rosenthal, 1987; Rosenthal & Rubin, 1978). These researchers found that a teacher's expectations about a child's academic ability may become a self-fulfilling prophecy, even when the expectations are groundless. That is, the teacher's expectations in themselves may lead to behavior that causes the expectations to be realized.

To demonstrate the power of teachers' expectations, Rosenthal and Lenore Jacobsen (1968) gave children in all six grades of an elementary school a test that, they told the teachers, would identify children who were likely to "bloom" intellectually during the coming year. After the testing, the researchers gave the teachers the names of those children who would supposedly show a spurt in intellectual development during the school year. In fact, the names of the predicted "bloomers" were chosen at random (with a few exceptions, to be described in due course).

At the end of the school year, the children were tested again. This time the researchers found that at the first- and second-grade levels there was in fact a difference between the "bloomers" and "nonbloomers": the children who had been randomly identified as likely candidates for rapid intellectual growth actually gained an average of 15 points on their IQ scores, while their classmates' IQ scores remained unchanged. In this study, the IQs of children in grades 3 through 6 did not change, but in a follow-up study Rosenthal and his colleagues found that older schoolchildren's performance on IQ tests could also be influenced by the teachers' expectations (Rosenthal et al., 1974). Since the children identified as those likely to bloom intellectually were chosen at random, Rosenthal and his colleagues concluded that teachers' expectations influence their own behavior and thus their students', making their teaching more effective with children they believe to be academically able.

A particularly provocative finding in Rosenthal and Jacobsen's study concerned race, ethnic, and class differences in academic performance. Teachers often have lower expectations regarding the academic performance of minority-group and poor children than they do regarding that of their white, middle-class counterparts (Minuchin & Shapiro, 1983). To test the possibility that these lowered expectations actually lower minority and poor children's academic performance, Rosenthal and Jacobsen included a group of poor Mexican-American children among those they identified as likely to bloom during the coming year. These children made particularly large gains in IQ test performance. In fact, the children whom the teachers identified as most "Mexican-looking" made the largest gains, perhaps because the teachers, recognizing that these students were the ones from whom they would ordinarily have expected the least, paid them all the more attention.

Such results immediately attracted the attention of researchers and the public at large. Hundreds of studies have since been conducted on the role of teachers' expectations in students' academic performance (Wineberg, 1987). Many school districts even have special training programs to ensure that their teachers are sensitive to the ways in which their expectations may negatively affect some children. However, despite general acceptance of the idea that teachers' expectations are a significant factor in children's academic performance, some psychologists and educators remain skeptical (Wineberg, 1987). One basis for doubt is that many studies fail to find any such effects. Why? When researchers attempted to find out by observing teachers and children in interaction in classrooms, they found that teachers differ in their approach to the children they expect little of. Some teachers ignore those children

the schools have to contend with several of the more than than 50 languages spoken by California schoolchildren.

Dealing Successfully with Diverse Student Populations

The evidence presented in this chapter should leave no doubt that schools are extremely important contexts of development in middle childhood. But they are also problematic contexts, which often fail to provide children with a strong foundation in the culturally valued skills they will need as adults.

The current demands for high levels of academic achievement for *all* children in an increasingly diverse student population have led many educators to explore new approaches to instruction at all levels—in individual lessons, in classrooms, in schools—and to create linkages between schools and homes in the local community. Some believe that children's academic performance can be improved simply by increasing the length of the school day and

and focus on the ones they consider more capable, but other teachers seem to give extra help and encouragement to those children (Good et al., 1973). This research also makes it clear that children are not passive recipients of teachers' expectations. Children influence those expectations by their own classroom behavior (Brophy, 1983).

Research by Carol Dweck and her colleagues (see also pp. 538–539) has shown one way in which the interplay between teachers' expectations and children's behavior may shape academic development. Dweck studied teachers' differing expectations for boys and girls. In general, girls are better behaved than boys during the elementary school years. Consequently, teachers expect boys to challenge classroom decorum and girls to support it. Dweck and her colleagues found that these differences in children's behavior and teachers' expectations led teachers to respond differently to boys and girls (Dweck & Bush, 1976; Dweck et al., 1978; Dweck & Goetz, 1978). Overall, teachers criticize boys more than girls. Often this criticism focuses on boys' lack of decorum, their failure to do their work neatly, or their inattentiveness. Their criticism of girls, by contrast, is likely to focus on ability and intellectual performance. At the same time, when teachers offer praise, its focus is likely to be girls' cooperative social behavior and boys' intellectual accomplishments.

These differences in teachers' expectations for boys and girls and in the kind of feedback they provide have been found to be related to the kinds of expectations that children form about their own behavior (Dweck & Elliott, 1983). When girls are told that they have failed, they usually believe that the teacher has correctly assessed their intellectual capacity, so they tend to stop trying. Boys interpret such criticism differently: they blame their poor performance on someone else, on their situation, or on bad luck and retain faith in their own ability to do better next time.

Evidence that children's school performance can be affected by teachers' expectations has led many schools to raise their standards for acceptable performance and to initiate programs like "math olympics" to encourage the ideal of academic excellence.

school year and by giving children more homework and academic work to do in their after-school hours. Others believe that instructional procedures must be improved if there is to be improvement in children's performance in school (Augusta & Hakuta, 1998). Whatever their particular emphasis, the most successful programs, each in its own way, draw on aspects of life and learning that the children understand and use at home. This approach provides a bridge from the child's everyday world to the increasingly abstract world of the school and its socially codified knowledge. Two influential studies illustrate the kinds of adjustments that have to be made to traditional classroom approaches for such programs to work.

An example of a minimal cultural adaptation that seemed to make a significant difference occurred in a classroom of students from the Odawa Indian tribe in Canada taught by an expert Odawa teacher (Erickson & Mohatt, 1982). On the surface, the teacher appeared to adhere to a recitation-script approach, talking for most of the lessons, asking many known-answer questions, and limiting the students' role to answering her questions. In fact, however, although the teacher engaged in recitation-script procedures, she did so in a special way consistent with the language use and cultural patterns employed in Odawa homes. When she was giving instruction, she organized students into small groups instead of rows, approximating the social organization of activities in the children's homes. She generally addressed the children as a group and did not single out individual children. Instead of saying "good" when she was giving the children feedback on their responses to her questions, she signaled her acceptance of students' answers by moving on to the next question. She never reprimanded students in public, but she did praise them in public, in accordance with Odawa norms against public criticism. This culture-sensitive way of implementing classroom lessons worked well.

A very different cultural adaptation of standard classroom lessons involved a successful reading program designed for low-income, traditionally underachieving, Hawaiian children (Au & Mason 1981). This program included instructional practices, classroom organization, and motivational management that were culturally congruent with native Hawaiian practices (Vogt et al., 1987). Teachers in this program had children work together in the classroom, allowing them to draw on familiar home-culture patterns of giving and seeking help from peers and siblings. Teachers did not praise the children simply for staying on task but instead praised or criticized the children for the quality of work done, again consciously modeling the cultural practices of the Hawaiian children's homes. The success of this program was demonstrated not only in higher reading-achievement scores but in greater student enthusiasm for, and engagement in, classroom activities.

These examples could be multiplied to encompass a wide variety of ethnic and social-class groups—wide enough to make a convincing case that it is possible to organize effective contexts for education by taking into account local variations in culture and social class (Tharp et al., 2000). At the same time, research is unanimous in showing that schools that provide a warm and friendly atmosphere combined with rigorous instruction, high expectations for success, and good communication with the home have the best chance of succeeding (Scheurich, 1998).

OUTSIDE OF SCHOOL

As important as schooling is to middle childhood, it is not the only extrafamilial context that influences children. There is also the new and important context of independent interactions with the peer group. On weekday afternoons and evenings, on weekends and holidays, children this age are likely to be found among their friends, engaged in activities of their own choosing. Some of these settings have an adult or two present, but in many cases, adults are not on the scene.

Participation in these peer groups provides a kind of preparation for adult life that is quite different from that organized by adults in classrooms and at home. At the same time, peer group experiences influence life at home and in school. Consequently, a full understanding of the nature of middle childhood requires investigation of peer contexts as well, so we turn to this important topic in Chapter 14.

SUMMARY

- School is a specialized socialization environment that is specific to certain societies and historical eras.

THE CONTEXTS IN WHICH SKILLS ARE TAUGHT

- Traditional hunter-gatherer and agricultural societies achieve the goals of education in the context of everyday activities. As societies become more complex, adults pay increasing attention to instructing children in the skills they will need as adults by organizing apprenticeships.
- Schooling arose coincident with the emergence of city-states as a means of training large numbers of scribes to keep the records on which complex societies depend.
- Formal education in schools differs from traditional training, such as apprenticeship, in the motives for learning as well as in the social relations, the social organization, and the medium of instruction.

LITERACY AND SCHOOLING IN MODERN TIMES

- Mastery of two basic symbol systems, written language and mathematics, is essential to the process of schooling.
- When schooling was extended to large segments of the population in industrialized countries in the nineteenth century, most students received "mass education," which focused on the basics of literacy and numeracy, while children of the economic and professional elites received a "liberal education," which included complex uses of literacy and numeracy.
- Reading an alphabetic language is a complex cognitive skill in which information the reader obtains by learning the correspondences between letters and sounds must be coordinated with higher-order information about the content of the text.
- Researchers are divided in their ideas about how reading should be taught.
    1. Those who favor the code-first approach believe that children should first be taught to decode fluently before concentrating instruction on comprehension.
    2. Those who favor the comprehension-first approach believe that from the outset decoding should be learned in the context of reading for meaning.
- Learning mathematics in school requires students to acquire and coordinate three kinds of knowledge:
    1. Conceptual knowledge, or the understanding of mathematical principles
    2. Procedural knowledge, or the ability to carry out sequences of actions to solve a problem
    3. Utilization knowledge, or the knowledge of when to apply particular procedures
- Theories of how best to teach both reading and mathematics vary between two extremes, one emphasizing the need for drill and practice, the other emphasizing the centrality of conceptual understanding. Most current teaching techniques attempt to balance drill with explanation.
- Classroom instruction occurs in settings characterized by specialized modes of social interaction and a special form of language use called instructional discourse.
    1. Traditional modes of classroom discourse follow a recitation script in which teachers ask known-answer questions and provide direct feedback on the basis of children's answers.

2. A great emphasis is placed on the use of correct linguistic forms in classroom discourse organized around a recitation script.
3. Alternative forms of classroom organization emphasize the role of small-group interaction and the use of tasks designed to be meaningful to the children.

THE COGNITIVE CONSEQUENCES OF SCHOOLING

- Research comparing the cognitive performances of schooled and unschooled children reveals that formal schooling in middle childhood enhances the development of certain cognitive skills, including logical problem solving, memory, and metacognition.
- There is no evidence that schooling enhances cognitive development in general.

APTITUDE FOR SCHOOLING

- Tests of aptitude for schooling first appeared when education was extended to the population at large. The earliest tests were designed to identify children who needed special support to succeed in school.
- Binet and Simon's key innovation in constructing their test of school aptitude was to sort test items according to the age at which children could typically cope with them, thus producing a scale of "mental age."
- The aptitude measure called IQ represents a child's mental age (as determined by the age at which average children answer each test item correctly) divided by chronological age, with the result multiplied by 100 (a number arbitrarily chosen to represent the average IQ): IQ = (MA/CA)100.
- IQ test scores have been found to be correlated significantly with later school success.
- An important unresolved question about intelligence tests is the degree to which the aptitudes they tap are general across all domains of human activity or are closely related to specialized activities, such as those involved in schooling and music.
- Persistent class, racial, and ethnic differences in IQ test performance have inspired fierce debates about whether such differences are the result of genetic or environmental factors.
- Modern research comparing the IQs of identical and fraternal twins indicates that IQ has a genetic component that accounts for perhaps 50 percent of the variation in test performance within groups.
- Large increases in IQ test performances of children around the world during the twentieth century indicates that average differences in IQ scores among groups are strongly influenced by environmental factors.

PERSONAL AND SOCIAL BARRIERS TO SCHOOL SUCCESS

- A variety of factors other than IQ have been shown to be related to school success.
  1. Some children who have normal tested intelligence are believed to suffer disabilities in school learning in areas such as reading and arithmetic.
  2. Children develop different responses to failure that help or hinder their learning and performance in school.

3. Children's school achievement is hindered when patterns of interaction and language use in the family do not match those of the school.
4. When mismatches are recognized, school curricula can be modified to take advantage of family interaction patterns.

➢ Schools with a strong academic emphasis, teachers skilled in classroom management, an emphasis on praise over punishment, and a welcoming attitude toward students all have positive effects on students' achievement in school.

KEY TERMS

academic motivation, p. 538
apprenticeship, p. 506
conceptual knowledge, p. 512
decoding, p. 509
education, p. 505
environmental hypothesis of intelligence, p. 531
initiation-reply-feedback sequence, p. 515
innatist hypothesis of intelligence, p. 531
instructional discourse, p. 515
intelligence quotient (IQ), p. 528
mental age (MA), p. 527
phonemic awareness, p. 509
procedural knowledge, p. 512
reciprocal teaching, p. 517
schooling, p. 507
school-cutoff strategy, p. 522
specific learning disabilities, p. 536
utilization knowledge, p. 512

THOUGHT QUESTIONS

1. When you look back over your own work and school experiences so far, what personal examples can you recall of the differences between learning in other contexts and learning in school?
2. What factors might give rise to the special language of schooling? What might account for the fact that aspects of this way of using language are also found in some homes?
3. Paraphrase Binet and Simon's contention (quoted on p. 527) that "life is not so much a conflict of intelligences as a combat of characters." How does this idea bear on disputes about the significance of IQ testing as a means of assessing cognitive development?
4. Suppose you were assigned the task of creating a culture-free intelligence test. How would you go about it? What major obstacles would you expect to encounter?
5. How might greater knowledge of children's home cultures be helpful in organizing effective classroom instruction?

CHAPTER 14

Social Development in Middle Childhood

We went home and when somebody said, "Where were you?" we said, "Out," and when somebody said, "What were you doing until this hour of the night," we said, as always, "Nothing."

But about this doing nothing: we swung on the swings. We went for walks. We lay on our backs in the backyards and chewed grass . . . and when we were done, he [my best friend] walked me home to my house, and when we got there I walked him back to his house, and then he—.

We watched things: we watched people build houses, we watched men fix cars, we watched each other patch bicycle tires with rubber bands . . . [we watched] our fathers playing cards, our mothers making jam, our sisters skipping rope, curling their hair. . . .

We sat in boxes; we sat under porches; we sat on roofs; we sat on limbs of trees.

We stood on boards over excavations; we stood on tops of piles of leaves; we stood under rain dripping from the eaves; we stood up to our ears in snow. We looked at things like knives . . . and grasshoppers and clouds and dogs and people.

We skipped and hopped and jumped. Not going anywhere—just skipping and hopping and jumping and galloping.

We sang and whittled and hummed and screamed.

What I mean, Jack, we did a lot of nothing.

Robert Paul Smith, *Where Did You Go? Out. What Did You Do? Nothing.*

Between the ages of 6 and 12, U.S. children typically spend more than 40 percent of their waking hours in the company of **peers,** children of their own age and status. This is twice the time they spent with peers during the preschool years, and it is accompanied by a corresponding decrease in time spent with parents (Zarbatany et al., 1990). In some of their peer interactions, children are brought together and supervised by adults, as in school, at church, or in organized sports. But sometimes they are together without direct adult oversight, often doing the kind of "nothing" that is referred to in the quotation that opens this chapter.

The opportunity to interact with peers without adult supervision affects children's behavior in two important ways. First, the *content* of peer activity is usually different. When adults preside over children's activities, some form of instruction or work is likely to be going on, whether it involves arithmetic homework, a piano lesson, or sliding into second base. When several children get together with no adults present, they will probably play a game or just "do nothing."

Second, the *forms of social control* in unsupervised peer activity are different. When children are under the watchful eyes of adults, either at home or in school, it is the adults who keep the peace and maintain social order. If a child takes an unfair share of ice cream or refuses to let another child on the swings, an adult is there to invoke society's rules ("Share and share alike"; "Everyone gets a turn") and to settle disputes. But when children are on their own in peer groups, they must establish authority and responsibility themselves. Sometimes the rule of "might makes right" prevails, as when an especially strong child dominates the group. However, authority is usually established through negotiation, compromise, and discussion, as well as conflict

peers Others of one's own age and status.

When children begin to play on their own, without adults being present to arbitrate disputes, they must learn the skills of negotiation and compromise for themselves. Sometimes the lessons are painful.

(Rubin et al., 1998). Authority within the group may also shift with the group's activities. A leader in making mischief on the playground may not be the leader in organizing an afternoon trip to the movies (Sherif & Sherif, 1956).

The increased time that children spend among their peers is both a cause and an effect of their development during middle childhood. Adults begin to allow their children to spend extensive time with friends because they recognize the children's greater ability to think and act for themselves. At the same time, the new experiences with peers challenge children to master new cognitive and social skills in order to hold on to their increased freedom of action (Rubin et al., 1998).

Children's sense of themselves and their relations with others also changes in middle childhood. As long as they spend their time primarily

These boys are playing in the ocean without any supervision by their parents, something that they would not have been allowed to do when they were younger.

among family members, their social roles and sense of self are more or less predefined. Their place in the social world is determined for them. When children spend more time among their peers, the sense of self they acquired in their families no longer suffices, and they must form new identities appropriate to the new contexts they inhabit (Harter, 1999). The child who seems fearless at home and who dominates her younger siblings may find that she needs to be more restrained on the playground with her peers.

Middle childhood also brings changes in the quality of children's relations with their parents. Parents can no longer successfully demand blind obedience from their children, nor can they easily just pick them up and remove them from danger or situations in which they are behaving badly. Parents can still monitor their children's whereabouts, but they must rely on their children's greater understanding of the consequences of their actions and on their desire to conform to adult standards to keep them out of harm's way and behaving appropriately. As a result, parents' socialization techniques become more indirect, and they increasingly have to rely on discussion and explanation to influence their children's behavior.

All of these changes are obviously of great interest to developmentalists. Unfortunately, current research methods cannot always do justice to the greatly increased diversity of experience that is so central during middle childhood. This limitation arises largely because, unlike younger children, school-age children are likely to behave differently with their peers when an adult observer appears on the scene than when they are playing on their own. Scientific knowledge about middle childhood is therefore fragmentary in several respects. We have extensive information about how children behave with peers in school and how they respond when researchers ask them to reason about hypothetical moral dilemmas, or to articulate their conceptions of friendship, or to solve a variety of intellectual puzzles. And we have experimental and observational findings on children in small-group interactions. But we have little systematic information about children's behavior in those settings where no adults are present and children are on their own.

To complement our discussion of school contexts in Chapter 13, in this chapter we will examine evidence about the social aspects of middle childhood chiefly through the lens of research on children's interactions in peer groups. Then we return to the question, raised in Chapters 12 and 13, of the ways in which middle childhood does and does not correspond to a distinctive stage of development.

GAMES AND GROUP REGULATION

The increasing prominence of peer groups among 6- to 12-year-olds raises a central question about middle childhood: How do children learn to regulate their social relations when adults are not present? The precise psychological mechanisms have not been identified with certainty, but it appears that one important arena for this development is game playing (Hughes, 1995; Nicolopoulou, 1993; Piaget, 1967).

GAMES AND RULES

Like 4- and 5-year-olds, children who have entered middle childhood engage in fantasy role play, with each child taking a part in an imaginary situation: cops chase robbers, shipwrecked families take up residence in tree houses, runaway children hide in secret forts (Singer & Singer, 1990). But in middle childhood, children also engage in a new form of play—games based on rules.

These games may vary widely from culture to culture. In West Africa, children divide into teams and challenge each other to remember the names

Games with rules are prominent in the lives of children during middle childhood.

of leaves gathered in the forest. In the United States, a children's game of mental challenges is more likely to take the form of Twenty Questions or Monopoly. But what these games all have in common are explicit rules that every player is expected to respect. In many children's games these rules can sometimes be formidably complex, as are, for example, the rules of what constitutes a "strike" in the game of baseball (Roopnarine et al., 1994). A strike in baseball occurs when a pitched ball is (a) swung at and missed; (b) delivered through the strike zone but not swung at; (c) hit foul but not caught (unless it is bunted when there are two strikes); (d) foul-tipped when there are two strikes and caught by the catcher. The ability to comprehend and behave in accordance with such complex sets of rules is a characteristic of middle childhood.

This is not to suggest that rules are totally absent from fantasy play in early childhood. When young children perform their fantasy roles, they typically follow implicit social rules. The pretend teacher tells the pretend students to sit quietly; the students do not tell the teacher what to do. In addition, young children use rules to negotiate the roles they adopt and to maintain the make-believe context: "Only girls are allowed to be Superwoman"; "Go away, Darth Vader, we're having a birthday party and spacemen are not allowed at birthday parties" (Paley, 1984).

However, at about the age of 7 or 8, rules become the essence of many games. The rules determine what roles are to be played and what one can and cannot do in playing those roles. Rules also enter differently into the content of the games of middle childhood. Whereas the rules in preschool fantasy play can change on a whim, the rules in the games characteristic of older children must be agreed upon ahead of time and consistently followed. Anyone who changes the rules without common consent is "cheating."

Rule-based games seem to require the same kinds of mental abilities that support the performance of the new tasks and responsibilities typically assigned to 6- and 7-year-olds (see Chapter 12). Children must be able to keep in mind the overall set of preestablished task requirements as they pursue the goals of the moment. At the same time, to be successful, they need to engage in social perspective taking, understanding the relation between the thoughts of the other players and their own actions ("If I move my checker to this square, she'll double-jump me").

Rule-based games have a different purpose than fantasy play. In fantasy play, the play's the thing. Satisfaction comes from exercising the imagination in the company of others. Imagination is not absent from rule-based play, but the explicit objective is to win through competition governed by rules.

Compared with the fantasy play of early childhood, rule-based games expand both the number of children who can play together and the likely duration of their joint activity. Typically, in early fantasy play, only two or three children play together at a time, and their play episodes are likely to last less than 10 minutes (Corsaro, 1985). When larger groups gather, it is almost certainly because an adult has deliberately coordinated their activity. School-age children, by contrast, often play games for hours in groups numbering up to 20 (Hartup, 1984). The increased duration and complexity of children's play provide evidence that, at least under some conditions, children who have entered middle childhood are capable of regulating their own behavior according to agreed-upon social rules.

GAMES AND LIFE

Developmentalists have long been interested in the links between the forms of children's play and their social behavior in general. In early childhood, the connections between pretend play and children's everyday lives are fairly obvious because children use adult roles and familiar scripts as the basis of their fantasy. It is less obvious how a game of baseball or checkers relates to social behavior in middle childhood and later life. Nonetheless, the idea that rule-based games are preparation for life has widespread appeal.

Piaget (1932/1965) believed that the appearance of rule-based games has a double significance for children's development. First, he saw the ability to engage in rule-based games as a *manifestation of concrete operations in the social sphere,* corresponding to decreasing egocentrism, the appearance of conservation, and other cognitive abilities discussed in Chapter 12. Second, he believed that such games are *models of society* because they create structured situations in which children practice balancing their own desires against the rules of the group.

Rule-based games are models of society for children in two closely related respects, Piaget argued. First, they are social institutions in that they remain basically the same as they are transmitted from one generation to the next. Thus, like other social institutions—a church service, for example—rule-based games provide an already existing structure of rules about how to behave in specific social circumstances.

Second, like all social institutions, rule-based games can exist only if people agree to their existence. In order to play a game such as hide-and-seek or marbles, children must learn to subordinate their immediate desires and behavior to a socially agreed-upon system. Piaget (1932/1965) linked this ability to play within a framework of rules to children's acquisition of respect for rules and a new level of moral understanding:

> All morality consists in a system of rules, and the essence of all morality is to be sought for in the respect which the individual acquires for these rules. . . . The rules of the game of marbles are handed down, just like so-called moral realities, from one generation to another, and are preserved solely by the respect that is felt for them by individuals. (pp. 13–14)

In Piaget's (1932/1965) view, it is through the give-and-take of negotiating plans, settling disagreements, making and enforcing rules, and keeping and breaking promises that children come to develop an understanding that social rules provide a structure that makes cooperation with others possible. As a consequence, peer groups can be self-governing, and their members are capable of autonomous moral thinking.

SOCIAL RULES, SOCIAL THINKING, AND SOCIAL BEHAVIOR

Piaget's suggestions concerning the way in which forms of play both reflect and make possible new forms of social interaction among peers have generated a great deal of interest among developmentalists (Rubin et al., 1998; Turiel, 1998). This work has focused on specifying how best to conceive of social rules, the ways that social rules relate to children's ideas about authority, and the mechanisms by which children come to follow (or ignore) the rules of their society (see Figure 14.1).

From: Leila Ciszewski
To: Alexander Cole
Subject: The rules in English

The rules:
Respect all people
1. No fighting
2. No bullying
3. Respect club dogs
4. Follow directions

Respect all things
1. No littering
2. No stealing
3. No breaking things
4. Do not touch things unless you are told to

Other rules
1. If you don't follow the rules, leave.

Dear Sasha,
These are the rules in English. Please send them back to me in Spanish.
Figure out the code, knwd, xntq cztfgsdq, Kdhkz

FIGURE 14.1
This is an e-mail message from our 9-year-old granddaughter to her father, Sasha. Leila has many Spanish-speaking kids on her block, and she wanted to make sure they understood her clubhouse rules.

RULES OF THE GAME AND SOURCES OF AUTHORITY: PIAGET'S ACCOUNT

On the basis of his observations of the way children play games, Piaget proposed a developmental progression in children's understanding of social rules. He found that very young children play marbles with little regard for the rules and with no notion of competition as a part of the game. Four-year-olds pile marbles up or roll them around to suit their fancy. At this stage, marbles is not a true game at all.

In middle childhood, marble players try to win according to preexisting rules. At first they tend to believe that the rules of the game have been handed down by such authority figures as older children, adults, or even God; therefore, the rules cannot be changed. Piaget (1932/1965) asked one 5½-year-old if it would be all right to allow little children to shoot their marbles from a position closer to the marbles they were trying to hit:

> "No," answered Leh, "that wouldn't be fair." "Why not?"—"Because God would make the little boy's shot not reach the marbles and the big boy's shot would reach them." (p. 58)

When Piaget asked Ben, age 10, if it would be possible to invent a new version of marbles, Ben agreed reluctantly that it would be possible to think up new rules, and he suggested one. Piaget (1932/1965) asked if others would accept such a new rule:

> *Piaget:* Then people could play that way?
> *Ben:* Oh, no, because it would be cheating.
> *Piaget:* But all your pals would like to, wouldn't they?
> *Ben:* Yes, they all would.
> *Piaget:* Then why would it be cheating?
> *Ben:* Because I invented it: it isn't a rule! It's a wrong rule because it's outside of the rules. A fair rule is one that is in the game. (p. 63)

Most children begin to treat the rules of games with less awe sometime between the ages of 9 and 11, according to Piaget. They realize that game rules are social conventions resulting from mutual consent. They understand that the rules must be respected if you want to play together, "but it is permissible to alter the rules as long as general opinion is on your side" (Piaget, 1932/1965, p. 28).

In Geneva, where Piaget lived, marbles was played almost exclusively by boys. Piaget wanted to show that the developmental progression he had encountered was universal, but he reported that he could not find any collective games played by girls that used as many rules and had as many fine-grained codifications as marbles. After observing many girls playing hopscotch, he remarked that girls seemed more interested in inventing new configurations of hopscotch squares than in elaborating the rules.

Piaget's observation that boys and girls not only play different games but play games differently has generated a good deal of controversy and subsequent research. When José Linaza (1984) observed English and Spanish

BOX 14.1

BOYS' GAMES, GIRLS' GAMES

Piaget's original observation that rules play a different function in boys' and girls' play has generated a good deal of research and controversy regarding possible gender differences in children's play during middle childhood. Much of this research has focused on differences in the complexity and competitiveness of the play activities that boys and girls typically engage in and on the possible developmental consequences of those differences.

In a widely cited study of American children, Janet Lever (1978) observed boys and girls in playgrounds, interviewed them, and had them keep diaries of their after-school play. She then rated the children's play according to its complexity. She defined complex games as those that require each player to take a different role (such as baseball); that require a relatively large number of participants; that require players to compete for an explicit objective, such as scoring a goal in soccer; that have a number of specified rules that are known by all the players before the game begins and whose violations are penalized; and that require teams.

According to Lever's data (see the accompanying table), both boys and girls engage in a wide variety of play activities, including complex games. But on the average, girls play what appear to be less complex games with fewer participants than do boys. Boys are also almost twice as likely as girls to engage in overtly competitive games, even when they are not playing team sports. To the casual observer, girls appear to play cooperatively. According to Lever, when girls' games involve explicit competition, as do jump-rope and jacks, competition is indirect: each player acts independently, competing by turn against the others' scores, rather than in face-to-face confrontations, as boys do.

Lever also found that boys' play groups tend to be larger than the play groups of girls. Team sports, which boys are more likely to engage in than girls, require from 10 to 25 participants to be played properly. Lever rarely observed girls playing in groups as large as 10; they favored such games as hopscotch and tag, which can be played with as few as two people and seldom include more than six. She reported that during their games, girls sometimes talked more than they played.

Lever conjectured that such differences provide girls and boys with markedly different sets of socialization experiences and social skills. Boys' games, she contended, provide them with the opportunity to deal with diversity, to coordinate with a large number of people, to work within impersonal rule systems, and to strive for collective as well as personal goals. Her conclusions mirror the widely held belief that participation in team sports furnishes boys with experience in leadership roles and teaches them to deal with competition in a depersonalized fashion, to engage in teamwork, and to think in more complex ways. However, later work challenges this belief.

For example, a decade after Lever's study, Katheryn Borman and Lawrence Kurdek (1987) replicated Lever's empirical finding that boys generally play games that require more players (such as soccer, baseball, and kickball), have more explicit rules, and are more overtly competitive than the games that girls play (such as hopscotch, four square, and tetherball). But when Borman and Kurdek gave children tests of social perspective taking, knowledge of rules, and logical reasoning, they found no consistent relation between playing complex games and children's cognitive abilities, a finding seriously undermin-

boys and girls playing marbles, he found that though the boys might play marbles more often and more skillfully than girls, there were no marked sex differences in the children's understanding of the rules of the game. Others, however, confirmed Piaget's finding that rules enter into the play of boys and girls differently (see Box 14.1). Overall, though, the research suggests that, despite some observed sex differences in game preferences, middle childhood is a time when play based on explicit rules begins to assume prominence in the interactions of children of both sexes (Thorne, 1993).

ALTERNATIVES TO PIAGET'S ACCOUNT OF SOCIAL DEVELOPMENT

An attractive feature of Piaget's theory of social rules, games, and moral development is that it connects many phenomena in a plausible way. That is, children's ability to think in terms of mental operations makes it possible for them to keep social rules in mind, and this ability, in turn, allows them to cooperate with each other in many contexts without a "rule enforcer" present. But his approach also has weaknesses that have been the focus of research by subsequent generations of researchers.

The first perceived weakness of Piaget's theory is that it recognizes only two states of understanding during childhood: in the first, all rules and authority come from powerful other people who must be given unilateral

PERCENTAGE OF TIME GIRLS AND BOYS WERE OBSERVED PLAYING GAMES OF VARIOUS DEGREES OF COMPLEXITY

	Girls	Boys
Complexity score 0 Roller skating, bike riding, listening to records	42%	27%
Complexity score 1 Singing, playing catch, bowling, racing electric cars	7	12
Complexity score 2 Indoor fantasy, jump-rope, tag, simple card games	31	15
Complexity score 3 Board games, checkers	8	15
Complexity score 4 Capture the flag	2	1
Complexity score 5 Team sports	10	30

Source: Lever, 1978.

ing Lever's speculations about the different socializing functions for boys' and girls' games.

The conclusion that the kinds of games boys play trains them to think more complexly than girls has also been severely criticized by developmentalists experienced in ethnographic observation. These scholars believe that the scholars who promote this idea have inaccurately described girls' game playing because they have not observed the games in question closely enough (Goodwin, 1995, 1997; Hughes, 1991). This criticism is supported by the work of Marjorie Goodwin (1995, 1998), who videotaped and tape-recorded girls' attention to rules and modes of argumentation in various situations, including games of hopscotch. She found that hopscotch is both more complex and more competitive than psychologists' observations had suggested: "As girls play, they do not simply rotate through various positions, but animatedly dispute, resist, and probe the boundaries of rules as referees and players together build the game event" (Goodwin, 1995, p. 261). Another ethnographer, Linda Hughes (1988), found that girls often engage in "competing in a cooperative mode": girls use the language of "being friends" and "being nice" while trying to eliminate players from the games. They also engage in extended disputes about rules, but not in the same obvious style as boys. This line of work leads to the conclusion that girls have as much practice and aptitude in playing games with rules and engaging in complex reasoning as boys do; what differs are the particular games and the styles of argumentation.

At present the difference in preferred games may be changing. In recent decades there has been a marked increase in girls' participation in team sports, further eroding the notion that girls and boys naturally engage in two distinct kinds of play with two distinct cognitive and social outcomes.

respect; in the second, children engage in interactions requiring mutual respect and begin to govern themselves. Further understanding, according to Piaget, does not come until adolescence or later, when individuals develop a more systematic and global grasp of the social rules of their society. However, as we saw in the research on cognitive development in Chapter 9, Piaget's stage theory of cognitive development has been challenged because in some cases young children appear to engage in forms of reasoning that he claimed develop only in middle childhood. Research on social development has found similar patterns of varying competence. Furthermore, young children do ***not*** always accord adults unilateral authority, a fact that undermines Piaget's claim that there is a clear-cut stagelike change from heteronomous to autonomous moral thinking (Chapter 10, p. 393).

The second perceived weakness of Piaget's theory is that while it may be that "all morality consists in a system of rules," as Piaget suggested, not all social rules involve moral issues in the same way or to the same degree. In general, killing someone is considered a greater moral wrong than hurting that person's feelings. Both of these concerns about Piaget's theory of social development have received considerable attention.

Distinguishing More Stages

A number of researchers who have studied children's moral thinking from an essentially Piagetian perspective have extended the number of stages children are said to pass through. They have also devised detailed methods for identifying the different forms of reasoning that apply at each stage. This work has addressed moral issues involving harm and justice, as well as fairness issues involving the distribution of resources.

Moral Reasoning about Harm and Justice The most influential attempt to build on Piaget's approach to moral development was carried out by Lawrence Kohlberg. In place of the two stages of moral reasoning proposed by Piaget, Kohlberg argued for the existence of a sequence of six stages extending from childhood into adolescence and adulthood. These six stages are grouped into three hierarchical levels of moral reasoning (Colby & Kohlberg, 1987; Kohlberg, 1969, 1976, 1984). We will focus here on the application of Kohlberg's ideas to middle childhood and postpone an overall evaluation of his approach until the discussion of adolescent moral development in Chapter 16. (Table 14.1 summarizes the first three stages, according to Kohlberg's theory.)

Kohlberg's method for studying moral reasoning was to present children with stories about people faced with dilemmas involving the value of human life and property, people's obligations to each other, and the meaning of laws and rules. In the manner of Piaget's clinical interview technique, Kohlberg would read the story, ask the child's opinion about how the protagonist should behave in response to the dilemma, and then probe the child's reasoning behind that opinion. Kohlberg's (1969) most famous story is the "Heinz dilemma":

> In Europe, a woman was near death from cancer. One drug might save her, a form of radium that a druggist in the same town had recently discovered. The druggist was charging $2,000, ten times what the drug cost him to make. The sick woman's husband, Heinz, went to everyone he knew to borrow the money, but he could get together only about half of what it cost. He told the druggist that his wife was dying and asked him to sell it cheaper or let him pay later. But the druggist said no. The husband got desperate and broke into the man's store to steal the drug for his wife. Should the husband have done that? Why? (p. 379)

In Kohlberg's theory of moral development, stage 1 coincides with the end of the preschool period and the beginning of middle childhood. Children at stage 1 adopt an egocentric point of view of right and wrong: they do not recognize the interests of others as distinct from their own. What is right or wrong for them must be right or wrong for others. Moreover, their judgments about the rightness and wrongness of an action are based on its objective outcome, which in this case is how authorities would respond to it. In stage 1, children might assert that Heinz must not steal the medicine because he will be put in jail.

In stage 2, which ordinarily appears around the age of 7 or 8, children continue to adopt a concrete, self-interested (egocentric) perspective but can recognize that other people have different perspectives. Justice is seen as an exchange system: you give as much as you receive. Kohlberg referred to the moral reasoning of children at this stage as **instrumental morality** because it assumes that it is perfectly acceptable to use others for one's own interests. Children at this stage might respond to the Heinz dilemma by saying that Heinz should steal the drug because someday he might have cancer and would want someone to steal it for him.

Stage 2 is the key transition associated with school-age children's ability to get along without adult supervision. Children no longer depend on a strong external source to define right and wrong; instead, their behavior is regulated by reciprocal relations between group members. Sometimes the resulting behaviors are desirable ("I'll help you with your model, if you help me with mine"); other times, they are less so ("I won't tell Mom you went to the arcade, if you don't tell her I got in a fight at school"). In either case, this form of thinking allows children to regulate their actions with each other.

instrumental morality In Kohlberg's theory, a form of moral reasoning in which children believe it is perfectly acceptable to use others for one's own interests.

In stage 3, which children begin to achieve around the age of 10 or 11, moral judgments are made on the basis of a social-relational moral perspective. At this stage, children see shared feelings and agreements, especially with people close to them, as more important than individual self-interest. One child quoted by Kohlberg (1984) said, "If I was Heinz, I would have stolen the drug for my wife. You can't put a price on love, no amount of gifts make love. You can't put a price on life either" (p. 629). Stage 3 is often equated with the golden rule (Treat others as you wish to be treated), a moral rule of reciprocity found in scriptures in all major religions.

prosocial moral reasoning The thinking that is involved in deciding whether to share with, help, or take care of other people when doing so may prove costly to oneself.

Prosocial Moral Reasoning **Prosocial moral reasoning** refers to the thinking that is involved in deciding whether to share with, help, or take care of

TABLE **14.1** KOHLBERG'S SIX MORAL STAGES

LEVEL AND STAGE	WHAT IS RIGHT	REASONS FOR DOING RIGHT	SOCIAL PERSPECTIVE
Level I–Preconventional			
Stage 1–Heteronomous morality	• Adherence to rules backed by punishment. • Obedience for its own sake. • Avoidance of physical damage to persons and property.	• Avoidance of punishment. • Superior power of authorities.	Egocentric point of view: doesn't consider the interests of others or recognize that they differ from one's own; doesn't relate two points of view. Actions are considered in physical terms rather than in terms of psychological interests of others. Confusion of authority's perspective with one's own.
Stage 2–Instrumental morality	• Following rules only when doing so is in one's immediate interest. • Acting to meet one's own interests and needs and letting others do the same. • Seeing fairness as an equal exchange.	• To serve one's own needs or interests in a world where other people have their own interests.	Concrete individualistic perspective: aware that all people have their own interests to pursue and these interests conflict, so that right is relative.
Level II–Conventional			
Stage 3–Good-child morality	• Living up to what is expected by people close to you. • Having good motives, and showing concern about others. • Keeping mutual relationships by such means as trust, loyalty, respect, and gratitude.	• The need to be a good person in one's own eyes and those of others. • Caring for others. • Belief in the Golden Rule. • Desire to maintain rules and authority that support stereotypical good behavior.	Perspective of an individual in relationships with other individuals: aware of shared feelings, agreements, and expectations. Ability to relate points of view through the Golden Rule.
Stage 4–Law-and-order morality	• Upholding the law.	• To keep the institution going as a whole.	Perspective of an individual in relation to the social group.
Level III–Postconventional, or Principled			
Stage 5–Social-contract reasoning	• Being aware that people hold a variety of values and opinions.	• A sense of obligation to law because of one's social contract to act for the welfare of the group.	Prior-to-society perspective: perspective of a rational individual aware of others' values and rights.
Stage 6–Universal ethical principles	• Following self-chosen ethical principles.	• A belief in the validity of universal moral principles.	Perspective of a moral point of view from which social arrangements derive.

Source: Adapted from Kohlberg, 1976.

other people when doing so may prove costly to oneself (Eisenberg & Fabes, 1998). According to Nancy Eisenberg (1992, 1998), prosocial moral reasoning goes through stagelike developmental changes similar to those proposed by Kohlberg for moral reasoning involving issues of harm and justice.

In her research on prosocial moral reasoning, Eisenberg used story dilemmas that generally included a conflict between immediate self-interest and the interest of others. For example, in one such story, a child is having a good time playing in his yard and sees a bully hurting another child when no adults are around. In another, the child has to choose between going to a birthday party or stopping to help a child who has injured his leg. The contrasts between a 5-year-old and a 10-year-old responding to the latter story illustrate the changes in reasoning typically observed between early and middle childhood:

> AGE 5 YEARS
> *Interviewer:* What do you think [Eric, the story protagonist] should do?
> *Child:* Go to the party.
> *Interviewer:* Why is that?
> *Child:* Because he doesn't want to be late.
> *Interviewer:* Why doesn't he want to be late?
> *Child:* Cause then it'd be over.
>
> AGE 10 YEARS
> *Interviewer:* What do you think Eric should do?
> *Child:* Go get the boy's parents.
> *Interviewer:* Why do you think he would want to get his parents for him?
> *Child:* Because he doesn't want him to have a broken leg and he wants him to get to the hospital real fast because he doesn't want him to get a broken leg or anything worse.
>
> (Eisenberg, 1992, p. 29)

Although many factors are involved in determining the sophistication of children's prosocial moral reasoning, reviews of the large literature on this topic show that as children get older, their reasoning reflects the trend in these two examples: young children's reasoning is focused on themselves, and helping others is justified in terms of what is to be gained personally. With increasing age, children express more empathy for the person in difficulty and a greater consideration of social norms.

Reasoning about Rules of Fairness A different but not entirely dissimilar account of stagelike moral development has been proposed by William Damon (1975, 1977, 1980). Damon investigated stages in children's developing conceptions of **positive justice,** that is, their ideas about how to divide resources or distribute rewards fairly. In order to study age-related changes in this form of reasoning, Damon adopted the technique of telling children a story and then asking them a series of questions designed to reveal their reasoning. One of his stories went like this:

> A classroom of children spent a day drawing pictures. Some children made a lot of drawings; some made fewer. Some children drew well; others did not draw as well. Some children were well-behaved and worked hard; others fooled around. The class then sold the drawings at a school bazaar and made a lot of money.
>
> The next day the children gathered to decide how the money should be distributed. One child said that the kids who did the most work should get the most money. Another child said that the kids who made the best pictures should get the most money. A third child said that the kids who were most cooperative should get the most money. How should the proceeds from the sale of the drawings be fairly distributed? (Adapted from Damon, 1975)

Damon probed the answers that children 4 to 12 years old gave to such questions, challenged them, and followed up with additional questions to

positive justice Moral reasoning about how to divide resources or distribute rewards fairly.

determine the reasoning behind them. He found that children's conceptions of positive justice develop through the sequence of levels shown in Table 14.2. Although his initial studies were conducted in the United States, Damon (1983) reported that the same sequence is found in Israel, Puerto Rico, and parts of Europe.

Before the age of 4, children do not give objective reasons for their choices; they simply state their wants. Most 4- and 5-year-olds still focus primarily on gratifying themselves, but now they begin to justify their decisions with appeals to such arbitrary characteristics as size and sex: "The biggest should get the most"; "We should all get some because we're girls."

Between the ages of 5 and 7, children begin to believe that all participants have an equal claim to the rewards. Their arguments recognize no mitigating circumstances; the only fair treatment is equal treatment.

From approximately the age of 8 onward, children begin to take particular circumstances into consideration, believing, for example, that some individuals within the group may have a legitimate claim to more than an equal share of the group's rewards if they contributed a greater share to the group's work or if they are handicapped in some way, such as by poverty or by a phys-

TABLE 14.2 LEVELS OF REASONING ABOUT POSITIVE JUSTICE

Level 0–A (Age 4 and Under)
Positive-justice choices derive from a wish that an act occur. Reasons simply assert the wishes rather than attempting to justify them ("I should get it because I want to have it").

Level 0–B (Ages 4 to 5)
Choices still reflect desires but are now justified on the basis of external, observable realities such as size, sex, or other physical characteristics of persons (e.g., "We should get the most because we're girls"). Such justifications, however, are invoked in a fluctuating, after-the-fact manner and are self-serving in the end.

Level 1–A (Ages 5 to 7)
Positive-justice choices derive from notions of strict equality in actions (i.e., that everyone should get the same). Equality is seen as preventing complaining, fighting, "fussing," or other types of conflict.

Level 1–B (Ages 6 to 9)
Positive-justice choices derive from a notion of reciprocity in actions: that persons should be paid back in kind for doing good or bad things. Notions of merit and deserving emerge.

Level 2–A (Ages 8 to 10)
A moral relativity develops out of the understanding that different persons can have different yet equally valid justifications for their claims to justice. The claims of persons with special needs (e.g., the poor) are weighed heavily. Choices are attempts to reconcile competing claims.

Level 2–B (Ages 10 and Up)
Considerations of equality and reciprocity are coordinated so that choices take account of more than one person's claims and the demands of the specific situation. Choices are firm and clear-cut, yet justifications reflect the recognition that all persons should be given their due (though, in many situations, this does not mean equal treatment).

Source: Damon, 1980.

ical disability. However, it is still difficult for 8-year-olds to balance all the competing considerations to produce a fair outcome. Changes after the age of 8 reflect children's increased sophistication at logically weighing multiple relevant factors (McGillicuddy-De Lisi et al., 1994).

Damon's description of changes in children's thinking about fairness has generally been confirmed by other investigators. However, consistent with evidence concerning children's problem-solving behaviors discussed in previous chapters, subsequent research also indicates that, in familiar contexts, children can make complex decisions about fairness at an earlier age than Damon's stage theory suggests. For example, Theresa Thorkildsen and her colleagues posed questions about the fairness involved in familiar events that children routinely encounter in school (Thorkildsen, 1989; Thorkildsen & Schmahl, 1997). Thorkildsen's initial study was conducted among 6- to 11-year-old European American middle-class children who attended a school in which there was a wide range of activities beyond standard recitation that were defined as "learning opportunities" and in which children were often encouraged to work together on interesting problems. Thorkildsen told the children a story about a classroom in which everyone is trying hard to learn how to read, but some children finish the assignments more quickly than others. She then asked her subjects if it is fair for those who already read well to help other children who are slower learners in each of three situations:

1. Is it fair for the teacher to ask the fast readers to help the slow readers during a reading lesson?
2. Is it fair for the good readers to help the slow readers by whispering answers during a spelling bee?
3. Is it fair for the good readers to help the slow readers during a test?

Children's judgments of fairness in these familiar events depended on the situation being described (see Figure 14.2). Most of the children thought that it was fair to have a reading lesson in which the good learners were told to help the slow learners. However, if the activity was a spelling bee or a test, independent work was seen as the only fair alternative, and one child helping another was considered cheating. Thorkildsen found no substantial differences between the judgments of the younger and older children, indicating that even 6-year-olds take the social context of an action into account when they judge fairness in circumstances with which they are familiar.

FIGURE 14.2
Children 6 to 11 years old were asked to rate the fairness of helping, competition, and independent work in three different school activities: reading practice, a spelling bee, and a test. A rating of 0 indicates unfair; a rating of 3 indicates fair. (From Thorkildsen, 1989.)

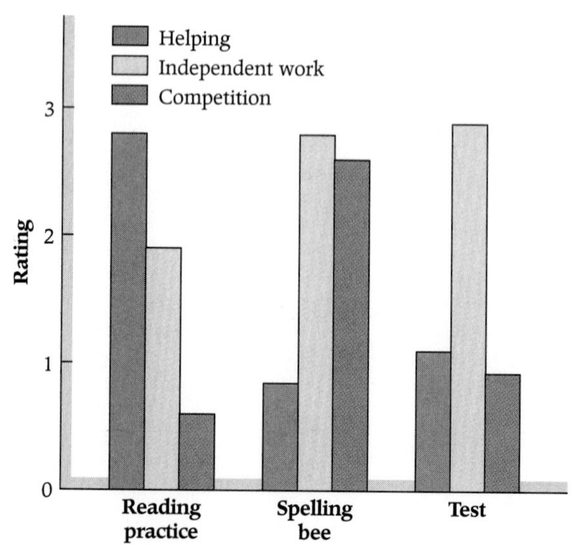

Thorkildsen and Cindy Schmahl (1997) repeated this study with working-class children from African American and Latino backgrounds who attended schools where traditional teacher-led lessons were the norm and there was no tradition of providing children with a variety of activities that were believed to be good "learning opportunities." These children responded to the questions about fairness in each of the three different situations much as the European American children did. However, there were some cultural differences. From interviews with the children, Thorkildsen and Schmahl found that the minority-group children, mirroring the practices of their classrooms, placed a higher value on working by oneself and were more likely to treat all forms of classroom lessons as a test. Thus, they were more likely than their middle-class peers to think that peer tutoring would be a form of cheating.

Development in Different Domains of Social Rules

As we noted earlier (p. 394), even 4- to 5-year-old children distinguish between breaking *moral rules* that result in harm to another person and breaking *social rules* that merely disrupt the social order, such as cheating in a game of basketball. This fact led Elliot Turiel and his colleagues to conclude that moral reasoning and reasoning about social conventions occur as independent domains (Turiel, 1983; Turiel & Wainryb, 1994).

In a series of studies, Turiel and his colleagues provided evidence that children's judgments about social conventions have their own criteria and undergo their own sequence of developmental transformations (Tisak & Turiel, 1988; Turiel, 1983; Turiel et al., 1987). They found, for example, that in the domain of moral rules involving harm and justice, children's judgments about who has the authority to stop someone from harming another person do not depend on who is involved: children regard a command from a child to other children to stop fighting to be legitimate even though the child has no special authority. Children also regard as illegitimate a command from an authority figure like a teacher to let the children keep on fighting (Kim, 1998; Laupa & Turiel, 1993). This result shows that reasoning about moral rules does not depend on context; fighting is perceived as wrong across contexts.

By contrast, children's judgments about problems involving social conventions do depend upon the context and who is in charge. Marta Laupa and Elliott Turiel (1993) asked children between the ages of 5 and 11 to judge whether a school principal could issue directives to children in different social contexts—the school, a public park, or a child's home. Children at all ages understood that principals have the right to make rules in their own school but not in children's homes. The only developmental change the researchers observed was that the youngest children were more inclined to think that principals have authority in a public park.

To study age-related changes in reasoning about social conventions, Turiel (1983) told children a story about a young boy who wants to become a nurse and care for infants when he grows up, but his father doesn't want him to. The following interview, based on the nurse story, illustrates the earliest stage of reasoning about social conventions. The child being interviewed seems to believe that conventions reflect the natural order of things and that to violate the convention would be to behave unnaturally:

> Joan (6 years, 5 months): *(Should he become a nurse?)* Well, no, because he could easily be a doctor and he could take care of babies in the hospital. *(Why shouldn't he be a nurse?)* Well, because a nurse is a lady and the boys, the other men would just laugh at them. *(Why shouldn't a man be a nurse?)* Well, because it would sort of be silly because ladies wear those kind of dresses and those kind of shoes and hats. . . . *(Do you think his father was right?)* Yes, because, well, a nurse, she typewrites and stuff and all that. *(The man should not do that?)* No, because he would look silly in a dress. (Turiel, 1978, pp. 62–63)

At the second level of reasoning about social conventions, evident around the age of 8 or 9, children realize that just because most doctors are men and most nurses are women, the empirical association between activities, roles, and modes of dress does not mean that other combinations are impossible. At this second level, children place no special value on the role of social conventions. They are even sophisticated enough to realize that traditional social conventions may mislead people:

> Emily (8 years, 11 months): *(Why do you think his parents see that job as for women only?)* Being a nurse—because not many men are nurses so they get used to the routine. I know a lot of ladies who are doctors, but I don't know a man who is a nurse, but it is okay if they want to. (Turiel, 1978, p. 64)

At level 3, achieved around 10 or 11 years of age, most children begin to believe that social conventions, arbitrary though they may be, have a legitimate role in the regulation of social life. Eventually, sometime in early adulthood, they come to view social conventions as a positive force because they facilitate the coordination of social interactions, which is essential to the functioning of any social group.

TABLE 14.3 Excerpts from Damon's Transcripts Comparing 6- and 10-Year-Olds' Reasoning about and Practice of Positive Justice

In return for making bracelets, each group of four children received ten candy bars; they discussed how to divide them.

Three 6-Year-Olds: Jay, Juan, and Susan

Experimenter: So what Jay said is he put them out, three for him and three for Juan, two for Susan and two for Jennifer *[not present]*. And Susan said that's OK too. That's the way she did it.

Jay: [to Juan] You should think that's fair too. You have three, and I have three, and they have two.

Juan: I don't think that's fair.

Jay: Why?

Juan: We shouldn't give the boys more than the girls. We should break them in half and give the girls two, the boys two, and then . . .

Jay: No. No. No. I said ours were the prettiest, and that's why we get more.

Juan: Wait a second. Whose is this?

Jay: Yours.

Juan: No, it isn't.

Jay: See, we made the prettiest. I say we made the prettiest. Do you think that's a nice one? And you made the nice ones, and we made the prettiest. I think that's fair because we made the prettiest. . . .

E: What do you think, Susan? Didn't you at one point say you thought we should split them in half?

Susan: That's what I said. Now I say . . . *[Susan gives them out—three, three, two, two, as Jay wishes]*

E: What? This way?

Jay: Yeah. Because she thinks that we made the prettiest.

Juan: She got some in her lunch box. Do you have candy? . . .

E: Susan says it's OK. How about Jennifer?

Jay: I think she would say it's OK.

Juan: If she didn't leave, I think it wouldn't be OK. . . .

Jay: Think that would be fair! She would have three, and we would all have three.

E: We don't have eleven, we have ten.

Jay: But she only made one, and it's not pretty.

Juan: It's good. She's only in kindergarten. She would think it's fair, I think. Yeah, she would.

E: What are you guys going to do?

Jay: If you think it's fair, and Susan thinks it's fair, and I think it's fair, she *[Jennifer]* might think it's fair.

E: Well, let's see what Juan thinks. What do you suggest, Juan? What's the best way? What's the best thing to do with the candy bars?

Juan: I think that's *[three, three, two, two]* the best way, if she's only in kindergarten.

Jay: She had two, and we have three.

Juan: You made the most.

Jay: You see I had four bracelets.

Juan: I had the second most. Give these two candy bars to her.

Jay: You see, what I was thinking was, Juan and I get three 'cause we, ours are pretty and I made the most. Susan already has one in her lunch box.

Juan: And Jennifer's only in kindergarten.

Jay: She doesn't get more, 'cause she just made one and it's not pretty.

E: Do you agree, Susan?

Susan: OK.

A current source of controversy among the developmental psychologists who study reasoning about social rules is whether children around the world think about social rules in the same way North American children do. Using culturally appropriate versions of Turiel's stories, researchers have replicated his basic findings in a wide variety of societies (summarized in Turiel, 1998). Others, using slightly different methods to elicit judgments, have concluded that people in at least some cultures are more likely than North Americans to consider breaches of social convention to be moral issues (Shweder et al., 1987). For example, in parts of India it is considered a serious moral infraction for a widow to eat fish two or three days a week, while such behavior would be considered a matter of personal choice in the United States. At present the issue of cultural variations in thinking about moral rules and social conventions is still in dispute. We will return to discuss this issue again in Chapter 16, because most of the relevant cross-cultural data have been collected from adolescents and adults, making it risky to draw conclusions about the role of cultural differences in such reasoning during middle childhood.

Three 10-Year-Olds: Craig, Norman, and Bonnie

E: . . . What do you think is the best way to give it out?

Craig: Would Dennis *[the younger child]* get some?

E: If you think so.

Norman: He has to be here too.

E: Well, you all decide among you.

Bonnie: I was thinking, we could give out one a bracelet, because Dennis did one and we all did three. Or give two and a half to everybody. That way everybody gets the same thing.

Craig: Maybe he *[Dennis]* should get one and we get three.

Norman: No. It ain't fair.

Bonnie: Also, Dennis is younger and he left earlier.

E: Well, what do you think? Is that the best way?

Norman: No.

E: Why not, Norman?

Norman: Because if he were here too, and he's a child too, so he should get even.

Bonnie: Yeah, well, lookit. His was bigger so it would have taken longer. And he used more black, but that made it shorter. But he left earlier, he's younger and, you know, didn't do it neat.

Norman: I know. That's beside the point. That means we don't expect much from him. . . .

Craig: Or give three to her *[Bonnie]*, three for Norman, and three for me, and one for Dennis.

E: And why do you think that is the best way, Craig?

Craig: *[No reply.]*

Norman: You're not putting his *[Dennis's]* mind into your little mind. . . .

Craig: Yes, I am.

Norman: Well, you're not reasoning about him. If we did that he would say *[mimics child's whining voice]* "Come, come, you guys got this and I only got this" and he'd start bawling his brains out.

Bonnie: Well, his isn't that neat or anything.

Norman: I know, but he is younger.

Bonnie: Well, wouldn't you say, supposing that you had a younger dog and an older dog, right? You could teach them both the same tricks. And if you had a box of dog bones, you'd give them a bone for every trick. Supposing the little one or even the big one just wanted the dog bones and he wouldn't do any tricks. you wouldn't give him one for that.

Norman: I know, but he did something. It's not like he didn't do anything. Least he did one. You're getting on the point like he didn't do anything.

Bonnie: No, I know he did something. He did the best he could.

Norman: Yeah, so he should get as much as we do.

Source: Damon, 1977.

FROM REASONING TO ACTING

Thus far the studies of moral reasoning we have discussed have been restricted to studies of how children reason about, and reach judgments about, hypothetical situations involving moral questions and social conventions. The question naturally arises: *How is children's reasoning about such issues related to their actions in a real-life situation?*

In an extensive survey of studies relating children's prosocial reasoning to their behavior, Nancy Eisenberg and colleagues (1998) found that higher levels of reasoning are positively related to higher levels of prosocial behavior. In one such study William Damon (1977) created a real-life sharing situation to focus on the relation between reasoning about fairness and actual behavior. He arranged for 144 children to be divided into groups of 4. Each group was asked to make bracelets, and at the end of the session each group was given ten candy bars, which the members were to divide among themselves as payment for their work. Damon interviewed the children about how the candy should be distributed, and then he noted what the children actually did when it came time to divide up the candy. As Table 14.3 indicates, the children's reasoning about fairness varied markedly depending on their age. In accord with other studies of reasoning about positive justice, the 6-year-olds insisted that fairness means equal shares for all, whereas the older children were better able to apportion the rewards according to the quantity and quality of a person's effort.

When Damon compared the children's hypothetical reasoning with their actual behavior, he found that in half the cases the children's behavior matched their reasoning and that in about 10 percent of the cases the children actually exhibited behavior that was more advanced than their hypothetical reasoning. The remaining 40 percent scored lower in their behavior than in their reasoning, having apparently succumbed to temptation. These children claimed more than they deserved according to the reasoning they had displayed in the hypothetical situation.

In a study of how reasoning about honesty relates to actual behavior, Eugene Subbotsky (1993) conducted an experiment with large numbers of Russian children between 3 and 12 years of age. The children experienced the same moral situation under three conditions: as a story, as an event they participated in, and as a more complicated event designed to tease out the reasons that they told the truth or lied in the second condition.

The first condition was a moral-dilemma story like those used by Kohlberg and Damon: children were told a story about a boy who was instructed by an adult to transfer Ping-Pong balls from a pail to a jar using an L-shaped shovel. The boy was told that under no condition was he allowed to touch the Ping-Pong balls but that if he successfully transferred the balls, he would receive a reward. The adult then left the room to do something. The boy could not move the balls using the shovel, so he moved the balls by hand. When the adult returned, the boy lied, saying that he had moved the balls with the shovel, and he was rewarded. After the children heard this story, they were asked to judge the boy's morality and say what they would do in the same circumstances.

In the second condition, Subbotsky observed the children's actual behavior in a situation very similar to the one described in the story, with one small, but critical, change. First he gave each of the children practice moving the balls from pail to jar with an L-shaped shovel that was convex—turned up so that the task was easy to perform. Then, as he left the room, he surreptitiously substituted an identical-looking *concave* shovel that slanted down slightly from the middle. This small change made the task impossible.

In condition 1, almost 100 percent of the children declared that the boy was wrong and that they would not deceive the adult to get the reward. In condition 2, about 40 percent of the children cheated.

FIGURE 14.3

Percentage of children who observed the moral rule in the "honesty" situation under different circumstances. (From Subbotsky, 1993.)

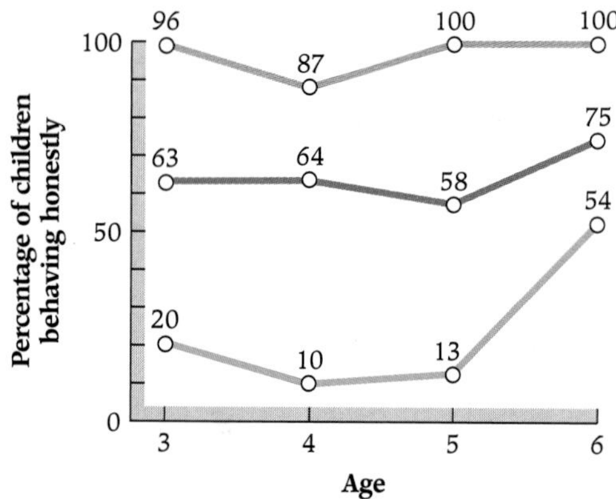

These results set the stage for condition 3, in which Subbotsky arranged for the children to witness another child breaking the "no touching" rule, lying about it, and getting the reward nevertheless. Then the children were put back in condition 2 for a second time, to see if they would cheat. Having seen another child cheat and get away with it, the younger children cheated with abandon (see Figure 14.3).

This pattern of behavior indicates that in condition 2 many of the children who did not cheat acted under a kind of imaginary social constraint arising from their fear that *somehow* the experimenter would know that they were lying. Once they saw that they would not be punished, the social constraint to be honest disappeared and they lied. Note that 10- and 11-year-old children were much less likely to cheat than the younger children, even after they learned that they could get away with it. Subbotsky argues that their honesty reflects the fact that they have thoroughly internalized the cultural norm to be honest.

The overall conclusion seems to be that moral judgment is important to moral action. But when conditions require one to resist temptation, some element of social control and a threat of punishment appear to be necessary for younger children to behave according to moral norms. The desire to behave morally despite the consequences is unlikely to be uniformly achieved at any age.

nomination procedure A method of assessing peer preferences in which children are asked to name those they would like to sit near, play with, or work with or to name their friends in the group.

rating scale A method of assessing peer preferences in which researchers ask children to rank every other child in the group according to a specific criterion, such as popularity or desirability as a friend or as a teammate in sports.

RELATIONS WITH OTHER CHILDREN

Once children begin to spend significant amounts of time among their peers, they must learn to create a satisfying place for themselves within the social group. Their greater appreciation of social rules and their increased ability to consider other people's points of view are essential resources for this developmental task. But no matter how sensitive or sophisticated they may be about social relations, there is no guarantee that they will be accepted by other children. In creating a life for themselves among peers, all children must learn to compete for social status, come to terms with the possibility that they may not be liked, and deal with the conflicts that inevitably arise.

PEER RELATIONS AND SOCIAL STATUS

Whenever a group of children exists over a period of time, a social structure emerges in which it is possible to identify a few members whom almost all the others like, others who enjoy less popularity, and some who are actively disliked by most of the group. Researchers who study the relative social status of group members usually begin by asking children how they feel about other children in the group. Two techniques are widely used for this purpose.

When investigators use a **nomination procedure,** they ask members of a group to name their friends in the group or the children they would like to sit near, play with, or work with. They may also ask children to name those whom they do not like. Alternatively, researchers may use a **rating scale,** asking children to rank every child in the group according to a specific criterion, such as popularity or desirability as a friend or as a teammate in sports. Sometimes researchers use both techniques in the same study as a means of evaluating the validity of the results

During middle childhood, acceptance by peers becomes a prime concern for children.

sociogram A graphic representation of how each child feels about every other child in a group.

The results from these assessment techniques can be compiled to create a **sociogram,** a graphic representation of how each child feels about every other child (Rubin et al., 1998) (see Figure 14.4). The picture of social relations given by the sociogram is then used to investigate how the children's individual characteristics are related to their group status.

Using these techniques, developmentalists have identified categories of social status defined by children's position in their social group (Rubin et al., 1999). The following list of categories has been compiled from several sources (Asher & Coie, 1990; Ladd, 1999; Rubin et al., 1998, 1999):

- *Popular children* are those who receive the most positive nominations or highest ratings from their peers.
- *Rejected children* are those who receive few positive nominations and many negative ones from their peers. They are actively disliked.
- *Neglected children* are those who receive few nominations of any kind. These children seem to be ignored by their peers rather than disliked.
- *Controversial children,* as the label suggests, are those who receive both positive and negative nominations.
- *Victimized children* are not necessarily rejected by the whole group but are selectively and actively harmed, psychologically and physically, by a limited minority of the peer group.
- *Bullies* are children who, without provocation, act aggressively to achieve domination over other children. They are often the "interactional partners" of victimized children.

Factors Relating to Sociometric Status

One of the most pervasive findings of sociometric research on *popular children* is that their popularity is related to physical attractiveness (Boyatzis et al., 1998). In one study, a group of boys was categorized into five subgroups according to their popularity among their peers. Then adult raters who did not know the boys were asked to judge their attractiveness from photographs (Langlois, 1986). In general, the lower the boys' attractiveness ratings, the lower the popularity standing of their subgroup was. Other research using similar methods has shown that attractiveness and popularity are also correlated among girls (Adams & Roopnarine, 1994; Boyatzis et al., 1998). Attractive children also appear to benefit from the stereotypic assumption that attractive individuals are generally superior.

However, there is more to popularity than good looks. Popular children are generally skilled at initiating and maintaining positive relationships. Kenneth Rubin and his colleagues comment that when popular children attempt to enter a group, "it is as if they ask themselves, 'What's going on?' and then, 'How can I fit in?'" They are also good at compromising and negotiating. Overall, their behavior appears to be socially competent (Rubin et al., 1999).

FIGURE 14.4

A sociogram of the relationships among a group of fifth-grade boys and girls. Note that the one boy who has a friendship with a girl is only marginally related to the two groups of boys. The girl in this friendship, by contrast, is part of a group of girls. Two girls and one boy are social isolates, while a pair of boys have chosen each other in isolation from the group. (Adapted from Gronlund, 1959.)

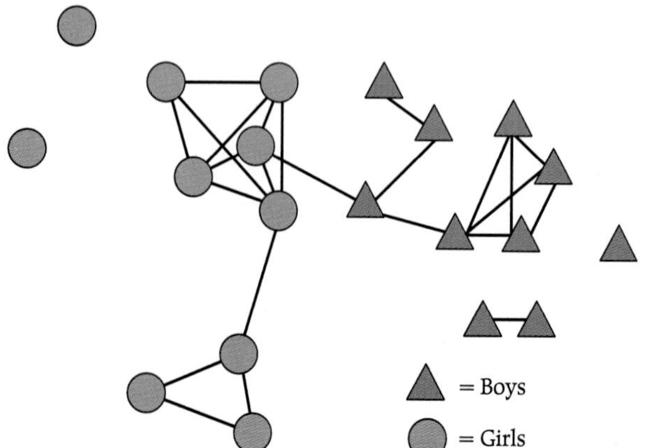

The factors associated with the status of *rejected children* appear to be more complicated. Studies of children who are rejected by their peers reveal that the most conspicuous cause of rejection is that the child is aggressive; children quite naturally do not like to be around others who behave unpleasantly or hurt them. Aggressive rejected children overestimate their social skills and competence and underestimate how much their peers dislike them (Cillessen et al., 1992; Hymel et al., 1993). They are also more likely to misinterpret an accidental injury from another as deliberate. As a consequence of these deficits in social information processing, they are often in conflict with the people around them. Rejection is especially likely to occur when aggressiveness is combined with lower levels of sociability and cognitive ability (Newcomb et al., 1993).

Once children are rejected, they may acquire a reputation as such and have a difficult time gaining acceptance by their peer group even if their behavior changes. In a study of first-, third-, and fifth-graders who had been rated either low or high on a sociometric questionnaire, researchers focused on children's attempts to gain entry to a group of children who were playing a game in the school playground. They noted little difference in the skill with which low-status and high-status children sought entry to the game, yet the low-status children were more than twice as likely to be ignored as the high-status children. In the familiar setting of a school playground, apparently, children may be rejected before they utter a word or make a move because the group has already formed a negative opinion of them (Putallaz & Wasserman, 1990).

Shelley Hymel and her colleagues found that when negative opinions about a child become general in a group, the child's reputation ("He is always hitting"; "She never gives anyone else a turn") can become self-perpetuating (Hymel et al., 1990). These researchers described a number of cases in which a peer group's expectations caused the members to interpret a child's behavior as aggressive or unfriendly even when, by objective standards, it was not. Such biased interpretations make the rejected child's task of winning acceptance more difficult and might even evoke the very behaviors (grabbing, hitting, tattling, or crying) that led to the child's being rejected in the first place.

Not all rejected children are aggressive, however. Some extremely shy children are also rejected (Bierman et al., 1993). These rejected withdrawn children value getting along with others as highly as do other children, and they are aware of their social failure (Asher et al., 1990). As a result, their rejection makes these shy children lonelier than other children, more dissatisfied with their social relations at school, and more distressed about them (Cassidy & Asher, 1992; Crick & Ladd, 1993).

Overall, the evidence indicates that rejection by one's peers is the result of a bundle of factors, each of which carries the potential to influence a child to interact in socially inappropriate ways. The consequences of this unhappy situation are that the child is socially isolated and lonely, and this only makes a difficult situation worse.

Neglected children, like rejected children, are less sociable than their peers but they are neither aggressive nor overly shy. A study conducted in Holland found that neglected children are more likely than rejected children to improve their social status among their classmates over the course of the school year (Cillessen et al., 1992). Neglected children also perform better academically than rejected children, are more compliant in school, and are better liked by their teachers (Wentzel & Asher, 1995).

Controversial children, who are unusual in that they are both highly accepted and highly rejected, and tend to behave even more aggressively than rejected children. However, they compensate for their aggression by joking around about it or by using other social and cognitive skills to keep their social partners from becoming angry enough to break off the relationship (Newcomb et al., 1993).

Controversial and neglected children tend not to be particularly distressed by their relative lack of social success. This may be the case because such children are usually liked by at least one other child, and these friendships may be sufficient to prevent loneliness. Children without best friends, no matter how well they are accepted by their classmates, are lonelier than children with best friends (Parker & Asher, 1993).

In recent years, special concern has been devoted to *victimized children,* who are the targets of other children's aggressive and demeaning behavior (Craig, 1998; Finnegan et al., 1998; Schwartz et al., 1998). Victimized children experience a variety of social difficulties in addition to the mistreatment they receive directly from their peers: in general, they lose their tempers easily, have difficulty regulating their attention, and act in an immature and dependent way.

Concern about victimized children is closely coupled with concern about *bullies,* their main tormentors. Bullying is not restricted to victimized children, however. In many industrialized countries, including the United States, as many as 40 to 50 percent of schoolchildren report that they have been bullied in the prior month (Smith et al., 1999).

The causes of bullying are more complicated than they may at first seem. Bullying is a form of aggression, so it seems reasonable to assume that bullies, like other aggressive children, suffer from a deficit in social information processing. However, unlike many children who act aggressively because they negatively misinterpret other children's behavior toward them, bullies are aggressive without provocation. Current evidence suggests that bullies behave as they do because the behavior is instrumental for them; that is, bullying is the means by which they control other people and get what they want. Some researchers argue that bullies often have quite well developed social information processing skills but differ from accepted children by using these skills in an antisocial way (Crick & Dodge, 1999; Sutton et al., 1999). This conclusion is supported by evidence that some bullies are also among the boys considered to be most popular by their 11- to 12-year-old classmates (Rodkin et al., 2000).

RELATIONS BETWEEN BOYS AND GIRLS

During middle childhood, children of all cultures spend a great deal of time in sexually segregated groups (Archer, 1992). In nonindustrialized societies, sexual segregation may stem from the kinds of chores that children are assigned by adults. The girls help their mothers around the village by fetching water, doing the wash, sweeping, and helping to prepare food, while the boys watch the herds, hunt, and fish (Edwards & Whiting, 1993). In industrialized societies, children's tendency to gather in same-sex groups appears to depend more on their preferences for different kinds of activities and styles of interac-

These children playing during recess demonstrate the kind of sex segregation that appears during middle childhood.

tion. Studies in the United States have found that when children are 6 years of age, roughly 68 percent choose a child of the same sex as a "best friend"; by the time children are 12, the figure has grown to about 90 percent (Daniels-Beirness, 1989; Graham et al., 1998)

In most cultures, sex segregation is by no means total during middle childhood (Best & Williams, 1997; Rogoff, 2000); its extent depends upon the setting (Archer, 1992). There is more mixing of the two sexes, for example, when children are in their neighborhoods than when they are in their schools (Ellis et al., 1981), when they are visiting an unfamiliar setting such as a museum (Luria & Herzog, 1991), or when the children live in a small village and thus do not have many choices of playmates (Edwards & Whiting, 1993).

At this age, relations between boys and girls in many settings, such as school playgrounds and summer camps, are not particularly friendly. Those who come in contact with members of the other sex may be teased by their friends, who act as if they have been polluted in some way. At the same time, there is fascination. Some of the meetings between the two sexes have the qualities of a foray into enemy territory. Others, such as chase-and-kiss games and teasing, have sexual overtones. But there are also occasions when the two sexes naturally merge in joint activities or just "fool around the block together" after school or on the weekends. Both age and sex segregation are diminished under these conditions (Adler et al., 1992; Ellis et al., 1981; Thorne, 1993) (see Box 14.2).

Boys' and girls' experiences with peers often differ considerably. Observational studies of children on playgrounds report that girls ordinarily congregate to talk or play in groups of two or three, whereas boys tend to play or run around in "swarms" (Daniels-Bierness, 1989). More recent work has shown that these generalizations apply primarily to the most conspicuous and often most popular children present. There is always a sizable proportion of both boys and girls who are not following the pattern of the dominant social group (Thorne, 1993). Nonetheless, it seems clear that for many children middle childhood is a time when boys and girls do not find each other attractive social partners.

COMPETITION AND COOPERATION AMONG PEERS

As they begin to spend more time among their peers, children must learn to balance the ways they compete with each other and the need to cooperate in order to get things done. How children learn these lessons is influenced by the values and beliefs of their cultural group, a fact that was neatly illustrated by Millard Madsen and his colleagues (Kagan & Madsen, 1971; Madsen & Shapira, 1970; Shapira & Madsen, 1969) in a study of two different groups of Israeli children (Shapira & Madsen, 1969).

One group was composed of children who lived in agricultural communes, or *kibbutzim;* the other group was made up of children from a middle-class urban neighborhood. Middle-class urban Israelis, like their U.S. counterparts, encourage their children to achieve as individuals. Kibbutzim, by contrast, prepare children from an early age to cooperate and work as a group. Kibbutz adults deliberately reward cooperation and punish failure to cooperate (Spiro, 1965). Competition is so discouraged that children may feel ashamed to be at the top of their class (Rabin, 1965).

Six- to ten-year-old children of both communities were brought together four at a time to play a game with the apparatus depicted in Figure 14.5. At the start of each round of the game, four children were seated at the corners of the board. In the center of the board was a pen connected to each corner by a string, which each child could pull to move the pen. The board itself was covered with a clean piece of paper, on which the pen left a mark as it moved.

FIGURE 14.5
Diagram of apparatus used to assess children's predispositions to compete or cooperate. The pen at the center of the board must be moved to the target circles, an act that requires changes in the lengths of the strings manipulated by four players. (From Shapira & Madsen, 1969.)

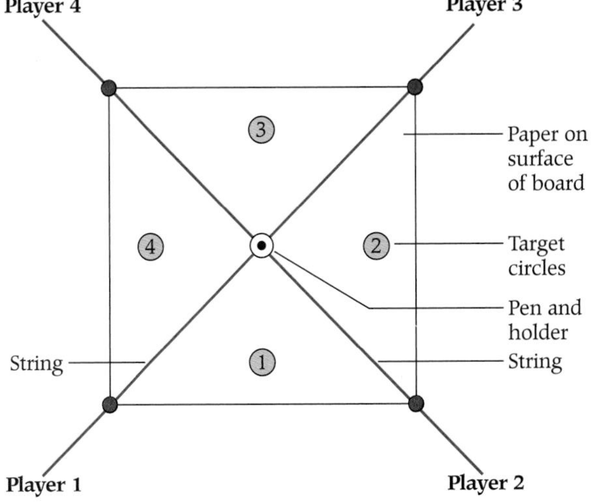

BOX 14.2

Border Work: Contact between the Sexes

When our son, Sasha, was 8 years old, we assigned him the task of looking after 6-year-old Tiana on the city bus that the two of them took to school. Tiana is the daughter of our closest friends, and Sasha had known her from infancy. They shared a baby-sitter and over the years had spent countless hours playing together. They chatted, argued, and even played tag as they walked across town with one or the other of us to catch the uptown bus. But once on the bus, they acted as if they didn't know each other. They never sat together or even spoke. When we found out about this, we asked them why. The only explanation they gave was that Tiana liked to sit up front and Sasha liked to sit way in the back.

In fact, Sasha and Tiana were displaying a kind of social behavior that is part of the code of behavior for school-age children—they were maintaining the public boundaries between the sexes (Thorne, 1993). They were by no means extreme in the way they did this. In fact, they were rather discreet in comparison with many of their peers. For example, when Courtney Cazden and Sarah Michaels (1985) introduced a computer mail system into a second-grade classroom in Boston as part of a 6-month study designed to promote children's writing, they found that throughout the study not one child wrote to a child of the other sex. Additional research finds that children become less willing to help children of the other sex in school during middle childhood (Nelson–Le Gall & De Cooke, 1987).

When gender boundaries are crossed, children often behave as though they have been contaminated just by being near a member of the other sex, and they engage in elaborate "cleansing rituals" to get rid of the "girl cooties" or the "boy germs." Alan Sroufe and his colleagues (1993) report that a boy at a day camp was seen leaving the girls' tent (where he had gone to retrieve his radio) and was bombarded with taunts from his peers like "Uuh, he's with the girls!" and "Did you kiss anyone, Charlie?" He had to chase and hit each taunter in turn to reestablish his place in the group.

From their own and others' observations of children in a variety of contexts in this same day camp, Sroufe and his co-workers abstracted a number of rules under which school-age children find it permissible to have contact with members of the other sex (see table). They then analyzed videotaped samples of the interactions between 47 9½- to 11½-year-old boys and girls at the camp, looking for violations of those rules. The researchers noted who each child's friends were, had the children rated for social skill by their counselors, and interviewed each child about the popularity of others in the group.

The researchers found that most children observed the rules for cross-sex contact. The children who violated the rules were those who were generally unpopular with the other children. They were also judged by their counselors to be less socially competent than their peers.

These strict gender boundaries are sometimes broken in interesting ways. Often, contact between the two sexes occurs in the form of "raids" into enemy territory. From time to time, the boys will run through an area where the girls are playing and try to get the girls to chase them, or a couple of girls, shrieking with laughter, will threaten to kiss a boy. Calling a boy on the telephone and leaving a pseudoromantic message on the family answering machine is another favorite border-crossing technique. These raids are accompanied by a lot of excitement.

Barrie Thorne and Zella Luria (1986) maintain that brief cross-sex encounters, which they refer to as "border work," are a rehearsal for adult romantic relationships. Cross-cultural researchers seem to agree. For example, when Brian Sutton-Smith and John Roberts (1973) examined ethnographic reports of border work in various societies to see who chased whom, they discovered that in societies where girls marry boys from their own communities, boys and girls chase each other. But in societies where girls marry outside their communities, boys do the chasing, the pattern one would expect when males must go outside their group in pursuit of a wife.

Knowing the Rules: Under What Circumstances Is It Permissible to Have Contact with the Other Gender in Middle Childhood?

Rule:	The contact is accidental.
Example:	You're not looking where you are going and you bump into someone.
Rule:	The contact is incidental.
Example:	You go to get some lemonade and wait while two children of the other gender get some. (There should be no conversation.)
Rule:	The contact is in the guise of some clear and necessary purpose.
Example:	You may say, "Pass the lemonade," to persons of the other gender at the next table. No interest in them is expressed.
Rule:	An adult compels you to have contact.
Example:	"Go get that map from X and Y and bring it to me."
Rule:	You are accompanied by someone of your own gender.
Example:	Two girls may talk to two boys, though physical closeness with your own partner must be maintained and intimacy with the others is disallowed.
Rule:	The interaction or contact is accompanied by disavowal.
Example:	You say someone is ugly or hurl some other insult or (more commonly for boys) push or throw something at the person as you pass by.

Source: Sroufe et al., 1991.

The game called for the children to move the pen to specific places on the game board marked by four small circles. To bring the pen to one of these circles, the children had to cooperate in pulling the strings; otherwise, the pen would remain in the center or move erratically.

Each group of children was asked to play the game six times. For the first three trials Madsen and Ariella Shapira told them that the object of the game was to draw a line over the four circles in 1 minute. If they succeeded, each of them would get a prize. If they covered the four circles twice, they would get two prizes, and so on. But if they covered fewer than four circles, no one would receive a prize. Under these circumstances, children from both kinds of communities responded similarly, in a generally cooperative manner (see Figure 14.6).

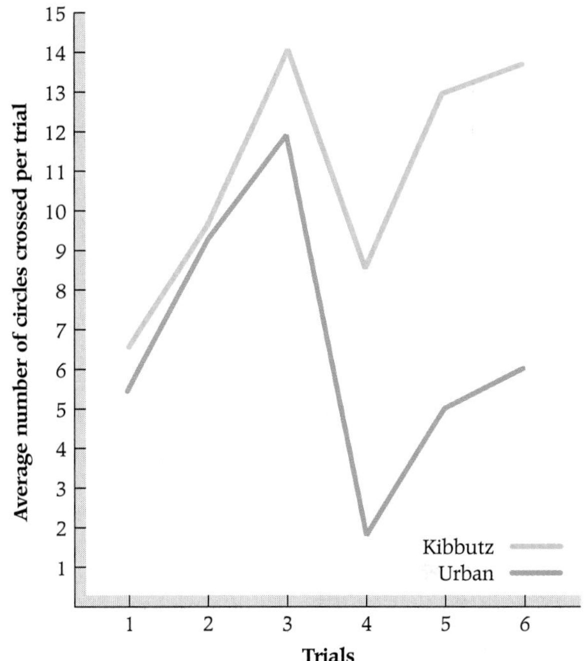

FIGURE 14.6

The average number of successful attempts to cross a target circle by urban Israeli children and by Israeli children raised in a kibbutz. On the first three trials, children were rewarded for cooperating. On the second three trials, rewards were distributed for individual achievement. Children raised on a kibbutz continued to cooperate and succeed after the first three trials, but urban children began to compete, lowering their success rate. (From Shapira & Madsen, 1969.)

After the first three trials, the experimenters changed the conditions for getting a prize. Now, a child received a prize whenever the pen crossed the circle to his or her right. Under these new conditions, a cultural difference quickly became apparent. Among the urban children, each started pulling the pen toward himself or herself. These children persisted in competing even on the fifth trial, by which time they had had ample opportunity to see that they were getting nowhere. In some cases the children would agree to cooperate, but the cooperation would break down as soon as one child pulled a little too hard on the string. As a result, their rate of success was greatly reduced.

In contrast, the children from kibbutzim responded by quickly setting up cooperative rules, saying such things as "Okay, gang, let's take turns." They also directed one another during the game with such suggestions as "We'll start here, then here." The kibbutz children were concerned that no one be rewarded more than the others, and they set up rules to see that they all shared equally in the prizes.

Using this same procedure, Madsen and his colleagues found that urban European American children, especially older ones, were far more competitive than children their own age from rural Mexico (Kagan & Madsen, 1972). When Ariela Friedman and her colleagues replicated this research in Kenya two decades later, they also found that urban children were more competitive than rural children (Friedman et al., 1995).

A similar pattern of results was obtained by George Domino (1992) when he compared the competitive and cooperative tendencies of European American children with those of children from China. In this study, the children were asked to exchange tokens for various prizes. In some cases the token could be obtained by working alone, while in other cases collaboration was required. Most of the U.S. children preferred to work alone so that they could obtain as many tokens as possible for themselves. By contrast, the Chinese children were more likely to favor collaboration with others over individual success.

At present there is no overarching explanation for what cultural factors, in particular, foster collaboration over competition. One leading possibility is that societies that value interdependence over independence also foster collaboration over competition (Kagitçibasi, 1997). But evidence of urban-rural differences in countries as unalike as the United States, Mexico, and Kenya suggest that relatively local cultural factors may be at work. (Box 14.3 addresses a related issue: What factors make it possible for different peer groups to work together?)

FRIENDSHIP: A SPECIAL FORM OF RELATIONSHIP

Friendship is generally described as a relationship of affection, reciprocity, and commitment between two people who see themselves more or less as equals (Ladd, 1999). Friendship relations differ from relations based only on social

BOX 14.3 COMPETITION AND CONFLICT BETWEEN GROUPS

In a single urban neighborhood there may be several peer groups—some based on common interests; some based on membership in a church or athletic team or, in some locales, a street gang; and some based simply on residence on the same block. Except in small, widely separated communities, peer groups are unlikely to be isolated from one another. Just as individual children must learn to get along with each other, so groups of children must find a way to regulate their interactions with other groups.

A classic series of studies by Muzafer and Carolyn Sherif (1953) provides the best evidence to date about the conditions that foster different kinds of interaction between peer groups. In the most famous of these studies, 11-year-old boys—all strangers to one another—were divided into two groups and brought to two separate summer camps in Robbers Cave State Park in Oklahoma. The boys all came from stable middle-class homes. They were all in the upper half of their class in academic standing, and all were judged to be physically healthy and well adjusted.

The boys in the two encampments went canoeing, swam, played ball, and engaged in other typical camp activities. To ensure that the boys at each encampment formed a cohesive group, the adults arranged for them to encounter problems they could solve only by cooperating. They provided the ingredients for each day's dinner, for example, but left it to the boys themselves to prepare and apportion the food. By the end of the week, friendships had formed and leaders had emerged within each group. Each group had adopted a name: they were the Rattlers and the Eagles.

When it was clear that both the Rattlers and the Eagles had formed a stable pattern of group interactions, the adults let each group know about the other. The two groups soon expressed a keen desire to compete against each other, and the adults arranged for a tournament between the two, with prizes for the winners. On the first day of competition, the Eagles lost a tug-of-war with the Rattlers. Stung by their defeat, they burned a Rattlers' flag that had been left behind. When the Rattlers returned the next morning and discovered the burned flag, they immediately seized the Eagles' flag. Scuffling and name-calling ensued. Over the next 5 days hostilities escalated. The Rattlers staged a raid on the Eagles' camp. The Eagles retaliated with a destructive raid of their own.

Once the intergroup hostility had reached a high level, the experimenters took steps to reverse it. First, they tried bringing the boys together in a series of pleasant social gatherings—joint meals, attendance at a movie, setting off firecrackers—but these attempts all failed miserably. The boys used these occasions to escalate hostilities by throwing food and calling names.

Next, the experimenters introduced a series of superordinate problems that affected the welfare of both groups equally, requiring them to combine efforts to reach a solution. The most successful application of this technique occurred during an overnight camping trip. The adults arranged for the truck that was to bring food to get stuck in a position where it could not be pushed. The boys came up with the idea of using their tug-of-war rope to pull the truck out of its predicament. The Sherifs (1956) describe the outcome:

> It took considerable effort to pull the truck. Several tries were necessary. During these efforts, a rhythmic chant of "Heave, heave" arose to accent the times of greatest effort. This rhythmic chant of "Heave, heave" had been used earlier by the Eagles during the tug-of-war contests in the period of intergroup competition and friction. Now it was being used in a cooperative activity involving both groups. When, after some strenuous efforts, the truck moved and started there was jubilation over the common success. (pp. 322–323)

After this joint achievement, the boys apparently saw no point in preparing separate meals. The two groups cooperated, making dinner without much discussion and with no outbreaks of name-calling or food throwing. The experimenters soon arranged for the truck to get stuck again. This time the boys immediately knew what to do, and the two groups mixed freely as they organized the rope pull.

By the end of the series of joint-activity problems, the boys' opinions of each other had changed significantly. Mutual respect had largely replaced hostility, and several of the boys had formed friendships in the opposite group.

The Sherifs' experiment carries an important lesson. Cooperation and competition are not fixed biological characteristics of individuals or of groups. They are forms of interaction that can be found at some time in all social groups and in all individuals; they can be, and are, heavily influenced by social context.

status. There are children who are generally rejected by their peers but who still have a best friend, and there are popular children who have no particularly close friends.

Researchers have identified several developmental functions of friendships (Hartup, 1992; Parker & Asher, 1993). These functions include providing children with

1. contexts in which to develop many basic social skills, including communication, cooperation, and the ability to resolve conflicts;

2. information about themselves, others, and the world;
3. companionship and fun that relieves the stress of everyday life; and
4. models of intimate relationships characterized by helping, caring, and trust.

Table 14.4 contains a sample set of items used to assess what children value in their friendships. It is clear from the table that friends make each other feel good about themselves, are easy to get along with, and provide mutual assistance, in addition to simple companionship (Parker & Asher, 1993).

The qualitative uniqueness and intensity of feeling that emerge from the valued characteristics of friendships shown in Table 14.4 were described by Harry Stack Sullivan (1953), a neo-Freudian who specialized in the study of interpersonal relationships:

> If you will look very closely at one of your children when he finally finds a chum . . . you will discover something very different in the relationship—namely, that your child begins to develop a new sensitivity to what matters to another person. And this is not in the sense of "what should I do to get what I want," but instead "what should I do to contribute to the happiness or to support the prestige and feeling of worth-whileness of my chum." So far as I have been ever able to discover, nothing remotely like this appears before the age of, say, 8½, and sometimes it appears decidedly later. (pp. 245–246)

Sullivan believed that children's tendency to pick out one or a few other children with whom they feel this kind of special affinity is the childhood precursor of the need for interpersonal intimacy that will be called love when it is encountered again in adolescence. He further claimed that the failure to form such friendships in childhood creates a social deficit that is difficult to remedy later. His general view of the importance of friendships is widely shared by developmentalists (Ladd, 1999; Rubin et al., 1998,1999).

Factors That Influence the Formation of Friendships

Before children can become friends, they have to spend time together, so it is no surprise that one of the major determinants of friendship between children is proximity (Meyer et al., 1998). But proximity cannot be the full story,

TABLE 14.4 CHILDREN'S VIEWS OF THE VALUES OF FRIENDSHIP

Validation and Caring
- Make each other feel important and special.
- Sticks up for me if others talk behind my back.

Conflict Resolution
- Make up easily when we fight.
- Talk about how to get over being mad at each other.

Help and Guidance
- Helps me so I can get things done quicker.
- Loan each other things all the time.

Companionship and Recreation
- Always sit together at lunch.
- Go to each other's houses.

Intimate Exchange
- Always tell each other our problems.
- Tell each other secrets.

Source: Parker & Asher, 1993, p. 615, table 1.

because most children are in the company of other children several hours every day and become friends with only a few of them.

Children tend to pick friends who are similar to themselves in a variety of ways (Rubin et al., 1994). Typically friends are the same age, the same race, the same sex, and the same general skill level in various activities. Friends are also likely to feel the same way about school (a child who likes school and gets good grades is likely to have a friend who also likes school and gets good grades) and to like the same sports, music, movies, books, and so on.

To determine how children go about becoming friends, John Gottman (1983) arranged for pairs of children of the same age to meet and play together in one of the children's homes for three sessions within the space of a month. Each session was videotaped. The children, who were strangers to each other at the start of the study, ranged from 3 to 9 years in age. In order to find out if the children became friends during the experiment, Gottman asked the host mothers to fill out a questionnaire that probed the strength and quality of the children's relationship. He then analyzed the tapes of the play sessions, comparing children who became friends with those who did not. Five aspects of the children's social interaction appeared to distinguish pairs who became friendly from those who did not:

1. *Common-ground activity.* The children who became friends were those who quickly found something they could do together. In addition, they explored their similarities and differences.
2. *Clear communication.* Children who became friends were likely to listen to each other, request clarification when they did not understand, and speak in ways that were relevant to the task at hand.
3. *Exchange of information.* Children who became friends both asked for and provided relevant information to their partners.
4. *Resolution of conflicts.* Children who became friends gave good reasons when they disagreed, and they were able to bring conflicts to a quick resolution.
5. *Reciprocity.* Children who became friends were likely to respond to their partners' positive behaviors with an appropriate positive contribution of their own.

In reviewing the tapes of the oldest children, Gottman also found that those who became friends were more attentive, emotionally positive, vocal, active, involved, relaxed, and playful with each other than were acquaintances. They were also more likely to share the same mood. These findings nicely mirror how children themselves talk about what they value in friendships.

What Do Friends Do Together?

As we saw in Chapter 10, in early childhood the focus of friendship is pretend play. Young children's descriptions of their actual friendships and of their beliefs about friendship in general reveal that they clearly place a premium on other children's potentials as playmates (Berndt, 1986). A good playmate is someone with whom the child can achieve a high level of coordination, leading to more fun, more solidarity, and more humor.

In middle childhood, belonging and social acceptance are the major themes of friendship. At this point in their lives, children recognize that their age-mates have different statuses and that play groups are hierarchically organized into leaders and followers. Children's awakened sensitivity to their relative status among their peers leads them to be particularly concerned about the possibility that they will be rejected or have their feelings hurt (Parker & Gottman, 1989).

As a result of their focus on acceptance and status within the group, one of the major things friends do is gossip together. Although gossip is often thought of as "malicious," it serves several purposes in keeping a friendship going, aside from providing entertainment. Children use it to regulate their friendships, affirm feelings of belonging, and establish cultural norms. It is, according to Jeffrey Parker and John Gottman (1989), "the mortar as well as much of the brick of friendship conversation during middle childhood" (p. 114). It is through gossip that children carry out the basic social reciprocities and information exchanges that are central to friendship.

Of course, childhood friends do more than just gossip. As they move toward adolescence, they increasingly exchange intimate personal knowledge. They are also more generous, cooperative, and helpful with each other. Friends also compete with each other, go to school together, and hang out after school engaging in all those forms of "doing nothing" that Robert Paul Smith described in the epigraph to this chapter.

Friendship and Social Competence

Many of the personal characteristics that are important for the development of peer relations in general are also important in the formation of friendships. Of particular importance is that children be able to understand how their friends think and feel, the capacity we described in Chapter 10 (p. 415) as *socioemotional competence.* Psychologists who study the development of friendship use a similar term, **social competence,** to refer to the set of skills that collectively result in successful social functioning with peers (Howes, 1987). According to Jacqueline Goodnow and Ailsa Burns (1985, p. 134), the most important elements of social competence for the formation of friendships include

1. knowing how to make successful overtures;
2. learning what is expected at various stages of friendship;
3. working out which people are unlikely candidates for friendship;
4. deepening one's relationships with people who are likely to be rewarding friends;
5. keeping things going in a manner pleasing to both parties;
6. making sure that each party puts a similar effort into the relationship, without keeping too close a tally;
7. avoiding the risk of placing too much trust in someone likely to prove fickle;
8. fighting off challenges from those who want to "steal" one's friends;
9. avoiding getting stuck with friends one no longer finds appealing;
10. avoiding a reputation for disloyalty and self-seeking;
11. avoiding being stranded without friends; and
12. achieving resilience in the face of being dumped.

One important aspect of social competence is **social perspective taking,** the ability to adopt another person's perspective in the social realm. To study its development, Robert Selman (1980) compared children's social perspective-taking skills (as revealed by their interpretations of specially constructed stories) with their understanding of friendship (as revealed by structured clinical interviews). He found that children who responded to social perspective-taking problems at a high level were also likely to have more sophisticated ideas about friendship. Table 14.5, which summarizes Selman's findings, shows that children's reasoning in each domain develops from uncoordinated, individualistic understanding, to understanding that coordinates two perspectives, and then to a stage in which individual perspectives are viewed in the context of a

social competence The set of skills that collectively result in successful social functioning with peers.

social perspective taking The ability to adopt another person's perspective in the social realm.

TABLE 14.5 HOW SELMAN RELATES DEVELOPMENTAL LEVELS OF PERSPECTIVE TAKING TO DEVELOPMENTAL LEVELS OF FRIENDSHIP

DEVELOPMENTAL LEVEL IN COORDINATION OF PERSPECTIVES	STAGE OF UNDERSTANDING REFLECTED IN CLOSE FRIENDSHIPS
Level 0 (Approximately Ages 3 to 7) *Egocentric or undifferentiated perspective.* Children do not distinguish their own perspective from that of others. They do not yet recognize that others may interpret the same social experience or course of action differently from the way they do.	**Stage 0** *Momentary playmates.* A close friend is someone who lives close by and with whom one is playing.
Level 1 (Approximately Ages 4 to 9) *Subjective or differentiated perspectives.* The child understands that others' perspectives may differ from her own.	**Stage 1** *One-way assistance.* A friend does what one wants. A close friend is someone who shares the same dislikes and likes.
Level 2 (Approximately Ages 6 to 12) *Self-reflective or reciprocal perspective.* The child is now able to view his own thoughts and feelings from another's perspective.	**Stage 2** *Fair-weather cooperation.* With their new awareness of the reciprocal nature of personal perspectives, children become concerned with coordinating their thoughts and actions, rather than adjusting them to a fixed standard, as they did before. Relationships depend on adjustment and cooperation and fall apart over arguments.
Level 3 (Approximately Ages 9 to 15) *Third-person or mutual perspective.* The child at this level can step outside of an interaction and take the perspective of a third party.	**Stage 3** *Intimate and mutually shared relationships.* Friendships are seen as the basic means of developing mutual intimacy and mutual support. At this stage friendship transcends momentary interactions, including conflicts. The primary limitation of this stage is possessiveness and jealousy.
Level 4 (Approximately Ages 12 to Adulthood) *Societal or in-depth perspective.* Children at this level are able to take the generalized perspective of society, the law, or morality.	**Stage 4** *Autonomous, interdependent friendships.* This stage is characterized by an awareness of the interdependence of friends for support and a sense of identity and at the same time an acceptance of the other's need to establish relations with other people.

Source: Adapted from Selman, 1981.

more complex system. This sequence fits closely with Piaget's theory that young children's egocentricity restricts them to their own point of view, whereas older children can keep two aspects of a problem in mind at the same time (see Chapter 9, p. 339, and Chapter 12, pp. 476–486).

Overall it appears that higher levels of reasoning about interpersonal relationships, including friendships, provide children with a variety of resources for dealing with their social environment. They are more skilled at the use of **social repair mechanisms,** strategies that allow friends to remain friends even when serious differences temporarily drive them apart. Social repair mechanisms take on importance in middle childhood because of children's changed social circumstances. When no caregiver is present, children must settle conflicts on their own. Examples of social repair mechanisms include disengaging before a disagreement escalates into a fight, staying nearby after a fight to smooth things over, and minimizing the importance of a conflict once it is over. Each of these strategies increases the likelihood that when the conflict is over, the children will still be friends.

social repair mechanisms Strategies that allow friends to remain friends even when serious differences temporarily drive them apart.

In this confluence of changed social circumstances and increased social competence, we see that neither the social nor the cognitive characteristics of middle childhood could emerge without the other. They are two facets of a single developmental process.

PARENTAL INFLUENCES ON CHILDREN'S PEER RELATIONS

While family life and peer relationships sometimes appear to be two separate social worlds, they are linked in at least two general ways. First, patterns of parent–child interaction, both in early childhood and later, provide working models for how people should interact with each other that carry over to interactions among peers. Second, the way parents keep track of, and organize, children's interactions with peers has a direct effect on the course of their peer relations (Collins & Laursen, 1999; Rubin et al., 1999).

With respect to the idea that early family relationships set the stage for peer relations, there is a considerable body of evidence indicating (as discussed in Chapter 7, p. 283) that secure attachment in infancy enhances development of peer relations in early childhood and leads to better personal relationships later in life (see Rubin et al., 1999, for an overview). Alan Sroufe and his colleagues (Sroufe et al., 1999) call this a "cascade effect,"

> wherein early family relationships provide the necessary support for effectively engaging the world of peers, which, in turn, provides the foundation for deeper and more extensive and complex peer relationships. Each phase supports the unfolding of subsequent capacities (p. 258).

The idea of a cascade effect also applies to negative forms of attachment, which lay the foundation for poor peer relations.

As appealing as the logic of this analysis is, we need to keep in mind the evidence presented in Chapter 7 (p. 284), indicating that early family interactions do not necessarily have discernible long-lasting consequences (Kagan, 1998; Lewis, 1997). Whether or not the developmental cascade that Sroufe describes actually takes place depends critically on the stability of the environmental conditions with which early family interactions are associated.

There is ample evidence with respect to the idea that current parent–child relations in the family influence peer relations (Rubin et al., 1998). Aggressive behavior is a good case in point. As we saw in Chapter 10, parents may unwittingly encourage their children to behave aggressively when they themselves engage in coercive, power-assertive modes of socialization. Since aggressive behavior in children is associated with rejection by their peers, a number of researchers have focused on coercive family interaction patterns as a possible source of low social status in middle childhood (Dishion et al., 1994; Hart et al., 1990; Putallaz & Heflin, 1990).

In one such study, Thomas Dishion (1990) collected information on the social status of over 200 boys between the ages of 9 and 10 by interviewing their teachers and classmates. Through interviews with the parents and the boys themselves, as well as home observations, he also obtained evidence about the children's family socialization patterns and their behavior in the family setting. Dishion found that the boys who were exposed to more coercive family experiences at home were the ones most likely to be rejected by their peers at school. These boys not only were more aggressive with their peers but also behaved badly in the classroom. Although boys from lower-income homes were more likely to fall within the rejected category, Dishion's data showed that socioeconomic class was not a direct cause of lower peer status or aggressive behavior. Rather, in accord with findings discussed in Chapter 11 (pp. 436–437), he found that poverty affected social status and behavior indirectly by increasing the general level of stress within the family. When parents coped well enough with the pressures of poverty to treat their

retrospective study A follow-back research method that starts with developmental outcomes in later childhood and looks back at the individual's early life for predictive signs of those later outcomes.

children in a noncoercive way, the children were less likely to have low social status among their peers. These results were replicated and supplemented in a study conducted in the People's Republic of China (Chen & Rubin, 1994).

In addition to influencing their children's peer relations indirectly through parent–child interactions, parents can have a direct effect on them in a number of ways. To begin with, they have considerable power to determine the contexts in which their children spend their time (Whiting, 1980). They choose, for example, the neighborhood in which they live and where their children go to school (and, hence, who their children have as potential playmates and who they go to school with). They also provide or deny their children opportunities to interact with other children in specific activities during nonschool hours (Parke & Ladd, 1992).

Another way in which parents directly influence their children's peer relations is by monitoring where their children are, who they are with, and what they are doing (Pettit et al., 1999). Children whose parents do not know where they are or who they are with are more likely to engage in antisocial behavior and to face rejection by their peers (see Ladd, 1999, for a review of this evidence).

THE SIGNIFICANCE OF PEER RELATIONS FOR CHILDREN'S DEVELOPMENT

What significance do peer relations have for children's development? The current thinking among developmentalists is that "children who are successful with peers are on track for adaptive and psychologically healthy outcomes, whereas those who fail to adapt to the peer milieu are at risk for maladaptive outcomes" (Parker et al., 1995, p. 96).

A great deal of research supports this view. Differences in peer-group relations in middle childhood are clearly related to later differences in children's cognitive and social development, their achievement in school, their success in forming good social relations in adolescence, and their own personal sense of well-being (see Figure 14.7). However, the processes that produce these kinds of outcomes are only partially understood (Collins & Laursen, 1999; Ladd, 1999; Rubin et al., 1998, 1999).

Researchers have used two methods for tracking this potential cascade effect of peer-group relationships. **Retrospective studies** use a "follow-back" method that starts with developmental outcomes in later childhood and beyond and looks back at the individual's early life for predictive signs of those outcomes. For example, a psychologist might examine the records of people who become school dropouts or criminals to see if there are any signs in their early lives that might have predicted these outcomes.

Perhaps the most convincing retrospective evidence for the importance of childhood peer relationships on later development comes from a study by Emory Cowen and his colleagues (Cowen, 1973). These researchers, who initially were interested in the long-term consequences of children's social status, asked third-graders to select classmates they thought would fit certain roles (such as the hero/heroine or the villain) in a hypothetical class play. Over a decade later, a county psychiatric registry was created that contained the names of everyone who had come in contact with a psychiatric facility in that county. The existence of this registry made it possible for Cowen and his colleagues to conduct a retrospective analysis by identifying all the third-graders in their study whose names appeared in the registry and then checking to see what their social status had been. They found that as third-graders these chil-

FIGURE 14.7
A letter from a friendless man giving his account of the importance of childhood friendships for development. (From Hartup, 1978.)

DEAR DR

I read the report in the Oct. 30 issue of ____________ about your study of only children. I am an only child, now 57 years old and I want to tell you some things about my life. Not only was I an only child but I grew up in the country where there were no nearby children to play with. My mother did not want children around. She used to say 'I don't want my kid to bother anybody and I don't want nobody's kids bothering me.'

. . . From the first year of school I was teased and made fun of. For example, in about third or fourth grade I dreaded to get on the school bus to go to school because the other children on the bus called me 'Mommy's baby.' In about the second grade I heard the boys use a vulgar word. I asked what it meant and they made fun of me. So I learned a lesson–don't ask questions. This can lead to a lot of confusion to hear talk one doesn't understand and not be able to learn what it means . . .

I never went out with a girl while I was in school–in fact I hardly talked to them. In our school the boys and girls did not play together. Boys were sent to one part of the playground and girls to another. So, I didn't learn anything about girls. When we got into high school and the boys and girls started dating I could only listen to their stories about their experiences.

I could tell you a lot more but the important thing is I have never married or had any children. I have not been very successful in an occupation or vocation. I believe my troubles are not all due to being an only child, but I do believe you are right in recommending playmates for preschool children and I will add playmates for the school agers and not have them strictly supervised by adults. I believe I confirm the experiments with monkeys in being overly timid sometimes and overly aggressive sometimes. Parents of only children should make special efforts to provide playmates for [their children].

Sincerely yours,

dren were likely to have been chosen by their classmates for the less desirable roles in the play.

Although children who are rejected because they are aggressive are at much greater risk for long-time difficulties than withdrawn rejected children, being frozen out of the group for being shy or merely different can be a very distressful experience.

The second method used to trace the outcomes associated with different peer statuses is the **prospective study**, in which children are studied as they grow older. Developmentalists prefer to use this forward-looking, longitudinal approach because they can be sure that the data were gathered with the goal of testing a particular hypothesis about developmental trajectories.

The prospective evidence that peer relations affect later life is considerably more detailed than the retrospective evidence, but the major conclusion is the same: Peer status and friendship in middle childhood predict a good deal about what kinds of successes and difficulties children will have in later years.

A few studies give a representative sample of these findings. For example, John Coie and his colleagues (Coie et al., 1992) conducted a 3-year prospective study during which children graduated from elementary school and began attending middle school. The junior high teachers of the children who were rejected in elementary school reported that many of these children misbehaved in class, were aggressive and physically uncontrolled, and had short attention spans. The children themselves reported their own sense of being rejected. They were more likely than other children to fail a grade and experienced more difficulties in the transition to middle school. They were also more likely to drop out of school. In another study, 25 percent of low-accepted children later dropped out of school, compared with 8 percent of children who were not rejected by their peers (Ollendick et al., 1992).

Rejected children experience difficulties that extend beyond the classroom into everyday life. They show higher levels of delinquency, substance abuse, and psychological disturbances than children who are accepted by their peers, and, unsurprisingly, they are almost twice as likely to be arrested as juvenile delinquents (Kupersmidt & Coie, 1990; Ollendick et al., 1992).

Recall, however, that not all forms of rejection are the same. Across studies, it appears that a combination of aggressiveness and rejection in peer interactions is especially perilous for children. Rejected aggressive children are the ones most likely to come into contact with law enforcement or spend time in a psychiatric ward (Ladd, 1999; Rubin et al., 1998). A similar fate awaits bullies. One influential study found that bullies were four times as likely as other children to have criminal records as young adults (Olweus, 1993).

CHANGING RELATIONS WITH PARENTS

As children grow older, the nature of parent–child interactions changes in a number of ways. For one thing, there is an overall decrease in overt affection (Collins et al., 1997). Parents no longer act as if their children are adorable; they expect them to behave themselves and perform appropriately. The children, for their part, are often embarrassed when their parents do show them open affection in public because they don't want to be "treated like a baby." They are also less likely to use such coercive behaviors such as whining, yelling, or hitting: now they argue with their parents and point out their parents' inconsistencies.

Parents are also more severe with older children and are more critical of the mistakes they make (Maccoby, 1984). Two related factors combine to account for this change in parental standards and behavior as children enter middle childhood. First, parents all over the world believe that the children should now be more capable and responsible. Second, the strategies parents adopt to influence their children's good behavior and correct their bad behavior change as children's competence increases (Goodnow, 1998; Lamb et al., 1999).

prospective study A forward-looking research method in which children are studied as they grow older.

For children in all cultures, middle childhood brings an increase in what adults expect of them. In many cultures, children, like this Inuit girl, are expected to attain competence in activities that contribute to the family's means of subsistence.

The precise ages at which parents expect children to be able to display behavioral competence in different areas varies across cultures. Jacqueline Goodnow and her colleagues asked Japanese, American, Australian, and Australian Lebanese mothers at what approximate age—before the age of 4 years, between 4 and 6 years, or after 6 years of age—they expected children to be capable of each of 38 kinds of behavior (Goodnow et al., 1984). As Table 14.6 indicates, Japanese mothers expected their children to display emotional maturity, compliance, and ritual forms of politeness at an earlier age than mothers in the other three groups. (Note that the numbers in the table columns represent not ages but the means for three age categories, with 1 representing 6 or older, 2 representing age 4 to 5, and 3 representing under age 4. Thus, the lower the number, the later the children are expected to show competence.) The American and Australian mothers expected their children to develop social skills and the ability to assert themselves verbally relatively early. The Australian Lebanese mothers were distinctive in their willingness to let the children attain the needed competencies in their own good time; their developmental timetables were usually later than those of the other groups. Despite cultural variations in the precise age at which the various competencies were expected to be achieved, all the parents expected their children to master these basic competencies sometime during middle childhood.

Related to this change in parents' expectations is a change in the issues that arise between parents and children. According to Eleanor Maccoby (1980), parents of young children are concerned with establishing daily routines and controlling temper tantrums and fights, as well as teaching children to care for, dress, feed, and groom themselves. While some of the issues of early childhood, especially fights among siblings, are still of concern during the years from 6 to 12, a whole new set of issues crop up when children start to take responsibility for chores at home, attend school, work, and spend increasing time away from adult supervision.

In economically developed countries, school is a prominent arena in which children's achievement is judged by parents. Parents worry about how involved they should become in their child's schoolwork, what they should do if a child has academic problems, and how they should deal with school behavior problems. Other matters of concern to parents during middle childhood include the extent to which they should monitor their children's social

TABLE 14.6 MEAN AGES AT WHICH MOTHERS IN FOUR CULTURAL GROUPS EXPECT THEIR CHILDREN TO ATTAIN VARIOUS COMPETENCIES

(1 = 6 years or older; 2 = 4–5 years; 3 = younger than 4 years)

Item	Japan	United States	Australia	
			A*	B†
Emotional Maturity				
Does not cry easily	2.49	2.08	1.66	1.95
Can get over anger by self	2.67	1.69	1.93	1.38
Stands disappointment without crying	2.34	1.97	1.83	1.65
Does not use baby talk	2.07	1.91	2.66	2.76
Compliance				
Comes or answers when called	2.66	2.21	1.79	1.13
Stops misbehaving when told	2.57	2.33	2.28	1.57
Gives up reading/TV to help mother	1.33	1.54	1.59	1.51
Politeness				
Greets family courteously	2.90	2.22	2.69	2.38
Uses polite forms (please) to adults	2.08	2.37	2.76	2.73
Independence				
Stays home alone for an hour or so	1.78	1.04	1.10	1.05
Takes care of own clothes	2.17	1.87	1.55	1.35
Makes phone calls without help	1.41	1.21	1.14	1.21
Sits at table and eats without help	2.95	2.76	2.79	2.59
Does regular household tasks	2.03	1.97	2.07	1.32
Can entertain self alone	2.74	2.78	2.72	1.78
Plays outside without supervision	1.98	2.19	2.38	1.40
Social Skills				
Waits for turn in games	2.31	2.12	1.97	1.89
Shares toys with other children	2.62	2.72	2.72	1.73
Sympathetic to feelings of children	1.86	2.13	1.79	1.22
Resolves disagreement without fighting	1.41	1.70	1.45	1.11
Gets own way by persuading friends	1.40	1.94	1.97	1.30
Takes initiative in playing with others	1.59	2.48	2.24	1.73
Verbal Assertiveness				
Answers a question clearly	2.10	1.98	2.14	1.46
States own preference when asked	1.72	2.25	2.00	1.30
Asks for explanation when in doubt	1.71	2.30	2.21	1.38
Can explain why s/he thinks so	1.48	2.09	1.76	1.32
Stands up for own rights with others	1.62	2.27	2.10	1.24
Miscellaneous				
Uses scissors without supervision	2.00	1.54	1.52	1.11
Keeps feet off furniture	2.74	2.30	2.31	2.05
Disagrees without biting or throwing	2.43	2.34	2.38	1.92
Answers phone properly	1.52	1.49	2.10	1.98
Resolves quarrels without adult help	1.52	1.73	1.52	1.46

* Born in Australia.
† Born in Lebanon.
Source: Goodnow et al., 1984.

life and whether they should require their children to do chores around the house and, if so, what standards of performance to expect of them and whether to pay them (Goodnow, 1998). In less developed countries, where a family's survival often depends on putting children to work as early as possible, parents worry about their children's ability to take care of younger kin in the absence of adult supervision and to carry out important economic tasks such as caring for livestock or hoeing weeds (Weisner, 1996).

As children grow older and are increasingly held responsible for themselves, parents attempt to influence their behavior by reasoning with them, appealing to their self-esteem ("You wouldn't do anything that stupid") or to their sense of humor, and arousing their sense of guilt. In many societies, when school-age children break rules, their parents are less likely to spank them than to deprive them of privileges or ground them (Lamb et al., 1999).

In sum, parents increasingly share their control over their children's lives with the children themselves (Collins et al., 1997). Maccoby (1984) terms this sharing of responsibility **coregulation.** Coregulation is built on parent–child cooperation. It requires that parents work out methods of monitoring, guiding, and supporting their children when adults are not present, using the time they are together to reinforce their children's understandings of right and wrong, what is safe and unsafe, and when they need to come to adults for help. For coregulation to succeed, children must be willing to inform their parents of their whereabouts, their activities, and their problems.

A NEW SENSE OF SELF

The significant rearrangement of children's social lives that takes place in the transition from early to middle childhood is accompanied by equally striking developments in how children think about themselves, the emergence of a new level of sensitivity to their personal standing among their peers, and their resulting efforts to maintain their self-esteem.

CHANGING CONCEPTS OF THE SELF

A sizable body of evidence suggests that as children move from early childhood to middle childhood and then to adolescence their sense of self undergoes marked changes that parallel the changes occurring in their cognitive and social processes (Harter, 1999; Mascolo & Fischer, 1998).

To understand how children's conceptions of themselves change as they grow older, William Damon and Daniel Hart (1988) asked children between 4 and 15 years of age to describe themselves. They found that all the children referred to their appearance, their activities, their relations to others, and their psychological characteristics, but both the importance they attached to these various characteristics and the complexity of their self-concepts changed with age. As the data in Table 14.7 show, children between the ages of 4 and 7 years make categorical statements about aspects of themselves that place them in socially recognized categories ("I'm 6 years old"), but they seldom make comparative judgments. According to these data, comparative judgments relating one's own characteristics to those of others make their appearance sometime between the ages of 8 and 11 years (see Figure 14.8 for a self-description from a 7½-year-old girl).

Subsequent research has supported the picture of a general trend from self-concepts based on limited, concrete characteristics to more abstract and stable conceptions arrived at through **social comparison,** the process of defining oneself in relation to one's peers (Ruble & Frey, 1991).

There is no mystery as to why social comparison begins to play a significant role in children's sense of themselves during middle childhood. The

coregulation A form of indirect social control in which parents and children cooperate to reinforce the children's understandings of right and wrong, what is safe and unsafe, when they are not under direct adult control.

social comparison The process of defining oneself in relation to one's peers.

TABLE 14.7 A Developmental Model of Self-Concept

Level of Self-Concept	Area of Evaluation: Physical	Activity-Based	Social	Psychological
1. Categorical identification (4–7 years)	I have blue eyes. I'm 6 years old.	I play baseball. I play and read a lot.	I'm Catholic. I'm Sarah's friend.	I get funny ideas sometimes. I'm happy.
2. Comparative assessments (8–11 years)	I'm bigger than most kids. I have really light skin, because I'm Scandinavian.	I'm not very good at school. I'm good at math, but I'm not so good at art.	I like it when my mom and dad watch me play baseball. I do well in school because my parents respect me for it.	I'm not as smart as most kids. I get upset more easily than other kids.
3. Interpersonal implications (12–15 years)	I am a four-eyed person. Everyone makes fun of me. I have blonde hair, which is good because boys like blondes.	I play sports, which is important because all kids like athletes. I treat people well so I'll have friends when I need them.	I am an honest person, so people trust me. I'm very shy, so I don't have many friends.	I understand people, so they come to me with their problems. I'm the kind of person who loves being with my friends; they make me feel good about being me.

Source: After Damon & Hart, 1988.

increased time they spend with their peers and their greater ability to understand others' points of view lead children to engage in a new kind of questioning about themselves. Depending on the setting, they must decide on such questions as "Am I good at sports?" "Am I a good friend?" "Do the other kids like me?" "Am I good at math?" Such questions have no absolute answer because there are no absolute criteria of success. Rather, success is measured in relation to the performance of others in the social group. The many comparisons children make in a wide variety of settings provide them with a new overall sense of themselves.

The process of social comparison can be quite complex. When deliberate and pervasive social comparison becomes important at around 8 years of age, children are initially inclined to make overt social comparisons in interaction with their peers, saying such things as "My picture is the best one." But they soon discover that this kind of comparison is perceived as bragging and is likely to evoke negative reactions. As a consequence, they begin to develop more subtle ways of making social comparisons: instead of telling another child that they are faster at doing math or better at a video game, they will ask the other child, "What problem are you on?" or "What was your highest

All About Me

Hi, my name is Leila. There are many good things and bad things about me. I'm spunky, mischievous girl. I have brown hair and brown eyes. My eyes are dark and my hair is never the same length for over a year. My hair is sometimes curly, and sometimes straight. I am a Jewish girl.

FIGURE 14.8
A self description written by Leila after reading the descriptions of the heroines on the back of "The American Girl" books. She was 7½ at the time.

Social comparison is an integral part of these children's daily lives, allowing them to compare aspects of their personalities, abilities, and social circumstances with those of their peers.

score?" (Pomerantz et al., 1995). Overt expressions of superiority are more likely to be used to intentionally make another child feel bad.

Sometime around the age of 7 or 8, children also begin to describe themselves in terms of more general, stable traits. Instead of saying "I can kick a ball far" or "I know my ABC's," they begin to say "I am a good athlete" or " I am smart." At the same time, they begin to assume more consistently that other people also have stable traits that can be used to anticipate what they will do in a variety of contexts (Ruble & Dweck, 1995). Taken as a whole, studies in this area indicate that children begin to attribute stability to the psychological states of others at about the same time they begin to think about themselves as having stable traits.

FIGURE 14.9
A sample item used to elicit information about children's self-esteem. Children were asked to indicate which picture corresponded most closely to themselves by marking the appropriate circle. The small circle means that the picture applies a little, the large circle that it applies a lot. (From Harter & Pike, 1984.)

SELF-ESTEEM

As we mentioned in Chapter 10 (p. 399), Erik Erikson (1963) thought of middle childhood as the time when children have to resolve the crisis of industry versus inferiority. If children judge themselves (and are judged by others) as being industrious and meeting the new assignments they are given by adults at work and at school, then they are able to maintain positive **self-esteem,** that is, a positive self-evaluation of one's own worth; but if they fail to demonstrate that they are capable, they feel "inferior" and, as a result, their self-esteem suffers.

Susan Harter, a developmental researcher and clinician, has been intrigued by the question of children's evaluations of themselves and their development of self-esteem for more than 20 years. Her research has shown that self-esteem is an important index of mental health. High self-esteem during childhood has been linked to satisfaction and happiness in later life, while low self-esteem has been linked to depression, anxiety, and maladjustment both in school and in social relations.

To study the basis on which children's evaluations of themselves change in the transition from early to middle childhood, Harter and Robin Pike (1984) presented 4-, 5-, 6-, and 7-year-olds with pairs of pictures like those in Figure 14.9 and asked them to say whether each picture was a lot or a little like them. Each picture was selected to tap the children's judgments in one of four domains important to self-esteem: cognitive competence, physical

Really true for me	Sort of true for me	Some kids often forget what they learn	but	Other kids can remember things easily	Sort of true for me	Really true for me
☐	☐				☐	☐

FIGURE 14.10

A sample item from Harter's scale of self-esteem. Choices to the left of center indicate degrees of poor self-esteem. Choices to the right indicate degrees of positive self-esteem. (From Harter, 1982.)

competence, peer acceptance, and maternal acceptance. All the items presented to the children were age-appropriate and comparable. For example, an item such as "Knows the alphabet," used to assess cognitive competence in the 4- and 5-year-olds, corresponded to the item "Can read alone" for the 6- and 7-year-olds.

The pattern of children's responses to these self-evaluation tasks revealed that they judged their own worth in terms of two broad categories—competence and acceptance. Statistical analysis revealed that the children lumped cognitive and physical competence together in a single category of competence and combined peer and maternal acceptance in the single category of acceptance. Nevertheless, the scale seemed to tap children's feelings of self-worth in a realistic way. Harter and Pike found, for example, that the picture selections of children who had been held back a grade reflected a self-evaluation of low competence while the picture selections of newcomers to a school reflected a self-evaluation of low acceptance.

In research on somewhat older children (8 to 12 years old), Harter (1982) assessed self-esteem using the written format shown in Figure 14.10. She found that these older children made more differentiated self-evaluations; for example, they distinguished between cognitive, social, and physical competence (Harter, 1987). (Table 14.8 shows the content of sample items in each domain of self-esteem included in Harter's scale for 8- to 12-year-olds.)

At the same time that older children's self-evaluations become more differentiated, a new level of integration in the components of self-esteem appears, enabling children to form an overall sense of their general self-worth (see Table 14.8) (Harter, 1999).

Another aspect of children's changing ideas about themselves in middle childhood is that they begin to form representations of the kind of person they would like to be—an "ideal self" against which they measure their "actual self," that is, the person they actually believe they are. The fact that there is likely to be a discrepancy between childrens' actual and ideal selves can be

TABLE 14.8 HARTER SELF-ESTEEM SCALE FOR 8- TO 12-YEAR-OLDS

AREA OF SELF-EVALUATION	CONTENT OF SAMPLE ITEMS
Cognitive competence	Good at schoolwork, can figure out answers, remember easily, remember what is read
Social competence	Have a lot of friends, popular, do things with kids, easy to like
Physical competence	Do well at sports, good at games, chosen first for games
General self-worth	Sure of myself, do things fine, I am a good person, I want to stay the same

Source: Harter, 1982.

self-esteem One's evaluation of one's own self-worth.

either a source of motivation toward self-improvement or a source of distress and discouragement, depending on the perceived degree of discrepancy.

Of course, not all discrepancies between the actual and ideal selves are equally important. If, for example, being athletic is not important to a child, then her self-worth will not be much affected by her feelings that she isn't a good athlete and will never become one. On the other hand, if her athletic ability is a core part of her sense of self, then it can be devastating to know that she will never be much good at sports (Harter, 1998).

Harter and others also report that there is an age-related change in the extent to which children's self-evaluations fit the views of others (Harter, 1999). Younger children's rating of their peers' "smartness" at school generally agrees with teachers' evaluations. Their ratings of their own smartness, however, do not correlate with either their teachers' or their peers' ratings. Around the age of 8, children's self-evaluations begin to fit with the judgments of both their peers and their teachers. This pattern of results fits nicely with the conclusion presented above that an overall sense of oneself in relation to others arises around the age of 8. It also fits with the evidence presented in this chapter (p. 582) that social perspective taking undergoes a marked improvement during the transition to middle childhood.

Foundations of Self-Esteem

Self-esteem has been linked to patterns of child rearing (Coopersmith, 1967; Feiring & Taska, 1996). In an extensive study of 10- to 12-year-old boys, Stanley Coopersmith found that parents of boys with high self-esteem (as determined by their answers to a questionnaire and their teachers' ratings) employed a style of parenting strikingly similar to the "authoritative" pattern described by Diana Baumrind in her study of parenting (see Chapter 11). Recall that authoritative parents are distinguished by their mixture of firm control, promotion of high standards of behavior, encouragement of independence, and willingness to reason with their children. Coopersmith's data suggest that three parental characteristics combine to produce high self-esteem in late middle childhood:

1. *Parents' acceptance of their children.* The mothers of sons with high self-esteem had closer, more affectionate relationships with their children than did mothers of children with low self-esteem. The children seemed to appreciate this approval and to view their mothers as supportive. They also tended to interpret their mothers' interest as an indication of their personal importance, as a consequence of which they came to regard themselves favorably. "This is success in its most personal expression—the concern, attention, and time of significant others" (Coopersmith, 1967, p. 179).
2. *Parents' setting of clearly defined limits.* Parents' imposition and enforcement of strict limits on their children's activities appeared to give the children a sense that norms are real and significant and contributed to their self-definition.
3. *Parents' respect for individuality.* Within the limits set by the parents' sense of standards and social norms, the children with high self-esteem were allowed a great deal of individual self-expression. Parents showed respect for these children by reasoning with them and considering their points of view.

Taken together, contemporary evidence suggests that the key to high self-esteem is the feeling, transmitted in large part by the family, that one has some ability to control one's own future by controlling both oneself and one's environment (Harter, 1998). This feeling of control is not without bounds. As Coopersmith's data suggest, children who have a positive self-image know their boundaries, but this awareness does not detract from their feeling of effectiveness. Rather, it sets clear limits within which the person feels considerable assurance and freedom.

MIDDLE CHILDHOOD RECONSIDERED

With the evidence from this and the preceding two chapters before us, it is appropriate to return to the question of whether the transition from early to middle childhood constitutes a bio-social-behavioral shift. Is middle childhood a stage of development characterized by a common set of features in every culture?

Table 14.9 summarizes the changes that appear to distinguish middle childhood from early childhood. We have placed the social domain at the top because surveys of the world's cultures make it clear that adults everywhere assign 6- and 7-year-olds to a new social category and require that they behave themselves in new (and sometimes stressful) contexts. Whether individual children are fully prepared or not, they must adapt to their new duties and roles or face the displeasure of their parents and the scorn of their peers.

Another universal characteristic of middle childhood is the rise of the peer group as a major context for development. For the first time, children must define their status within a group of relative equals without the intervention of adults. In many cultures, interactions with peers become coordinated, with games governed by rules serving as surrogates for adult control. The experience of negotiating these interactions and comparing themselves with peers contributes to children's mastery of the social conventions and moral rules that regulate their communities. Peer interactions also provide crucial contexts within which children arrive at a new, more complex, and global sense of themselves.

The new cognitive capacities that develop at this time are less obvious than changes in the social domain but are no less important in creating a qualitatively distinct stage of development. As we saw in Chapters 12 and 13, thought processes in middle childhood become more logical, deliberate, and consistent. Children become more capable of thinking through actions and

TABLE 14.9 THE BIO-SOCIAL-BEHAVIORAL SHIFT THAT INITIATES MIDDLE CHILDHOOD

Social Domain
- Peer-group participation
- Rule-based games without direct adult supervision
- Deliberate instruction
- Golden Rule morality
- Coregulation of behavior between parent and child
- Social comparison

Behavioral Domain
- Increased memory capacity; strategic remembering
- Concrete operations
- Logical classification
- Decreased egocentrism and improved perspective taking

Biological Domain
- Loss of baby teeth and gain of permanent teeth
- Growth spurt in frontal lobes and in overall brain size
- Sharp increase in EEG coherence

their consequences; they are able to engage in concentrated acts of deliberate learning in the absence of tangible rewards; they keep in mind the points of view of other people in a wider variety of contexts; and they learn to moderate their emotional reactions in order to facilitate smooth relations with their parents and their peers. As we have emphasized several times, these cognitive changes must be considered as both cause and effect of the social changes discussed in this chapter.

Least visible are the biological changes that underpin children's apparent new mental capacities and modes of social interaction. The fact that children are bigger, stronger, and better coordinated is obvious enough. But only recently has modern anatomical and neurophysiological research provided evidence of such subtle changes as the proliferation of brain circuitry, changing relations between different kinds of brain-wave activity, and the greatly expanded influence of the brain's frontal lobes. Without such biological changes, the cognitive and social changes we have reviewed would not be possible. By the same token, when children are deprived of experience, such biological changes do not occur normally.

If we were to consider each element in the transition to middle childhood separately, it would be difficult to sustain the argument that it is initiated by a bio-social-behavioral shift and represents a qualitatively stagelike change from earlier periods. After all, preschoolers, in the company of older children, sometimes play without adult supervision; they have been shown to exhibit logical thinking and the use of memory strategies in some contexts; and their play contains elements of rules as well as social roles. But the changes we have documented do not occur separately; they occur in the kind of loosely coordinated ensemble that we have come to expect of a bio-social-behavioral shift. Although the details vary from one culture and one child to the next, the overall pattern is consistent and thus suggests a distinctive stage of life.

The existence of a universal pattern of changes associated with middle childhood in no way contradicts the fact that there are significant variations among cultures in the particular ways they conceive of and organize 6- to 12-year-old children's lives. Societies in which formal schooling is a central arena for children's development are especially likely to encourage uniformity in the age at which children begin to enter into the mode of life typical of middle childhood. Rural agrarian societies, in which the change in children's activities is less extreme, are less precise in the specific age at which a child is accorded the responsibilities and rights of middle childhood. But a few months' variation in the occurrence of various elements in the bio-social-behavioral shift does not substantially change their significance in the overall process of development.

SUMMARY

GAMES AND GROUP REGULATION

- Between the ages of 6 and 12, children begin to spend significant amounts of time beyond direct adult control, in the company of children roughly their own age.
- During middle childhood the nature of children's play changes from role-based fantasy to games that require adherence to rules.
- Rule-based games serve as a model of society: they are transmitted from one generation to the next, and they exist only through mutual agreement.

SOCIAL RULES, SOCIAL THINKING, AND SOCIAL BEHAVIOR

- Piaget proposed a two-stage developmental sequence in children's thinking about social rules. Initially their rules are based on unilateral respect for authority, and then they become based on mutual respect. This change allows children to govern themselves.
- Piaget's account of the development of thinking about social rules has been challenged in two ways:
  1. His theory has been refined to include more stages of development.
  2. Children's thinking about moral issues has been shown to depend upon the domain of morality involved and the context in which the issues occur.
- Kohlberg has proposed that moral reasoning changes during middle childhood from a belief that right and wrong are based on a powerful outside authority (heteronomous morality) to an instrumental morality based on mutual support and, in some cases, to a belief in reciprocal responsibility (the Golden Rule).
- Ideas about the fair distribution of resources change from reliance on arbitrary criteria to a recognition of the rights of all to share in the group's resources. Further development consists of children's increasingly sophisticated ability to appreciate the legitimacy of distributing resources unequally under certain conditions.
- When children first reason about social conventions, they treat conventions as more or less equivalent to natural laws. With increased sophistication they begin to separate empirical associations ("Most nurses are women") from necessity ("A nurse has to be a woman"). Finally, children come to appreciate the usefulness of social conventions in the regulation of social interaction.
- Children's actual behavior is only loosely related to their reasoning about social rules. Whether they behave morally or not depends upon both how they reason and what they perceive the consequences of their behavior to be.

RELATIONS WITH OTHER CHILDREN

- Whenever a peer group forms, a social structure emerges.
- Developmentalists have identified several categories of peer-group status: children who are popular, rejected, neglected, controversial, victimized, and bullies.
- Physical attractiveness is one factor in shaping social status, but relevant social skills—such as making constructive contributions to group activity, adopting the group's frame of reference, and understanding social rules—also play important roles.
- Middle childhood is a period of relative segregation of the sexes.
- Cultures vary in the value they place on cooperation versus competition in peer interactions.
- Children's friendships develop from an emphasis on participating in joint activities to an emphasis on sharing interests, building mutual understanding, and creating trust.
- While spending time together, friends not only play but also gossip and exchange personal knowledge.

- The development of conceptions of friendship is closely associated with an increased ability to adopt other people's points of view and to repair misunderstandings when they arise.
- Parents both set the stage for children's peer interactions and influence the quality of their children's peer relations by the way in which they monitor ongoing relationships and activities.
- Participation in peer groups is important to later development. Peer interactions can foster the ability to communicate, to understand others' points of view, and to get along with others. Rejected children are at risk for negative outcomes in later life.

CHANGING RELATIONS WITH PARENTS

- As children begin to participate in peer groups, their relationship with their parents undergoes significant changes:
    1. Parents become more demanding of their children, with respect to both their domestic duties and their achievement in school.
    2. Parents shift from direct to indirect methods of control—to reasoning, humor, appeals to self- esteem, and the arousal of guilt.

A NEW SENSE OF SELF

- Children's increased time spent among peers is accompanied by a changing sense of themselves. Initially children think of themselves in concrete terms associated with distinct areas of activity. With age, their conceptions develop, becoming more inclusive and complex.
- Special challenges to the sense of self arise from the process of social comparison, which occurs when children compete in games and in school.
- During middle childhood children begin to believe that their psychological characteristics and those of other people are stable, so they come to expect consistency in their own and others' behavior in different contexts.
- A strong sense of self-esteem is important to mental health. Family practices that emphasize acceptance of children, clearly defined limits, and respect for individuality are most likely to give rise to a firm sense of self-worth.

MIDDLE CHILDHOOD RECONSIDERED

- Social development is an essential part of the bio-social-behavioral shift that occurs in the years between 5 and 7. Understood as a unique configuration of biological, social, and behavioral characteristics, middle childhood appears to be a universal stage of human development.

KEY TERMS

coregulation, 588
instrumental morality, 562
nomination procedure, 571
peers, 554
positive justice, 564
prosocial moral reasoning, 563
prospective study, 585
rating scale, 571
retrospective study, 584
self-esteem, 590
social comparison, 588
social competence, 581
social perspective taking, 581
social repair mechanisms, 582
sociogram, 572

THOUGHT QUESTIONS

1. Developmentalists link the emergence of rule-based games in middle childhood to the willingness of adults to allow children to spend time without supervision. What is the psychological connection between these two aspects of development?
2. Piaget asserted that "all morality consists in a system of rules, and the essence of all morality is to be sought for in the respect which the individual acquires for these rules" (p. 558). What are the implications of this view for the relationship between moral and cognitive development?
3. Make up a moral dilemma based on your everyday experience that is logically equivalent to Kohlberg's "Heinz dilemma" (p. 562). Present yours and Kohlberg's version to a friend. How is the reasoning produced by the two versions of the dilemma the same, and how does it differ? What gives rise to the differences?
4. Evidence shows that children tend to choose friends who are similar to themselves.
   (a) What might be the psychological basis for this convergence?
   (b) Think of two friends from your own childhood, one who is like you and one who is quite different. What qualities of the two friendships were different? Why?

PART V

Adolescence

Puberty, the cascade of biochemical events that begins around the end of the first decade of life, alters the body's size, shape, and functioning. The most revolutionary of these alterations is the development of an entirely new potential, the ability to engage in biological reproduction. This biological fact has profound interpersonal implications for the simple reason that reproduction involves partners from each sex. As their reproductive organs reach maturity, boys and girls begin to engage in new forms of social behavior because of the emergence of sexual attractions.

There is a great deal more to adolescence than a new capacity for biological reproduction, however. Central to the course of human development is the extended process of *cultural* reproduction, in which the "designs for living" evolved by the group are acquired and modified by the next generation. Much of this cultural reproduction takes place during adolescence. In addition to mastering the skills necessary for economic survival, young people must achieve new and more mature relations with age-mates of both sexes, learn the appropriate social roles associated with adult status, develop emotional independence from parents and other adults, acquire a deeper understanding of their culture's values and ethical system, and learn to behave in a socially responsible manner (Grotevant, 1998).

An analysis of information from 175 societies around the world has found that a social stage corresponding to adolescence is widespread, if not universal (Schlegel & Barry, 1991). Wherever it is encountered, adolescence is a time when social relations are in the process of being restructured. The changes in responsibilities and social roles that occur at this time naturally give rise to psychological uncertainties and disruptions as younger and older generations renegotiate their social relations.

The length of adolescence and the degree to which it is associated with social and psychological disruptions varies greatly from one society to the next. In the United States and other industrialized societies, a gap of 7 to 9 years typically separates the biological changes that mark the onset of sexual maturity from the social changes that confer adult status (such as the right to marry without parental consent or to run for elective office). This lengthy period is necessary because it takes young people many years to acquire the knowledge and skills they will need to achieve independence and to contribute to the perpetuation of their society.

By contrast, in some societies there is only a brief delay between the beginning of sexual maturity and the beginning of adulthood (Whiting et

al., 1986). These are usually societies in which biological maturity occurs late by Western standards and in which the level of technology is relatively low. By the time biological reproduction becomes possible, at about the age of 15 in many nonindustrial societies, young people already know how to perform the basic tasks of their culture, such as farming, weaving cloth, preparing food, and caring for children.

We will return to the question of cultural variations in the length and content of adolescence as a distinctive developmental stage at the end of Chapter 16. First, however, in Chapter 15, we examine the advent of biological maturity and its intimate links with changes in social life. These include changes in the nature of interactions with peers, friends, and one's family, as well as with entry into the workforce. Chapter 16 concentrates on what have traditionally been thought of as the psychological characteristics of adolescence: the new modes of thought that are needed to perform the economic tasks and fulfill the social responsibilities of adulthood; the changed sense of personal identity that is occasioned by a transformed physique and altered social relationships; and the new beliefs about morality and the social order that accompany the transition to adulthood.

CHAPTER 15

Biological and Social Foundations of Adolescence

How is it that, in the human body, reproduction is the only function to be performed by an organ of which an individual carries only one half so that he has to spend an enormous amount of time and energy to find another half?

—François Jacob, *The Possible and the Actual*

One of the most poignant accounts of what it feels like to enter adolescence appears in the diary of Anne Frank, a Jewish girl who lived in hiding with her family in Holland during the German occupation of World War II. Unable to leave her hiding place and go outside for fear of being captured, Anne turned her diary into the friend she longed for. The entries quoted here were written shortly before Anne and her family were discovered and sent to their deaths in a concentration camp.

WEDNESDAY, 5 JANUARY 1944

Yesterday I read an article about blushing by Sis Heyster. This article might have been addressed to me personally. Although I don't blush very easily, the other things in it certainly all fit me. She writes roughly something like this—that a girl in the years of puberty becomes quiet within and begins to think about the wonders that are happening to her body.

I experience that, too, and that is why I get the feeling lately of being embarrassed about Margot, Mummy, and Daddy. Funnily enough, Margot, who is much more shy than I am, isn't at all embarrassed.

I think what is happening to me is so wonderful, and not only what can be seen on my body, but all that is taking place inside. I never discuss myself or any of these things with anybody; that is why I have to talk to myself about them.

Each time I have a period—and that has only been three times—I have the feeling that in spite of all the pain, unpleasantness, and nastiness, I have a sweet secret, and that is why, although it is nothing but a nuisance to me in a way, I always long for the time that I shall feel that secret within me again. (1975, pp. 116–117)

THURSDAY, 6 JANUARY 1944

My longing to talk to someone became so intense that somehow or other I took it into my head to choose Peter. [a teenager hiding in the same house as the Franks]

Sometimes if I've been upstairs into Peter's room during the day, it always struck me as very snug, but because Peter is so retiring and would never turn anyone out who became a nuisance, I never dared stay long, because I was afraid he might think me a bore. I tried to think of an excuse to stay in his room and get him talking, without it being too noticeable, and my chance came yesterday. Peter has a mania for crossword puzzles at the moment and hardly does anything else. I helped him with them and we sat opposite each other at his little table, he on the chair and me on the divan.

It gave me a queer feeling each time I looked into his deep blue eyes, and he sat there with that mysterious laugh playing round his lips. I was able to read his inward thoughts. I could see on his face that look of helplessness and uncertainty as to how to behave, and at the same time, a trace of his sense of manhood. I noticed his shy manner and it made me feel very gentle; I couldn't refrain from meeting those dark eyes again and again, and with my whole heart I almost beseeched him: oh, tell me, what is going on inside you, oh can't you look beyond this ridiculous chatter?

But the evening passed and nothing happened, except that I told him about blushing—naturally not what I have written, but just that he would become more sure of himself as he grew older. (pp. 118–119)

These diary entries, written less than 24 hours apart when Anne was 14½ years old, vividly reveal the intimate connection between the physical changes of puberty and the social characteristics of adolescence. They touch on many aspects of the bio-social-behavioral shift that marks the end of middle childhood. First, the biological changes of puberty transform the size and shape of young people's bodies and evoke new, initially strange feelings. These changes are accompanied by changes in social life: after many years of relatively little interest in the other sex, most boys and girls begin to find each other attractive, and their mutual attraction brings about changes in their interactions with peers and close friends. Simultaneously, their relationships with their parents change, as if in recognition of the fact that independence, work, and the responsibility of caring for others must replace reliance on their parents' support. Lastly, the combination of biological and social developments is accompanied by changes in the way young people think about themselves and the world, as we shall see in Chapter 16.

In attempting to gain a comprehensive picture of development during adolescence, developmental researchers face a particular difficulty. Although adolescents are able to talk more reflectively and coherently about their feelings, behaviors, and thought processes than are younger children, they are usually reluctant to talk about many of the topics that preoccupy them. In addition, adolescents' behavior is much less accessible to direct observation than younger children's. As a result, the actual facts of adolescents' behavior are difficult to document. Despite this difficulty, interested scholars have long sought to understand the nature of adolescence, both as a transition from middle childhood to adulthood and as a stage of development in its own right.

The "nature of adolescence" is shaped by the views the society (including its interested scholars) has of it. Social beliefs about adolescence determine the demands that are made on young people, the rights they are permitted to exercise, and the ways in which their behavior is interpreted. If adolescents live in a society that considers puberty to be the onset of adulthood, they will be expected to maintain themselves economically, to care for others, and to be legally responsible for their actions. Conversely, if they live in a society that considers 15- and 16-year-olds to still be children, they will be cared for by others and will remain free of many of the responsibilities adults must accept. But they will also be expected to acquiesce to adult demands as the price for their continued dependence.

Trying to find out what adolescents really think and feel poses a considerable challenge to developmentalists, as well as to parents. Although teenagers may readily share their innermost confidences with trusted peers, they are often reluctant to reveal themselves fully to adults.

CONCEPTIONS OF ADOLESCENCE

The English word "adolescence" comes from the Latin word *adelesco,* which means "to grow up." The historical record and cross-cultural comparisons document clearly that many of the characteristics we currently associate with adolescence have a long history and are widespread in human societies.

HISTORICAL PRECURSORS

The Greek philosopher Aristotle described adolescents in the fourth century as "passionate, irascible, and apt to be carried away by their impulses.

. . . They regard themselves as omniscient and are positive in their assertions; this is, in fact, the reason for their carrying everything too far" (quoted in Kiell, 1964, pp. 18–19). Many centuries later, William Shakespeare's story of Romeo and Juliet presented a strikingly similar vision of adolescents whose uncontrolled emotions and desires dim their reason and lead to tragedy.

The first great theorist of adolescence, Jean-Jacques Rousseau (see Chapter 1, pp. 12–13), saw this period of life in much the same light. In *Emile* (1762/1911), his treatise on human nature and education, Rousseau suggested three features of adolescence that continue to play a prominent role in current discussions of this period:

1. Adolescence is a period of heightened instability and emotional conflict that is brought on by biological maturation. As Rousseau phrased it:

   > As the roaring of the waves precedes the tempest so the murmur of rising passions announces this tumultuous change, a suppressed excitement warns us of the approaching danger. A change of temper, frequent outbreaks of anger, a perpetual stirring of the mind, make the child almost ungovernable. He becomes deaf to the voice he used to obey; he is a lion in a fever; he distrusts his keeper and refuses to be controlled. (p. 172)

2. The biological and social changes that figure prominently in adolescence are accompanied by a fundamental change in psychological processes. Rousseau believed that the transition to adolescence brought with it self-conscious thought and the ability to reason logically.
3. In important respects, the changes that occur during adolescence are a "rebirth." According to this view, adolescence **recapitulates**—that is, repeats in condensed form—the earlier stages of life through which the child has passed. In Rousseau's words, "We are born, so to speak, twice over; born into existence, and born into life; born a human being and born a man" (p. 172).

In the late eighteenth and early nineteenth centuries, as education for children became more widespread and extensive, older children attracted increased social attention because they tended to get into trouble and were difficult to control. When developmental psychologists began to turn their attention to the phenomenon of adolescence at the end of the nineteenth century, many picked up and modified Rousseau's ideas. Among them was G. Stanley Hall, the first president of the American Psychological Association and a major figure in the shaping of developmental psychology (Cairns, 1998).

Hall (1904), like Rousseau, described adolescence as a time of heightened emotionality and stress: stratospheric highs, deep depressions, and love of excitement, "suggestive of some ancient period of storm and stress" (p. xiii). He also believed adolescence to be a period of rebirth after childhood, but a rebirth that went beyond Rousseau's idea of recapitulation. Like many scholars at the time who were inspired by Darwin's evolutionary ideas, Hall believed that every child's individual development repeats the entire evolutionary history of our species. This idea was so popular that it inspired the tongue-twisting aphorism "Ontogeny recapitulates phylogeny."

According to Hall, middle childhood corresponds to an ancient period of historical development when human reason, morality, feelings of love toward others, and religion were underdeveloped by modern standards. He believed that it is only when they reach adolescence that young people can go beyond the biologically predetermined past. As a consequence, adolescence is more flexible than any other period of development. It provides a "once in a lifetime" opportunity for creativity.

recapitulate To repeat in condensed form earlier stages of life through which the child has passed.

MODERN BIOSOCIAL APPROACHES TO ADOLESCENCE

In modified form, Hall's ideas continue to influence developmental research on adolescence (Arnett, 1999). The idea that new evolutionary forms arise late in ontogeny has attracted new interest, and Hall's description of adolescence as a period of storm and stress, as reflected in adolescents' conflicts with their parents, their widely fluctuating moods, their innovativeness, and their risky behavior, is widely accepted. There is, however, continuing dispute over the degree to which adolescence is characterized by stress and conflict (McKinney, 1998).

Building on these ideas, modern theorists of adolescence attempt to explain how biological, social, behavioral, and cultural factors are interwoven in the transition from childhood to adulthood. As with earlier periods of development, each of the four theoretical perspectives we have been examining offers insights essential to gaining an integrated understanding of this transition, but as yet there is no widely accepted, unified theory of adolescence.

In this chapter, we begin by examining theoretical approaches that emphasize the biological changes associated with adolescence. However, we cannot go very far in discussing biological changes without considering their social consequences. As John Conger and Ann Peterson (1984) comment, it seems that adolescence "begins in biology and ends in culture." We therefore conclude the chapter with a discussion of how the changes of puberty initiate a reorganization of the child's social life.

The hallmark of biological approaches to adolescence is their emphasis on the idea that development is highly constrained and canalized by the evolutionary history of *Homo sapiens.* As a result, the developmental changes associated with adolescence will occur "naturally" within a very broad range of particular environmental circumstances. This applies not only to physical and social development, our topic in this chapter, but to cognitive and personality development, which is our topic in the next chapter.

Two early modern biological theorists whose ideas have influenced contemporary research on adolescence are Arnold Gesell and Sigmund Freud.

Arnold Gesell

Gesell shared Hall's idea that adolescents have completed the evolutionarily prescribed path of development. He asserted that the "higher human traits," such as abstract thinking, imagination, and self-control, make their appearance late in the development of the individual because they were acquired late in the history of the species. He admitted that the environment may exert a more powerful influence during adolescence than it did earlier in life, but he still maintained that environmental conditions do not alter the basic pattern of development in any fundamental way:

> Neither he [the adolescent] nor his parents in their zeal can transcend the basic laws of development. He continues to grow essentially in the same manner in which he grew as he advanced from the toddling stage of two years through the paradoxical stage of two and a half, and the consolidating stage of three. (Gesell & Ilg, 1943, p. 256)

Sigmund Freud

As we saw in Chapter 1 (p. 34), Freud's psychoanalytic theory is often best thought of as reflecting a maturational position with respect to the sources of development. In accord with the biological-maturational position, Freud viewed adolescence as a distinctive stage of development during which human beings can at last fulfill the biological imperative to reproduce themselves and hence the species. This evolutionary assumption underlay Freud's emphasis on sex as the master motive for all human behavior, even in the earliest stages of life. He called adolescence the **genital stage** because this is the period during which sexual intercourse becomes a major motive of behavior.

genital stage In Freudian theory, the developmental stage during which sexual intercourse becomes a major motive of behavior.

In Freud's theory, the emotional storminess associated with adolescence is the culmination of a psychological struggle among the three parts of the personality: the *id,* the *ego,* and the *superego* (see Chapter 10, pp. 378–379). As Freud saw it, the upsurge in sexual excitation that accompanies puberty reawakens primitive instincts, increases the power of the id, and upsets the psychological balance achieved during middle childhood. This imbalance produces psychological conflict and erratic behavior. The main developmental task of adolescence is therefore to reestablish the balance of psychological forces by reintegrating them in a new and more mature way that is compatible with the individual's new sexual capacities.

Freud, like Hall, was greatly influenced by the doctrine of recapitulationism. He argued, for example, that when sexual maturation reawakens the oedipal urges that were repressed at the start of middle childhood, the young person must rework this old conflict under the new conditions of social life that attend sexual maturity.

Although Freud's theory of adolescence is rooted in biology, it does not ignore the social world. The superego is, after all, the internal representation of society, and the ego mediates between the social world embodied in the superego, on the one hand, and the demands of the id, on the other.

Evolutionary and Ethological Approaches

A recent trend in the study of adolescence has been a growing interest in applying theories and methods of ethology and evolutionary biology to the study of human development (Weisfeld, 1999). As we saw in our discussion of social development in early childhood (Chapter 10, p. 402), there are striking similarities between the social interactions of young children and those of several nonhuman species in terms of the development of dominance relations. These similarities in social behaviors between species (chimpanzees and children, for example) provide the foundation for hypothesizing common biological mechanisms underpinning their development (Scott, 1997). Research on the development of social hierarchies and aggressive behavior among teenagers indicates the continued importance of such biologically influential social control mechanisms throughout human development (Weisfeld, 1999).

In his study of the evolution of distinctive periods within the human life cycle, Barry Bogin found that *Homo sapiens* is the only primate that experiences a growth spurt following childhood. This growth spurt is a key indicator of the onset of puberty. Echoing the perspective discussed in the introduction to Part V (p. 600), Bogin (1999) argues that "adolescence became a part of human life history because it conferred significant reproductive advantages to our species, in part, by allowing the adolescent to learn and practice adult economic, social, and sexual behavior before reproducing" (p. 216). Bogin refers to this view as a "biocultural model of adolescence."

PUBERTY

During the second decade of life, the series of biological developments known as **puberty** transforms young people from a state of physical immaturity to one in which they are biologically mature and capable of sexual reproduction. Puberty begins with a chemical signal from the hypothalamus, located at the base of the brain, that activates the pituitary gland, a pea-size organ appended to the hypothalamus. The pituitary then increases its production of growth hormones, which in turn stimulate the growth of all body tissue. The pituitary gland also releases hormones that trigger a great increase in the manufacture of two gonadotrophic ("gonad-seeking") hormones. The **gonads,** or primary sex organs, are the ovaries in females and the testes in males. In females these gonadotrophic hormones stimulate the ovaries to manufacture estrogen and

puberty The series of biological developments that transforms individuals from a state of physical immaturity to one in which they are biologically mature and capable of sexual reproduction.

gonads The primary sex organs; the ovaries in females and the testes in males.

progesterone. These two hormones trigger the numerous physical events, including the release of mature ova from the ovaries, that eventually allow for reproduction. In males, gonadotrophic hormones stimulate the testes and adrenal glands to manufacture the hormone testosterone, which brings about the manufacture of sperm (Bogin, 1999) (see Figure 15.1). While estrogen is usually considered to be the female hormone and testosterone the male hormone, both hormones are present in the two sexes. During puberty, both sexes experience an increase in these hormones, but the rate of increase is specific to each sex. Testosterone in boys increases to 18 times its level in middle childhood, while estrogen undergoes an eightfold increase in girls (Malina & Bouchard, 1991).

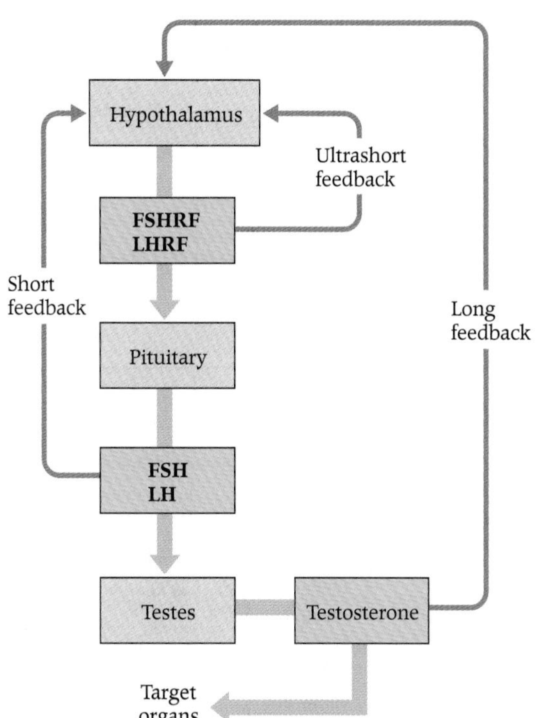

FIGURE 15.1
Puberty in males is initiated by complex interactions among the hypothalamus, the pituitary gland, and the testes. When the hypothalamus releases gonadotropin releasing factors (FSHRF, LHRD), it causes the pituitary to discharge the gonadotropins FSH and LH into the blood. These hormones stimulate the testes, promoting the production of testosterone, which in turn stimulates changes in other body organs and provides feedback to the hypothalamus. (From Katchadourian, 1977.)

THE GROWTH SPURT

As noted above, one of the first visible signs of puberty is a spurt in the rate of physical growth. Boys and girls grow more quickly now than at any other time since they were babies. During the 2 to 3 years of the growth spurt, a boy may grow as much as 9 inches taller and a girl as much as 6 to 7 inches taller. Although adolescents continue to grow throughout puberty, they reach 98 percent of their ultimate adult height by the end of the growth spurt (Sinclair & Dangerfield, 1998).

The rate of growth during adolescence varies for different parts of the body. As a rule, leg length reaches its peak first, followed 6 to 9 months later by trunk length. Shoulder and chest breadths are the last to reach their peak. As James Tanner (1978) has quipped, "A boy stops growing out of his trousers (at least in length) a year before he stops growing out of his jackets" (p. 69). Even the head, which has grown little since the age of 2, participates in the growth spurt. The skull bones thicken, lengthening and widening the head. The brain, which attains 90 percent of its adult weight by the age of 5, grows little during this period (Sinclair & Dangerfield, 1998).

Changes in physical size are accompanied by changes in overall shape. During puberty, males and females acquire the distinctive physical features that characterize the two sexes. Girls develop breasts, and their hips expand. Boys acquire wide shoulders and a muscular neck. Boys also lose fat during adolescence, and so appear more muscular and angular than girls. Girls continue to have a higher ratio of fat to muscle, so they have a rounder, softer look.

Most boys not only appear to be stronger than girls after puberty; they are stronger. Before puberty, boys and girls of similar size differ little in strength. But by the end of this period, boys can exercise for longer periods and can exert more force per ounce of muscle than girls of the same size. Boys develop relatively larger hearts and lungs, which give them higher blood pressure when their heart muscles contract, a lower resting heart rate, and a greater capacity for carrying oxygen in the blood, which neutralizes the chemicals that lead to fatigue during physical exercise (Weisfeld, 1999).

The physiological differences between males and females may help to explain why males have traditionally been the warriors, hunters, and heavy laborers throughout human history. They also help to explain why most superior male athletes can outperform superior female athletes. In some important respects, however, females exhibit greater physical prowess than males: they are, on the average, healthier, live longer, and are better able to tolerate long-term stress (Hayflick, 1994).

SEXUAL DEVELOPMENT

During puberty all the **primary sex organs**, the organs involved in reproduction, enlarge and become functionally mature. In males the testes begin to

primary sex organs The organs involved in reproduction.

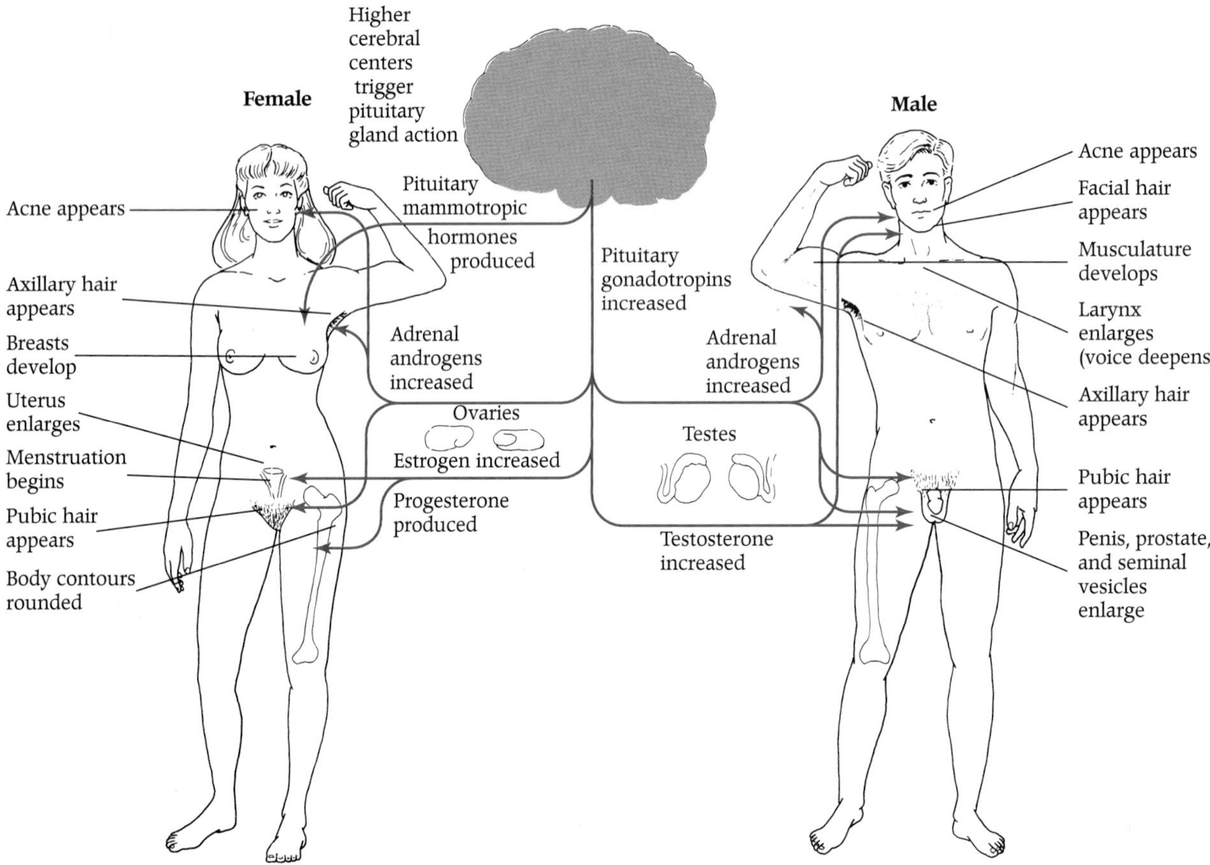

FIGURE 15.2

The hormonal changes that accompany puberty cause a wide variety of physical changes in both females and males. (Adapted from Netter, 1965.)

produce sperm cells, and the prostate begins to produce semen, the fluid that carries the sperm. Sperm and semen come together in the vas deferens. In females the ovaries begin to release mature ova into the fallopian tubes. When conception does not take place, menstruation occurs.

Secondary sex characteristics, the anatomical and physiological signs that outwardly distinguish males from females, appear at the same time that the primary sex organs are maturing (see Figure 15.2). The first signs that boys are entering puberty are an enlargement of the testes, a thickening and reddening of the skin of the scrotum, and the appearance of pubic hair. These changes usually occur about 3 years before boys reach the height of their growth spurt. About the time the growth spurt begins, the penis begins to grow, continuing to do so for about 2 years. About a year after the penis begins to grow, boys become able to ejaculate semen. **Semenarche,** the first ejaculation, often occurs spontaneously during sleep and is called a nocturnal emission. For the first year or so after semenarche, the sperm in the semen are less numerous and less fertile than sperm in adult males (Katchadourian, 1977).

Underarm and facial hair usually appear about 2 years after a boy's pubic hair begins to grow, but in some individuals underarm and facial hair may appear first. Most men do not develop a hairy chest until late adolescence or early adulthood. A boy's voice usually does not deepen until late in puberty and then does so gradually as the larynx expands and the vocal cords lengthen. During this process, cracks in a boy's voice announce to the world the changes that are taking place in his body. Near the end of puberty, boys also experience a marked increase in muscle development (Bogin, 1999).

The first visible sign that a girl is beginning to mature sexually is often the appearance of a small rise around the nipples called the breast bud. Pubic hair usually appears a little later, just before the growth spurt begins. About

secondary sex characteristics The anatomical and physiological signs that outwardly distinguish males from females; they appear at the same time that the primary sex organs are maturing.

semenarche The first ejaculation. It often occurs spontaneously during sleep and is called a nocturnal emission.

the same time that girls' outward appearance is beginning to change, their ovaries enlarge, and the cells that eventually will evolve into ova begin to ripen. The uterus begins to grow, and the vaginal lining thickens. The pelvic inlet, the bony opening of the birth canal, grows more slowly. It does not reach adult size until girls are about 18 years of age, which makes childbirth more difficult and potentially more dangerous for young adolescents (Bogin, 1999).

Girls' secondary sex characteristics develop throughout puberty. The breasts continue to grow with the development of the mammary glands, which allow for lactation, and the accumulation of adipose (fatty) tissue, which gives them their adult shape.

Usually **menarche**—the first menstrual period—occurs relatively late in puberty, about 18 months after the growth spurt has reached its peak velocity. Early menstrual periods tend to be irregular, and they often occur without ovulation—the release of a mature egg. Ovulation typically begins about 12 to 18 months after menarche (Bogin, 1999).

When she reaches puberty, this girl from Kathmandu, Nepal will face a dramatic change in life. Since she was four, she has been the personification of the goddess Kumari and except for religious festivals, she has spent her childhood secluded in a temple, but as soon as she reaches puberty another four-year-old girl will be chosen and this one will return to her family.

menarche The first menstrual period.

THE TIMING OF PUBERTY

A glance around a seventh-grade classroom is sufficient to remind even the most casual observer of the wide variations in the age at which puberty begins. Some of the 12- and 13-year-old boys may look much as they did at the age of 9 or 10, whereas others may have the gangly look that often characterizes the growth spurt. Among the girls, who on the average begin to mature sexually somewhat earlier, some may look like mature women with fully developed breasts and rounded hips, some may still have the stature and shape of little girls, and some may be somewhere in between.

Like all events in development, the timing of the changes of puberty depends on complex interactions between genetic and environmental factors. The importance of genetic factors is demonstrated by comparisons of identical and fraternal twins. The average difference in the age at which menarche occurs in identical twin sisters is only 2 months, whereas the average difference for fraternal twin sisters is 8 months (Marshall & Tanner, 1974).

Several studies have documented the importance of environmental factors in the timing of menarche. One critical factor is caloric intake. The onset of menstruation is associated with increases in body fat, so when calorie intake is insufficient to produce a certain level of body fat, menstruation is delayed or may cease once it has begun. This explains why many lean adolescent dancers and girls who participate in a high level of physical exercise reach menarche later than other girls (Calabrese et al., 1983; Warren et al., 1991).

A variety of other environmental factors, such as health, nutrition, stress, and psychological depression, also influence the age of menarche. One important stress factor is family conflict. Studies in the United States and New Zealand have found that adolescents who experience a high level of family conflict go through menarche earlier than those who live in more harmonious families (Graber et al., 1995; Moffit et al., 1992). There is broad agreement that environmental stress affects children's developing hormonal systems. However, the exact mechanisms of these effects and the importance of the time at which they occur remain uncertain.

The age at which menarche is reached has also undergone striking historical changes. In industrialized countries and in some developing countries as well, the age when menstruation begins has been declining among all social groups (Graham et al., 1999) (see Figure 15.3). In the 1840s the average age of menarche among European women was between 14 and 15 years, whereas today it is

FIGURE 15.3
The age of menarche has been declining in many countries during the past 150 years. (Adapted from Katchadourian, 1977.)

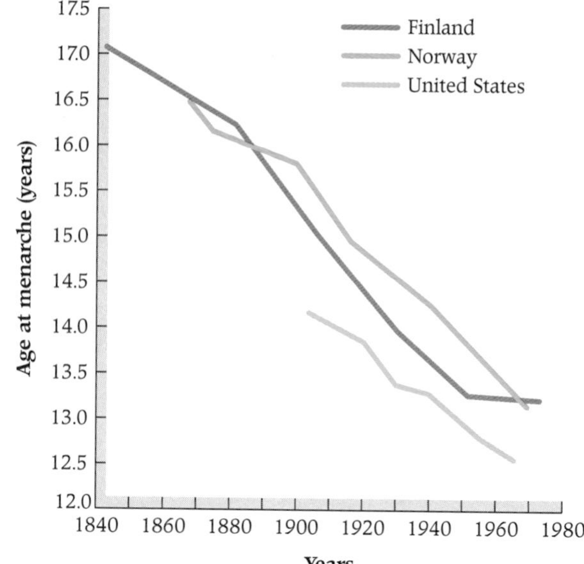

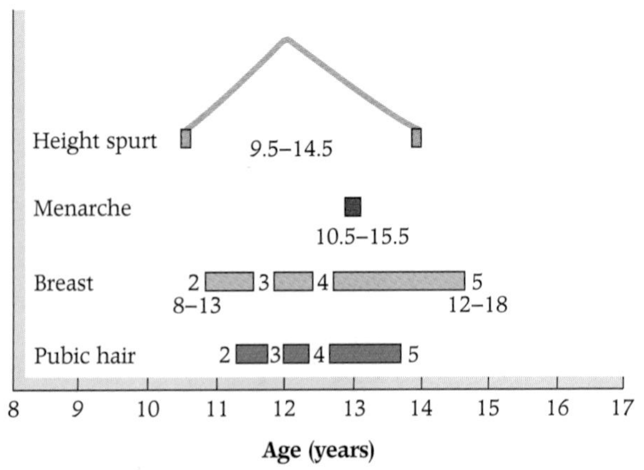

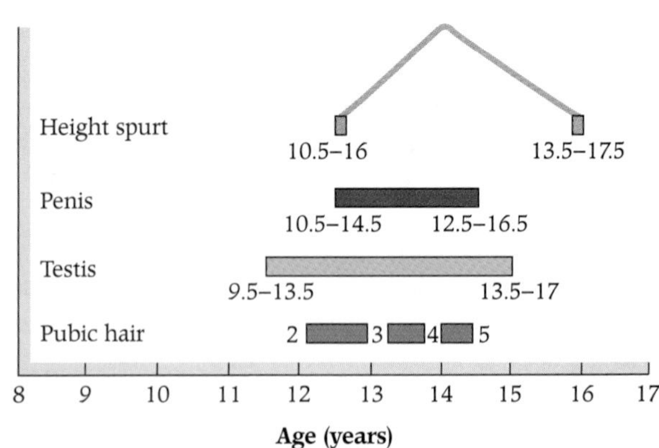

FIGURE 15.4

Diagram of the sequence of events at puberty in girls (left) and boys (right). (From Tanner, 1990.)

between 12 and 13 (Bullough, 1981). A similar trend is apparent in the United States, where menarche occurs more than 2 years earlier than it did in 1890.

Puberty also seems to be occurring earlier among males, but the evidence for this change is less direct. Fifty years ago the average American male gained his maximum height at the age of 26; now this marker of the end of puberty occurs, on average, at the age of 18 (Marshall & Tanner, 1974).

Studies of the physical changes associated with puberty indicate that it ordinarily lasts about 4 years (Tanner, 1990) (see Figure 15.4). The duration of puberty, however, is as variable as the age at which it begins. One boy may go through all the events of puberty in the time it takes another's genitals to develop.

THE DEVELOPMENTAL IMPACT OF PUBERTY

In all societies the biological changes associated with puberty have profound social and psychological significance, both to the young people themselves and to their community. However, the specific psychological and social consequences of puberty vary with cultural circumstances and personal characteristics of the children.

Psychological Responses to Pubertal Events

In a series of studies (summarized in Brooks-Gunn & Reiter, 1990), Jeanne Brooks-Gunn and her colleagues found that girls' attitudes and beliefs about menstruation are only in part a result of their own direct experience of menstruation. How they perceive menstruation is influenced by the attitudes and beliefs of those around them. The influence of girls' social context on their experience of menarche is borne out by the finding that a girl's physical symptoms during menstruation are often correlated with the expectations she had before menarche. Girls who reported unpleasant symptoms were more likely to have been unprepared for menarche, to have matured early, and to have been told about menstruation by someone they perceived negatively.

Similarly, boys' responses to their first ejaculation (semenarche) depend on the context in which it occurs. When semenarche occurs as a nocturnal emission ("wet dream"), boys report that their primary reactions are surprise and confusion. One boy recalled, "It reminded me of peeing in my pants—that was my first reaction even though I'd never done it" (Stein & Reisser, 1994, p. 377). If semenarche occurs during masturbation, the predominant reaction is more positive.

One of the physical changes associated with the growth spurt during puberty is an increase in weight. For boys this increase comes largely from an increase in muscle mass. For girls the increase comes largely from the accumulation of fat in their subcutaneous tissues. It has been estimated that during

Every society has evolved customs that mark the end of childhood and the transition to adult status. Here Karla Cahvez celebrates her quinceanera, her fifteenth birthday, in Houston with a Mass followed by a dance.

adolescence the average girl gains a little over 24 pounds in the form of body fat (Bogin, 1999).

These changes are perfectly normal, but insofar as they result in a body size and shape that deviates from cultural ideals, they can be the source of significant psychological distress (Abell & Richards, 1996; Guinn et al., 1997; Stattin & Magnusson, 1990). As noted in Chapter 12 (p. 474), in the United States, a thin, prepubertal body shape is taken as the ideal for women, an ideal that is reflected in everything from television, movie, and magazine images to the shapes of dolls given to young girls (Botta, 1999). Reinforcing the ideal is the media's frequent representation of heavy-set people as unhappy, unattractive individuals who lack self-control and are undeserving of respect or admiration. It is no wonder, then, that most adolescent girls in our society are afraid of becoming even slightly overweight, let alone fat. They want to be beautiful; they want to look like models and actresses.

For better or for worse, the thin, prepubertal body shape idealized by the media is unattainable for most females after puberty. As a consequence, many adolescent girls are dissatisfied with their new, more mature bodies. They see themselves as being "overweight" and "ugly" (Rosenblum & Lewis, 1999) (see Figure 15.5), and many of them go to great lengths to lose weight (see Box 15.1).

FIGURE 15.5
The relationship of pubertal change to body image. While boys retain a basically positive image of their bodies as they go through puberty, girls' self-image declines precipitously. (From Brooks-Gunn & Petersen, 1983.)

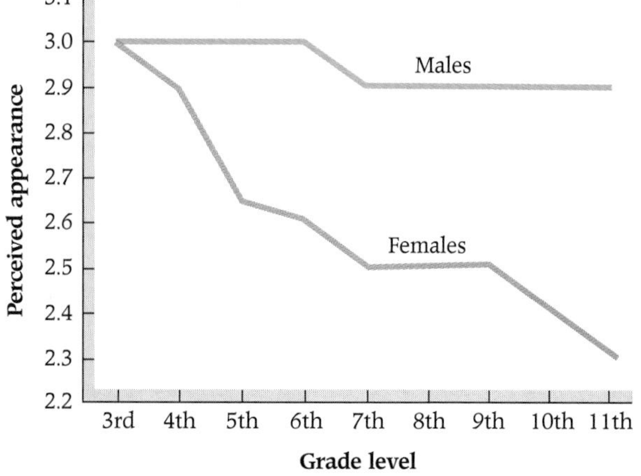

The extent to which girls become satisfied or dissatisfied with their bodies is influenced not only by the media but also by how peers and family members respond to their appearance, and these responses, in turn, are influenced by the cultural contexts in which the peers and family members participate (Alsaker, 1996). Girls from African American and Mexican American families, for example, are less likely than American girls of European descent to perceive themselves as overweight when their weight is normal, primarily because their respective cultures value a larger body size than the one promoted by the Anglo culture (Guinn et al., 1997; Parker et al., 1995).

Even the atmosphere at school can make a difference in how satisfied girls are with their bodies. Marsye Richards and her colleagues compared the extent to which sixth- to eighth-grade girls in

BOX 15.1

EATING DISORDERS

Gena was a chubby clarinet player who liked to read and play chess. She was more interested in computers than makeup and in stuffed animals more than designer clothes. She walked to her first day of junior high with her pencils sharpened and her notebooks neatly labeled. She was ready to learn Spanish and algebra and to audition for the school orchestra.

She came home sullen and shaken. The boy whose locker was next to hers had smashed into her with his locker door and sneered, "Move your fat ass." That night she told her mother, "I hate my looks. I need to go on a diet." Her mother thought, Is that what this boy saw? When he looked at my musical, idealistic Gena, did he see only her behind? (adopted from Pipher, 1994, p. 55)

Gena is not the only young adolescent who has decided she hates the way she looks because of a boy's comment. However, boys are by no means the only ones delivering the message that being beautiful in our society means being thin. Images of tall, lithe models with slim figures are ubiquitous in advertisements and fashion magazines. Thin young actresses are the objects of desire in popular movies and television shows. In attempts to achieve this ideal figure, many young women go on fad diets that may cut out entire classes of food, such as fats or carbohydrates; take drugs to suppress their appetites; or induce vomiting and take laxatives to avoid gaining weight (Striegel-Moore & Cachelin, 1999). All these practices endanger their health and, in extreme forms, can lead to psychiatric conditions known as *eating disorders.*

One eating disorder that has received a great deal of attention from the psychiatric community is *anorexia nervosa,* a condition in which girls (and only rarely boys) starve themselves, losing up to 25 percent or more of their body weight. Girls suffering from this condition consider themselves to be fat even when, by objective standards, they are painfully thin. To enhance their weight loss, they may exercise feverishly even when they weigh well under 100 pounds. Anorexia poses numerous health threats, including serious malnutrition, manifested in such symptoms as cessation of menstruation, pale skin, the appearance of fine black hairs on the body, and extreme sensitivity to cold. About 4 to 6 percent of anorexia victims die due to kidney failure or heart damage (Sullivan, 1995). Anorexia is estimated to afflict approximately 5 in every 100,000 adolescent American girls, but it is much more prevalent among the white middle and upper classes, where the incidence is as high as 1 in every 100 girls (Hendren & Berenson, 1997).

A more common eating disorder is *bulimia nervosa,* which is found in all classes. Estimates are that 5 percent of all girls (and a smaller percentage of boys) are afflicted with this disorder (Graber et al., 1994). Girls suffering from bulimia are usually obsessed by their weight. They try to keep it at a suboptimal level by starving themselves, but this effort is broken by periods of "binge eating," during which they eat abnormal amounts. Typically these binges are followed by self-induced vomiting or the use of heavy doses of laxatives. Bulimia usu-

two different schools were comfortable with their bodies (Richards et al., 1993). Although there were many similarities between the two groups of girls and the communities they lived in, the atmosphere of the schools they attended differed in two respects. In one school, most girls said they felt accepted by their schoolmates and participated in school activities. In the second school, many of the girls reported that they felt excluded by certain cliques and were less likely to participate in school activities. While the girls in both schools indicated that they felt most satisfied with their weight when they perceived themselves to be underweight and were increasingly dissatisfied the heavier they perceived themselves to be, the extent to which they felt dissatisfied was significantly greater for the girls in the school where they felt excluded.

Consequences of Early and Late Maturation

Several studies have sought to determine what effects relatively early or late sexual maturation might have on young people's peer relations, personality, and social adjustment. This research has produced a mixed picture (Alsaker, 1996; Graber et al., 1997).

One of the earliest studies of this kind, conducted by Mary Cover Jones and Nancy Bayley (1950), reported that early-maturing boys experience adolescence differently than late-maturing boys. Using an X-ray analysis of bone growth, these researchers identified 16 adolescent boys who were maturing late and 16 who were maturing early. They then asked adults and peers who knew the boys to rate them on a variety of social and personality scales to see if the boys' state of physical maturation affected other people's perceptions of them.

ally begins when a girl is in late adolescence, often when she leaves home for college, and continues into her twenties.

Unlike girls suffering from anorexia, bulimic girls are near normal weight and thus are not in danger of starving themselves to death. However, they are at risk for a variety of health problems, including gastrointestinal damage and heart failure due to electrolyte imbalance. In addition, bulimia has been closely linked with substance abuse (Peveler & Fairburn, 1990). One study of 2016 Canadian high school students found that binge eaters, particularly girls who then compensate for their eating binges by taking laxatives or vomiting, were more likely than their peers to smoke, use marijuana and other illegal drugs, and consume alcohol (Ross & Ivis, 1999).

To determine the factors that lead to these and other eating problems, Julia Graber and her colleagues conducted a longitudinal study that followed 116 adolescent girls from the ages of 14 to 22 (Graber et al., 1994). This age range spans the period when many girls of normal weight begin to diet. The girls, who all attended private schools in a major metropolitan area, filled out questionnaires about their attitudes toward food, their satisfaction with the way they looked, and their perception of social pressures to gain or lose weight. Their physical development and family relationships were also assessed.

The researchers found that several factors were at work when girls developed an obsession with weight and eating after the onset of puberty. First, as might be expected, girls with the highest percentage of body fat were most likely to exhibit chronic eating disorders. But pubertal timing, body image, and family relationships also contributed to the onset of eating disorders. Among girls who entered puberty relatively early and who had poor body images, those who were in conflict with their families were at increased risk for chronic eating disorders. Personality factors also played a role: girls who tended toward high levels of psychological depression were more likely than their peers to develop an eating disorder. The link between eating disorders and depression has been confirmed by a number of other studies (Dancyger & Garfinkel, 1995; Ross & Ivis, 1999).

No single treatment has proved to be effective in the case of either of these chronic, frequently relapsing eating disorders (Hendren & Berenson, 1997). Because of the potentially fatal consequences of anorexia nervosa, and because most adolescents suffering from this condition deny that there is anything wrong with them, the first step in treating many victims of anorexia is to hospitalize them in an attempt to restore their body weight to a more normal level. Individual, group, family, and cognitive-behavioral therapies have all been used to help anorexic girls overcome their distorted body image. Most adolescents suffering from bulimia are treated as outpatients with a combination of antidepressant drugs and psychological counseling (Hendren & Berenson, 1997).

Both adults and peers rated the early-maturing boys as more psychologically and socially mature. These boys did not appear to need to strive for status, and they were the group from which school leaders emerged. The boys who were slower to mature physically were rated as less mature psychologi-

Differences in the timing of puberty can result in startling differences in size between adolescents who are close in age.

cally and socially. Both adults and peers thought that these boys often sought attention to compensate for their late development and that some of them tended to withdraw from social interaction. Subsequent studies have confirmed some parts of this picture. In general, early-maturing boys seem to have a more favorable attitude toward their bodies, largely because their greater size and strength make them more capable athletes, and athletic prowess brings them social recognition (Graber et al., 1997; Simmons & Blyth, 1987).

However, not all the effects of early maturation are positive for boys. On the basis of data from a longitudinal study that used a personality test to measure maturity, instead of ratings by other people, Harvey Peskin (1967) found that, after the onset of puberty, early-maturing boys become significantly more somber, temporarily more anxious, less exploratory, less intellectually curious, and less active than do late-maturing boys. He argued that early-maturing boys are actually handicapped by the early end to their childhood because they are less prepared for the hormonal and social changes taking place. Thus the experience of puberty is more intense and less manageable for them than it is for those who mature more slowly.

Peskin's conclusions are supported by later research that associates early sexual maturation with lower self-control and less emotional stability, as measured by psychological tests (Sussman et al., 1985). Adolescent boys who reach puberty at a relatively early age are also more likely to smoke, drink, use drugs, and get in trouble with the law (Duncan et al., 1985).

The picture for girls is also mixed, but the overall effect of early maturation appears to be generally negative (Brooks-Gunn & Petersen, 1983; Simmons & Blyth, 1987; Stattin & Magnusson, 1990). In elementary school, girls who develop before their peers are often embarrassed about the changes in their body and may take to wearing big shirts and slouching to hide their breasts. Later, they are more likely than their late-maturing peers to be dissatisfied with their bodies. This is because early-maturing children tend to weigh more and to be slightly shorter than late-maturing children when they finish puberty, and this difference persists throughout life (Brooks-Gunn & Reiter, 1990). Thus early-maturing girls are less likely to approximate the ideal body shape promoted in most Western cultures.

For some girls, early maturation brings greater social prestige based on sexual attractiveness. One study found that girls who had reached puberty by the sixth or seventh grade considered themselves more popular with boys and were more likely to be dating than girls who had not yet reached puberty (Simons et al., 1987). But this increased social prestige may carry potential risks. A longitudinal study of Swedish adolescent girls found that early-maturing girls were more likely to be in sexual relationships by midadolescence than girls who matured later. They were also more likely to experience a decline in their academic performance and engage in such problem behaviors as truancy, drug and alcohol use, shoplifting, and running away (Stattin & Magnusson, 1990). Studies in the United States have found that early-maturing girls tend to have somewhat lower emotional stability and self-control, perhaps as a result of social and psychological stress associated with their sexual maturity (Richards et al., 1993).

In contrast, a relatively late passage through puberty may be a negative experience for girls at first, but the overall consequences are more likely to be positive. Late-maturing sixth-grade girls in the United States report dissatisfaction with their appearance and their lack of popularity, but in a few years they may actually be more satisfied with their appearance and more popular than their early-maturing peers (Simmons & Blyth, 1987).

It is important to keep in mind that these effects of early and later onset of puberty are not the inevitable outcome of biological processes. Rather, such outcomes are mediated by the social context in which early maturation takes place and by the way others respond to the physical changes young people are experiencing. Avshalom Caspi and his colleagues compared the behavior of early- and late-maturing girls who attended either an all-girls or a coed secondary school in New Zealand (Caspi, 1995; Caspi et al., 1993). They found that the girls who attended an all-girls school had higher academic performance and lower rates of delinquent behavior than did girls attending a coed school. They attributed the better outcomes at the all-girls school to the absence of boys, because it is boys who most often are the instigators of girls' socially disapproved behavior.

Evidence concerning the impact of the timing of puberty on later life is inconclusive. On the basis of her study following early-maturing and late-maturing boys into their early thirties, Mary Cover Jones (1965) concluded that early maturation has positive psychological benefits that continue into manhood. She found the early-maturing boys to be poised, cooperative, and responsible; they held good positions at work and were leaders in their social organizations. The late developers were more likely to be impulsive, touchy, and nonconforming; they were not so successful, and some felt rejected and inferior. When John Clausen (1975) tested the same men at the age of 38, however, he could find only two differences between the groups: the early maturers took more pride in being objective and in being seen as conventional than did those who matured late. Norman Livson and Harvey Peskin (1967) reported partly converging findings. In adulthood the late-maturing boys they studied were sometimes viewed as impulsive and nonconformist but also creative; the early-maturing boys tended to be regarded as conventional and inflexible.

The evidence concerning long-term effects of pubertal timing on girls is also inconsistent. An early study by Peskin (1973) reported that early-maturing girls develop coping skills in adolescence that make them flexible in adulthood. However, in the previously cited study of Swedish girls, Hakan Stattin and David Magnusson (1990) found that the early-maturing girls were likely to have children at younger ages and to complete fewer years of school than other girls their age, factors which had a negative impact on their later development.

The fact that long-term effects of pubertal timing are difficult to pin down should not be surprising. As we noted in Chapter 7 (p. 275), development is a transactional process: whether early or late experience of puberty has lasting effects, and what those effects are, depend on how the changes are responded to by others when they occur, how the individual reacts to those responses, and the consequences that follow from those interactions.

THE REORGANIZATION OF SOCIAL LIFE

The marked changes that young people experience in their biological capacities during adolescence are associated with equally marked changes in the way they interact with their families and their peers.

A NEW RELATIONSHIP WITH PEERS

As children enter adolescence, their social relationships with their peers undergo a marked reorganization. According to B. Bradford Brown (1990), in technologically developed societies, this reorganization involves at least four major changes:

1. Peer interaction increases even more than it did during middle childhood. High school students spend twice as much time with their peers outside school as they do with their parents or other adults. In

The driving force behind the shifts that occur in peer relationships during adolescence is gender reorientation.

the United States, teenagers spend an average of approximately 20 hours a week with their peers outside of school (Csikszentmihalyi & Larson, 1984; Fuligni & Stevenson, 1995). Correspondingly, the amount of time they spend with their families drops by approximately 50 percent between the fifth and ninth grades (Larson & Richards, 1991).

2. Adolescent peer groups function with less guidance and control from adults than do the peer groups of younger children. Instead of being confined to local neighborhoods, adolescent peer groups draw their members from many neighborhoods, and they are more likely to find ways to ensure that no parents or other adult authorities are observing their actions.
3. As adolescents increasingly distance themselves from adults, most seek out members of the other sex. This gender reorientation is a major reason for the reorganization of peer groups during adolescence.
4. Peer groups increase in size at the same time that friendships and other close relationships increase in intensity.

Friendships

Several large-scale studies conducted in the United States and other industrialized countries document the changing basis of friendships as children enter adolescence (Berndt, 1988; Cottrell, 1996; Schneider & Stevenson, 1999). As Table 15.1 indicates, between the ages of 6 and 12 (grades 1 to 6), participation in common activities, including organized play, is a major reason given for considering a peer to be a friend. This criterion does not disappear in adolescence but is supplemented by other factors. In grade 7 (12 to 13 years of age), for example, common interests, similarity of attitudes and values, loyalty, and intimacy become important to friendship.

Indeed, though adolescents in the United States are more mobile than younger children, attend larger schools, and have more opportunities to meet peers of other social classes and ethnic backgrounds, their close friends tend to be even more similar to them than they were in elementary school, a trend that continues all during adolescence (Berndt & Keefe, 1995). Teenagers choose friends who share their interests, values, beliefs, and attitudes because such friends are more likely to be supportive and understanding in times of need (Youniss & Smollar, 1985). High school friends tend to be similar in their views of school, their academic achievement, and their dating and other leisure-time activities (Berndt & Keefe, 1995; Berndt & Savin-Williams, 1993).

TABLE 15.1 INCIDENCE OF VARIOUS TYPES OF FRIENDSHIP, BY GRADE LEVEL (PERCENT)

	Grade Level*							
Type	**1**	**2**	**3**	**4**	**5**	**6**	**7**	**8**
Help (friend as giver)	5	12†	14	7	14	25	33	35
Common activities	3	7	32	52	24	40	60	60
Propinquity	7	5	9	12	12	20	38	32
Stimulation value	2	3	12	23	30	51	52	61
Organized play	2	0	15	26	9	10	17	20
Demographic similarity	0	3	7	35	15	15	10	23
Evaluation	2	5	13	13	17	33	21	30
Acceptance	3	0	5	9	9	18	18	38
Admiration	0	0	5	23	17	24	32	41
Incremental prior interaction	2	7	4	10	10	17	32	34
Loyalty and commitment	0	0	2	5	10	20	40	34
Genuineness	0	3	0	2	5	12	10	32
Help (friend as receiver)	2	5	3	5	2	12	13	25
Intimacy potential	0	0	0	0	0	0	8	20
Common interests	0	0	5	7	0	5	30	18
Similarity of attitudes and values	0	0	0	0	2	3	10	8

*At each grade level, the number of subjects (n) = 60.
†An underlined score indicates the grade level at which the incidence of the type of friendship first becomes significant.
Source: Bigelow & La Gaipa, 1975.

They also tend to have similar feelings about drug use, drinking, and delinquency (Akers et al., 1998; Urberg et al., 1998).

It is not difficult to understand why intimacy and loyalty become major criteria of friendships in adolescence. It is in the context of intimate, self-disclosing conversations with close friends that teenagers define themselves and explore their identities (see Figure 15.6). As evidence, John Gottman and Gwendolyn Mettetal (1989) offer the following excerpt from a conversation between two teenagers:

> *A:* *(joking)* I think you should take Randy to court for statutory rape.
> *B:* I don't. I'm to the point of wondering what "that kind of girl" is. . . . I don't know about the whole scene.
> *A:* The thing is . . .
> *B:* It depends on the reasoning. And how long you've been going out with somebody.
> *A:* Yeah. I'm satisfied with my morals.
> *B:* As long as you're satisfied with your morals, that's cool.
> *A:* Yeah, but other people . . .
> *B:* And I am pretty, I'm pretty sturdy in mine.
> *A:* Yeah *(giggle),* I know that. Mine tend to bend too easily.
>
> *(p. 119)*

Obviously no one would want to have such a conversation with someone who was not loyal or who might gossip. Nor would one want to share such confidences with a person who was not understanding and supportive.

While friends are important to both boys and girls during adolescence, there are differences in the quality of their friendships. Adolescent girls' friendships have been found to be more intense than friendships among boys (Brown et al., 1999). In middle adolescence, girls' friendships tend to have a feverish, jealous quality about them. At this stage, girls who are close friends

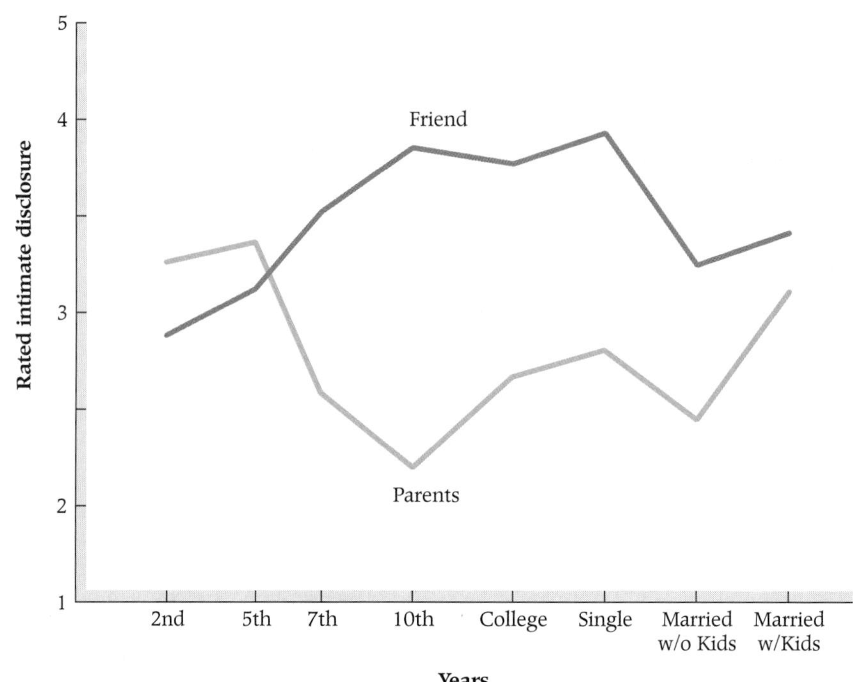

FIGURE 15.6
Age trends in reported self-disclosure to parents and friends. (Buhrmester, 1998.)

often watch each other's every move, calling each other on the telephone several times a day to report to each other and check up on one another. They also copy each other's behavior. If one girl has a boyfriend, her best friend will try to acquire a boyfriend, too. This intense, competitive aspect of girls' friendships tends to wane by late adolescence, perhaps because, as Elizabeth Douvan and Joseph Adelson (1966) suggest, girls are "less haunted by fears of being abandoned and betrayed" (p. 192). This trend is consistent with the sequence of Selman's developmental stages of friendship (see Chapter 14, p. 582). According to Selman's (1981) evidence, there is a shift during adolescence from stage 3, in which friendships are seen as a means of developing mutual intimacy and support, to stage 4, which is characterized by a new acceptance of a friend's need to establish relations with other people.

The friendships of boys between the ages of 14 and 16 years are likely to be less close, and more numerous, than those of girls because boys, more than girls, are concerned with establishing independence from parents and other adults and need the alliance of a group of friends to do so (Douvan & Adelson, 1966). Duane Buhrmester and Wyndol Furman (1987) suggest that these sex differences in friendship are more a matter of style than of substance. They have found that boys form friendships "in which sensitivity to needs and validation of worth are achieved through actions and deeds, rather than through interpersonal disclosure of personal thoughts and feelings" (pp. 111–112). Their view is supported by findings that boys are generally less articulate than girls about the nature and meaning of friendship. Like girls of 11 to 13, the 14- to 16-year-old boys studied by Douvan and Adelson (1966) said that they wanted their friends to be amiable and cooperative, to be able to control their impulses, and to share their interests. Like girls in their late teens, they said that they expected their friends to help them in times of trouble. What differed between the sexes was the kind of trouble they expected and therefore the kind of friendly support they sought.

Overall, the friendship circles of adolescent boys tend to be larger and less intimate than those of adolescent girls. Male friends are much more likely to discuss their thoughts about sports, cars, and girls in general than they are to reveal their self-doubts and anxieties or their feelings for a particular girl.

Girls wanted their friends to be people they could confide in about their relations with boys, whereas boys wanted their friends to support them when they got into trouble with their parents, teachers, and other authority figures.

For both boys and girls, adolescent friendships play a developmental role similar in certain respects to the role of attachment in infancy. As we saw in Chapters 5 and 6, during infancy babies engage in "social referencing"—continually looking to their caregivers to see how they evaluate what is going on—and they use their caregivers as a "secure base" to which they can retreat when they feel threatened as they explore their environment. During adolescence, friends look to each other for help in confronting and making sense of uncertain and often anxiety-provoking situations. The first time a boy calls up a girl for a date, his best friend may well be standing at his elbow providing support and maybe some coaching. And no sooner has the girl hung up than she is likely to call her best friend to tell her about the conversation and get her opinion. The two pairs of friends will decide together if the call was a success or a failure and will lay plans for the next move. For both the infant and the adolescent, the attachment bond is gradually modified by successful interaction with the world "out there." Eventually, just as the baby relies less on the mother, the adolescent will begin to depend less on the best friend.

Evidence from a number of studies (Berndt & Savin-Williams, 1993; Newcomb & Bagwell, 1996) indicates that close friendships have a positive influence on adolescents' social and personality development. Adolescents who perceive their friends as supportive report fewer school-related and psychological problems, greater confidence in their social acceptance by peers, and less loneliness. Difficulty in making friends during adolescence is part of a broader syndrome of poor social adjustment.

clique A group of several young people that remains small enough to enable its members to be in regular interaction with one another and to serve as the primary peer group.

Cliques and Crowds

A friendship is the smallest unit of peer interaction, a group of two. As children in some industrialized countries move into adolescence, two additional, more inclusive kinds of peer groups become prominent—*cliques* and *crowds*. A **clique** is a group of several young people that remains small enough to enable its members to be in regular interaction with one another and to serve as the primary peer group (Brown, 1999). Members of cliques are often friends of the same sex who dress alike and share similar interests (Cottrell, 1996). According to John Cottrell (1996), "Cliques are the building blocks of peer society, the anchor of social activities, and the access route for making new friends" (p. 24).

Dexter Dunphy (1963), one of the first researchers to study cliques, noted that they are about the size of a two-child family with the grandparents present. "Their similarity in size to a family," Dunphy wrote, "facilitates the transference of the individual's allegiance to them and allows them to provide an alternative center of security" (p. 233).

Cliques differ from families in at least one important respect: they are voluntary groups that adolescents are free to leave. The element of choice in clique membership reflects the increased control adolescents have in choosing the settings in which they find themselves, the people with whom they associate, and the things they do.

Adolescents may belong to several cliques made up of different members who see each other at different times of the day in different settings. For example, an adolescent may be a member of one clique in science class, another during lunch hour, and still another in the neighborhood on the weekends. In this respect, cliques differ from friendships, which are not restricted to a particular setting (Cottrell, 1996).

Teenage girls often rely on each other for social support, and especially for advice about their new interest in boys.

crowd A type of peer group. One kind of crowd grows out of preexisting cliques and friendship groups; a second kind, referred to as a *reputation-based crowd,* is most likely to be encountered in the high school setting, and its members may or may not be friends.

The second type of peer group is the **crowd.** The word "crowd" appears to have two meanings corresponding to different ways in which crowds arise and the social settings in which they are prominent. One kind of crowd grows out of preexisting cliques and friendship groups. A second form of crowd, referred to as a *reputation-based crowd,* is most likely to be encountered in the high school setting, and the members of the crowd may or may not be friends (Brown, 1999). Members of reputation-based crowds are perceived to behave in particular ways and to share common interests, beliefs, and values with other members.

Although the labels differ from one locale to another, a relatively small set of stereotypic names are repeatedly encountered in the descriptions adolescents use to differentiate among reputation-based crowds: jocks, brains, loners, druggies, nerds, and so on (Brown & Huang, 1995; Eckert, 1995). In schools with a diverse ethnic population, ethnicity has been found to be an important factor in crowd formation (Brown & Huang, 1995). In such cases, studies have found that one-half to two-thirds of minority-group students were identified by their peers as members of ethnically defined crowds (African Americans, Latinos, Asians, etc.).

As names such as "jocks" or "brains" indicate, the norms and values of some crowds like "student government" or "born-again Christians" fit closely with those of the adult community. Other crowds, like the "druggies," adhere to lifestyles that are in opposition to dominant adult values and foster behaviors that are socially problematic. These differences are seen clearly in Table 15.2, which summarizes differences among high school crowds studied by Brown and Bih-Hu Huang (1995) with respect to four characteristics: grades, the importance attached to schooling, drug use, and delinquency.

B. Bradford Brown and his colleagues point to three ways in which crowds influence adolescent social life. First, crowds and the way they are categorized help adolescents learn about the alternative social identities that are available to them. Second, the crowd adolescents belong to strongly influences whom they are likely to meet and spend time with. Third, crowds shape their members' interpersonal relations (Brown et al., 1994).

In addition, being identified as a member of a particular crowd has a significant impact on an adolescent's social status. In a classic study of the relationship between individual status and crowd association, James S. Coleman (1962) analyzed questionnaires distributed to thousands of U.S. students at ten high schools in small towns, small cities, large cities, and suburbs. In every school he studied, Coleman found that students could identify a "leading crowd" against which they evaluated themselves. The responses he obtained to the question "What does it take to get into the leading crowd in this school?" reveal some of the values American adolescents held at the time and the characteristics they considered important to be a success within the crowd (see Figure 15.7). Coleman found that both boys and girls said a "good personality" was the most important characteristic of people in the leading group. For boys, the next most important characteristics were having a good reputa-

TABLE 15.2 CROWD DIFFERENCES IN MEAN SCORES ON OUTCOME MEASURES

Outcome	Total	Jock	Popular	Druggie	Outcast	Brain	Normal	Floater	Outsider
GPA	3.06	3.26	3.18	2.82	2.87	3.61	3.19	3.13	2.65
Importance of schooling	3.86	4.22	3.95	3.34	3.84	4.23	4.10	4.02	3.42
Drug use	1.62	1.33	1.43	2.61	1.28	1.11	1.27	1.34	2.02
Minor delinquency	1.41	1.33	1.34	1.77	1.31	1.15	1.21	1.29	1.64

Note. Values are adjusted for the effects of gender and grade level. Higher scores indicate higher levels of the construct described by the scale.
Source: Brown & Huang, 1995.

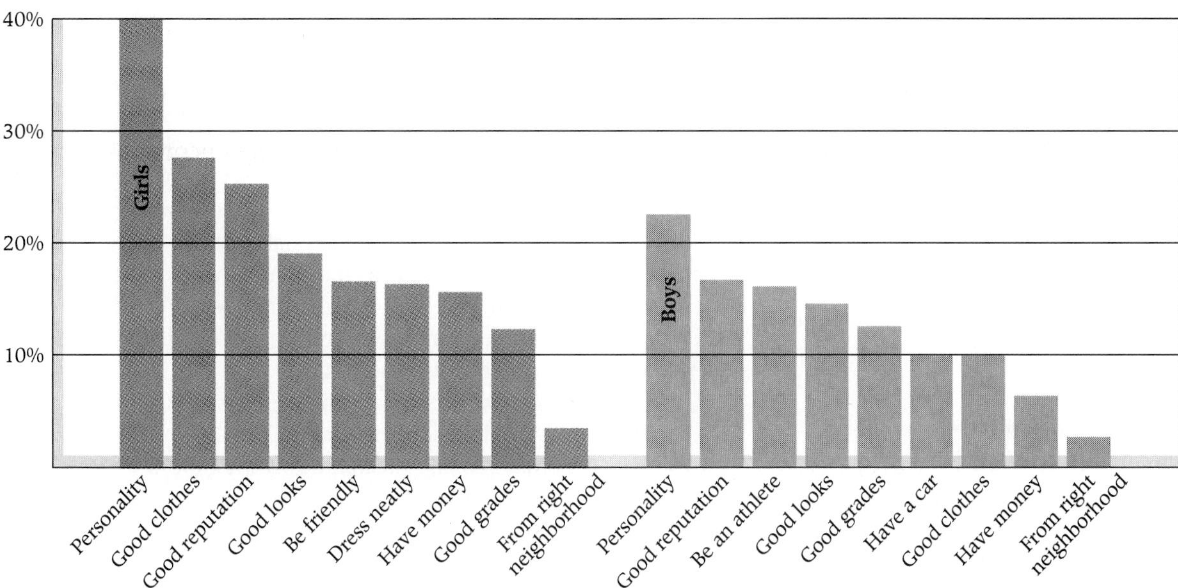

FIGURE 15.7
The average ranks given by boys and girls to major criteria of popularity. (Adapted from Coleman, 1962.)

tion, being a good athlete, being good-looking, wearing good clothes, and getting good grades. For girls, the most important characteristics after a good personality were good looks, good clothing, and a good reputation. Although Coleman's research was conducted many years ago, later research has confirmed his general finding that there is a leading crowd in middle and high schools to which others are oriented (Brown et al., 1994; Cottrell, 1996).

The leading crowd seems to have great influence in adolescents' lives, primarily because being a member of the leading crowd is associated with greater popularity. When Coleman's subjects were asked to respond to the statement "If I could trade, I would be someone different from myself," one out of five boys and girls expressed a desire to change themselves so that they would be accepted by the leading crowd.

The popularity derived from being associated with groups other than the leading crowd seems to vary. For example, as a rule, "brains" occupy a status somewhere between the elite groups and groups that are disparaged. However, in some groups, academic achievement leads to a decided decrease in popularity (Ishiyama & Chabassol, 1985). In some working-class African American communities, for example, being labeled a "brain" can lead to being ostracized, and academically able young people try to mask their abilities in order to avoid this fate (Ogbu, 1997).

Peer Pressure to Conform

For many decades developmentalists have worried that it may be unhealthy for adolescents to spend excessive time with their peers, beyond the observation and control of adults. The core of this concern was expressed by Urie Bronfenbrenner (1970): "If children have contact only with their own age-mates, there is no possibility for learning culturally-established patterns of co-operation and mutual concern" (p. 121). In short, the belief was that, left to themselves, adolescents are likely to engage in antisocial behavior.

There is a lot of evidence to support this belief. For example, Thomas Berndt and Keunho Keefe (1995) asked a large group of seventh- and eighth-graders to fill out a questionnaire about their involvement in school and any disruptive behaviors they engaged in. They were also asked to identify their friends. Their teachers were asked to fill out a questionnaire about each participant to check on the validity of the self-reports. The questionnaires were given both in the fall and in the spring of the school year.

BOX 15.2

Risk Taking and Social Deviance during Adolescence

While the extent of psychological storm and stress during adolescence continues to be debated, there is little doubt that in modern industrial societies, adolescents engage in an exceptional level of socially disapproved behaviors that pose risks to their long-term well-being (Arnett, 1999; Centers for Disease Control and Prevention, 1998):

- One in four sexually active U.S. adolescents contract a sexually transmitted disease; this level is twice that of people in their twenties.
- One in five adolescents report having seriously considered committing suicide in the past year.
- Driving under the influence of alcohol is reported by 17 percent of high school students, and one in three report that they have participated in "binge drinking" (having five or more drinks on a single occasion) within the prior month.
- Adolescents commit a disproportionate number of petty crimes.

These kinds of statistics, coupled with the fact that the levels of such behaviors seem to have risen sharply in recent years, have spurred efforts to determine the causes of adolescent risk taking and social deviance (Carnegie Council on Adolescent Development, 1995).

One insight into the problem comes from cross-cultural evidence, which indicates that high levels of risk taking and antisocial behavior are not a universal outcome of the transition to adulthood (Schlegel & Barry, 1991). Two features distinguish societies where antisocial behavior is common from those where it is not. First, when adolescent boys spend most of their time with adult men at work and during leisure hours, antisocial behavior is absent. When boys spend most of their time in peer groups, the level of antisocial behavior is significantly elevated. Second, the nature of the interactions in a given peer group makes a difference. When peer groups are organized for competition and given special names, antisocial behavior is significantly higher than it is when peer relations are less formally organized and are noncompetitive. These results immediately indicate why high levels of antisocial behavior could be expected in industrialized societies such as Canada and the United States, where adolescents spend a great deal of time in peer groups that are often highly organized and competitive, schools, gangs, and sports teams being prominent examples. Pierre Dasen (1999) points out that in rapidly changing societies in Africa, where traditional authority structures are eroding and thus adolescent males no longer spend their days with older men, one can see the emergence of the kinds of problematic risk-taking behaviors that are a significant social problem in the industrialized world.

Cross-cultural comparisons identify the social conditions that promote adolescent risk taking, but they do not explain what it is that actually precipitates risk taking in those conditions. One frequently offered explanation is that adolescents ignore or greatly underestimate the risks they are taking. In effect, according to this view, adolescents feel invulnerable and don't believe that anything bad can happen to them. To evaluate this possibility, Marilyn Quadrel and her colleagues conducted a study of adults and their adolescent children, as well as adolescents who were living in treatment homes because they had gotten into trouble through risky, antisocial behavior (Quadrel et al., 1993). Subjects in all three groups were asked to estimate their risk of experiencing such events as an automobile accident, an unplanned pregnancy, and alcohol dependency. In all three groups, the subjects thought that they were at less risk than other people, but the two groups of adolescents were no more likely to make such judgments than the adults. These results speak against the idea that adolescents are especially prone to viewing themselves as invulnerable to risk.

Other evidence suggests that an important psychological characteristic underpinning adolescent risk taking is sensation seeking, defined as "a personality trait characterized by the extent of a person's desire for novelty and intensity of sensory stimulation" (Arnett, 1999). James Arnett (1996) and others have repeatedly found significant correlations between measures of sensation seeking and a variety of risk behaviors, including promiscuous sexual activity, drinking, drug use, and antisocial behavior. Marvin Zuckerman (1990), who has studied individual differences in sensation-seeking behaviors, reports that adolescents who score high on tests of sensation seeking also respond strongly to novel stimuli as measured by

As one might expect, Berndt and Keefe found that boys and girls whose friends engaged in a high level of disruptive behavior in the fall reported an increase in the level of their own disruptive behavior in the spring, with the girls being more susceptible to such influence. Other studies show that if an adolescent's close friends smoke cigarettes, drink alcohol, use illegal drugs, are sexually active, or break the law, sooner or later the adolescent is likely to do these things, too (see Box 15.2) (Cairns & Cairns, 1994; Reed & Roundtree, 1997).

Such findings, however, are not sufficient to demonstrate that direct social pressure from one's peers *causes* young people to behave in a particular

These girls were photographed inhaling air freshener in the bathroom of their high school. Inexpensive and readily available, inhalants are an increasingly popular avenue to drug abuse among adolescents.

electrical activity of the brain and heart rate. This kind of evidence suggests that sensation-seeking and risk-taking tendencies are biologically rooted and thus to be found in all societies. What differs across societies is the extent to which adolescents continue to spend their time with adults who act as a counterforce to those tendencies.

While the sensation-seeking hypothesis may apply to some kinds of adolescent risk taking, in some contexts, it does not seem applicable to many others. Richard Jessor (1992) is critical of the sensation-seeking hypothesis. He argues:

> Playing the game of "Chicken" on the highway, taking chances on avoiding detection during certain delinquent acts, or pursuing activities like rock climbing may be exemplars [of sensation-seeking behaviors]. But the larger class of adolescent risk behavior does not lend itself to that kind of analysis. Few adolescents continue cigarette smoking for the thrill of seeing whether or not they can avoid pulmonary disease; few engage in unprotected sexual intercourse for the thrill of beating the odds of contracting a sexually transmitted disease or becoming pregnant. Indeed a key concern of health educators is to make adolescents aware that there are risks associated with many of the behaviors they engage in. (p. 379)

Against the prevailing negative view of adolescent risk taking, Cynthia Lightfoot (1997) maintains that some risk taking in adolescence is natural and necessary for normal development. On the basis of interviews with 41 teenagers, 15 to 17 years old, she concluded that risk taking is often a mode of play that helps to create bonds between friends, to test the limits of adult authority, and to test oneself. For example, one 17-year-old answered her question about the attractions of taking risks this way:

> What's appealing? I think growth—inner growth. And a feeling of independence and maturity in trying something new. Even if I fail, I still kind of pat myself on the back and say, "hey, you tried it, and no one can blame you for sitting back and not participating." I want to be a participant. (Lightfoot, 1994, p. 5)

At present developmentalists have no fully satisfactory explanation or solution for difficulties caused by adolescent risk taking. While it is clear that the social and cultural organization of modern life greatly increases adolescent risk taking and antisocial behavior, the complex ways in which these contextual factors contribute to risk taking make it a very difficult pattern of behavior to explain or to deal with.

manner. As we have seen, social influence is a mutual process. Adolescents not only influence their friends but are being influenced by them at the same time; they also choose friends who are like them. Moreover, adolescent peer relationships are not particularly stable. When adolescents behave in ways that their peers are uncomfortable with, the bonds of friendship may loosen (Cairns & Cairns, 1994). All these factors make it hard to determine how much of an adolescent's behavior is influenced by peer relations.

An earlier study by Thomas Berndt (1979) found that teenagers may not be as susceptible to peer pressure as adults assume they are. In a study with third- through twelfth-graders, Berndt posed several hypothetical situations in

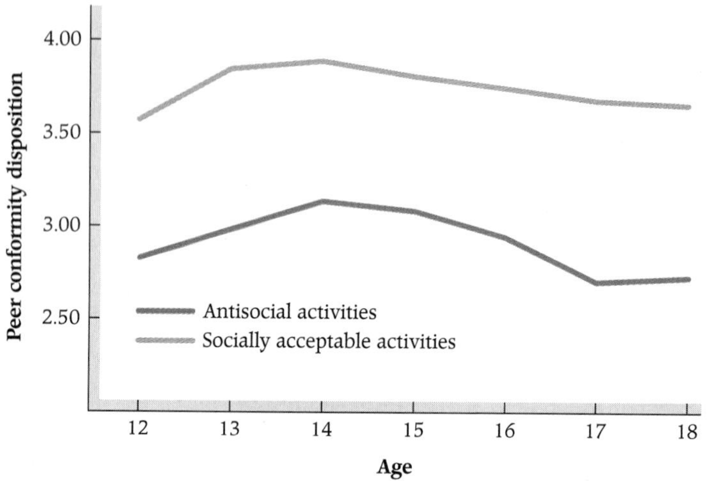

FIGURE 15.8

Average scores on a measure of susceptibility to peer pressure. Higher scores indicate greater conformity. A score of 3.50 indicates that the tendencies to conform and to reject peer pressure are equal. Note that while susceptibility to peer pressure increases slightly in early adolescence, pressure to conform to antisocial activities is significantly less than pressure to conform to socially acceptable forms of behavior. (After Brown et al., 1986, Fig. 1.)

which the adolescent could either choose to go along with the group or refuse to. Some of the situations involved neutral behavior, while others involved more questionable behavior, such as the following:

> You are with a couple of friends on Halloween. They're going to soap windows, but you're not sure whether you should or not. Your friends all say you should, because there is no way you could get caught. What would you really do? (p. 610)

Berndt found that the level of conformity to peer pressure, especially with regard to engaging in antisocial acts, increased between the third and ninth grades (roughly between the ages of 9 and 15) and then decreased, a pattern that has been found by other investigators (Brown et al., 1986). (See Figure 15.8.) Note two points, however: First, the overall level of conformity to peer pressure is lower for antisocial acts than for neutral ones. Second, the students were, overall, more likely to say that they would not go along with their peers than to say that they would.

Berndt also asked his subjects to evaluate the seriousness of various kinds of antisocial behaviors, such as stealing candy from a store. He found that the adolescents evaluated antisocial behaviors as being less bad than third-graders did. Third-graders were likely to say that stealing candy from a store is very bad, whereas ninth-graders did not seem to think it was particularly bad at all. Consequently, the increase in going along with peers displayed in Figure 15.8 may reflect decreased concern that the action is wrong rather than an increase in the influence of peers. As Berndt (1979) comments, the results "suggest that mid-adolescence is the period of least acceptance of conventional standards of behavior" (p. 613).

Even with regard to the evidence showing that older adolescents are increasingly likely to drink alcoholic beverages, smoke cigarettes, and become sexually active if their friends do, it is not clear if such increases are the result of peer pressure or simply a part of the reorientation associated with becoming an adult. Adults disapprove of such activities for young people, though they think nothing of drinking or having sexual relations themselves. This situation has led some developmentalists to argue that age-related increases in drinking and other "grown-up" activities that some people might consider risky should be viewed not as social deviance or susceptibility to peer pressure but as an attempt to model accepted adult behavior (Jessor, 1998).

Peer-Group Organization and the Transition to Sexual Relationships

In many cultures, a key function of the peer group is to provide a context for the transition to sexual relationships. Two large studies conducted in Australia suggest how this function is carried out (Cottrell, 1996; Dunphy, 1963). Despite the fact that the observations were made many years apart, they agree in the picture they yield of how young people's peer interactions often shift gradually from same-sex cliques to heterosexual crowds during the course of adolescence. The following description is synthesized from observations made by John Cottrell and his students in shopping malls and reported by Cottrell (1996).

On a weekend evening, groups of five to ten teenagers can be observed "hanging out" at the shopping mall. The cliques of girls are window shopping; the cliques of boys position themselves to watch the cliques of girls. Within each clique there is a continual stream of loud talking and joking as the members covertly look over those in the other cliques around them. Often they seem to be acting up in ways calculated to get the attention of another clique. As the evening progresses, the cliques start to make direct contact with each other, interacting in a nonchalant manner that contrasts with the attention-getting behavior they had engaged in earlier. Cottrell likens the interaction among cliques of 13- to 14-year-old adolescents to a "marshaling area" in which several cliques eventually merge into a single crowd before the entire group goes off to watch a movie or go dancing at a disco.

The initial behavior of the 15- to 16-year-olds is similar, but instead of simply merging into a crowd, male and female cliques begin to interact with each other. As Cottrell puts it, what begins as apparently casual glances between members of two cliques is supplemented by body language that "becomes intense." At some point, one of the boys, usually someone who enjoys high status within his clique, walks over to the girls and begins talking to them. The two cliques remain where they met, and later in the evening, instead of going to some larger public event, they become organized into smaller subgroups composed of members of both sexes.

Dexter Dunphy, whose earlier study yielded a similar pattern of behavior, diagrammed the stages of this transition from small, same-sex cliques to larger, heterosexual crowds, as shown in Figure 15.9. At stage 1 there are as yet no crowds, only isolated same-sex cliques. These cliques are, in effect, a continuation from the days of middle childhood.

Stage 2 represents the first movement toward heterosexual peer relations. At first the cliques begin to interact and to form crowds in which anonymity precludes the likelihood of intimacy, which the clique members fear.

In stage 3 the members of the crowd with the highest status initiate heterosexual contacts across cliques while still maintaining membership in their same-sex cliques.

During stages 2 and 3, social events that require more intimate interaction, such as dances and parties, become prominent. Here again the size of the crowd is important, since there *is* safety in numbers! The presence of others makes it less likely that anyone will overstep the bounds of propriety.

In stage 4, same-sex cliques are transformed into heterosexual cliques, whose members are often paired. These arrangements allow a greater degree of intimacy, should the pair want it, but also provide a group of co-conspirators with whom each member can talk about what is going on.

Stage 5 sees the slow disintegration of the crowd as its members begin to take on adult roles.

Although the general pattern of changes reported in these studies provides convincing evidence of cultural continuity over time, there are important cultural and historical variations in adolescent social relationships (Berndt & Savin-Williams, 1993; Brown et al., 1994). On the basis of the data he collected in the late 1950s, Dunphy reported that the crowd disintegrated into groups of couples who were going steady or were engaged to get married. Fifty years later this pattern may continue in some parts of the world, but it does not appear to be generally characteristic of contemporary industrialized societies. Instead, marriage is often postponed until several years after the initiation of sexual activity (see Figure 5.10).

FIGURE 15.9

The stages of group development during adolescence. At the start of this period, peer-group interactions are largely segregated by sex; at the end, there is far more heterosexual peer-group interaction. (Adapted from Dumphy, 1963.)

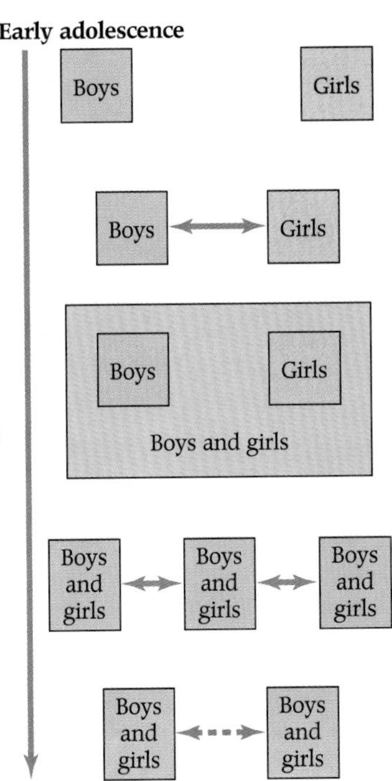

SEXUAL ACTIVITY

Adolescent sexual activity varies according to contextual factors including the prevailing behavioral patterns in the culture and historical times in question. For example, in a survey of 114 societies, it was found that among girls, adolescent sexual activity was universal in 49

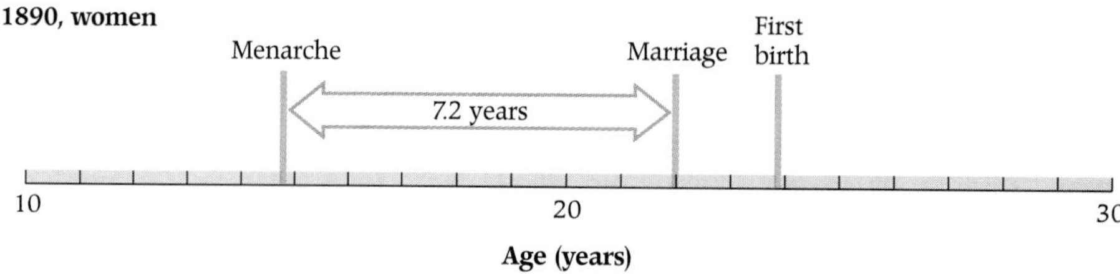

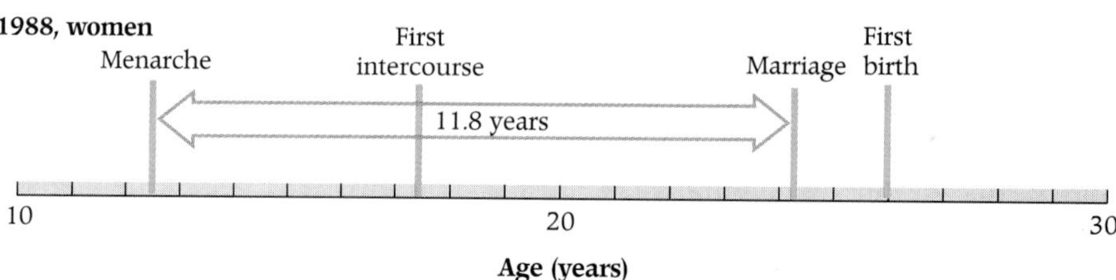

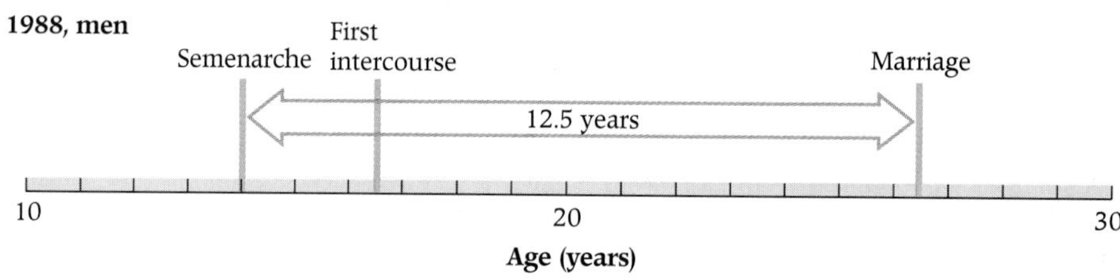

FIGURE 15.10
The length of time between puberty, initiation of sexual activity, and marriage in the United States, 1890 and 1988. (Reproduced with the permission of The Alan Guttmacher Institute from Sex and America's Teenagers, *1994, The Alan Guttmacher Institute, New York.)*

percent of the societies, common in 17 percent, occasional in 14 percent, and uncommon in 20 percent (Broude & Greene, 1976). The variability among societies in regard to adolescent sexual activity ranges from the customs of many Middle Eastern cultures that prohibit girls from having any contact with males outside their families after they reach puberty to the expectation among certain groups in the Philippines that sexual activity will naturally occur. The situation in the contemporary United States is contradictory. A great deal of official public rhetoric discourages teenage sexual activity at the same time that the mass media often make it appear desirable and common.

FIGURE 15.11
Percentage of teenagers who had sexual intercourse at different ages, 1995. (Source: Alan Guttmacher Institute, 1999.)

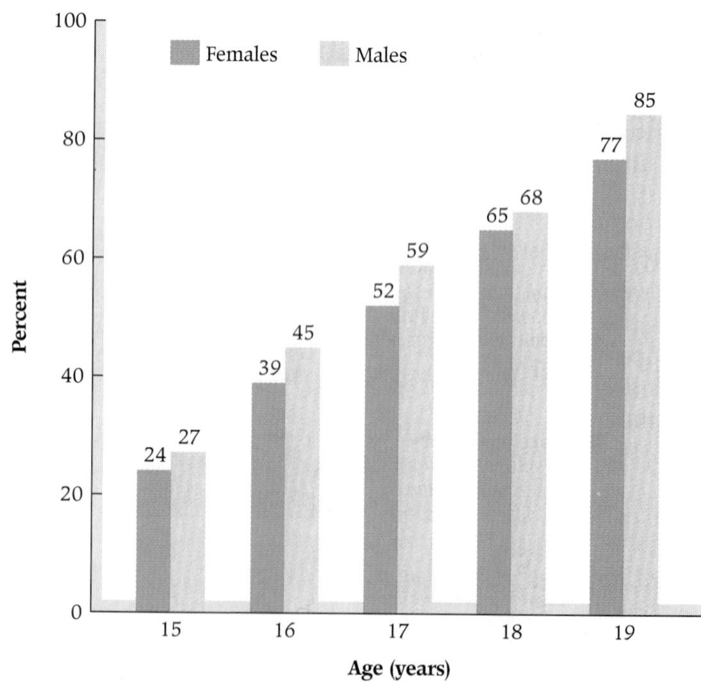

According to the most recent data available, most U.S. adolescents 15 and under have not had sexual intercourse. The likelihood of teenagers having sexual intercourse increases steadily with age. Over half of 17-year-olds have had intercourse (see Figure 15.11) (Alan Guttmacher Institute, 1999).

It should be clear by now that a great deal of the social behavior associated with sex roles is learned from observation and practice, consistent with environmental-learning approaches to development. Less obvious, perhaps, is the fact that the act of uniting with another person sexually also requires a good deal of learning. Moreover, because boys and girls have different biological roles and social histories, the processes by which they learn to engage in sexual intercourse—often referred to as *coitus,* from a Latin word meaning "to come together"—differ in important respects.

Among human beings, there is ample evidence for the role of learning in the initiation of sexual activity because the appropriate behaviors vary according to such factors as culture, historical circumstances, and social class (Michael et al., 1994; Peplau et al., 1999) (see Box

BOX 15.3 **THE TRADITIONAL KIKUYU SCRIPT FOR ADOLESCENT SEX**

Among the Kikuyu people of central Kenya at the turn of the century, boys and girls underwent an initiation ceremony, or rite of passage, just before the start of puberty, after which the boys were considered to be junior warriors and the girls were considered to be maidens (Worthman & Whiting, 1987). For the next several years, approved sexual relations between the young men and women followed a script that differed in many ways from the scripts typically followed by teenagers in the United States.

In addition to helping their mothers with household chores and gardening, Kikuyu maidens were expected to strengthen the social cohesion of the group by entertaining the bachelor friends of their older brothers. The entertainment included not only dancing and feasting but a kind of lovemaking called *ngweko.* Jomo Kenyatta (1938), the first president of Kenya after it won its independence in 1962, described *ngweko* in the following manner:

> The girls visit their boy-friends at a special hut, *thingira,* used as a rendezvous by the young men and women. . . .
>
> Girls may visit the *thingira* at any time, day or night. After eating, while engaged in conversation with the boys, one of the boys turns the talk dramatically to the subject of *ngweko.* If there are more boys than girls, the girls are asked to select whom they want as their companion. The selection is done in the most liberal way. . . . In such a case it is not necessary for girls to select their most intimate friends, as this would be considered selfish and unsociable. . . . After the partners have been arranged, one of the boys gets up, saying *"ndathie kwenogora"* (I am going to stretch myself). His girl partner follows him to the bed. The boy removes all his clothing. The girl removes her upper garment . . . and retains her skirt, *motheru,* and her soft leather apron, *mwengo,* which she pulls back between her legs and tucks in together with her leather skirt, *motheru.* The two V-shaped tails of her *motheru* are pulled forward between her legs from behind and fastened to the waist, thus keeping the *mwengo* in position and forming an effective protection of her private parts. In this position, the lovers lie together facing each other, with their legs interwoven to prevent any movement of their hips. They begin to fondle each other, rubbing their breasts together, whilst at the same time engaged in love-making conversation until they gradually fall asleep. (pp. 157–158)

Sexual intercourse was explicitly forbidden as a part of this premarital sexual activity. In fact, both the boys and the girls were taught that if either of them directly touched the genitals of the other, they would become polluted and have to undergo an expensive purification rite. Boys who did not adhere to this restriction were ostracized by their peers. Not until marriage was sexual intercourse sanctioned.

15.3). One example of a behavior that has changed over time is petting—erotic caressing that does not include the union of male and female genitals. According to Dr. Alfred Kinsey and his associates, whose famous surveys of sexual behavior were published in the middle of the twentieth century (Kinsey et al., 1948, 1953), the practice of petting increased substantially among Americans born after 1900. More recent surveys indicate that petting has continued to increase in the decades since Kinsey gathered his data (Michael et al., 1994). A good example of a sexual practice that varies markedly from one cultural group to another is oral sex. Among some groups (for example, college-educated European Americans), oral sex is relatively common, whereas in other groups (Hispanic Americans, African Americans, and older Americans), it is much less common (Michael et al., 1994).

Sex as a Scripted Activity

Researchers who study the development of sexual activity use the concept of scripts to describe the sequence of behaviors that precede first intercourse (Michael et al., 1994). In recent years in the United States and Australia (two countries for which data are available), the typical pattern of discrete "steps" that precedes the initiation of first intercourse proceeds from lip kissing to tongue kissing to caressing breasts through clothing to fondling breasts under the clothing to touching the genitals through clothing to touching genitals directly, and finally to genital contact. Oral sex, if it is a part of this sequence, may or may not precede coitus (Katchadourian, 1990; Rosenthal et al., 1999).

BOX 15.4

Teenage Pregnancy

About 1 million American teenagers become pregnant each year, giving the United States the highest teenage pregnancy rate among developed countries (U.S. Dept. of Health and Human Services Control, 1998). U.S. teenagers are no more sexually active than those in the other countries surveyed, so it seems clear that American adolescents use contraception far less often than do adolescents in other developed countries (Alan Guttmacher Institute, 1999). One reason for the difference in the use of contraceptives may be that adults in many other industrialized countries have a more realistic view of the likelihood of teenage sexual activity and thus better prepare their adolescent children for dealing with their sexuality. In the United States, by contrast, sex education is still controversial in many communities and contraceptive use by teenagers is sporadic.

Of the million teenage pregnancies that occur in the United States each year, 95 percent are unintended. Almost one-third of the teenage pregnancies end in voluntary abortions, and another 14 percent are miscarried (U. S. Dept. of Health and Human Services, 1998). Of the 55 percent of pregnant girls who go on to give birth, 76 percent are unmarried. Unlike unwed mothers of earlier decades, these girls are more likely to keep and raise their babies than to give them up for adoption (U.S. Dept. of Health and Human Services, 1998).

Race, social class, education, and the strength of religious beliefs all affect a teenager's decision about whether or not to have and keep her child (Coley & Chase-Lansdale, 1998). African American teenagers are more likely than European American teenagers to become single mothers. According to government statistics, 83 percent of the teenagers who give birth come from poor or low-income families (U.S. Dept. of Health & Human Services, 1998). The more education a pregnant teenager's mother has (which is an indirect measure of her social class) and the better the teenager is doing in school, the more likely she is to decide to abort the pregnancy. In fact, one-third of all teenagers who become mothers drop out of school before they become pregnant (Aber et al., 1995). Teenagers with strong religious convictions are likely to have and keep their babies, no matter what their race or social class (Eisen et al., 1983).

While many of the negative outcomes that follow from teenage pregnancy, such as poverty and low educational achievement, also precede pregnancy, teenage childbearing serves to further limit the futures of girls who are already disadvantaged. Compared with women who delay their childbearing, women who give birth while in their teens are, on the average, more likely to drop out of school, to divorce, to continue to have children outside of marriage, to change jobs more frequently, to be on welfare, and to have health problems (Coley & Chase-Lansdale, 1998). They are also more likely to have low-birth-weight babies who are susceptible to illness and infant mortality.

Despite these grim findings, not every girl who bears a child while still in her teens ends up quitting school or living in poverty. Longitudinal studies of mothers who became pregnant as teenagers have found that some of these women eventually complete high school and become economically self-sufficient. Long-term success for these women was predicted by their being at grade level when they become pregnant, coming from smaller families that were not on welfare, and having families that had high expectations for their future and communicated those expectations to them (Furstenberg et al.,1992).

The limited information about teenage boys who become fathers indicates that, like the girls who become mothers, they are often from poor families who live in low-income communities and have low educational achievement. Because of their own poverty, young fathers usually cannot provide stable, adequate economic support for their children even when they wish to. Initially, many young fathers have extensive contact with their children, but as time passes this contact tends to decrease (Coley & Chase-Lansdale, 1998).

Although it is difficult for adolescent mothers to keep up with the demands of a new baby and school work, many school districts have established special programs to ensure that teenage mothers have an opportunity to continue their education.

This scripted sequence is also culturally variable. It describes the behavior of European American adolescents but not that of African American teenagers, who are likely to move toward intercourse earlier and with fewer intervening steps (Smith & Udry, 1985).

In Chapter 9 we saw that the concept of scripts is important for understanding the mental development of preschool children. Scripts allow small children, who do not understand fully what is expected of them, to participate with adults in such activities as eating in a restaurant, attending a birthday party, and drawing a picture. A similar use of scripts is evident among adolescent boys and girls who are engaging in sexual activity for the first time. Their peer-group experiences, their observations of adults, and their general cultural knowledge provide them with a rough idea of the scripts they are supposed to follow and the roles they are supposed to play. In the United States, for example, the male is traditionally active and controls the interaction, while the female responds.

A script also gives sexual meaning to individual acts that may have no such meaning in other contexts. Hand-holding, kissing, and unzipping one's pants are not inherently sexual acts; each occurs often in nonsexual contexts. It is only within the context of the larger script of dating or of coitus that these acts take on sexual meanings and give rise to sexual excitement.

Motives for Initiating Sexual Activity

Evidence from a wide variety of sources indicates that males and females initiate sexual activity for different reasons (Beal, 1994). To begin with, biological differences between the two sexes set the stage for males and females to have divergent experiences with the erotic potential of their own bodies.

Sexual arousal is more obvious in males than in females because of its expression in clearly visible penile erection. In addition, most males experience orgasm within a few years of the onset of puberty, usually through masturbation (Graber et al., 1998). Not only is sexual arousal more ambiguous in females than in males, but females usually experience their first orgasm much later than males do. Part of the reason is that the clitoris, the center of female sexual pleasure, is small and hidden within the vulva, so girls are less likely to discover its erotic possibilities. Robert Michael and his colleagues report that adolescent girls masturbate considerably less frequently than do boys. Many women begin to masturbate only after they have begun having sexual intercourse (Michael et al., 1994).

According to John Gagnon and William Simon (1973), differences in the masturbatory behavior of boys and girls have consequences for later sexual behavior. First, masturbating to orgasm reinforces males' commitment to sexual behavior early in adolescence. Second, experience with masturbation tends to focus the male's feelings of sexual desire on the penis, whereas most females, lacking such experiences, do not localize their erotic responses in their genitals until much later, and then primarily as a result of sexual contacts with males.

This conclusion is bolstered by the fact that most teenage boys say that their first experience of sexual intercourse was motivated primarily by curiosity and only secondarily by affection for their partners. Girls, by contrast, rank affection for their partners as the major reason for engaging in sexual intercourse and curiosity as secondary. This difference in orientation between boys and girls led Gagnon and Simon (1973) to comment, "Dating and courtship may well be considered processes in which persons train members of the opposite sex in the meaning and content of their respective commitments"(p. 74).

In general, boys respond more positively than girls to their first experience of intercourse. In one survey, very few boys said they were sorry about having had intercourse, but the girls were more likely to say that they experienced pain and to express ambivalence about the event (Michael et al., 1994). Many girls are less positive about their initial experience of intercourse for a good reason: they were coerced into having sex. About 60 percent of the girls who had

Even before they reach sexual maturity, children in many countries are the objects of sexual exploitation. These young Thai girls have been sold into prostitution.

sex before they were 15 years old say that they did so involuntarily (Alan Guttmacher Institute, 1999).

CHANGING PARENT–CHILD RELATIONS

The increasing time that adolescents spend with their peers and the importance they place on peer relationships inevitably change the relationships between parents and their children. At the most general level, adolescents become more distant from their parents and are more likely to turn to their peers than to their parents for advice on a variety of questions about how to conduct themselves in a wide variety of contexts (Paikoff & Brooks-Gunn, 1991; Steinberg & Silverberg, 1986). However, extensive research shows that the ways in which parent–child relationships change depend on a host of factors.

The Content and Severity of Adolescent–Parent Conflicts

When developmentalists describe adolescence as a period of "storm and stress," they usually are thinking about the conflicts between adolescents and their parents. On the basis of a review of a large number of studies carried out over the past several decades, Brett Laursen and his colleagues found that patterns of conflict between families and their children do indeed change over the course of adolescence (Laursen et al., 1998). First, they found that the *frequency* of conflict between adolescents and their parents is highest early in adolescence and then decreases. This decreased frequency is difficult to interpret because adolescents tend to spend less time at home as they grow older and thus it may be that in relation to the actual time they spend with parents, the amount of parent–child conflict remains the same.

Adolescents display conspicuous styles of dress and behavior. These styles change from one cohort (and one generation) to the next, but they are consistently at odds with adult norms.

Second, Laursen and his colleagues found that the *intensity* of the conflicts between parents and their adolescent children increases from early to midadolescence before declining. The trend toward increased intensity of conflict coincides with the period when adolescents are spending less and less time at home and shifting their emotional attachments to their peers. Their parents are aware of this change and the risks that go with it, which they find worrisome.

In addition to their concerns about their children, parents have concerns of their own. They are reaching an age where they are likely to have increased responsibilities at work; their own parents are aging and are likely to need special care; and their own physical powers are beginning to decline. Given the stress that both parents and their adolescent children feel, it should come as no surprise that there is an escalation in the intensification of conflicts that arise between them (Holmbeck et al., 1995). However, although the conflicts between parents and their adolescent children may be intensely stormy, only rarely do they lead to a serious breakdown in relations (Schneider & Stevenson, 1999).

Whatever their disagreements, adolescents continue to discuss a variety of important life issues with their parents, although the topics they discuss with their fathers are not those they discuss with their mothers (Smetana, 1989; Youniss & Smollar, 1985). James Youniss and Jacqueline Smollar describe a "family division of labor" in which fathers are authority figures who are responsible for providing their adolescent children with long-range goals. They are brought into personal matters only when special advice is needed. By contrast, adolescents talk to their mothers about personal topics both to obtain practical advice and to validate their feelings and impressions.

Of course, conversations with parents are also opportunities for conflict to arise. The adolescents interviewed and observed in recent research reported that most often their arguments with their parents were over such matters as household responsibilities and privileges, dating, involvement in athletics, and

Date: 5/15/77 Time Beeped: 3:20 am (pm) Time Filled Out: 3:20

AS YOU WERE BEEPED

What were you thinking about? that my mom belongs in a mental institution

Where were you? in my house

What was the MAIN thing you were doing? my homework

What other things were you doing? thinking that she's awfully nutty in the head

	not at all		some what		quite		very
How well were you concentrating?			(3)				
Was it hard to concentrate?							(9)
How self-conscious were you?	(0)						
Were you in control of your actions?							(9)

0 1 2 3 4 5 6 7 8 9

Describe your mood as you were beeped:

	very	quite	some	neither	some	quite	very	
alert	0	o	.	-	(.)	o	0	drowsy
happy	0	o	.	-	.	o	(0)	sad
irritable	(0)	o	.	-	.	o	0	cheerful
strong	(0)	o	.	-	.	o	0	weak
angry	(0)	o	.	-	.	o	0	friendly
active	0	o	.	-	(.)	o	0	passive
lonely	0	o	.	(-)	.	o	0	sociable
detached	0	o	.	(-)	.	o	0	involved
free	0	o	.	-	(.)	o	0	constrained
excited	0	o	.	-	.	o	(0)	bored
open	0	o	.	-	.	o	(0)	closed
confused	(0)	o	.	-	.	o	0	clear
satisfied	0	o	.	-	.	o	(0)	dissatisfied

Challenges of the activity — low ... high (4)

Your Skills in the activity — low ... high (5)

Do you wish you had been doing something else? — not at all ... very much (9)

Was anything at stake for you in the activity? — (n)othing ... very much

0 1 2 3 4 5 6 7 8 9

Time was passing: fast 0 o (.) - as usual . o 0 slow

Think back on how you got into this activity.

How much choice did YOU have in selecting this activity? (How easily could you have chosen to do something else?)
1) None 2) A little 3) Some 4) Pretty much (5) Very much

Did you do it for
Your family? 1) Yes (2) No
Your friends? 1) Yes (2) No
Your future? 1) Yes (2) No

Were there other things available that you wanted to do? (1) Yes 2) No

Would you do it if you didn't have to? 1) Yes (2) No

Who were you with?
( ) brother(s), sister(s) ( ) friend(s)
(X) parent(s) mother (bitch) (crazy person) number ___ (initials ___,___,___)
( ) strangers 1) male(s) 2) female(s) 3) both
( ) alone ( ) other ______

Answer the following questions only if you were with other people:

Was somebody being the leader? 1) Yes (2) No she deliberately plays on my hurt
Was it you? 1) Yes (2) No

Was talk: Serious 0 o . . o (0) Joking mentally

In your activity the go[als of the others] were: the same as yo[urs] . . o (0) different from yours

In this situatio[n] ... to get negative or positive feedback from the [...] (0) . . o 0 positive

Great thoughts, nasty cr[...] and jokes, excuses

help me I hate her so guts etc. I hate her she broke my eardrum help me please I can't much she's even I stand her mentally insane retarded she's helpless

FIGURE 15.12
A self-report filled out by a teenager at the time she was "beeped." (From Csikszentmihalyi & Larson, 1984.)

financial independence. Arguments over religion and politics were less common (Holmbeck, 1996).

Although it may appear from the outside that the issues involved in adolescent–parent conflict are not particularly serious, when we stop to consider how the conflicts feel to the participants, the picture changes. In a well-known study, Mihaly Csikszentmihalyi and Reed Larson (1984) asked adolescents to carry an electronic beeper with them for a week, from the time they got up in the morning until they went to sleep at night. At a randomly chosen moment every 2 hours or so, the subjects were "beeped," at which point they filled out a standard report about what they were doing and experiencing (see Figure 15.12). In this way the researchers gained detailed information—unfiltered by memory—about the kinds of activities adolescents engage in at home, as well as their thoughts about their parents.

The following sample of the responses to the question "As you were beeped, what were you thinking about?" gives some sense of the emotions aroused by conflicts between young people and their parents:

- Why my mother manipulates the conversation to get me to hate her.
- How much of a bastard my father is to my sister.
- How ugly my mom's taste is.
- How incompetent my mom is.

- ➢ My bitchy mom.
- ➢ How pig-headed my mom and dad are.
- ➢ About my mom getting ice cream all over her.
- ➢ How f—-ing stupid my mom is for making a big f—-ing fuss.

Very often, virulent comments like these are inspired by seemingly trivial events—a parent's insisting the adolescent's room be kept neat, or grounding the adolescent for missing a curfew, or questioning the value of some activity the adolescent is engaged in. But as the authors point out, the appearance of triviality can be misleading:

> Asking a boy who has spent many days practicing a song on the guitar Why are you playing that trash? might not mean much to the father, but it can be a great blow to the son. The so-called "growth pains" of adolescence are no less real just because their causes appear to be without much substance to adults. In fact, this is exactly what the conflict is all about: What is to be taken seriously? (Csikszentmihalyi & Larson, 1984, p. 140)

Adults naturally try to structure adolescents' realities to correspond to their notions of how the world works. And adolescents, who are at the threshold of adulthood, can see the shortcomings of their parents' realities. In large and small ways, adolescents resist having their own realities defined for them on their parents' terms and try to assert their own preferences. At the same time, adolescents realize that they are dependent on their parents.

Here we see the real dilemma of adolescence and the major source of conflict between adolescents and their parents. Teenagers are caught between two worlds, one of dependence, the other of responsibility. Quite naturally, they would like to have the best of both worlds. But their parents, who pay the bills and pick up the clothing tossed on the floor, demand that independence be matched by responsibility. Once we realize that conflicts over "little things" are also disagreements about the major issues of growing up—the power to decide for oneself and to take responsibility for oneself—the issue of adolescent–parent conflict is brought into proper focus.

Continuing Parental Influences

It seems clear from the evidence that parents continue to play a very important role in their children's lives. This continuing influence extends well beyond providing shelter, food, and advice: parents influence whom their adolescent children interact with and to some extent the timing and content of those interactions, including the kinds of crowds their children are likely to become associated with (Brown & Huang, 1995; Holmbeck et al., 1996).

One indication of how parental behaviors influence adolescent experiences with their peers comes from a study of sixth- and seventh-graders by Andrew Fuligni and Jacqueline Eccles (1993). Fuligni and Eccles asked these young adolescents to answer a questionnaire about their parents' strictness, their opportunities to make decisions on their own, and the extent to which their parents monitored their behavior (see Table 15.3). The questionnaire also included questions about the extent to which the adolescents turned to peers rather than to their parents for support, as well as their adjustment to junior high school.

Fuligni and Eccles found that the extent to which the adolescents spent time with their peers and turned to them for advice depended on how their parents' behavior changed in response to their growing up. When children perceived their parents as becoming stricter as they progressed into adolescence, they responded by turning to their peers. When they saw their parents

TABLE 15.3 SAMPLE ITEMS MEASURING RELATIONSHIPS BETWEEN 6TH- AND 7TH-GRADERS AND THEIR PARENTS

How does each of the following questions and statements apply to your situation?

Parental Strictness
My parents want me to follow their directions even if I disagree with them.
I have to ask my parents' permission to do most things.
My parents worry that I am up to something they won't like.

Decision-Making Opportunities
How often do you take part in family decisions concerning yourself?
My parents encourage me to give my ideas and opinions even if we might disagree.

Parental Monitoring
When you go out at night, do you have a curfew?
When you are late getting home, do you have to call home?
Do your parents warn you it is dangerous to go out alone?

Source: Fuligni & Eccles, 1993.

as including them in family decisions and encouraging them to express their ideas, they did not orient as much to their peers. At the same time, the children whose parents set a curfew for them and asked them to call if they were going to be late coming home were less peer-oriented than those whose parents did not monitor their behavior.

In a comprehensive review of research on the influence of parenting styles on adolescent behavior, Grayson Holmbeck and his colleagues report that the developmental outcomes for adolescents are most favorable when parents do the following (Holmbeck et al., 1996):

1. Set clear standards for behavior.
2. Enforce rules in ways that are firm but not coercive.
3. Discipline their children in a consistent way.
4. Explain the basis for their decisions.
5. Permit real discussion of contentious issues.
6. Monitor their adolescents' whereabouts without being overprotective.
7. Provide a warm family environment.
8. Provide information and help their adolescents to develop social skills.
9. Respond flexibly to the changing circumstances of their children.

This finding corresponds to evidence presented earlier that adolescent children of authoritative parents are more competent in school and less likely to get into trouble than are peers from authoritarian or rejecting-neglecting families. Moreover, these positive effects of authoritative parenting apply across different kinds of peer groups, whether the adolescents in question are classified as "jocks," "druggies," "nerds," or "brains" (Brown & Huang, 1995). These effects even extend to the adolescents' friends, whose school performance and behavior are likely to improve as an indirect result of the effective parenting of their friends' parents (Fletcher et al., 1995).

On the whole, current evidence strongly supports the notion that adolescents' conflicts with their parents increase relative to middle childhood, while their feelings of family solidarity and warmth decrease (Conger & Ge, 1999; Laursen et al., 1998). Some adolescents really do break away and establish relationships outside the family that remove them from their parents both physically and emotionally; but the more common pattern is for adolescents and their parents to negotiate a new form of interdependence that grants the adolescent increasingly equal rights and more nearly equal responsibilities.

WORK

Another vital factor in the changing relations between parent and child is the young person's gradual assumption of adult work responsibilities. Until young people can participate in adult work—work that sustains them and their family—they will not gain adult status.

In many countries, including the United States, access to adult jobs and adult status comes only after a long period of preparation during which young people learn how to work in general and then acquire the skills that particular jobs require. American children's first work experience often consists of doing household chores, such as setting the table, washing dishes, and caring for pets. At about the age of 12 years, many children begin to work at odd jobs around the neighborhood—baby-sitting, delivering newspapers or groceries, mowing lawns. Usually the money they earn from these jobs is theirs to spend with less parental supervision than they would encounter if they were receiving an allowance (Manning, 1990). By the age of 15, many adolescents have progressed from working in casual jobs to regular part-time employment (Finch et al., 1997).

Each successive job that an adolescent holds tends to be more substantial and more responsible. It also provides greater exposure to the options in the labor market. After high school, many adolescents gradually enter jobs in which they stay long enough to learn a skill, either formally or informally. Others seek career training in professional schools, colleges, public programs, or the military. By the time they are in their mid-twenties, most young people have acquired vocational competence and are beginning to work in an adult career. (Figure 15.13 shows the long transition from school to full-time work.)

FIGURE 15.13
The slow transition to full-time work. (Reproduced with the permission of The Alan Guttmacher Institute from Sex and America's Teenagers, *1994, The Alan Guttmacher Institute, New York.)*

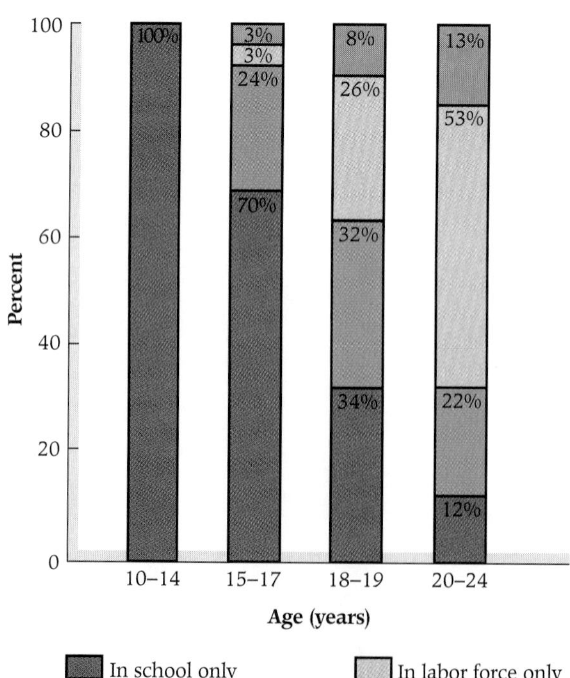

Some young people drop out of high school and plunge directly into the full-time labor market. According to the U.S. Bureau of the Census (1999), 4.3 percent of students in the tenth through twelfth grades dropped out of high school in 1997, with the figure being considerably higher for adolescents of Hispanic origin.

According to official counts, more than one-third of all 16- to 19-year-old students work at least part-time (U.S. Census Bureau, 1998). (The actual number is probably much higher because many teenagers work in jobs that the Labor Department does not monitor and because some are paid "off the books"). A survey conducted in high schools in St. Paul, Minnesota, found that as many as 70 percent of the eleventh- and twelfth-graders worked during the school year (Finch et al., 1997).

The number of hours that teenagers work each week varies with their social class and grade level. When teenagers from minority and less advantaged homes find jobs, they tend to work longer hours than do middle-class youths. High school freshmen typically work 11 to 12 hours a week, while seniors work approximately 20 hours a week. Many teenagers work longer hours during school vacations (Finch et al., 1997).

It was once widely believed that extensive work experience during adolescence is all to teenagers' benefit, but more recent research has cast doubt on this conclusion. In the 1970s and 1980s, government policy advisers contended that work complements school. Holding a job, so the argument went, teaches adolescents to be responsible, develops positive attitudes toward work, provides on-the-job training, brings youngsters into contact with adults from whom they can learn, and keeps them out of trouble (Carnegie Commission on Policy Studies in Higher Education, 1980; National Commission on Youth, 1980). This view was supported by high school students' responses to questionnaires, which indicated that students acquire many practical skills and insights at their part-time jobs, including how to find and hold a job, how to manage money, and how the business world functions. Students also reported that their jobs taught them to be punctual and dependable, to budget their time, to take personal responsibility, and to assess their goals (such as whether it was more important to work a few more hours a week or get good grades) (Greenberger & Steinberg, 1986).

Part-time jobs do not usually provide young people with on-the-job training that will prove useful in adulthood, but they do provide young people with some practical knowledge about work in addition to giving them spending money and a sense of accomplishment.

At present the picture appears to be more complicated. On the positive side, when they handle work situations well, young workers say they feel proud and have a sense of accomplishment. Not surprisingly, even when they disliked their jobs, most adolescents reported that they enjoyed the sense of power and independence they got from earning their own money (Mortimer et al., 1994). Dating and other social activities can be expensive, so for most boys and for some girls, earning their own money is an essential prerequisite for participation in the social scene.

On the negative side, and contrary to the beliefs of many advocates of adolescent work experience, part-time jobs do *not* typically provide students with on-the-job training that will prove useful in adulthood, nor do they usually bring adolescents into contact with many adults. The vast majority of employed adolescents work in jobs that pay the minimum wage, offer no job protection, and provide few opportunities for advancement (Schneider & Stevenson, 1999). They are jobs that few adults can afford to work in. As a result, adolescents frequently work with other adolescents in segregated sections of the labor market, such as food service, retail sales, clerical work, and manual labor—all jobs that offer little formal instruction in work-related skills.

In addition, part-time employment does not, as its advocates assume, necessarily keep teenagers out of trouble. A number of studies have found that extensive part-time employment is associated with higher rates of alcohol use, illegal drug use, psychological distress, and health problems, as well as more frequent delinquency (Mortimer et al., 1996; Steinberg et al., 1993). It also distances adolescents from their families (Manning, 1990).

Given the close correlation between years of schooling and the ability to find work as an adult, the data with perhaps the most serious negative developmental implications are those showing that adolescents who work are generally less involved in school than their classmates (D'Amico, 1984; Mortimer & Johnson, 1998). Many researchers believe that it is not the mere fact of working that causes the grades of teenagers to fall but rather the number of hours they work. They argue that working too many hours reduces the time teenagers have available for homework and disengages them from school (Bachman & Schulenberg, 1993; Finch et al., 1997; Steinberg et al., 1993). Sophomores and juniors who work more than 20 hours a week during the school year are more likely to drop out of school than are their classmates who do not work as much. They also report being absent more and enjoying school less.

Jeylan Mortimer and her associates acknowledge that high levels of work are related to lower levels of school achievement, but they disagree that working is the main *cause* of lower grades (Finch et al., 1997; Mortimer & Johnson, 1998). On the basis of the data from a large longitudinal study, they argue that many of the students who work long hours and do poorly in school were less committed to academic work even before they began working. Among students who begin high school with a good record of achievement and a positive orientation to schooling, moderate levels of time spent at work may even lead to higher levels of academic achievement in later adolescence.

One conclusion seems clear: The more time students spend working, the greater independence they achieve. Whether this increased independence is good or bad for their subsequent development depends on how the adolescent uses it.

THE BIOSOCIAL FRAME AND ADOLESCENT DEVELOPMENT

The basic biosocial dilemma of adolescence is clear. Because biological maturity fundamentally changes the power relations between children and their parents, adolescence is a transition that one would expect to be difficult. It is especially difficult in societies where the assumption of adult rights and responsibilities is delayed well beyond puberty. Young people must then cope with bodies that allow mature sexual activity but social circumstances that keep them in a state of dependence and immaturity. Parents continue to exert considerable influence over their children, but this influence must be renegotiated—because, in a phrase, the children are "too big to be spanked."

In modern industrialized societies such as the United States and Canada, the transition to adulthood is further complicated by two interrelated facts. First, the earlier onset of puberty and the increasingly longer years of education required for economic productivity have combined to lengthen adolescence compared with its duration in earlier eras. Second, the ways in which schooling and work are organized separate adolescents and adults, increasing the influence of peers and dividing generations.

Taken together, the biological and social reorganizations that define modern adolescence provide essential conditions for the psychological changes that characterize this developmental period. In Chapter 16 we will first examine the special qualities of mind that develop as young people struggle to understand their new circumstances and to master the complex systems of technical knowledge that will structure their adult work lives. Then we will consider all three domains of developmental change—the biological, the social, and the psychological—simultaneously as an interacting system of influences in a cultural context.

SUMMARY

CONCEPTIONS OF ADOLESCENCE

- For the past 300 years, three key issues have preoccupied those who theorize about adolescence:
  1. The degree to which rapid biological changes increase psychological instability.
  2. The possibility that development in adolescence recapitulates earlier stages in achieving an integration appropriate to adulthood.
  3. The relation of biological and social changes to cognitive changes.
- Common to all theories of adolescence is recognition of the child's need to integrate new biological capacities with new forms of social relations. Theories vary in this regard as they do in respect to earlier periods:
  1. Biosocial theories emphasize that the universal physical changes in children's bodies are the central causes of changes in adolescent social behavior.
  2. Arnold Gesell believed that advanced forms of behavior make their appearance late in the development of individuals because they were acquired late in the history of the human species.

3. Sigmund Freud attributed the characteristics of adolescence to increases in sexual excitation that upset the psychological balance between the id, the ego, and the superego established during middle childhood.
4. Ethologists and evolutionary biologists maintain that adolescence arose among human beings because it confers a reproductive advantage over other species.

PUBERTY

- Puberty, the sum of the biological changes that lead to sexual maturity, is accompanied by a growth spurt during which boys and girls attain approximately 98 percent of their adult size. During puberty the bodies of males and females take on their distinctive shapes.
- Menarche, or the first menstrual period, usually occurs late in a girl's puberty, after her growth spurt has reached its peak. Among males, semenarche, the ability to ejaculate semen, signals the maturation of the primary sex organs.
- Both genetic and environmental factors affect the onset of puberty. For example, high levels of physical exercise delay the onset of menarche, while family stress is associated with early menarche.
- The age at which biological maturation occurs influences a child's social standing with peers and adults.
- In general, the impact of early sexual maturation is negative for girls and positive for boys, although the impact varies with cultural and personal circumstances.

THE REORGANIZATION OF SOCIAL LIFE

- Four major changes occur as part of the reorganization of social life during adolescence:
    1. A great deal more time is spent with peers.
    2. Adult guidance is reduced and becomes more indirect.
    3. Cross-sex interactions increase markedly.
    4. Participation in large social groups becomes important.
- The dominant mode of peer relations at the start of adolescence is same-sex friendship focused on shared activities. As adolescence proceeds, same-sex friendship is increasingly characterized by an emphasis on trust, loyalty, and mutual understanding.
- Boys and girls have somewhat different expectations of friends. Girls seek confidantes with whom to share intimate knowledge and feelings, while boys seek support when they come in conflict with authority.
- Two new forms of peer group come to prominence in adolescence, cliques and crowds. Two kinds of crowds are developmentally significant: activity-based crowds which are associated with the transition to sexual activity, and reputation-based crowds, which are focused on social identity.
- Social status within one's peer group depends on social factors, such as membership in the leading crowd, and personal factors, such as girls' physical attractiveness and boys' athletic ability.
- Special susceptibility to peer pressure, especially antisocial peer pressure, is commonly believed to characterize adolescent behavior. Evidence for this concern is mixed.

- Sensitivity to peer pressure seems to peak around the age of 15.
- Most adolescents report that they are more likely to go along with peer pressure that is prosocial than with pressure to misbehave. The more pressure adolescents feel to engage in antisocial behavior, however, the more likely they are to do so.
- The transition to two-person heterosexual relations goes through a number of stages. It begins with membership in small same-sex cliques and participation with the other members in social events that draw heterosexual activity-based crowds. Within these crowds, heterosexual cliques are formed, and couples begin the process of pairing off. As adult sexual relationships emerge, crowds become less prominent in adolescents' social lives.
- Sexual behavior requires the learning of culturally specified scripts and forms of behavior as well as biological maturation.
- The transition to heterosexual relations proceeds in opposite directions for males and females in our culture because of differences in their histories. Males begin with the highly developed goal of sexual satisfaction and only gradually learn to include a deeper social and emotional commitment in their heterosexual relations. Females begin with the highly developed goal of social and emotional affiliation and only gradually acquire the goal of sexual satisfaction.
- Biological maturation and the increasing time spent with peers alter parent–child relations. Parents' authority decreases in relation to the influence of peers, and they must now exercise their authority even more through persuasion than they did earlier.
- Contrary to the hypothesis of a separate youth culture, most adolescents share their parents' values. Dialogue, rather than outright conflict or rejection, is the major method of resolving disagreements between adolescents and their parents.
- Parents continue to exert an important influence on their children's development throughout adolescence. As in earlier years, authoritative parents have children who are more competent in school and less likely to engage in antisocial behavior.
- Conflicts with parents during adolescence seem to center on matters of taste, though often they are actually about larger issues of control.
- Evidence concerning the developmental impact of work experience in the United States is mixed. Moderate amounts of work enhance feelings of independence and efficacy, but too much work is associated with reduced achievement in school.

THE BIOSOCIAL FRAME AND ADOLESCENT DEVELOPMENT

- The biosocial shift to adulthood is complicated by the fact that sexual maturity does not necessarily coincide with adult status. The resulting conflict between biological and social forces gives this transition its unique psychological characteristics.

KEY TERMS

clique, p. 621
crowd, p. 622
genital stage, p. 607
gonads, p. 608
menarche, p. 611
primary sex organs, p. 609
puberty, p. 608
recapitulate, p. 606
secondary sex characteristics, p. 610
semenarche, p. 610

THOUGHT QUESTIONS

1. It is clear from the preceding material that there is more to human reproduction than sex. What more is there, and what significance does your answer have for how you think about adolescence as a stage of development?
2. François Jacob calls reproduction the only bodily function for which the individual possesses only one-half of the necessary bodily organs. What might the consequences of this unique situation be?
3. According to the idea of a bio-social-behavioral shift, the biological changes associated with puberty, such as the growth spurt and the appearance of secondary sexual characteristics, are simultaneously relevant to social and behavioral change. Argue for or against this idea.
4. Provide several reasons for questioning the literature on peer influence during adolescence. What kind of research strategies would you propose to overcome these doubts?
5. Argue for or against the following proposition: For adolescents to complete childhood development effectively, conflict between them and their parents is essential.

CHAPTER 16

The Psychological Achievements of Adolescence

RESEARCH ON ADOLESCENT THOUGHT
- Formal Operations
- Alternative Approaches to Explaining Adolescent Thought

ADOLESCENT THINKING ABOUT THE SOCIAL ORDER
- Thinking about Moral Issues
- Thinking about and Participating in Politics

INTEGRATION OF THE SELF
- Changing Attributes of the Self
- Adolescent Self-Esteem
- Resolving the Identity Crisis
- Gender Differences in Identity Formation
- Formation of a Sexual Identity
- Minority-Group Status and Identity Formation
- Cross-Cultural Variations in Identity Formation

THE TRANSITION TO ADULTHOOD
- Adolescence in Modern Societies
- Looking Ahead

Now I look into myself and see the I of me, the weak and aimless thing which makes me. I is not strong and needs be, I needs to know direction, but has none. My I is not sure, there are too many wrongs and mixed truths within to know. I changes and does not know. I knows little reality and many dreams. What I am now is what will be used to build the later self. What I am is not what I want to be, although I am not sure what this is which I do not want.

But then what is I? My I is an answer to every all of every people. It is this which I have to give to the waiting world and from here comes all that is different.

I is to create.

John D., age 17,
Quoted in Peter Blos, *On Adolescence*

Theorists of adolescence have long agreed that the transition from middle childhood to adulthood is accompanied by the development of a new quality of mind, characterized by the ability to think systematically, logically, and hypothetically. This new quality of mind is thought to arise from the same combination of changes that accounts for the bio-social-behavioral shift we examined in Chapter 15: the emergence of the capacity for biological reproduction accompanied by changes in social relations that propel young people into a new social status, with new rights and responsibilities. These same changes make it both possible and necessary for adolescents to engage in the complex forms of economic and sociopolitical activity on which the welfare of the community depends. In turn, both the new forms of social relations and the new sociopolitical and economic responsibilities require more complex forms of thinking.

One manifestation of this new mode of thinking is adolescents' tendency to become critical of received wisdom and even more critical of the discrepancies between the ideals adults espouse and the behaviors in which they actually engage. Arnold Gesell and Francis Ilg suggest that in response to this disillusionment with adult behavior, the adolescent seeks out adult

> models to imitate; heroes to worship. He also seeks out heroes of history and of biography. . . . Literature, art, religion take on new meanings and may create new confusions in his thinking. He has a strangely novel interest in abstract ideas. He pursues them in order to find himself. (Gesell & Ilg, 1943:256)

In the end, young people must reconcile their own emerging ideals with the world as it actually is. They must also reconcile their view of who they want to be with who they are and have been. In the process, they arrive at their own personal sense of self and identity. Viewed in this way, adolescents' thinking is, on the one hand, their most important psychological means of coming to grips with the tasks of adult life and, on the other hand, a result of their struggles to reconcile competing social and psychological demands of adult life.

We begin this chapter by examining the experimental evidence for the idea that young people's thought processes become more systematic and logical as they begin the transition to adulthood. This evidence raises a number of questions: No one is systematically logical *all* the time, so under what circumstances do adolescents engage in systematic, logical thinking? How does the quality of adolescents' thinking depend upon the content of what is being thought? Is the quality of adolescents' thinking the same when they are analyzing the results of a scientific experiment, debating laws that govern society, confronting moral dilemmas, or trying to arrive at their own personal sense of identity? And finally, when the entire pattern of biological, social, and cognitive changes is examined in different cultural contexts, does it support the idea that adolescence is a universal stage of development?

RESEARCH ON ADOLESCENT THOUGHT

Developmentalists who focus on adolescent thought processes emphasize several characteristics that distinguish adolescent thinking from the thinking that is typical of middle childhood (Keating, 1990; Moshman, 1999):

1. *Reasoning hypothetically* Adolescents are more likely than younger children to engage in thinking that requires them to generate and mentally test hypotheses and to think about situations that are contrary to fact. In thinking about going to a beach party with a boy she does not know well, a teenage girl may reason, "What if they get drunk and crazy? What will I do? I guess if things get out of hand, I can always ask someone to take me home. But then they'll think I'm a drag." In an analogous situation, a younger child would make a decision without contemplating the wide range of possible scenarios first.
2. *Thinking about thinking* During adolescence, thinking about one's own thought processes—the metacognitive thinking we described in Chapter 12—becomes increasingly complex. At the same time, adolescents can think more systematically and deeply than younger children about other people's points of view, a development that is reflected in the changing nature of adolescent friendships (see Chapter 15, pp. 618–620).
3. *Planning ahead* Adolescence is a time when young people start thinking about what they will do when they grow up. Adolescents by no means always plan ahead, but they do so more often and more systematically than younger children. Contemplating the upcoming summer holiday, an adolescent might think, "Well, I could relax and just goof around with my friends, or I could work on raising that D in algebra, which isn't going to look too good when I apply to college." A younger child would be more likely to focus only on having a good time and forget other responsibilities.
4. *Thinking beyond conventional limits* Adolescents use their more sophisticated cognitive abilities to rethink fundamental issues of social relations, morality, politics, and religion—issues that have perplexed human beings since the dawn of history. Now acutely aware of the disparities between the ideals of their community and the behavior of individual adults around them, adolescents are highly motivated to figure out how to "do it right." Arnold Gesell and Frances Ilg, as quoted earlier, link this aspect of adolescent thought to youth's idealism and search for heroes.

One can certainly find adolescents around the world displaying these characteristic cognitive abilities. However, as we have seen in previous chapters, the quality of a person's thinking can vary depending on its specific content and the context in which it occurs. As David Moshman notes, it appears that "qualitatively distinct forms of thought and knowledge routinely coexist in the same mind" (1998:950).

Extensive evidence indicates that such variation is characteristic of adolescent thinking, raising basic questions about both the distinctiveness and the universality of cognitive development during adolescence. Many developmentalists continue to believe that adolescent thought processes can be characterized by a small set of general properties such as those

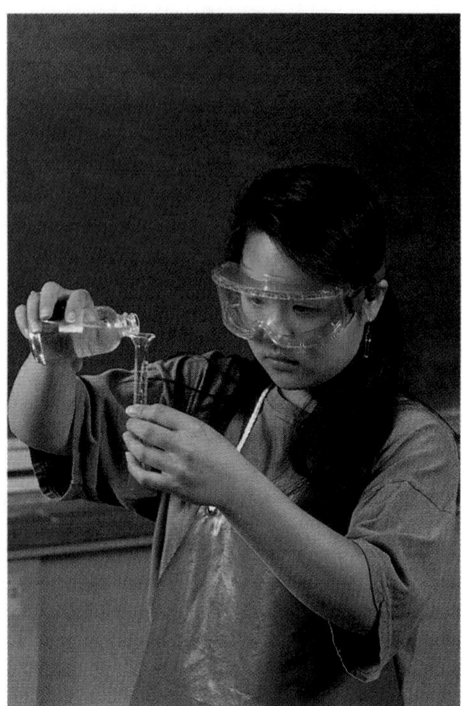

This young woman is engaged in a task that requires her to combine variables in a manner that makes use of formal operations.

listed above. But the fact that the quality of adolescent thinking is variable according to content and contexts has led others to doubt that the transition from middle childhood to adolescence brings about stagelike changes in cognition.

The difficulty of deciding how best to characterize changes in cognition associated with adolescence is nowhere more apparent than in current research on formal operational thinking.

FORMAL OPERATIONS

It was Piaget's contention that changes in the way adolescents think about themselves, their personal relationships, and the nature of their society have a common source: the development of a new logical structure that he called **formal operations** (see Table 16.1). As you will recall, an "operation" in Piaget's terminology is a mental action that fits into a logical system. Inhelder and Piaget distinguished formal operations from the concrete operations characteristic of middle childhood in this way:

> Although concrete operations consist of organized systems (classifications, serial ordering, correspondences, etc.), [children in the concrete operational stage] proceed from one partial link to the next in step-by-step fashion, without relating each partial link to all the others. Formal operations differ in that all of the possible combinations are considered in each case. Consequently, each partial link is grouped in relation to the whole; in other words, reasoning moves continually as a function of a "structured whole." (Inhelder & Piaget, 1958, p. 16)

Formal operational thinking is the kind of thinking needed by anyone who has to solve problems systematically. This new ability is needed by the owner of a gasoline station who, in order to make a profit, has to take into account the price he or she pays for gasoline, the kinds of customers who pass by the station, the kinds of services the station needs to offer, the hours it needs to stay open, and the cost of labor, supplies, rent, and utilities. Formal operational thinking is also needed by lawyers when they consider a wide variety of alternative strategies, legal precedents, and possible consequences in deciding how best to present a case and counter the arguments of the attorney on the opposing side.

Reasoning by Manipulating Variables

Inhelder and Piaget's studies of formal operational thinking focused on very basic versions of the kinds of problems encountered in scientific laboratories. Typically these problems require subjects to hold one variable of a complex system constant while systematically searching mentally through all the other variables.

An example of the "combination-of-variables" problems that Piaget and his colleagues used to study the development of formal operational thinking is the balance-beam problem, discussed in Chapter 12 (p. 490). The correct solution to the balance-beam problem exemplifies the key properties of formal operational thinking because this problem requires the values of two key variables—weight and distance from the fulcrum—to be varied and combined systematically.

Perhaps the most widely cited example of a Piagetian problem designed to illustrate the nature of formal operations is the combination-of-chemicals problem, which requires the ability both to combine variables and to create in one's mind a "structured, psychological whole," the key characteristics of formal operational thinking. At the start of the task, four large bottles, one indicator bottle, and two beakers are arrayed on a table in front of the child, as in Figure 16.1. Each bottle contains a clear liquid. The liquids are such that when the liquids from bottles 1 and 3 are combined in a beaker and then a drop of

formal operations In Piaget's terms, a kind of mental operation in which all possible combinations are considered in solving a problem. Consequently, each partial link is grouped in relation to the whole; in other words, reasoning moves continually as a function of a structured whole.

TABLE 16.1 PIAGET'S STAGES OF COGNITIVE DEVELOPMENT: FORMAL OPERATIONAL

Age (years)	Stage	Description	Characteristics and Examples
Birth to 2	SENSORIMOTOR	Infants' achievements consist largely of coordinating their sensory perceptions and simple motor behaviors. As they move through the 6 substages of this period, infants come to recognize the existence of a world outside themselves and begin to interact with it in deliberate ways.	Formal operational reasoning, in which each partial link in a chain of reasoning is related to the problem as a whole • Young people solve the combination-of-chemicals problem by systematically testing all possible combinations. • In forming a personal identity, young people take into account how they judge others, how others judge them, how they judge the judgment process of others, and how all this corresponds to social categories available in the culture. Application of formal operational thinking to a wide variety of life's problems • Young people think about politics and law in terms of abstract principles and are capable of seeing the beneficial, rather than just the punitive, side of laws. • Young people are interested in universal ethical principles and critical of adults' hypocrisies.
2 to 6	PREOPERATIONAL	Young children can represent reality to themselves through the use of symbols, including mental images, words, and gestures. Objects and events no longer have to be present to be thought about, but children often fail to distinguish their point of view from that of others, become easily captured by surface appearances, and are often confused about causal relations.	
6 to 12	CONCRETE OPERATIONAL	As they enter middle childhood, children become capable of mental operations, internalized actions that fit into a logical system. Operational thinking allows children mentally to combine, separate, order, and transform objects and actions. Such operations are considered concrete because they are carried out in the presence of the objects and events being thought about.	
12 to 19	FORMAL OPERATIONAL	In adolescence the developing person acquires the ability to think systematically about all logical relations within a problem. Adolescents display keen interest in abstract ideas and in the process of thinking itself.	

the chemical from the indicator bottle (g) is added, the mixture turns yellow. If the chemical in bottle 2 is added to a beaker containing liquid from both 1 and 3, the mixture remains yellow, but if the liquid in bottle 4 is then added, the mixture turns clear again.

The experimenter begins with two beakers already full of liquid. One contains liquid from bottles 1 and 3, the other, liquid from bottle 2. The experimenter puts a drop from bottle g in each beaker, demonstrating that it produces a yellow color in one case but not in the other. Now the child is invited to try out various combinations in an attempt to determine which combination of chemicals will transform the color of the liquid.

Interviews with two of Inhelder and Piaget's subjects, 7- and 14-year-old boys, are shown at the bottom of Figure 16.1. The 7-year-old does not have the kind of overall conceptual grasp of the problem that indicates the presence of a **structured whole,** that is, a system of relationships that can be logi-

structured whole A system of relationships that can be logically described and thought about.

Full set of chemicals to be combined

Experimenter's demonstration

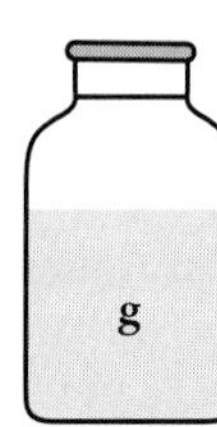

[Ren (7.1 years old) tries 4 × g, then 2 × g, and 3 × g.]

Ren: I think I did everything. I tried them all.

Exp [Experimenter]: What else could you have done?

Ren: I don't know. *[He is given the glasses again. He repeats 1 × g, etc.]*

Exp: You took each bottle separately. What else could you have done?

Ren: Take two bottles at a time? *[He tries 1 × 4 × g, then 2 × 3 × g, thus failing to cross over between the two sets of bottles. When we suggest that he add others, he puts 1 × g in the glass already containing 2 × 3, which results in the appearance of the color.]*

Exp: Try to make the color again.

Ren: Do I put two or three? *[He tries 2 × 4 × g, then adds 3, then tries it with 1 × 4 × 2 × g.]*

Ren: No, I don't remember anymore.

[Eng (14.6 years old) begins with 2 × g, 1 × g, 3 × g, and 4 × g.]

Eng: No it doesn't turn yellow. So you have to mix them. *[He goes on to the six two–by–two combinations and at last hits 1 × 3 × g.]*

Eng: This time I think it works.

Exp: Why?

Eng: It's 1 and 3 and some water.

Exp: You think it's water?

Eng: Yes, no difference in odor. I think that it's water.

Exp: Can you show me? *[He replaces g with some water: 1 × 3 × water.]*

Eng: No it's not water. It's a chemical product: it combines with 1 and 3 and then it turns into a yellow liquid. *[He goes on to three–by–three combinations beginning with the replacement of g by 2 and by 4–i.e., 1 × 3 × 2 and 1 × 3 × 4.]*

Eng: No, these two products aren't the same as the drops: they can't produce color with 1 and 3 *[Then he tries 1 × 3 × g × 4.]*

Eng: It turns white again: 4 is the opposite of g because 4 makes the color go away while g makes it appear.

FIGURE 16.1

A 7-year-old and adolescent tackle the combination-of-chemicals task. Note that the 7-year-old starts by testing only one chemical at a time. When it is suggested that he try working with two chemicals at a time, he becomes confused. The 14-year-old also starts with one chemical at a time but quickly realizes that he must create more complicated combinations, which he does in a systematic way until he arrives at the solution to the problem. (From Inhelder & Piaget, 1958.)

cally described and thought about; the 14-year-old does. The younger child is unsystematic in his sampling of possible combinations, even with hints from the experimenter. The adolescent sets about his task systematically. He starts with the simplest possibility (that one of the chemicals, when combined with g, turns yellow), then proceeds to the next level of complexity—the possibility that two, and later three, chemicals must be combined. When he combines pairs, he discovers that when g is added to a mixture of 1 and 3, the yellow color appears, but because he is methodical in exploring all the logical possibilities, he also discovers that 4 counteracts g, thereby arriving at a systematic understanding of the miniature chemical system that Inhelder and Piaget had arranged for him. The adolescent is exhibiting formal operational thinking par excellence.

deductive reasoning A form of reasoning that moves from a general premise to a specific instance of that premise, followed by a conclusion. If the premises are true, the conclusion must logically follow.

Reasoning by Logical Necessity

According to Piaget (1987), one of the consequences of acquiring formal operational thinking is the ability to construct logical proofs in which conclusions follow from logical necessity. This ability underlies **deductive reasoning,** one of the central processes in scientific work. The simplest form of deductive reasoning begins with the statement of a general premise followed by the state-

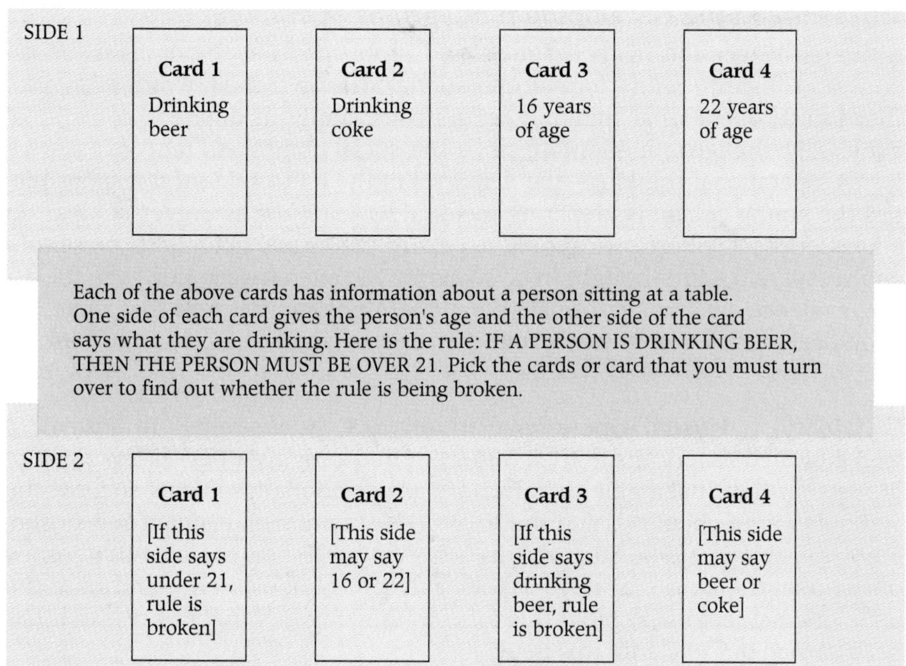

FIGURE 16.2
One of the deductive reasoning problems used by Willis Overton and his colleagues to study the development of formal operation thinking.

ment of a particular specific premise and then by a conclusion. If the premises are true, the conclusion must also be true. Willis Overton (1990), who has studied the development of formal deductive reasoning, gives the following example of such a problem:

General premise: All trains to Washington stop in Baltimore.

Specific premise: The train on track 6 goes to Washington.

Conclusion: Therefore, the train on track 6 stops in Baltimore.

To study developmental changes in formal logical reasoning, Overton and his colleagues have used a task in which children and adolescents must gauge whether an explicit rule is being followed or broken in a series of specific cases. In these tasks, the way children select the information with which to make a judgment provides the critical evidence about their use of deductive reasoning (Müller et al., 1999; Ward & Overton, 1990).

A sample problem is shown in Figure 16.2. An adolescent subject is given four cards that contain information about a person sitting at a table and drinking a beverage. Below the four pictured cards are instructions (1) informing the subject of a rule that a person must be over age 21 to drink beer and (2) asking the subject to select the cards that are needed to determine if the person drinking at the table is breaking that rule. To perform this task according to formal logic, it is necessary to turn over cards 1 and 3. Information from the other cards is logically irrelevant to the question of whether or not the rule is being broken.

Several studies using this or similar procedures (summarized by Müller et al., 1999) find a steady increase in the percentage of subjects who display logical reasoning between the fourth and twelfth grades (roughly, between 10 and 18 years of age) (see Figure 16.3). Note that formal deductive reasoning is very rare before the sixth grade (11 to 12 years). On the basis of such results, Overton and his colleagues argue that competence in reasoning deductively emerges early in adolescence (Ward & Overton, 1990).

FIGURE 16.3
The development of formal operational reasoning ability as indicated by responses to deductive reasoning problems in four experiments by Overton and his colleagues. Note how closely the different experiments replicate each other. (From Ward & Overton, 1990.)

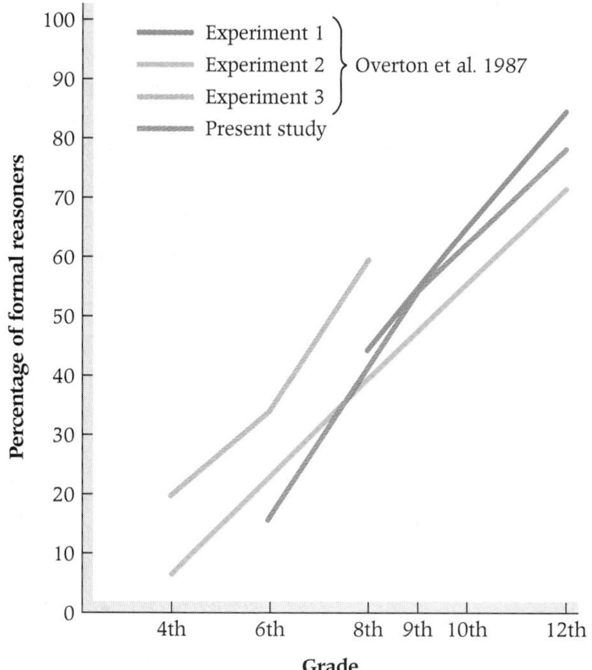

Variability in the Development of Formal Operations

Although Piaget and his colleagues used problems from the domains of science and logic to study formal operational thinking, their writings suggest that formal operational thinking occurs consistently in different domains of adolescent thought. In addition, since the social conditions that give rise to formal operational thinking—the demands of the adult roles and responsibilities the young person is preparing to shoulder—are just as universal a part of adolescence as puberty, we should expect to see formal operations present in adolescent and adult thought in all societies. As noted earlier, however, the actual evidence concerning formal operational thinking indicates that there is a good deal of variation in when, and under what circumstances, such thinking is displayed.

Variability in Formal Operations among U.S. Adolescents In studies of well-educated Americans in their late teens and early twenties, as few as 30 to 40 percent have been able to solve formal operational problems such as the combination-of-chemicals and the balance-beam problem (Dimant & Bearison, 1991; Moshman, 1998). Such results bring into question the idea that formal operational thinking is a universal achievement of adolescence and raise the issue of what factors promote this form of thinking. A variety of research has been carried out to clarify this issue.

Robert Siegler and Robert Liebert (1975), for example, designed an experiment to see if systematic training could promote the use of formal operational thinking. They created a combination-of-variables problem in which children ranging in age from 10 to 13 were asked to find the combination of open and closed positions on four switches that was needed to make a model train go along a track. This problem is logically similar to the combination-of-chemicals problem shown in Figure 16.1.

After introducing the children to the problem, the experimenters tested some of them directly afterward; others they tutored, using one of two supplementary procedures. In the first supplementary procedure, they showed the children a systematic way to check through the various combinations of open and closed switches. In the second supplementary procedure, they showed the children the checking method and then coached them on two problems that were logically equivalent to the one they would be asked to solve. Siegler and Liebert then compared the performances of the three groups of children.

With no training or tutoring, none of the 10-year-olds and only 20 percent of the 13-year-olds systematically tried all the alternatives, as formal operational thinkers are supposed to do. With training in checking but no tutoring in similar problems, the 13-year-olds showed only modest improvement and the 10-year-olds showed none at all. All the children who received both training and tutoring in analogous problems solved the problem correctly.

A different approach to eliciting "latent" formal operational thinking through training was demonstrated by Rose Dimant and David Bearison with college English students (40 percent of the class) who failed on the combination-of-chemicals test. Rather than tutoring these students, Dimant and Bearison provided them with six sessions during which they worked through a series of increasingly difficult combinatorial problems. In some cases the students worked alone. In other cases they worked with another student. Analysis of videotapes of the sessions in which two students worked together revealed that the quality of the students' conversation about the problems was the key to developing formal operational abilities on this task. Students who actively engaged the task and worked cooperatively showed significantly greater gains when retested than did students who worked alone or students who worked in pairs but did not engage in collaborative problem-solving actions.

Overall, the evidence indicates that children on the threshold of adolescence are *capable* of the kind of systematic, logical manipulation of variables that is the hallmark of formal operations and can demonstrate this kind of thinking *if they are given proper instruction and if the benefits of the systematic manipulation are made clear.*

Gender Differences in Formal Operations? A good deal of research has sought to determine whether there are gender differences in the ability to engage in formal operational thought. The reasons for this interest are social as well as scientific because the results directly affect educational policies and young people's possible career paths. There is a pervasive popular belief that males have greater talent in such areas as mathematics, science, and engineering, fields that appear to require formal operational thinking. This stereotype is bolstered by (and bolsters) the fact that more men than women currently work in these fields. Yet if formal operational thinking is a universal capacity, both sexes can acquire this kind of reasoning and boys and girls should receive equal support to do so.

To address this issue, Marcia Linn and Janet Hyde (1991) reviewed the results of several studies conducted during the 1970s and 1980s that compared the performances of males and females on spatial and mathematical tests that required formal operational thought. Linn and Hyde reported that in many of the studies, *no* sex differences in performance were found. When gender differences were found, they generally favored males, but they also were generally small and confined to certain content areas. Linn and Hyde also found that gender differences in performance declined over the 20 years of research they surveyed. Reviewing the same issues a decade later, David Moshman concluded that gender differences in formal operational thinking are "minimal if they are found at all" (Moshman, 1998, p. 970).

Current evidence favors the idea that the capacity to solve formal operational problems develops equally in males and females. This conclusion, as we will see, is supported by evidence from the other line of research on the universality of formal operations, which compares the performances of children from different cultures.

Cultural Variations in Formal Operations In Chapters 12 and 13 we reviewed research on cultural variability in the development of concrete operations in middle childhood. Some of the studies suggested that children who grow up without attending school are delayed in the age at which they begin to use concrete operational reasoning to solve conservation problems. We also saw, however, that this variability seems to result from relatively superficial difficulties the children had in understanding the tasks because of their specific content or the ways they were presented. Concrete operational ability appears to be universal and does not depend on schooling for its appearance.

Evidence concerning the development of formal operations in different cultures offers a more difficult challenge to the idea that the stages of cognitive development proposed by Piaget are universal. Unless they are among the relatively small part of the population that have attended high school or college, people in small, technologically unsophisticated societies rarely seem to use formal operations when they are tested with Piagetian methods (Hollos & Richards, 1993; Segall et al., 1999). But is it correct to conclude that they are incapable of this level of thinking?

Piaget's own final conclusion on this question was that all normal people attain the level of formal operations. "However," he wrote, "they reach this stage in different areas according to their aptitudes and their professional specializations (advanced studies or different types of apprenticeship for the various trades): the way in which these formal structures are used, however, is not necessarily the same in all cases" (1972:10). In other words, while a lawyer might think in a formal manner about law cases, and a football coach might use formal thinking to call for particular plays in particular situations, both might fail to use formal reasoning in the combination-of-chemicals task.

Evidence in favor of this conclusion, which fits well with a cultural-context approach to cognitive development, comes from studies of a popular board game known as the "national game of Africa," in which players try to capture seeds from their opponents according to a complex set of rules (Cole et al., 1971; Retschitzki, 1989). The game is usually played by men and older boys. Analysis of the sequence of moves used by skilled players demonstrates that a good memory is not sufficient for mastery of the game. Rather, mastery of the game requires a player to anticipate the possible moves for several coming turns, balance defensive and offensive moves, and calculate complex trade-offs. On the basis of detailed clinical interviews with skilled players from Ivory Coast, Jean Retschitzki (1989) concluded that the strategies described by the players require the kind of logical thinking characteristic of formal operations. Yet when presented with typical Piagetian formal operations problems, these same people rarely solve them (Segall et al., 1999).

A different kind of evidence concerning cultural differences in the development of formal operational thinking comes from two studies by André Flieller, who compared the performances of French adolescents tested on standard Piagetian tasks in 1967 or 1972 with those of same-age adolescents tested 19 years later (Flieller, 1999). Flieller found that there was a significant overall increase in adolescents' levels of formal operational thinking over the 19-year interval between tests. The cause for this change, like the causes of the "Flynn effect" for rising IQ scores (Chapter 13, p. 532), is difficult to pinpoint, but cultural factors must be involved since there is no possibility of genetic change occurring over such a short period in the French population as a whole.

ALTERNATIVE APPROACHES TO EXPLAINING ADOLESCENT THOUGHT

Investigators who question Piaget's account of adolescent cognition, like those who questioned his account of cognition at early ages, have sought alternative explanations for the kinds of results presented in the preceding sections. Neo-Piagetian theorists focus on the way that changing memory capacities permit the development of more complex "central conceptual structures" and systematic thinking. Information-processing theorists also emphasize cumulative changes in memory capacity to explain adolescent thought processes, but in addition they focus on the adolescent's expanding knowledge base, the development of more effective problem-solving strategies, and increasing metacognitive understanding. Those who emphasize the importance of cultural context have pursued the path that Piaget himself suggested, concentrating on the way specialized practice in particular domains of experience gives rise to the kind of systematic thought that appears to underlie the new quality of adolescent cognition.

Neo-Piagetian Approaches

In the view of Robbie Case, adolescents' ability to think systematically arises from their having a larger working memory. Working memory increases from infancy through adolescence up until the age of 16 (Case, 1995,1998). Case estimates that 9- to 10-year-olds, who still reason in terms of concrete operations, can hold about five items in working memory, whereas 15- to 16-year-olds can hold and work with as many as seven items. In problem solving, this increased capacity makes it possible for older adolescents to coordinate several different factors at once, keep intermediate results in mind, and come up with a solution that is comprehensive and consistent. For example, as we noted in Chapter 12, even after they have presumably become capable of formal operational thinking, many younger teenagers do not give correct responses to the balance-beam problem, which requires them to calculate the trade-offs between the amount of weight placed on each side of the beam and the distance of those weights from the fulcrum. Case argues that mature performance of difficult balance-beam problems requires a number of complex subcomponents, including the calculation and comparison of ratios of weight to distance on each side. This intellectual feat requires the expanded working memory capacity that becomes available only in later adolescence.

Information-Processing Approaches

The explanations that information-processing theorists give of adolescent thinking are a direct extension of the explanations they give for the development of thought during earlier periods of life. According to this view, adolescents, in comparison with younger children, have developed more efficient strategies for solving problems and have become better able to retain information in memory while relating the components of a task to one another.

In Chapter 12 we discussed the application of Robert Siegler's information-processing approach to Inhelder and Piaget's balance-beam problem (Siegler, 1996). The impression one gets from Inhelder and Piaget's account of this problem is that it is a single logical puzzle that older children are able to master by applying more powerful logic. Siegler demonstrated, however, that what seems to be a single logical problem can also be viewed as a collection of more specific problems, each of which makes its own cognitive demands. Moreover, he found that only a quarter of the 17-year-olds he studied demonstrated the ability to solve the balance-beam problem in all its forms.

Siegler's evidence suggests that rather than seeing the increased problem-solving skills of adolescents as a global, qualitative change in modes of thinking, these improved skills are better explained as the result of a gradual acquisition and implementation of more powerful rules or strategies that can then be applied to particular problem-solving situations with increasing, but still incomplete, reliability.

Support for this view comes from a series of studies by Deanna Kuhn and her colleagues (1995), who examined the role of repeated experience on the ability of 10-year-olds and young adults to engage in logical inductive reasoning. The researchers presented their subjects with four sets of problems, two from the domain of physical problems, such as the factors related to how fast a boat goes, and two from the domain of social problems, such as the factors that lead to successful achievement in school. Each problem was presented with a specific set of variables that were potentially relevant to the outcome in question. For example, the problem focused on schooling required subjects to consider five school variables as potentially relevant to achievement:

- The sex of the principal
- Whether classrooms were noisy or quiet
- Whether the school used teaching assistants (TAs)
- Whether the teachers were in the teachers' lounge or on the playground during recess
- The size of the classes

The problems were designed so that some variables exerted a direct causal influence (for example, in the school problem, having a TA made a difference), while other variables either had no effect or had an effect only in combination with other variables (for example, the effect of a teacher's whereabouts during recess depended on whether or not there was a TA).

The subjects worked on these multivariate problems in 20 sessions over a 10-week period. When the problems were first presented, the subjects were asked to say what they thought the effect of each variable would be and were probed about the reasoning strategies they used to arrive at their answers. The first session served as a baseline against which to measure individual cognitive change. In subsequent sessions, the subjects were given sample cases, which they were to use to draw inferences about the possible relevance of the variables to the outcome. In the school achievement problem, for example, they were given an extensive series of hypothetical "student records" that included the student's achievement score as well as descriptions of the school situation (for example, no TAs, male principal, noisy classrooms, teachers on playground during recess, medium class size). The particular values of each variable changed from one problem to the next.

Over time, as the subjects gained experience in comparing variables and drawing inferences about outcomes for each of the problems, subjects in both groups came to use more sophisticated strategies—such as making systematic logical tests to rule out a variable as a causal factor or establishing covariation between variables—to pin down the causal relations involved. These results provide additional evidence in support of the information-processing view that the development of reasoning is more a matter of learning to select and implement logical strategies consistently than of acquiring a new quality of thought. However, neither the children nor the adults were always logically consistent in making inferences about either the same problem over time or different problems. In line with the results of Siegler's work with the balance beam described in Chapter 12, the *mixture* of logical strategies changed as the subjects got more and more practice, and the older children differed from younger children in the richer mix of high-level strategies that they used.

The Cultural-Context Perspective

The cultural-context approach to adolescent thought begins with an observation similar to Inhelder and Piaget's: New modes of thought become prominent as teenagers prepare to adopt adult roles. Both approaches start by analyzing the structure of adult activity. However, whereas Piaget sought a single new logic underlying all adult thought, cultural-context theorists emphasize the heterogeneity of adult thought processes that arises from variation in the contexts of adult activity. As in earlier periods of development, these theorists believe that in order to understand adolescent thought processes, it is necessary to analyze the structure of activity and the scripts encountered in the various kinds of settings that adolescents are called upon to reason about (see Box 16.1).

As we have seen, Piaget's research on formal operational thinking is based on the kinds of activity that scientists are assumed to engage in and that schoolchildren are exposed to when they are taught principles of science. From a cultural-context perspective, it is inappropriate to use Piaget's specialized scientific procedures as the standard for assessing formal operations *in general.* Instead, formal operational thinking, like all other forms of thinking, should be regarded as dependent on the specific properties of an activity and the context in which it is occurring. In this view, it is possible to find a wide variety of situations in which individuals exhibit reasoning that is formal operational in nature even though it doesn't appear similar to the standard Piagetian procedures.

Consider, for example, the reasoning involved in the common event called "planning a holiday meal." On the holiday in question it is customary in many cultures to eat one of several main dishes: turkey, goose, or ham. The choice of the main course depends on several variables: What is available? How expensive is each of the alternatives? Is anyone coming to the meal on a low-cholesterol diet? Is anyone a vegetarian? Do the guests like to try new dishes, or are they meat-and-potatoes people? If turkey is on sale and a lot of people are expected, turkey can be very tempting. Goose, on the other hand, is more unusual, but the fattiness may bother guests who worry about cholesterol.

These calculations do not stop with the main course. If turkey is to be served, there has to be cranberry sauce; if ham is served, Cumberland sauce is essential. What about starches? Stuffing? Rice? Potatoes? Sweet potatoes? What about the soup? Clam chowder goes with turkey, but will it go with goose, or would a clear broth be better?

Social factors also have to be taken into account. First, who is coming to dinner? Are all the guests old friends who expect the usual turkey, or are there going to be some "important personages" who might anticipate something fancier? Social factors also include such elements as how to present and serve the food and how to keep everyone happy (who will sit next to chatty Aunt Betty or deaf Uncle Norm?).

The ability of a cook to engage in such thinking while planning the meal illustrates several essential features of formal operational thinking. First, the cook is able to sort through several variables, holding one constant while working on the others ("Hmmmm, ham? That means candied sweet potatoes. Brussels sprouts. . . . uh-oh, Martha hates brussels sprouts, that means gotta start over again. . . . Besides, John keeps begging for goose, but will one goose be enough for 12 people? Two would make dinner too expensive. Well, let's see . . . "). Second, this kind of thinking clearly is a form of planning that involves a "structured whole" organized by concepts significant to the cook, in this case, the concept of the "holiday meal." Finally, the cook is able to reflect on and describe thought processes being engaged in.

This example differs from Piaget's characterization of formal operations in that the cook fails to consider literally *all* of the possible combinations of relevant factors. Instead, he or she pursues each of the variables in the problem only long enough to come up with a usable solution. Nevertheless, the process of planning clearly involves the kind of systematic variation of alternatives indicative of formal operations.

Experimental studies that model both "scientific" and "everyday" situations suggest that it is quite common for people to reason differently in everyday situations than they do in formal experiments designed as logical puzzles (Lave, 1988; Linn, 1983; Tschirgi, 1980). Marcia Linn and her colleagues (1982) tested a sample of adults on their ability-to-reason performance in Piagetian-style problems and on their ability to reason about the truthfulness of advertising. The researchers were questioning Piaget's hypothesis that once individuals can engage in formal reasoning, it becomes a general characteristic of their thinking. They found virtually no correlation between the quality of reasoning used in the Piagetian problems and that used in the advertising problems. Apparently, then, the participants did not use one single characteristic mode of thinking.

Experiments by Judith Tschirgi (1980) found that even when two problems are analogous, the kind of reasoning used to solve each one depends on whether the outcome of the situation is one the person views as positive (and hence wants to maintain) or negative (and hence wants to change). In one of these experiments, the positive-outcome problem involves a boy who has baked a cake with margarine, honey, and whole wheat flour, and the cake is a great success because it is so moist. The boy hypothesizes that the cause of the success is the honey. The question is: What should he change when he bakes another cake to check his hypothesis? In the negative-outcome version of the problem, the cake is too runny and the boy again hypothesizes that honey is the crucial factor. The question remains: What must be done to test this hypothesis?

The logic of these problems is the same. In each case, the best way to test the hypothesis is to hold the kind of shortening and flour constant while varying the kind of sweetener (see Figure 16.4). But in this experiment, only when the cake was a failure did participants agree that the boy should substitute sugar for honey. When the cake was a success, they kept honey constant and changed other factors. College students were as likely to follow this pattern as second-graders, an indication that this illogical pattern may be a general characteristic of human reasoning. As Tschirgi comments, when people

BOX 16.1 FORMAL OPERATIONS IN A NONLITERATE CULTURE

In a great many of the situations that seem to call for the use of formal operations in our everyday lives, most of us use written notes as a means of keeping track of our thoughts. Even scientists, who are likely candidates for having achieved the stage of formal operations, routinely resort to paper and pencil or a computer when they have to sort through a large number of variables to solve a problem. Only rarely, as in a chess game or a psychological test, does formal thinking have to go on entirely inside a person's head.

Attempts to determine the universality of a new mode of thinking associated with the transition to adulthood are undermined by the fact that many cultures do not have writing systems or the formal scientific procedures that tests of formal operations typically model. Consequently, "standardized" test procedures are completely alien to many cultures. Fortunately, however, research by anthropologists familiar with psychological theories has provided evidence on complex problem solving in a variety of settings (Hutchins, 1980; Rogoff & Lave, 1984).

An interesting instance of complex problem solving in a nonscientific culture is seen in the navigational practices of South Sea islanders (Gladwin, 1970; Goodenough, 1953). Until such devices as magnetic compasses became readily available after World War II, natives of Polynesia and Micronesia, groups of islands northeast of New Guinea, sailed their small outrigger canoes over hundreds of miles of ocean to get from one tiny island to another without the help of conventional instruments. Even very experienced sailors from other parts of the world would not presume to sail such distances without a compass for fear of sailing off into the vast Pacific and probable death.

The technique the islanders have developed for finding their way over the sea requires an external record-keeping system, a hypothetical reference point, and constant estimates of speed—all combined in a single problem-solving process that lasts as long as the voyage itself. It depends heavily on 14 distinctive "star paths," that is, a set of stars that always rise from the same point on the eastern horizon and set at the same place in the west, appearing to move in an unvarying arc across the sky. Instruction in how to navigate with this system begins in adolescence and continues for several years. A practiced navigator is able to construct the entire "star compass" mentally from a glimpse of two or three stars on the horizon (see diagram). As Edwin Hutchins phrases it, "the star compass is an abstraction which can be oriented as a whole by determining the orientation of any part" (1983, p. 195).

The star compass is only one element of the navigator's mental model of the voyage. An essential additional element is a "reference island" whose bearing on the star compass is

Navigators from one of the Caroline Islands conduct a lesson in how to use the star compass.

are confronted with an everyday problem, their expectations about the outcome, rather than their underlying cognitive competencies, control the way they reason (see also Linn, 1983).

The shortcuts taken by the hypothetical cook and the errors of the participants in Tschirgi's study do not conform to Piaget's idealized scientific solution. Even studies of the way experts solve problems suggest that such unscientific habits are typical (Daley, 1999). In fact, the systematic reasoning of the cook displays more aspects of formal operations than skilled adults often display when they solve highly demanding intellectual problems. Expert chess players, for example, do not usually run through all possible combinations of moves, preferring instead to match the overall board pattern to a successful pattern they recall from past experience (Chase & Simon, 1973). Similarly, scientists follow their intuitions and take shortcuts that clearly violate the canons of scientific reasoning (Latour, 1987).

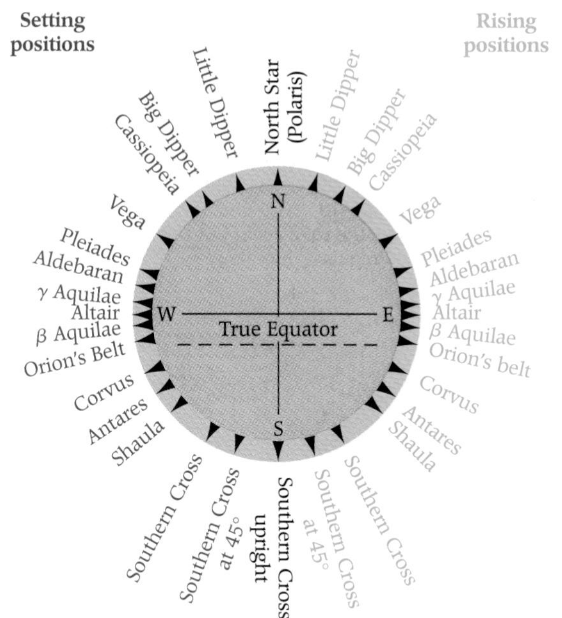

A schematic representation of the star compass used by navigators in the Caroline Islands to guide their outrigger canoes form one island to another. (From Goodenough, 1953.)

known in relation to any island from which a boat might set out. The term "reference island" is placed in quotation marks because in many cases the island is purely hypothetical, a reference point needed only to make calculations of relative distance from the destination.

In the actual process of sailing, navigators mentally combine the information about the star paths, the location of the reference island, and their rate of speed in order to discover their current position and distance from their destination. So skillful are they at making these calculations that they can tack away from their destination to catch the wind and still keep track of their location.

Some of the earlier researchers who investigated this kind of navigation believed that the navigators could not talk logically about the system they were using (Gladwin, 1970). Their explanations seemed to be inconsistent with the anthropologists' analysis of their navigational system. If they were indeed incapable of describing their own thought processes, the claim that their problem solving demonstrated formal operations would be considerably weakened.

Hutchins (1983) showed, however, that the navigators' explanations were perfectly logical for the system they were using. The apparent illogic arose from a basic cultural difference in the way people think about compasses and relative motion. It seemed obvious to the anthropologists who had first studied Micronesian navigation that the canoe moved across the water while the reference island remained stationary. The navigators, however, had developed their system by imagining that the boat stood still while the reference island moved. When Hutchins took their accounts completely seriously, he was able to show that the anthropologists had simply failed to work out the full system.

Although Micronesian navigators were clearly able to engage in formal operational thought when voyaging, they showed no such ability when they were presented with a standard Piagetian combination-of-variables task (Gladwin, 1970). When adolescents and adults were given stacks of poker chips of many different colors and asked to find all the possible combinations of colors, even expert navigators performed at a very low level: most paired only a few colors, falling far short of the formal operational ideal. Only a few young men who had attended high school managed to display some aspects of systematic combinatorial activity.

These results suggest that formal operational thinking may occur far more widely than the evidence from typical experiments suggests, and that this type of thinking may indeed be universal in human groups. At the same time, the data make it clear that formal operational thinking does not uniformly replace earlier modes of thought. Its use remains highly restricted to contexts in which the individual has had considerable experience.

These data fit with a suggestion that Piaget made late in his life—that the acquisition of formal operations is context-specific (Piaget, 1972). They suggest that it is more appropriate to think of Piaget's theory as focused on the development of the underlying competence to engage in formal operational thinking, while the cultural-context approach focuses more on the conditions under which such competence is realized (Chapell & Overton, 1998).

Overall, the evidence from the information-processing and cultural-context perspectives regarding the variability of performance on formal operations tasks would seem to weaken the idea, central to traditional Piagetian theory, of a sharp discontinuity in cognitive development between middle childhood and adolescence. According to these perspectives, the improvements in cognitive ability during this transition may appear either continuous or discontinuous, depending on the depth of the young person's knowledge about a particular context or problem. Only if a qualitatively new mode of thinking appears across a broad range of contexts is it le-

Problem

John decided to bake a cake. But he ran out of some ingredients. So:

- He used margarine instead of butter for the shortening
- He used honey instead of sugar for the sweetening and
- He used brown whole wheat flour instead of regular white flour.

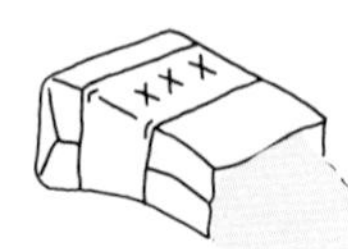

The cake turned out great because it was so moist.

John thought that the reason the cake was so great was the honey. He thought that the type of shortening (butter or margarine) or the type of flour really didn t matter.

= Great cake

What should he do to prove this point?

Possible strategies

1 He can bake the cake again but use sugar instead of honey, and still use margarine and brown whole wheat flour.

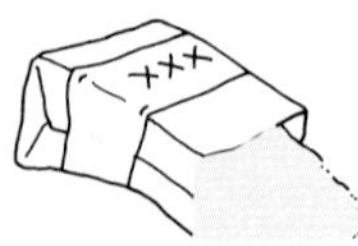

2 He can bake the cake again but this time use sugar, butter, and regular white flour.

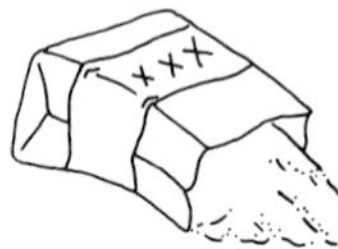

3 He can bake the cake again still using honey, but this time using butter and regular white flour.

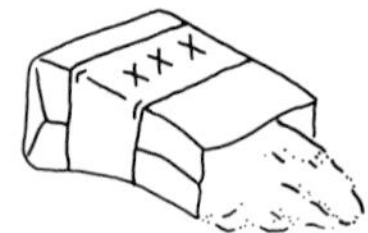

FIGURE 16.4

A combination-of-variables task involving an everyday situation. Subjects were asked to choose one of the three problem-solving strategies. When the outcome of the original hypothetical event was positive, as in this case, neither children nor adults used rigorously logical testing procedures. (From Tschirgi, 1980.)

gitimate to conclude that a stagelike change has taken place. Consequently, to resolve the question whether thinking undergoes a stagelike change in adolescence, we turn now to assess the extent to which adolescent thinking is more systematic than younger children's thinking in a variety of social contexts and content areas.

ADOLESCENT THINKING ABOUT THE SOCIAL ORDER

Following a pattern that we have seen repeat itself since infancy, evidence of increased cognitive capacity during adolescence is manifested in new ways of thinking about oneself in relation to other people (Alsaker & Flammer, 1999; Flanagan et al., 1998). In adolescence, these new ways of thinking apply to issues such as how to balance one's responsibilities to others against one's personal rights; what it means to be a moral person in a world where immoral behavior is so prevalent; why one's society is organized as it is; what might be done to improve society and oneself. How young people think about themselves in relation to other people takes on added urgency at the onset of adolescence because they must soon begin to take on adult responsibilities and make decisions that have far-reaching implications for themselves and others.

THINKING ABOUT MORAL ISSUES

Regardless of their theoretical orientation, developmentalists agree that adolescence is a time when questions of moral behavior take on special importance for young people: What is right? What is wrong? What principles should I base my behavior on and use to judge the behavior of others? Evidence suggests that the processes used to think about such questions, like those used to think about science problems and politics, undergo important changes between the ages of 12 and 19 years (Moshman, 1999; Turiel, 1998).

Kohlberg's Theory of Moral Reasoning

As we noted in Chapter 14 (p. 562), the study of moral development during middle childhood and adolescence has been greatly influenced by Lawrence Kohlberg, who suggested that moral reasoning progresses through three broad levels during childhood and adolescence, each consisting of two stages (Table 16.2 summarizes these levels and stages). As they develop from one stage to the next, children make more complex analyses of both the moral obligations that prevail among individuals and the obligations that exist between individuals and their social groups.

Their increased understanding of the social order motivates teenagers to question the status quo and support social causes.

According to Kohlberg, moral reasoning at the start of middle childhood is at the *preconventional* level; that is, it is not based on social conventions or laws. Rather, in stages 1 and 2, children judge actions in the light of their own wants and fears and do not yet take into account the fact that social life requires shared standards of behavior. Toward the end of middle childhood, children attain the second level—the *conventional* level—in which they begin to take social conventions into account and recognize the existence of shared standards of right and wrong. Kohlberg called stage 3 reasoning (the first stage at this level) "good-child morality," because he believed that for the child in stage 3, being moral means living up to the expectations of one's family, teachers, and other significant people in one's life.

Moral reasoning at stage 4 is like that at stage 3 except that its focus shifts from relations between individuals to relations between the individual and the group. People who reason at stage 4 believe that society has legitimate authority over individuals, and they feel an obligation to accept its laws, customs, and standards of decent behavior. Moral behavior from this point of view is behavior that maintains the social order. For this reason, stage 4 is sometimes referred to as the "law-and-order stage" (Brown & Herrnstein, 1975:289). Stage 4 reasoning begins to appear during adolescence, but stage 3 is still the dominant mode of reasoning about moral questions until people reach their mid-twenties (see Figure 16.5) (Colby et al., 1983).

Kohlberg believed that moral thinking at stages 3 and 4 depends on a partial ability to engage in formal operational reasoning—specifically, the ability to consider simultaneously the various *existing* factors relevant to moral choices (Kohlberg, 1984). People who are reasoning at stages 3 and 4, however, are still reasoning concretely insofar as they do not yet simultaneously consider all *possible* relevant factors or form abstract hypotheses about what is moral.

FIGURE 16.5

Mean percentage of moral reasoning of U.S. citizens at each of Kohlberg's stages, by age group. (Adapted from Colby et al., 1983.)

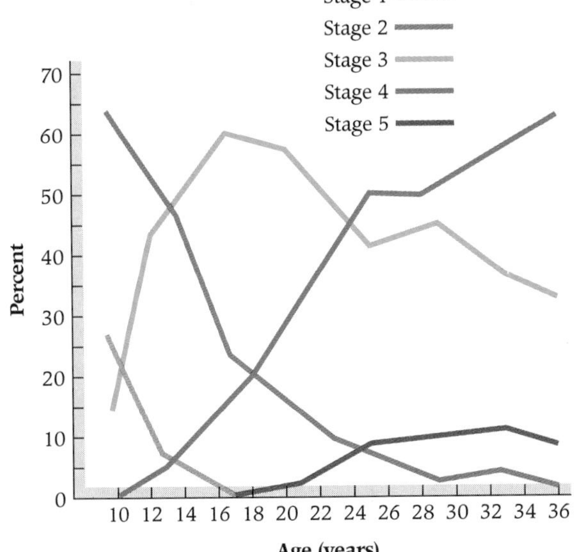

With the transition from stage 4 to stage 5 comes another basic shift in the level of moral judgment. Reasoning at stage 5 requires people to go beyond existing social conventions to consider more abstract principles of right and wrong. This perspective, which Kohlberg called *postconventional,* requires moral reasoning to be based on the idea of a society as bound by a social contract. People still accept and value the social system, but instead of insisting on maintaining society as it is, they are open to democratic processes of change and to continual exploration of possibilities for improving on the existing social contract. Recognizing that laws are sometimes in conflict with moral principles, they become creators as well as maintainers of laws. Kohlberg found that stage 5 moral reasoning does not appear until early adulthood, and then only rarely.

People reach stage 6 in Kohlberg's system when they make moral judgments in accordance with ethical principles that they believe transcend the rules of individual societies. Kohlberg and his colleagues failed to observe stage 6 reasoning in their research on moral dilemmas, and Kohlberg eventually concluded that this stage is more usefully thought of as a philosophical ideal than as a psychological reality. Nonetheless, under extraordinary circumstances, otherwise ordinary people have put their lives at risk because of moral beliefs guided by

TABLE 16.2 Kohlberg's Six Moral Stages

Level and Stage	What Is Right	Reasons for Doing Right	Social Perspective
Level I—Preconventional			
Stage 1—Heteronomous morality	• Adherence to rules backed by punishment; obedience for its own sake.	• Avoidance of punishment.	Egocentric point of view.
Stage 2—Instrumental morality	• Acting to meet one's own interests and needs and letting others do the same.	• To serve one's own needs or interests.	Concrete individualistic perspective: Right is relative, an equal exchange, a deal, an agreement.
Level II—Conventional			
Stage 3—Good-child morality	• Living up to what others expect.	• The need to be a good person in one's own eyes and those of others.	Perspective of the individual sharing feelings, agreements, and expectations with others.
Stage 4—Law-and-order morality	• Fulfilling the actual duties to which one has agreed. • Upholding laws except in extreme cases when they conflict with other fixed social duties. • Contributing to society, group, or institution.	• To keep the institution going as a whole. • What would happen "if everyone did it"? • The imperative of conscience to meet one's defined obligations (easily confused with stage 3 belief in rules and authority).	Perspective of an individual in relation to the social group: takes the point of view of the system that defines roles and rules.
Level III—Postconventional or Principled			
Stage 5—Social-contract reasoning	• Being aware that people hold a variety of values and opinions, most of which are relative to the group that holds them. • Upholding relative rules in the interest of impartiality and because they are the social contract. • Nonrelative values and rights such as *life,* and *liberty,* must be upheld in any society, regardless of majority opinion.	• A sense of obligation to law because of one's social contract to make and abide by laws for the welfare of all and for the protection of all people's rights. • A feeling of contractual commitment, freely entered upon, to family, friendship, trust, and work obligations. • Concern that laws and duties be based on rational calculation of overall utility, "the greatest good for the greatest number."	Prior-to-society perspective: Perspective of a rational individual aware of values and rights prior to social attachments and contracts. Integrates perspectives by mechanisms of agreement, formal contract, objective impartiality, and due process. Considers moral and legal points of view; recognizes that they sometimes conflict and finds it difficult to integrate them.
Stage 6—Universal ethical principles	• Following self-chosen ethical principles because they are universal principles of justice: the equality of human rights and respect for the dignity of human beings as individual persons. • Judging laws or social agreements by the extent to which they rest on such principles. • When laws violate principles, acting in accordance with the principle.	• A belief in the validity of universal moral principles. • A sense of personal commitment to those principles.	Perspective of a moral point of view from which social arrangements derive: Perspective is that of any rational individual recognizing the nature of morality or the fact that persons are ends in themselves and must be treated as such.

Source: Adapted from Kohlberg, 1976.

Both the experience of helping other people and formal instruction in issues of morality have been found to enhance moral development. The young people in the upper photo are volunteering at a food bank, while those in the lower photo are among a group of animal-rights advocates arrested during a protest demonstration.

stage 6 reasoning. Such was the case during World War II, when many European gentiles rescued Jews destined for extermination. According to Samuel and Pearl Oliner (1988), most of them were motivated by ethical principles that they believed apply to all of humanity, the hallmark of stage 6 moral reasoning.

Evaluating Kohlberg's Theory of Moral Reasoning during Adolescence

By and large, researchers who have used Kohlberg's methods and criteria for assigning people to different stages of moral reasoning have confirmed that children progress through the sequence proposed by Kohlberg in the predicted order (Rest et al., 1999; Walker, 1989). However, Kohlberg's approach is not without its difficulties.

One problem area concerns the procedures used to score the answers to Kohlberg's questions. Recall from Chapter 14 that Kohlberg presented dilemmas in the form of stories and asked children to reason about them in a give-and-take interview session. Some investigators have reported having trouble sorting interview answers reliably into Kohlberg's six categories (Kurtines & Gewirtz, 1984). Others wonder if children and adolescents might be able to reason at higher levels than they can articulate.

In response to these difficulties, James Rest and his colleagues created the *Defining Issues Test* (DIT) in order to make it easier for people to respond to moral dilemmas and easier for the researchers to score their responses reliably (Rest, 1986; Rest et al., 1999). Rest and his colleagues presented children and adolescents with moral dilemmas like Kohlberg's "Heinz dilemma" (about the man who is tempted to steal the drug that can save his wife's life; see Chapter 14, p. 562) and asked them how the dilemma should be resolved. But instead of using clinical interviews to probe people's moral reasoning, these researchers asked their subjects to elaborate on their reasoning by choosing from a set of ready-made justifications that fit Kohlberg's various levels of moral reasoning. The problems were presented in written form along with a scoring sheet on which subjects were to indicate the relative moral appropriateness of the different justifications. In addition, each person had to rank the four most important factors to consider among the choices they were given (see Table 16.3, which illustrates alternatives presented for the Heinz dilemma).

The results from a large number of studies that used the Defining Issues Test show a regular increase in the level of moral reasoning from early adolescence to adulthood that accords with the general sequence he proposed (Rest et al., 1999) (see Figure 16.6). But in one important way the results obtained using the Defining Issues Test differ from results using Kohlberg's procedures: a significant number of adolescents and young adults made moral choices that reflected Kohlberg's stages 5 and 6, the postconventional stage. Rest argues that these higher stages were reached because the Defining Issues Test does not require young people to produce complex arguments but rather taps into their ability to recognize which moral arguments they think are most appropriate.

Are There Gender Differences in Moral Reasoning?

In some of the first tests of adolescents' moral reasoning using Kohlberg's methods, boys appeared to score higher than girls (Haan et al., 1976; Holstein, 1976). The data in Figure 16.7, taken from Constance Holstein's (1976) study of moral reasoning, show the pattern of results. Adolescent boys were frequently scored at stage 4, whereas adolescent girls most frequently scored at stage 3.

As might be expected, such findings ignited a heated controversy. Carol Gilligan and her colleagues asserted that Kohlberg's treatment of moral issues left out a key dimension of moral thinking that is of particular concern to females (Gilligan, 1982, 1986; Gilligan & Attanucci, 1988). According to Gilligan, female moral thinking is oriented toward interpersonal relationships, coupled with an ethic of caring and responsibility for other people. Male moral reasoning, in contrast, is oriented toward the question of individual rights and justice. On Kohlberg's tests, Gilligan claimed, this difference in "moral orientation" inclines females to suggest moral choices involving altruism and self-sacrifice rather than choices that invoke rights and rules, and thus puts females at a disadvantage in Kohlberg's scoring system.

Recent research has quieted this controversy considerably. Not only has it found few gender differences in levels of moral reasoning than earlier studies did, but when such differences do appear, they are small and may be in favor of females (Turiel, 1998; Walker et al., 1995). In addition, this research has

TABLE 16.3 Responses to Heinz Dilemma Using Defining Issues Test

_______ Should steal it _______ Can't decide _______ Should not steal it

Importance:

Great	Much	Some	Little	No	
					1. Whether a community's laws are going to be upheld.
					2. Isn't it only natural for a loving husband to care so much for his wife that he'd steal?
					3. Is Heinz willing to risk getting shot as a burglar or going to jail for the chance that stealing the drug might help?
					4. Whether Heinz is a professional wrestler, or has considerable influence with professional wrestlers.
					5. Whether Heinz is stealing for himself or doing this solely to help someone else.
					6. Whether the druggist's rights to his invention have to be respected.
					7. Whether the essence of living is more encompassing than the termination of dying, socially and individually.
					8. What values are going to be the basis for governing how people act toward each other.
					9. Whether the druggist is going to be allowed to hide behind a worthless law that only protects the rich anyway.
					10. Whether the law in this case is getting in the way of the most basic claim of any member of society.
					11. Whether the druggist deserves to be robbed for being so greedy and cruel.
					12. Would stealing in such a case bring about more total good for the whole society or not.

From the list of questions above, select the four most important:

Most important _______

Second most important _______

Third most important _______

Fourth most important _______

Source: From Rest, 1986, pp. 187–188.

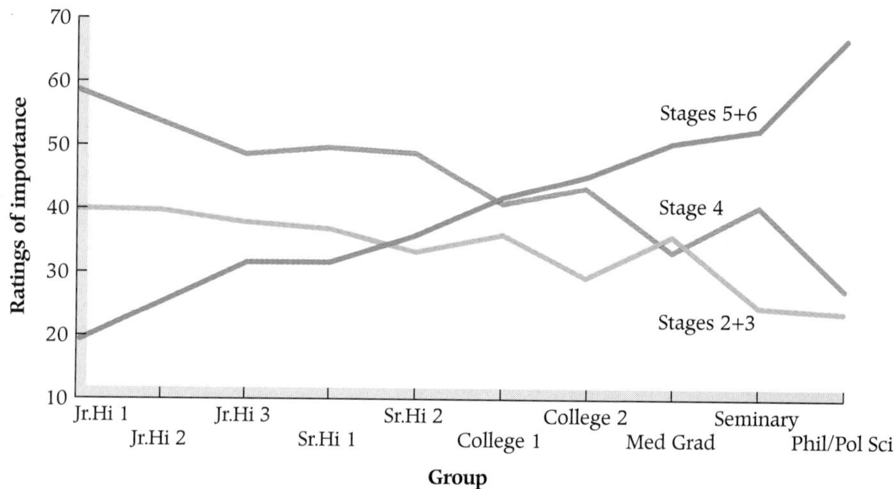

FIGURE 16.6
Average ratings of the importance of moral arguments clustered by stage sophistication by age/education subgroup. (From Rest et al., 1999.)

shown that although females may be more inclined than males to emphasize considerations of care and empathy for some of the dilemmas posed to them, these differences seem to appear when subjects are presented with real-life dilemmas rather than hypothetical dilemmas. This finding suggests that when constructing their answers to real-life dilemmas, males and females draw on objectively existing differences in their daily life experiences, such as the fact that women continue to be the primary caretakers—of children, spouses, and ailing parents (Wark & Krebs, 1996). Thus, even if there were gender-related differences in dominant moral concerns, they do not support the idea that one sex is more capable of reasoning morally about issues of care or justice than the other.

Cultural Variations in Moral Reasoning

Standard studies of cross-cultural variability in moral reasoning using Kohlbergian dilemmas, like the cross-cultural variability of formal operational reasoning, reveal greater differences between cultural groups than between the two sexes (Kohlberg, 1969; Turiel, 1998). Although there are some exceptions (Shweder et al.,1987), most studies show that people who live in relatively small, face-to-face communities in technologically unsophisticated societies, and who have not received high levels of schooling that take them outside of the traditional way of life, rarely reason beyond stage 3 on Kohlberg's scale. Most often they justify their moral decisions at the level of stage 1 or 2, although people in roles of special responsibility may reason at stage 3 (Snarey, 1995; Tietjen & Walker, 1985). This difference can be seen by comparing the scores in Figure 16.8 with those in Figure 16.5).

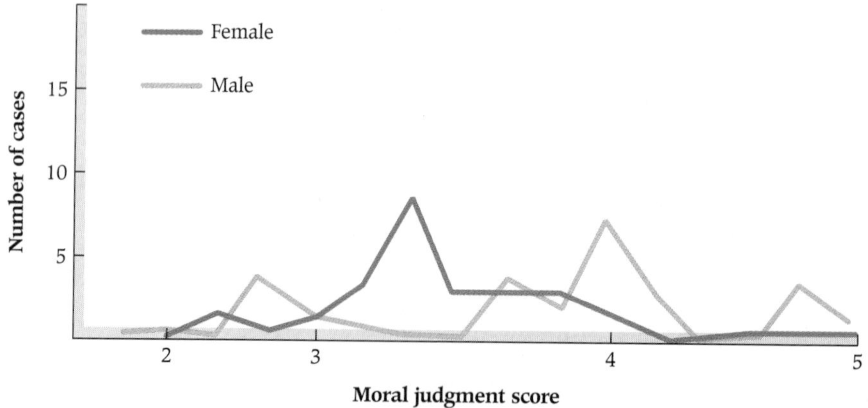

FIGURE 16.7
The distribution of moral judgment scores for a sample of male and female 16-year-olds. Note that the most frequent score for girls is near level 3, whereas the most frequent score for boys is in the range of level 4. (From Holstein, 1976.)

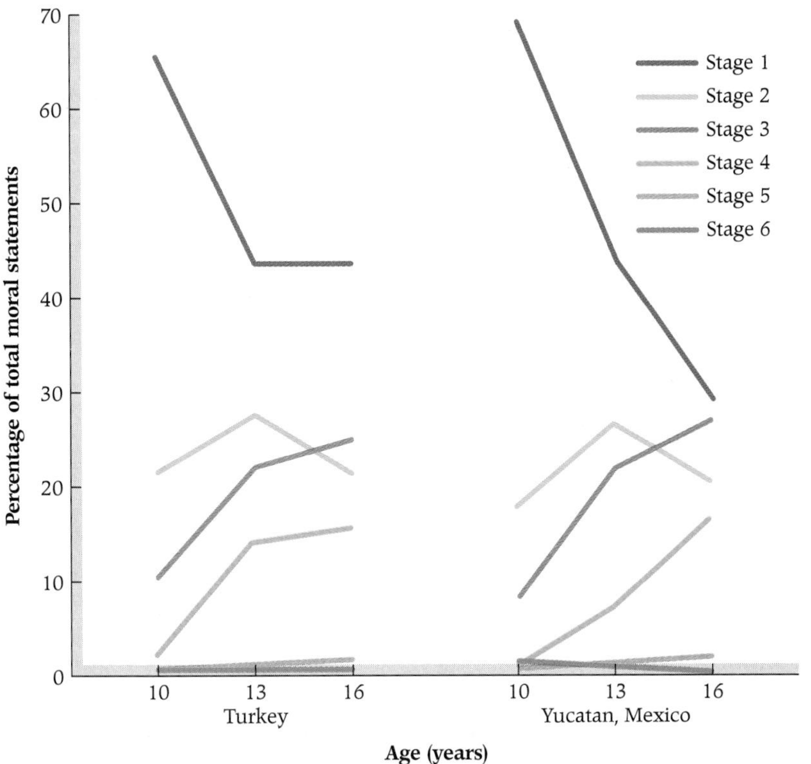

FIGURE 16.8
Age trends in the moral judgments of boys in small isolated villages in two nations. Note the continuing high incidence of stage 1 responses even by 16-year-olds. (From Kohlberg, 1969.)

Kohlberg explained cross-cultural data such as those in Figure 16.8 by suggesting that cultural differences in social stimulation produce differences in moral reasoning. However, several developmentalists have argued that culture-specific value judgments are built directly into Kohlberg's stage sequence, making it no more than a justification for the special cultural perspective of Anglo males, inheritors of the political ideology of liberal democracy (Shweder, 1982; Tappan, 1997). Are we to believe, such critics ask, that people who grow up in a traditional Third World village are less moral than the residents of a city in an industrially advanced country (Simpson, 1974)? Isn't it more reasonable to assume that because, say, Turkish villagers live in face-to-face contact with the people who share their fate, they are bound to give the greatest moral value to the Golden Rule, a morality of caring and responsibility?

The historian Howard Kaminsky (1984) expresses the same doubts in a different form:

> Is a Stage 6 refusal to support a friend who is wrong superior to a Stage 3 loyalty to that friend? A medieval nobleman would say no, and history suggests to us that if we repudiate the nobleman's sense of right, we are also repudiating the civilization created in resonance with his mentality, as well as those elements of the aristocratic ideal that have formed the modern sense of individuality. . . . [P]ersonal loyalty has obvious virtues that are lost when friendship or affection is made conditional on abstract rightness. (p. 410)

Kohlberg (1984) denied that bias in his scales fosters the conclusion that some societies, the United States among them, are more moral than others. He echoed the classical position of modern anthropology, that cultures should be thought of as unique configurations of beliefs and institutions that help the social group adapt to both local conditions and universal aspects of life on earth (Boas, 1911; Geertz, 1984). In this view, a culture in which stage 3 was the height of moral reasoning would be considered "morally equivalent" to a culture dominated by stage 5 or 6 reasoning, even though the specific reasoning practices could be scored as less "developed" according to Kohlberg's universal criteria.

Nevertheless, other approaches to moral reasoning have produced results that depart markedly from those obtained using Kohlberg's methods. Cross-cultural studies using Rest's Defining Issues Test, for example, have reported that by adulthood a shift from conventional to postconventional moral reasoning is quite widespread if not universal (Gielen & Markoulis, 1994). In cases where differences appear between countries, the level of education provided to the populations in question appears to be the critical factor.

Similarly, Elliott Turiel and his colleagues, in accordance with their emphasis on the need to separate moral issues from issues involving social convention and personal choice (see p. 567), provide evidence that the pattern of development for moral reasoning is cross-culturally universal. When cultural differences do appear, these researchers contend, the differences are related to issues concerning social conventions and personal choice, the importance of obedience to authority, and the nature of interpersonal relations (Turiel, 1998; Wainryb, 1995). In one extensive study, Cecilia Wainryb compared judgments about social conflicts given by a large sample of Israeli 9- to 17-year-olds. Half the participants were Jews from a secular, Westernized part of the Israeli population. The other half were from Druze Arabic villages, where the cultural norms emphasize hierarchical family structures, fixed social roles, and severe punishment for violating traditional duties and customs. The study pitted questions about justice and personal choice against questions about authority and interpersonal considerations (see Table 16.4).

Wainryb found that, in response to questions involving justice, there were no cultural or age differences. For example, an overwhelming percentage of participants at all ages said that a boy who saw someone lose money should return it, even though his father said to keep the money. Jewish children were slightly more likely than Druze children to choose personal consid-

TABLE 16.4 Questions Pitting One Kind of Social Conflict Against Another

Justice versus Authority (J–A)

Hannan and his father were shopping and they saw that a young boy inadvertently dropped a 10 shekel bill.

J Hannan told his father that they should return the money to the boy.

A His father told him to keep it.

Justice versus Interpersonal (J–I)

On a field trip, Kobby realized that the school did not provide enough soft drinks for all the children.

I Kobby had to choose between taking two drinks for his two younger brothers who were very thirsty or

J Alerting the teachers so that the drinks could be distributed equally among all children.

Personal versus interpersonal (P–I)

P Dalya was invited to a party.
She was looking forward to going there with her friends.

I Her young sister sprained her ankle and asked Dalya to stay home with her and keep her company.

Personal versus Authority (P–A)

Anat loves music.

P She wants to participate in an after-school music class.

A Her father does not like music; he tells her not to participate in the music class and take another class instead.

Source: Wainryb, 1995.

erations over interpersonal considerations, but the variability within each cultural group was far larger than the variation between them. The only really significant cultural difference was that Jewish children were much more likely to assert personal rights over authority than the Druze children. This result was in line with the hierarchical family structure in Druze culture in which obedience to authority is a central value. Nonetheless, there was wide variation in the responses of Druze youngsters. Wainryb (1995) concluded:

> Although Druze children appeared more oriented to obedience to authority, this tendency was not overriding across contexts: Considerations of obedience clearly did not take precedence over matters of justice, and concerns with personal choice were often given priority over interpersonal considerations. (pp. 397–398)

In a similar vein, Joan Miller and her colleagues found that while people from India and the United States may differ in where they draw the line between moral infractions and personal conventions, members of both groups make this distinction (Bersoff & Miller, 1993). For example, both Indians and Americans judged the violation of dress codes in terms of social conventions, not moral issues, and members of both societies judged theft to be a moral issue, not a matter of social convention. These studies suggest that by dividing up questions of morality into separate domains, it is possible to obtain a more subtle picture of cultural influences on moral reasoning in which there are both universal and culture-specific elements.

The Relation between Moral Reasoning and Moral Action

As we saw in Chapter 14 (p. 570), children may say they would behave one way in a hypothetical moral situation but actually behave in quite a different way. Although the correspondence between moral reasoning and moral behavior continues to be far from perfect in adolescence, there is evidence of a generally positive, if modest, relationship between the two: the higher the individual's score on tests of moral reasoning, the more likely he or she is to behave in a morally appropriate way. It has been found, for example, that adolescents who score at higher levels of moral reasoning are less likely to cheat in school or come in contact with the law and are more likely to engage in prosocial acts such as helping someone in distress or defending victims of oppression (Blasi, 1994; Rest, 1986; Turiel, 1990).

In some cases, the links between levels of moral reasoning and levels of moral action appear to be quite close. For example, in a study that presented moral dilemmas to children in the fourth to eighth grades (roughly, 9 to 14 years of age), Herbert Richards and his colleagues found that the level of children's moral reasoning was related to the quality of their classroom behavior in a way that makes good sense in terms of Kohlberg's theory (Richards et al., 1992). Children who responded at stage 1 (reasoning based on obedience and punishment) or stage 3 (reasoning based on acceptance of shared social norms) were the best-behaved children in the classroom. Those who responded at stage 2 (reasoning based on immediate interest) were the ones most likely to misbehave. This finding fits with other studies reporting that stage 2 reasoning is the most common form of moral reasoning encountered among juvenile delinquents (Gregg et al., 1994; Trevethan & Walker, 1989).

Often, however, the links between moral judgments and moral action are not particularly close because, as many of the young people in one study commented, the moral dilemmas they had to deal with in their real-life experience were not so clear-cut as those posed in hypothetical dilemmas (Walker et al., 1995). If you happen upon two people engaged in a fight, you might be uncertain who is in the wrong and afraid that you yourself will be hurt if you intervene. As one high school student told the researchers, "Like, you can't separate sort of totally moral principles from reality and sort of practical issues" (Walker et al., 1995:382).

As a consequence of the competing factors that enter into moral choices, there is often some kind of gap between people's moral judgments and their actions. At the same time, the ability to reason about moral issues provides the minimal level of understanding required for moral action. Another factor that helps adolescents to act morally is their increasing ability to understand the plight of others and to reason prosocially (Eisenberg & Fabes, 1998). As we discuss below, adolescents are increasingly focused on their sense of identity and more mindful of the need to be true to themselves as well as to others.

THINKING ABOUT AND PARTICIPATING IN POLITICS

Because young people are on the threshold of moving into positions of political leadership, it is vital to every society that they think about and participate in the political life of their countries. Yet existing evidence shows that adolescents' thinking about political matters is, for the most part, immature. In addition, many adolescents, especially those who feel excluded from national life because they are poor, or from a minority religious or ethnic group, show little interest in political life. This situation is an obvious matter of social concern.

Evidence on the development of adolescents' reasoning about political issues is based primarily on reasoning about hypothetical situations and interviews concerning real-life dilemmas that are of importance in the larger society.

In one study, Joseph Adelson and his colleagues proposed a hypothetical society as the basis for eliciting modes of reasoning. They asked middle-class young people 11 to 18 years old in the United States, Germany, and Great Britain to imagine that a thousand people who have become socially and politically disgusted with their country move to a Pacific island to set up a new society. The researchers then presented their subjects with a series of questions about how they thought the new society should be organized.

The results revealed a major change in adolescents' reasoning about politics sometime around the age of 14 (Adelson, 1991; Adelson et al., 1969). This change, which occurred for members of both sexes and in all three countries, was particularly evident in three areas: the way adolescents reasoned about laws; the level of social control they considered appropriate; and the increasing frequency with which they invoked overarching political ideals when they expressed their views.

Laws

In response to questions about society and its laws, the 12- to 13-year-olds in Adelson's research answered in terms of concrete people and events, whereas 15- to 16-year-olds answered in terms of abstract principles. Here are some typical responses, for example, to the question "What is the purpose of laws?" (Adelson, 1986:207):

12- to 13-year-olds' answers

- "They do it, like in school, so that people don't get hurt."
- "If we had no laws, people could go around killing people."
- "So people don't steal or kill."

15- to 16-year-olds' answers

- "To ensure safety and enforce the government."
- "To limit what people can do."
- "They are basically guidelines for people."

Correspondingly, when adolescents were asked questions about whether the government should be allowed to take private property for public use, the older adolescents demonstrated that they could reason hypothetically, taking many aspects of the problem into account. In response to a case in which the government wanted to build a highway through land that an owner refused to sell, an older adolescent answered:

> If it's a strategic point like the only way through a mountain maybe without tunneling, then I'm not too sure what I'd do. If it's a nice level stretch of plain that if you didn't have it you'd have to build a curve in the road, I think that the government might go ahead and put a curve in the road. (p. 212)

Social Control

The ways 12- to 13-year-olds think about social control became evident when they were asked about crime, punishment, and retribution. In response after response, the youngest adolescents suggested that severe punishment is the best way to deal with lawbreakers, leading Adelson to conclude that "the young adolescent's views on crime and punishment reflect a . . . pervasive authoritarian bias" (p. 214). One 13-year-old boy who was asked how to teach people not to commit crimes in the future answered:

> Jail is usually the best thing, but there are others. . . . In the nineteenth century they used to torture people for doing things. Now I think the best place to teach people is in solitary confinement. (p. 213)

As adolescents grow older, this authoritarian way of thinking declines. Adelson reports that when asked what should be done when a law isn't working, 13-year-olds suggest that the law should be enforced more strictly. Older adolescents are more likely to suggest that perhaps the law should be changed. And when a proposed law, or a change in social policy is suggested, older adolescents are more likely to consider if there is more to the situation than meets the eye. They start to consider such factors as who is likely to benefit or be hurt by the changes, who has the advantage and who is in need of special consideration. Older adolescents also conceive of the beneficial side of laws, such as allowing people to get along together, whereas younger ones think of laws only as a way of keeping people from behaving badly.

Overall it seems that the younger adolescents in Adelson's study find it difficult to conceive of social and political regulation as a continually evolving process, assuming instead that "what is, has been; what is, will be." What "has been" for them is a world in which they were told what to do, so they project this regime into the future. The older adolescents, perhaps because they have experienced the need to be responsible for their own good behavior, seem capable of reasoning about a world in which they must formulate their own personal code of ethics.

Adelson points out that this shift in reasoning about politics corresponds to changes that Inhelder and Piaget found in their studies of scientific problem solving. He suggests that this correspondence is due to the fact that conceptualizing modifiable, flexible, well-balanced political systems requires formal operational thinking.

An interesting outcome of Adelson's research was the discovery that the changes he observed over the course of adolescence were very similar from one country to the next. These similarities led him to remark that "a twelve-year-old German youngster's ideas of politics are closer to those of a twelve-year-old American than to those of his fifteen-year-old brother" (Adelson, 1986:206).

Developmental changes are also apparent when adolescents are asked to apply their moral reasoning abilities to real-life questions about the fair distribution of resources, such as widespread poverty, homelessness, and unemployment (Flanagan, 1995; Flanagan & Tucker, 1999). Connie Flanagan (1995) asked adolescents ranging in age from 12 to 14 years and from 15 to 18 years such questions as, "If you had to explain why some people are homeless, what would you say?" The answers of the younger adolescents differed in two ways from those of the older ones. First, the younger group answered as if there were only one legitimate view, evaluating the issue in all-or-nothing terms without considering possible exceptions or qualifications. Second, they tended to offer individual traits, such as laziness, as the basis of explanation. One young adolescent, for example, wrote, "I would tell them that it is many of their own faults and that they chose that lifestyle when they didn't take school work or whatever seriously."

In general, older adolescents offered explanations for homelessness that included both individual and social factors in their explanations, often proposing that both factors could be at work at the same time. This more complex thinking is reflected in answers such as, "I would say that a lot of them got laid off and couldn't afford their homes anymore. Some of them were on welfare and got cut off, and the rest would be people who got into drugs and alcohol, and some who ran away from home."

Political Idealism and Community Involvement

According to many influential theories of adolescence, young people are both pushed and pulled toward ideologies, systems of ideas on which particular political systems are formed (Adelson, 1991; Erikson, 1963; Inhelder & Piaget, 1958). They are pushed by their desire to become independent of their parents and to show that they can govern their own affairs; they are pulled by a seemingly coherent system that the ideology offers as an alternative to the imperfections of the adult world.

Since no ideal political system has yet appeared on Earth, adolescents' newly adopted ideologies are frequently utopian or religious. This idealism was especially visible in the civil rights and commune movements of the 1960s, both of which drew heavily for support on adolescents who saw in them a consistent alternative to the imperfect society in which they lived (Berger, 1981). This same tendency to seek ideal systems of life is reflected currently in the attraction that various cults hold for their adolescent followers (Miller et al., 1999) and in the appeal of the environmental movement (Read, 1997).

Although adolescents may show a proclivity to think about ideal systems, most teenagers have not worked out any systematic alternatives to the existing political order for themselves. When Joseph Adelson (1986) asked adolescents to imagine an ideal society, his teenage respondents came up with such platitudes as these:

> A society that everyone gets along and knows each other's problems and try to sit down and figure out each other's problem and get along like that.
>
> I think right now that the only society I would have would be the exact same one as we have now, although it does have its faults, I think we do have a good government now.
>
> Well, I would set up a society of helping out people like when there would be crime. (pp. 74–75)

Concerned that too many adolescents reach adulthood unable to reason more effectively about politics and society, some developmentalists have urged that high schools offer classes that allow young people to confront social problems through personal experience in addition to reading about them in textbooks. For example, Miranda Yates and James Youniss studied the effect that helping out at a soup kitchen for the homeless had on a large group of African American high school juniors (Yates & Youniss, 1999; Youniss & Yates, 1999). On the basis of group discussion sessions and essays written by the students before and after their experiences, Youniss and Yates found that the direct experience of severe social problems not only stimulated the students to think more deeply about social problems but resulted in more complex reasoning over the course of time as they made increasingly clear connections between different social problems. For example, students who were angered that young children had to come to the soup kitchen for their meals also drew connections between the need for the soup kitchen and the absence of affordable housing in the area.

Many young people become cynical about political processes (Torney-Purta, 1990). This problem is especially acute among minorities and the poor for obvious reasons: the political process routinely works to their disadvantage. They can see the problems and inconsistencies in political life, but they are unable to work out practical solutions. Figure 16.9 shows adolescents' increasingly pessimistic responses to the question, "Would it ever be possible to eliminate crime? poverty? racial prejudice?" In general, the older adolescents are pretty certain that political solutions to the world's ills are unlikely. At the same time, since they are in the process of defining themselves in contrast to their parents' generation, they are still attracted to the promises of someone who declares that, given the right beliefs and behavior, a more rational organization of life on Earth is possible.

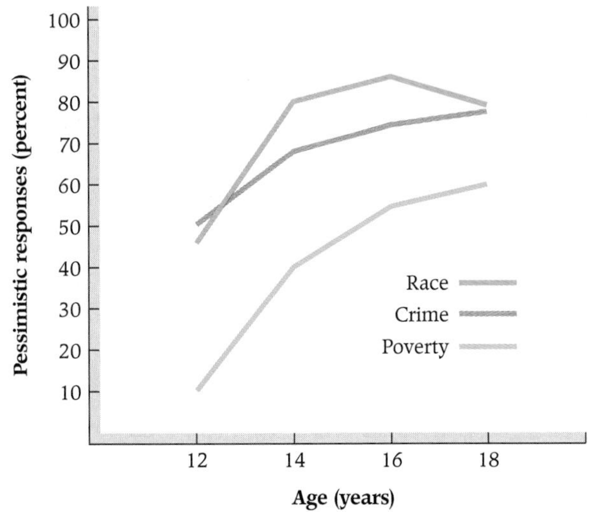

FIGURE 16.9

Data indicating the increasing pessimism of young people about society's ability to eliminate crime, poverty, and racial prejudice. (From Torney-Purta, 1990.)

INTEGRATION OF THE SELF

One of the most widely held ideas about adolescence is that this is the period when the individual forges the basis for a stable adult personality. Teenagers' ability to take several factors into account at the same time when they think about a problem, their broader and deeper knowledge of their society's norms and moral codes, and their increasing awareness that adulthood is approaching all contribute to the establishment of an integrated sense of self and identity.

CHANGING ATTRIBUTES OF THE SELF

In Chapter 14 we saw that at about the age of 6, when American children enter school, they begin to think of themselves in comparative terms: instead of saying (for example), "I am a girl who likes to skate," they begin to provide such self-descriptions as "I am a better skater than most of my class." A little later they begin explicitly to include the interpersonal consequences of their attributes: "I am a good skater, so lots of kids like to skate with me" (see Table 14.7, p. 589).

During adolescence, a new kind of self-description makes its appearance, in which personal identity is expressed in terms of general beliefs, values, and life plans, as in the following dialogue:

> *Interviewer:* What kind of person are you?
> *Adolescent:* I am someone who believes that everybody is created equal.
> *Interviewer:* Why is that important?
> *Adolescent:* Because I want to work for equal rights for everybody.
> *Interviewer:* What do you mean?
> *Adolescent:* I am going to be a lawyer and take cases and see that everyone gets rights, even if he's very poor or the wrong color or something. (Damon & Hart, 1988:69)

As children enter adolescence, their self-descriptions also shift from relatively concrete attributes (for instance, "I'm a good listener" or "I am easygoing") to more inclusive, higher-order concepts ("I am tolerant"). As Susan Harter (1990b) points out, "to consider oneself sensitive, one must potentially combine such attributes as being understanding, friendly, and caring" (p. 355).

Another feature that distinguishes the self-concepts of adolescents from those of younger children is the greater variety of attributes they include. In middle childhood, children describe themselves in terms of either their cognitive, physical, and social competence or a global notion of their self-worth

(Harter, 1999). Adolescents describe themselves in terms of characteristics from many domains: scholastic competence, athletic competence, job competence, physical appearance, social acceptance, close friendship, romantic appeal, and so on. These categories overlap but are not identical to those that are prominent in middle childhood.

Adolescents are also more likely to think of themselves with respect to the particular context they are being asked about. If they are asked what they are like when they are with their friends or in a class at school, their answers will differ from those they give when they are asked to describe what they are like when they are having dinner at home.

The appearance of "multiple selves" in adolescents' descriptions of themselves makes it necessary for them to deal with the fact that they are, in some sense, different people in different contexts. It is at this point that the question "Who is the real me?" becomes personally compelling.

On the basis of research among American adolescents, Susan Harter (1986) reports that the appearance of several selves, each depending on whom one is with and what role one is playing, is especially difficult for young adolescent Americans. When asked about the contradiction between being nice to some people but not to others, a 13-year-old responded, "I guess I just think about one thing about myself at a time and don't think about the other until the next day" (p. 45). By contrast, an older adolescent, when asked about problems in a romantic relationship, replied in a way that indicates her sensitivity to variations in herself when she is with her boyfriend and when she is in other situations: "I hate the fact that I get so nervous! I wish I wasn't so inhibited. The real me is talkative: I want to be natural, but I can't" (p. 45).

As young people move into late adolescence, they become increasingly better at formulating self-descriptions that apply to several contexts, allowing them to integrate the contradictory selves that they see themselves to be. For example, a young person who is both intelligent and forgetful might use a more inclusive category and think of himself as "inconsistent," or someone who is sometimes cheerful and sometimes depressed might coordinate these two opposing tendencies by using the general concept of "moody." According to Harter (1998:574), "such higher-order abstractions provide self-labels that bring meaning and therefore legitimacy to what formerly appeared to be troublesome contradictions within the self."

Concern with personal appearance is part of the formation of identity and self-esteem typical of the adolescent years.

ADOLESCENT SELF-ESTEEM

When adolescents routinely begin to notice the disparities between the way they actually behave and the way they ought to behave if they were being true to their "real selves," they begin to become preoccupied with what their "true" self is. Once they start dwelling on their own characteristics, they are confronted with the question "How much do I like myself?" To a considerable degree, attributes associated with high self-esteem in adolescents are the same ones they attribute to popular peers in earlier years. Attractiveness heads the list, especially for girls, followed by peer acceptance. All other characteristics trail behind.

This heavy emphasis on attractiveness has an unfortunate impact on the self-esteem of girls, because many of them consider themselves to be unattractive. At least in part, this negative self-perception helps explain why studies in a wide range of countries have found that, on average, girls have a lower sense of self-esteem than boys do (Harter, 1999; Wichstrom, 1998).

Studies in the United States show a marked decline in overall self-esteem in early adolescence followed by a steady increase after the age of 14 or 15 (Harter, 1999). Researchers believe that this early decline in self-esteem is due in part to the transition from elementary school to junior high school, which confronts children with increased academic and social demands at the same time that it puts them at the bottom of the school social ladder (Eccles et al., 1996). The steady increase in self-esteem thereafter is less well understood; it may reflect the increasing freedom young people have to choose their friends, contexts, and activities as they grow older, so that they can establish and live up to their own standards; or it may indicate that they are bringing their image of their ideal selves more into line with reality.

identity formation The process of forming a secure sense of self, which, according to Erikson, involves the integration of the individual self and the social self into a single identity.

RESOLVING THE IDENTITY CRISIS

The fact that adolescents are troubled by the feeling that they are, in some sense, different people depending on the roles they play in the increasingly diverse contexts of their lives makes the search for one's "true self" one of the dominant developmental tasks of adolescence (Muuss & Porton, 1998). According to Erik Erikson, the need to create a unified sense of identity is the final developmental crisis before adulthood; adolescents must either resolve the crisis by achieving a secure sense of personal identity or confront a variety of psychological problems in later life (Erikson, 1968a).

As we noted earlier, Erikson saw the process of **identity formation** as involving the integration of more than the individual's personality. In order to forge a secure sense of self, adolescents must resolve their identities in both the individual and the social spheres, or, as Erikson put it, establish "the identity of these two identities" (p. 22). Some idea of the cognitive complexity of this task can be gleaned from Erikson's attempt to specify the thought processes required to achieve identity formation:

> In psychological terms, identity formation employs a process of simultaneous reflection and observation, a process taking place on all levels of mental functioning, by which the individual judges himself in the light of what he perceives to be the way in which others judge him in comparison to themselves and to a typology significant to them; while he judges their way of judging him in the light of how he perceives himself in comparison to them and to types that have become relevant to him. (pp. 22–23)

Adolescents often seek out heroes to adulate and imitate. In the United States, many identify with popular musicians. These young people are waiting outside a funeral home to pay tribute to the platinum-selling rapper known as Big Pun.

During the transition from chilhood to adulthood, adolescents are at an increased risk for suicide and depression.

Although Erikson's description of the kind of thinking required to achieve a sense of an integrated identity may seem unnecessarily convoluted, this passage is worth careful study. It corresponds closely to Piaget's descriptions of formal operational thinking, suggesting a link between Piagetian and neo-Piagetian theories of cognitive development and Erikson's theory of personality development.

Erikson's core idea is that adolescents engage in an identity-forming process that depends on:

- How they judge others
- How others judge them
- How they judge the judgment processes of others
- Their ability to keep in mind relevant social categories (Erikson's "typologies") available in the culture when they form judgments about other people

Note that it is not enough to take only one or two of these elements into account—say, the fact that you base judgments of others on social categories of importance to you: "Sam is a jerk for allowing himself to be caught smoking a joint behind the gym." If your judgment of Sam is to be complete with respect to your own identity, you must simultaneously consider both your own and other people's judgments, plus the perspective of society (embodied in the social categories, such as "jerk," used to formulate the judgments). Sam may have been caught smoking marijuana, but if you too smoke marijuana or if you sometimes cut class, does that make you a jerk too? Or is getting caught what makes him a jerk? And wouldn't Sam think you were a jerk for volunteering to be on the prom committee? And what would your teacher think if he knew what you were doing and with whom at 11:30 last night?

Viewed in this way, Erikson's ideas about the mental processes involved in resolving the identity crisis of adolescence fit not only with research on the development of formal operational thinking but also with the findings of a variety of studies on the development of self-understanding during adolescence. As we noted earlier, adolescents begin to describe the self primarily in abstract, general terms, to be more self-reflective, and to show concern for integrating their past selves with an imagined future self.

Erikson's characterization of the developmental tasks of adolescence also makes it clear that the process of identity formation is likely to be difficult for families and friends as well as for adolescents themselves. Young people who are in the midst of working out a coherent notion of themselves sometimes take out their confusion on themselves and others, and the result can be antisocial, sometimes self-destructive, behavior (see Figure 16.10). As Erikson

crisis/exploration A stage in the process of identity formation during which adolescents actively examine their future opportunities in life, reexamine the choices their parents have made, and begin to search for alternatives that they find personally satisfying.

commitment The final phase in identity formation during which individuals are committed to the goals, values, beliefs, and future occupation that they have adopted for themselves.

FIGURE 16.10
The causes of death for adolescents when compared with those for aduls reflect the kinds of adolescent behavior that are of great concern to developmentalists and society at large.

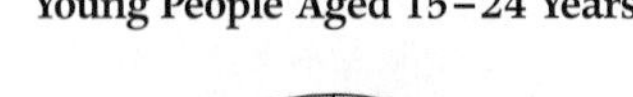

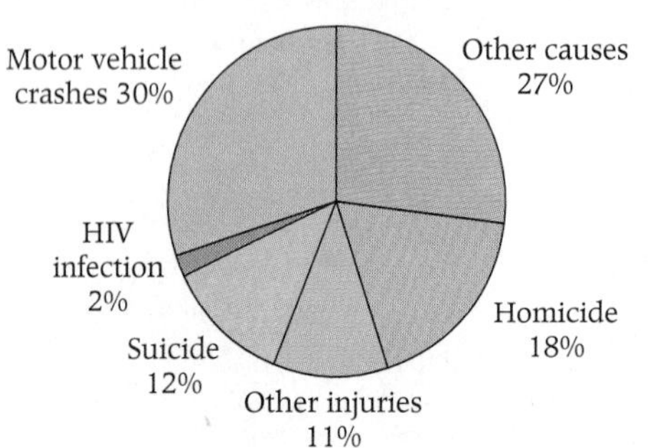

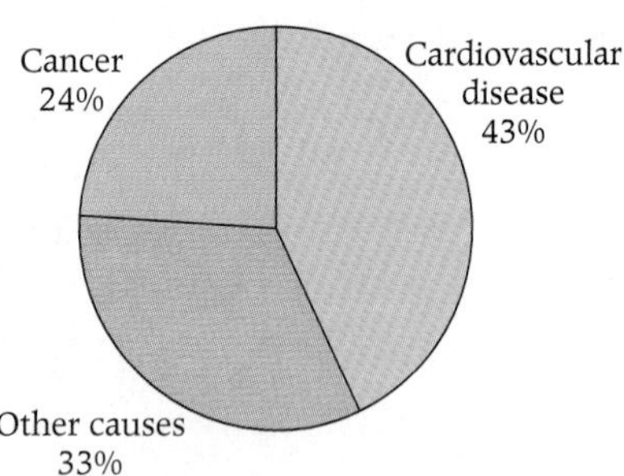

Souce: Centers for Disease Control and Prevention, 1998.

(1968a) summarized it, a frequent result of identity confusion among adolescents is that

> youth after youth, bewildered by the incapacity to assume a role forced on him by the inexorable standardization of American adolescence, runs away in one form or another, dropping out of school, leaving jobs, staying out all night, or withdrawing into bizarre and inaccessible moods. (p. 132)

Here we have the Eriksonian version of Hall's and Freud's visions of an emotionally stormy adolescence, clothed in more modern terminology (see Chapter 15, pp. 606, 608).

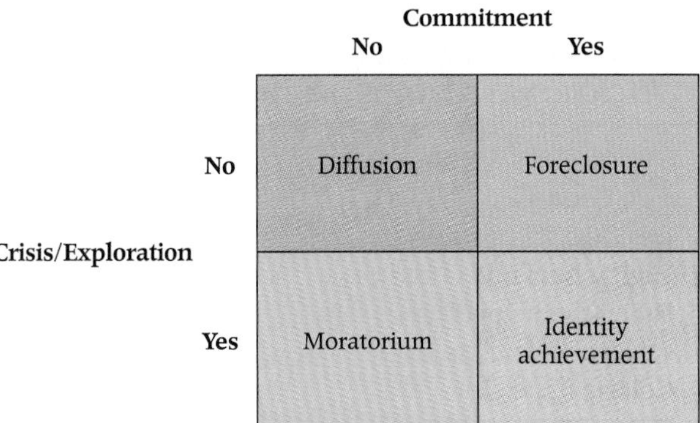

FIGURE 16.11
When the combinations of Erickson's two processes of identity formation, crisis/exploration and commitment, are considered together, the result is the four states of adolescent identity formation proposed by Marcia.

The Path to Identity Formation

The popularity of Erikson's ideas created a demand for an assessment method that could both depict an identity in the process of being formed and provide quantitative measures of the different states of identity formation (Grotevant, 1998; Grotevant & Cooper, 1998; Marcia, 1999). In an early and influential effort at such an assessment method, James Marcia (1966) focused on two factors identified by Erikson as essential to achieving a mature identity: crisis/exploration and commitment. **Crisis/exploration** refers to the process through which adolescents actively examine their future opportunities in life, reexamine the choices their parents have made, and begin to search for alternatives that they find personally satisfying. **Commitment** refers to individuals' personal involvement in, and allegiance to, the goals, values, beliefs, and future occupation that they have adopted for themselves.

Marcia interviewed male college students about two life domains that play a central role in identity formation according to Erikson: their choice of occupation and their commitment to beliefs about religion and politics. His questions were designed to elicit information on the degree to which individuals have adopted and fully committed themselves to a point of view.

Marcia (1966, 1999) identified four patterns of coping with the task of identity formation that arise from four possible patterns of crisis/exploration and commitment (see Figure 16.11):

1. *Identity achievement* Adolescents who display this pattern have gone through a period of decision making about their choice of occupation, for example, or their political or religious commitment. They are now actively pursuing their own goals. When people in this group were asked about their political beliefs, they responded with such answers as "I've thought it over, and I've decided to be a ______ . Their program is the most sensible one for the country to be following."
2. *Foreclosure* Young people who display this pattern are also committed to occupational and ideological positions, but they show no signs of having gone through an identity crisis. In a sense they never really undergo a personality reorganization. Instead, they just take over patterns of identity from their parents. They respond to questions about their political beliefs with such answers as "I really never gave politics much thought. Our family always votes ______ , so that's how I vote."
3. *Moratorium* This pattern is displayed by adolescents currently in an identity crisis. They are likely to answer a question about their political beliefs by saying, "I'm not sure. Both parties have their good points, but neither one seems to offer a better chance for my economic future."
4. *Identity diffusion* Adolescents who manifest this pattern have tried out several identities without being able to settle on one. They are likely to take a cynical attitude toward the issues confronting them, so they may answer questions about political commitment by declaring, "I stopped thinking about politics ages ago. There are no parties worth supporting."

For many adolescents, the search for identity involves a good deal of introspective solitude.

TABLE 16.5 Percentage of Students Manifesting Four Identity Statuses in the Domain of Vocational Choice, by Age Group

Age Group	Identity Achievement	Moratorium	Foreclosure	Identity Diffusion
Pre–high school years	5.2%	11.7%	36.6%	46.4%
High school underclass years	9.0	14.6	37.1	39.3
High school upperclass years	21.3	13.5	36.0	29.2
College underclass years	22.8	28.3	25.7	23.2
College upperclass years	39.7	15.5	31.3	13.5

Source: Waterman, 1985.

Subsequent researchers have extended Marcia's methods to incorporate additional domains of experience, including family life, friendships, dating, and sex roles (Grotevant, 1998). By and large these studies have shown that the proportion of identity achievers increases steadily from the years before high school to the late college years, while the proportion of young people manifesting identity diffusion decreases (Grotevant & Cooper, 1998; Kroger, 1996; Moshman, 1999) (See Table 16.5 for typical results showing how identity status grows in the occupational category.)

Because identity achievement is considered so important to normal adolescent development, researchers have given special effort to identifying factors that facilitate or retard identity formation and to determining how the process might differ for boys and girls.

The Role of Family and Friends in Identity Formation

Research has shown that both the immediate family and the adolescent's peer relations influence the process of identity formation. Futhermore, the two contexts of experience influence each other.

Harold Grotevant and Catherine Cooper conducted several studies focused on the special role that social relationships within families play in shaping the process of identity formation (Grotevant & Cooper, 1985, 1998). They constructed a "family interaction task" to evaluate the way that patterns of family interaction influence the process of identity exploration (Grotevant & Cooper, 1985). In this task, a mother, a father, and their adolescent are asked to make plans for a 2-week vacation together. They have 20 minutes to arrive at a day-by-day plan that covers both the location and the activity for each day. The discussions are scored according to the way the family members express their individuality (for example, by stating their own point of view or by disagreeing with another family member) and their connectedness (as displayed by their responsiveness and sensitivity to others' points of view).

Grotevant and Cooper also interviewed the adolescents in these families to find out how thoroughly they had explored a variety of options for their futures. They hypothesized that identity exploration would be related to individuality (the adolescent had to learn how to develop a distinctive point of view) and connectedness (the family had to provide a secure base from which the adolescent could explore).

In this and subsequent studies, Grotevant and Cooper found that adolescents who scored higher on measures of identity exploration lived in families that supported their right to express their own points of view (Grotevant, 1998). They also found that the role of family relationship patterns in identity formation differed for sons and daughters. For sons, greater identity exploration was associated with their father's willingness to allow disagreement, to compromise, and to modify his own suggestions in light of theirs—in short, to engage in genuine give-and-take. For daughters, a higher degree of identity exploration was associated with assertiveness, as manifested in their expressions of disagreement with their parents and the assertiveness with which they made suggestions. Despite these somewhat different patterns for boys and girls, it appears safe to say that the family systems that are most effective in promoting identity achievement are those that offer adolescents support and security while encouraging them to create a distinct identity.

Friendships play a complementary role in the process of identity formation as shown by Wim Meeus and Maja Deković, who conducted a study of almost 3000 Dutch subjects between the ages of 12 and 24. In addition to collecting data about levels of identity achievement, these researchers asked their subjects to indicate the extent to which they felt supported by key people in their lives—father, mother, siblings, friends, and classmates in their social relations, school, and work. They found that the support of classmates and friends was rated as more important than the support of family members in promoting identity achievement (Meeus & Deković, 1995).

GENDER DIFFERENCES IN IDENTITY FORMATION

Erikson sparked debate on the question of possible gender differences in identity formation by proposing that women cannot complete their identity formation process until they have married and become mothers (Erikson, 1968). That conclusion may have had some validity for the cultural conditions in which Erikson himself grew up, but it was highly debatable for many young women in the 1960s and is certainly of dubious validity in most Western cultures today.

Recent studies using identity-status interviews like that developed by Marcia have found little evidence of general gender differences in identity formation. However, some gender differences have been found in particular domains. For example, reviewing 56 studies that used Marcia's methods, Jane Kroger concluded that there is "strong evidence for the similarity of style that both men and women use to approach identity-defining questions during adolescence and adulthood" (Kroger, 1997:750). However, she also reported that in some studies, sexuality and family roles were a more salient dimension of identity formation for woman than they were for men.

War creates the conditions under which many adolescent males begin to assume an adult identity. These young adolescents are learning how to look and act like soldiers.

TABLE 16.6 VIEWS OF ADOLESCENT GIRLS AND BOYS ON FAMILY AND CAREER PRIORITIES

Girls' Views

I might be a mother and a wife. Having a husband is just like your father. You can't go out, can't do anything. You have to cook, clean, take care of the children and still work.

If I have a career and a husband who doesn't want me to work, I'll do what I want.

I intend to have a career. Being a wife is okay; it's not so much of a strain. Kids are a strain. Maybe I can talk him into adopting a 5-year-old; or stop my career. If I am into my career, especially at my peak, it would really hurt.

Boys' Views

If I was into sports, my wife and kids would have to travel and stay in a little room—but there's nothing that couldn't be worked out.

If I am a musician, on tour, my wife's going to get worried. I wouldn't try to bring it home. We'd talk and just give it some time. Sometimes it shouldn't interfere.

I would enjoy something like marriage and family. I'd love to have my own kid at the right time. I look forward to it. You have a wife to be with and share time with. Helping each other out. But you're tied down. Can't go out with the guys.

Source: Archer, 1985.

Others have also found gender differences in the particular domains in which boys or girls most quickly achieve identity. Meuss and Deković (1995), for example, reported that adolescent girls score at higher levels of identity achievement than boys in the domain of friendship, and Sally Archer (1985) found that girls score higher in the domain of choices about combining career and family. Archer's interviews also reveal American girls' ambivalence as they confront the dilemmas that are inherent in the cultural expectations and standard social roles that await them (see Table 16.6).

Several theorists have suggested that personal relationships may play a greater role in self-definition for females than for males. In this view, females' first priority in achieving identity is to establish and maintain their close relationships. To explore this issue, Arlene Lacombe and Judith Gay (1998) asked 15- to 16-year-old students to respond to dilemmas involving issues of identity where the quality of the education they would receive was pitted against the value they placed on an intimate relationship. The students were asked to respond to the following dilemma:

> Allison has been accepted at a very prestigious college with a reputation for a high quality English Department. She knows she wants to major in English. The main drawback is that the college is a six hour drive from her boyfriend. She also has been accepted to a college an hour from her boyfriend, which has an average English Department. She is unsure of which to choose.
>
> How much consideration should she give to each of the following issues in resolving the dilemma?
>
> (a) the quality of the program
> (b) the distance from her boyfriend
> Why?

More than 50 percent of the time, both boys and girls chose responses that favored educational identity over those that involved intimacy, and, contrary to expectations, boys chose more intimacy resolutions than girls did.

However, girls' explanations of their choices were more likely than boys' to combine concerns with educational identity and intimacy (Lacombe & Gay, 1998).

Although the data on gender differences in the process of identity formation are not entirely consistent, the bulk of the evidence indicates that adolescent girls, like adolescent boys, go through psychologically similar processes, despite some variations in the domains that are most important to them.

sexual orientation Refers to the sex toward which one has erotic feelings.

FORMATION OF A SEXUAL IDENTITY

The vast bulk of research on the formation of sexual identity assumes that the identity eventually arrived at will be a heterosexual one, that is, one centered on a sexual preference for members of the other sex. However, a sizable number of people exhibit nonheterosexual preferences—that is, a preference for members of their own sex as sexual partners. Therefore, in order to address the question of sexual identity, we need first to consider the question of sexual orientation.

Sexual orientation refers to the sex toward which one has erotic feelings. Estimates vary, but it appears that a vast majority of adults in the United States and societies around the world have heterosexual orientations (Kinsey et al., 1953; Michaels, 1996). However, a significant proportion of adults have a *non*heterosexual orientation, one that is homosexual or bisexual.

Sexual orientation is clearly important to sex-role identity, but it cannot be considered to *determine* sexual identity. Sexual identity is also influenced by the categories of sexuality present in one's culture and the culture's attitudes toward people who fit into those categories. Both cultural categories of sexuality and cultural attitudes toward them vary widely across societies and within societies over time (Bem, 1996).

Heterosexual Identity Formation

During the years of middle childhood, when most young people strongly prefer to spend time with members of their own sex, children's sense of self usually depends heavily on how other children of the same sex respond to them. For the most part, children during this period are indifferent or hostile to members of the other sex. Later, as a result of the changes brought on by puberty, their orientation to the other sex changes from one based on indifference or antagonism to one based on attraction.

The work of Sigmund Freud has had an enduring influence on psychologists' thinking about this process. As we noted in Chapter 15 (p. 608), Freudian psychologists view adolescence as a period when children reexperience the conflicts of earlier stages in new guises (Blos, 1972). In their view, unless these problems are worked through and resolved, the adult personality will be distorted. Central among the early developmental problems that must be reworked, according to Freud, is the child's primitive desire to possess the parent of the other sex. The way young children resolve this conflict, which Freud called the Oedipus conflict, is to repress illicit desire by identifying with the same-sex parent. Freud maintained that this infantile resolution is essential to proper sex-role identification (see Chapter 10, p. 380).

These early Oedipal feelings are encountered again in adolescence, but repression and identification with members of the same sex are no longer the adaptive responses that they were at the end of infancy. Puberty, Freud argued, reawakens sexual desire at a time when adolescents are fully capable both of carrying out the forbidden acts and of understanding the incest taboo that denies them the parent as a sexual partner.

Freud held that the combination of awakened desire and social constraint leads the adolescent to search for people outside the family to love.

The basis for this search formed during the peer-group experience of middle childhood, but the adolescent's reorientation is nonetheless fraught with difficulties. To begin with, the young person has had little experience of friendship with other-sex peers and virtually no experience interacting with peers as sex partners; new modes of social behavior will have to be learned. Second, a shift in the object of affection from a parent to a peer requires emotional disengagement from the family, which has been the bedrock of emotional security since birth. Recognizing the difficulty of this task, Freud (1905/1953a) referred to the adolescent's reorientation of affection as "one of the most painful psychical achievements of the pubertal period" (p. 227).

In recent years, attempts have been made to formulate theories of sexual identity that are based on biological events that occur early in life (see Chapter 10, p. 385). For example, Daryl Bem (1996) proposed that

> biological variables, such as genes, prenatal hormones, and brain neuroanatomy, do not code for sexual orientation per se but for childhood temperaments that influence a child's preferences for sex-typical or sex-atypical activities in peers. These preferences lead children to feel different from opposite- or same-sex peers—to perceive them as dissimilar, unfamiliar, and exotic. This, in turn, produces heightened nonspecific autonomic arousal that subsequently gets eroticized to that same class of dissimilar peers: Exotic becomes erotic. (p. 320)

Thus, once an adolescent focuses his or her sexual feelings and arousal on one sex or the other, these feelings become the foundation for constructing a sexual identity.

Nonheterosexual Identity Formation

When addressing the issue of same-sex sexual orientation, the first question that arises is, What causes a person to be sexually oriented toward others of the same sex? Two biological explanations for same-sex sexual orientations have attracted the most attention among developmentalists. The first is that a nonheterosexual orientation is genetically based. Findings that seem to support this supposition come from twin studies: the chances of *both* members of a twin pair being homosexual is 2 to 5 times greater among monozygotic twins than among dizygotic twins (Bailey & Bell, 1993; Ellis, 1996a; Whitam et al., 1993). Another finding that lends support to the genetic hypothesis is that both lesbian women and gay men have higher proportions of brothers and sisters who also express same-sex preferences than do heterosexual men and women (Bailey et al., 1999). Both these results seem to indicate that genetic factors play a role in determining an individual's sexual orientation. However, if genes were the whole story, one would expect *all* monozygotic twins to be alike on this trait, and such is not the case. What is more, the data do not explain how genes operate to influence a person's sexual orientation.

The second biological explanation for a nonheterosexual orientation that has received wide attention focuses on the role of hormones in prenatal development. As we saw in Chapter 3 (p. 87), the influence of male hormones, or androgens, on the developing fetus is not limited to the gonads and the genital tract. During the last 6 months of prenatal development, the presence of testosterone serves to suppress the natural rhythmic activity of the brain. If testosterone is absent, the pituitary gland establishes the cyclical pattern of hormone secretion that is characteristic of the female. In most cases, the effects of androgens on the fetal brain are complementary with the fetus's genital sex. However, if for some reason the male fetus is insensitive to androgens, or if the female fetus is exposed to androgens during the critical period when certain neural pathways are forming, it may be that a same-sex preference in sexual partners becomes more likely.

A good deal of the research conducted to demonstrate the effects of sex hormones on the brain and on subsequent sexual behavior has been conducted with animals (Bohan, 1996). Female animals who have been exposed to androgens in utero are more active than other females, and they attempt to mount other animals. Male animals who are androgen-deprived show female mating behaviors and present themselves to be mounted.

A recent study of adult women who were exposed to the drug DES (diethylstilbestrol) in utero lends additional support to this hypothesis (Meyer-Bahlberg et al., 1995). DES, which is now banned because of its cancer-causing side effects, is a synthetic hormone that was given to pregnant women who were in danger of miscarrying. Suspicion that the drug affected sexual development by increasing the production of masculinizing androgens during the period of fetal brain organization led researchers to compare women who had been exposed to the drug in utero with a group of women of similar age and medical history who had not been exposed to the drug. As expected, women who had been exposed to DES in utero scored higher on measures of same-sex and bisexual orientation than their peers who had not been exposed to the drug.

Environmental explanations of a nonheterosexual orientation have also been offered, focusing on ways that sexual orientation is learned. One old hypothesis was that adolescents may assume a nonheterosexual orientation because they were seduced when they were young by an older gay, lesbian, or bisexual individual. While some lesbians, gay men, or bisexuals may have been seduced by a person of the same sex when they were young, interviews with lesbians and gay men find that most do not participate in same sex-activity until *after* they become aware of their attraction to other members of their sex (Bell et al., 1981). A related hypothesis is that a nonheterosexual orientation is the result of a kind of sexual "imprinting." According to this theory, if a person's first sexual encounters are with someone of the same sex, sexual arousal will become associated with members of one's own sex (Bohan, 1996). Since, in fact, many people's first sexual explorations occur with members of their own sex, this hypothesis fails to explain why most people develop a heterosexual orientation.

While nonheterosexual activity is believed to be widespread, only a small number of the people who engage in it identify themselves as gay, lesbian, or bisexual (Michael et al., 1994). Because of such disparities, several contemporary researchers make a distinction between (1) having a nonheterosexual *orientation,* (2) engaging in same-sex *sexual behavior,* and (3) assuming a nonheterosexual *identity.* In their view, a nonheterosexual identity involves an enduring integration of sexual orientation and sexual behavior into a sense of oneself as a gay man, a lesbian, or a bisexual. Most contemporary scholars believe that sexual orientation, sexual behavior, and sexual identity, like most human behaviors, are the result of the interaction of biology and environmental influences.

One interactionist theory that has received attention focuses on self-labeling. According to this view, "children whose appearance and mannerisms resemble those of the opposite sex become confused about their sexual identity and this confusion increases their chances of being attracted to members of their own sex" (Ellis, 1996b:25). That is, boys whose behavior is perceived by others as "feminine," and girls who are viewed as "tomboys" and whose behavior is not considered "feminine," are more likely to come to think of themselves as different from other members of their sex. Because of this difference, they come to label themselves as gay or lesbian or bisexual. In support of this hypothesis, research has shown that many very feminine boys become gay or bisexual men. While there is less research on masculine girls, the existing research suggests that though most will become heterosexual, they have a higher-than-average chance of becoming lesbians (Bailey, 1996; Bailey & Zucker, 1995).

Several scholars maintain that, given the enormous diversity among nonheterosexual individuals, it is reasonable to assume that the origin and de-

Because of homophobic attitudes in many segments of the U.S. population, the decision to "come out" is often agonizing and sometimes dangerous. However, in some communities and schools, open nonheterosexual relationships are much more likely to be accepted.

velopment of sexual orientation and identity vary widely from one person to the next (Bohan, 1996; Ellis, 1996). For some nonheterosexual individuals, biology might play a major role; for others, learning, or the social milieu they find themselves in at a particular time in their lives may be the key factor.

Stages of Nonheterosexual Identity Formation

Developmental regularities in the sequence through which a person forms a nonheterosexual identity in many societies have inspired attempts to describe stages in the process (Cass, 1984, 1996; Troiden, 1988, 1993). Richard Troiden has offered a stage model of identity formation that fits the experience of many North American gay men in recent decades.

Stage 1: Sensitization; feeling different In retrospective reports, men with a homosexual orientation often say that during middle childhood they had social experiences that made them feel different from other children and that served later to make homosexuality personally relevant to them, although they assumed at the time that they were heterosexual (Bell et al.,1981). Typical comments are: "I couldn't stand sports, so naturally that made me different. A ball thrown at me was like a bomb" (p. 74); "I just didn't feel like I was like other boys. I was very fond of pretty things like ribbons and flowers and music" (p. 86).

Stage 2: Self-recognition; identity confusion When such boys enter puberty, they realize that they are attracted to members of the same sex and begin to label such feelings as homosexual. This recognition is the source of considerable inner turmoil and identity confusion; they can no longer take their heterosexual identities as given, and they know that homosexual individuals are stigmatized. Typically they feel that

> you are not sure who you are. You are confused about what sort of person you are and where your life is going. You ask yourself the questions, "Who am I? Am I a homosexual? Am I really a heterosexual?" (Cass, 1984:156)

By middle or late adolescence they begin to believe that they are probably homosexual because they are uninterested in the heterosexual activities of their peers. Many homosexual adults recall adolescence as a time when they were loners and social outcasts. This upsetting psychological and social situation provokes denial and attempts to rationalize their different sexual orientation in socially approved ways.

Stage 3: Identity assumption Some young people who have had homosexual experiences and who recognize that they prefer sexual relations with members of their own sex do not act on their preference. Many others, however, move from private acknowledgment of their homosexual preference to admitting it openly, at least to other homosexuals. Although homosexual identity is assumed during the early stages of this process, it is often not fully accepted. Vivienne Cass (1984) describes people at this stage of identity formation:

> You feel sure you're a homosexual and you put up with, or tolerate this. You see yourself as homosexual for now, but you are not sure of how you will be in the future. You usually take care to put across a heterosexual image. You sometimes mix socially with homosexuals, or would like to do this. You feel a need to meet others like yourself. (p. 156)

Young people who have achieved this level of homosexual identity deal with it in a variety of ways. Some try to avoid homosexual contacts and attempt to pass as heterosexual because they are afraid of being stigmatized. Others adopt the broader society's stereotypes of homosexuals and behave in extreme ways that fit those stereotypes. Still others begin to align themselves with the homosexual community in an unobtrusive way.

Stage 4: Commitment; identity integration This final level is reached by those who adopt homosexuality as a way of life. Identity integration is indicated by a fusion of one's sexuality and emotional commitments, by expressions of satisfaction with one's orientation, and by public disclosure of one's homosexual identity.

Troiden notes that commitment to a homosexual identity may vary from weak to strong, depending on such factors as the individual's success in forging satisfying personal relationships, being accepted by his family, and functioning well at work or in a career.

It needs to be emphasized that a sequence of changes in sexual identity like the one described by Troiden should not be considered universal. In some societies, and at other times in history, adolescent same-sex sexual behavior has not been viewed as an expression of a life-long sexual identity. Rather, it has been variously interpreted as a necessary response to a culture's practice of sex segregation, as a way to learn about sex, as part of the ritual of becoming an adult, or as a playful acting out of the sex drive by young people who have excess sexual energy (Gonsiorek & Weinrich, 1991; Herdt, 1989; Savin-Williams, 1990).

MINORITY-GROUP STATUS AND IDENTITY FORMATION

The process of identity formation is particularly complicated among ethnic minority-group children in the United States for several reasons (Phinney, 1996). First, in cases where the values, beliefs, and customs of the minority group differ from those of the majority population, minority-group youth face the task of reconciling two different identities, one based on their own cultural heritage, the other on the cultural heritage of the majority group. In effect, they have at least twice as much psychological work to do. Second, these young people often face prejudice, discrimination, and accompanying barriers to economic opportunity, all of which further complicates their task.

As we saw in Chapter 10 (pp. 389–390), ethnic minority-group children entering middle childhood have acquired an awareness of their ethnic identity in the sense that they know the labels and attributes that apply to their own ethnic group and have developed basic attitudes concerning their ethnicity. During middle childhood and adolescence, children in ethnic minority groups undergo three additional stages of ethnic identity formation (Cross & Phagen-Smith, 1996; Phinney, 1993). Although researchers apply different labels to these stages, they agree on the basic content of each stage and the general kinds of experiences associated with movement from one stage to the next (see Table 16.7). In this discussion, we have adopted the labels suggested by Jean Phinney because she explicitly links the stages to those used by Marcia, whose methods (described on p. 675) have been widely generalized to the study of ethnic identity.

Unexamined Ethnic Identity In this initial stage, children still accept and show a preference for the cultural values of the majority culture in which they find themselves. This acceptance may include a negative evaluation of their own group (see Chapter 10, p. 390). In some cases, this initial stage appears to correspond to Marcia's category of foreclosure, because the person refuses to consider the relevant issues and adopts the views of others unquestioningly. One Mexican American male told Phinney, "I don't go looking for my culture. I just go by what my parents say and do, and what they tell me to do, the way they are" (p. 68). In other cases, the failure to examine questions of ethnic identity is more similar to identify diffusion. An example is provided by a young African American female, who responded, "Why do I need to learn

TABLE 16.7 Labels for Stages of Ethnic Identity Formation According to Different Researchers

Researcher	Stage 1	Stage 2	Stage 3
Phinney (1989)	Unexamined ethnic identity	Ethnic identity search	Achieved ethnic identity
Cross (1978)	Preencounter	Encounter and immersion	Internalization
Kim (1981)	White-identified	Awakening to sociopolitical awareness and redirection to Asian consciousness	Incorporation

Source: De Vries et al., 1982. Adapted by permission.

about who was the first black woman to do this or that? I'm just not too interested" (p. 68).

Ethnic Identity Search Movement beyond stage 1 is often initiated by a shocking experience in which the young person is rejected or humiliated because of his or her ethnic background. The specifics of such encounters are quite varied (Cross & Strauss, 1998; Fordham & Ogbu, 1986). A minority student may be accused of cheating when he or she does outstanding work, simply because the teacher assumes that members of the student's ethnic group are incapable of such work; or a boy and girl who have been friends for years may be forbidden to socialize with each other romantically because they have different skin colors, ethnic backgrounds, or religions. However, a shocking encounter is not necessary for young people to begin pondering their ethnic identity; for some, a growing awareness that the values of the dominant group are not beneficial to ethnic minorities is sufficient to move them into stage 2.

In stage 2, young people show an intense concern for the personal implications of their ethnicity. They often engage in an active search for information about their own group. They are likely to become involved in social and political movements in which ethnicity is a core issue. They may also experience intense anger at the majority group and glorify their own heritage.

Signithia Fordham and John Ogbu (1986) describe several cases in which African American adolescents go through a process of **oppositional identity formation,** rejecting the patterns of dress, speech, mannerisms, and attitudes associated with European American society and adopting an identity that opposes them. These researchers believe that the process of oppositional identity formation provides one of the major explanations for the school failure of African American children. For many of these young people, who feel automatically shut out of the economic opportunities of the majority culture, successful identity formation requires that they find school and the academic activities that go on there to be irrelevant to their lives. Evidence suggests that similar identity processes are at work in the development of adolescents of many minority groups (Phinney, 1995).

Ethnic Identity Achievement Individuals who achieve a mature ethnic identity have resolved the conflicts characteristic of the prior stage and now accept their own ethnicity and have a positive self-concept. At this stage, which William Cross and P. Phagen-Smith have termed *internalization,* "tension, emotionality, and defensiveness are replaced by calm, secure demeanor" (Cross, 1978; Cross & Phagen-Smith, 1996). The individual displays "ideological flexibility, psychological openness, and self-confidence" about his or her ethnicity (p. 18).

A word of caution is needed in regard to these findings. The economic inequalities that go with some minority-group statuses make it very difficult to isolate minority-group membership as the crucial variable in the development of members' personal and social identities. (We saw the same problem

oppositional identity An identity forged by members of racial or ethnic minorities, in which they reject the patterns of dress, speech, mannerisms, and attitudes associated with mainstream white American society.

with regard to group differences in IQ in Chapter 13, p. 535.) As a consequence, we cannot be certain why foreclosure occurs more frequently among minority-group adolescents or why some of them appear to identify less with their own ethnic or racial group than with that of the dominant group in American society.

independent sense of self A sense of self oriented to being unique, to promoting one's own individual goals, and to expressing one's own thoughts and opinions.

interdependent sense of self A sense of self oriented to fitting into the group, to promoting the goals of others (that is, of the group), and to developing the ability to "read" the minds of others.

Cross-Cultural Variations in Identity Formation

Many researchers have claimed that cross-cultural differences in identity formation can be profound (Markus & Kitayama, 1998; Miller, 1997; Shweder et al., 1998). In discussions of cultural variations in concepts of the self, it is common for cultures to be considered along a continuum describing the degree to which either individuals or social groups provide the anchor for concepts of the self and identity (Greenfield, 1997; Kagitçibasi, 1997). At one end are cultures whose members see themselves primarily as individuals, as middle-class Americans do. At the other end are cultures, such as Japan's, whose members see themselves primarily in relation to the larger social group. Members of the first kind of culture are said to perceive themselves as independent, while members of the second kind see themselves as interdependent.

According to Hazel Markus and Shinobu Kitayama, people whose cultures encourage an **independent sense of self** are oriented to being unique, to promoting their individual goals, and to expressing their own thoughts and opinions. People whose cultures emphasize an **interdependent sense of self,** by contrast, seek to fit into the group, to promote the goals of others (that is, of the group), and to develop the ability to "read" the minds of others (see Table 16.8).

As Markus and Kitayama point out, this difference in orientation to the self creates different sets of problems for the young person who is forging a unified sense of identity. For one thing, the American emphasis on the autonomous self presupposes that identity formation is an individual, personal process. In societies where the self is seen in relation to others, by contrast, others are included as an integral part of the self. Thus adolescents in collectivist societies do not have to make many of the decisions and choices that American adolescents must face in order to resolve their identity. It makes little sense to assert that healthy identity formation requires adolescents to make a "commitment to a sexual orientation, an ideological stance, and a vo-

TABLE 16.8 Key Differences between an Independent and an Interdependent Construal of Self

Feature Compared	Independent	Interdependent
Definition	Separate from social context	Connected with social context
Structure	Bounded, unitary, stable	Flexible, variable
Important features	Internal, private (abilities, thoughts, feelings)	External, public (statuses, roles, relationships)
Tasks	Be unique	Belong, fit in
	Express self	Occupy one's proper place
	Realize internal attributes	Engage in appropriate action
	Promote own goals	Promote others' goals
	Be direct; "say what's on your mind"	Be indirect; "read other's mind"
Role of others	Self-evaluation: others important for social comparison, reflected appraisal	Self-definition: relationships with others in specific contexts define the self
Basis of self-esteem*	Ability to express self, validate internal attributes	Ability to adjust, restrain self, maintain harmony with social context

*Esteeming the self may be primarily a Western phenomenon, and the concept of self-esteem should perhaps be replaced by self-satisfaction or by a term that reflects the realization that one is fulfilling the culturally mandated task.
Source: Markus & Kitayama, 1991.

cational choice" (Marcia, 1980:160) in societies in which marriages are arranged by the family, one's vocation is whatever one's father or mother does, and strict subordination to one's elders is a moral imperative (Grotevant, 1998).

Unfortunately, there is little cross-cultural research on the development of identity except in industrialized societies or in those small segments of the population in nonindustrial societies that have entered the modern, industrialized sector (Marcia, 1999). Consequently we have to turn to the reports of anthropologists who have concerned themselves with identity formation in small hunter-gatherer or agricultural societies, such as those found in parts of West Africa, the Arctic regions, and New Guinea (Schlegel & Barry, 1991). The most distinctive fact about identity formation in such groups is that, as in the collectivist societies discussed by Markus and Kitayama, it involves little of the cognitive deliberation and personal choice that play such large roles in accounts of identity formation in Western cultures. There are so few distinct adult roles in such societies that a young person has few decisions to make. The transition to adult identity in such societies is often made in ritual initiation ceremonies that are obligatory and painful (see Box 16.2). These circumstances must certainly influence identity formation, but existing research does not permit us to draw conclusions about the processes involved.

THE TRANSITION TO ADULTHOOD

As we commented in the introduction to our discussion of adolescence, no developmental transition after birth is so well marked as the end of middle childhood. Profound changes in the size and shape of children's bodies are unmistakable signs that they are "ripening." Certainty about the end of middle childhood, however, is not the same as certainty that a distinctive stage intervenes between middle childhood and adulthood. Is adolescence really a stage in the same way that infancy or middle childhood is, or is it more like an uneven transition between stages, as Piaget sometimes conceived early childhood to be?

In examining the data in Chapter 15 concerning physical and social changes of adolescence, as well as the data in this chapter concerning cognitive and personality changes, we saw evidence from various cultures suggesting that the transition to adult status universally involves conflict, anxiety, and uncertainty. At the same time, however, the data suggest equally strongly that adolescence is rarely as fraught with conflicts as the Western stereotype suggests. Moreover, the highly elaborated stage of adolescence encountered in modern industrial societies exists only under particular cultural circumstances (Whiting et al., 1986). When researchers assume that adolescence exists in societies that have no concept of it and no set of social practices corresponding to it, they do violence to the facts.

The Inuit of the Canadian Arctic at the turn of the century, for example, used special terms to refer to boys and girls when they entered puberty, but these terms did not coincide with the usual notion of adolescence (Condon, 1987). Young women were considered adult at menarche, a change in status marked by the fact that they were likely to be married by this time and ready to start bearing children. Young men were not considered fully grown until they were able to build a snow house and kill large game unassisted. They might be able to do both shortly after the onset of puberty, but boys usually achieved adult status somewhat later because they had first to prove that they could support themselves and their families. In view of the life circumstances of these people, it is not surprising that they developed no special concept corresponding to adolescence that applied to boys and girls alike; such a concept did not correspond to their reality.

BOX 16.2

Rites of Passage

In many societies a rite of passage, a ritual or series of events intended to give structure and special meaning to important life transitions, marks the shift from childhood to adulthood (Scott, 1998; Delaney, 1995). Although the particular content and length of rites of passage differ markedly among cultures, they all share certain common elements. These include separation from society, preparation or instruction from an elder, a transitional ceremony or special set of activities, and reentry into society with a new social status. These ceremonies are often public events that herald the contributions to society the young person is expected to make in his or her adult life (Schlegel & Barry, 1991).

A classic example of a rite of passage was provided by Margaret Mead in her study of the Arapesh of New Guinea in the 1930s. At their first menstruation, Arapesh girls were put through ceremonial rites that symbolized their emergence as women ready to become productive members of the community. Here Mead describes the preparations for the ceremony, which takes place in the girl's husband's home:

> Her woven arm and leg bands, her earrings, her old lime gourd and lime spatula are taken from her. Her woven belt is taken off. If these are fairly new they are given away; if they are old they are cut off and destroyed. There is no feeling that they themselves are contaminated, but only the desire to cut the girl's connection with her past.
>
> The girl is attended by older women who are her own relatives or relatives of her husband. They rub her all over with stinging nettles. They tell her to roll one of the large nettle-leaves into a tube and thrust it into her vulva: this will ensure her breasts growing large and strong. The girl eats no food, nor does she drink water. On the third day, she comes out of the hut and stands against a tree while her mother's brother makes the decorative cuts on her shoulders and buttocks. . . . Each day the women rub the girl with nettles. It is well if she fasts for five or six days, but the women watch her anxiously, and if she becomes too weak they put an end to it. Fasting will make her strong, but too much of it might make her die, and the emergence ceremony is hastened. (1935:92–93)

Among the Kpelle in Liberia and in several other West African tribes, boys undergo a ceremonial "death" at puberty and are then spirited away by older men to an isolated grove deep in the forest. There they are taught the secret lore of the men, as well as the farming and other skills they will need to earn a living. When they emerge from "behind the fence," in some cases several years later, they have a new name and a new identity (Gay, 1984).

Contemporary cultures in the United States practice a variety of rites of passage associated with the transition to adulthood, among which high school and college graduations are the most widespread. But there are also special rituals associated with different ethnic group and religious traditions, such as *quinceaneras* marking the fifteenth birthday and the transition to adult status of Latina girls, and bar mitzvahs and bat mitzvahs marking the transition to adult religious status for Jewish boys and girls on their thirteenth birthdays.

In recent years, various cultural and ethnic groups in the United States have reinvigorated traditional rites of passage as a means of supporting their young people's ethnic identity development (Brookins, 1995; Delaney, 1995). Craig Brookins describes various special activities organized for African American adolescents in order to help them cope with the racism they encounter in their schools and communities. Through ceremonies and special educational activities, these programs attempt to instill knowledge of African American history, belief in the special strengths and abilities of African Americans, important practical skills they will need in later life, and a commitment to the African American community.

Graduation is an important event shaping one's sense of identity, regardless of one's ethnic background.

ADOLESCENCE IN MODERN SOCIETIES

Granted that a social category corresponding to adolescence may arise only in certain cultural circumstances, we are still left with the problem of understanding the developmental dynamics of young people who fit this category in modern industrialized societies. If we want to claim that adolescence is a stage of development in modern societies, we must determine whether it adheres to the same rules of organization and transition as earlier stages or is unique in important respects.

When its historical roots in the United States and other modern industrialized societies are traced, adolescence appears to be closely associated with apprenticeship training or formal schooling; or with a period of waiting until the designated adult role becomes available, through either a marriage proposal or an inheritance (Kett, 1977; Muuss & Porton, 1996). Although scattered instances of the concept of adolescence can be found in records of ancient civilizations, it was only during the nineteenth century, when mass education was introduced, that adolescence became a generally recognized and pervasive category defining children of a certain age regardless of sex and social class.

Two crucial factors were introduced by formal schooling. One is a long delay in achieving economic self-sufficiency. The other is prolongation of social experiences that take place in such contexts as a school or a community sports program, which are institutionally separated from the activities of adult life. In the United States, for example, young people are expected to attend school for 12 or more years and to abstain from starting a family until after they have graduated from high school. In these circumstances, there can be no doubt that adolescence as a stage of development is a social reality.

In fact, adolescence has been elaborated in such detail in the United States and other industrially advanced societies that developmentalists who specialize in this developmental stage often distinguish three substages: early adolescence (11 to 14 years), middle adolescence (15 to 18 years), and late adolescence (18 to 21 years). As several commentators have noted, these divisions correspond to the way modern societies group children in schools: early adolescence frequently corresponds roughly to middle or junior high school, middle adolescence to high school, and late adolescence to college (Hendry et al., 1994; Steinberg,1989).

This correspondence between age and the context of development presents analysts of adolescence with a problem: they can show that younger adolescents are more susceptible to peer pressure than older adolescents (Figure 15.8, p. 626) and reason differently about political processes (p. 668), but it is difficult to determine why. The differences may arise from some factor closely associated with age (such as density of brain cells or greater social experience) or perhaps from the differences in experience afforded by the various ways children's school life is organized.

A distinctive fact about adolescence in societies such as the United States is that not all aspects of the bio-social-behavioral shift that initiates it coincide as they do in earlier stages. To be sure, biological maturation simultaneously gives rise to new desires and emotions and to new forms of social relationships. Intimate friendships with peers are supplemented by, and in some cases supplanted by, intimate love relationships. As these relationships develop, family ties loosen.

Yet an important element in the "social" part of the bio-social-behavioral shift that defines the transition to adulthood for Piaget and other stage theorists (see Table 16.9) is the partial failure of the social system to change at the expected time. With some exceptions (such as peripheral participation in adult work), modern young people are offered carefully arranged substitutes for real adult roles. Instead of responsibility for conducting real chemistry experiments, students are given exercises that model the ideal practice of chemists. Instead of having responsibility for running their own school, students are given a student government with elected officers, laws, and legislatures but no power. Instead of

TABLE 16.9 THE BIO-SOCIAL-BEHAVIORAL SHIFT: TRANSITION TO ADULTHOOD

Biological Domain
- Capacity for biological reproduction
- Development of secondary sex characteristics
- Attainment of adult size

Behavioral Domain
- Achievement of formal operations in some areas (systematic thinking)
- Formation of identity

Social Domain
- Sexual relations
- Shift toward primary responsibility for oneself
- Beginning of responsibility for next generation

responsibility for informing the community of important events, students are allowed to run student newspapers whose topics are carefully circumscribed by rule and custom. If modern adolescence is to be considered a separate stage of development, we must admit that it combines biological, social, and behavioral factors in a way we have not seen in any of the stages that precede it.

When adolescents throw themselves into an activity as if it were a lifetime commitment, or in those rare instances when they are allowed or required to take on an adult role (in a work situation, say, or when a parent falls ill), they may display the formal operational cognitive ability that is supposed to appear at this time. In many other situations, however, both their social roles and their thought processes can be expected to remain distinctly "adolescent."

LOOKING AHEAD

The modern trend toward extending and intensifying adolescence springs from the same forces that made adolescence a source of social concern and scientific interest in the first place. It is a virtual certainty that in the decades to come, as high technology increasingly comes to dominate the economic sector, young people will be expected to achieve higher levels of learning than ever before. This increased achievement will be sought in part through intensification of education in the lower grades, longer school hours, and more days of schooling per year. But to gain access to higher-paying and more secure jobs, young people will also be required to spend more years in school, which will further delay their independent working lives and prolong their economic dependence. These economic factors will mean that the transition to full adult status for many adolescents will be delayed longer and longer, with uncertain social and psychological consequences (Coté & Allahar, 1996).

SUMMARY

RESEARCH ON ADOLESCENT THOUGHT

- The thinking of adolescents often manifests four characteristics not usually observed in the thinking of younger children:
  1. Reasoning hypothetically
  2. Thinking about thinking
  3. Planning ahead
  4. Thinking beyond conventional limits

- Piagetian theory attributes these characteristics to the emergence of formal operations, in which all possible logical aspects of a problem are thought about as a structured whole. The core of Piaget's evidence comes from observations of adolescents working on problems modeled on scientific experiments and formal logical reasoning.
- Not everyone proves capable of solving Piagetian formal operational tasks consistently, even in adulthood.
- Studies of sex differences in formal operational thinking over several decades indicate that differences favoring males have all but disappeared in recent years.
- Large cultural variations in formal operational thinking have been observed in traditional, nontechnological societies among children who have not experienced relatively high levels of education. However, ability to reason in terms of formal operations appears in specific culturally valued domains in all cultures.
- Difficulties with Piaget's explanations of adolescent thought processes have inspired attempts at alternative explanations.
    1. Neo-Piagetian approaches emphasize increased memory-processing capacity that makes it possible to keep in mind several aspects of a problem at the same time.
    2. Information-processing theorists hypothesize that increased memory capacity and increased efficiency in the use of strategies and rules, rather than changes in the logic of thought, account for adolescents' new thought processes.
    3. Cultural-context theorists propose that involvement in new activities creates the conditions for a new level of systematic thought. Systematic thought is assumed to occur in all societies but is always bound to the demands of particular contexts.

ADOLESCENT THINKING ABOUT THE SOCIAL ORDER

- Adolescents' thinking about the social order undergoes several changes.

    With respect to thinking about moral issues:

    a. The ability to reason about all *existing* factors relevant to moral choices is supplemented by the ability to think about all *possible* factors.

    b. Reasoning about moral issues begins to go beyond social conventions to encompass more abstract principles of right and wrong.
- Variability in the way males and females respond to some moral-reasoning problems has led to proposals that there are sex differences in moral orientations rather than a single sequence of moral development. The current consensus is that both sexes are equally capable of reasoning from different moral orientations.
- Members of small, face-to-face, traditional cultures generally do not engage in postconventional reasoning about moral issues but sometimes do attain the level associated with the Golden Rule.
- Adolescents in all cultures distinguish moral issues from social conventions and personal issues, but the border between these categories of social rules varies from one culture to the next.
- Though some developmental psychologists assume that increased intellectual capacity results in a higher level of moral and political behavior, the evidence linking reasoning ability with actual behavior shows that many other factors are involved.

With respect to thinking about politics:

a. Conceptions of the law become more abstract.
b. An appreciation of the positive value of laws appears.
c. Adolescents show increasing ability to consider both individual and social contributions to conditions such as poverty and homelessness.
d. Adolescents desire ideal political systems, but at the same time they are increasingly cynical about the possibilities of solving social problems.

INTEGRATION OF THE SELF

- Personality development during adolescence requires that new sexual capacities and new social relations be integrated with the personality characteristics accumulated since birth.
- Adolescents describe themselves in more varied, generalized, and abstract ways than they did during middle childhood, an indication of the need to reconcile their "multiple selves."
- In the United States, self-esteem declines at the onset of adolescence, especially among girls, reflecting the difficulties of adjusting to social and biological changes. It then rises throughout the remainder of adolescence.
- According to Erikson, adolescence is the time when individuals must initiate the process of identity formation, attempting to resolve their identity in both the personal and social spheres in order to form an adult identity.
- Marcia divided the process of identity formation into four categories arising from the possible combinations of crisis/exploration and commitment: identity achievement, foreclosure, moratorium, and identity diffusion.
- Families that encourage adolescents to express their own views enhance their children's identity formation.
- Supportive friendships enhance identity formation.
- There is little evidence for the existence of sex differences in the sequence of changes that lead to identity formation, although there are sex differences in the salience of different domains of experience within which identities are formed.
- A key issue in the process of forming a sexual identity is one's sexual orientation.
- According to the Freudian view, the adolescent's shift from indifference to attraction regarding opposite-sex peers begins when new sexual desires reawaken the Oedipus complex, requiring the individual to find an appropriate person to love.
- There is currently considerable uncertainty about the factors leading to nonheterosexual identity formation. Both heredity and experience, including exposure to androgens during the prenatal period and to socializing experiences during childhood, have been implicated in nonheterosexual identity formation.
- The formation of nonheterosexual identity appears to go through four stages:
    1. Sensitization: a feeling of being different
    2. Self-recognition and identity confusion

3. Identity assumption
4. Commitment

- The formation of ethnic identity in adolescence appears to go through three stages:
    1. Unexamined ethnic identity
    2. Ethnic identity search
    3. Ethnic identity achievement
- There is ample evidence that the process of identity formation varies with sociocultural circumstances.

THE TRANSITION TO ADULTHOOD

- Historical and cultural variations in the organization of young people's lives after middle childhood raises the question of whether adolescence is a universal stage of development. While the transition to adulthood is marked by additional social and psychological stresses, adolescence as a social category is most prominent where there is a gap between the ability to reproduce biologically and the ability to reproduce culturally.
- In modern industrial societies, where adolescence is an institutionalized stage of development, the discoordination of biological, social, and psychological changes creates a developmental configuration unlike those of earlier stages of development.

KEY TERMS

commitment, p. *675*
crisis/exploration, p. *675*
deductive reasoning, p. *648*
formal operations, p. *646*
identity formation, p. *673*
independent sense of self, p. *685*
interdependent sense of self, p. *685*
oppositional identity formation, p. *684*
sexual orientation, p. *679*
structured whole, p. *647*

THOUGHT QUESTIONS

1. What are the key features that distinguish formal operational thinking from concrete operational thinking?
2. Why is reasoning more likely to be logical in familiar situations than in contexts unrelated to one's everyday experience?
3. Monitor your activities for a day and make a list of all those in which you engaged in formal operational thinking to any extent. What characteristics seem to differentiate the contexts in which you use formal operational thinking from those in which you don't?
4. Draw comparisons between Troiden's stages of homosexual identity formation, Erikson's four preadolescent developmental crises, and Marcia's four patterns of identity development. What accounts for the similarities and differences among them?
5. Increasing numbers of young adults in the United States are remaining in their parents' homes long after they have finished college and found employment. On the basis of material covered in Chapters 15 and 16, what can you hypothesize about the psychological consequences of this trend?

Epilogue: Putting It Together

Now that you have traced the process of development from conception to the threshold of adulthood, it is time to consider some of the general lessons you have learned. As we noted in the Preface, it is our conviction that knowledge about the process of development is not only of practical use to people who become responsible for children; it is useful in everyday life to anyone who comes in contact with children at all.

RELATING THEORY TO PRACTICE

Developmentalists cannot rely heavily on precise scientific formulas to explain and solve problems the way physicists can. The application of principles of development to events in the world is more comparable to the craft of the traditional family doctor—the doctor who made house calls carrying a black bag equipped with simple diagnostic tools, a small array of medications, and a vast store of understanding and experience. Developmentalists come to the practice of studying development and promoting the well-being of children with a tool kit of theoretical principles, diagnostic procedures, and remedial techniques. They then need to combine these principles and tools with their own practical experience to deal with the situation at hand.

A PRELIMINARY TOOL KIT

Looking back over the contents of this book, it is possible to identify several principles that qualify for the "black bag" of the practicing developmentalist. The following list, by no means comprehensive, consists of six concepts that in our view are indispensable to an understanding of human development.

Sequence Is Fundamental At the core of the definition of development we offered in Chapter 1 (p. 5) is the idea that developmental changes follow one another in an orderly sequence: there must be one cell before there can be two; muscles and bones must be present before nerves can coordinate arm and leg movement; gonads must secrete testosterone before the genitalia characteristic of genetically male embryos can emerge. The same principle is equally apparent after birth. The primary emotions evident near or at birth must be present in order for the secondary emotions to arise with the acquisition of language. Children must be able to think operationally before they can develop the ability to think formally.

Owing to the sequential nature of development, the old proverb that "an ounce of prevention is worth a pound of cure" is especially relevant where children are concerned. When expectant mothers receive inadequate health care and give birth to premature and underweight babies, or when children begin their schooling without benefit of appropriate intellectual socialization at home, the long-term costs to society, as well as to the children, are vastly greater than the costs of preventing the problem in the first place.

Timing Is Important Recall that fetuses who were exposed to thalidomide later than 3 months after conception were unlikely to be affected by the drug, whereas many of those exposed during the first 2 to 3 months of pregnancy experienced disastrous developmental effects. The timing of developmental change after birth is just as important. Children's ability to acquire language depends critically on their having linguistic input during the first few years of life. In modern societies, adolescents' self-esteem depends in part upon the timing of their experience of puberty relative to their peers' and of their transition from elementary to middle to high school. Timing is also significant in a broader sense, in that the developmental impact of many life events—from a change in residence to the loss of a parent—is affected by when in the child's life those events occur.

Development Involves Differentiation and Integration This principle is evident within hours of conception when the single cell of the zygote gives rise to the many apparently identical cells of the morula. These cells then differentiate into two distinct *kinds* of cells whose different shapes and functions become integrated into a new pattern in the blastocyst. Later cycles of differentiation and integration transform arm buds into the complex structure of the human hand.

After birth this double-sided process of differentiation and integration characterizes psychological development as well as physical development. Single-word utterances that stand for complete sentences are replaced by multiword sequences that are then integrated into the complex patterns of a language's grammar; the one-sided, egocentric thinking of preschoolers opens up to include the viewpoints of others and becomes reintegrated into a new way of thinking and solving problems.

Development Is Patterned In Chapter 1 we noted that one of the fundamental issues debated by developmentalists is the relative importance of stagelike changes versus gradual cumulative change in the process of development (the continuity–discontinuity issue). Our review of the current evidence makes it clear that development is characterized by *both* qualitative, stagelike changes *and* quantitative, continuous change.

In part the argument between the two positions is a matter of scale. When you encounter your niece 6 years after last meeting her as a 2-year-old, it is crystal clear that the schoolgirl standing before you is a qualitatively different kind of person than she was as a toddler. But to someone who saw that child every day (such as her mother, father, live-in grandparent, or sibling), the process of change would have seemed almost seamlessly continuous and incremental.

The relative prominence of continuous and discontinuous change also depends on the phase of development that is the focus of interest. During prenatal development, major changes both in the appearance of the organism and in its interactions with the environment occur with stunning rapidity. Soon after implantation, for example, the embryo is altogether different from the blastocyst, giving rise to new, still more complicated physical forms. When such dramatic changes occur over a relatively short period of time, development indeed appears to be dominated by qualitative, stagelike episodes of change.

After birth the situation is more mixed; both qualitative and quantitative changes command our attention. The progression of changes that leads to walking, for example, has been described as a sequence of stagelike changes—from creeping to rocking on hands and knees to crawling and, finally, to upright walking. Each of these forms of motion uses different combinations of muscles and skills and each results in qualitatively different interactions with the environment. Such stagelike changes appear in social behavior as well: the symbolic play of 4-year-olds requires a form of interaction with other persons that differs qualitatively from both the solitary motor play of infancy and the rule-bound games of school-age children.

Sequences of psychological changes, however, are not so clear-cut. It seems that for every claim of an abrupt stagelike change in the ability to remember, to think logically, or to classify, there is a counterclaim showing that the corresponding process of change is actually gradual and continuous. Moreover, for every claim that a child's psychological behavior in a given stage is uniform, someone can point to instances when the child remembered, reasoned, or classified according to one stage under some circumstances and according to another stage in other circumstances. This unevenness is particularly apparent in early childhood, as we noted in Chapter 9, but it is evident in other periods as well.

Development Emerges from Multiple Sources Just as the study of development pushes us to the view that development is both continuous and discontinuous, studies of the causes of development argue strongly for the view that *change emerges from the influence of multiple forces acting more or less simultaneously and interactively.*

This view is particularly pertinent when considering the traditional form of the nature–nurture debate. As data presented in Chapters 2 and 13 indicate, when statistical procedures are used to tease apart genetic and environmental contributions to an individual trait such as personality or intelligence, roughly half of the observed variations are attributed to genetic factors and half to the specific environments that individuals encounter after birth. Even these kinds of estimates are fraught with uncertainty, because they assume those two sources of variation to be independent contributors to development when in reality each contributes in subtle ways to the other.

Our use of the notion of a bio-social-behavioral shift to describe apparent turning points in development emphasizes the erroneousness of assigning causal priority to one or another source of development. It is tempting, for example, to envision the appearance of social smiling as the result of a sequence of factors: first, biological changes in the infant's visual system reorder the potential for social interaction; then smiles become linked to social feedback; then changes occur in the emotional tone of child–caregiver relations. However, when Robert Emde and his colleagues examined the relation between changes in brain waves and the advent of social smiling, they could find no strict sequence. Each kind of change—biological, cognitive, and social—is necessary for the others to occur.

Development Is Culturally Mediated The development of every human being occurs within the medium of culture. Even before birth, culture contributes to development of children through such factors as the food to which the mother has access and the speech patterns that filter through her body. After birth, culture occupies a central role in children's experience because they are highly dependent upon others to support their continued development. As infants, all their interactions with the world are mediated by culture because the ways they are fed and cared for are woven into a vast array of distinct cultural practices that make up their society's design for living. Born into one culture, they may have a long, almost exclusive relationship with their mothers during the day but sleep in a crib by themselves at night, requiring them to wake their caregivers with their cries before they are fed. Born into another culture, their days may soon come to be spent under the care of older siblings and other family members, while they spend their nights nestled in their mother's arms, nursing at will while their mothers continue to sleep or nurse drowsily. Every cultural pattern sets up a workable means of coordinating infants' and essential adult activities, but each does so in a fashion consistent with the particular demands and customs of the local group.

All during the early years of development, children spend their time engaged in activities that have been scripted for them by adults who have well-fixed ideas about what sorts of roles, skills, knowledge, and values children should be expected to have mastered by the time they reach adulthood. The experiences arranged for young children growing up in a technologically advanced "information society" that emphasizes individualism and competition are vastly different from those arranged for children growing up in an agrarian or nomadic society that emphasizes interdependence and cooperation. These different sets of experiences have important differential consequences for the course of development.

Despite vastly different specifics of experience depending upon one's cultural origins and one's role within the cultural group, the principle that the development of every human being occurs within the medium of culture is universal. In short, culture shapes our very sense of self as well as our relations with the other members of our society and the way in which we experience the world.

USING THE TOOL KIT IN EVERYDAY LIFE

The ways in which we put developmental theory into practice depend, of course, very much on each particular situation and our role in it. In our roles as citizens, for example, the tool kit provided by developmentalists helps us to think critically about the constant stream of information concerning children that greets us daily when we open our newspaper or turn on the television set. When experts argue about the influence of television on children's behavior, we know that their failure to reach agreement is the result of their inability, for perfectly legitimate ethical reasons, to create the necessary conditions for a proper experimental study of the issue. When a politician advocates a simple plan for improving the reading scores of schoolchildren, we know that the children's performance is the result of a convergence of factors and is not likely to improve in response to any one-dimensional program. The tool kit of developmentalists cannot solve every problem, but it can help prevent our wasting time and resources on policies that are poorly conceived.

The realization that children's lives are greatly affected by the developmental niches that they inhabit and the larger social contexts that shape those niches puts the tool kit to use at a broader level of social policy. For example, developmental research has shown that when adults are under stress, their ability to provide optimal conditions for their children's development suffers. This understanding gives added importance to programs based on contemporary research that are designed to provide parents with employment, safe housing, good health care, and supportive social networks.

The people who assume professional responsibility for promoting children's development—those who work in schools, hospitals, clinics, youth clubs, family services, and the like—must use information from developmental studies in a different way. These are the child-development practitioners who most closely fit the model of the old-fashioned family doctor with the satchel full of tools. Psychologists who work with visually impaired children, for example, have a variety of physical tools at their disposal: ways to test vision, intellectual development, language development, and so on. In this case, if they also know that a child's development of social smiling depends on her getting the right kind of feedback regardless of the sensory medium, and that well-timed tickling can be an adequate feedback substitute for the sight of a smiling face, they then have a flexible tool for preventing a different kind of deficit. They can also draw on other developmental research for guidance in organizing the child's social life, literacy instruction, and access to other valued cultural resources.

In the end, however, the effectiveness of the therapies prescribed by the specialist in the development of visually impaired children, like the effectiveness of the old-fashioned doctor's prescription for a cure, will depend on the specific case in question. Just how sick is the patient? Is the medicine known to work in such cases? Is the patient taking the medicine according to instructions? Are the surroundings otherwise healthful? Is the family doing all they can to help? In the face of the fact that every individual experiences a unique combination of such factors, science is silenced because its methods depend on knowing how each individual is *like* all the rest. And inevitably every one of us is unique. It is at this point that the art of the developmental practitioner must take over.

It is our hope that reading this book has helped readers to think more systematically about all of these issues. Beyond the potential practical utility of knowing more about the study of development, however, we also hope our readers will find our discussions useful in thinking about their own development, past, present, and future. Reading about adolescence may give them another perspective on the idealism, longing, self-consciousness, and conflicts that they themselves experienced during this period. Reading about sibling relationships may help them to understand the behaviors of their own brothers and sisters, as well as themselves.

As parents and grandparents we know from personal experience that the more one knows about processes of development, the more interesting interacting with children becomes. Raising children is often tiring and discouraging. When a 2-year-old screams in defiance, a 4-year-old refuses to go to bed without the lights on, a 9-year-old cannot seem to concentrate on her spelling lesson, or a teenager appears hypersensitive to criticism, it helps to understand the larger pattern of changes that the crisis of the moment fits into.

Finally, an appreciation of the process of development can be a direct source of pleasure. During a recent holiday visit, our granddaughter was just old enough to be entering the bio-social-behavioral shift at 10 weeks described in Chapter 4. We had not yet seen her exhibit social smiling, although her parents claimed that she sometimes smiled when they picked her up to feed her or to change her diaper. Knowing that she was on the threshold of social smiling, we repeatedly found ourselves trying to amuse her. When she seemed alert and contented, one of us would bend over her crib or pick her up and start bobbing our heads in an eye-catching way, while at the same time smiling at her and talking to her in exaggerated, high-pitched "motherese." And sure enough, the baby soon reciprocated, signaling the advent of a new level of social contact and delighting her grandparents no less than her parents.

Appendix: Guide to Discussions of Specific Aspects of Development

GUIDE 1 Discussions of Physical Development

Period	Characteristic	Page Numbers
Early infancy	Hearing capacities at birth	pp. 133–134
	Early visual capacities	pp. 135–138
	Taste and smell	pp. 137–138
	Detection of touch, temperature, and position	p. 138
	Reflexes present at birth	pp. 139–141
	Maturation of sleeping patterns	pp. 147–149
	Maturation of the nervous system	pp. 154–161
	Growth and weight gain in first year	pp. 181–183
	Sex differences in rate of growth	p. 183
	Brain development in first year	p. 183
	Development of reaching and grasping	pp. 184–185
	Development of locomotion	pp. 185–186
	Effect of practice on early motor development	p. 188
Later infancy	Height and weight during second year	p. 219
	Changes in brain during second year	p. 219
	Transition from crawling to walking	pp. 219–222
	Manual dexterity during second year	p. 222
	Control during elimination	pp. 223–224
	Biological prerequisites for language	pp. 319–320
Early childhood	Brain maturation	pp. 353–354
Middle childhood	Physical growth	pp. 470–473
	Motor development	p. 473
	Brain maturation	pp. 474–476
Adolescence	Puberty	pp. 608–612

GUIDE 2 Discussions of Social Development

Period	Characteristic	Page Numbers
Early infancy	Infant's preference for facelike figures	p. 137
	Coordination of infant's needs and caretaker's responses	pp. 147–152
	Role of mother's response in sensorimotor substages	pp. 165–166
	Emergence of social smiling	pp. 171–173
Later infancy	Help-seeking behavior in infants	p. 207
	The origins of social play	pp. 228–229
	Consequences of different patterns of attachment	pp. 239–241
	Self-recognition	pp. 248–249
	Self-reference	p. 249
	Developing a sense of standards	pp. 249–250
	Optimal conditions for development	pp. 259–262
	Effects of separation from parents	pp. 262–267
	Effects of isolation	pp. 269–270
	Effects of maternal depression	p. 274
	Recovery from deprivation	pp. 277–279
	Environmental support of language	pp. 321–327
Early childhood	Scripts	pp. 359–360
	Cultural and social influences on development	pp. 359–362
	Sociodramatic play	pp. 362–363
	Mechanisms of identification	pp. 376, 378–389
	Acquiring a sex-role identity	pp. 376–378, 385–389
	Acquiring an ethnic or racial identity	pp. 389–390
	Self-regulation	pp. 392–397, 414
	Morality of constraint	p. 393
	Aggression	pp. 397–408
	Prosocial behavior	pp. 408–412
	Social competence	p. 581
	Relations with siblings	pp. 424–425
	Effects of media	pp. 440–449
	Day care	pp. 450–453
	Preschool	pp. 453–455
Middle childhood	Education and apprenticeship	pp. 505–506
	Rule-based games	pp. 556–558
	Rules of behavior	pp. 559–561
	Thinking about morality	pp. 562–569
	Peer relations	pp. 571–585
	Relations with parents	pp. 585–588
	Self-concept	pp. 588–590
	Social comparison	p. 589
	Self-esteem	pp. 590–593
Adolescence	Rites of passage	p. 687
	Consequences of early and late maturation	pp. 614–617
	Peer relations	pp. 617–627
	Sexual activity	pp. 627–632
	Relations with parents	pp. 632–636
	Work	pp. 636–638
	Thinking about the social order	pp. 658–660
	Thinking about morality	pp. 658–668
	Identity formation	pp. 675–679
	Self-esteem	pp. 672–673
	Sexual variations in identity formation	pp. 679–684
	Minority-group status and identity formation	pp. 684–686
	Adolescence in modern societies	pp. 688–689

GUIDE 3 DISCUSSIONS OF LANGUAGE DEVELOPMENT

Period	Characteristic	Page Numbers
General	Questions about language acquisition	pp. 295–298
	Language subsystems	pp. 298–313
	Theories of language acquisition	pp. 313–319
	Biological prerequisites	pp. 319–320
	Social prerequisites	pp. 321–327
	Relation between language and thought	pp. 327–330
	Cultural influences	pp. 329–330
Infancy	Language preferences at birth	p. 133
	Distinguishing phonemic differences	p. 299
	First words	pp. 301–303
Later infancy	Intersubjectivity and social referencing	p. 209
	Beginnings of speech: cooing, babbling, jargoning	pp. 210–211
	Pointing	p. 310
Early childhood	Earliest vocabulary	pp. 301–302
	Early word meanings	pp. 302–306
	Constructing sentences	pp. 306–309
	Learning the uses of language	pp. 309–313
	Associations between early language development and early cognitive development	pp. 327–329
Middle childhood	Language of schooling	p. 515

GUIDE 4 DISCUSSIONS OF EMOTIONAL DEVELOPMENT

Period	Characteristic	Page Numbers
General	Vulnerability and resilience	pp. 270–277
Early infancy	Evidence of emotions at birth	pp. 142–143
	Differentiation approach to emotional development	p. 143
	Evidence of temperament differences at birth	pp. 143–147
	Crying and parents' responses	pp. 151–152
Later infancy	The onset of wariness	pp. 205–208
	Beginnings of attachment	pp. 208–209
	Explanations of attachment	pp. 235–238
	Patterns of attachment	pp. 239–248
	Emergence of secondary emotions	pp. 250–251
Early childhood	Regulation of emotions	pp. 395, 414–415
	Development of emotions	pp. 397, 412–414
	Beginnings of empathy	p. 397
	Socio-emotional competence	p. 415
Middle childhood	Emotional control and social status	p. 573
	Emotional maturity	p. 587
Adolescence	Traditional and modern conceptions of adolescents' emotions	pp. 605–608
	Psychological responses to puberty	pp. 612–614
	Emotional consequences of early and late maturation	pp. 614–617

GUIDE 5 DISCUSSIONS OF CULTURAL INFLUENCES ON DEVELOPMENT

Period	Characteristic	Page Numbers
General	Culture in language development	pp. 329–331
	Family organization	pp. 424–428
	Socialization practices	pp. 428–433
	Social networks	p. 440
Early infancy	Coordination of feeding and sleep schedules	pp. 147–150
	Nursing behaviors	pp. 167–169
	Adults' view and expectations of young infants	p. 169
Later infancy	Maternal responsiveness	p. 244
	Attachment patterns	pp. 246–247
	Effects of temperamental traits	pp. 260–261, 273
	Language instruction	pp. 324–327
Early childhood	Social co-construction	p. 363
	Scripts	pp. 357, 359–360
	Unevenness of development	p. 359
	Guided participation	pp. 360–361
	Sociodramatic play	pp. 362–363
	Acquiring a sex-role identity	pp. 376–378, 385–389
	Acquiring ethnic and racial identity	pp. 389–390
	Internalization of adult standards	p. 396
	Causes of aggression	pp. 400–403
	Media	pp. 440–449
	Day care	pp. 449–453
	Variations in preschool environments	p. 455
Middle childhood	Physical growth	pp. 471–473
	Concrete operations	pp. 477–481
	Memory development	pp. 482–485, 523–524
	Schooling	pp. 522–525, 542–543
	Intelligence testing	pp. 526–529
	Competition and cooperation among peers	pp. 575–577
Adolescence	Adolescence as a product of culture	pp. 688–689
	Rites of passage	p. 687
	Sex as scripted activity	pp. 629–631
	Formal operations	pp. 646–648, 650–652, 656–657
	Moral reasoning	pp. 562–566, 659–668
	Identity formation	pp. 675–679

Guide 6 Discussions of Cognitive Development

Period	Characteristic	Page Numbers
Early infancy	Imitation in newborns	pp. 158–159
	Learning	pp. 156–166
	Piagetian substages 1 and 2	pp. 162–164
	Piagetian substages 3 and 4	pp. 188–190
	Appearance of object permanence	pp. 191–192
	Stages of object permanence	p. 192
	Cross modal perception	p. 195
	Perception of number	p. 196
	Categorizing by perceptual features	pp. 202–203
	Memory	pp. 203–206
Later infancy	Piagetian substages 5 and 6	pp. 224–225
	Mastery of object permanence	pp. 226–227
	The beginnings of systematic problem solving	pp. 227–228
	The origins of symbolic play	pp. 228–229
	Deferred imitation	pp. 229–230
	Categorizing by conceptual features	pp. 231–232
	The ability to create categories	p. 232
	The ability to use models	p. 232
	The influence of language on thought	pp. 233–234
	Effects of extended separation and isolation	pp. 262–267
	Studies of cognitive continuity between infancy and childhood	pp. 284–285
Early childhood	Preoperational thinking	pp. 338–343
	Egocentrism	pp. 339–341
	Theory of mind	p. 341
	Confusing appearance and reality	pp. 341–343
	Precausal reasoning	p. 343
	Uneven levels of performance	pp. 344–348
	Memory	pp. 351–353
	Mental modules	pp. 354–355
	Role of sociodramatic play	pp. 362–363
	Cognitive basis of empathy	pp. 409–410
Middle childhood	Concrete operations	pp. 477–486
	Logical problem solving	pp. 487–492
	Changes in remembering processes	pp. 483–487
	Learning to read	pp. 509–512
	Learning disabilities	pp. 536–538
	Learning arithmetic	pp. 512–514
	Effects of schooling on cognition	pp. 521–525
	Reasoning about rules and morality	pp. 562–569
	Cultural influences on learning	pp. 540–543
	Aptitude for schooling (intelligence)	pp. 525–526
	Social influences on learning	p. 548
	Ability to play rule-based games	pp. 556–558
	Cognitive importance of peer interactions	pp. 584–585
Adolescence	Formal operations	pp. 646–648, 650–652, 656–657
	Information-processing explanations for adolescent thought	pp. 653–654
	Cultural-context explanations for adolescent thought	pp. 654–658

Glossary

accommodation In Piagetian terms, a modification of a previous schema so that it can be applied to both old and new experiences.

adaptation Piaget's term for the twofold process involving assimilation and accommodation.

adoption study A study in which genetically related individuals who are raised in different family environments are compared to determine the extent to which heredity or environment controls a given trait.

affordances Properties of an object that support, or lend themselves, to particular ways of interacting with that object.

aggression The committing of an act intended to hurt another.

allele An alternate form of a gene coded for a particular trait.

amnion A thin, tough, transparent membrane that holds the amniotic fluid.

anxious/avoidant attachment The attachment pattern in which infants are indifferent to where their mothers are sitting, may or may not cry when their mother leaves, are as likely to be comforted by strangers as by their mothers, and are indifferent when their mother returns to the room.

anxious/resistant attachment The attachment pattern in which infants stay close to their mothers and appear anxious even when their mothers are near. They become very upset when their mothers leave but are not comforted by their return. They simultaneously seek renewed contact with their mothers and resist their efforts to comfort them.

Apgar Scale A quick, simple test used to diagnose the physical state of newborn infants.

apprenticeship A form of activity combining instruction and productive labor that is intermediate between the implicit socialization of family and community life and the explicit instruction of formal education.

assimilation Piaget's term for the process by which various experiences are mentally taken in by the organism and incorporated into existing schemas.

attachment An enduring emotional bond between babies and specific people.

authoritarian parenting pattern A parenting pattern in which the parents try to shape, control, and evaluate the behavior and attitudes of their children according to a set standard. They stress the importance of obedience to authority and favor punitive measures to bring about their children's compliance.

authoritative parenting pattern A parenting pattern in which the parents take it for granted that children also have rights. They attempt to control their children by explaining their rules or decisions and by reasoning with the children. They are willing to consider the child's point of view, even if they do not always accept it. They set high standards for their children's behavior.

autobiographical memory A personal narrative that helps children acquire an enduring sense of themselves.

autonomous morality Morality that is based on an understanding of rules as arbitrary agreements that can be changed if everyone agrees.

axon The main protruding branch of a neuron that carries messages to other cells in the form of electrical impulses.

babbling A form of vocalizing by babies that includes consonant and vowel sounds like those in speech.

baby biography A parent's detailed record of an infant's behavior over an extended period of time.

behavioral geneticist A researcher who studies how genetic and environmental factors combine to produce individual differences in behavior.

bio-social-behavioral shift A transition point in development during which a convergence of biological, social, and behavioral changes converge to cause distinctively new forms of behavior.

biological drives States of arousal, such as hunger or thirst, that urge the organism to obtain the basic prerequisites for its survival.

blastocyst The hollow sphere of cells that results from the differentiation of the morula into the trophoblast and the inner cell mass.

brain stem The base of the brain, which controls such elementary reactions as blinking and sucking, as well as such vital functions as breathing and sleeping.

Brazelton Neonatal Assessment Scale A scale used to assess the newborn's neurological condition.

canalization The process that makes some traits relatively invulnerable to environmental events.

categorizing The process of responding to different things as equivalent because of a similarity between them.

catharsis A general term for the release of fear, tension, or other intense negative emotions.

central conceptual structure The mental equivalent of knowledge common to a broad range of examples within a domain.

cephalocaudal pattern The pattern of development that proceeds from the head down.

cerebral cortex The brain's outermost layer. The networks of neurons in the cerebral cortex integrate information from several sensory sources with memories of past experiences, processing them in a way that results in human forms of thought and action.

child development The sequence of physical, cognitive, and psychological and social changes that children undergo as they grow older.

chorion One of the membranes that develops out of the trophoblast. It forms the fetal component of the placenta.

chromosome A threadlike structure made up of genes. In humans, there are 46 chromosomes in every cell, except sperm and ova.

classical conditioning Learning in which previously existing behaviors come to be elicited by new stimuli.

cleavage The mitotic division of the cells in the zygote.

clinical method A research method in which questions are tailored to the individual, with each question depending on the answer to the preceding one.

clique A group of several young people that remains small enough to enable its members to be in regular interaction with one another and to serve as the primary peer group.

codominance A trait that is determined by two alleles but is different from the trait produced by either of the contributing alleles alone.

coevolution The combined process that emerges from the interaction of biological evolution and cultural evolution.

cognitive processes Psychological processes through which children acquire, store, and use knowledge about the world.

cohort A group of persons born about the same time who are therefore likely to share certain experiences.

cohort sequential design An experimental design in which the longitudinal method is replicated with several cohorts.

collective monologue Exchanges between preschoolers in which their remarks actually focus on what they are doing by themselves, with no real regard for their partner and with no apparent intent to communicate.

commitment The final phase in identity formation during which individuals are committed to the goals, values, beliefs, and future occupation that they have adopted for themselves.

compensation A mental process in which changes in one aspect of a problem are compared with and compensated for by changes in another.

conceptual categorization Categorization based on such features as what things do and how they become the way they are.

conceptual knowledge The ability to understand the principles that underpin a problem.

concrete operations Coordinated mental actions that fit into a logical system in a way that creates greater unity of thinking.

conditional response (CR) In classical conditioning, a response to the conditional stimulus (CS).

conditional stimulus (CS) In classical conditioning, a stimulus that elicits a behavior that is dependent on the way it is paired with the unconditional stimulus.

conscience The facet of the personality that emerges once children have developed generalizable, internalized standards for how to behave.

conservation Piaget's term for the understanding that some properties of an object or substance remain the same even when its appearance is altered in some superficial way.

control group The group in an experiment that is treated as much as possible like the experimental group except that it does not participate in the experimental manipulation.

conversational acts Actions that achieve goals through language.

cooperative principle The conversational maxim to make your contributions to conversation at the required time and for the accepted purpose of the talk exchange.

coregulation A form of indirect social control in which parents and children cooperate to reinforce the children's understandings of right and wrong, what is safe and unsafe, when they are not under direct adult control.

correlation The condition that exists between two factors when changes in one factor are associated with changes in the other.

crisis/exploration A stage in the process of identity formation during which adolescents actively examine their future opportunities in life, reexamine the choices their parents have made, and begin to search for alternatives that they find personally satisfying.

critical period A period during which specific biological or environmental events are required for normal development to occur.

cross-modal perception The understanding that certain features of an object perceived in one sensory mode go together with features perceived in a different sensory mode.

cross-sectional design A research design in which children of various ages are studied at the same time.

crossing over The process in which genetic material is exchanged between chromosomes containing genes for the same characteristic.

crowd A type of peer group. One kind of crowd grows out of preexisting cliques and friendship groups; a second kind, referred to as a *reputation-based collective,* is most likely to be encountered in the high school setting, and its members may or may not be friends.

culture A people's design for living as encoded in their language, and seen in the physical artifacts, beliefs, values, customs, and activities that have been passed down from one generation to the next.

day-care center An organized child-care facility supervised by licensed professionals.

decoding The process of establishing letter-sound correspondences when reading.

deductive reasoning A form of reasoning that moves from a general premise to a specific instance of that premise, followed by a conclusion. If the premises are true, the conclusion must logically follow.

deep structure In Chomskian terms, the basic set of rules of a language from which the actual sentences that people produce are derived.

deferred imitation The ability to imitate an action observed in the past.

dendrite The protruding part of a neuron that receives messages from the axons of other cells.

deoxyribonucleic acid (DNA) A long double-stranded molecule that makes up chromosomes.

developmental niche The physical and social context in which a child lives, including the child-rearing and educational practices of the society and the psychological characteristics of the parents.

developmental stage A qualitatively distinctive, coherent pattern of behavior that emerges during the course of development.

dialogic reading Reading in which the adult listens actively, asking questions, adding information of interest, and prompting children to increase the complexity of their contributions until they are retelling the story in their own way.

disattachment The state of indifference to others that children manifest when there is a continuing separation from their caregiver.

dishabituation The term used to describe the situation in which an infant's interest is renewed after a change in the stimulus.

dizygotic twins Twins that come from two zygotes.

dominance hierarchy A hierarchical social structure in which some members have dominant status and others have subordinate status.

dominant allele The allele that is expressed when an individual possesses two different alleles for the same trait.

ecology The range of situations in which people are actors, the roles they play, the predicaments they encounter, and the consequences of those encounters.

ectoderm Cells of the inner cell mass that develop into the outer surface of the skin, the nails, part of the teeth, the lens of the eye, the inner ear, and the central nervous system.

education A form of socialization in which adults engage in deliberate teaching of the young to ensure that they acquire specialized knowledge and skills.

EEG coherence The synchronization of electrical activity in different areas of the brain.

ego In Freudian theory, this is the mental structure that develops out of the id as the infant is forced by reality to cope with the social world. The ego's primary task is self-preservation, which it accomplishes through voluntary movement, perception, logical thought, adaptation, and problem solving.

egocentrism In Piaget's terms, to "center on oneself," to consider the world entirely in terms of one's own point of view.

elaboration A memory strategy in which children identify or make up connections between two or more things they have to remember.

emotion A feeling state produced by the distinctive physiological responses and cognitive evaluations that motivate action.

empathy The sharing of another's emotions and feelings. Empathy is widely believed to provide the essential foundations for prosocial behavior.

endoderm Cells of the inner cell mass that develop into the digestive system and the lungs.

endogenous The term applied to causes of development that arise as a consequence of the organism's biological heritage.

environment The totality of conditions and circumstances that surround the organism.

environmentalist hypothesis of intelligence The hypothesis that intelligence is both specific and heavily dependent on experience.

epigenesis The process by which new forms emerge through the interactions of the preceding form and its current environment.

equilibration The Piagetian term for the back-and-forth process of the child's seeking a fit between existing schemas and new environmental experiences.

ethnographers Scholars who study the cultural organization of behavior.

ethology An interdisciplinary science that studies the biological and evolutionary foundations of behavior.

eugenics A policy of attempting to rid the gene pool of genes considered undesirable by preventing individuals who have the genes from reproducing, thereby ensuring that these genes are not passed on to the next generation.

exogenous The term applied to causes of development that come from the environment, particularly from the adults who shape children's behavior and beliefs.

experiment In psychology, research in which a change is introduced in a person's experience and the effect of that change is measured.

experimental group The persons in an experiment whose experience is changed as part of the experiment.

explicit modeling The kind of modeling in which adults behave in ways they desire the child to imitate.

extended family A family in which not only parents and their children but other kin–grandparents, cousins, nephews, or more distant family relations–share a household.

exuberant synaptogenesis The rapid growth in synaptic density that occurs between 3 and 12 months of age.

family care Child care provided in someone else's home, that of either a relative or a stranger.

family study A study that compares members of the same family to determine how similar they are on a given trait.

fast mapping The way in which children quickly form an idea of the meaning of an unfamiliar word they hear in a familiar and highly structured social interaction.

fetal alcohol syndrome A syndrome found in babies whose mothers were heavy consumers of alcohol while pregnant. Symptoms include an abnormally small head and underdeveloped brain, eye abnormalities, congenital heart disease, joint anomalies, and malformations of the face.

fetal growth retardation The term for newborns who are especially small for their gestational age.

formal operations In Piaget's terms, a kind of mental operation in which all possible combinations are considered in solving a problem. Consequently, each partial link is grouped in relation to the whole; in other words, reasoning moves continually as a function of a structured whole.

format Recurrent socially patterned activities in which adult and child do things together.

gender schema A mental model containing information about males and females that is used to process gender-relevant information.

gene pool The total genetic information possessed by a sexually reproducing population.

genes The segments on a DNA molecule that act as hereditary blueprints for the organism's development.

genital stage In Freudian theory, the developmental stage during which sexual intercourse becomes a major motive of behavior.

genotype The genetic endowment of an individual.

germ cells The sperm and ova, which are specialized for sexual reproduction and have half the number of chromosomes normal for a species.

germinal period The period from fertilization until implantation of the developing organism in the wall of the uterus.

gestational age The time that has passed between conception and birth. The normal gestational age is between 37 and 43 weeks.

gonads The primary sex organs; the ovaries in females and the testes in males.

grammar The rules of a given language for the sequencing of words in a sentence and the ordering of parts of words.

grammatical morphemes Words and parts of words that create meaning by showing the relations between other elements within the sentence.

guided participation The ways that adults and children collaborate in routine problem-solving activities so that children receive help in adapting their understanding to new situations, in structuring their problem-solving attempts, and eventually in achieving mastery.

habituation The process in which attention to novelty decreases with repeated exposure.

heritability A measure of the degree to which a variation in a particular trait among individuals in a specific population is related to genetic differences among those individuals.

heterochrony Variability in the rates of development of different parts of the organism.

heterogeneity Variability in the levels of development of different parts of the organism at a given time.

heteronomous morality A kind of morality that is based on externally imposed controls.

heterozygous Having inherited two genes of different allelic form for a trait.

holophrase A term for babies' simple-word utterances that some believe stand for entire phrases or sentences.

home care Child care provided in the child's own home, primarily by the father or a grandmother–while the mother is at work.

homozygous Having inherited two genes of the same allelic form for a trait.

horizontal décalage Variations in performance from one version of a problem to another, even though the problems seem to require the same logical operations.

hostile aggression Ordinarily referred to as "bullying," aggression that is aimed at hurting another person as a way of establishing dominance, which may gain the aggressor possessions in the long run.

id In Freudian theory, the mental structure present at birth that is main source of psychological energy. It is unconscious and pleasure-seeking and demands that bodily drives be satisfied.

identification A psychological process in which children try to look, act, feel, and be like significant people in their social environment.

identity A mental operation in which the child realizes that a change limited to outward appearance does not change the substances involved.

identity formation The process of forming a secure sense of self, which, according to Erikson, involves the integration of the individual self and the social self into a single identity.

implantation The process by which the blastocyst becomes attached to the uterus.

independent sense of self A sense of self oriented to being unique, to promoting one's own individual goals, and to expressing one's own thoughts and opinions.

induction A means of promoting children's prosocial behavior in which adults give explanations of what needs to be done and why children should behave in a prosocial manner.

information-processing approach A strategy for explaining cognitive development based on an analogy with the workings of a digital computer.

initiation-reply-feedback sequence An instructional discourse pattern in which the teacher initiates an exchange, usually by asking a question; a student replies; and then the teacher provides feedback.

innatist hypothesis of intelligence The hypothesis that some people are born generally smarter than others and no amount of training or variation in the environment can alter this fact.

inner cell mass The collection of cells inside the blastocyst that eventually becomes the embryo.

instructional discourse A distinctive way of talking and thinking that is typical in school but rarely encountered in everyday interactions in the community or home.

instrumental aggression Aggression that is directed at obtaining something.

instrumental morality In Kohlberg's theory, a form of moral reasoning in which children believe it is perfectly acceptable to use others for one's own interests.

intelligence quotient (IQ) The ratio of mental age to chronological age, calculated as IQ = (MA/CA)100. Calculation of IQ in this fashion ensures that when children are performing precisely as expected for their age, the resulting score will be 100; thus 100 is an "average IQ" by definition.

intentionality The ability to engage in behaviors directed toward achieving a goal.

interdependent sense of self A sense of self to fitting into the group, to promoting the goals of others (that is, of the group), and to developing the ability to "read" the minds of others.

internal working model A mental model that children construct as a result of their experiences with their caregivers that they use to guide their interactions with their caregivers and others.

internalization The process by which external, culturally organized experience becomes transformed into internal psychological processes that, in turn, organize how people behave.

jargoning Babbling with the stress and intonation of actual utterances in the language that the baby will eventually speak.

knowledge base The store of information that children can draw on to deal with a new situation.

language acquisition device (LAD) Chomsky's term for an innate language-processing capacity that is programmed to recognize the universal rules that underlie any particular language that a child might hear.

language acquisition support system (LASS) Bruner's term for the parental behaviors and formatted events within which children acquire language. It is the environmental complement to the innate, biologically constituted LAD.

latency stage In Freudian theory, the period of middle childhood when children's sexual desires are suppressed as a defense against the dangerous feelings they evoke and children display a great interest in learning the skills possessed by adults.

learning A relatively permanent change in behavior brought about by experience of events in the environment or the process by which an organism's behavior is modified as a result of experience.

locomotion The ability to move around on one's own.

long-term memory Memory that is retained over a long period of time.

longitudinal design A research design in which data are gathered from the same group of children as they grow older over an extended period of time.

low birth weight The term for babies weighing 2500 grams or less at birth whether or not they are premature.

maturation A sequence of changes that are strongly influenced by genetic inheritance and that occur as individuals grow older.

meiosis The process that produces sperm and ova, each of which contains only half of the parent cell's original complement of 46 chromosomes.

memory organization A memory strategy in which children mentally group the materials to be remembered in meaningful clusters of closely associated items.

memory span The number of randomly presented items of information that can be repeated immediately after they are presented.

menarche The first menstrual period.

mental age (MA) The measure of intelligence proposed by Binet and Simon to describe the test performance of an average child of a given age.

mental module A highly specific mental faculty that is tuned to particular kinds of environmental input.

mental operations In Piaget's theory, the mental process of combining, separating, or transforming information in a logical manner.

mental perspective taking The ability to think about what goes on in another person's mind and to take their perspective.

mesoderm The cells of the inner cell mass that give rise to the muscles, the bones, and the circulatory system.

metacognition The ability to think about one's own thought processes.

metamemory The ability to think about one's memory processes.

microgenetic method A research method in which children's development is studied intensively over a relatively short period of time.

mitosis The process of cell duplication and division that generates all the individual's cells except sperm and ova.

modularity theory The belief that many cognitive processes consist of separate systems, each with their own properties, that are present at birth and do not need special tutoring in order to develop.

monozygotic twins Twins that come from one zygote and therefore have identical genotypes.

morpheme The smallest unit of meaning in the words of a language.

morula The cluster of cells inside the zona pellucida.

motherese Speech directed to young children that is characterized by a special high-pitched voice, an emphasis on the boundaries between idea-bearing clauses, and a simplified vocabulary.

motivation The ability to try hard and persist at school tasks in the face of difficulties.

mutation An error in the process of gene replication that results in a change in the molecular structure of the DNA.

myelin A sheath of fatty cells that insulates axons and speeds transmission of nerve impulses from one neuron to the next.

naturalistic observation Observation of the actual behavior of people in the course of their everyday lives.

nature The inherited biological predispositions of the individual.

neuron A nerve cell.

neurotransmitter A chemical secreted by the cell sending a message that carries the impulse across the synaptic gap to the receiving cell.

nomination procedure A method of assessing peer preferences in which children are asked to name those they would like to sit near, play with, or work with or to name their friends in the group.

nuclear family A family consisting of a husband, a wife, and their children.

nurture The influence of the social and cultural environment on the individual.

object permanence The understanding that objects have substance, maintain their identities when they change location, and ordinarily continue to exist when out of sight.

objectivity The requirement that scientific knowledge not be distorted by the investigator's preconceptions.

Oedipus complex In Freudian theory, the fear, guilt, and conflict evoked by a little boy's desire to get rid of his father and take the father's place in his mother's affections.

ontogeny The development of an individual organism during its lifetime.

operant conditioning Learning in which changes in behavior are shaped by the consequences of that behavior, thereby giving rise to new and more complex behaviors.

oppositional identity An identity forged by members of racial or ethnic minorities, in which they reject the patterns of dress, speech, mannerisms, and attitudes associated with mainstream white American society.

overextension A term for the error of applying verbal labels too broadly.

peers Others of one's own age and status.

perceptual categorization Categorization based on how things look, feel, sound, and taste.

period of the embryo The period that begins when the organism becomes attached to the uterus and lasts until the end of the eighth week, when the major organs have taken shape.

period of the fetus The period from 9 weeks after conception until birth.

permissive parenting pattern A parenting pattern in which the parents exercise less explicit control over their children's behavior. They give their children a lot of leeway to determine their own schedules and activities, and they often consult them about family policies. They do not demand the same levels of achievement and mature behavior that authoritative and authoritarian parents do.

personality The unique pattern of temperament, emotions, interests, and intellectual abilities that a child develops as the child's innate propensities and capacities are shaped by his or her social interactions with kin and community.

phallic stage In Freudian theory, the period around the fourth year when children begin to regard their own genitals as a major source of pleasure.

phenotype The organism's observable characteristics that result from the interaction of the genotype with the environment.

phonemes The smallest sound categories in human speech that distinguish meanings. Phonemes vary from language to language.

phonemic awareness The ability to "hear phonemes" (for example, to recognize that "balloon," begins with a *b*).

phylogeny The evolutionary history of a species.

placenta An organ made up of tissue from both the mother and the fetus that serves as a barrier and filter between their bloodstreams.

polygenic trait A genetic trait that is determined by the interaction of several genes.

positive justice Moral reasoning about how to divide resources or distribute rewards fairly.

pragmatic uses of language The ability to select words and word orderings that are appropriate to their actions in particular contexts.

precausal thinking Piaget's description of the reasoning of young children that does not follow the procedures of either deductive or inductive reasoning.

preoperational stage According to Piaget, the stage of thinking between infancy and middle childhood in which children are unable to decenter their thinking or to think through the consequences of an action.

preterm The term for babies born before the 37th week of pregnancy.

primacy The idea that children's earliest experiences determine their later development.

primary circular reaction The term Piaget used to describe the infant's tendency to repeat pleasurable bodily actions for their own sake.

primary identification In Freud's terms, the recognition by infants that some objects in the external world are like themselves.

primary intersubjectivity The emotional sharing that occurs between very young infants and their caregivers. It is restricted to face-to-face communication.

primary motor area The area of the brain responsible for nonreflexive, or voluntary, movement.

primary sensory areas The areas of the cerebral cortex responsible for the initial analysis of sensory information.

primary sex organs The organs involved in reproduction.

procedural knowledge The ability to carry out a sequence of actions to solve a problem.

prosocial behaviors Behaviors such as sharing, helping, caregiving, and showing compassion.

prosocial moral reasoning The thinking that is involved in deciding whether to share with, help, or take care of other people when doing so may prove costly to oneself.

prospective study A forward-looking research method in which children are studied as they grow older.

protective factors Environmental and personal factors that are the source of children's resilience in the face of hardship.

proximodistal pattern The pattern of development from the middle of the organism out to the periphery.

puberty The series of biological developments that transforms individuals from a state of physical immaturity to one in which they are biologically mature and capable of sexual reproduction.

range of reaction All the possible phenotypes for a single genotype that are compatible with the continued life of the organism.

rating scale A method of assessing peer preferences in which researchers ask children to rank every other child in the group according to a specific criterion, such as popularity or desirability as a friend or as a teammate in sports.

recapitulate To repeat in condensed form earlier stages of life through which the child has passed.

recessive allele The allele that is not expressed when an individual possesses two different alleles for the same trait.

reciprocal teaching A method of teaching reading in which teachers and children take turns reading text in a manner that integrates decoding and comprehension skills.

recursion The embedding of sentences within each other.

reflex A specific, well-integrated, automatic (involuntary) response to a specific type of stimulation.

rehearsal The process of repeating to oneself the material that one is trying to memorize.

reinforcement A consequence such as a reward that increases the likelihood that a behavior will be repeated.

relational aggression A form of aggression in which harm is done to another child's friendships or a child is excluded from the group.

reliability The scientific requirement that when the same behavior is measured on two or more occasions by the same or different observers, the measurements be consistent with each other.

replicability The scientific requirement that other researchers can use the same procedures as an initial investigator did and obtain the same results.

representative sample A sample of people that reflects all the characteristics of the overall population that the researcher is interested in learning about.

resilience The ability to recover quickly from the adverse effects of early experience or persevere in the face of stress with no apparent special negative psychological consequences.

retrospective study A follow-back research method that starts with developmental outcomes in later childhood and looks back at the individual's early life for predictive signs of those later outcomes.

reversibility A mental operation in which the child realizes that one operation can be negated, or reversed, by the effects of another.

risk factors Personal characteristics or environmental circumstances that increase the probability of negative outcomes for children. Risk is a statistic that applies to groups, not individuals.

schema In Piagetian terms, a mental structure that provides an organism with a model for action in similar or analogous circumstances.

school-cutoff strategy A means of assessing the impact of education while controlling for age by comparing children who are almost the same age but begin schooling a year apart because of school rules that set a specific cutoff date for starting school.

schooling A form of education that is characterized by special forms of motivation, social relations, social organization, and communication using written language.

scientific hypothesis An assumption that is precise enough to be tested and can be shown to be incorrect.

scripts Event schemas that specify who participates in an event, what social roles they play, what objects they are to use during the event, and the sequence of actions that make up the event.

secondary circular reactions The behavior characteristic of the third substage of Piaget's sensorimotor stage in which babies repeat actions to produce interesting changes in their environment.

secondary emotions Emotions such as embarrassment, pride, shame, guilt, and envy that depend on children's ability to recognize, talk about, and think about themselves in relation to others.

secondary identification In Freudian terms, the effort of a child to take on the qualities and copy the behavior of a person with whom he or she identifies.

secondary intersubjectivity The sharing between infants and their caregivers of understandings and emotions that refer beyond themselves to objects and other people.

secondary sex characteristics The anatomical and physiological signs that outwardly distinguish males from females; they appear at the same time that the primary sex organs are maturing.

secure attachment A pattern of attachment in which children play comfortably and react positively to a stranger as long as their mothers are present. They become upset when their mothers leave and are unlikely to be consoled by a stranger, but they calm down as soon as their mothers reappear.

secure base Bowlby's term for the people whose presence provides the child with the security that allows him or her to make exploratory excursions.

self-concept The way in which children come to conceive of themselves in relation to other people.

self-control The capacity of children to act in accordance with the expectations of their caregivers, even when they do not want to and are not being directly monitored.

self-esteem One's evaluation of one's own self-worth.

self-report A method of gathering data in which people report on their own psychological states and behavior.

semenarche The first ejaculation. It often occurs spontaneously during sleep and is called a nocturnal emission.

sensitive period An optimal time for certain developments to occur because environmental events are most effective for fostering their development at that time.

sensorimotor stage Piaget's term for the stage of infancy during which the process of adaptation consists largely of coordinating sensory perceptions and simple motor behaviors to acquire knowledge of the world.

sensory register That part of the information-processing system that stores incoming information for a fraction of a second before it is selectively processed.

separation anxiety The distress that babies show when the person to whom they are attached leaves.

sex-linked characteristics Traits determined by genes that are found on only the X or the Y chromosome.

sexual orientation Refers to the sex toward which one has erotic feelings.

short-term (working) memory That part of the information-processing system that holds incoming sensory information until it is taken up into long-term memory or forgotten.

skeletal principles Domain-specific principles that get particular cognitive processes started and provide some initial direction, but require subsequent experience in order to realize their potential.

social comparison The process of defining oneself in relation to one's peers.

social competence The set of skills that collectively result in successful social functioning with peers.

social development A two-sided process in which children simultaneously become integrated into the larger social community and differentiated as distinctive individuals.

social perspective taking The ability to adopt another person's perspective in the social realm.

social referencing Babies' tendency to look at their caregivers for some indication of how they should feel and act when they encounter something unfamiliar.

social repair mechanisms Strategies that allow friends to remain friends even when serious differences temporarily drive them apart.

social roles The social categories such as son, daughter, and student that specify a person's relations to the social group and the person's rights, duties, and obligations in that role.

socialization The process by which children acquire the standards, values, and knowledge of their society.

sociodramatic play Make-believe play in which two or more participants enact a variety of social roles.

socioemotional competence The ability to behave appropriately in social situations that evoke strong emotions.

sociogram A graphic representation of how each child feels about every other child in a group.

somatic (body) cells All the cells in the body except for the germ cells (ova and sperm).

specific learning disabilities A term used to refer to the academic difficulties of children who fare poorly in school despite having normal intelligence.

spinal cord The part of the central nervous system that extends from the waist to the base of the brain.

strange situation A procedure designed to assess children's attachment on the basis of their responses to a stranger when they are with their mothers, when they are left alone, and when they are reunited with their mothers.

strategy A deliberate, controllable cognitive operation performed for the purpose of attaining a particular goal.

structured whole A system of relationships that can be logically described and thought about.

superego In Freudian terms, the conscience. It represents the authority of the social group and sits in stern judgment of the ego's efforts to hold the id in check. It becomes a major force in the personality in middle childhood.

surface structure In Chomskian terms, the actual sentences that people produce.

symbolic play (pretend, fantasy play) Play in which one object stands for, or represents, another.

symbolic thought (representation) The mental ability to have one thing represent, or stand for, another.

synapse The tiny gap between axons and dendrites.

temperament The term for the individual modes of responding to the environment that appear to be consistent across situations and stable over time. Typically included under the rubric of temperament are such characteristics as children's activity level, their intensity of reaction, the ease with which they become upset, their characteristic responses to novelty, and their sociability.

teratogens Environmental agents that cause deviations from normal development and lead to abnormalities or death.

tertiary circular reactions The fifth stage of sensorimotor period, which is characterized by the deliberate variation of action sequences to solve problems and explore the world.

theory A broad framework or set of principles that can be used to guide the collection and interpretation of a set of facts.

theory of mind The ability to think about other people's mental states and form theories of how they think.

transactional models Models of development that trace the ways in which the characteristics of the child and the characteristics of the child's environment interact across time ("transact") to determine developmental outcomes.

trophoblast The outer layer of cells of the blastocyst that develop into the membranes that protect and support the embryo.

twin study A study in which groups of monozygotic (identical) and dizygotic (fraternal) twins of the same sex are compared with each other and to other family members for similarity on a given trait.

umbilical cord A soft tube containing blood vessels that connects the developing organism to the placenta.

unconditional response (UCR) In classical conditioning, the response, such as salivation, that is invariantly elicited by the unconditional stimulus (UCS).

unconditional stimulus (UCS) In classical conditioning, the stimulus, such as food in the mouth, that invariably causes the unconditional response (UCR).

underextension A term used for applying verbal labels in a narrower way than adults do.

utilization knowledge The ability to know when to apply particular problem-solving procedures.

validity The scientific requirement that data being collected actually reflect the phenomenon being studied.

X and Y chromosomes The two chromosomes that determine the sex of the individual. Normal females have two X chromosomes, while normal males have one Y chromosome inherited from their fathers and one X chromosome inherited from their mothers.

zona pellucida The thin envelope that surrounds the zygote and later the morula.

zone of proximal development The gap between what children can accomplish independently and what they can accomplish when they are interacting with others who are more competent.

zygote The single cell formed at conception from the union of the sperm and the ovum.

References

Abbott, S. (1992). Holding on and pushing away: Comparative perspectives on an Eastern Kentucky child rearing practice. *Ethos, 20*, 33–65.

Abell, S. C., & Richards, M. H. (1996). The relationship between body shape satisfaction and self-esteem: An investigation of gender and class differences. *Journal of Youth & Adolescence, 25*(5), 691–703.

Aber, J. L., Brooks-Gunn, J., & Maynard, R. A. (1995). Effects of welfare reform on teenage parents and their children. *Future of Children, 5*(2), 53–71.

Abramovitch, R., Pepler, D., & Corter, C. (1982). Patterns of sibling interaction among pre-school-aged children. In M. Lamb & B. Sutton-Smith (Eds.), *Sibling relationships: Their nature and significance across the lifespan.* Hillsdale, NJ: Erlbaum.

Abramovitch, R., Corter, C., Pepler, D., & Stanhope, L. (1986). Sibling and peer interaction: A final follow up and comparison. *Child Development, 57*, 217–229.

Abrams, R. M., Gerhardt, K. J., & Peters, A. J. M. (1995). Transmission of sound and vibration to the fetus. In J. P. Lecanuet, W. P. Fifer, N. A. Krasnegor, & W. P. Smotherman (Eds.), *Fetal development: A psychobiological perspective* (pp. 315–330). Hillsdale, NJ: Erlbaum.

Abrams, S. M., Field, T., Scafidi, F., & Prodromidis, M. (1995). Newborns of depressed mothers. *Infant Mental Health Journal, 16*(3), 223–239.

Abravanel, E., Levan-Goldschmidt, E., & Stevenson, M. B. (1976). Action imitation: The early phase of infancy. *Child Development, 47*, 1032–1044.

Abravanel, E., & Sigafoos, A. D. (1984). Exploring the presence of imitation during early infancy. *Child Development, 55*, 381–392.

Adair, L. S. (1987). *Nutrition in the reproductive years.* New York: Alan R. Liss.

Adams, G. R., & Roopnarine, J. L. (1994). Physical attractiveness, social skills, and same-sex peer popularity. *Journal of Group Psychotherapy, Psychodrama & Sociometry, 47*(1), 15–35.

Adams, M. J. (1990). *Learning to read: Thinking and learning about print.* Cambridge, MA: MIT Press.

Adams, M. J., Treiman, R., & Pressley, M. (1998). Reading, writing, and literacy. In W. Damon, I. E. Sigel & K. A. Renninger (Eds.), *Handbook of child psychology* (5th ed.)*: Vol. 4: Child psychology in practice* (pp. 275–355). New York: Wiley.

Adamson, L. B. (1995). *Communication development during infancy.* Madison, WI: Brown & Benchmarks.

Adelson, J. (1986). *Inventing adolescence : The political psychology of everyday schooling.* New Brunswick, NJ: Transaction Books.

Adelson, J. (1991). Political development. In R. Lerner, A. C. Petersen, & J. Brooks-Gunn (Eds.), *Encyclopedia of adolescence.* New York: Garland Publishers.

Adelson, J., Green, B., & O'Neil, R. P. (1969). Growth of the idea of law in adolescence. *Developmental Psychology, 1*, 327–332.

Adler, P. A., Kless, S. J., & Adler, P. (1992). Socialization to gender roles: Popularity among elementary school boys and girls. *Sociology of Education, 65*, 169–187.

Adolph, K. (1997). Learning in the development of infant locomotion. *Monographs of the Society for Research in Child Development, 62*(3), 1–140.

Adolph, K. E., Eppler, M. A., & Gibson, E. J. (1993). Crawling versus walking infants: Perceptions of affordances for locomotion over sloping surfaces. *Child Development, 64*, 1158–1174.

Adolph, K. E., Vereijken, B., & Denny, M. A. (1998). Learning to crawl. *Child Development, 69*(5), 1299–1312.

Ahadi, S. A., & Rothbart, M. K. (1993). Children's temperament in the US and China: similarities and differences. *European Journal of Personality, 7*, 359–377.

Ainsworth, M. D. S. (1967). *Infancy in Uganda: Infant care and the growth of love.* Baltimore, MD: Johns Hopkins University Press.

Ainsworth, M. D. S. (1982). Attachment: Retrospect and prospect. In C. M. Parkes & J. Stevenson-Hinde (Eds.), *The place of attachment in human behavior.* New York: Basic Books.

Ainsworth, M. D. S. (1993). Attachment as related to the mother-infant interaction. In C. Rovee-Collier & L. P. Lipsett (Eds.), *Advances in infancy research* (Vol. 8). Norwood, NJ: Ablex.

Ainsworth, M. D. S., & Bell, S. M. (1969). Some contemporary patterns of mother-infant interaction in the feeding situation. In A. Ambrose (Ed.), *Stimulation in early infancy.* New York: Academic Press.

Ainsworth, M. D. S., & Wittig, B. A. (1969). Attachment and exploratory behavior of one-year-olds in a strange situation. In B. M. Foss (Ed.), *Determinants of infant behavior* (Vol. 4). London: Methuen.

Ainsworth, M. D. S., Bell, S. M., & Stayton, D. J. (1971). Individual differences in strange-situation behavior of one-year-olds. In H. R. Schaffer (Ed.), *The origins of human social relations.* New York: Academic Press.

Ainsworth, M. D. S., Blehar, M. C., Waters, E., & Wall, S. (1978). *Patterns of attachment: A psychological study of the strange situation.* Hillsdale, NJ: Erlbaum.

Akers, J. F., Jones, R. M., & Coyl, D. D. (1998). Adolescent friendship pairs: Similarities in identity status development, behaviors, attitudes, and intentions. *Journal of Adolescent Research, 13*(2), 178–201.

Aldrich, C. A., & Hewitt, E. S. (1947). A self-regulating feeding program for infants. *Journal of the American Medical Association, 35*, 341.

Alan Guttmacher Institute (1994). *Sex and America's teenagers.* New York.

Alan Guttmacher Institute. (1999). *Teen sex and pregnancy.* Facts in brief. Available: http://www.agi-usa.org/pubs/fb_teen_sex.html.

Allen, K. E., Turner, K. D., & Everett, P. M. (1970). A behavior modification classroom for Head Start children with problem behavior. *Exceptional Children, 37*, 119–127.

Allesandri, S. M., Sullivan, M. W., Imaizumi, S., & Lewis, M. (1993). Learning and emotional responsivity and cocaine-exposed infants. *Developmental Psychology, 29*, 989–997.

Allport, G. (1937). *Personality: A psychological interpretation.* New York: Holt, Rinehart and Winston.

Alsaker, F. D. (1996). Annotation: The impact of puberty. *Journal of Child Psychology and Psychiatry and Allied Disciplines, 37*(3), 249–258.

Alsaker, F. D., & Flammer, A. (1999). *The adolescent experience: European and American adolescents in the 1990s.* Mahwah, NJ: Erlbaum.

Amato, P. R., & Keith, B. (1991). Parental divorce and the well-being of children: A meta-analysis. *Psychological Bulletin, 110*, 26–46.

American Association of Childhood and Adolescent Psychiatry. (2000). Children and TV Violence. Available: http://www.parenthoodweb.com/articles/phw247.htm.

Ampofo-Boateng, K., Thornson, J. A., Grieve, R., Pitcairn, T., Lee, D. N., & Demetre, J. D. (1993). A developmental training study of children's ability to find safe routes to cross the road. *British Journal of Developmental Psychology, 11*, 31–45.

Anderson, R. E., & Ronnkvist, A. (1999). *Teaching, learning, and computing: 1998 National Survey* (2). Irvine, CA: University of California, Irvine: Center for Research on Information Technology and Organizations.

Anglin, J. M. (1977). *Word, object, and conceptual development.* New York: W. W. Norton.

Anglin, J. M. (1985). The child's expressible knowledge of word concepts: What preschoolers can say about the meanings of some nouns and verbs. In K. E. Nelson (Ed.), *Children's language* (Vol. 5). Hillsdale, NJ: Erlbaum.

Anglin, J. (1993). Vocabulary development: A morphological analysis. *Monographs of the Society for Research in Child Development, 58* (10, Serial No. 238).

Annis, R. C., & Corenblum, B. (1987). Effect of test language and experimenter race on Canadian Indian children's racial and self-identity. *Journal of Social Psychology, 126*, 761–773.

Antonov, A. N. (1947). Children born during the siege of Leningrad in 1942. *Journal of Pediatrics, 30*, 250.

Apfel, R. J., & Bennett, S. (Eds.). (1996). *Mind fields in their hearts: The mental health of children in war and communal violence.* New Haven: Yale University Press.

Apgar, V. (1953). A proposal for a new method of evaluation of the newborn infant. *Current Researches in Anesthesia and Analigesics, 32*, 260–267.

Archer, S. L. (1985). Identity and the choice of social roles. In A. S. Waterman (Ed.), *Identity in adolescence: Processes and contents (New directions for child development, No. 30).* San Francisco: Jossey-Bass.

Archer, J. (1992). Childhood gender roles: Social context and organisation. In H. McGurk (Ed.), *Childhood social development: Contemporary perspectives* (pp. 31–61). Hove, England: Erlbaum.

Arey, L. B. (1974). *Developmental anatomy: A textbook and laboratory manual of embryology*, 7th ed. Philadelphia: Saunders.

Arias-Camison, J. M., Lau, J., Cole, C. H., & Frantz, I. D. (1999). Meta-analysis of dexamethasone therapy started in the first 15 days of life for prevention of chronic lung disease in premature infants. *Pediatric Pulmonology, 28*(3), 167–174.

Arnett, J. J. (1996). Sensation seeking, aggressiveness, and adolescent reckless behavior. *Personality and Individual Differences, 20*(6), 693–702.

Arnett, J. J. (1999). Adolescent storm and stress. *American Psychologist, 54*(5), 317–326.

Ashem, B., & Janes, M. D. (1978). Deleterious effects of chronic undernutrition on cognitive abilities. *Journal of Child Psychology and Psychiatry and Allied Disciplines, 19*(1), 23–31.

Asher, S. R., & Coie, J. D. (Eds.). (1990). *Peer rejection in childhood.* New York: Cambridge University Press.

Asher, S. R., Parkhurst, J. T., Hymel, S., & Williams, G. (1990). Peer rejection and loneliness in childhood. In S. R. Asher & J. D. Cole (Eds.), *Peer rejection in childhood.* New York: Cambridge University Press.

Aslin, R. N., Jusczyk, P.W., & Pisoni. (1998). Speech and auditory processing during infancy: Constraints on and precursors to langauge. In W. Damon, D. Kuhn, & R. Siegler (Eds.), *Handbook of child psychology* (5th ed.), *Vol. 2: Cognition, perception, and language.* New York: Wiley.

Aspendorf, J. B., & Valsiner, J. (1992). *Stability and change in development.* Newbury Park: Sage.

Astington, J. W. (1993). *The child's discovery of the mind.* Cambridge, MA: Harvard University Press.

Atkinson, C. C. (1997). Another baby walker injury. *Journal of Emergency Nursing, 23*(4), 302–325.

Atkinson, J. (1998). The "where and what" or '"who and how" of visual development. In F. Simion & G. Butterworth (Eds.), *The development of sensory, motor and cognitive capacities in early infancy: From perception to cognition.* Hove, England: Psychology Press/Erlbaum.

Atkinson, R. C., & Shiffrin, R. M. (1968). Human memory: A proposed system and its control processes. In K. W. Spence & J. T. Spence (Eds.), *The psychology of learning and motivation: Advances in research and theory* (Vol. 2). Orlando, FL: Academic Press.

Atran, S. (1998). Folk biology and the anthropology of science: Cognitive universals and cultural particulars. *Behavioral & Brain Sciences, 21*(4), 547–609.

Au, K. H., & Mason, J. (1981). Social organizational factors in learning to read: The balance of rights hypothesis. *Reading Research Quarterly, 17*(1), 115–152.

Augusta, D., & Hakuta, K. (1998). *Educating language-minority children.* Washington, D.C: National Academy Press.

Augustine, St. (1961). *Confessions ; translated with an introduction by R.S.* New York: Pine-Coffin.

Azmitia, M., & Hesser, J. (1993). Why siblings are important agents of cognitive development: A comparison of siblings and peers. *Child Development, 64*, 430–444.

Bachman, J. G., & Schulenberg, J. (1993). How part-time work intensity relates to drug use, problem behavior, time use, and satisfaction among high school seniors: Are there consequences or merely correlates? *Developmental Psychology, 29*, 220–235.

Bailey, J. M. (1996). Gender identity. In R. C. Savin-Williams & K. M. Cohen (Eds.), *The lives of lesbians, gays, and bisexuals: Children to adults.* (pp. 71–93). Ft. Worth, TX,: Harcourt Brace College Publishers.

Bailey, J. M., & Bell, A. P. (1993). Familiality of female and male homosexuality. *Behavioral Genetics, 23*, 313–322.

Bailey, J. M., & Zucker, K. J. (1995). Childhood sex-typed behavior and sexual orientation: A conceptual analysis and quantitative review. *Developmental Psychology, 31*(1), 43–55.

Bailey, J. M., Pillard, R. C., Dawood, K., Miller, M. B., Farrer, L. A., Trivedi, S., & Murphy, R. L. (1999). A family history study of male sexual orientation using three independent samples. *Behavior Genetics., 29*(2), 79–86.

Baillargeon, R. (1984). Object permanence in 36- and 48-month old infants. *Developmental Psychology, 23*, 655–664.

Baillargeon, R. (1993). The object concept revisited: New direction in the investigation of infants' physical knowledge. In C. Granrud (Ed.), *Visual perception and cognition in infancy. Carnegie Mellon symposia on cognition.* Hillsdale, NJ: Erlbaum.

Baillargeon, R. (1998). Infants' understanding of the physical world. In M. Sabourin & F. Craik (Eds.), *Advances in psychological science, Vol 2: Biological and cognitive aspects* (pp. 503–529). Hove, England: Taylor & Francis.

Baillargeon, R., Spelke, E., & Wasserman, S. (1985). Object permanence in five-month-old infants. *Cognition, 20*, 191–208.

Baker, M. (1993). Long term love: Discover the magic. *Parents, 73*, 89–91.

Baker-Ward, L., Gordon, B. N., Ornstein, P. A., Larus, D. M., & Clubb, P. A. (1993). Young children's long-term retention of a pediatric examination. *Child Development, 64*, 1519–1533.

Baldwin, J. M. (1902). *Social and ethical interpretations in mental development* (3rd ed.). New York: Macmillan.

Bandura, A. (1965). Influence of models' reinforcement contingencies on the acquisition of imitative responses. *Journal of Personality and Social Psychology, 1*, 587–595.

Bandura, A. (1969). Social-learning theory of identificatory processes. In D. A. Goslin (Ed.), *Handbook of socialization theory and research.* Chicago: Rand McNally.

Bandura, A. (1973). *Aggression: A social learning analysis.* Englewood Cliffs, NJ: Prentice-Hall.

Bandura, A. (1977). *Social learning theory.* Englewood Cliffs, NJ: Prentice-Hall.

Bandura, A. (1986). *Social foundations of thought and action: A social cognitive theory.* Englewood Cliffs, NJ: Prentice-Hall.

Bandura, A., Ross, D., & Ross, S. A. (1963). Imitation of film-mediated aggressive models. *Journal of Abnormal and Social Psychology, 66,* 3–11.

Barcus, F. E. (1986). The nature of television advertising to children. In E. L. Palmer & A. Dorr (Eds.), *Children and the faces of television* (pp. 273–285). New York: Academic Press.

Bargelow, P., Vaughn, B. E., & Molitor, N. (1987). Effects of maternal absence due to employment on the quality of infant-mother attachment in a low-risk sample. *Child Development, 58,* 945–953.

Barker, D. J. P. (1995). The Wellcome Foundation Lecture, 1994. The fetal origins of adult disease. *Proceedings of the Royal Society of London. Series B: Biological Sciences,, 262,* 37–43.

Barker, R. G., & Wright, H. F. (1951). *One boy's day: A specimen record of behavior.* New York: Harper Brothers.

Barker, R. G., & Wright, H.F. (1955). *One boy's day: A specimen record of behavior.* New York: Harper Brothers.

Barnett, D., Manly, J. T., & Cicchetti, D. (1993). Defining child maltreatment. In D. Cicchetti & S. L. Toth (Eds.), *Child abuse, child development, and social policy: Advances in applied developmental psychology* (Vol. 8). Norwood, NJ: Ablex.

Barnett, O. W., Miller-Perrin, C. L., & Perrin, R. D. (1997). Physical child abuse. In O. W. Barnett (Ed.), *Family violence across the lifespan: An introduction.* (pp. 39–67). Thousand Oaks, CA,: Sage.

Barnett, W. S. (1995). Long-term effects of early childhood programs on cognitive and school outcomes. *The Future of Children, 5*(3), 25–50.

Barr, R., Dowden, A., & Hayne, H. (1996). Developmental changes in deferred imitation by 6– 24-month-old infants. *Infant Behavior and Development, 19*(2), 159–170.

Barr, R. G. (1990). The normal crying curve: what do we really know? *Developmental Medicine and Child Neurology, 32,* 356–362.

Barrett, K. C. (1995). A functionalist approach to shame and guilt. In J. P. Tangney & K. W. Fischer (Eds.), *Self-conscious emotions: The psychology of shame, guilt, embarrassment, and pride.* New York: Guilford Press.

Barrett, M. (1995). Early lexical development. In P. Fletcher & B. McWhinney (Eds.), *The handbook of child language* (pp. 362–392). Cambridge, MA.: Blackwells.

Barth, R. P. (1998). Abusive and neglecting parents and the care of their children. In M. A. Mason & A. Skolnick (Eds.), *All our families: New policies for a new century* (pp. 217–235). New York: Oxford University Press.

Bartlett, E. (1977). The acquisition of the meaning of color terms. In P. T. Smith & R. N. Campbell (Eds.), *Proceedings of the Sterling Conference on the psychology of language.* New York: Plenum Press.

Bates, E. (1976). *Language and context: The acquisition of pragmatics.* New York: Academic Press.

Bates, E. (1999). On the nature and nurture of language. In E. Bizzi & P. Calissano & V. Volterra (Eds.), *Frontiere della biologia [Frontiers of biology].* Rome: Giovanni Trecanni.

Bates, E., & Goodman, J. (1999). On the emergence of grammar from the lexicon. In B. MacWhinney (Ed.), *The emergence of language.* Mahwah, NJ: Erlbaum.

Bates, E., Camaioni, L., & Volterra, V. (1975). The acquisition of performatives prior to speech. *Merrill Palmer Quarterly, 21,* 205–226.

Bates, E., Benigni, L., Bretherton, I., Camaioni, L., & Volterra, V. (1979). *The emergence of symbols: Cognition and communication in infancy.* New York: Academic Press.

Bates, E., O'Connell, B., & Shore, C. (1987). Language and communication. In J. D. Osofsky (Ed.), *Handbook of infant development* (2nd ed.). New York: Wiley.

Bates, J. E., Maslin, C. A., & Frankel, K. A. (1985). Attachment, security, and temperament as predictors of behavior: Problem ratings at three years. *Monographs of the Society for Research in Child Development, 50* (Serial No. 209).

Bates, J. E., Marvinncy, D., Kelly, T., Dodge, K. A., Bennett, D. S., & Pettit, G. S. (1994). Childcare history and kindergarten adjustment. *Developmental Psychology, 30,* 690–700.

Baumrind, D. (1971). Current patterns of parental authority. *Developmental Psychology Monographs, 4 (1, Part 2).*

Baumrind, D. (1980). New directions in socialization research. *American Psychologist, 35,* 639–652.

Beal, C. R. (1994). *Boys and girls: The development of gender roles.* New York, NY: McGraw Hill.

Beeghly, M., Brazelton, T. B., Flannery, K. A., Nugent, J. K., Barrett, D. E., & Tronick, E. Z. (1995). Specificity of Preventative Pediatric Intervention Effects in Early Infancy. *Developmental and Behavioral Pediatrics, 16*(3), 158–166.

Behl-Chadha, G., & Eimas, P. D. (1995). Infant categorization of left-right spatial relations. *British Journal of Developmental Psychology, 13*(1), 69–79.

Bell, A. P., Weinberg, M. S., & Hammersmith, S. K. (1981). *Sexual preference: Its development in men and women.* Bloomington, IN: Indiana University Press.

Bell, M. A., & Fox, N. A. (1997). Individual differences in object permanence performance at 8 months: Locomotor experience and brain electrical activity. *Developmental Psychobiology, 31*(4), 287–297.

Bellugi, U., Lichtenberg, L., Mills, D., & Galaburda, A. (1999). Bridging cognition, the brain, and molecular genetics: Evidence from Williams syndrome. *Trends in Neurosciences, 22*(5), 197–207.

Belsky, J. (1986). Infant day care: A cause for concern? *Zero to Three, 7*(1), 1–7.

Belsky, J. (1993). Etiology of child maltreatment: A developmental-ecological analysis. *Psychological Bulletin, 114,* 413–434.

Belsky, J. (1996). Parent, infant, and social-contextual antecedents of father-son attachment security. *Developmental Psychology, 32*(5), 905–913.

Belsky, J., & Isabella, R. (1988). Maternal, infant, and social-contextual determinants of attachment security. In J. Belsky & T. Nezworski (Eds.), *Clinical implications of attachment* (pp. 41–94). Hillsdale, NJ: Erlbaum.

Belsky, J., Steinberg, L. D., & Walker, A. (1982). The ecology of day care. In M. E. Lamb (Ed.), *Nontraditional families: Parenting and child development.* Hillsdale, NJ: Erlbaum.

Belsky, J., Gilstrap, B., & Rovine, M. (1984). The Pennsylvania infant and family development project: I. Stability and change in mother-infant and father-infant interaction in a family setting at one, three, and nine months. *Child Development, 55*(3), 692–705.

Belsky, J., Woodworth, S., & Crnic, K. (1996). Trouble in the second year: Three questions about family interaction. *Child Development, 67*(2), 556–578.

Bem, D. J. (1996). Exotic becomes erotic: A developmental theory of sexual orientation. *Psychological Review., 103*(2), 320–335.

Bem, S. L. (1989). Genital knowledge and gender constancy in preschool children. *Child Development, 60,* 649–662.

Bemak, F., & Young, M. E. (1998). Role of catharsis in group psychotherapy. *International Journal of Action Methods, 50*(4), 166–184.

Bendersky, M., & Lewis, M. (1998). Arousal modulation in cocaine-exposed infants. *Developmental Psychology, 1998*(34), 3.

Berg, W. K., & Berg, K. M. (1987). Psychophysiological development in infancy: State, startle, and attention. In J. D. Osofsky (Ed.), *Handbook of infant development* (2nd ed.). New York: Wiley.

Berger, B. M. (1981). *The survival of a counterculture: Ideological work and everyday life among rural communards.* Berkeley: University of California Press.

Berk, L. B., & Friman, P. C. (1990). Epidemiologic aspects of toilet training. *Clinical Pediatrics, 29,* 278–282.

Bernal, J. F. (1972). Crying during the first few days and maternal responses. *Developmental Medicine and Child Neurology, 14,* 362–372.

Berndt, T. J. (1979). Developmental changes in conformity to peers and parents. *Developmental Psychology, 15,* 608–616.

Berndt, T. J. (1986). Children's comments about their friendships. In M. Perlmutter (Ed.), *Minnesota symposia on child psychology* (Vol. 18: Cognitive perspectives on children's social and behavioral development). Hillsdale, NJ: Erlbaum.

Berndt, T. J. (1988). The nature and significance of children's friendships. In R. Vasta (Ed.), *Annals of Child Development* (Vol. 5). Greenwich, CT: JAI Press.

Berndt, T. J., & Savin-Williams, R. C. (1993). Peer relations and friendships. In P. H. Tolan & B. J. Cohler (Eds.), *Handbook of clinical research and practice with adolescents.* New York: Wiley.

Berndt, T. J., & Keefe, K. (1995). Friend's influence on adolescent's adjustment in school. *Child Development, 66*, 1312–1329.

Berry, J. W. (1976). *Human ecology and cultural style.* New York: Sage-Halstead.

Bersoff, D. M., & Miller, J. G. (1993). Culture, context, and the development of moral accountability judgments. *Developmental Psychology, 29*(4), 664–676.

Bertenthal, B. I., & Fischer, K. W. (1978). Development of self-recognition in the infant. *Developmental Psychology, 14*, 44–50.

Bertenthal, B. I., Campos, J. J., & Barrett, K. C. (1984). Self-produced locomotions: An organizer of emotional, cognitive, and social development in infancy. In R. Emde & R. Harmon (Eds.), *Continuities and discontinuities in development.* New York: Plenum Press.

Best, D. L., & Williams, J. E. (1997). Sex, gender, and culture. In M. H. Segall, J.W. Berry, & C. Kagitçibasi (Eds.), *Handbook of cross-cultural psychology, Vol. 3: Social and behavioral application* (pp. 163–212). Boston: Allyn & Bacon.

Bettelheim, B. (1977). *The uses of enchantment: The meaning and importance of fairytales.* New York: Vintage Books.

Beuf, A. H. (1977). *Red children in white America.* Philadelphia: University of Pennsylvania Press.

Biederman, J., Rosenbaum, J. F., Chaloff, J., & Kagan, J. (1995). Behavioral inhibition as a risk factor for anxiety disorders. In J. S. March (Ed.), *Anxiety disorders in children and adolescents.* New York: Guilford Press.

Bierman, K. L., Smoot, D. L., & Aumiller, K. (1993). Characteristics of aggressive-rejected, aggressive (nonrejected), and rejected (nonaggressive) boys. *Child Development, 64*, 139–151.

Bigelow, B. J., & Lagaipa, J. J. (1975). Children's written descriptions of friendship: A multi-dimensional analysis. *Developmental Psychology, 41*, 857–858.

Bijou, S. W., & Baer, D. M. (1966). *Child development: Vol. 2. The universal stage of infancy.* New York: Appleton-Century-Crofts.

Binet, A., & Simon, T. (1916). *The development of intelligence in children.* Vineland, NJ: Publications of the Training School at Vineland (reprinted by Williams Publishing Co., Nashville, TN, 1980.).

Birnstiel, M. L. (1996). Gene therapy. *European Review, 4*, 335-336.

Bisanz, J., & Lefevre, J. (1990). Mathematical cognition: Strategic processing as interactions among sources of knowledge. In D. P. Bjorkland (Ed.), *Children's strategies: Contemporary views of cognitive development.* Hillsdale, NJ: Erlbaum.

Bisanz, J., Morrison, F. J., & Dunn, M. (1995). Effects of age and schooling on the acquisition of elementary cognitive skills. *Developmental Psychology, 31*, 221–236.

Bjorklund, D. F., & Miller, P. H. (1997). New themes in strategy development. *Developmental Review, 17*(4), 407–410.

Bjorklund, D. F., Schneider, W., Cassel, W. S., & Ashley, E. (1994). Training and extension of a memory strategy: Evidence for utilization deficiencies in the acquisition of an organizational strategies in high- and low-IQ children. *Child Development, 65*, 951–965.

Blachman, B. A. (1987). An alternative classroom reading program for learning disabled and their low-achieving children. In W. Ellis (Ed.), *Intimacy with language: A forgotten basic in teacher education.* Baltimore: Orton Dyslexia Society.

Blake, J., & De Boysson-Bardies, B. (1992). Patterns in babbling: A cross-linguistic study. *Journal of Child Language, 19*, 51–74.

Blakemore, C., & Mitchell, D. E. (1973). Environmental modification of the visual cortex and the neural basis of learning and memory. *Nature, 241*, 467–468.

Blass, E. M., & Smith, B. A. (1992). Differential effects of sucrose, fructose, glucose, and lactose on crying in 1- to 3-day-old human infants: Qualitative and quantitative considerations. *Developmental Psychology, 28*, 804–810.

Blass, E. M. (1997). Infant formula quiets crying human newborns. *Journal of Developmental and Behavioral Pediatrics, 18*(3), 162–165.

Blass, E. M., Ganchrow, J. R., & Steiner, J. E. (1984). Classical conditioning in newborn humans 2–48 hours of age. *Infant Behavior and Development, 7*, 223–235.

Bleichfeld, B., & Moely, B. (1984). Psychophysiological response to an infant cry: Comparison of groups of women in different phases of the maternal cycle. *Developmental Psychology, 20*, 1082–1091.

Block, J. H., Block, J., & Morrison, A. (1981). Parental agreement-disagreement on child-rearing orientations and gender-related personality correlates in children. *Child Development, 52, 965–974.*

Block, J. H., Block, J., & Gjerde, P. (1986). The personality of children prior to divorce: A prospective study. *Child Development, 57*, 827–840.

Bloom, L. (1973). *One word at a time: The use of single word utterances before syntax.* The Hauge: Mouton.

Bloom, L. (1993). *The transition from infancy to language: Acquiring the power of expression.* Cambridge: Cambridge University Press.

Bloom, L., Lifter, K., & Broughten, J. (1985). The convergence of early cognition and language in the second year of life: Problems in conceptualization and measurement. In M. Barrett (Ed.), *Children's single word speech.* New York: Wiley.

Bloom, P. (1998). Some issues in the evolution of language and thought. In D. D. Cummins & C. Allen (Eds.), *The evolution of mind* (pp. 204–233). New York: Oxford University Press.

Blos, P. (1962). *On adolescence.* New York: Free Press.

Blos, P. (1972). The child analyst looks at the young adolescent. In J. Kagan & R. Coles (Eds.), *Twelve to sixteen: Early adolescence.* New York: W. W. Norton.

Boaler, J. (1997). *Experiencing school mathematics : teaching styles, sex, and setting.* Buckingham, England: Open University Press.

Boas, F. (1911). *The mind of primitive man.* New York: Macmillan.

Boer, F. (1990). *Sibling relationships in middle childhood.* Leiden: DSWO University of Leiden Press.

Bogartz, R. S., Shinskey, J. L., & Speaker, C. J. (1997). Interpreting infant looking: The event set design. *Developmental Psychology, 33*(3), 408–422.

Bogin, B. (1999). *Patterns of human growth* (2nd ed.). New York: Cambridge University Press.

Bohan, J. S. (1996). *Psychology and sexual orientation: Coming to terms.* New York: Routledge.

Bohannon, J. N., III, & Warren-Leubecker, A. (1988). Recent developments in child-directed speech: We've come a long way baby-talk. *Language Sciences, 10*, 89–110.

Bohlin, G., Hagekull, B., Germer, M., Andersson, K., & Lindberg, L. (1989). Avoidant and resistant reunion behaviors as predicted by maternal interactive behavior and infant temperament. *Infant Behavior and Development, 12*, 105–118.

Bolger, K. E., Patterson, C. J., Thompson, W. W., & Kupersmidt, J. B. (1995). Psychosocial adjustment among children experiencing persistent and intermittent family economic hardship. *Child Development, 66*(4), 1107–1129.

Borke, H. (1975). Piaget's mountains revisited: Changes in the egocentric landscape. *Developmental Psychology, 11*, 240–443.

Borman, K. M., & Kurdek, L. A. (1987). Grade and gender differences in and the stability and correlates of the structural complexity of children's playground games. *International Journal of Behavioral Development, 10*(2), 241–251.

Bornstein, P., Duncan, P., D'Ari, A., & Pieniadz, J. (1996). Family and parenting behaviors predicting middle school adjustment: A longitudinal study. *Family Relations: Journal of Applied Family & Child Studies, 45*, 415–426.

Botta, R. A. (1999). Television images and adolescent girls' body image disturbance. *Journal of Communication, 49*(2), 22–41.

Bouchard, C. (1997). Obesity in adulthood–the importance of childhood and parental obesity. *New England Journal of Medicine, 337*(13), 926–927.

Bouchard, T. J., Jr. (1994). Genes, environment, and personality. *Science, 264*, 1700–1701.

Bouè, A. (1995). *Maternal infection in fetal medicine: Prenatal diagnosis and management.* Oxford, England: Oxford University Press.

Boukydis, C. F. Z., & Burges, R. L. (1982). Adult physiological response to infant cries: Effects of temperament of infant, parental status, and gender. *Child Development, 53*, 1291–1298.

Boulton, M. J. (1996). A comparison of 8- and 11-year-old girls' and boys' participation in specific types of rough and tumble play and aggressive fighting: Implications for functional hypotheses. *Aggressive Behavior, 22*(4), 271–287.

Bower, T. G. R. (1979). *Human development.* San Francisco: W. H. Freeman.

Bower, T. G. R. (1982). *Development in human infancy.* New York: W. H. Freeman.

Bowlby, J. (1969). *Attachment and loss: Vol. 1. Attachment.* New York: Basic Books.

Bowlby, J. (1973). *Attachment and loss: Vol. 2. Separation.* New York: Basic Books.

Bowlby, J. (1980). *Attachment and loss: Vol. 3. Loss, sadness, and depression.* New York: Basic Books.

Boyatzis, C. J., Baloff, P., & Durieux, C. (1998). Effects of perceived attractiveness and academic success on early adolescent peer popularity. *Journal of Genetic Psychology, 159*(3), 337–344.

Bradbard, M. R., Martin, C. L., Endsley, R. C., & Halverson, C. F. (1986). Influence of sex stereotypes on children's exploration and memory: A competence versus performance distinction. *Developmental Psychology, 22*, 481–486.

Bradley, R. H., & Whiteside-Mansell. (1998). Home environment and children's development: Age and demographic differences. In M. Lewis & C. Feiring (Eds.), *Families, risk, and competence* (pp. 133–157). Mahwah, NJ: Earlbaum.

Braine, M. D. S. (1963). The ontogeny of English phrase structure: The first phase. *Language, 39*, 3–13.

Bransford, J. D., Brown, A. L., & Cocking, R. R. (Eds.). (1999). *How people learn: Brain, mind, experience, and school.* Washington, DC: National Academy Press.

Brazelton, T. B. (1984). *Neonatal behavioral assessment scale (2nd ed.).* London: Spastics International Medical Publications.

Brazelton, T. B. (1990). Saving the bathwater. *Child Development, 61*, 1661–1671.

Brazelton, T. B., Koslowski, B., & Main, M. (1974). The origin of reciprocity: The early mother-infant interaction. In M. Lewis & L. Rosenblum (Eds.), *The effect of the infant on its caretaker.* New York: Wiley.

Brazelton, T. B., Nugent, K. J., & Lester, B. M. (1987). Neonatal behavioral assessment scale. In J. D. Osofsky (Ed.), *Handbook of infant development* (2nd ed.). New York: Wiley.

Bretherton, I. (1984). Representing the social world in symbolic play: Reality and fantasy. In I. Bretherton (Ed.), *Symbolic play: The development of social understanding.* New York: Academic Press.

Bretherton, I. (1985). Attachment theory: Retrospect and prospect. *Monographs of the Society for Research in Child Development, 50*(1–2, Serial No. 209).

Bretherton, I. (1993). From dialogue to internal working models: The co-construction of self in relationships. In C. A. Nelson (Ed.), *Memory and affect in development* (pp. 237–263). Hillsdale, NJ: Erlbaum.

Bretherton, I., & Bates, E. (1985). The development of representation from 10 to 28 months: Differential stability of language and symbolic play. In R. N. Emde & R. J. Harmon (Eds.), *Continuities and discontinuities in development.* New York: Plenum Press.

Bretherton, I., & Waters, E. E. (1985). Growing points in attachment theory. *Monographs of the Society for Research in Child Development, 50*(1–2, Serial No. 209).

Bretherton, I., Fritz, J., Zahn-Waxler, C., & Ridgeway, D. (1986). Learning to talk about emotions. *Child Development, 57*, 529–548.

Brewin, C. R., Andrews, B., & Gotlib, I. H. (1993). Psychopathology and early experience: A reappraisal of retrospective reports. *Psychological Bulletin, 113*, 82–98.

Bridges, L. J., & Grolnick, W. S. (1995). The development of emotional self-regulation in infancy and early childhood. In N. Eisenberg (Ed.), *Social development: Review of personality and social psychology.* Thousand Oaks, CA: Sage Publications.

Brody, G. H. (1998). Sibling relationship quality: Its causes and consequences. *Annual Review of Psychology, 49*, 1–24.

Brody, G. H., Stoneman, Z., McCoy, J. K., & Forehand, R. (1992). Contemporaneous and longitudinal associations of sibling conflict with family relationship assessments and family discussions about sibling problems. *Child Development, 63*, 391–400.

Bronfenbrenner, U. (1970). *Two worlds of childhood: U.S. and U.S.S.R.* New York: Russell Sage Foundation.

Bronfenbrenner, U. (1979). *The ecology of human development.* Cambridge, MA: Harvard University Press.

Bronfenbrenner, U., & Ceci, S. J. (1993). Heredity, environment, and the question, "How?": A first approximation. In R. Plomin & G. McClearn (Eds.), *Nature, nurture, and psychology.* Washington, DC: American Psychological Association.

Bronfenbrenner, U., & Morris, P. A. (1998). The ecology of developmental processes. In R. M. Lerner (Ed.), *Handbook of child psychology: Theoretical models of human development* (Fifth ed., Vol. 1, pp. 993–1028). New York: Wiley.

Bronson, G. (1991). Infant differences in rate of visual encoding. *Child Development, 62*, 44–54.

Bronson, G. W. (1994). Infants' transitions toward adult-like scanning. *Child Development, 65*, 1243–1261.

Bronson, G. W. (1997). The growth of visual capacity: Evidence from infant scanning patterns. *Advances in Infancy Research, 11*, 109–141.

Bronson, W. C. (1975). Development of behavior with age-mates during the second year of life. In M. Lewis & L. A. Rosenblum (Eds.), *The origins of behavior: Friendship and peer relations.* New York: Wiley.

Brooke, J. (1991, June 15). Cubato journal: Signs of life in Brazil's industrial valley of death. *New York Times*, pp. Pt. 1, p. 2.

Brookins, C. C. (1996). Promoting ethnic identity development in African American youth: The role of rites of passage. *Journal of Black Psychology, 22*, 388–417.

Brooks-Gunn, J., & Petersen, A. (Eds.). (1983). *Girls at puberty: Biological and psychosocial perspectives.* New York: Plenum Press.

Brooks-Gunn, J., & Reiter, E. O. (1990). The role of pubertal processes in the early adolescent transition. In S. Feldman & G. Elliot (Eds.), *At the threshold: The developing adolescent.* Cambridge, MA: Harvard University Press.

Brooks-Gunn, J., Klebanov, P. K., Liaw, F. R., & Spiker, D. (1993). Enhancing the development of low-birthweight premature infants: Changes in cognition and behavior over the first three years. *Child Development, 64*, 736–753.

Brooks-Gunn, J., Klebanov, P. K., & Duncan, G. J. (1996). Ethnic differences in children's intelligence test scores: Role of economic deprivation, home environment, and maternal characteristics. *Child Development, 67*(2), 396–408.

Brooks-Gunn, J., Duncan, G. J., & Aber, J. L. (Eds.). (1997). *Neighborhood poverty: Context and consequences for young children* (Vol. 1). New York: Russell-Sage.

Brophy, J. E. (1983). Research on the self-fulfilling prophecy ad teacher expectation. *Journal of Educational Psychology, 75*, 631–661.

Broude, G. J., & Green, S. J. (1976). Cross-cultural codes on twenty sexual attitudes and practices. *Ethnology, 15*, 409–429.

Brown, A. L. (1992). Design experiments: Theoretical and methodological challenges in creating complex interventions in classroom settings. *The Journal of Learning Sciences, 2,* 141–178.

Brown, A. L. (1997). Transforming schools into communities of thinking and learning about serious matters. *American Psychologist, 52*(4), 399–413.

Brown, A. L. & Palinscar, A.S. (1982). Inducing strategic learning from text by means of informed, self-control training. *Topics in Learning and Learning Disabilities, 2,* 1–17.

Brown, A. L., Campione, J. C., Reeve, R. A., Ferrara, R. A., & Palincsar, A. S. (1992). Interactive learning and individual understanding: The case of reading and mathematics. In L. T. Landsmann (Ed.), *Culture, schooling, and psychological development.* Hillsdale, NJ: Erlbaum.

Brown, B. B. (1990). Peer groups and peer cultures. In S. S. Feldman & G. R. Elliott (Eds.), *At the threshold: The developing adolescent.* Cambridge, MA: Harvard University Press.

Brown, B. B. (1999). Measuring the peer environment of American adolescents. In S. L. Friedman & T. D. Wachs (Eds.), *Measuring environment across the life span.* Washington, DC: American Psychological Association.

Brown, B. B., & Huang, B. (1995). Examining parenting practices in different peer contexts: Implications for adolescent trajectories. In L. J. Crockett & A. C. Crouter (Eds.), *Pathways through adolescence: Individual development in relation to social contexts* (pp. 151–174). Mahwah, NJ: Erlbaum.

Brown, B. B., Clasen, D. R., & Eicher, S. A. (1986). Perception of peer pressure, peer conformity dispositions, and self reported behavior among adolescents. *Developmental Psychology, 22,* 521–530.

Brown, B. B., Mory, M. S., & Kinney, D. (1994). Casting adolescent crowds in a relational perspective: Caricature, channel, and context. In R. Montemayor & G. Adams & T. Gullotta (Eds.), *Personal relationships in adolescence: Advances in adolescent development* (Vol. 6). Thousand Oaks, CA: Sage.

Brown, J. R., & Dunn, J. (1991). "You can cry mum": The social and developmental implications of talk about internal states. *British Journal of Developmental Psychology, 9,* 237–256.

Brown, L. M., Way, N., & Duff, J. L. (1999). The others in my I: Adolescent girls' friendships and peer relations. In N. G. Johnson, M. C. Roberts & J. Worell (Eds.), *Beyond appearance: A new look at adolescent girls.* Washington, DC: American Psychological Association.

Brown, P., & Elliot, R. (1965). Control of aggression in a nursery school class. *Journal of Experimental Child Psychology, 2,* 103–107.

Brown, R. (1973). *A first language: The early stages.* Cambridge, MA: Harvard University Press.

Brown, R., & Bellugi, U. (1964). Three processes in the child's acquisition of syntax. *Harvard Educational Review, 34,* 133–151.

Brown, R., & Hanlon, C. (1970). Derivational complexity and the order of acquisition of child speech. In J. R. Hayes (Ed.), *Cognition and the development of language.* New York: Wiley.

Brown, R., & Herrnstein, R. J. (1975). *Psychology.* Boston: Little, Brown.

Brown v. Board of Education of Topeka. (1954). Paper presented at the 347 U.S. 483; 7455 Ct. 686, Kansas.

Browne, S. T. (1642/1964). *Religio Medici.* London: Oxford University Press.

Bruner, J. S. (1966). On cognitive growth. In J. S. Bruner & R. R. Olver & P. M. Greenfield (Eds.), *Studies in cognitive growth.* New York: Wiley.

Bruner, J. S. (1968). *Process of cognitive growth: Infancy.* Worcester, MA: Clark University Press.

Bruner, J. S. (1982). Formats of language acquisition. *American Journal of Semiotics, 1,* 1–16.

Bruner, J. S. (1983). *Child's talk.* New York: W.W. Norton.

Bruner, J. S. (1983). *In search of mind.* New York: Harper and Row.

Bruner, J. S. (1996). *The culture of education.* Cambridge, MA: Harvard University.

Bryant, P. (1993). Reading in development. In C. Pratt & A. F. Garton (Eds.), *Systems of representation in children.* Chichister, England: Wiley.

Bryant, P., & Nunes, T. (1998). Learning about the orthography: A cross-linguistic approach. In S. G. Paris & H. M. Wellman (Eds.), *Global prospects for education: Development, culture, and schooling* (pp. 171–191). Washington, DC: American Psychological Association.

Bugental, D. B., & Goodnow, J. J. (1998). Socialization processes. In W. Damon & N. Eisenberg (Eds.), *Handbook of child psychology (5th ed.), Vol 3: Social, emotional, and personality development* (pp. 389–462). New York: Wiley.

Buhrmester, D. (1996). Need fulfillment, interpersonal competence, and the developmental contexts of early adolescent friendship. In W. M. Bukowski & A. F. Newcomb & W. W. Hartup (Eds.), *The company they keep: Friendship in childhood and adolescence.* (pp. 158–185). New York: Cambridge University Press.

Buhrmester, D. (1998). Need fulfillment, interpersonal competence, and the developmental contexts of early adolescent friendship. In W. M. Bukowski & A. F. Newcomb (Eds.), *The company they keep: Friendship in childhood and adolescence* (pp. 158–185). New York: Cambridge University Press.

Buhrmester, D., & Furman, W. (1987). The development of companionship and intimacy. *Child Development, 58,* 1101–1113.

Bullock, M. (1984). Preschool children's understandings of causal connections. *British Journal of Developmental Psychology, 2,* 139–142.

Bullock, M., & Gelman, R. (1979). Preschool children's assumptions about cause and effect: Temporal ordering. *Child Development, 50, 89–96.*

Bullock, M., & Lutkenhaus, P. (1989). The development of volitional behavior in the toddler years. *Child Development, 59,* 664–674.

Bullough, V. (1981). Age of menarche: A misunderstanding. *Science, 213,* 365–366.

Bushnell, I. W. R. (1998). The origins of face perception. In F. Simion & G. Butterworth (Eds.), *The development of sensory, motor and cognitive capacities in early infancy: From perception to cognition.* Hove, England: Psychology Press/Erlbaum.

Bushnell, I. W. R., Sai, F., & Mullin, J. T. (1989). Neonatal recognition of the mother's face. *British Journal of Developmental Psychology, 7,* 3–15.

Buss, A. H., & Plomin, R. (1984). *Temperament: Early developing personality traits.* Hillsdale, NJ: Erlbaum.

Bussey, K., & Bandura, A. (1992). Self regulatory mechanisms governing gender development. *Child Development, 63,* 1236–1250.

Butterworth, G. (1998). What is special about pointing in babies? In F. Simion & G. Butterworth (Eds.), *The development of sensory, motor and cognitive capacities in early infancy: From perception to cognition* (pp. 171–190). Hove, England: Psychology Press/Erlbaum.

Butterworth, G., & Jarrett, N. (1991). What minds have in common in space: Spatial mechanisms serving joint visual attention in infancy. *British Journal of Developmental Psychology, 9,* 55–72.

Butterworth, G., & Morissette, P. (1996). Onset of pointing and the acquisition of language in infancy. *Journal of Reproductive & Infant Psychology, 14*(2), 219-231.

Cairns, R. B. (1979). *Social development: The origins of interchanges.* New York: W. H. Freeman.

Cairns, R. B. (1998). The making of developmental psychology. In W. Damon & R. M. Lerner (Eds.), *Handbook of child psychology (5th ed.): Vol. 1: Theoretical models of human development.* New York: Wiley.

Cairns, R. B., & Cairns, B. D. (1994). *Lifelines and risks: Pathways of youth in our times.* Cambridge: Cambridge University Press.

Cairns, R., Xie, H., & Leung, M.-C. (1998). The popularity of friendship and the neglect of social networks: Toward a new balance. In W. M. Bukowski & A. H. Cillessen (Eds.), *Sociometry then and now: Building on six decades of measuring children's experiences with the peer group.* San Francisco: Jossey-Bass.

Calabrese, L. H., Kirkendall, D. T., Floyd, M., Rapoport, S., Williams, G. W., Weiker, G. F., & Bergfeld, J. A. (1983). Menstrual abnormalities, nutritional patterns and body composition in female classical ballet dancers. *Physician and Sports Medicine, 11*, 86–98.

Caldera, Y. M., Huston, A. C., & O'Brien, M. (1989). Social interactions and play patterns of parents and toddlers with feminine, masculine, and neutral toys. *Child Development, 60*, 70–76.

Campbell, F. A., & Ramey, C. T. (1994). Effects of early intervention on intellectual and academic achievement: A follow-up study of children from low-income families. *Child Development, 64*, 684–698.

Campbell, S. B., Cohn, J. F., & Meyers, T. (1995). Depression in first-time mothers: Mother-infant interaction and depression chronicity. Special Section: Parental depression and distress: Implications for development in infancy, childhood, and adolescence. *Developmental Psychology, 31*, 349–357.

Campos, J. J., Kermoian, R., Witherington, D., Chen, H., & al., e. (1997). Activity, attention, and developmental transitions in infancy. In P. J. Lang & R. F. Simons (Eds.), *Attention and orienting: Sensory and motivational processes.* (pp. 393–415). Mahwah, NJ: Erlbaum.

Campos, J. J., & Sternberg, C. G. (1981). Perception, appraisal, and emotion: The onset of social referencing. In M. E. Lamb & R. Sherrod (Ed.), *Infants' social cognition: Empirical and social considerations.* Hillsdale, NJ: Erlbaum.

Campos, J. J., Benson, J., & Rudy, L. (1986). *The role of self-produced locomotion in spatial behavior.* Unpublished Posterpaper presented at the meeting of the International Conference for Infant Studies, Beverly Hills, CA.

Campos, J. J., Kermoian, R., & Zumbahlen, M. R. (1992). Socioemotional transformations in the family system following infant crawling onset. In N. Eisenberg & R. A. Fabes (Eds.), *Emotion and its regulation in early development (New directions for child development, 55).* San Francisco: Jossey-Bass.

Campos, J., Anderson, D. I., Barbu-Roth, M. A., Hubbard, E. M., Hertenstein, M. J., & Witherington, D. (2000). Travel Broadens the Mind. *Infancy.*

Caplan, N., Whitmore, J. K., & Choy, M. H. (1989). *The boat people and achievement in America: A study of family life, hard work, and cultural values.* Ann Arbor: University of Michigan Press.

Carey, S. (1978). The child as word learner. In M. Halle & J. Bresnan & G. A. Miller (Eds.), *Linguistic theory and psychological reality.* Cambridge, MA: MIT Press.

Carey, S. (1985). *Conceptual change in childhood.* Cambridge, MA: MIT Press.

Carey, W. B., & McDevitt, S. C. (1995). *Coping with children's temperament: A guide for professionals.* New York: Basic Books.

Carnegie Commission on Policy Studies in Higher Education. (1980). *Giving youth a better chance.* San Francisco: Jossey-Bass.

Carnegie Council on Adolescent Development (1995). *Great transitions: Preparing adolescents for a new century: Concluding report of the Carnegie Council on Adolescent Development.* New York: Carnegie Corporation.

Carro, M. G., Grant, K. E., Gotlib, I. H., & Compas, B. E. (1993). Postpartum depression and child development: An investigation of mothers and fathers as sources of risk and resilience. *Developmental Psychopathology, 5*, 567–579.

Case, R. (1992). The role of the frontal lobes in the regulation of cognitive development. *Brain and Cognition, 20*(1), 51–73.

Case, R. (1995). Capacity based explanations of working memory growth: A brief history and reevaluation. In F. M. Weinazt & W. Schneider (Eds.), *Memory performance and competencies: Issues in growth and development.* Mahwah, NJ: Erlbaum.

Case, R. (1998). The development of conceptual structures. In D. Kuhn & R. S. Siegler (Eds.), *Handbook of child psychology (5th ed.), Vol 2: Cognition, perception and language* (pp. 745–800). New York: Wiley.

Case, R., & Okamoto, Y. (1995). The role of central conceptual structures in the development of children's thought. *Monographs of the Society for Research in Child Development, 61*(1–2, Serial No. 246).

Case, R., & Okamoto, Y. (1996). The role of central conceptual structures in the development of children's thought. *Monographs of the Society for Research in Child Development, 61*(1–2).

Case, R., Kurland, D. M., & Goldberg, J. (1982). Operational efficiency and growth of short-term memory span. *Journal of Experimental Child Psychology, 33*, 386–404.

Case, R., Marini, Z., McKeough, A., Dennis, S., & Goldberg, J. (1986). Horizontal structure in middle childhood: Cross domain parallels in the course of cognitive growth. In I. Levin (Ed.), *Stage and structure: Reopening the debate.* Norwood, NJ: Ablex.

Cashon, C. H., & Cohen, L. B. (2000). Eight-month-old infant's perception of possible and impossible events. *Infancy, 1*, in press.

Casper, C. (1997). *The reconstruction.* New York: St. Martin's Press.

Casper, R. C. (1996). Carbohydrate metabolism and its regulatory hormones in anorexia nervosa. *Psychiatry Research, 62*(1), 85–96.

Caspi, A. (1995). Puberty and the gender organization of schools: How biology and social context shape the adolescent experience. In L. J. Crockett & A. C. Crouter (Eds.), *Pathways through adolescence: Individual development in relation to social contexts* (pp. 57–74). Mahwah, NJ: Erlbaum.

Caspi, A. (1998). Personality development across the life course. In W. Damon & N. Eisenberg (Eds.), *Handbook of child psychology (5th ed.), Vol. 3: Social, emotional, and personality development* (pp. 311–388). New York: Wiley.

Caspi, A., Lynam, D., Moffitt, T. E., & Silva, P. A. (1993). Unraveling girls' delinquency: Biological, dispositional, and contextual contributions to adolescent misbehavior. *Developmental Psychology, 29*, 19–30.

Cass, V. (1996). Sexual orientation identity formation: A Western phenomenon. In R. P. Cabaj & T. S. Stein (Eds.), *Textbook of homosexuality and mental health* (pp. 227–251). Washington, DC: American Psychiatric Press.

Cass, V. C. (1984). Homosexual identity formation: Testing a theoretical model. *Journal of Sex Research, 20*, 143–167.

Cassidy, J., & Asher, S. R. (1992). Loneliness and peer relations in young children. *Child Development, 63*, 350–365.

Cattell, R. B. (1949). *The culture free intelligence test.* Champaign, IL: Institute for Personality and Ability Testing.

Caudill, W., & Plath, D. (1966). Who sleeps by whom?: Parent-child involvement in urban Japanese families. *Psychiatry, 29*, 344–366.

Caughy, M. O., Dipietro, J. A., & Strobino, D. M. (1994). Daycare participation as a protective factor in the cognitive development of young children. *Child Development, 65*, 457–471.

Cazden, C. (1986). Classroom discourse. In M. C. Wittrock (Ed.), *Handbook of research on teaching* (3rd ed., pp. 432–463). New York: Macmillan Publishing Co.

Cazden, C. B. (1965). *Environmental assistance to the child's acquisition of grammar.* Unpublished doctoral dissertation, Harvard University.

Cazden, C. B. (1988). *Classroom discourse: The language of teaching and learning.* Portsmouth, NH: Heinemann Educational Books, Inc.

Cazden, C. B., & Michaels, S. (1985). *Gender differences in sixth grade children's letters in an electronic mail system.* Paper presented at the Paper presented at the Boston University Child Language Conference, Boston, MA.

Ceci, S. J., & Bruck, M. (1993). Suggestibility of child eyewitnesses: A historical review and synthesis. *Psychology Bulletin, 113*, 403–439.

Ceci, S. J., & Bruck, M. (1998). The ontogeny and durability of true and false memories: A fuzzy trace account. *Journal of Experimental Child Psychology, 71*(2), 165–169.

Ceci, S. J., & Hembrooke, H. A. (1995). A bioecological model of intellectual development. In P. Moen & J. G. H. Elder & K. Luscher (Eds.), *Examining lives in context: Perspectives on the ecology of human development.* Washington, DC: American Psychological Association.

Centers for Disease Control and Prevention. (1998)., *CDC Surveillance Summaries.*

Centers for Disease Control (1999b). Achievements in public health, 1900–1999: Healthier mothers and babies. *Mortality and Morbidity Weekly Report, 48*(38), 849–858.

Centers for Disease Control (2000). Trends in the attendant, place, and timing of births and in the use of obstetric interventions in the United States, 1989–1997. *Mortality and Morbidity Weekly Report, 49.*

Centers for Disease Control. (1999a). Infant mortality statistics from the linked birth/infant death data set–1997 period data. *Mortality and Morbidity Weekly Report, 48.*

Chan, A., McCaul, K. A., Keane, R. J., & Haan, E. A. (1998). Effect of parity, gravidity, previous miscarriage, and age on risk of Down's syndrome: population based study. *Bmj (Clinical Research Ed.), 3*(17), 923–924.

Chao, R. K. (1994). Beyond parental control and authoritarian parenting style: Understanding Chinese parenting through the cultural notion of training. *Child Development, 65*, 1111–1119.

Chao, R. K. (1996). Chinese and European American mothers' beliefs about the role of parenting in children's school success. *Journal of Cross-Cultural Psychology, 27*(4), 403–423.

Chapell, M. S., & Overton, W. F. (1998). Development of logical reasoning in the context of parental style and test anxiety. *Merrill-Palmer Quarterly, 44*(2), 141–156.

Chapman, R. S. (1995). Language development in children and adolescents with Down syndrome. In P. Fletcher & B. MacWhinney (Eds.), *Handbook of child language* (pp. 641–663). Oxford: Blackwell.

Chase-Lansdale, P. L. (1994a). Families and maternal employment during infancy: New linkages. In R. D. Parke & S. G. Kellam (Eds.), *Exploring family relationships with other social contexts.* Family research consortium: Advances in family research: Hillsdale, NJ: Erlbaum.

Chase-Lansdale, P. L., & Hetherington, E. M. (1990). The impact of divorce on life-span development: Short- and long-term effects. In P. B. Baltes, D. L. Featherman & R. M. Lerner (Eds.), *Life-span development and behavior.* Volume 10: Hillsdale, NJ: Erlbaum.

Chase-Lansdale, P. L., Brooks-Gunn, J., & Zamsky, E. S. (1994b). Young African-American multigenerational families in poverty: Qualities of mothering and grandmothering. *Child Development, 65*, 394–403.

Chen, C., & Stevenson, H. W. (1988). Cross-linguistic differences in digit span of preschool children. *Journal of Experimental Child Psychology, 46*, 150–158.

Chen, X., & Rubin, K. H. (1994). Family conditions, parental acceptance, and social competence and aggression in Chinese children. *Social Development, 3*(3), 269–290.

Cherlin, A. J., Furstenberg, F. F. J., Chase-Lansdale, P. L., Kiernan, K. E., Robins, P. K., Morrison, D. R., & Teitler, J. O. (1991). Longitudinal studies of the effects of divorce on children in Great Britain and the United States. *Science, 252*(5011), 1386–1389.

Chess, S., & Thomas, A. (1982). Infant bonding: Mystique and reality. *American Journal of Orthopsychiatry, 52*, 213–221.

Chi, M. T. H. (1978). Knowledge structures and memory development. In R. S. Siegler (Ed.), *Children's thinking: What develops?* Hillsdale, NJ: Erlbaum.

Chi, M. T. H., & Koeske, R. D. (1983). Network representation of a child's dinosaur knowledge. *Developmental Psychology, 19*, 29–39.

Chi, M. T., Hutchinson, J. E., & Robin, A. F. (1989). How inferences about novel domain-related concepts can be constrained by structured knowledge. *Merrill-Palmer Quarterly, 35*(1), 27-62.

Chisholm, K. (1998). A three year follow-up of attachment and indiscriminate friendliness in children adopted from Romanian orphanages. *Child Development, 69*(4), 1092–1106.

Chodorow, N. (1974). Family structure and feminine personality. In M. Z. Rosaldo & L. Lamphere (Eds.), *Women, culture and society.* Stanford, CA: Stanford University Press.

Choi, S., & Gopnik, A. (1995). Early acquisition of verbs in Korean: A cross-linguistic study. *Journal of Child Language, 22*(3), 497–529.

Chomsky, C. (1969). *Acquisition of syntax in children from 5 to 10.* Cambridge, MA: MIT Press.

Chomsky, N. (1959). Review of verbal behavior by B. F. Skinner. *Language, 35*, 26–58.

Chomsky, N. (1975). *Reflections on language.* New York: Pantheon Books.

Chomsky, N. (1980). Initial states and steady states. In M. Piatelli-Palmerini (Ed.), *Language and learning: The debate between Jean Piaget and Noam Chomsky.* Cambridge, MA: Harvard University Press.

Chomsky, N. (1986). *Knowledge of language: Its nature, origins, and use.* New York: Praeger.

Chomsky, N. (1988). *Language and problems of knowledge.* Cambridge, MA: MIT Press.

Christian, K., Bachman, H. J., & Morrison, F. J. (2000). Schooling and cognitive development. In R. J. Sternberg & R. L. Grigorenko (Eds.), *Environmental effects on cognitive abilities.* Mahwah, NJ: Erlbaum.

Chugani, H. T. (1998). The ontogeny of cerbral metabolism. In B. Garreau (Ed.), *Neuroimaging in child neuropsychiatric disorders* (pp. 89–96). Berlin: Springer-Verlag.

Chugani, H. T., & Phelps, M. E. (1986). Maturational changes in cerebral function determined by 18FDG positron emission tomography. *Science, 231*, 840–843.

Chukovsky, K. (1968). *From two to five.* Berkeley: University of California Press.

Cicchetti, D., & Carlson, V. (Eds.). (1989). *Child Maltreatment: Theory and research on the causes and consequences of child abuse and neglect.* Cambridge: Cambridge University Press.

Cicchetti, D., & Toth, S. L. (1993). Child maltreatment research and social policy: The neglected nexus. In D. Cicchetti & S. L. Toth (Eds.), *Advances in applied developmental psychology series: Vol. 8. Child abuse, child development, and social policy.* Norwood, NJ: Ablex.

Cicchetti, D., & Toth, S. L. (1998). The development of depression in children and adolescents. *American Psychologist, 53*(2), 221–241.

Cicchetti, D., Toth, S. L., & Maughm, A. (2000). An ecological-transactional model of child maltreatment. In A. Sameroff & M. Lewis & J. Miller (Eds.), *Handbook of developmental psychology* (2nd ed.). New York: Plenum.

Cillessen, A. H. N., Vanijzendoorn, H. W., Van Lieshorst, C. F. M., & Hartup, W. W. (1992). Heterogeneity among peer-rejected boys: Subtypes and stabilities. *Child Development, 63*, 893–905.

Clahsen, H., & Almazan, M. (1998). Syntax and morphology in Williams syndrome. *Cognition, 68*(3), 167–198.

Clark, E. V. (1995). Later lexical development and word formation. In P. Fletcher & B. MacWhinney (Eds.), *The handbook of child language.* Cambridge, MA: Basil Blackwell.

Clark, J. E., & Phillips, S. J. (1993). A longitudinal study of intralimb coordination in the first year of independent walking: A dynamical systems analysis. Special section: Developmental biodynamics: Brain, body, behavior, connections. *Child Development, 64*, 1143–1157.

Clark, K. B., & Clark, M. P. (1939). The development of consciousness of self and the emergence of racial identity in Negro pre-school schoolchildren. *Journal of Social Psychology, 10*, 591–599.

Clark, K. B., & Clark, M. P. (1950). Emotional factors in racial identification and preference in Negro children. *Journal of Negro Education, 19*, 341-350.

Clarke, A. M., & Clarke, A. D. B. (1986). Thirty years of child psychology: A selective review. *Journal of Child Psychology and Psychiatry, 27*, 719–759.

Clarke-Stewart, A. (1982). *Daycare* (2nd ed.). Cambridge, MA: Harvard University Press.

Clarke-Stewart, A. (1984). Day-care: A new context for research and development. In M. Perlmutter (Ed.), *Parent-child interaction and parent-child relations in child development: The Minnesota Symposia on Child Psychology* (Vol. 17). Hillsdale, NJ: Erlbaum.

Clarke-Stewart, A., & Fein, G. G. (1983). Early childhood programs. In P. H. Mussen (Ed.), *Handbook of child psychology* (4th ed.)*: Vol. 2: Infancy and developmental psychobiology.* New York: Wiley.

Clarke-Stewart, A., & Koch, J. B. (1983). *Children: Development through adolescence.* New York: Wiley.

Clausen, J. A. (1975). The social meaning of differential physical and sexual maturation. In S. E. Dragastin & J. G. E. Elder (Eds.), *Adolescence in the life cycle.* Washington, DC: Hemisphere Press.

Clement, P. F. (1997). *Growing pains: Children in the industrial age, 1850–1890.* New York: Twayne Publishers.

Clifton, R. K., Muir, D. W., Ashmead, D. H., & Clarkson, M. G. (1993). Is visually guided reading in early infancy a myth? *Child Development, 64,* 1099–1110.

Coates, S., & Wolfe, S. (1997). Gender identity disorders in children. In P. F. Kernberg & J. R. Bemporad (Eds.), *Handbook of child and adolescent psychiatry* (Vol. 2, pp. 595–609). New York: Wiley.

Cobb, P., Gravemeijer, K., Yackel, E., McClain, K., & Whitenack, J. (1997). Mathematizing and symbolizing: The emergence of chains of signification in one first-grade classroom. In D. Kirshner & J. A. Whitson (Eds.), *Situated cognition: Social, semiotic, and psychological perspectives* (pp. 151–234). Mahwah, NJ: Erlbaum.

Cochran, M., & Niego, S. (1995). Parenting and social networks. In E. Marc H. Bornstein (Ed.), *Handbook of parenting, Vol. 3: Status and social conditions of parenting* (pp. 393–418). Mahwah, NJ: Erlbaum.

Cognition and Technology Group. (1996a). MOST environments for accelerating literacy development. In S. Vosniadou & E. De Corte (Eds.), *International perspectives on the design of technology-supported learning environments* (pp. 223–255). Mahwah, NJ: Erlbaum.

Cognition and Technology Group at Vanderbilt. (1996b). Looking at technology in context: A framework for understanding technology and education research. In D. Berliner & E. R. Calfee (Eds.), *Handbook of educational psychology.* New York: John Wiley.

Cohen, L. B. (1998). An information-processing approach to infant perception and cognition. In F. Simion & G. Butterworth (Eds.), *The development of sensory, motor and cognitive capacities in early infancy: From perception to cognition* (pp. 277–300). Hove, England: Psychology Press/Erlbaum.

Coie, J. D., & Dodge, K. A. (1998). Aggression and antisocial behavior. In N. Eisenberg (Ed.), *Handbook of child psychology* (5th ed.), *Vol. 3: Social, emotional, and personality* (pp. 779–882). New York: Wiley.

Coie, J. D., Lochman, J. E., Terry, R., & Hyman, C. (1992). Predicting early adolescent disorder from childhood aggression and peer rejection. *Journal of Consulting & Clinical Psychology, 60*(5), 783–792.

Colby, A., & Kohlberg, L. (1987). *The measurement of moral judgment.* New York: Cambridge University Press.

Colby, A., Kohlberg, L., Gibbs, J., & Lieberman, M. (1983). A longitudinal study of moral development. *Monographs of the Society for Research in Child Development, 48* (1–2, Serial No. 200).

Cole, M., & Means, B. (1981). *Comparative studies of how people think.* Cambridge, MA: Harvard University Press.

Cole, M. (1996). *Cultural psychology: A once and future discipline.* Cambridge, MA: Belknap Harvard.

Cole, M., & Scribner, S. (1977). Cross-cultural studies of memory and cognition. In R. V. Kail & J. W. Hagen (Eds.), *Perspectives on the development of memory and cognition.* Hillsdale, NJ: Erlbaum.

Cole, M., Gay, J., Glick, J. A., & Sharp, D. W. (1971). *The cultural context of learning and thinking.* New York: Basic.

Cole, P. M. (1986). Children's spontaneous control of facial expression. *Child Development, 57*(6), 1309–1321.

Coleman, J. S. (1962). *The adolescent society.* Glencoe, IL: Free Press.

Coles, C. D. (1993). Saying "goodbye" to the "crack baby". *Neurotoxicology and Teratology, 15,* 290–292.

Coley, R. L., & Chase-Lansdale, P. L. (1998). Adolescent pregnancy and parenthood. *American Psychologist, 53*(2), 152–166.

Collins, W. A., & Laursen, B. (1999). *Relationships as developmental contexts.* Mahwah, NJ: Erlbaum.

Collins, W. A., Laursen, B., Mortensen, N., Luebker, C., & others. (1997). Conflict processes and transitions in parent and peer relationships: Implications for autonomy and regulation. *Journal of Adolescent Research, 12*(2), 178–198.

Collins, W. A., Maccoby, E. E., Steinberg, L., Hetherington, E. M., & Bornstein, M. H. (2000). Contenporary research on parenting: The case for nature and nurture. *American Psychologist, 55*(218–232).

Comstock, G., & Scharrer, E. (1999). *Television: What's on, who's watching, and what does it mean?* New York: Academic Press.

Condon, R. G. (1987). *Inuit youth.* New Brunswick, NJ: Rutgers University Press.

Conel, J. L. (1939/1967). *The postnatal development of the human cerebral cortex (8 vols.).* Cambridge, MA: Harvard University Press.

Conger, J. J., & Petersen, A. C. (1984). *Adolescence and youth: Psychological development in a changing world.* New York: Harper & Row.

Conger, K. J., & Conger, R. D. (1994). Differential parenting and change in sibling differences in delinquency. *Journal of Family Psychology, 8*(3), 287–302.

Conger, R. D., & Ge, X. (1999). Conflict and cohesion in parent-adolescent relations: Changes in emotional expression from early to midadolescence. In M. J. Cox & J. Brooks-Gunn (Eds.), *Conflict and cohesion in families.* Mahwah, NJ: Erlbaum.

Connolly, K., & Dalgleish, M. (1989). The emergence of a tool using skill in infancy. *Developmental Psychology, 25,* 539–549.

Connor, J. M., & Ferguson-Smith, M. A. (1991). *Essential medical genetic* (3rd ed.). London: Blackwell Scientific Publications.

Consortium for Longitudinal Studies. (1983). *As the twig is bent.* Hillsdale, NJ: Erlbaum.

Coopersmith, S. (1967). *The antecedents of self-esteem.* New York: W. H. Freeman.

Corbin, P. F., & Bickford, R. G. (1955). Studies of the electroencephalogram of normal children. *Electroencephalography and Clinical Neurology, 7,* 15–28.

Cornell, E. H., Heth, C. D., & Broda, L. S. (1989). Childrens' wayfinding: Response to instructions to use environmental landmarks. *Developmental Psychology, 25,* 755–764.

Cornell, E. H., Heth, C. D., & Rowat, W. L. (1992). Wayfinding by children and adults: Response to instructions to use look-back and retrace strategies. *Developmental Psychology, 28,* 328–336.

Corsaro, W. A. (1985). *Friendship and peer culture in the early years.* Norwood, NJ: Ablex.

Cost, Q., & Child Outcomes Study Team. (1995). *Cost, quality, and child outcomes in child care centers, executive summary* (2nd ed.). Denver: Economics Department, University of Colorado at Denver.

Coté, J. E., & Allahar, A. L. (1996). *Generation on hold : Coming of age in the late twentieth century.* New York: New York University Press.

Cottrell, J. (1996). *Social networks and social influences in adolescence.* London: Routledge.

Cowan, W. M. (1979). The development of the brain. *Scientific American, 241,* 112–133.

Cowen, E. (1973). Long-term follow-up of early detected vulnerable children. *Journal of Consulting & Clinical Psychology., 41*(3), 438–446.

Cox, M., Owen, M. T., Lewis, J. M., & Henderson, V. K. (1989). Marriage, adult adjustment, and early parenting. *Child Development, 60*(5), 1015–1024.

Cox, M. J., Owen, M. T., Henderson, V. K., & Margand, N. A. (1992). Prediction of infant-father and infant-mother attachment. *Developmental Psychology, 28,* 474–483.

Coy, M. (1989). *Apprenticeship: From theory to method and back again.* Albany, NY: SUNY Press.

Craig, W. M. (1998). The relationship among bullying, victimization, depression, anxiety, and aggression in elementary school children. *Personality & Individual Differences, 24*(1), 123–130.

Crick, N. R., & Dodge, K. A. (1999). "Superiority" is in the eye of the beholder: A comment on Sutton, Smith and Swettenham. *Social Development, 8*(1), 128–131.

Crick, N. R., & Ladd, G. W. (1993). Children's perceptions of their peer experiences: Attributions, loneliness, social anxiety and social avoidance. *Developmental Psychology, 29,* 244–254.

Crick, N. R., Casas, J. F., & Mosher, M. (1997). Relational and overt aggression in preschool. *Developmental Psychology, 33*(4), 579–588.

Crockenberg, S. (1987). Support for adolescent mothers during the postnatal period. In C. Boukydis (Ed.), *Research on support for parents and infants in the postnatal period.* Norwood, NJ: Ablex.

Crook, C. (1987). Taste and Olfaction, *Handbook of Infant Perception* (Vol. 1, pp. 237–264). New York: Academic Press.

Crook, C. (1996). Schools of the future. In T. Gill (Ed.), *Electronic children : How children are responding to the information revolution*. London: National Children's Bureau.

Cross, W. E., & Phagen-Smith, P. (1996). Nigrescence and ego identity development. In P. B. Pedersen & J. G. Draguns & W. J. Lonner & J. E. Trimble (Eds.), *Counselling across cultures* (pp. 108–123). Thousand Oaks, CA.: Sage.

Cross, W. J. (1978). The Thomas and Cross models of psychological nigrescence: A review. Journal of Black psychology. *Journal of Black Psychology, 5*, 13–31.

Cross, W. E. J., & Strauss, L. (1998). The everyday functions of African American identity. In J. K. Swim & C. Stangor (Eds.), *Prejudice: The target's perspective* (pp. 267–279). San Diego: Academic Press, Inc.

Crouter, A. (1994). Processes linking families and work: Implications for behavior and development in both settings. In R. D. Parke & S. G. Killam (Eds.), *Exploring family relationships with other social contexts*. Hillsdale, NJ: Erlbaum.

Crowley, K., & Siegler, R. S. (1993). Flexible strategy use in young children's tic-tac-toe. *Cognitive Science, 17*(4), 531–561.

Crystal, D. (1995). Postilion sentences. *Child Language Teaching & Therapy, 11*(1), 79–90.

Csikszentmihalyi, M., & Larson, R. (1984). *Being adolescent: Conflict and growth in the teenage years*. New York: Basic Books.

Cunningham, F. G., MacDonald, P. C., Gant, N. F., Leveno, K. J., Gilstrap, L. C., III, Hankins, G. D. V., & Clark, S. L. (1997). *Williams Obstetrics* (20 ed.). Stamford, CN: Appleton & Lange.

Curtis, H. (1979). *Biology*. New York: Worth.

D'Amico, R. (1984). Does employment during high school impair academic progress? *Sociology of Education, 57*, 152–164.

D'Andrade, R. G. (1974). Memory and assessment of behavior. In J. H. M. Blalock (Ed.), *Measurement in the social sciences*. Chicago: Aldine.

D'Andrade, R., & Morin, P. A. (1996). Chimpanzee and human mitochondrial DNA. *American Anthropologist, 98*, 352–370.

Daley, B. J. (1999). Novice to expert: An exploration of how professionals learn. *Adult Education Quarterly, 49*(4), 133–147.

Damerow, P. (1998). Prehistory and cognitive development. In J. Langer & M. Killen (Eds.), *Piaget, evolution, and development* (pp. 247–270). Mahwah, NJ: Erlbaum.

Damon, W. (1975). Early conceptions of positive justice as related to the development of logical operations. *Child Development, 46*, 301–312.

Damon, W. (1977). *The social world of the child*. San Francisco: Jossey-Bass.

Damon, W. (1980). Patterns of change in children's social reasoning: A two-year longitudinal study. *Child Development, 51*, 1010–1017.

Damon, W. (1983). *Social and personality development: Infancy through adolescence*. New York: W. W. Norton.

Damon, W., & Hart, D. (1988). *Self-understanding in childhood and adolescence*. Cambridge: Cambridge University Press.

Dancyger, I. F., & Garfinkel, P. E. (1995). The relationship of partial syndrome eating disorders to anorexia and bulimia nervosa. *Psychological Medicine, 25*(5), 1019–1025.

Daniels-Beirness, T. (1989). Measuring peer status in boys and girls: A problem of apples and oranges. In B. H. Schneider & G. Attili & J. Nadel & R. P. Weissberg (Eds.), *Social competence in developmental perspective*. Boston: Kluwer Academic Publishers.

Danziger, K. (1990). *Constructing the subject: Historical origins of psychological research*. New York: Cambridge University Press.

Darwin, C. (1859/1958). *The origin of species*. New York: Penguin.

Darwin, C. (1877). A biographical sketch of an infant. *Mind, 2*, 285–294.

Dasen, P. (1999). Rapid social change and turmoil in adolescence: A cross-cultural perspective. *World Psychology, 5*.

Dasen, P. R. (1972). Cross-cultural Piagetian research: A summary. *Journal of Cross-cultural psychology, 3*, 29–39.

Dasen, P. R. (1973). Preliminary Study of Sensori-Motor Development in Baoule Children. *Early Child Development & Care,, 2*(3), 345–354.

Dasen, P. R., Lavallee, M., & Retschitzki, J. (1979). Training conservation of quantity (liquids) in West Africa (Baoule) children. *International Journal of Psychology, 14*(1), 57–68.

Dasen, P. R., Dembélé, B., Koffi, D. A., & N'guessan, A. (1985). N'glouèlê, l'intelligence chez les Baoulé. *Archive de Psychologie, 53*, 293–324.

David, H. P. (1981). Unwantedness: Longitudinal studies of Prague children born to women twice denied abortions for the same pregnancy and matched controls. In P. Ahmed (Ed.), *Pregnancy, childbirth, and parenthood*. New York: Elsevier.

Davies, M. M. (1997). *Fake, fact, and fantasy: Children's interpretations of television reality*. Mahwah, NJ: Erlbaum.

Davis, A. (1948). *Social class differences in learning*. Cambridge, MA: Harvard University Press.

Davydov, V. V. (1999). A new approach to the interpretation of activity structure and content. In S. Chaiklin & E. Hedegaard (Eds.), *Activity theory and social practice* (pp. 39–50). Aarhus, Denmark: Aarhus University Press.

De Casper, A., Leccnuet, J.-P., Busnel, M.-C., Granier-Deferre, C., & others (1994). Fetal reactions to recurrent maternal speech. *Infant Behavior & Development, 17*(2), 159–164.

De Casper, A. J., & Fifer, W. P. (1980). Of human bonding: Newborns prefer their mother's voices. *Science, 208*, 1174–1176.

De Casper, A. J., & Sigafoos, A. D. (1983). The intrauterine heartbeat: A potent reinforcer for newborns. *Infant Behavior and Development, 6*, 19–25.

De Casper, A. J. S., M.J. (1986). Prenatal maternal speech influences newborn's perceptions of speech sounds. *Infant Behavior and Development, 3*, 133–150.

De Villiers, J. G., & de Villiers, P. A. (1978). *Language acquisition*. Cambridge, MA: Harvard University Press.

De Villiers, J. G., & De Villiers, P. A. (1979). *Early language*. Cambridge, MA: Harvard University Press.

de Vos, H., & Zeggelink, E. (1997). Reciprocal altruism in human social evolution: The viability of reciprocal altruism with a preference for "old-helping-partners." *Evolution and Human Behavior, 18*(4), 261–278.

De Vries, J. I. P. (1992). The first trimester. In J. G.Nijhuis (Ed.), *Fetal behavior: Developmental and perinatal aspects*. New York: Oxford University Press.

De Vries, J. I., Hay V. G., & Prechtl, H. F. (1982). The emergence of fetal behaviour. I. Qualitative aspects. *Early Human Development, 7*(4), 301–322.

De Vries, M. (1987). Cry babies, culture, and catastrophe: Infant temperament among the Masai. In N. Scheper-Hughes (Ed.), *Child survival: Anthropological approaches to the treatment and maltreatment of children*. Boston: Reidel.

De Vries, M. W. (1994). Kids in context: Temperament in cross-cultural perspective. In W. B. Carey & S. C. Devitt (Eds.), *Prevention and early intervention: Individual differences as risk factors for the mental health of children*. New York: .: Brunner/Mazel.

De Vries, R. (1969). Constancy of genetic identity in the years three to six. *Monographs of the Society for Research in Child Development, 34*(Serial No. 127).

de Vrijer, B., Harthoorn-Lasthuizen, E. J., & Oosterbaan, H. P. (1999). The incidence of irregular antibodies in pregnancy: a prospective study in the region of the 's-Hertogenbosch. *Nederlands Tijdschrift voor Geneeskunde, 143*(5), 2523–2527.

De Wolff, M., & van Ijzendoorn, M. H. (1997). Sensitivity and attachment: A meta-analysis on parental antecedents of infant attachment. *Child Development, 68*(4), 571–591.

Decarie, T. G. (1969). A study of the mental and emotional development of the thalidomide child. In B. M. Foss (Ed.), *Determinants of infant behavior* (Vol. 4). London: Methuen.

Delaney, C. H. (1995). Rites of passage in adolescence. *Adolescence, 30*, 891–897.

DeFries, J. C., Plomin, R., & Fulker, D. W. (Eds.). (1994). *Nature and nurture during middle childhood.* Cambridge, MA: Blackwell.

DeLoache, J. S. (1987). Rapid change in the symbolic functioning of very young children. *Science, 238*, 1556–1557.

DeLoache, J. S. (1995a). Early symbolic reasoning. In D. Medin (Ed.), *The Psychology of Learning and Motivation* (Vol. 32). New York: Academic Press.

DeLoache, J. S. (1995b). Early understanding and use of symbols: The model model. *Current Directions in Psychological Science, 4*, 109–113.

DeLoache, J. S., & Burns, N. M. (1994). Symbolic functioning in preschool children. *Journal of Applied Developmental Psychology, 15*(4), 513–527.

DeLoache, J. S., Cassidy, D. J., & Brown, A. L. (1985). Precursors of mnemonic strategies in young children. *Child Development, 56*, 125–137.

DeLoache, J. S., Miller, K. F., & Pierroutsakos, S. L. (1998). Reasoning and problem solving. In D. Kuhn & R. S. Siegler (Eds.), *Handbook of child psychology* (5th ed.)*: Vol. 2: Cognition, perception, and language* (pp. 801–850). New York: Wiley.

Dennis, M., Sugar, J., & Whitaker, H. A. (1982). The acquisition of tag questions. *Child Development, 53*, 1254–1257.

Dennis, W. (1973). *Children of the creche.* New York: Appleton-Century-Crofts.

Dennis, W., & Dennis, M. (1940). The effect of cradling practices upon the onset of walking in Hopi children. *Journal of Genetic Psychology, 56*, 77–86.

Dent-Read, C. (1997). A naturalistic study of metaphor development: Seeing and seeing as. In C. Dent-Read & P. Zukow-Goldring (Eds.), *Evolving explanations of development* (pp. 255–296). Washington, DC: American Psychological Association.

Devaney, B. L., Ellwood, M. R., & Love, J. M. (1997). Programs that mitigate against poverty. *The Future of Children, 7*(2), 88–112.

Diamond, A. (1990a). Introduction. *Annals of the New York Academy of Sciences, 608*, xiiii–vi.

Diamond, A. (1990b). The development and neural basis of higher cognitive functions. *Annals of the New York Academy of Sciences, 608*, 267–317.

Diamond, A., Cruttenden, L., & Neiderman, L. (1994). AB with multiple wells: 1. Why are multiple wells sometimes easier than two wells? 2. Memory or memory and inhibition. *Developmental Psychology, 30*, 195–205.

Diamond, A., Prevor, M. B., Callendar, G., & Druin, D. P. (1997). Prefrontal cortex cognitive deficits in children treated early and continuously for PKU. *Monographs of the Society for Research in Child Development, 62*(4), Serial No. 252.

Dias, M. G., & Harris, P. L. (1988). The effect of make-believe play on deductive reasoning. *British Journal of Developmental Psychology, 6(3)*, 207–221.

Dias, M. G., & Harris, P. L. (1990). The influence of the imagination on reasoning by young children. *British Journal of Developmental Psychology, 8*, 305–318.

Dietz, W. H., & Gortmacher, S. L. (1985). Do we fatten our children at the television set: Obesity and television viewing in children and adolescents. *Pediatrics, 75*, 807–812.

Dillard, A. (1987). *An American childhood.* New York: Harper & Row.

Dimant, R. J., & Bearison, D. J. (1991). Development of formal reasoning during successive peer interactions. *Developmental Psychology, 27*(2), 277–284.

Dishion, T. J. (1990). The family ecology of boys' peer relations in middle childhood. *Child Development, 61*, 874–892.

Dishion, T. J., Duncan, T. E., Eddy, M. J., Fagot, B. I., & Etrow, R. (1994). The world of parents and peers: Coercive exchanges and children's social adaption. *Social Development, 3*, 255–268.

Dlugosz, L., & Bracken, M. B. (1992). Reproductive effects of caffeine: A review and theoretical analysis. *Epidemiologic Reviews, 14*, 83–100.

Dobbs, S. E. (1992). Conceptions of giftedness and talent: A Q-methodological study. *Dissertation Abstracts International, 52*(7).

Dodge, K. A. (1990). Developmental psychopathology in children of depressed mothers. *Developmental Psychology, 26*, 3–6.

Dodge, K. A. (1994). Studying mechanisms in the cycle of violence. In C. Thompson & P. Cowas (Eds.), *Violence: Basic and clinical science.* Oxford: Butterworth-Hernemas.

Domino, G. (1992). Cooperation and competition in Chinese and American children. *Journal of Cross-Cultural Psychology, 23*(4), 456–467.

Donald, M. (1991). *Origins of the modern mind: Three stages in the evolution of culture and cognition.* Cambridge, MA: Harvard University Press.

Dondi, M., Simion, F., & Caltran, G. (1999). Can newborns discriminate between their own cry and the cry of another newborn infant? *Developmental Psychology, 35*(3), 323–334.

Donlan, C. (Ed.). (1998). *The development of mathematical skills.* Hove, England: Psychology Press/Taylor & Francis.

Dore, J. (1979). Conversational acts and the acquisition of language. In E. Ochs & B. B. Schieffelin (Eds.), *Developmental Pragmatics.* New York: Academic Press.

Dore, J., Gearhart, M., & Newman, D. (1979). The structure of nursery school conversation. In K. E. Nelson (Ed.), *Children's language* (Vol. 1). Hillsdale, NJ: Erlbaum.

Dornbusch, S. M., Ritter, P. L., Leiderman, P. H., Roberts, D. F., & Fraleigh, M. J. (1987). The relation of parenting style to adolescent school performance. *Child Development, 58*, 1244–1257.

Dorr, A. (1983). No shortcuts to judging reality. In P. E. Bryant & S. Anderson (Eds.), *Watching and understanding TV: Research on children's attention and comprehension.* New York: Academic Press.

Dorval, B. (Ed.). (1990). *Conversational organization and its development.* Norwood, NJ: Ablex.

Douvan, E., & Adelson, J. (1966). *The adolescent experience.* New York: Wiley.

Downey, J., Elkin, E. J., Ehrhardt, A. A., & Meyer-Bahlburg, H. F. (1991). Cognitive ability and everyday functioning in women with Turner syndrome. *Journal of Learning Disabilities, 24*(1), 32–39.

Dreher, M. C., Nugent, K., & Hudgins, R. (1994). Prenatal marijuana exposure and neonatal outcomes in Jamaica: An ethnographic study. *Pediatrics, 93*(2), 254–260.

Dufresne, E. (Ed.). (1997). *Freud under analysis: History, theory, and practice.* Northvale, NJ: Jason Aronson, Inc.

Duncan, G. J., & Brooks-Gunn, J. (Eds.). (1997). *Consequences of growing up poor.* New York: Russell Sage Foundation.

Duncan, P. D., Ritter, P. L., Dornbusch, S. M., Gross, R. T., & Carlsmith, J. M. (1985). The effects of pubertal timing on body image, school behavior, and deviance. *Journal of Youth and Adolescence, 14*, 227–235.

Dunn, J. (1984). *Sisters and brothers.* Cambridge, MA: Harvard University Press.

Dunn, J. (1988). *The beginnings of social understanding.* Cambridge, MA: Harvard University Press.

Dunn, J., & Kendrick, C. (1979). Young siblings in the context of family relationships. In M. Lewis & L. A. Rosenblum (Eds.), *The child and its family.* New York: Plenum Press.

Dunn, J., & McGuire, S. (1992). Sibling and peer relationships in childhood. *Journal of Child Psychology & Psychiatry & Allied Disciplines, 33*(1), 67–105.

Dunn, J., & McGuire, S. (1994). Young children's nonshared experience: A summary of studies in Cambridge and Colorado. In E. M. Hethrington & D. Reiss & R. Plomin (Eds.), *Separate social worlds of siblings: The impact of nonshared environment on development.* Hillsdale, NJ: Erlbaum.

Dunn, J., & Plomin, R. (1990). *Separate lives: Why siblings are so different.* New York: Basic Books.

Dunn, J., & Shatz, M. (1989). Becoming a conversationalist despite (or because of) having a sibling. *Child Development, 60*, 399–410.

Dunn, J., Deater-Deckard, K., Pickering, K., & O'Connor, T. G. (1998). Children's adjustment and prosocial behavior in step-, single-parent, and non-stepfamily settings: Findings from a community study. *Journal of Child Psychology and Psychiatry & Allied Disciplines, 39*(8), 1083–1095.

Dunphy, D. C. (1963). The social structure of urban adolescent peer groups. *Sociometry, 26*, 230–246.

Durrett, M. E., Otaki, M., & Richards, P. (1984). Attachment and mothers' perception of support from the father. *Journal of the International Society for the Study of Behavioral Development, 7*, 167–176.

Dweck, C. S. (1991). Self-theories and goals: Their role in motivation, personality, and development. In R. A. Dienstbier (Ed.), *Nebraska Symposium on Motivation, 1990: Perspectives on motivation.* (pp. 199–235). Lincoln, NE: University of Nebraska Press.

Dweck, C. S. (1999). Self-theories: Their role in motivation, personality, and development. Philadelphia, PA: Psychology Press/Taylor & Francis,.

Dweck, C. S., & Bush, E. S. (1976). Sex differences in learned helplessness: I. Differential debilitation with peer and adult evaluators. *Developmental Psychology, 12*, 147–156.

Dweck, C. S., & Elliot, E. S. (1983). Achievement motivation. In P. H. Mussen (Ed.), *Handbook of child psychology (4th ed.): Vol. 4. Socialization, personality and social development.* New York: Wiley.

Dweck, C. S., & Goetz, T. E. (1978). Attributions and learned helplessness. In J. H. Harvey & W. Ickles & R. F. Kidd (Eds.), *New directions in attribution research* (Vol. 2). Hillsdale, NJ: Erlbaum.

Dweck, C. S., Davidson, W., Nelson, S., & Enna, B. (1978). Sex differences in learned helplessness: II. The contingencies of evaluative feedback in the classroom. III. An experimental analysis. *Developmental Psychology, 14*, 268–276.

Eaton, W. O. (1994). Methodological implications of the impending engagement of temperament and biology. In J. E. Bates & T. D. Wachs (Eds.), *Temperament: Individual differences at the interface of biology and behavior.* Washington, DC: American Psychological Association.

Eaton, W. O., & Yu, A. P. (1989). Are sex differences in child motor activity level a function of sex differences in maturational status. *Child Development, 60*, 1005–1011.

Eccles, J. S., Lord, S., & Buchanan, C. M. (1996). School transitions in early adolescence: What are we doing to our young people? In J. A. Graber & J. Brooks-Gunn (Eds.), *Transitions through adolescence: Interpersonal domains and contex* (pp. 251–284). Mahwah, NJ: Erlbaum,

Eckenrode, J., Laird, M., & Doris, J. (1993). School performance and disciplining problems among abused and neglected children. *Developmental Psychology, 29*, 53–62.

Eckerman, C. D., Sturm, L. A., & Gross, S. J. (1985). Different developmental courses for very-low-birth-weight infants differing in early head growth. *Developmental Psychology, 21*, 813–827.

Eckert, P. (1995). Trajectory and forms of institutional participation. In L. J. Crockett & A. C. Crouter (Eds.), *Pathways through adolescence: Individual development in relation to social contexts* (pp. 175–195). Mahwah, NJ: Erlbaum.

Edelman, G. M. (1992). *Bright air, brilliant fire: On the matter of the mind.* New York: Basic Books.

Eder, R. A. (1989). The emergent personologist: The structure and content of 3-, 5-, and 7-year-olds' concepts of themselves and other persons. *Child Development, 5*(1218–1228).

Edwards, C. P., & Whiting, B. B. (1993). "Mother, older sibling and me": The overlapping roles of caregivers and companions in the social world of two- to three-year-olds in Ngeca, Kenya. In K. MacDonald (Ed.), *Parent-child play: Descriptions and implications* (pp. 305–329). Albany, NY: State University of New York Press.

Eimas, P. D. (1985). The perception of speech in early infancy. *Scientific American, 252* (1), 66–72.

Eimas, P. D., & Quinn, P. C. (1994). Studies on the formation of perceptually based-level categories in young infants. *Child Development, 65*, 903–917.

Eisen, M., Zellman, G. I., Leibowitz, A., Chow, W. K., & Evans, J. R. (1983). Factors discriminating pregnancy resolution decisions of unmarried adolescents. *Genetic Psychology Monographs, 108*, 69–95.

Eisenberg, N. (1992). *The caring child.* Cambridge, MA: Harvard University Press.

Eisenberg, N., & Fabes, R. (1998). Prosocial Development. In W. Damon & N. Eisenberg (Eds.), *Handbook of child psychology* (5th ed.) *Vol. 3: Social, emotional, and personality development* (pp. 701–778). New York: Wiley.

Eisenberg, N., Fabes, R. A., Bernzweig, J., Karbon, M., Poulin, R., & Hanish, L. (1993). The relation of emotionality and regulation to preschooler's social skills and soicometric status. *Child Development, 64*, 1418–1438.

Ekman, P. (1994). Strong evidence for universal in facial expressions: A reply to Russell's mistaken critique. *Psychological Bulletin, 115*, 268–287.

Ekman, P. (1997). Expression or communication about emotion. In N. L. Segal & G. E. Weisfeld (Eds.), *Uniting psychology and biology: Integrative perspectives on human development.* (pp. 315–338). Washington DC: American Psychological Association.

Elder, G. H. J. (1998). The life course and human development. In W.Damon & R. M. Lerner (Eds.), *Handbook of child psychology* (5th ed.), *Vol 1: Theoretical models of human development* (pp. 939–992). New York: Wiley.

Eley, T. C., Lichtenstein, P., & Stevenson, J. (1999). Sex differences in the etiology of aggressive and nonaggressive antisocial behavior: Results from two twin studies. *Child Development, 70*(1), 155–168.

Eliot, T. S. (1971). East Coker, *The complete poems and plays: 1909 to 1950.* Orlando, FL: Harcourt Brace Jovanovich.

Ellis, L. (1996a). The role of perinatal factors in determining sexual orientation. In R. C. Savin-Williams & K. M. Cohen (Eds.), *The lives of lesbians, gays, and bisexuals: Children to adults.* (pp. 35–70). Fort Worth, TX: Harcourt-Brace College Publishers.

Ellis, L. (1996b). Theories of homosexuality. In R. C. Savin-Williams & K. M. Cohen (Eds.), *The lives of lesbians, gays, and bisexuals: Children to adults.* (pp. 11–34). Fort Worth, TX: Harcourt-Brace College Publishers.

Ellis, S. A., & Gauvain, M. (1992). Social and cultural influences on children's collaborative interactions. In L. T. Winegar & J. Valsiner (Eds.), *Children's development within social context,* (pp. 155-180). Hillsdale, NJ: Erlbaum.

Ellis, S., & Siegler, R. S. (1997). Planning as a strategy choice, or why don't children plan when they should? In S. L. Friedman & E. K. Scholnick (Eds.), *The developmental psychology of planning: Why, how, and when do we plan?* (pp. 183–208). Mahwah, NJ: Erlbaum.

Ellis, S., Rogoff, B., & Cromer, C. (1981). Age segregation in children's interactions. *Developmental Psychology, 17*, 399–407.

Elman, J., & others (1996). *Rethinking innateness: A connectionist perspective on development.* Cambridge, Mass: MIT Press.

Emde, R. N. (1992). Individual meaning and increasing complexity: Contributions of Sigmund Freud and Rene Spitz to developmental psychology. *Developmental Psychology, 28*, 347–359.

Emde, R. N., & Robinson, J. (1979). The first two months: Recent research in developmental psychobiology and the changing view of the newborn. In J. Noshpitz & J. Call (Eds.), *Basic handbook of child psychiatry.* New York: Basic Books.

Emde, R. N., Gaensbauer, T. J., & Harmon, R. J. (1976). Emotional expression in infancy: A behavioral study. *Psychological Issues Monograph Series, 10*(1, Serial No. 37).

Emery, R. E., & Forehand, R. (1994). Parental divorce and children's well-being: A focus on resilience. In R. J. Haggerty & L. R. Sherrod & N. Garmezy & M. Rutter (Eds.), *Stress, risk, and resilence in children and adolescents* (pp. 64–99). Cambridge: Cambridge University Press.

Engen, T., Lipsitt, L. P., & Kaye, H. (1963). Olfactory responses and adaptation in the human neonate. *Journal of Comparative and Physiological Psychology, 56*, 73–77.

Epstein, L. H., McCurley, J., Wing, R. R., & Valoski, A. (1990). A five-year follow-up of family-based behavioral treatments for childhood obesity. *Journal of Consulting and Clinical Psychology, 58*, 661–664.

Epstein, L. H., Valoski, A., & McCurley, J. (1993). Compliance and long-term follow-up for childhood obesity: Retrospective analysis. In N. A. Krasnegor & L. H. Epstein & S. B. Johnson & S. J. Yaffe (Eds.), *Developmental aspects of health compliance behavior.* Hillsdale, NJ: Erlbaum.

Erel, O., Margolin, G., & Joh, R. S. (1998). Observed sibling interaction: Links with the marital and mother-child relationship. *Developmental Psychology, 34*(2), 288–298.

Erickson, F., & Mohatt, G. (1982). Cultural organization of participation structures in two classrooms of Indian students. In G. Spindler (Ed.), *Doing the ethnography of schooling: Educational anthropology in action* (pp. 132–175). Prospect Heights, IL: Waveland Press.

Erikson, E. H. (1963). *Childhood and society* (2nd ed.). New York: W.W. Norton.

Erikson, E. H. (1968a). *Identity: Youth and crisis.* New York: W. W. Norton.

Erikson, E. H. (1968b). Life cycle. In D. L. Sills (Ed.), *International encyclopedia of the social sciences* (Vol. 9). New York: Crowell, Collier.

Erikson, M. F., Sroufe, L. A., & Egeland, B. (1985). The relationship between the quality of attachment and behavior problems in preschool in a high-risk sample. *Monographs of the Society for Research in Child Development, 50,* 1–2, Serial No. 209.

Eron, L., Walder, L., & Lefkowitz, M. (1971). *Learning of aggression in children.* Boston: Little, Brown.

Estes, D. (1998). Young children's awareness of their mental activity: The case of mental rotation. *Child Development, 69*(5), 1345–1360.

Eveleth, P. B., & Tanner, J. M. (1990). *Worldwide variation in human growth* (2nd ed.). Cambridge: Cambridge University Press.

Eyer, D. E. (1992). *Mother-infant bonding: A scientific fiction.* New Haven, CT: Yale University Press.

Fabes, R. A., & Eisenberg, N. (1992). Young children's coping with interpersonal anger. *Child Development, 63,* 116–128.

Fabricus, W. V., & Hagen, J. W. (1984). Use of casual attributions about recall performance to assess metamemory and predict strategic memory behavior in young children. *Developmental Psychology, 20,* 975–987.

Fagot, B. I. (1978a). The influence of sex of child on parental reactions to toddler children. *Child Development, 49,* 459–465.

Fagot, B. I. (1978b). Reinforcing contingencies for sex role behaviors: Effect of experience with children. *Child Development, 49,* 30–36.

Fagot, B. I. (1995). Psychosocial and cognitive determinants of early gender-role development. *Annual Review of Sex Research, 6,* 1–31.

Fagot, B. I., & Leinbach, M. D. (1989). The young child's gender schema: Environmental input, internal organization. *Child Development, 60,* 663–672.

Fagot, B. I., Leinbach, M. D., & Hagen, R. (1986). Gender labeling and adoption of sex-typed behaviors. *Developmental Psychology, 22,* 440–443.

Fanaroff, A. A., & Martin, R. J. (Eds.). (1997). *Neonatal-perinatal medicine: Diseases of the fetus and infant.* St. Louis: Mosby.

Fantz, R. L. (1961). The origins of form perception. *Scientific American, 204* (5) 66–72.

Fantz, R. L. (1963). Pattern vision in newborn infants. *Science, 140,* 296–297.

Fantz, R. L., Ordy, J. M., & Udelf, M. S. (1962). Maturation of pattern vision in infants during the first six months. *Journal of Comparative Physiological Psychology, 55,* 907–917.

Farrar, M. J. (1992). Negative evidence and grammatical morpheme acquisition. *Developmental Psychology, 28,* 90–98.

Farver, J. A. M. (1999). Activity setting analysis: A model for examining the role of culture in development. In A. Goencue (Ed.), *Children's engagement in the world: Sociocultural perspectives* (pp. 99–127). New York, NY: Cambridge University Press.

Farver, J. M., & Branstetter, W. H. (1994). Preschoolers' prosocial responses to their peers' distress. *Developmental Psychology, 30,* 334–341.

Farver, J. M., & Wimbarti, S. (1995). Indonesian children's play with their mothers and older siblings. *Child Development, 66,* 1493–1503.

Fearon, I., Kisilevsky, B. S., Hains, S. M. J., Muir, D. W., & and others. (1997). Swaddling after heel-lance: Age-specific effects on behavioral recovery in preterm infants. *Journal of Developmental & Behavioral Pediatrics, 18*(4), 222–232.

Feiring, C., & Taska, L. S. (1996). Family self-concept: Ideas on its meaning. In B. A. Bracken (Ed.), *Handbook of self-concept: Developmental, social, and clinical considerations.* New York: Wiley.

Feldman, D. H. (1994). *Beyond universal in cognitive development* (2nd ed.). Norwood, NJ: Ablex.

Feldman, D. H. (1999). A developmental, evolutionary perspective on gifts and talents. *Journal for the Education of the Gifted, 22*(2), 159–167.

Feldman, H., Goldin-Meadow, S., & Gleitman, L. (1978). Beyond Herodotus: The creation of language by linguistically deprived, deaf children. In A. Lock (Ed.), *Action, symbol, and gesture: The emergence of language.* New York: Academic Press.

Fendrick, M., Warner, V., & Weissman, M. M. (1990). Family risk factors, parental depression, and psychopathology in offspring. *Developmental Psychology, 26,* 40–50.

Fenson, L., Dale, P. S., Reznick, J. S., Bates, E., Thal, O. J., & Pettnick, S. J. (1994). Variability in early communicative development. *Monographs for Research in Child Development, 59*(5, Serial No. 242).

Fernald, A. (1991). Prosody in speech to children: Prelinguistic and linguistic functions. In R. Vasta (Ed.), *Annals of child development* (Vol. 8). London: Kingley.

Field, T. (1990). *Infancy.* Cambridge, MA: Harvard University Press.

Field, T. (1997). The treatment of depressed mothers and their infants. In L. Murray & P. J. Cooper (Eds.), *Postpartum depression and child development* (pp. 221–236). New York, NY: Guilford Press.

Field, T. M., Woodson, R., Greenberg, R., & Cohen, D. (1982). Discrimination and imitation of facial expressions by neonates. *Science, 218,* 179–182.

Fiese, B. H. (1990). Playful relationships: A contextual analysis of mother-toddler interaction and symbolic play. *Child Development, 61,* 1648–1656.

Fifer, W. P., & Moon, C. M. (1995). The effects of fetal experience with sound. In J. P. Lecanuet & W. P. Fifer & N. A. Krasnegor & W. P. Smotherman (Eds.), *Fetal development: A psychobiological perspective.* Hillsdale, NJ: Erlbaum.

Finch, M. D., Mortimer, J. T., & Ryu, S. (1997). Transition into part-time work: Health risks and opportunities. In J. Schulenberg & J. L. Maggs (Eds.), *Health risks and developmental transitions during adolescence* (pp. 321–344). New York: Cambridge University Press.

Finkelhor, D. (1994). The international epidemiology of child sexual abuse. *Child Abuse and Neglect, 18,* 409–417.

Finkelhor, D., & Dziuba-Leatherman, J. (1995). Victimization prevention programs: A national survey of children's exposure and reactions. *Child Abuse & Neglect, 19*(2), 129–139.

Finnegan, R. A., Hodges, E. V. E., & Perry, D. G. (1998). Victimization by peers: Associations with children's reports of mother-child interaction. *Journal of Personality & Social Psychology, 75*(4), 1076–1086.

Fischer, K. W., & Bidell, T. R. (1998). Dynamical development of psychological structures in action and thought. In W. Damon & R. M. Lerner (Eds.), *Handbook of child psychology* (5th ed.), *Vol 1: Theoretical models of human development* (pp. 467–562). New York: Wiley.

Fischer, K. W., & Rose, S. P. (1994). Dynamic development of coordination of components in brain and behavior: A framework for theory and research. In G. Dawson & K. W. Fischer (Eds.), *Human behavior and the developing brain* (pp. 3–66). New York: Guilford Press.

Fischer, K. W., Shaver, P. R., & Carnochan, P. (1989). A skill approach to emotional development: From basic-to-subordinate-category emotions. In W. Damon (Ed.), *Child development today and tomorrow.* San Francisco: Jossey-Bass.

Fischer, K. W., & Rose, S. P. (1995). Dynamic growth cycles of brain and cognition development. In R. W. Thatcher & G. R. Lyon & J. Ramsey & N. Krasnegor (Eds.), *Developmental neuroimaging: Mapping the development of brain and behavior.* New York: Academic Press.

Fischer, K. W., & Rose, S. P. (1996). Dynamic growth cycles of brain and development. In R. Thatcher & G. R. Lyon & J. Rumsey & N. Krasnegor (Eds.), *Developmental neuroimaging: Mapping the development of brain and behavior.* New York: Academic Press.

Fishbein, H. D. (1976). *Evolution, development and children's learning.* Pacific Palisades, CA: Goodyear.

Fivush, R. (1998). Gendered narratives: Elaboration, structure, and emotion in parent-child reminiscing across the preschool years. In P. Thompson & D. J. Herrmann (Eds.), *Autobiographical memory: Theoretical and applied perspectives* (pp. 79–103). Mahwah, NJ: Erlbaum.

Fivush, R., Haden, C., & Reese, E. (1996). Remembering, recounting, and reminiscing: The development of autobiographical memory in social context. In D. C. Rubin (Ed.), *Remembering our past: Studies in autobiographical memory* (pp. 341–359). New York: Cambridge University Press.

Flanagan, C. (1995, March). *Adolescents' explanations for poverty, unemployment, homelessness, and wealth.* Paper presented at the Paper presented at the biennial meetings of the Society for Research On Child Development, Indianapolis, Indiana.

Flanagan, C. A., & Tucker, C. J. (1999). Adolescents' explanations for political issues: Concordance with their views of self and society. *Developmental Psychology, 35*(5), 1198–1209.

Flanagan, C. A., Bowes, J. M., Jonsson, B., Csapo, B., & Sheblanova, E. (1998). Ties that bind: Correlates of adolescents' civic commitments in seven countries. *Journal of Social Issues., 54*(3), 457–475.

Flavell, J. H. (1971). Stage-related properties of cognitive development. *Cognitive Psychology, 2*, 421–453.

Flavell, J. H. (1990b June 2). *Perspectives on perspective-taking.* Paper presented at the Paper presented at the 20th Annual Symposium of the Jean Piaget Society, Philadelphia.

Flavell, J. H., & Miller, P. H. (1998). Social cognition. In D. Kuhn & R. S. Siegler (Eds.), *Handbook of child psychology* (5th ed.), *Vol. 2: Cognition, perception, and language* (pp. 851–898). New York: Wiley.

Flavell, J. H., Friedrichs, A. G., & Hoyt, J. D. (1970). Developmental changes in memorization processes. *Cognitive Psychology, 1*, 324–340.

Flavell, J. H., Flavell, E. R., & Green, F. L. (1983). Development of the appearance-reality distinction. *Cognitive Psychology, 15*, 95–120.

Flavell, J. H., Green, F. L., & Flavell, E. R. (1986). Development of knowledge about the appearance-reality distinction. *Monographs of the Society for Research in Child Development, 51*(1, Serial No. 212).

Flavell, J. H., Green, F. L., Wahl, K. R., & Flavell, E. R. (1987). The effects of question clarification and memory aids on young children's performance on appearance-reality tasks. *Cognitive Development, 2*, 127–144.

Flavell, J. H., Green, F. L., & Flavell, E. R. (1990a). Developmental changes in young children's knowledge about the mind. *Cognitive Development, 5*, 1–27.

Flavell, J. H., Flavell, E. R., Green, F. L., & Korfmacher, J. E. (1990c). Do young children think of television images as pictures or real objects? *Journal of Broadcasting & Electronic Media, 34*, 339–419.

Flavell, J. H., Miller, P. H., & Miller, S. A. (1993). *Cognitive development* (3rd ed.). Englewood Cliffs, NJ: Prentice Hall.

Flavell, J. H., Green, F. L., & Flavell, E. R. (1995). Young children's knowledge about thinking. *Monographs of the Society for Research in Child Development, 60*(1, Serial No. 243), 1–95.

Fletcher, A. C., Darling, N. E., Steinberg, L., & Dornbusch, S. (1995). The company they keep: Relation of adolescents' adjustment and behavior to their friends; perceptions of authoritative parenting in the social network. *Developmental Psychology, 31*, 300–310.

Flieller, A. (1999). Comparison of the development of formal thought in adolescent cohorts aged 10 to 15 years (1967–1996 and 1972–1993). *Developmental Psychology.*

Flynn, J. R. (1999). Searching for justice: The discovery of IQ gains over time. *American Psychologist, 54*(1), 5–20.

Fodor, J. (1983). *The modularity of mind.* Cambridge, MA: MIT Press.

Fordham, S., & Ogbu, J. U. (1986). Black students school success: Coping with the "burden of 'acting white.' "*Urban Review, 18(3)*, 176–206.

Foreman, N., Fielder, A., Minshell, C., Hurrion, E., & Sergienko, E. (1997). Visual search, perception, and visual-motor skill in "healthy" children born at 27–32 weeks' gestation. *Journal of Experimental Child Psychology, 64*(1), 27–41.

Forgatch, M. S., & Patterson, G. R. (1998). Behavioral family therapy. In F. M. Dattilio (Ed.), *Case studies in couple and family therapy: Systemic and cognitive perspectives* (pp. 85–107). New York: Guilford Press.

Forgays, D. G., & Forgays, J. W. (1952). The nature of the effect of free-environmental experience in the rat. *Journal of Comparative and Physiological Psychology, 45*, 322–328.

Fox, N., & Bell, M. A. (1990). Electrophysiological indices of frontal lobe development. *Annals of the New York Academy of Sciences, 608*, 677–704.

Fox, N., Kagan, J., & Weiskopf, S. (1979). The growth of memory during infancy. *Genetic Psychology Monographs, 99*, 91–130.

Fraiberg, S. (1977). *Every child's birthright: In defense of mothering.* New York: Basic Books.

Fraiberg, S. H. (1959). *The magic years: Understanding and handling the problems of early childhood.* New York: Scribner.

Fraiberg, S. H. (1974). Blind infants and their mothers: An examination of the sign system. In M. Lewis & L. Rosenblum (Eds.), *The effect of the infant on its caregiver.* New York: Wiley.

Franco, F., & Butterworth, G. (1991, April). *Infant pointing: Prelinguistic reference and co-reference.* Paper presented at the Society for Research in Child Development Biennial Meeting, Seattle, WA.

Frank, A. (1975). *The diary of a young girl.* New York: Pocket Books.

Frankel, K., & Bates, J. (1990). Mother-toddler problem solving: Antecedents in attachment, home behavior,and temperament. *Child Development, 61*, 810–819.

Frankenburg, W. K., & Dodds, J. B. (1967). The Denver developmental screening test. *The Journal of Pediatrics, 71*, 181–191.

Frankenburg, W. K., Fandal, A. W., Sciarillo, W., & Burgess, D. (1981). The newly abbreviated and revised Denver Developmental Screening Test. *Behavioral Pediatrics, 99*(6), 995-999.

Franscino, R. J. (1995). Changing Face of HIV/AIDS Care–Mother-Fetal and Maternal-Child HIV Transmissions. *Western Journal of Medicine, 163*(4), 368–369.

Freed, K. (1983, March 14). Cubatao–a paradise lost to pollution. *Los Angeles Times*, pp. pp. 1, 12, 13.

Fremgen, A., & Fay, D. (1980). Overextensions in production and comprehension: A methodological clarification. *Journal of Child Language, 7*, 201–211.

Frenkiel, N. (1993, November 11). Planning a family, down to a baby's sex. *New York Times*, pp. B1, B4.

Freud, A. (1942). *The ego and the mechanisms of defence.* London: Hogarth Press, and the Institute of Psycho-analysis.

Freud, S. (1905/1953a). Three essays on the theory of sexuality. In J. Strachey (Ed.), *The standard edition of the complete psychological works of Sigmund Freud* (Vol. 7). London: Hogarth Press.

Freud, S. (1920/1955). Beyond the pleasure principle. In J. Strachey (Ed.), *The standard edition of the complete psychological works of Sigmund Freud* (Vol. 18). London: Hogarth Press.

Freud, S. (1921/1949). Group psychology–The analysis of the Ego. In J. Strachey (Ed.), *The standard edition of the complete psychological works of Sigmund Freud* (Vol. 18). London: Hogarth Press.

Freud, S. (1925/1961). Some psychical consequences of the anatomical distinctions between the sexes. In J. Strachey (Ed.), *The standard edition of the complete psychological works of Sigmund Freud* (Vol. 19). London: Hogarth Press.

Freud, S. (1930/1961). *Civilization and its discontents.* New York: W. W. Norton.
Freud, S. (1933/1964). *New introductory lectures in psychoanalysis.* New York: W. W. Norton.
Freud, S. (1940/1964). An outline of psychoanalysis. In J. Strachey (Ed.), *The standard edition of the complete psychological works of Sigmund Freud* (Vol. 23). London: Hogarth Press.
Frid, C., Drott, P., Lundell, B., Rasmussen, F., & Anneren, G. (1999). Mortality in Down's syndrome in relation to congenital malformations. *Journal of Intellectual Disability Research, 43*(3), 234–241.
Friedman, A., Todd, J., & Kariuki, P. W. (1995). Cooperative and competitive behavior of urban and rural children in Kenya. *Journal of Cross-Cultural Psychology, 26*(4), 374–383.
Friedman, H. S., Tucker, J. S., Schwartz, J. E., Tomlinson-Keasey, C., Martin, L. R., Wingard, D. L., & Criqui, M. H. (1995). Psychosocial and behavioral predictors of longevity. *American Psychologist, 50(2), 69–78.*
Frith, U. (1989). *Autism.* Oxford: Oxford University Press.
Frodi, A. (1985). When empathy fails: Aversive infant crying and children abuse. In B. M. Lester & C. F. Z. Boukydis (Eds.), *Infant crying: Theoretical and research prospectives.* New York: Plenum Press.
Frost, R. (1916/1969). The road not taken. In E. C. Lathem (Ed.), *The poetry of Robert Frost.* New York: Holt, Rinehart and Winston.
Fry, D. P. (1988). Intercommunity differences in aggression among Zapotec children. *Child Development, 59,* 1008–1018.
Fukushima, O., & Kato, M. (1976). The effects of vicarious experiences on children's altruistic behavior. *Bulletin of Tokyo Gakuge University, 27* (Series 1), *90–94.*
Fuligni, A. J., & Eccles, J. S. (1993). Perceived parent-child relationships and early adolescents' orientation toward peers. *Developmental Psychology, 29,* 622–632.
Fuligni, A. J., & Stevenson, H. W. (1995). Time use and mathematics achievement among American, Chinese, and Japanese high school students. *Child Development, 66*(3), 830–842.
Fullard, W., & Reiling, A. M. (1976). An investigation of Lorenz's babyness. *Child Development, 47,* 1191–1193.
Furman, W., Rahe, D. F., & Hartup, W. W. (1979). Rehabilitation of socially withdrawn preschool children through mixed-age and same-age socialization. *Child Development, 50(4),* 915–922.
Furstenberg, F. F., Jr., & Cherlin, A. J. (1991). *Divided families: What happens to children when parents part.* Cambridge, MA: Harvard University Press.
Furstenberg, F. F., Jr., Hughes, M. E., & Brooks-Gunn, J. (1992). The next generation: The children of teenage mothers grow up. In M. Rosenheim & M. F. Testa (Eds.), *Early parenthood and coming of age in the 1990's.* New Brunswick, NJ: Rutgers University Press.
Futuyma, D. J. (1998). *Evolutionary biology* (3rd ed.). Sunderland, MA: Sinauer Associates.

Gagnon, J. H., & Simon, W. (1973). *Sexual conduct: The social sources of human sexuality.* Chicago: Aldine.
Galinsky, E., Howes, C., Kontos, S., & Shinn, M. (1994). *The study of children in family child care and relative care: Highlights of the findings.* New York: Families and Work Institute.
Gallego, M. A., Cole, M., & Cognition, L. o. C. H. (2000). Classroom culture and culture in the classroom. In V. Richardson (Ed.), *The Handbook of Research on Teaching.* Washington, DC: American Educational Research Association.
Gallup, G. G. J. (1970). Chimpanzees: Self-recognition. *Science, 167,* 86–87.
Gamper, E. (1926). Bau and Leistungen eines menschichen Mitteilhirnwesens (Arhinencephalie mit Encephalocele). Zugleich ein Beitrag zu Teratologie und Fasersystematik. *Zeitschr. f.d.ges. Neurol. u. Psychiat, vii*(154, civ. 149).
Gardner, D. P., & others. (1983). *A nation at risk: The imperative for educational reform. An open letter to the American people* (50226006). Washington, DC: National Commission on Excellence in Education.
Gardner, H. (1980). *Artful scribbles: The significance of children's drawings.* New York: Basic Books.
Gardner, H. (1983). *Frames of mind: The theory of multiple intelligences.* New York: Basic Books.
Gardner, H., Wolf, D., & Smith, A. (1982). Max and Molly: Individual differences in early artistic symbolization. In H. Gardner (Ed.), *Art, mind and brain: A cognitive approach to creativity.* New York: Basic Books.
Gardner, W., & Rogoff, B. (1990). Children's deliberateness of planning according to task circumstances. *Developmental Psychology, 26,* 480–487.
Garmezy, N., & Rutter, M. (Eds.). (1988). *Stress, coping, and development in children.* Baltimore: Johns Hopkins Press.
Garner, P. W., Jones, D. C., & Palmer, D. J. (1994). Social cognitive correlates of preschool children's sibling caregiving behavior. *Developmental Psychology, 30,* 905–911.
Garton, A., & Pratt, C. (1998). *Learning to be literate: The development of spoken and written language.* Oxford: Blackwell.
Garvey, C. (1990). *Play.* Cambridge, MA: Harvard University Press.
Gaskins, S. (1990). *Exploratory play and development in Maya infants.* Unpublished doctoral dissertation, University of Chicago.
Gaskins, S. (1999). Children's daily lives in a Mayan village: A case study of culturally constructed roles and activities. In A. Göncü (Ed.), *Children's engagement in the world: Sociocultural perspectives* (pp. 25–61). New York: Cambridge University Press.
Gatty, H. (1958). *Nature in your guide.* London: Collins.
Gay, J. (1984). *Red dust on the green leaves: A Kpelle twins' childhood.* Yarmouth, Me: Intercultural Press.
Gay, J., & Cole, M. (1967). *The new mathematics and an old culture.* New York: Holt, Rinehart, & Winston.
Gearhart, M., & Newman, D. (1980). Learning to draw a picture: The social context of individual activity. *Discourse Processes, 3,* 169–184.
Geertz, C. (1984). From the native's point of view: On the nature of anthropological understanding. In R. Shweder & R. Levine (Eds.), *Culture theory.* Cambridge: Cambridge University Press.
Gelman, R. (1990). First principles affect learning and transfer in children. *Cognitive Science, 14, 79–107.*
Gelman, R. (1998). Domain specificity in cognitive development: Universals and nonuniversals. In M. Sabourin & F. Craik (Eds.), *Advances in psychological science, Vol. 2: Biological and cognitive aspects* (pp. 557–579). Hove, England: Psychology Press/Erlbaum.
Gelman, R., & Williams, E. M. (1998). Enabling constraints for cognitive development and learning: Domain specificity and epigenesis. In D. Kuhn & R. S. Siegler (Eds.), *Handbook of child psychology,* (5th ed.), *Vol 2: Cognition, perception and language* (pp. 575–630). New York: Wiley.
Gelman, R., Meck, E., & Merkin, S. (1986). Young children's mathematical competence. *Cognitive Development, 1,* 1–29.
Gelman, S. A., & Wellman, H. M. (1991). Insides and essence: Early understandings of the non-obvious. *Cognition, 38*(3), 213-244.
Genovese, E. D. (1976). *Role, Jordan, roll.* New York: Random House.
Gentile, D. A. (1993). Just what are sex and gender, anyway? A call for a new terminological standard. *Psychological Science, 4*(2), 120–122.
Gergely, G., Nadasdy, Z., Csibra, G., & Biro, S. (1995). Taking the intentional stance at 12 months of age. *Cognition, 56,* 165–193.
Gesell, A. (1929). *Infancy and human growth.* New York: Macmillan.
Gesell, A. (1940). *The first five years of life* (9th ed.). New York: Harper & Row.
Gesell, A., & Ilg, F. L. (1943). *Infant and child in the culture of today.* New York: Harper & Row.
Gewirtz, J. L., & Pelaez-Nogueras, M. (1992). B. F. Skinner's legacy in human infant behavior and development. *Americn Psychologist, 47*(11), 1411–1422.
Gibson, E. J. (1988). Exploratory behavior in the development of perceiving, acting, and the acquiring of knowledge. *Annual Review of Psychology, 39,* 1–41.

Gibson, E. J., & Walker, A. S. (1984). Development of knowledge of visual-tactual affordances of substances. *Child Development, 55*(2), 453–460.

Gibson, M. (1997). Exploring and explaining the variability: Cross-national perspectives on the school performance of minority students. *Anthropology & Education Quarterly, 28*(3), 318–329.

Gielen, U. P., & Markoulis, D. C. (1994). Preference for principled moral reasoning: A developmental and cross-cultural perspective. In L. L. Adler & U. P. Gielen (Eds.), *Cross-cultural topics in psychology* (pp. 73–87). Westport, CT: Praeger Publishers/Greenwood Publishing Group, Inc.

Gilbert, S. F. (1991). *Developmental biology* (3rd ed.). Sunderland, MA: Sinaver.

Gilbert, S. F., & Raunio, A. M. (Eds.). (1997). *Embryology: Constructing the organism.* Sunderland, MA: Sinauer Associates.

Gilligan, C. (1977). In a different voice: Women's conceptions of the self and of morality. *Harvard Educational Review, 47,* 481–517.

Gilligan, C. (1982). *In a different voice: Psychological theory and women's development.* Cambridge, MA: Harvard University Press.

Gilligan, C. (1986). Remapping the moral domain: New images of the self in relationship. In J. C. Heller & M. Sosna & D. E. Wellberg (Eds.), *Reconstructing individualism: Autonomy, individuality, and self in Western thought.* Stanford, CA: Stanford University Press.

Gilligan, C., & Attanucci, J. (1988). Two moral orientations: Gender differences and similarities. *Merrill-Palmer Quarterly, 34,* 223–237.

Ginsberg, B. G. (1993). Catharsis. In C. E. Schaefer (Ed.), *Therapeutic powers of play* (pp. 107–141). Northvale, NJ: Jason Aronson, Inc.

Ginsberg, H. (1977). *Children's arithmetic.* New York: Van Nostrand.

Gladwin, E. T. (1970). *East is a big bird.* Cambridge, MA: Harvard University Press.

Gleitman, H. (1963). *Psychology.* New York: W. W. Norton.

Gleitman, L., Newport, E., & Gleitman, H. (1984). The current status of the motherese hypothesis. *Journal of Child Language, 11,* 43–80.

Godfrey, K. M. (1998). Maternal Regulation of fetal development and health in adult life. *European Journal of Obstetrics & Gynecology and Reproductive Biology, 78,* 141–150.

Goelman, H. (1988). The relationship between structure and process variables in home and day care settings on children's language development. In A. R. Pence (Ed.), *Ecological research with children and families.* New York: Teachers College Press.

Golan, M., Fainaru, M., & Weizman, A. (1998). Role of behaviour modification in the treatment of childhood obesity with the parents as the exclusive agents of change. *International Journal of Obesity and Related Metabolic Disorders, 22*(12), 1217–1224.

Goldin-Meadow, S. (1985). Language development under atypical learning conditions. In K. E. Nelson (Ed.), *Children's language* (Vol. 5). Hillsdale, NJ: Erlbaum.

Goldin-Meadow, S. (1997). The resilience of language in humans. In C. T. Snowdon & M. Hausberger (Eds.), *Social influences on vocal development.* Cambridge: Cambridge University Press.

Goldin-Meadow, S., & Mylander, C. (1998). Spontaneous sign systems created by deaf children in two cultures. *Nature, 391,* 279–281.

Goldsmith, H. H., & Campos, J. J. (1982). Toward a theory of infant temperament. In R. N. Emde & R. Harmon (Eds.), *The development of attachment and affiliative systems.* New York: Plenum Press.

Goldsmith, H. H., & Gottesman, I. I. (1981). Origins of variation in behavior style: A longitudinal study of young twins. *Child Development, 52,* 91–103.

Goldsmith, H. H., & Rothbart, M. K. (1991). Contemporary instruments for assessing early temperament by questionnaire and in the laboratory. In J. Strelau & A. Angleitner (Eds.), *Explorations in temperament: International perspectives on theory and measurement.* (pp. 249–272). New York: Plenum Press.

Golinkoff, R. M., Mervis, C. B., & Hirsh-Pasek, K. (1994). Early object labels: The case for a developmental lexical principles framework. *Journal of Child Language, 21,* 125–155.

Golinkoff, R. M., Hirsh-Pasek, K., & Schweisguth, M. A. (1999). A reappraisal of young children's knowledge of grammatical morphemes. In J. Weissenborn & B. Hoehle (Eds.), *Approaches to bootstrapping: Phonological, syntactic, and neurophysiological aspects of early language acquisition.*

Golinkoff, R. M., Shuff-Bailey, M., Olguin, R., & Ruan, W. (1995). Young children extend novel words at the basic level: Evidence for the principle of categorical scope. *Developmental Psychology, 31*(3), 494–507.

Golomb, C. (1974). *Young children's sculpture and drawing.* Cambridge, MA: Harvard University Press.

Gomes-Schwartz, B., Horowitz, J. M., & Cardarelli, A. P. (1990). *Child sexual abuse: Initial effects.* Newbury Park, CA: Sage Publications.

Goncu, A. & Kessel, F. S. (1988). Preschoolers' collaborative construction in planning and maintaining imaginative play. *International Journal of Behavioral Development, 11,* 327–344.

Goncu, A. E. (Ed.). (1999). *Children's engagement in the world: Sociocultural perspectives.* New York: Cambridge University Press.

Gonsiorek, J. C., & Weinrich, J. D. (Eds.). (1991). *Homosexuality: Research implications for public policy.* Newbury Park, CA: Sage Publications.

Good, T. L., Sikes, J., & Brophy, J. (1973). Effects of teacher sex and student sex on classroom interaction. *Journal of Educational Psychology, 65,* 74–87.

Goodenough, F. L. (1936). The measurement of mental functions in primitive groups. *American Anthropologist, 38,* 1–11.

Goodenough, W. H. (1953). *Native astronomy in the Central Carolines. Museum Monographs.* Philadelphia: University Museum, University of Pennsylvania.

Goodman, G. S., Rudy, L., Bottoms, B. L., & Aman, C. (1990). Children's concerns and memory: Issues of ecological validity in the study of children's eyewitness testimony. In R. Fivush & J. A. Hudson (Eds.), *Knowing and remembering in young children.* New York: Cambridge University Press.

Goodman, G. S., Emery, R. E., & Haugaard, J. J. (1998). Developmental psychology and the law: Divorce, child maltreatment, foster care, and adoption. In I. E. Sigel & K. A. Renninger (Eds.), *Handbook of child psychology* (5th ed.), *Vol 4: Child psychology in practice* (pp. 775–876). New York: Wiley.

Goodman, K. S. (1996). *On reading.* Portmouth, NH: Heinemann.

Goodman, K. S. (1998). Reading, writing, and written texts: A transactional sociopsycholinguistic view. In R. B. Ruddell & M. R. Ruddell (Eds.), *Theoretical models and processes of reading* (4th ed., pp. 1093–1130). Newark, DE: International Reading Association.

Goodnow, J. J. (1977). *Children drawing.* Cambridge, MA: Harvard University Press.

Goodnow, J. J. (1998). Beyond the overall balance: The significance of particular tasks and procedures for perceptions of fairness in distributions of household work. *Social Justice Research, 11*(3), 359–376.

Goodnow, J. J., & Collins, W. A. (1990). *Development according to parents: The nature, sources, and consequences of parents' ideas.* Hillsdale, NJ: Erlbaum.

Goodnow, J. J., Cashmore, J., Cotton, S., & Knight, R. (1984). Mothers' developmental timetables in two cultural groups. *International Journal of Psychology, 19,* 193–205.

Goodwin, M. H. (1995). Co-construction in girls' hopscotch. *Research on Language and Social Interaction, 28*(3), 261–281.

Goodwin, M. H. (1997). Crafting activities: Building social organization through language in girls' and boys' groups. In C. T. Snowdon & M. Hausberger (Eds.), *Social influences on vocal development.* (pp. 328–341). Cambridge, England: Cambridge University Press.

Goodwin, M. H. (1998). Games of stance: conflict and footing in hopscotch. In M. H. Goodwin (Ed.), *Kids talk: Strategic language use in later childhood* (pp. 23–46). New York: Oxford University Press.

Goody, E. N. (1989). Learning, apprenticeship, and the division of labor. In M. Coy (Ed.), *Apprenticeship: From theory to method and back again.* Albany, NY: SUNY Press.

Gopnik, A., & Astington, J. W. (1988). Children's understanding of representational change and its relation to the understanding of false belief and the appearance-reality distinction. *Child Development, 59*(1), 26–37.

Gopnik, A., & Choi, S. (1990). Do linguistic differences lead to cognitive differences? A cross-linguistic study of semantic and cognitive development. *First Language, 10*(3), 199–215.

Gopnik, A., & Meltzoff, A. N. (1986). Words, plans, things, and locations: Interactions between semantic and cognitive development at the one-word stage. In S. R. Kuczaj & M. D. Barrett (Eds.), *The development of word meaning.* New York: Springer-Verlag.

Gopnik, A., & Meltzoff, A. N. (1997). *Words, thoughts, and theories.* Cambridge, MA: MIT Press.

Gortmaker, S. L., Must, A., Perrin, J. M., & Sobol, A. M. (1993). Social and economic consequences of overweight in adolescence and young adulthood. *New England Journal of Medicine, 329*(14), 1008-1012.

Gortmaker, S. L., Must , A., Sobol , A. M., Peterson, K., Colditz, G. A., & Dietz, W. H. (1996). Television viewing as a cause of increasing obesity among children in the United States, 1986–1990. *Archives of Pediatrics and Adolescent Medicine, 150*(4), 356–362.

Goswami, U. (1999). The relationship between phonological awareness and orthographic representation in different orthographies. In M. Harris & G. Hatano (Eds.), *Learning to read and write: A cross-linguistic perspective.* New York: Cambridge University Press.

Gottesman, I. I. (1991). *Schizophrenia genesis: The origins of madness.* New York: W. H. Freeman.

Gottlieb, G. (1997). *Synthesizing nature-nurture: Prenatal roots of instinctive behavior.* Mahwah, NJ: Erlbaum.

Gottlieb, G., Wahlsten, D., & Lickliter, R. (1998). The significance of biology for human development: A developmental psychobiological view. In W. Damon & R. M. Lerner (Eds.), *Handbook of child psychology* (5th ed.), *Vol. 1: Theoretical models of human development* (pp. 233–274). New York: Wiley.

Gottman, J., & Mettetal, G. (1989). Speculations about social and affective development: Friendship and acquaintanceship in adolescence. In J. M. Gottman & J. G. Parker (Eds.), *Conversations of friends: Speculations on affective development* (pp. 192–237). New York: Cambridge University Press.

Gottman, J. M. (1983). How children become friends. *Monographs of the Society for Research in Child Development, 48*(3, Serial No. 201).

Gould, S. J. (1977). *Phylogeny and ontogony.* Cambridge, MA: Harvard University Press.

Graber, J. A., Brooks-Gunn, J., Paikoff, R. L., & Warren, M. P. (1994). Prediction of eating problems: An 8--year study of adolescent girls. *Developmental Psychology, 30,* 823–834.

Graber, J. A., Brooks-Gunn, J., & Warren, M. (1995). The antecedents of menarcheal age: Heredity, family environment, and stressful life events. *Child Development, 66,* 346–359.

Graber, J. A., Lewinsohn, P. M., Seeley, J. R., & Brooks-Gunn, J. (1997). Is psychopathology associated with the timing of pubertal development? *Journal of the American Academy of Child & Adolescent Psychiatry, 36*(12), 1768–1776.

Graber, J. A., Brooks-Gunn, J., & Galen, B. R. (1998). Betwixt and between: Sexuality in the context of adolescent transitions. In R. Jessor (Ed.), *New perspectives on adolescent risk behavior* (pp. 270–316). New York: Cambridge University Press.

Graham, F. K., Leavitt, L. A., Stroch, B. D., & Brown, J. W. (1978). Precocious cardiac orienting in human anencephalic Infants. *Science, 199,* 322–324.

Graham, J. A., Cohen, R., Zbikowski, S. M., & Secrist, M. E. (1998). A longitudinal investigation of race and sex as factors in children's classroom friendship choices. *Child Study Journal, 28*(4), 245–266.

Graham, M. J., Larsen, U., & Xu, X. (1999). Secular trend in age at menarche in China: A case study of two rural counties in Anhui province. *Journal of Biosocial Science, 31*(2), 257–267.

Gralinski, H. J., & Kopp, C. B. (1993). Everyday rules for behavior: Mother's requests to young children. *Developmental Psychology, 29,* 573–584.

Graves, Z., & Glick, J. A. (1978). The effect of context on mother-child interaction: A progress report. *Quarterly Newsletter of the Laboratory of Comparative Human Cognition, 2,* 41–46.

Greco, C., Rovee-Collier, C., Hayne, H., & Griesler, P. (1986). Ontogeny of early event memory: I. Forgetting and retrieval by 2- and 3-month-olds. *Infant Behavior Development, 9,* 441–460.

Green, G. (1984). On the appropriateness of adaptations in primary-level basal readers: Reactions to remarks by Bertran Bruce. In R. C. Anderson & J. Osborn & R. J. Tierney (Eds.), *Learning to read in American schools.* Hillsdale, NJ: Erlbaum.

Greenberg, B. S., & Brand, J. E. (1994). Minorities and the mass media. In J. Bryant & D. Zillman (Eds.), *Media effects: Advances in theory and research.* Hillsdale, NJ: Erlbaum.

Greenberger, E., & Steinberg, L. (1986). *When teenagers work: The psychological and social costs of adolescent employment.* New York: Basic Books.

Greenberger, E., O'Neil, R., & Nagel, S. K. (1994). Linking workplace and homeplace: Relations between the nature of adult's work and their parenting behaviors. *Developmental Psychology, 30,* 990–1002.

Greene, L. S., & Johnston, F. E. (Eds.). (1980). *Social and biological predictors of nutritional status, physical growth and neurological development.* New York: Academic Press.

Greenfield, P. M. (1984). *Mind and media: The effects of television, video, games and computers.* Cambridge, MA: Harvard University Press.

Greenfield, P. M. (1997). Culture as process: Empirical methods for cultural psychology. In J. W. Berry, Y. H. Poortinga & J. Pandey (Eds.), *Handbook of cross-cultural psychology : Theory and method* (Vol. 1). Boston: Allyn & Bacon.

Greenfield, P. M., & Cocking, R. R. (Eds.). (1994). *Cross-cultural roots of minority child development.* Hillsdale, NJ: Erlbaum.

Greenfield, P. M., & Savage-Rumbaugh, E. S. (1990). Grammatical combination in Pan paniscus: Processes of learning and invention in the evolution and development of language. In S. T. Parker & K. R. Gibson (Eds.), *Language and intelligence in monkeys and apes.* Cambridge, England: Cambridge University Press.

Greenfield, P. M., & Smith, J. H. (1976). *The structure of communication in early language development.* New York: Academic Press.

Greenfield, P. M., Brazelton, T. B., & Childs, C. P. (1989). From birth to maturity in Zinacantan: Ontogenesis in cultural context. In V. Bricker & G. Gossen (Eds.), *Ethnographic encounters in southern Mesoamerica: Celebratory essays in honor of Evon Z. Vogt.* Albany: Institute of Mesoamerican Studies, State University of New York.

Gregg, N. M. (1941). Cogenital cataracts following German measles in mothers. *Transcripts of the Ophthalmological Society of Australia, 3,* 35.

Gregg, V., Gibbs, J. C., & Basinger, K. S. (1994). Patterns of developmental delay in moral judgment by male and female delinquents. *Merrill-Palmer Quarterly, 40*(4), 538–553.

Gregor, J. A., & McPherson, D. A. (1966). Racial preference and ego identity among White and Bantu children in the Republic of South Africa. *Genetic Psychology Monographs, 73,* 218–253.

Grice, H. P. (1975). Logic and conversation. In P. Cole & J. L. Morgan (Eds.), *Syntax and semantics: Vol. 3. Speech acts.* New York: Academic Press.

Griffin, P. (1983). *Personal communication.*

Griswold Del Castillo, R. (1984). *La familia: Chicano families in the urban southwest, 1848 to the present.* Notre Dame, IN: University of Notre Dame Press.

Grolnick, W. S., McMenamy, J. M., & Kurowski, C. O. (1999). Emotional self-regulation in infancy and toddlerhood. In L. Balter & C. S. Tamis-LeMonda (Eds.), *Child psychology: A handbook of contemporary issues.* Philadelphia, PA: Psychology Press/Taylor & Francis.

Gronlund, N. E. (1959). *Sociometry in the classroom.* New York: Harper Brothers.

Grossman, K. E., & Grossman, K. (1990). The wider concept of attachment in cross-cultural research. *Human Development, 33,* 31–47.

Grossmann, K. E., & Grossmann, K. (1997). *The development of attachment and psychological adaptation from the cradle to the grave.* Paper presented at the 8th European Conference on Developmental Psychology, Rennes, France.

Grossmann, K., Grossmann, K. E., Spangler, S., Suess, G., & Unzner, L. (1985). Maternal sensitivity and newborn orientation responses as related to quality of attachment in northern Germany. In I. Bretherton & E. Waters (Eds.), *Growing points of attachment theory. Monographs of the society for research in child development* (Vol. 50 (1–2 Serial No. 209)).

Grotberg, E. (1969). *Review of Head Start research, 1965–1969* (Vol. OEO Pamphlet 1608:13 ED02308). Washington, DC.

Grotevant, H. (1998). Adolescent development in family contexts. In W. Damon & N. Eisenberg (Eds.), *Handbook of child psychology* (5th ed.), *Vol 3: Social, emotional, and personality development.* (pp. 1097–1150). New York: Wiley.

Grotevant, H., & Cooper, C. (1985). Patterns of interaction in family relationships and the development of identity exploration in adolescence. *Developmental Psychology, 56*, 415–428.

Grotevant, H. D., & Cooper, C. R. (1998). Individuality and connectedness in adolescent development: Review and prospects for research on identity, relationships, and context. In E. E. A. Skoe & A. L. von der Lippe (Eds.), *Personality development in adolescence: A cross national and life span perspective* (pp. 3–37). New York: Routledge.

Grusec, J. E. (1991). Socializing concern for others in the home. *Developmental Psychology, 27*, 338–342.

Grych, J. H., & Fincham, F. D. (1997). Children's adaptation to divorce. In S. A. Wolchik & I. N. Sandler (Eds.), *Handbook of children's coping: Linking theory and intervention* (pp. 159–193). New York: Plenum.

Guilford, J. P. (1967). *The nature of human intelligence.* New York: McGraw-Hill.

Guinn, B., Semper, T., & Jorgensen, L. (1997). Mexican American female adolescent self-esteem: The effect of body image, exercise behavior, and body fatness. *Hispanic Journal of Behavioral Sciences, 19*(4), 517–526.

Guttler, F. (1988). Epidemiology and natural history of phenylketonuria and other hyperphenylalaninemias. In R. J. Wurtman & E. Ritter-Walker (Eds.), *Dietary phenylaline and brain function.* Boston: Birkhauser.

Haan, N., Langer, J., & Kohlberg, L. (1976). Family patterns of moral reasoning. *Child Development, 47*, 1204–1206.

Hagen, J. W., Meacham, J. A., & Mesibov, G. (1970). Verbal labeling, rehearsal, and short-term memory. *Cognitive Psychology, 1*, 47–58.

Haith, M. M. (1980). *Rules that babies look by: The organization of newborn visual activity.* Hillsdale, NJ: Erlbaum.

Haith, M., & Benson, J. B. (1998). Infant cognition. In D. Kuhn & R. S. Siegler (Eds.), *Handbook of child development* (5th ed.), *Vol 2: Cognition, perception, and language* (pp. 199–254). New York: Wiley.

Hall, G. S. (1904). *Adolescence.* New York: D. Appleton.

Halpern, R. (1990). Poverty and early childhood parenting: Toward a framework for intervention. *American Journal of Orthopsychiatry, 60(1)*, 6–18.

Hammen, C. (1991). *Depression runs in families: The social context of risk and resilience in children of depressed mothers.* New York: Springer-Verlag.

Hanna, E., & Meltzoff, A. N. (1993). Peer imitation by toddlers in laboratory, home, and day-care contexts: Implications for social learning and memory. *Developmental Psychology, 29*(4), 701–710.

Harkness, S. (1990). A cultural model for the acquisition of language: Implications for the innateness debate. *Developmental Psychobiology, 23*, 727–740.

Harkness, S., & Super, C. M. (1983). The cultural construction of child development: A framework for the socialization of emotion. *Ethos, 11*, 221–231.

Harkness, S., & Super, C. M. (1996). *Parent's cultural belief systems: Their origins, expressions, and consequences.* New York: Guilford Press.

Harlow, H. (1959). Love in infant monkeys. *Scientific American, 200(6)*, 68–74.

Harlow, H. F., & Harlow, M. K. (1962). Social deprivation in monkeys. *Scientific American, 207*(5), 136–146.

Harlow, H. F., & Harlow, M. K. (1969). Effects of various mother-infant relationships on rhesus monkey behaviors. In B. M. Foss (Ed.), *Determinants of infant behavior* (4th ed., Vol. 4). London: Methuen.

Harlow, H. F., & Novak, M. A. (1973). Psychopathological perspectives. *Perspectives in Biology and Medicine, Spring*, 461–478.

Harlow, H. F., & Zimmerman, R. (1959). Affectional responses in the infant monkey. *Science, 130*, 421–432.

Harman, C., & Fox, N. A. (1997). Frontal and attentional mechanisms regulating distress experience and expression during infancy. In N. A. Krasnegor & G. Reid Lyon (Eds.), *Development of the prefrontal cortex: Evolution, neurobiology, and behavior* (pp. 191–208). Baltimore: Paul H. Brookes.

Harrington, M. (1963). *The other America: Poverty in the United States.* New York: Macmillan.

Harris, H. W., Blue, H. C., & Griffith, E. H. (Eds.). (1995a). *Racial and ethnic identity: Psychological development and creative expression.* New York: Routledge.

Harris, J. R. (1998). *The nurture assumption : Why children turn out the way they do.* New York: Free Press.

Harris, P. L., & Gross, D. (1988). Children's understanding of real and apparent motion. In J. W. Astington, P. L. Harris & D. R. Olson (Eds.), *Developing theories of mind.* New York: Cambridge University Press.

Harrison, A. O., Wilson, M. N., Pine, C. J., Chan, S. Q., & Buriel, R. (1990). Family ecologies of ethnic minority children. *Child Development, 61*, 347–362.

Hart, B., & Tisley, R. (1995). *Meaningful differences in the everyday experience of young American children.* Baltimore MD: P.H. Brookes.

Hart, C. H., Ladd, G. W., & Burleson, B. R. (1990). Children's expectations of the outcomes of social strategies: Relations with sociometric status and maternal disciplinary styles. *Child Development, 61*, 127–137.

Hart, S., Field, T., & Roitfarb, M. (1999). Depressed mothers' assessments of their neonates' behaviors. *Infant Mental Health Journal, 20*(2), 200–210.

Harter, S. (1982). The perceived competence scale for children. *Child Development, 53*, 87–97.

Harter, S. (1986). Cognitive-developmental processes in integration of concepts about emotion and the self. *Social Cognition, 4*, 119–151.

Harter, S. (1987). The determinants and mediational role of global self-worth in children. In N. Eisenberg (Ed.), *Contemporary topics in developmental psychology.* New York: Wiley.

Harter, S. (1998). The development of self-representation. In N. Eisenberg (Ed.), *Handbook of child psychology* (5th ed.), *Vol 3: Social, emotional, and personality development* (pp. 553–617). New York: Wiley.

Harter, S. (1999). *The construction of the self: A developmental perspective.* New York: Guilford Press.

Harter, S., & Pike, R. (1984). The pictorial scale of perceived competence and social acceptance for young children. *Child Development, 55*, 1969–1982.

Hartshorn, K., & Rovee-Collier, C. (1997). Infant learning and long-term memory at 6 months: A confirming analysis. *Developmental Psychobiology, 30*(1), 71–85.

Hartshorn, K., Rovee-Collier, C., Gerhardstein, P., Bhatt, R. S., Wondoloski, T. L., Klein, P., Gilch, J., Wurtzel, N., & Campos-de-Carvalho, M. (1998). The ontogeny of long-term memory over the first year-and-a-half of life. *Developmental Psychobiology, 32*(2), 69–89.

Hartup, W. W. (1974). Aggression in childhood: Developmental perspectives. *American Psychologist, 29*, 336–341.

Hartup, W. W. (1978). Children and their friends. In H. McGurk (Ed.), *Issues in childhood social development.* London: Methuen.

Hartup, W. W. (1984). The peer context in middle childhood. In A. Collins (Ed.), *Development during middle childhood: The years from six to twelve.* Washington, DC: National Academy Press.

Hartup, W. W. (1992). Friendships and their developmental significance. In H. McGurk (Ed.), *Childhood social development: Contemporary perspectives.* London: Erlbaum.

Hashima, P. Y., & Amato, P. R. (1994). Poverty, social support, and parental behavior. Special issue: Children and poverty. *Child Development, 65,* 394–403.

Haskett, M. E., & Kistner, J. A. (1991). Social interactions and peer perception in young physically abused children. *Child Development, 62,* 979–990.

Haskins, R. (1989). Beyond metaphor: The efficacy of early childhood education. *American Psychologist, 44,* 274–282.

Hatano, G., & Inagaki, K. (1996). Cultural contexts of schooling revisited: A review of *The Learning Gap* from a cultural psychological perspective. In S. G. Paris & H. M. Wellman (Eds.), *Global prospects for education: Development, culture, and schooling.* Washington, DC: American Psychological Association.

Hayes, K., & Hayes, C. (1951). The intellectual development of a home-raised chimpanzee. *Proceedings of the American Philosophical Society, 95,* 105–109.

Hayflick, L. (1994). *How and why we age.* New York: Ballantine Books.

Hayne, H., & Rovee-Collier, C. (1995). The organization of reactivated memory in infancy. *Child Development, 66,* 893–906.

Hayne, H., Rovee-Collier, C., & Perris, E. E. (1987). Categorization and memory retrieval by three-month-olds. *Child Development, 58*(3), 750–767.

Heath, S. B. (1983). *Ways with words: Language, life, and work in communities and classrooms.* Cambridge, England: Cambridge University Press.

Hedegaard, M., Henriksen, T. B., & Sabroe, S. (1993). Psychological distress in pregnancy and preterm delivery. *British Medical Journal, 307,* 234–238.

Held, R. (1965). Plasticity in sensory-motor systems. *Scientific American, 213*(5), 84-94.

Held, R., & Hein, A. (1963). Movement-produced stimulation and the development of visually guided behaviors. *Journal of Comparative and Physiological Psychology, 56,* 872–876.

Heller, J. (1987). What do we know about the risks of caffeine consumption in pregnancy? *British Journal of Addiction, 82,* 885–889.

Hendren, R. L., & Berenson, C. K. (1997). Adolescent impulse control disorders: Eating disorders and substance abuse. In L.T. Flaherty & R. M. Sarles (Eds.), *Handbook of child and adolescent psychiatry, Volume 3: Adolescence: Development and syndromes.* New York: Wiley.

Hendry, L. B., Glendenning, A., Shucksmith, J., Love, J., & Scott, J. (1994). The developmental context of adolescent life-styles. In R. K. Silbereisen & E. Todt (Eds.), *Adolescence in context: The interplay of family, school, peers, and work in adjustment* (pp. 66–81). Berlin: Springer-Verlag.

Henington, C., Hughes, J. N., Cavell, T. A., & Thompson, B. (1998). The role of relational aggression in identifying aggressive boys and girls. *Journal of School Psychology, 36*(4), 457–477.

Hennessy, K. D., Rabideau, G., Cicchetti, D., & Cummings, E. M. (1994). Responses of physically abused and nonabused children to different forms of interadult anger. *Child Development, 65,* 815–828.

Hepper, P. G., & Shahidullah, S. (1994). The beginnings of mind: Evidence from the behavior of the fetus. *Journal of Reproductive and Infant Psychology, 12*(3), 143–154.

Herdt, G. (Ed.). (1989). *Gay and lesbian youth.* New York: Harrington Park Press.

Herman, M. R., Dornbusch, S. M., Herron, M. C., & Herting, J. R. (1997). The influence of family regulation, connection, and psychological autonomy on six measures of adolescent functioning. *Journal of Adolescent Research, 12*(1), 34–67.

Herrnstein, R. J., & Murray, C. (1994). *The Bell Curve: Intelligence and class structure in American life.* New York: Free Press.

Herskovitz, M. J. (1948). *Man and his works: The science of cultural anthropology.* New York: Knopf.

Heth, C. D. (1997). Differential use of landmarks by 8- and 12-ye old children during route reversal navigation. *Journal of Environmental Psychology, 17,* 199–213.

Hetherington, E. M. (1988). Parents, children, and siblings: Six ye after divorce. In R. A. Hinde & J. Stevenson-Hinde (Eds.), *Relationships within families: Mutual influences.* Oxford: Oxfor University Press.

Hetherington, E. M. (1989). Coping with family transitions: Winn losers, and survivors. *Child Development, 60,* 1–14.

Hetherington, E. M., Cox, M., & Cox, R. (1982). Long-term effects divorce and remarriage on the adjustment of children. *Journa the American Academy of Child Psychiatry, 24,* 518–530.

Hetherington, E. M., Reiss, D., & Plomin, R. (Eds.). (1994). *Separat social worlds of siblings: The impact of nonshared environment development.* Hillsdale, NJ: Erlbaum.

Hetherington, E. M., Bridges, M., & Insabella, G. M. (1998). What matters? What does not?: Five perspectives on the association between marital transitions and children's adjustment. *Americ Psychologist, 53*(2), 167–184.

Hetherington, E. M., Collins, W. A., & Laursen, E. (1999). Social ca and the development of youth from nondivorced, divorced an remarried families. In W. A. Collins (Ed.), *Relationships as developmental contexts* (pp. 177–209). Mahwah, NJ: Erlbaum.

Hewlett, B. S. (1992). The parent-infant relationship and socio-emotional development among Aka pygmies. In J. L. Roopnarin D. B. Carter (Eds.), *Parent-child socialization in diverse cultures* (5, pp. 223–244). Norwood, NJ: Ablex.

Heyman, G. D., & Dweck, C. S. (1998). Children's thinking about traits: Implications for judgments of the self and others. *Child Development, 69*(2), 391–403.

Hicks, L. E., Langham, R. A., & Takenaka, J. (1982). Cognitive and health measures following early nutritional supplementation: A sibling study. *American Journal of Public Health, 72,* 1110–1118

Hill, W. H., Borovsky, O. L., & Rovee-Collier, C. (1988). Continuities infant memory development over the first half-year. *Developmental Psychologybiology, 21,* 43–62.

Hinde, R. A. (1982). Attachment: Some conceptual and biological issues. In C. Parkes & J. Stevenson-Hinde (Eds.), *The place of attachment in human behavior.* New York: Basic Books.

Hinde, R. A. (1987). *Relationships and culture: Links between etholog and the social sciences.* Cambridge: Cambridge University Press.

Hirsch, H. V. B., & Spinelli, D. N. (1971). Modification of the distribution of receptive field orientation in cats by selective visu exposure during development. *Experimental Brain Research, 13,* 509–527.

Hirschfeld, L. A., & Gelman, S. (Eds.). (1994). *Mapping the mind: Domain specificity in cognition and culture.* New York: Cambridge University Press.

Hirsh-Pasek, K., & Golinkoff, R. M. (1996). *The origins of grammar: Evidence from early language comprehension.* Cambridge, MA.: MIT Press.

Ho, C. S., & Bryant, P. (1997). Phonological skills are important in learning to read Chinese. *Developmental Psychology, 33*(6), 946–951.

Hodges, J., & Tizard, B. (1989a). IQ and behavioral adjustments of ex-institutional adolescents. *Journal of Child Psychology and Psychiatry, 30,* 53–75.

Hodges, J., & Tizard, B. (1989b). Social and family relationships of ex-institutional adolescents. *Journal of Child Psychology and Psychiatry, 30,* 77–97.

Hodgkinson, S., Mullan, M., & Murray, R. M. (1991). The genetics of vulnerability to alcoholism. In P. M. R. Murray (Ed.), *The new genetics of mental illness.* London: Mental Health Foundation.

Hoff-Ginsberg, E., & Tardif, T. (1995). Socioeconomic status and parenting. In M. H. Bornstein (Ed.), *Handbook of parenting: Biology and ecology of parenting* (Vol. 2, pp. 161–188). Mahwah, NJ: Marc H. Bornstein.

Hoffman, M. L. (1975). Altruistic behavior and the parent-child relationship. *Journal of Personality and Social Psychology, 31,* 937–943.

Hoffman, M. L. (1991). Empathy, social cognition, and moral action. In M. K. Kurtines & J. L. Gewirtz (Eds.), *Handbook of moral behavior and development,* (Vol. 1, pp. 271-301): Erlbaum.

Hofstader, D. (1979). *Godel, Escher, Bach: An eternal golden braid.* New York: Basic Books.

Hogge, A. W. (1990). Teratology. In I. R. Merkatz & J. E. Thompson (Eds.), *New perspectives on prenatal care.* New York: Elsevier.

Holden, G. W., & Zambarano, R. J. (1992). The origins of parenting: Transmission of beliefs about physical punishment. In I. E. Sigel, A. V. McGillicuddy & J. J. Goodnow (Eds.), *Parental belief systems: The psychological consequences for children.* Hillsdale, NJ: Erlbaum.

Hollos, M., & Richards, F. A. (1993). Gender-associated development of formal operations in Nigerian adolescents. *Ethos, 21,* 24–52.

Holmbeck, G. N., Paikoff, R. L., & Brooks-Gunn, J. (1995). Parenting adolescents. In M. H. Bornstein (Ed.), *Handbook of parenting: Children and parenting* (Vol. 1, pp. 91–118). Mahwah, NJ: Erlbaum.

Holmbeck, G. N. (1996). A model of family relational transformations during the transition to adolescence: Parent-adolescent conflict and adaptation. In J. A. Graber & J. Brooks-Gunn (Eds.), *Transitions through adolescence: Interpersonal domains and context* (pp. 167–199). Mahwah, NJ: Erlbaum.

Holstein, C. (1976). Development of moral judgment: A longitudinal study of males and females. *Child Development, 47,* 51–61.

Honig, A. S., & Park, K. J. (1993). Effects of day care on preschool sex-rate development. *American Journal of Orthopsychiatry, 36,* 481–486.

Hook, E. B. (1982). Epidemiology of Down Syndrome. In S. M. Pueschel & J. E. Rynders (Eds.), *Advances in biomedicine and behavioral sciences.* Cambridge, MA: Ware Press.

Hooker, D. (1952). *The prenatal origins of behavior.* Lawrence: University of Kansas Press.

Hopkins, B., & Westen, T. (1988). Maternal handling and motor development: An intracultural study. *Genetic Psychology Monographs, 14,* 377–420.

Howe, N. (1991). Sibling-directed internal state language, perspective taking, and affective behavior. *Child Development, 62,* 1503–1512.

Howes, C. (1987). Peer interaction of young children. *Monographs of the Society for Research in Child Development, 53*(1, Serial No. 217).

Howes, C., Unger, O, & Seider, L. B. (1989). Social pretend play in toddlers: Parallels with social play and with solitary pretend. *Child Development, 60,* 77–84.

Howes, C., Phillips, D. A., & Whitebook, M. (1992). Thresholds of quality implications for the social development of children in center-based child care. *Child Development, 63,* 447–460.

Hrdlicka, A. (1931). *Children who run on all fours, and other animal-like behaviors in the human child.* New York: Whittlesey House/McGraw Hill.

Hsi, B. L., & Adinolfi, M. (1997). Prenatal sexing of human fetuses and selective abortion. *Prenatal Diagnosis, 17*(1), 1–3.

Hubel, D. H., & Wiesel, T. N. (1979). Brain mechanisms of vision. *Scientific American, 241,* 130–139.

Hughes, F. P. (1991). *Children, play, and development.* Boston, MA: Allyn & Bacon, Inc.

Hughes, F. P. (1995). *Children, play, & development* (2nd ed.). Boston: Allyn & Bacon.

Hulme, C., & Joshi, R. M. (Eds.). (1998). *Reading and spelling: Development and discourse.* Mahwah, NJ: Erlbaum.

Humphreys, A. P., & Smith, P. K. (1987). Rough and tumble friendships and dominance in school children: Evidence for continuity and change with age. *Child Development, 58,* 201–212.

Huston, A. C., & Wright, J. C. (1996). Television and socialization of young children. In T. M. MacBeth (Ed.), *Tuning in to young viewers: Social science perspectives on television* (pp. 37–60). Thousand Oaks: Sage Publications, Inc.

Hutchins, E. (1980). *Culture and inference.* Cambridge, MA: Harvard University Press.

Hutchins, E. (1983). Understanding Micronesian navigation. In D. Genter & L. Sevens (Eds.), *Mental Models.* Mahwah, NJ: Erlbaum.

Huttenlocher, P. R. (1990). Morphometric study of human cerebral cortex development. *Neuropsychologia, 28,* 517–527.

Huttenlocher, P. R. (1994). Synaptogenesis in human cerebral cortex. In G. Dawson & K. W. Fischer (Eds.), *Human behavior and the developing brain.* New York: Guilford Press.

Huttenlocher, P. R., & Dabholkar, A. S. (1997). Regional differences in synaptogenesis in human cerebral cortex. *Journal of Comparative Neurology, 387*(2), 167–178.

Hymel, S., Wagner, E., & Butler, L. J. (1990). Reputational bias: View from the peer group. In S. R. Asher & J. D. Coie (Eds.), *Peer rejection in childhood.* Cambridge: Cambridge University Press.

Hymel, S., Bowker, A., & Woody, E. (1993). Aggressive versus withdrawn unpopular children: Variations in peer and self-perceptions in multiple domains. *Child Development, 64*(3), 879–896.

Inagaki, K., & Hatano, G. (1987). Young children's spontaneous personification as analogy. *Child Developmen, 58*(4), 1013-1020.

Inhelder, B., & Piaget, J. (1958). *The growth of logical thinking from childhood to adolescence.* New York: Basic Books.

Inhelder, B., & Piaget, J. (1964). *The early growth of logic in the child.* New York: Harper & Row.

Irvine, S. H., & Berry, J. W. (1987). *Human abilities in cultural context.* New York: Cambridge University Press.

Isaacs, S. (1966). *Intellectual growth in young children.* New York: Schocken.

Isabella, R. A. (1995). The origins of infant-mother attachment: Maternal behavior and infant development. In R. Vasta (Ed.), *Annals of child development* (Vol. 10, pp. 57–82). London: Jessica Kingsley.

Ishiyama, F. I., & Chabassol, D. J. (1985). Adolescents' fear of social consequences of academic success as a function of age and sex. *Adolescence, 14,* 37–46.

Itard, J. M. G. (1801/1982). *The wild boy of Aveyron.* New York: Appleton-Century-Crofts.

Izard, C. (1994). Innate and universal facial expressions. *Evidence from developmental and cross-cultural research, Psychological Bulletin,* 115.

Izard, C. E., Huebner, R. R., Risser, D., & McGinnes, G. C., Dougherty, L. M. (1980). The young infant's ability to produce discrete emotion expressions. *Developmental Psychology, 16,* 132–140.

Jacklin, C. N., & Maccoby, E. E. (1978). Social behavior at 33 months in same-sex and mixed-sex dyads. *Child Development, 49,* 557–569.

Jackson, J. S., McCullough, W. R., & Gurin, G. (1997). Family, socialization environment, and identity development in Black Americans. In H. P. McAdoo (Ed.), *Black Families* (Third ed., pp. 251–266). Thousand Oaks, CA.: Sage.

Jacob, F. (1982). *The possible and the actual.* New York: Pantheon Books.

Jacobson, S. W., Jacobson, J. L., Sokol, R. J., Martier, S. S., & Ager, J. W. (1993). Prenatal alcohol exposure and infant information processing ability. *Child Development, 64,* 1706–1721.

Jahoda, G. (1980). Theoretical and systematic approaches in cross-cultural psychology. In H. C. Triandis & W. W. Lambert (Eds.), *Handbook of cross-cultural psychology* (Vol. 1). Boston: Allyn & Bacon.

James, W. T. (1890). *The principles of psychology.* New York: Holt, Rinehart and Winston.

James, W. T. (1951). Social organization among dogs of different temperaments: Terriers and beagles reared together. *Journal of Comparative and Physiological Psychology, 44,* 71–77.

James, D., Pillai, M., & Smoleniec, J. (1995). Neurobehavioral development in the human fetus. In J. P. Lecanuet & W. P. Fifer (Eds.), *Fetal development: A psychobiological perspective* (pp. 101–128). Hillsdale, NJ: Erlbaum.

Janowsky, J. S., & Carper, R. (1996). Is there a neural basis for cognitive transitions in school-age children? In Arnold J. Sameroff & M. M. Haith (Eds.), *The five to seven year shift: The age of reason and responsibility.* Chicago, IL: University of Chicago Press.

Jason, L., & Hanaway, L. K. (1997). *Remote control: A sensible approach to kids, TV, and the new electronic media.* Sarasota, FL: Professional Resource Press.

Jessor, R. (1992). Risk behavior in adolescence: A psychosocial framework for understanding and action. *Developmental Review, 12*, 374–390.

Jessor, R. (1998). *New perspectives on adolescent risk behavior.* New York: Cambridge University Press.

John, V. P. (1972). Styles of learning–styles of teaching: Reflections on the education of Navajo children. In C. Cazden, V. P. John & D. Hymes (Eds.), *Functions of language in the classroom* (pp. 331–343), New York: Teachers College Press.

Johnson, F. E., Borden, M., & MacVean, R. B. (1973). Height, weight, and their growth velocities in Guatemalan private school children of high socioeconomic class. *Human Biology, 45*, 627–641.

Johnson, J. S., & Newport, E. L. (1989). Critical period effects in second language learning: The influence of maturational state on the acquisition of English as a second language. *Cognitive Psychology, 21*(1), 60–99.

ohnson, M. H. (1999). Developmental Neuroscience. In M. H. Bornstein & M. E. Lamb (Eds.), *Developmental psychology: An advanced textbook* (4th ed., pp. 199–230). Mahwah, NJ: Erlbaum.

Johnson, W., Emde, R. N., Pannebecker, B., Stenberg, C., & Davis, M. (1982). Maternal perception of infant emotion from birth through 18 months. *Infant Behavior and Development, 5*, 313–322.

Jolly, A. (1999). *Lucy's legacy: Sex and intelligence in human evolution.* Cambridge, MA: Harvard University Press.

Jones, C. L., & Lopez, R. E. (1990). Drug abuse and pregnancy. In I. R. Merkatz & J. E. Thompson (Eds.), *New perspectives on prenatal care.* New York: Elsevier.

Jones, M. C., & Bayley, N. (1950). Physical maturing among boys as related to behavior. *Journal of Educational Psychology, 41*, 129–184.

Jones, M. C. (1965). Psychological correlates of somatic development. *Child Development, 36*, 899–911.

Jones, P. R. (1992). Play therapy training in residential school children with emotional and behavioral problems. *British Journal of Projective Psychology, 37*(2), 8–25.

Jones, R. E. (1997). *Human reproductive biology.* San Diego: Academic Press.

Jordan, B. (1983). *Birth in four cultures.* Montreal: Eden Press.

Jorde, L. B., Carey, J. C., Bamshad, M. J., & White, R. L. (1999). *Medical Genetics.* St. Louis: Mosby.

Joshi, M. S., & MacLean, M. (1994). Indian and English children's understanding of the distinction between real and apparent emotion. *Child Development, 65*(5), 1372–1384.

Jusczyk, P. W. (1997). *The discovery of spoken language.* Cambridge, MA: MIT Press.

Kafai, Y., & Resnick, M. (1996). *Constructionism in practice: Designing, thinking, and learning in a digital world.* Mahwah, NJ: Erlbaum.

Kagan, J. (1981). *The second year.* Cambridge, MA: Harvard University Press.

Kagan, J. (1982). *Psychological research on the human infant: An evaluative summary.* New York: William T. Grant Foundation.

Kagan, J. (1984). *The nature of the child.* New York: Basic Books.

Kagan, J. (1994). *Galen's prophecy: Temperament in human nature.* New York: Basic Books.

Kagan, J. (1998). *Three seductive ideas.* Cambridge, MA: Harvard University Press.

Kagan, J., Kearsley, R. B., & Zelazo, P. (1978). *Infancy: Its place in human development.* Cambridge, MA: Harvard University Press.

Kagan, S., & Madsen, M. C. (1971). Cooperation and competition of Mexican, Mexican-American, and Anglo-American children of two ages under four instructional sets. *Developmental Psychology, 5*, 32–39.

Kagan, S., & Madsen, M. C. (1972). Experimental analyses of cooperation and competition of Anglo-American and Mexican children. *Developmental Psychology, 6*(1), 49–59.

Kagitçibasi, C. (1997). Individualism and collectivism. In J. Berry & M. H. Segall & C. Kagitçibasi (Eds.), *Handbook of cross-cultural psychology* (Vol. 3, pp. 1–50). Needham Heights, MA: Allyn & Bacon.

Kail, R. (1991). Processing time declines exponentially during childhood and adolescence. *Developmental Psychology, 27*, 259–266.

Kail, R., & Park, Y. (1994). Processing time, articulation time, and memory span. *Journal of Experimental Child Psychology, 57*, 281–291.

Kaitz, M., Meschulach-Sarfaty, O., Auerbach, J., & Eidelman, A. (1988). A reexamination of newborns' ability to imitate facial expressions. *Developmental Psychology, 24*, 3–7.

Kaltenbach, K., Berghella, V., Finnegan, L., & Woods, J. R., Jr. (1998). Opoid dependence during pregnancy: effects and management in Substance Abuse in Pregnancy. *Obstetrics and Gynecology Clinics of North America, 25*(1), 139–152.

Kalverboer, A. F., Hopkins, B., & Geuze, R. H. (1993). *Motor development in early and later childhood: Longitudinal approaches.* Cambridge, England: Cambridge University Press.

Kamara, A. I., & Easley, J. A. (1977). Is the rate of cognitive development uniform across cultures? A methodological critique with new evidence from Themne children. In P. R. Dasen (Ed.), *Piagetian psychology: Cross-cultural contributions.* New York: Gardner.

Kaminsky, H. (1984). Moral development in historical perspective. In W. M. Kurtines & J. L. Gewirtz (Eds.), *Morality, moral behavior, and moral development.* New York: Wiley.

Kang, A., Zamora, S. A., Scott, R. B., & Parsons, H. G. (1998). Catch-up growth in children treated with home enteral nutrition. *Pediatrics, 102*(4 Pt 1), 951–955.

Kaplan, H., & Dove, H. (1987). Infant development among the Ache of Eastern Paraguay. *Developmental Psychology, 23*, 190–198.

Kaplan, M., Eidelman, A. I., & Aboulafia, Y. (1983). Fasting and the precipitation of labor: The Yom Kippur effect. *Journal of the American Medical Association, 250 (10)*(Sept. 9), 1317–1318.

Karniol, R. (1989). The role of manual manipulative stages in the infant's acquisition of perceived control over object. *Developmental Review, 9*, 205–233.

Katchadourian, H. A. (1977). *The biology of adolescence.* New York: W. H. Freeman.

Katchadourian, H. A. (1989). *Fundamentals of human sexuality* (5th ed.). Fort Worth, TX: Holt, Rinehart & Winston.

Kaufman, J., & Zigler, E. (1989). The intergenerational transmission of child abuse. In D. Cicchetti & V. Carlson (Eds.), *Child maltreatment: Theory and research on the causes and consequences of child abuse and neglect.* Cambridge: Cambridge University Press.

Kaye, K. (1982). *The mental and social life of babies.* Chicago: University of Chicago Press.

Keating, D. (1990). Adolescent thinking. In S. S. Feldman & G. R. Elliott (Eds.), *At the threshold: The developing adolescent.* Cambridge, MA: Harvard University Press.

Keeney, T. J., Cannizzo, S. D., & Flavell, J. H. (1967). Spontaneous and induced verbal rehearsal in a recall task. *Child Development, 38*, 935–966.

Kellman, J. (1998). Narrative and the art of two children with autism. *Visual Arts Research, 24*(2), 38–48.

Kellogg, W. N., & Kellogg, L. A. (1933). *The ape and the child: A study of environmental influences upon early behavior.* New York: Whittlesey House.

Kempe, C., Silverman, E., Steele, B., Droegemueller, W., & Silver, H. (1962). The battered child syndrome. *Journal of the American Medical Association, 181*, 17–24.

Kendall-Tackett, K. A., Williams, L. M., & Finkelhor, D. (1993). Impact of sexual abuse on children: A review and synthesis of recent empirical studies. *Psychological Bulletin, 113*, 164–180.

Kennell, J. H., Jerauld, R., Wolfe, H., Chester, D., Kreger, N., McAlpine, W., Steffa, M., & Klaus, M. H. (1974). Maternal behavior one year after early and extended post-partum contact. *Developmental Medicine and Child Neurology, 16*, 172–179.

Kennell, J. H., Voos, D. K., & Klaus, M. H. (1979). Parent-infant bonding. In J. D. Osofsky (Ed.), *Handbook of infant development.* New York: Wiley.

Kenyatta, J. (1938). *Facing Mt. Kenya: The tribal life of the Kikuyu.* London: Secker & Warburg.

Kessen, W. (1965). *The child.* New York: Wiley.

Kett, J. F. (1977). *Rites of passage: Adolescence in America 1790 to the present.* New York: Basic Books.

Kiell, N. (1964). *The universal experience of adolescence.* New York: International Universities Press.

Kim, J. M. (1998). Korean children's concepts of adult and peer authority and moral reasoning. *Developmental Psychology, 34*(5), 947–955.

Kinsey, A. C., Pomeroy, W. B., & Martin, C. E. (1948). *Sexual behavior in the human male.* Philadelphia: Saunders.

Kinsey, A. C., Pomeroy, W. B., Martin, C. E., & Gebhard, P. H. (1953). *Sexual behavior in the human female.* Philadelphia: Saunders.

Kisilevsky, B. S., & Low, J. A. (1998). Human fetal behavior: 100 years of study. *Developmental Review, 18,* 1–29.

Kitcher, P. (1985). *Vaulting ambition: Sociobiology and the quest for human nature.* Cambridge, MA: MIT Press.

Klahr, D. (1982). Nonmonotone assessment of monotone development: An information processing analysis. In S. Strauss (Ed.), *U-shaped behavioral-growth.* New York: Academic Press.

Klaus, M. H., & Kennell, J. H. (1976). *Maternal-infant bonding: The impact of early separation or loss on family development.* St. Louis: Mosby.

Klaus, M. H., Kennell, J. H., Plumb, N., & Zuehlke, S. (1970). Human maternal behavior at the first contact with her young. *Pediatrics, 46,* 187.

Klaus, M. H., Kennell, J. H., & Klaus, P. H. (1995). *Bonding: Building the foundations of secure attachment and independence.* Reading, Mass.: Addison-Wesley.

Kleitman, N. (1963). *Sleep and wakefulness.* Chicago: University of Chicago Press.

Klesges, R. C., Klesges, L. M., Eck, L. H., & Shelton, M. L. (1995). A longitudinal analysis of accelerated weight gain in preschool children. *Pediatrics, 95 (1),* 126–130.

Klineberg, O. (1935). *Race differences.* New York: Harper & Row.

Klineberg, O. (1980). Historical perspectives: Cross-cultural psychology before 1960. In H. Triandis & W. Lambert (Eds.), *Handbook of cross-cultural psychology* (Vol. 1). Boston: Allyn & Bacon.

Klopfer, P. H., Adams, D. K., & Klopfer, M. S. (1964). Maternal imprinting in goats. *Proceedings of the National Academy of Sciences, 52,* 911–914.

Kluckhohn, C., & Kelly, W. H. (1945). The concept of culture. In R. Linton (Ed.), *The science of man in the world crisis.* New York: Columbia University Press.

Kochanska, G., & Askan, N. (1995). Mother-child mutually positive affect, the quality of child compliance to requests, and prohibitions, and maternal control as correlates of early internalization. *Child Development, 66,* 236–254.

Kochanska, G., & Thompson, R. A. (1997). The emergence and development of conscience in toddlerhood and early childhood. In J. E. Grusec & R. A. Thompson (Eds.), *Parenting and children's internalization of values* (pp. 53–77). New York: Wiley.

Kochanska, G., Padavich, D. L., & Koenig, A. L. (1996). Children's narratives about hypothetical moral dilemmas and objective measures of their conscience: Mutual relations and socialization antecedents. *Child Development, 67,* 1420–1436.

Koedinger, K. R., & Anderson, J. R. (1998). Illustrating principled design: The early evolution of a cognitive tutor for algebra symbolization. *Interactive Learning Environments, 5,* 161–180.

Kohlberg, L. (1966). A cognitive-developmental analysis of children's sex role concepts and attitudes. In E. E. Maccoby (Ed.), *The development of sex differences.* Stanford, CA: Stanford University Press.

Kohlberg, L. (1969). Stage and sequence: The cognitive-developmental approach to socialization. In D. A. Goslin (Ed.), *Handbook of socialization theory and research.* Chicago: Rand McNally.

Kohlberg, L. (1976). Moral stages and moralization: The cognitive-developmental approach. In J. Lickona (Ed.), *Moral development behavior: Theory, research and social issues.* New York: Holt, Rinehart and Winston.

Kohlberg, L. (1984). *The psychology of moral development: The nature and validity of moral stages* (Vol. 2). New York: Harper & Row.

Kohlberg, L., Yaeger, J., & Hjertholm, E. (1968). Private speech: Four studies and a review of theories. *Child Development, 39,* 691–736.

Kohn, M. L. (1977). *Class and conformity* (2nd ed.). Chicago: University of Chicago Press.

Kolata, G. (1986). Obese children: A growing problem. *Science, 232,* 20–21.

Kolb, B., & Whishaw, I. Q. (1996). *Fundamentals of human neuropsychology* (4th ed.). New York: W.H. Freeman.

Koluchova, J. (1972). Severe deprivation in twins: A case study. *Journal of Child Psychology and Psychiatry, 13,* 107–114.

Koluchova, J. (1976). A report on the further development of twins after severe and prolonged deprivation. In A. M. Clarke & A. D. B. Clarke (Eds.), *Early experience: Myth and evidence.* London: Open Books.

Konner, M. (1977). Evolution in human behavior development. In P. H. Leiderman & S. Tulkin & A. Rosenfeld (Eds.), *Culture and infancy: Variations in human experience.* New York: Academic Press.

Kopp, C., & McIntosh, J. M. (1997). High-risk environments and young children. In S. Greenspan, S. Wieder & J. Osofsky (Eds.), *Handbook of child and adolescent psychiatry* (Vol. 1. Infants and preschoolers: Development and syndromes, pp. 160–176). New York: Wiley.

Kopp, C. B., & McCall, R. B. (1982). Predicting later mental performance for normal, at-risk, and handicapped infants. In P. B. Baltes & O. G. Brim (Eds.), *Life span development and behavior* (Vol. 4). New York: Academic Press.

Kopp, C. B., & Wyer, N. (1994). Self-regulation in normal and atypical development. In D. Cicchetti & S. L. Toth (Eds.), *Disorders and dysfunctions of the self.* Rochester, NY: University of Rochester Press.

Korner, A. F. (1987). Preventive intervention with high-risk newborns: Theoretical conceptual and methodological perspectives. In J. D. Osofsky (Ed.), *Handbook of infant development* (2nd ed.). New York: Wiley.

Korner, A. F., & Thoman, E. (1970). Visual alertness in neonates as evoked by maternal care. *Journal of Experimental Child Psychology, 10,* 67–78.

Koschmann, T. (1996a). Paradigm shifts and instructional technology: An introduction. In T. Koschmann (Ed.), *CSCL: Theory and practice of an emerging paradigm* (pp. 1–24). Mahwah, NJ: Erlbaum.

Koschmann, T. (Ed.). (1996b). *CSCL: Theory and practice of an emerging paradigm.* Mahwah, NJ: Erlbaum.

Kotelchuck, M. (1976). The infant's relationship to the father: Experimental evidence. In M. E. Lamb (Ed.), *The role of the father in child development.* New York: Wiley.

Kowal, A., & Kramer, L. (1997). Children's understanding of parental differential treatment. *Child Development, 68*(1), 113–126.

Krashen, S. (1996). *Under attack: The case against bilingual education.* Culver City, CA: Language Education Associates.

Krasnegor, N. A., & Lecanuet, J. P. (1995). Behavioral development of the fetus. In J. P. Lecanuet & W. P. Fifer & N. A. Krasnegor & W. P. Smotherman (Eds.), *Fetal development: A psychobiological perspective* (pp. 3–14). Hillsdale, NJ: Erlbaum.

Krasnogorski, N. I. (1907/1967). The formation of artificial conditioned reflexes in young children. In Y. Brackbill & G. G. Thompson (Eds.), *Behavior in infancy and early childhood: A book of readings.* New York: Free Press.

Krauss, R. M., & Glucksberg, S. (1969). The development of communication: Competence as a function of age. *Child Development, 42,* 255–266.

Kreutzer, M. A., Leonard, S. C., & Flavell, J. H. (1975). An interview study of children's knowledge about memory. *Monographs of the Society for Research in Child Development, 40*(1, Serial No. 159).

Kroger, J. (1996). Identity, regression and development. *Journal of Adolescence, 19*(3), 203–222.

Kroger, J. (1997). Gender and identity: The intersection of structure, content and context. *Sex Roles, 36*(11–12), 747–770.

Kuhl, P. K., & Miller, J. D. (1978). Speech perception by the chinchilla: Identification functions for synthetic VOT stimuli. *Journal of the Acoustical Society of America, 63,* 905–917.

Kuhl, P. K., Williams, K. A., Lacerda, F., Stevens, K. N., & Lindblom, B. (1992). Linguistic experiences alters phonetic perception in infants by 6 months of age. *Science, 255,* 606–608.

Kuhn, D., Garcia-Mila, M., Zohar, A., & Anderson, C. (1995). Strategies of knowledge acquisition. *Monographs of the Society for Research in Child Development, 60*(Serial No. 245, 4).

Kundera, M. (1988). *The art of the novel.* New York: Grove Press.

Kunzel, W. (1994). Recommendations of the FIGO committee on perinatal health on guidelines for the management of a breech delivery. *Journal Gynaecalogical Obstetrics, 44,* 297.

Kupersmidt, J. B., Coie, J. D., & Dodge, K. A. (1990). The role of poor peer relationships in the development of disorder. In S. R. Asher & J. D. Coie (Eds.), *Peer rejection in childhood.* New York: Cambridge University Press.

Kurtines, W. M., & Gewirtz, J. L. (Eds.). (1984). *Morality, moral behavior, and moral development.* New York: Wiley.

Laboratory of Comparative Human Cognition. (1983). Culture and cognitive development. In P. Mussen (Ed.), *Handbook of child psychology* (4th ed.), *Vol. 1: History, theory, and methods.* New York: Wiley.

Lacombe, A. C., & Gay, J. (1998). The role of gender in adolescent identity and intimacy decisions. *Journal of Youth & Adolescence, 27*(6), 795–802.

Ladd, G. W. (1999). Peer relationships and social competence during early and middle childhood. *Annual Review of Psychology, 50,* 333–359.

Lagercrantz, H., & Slotkin, T. A. (1986). The "stress" of being born. *Scientific American, 254,* 100–107.

Lamb, M. (1998). Nonparental child care: context, quality, correlates, and consequences. In I. E. Sigel & K. A. Renninger (Eds.), *Handbook of child psychology* (5th ed.), *Vol 4: Child psychology in practice* (pp. 73–133). New York: Wiley.

Lamb, M. E. (1979). Paternal influences and the father's role: A personal perspective. *American Psychologist, 34,* 938–943.

Lamb, M. E. (Ed.). (1987). *The father's role: Cross-cultural perspectives.* Hillsdale, NJ: Erlbaum.

Lamb, M. E., Pleck, J. H., Charnov, E. L., & Levine, J. A. (1987). A biosocial perspective on paternal behavior and involvement. In J. B. Lancaster & J. Altmann & A. Rossi & L. R. Sherrod (Eds.), *Parenting across the lifespan: Biosocial perspectives.* Hawthorne, NY: Aldine de Gruyter.

Lamb, M. E., Hwang, C. P., Ketterlinus, R. D., & Fracasso, M. P. (1999). Parent-child relationships: Development in the context of the family. In M. H. Bornstein & M. E. Lamb (Eds.), *Developmental psychology: An advanced textbook* (pp. 411–450). Mahwah, NJ: Erlbaum.

Lamborn, S. D., Dornbusch, S. M., & Steinberg, L. (1996). Ethnicity and community context as moderators of the relations between family decision making and adolescent adjustment. *Child Development, 67*(2), 283–301.

Lampert, M. (1998). Studying teaching as a thinking practice. In J. G. Greeno & S. V. Goldman (Eds.), *Thinking practices in mathematics and science learnin* (pp. 53–78). Mahwah, NJ: Erlbaum.

Lampert, M., & Blunc, M. L. (Eds.). (1998). *Talking mathematics in school : studies of teaching and learning.* Cambridge, U.K: Cambridge University Press.

Lane, H. (1976). *The wild boy of Aveyron.* Cambridge, MA: Harvard University Press.

Lange-Küttner, C., & Thomas, G. V. (Eds.). (1995). *Drawing and looking: Theoretical approaches to pictorial representation in children.* London, England: Harvester Wheatsheaf.

Langlois, J. (1986). From the eye of the beholder to behavioral reality: Development of social behaviors and social relations as a function of physical attractiveness. In C. P. Herman, M. P. Zanna & E. T. Higgins (Eds.), *Physical appearance, stigma, and social behavior: The Ontario Symposium* (Vol. 3). Hillsdale, NJ: Erlbaum.

Langlois, J. H., Ritter, J. M., Casey, R. J., & Sawin, D. B. (1995). Infant attractiveness predicts maternal behaviors and attitudes. *Developmental Psychology, 31,* 464–472.

Largo, R. H., Molinari, L., von Siebenthal, K., & Wolfensberger, U. (1996). Does a profound change in toilet-training affect development of bowel and bladder control? *Developmental Medicine and Child Neurology, 38,* 1106–1116.

Larson, R., & Richards, M. (1991). Daily companionship in late childhood and early adolescence: Changing developmental contexts. *Child Development, 62,* 284–300.

Larson, R., & Richards, M. (1998). Waiting for the weekend: Friday and Saturday nights as the emotional climax of the week. In A. C. Crouter & R. Larson (Eds.), *Temporal rhythms in adolescence: Clocks, calendars, and the coordination of daily life* (pp. 37-51). San Francisco, CA: Jossey-Bass.

Latour, B. (1987). *Science in action.* Cambridge, MA: Harvard University Press.

Laupa, M., & Turiel, E. (1993). Children's concepts of authority and social contexts. *Journal of Educational Psychology, 85*(1), 191–197.

Laursen, B., Coy, K. C., & Collins, W. A. (1998). Reconsidering changes in parent-child conflict across adolescence: A meta-analysis. *Child Development (Chicago), 69*(3), 817–832.

Lave, J. (1988). *Cognition in practice: Mind, mathematics, and culture in everyday life.* Cambridge: Cambridge University Press.

Lave, J., & Wenger, E. (1991). *Situated learning: Legitimate peripheral practice.* New York: Cambridge University Press.

Lavigne, M. (1982). Rubella's disabled children: Research and rehabilitation. *Columbia, 7,* 10–17.

Lemaire, P., & Siegler, R. S. (1995). Four aspects of strategic change: Contributions to children's learning of multiplication. *Journal of Experimental Psychology: General, 124,* 83–97.

Leach, P. (1994). *Children first: What our society must do–and is not doing–for our children today.* New York: Knopf.

Leaper, C. (Ed.). (1994). *Childhood gender segregation: Causes and consequences. New directions for child development, No. 65.* San Francisco: Jossey-Bass.

Lebra, T. S. (1994). Mother and child in Japanese socialization: A Japan–U.S. comparison. In P. M. Greenfield & R. R. Cocking (Eds.), *Cross-cultural roots of minority child development* (pp. 259–274). Hillsdale, NJ: Erlbaum.

Lecanuet, J. P., & Schaal, B. (1996). Fetal sensory competencies. *European Journal of Obstetrics, Gynecology, and Reproductive Biology.*

Lecanuet, J. P., Fifer, P., Krasnegor, N. A., & Smotherman, W. P. (Eds.). (1995). *Fetal development: A psychobiological perspective.* Hillsdale, NJ: Erlbaum.

Lecours, A. R. (1982). Correlates of developmental behavior in brain maturation. In T. Bever (Ed.), *Regressions in mental development.* Hillsdale, NJ: Erlbaum.

Lee, L. (1965). *Cider with Rosie.* London: Hogarth Press.

Lee, M., & Woods, J. R., Jr. (1998). Marijuana and tobacco use in pregnancy in substance abuse in pregnancy. *Obstetrics and Gynecology Clinics of North America, 25*(1), 65–83.

Lee, S.-Y. (1996). Mathematics learning and teaching in the school context: Reflections from cross-cultural comparisons. In S. G. Paris & H. M. Wellman (Eds.), *Global prospects for education: Development, culture, and schooling.* Washington DC: American Psychological Association.

LeGault, F., & Strayer, F. F. (1990). The emergence of sex-segregation in preschool peer groups. In F. F. Strayer (Ed.), *Social interaction and behavioral development during early childhood.* Montreal: La Maison D'Ethologie de Montreal.

Leighton, D., & Kluckhohn, C. (1947/1969). *Children of the people; the Navaho individual and his development.* Cambridge: Harvard University Press.

Lemish, D., & Rice, M. L. (1986). Television as a talking picture book: A prop for language acquisition. *Journal of Child Language, 13,* 251–274.

Lenneberg, E. H., Rebelsky, F. G., & Nichols, I. A. (1965). The vocalizations of infants born to hearing and deaf parents. *Human Development, 8*, 23–27.

Leonard, L. B., Chapman, K., Rowan, L. E., & Weiss, A. L. (1983). Three hypotheses concerning young children's imitations of lexical items. *Developmental Psychology, 19*, 591–601.

Leoni, L. (1964). *Tico and the golden wings.* New York: Pantheon.

Lerner, M. I., & Libby, W. J. (1976). *Heredity, evolution, and society.* New York: W. H. Freeman.

Leslie, A. M. (1994). To MM, to BY, and agency: Core architecture and domain specificity. In L. A. Hirschfeld & S. Gelman (Eds.), *Mapping the mind: Domain specificity in cognition and culture.* New York: Cambridge University Press.

Leslie, A. M., & Keeble, S. (1987). Do six month old infants perceive causality? *Cognition, 25*, 265–288.

Lesser, G. S. (1974). *Children and television.* New York: Random House.

Lester, B. M., & Tronick, E. Z. (1994). The effects of prenatal cocaine exposure and child outcome. Special Issue: Prenatal drug exposure and child outcome. *Infant Mental Health Journal, 15*, 107–120.

Lester, B. M., Boukydis, C. Z., Garcia-Coll, C. T., Hole, W., & others. (1992). Infantile colic: Acoustic cry characteristics, maternal perception of cry, and temperament. *Infant Behavior & Development, 15*(1), 15–26.

Lever, J. (1978). Sex differences in the complexity of children's play and games. *American Sociological Review, 43*, 471–483.

Levin, J. A., Kim, H., & Riel, M. (1990). Analyzing instructional interactions on electronic message networks. In L. Harasim (Ed.), *On-line education: Perspectives on a new environment.* New York: Praeger.

Le Vine, R. A. (1974). Parental goals: A cross-cultural view. In H. J. Leichter (Ed.), *The family as educator.* New York: Teachers College Press.

Le Vine, R. A. (1988). Human parental care: Universal goals, cultural strategies, individual behavior. In R. A. Le Vine & P. M. Miller & M. M. West (Eds.), *Parental behavior in diverse societies. New directions for child development, No. 40: The Jossey-Bass social and behavioral sciences series.* San Francisco, CA: Jossey-Bass, Inc.

Le Vine, R. A., Dixon, S., Le Vine, S., & Richman, A. (1994). *Child care and culture: Lessons from Africa.* New York: Cambridge University Press.

Le Vine, R. A., Miller, P., Richman, A., & Le Vine, S. (1996). Education and Mother-infant interaction: A Mexican case study. In S. Harkness & C. Super (Eds.), *Parents' cultural belief systems: Their origins, expressions, and consequences.* New York: Guilford Press.

Levy, G. D., & Fivush, R. (1993). Scripts and gender: A new approach for examining gender-role development. *Developmental Review, 13*, 126–146.

Lewis, M. (1993). Self-conscious emotions: Embarrassment, pride, shame and guilt. In M. Lewis & J. M. Haviland (Eds.), *Handbook of Emotions.* New York: Guilford Press.

Lewis, M. (1997). *Altering fate: Why the past does not predict the future.* New York, NY: Guilford Press.

Lewis, M., & Brooks-Gunn, J. (1979). *Social cognition and the acquisition of self.* New York: Plenum Press.

Lewis, M., & Feiring, C. (1989). Infant, mother, and mother-infant interaction behavior and subsequent attachment. *Child Development, 60*, 831–837.

Lewis, M., & Ramsay, D. S. (1999). Effect of maternal soothing on infant stress response. *Child Development, 70*(1), 11–20.

Lewontin, R. C. (1976). Race and intelligence. In N. J. Block & G. Dworkin (Eds.), *The IQ controversy.* New York: Pantheon.

Lewontin, R. C. (1994). *Inside and outside: Gene, environment and organisms.* Worcester, MA: Clark University Press.

Liaw, F. R., & Brooks-Gunn, J. (1993). Patterns of low-birthweight children's cognitive development. *Developmental Psychology, 29*, 1024–1035.

Licht, B. G., & Dweck, C. S. (1984). Determinants of academic achievement: The interaction of children's achievement orientations with skill area. *Developmental Psychology, 20*(4), 628–636.

Lichter, S. R. (1994). Distorted reality: Hispanic characters in TV entertainment. In Center for Media and Public Affairs Monoraph, available on line at http://www.cmpa.com/archive/hisp1/htm

Lieberman, P. (1991). *Uniquely human: The evolution of speech, thought, and selfless behavior.* Cambridge, MA: Harvard University Press.

Lifter, K., & Bloom, L. (1989). Object knowledge and the emergence of language. *Infant Behavior and Development, 12*, 395–424.

Lightfoot, C. (1994). *Playing with desire: An interpretive perspective on adolescent risk-taking.* Paper presented at the 1994 annual meeting of the American Educational Research Association, New Orleans, LA.

Lightfoot, C. (1997). *The culture of adolescent risk taking.* New York: Guilford Press.

Linaza, J. (1984). Piaget's marbles: The study of children's games and their knowledge of rules. *Oxford Review of Education, 10*, 271–274.

Linn, M. C. (1983). Content, context, and process in reasoning. *Journal of Early Adolescence, 3*, 63–82.

Linn, M. C., & Hyde, J. S. (1991). Cognitive and psychosocial gender differences trends. In R. Lerner, A. C. Petersen & J. Brooks-Gunn (Eds.), *Encyclopedia of Adolescence.* New York: Garland Publishers.

Linn, M. C., De Benedictus, T., & Delucchi, K. (1982). Adolescent reasoning about advertisements: Preliminary investigations. *Child Development, 53*, 1599–1613.

Lino, M. (1993). Expenditure on a child by families. *Family Economic Review, 7*, 2–19.

Literacy, C. f. M. (1999). Beyond blame: Challenging violence in the media. World Wide Web: Center for Media Literacy.

Littleton, K., & Light, P. (1999). *Learning with computers: Analyzing productive interaction.* New York: Routledge.

Livson, N., & Peskin, H. (1967). Prediction of Adult Psychological Health in A Longitudinal Study. *Journal of Abnormal Psychology, 72*(6), 509-518.

Locke, J. (1938). *Some thoughts concerning education.* London: Churchill (Original work published 1699).

Loeber, R., & Hay, D., (1993). Developmental approach to aggression and conduct problems. In M. Rutter & D. Hay (Eds.), *Development through life: A handbook for clinicians* (pp. 488–516). Oxford, England: Blackwell.

Loehlin, J. C. (1992). *Genes and environment in personality development* (Vol. 2). Newbury Park, CA: Sage Publications.

Loftus, E. F. (1996). *Eyewitness testimony.* Cambridge, MA: Harvard University Press.

Lomax, E. M., Kagan, J., & Rosenkrantz, B. G. (1978). *Science and patterns of child care.* New York: W. H. Freeman.

Lonigan, C. J., & Whitehurst, G. J. (1998). Relative efficacy of parent and teacher involvement in a shared-reading intervention for preschool children from low-income backgrounds. *Early Childhood Research Quarterly, 13*(2), 263–290.

Lorch, E. P. (1994). Measuring children's cognitive processing of television. In A. Lang (Ed.), *Measuring psychological responses to media.* Hillsdale, NJ: Erlbaum.

Lorenz, K. (1943). Die Angebornen Formen mogicher Erfahrung. *Zeitschrift fur Tierpsychologie, 5*, 233–409.

Lorenz, K. (1966). *On aggression.* New York: Harcourt, Brace & World.

Lou, H. C., Hansen, D., & Nordenfoft, M. (1994). Prenatal stressors of human life affect fetal brain development. *Developmental Medicine and Child Neurology, 24*, 832–862.

Lourenco, O., & Machado, A. (1996). In defense of Piaget's theory: A reply to 10 common criticisms. *Psychological Review, 103*(1), 143–164.

Lucas, C. J. (1972). *Our western educational heritage.* New York: The Macmillan Company.

Luke, B., Johnson, T. R. B., & Petrie, R. H. (1993). *Clinical maternal-fetal nutrition.* Boston: Little, Brown, & Company.

Luria, A. R. (1973). *The working brain.* New York: Basic Books.

Luria, A. R. (1976). *Cognitive development: Its cultural and social foundations.* Cambridge, MA: Harvard University Press.

Luria, A. R. (1981). *Language and cognition.* New York: Wiley.

Luria, Z., & Herzog, E. W. (1991). Sorting gender out in a children's museum. *Gender and Society, 5*(2), 224–232.

Lutz, C. (1987). Goals, events, and understanding Ifaluk emotion theory. In D. Holland & N. Quinn (Eds.), *Cultural models in language and thought.* Cambridge: Cambridge University Press.

Lynn, R. (1982). IQ in Japan and the United States shows a growing disparity. *Nature, 297*, 222–223.

Maas, H. (1963). The young adult adjustment of twenty wartime residential nursery children. *Child Welfare, 42*, 57–72.

Maccoby, E. E. (1980). *Social development: Psychological growth and the parent-child relationship.* New York: Harcourt Brace Jovanovich.

Maccoby, E. E. (1984). Middle childhood in the context of the family. In W. A. Collins (Ed.), *Development during middle childhood: The years from six to twelve.* Washington, DC: National Academy Press.

Maccoby, E. E. (1988). Gender as a social category. *Developmental Psychology, 24*(6), 755–765.

Maccoby, E. E. (1998). *The two sexes.* Cambridge, MA: Havard Univeristy Press.

Maccoby, E. E., & Martin, J. A. (1983). Socialization in the context of the family: Parent-child interaction. In P. H. Mussen (Ed.), *Handbook of child psychology* (4th ed.)*: Vol. 4. Socialization, personality, and social behavior.* New York: Wiley.

MacFarlane, A. (1975). Olfaction in the development of social preferences in the human neonate. *Parent-infant interaction (CIBA Foundation symposium 33).* New York: Elsevier.

MacFarlane, A. (1977). *The psychology of childbirth.* Cambridge, MA: Harvard University Press.

Mack, K. J., & P.A., M. (1992). Introduction of transcription factors in somatosensory cortex after tactile stimulation. *Molecular Brain Research, 12*, 141–149.

Mackintosh, N. J. (1998). *IQ and human intelligence.* Oxford: Oxford University Press.

Madsen, M. C., & Shapira, A. (1970). Cooperative and competitive behavior of urban Afro-American, Anglo-American, Mexican-American, and Mexican village children. *Developmental Psychology, 3*, 16–20.

Main, M., & Solomon, J. (1990). Procedures for identifying infants as disorganized/disoriented during the Ainsworth strange situation. In M. Greenberg, D. Cicchetti & E.M. Cummings (Eds.), *Attachment in the preschool years: Theory, research, and intervention* (pp. 121–160). Chicago: University of Chicago Press.

Malina, R. M. (1998). Motor development and performance. In S. J. Ulijaszek, F. E. Johnston & M. A. Preece (Eds.), *The Cambridge encyclopedia of human growth and development* (pp. 247–250). Cambridge: Cambridge University Press.

Malina, R. M., & Bouchard, C. (1991). *Growth, maturation and physical activity.* Champaign, IL: Human Kinetics Books.

Mallick, S. K., & McCandless, B. R. (1966). A study of catharsis of aggression. *Journal of Personality and Social Psychology, 4*, 590–596.

Mandler, J. M., Scribner, S., Cole, M., & de Forest, M. (1980). Cross-cultural invariance in story recall. *Child Development, 51*, 19–26.

Mandler, J. M. (1984). Representation and recall in infancy. In M. Moscovitch (Ed.), *Infant memory.* New York: Plenum.

Mandler, J. M. (1998). Representation. In D. Kuhn & R. S. Siegler (Eds.), *Handbook of child psychology* (5th ed.)*:Vol. 2: Cognition, perception and language* (pp. 255–308). New York: Wiley.

Mandler, J. M., & Bauer., P. J. (1988). The cradle of categorization: Is the basic level basic? *Cognitive Development, 3*, 247–264.

Mandler, J. M., & McDonough, L. (1993). Concept formation in infancy. *Cognitive Development, 8*, 291–318.

Mandler, J., & McDonough, L. (1995). Long-term recall of event sequences in infancy. Special Issue: Early memory. *Journal of Experimental Child Psychology, 59*, 457–474.

Mandoki, M. W., Sumner, G. S., Hoffman, R. P., & Riconda, D. L. (1991). A review of Klinefelter's syndrome in children and adolescents. *Journal of the American Academy of Child & Adolescent Psychiatry, 30*(2), 167–172.

Manning, W. D. (1990). Parenting employed teenagers. *Youth and Society, 22*(2), 184–200.

Manns, W. (1997). Supportive roles of significant others in African American families. In H. P. McAdoo (Ed.), *Black families* (3rd ed., pp. 198–213). Thousand Oaks, CA: Sage.

Manstead, A. S. R. (1995). Children's understanding of emotion. In J. A. Russell & J. M. Fernandez-Dols (Eds.), *Everyday conceptions of emotion: An introduction to the psychology, anthropology and linguistics of emotion:* Boston: Kluwer Academic Publishers.

Maratos, O. (1998). Neonatal, early and later imitation: Same order phenomena? In F. Simion & G. Butterworth (Eds.), *The development of sensory, motor and cognitive capacities in early infancy: From perception to cognition.* Hove, England: Psychology Press/Erlbaum.

Maratsos, M. (1973). Nonegocentric communication abilities in preschool children. *Child Development, 44*, 697–700.

Marcia, J. E. (1966). Development and validation of ego identity status. *Journal of Personality and Social Psychology, 3*, 551–558.

Marcia, J. E. (1980). Identity in adolescence. In J. Adelson (Ed.), *Handbook of Adolescent Psychology.* New York: Wiley.

Marcia, J. E. (1999). Representational thought in ego identity, psychotherapy, and psychosocial developmental theory. In I. E. Sigel (Ed.), *Development of mental representation: Theories and applications.* (pp. 391–414). Mahwah, NJ: Erlbaum.

Marcus, G. F., Vijayan, S., Bandi Rao, S., & Vishton, P. M. (1999). Rule learning by seven-month-old infants. *Science, 283*, 77–79.

Markus, H. R., & Kitayama, S. (1991). Culture and the self: Implications for cognition, emotion, and motivation. *Psychological Review, 98*, 224–253.

Markus, H. R., & Kitayama, S. (1998). The cultural psychology of personality. *Journal of Cross-cultural Psychology, 29*(1), 63–87.

Marquis, D. (1931). Can conditioned reflexes be established in the newborn infant? *Journal of Genetic Psychology, 39*, 479–492.

Marshall, W. A., & Tanner, J. M. (1974). Puberty. In J. A. Davis & J. Dobbing (Eds.), *Scientific foundations of pediatrics.* Philadelphia: Saunders.

Martin, C. B., Jr. (1998). Electronic fetal monitoring: A brief summary of its development, problems and prospects. *European Journal of Obstetrics & Gynecology and Reproductive Biology, 78*, 133–140.

Martin, C. H., & Halverson, C. F. (1981). A schematic processing model of sextyping and stereotyping in children. *Child Development, 52*, 1119–1134.

Martin, C. H., & Halverson, C. F. (1987). The roles of cognition in sex role acquisition. In D. B. Carter (Ed.), *Current conceptions of sex roles and sex typing: Theory and research.* New York: Praeger Publishers.

Marx, K. (1845/1969). Theses on Feurbach. In L. D. Easton & K. H. Guddat (Eds.), *Writings of the young Marx on philosophy and society.* Garden City: Doubleday and Co./Anchor Books.

Mascolo, M. F., & Fischer, K. W. (1998). The development of self through the coordination of component systems. In M. D. Ferrari & R. J. Sternberg (Eds.), *Self-awareness: Its nature and development.* (pp. 332–384). New York: Guilford Press.

Mason, M. A., Skolnick, A., & Sugarman, S. D. (1998). *All our families: New policies for a new century.* New York: Oxford University Press.

Massey, C. M., & Gelman, R. (1988). Preschooler's ability to decide whether a photographed unfamiliar object can move itself. *Developmental Psychology, 24*(3), 307–317.

Massoni, G. A., Vannuccci, M., & Loftus, E. F. (1999). Misremembering story material. *Legal & Criminological Psychology, 4*(1), 93–110.

Mathew, A., & Cook, M. (1990). The control of reaching movements by young infants. *Child development, 61*, 1238–1257.

Mayes, L. C., Grillon, C., Granger, R., & Schottenfeld, R. (1998). Regulation of arousal and attention in preschool children exposed to cocaine prenatally. *Annals of the New York Academy of Sciences, 846*, 126–143.

Mazur, A., & Booth, A. (1998). Testosterone and dominance in men. *Behavioral & Brain Sciences, 21*(3), 353–397.

McAdoo, H. P. (1985). Racial attitude and self-concept of young black children over time. In H. P. McAdoo & J. L. McAdoo (Eds.), *Black children: Social, educational, and parental environments.* Beverly Hills: Sage.

McCall, R. B. (1981). Nature, nurture and the two realms of development: A proposed integration with respect to mental development. *Child Development, 52*, 1–12.

McCollam, K. M., Embretson, S. E., Mitchell, D. W., & Horowitz, F. D. (1997). Using confirmatory factor analysis to identify newborn behavior structure with the NBAS. *Infant Behavior and Development, 20*(2), 123–131.

McCune-Nicolich, L., & Bruskin, C. (1982). Combinatorial competency in symbolic play and language. In D. J. Pepler & K. H. Rubin (Eds.), *The play of children: Current theory and research.* Basal: S. Krieger.

McDonough, L., & Mandler, J. M. (1994). Very long-term memory in infancy: Infantile amnesia reconsidered. *Memory, 2*, 339–352.

McGillicuddy-De Lisi, A. V. (1992). Parental beliefs. In I. E. Sigel, A. V. McGillicuddy-De Lisi, & J. J. Goodnow (Eds.), *Parental belief systems: The psychological consequences for children* (2nd ed.). Hillsdale, NJ: Erlbaum.

McGillicuddy-De Lisi, A. V., & Sigel, I. E. (1995). Parental beliefs. In M. H. Bornstein (Ed.), *Handbook of parenting* (Vol. 3, pp. 333–358). Mawah, NJ: Erlbaum.

McGillicuddy-DeLisi, A. V., Watkins, C., & Vinchur, A. J. (1994). The effect of relationship on children's distributive justice reasoning. *Child Development, 65*, 1694–1700.

McGilly, K., & Siegler, R. S. (1989). How children choose among serial recall strategies. *Child Development, 60*(1), 172–182.

McGraw, M. B. (1975). *Growth: A study of Johnny and Jimmy.* New York: Arno Press (Original work published 1935).

McGue, M. (1993). From proteins to cognitions: The behavioral genetics of alcoholism. In R. Plomin & G. E. McClearn (Eds.), *Nature, nurture & psychology* (pp. 245–268). Washington DC: American Psychological Association.

McGue, M. (1995). Mediators and moderators of alcoholism inheritence. In J. R. Turner & L. R. Cardon & J. K. Hewitt (Eds.), *Behavior genetic approaches to behavioral medicine* (pp. 17–44). New York: Plenum Press.

McGuire, S., Neiderhiser, J. M., Reiss, D., & Hetherington, E. M. (1994). Genetics and environmental influences on perceptions of self-worth and competence in adolescence: A study of twins, full siblings, and step-siblings. *Child Development, 65*, 785–799.

McGuire, S., Dunn, J., & Plomin, R. (1995). Maternal differential treatment of siblings and children's behavioral problems: A longitudinal study. *Development & Psychopathology, 7*(3), 515–528.

McHale, S. M., & Pawletko, T. M. (1992). Differential treatment of siblings in two family contexts. *Child Development, 63*(1), 68–81.

McKinney, M. L. (1998). Cognitive evolution by extending brain development: On recapitulation, progress, and other heresies. In J. Langer & M. Killer (Eds.), *Piaget, evolution, and development.* Mahwah, NJ: Erlbaum.

McKusik, V. A. (1975). *Mendelian inheritance in man: Catalog of autosomal dominant, autosomal recession and x-linked phenotype* (4th ed.). Baltimore: Johns Hopkins University Press.

McLoyd, V. (1990). The impact of economic hardship on black families and children: Psychological distress, parenting, and socioemotional development. *Child Development, 61*, 311–346.

McLoyd, V. C. (1998a). Children in poverty: Development, public policy, and practice. In I. E. Sigel & K. A. Renninger (Eds.), *Handbook of child psychology* (5th ed.), *Vol. 4: Child psychology in practice* (pp. 135–210). New York: Wiley.

McLoyd, V. C. (1998b). Socioeconomic disadvantage and child development. *American Psychologist, 53*(2), 185–204.

McNeill, D. (1970). *The acquisition of language: The study of developmental psycholinguistics.* New York: Harper & Row.

McPhee, C. (1970). Children and music in Bali. In J. Belo (Ed.), *Traditional Balinese culture* (pp. 212–239). New York.

Mead, M. (1935). *Sex and temperament in three primitive societies.* New York: William Morrow.

Mead, M., & Macgregor, F. C. (1951). *Growth and culture.* New York: Putnam.

Meeus, W., & Dekovic, M. (1995). Identity development, parental and peer support in adolescence: Results of a national Dutch survey. *Adolescence, 30*(120), 931–944.

Mehan, H. (1979). *Learning lessons.* Cambridge, MA: Harvard University Press.

Mehan, H. (1979). What time is it, Denise? Asking known information questions in classroom discourse. *Theory into Practice, 18*, 285–294.

Mehan, H. (1997). *The study of social interaction in educational settings: Accomplishments and unresolved issues.* Unpublished Manuscript, University of California at San Diego, La Jolla, CA.

Mehan, H. (1998). The study of social interaction in educational settings: Accomplishments and unresolved issues. *Human Development, 41*(4), 245–268.

Meisel, J. M. (1995). Parameters in acquisition. In P. Fletcher & B. MacWhinney (Eds.), *The handbook of child language.* Oxford: Blackwell.

Mello, C. V., Vicario, D. S., & Clayton, D. F. (1992). *Song presentation induces gene experession in the songbird forebrain.* Paper presented at the Proceedings of the National Academy of Sciences, USA.

Melot, A., & Houde, O. (1998). Categorization and theories of mind: The case of the appearance/reality distinction. *Cahiers de Psychologie Cognitive, 17*(1), 71–993.

Meltzoff, A. N. (1988a). Imitation of televised models by infants. *Child Development, 59*, 1221–1229.

Meltzoff, A. N. (1988b). Infant imitation and memory: Nine-month-olds in immediate and deferred tests. *Child Development, 59*, 217–225.

Meltzoff, A. N. (1990). Towards a developmental cognitive science: The implications of cross-modal matching and imitation for the development of representation and memory in infancy. *Annals of the New York Academy of Sciences, 608*, 1–37.

Meltzoff, A. N. (1995). Understanding the intentions of others: Re-enactment of intended acts by 18-month-old children. *Development Psychology, 66*, 838–850.

Meltzoff, A. N., & Moore, M. K. (1977). Imitation of facial and manual gestures by human neonates. *Science, 198*, 75–78.

Meltzoff, A. N., & Moore, M. K. (1994). Imitation, memory, and the representation of persons. *Infant Behavior and Development, 17*, 83–99.

Meltzoff, A. N., & Moore, K. M. (1998). Object representation, identity, and the paradox of early permanence: Steps towards a new framework. *Infant Behavior and Development, 21*, 201–235.

Mervis, C. B., & Rosch, E. (1981). Categorization of natural objects. *Annual Review of Psychology, 32*, 89–115.

Merzenich, M. M., Jenkins, W. M., Johnston, P., Schreiner, C. (1996). Temporal processing deficits of language-learning impaired children ameliorated by training. *Science, 271*(5245), 77–81.

Messer, S. B. (1976). Reflection-impulsivity: A review. *Psychological Bulletin, 83*, 1026–1052.

Meyer, L. H., Park, H.-S., Grenot-Scheyer, M., Schwartz, I. S., & Harry, B. (1998). *Making friends.* Baltimore: Paul H. Brooks.

Meyer-Bahlburg, H. F. L., Ehrhardt, A. A., Rosen, L. R., & Gruen, R. S. (1995). Prenatal estrogens and the development of homosexual orientation. *Developmental Psychology, 31*(1), 12–21.

Michael, R. T. (1994). *Sex in America: A definitive survey.* Boston: Little Brown.

Michaels, S. (1996). The prevalence of homosexuality in the United States. In R. P. Cabaj & T. S. Stein (Eds.), *Textbook of homosexuality and mental health.* (pp. 43–63). Washington, DC: American Psychiatric Press.

Michalson, L., & Lewis, M. (1985). What do children know about emotions and when do they know it? In M. Lewis & C. Saarni (Eds.), *The socialization of emotions.* New York: Plenum Press.

Miller, G. A. (1981). *Language and speech.* New York: W. H. Freeman.

Miller, G. A. (1991). *The science of words.* New York: Scientific American Library.

Miller, J. G. (1997). Theoretical issues in cultural psychology. In J. W. Berry & Y. H. Poortinga (Eds.), *Handbook of cross-cultural psychology: Theory and method* (pp. 85–128). Boston, MA: Allyn & Bacon.

Miller, N. E., & Dollard, J. (1941). *Social learning and imitation.* New Haven: Yale University Press.

Miller, P. (1982). *Amy, Wendy and Beth: Learning language in south Baltimore.* Austin, TX: University of Texas Press.

Miller, P. H. (1990). The development of strategies of selective attention. In D. F. Bjorklund (Ed.), *Children's strategies: Contemporary views of cognitive development* (pp. 157-184). Hillsdale, NJ: Erlbaum.

Miller, P. H., & Coyle, T. R. (1999). Developmental change: Lessons from microgenesis. In E. K. Scholnick & K. Nelson (Eds.), *Conceptual development: Piaget's legacy* (pp. 209–239). Mahwah, N.J.: Erlbaum.

Miller, S. L., & Tallal, P. (1995). A behavioral neuroscience approach to developmental language disorder: Evidence for a rapid temporal processing deficient. In C. D. Cicchetti & D. J. Cohen (Eds.), *Developmental psychopathology: Vol. 2. Risk, disorder, and adaption.* New York: Wiley.

Minton, H. L. & Schneider, F. W. (1980). *Differentail psychiatry.* Monterey, CA: Brooks/Cole.

Minoura, Y. (1992). A sensitive period for the incorporation of a cultral meaning system: A study of Japanese children growing up in America. *Ethos, 20,* 304–339.

Minuchin, P. P., & Shapiro, E. K. (1983). The school as a context of social development. In P. H. Mussen (Ed.), *Handbook of child psychology* (4th ed.), *Vol. 4: Socialization, personality, and social development.* New York: Wiley.

Mischel, W. (1966). A social learning view of sex differences in behavior. In E. M. Maccoby (Ed.), *The development of sex differences.* Stanford: Stanford University Press.

Miyake, K., Chen, S., & Campos, J. J. (1985). Infant temperament, mother's mode of interaction, and attachment in Japan. An interim report. *Monographs of the Society for Research in Child Development, 50*(1–2, Serial No. 209).

Miyaki, K., Campos, J., Bradshaw, D. L., & Kagan, J. (1986). Issues in socioemotional development. In H. Stevenson & H. Azuma & K. Hakuta (Eds.), *Child development and education in Japan.* New York: W. H. Freeman.

Mizukami, K., Kobayashi, N., Ishii, T., & Iwata, H. (1990). First selective attachment begins in early infancy: A study using telethermography. *Infant Behavior and Development, 13,* 257–273.

Moely, B. E., Santulli, K. A., & Obach, M. S. (1995). Strategy instruction, metacognition, and motivation in the elementary school classroom. In F. E. Weinert & W. Schneider (Eds.), *Memory performance and competencies: Issues in growth and development* (pp. 301–321). Hillsdale, NJ: Erlbaum.

Moffit, T. E., Caspi, A., Belsky, J., & Silva, P. A. (1992). Childhood experience and the onset of menarche: A test of a sociobiological model. *Child Development, 63,* 47–58.

Mondloch, C. J., Lewis, T. L., Budreau, D. R., Maurer, D., Dannemiller, J. L., Stephens, B. R., & Kleiner-Gathercoal, K. A. (1999). Face perception during early infancy. *Psychological Science, 10*(5), 419–422.

Moon, C., & Fifer, W. P. (1990). Syllables as signals for 2-day-old infants. *Infant Behavior and Development, 13,* 377–390.

Moon, C., Cooper, R. P., & Fifer, W. P. (1993). Two day olds prefer their native language. *Infant Behavior Development, 16,* 495–500.

Moore, K. L., & Persaud, T. V. N. (1993). *The developing human: Clinically oriented embryology* (5th ed.). Philadelphia: Saunders.

Moore, K. L., Persaud, T. V. N., & Shiota, K. (1994). *Color atlas of clinical embryology.* Philadelphia: Saunders.

Moore, R., & Young, D. (1978). Childhood outdoors: Toward a social ecology of the landscape. In I. Altman & J. Wahlwill (Eds.), *Human behavior and environment* (Vol. 3). New York: Plenum Press.

Moore, T. R., Origel, W., Key, T. C., & Resnik, R. (1986). The perinatal and economic impact of prenatal care in a low socioeconomic population. *American Journal of Obstetrics and Gynecology, 154,* 29–33.

Morelli, G. A., Rogoff, B., Oppenheim, D., & Goldsmith, D. (1992). Cultural variation in infants sleeping arrangements: Questions of independence. *Developmental Psychology, 28,* 604–613.

Morelli, G. A., Tronick, E., & Beeghly, M. (1999). *Is there security in numbers? Child care in a hunting and gathering community and infants' attachment relationships.* Albuquerque, NM: Society for Research in Child Development.

Morris, K. (1998). Short course of AZT halves HIV–1 perinatal transmission. *Lancet, 351*(9103), 651.

Morrison, F. J., Smith, L., & Dow-Ehrensberger, M. (1995). Education and cognitive development: A natural experiment. *Developmental Psychology, 31,* 789–799.

Morrison, F. J., Alberts, D. M., & Griffith, E. M. (1997). Nature-nurture in the classroom: Entrance age, school readiness, and learning in children. *Developmental Psychology, 33*(2), 254–262.

Morrongiello, B. A., Fenwick, K. D., Hillier, L., & Chance, G. (1994). Sound localization in newborn human infants. *Developmental Psychobiology, 27*(8), 519–538.

Mortality and Morbidity Weekly Report. (1995). Cesarean delivery in the United States in 1993. *44, No.15*(April 21), 303–304.

Mortimer, J. T., & Johnson, M. K. (1998). Adolescent part-time work and educational achievement. In K. Borman & B. Schneider (Eds.), *The adolescent years: social influences and educational challenges* (pp. 183–206). Chicago: National Society for the Study of Education.

Mortimer, J. T., Shanahan, M., & Ryu, S. (1994). The effects of adolescent employment on school-related orientation and behavior. In R. K. Silbereisen & E. Todt (Eds.), *Adolescence in context: The interplay of family, school, peers and work in adjustment.* New York: Springer-Verlag.

Mortimer, J. T., Finch, M. D., Ryu, S., & Shanahan, M. J. (1996). The effects of work intensity on adolescent mental health, achievement, and behavioral adjustment: New evidence from a prospective study. *Child Development, 67*(3), 1243–1261.

Morton, J., & Johnson, M. H. (1991). Conspec and Conlearn: A two-process theory of infant face recognition. *Psychological Review, 98,* 164–181.

Moshman, D. (1998). Cognitive development beyond childhood. In D. Kuhn & R. S. Siegler (Eds.), *Handbook of child psychology* (5th ed.), *Vol. 2: Cognition, perception, and language.* (pp. 947–978). New York: Wiley.

Mosier, C. E., & Rogoff, B. (1994). Infant's instrumental use of their mother's to achieve their goals. *Child Development, 65,* 70–79.

Moss, N. E., & Carver, K. (1998). The effect of WIC and Medicaid on infant mortality–the United States. *American Journal of Public Health, 88,* 1354–1361.

Motulsky, V. (1986). *Human genetics: Problems and approaches* (2nd ed.). New York: Springer-Verlag.

Mowrer, O. H. (1950). *Learning theory and personality.* New York: Ronald Press.

Munn, P., & Dunn, J. (1988). Temperament and the developing relationship between siblings. *International Journal of Behavioral Development, 12,* 433–451.

Munroe, R. H., & Munroe, R.L. (1994). Behavior across cultures: Results from observational studies. In W. J. Lonner & R. Malpass (Eds.), *Psychology and culture* (pp. 107–111). Boston: Allyn & Bacon.

Murdock, G. P. (1949). *Social structure.* New York: Macmillan.

Murray, L., & Cooper, P. J. (1997). Postpartum depression and child development. *Psychological Medicine, 27*(2), 253–260.

Muuss, R., & Porton, H. (1998). *Theories of adolescence* (7th ed.). New York: McGraw-Hill.

Müller, U., Sokol, B., & Overton, W. F. (1999). Developmental sequences in class reasoning and propositional reasoning. *Journal of Experimental Child Psychology, 74,* 69–106.

Naeye, R. L. (1978). Effects of maternal cigarette smoking on the fetus and placenta. *Journal of Obstetrics and Gynecology of the British Commonwealth, 85,* 732–735.

Naigles, L. G., & Gelman, S. A. (1995). Overextensions in comprehensions and production revisited: Preferential-looking in a study of dog, cat, and cow. *Journal of Child Language, 22(1),* 19–46.

Natali, R., Nasello-Paterson, C., & Conners, G. (1988). Patterns in fetal breathing activity in the human fetus at 24 to 28 weeks of gestation. *American Journal of Obstetrics and Gynecology, 158,* 317–321.

National Academy of Sciences: Committee on Dietary Allowances, and Nutrition Board, National Research Council. (1989). *Recommended dietary allowances.* Washington, DC: National Academy of Sciences.

National Center for Educational Statistics. (1993). *Adult literacy in America.*: Princeton, NJ: Educational Testing Service.

National Clearinghouse on Child Abuse and Neglect (NCCAN). (1997). *National Child Abuse and Neglect Data System.* Available: http://www.acf.dhhs.gov/programs/cb/ stats/ncands97/cm97.htm.

National Clearinghouse on Child Abuse and Neglect (NCCAN). (1999). *National Clearing House on Child Abuse and Neglect Data System.* Available: http://www.calib.com/nccanch/pubs/factsheets/infact.htm.

National Council of Teachers of Mathematics (NCTM). (1995). *Assessment standards for teaching mathematics.* Reston, VA: National Council of Teachers of Mathematics.

National Commission on Youth. (1980). *The transition of youth to adulthood: A bridge too long.* Boulder, CO: Westview Press.

Needham, J. (1968). *Order and life.* Cambridge, MA: MIT Press.

Neisser, U. (1976). *General, academic, and artificial intelligence.* Hillsdale, NJ: Erlbaum.

Neisser, U. & others (1996). Intelligence: Knowns and unknowns. *American Psychologist, 51,* 77–101.

Neisser, U. (1998). *The rising curve: Long-term gains in IQ and related measures.* Washington, DC: American Psychological Association.

Nelson, C. A., & Bloom, F. E. (1997). Child and neuroscience. *Child Development (68) 5, 970–987.*

Nelson, K. (1973). Structure and strategy in learning to talk. *Monographs of the Society for Research in Child Development, 38*(2, Serial No. 149).

Nelson, K. (1976). Facilitating syntax acquisition. *Developmental Psychology, 13,* 101–107.

Nelson, K. (1977). The syntagmatic-paradigmatic shift revisited: A review of research and theory. *Psychological Bulletin, 84,* 93–116.

Nelson, K. (1981). Social cognition in a script framework. In J. H. Flavell & L. Ross (Eds.), *Social cognitive development.* Cambridge: Cambridge University Press.

Nelson, K. (1988). Constraints on word learning? *Cognitive Development, 3,* 221–246.

Nelson, K. (1993). The psychological and social origins of autobiographical memory. *Psychological Science, 4*(1), 7–14.

Nelson, K. (1996). *Language in cognitive development.* New York: Cambridge University Press.

Nelson-Le Gaull, S., & De Cooke, P. A. (1987). Same-sex and cross-sex help exchanges in the classroom. *Journal of Educational Psychology, 79,* 67–71.

Netter, F. H. (1965). *The CIBA collection of medical illustrations.* Summit, NJ: CIBA Pharmaceutical Products.

Newcomb, A. F., Bukowski, W. M., & Pattee, L. (1993). Children's peer relations: A meta-analytic review of popular, rejected, controversial and average sociometric status. *Psychological Bulletin, 113,* 99–128.

Newman, D. L., Caspi, A., Moffitt, T. E., & Silva, P. A. (1997). Antecedents of adult interpersonal functioning: Effects of individual differences in age 3 temperament. *Developmental Psychology, 33*(2), 206–217.

Newton, N., & Newton, M. (1972). Lactation: Its psychological component. In J. G. Howells (Ed.), *Modern perspectives in psycho-obstetrics.* New York: Brunner/Mazel.

NICHD Early Child Care Research Network. (1996). Characteristics of infant child care: Factors contributing to positive caregiving. *Early Childhood Research Quarterly, 11,* 296–307.

NICHD Early Child Care Research Network. (1997). Familial factors associated with the characteristics of nonmaternal care for infants. *Journal of Marriage & the Family, 59*(2), 389–408.

NICHD Early Child Care Research Network. (1998a). Characteristics and quality of child care for toddlers and preschoolers. *Applied Developmental Science.*

NICHD Early Child Care Research Network. (1998b). Relations between family predictors and child outcomes: Are they weaker for children in child care. *Developmental Psychology, 34*(5), 1198–1128.

NICHD Early Child Care Research Network. (1998c). Early child care and self-control, compliance, and problem behavior at twenty-four and thirty-six months. *Child Development, 69*(4), 1145–1170.

Nicolopoulou, A. (1993). Play, cognitive development, and the social world: Piaget, Vygotsky, and beyond. *Human Development, 36,* 1–23.

Niebyl, J. R. (1994). Teratology and drug use during pregnancy and lactation. In J. R. Scott & P. J. DiSaia & C. B. Hammond & W. N. Spellacy (Eds.), *Dansforth's obstetrics and gynecology* (7th ed.). Philadelphia: J.B. Lippincott.

Nightingale, E. O., & Meister, S. B. (1987). *Prenatal screening, policies and values: The example of neural tube defects.* Cambridge, MA: Harvard University Press.

Nijhuis, J. G. (Ed.). (1992). *Fetal behavior: Developmental and perinatal aspects.* New York: Oxford University Press.

Nikken, P., & Peters, A. L. (1988). Children's perceptions of TV reality. *Journal of Broadcasting and Electronic Media, 32*(4), 441–452.

Ninio, A., & Snow, C. E. (1999). The development of pragmatics: Learning to use language appropriately. In W. C. Ritchie & T. K. Bhatia (Eds.), *Handbook of child language acquisition* (pp. 347–383). San Diego, CA: Academic Press.

Nino, A., & Bruner, J. (1978). The achievement and antecedents of labeling. *Journal of Child Development, 5,* 1–15.

Niswander, K. R., & Evans, A. T. (Eds.). (1996). *Manual of obstetrics* (5th ed.). Boston: Little Brown.

Nucci, L. (1996). Morality and the personal sphere of actions. In E. Reed, E. Turiel & T. Brown (Eds.), *Values and knowledge* (pp. 41–60). Hillsdale, NJ: Erlbaum.

Nünes, T., Schliemann, A. D., & Carraher, D. W. (1993). *Street mathematics and school mathematics.* Cambridge: Cambridge University Press.

Nyiti, R. M. (1976). The development of conservation in the Meru children of Tanzania. *Child Development, 47,* 1122–1129.

Nyiti, R. M. (1982). The validity of "cultural differences explanations" for cross-cultural variation in the rate of Piagetian cognitive development. In D. Wagner & H. Stevenson (Eds.), *Cultural perspectives on child development.* New York: W. H. Freeman.

O'Brien, M., & Huston, A. C. (1985a). Development of sex-typed play behavior in toddlers. *Developmental Psychology, 21,* 866–871.

O'Brien, M., & Huston, A. C. (1985b). Activity level and sex-stereotyped toy choice in toddler boys and girls. *Journal of Genetic Psychology, 146*(4), 527–533.

Ochs, E. (1982). Talking to children in Western Samoa. *Language in Society, 11,* 77–104.

Ochs, E., & Schieffelin, B. (1984). Language acquisition and socialization. Three developmental stories and their implications. In R. Shweder & R. Le Vine (Eds.), *Culture theory.* Cambridge: Cambridge University Press.

Ochs, E., & Schieffelin, B. (1995). The impact of language socialization or grammatical development. In P. Fletcher & B. MacWhinney (Eds.), *The handbook of child language.* Cambridge, MA: Basil Blackwell.

Ogbu, J. U. (1997). Understanding the school performance of urban Blacks: Some essential background knowledge. In H. J. Walberg & O. Reyes (Eds.), *Children and youth: Interdisciplinary perspectives* (pp. 190–222). Thousand Oaks, CA: Sage Publications, Inc.

Okamoto, Y., & Case, R. (1996). Exploring the microstructure of children's central conceptional structures on the domain of numbers. *Monographs of the Society for Research on Child Development, 61*(1–2), 27–58.

Oliner, S. B., & Oliner, P. (1988). *The altruistic personality: Rescuers of Jews in Nazi Germany.* New York: Macmillan.

Ollendick, T. H., Weist, M. D., Borden, M. C., & Greene, R. W. (1992). Sociometric status and academic, behavioral, and psychological adjustment: A five-year longitudinal study. *Journal of Consulting & Clinical Psychology, 60*(1), 80–87.

Olson, D. R. (1994). *The world on paper.* New York: Cambridge University Press.

Olson, H. C., Streissguth, A. P., Sampson, P. D., & Barr, H. M. (1997). Association of prenatal alcohol exposure with behavioral and learning problems in early adolescence. *Journal of the American Academy of Child and Adolescent Psychiatry, 36*(9), 1187–1194.

Olweus, D. (1993). *Bullying at school: What we know and what we can do.* Oxford, England: Blackwells.

Ommen, G. S. (1978). Prenatal diagnosis of genetic disorders. *Science, 200,* 952—958.

Oppenheim, R. W. (1981). Ontogenetic adaptation and retrogressive processes in the development of the nervous system and behavior: A neuroembryological perspective. In K. J. Connolly & H. F. R. Prechtl (Eds.), *Maturation and development: Biological and psychological perspectives.* Philadelphia: Lippincott.

Ornstein, P. A., Shapiro, L. R., Clubb, P. A., Follmer, A., & Baker-Ward, L. (1997). The influence of prior knowledge on children's memory for salient medical experiences. In N. Stein & P. A. Ornstein & B. Tversky & C. J. Brainerd (Eds.), *Memory for everyday and emotional events* (pp. 83–112). Hillsdale, NJ: Erlbaum.

Ortony, A. (1993). *Metaphor and thought* (2nd ed.). New York: Cambridge University Press.

Overton, W. F. (1990). Competence and procedures: Constraints on the development of logical reasoning. In W. F. Overton (Ed.), *Reasoning, necessity and logic: Developmental perspectives.* Hillsdale, NJ: Erlbaum.

Packer, M. (1994). Cultural work on the kindergarten playground. *Human Development, 37,* 259–276.

Padden, C., & Humphries, T. (1989). *Deaf in America: Voices from a culture.* Cambridge, MA: Harvard University Press.

Paikoff, R. L., & Brooks-Gunn, J. (1991). Do parent-child relationships change during puberty? *Psychological Bulletin, 110,* 47–66.

Paley, V. G. (1981). *Wally's stories.* Cambridge, MA: Harvard University Press.

Paley, V. G. (1984). *Boys & girls: Superheroes in the doll corner.* Chicago: The University of Chicago Press.

Paley, V. G. (1986). *Mollie is three: Growing up in school.* Chicago: University of Chicago Press.

Papert, S. (1980). *Mindstorms, children, computers and powerful ideas.* New York: Basic Books.

Papert, S. (1996). A word for learning. In Y. B. Kafai & M. Resnick (Eds.), *Constructionism in practice: Designing, thinking, and learning in a digital world.* Mahwah, NJ: Erlbaum.

Parke, R. D. (1979). Perspectives on father-infant interaction. In J. Osofsky (Ed.), *A handbook of infant development* (pp. 549–590). New York: Wiley.

Parke, R. D., & Ladd, G. W. (1992). Family-peer relationships. *Merrill-Palmer Quarterly, 40,* 1–20.

Parke, R. D. (1995). Fathers and families. In M. H. Bornstein (Ed.), *Handbook of parenting: Status and social conditions of parenting* (Vol. 3, pp. 27–66). Mahwah, NJ: Erlbaum.

Parke, R. D., & Buriel, R. (1998). Socialization in the family: Ethnica and ecological perspectives. In W. Damon & N. Eisenberg (Eds.), *Handbook of child development* (5th ed.), *Vol 3: Social, emotional, and personality development* (pp. 463–552). New York: Wiley.

Parker, J. G., & Gottman, J. M. (1989). Social and emotional development in a relational context: friendship interactions from early childhood to adolescence. In T. J. Berndt & G. W. Ladd (Eds.), *Peer relationships in child development.* New York: Wiley.

Parker, J. G., & Asher, S. R. (1993). Friendship and friendship quality in middle childhood: Links with peer acceptance and feelings of loneliness and social dissatisfaction. *Developmental Psychology, 29,* 611–621.

Parker, J. G., Rubin, K. H., Price, J. M., & De Rosier, M. E. (1995). Peer relationships, child development, and adjustment: A developmental psychopathology. In D. Cicchetti & D. J. Cohen (Eds.), *Developmental Psychopathology.* New York: Wiley.

Parker, S., Nichter, M., Nichter, M., Vuckovic, N., Sims, C., & Ritenbaught, C. (1995). Body image and weight concerns among African American and White adolescent females: Differences that make a difference. *Human Organization, 54,* 103–114.

Parmalee, A. H., Jr., Akiyama, Y., Schultz, M. A., Wenner, W. H., Schulte, F. J., & Stern, E. (1968). The electroencephalogram in active and quiet sleep in infants. In P. Kellaway & I. Petersen (Eds.), *Clinical electroencephaly of children.* New York: Grune & Stratton.

Pascalis, O., De Schonen, S., Morton, J., & Deruelle, C. (1995). Mother's face recognition by neonates: A replication and an extension. *Infant Behavior and Development, 18,* 79–85.

Patterson, G. R., Littman, R. A., & Bricker, W. (1967). Assertive behavior in young children: A step toward a theory of aggression. *Monographs of the Society for Research for Child Development, 32*(Serial No. 113).

Patterson, G. R. (1976). The aggressive child: Victim and architect of a coercive system. In E. J. Marsh & L. A. Hamerlynk & L. C. Handy (Eds.), *Behavior modification and families: Vol. 1. Theory and research.* New York: Brunner/Mazel.

Patterson, G. R. (1979). A performance theory of coercive family interaction. In R. Cairns (Ed.), *Social interaction: Methods.* Hillsdale, NJ: Erlbaum.

Patterson, G. R. (1982). *Coercive family processes.* Eugene, OR: Castalia Press.

Patterson, G. R., & Crosby, L. V., S. (1992). Predicting risk for early police arrest. *Journal of Quantitative Criminology, 8*(4), 335–355.

Patterson, G. R. (1995). Coercion–a basis for early onset of arrest. In J. McCord (Ed.), *Coercion and punishment in long term perspective* (pp. 81–105). New York: Cambridge University Press.

Patterson, G. R., Reid, J. B. & Dishion, T. J. (1998). Antisocial boys. In J. M. Jenkins, K. Oatley, & N. L. Stein (Eds.), *Human emotions: A reader* (pp. 330–336). Malden, MA: Blackwell Publishers.

Pavlov, I. P. (1927). *Conditioned reflexes.* Oxford, England: Oxford University Press.

Pea, R. D., Kurland, D. M., & Hawkins, J. (1987). Logo and the development of thinking skills. In R. D. Pea & K. Sheingold (Eds.), *Mirrors of minds: Patterns of experience in educational computing.* (pp. 178–197). Norwood, NJ: Ablex.

Pedlow, R., Sanson, A., Prior, M., & Oberklaid, F. (1993). Stability of maternally reported temperament from infancy to 8 years. *Developmental Psychology, 29*(6), 998–1007.

Peplau, L. A., DeBro, S. C., Veniegas, R. C., & Taylor, P. L. (1999). *Gender, culture, and ethnicity: Current research about women and men.* Mountain View, CA: Mayfield Publishing Co.

Percy, W. (1975). *The message in the bottle.* New York: Farrar, Straus & Giroux.

Perez-Granados, D. R., & Callanan, M. A. (1997). Parents and siblings as early resources for young children's learning in Mexican-descent families. *Hispanic Journal of Behavioral Sciences.,* 3–33.

Perner, J., Leekam, S. R., & Wimmer, H. (1987). Three-year-olds' difficulty with false belief: The case for a conceptual deficit. *British Journal of Developmental Psychology, 5*(2), 125–137.

Perner, J., Ruffman, T., & Leekam, S. R. (1994). Theory of mind is contageous: You catch it from your sibs. *Child Development, 65,* 1228–1238.

Perry, D. G., & Bussey, K. (1984). *Social development.* Englewood Cliffs, NJ: Prentice-Hall.

Persaud, T. V. N. (1977). *Problems of birth defects: From Hippocrates to thalidomide and after.* Baltimore: University Park Press.

Pescosolido, B. A., Grauerholz, E., & Milkie, M. A. (1997). Culture and conflict: The portrayal of Blacks in U.S. children's picture books through the mid- and late-twentieth century. *American Sociological Review, 62*(3), 443–464.

Peskin, H. (1967). Pubertal onset and ego functioning. *Journal of Abnormal Psychology, 72*, 1–15.

Peskin, H. (1973). Influence of the developmental schedule of puberty on learning and ego functioning. *Journal of Youth & Adolescence, 2*(4), 273–290.

Pettit, G. S., Bates, J. E., Dodge, K. A., & Meece, D. W. (1999). The impact of after-school peer contact on early adolescent externalizing problems is moderated by parental monitoring, perceived neighborhood safety, and prior adjustment. *Child Development, 70*(3), 768–778.

Pettito, L. A., & Marentette, P. F. (1991). Babbling in the manual mode: Evidence for the onotogeny of language. *Science, 251*, 1493–1496.

Peveler, R., & Fairburn, C. (1990). Eating disorders in women who abuse alcohol. *British Journal of Addiction, 85*(12), 1633–1638.

Phinney, J. S. (1993). A three-stage model of ethnic identity development in adolescence. In M. E. Bernal & G. P. Knight (Eds.), *Ethnic identity: Formation and transmission among hispanics and other minorities*. Albany, NY: SUNY Press.

Phinney, J. S. (1995). Ethnic identity and self-esteem: A review and integration. In A. M. Padilla (Ed.), *Hispanic psychology: Critical issues in theory and research*. Thousand Oaks, CA: Sage.

Phinney, J. S. (1996). When we talk about American ethnic groups, what do we mean? *American Psychologist, 51*(9), 918-927.

Piaget, J. (1926). *The language and thought of the child*. New York: Meridian Books.

Piaget, J. (1928). *Judgment and reasoning in the child*. London: Routledge & Kegan Paul.

Piaget, J. (1929/1979). *The child's conception of the world*. New York: Harcourt Brace.

Piaget, J. (1930). *The child's conception of physical causality*. New York: Harcourt Brace.

Piaget, J. (1932/1965). *The moral judgment of the child*. New York: Free Press (Original work published 1932).

Piaget, J. (1952a). *The child's conception of number*. New York: W. W. Norton.

Piaget, J. (1952b). *The origins of intelligence in children*. New York: International Universities Press.

Piaget, J. (1954). *The construction of reality in the child*. New York: Basic Books.

Piaget, J. (1962). *Play, dreams and imitation*. New York: W. W. Norton.

Piaget, J. (1964). Development and learning. In R. E. Ripple & V. N. Rockcastle (Eds.), *Piaget rediscovered. Conference on cognitive studies and curriculum development*. Cornell University and University of California.

Piaget, J. (1966/1974). Need and significance of cross-cultural studies in genetic psychology. In J. W. B. P. R. Dasen (Ed.), *Culture and cognition: Readings in cross-cultural psychology*. London: Metheun.

Piaget, J. (1967). *Six psychological studies*. New York: Random House.

Piaget, J. (1972). Intellectual evolution from adolescence to adulthood. *Human Development, 15*, 1–12.

Piaget, J. (1973). *The psychology of intelligence*. Totowa, NJ: Littlefield & Adams.

Piaget, J. (1977). *The development of thought: Equilibration of cognitive structure*. New York: Viking.

Piaget, J. (1983). Piaget's theory. In P. H. Mussen (Ed.), *Handbook of child psychology* (4th ed.), *Vol. 1: History, theory and methods*. New York: Wiley.

Piaget, J. (1987). *Possibility and necessity: Vol. 1. The role of possibility in cognitive development*. Minneapolis, MN: University of Minnesota Press.

Piaget, J., & Inhelder, B. (1956). *The child's conception of space*. London: Routledge & Kegan Paul.

Piaget, J., & Inhelder, B. (1969). *The psychology of the child*. New York: Basic.

Piaget, J., & Inhelder, B. (1973). *Memory and intelligence*. New York: Basic Books.

Pianta, R., Egeland, B., & Erickson, M. F. (1989). Results of the mother-child interaction research project. In D. Cicchetti & V. Carlson (Eds.), *Child maltreatment: Theory and research on the causes and consequences of child abuse and neglect*. Cambridge: Cambridge University Press.

Pick, A. D. (1997). Perceptual learning, categorizing, and cognitive development. In C. Dent-Read & P. Zukow-Golding (Eds.), *Evolving explanations of development: Ecological approaches to organism environment systems* (pp. 335–370). Washington, DC: American Psychological Association.

Pinker, S. (1994). *The language instinct*. New York: William Morrow and Company.

Pipher, M. (1994). *Reviving Ophelia: Saving the selves of adolescent girls*. New York: G.P. Putnam's Sons.

Pittman, R., & Oppenheim, R. W. (1979). Cell death of motoneurons in the chick embryo spinal cord. *Journal of Comparative Neurology, 187*, 425–446.

Plath, D. W. (1980). *Long engagements: Maturity in moder Japan*. Stanford, CA: Stanford University Press.

Plato. (1945). *The republic*. London: Oxford University Press.

Plomin, R. (1997). Identifying genes for cognitive abilities and disabilities. In R. J. Sternberg & E. L. Grigorenko (Eds.), *Intelligence, heredity, and environment* (pp. 89–104). New York: Cambridge University Press.

Plomin, R., & Bergeman, C. S. (1991). The nature of nurture: Genetic influence on "environmental" measures. *Behavioral and Brain Sciences, 14*, 373–305.

Plomin, R., & De Fries, J. C. (1983). The Colorado adoption project. *Child Development, 54*, 276–289.

Plomin, R., De Fries, J. C., & McClearn, G. (1990). *Behavioral genetics: A primer* (2nd ed.). New York: W. H. Freeman.

Plomin, R., Emde, R. N., Braungart, J. M., & Campos, J. (1993). Genetic change and continuity from fourteen to twenty months: The MacArthur longitudinal twin study. *Child Development, 64*, 1354–1376.

Plomin, R., De Fries, J. C., McClearn, G. E. & Rutter, M. (1997). *Behavioral genetics: A primer* (3rd ed.). New York: W. H. Freeman.

Pollitt, E. (1994). Poverty and child development: Relevance of research in developing countries to the United States. Special issue: Children and poverty. *Child Development, 65*, 283–295.

Pollitt, E., Gorman, K. S., Engle, P. L., Martorell, R., & Rivera, J. (1993). Early supplementary feeding and cognition. *Monographs of the Society for Research in Child Development, 58*(7, Serial No. 235).

Pomerantz, E. M., Ruble, D. N., Frey, K. S., & Greulich, F. (1995). Meeting goals and confronting conflict: Children's changing perceptions of social comparison. *Child Development, 66*, 723–738.

Poulin-Dubois, D. (1995). Object parts and the acquisition of the meaning of names. In K. Nelson & Z. Réger (Eds.), *Children's language, Vol. 8*. Hillsdale, NJ: Erlbaum.

Povenelli, D. J. (1995). The unduplicated self. In P. Rochat (Ed.), *The self in infancy: Theory and research* (pp. 161–192). Amsterdam: Elsevier.

Pratt, H. (1954). The neonate. In L. Carmichael (Ed.), *Manual of child psychology* (2nd ed.). New York: Wiley.

Prechtl, H. (1977). *The neurological examination of the full-term newborn infant* (2nd ed.). Philadelphia: Lippincott.

Preisser, D. A., Hodson, B. W., & Paden, E. P. (1988). Developmental phonology: 18–29 months. *Journal of Speech and Hearing Disorders, 53*, 125–130.

Prescott, E., & Jones, E. (1971). Day care of children—assets and liabilities. *Children, 18*, 54–58.

Price-Williams, D., Gordon, W., & Ramirez, M. (1969). Skill and conservation: A study of pottery-making children. *Developmental Psychology, 1*, 769.

Pritchard, J. A., & MacDonald, P. C. (1980). *Williams' Obstetrics* (16th ed.). New York: Appleton-Century-Crofts.

Pueschel, S. M., Craig, W. Y., & Haddow, J. E. (1992). Lipids and lipoproteins in persons with Down's syndrome. *Journal of Intellectual Disability Research, 36*(4), 365–369.

Purcell-Gates, V. (1996). Stories, coupons, and the TV Guide: Relationships between home literacy experiences and emergent literacy knowledge. *Reading Research Quarterly, 31*, 406–428.

Putallaz, M., & Heflin, A. H. (1990). Parent-child interaction. In S. R. Asher & J. D. Coie (Eds.), *Peer rejection in childhood.* New York: Cambridge University Press.

Putallaz, M., & Wasserman, A. (1990). Children's entry behavior. In S. R. Asher & J. D. Coie (Eds.), *Peer rejection in childhood: Cambridge studies in social and emotional development.* New York: Cambridge University Press.

Quadrel, M. J., Fischoff, B., & Davis, W. (1993). Adolescent (in) vulnerability. *American Psychologist, 48*, 102–116.

Quinn, P. C., & Eimas, P. D. (1996). Perceptual organization and categorization in young infants. In C. Rovee-Collier & L. P. Lipsitt (Eds.), *Advances in infancy research* (Vol. 10, pp. 1–36). Norwood, NJ: Ablex.

Quinn, P., & Eimas, P. D. (1997). A reexamination of the perceptual-to-conceptual shift in mental representation. *Review of General Psychology, 1*(3), 271–287.

Quinn, P. C., & Eimas, P. D. (1998). Evidence for a global categorical representation of humans by young infants. *Journal of Experimental Child Psychology, 69*(3), 151–174.

Quinton, D., & Rutter, M. (1976). Early hospital admissions and later disturbances of behavior: An attempted replication of Douglas' findings. *Developmental Medicine and Child Neurology, 18*, 447–459.

Quinn, P. C., Eimas, P. D., & Rosenkrantz, S. L. (1993). Evidence for representations of perceptually similar natural categories by 3-month-old and 4-month-old infants. *Perception, 22*, 463–475.

Quinton, D., & Rutter, M. (1985). Parenting behavior of mothers raised "in care." In A. R. Nicol (Ed.), *Longitudinal studies in child psychology and psychiatry: Practical lessons from research experience.* New York: Wiley.

Rabin, A. J. (1965). *Growing up in the kibbutz.* New York: Springer-Verlag.

Rank, O. (1929). *The trauma of birth.* New York: Harcourt Brace.

Ravaglia, R., Suppes, P., Stillinger, C., & Alper, T. M. (1995). Computer-based mathematics and physics for gifted students. *Gifted Child Quarterly, 39*(1), 7–13.

Raven, J. C. (1962). *Coloured progressive matrices.* London: H. K. Lewis & Co., Ltd.

Raybaud, C., & Girard, N. (1998). Cerebral development and MRI. In B. Garreau (Ed.), *Neuroimaging in child neuropsychiatric disorders* (pp. 59–88). Berlin: Springer-Verlag.

Read, M. (1960/1968). *Children of their fathers: Growing up among the Ngoni of Malawi.* New York: Holt, Rinehart & Winston.

Rebok, G. W., Smith, C. B., Pascualvaca, D. M., & Mirsky, A. F. (1997). Developmental changes in attentional performance in urban children from eight to thirteen years. *Child Neuropsychology, 3*(1), 28–46.

Reed, M. D., & Roundtree, P. W. (1997). Peer pressure and adolescent substance abuse. *Journal of Quantitative Criminology, 13*(2), 143–180.

Reese, E., & Cox, A. (1999). Quality of adult book reading affects children's emergent literacy. *Developmental Psychology, 35*(1), 20–28.

Reichel-Domatoff, G., & Reichel-Domatoff, A. (1961). *The people of Aritama.* London: Routledge & Kegan Paul.

Resnick, D. P., & Resnick, L. D. (1977). The nature of literacy: A historical exploration. *Harvard Educational Review, 47*, 370–385.

Resnick, L. B. (1989). Developing mathematical knowledge. *American Psychologist, 44*(2), 162–169.

Resnick, M. (1998). Technologies for Lifelong Kindergarten. *Educational Technology Research and Development, 46*(4), 43–55.

Rest, J. R. (1986). *Moral development: Advances in research and theory.* New York: Praeger.

Rest, J., Narvaez, D., Bebeau, M. l. J., & Thoma, S. J. (1999). *Postconventional moral thinking: A neo-Kohlbergian approach.* Mahwah, NJ: Erlbaum.

Retschitzki, J. (1989). Evidence of formal thinking in Baoule airele players. In D. M. Keats & D. Munro & L. Mann (Eds.), *Heterogeneity in cross-cultural psychology.* Amsterdam: Swets & Zeitlinger.

Rheingold, H. L. (1982). Little children's participation in the work of adults, a nascent prosocial behavior. *Child Development, 53*, 114–125.

Rice, M. L. (1990). Preschooler's QUIL: Quick incidental learning of words. In G. C. Ramsden & C. E. Snow (Eds.), *Children's language* (Vol. 7). Hillsdale, NJ: Erlbaum.

Rice, C., Koinis, D., Sullivan, K., & Tager-Flusberg, H. (1997). When 3-year-olds pass the appearance-reality test. *Developmental Psychology, 33*(1), 54–61.

Richards, H. C., Bear, G. G., Stewart, A. L., & Norman, A. D. (1992). Moral reasoning and classroom conduct: Evidence of a curvilinear relationship. *Merrill-Palmer Quarterly, 38*, 176–190.

Richards, J. E., & Rader, N. (1983). Affective, behavioral, and avoidance responses on the visual cliff: Effects of crawling onset age, crawling experience, and testing age. *Psychophysiology, 20*, 633–642.

Richards, M. H., Abell, S. N., & Petersen, A. C. (1993). Biological development. In P. H. Tolan & B. J. Cohler (Eds.), *Handbook of clinical research and practice with adolescents.* New York: Wiley.

Richters, J. E., & Martinez, P. E. (1993). Violent communities, family choices, and children's chances: An algorithm for improving the odds. Special issue: Milestones in the development of resilience. *Development & Psychopathology, 5*, 609–627.

Riel, M. (1998). Learning communities through computer networking. In G. James & S. V. Goldman (Eds.), *Thinking practices in mathematics and science learning* (pp. 369–398). Mahwah, NJ: Erlbaum.

Riesen, A. H. (1950). Arrested vision. *Scientific American, 183*, 16–19.

Rimoin, D. L., Connor, J. M., & Pyeritz, R. E. (1997). *Emery and Rimoin's Principles and Practice of Medical Genetics* (3 ed.). New York: Churchill Livingstone.

Rivera, S. M., Wakeley, A., & Langer, J. (1999). The drawbridge phenomenon: Representational reasoning or perceptual preference? *Developmental Psychology, 35*(2), 427–435.

Robbins, W. J., Brody, S., Hogan, A. G., Jackson, C. M., & Greene, C. W. (Eds.) (1929). *Growth.* New Haven, CT: Yale University Press.

Robson, K. S., & Moss, H. A. (1970). Patterns and determinants of maternal attachment. *Journal of Pediatrics, 77*, 976–985.

Rochat, P. (1997). Early development of the ecological self. In C. Dent-Read, & P. Zukow-Goldring, (Ed.), *Evolving explanations of development: Ecological approaches to organism-environment systems* (pp. 91–122). Washington, DC: American Psychological Association.

Rochat, P. (2000). *The infant world: Self, objects, people.* Cambridge, MA: Harvard University Press.

Rodkin, P. C., Farmer, T. W., Pearl, R., & Van Acker, R. (2000). Heterogeneity of popular boys: Antisocial and prosocial configurations. *Developmental Psychology, 36*(1), 14–24.

Rogoff, B. (1981). Schooling and the development of cognitive skills. In H. C. Triandis & A. Heron (Eds.), *Handbook of cross-cultural psychology* (Vol. 4). Boston: Allyn & Bacon.

Rogoff, B. (1982). Integrating context and cognitive development. In M. E. Lamb & A. L. Brown (Eds.), *Advances in developmental psychology* (Vol. 2). Hillsdale, NJ: Erlbaum.

Rogoff, B. (1990). *Apprenticeship in thinking: Cognitive development in social context.* Oxford: Oxford University Press.

Rogoff, B. (1998). Cognition as a collaborative process. In D. Kuhn & R. S. Siegler (Eds.), *Handbook of child psychology* (5th ed.), *Vol. 2: Cognition, perception, and language* (pp. 679–744). New York: Wiley.

Rogoff, B. (2000). *Culture and development.* New York: Oxford University Press.

Rogoff, B., & Lave, J. (1984). *Everyday cognition.* Cambridge, MA: Harvard University Press.

Rogoff, B., & Waddell, K. J. (1982). Memory for information organized in a scene by children from two cultures. *Child Development, 53*, 1224–1228.

Roguer, J. M., Figueras, J., Botet, F., & Jimenez, R. (1995). Influence on fetal growth of exposure to tobacco smoke during pregnancy. *Acta Paediatrica, 84*(2), 118–121.

Roopnarine, J. L., & Carter, D. B. (Eds.). (1992). *Parent-child socialization in diverse cultures* (Vol. 5). Norwood, NJ: Ablex.

Roopnarine, J. L., Johnson, J. E., & Hooper, F. H. (1994). *Children's play in diverse cultures.* Albany, NY: State University of New York Press.

Roopnarine, J. L., Lasker, J., Sacks, M., & Stores, M. (1998). The cultural contexts of children's play. In O. N. Saracho & B. Spodek (Eds.), *Multiple perspectives on play in early childhood education.* Albany, NY: State University of New York Press.

Rosaldo, M. Z., & Lamphere, L. (Eds.). (1974). *Women, culture, and society.* Stanford: Stanford University Press.

Rose, S. A., & Ruff, H. A. (1987). Cross-modal abilities in human infants. In J. D. Osofsky (Ed.), *Handbook of infant development* (2nd ed.). New York: Wiley.

Rose, S. A., & Feldman, J. F. (1996). Memory and processing speed in preterm children at eleven years: A comparison with full-terms. *Child Development, 67*(5), 2005–2021.

Rose, S. A., & Feldman, J. F. (1997). Memory and speed: Their role in the relation of infant information processing to later IQ. *Child Development, 68*(4), 630–641.

Rosen, W., Adamson, L., & Bakemos, R. (1992). Experimental investigation of infant social referencing: Mother's messenger and sender. *Developmental Psychology, 28,* 1172–1178.

Rosenblatt, R. A., Dobie, S. A., Hart, L. G., Schneeweiss, R., Gould, D., Raine, T. R., Benedetti, T. J., Pirani, M. J., & Perrin, E. B. (1997). Interspecialty differences in the obstetric care of low-risk women. *American Journal of Public Health, 87*(3), 344–351.

Rosenblum, G. D., & Lewis, M. (1999). The relations among body image, physical attractiveness, and body mass in adolescence. *Child Development, 70*(1), 50–64.

Rosenshine, B., & Meister, C. (1994). Reciprocal Teaching: A review of the research. *Review of Educational Research, 64,* 479–530.

Rosenstein, D., & Oster, H. (1988). Differential facial responses to four basic tastes in newborns. *Child Development, 59,* 1555–1568.

Rosenthal, R., & Jacobsen, L. (1968). *Pygmalion in the classroom: Teacher expectation and pupils' intellectual development.* New York: Holt, Rinehart & Winston.

Rosenthal, R., Baratz, S. S., & Hall, C. M. (1974). Teacher behavior, teacher expectations, and gains in pupils' rated creativity. *Journal of Genetic Psychology, 124,* 115–121.

Rosenthal, R., & Rubin, D. B. (1978). Interpersonal expectancy effects: The first 345 studies. *Behavioral and Brain Sciences, 3,* 377–415.

Rosenthal, R. (1987). Pygmalion effects: Existence, magnitude, and social importance. *Educational Researcher, 16(9),* 37–41.

Rosenthal, D. A., & Smith, A. M. A. (1997). Adolescent sexual timetable. *Journal of Youth & Adolescence, 26*(5), 619–636.

Rosenzweig, M. R., Bennett, E. L., & Diamond, M. C. (1972). Brain changes in response to experience. The nature and nurture of behavior: Development psychobiology, *Scientific American.* New York: W. H. Freeman.

Rosenzweig, M. R. (1984). Experience, memory, and the brain. *American Psychologist, 39,* 365–376.

Rosenzweig, M. R. (1996). Aspects of the search for neural mechanisms of memory. *Annual Review of Psychology, 47,* 1–32.

Ross, H. E., & Ivis, F. (1999). Binge eating and substance use among male and female adolescents. *International Journal of Eating Disorders, 26*(3), 245–260.

Rossell, C. H., & Baker, K. (1996). The educational effectiveness of bilingual education. *Research in the Teaching of English, 30*(1), 7–74.

Rossner, S. (1998). Childhood obesity and adulthood consequences. *Acta Paediatrica, 87*(1), 1–5.

Rosso, P. (1990). *Nutrition and metabolism in pregnancy.* Oxford: Oxford University Press.

Rothbart, M. K. (1988). Temperament and the development of inhibited approach. *Child Development, 59,* 1241–1250.

Rothbart, M. K., & Bates, J. E. (1998). Temperament. In W. Damon & N. Eisenberg (Eds.), *Handbook of child psychology (*5th ed.*), Vol. 3: Social, emotional, and personality development* (pp. 105–176). New York: Wiley.

Rousseau, J. J. (1762/1911). *Emile; Or on education.* London: Dent.

Rovee-Collier, C. (1987). Learning and memory. In J. D. Osofsky (Ed.), *Handbook of infant development* (2nd ed.). New York: Wiley.

Rovee-Collier, C. (1997). Dissociations in infant memory: Rethinking the development of implicit and explicit memory. *Psychological Review, 104*(3), 467–498.

Rovee-Collier, C., & Boller, K. (1995). Interference or facilitation in infant memory? In F. N. Dempster & C. J. Brainerd (Eds.), *Interference and inhibition in cognition.* San Diego, CA.: Academic Press.

Rovee-Collier, C. (1999). The development of infant memory. *Psychological Science, 8*(3), 80–85.

Rovee-Collier, C., Sullivan, M. W., Enright, M., Lucas, D., & Fagan, J. W. (1980). Reactivation of infant memory. *Science, 208,* 1159–1161.

Rubin, J. Z., Provezano, F. J., & Luria, Z. (1974). The eye of the beholder: Parents' view on sex of newborns. *American Journal of Orthopsychiatry, 44,* 512–519.

Rubin, K. H., Lynch, D., Coplan, R., Rose-Krasnor, L., & Booth, C. L. (1994). "Birds of a feather...": Behavioral concordance and preferential personal attraction in children. *Child Development, 64,* 1778–1785.

Rubin, K. H., Bukowski, W., & Parker, J. G. (1998). Peer interactions, relationships, and groups. In W. Damon & N. Eisenberg (Eds.), *Handbook of child psychology* (5th ed.), *Vol. 3: Social, emotional, and personality development* (pp. 619–700). New York: Wiley.

Rubin, K. H., Coplan, R. J., Nelson, L. J., & Cheah, C. S. L. (1999). Peer relationships in childhood. In M. H. Bornstein & M. E. Lamb (Eds.), *Developmental psychology: An advanced textbook* (4th ed., pp. 451–501). Mahwah, NJ: Erlbaum.

Ruble, D. N., & Frey, K. S. (1991). Changing patterns of comparative behavior as skills are acquired: A functional model of self-evaluation. In J. Suls & T. H. Wells (Eds.), *Social comparison: Contemporary theory and research.* Hillsdale, NJ: Erlbaum.

Ruble, D. N., & Dweck, C. S. (1995). Self conceptions, person conceptions, and their development. In N. Eisenberg (Ed.), *Review of personality and social psychology* (Vol. 15). Thousand Oaks, CA: Sage Publications.

Ruble, D. N., & Martin, C. L. (1998). Gender development. In W. Damon & N. Eisenberg (Ed.), *Handbook of Child Development: Social, emotional, and personality development* (Vol. 5, pp. 933–1016). New York: Wiley.

Ruff, H. A., & Lawson, K. R. (1990). Development of sustained, focused attention in young children during free play. *Developmental Psychology, 26*(1), 85–93.

Ruffman, T., Perner, J., Naito, M., Parkin, L., & Clements, W. A. (1998). Older (but not younger) siblings facilitate false belief understanding. *Developmental Psychology, 34*(1), 161–174.

Rumbaugh, D. M., Savage-Rumbaugh, E. S., & Sevcik, R. A. (1994). Biobehavioral roots of language: A comparative perspective on chimpanzee, child, and culture. In R. W. Wrangham & W. C. McGrew & F. B. M. de Waal & P.G. Helthe (Eds.), *Chimpanzee cultures.* Cambridge, MA: Harvard University Press.

Rutter, M., Yule, B., Quinton, D., Rowland, O., Yule, W., & Berger, M. (1975). Attainment and adjustment in two geographical areas: III. Some factors accounting for area differences. *British Journal of Psychiatry, 126,* 520–533.

Rutter, M. (1976). Maternal deprivation 1972–1978: New findings, new concepts, new approaches. *Child Development, 50,* 283–305.

Rutter, M., & Garmezy, N. (1983). Developmental psychopathology. In P. H. Mussen (Ed.), *Handbook of child psychology: Vol. 4. Socialization, personality, and social development.* New York: Wiley.

Rutter, M., & Hersov, L. (1985). *Child and adolescent psychiatry: Modern approaches* (2nd ed.). Oxford: Blackwell.

Rutter, M. (1987). Continuities and discontinuities from infancy. In J. D. Osofsky (Ed.), *Handbook of infant development* (2nd ed.). New York: Wiley.

Rutter, M., Quinton, D., & Hill, J. (1990). Adult outcome of institution-reared children. In L. Robins & M. Rutter (Eds.), *Straight and devious pathways from childhood to adulthood.* Cambridge: Cambridge University Press.

Rutter, M., Dunn, J., Plomin, R., & Simonoff, E. (1997). Integrating nature and nurture: Implications of person-environment correlations and interactions for developmental psychopathology. *Development & Psychopathology,, 9*(2), 335–364.

Rymer, R. (1993). *Genie: A scientific tragedy.* New York: Harper Collins.

Rzepnicki, T. L., Schuerman, J. R., Littell, J. H., Chak, A., & Lopez, M. (1994). An experimental study of family preservation services: Early findings from a parent survey. In R. P. Barth & J. D. Berrick (Eds.), *Child welfare research review* (Vol. 1, pp. 60–82). New York: Columbia University Press.

Saarni, C. (1998). Issues of cultural meaningfulness in emotional development. *Developmental Psychology, 34*(4), 647–652.

Saarni, C. (1999). *The development of emotional competence.* New York: Guilford Press.

Sachs, J., & Devin, J. (1973). *Young children's knowledge of age-appropriate speech styles.* Paper presented to the Linguistic Society of America.

Sachs, J., Bard, B., & Johnson, M. (1981). Language learning with restricted input; Case studies of two hearing children of deaf parents. *Applied Psycholinguistics, 2*, 33–54.

Sacks, O. (1995). *An anthropologist on Mars.* New York: Knopf.

Sagi, A., Lamb, M. E., Lewkowicz, K. S., Shoham, R., Dvir, R., & Estes, D. (1985). Security of infant-mother, -father, and metapelet attachments among kibbutz reared Israeli children. *Monographs of the Society for Research in Child Development, 50*(1–2, Serial No. 209).

Sagi, A., Van Ijzendoorn, Aviezer, O., Donnell, F., & Mayseless, O. (1994). Sleeping out of home in a kibbutz communal arrangement: It makes a differences for mother-infant attachment. *Child Development, 65*, 992–1004.

Sale, R. (1978). *Fairy tales and after.* Cambridge, MA: Harvard University Press.

Salk, L. (1973). The role of the heartbeat in the relationship between mother and infant. *Scientific American, 228 (3)*, 24–29.

Salkind, N. J., & Nelson, C. F. (1980). A note on the developmental nature of reflection-impulsivity. *Developmental Psychology, 16*, 237–238.

Salomon, G. L. (1984). Television is "easy" and print is "tough": The differential investment of mental effort in learning as a function of perceptions and attributions. *Journal of Educational Psychology, 76*, 647–658.

Salvolini, E., Lucarini, G., Cester, N., Arduini, D., & Mazzanti, L. (1998). Growth retardation and discordant twin pregnancy. An immunomorophological and biochemical characterization of the human umbilical cord. *Biochemistry and Molecular Biology International, 46*(4), 794–805.

Salzinger, S. (1990). Social networks in child rearing and child development. In S. M. Pfafflin & J. A. Sechzer & J. M. Fish & R. L. Thompson (Eds.), *Psychology: Perspectives and practice.* New York: New York Academy of Science.

Salzinger, S., Feldman, R. S., Hammer, M., & Rosario, M. (1993). The effects of physical abuse on children's social relationships. *Child Development, 64*, 169–187.

Sameroff, A. (1978). Organization and stability of newborn behavior: A commentary on the Brazelton Neonatal Behavior Assessment Scale. *Monographs of Society for Research in Child Development, 43*(5–6, Serial No. 177).

Sameroff, A. J. (1983). Developmental systems: Contexts and evolutions. In P. H. Mussen (Ed.), *Handbook of child psychology: Vol. 1. History, theory and methods.* New York: Wiley.

Sameroff, A. J., Seifer, R., Baldwin, A., & Baldwin, C. (1993). Stability of intelligence from preschool to adolescence: The influence of social and family risk factors. *Child Development, 64*, 80–97.

Sameroff, A. J., & Haith, M. M. (1996). *The five to seven year shift: The age of reason and responsibility.* Chicago, IL: University of Chicago Press.

Sameroff, A. J., Bartko, W. T., Baldwin, A., Baldwin, C., & Seifer, R. (1998). Family and social influences on the development of child competence. In M. Lewis & C. Feiring (Eds.), *Families, risk, and competence* (pp. 161–186). Mahwah, NJ.: Erlbaum.

Sandman, C. A., Wadhwa, P., Hetrick, W., Porto, M., & Peeke, H. V. S. (1997). Human fetal heart rate dishabituation between thirty and thirty-two weeks gestations. *Child Development, 68*, 1031–1040.

Sandven, K., & Resnick, M. (1990). Informal adoption among black adolescent mothers. *American Journal of Orthopsychiatry, 60*, 210–224.

Saudino, K. J., Gagne, J. R., Grant, J., & Ibatoulina, A., (1999). Genetic and environmental influences on personality in adult Russian twins. *International Journal of Behavioral Development, 23*(2), 375–389.

Savage-Rumbaugh, E. S., & Rumbaugh, D. M. (1993). The emergence of language. In K. R. Gibson & T. Ingold (Eds.), *Tools, language and cognition in human evolution.* Cambridge, England: Cambridge University Press.

Savage-Rumbaugh, S. (1998). Scientific schizophrenia with regard to the language act. In J. Langer & M. Killen (Eds.), *Piaget, evolution, and development* (pp. 145–169). Mahwah, NJ,: Erlbaum., Publishers.

Savage-Rumbaugh, S., Shanker, S. G., & Taylor, T. J. (1998). *Apes, language, and the human mind.* New York: Oxford University Press.

Savin-Williams, R. C. (1987). *Adolescence: An ethological perspective.* New York: Springer-Verlag.

Savin-Williams, R. C. (1990). *Gay and lesbian youth: Expressions of identity.* New York: Hemisphere.

Saxe, G. B. (1981). Body parts as numerals: A developmental analysis of numeration among the Oksapmin in Papua, New Guinea. *Child Development, 52*, 306–316.

Saxe, G. (1994). Studying cognitive developments in sociocultural context: The development of a practice-based approach. *Mind, Culture, and Activity, 1*, 135–157.

Saxon, L. (1993). *The individual, marriage, and the family* (8th ed.). Belmont, CA: Wadsworth.

Saxton, M. (1997). The contrast theory of negative input. *Journal of Child Language, 24*(1), 139–161.

Scarr, S. (1981). *Race, social class and individual differences in I.Q.* Hillsdale, NJ: Erlbaum.

Scarr, S., & Weinberg., R. A. (1983). The Minnesota adoption studies: Genetic differences and malleability. *Child Development, 54*, 260–267.

Scarr, S., & McCartney, K. (1983). How people make their own environments: A theory of genotype-environment effects. *Child Development, 54*, 424–435.

Schafer, G., & Plunkett, K. (1998). Rapid word learning by fifteen-month-olds under tightly controlled conditions. *Child Development, 69*(2), 309–320.

Schaffer, H. R. (1974). Cognitive components of infant's response to strangeness. In M. Lewis & L. Rosenblum (Eds.), *The origins of fear* (pp. 11–24). New York: Wiley.

Schaffer, R. (1977). *Mothering.* Cambridge, MA: Harvard University Press.

Schaller, S. (1991). *A man without words.* New York: Summit.

Scheinfeld, A. (1972). *Heredity in humans.* Philadelphia: Lippincott.

Scheper-Hughes, N. (1992). *Death without weeping: The violence of everyday life in Brazil.* Berkeley: University of California Press.

Scheurich, J. J. (1998). Highly Successful and Loving, Public Elementary Schools Populated Mainly by Low-SES Children of Color: Core Beliefs and Cultural Characteristics. *Urban Education, 33*(4), 451–491.

Schlegel, A., & Barry, H. (1991). *Adolescence: An anthropological inquiry.* New York: Free Press.

Schmandt-Besserat, D. (1996). *How writing came about.* Austin, TX: University of Texas Press.

Schmitt, K. L., Anderson, D. R., & Collins, P. A. (1999). Form and content: Looking at visual features of television. *Developmental Psychology, 35*(4), 1156–1167.

Schneider, W., Gruber, H., Gold, A., & Opwis, K. (1993). Class expertise and memory for chess positions in children and adults. *Journal of Experimental Child Psychology, 56*, 328–349.

Schneider, W., & Pressley, M. (1997). *Memory development between two and twenty* (2nd ed.). Mahwah, NJ: Erlbaum.

Schneider, W., & Bjorklund, D. F. (1998). Memory. In D. Kuhn & R. S. Siegler (Eds.), *Handbook of child psychology* (5th ed.), *Vol. 2: Cognition, perception, and language* (pp. 467–522). New York: Wiley.

Schneider, B., & Stevenson, D. (1999). *The ambitious generation: America's teenagers, motivated, but directionless.* New Haven: Yale University Press.

Scholes, R. J. (1998). The case against phonemic awareness. *Journal of Research in Reading, 21*(3), 177–218.

Schuler, M. E., & Nair, P. (1999). Frequency of maternal cocaine use during pregnancy and infant neurobehavioral outcome. *Journal of Pediatric Psychology, 24*(6), 511–514.

Schwartz, D., McFadyen-Ketchum, S. A., Dodge, K. A., & Pettit, G. S. (1998). Peer group victimization as a predictor of children's behavior problems at home and in school. *Development and Psychopathology, 10*(1), 87–99.

Scott, J. O. (1997). Genetic analysis of social behavior. In N. L. Siegel & G. E. Weisfeld & C. C. Weisfeld (Eds.), *Uniting psychology and biology: Integrative perspectives on human development.* Washington DC: American Psychological Association.

Scott, D. (1998). Rites of passage in adolescent development: A reappreciation. *Child and Youth Care Forum, 27*(5), 317–335

Scribner, S., & Cole, M. (1981). *The psychology of literacy.* Cambridge, MA: Harvard University Press.

Segall, M. H., Ember, C., & Ember, M. (1997). Aggression, crime, and warfare. In J. W. Berry & M. H. Segall & C. Kagitçibasi (Eds.), *Handbook of cross-cultural psychology, Vol. 3: Social and behavioral applications* (pp. 213–254). Boston: Allyn & Bacon.

Segall, M. H., Dasen, P. R., Berry, J. W., & Poortinga, Y. H. (1999). *Human behavior in global perspective: An introduction to cross-cultural psychology* (2nd ed.). New York: Pergamon Press.

Seifer, R., Schiller, M., Sameroff, A. J., Resnick, S., & Riordan, K. (1996). Attachment, maternal sensitivity, and infant temperament during the first year of life. *Developmental Psychology, 32*(1), 12–25

Selfe, L. (1983). *Normal and anomalous representational drawing ability in children.* New York: Academic Press.

Selman, R. L. (1980). *The growth of interpersonal understanding: Developmental and clinical analysis.* New York: Academic Press.

Selman, R. L. (1981). The child as a friendship philosopher. In S. R. Asher & J. M. Gottman (Eds.), *The development of children's friendships.* Cambridge: Cambridge University Press.

Serbin, L. A., O'Leary, K. D., Kent, R. N., & Tonick, I. J. (1973). A comparison of teacher response to the pre-academic and problem behavior of boys and girls. *Child Development, 44*, 796–804.

Serpell, R. (1993). *The significance of schooling: Life journeys in an African society.* Cambridge: Cambridge University Press.

Serpell, R., & Hatano, G. (1997). Education, schooling, and literacy. In J. W. Berry & P. R. Dasen & T. S. Saraswathi (Eds.), *Handbook of cross-cultural psychology (Vol 2).* Boston: Allyn & Bacon.

Sfard, A. (1999). Balancing the unbalanceable: What theories of learning have to say on NCTM Standards. In J. Kilpatrick (Ed.), *Research companion for NCTM Standards.* Ralston, VA: NCTM.

Shaffer, D. R. (1985). *Developmental psychology: Theory, research, and application.* Monterey, CA: Brooks/ Cole.

Shahidullah, S., & Hepper, P. G. (1993). The developmental origins of fetal responsiveness to an acoustic stimulus. *Journal of Reproductive & Infant Psychology, 11*(3), 135–142.

Shapira, A., & Madsen, M. C. (1969). Cooperative and competitive behavior of kibbutz and urban children in Israel. *Child Development, 4*, 609–617.

Shatz, M. (1994). *A toddler's life: Becoming a person.* New York: Oxford University Press.

Shatz, M., & Gelman, R. (1973). The development of communication skills: Modification in the speech of young children as a function of listener. *Monographs of the Society for Research in Child Development, 38(5)*, Serial No. 152.

Shatz, M. (1974). *The comprehension of indirect directives: Can you shut the door?* Paper presented at the Linguistics Society of America, Amherst, MA.

Shatz, M. (1978). Children's comprehension of question-directives. *Journal of Child Language, 5*, 39–46.

Shaw, G. B. (1963). *George Bernard Shaw on language.* London: Peter Owen.

Shaw, D. S., Vondra, J. I., Hommerding, K. D., & Keenan, K. D. (1994). Chronic family adversity and early child behavior problems: A longitudinal study of low income families. *Journal of Child Psychology and Psychiatry, 35*, 1109–1122.

Shaw, D. S., Winslow, E. B., Owens, E. B., & Hood, N. (1998). Young children's adjustment to chronic family adversity: A longitudinal study of low-income families. *Journal of the American Academy of Child and Adolescent Psychiatry, 37*(5), 545–553.

Sherif, M., & Sherif, C. W. (1956). *An outline of social psychology.* New York: Harper & Row.

Shopen, T. (1980). How Pablo says "love" and "store". In T. Shopen & J. M. Williams (Eds.), *Standards and dialects in English.* Cambridge: Winthrop.

Shostak, M. (1981). *Nissa: The life and words of a !Kung Woman.* Cambridge, MA: Harvard University Press.

Shweder, R. A. (1982). Liberalism as destiny. *Contemporary Psychology, 27*, 421–424.

Shweder, R. A., Mahapatpa, M., & Miller, J. G. (1987). Culture and moral development. In J. Kagan & S. Lamb (Eds.), *The emergence of morality in young children.* Chicago: University of Chicago Press.

Shweder, R. A., Jensen, L. A., & Goldstein, W. M. (1995). Who sleeps by whom revisited: A method for extracting the moral goods implicit in practice. *New Directions for Child Development, 67*, 21–39.

Shweder, R. A., Goodnow, J., Hatano, G., LeVine, R. A., Markus, H., & Miller, P. (1998). The cultural psychology of development: One mind, many mentalities. In R. M. Lerner (Ed.), *Handbook of Child Psychology* (5th ed.) *Vol. 1: Theoretical models of human development* (pp. 865–938). New York: Wiley.

Siegal, M. (1991b). *Knowing children: Experiments in conversation and cognition.* Hillsdale, NJ: Erlbaum.

Siegel, L. S., & Ryan, E. B. (1988). Development of grammatical-sensitivity, phonological, and short-term memory skills in normally achieving and learning disabled children. *Developmental Psychology, 24*(1), 28–37.

Siegel, L. S. (1993). Phonological processing deficits as the basis of a reading disability. *Developmental Review, 13*(3), 246–257.

Siegel, L. S. (1998). Phonological processing deficits and reading disabilities. In J. L. Metsala (Ed.), *Word recognition in beginning literacy* (pp. 141–160). Mahwah, NJ: Erlbaum

Siegler, R. S., & Liebert, R. M. (1975). Acquisition of formal scientific reasoning by 10- and 13-year-olds: Designing a factorial experiment. *Developmental Psychology, 11*, 401–402.

Siegler, R. S. (1976). Three aspects of cognitive development. *Cognitive Psychology, 8*, 481–520.

Siegler, R. S. (1991). *Children's thinking* (2nd ed.). Englewood Cliffs, NJ: Prentice Hall.

Siegler, R. S. (1995). How does change occur: A microgenetic study of number conservation. *Cognitive Psychology, 28*, 225–273.

Siegler, R. S. (1996). *Emerging minds: The process of change in children's thinking.* New York: Oxford University Press.

Siegler, R. S., & Stern, E. (1998). Conscious and unconscious strategy discoveries: A microgenetic analysis. *Journal of Experimental Psychology: General, 127*(4), 377–397.

Simion, F., Valenza, E., & Umilta, C. (1998). Mechanisms underlying face preference at birth. In F. Simion & G. Butterworth (Eds.), *The development of sensory, motor and cognitive capacities in early infancy: From perception to cognition* (pp. 87–101). Hove, England: Psychology Press/Erlbaum.

Simmons, R. G., Burgeson, R., & Carlton-Fordblyth, D. (1987). The impact of cumulative change in early adolescence. *Child Development, 58*, 1220–1234.

Simmons, R. G., & Blyth, D. A. (1987). *Moving into adolescence: The impact of pubertal change in school context.* New York: Aldine de Gruyter.

Simpson, E. L. (1974). Moral development research: A case of scientific cultural bias. *Human Development, 17*, 81–106.

Simpson, J. L., & Golbus, M. S. (1993). *Genetics in obstetrics and gynecology* (2nd ed.). Philadelphia: W. B. Saunders and Company.

Sinclair, D., & Dangerfield, P. (1998). *Human growth after birth.* New York: Oxford University Press.

Sinclair De Zwart, H. (1967). *Acquisition du langage et développement de la pensée.* Paris: Dunod.

Singer, D. G., & Singer, J. L. (1990). *The house of make believe.* Cambridge, MA: Harvard University Press.

Singleton, J. (Ed.). (1998). *Learning in likely places: Varieties of apprenticeship in Japan.* New York: Cambridge University Press.

Siqueland, E. R. (1968). Reinforcement patterns and extinction in human newborns. *Journal of Experimental Child Psychology, 6*, 431–432.

Skinner, B. F. (1938). *The behavior of organisms.* New York: Appleton-Century-Crofts.

Skinner, B. F. (1953). *Science and human behavior.* New York: Macmillan.

Skinner, B. F. (1957). *Verbal behavior.* New York: Appleton-Century-Crofts.

Skuse, D. (1984b). Extreme deprivation in early childhood: II. Theoretical issues and a comparative review. *Journal of Child Psychology and Psychiatry, 25*, 543–572.

Slabach, E., Morrow, J., & Wachs, T. D. (1991). Questionnaire measurement of infant and child temperament. In J. Strelau & A. Angleitner (Eds.), *Explorations in temperament.* New York: Plenum Press.

Slaby, R. G., & Frey, K. S. (1975). Development of gender constancy and selective attention to same-sex models. *Child Development, 46*, 849–856.

Smetana, J. G. (1989). Adolescents' and parents' reasoning about actual family conflict. *Child Development, 60*, 1052–1067.

Smetana, J. G. (1997). Parenting and the development of social knowledge: A social domain analysis. In J. E. Grusec & L. Kuczynski (Eds.), *Parenting and children's internalization of values* (pp. 162–192). New York: Wiley.

Smidt-Jensen, S. (1998). Transabdominal chorionic villus sampling. *Danish Medical Bulletin, 45*, 402–411.

Smiley, P. A., & Dweck, C. S. (1994). Individual differences in achievement goals among young children. *Child Development, 65*(6), 1723–1743.

Smith, E., & Udry, J. (1985). Coital and non-coital sexual behaviors of white and black adolescents. *American Journal of Public Health, 75*, 1200–1203.

Smith, P. K. (1988). Children's play and its role in early development: A re-evaluation of the "play ethos." In A. D. Pellegrini (Ed.), *Psychological bases for early education.* New York: Wiley.

Smith, P. K., Morita, Y., Junger-Tas, J., Olweus, D., Catalano, R., & Slee, P. (1999). *The nature of school bullying: A cross-national perspective.* London: Routledge.

Smith, R. P. (1958). *Where did you go? OUT. What did you do? Nothing.* New York: W. W. Norton.

Smyth, C. M., & Bremner, W. J. (1998). Klinefelter syndrome. *Archives of Internal Medicine, 158*(12), 1309–1314.

Snarey, J. R. (1995). Cross-cultural universality of social moral development: A critical review of Kohlbergian research. *Psychological Bulletin, 97*, 202–232.

Snow, C. E. (1972). Mother's speech to children learning language. *Child Development, 43*, 549–565.

Snow, C. (1995). Issues in the study of input: Finetuning, universality, individual and developmental differences, and necessary causes. In P. Fletcher & B. MacWhinney (Eds.), *The handbook of child language.* Oxford: Blackwell.

Snow, C. E., Burns, S., & Griffin, P. (Eds.). (1998). *Preventing reading difficulties in young children.* Washington, DC: National Academy Press.

Spear, N. (1978). *The processing of memories: Forgetting and retention.* New York: Wiley.

Spearman, C. (1927). *The abilities of man.* New York: Macmillan.

Speidel, G. E., & Nelson, K. E. (1989). A fresh look at imitation in language learning. In G. E. Speidel & K. E. Nelson (Eds.), *The many faces of imitation in language learning.* New York: Springer-Verlag.

Spelke, E. S. (1976). Infants' intermodal perception of events. *Cognitive Psychology, 8*, 553–560.

Spelke, E. S. (1984). The development of intermodal perception. In L. B. Cohen & P. Salapatek (Eds.), *Handbook of infant perception.* New York: Academic Press.

Spelke, E. S. (1990). Principles of object perception. *Cognitive Science, 14*, 29–56.

Spelke, E. S., & Newport, E. L. (1998). Nativism, empiricism, and the development of knowledge. In R. M. Lerner (Ed.), *Handbook of child development: Theoretical models of human development* (Vol. 1, pp. 275–340). New York: Wiley.

Spelke, E. S., & Van De Walle, G. A. (1993). Perceiving and reasoning about objects: Insights from infants. In N. Eilan & R. A. McCarthy & B. Brewer (Eds.), *Spatial representation: Problems in philosophy and psychology.* Oxford: Blackwell Publishers.

Spellacy, W. N. (1994). Fetal growth retardation. In J. R. Scott & P. J. DiSaia & C. B. Hammond & W. N. Spellacy (Eds.), *Dansforth's Obstetrics and Gynecology* (7th ed.). Philadelphia: J.B. Lippincott.

Spencer, M. B. (1988). Self-concept development. *New Directions for Child Development, 42*, 59–72.

Spencer, M. B., & Markstrom-Adams, C. (1990). Identity processes among racial and ethnic minority children in America. *Child Development, 61*, 290–310.

Spiro, M. E. (1965). *Children of the kibbutz.* New York: Schocken Books.

Spitz, H. H., Minsky, S. K., & Besselieu, C. L. (1985). Influence of planning time and first move strategy on Tower of Hanoi problem solving performance of mentally retarded young adults and nonretarded children. *American Journal of Mental Deficiency, 90*(1), 46–56.

Sroufe, L. A. (1979). Socioemotional development. In J. Osofsky (Ed.), *Handbook of infant development.* New York: Wiley.

Sroufe, L. A., & Fleeson, J. (1986). Attachment and the construction of relationships. In W. W. Hartup & Z. Rubin (Eds.), *Relationships and development.* Hillsdale, NJ: Erlbaum.

Sroufe, L. A., Bennett, C., Englund, M., Urban, J., & Shulman, S. (1993). The significance of gender boundaries in preadolescence: Contemporary correlates and antecedants of boundary violations and maintenance. *Child Development, 64*, 455–466.

Sroufe, L. A., Carlson, E., & Shulman, S. (1993). Individuals in relationships: Development from infancy through adolescence. In D. C. Funder & R. D. Parke & C. Tomlinson-Keasey & K. Widaman (Eds.), *Studying life through time:Personality and development.* Washington: American Psychological Association.

Sroufe, L. A., Egeland, B., & Carlson, E. A. (1999). One social world: The integrated development of parent-child and peer relationships. In W. A. Collins & B. Laursen (Eds.), *Relationships as developmental contexts* (pp. 241–261). Mahwah, NJ: Erlbaum.

Sroufe, L. A., Carlson, E. A., Levy, A. K., & Egeland, B. V. (1999). Implications of attachment theory for developmental psychopathology. *Development & Psychopathology, 11*(1), 1–13.

St. James-Roberts, I., & Plewis, I. (1996). Individual differences, daily fluctuations, and developmental changes in amounts of infant waking, fussing, crying, feeding, and sleeping. *Child Development, 67*(5), 2527–2540.

St. James-Roberts, I., Conroy, S., & Wilshir, K. (1996). Bases for maternal perceptions of infant crying and colic behavior. *Archives of Disease in Childhood, 75*, 375–381.

Staats, A. W. (1968). *Learning, language, and cognition.* New York: Holt, Rinehart & Winston.

Stanovich, K. E., & Stanovich, P. J. (1996). Rethinking the concept of learning disabilities: The demise of the aptitude/achievement discrepancy. In D. R. Olson & N. Torrance (Eds.), *The handbook of education and human development* (pp. 117–147). Oxford: Blackwell.

Stattin, H., & Magnusson, D. (1990). *Pubertal maturation in female development.* Hillsdale, NJ: Erlbaum.

Stauder, J. E., Molenaar, P. C., & Van Der Molen, M. W. (1993). Scalp topography of event-related brain potentials and cognitive transition during childhood. *Child Development, 64,* 769–788.

Stein, J. H., & Reiser, L. W. (1994). A study of white middle-class adolescent boys' responses to "semenarche" (the first ejaculation). *Journal of Youth and Adolescence, 23,* 373–384.

Stein, Z., Susser, M., Saenger, G., & Marolla, F. (1975). *Famine and development: The Dutch hunger winter of 1944—1945.* Oxford: Oxford University Press.

Steinberg, L., & Silverberg, S. B. (1986). The vicissitudes of autonomy and early adolescence. *Child Development, 57,* 841–851.

Steinberg, L. (1989). Pubertal maturation and parent-adolescent distance: An evolutionary perspective. In G. Adams & R. Montemayor & T. Gullota (Eds.), *Advances in adolescent development* (Vol. 1). Beverly Hills, CA: Sage Publications.

Steinberg, L., Fegley, S., & Dornbusch, S. M. (1993). Negative impact of part-time work on adolescent adjustment: Evidence from a longitudinal study. *Developmental Psychology, 29,* 171–180.

Steiner, J. E. (1979). Human facial expressions in response to taste and smell stimulation. In H. W. Reese & L. P. Lipsitt (Eds.), *Advances in child development and behavior* (Vol. 13). New York: Academic Press.

Stenberg, C. R., & Campos, J. J. (1990). The development of anger expressions in infancy. In N. L. Stein & B. Leventhal (Eds.), *Psychological and biological approaches to emotion.* Hillsdale, NJ: Erlbaum.

Stephan, C. W., & Langlois, J. H. (1984). Baby beautiful: Adult attributions of infant competence as a function of infant attractiveness. *Child Development, 55,* 576–585.

Stern, W. (1910). Abstracts of lectures on the psychology of testimony and on the study of individuality. *American Journal of Psychology, 21,* 273–282.

Stern, W. (1912). *Psychologische methoden der intelligenz-prufung.* Leipzig: Barth.

Stern, D. (1977). *The first relationship.* Cambridge, MA: Harvard University Press.

Stern, D. (1985). *The interpersonal world of the infant: A view from psychoanalysis and developmental psychology.* New York: Basic Books.

Sternberg, R. J. (1985). *Beyond IQ: A triarchic theory of human intelligence.* New York: Cambridge University Press.

Sternberg, R. J. (1990). *Metaphors of mind: Conceptions of the nature of intelligence.* New York: Cambridge University Press.

Sternberg, K. J. (1993). Child maltreatment: Implications for policy from cross cultural research. In D. Cicchetti & S. L. Toth (Eds.), *Child abuse, child development, and social policy: Advances in applied developmental psychology* (Vol. 8). Norwood, NJ: Ablex.

Sternberg, R. J. (1999). A triarchic approach to the understanding and assessment of intelligence in multicultural populations. *Journal of School Psychology,* 37(2), 145–159.

Stevenson, H. W., & Stigler, J. W. (1992). *The learning gap: Why our schools are failing and what we can learn from Japanese and Chinese education.* New York: Summit.

Stevenson, H. W., Stigler, J. W., Lee, S., Lucker, G. W., Kitamura, S., & Hsu, C. (1985). Cognitive performance and academic achievement of Japanese, Chinese, and American children. *Child Development,* 56, 718–734.

Stevenson, R. (1977). *The fetus and newly born infant: Influence of the prenatal environment.* 2nd ed.: St. Louis: Mosby.

Stewart, R. B., & Marvin, R. S. (1984). Sibling relations: The role of conceptual perspective taking in the ontogeny of sibling caregiving. *Child Development,* 55, 1322–1332.

Stigler, J. W., & Perry, M. (1990). Mathematics learning in Japanese, Chinese, and American classrooms. In J. W. Stigler & R. A. Shweder & G. Herdt (Eds.), *Cultural psychology: Essays on comparative human development.* New York: Cambridge University Press.

Stocker, C., Dunn, J., & Plomin, R. (1989). Sibling relationships: Links with child temperament, maternal behavior, and family structure. *Child Development,* 60, 715–727.

Stone, J. L., & Church, J. (1957). *Childhood and adolescence: A psychology of the growing person.* New York: Random House.

Stone, J. E., & Clements, A. (1998). Research and innovation: Let the buyer beware. In R. R. Spillane & R. Regnier (Eds.), *The superintendent of the future* (pp. 59–97). Gaithersburg, MD: Aspen Publishers.

Stratton, K., Howe, C., & Battaglia, F. (1996). *Fetal Alcohol Syndrome: Diagnosis, Epidemiology, Prevention, and Treatment.* Washington DC: National Academy Press.

Strauss, R. (1999). Childhood obesity. *Current Problems in Pediatrics,* 29(1), 1–29.

Strayer, F. F. (1980). Child ethology and the study of preschool social relations. In H. C. Foot & A. J. Chapman (Eds.), *Friendship and social relations in children* (pp. 235–265). New Brunswick, NJ.: Transaction Publishers.

Strayer, F. F. (1991). The development of agonistic and affiliative structures in preschool play groups. In J. Silverberg & P. Gray (Eds.), *To fight or not to fight: Violence and peacefulness in humans and other primates.* Oxford: Oxford University Press.

Strayer, F. F., & Santos, A. J. (1996). Affiliative structures in preschool peer groups. *Social Development, 5,* 117–130.

Streri, A., & Spelke, E. S. (1988). Haptic perception of objects in infancy. *Cognitive Psychology, 20,* 1–23.

Striegel-Moore, R. H., & Cachelin, F. M. (1999). Body image concerns and disordered eating in adolescent girls: Risk and protective factors. In N. G. Johnson & M. C. Roberts & J. Worell (Eds.), *Beyond appearance: A new look at adolescent girls.* Washington DC: American Psychological Association.

Stunkard, A. J., Sorenson, T. I., Hanis, C., Teasdale, T. W., Chakraborty, R., Schull, W. J., & Schulsinger, F. (1986). An adoption study of human obesity. *New England Journal of Medicine, 314,* 193–198

Subbotsky, E. V. (1991). A life span approach to object permanence. *Human Development, 34,* 125–137.

Subbotsky, E. V. (1993). *The birth of personality: the development of independent and moral behavior in preschool children.* New York: Harvester Wheatsheaf.

Sullivan, H. S. (1953). *The interpersonal theory of psychiatry.* New York: W. W. Norton.

Sullivan, K., & Winner, E. (1993). Three-year-olds' understanding of mental states: The influence of trickery. *Journal of Experimental Child Psychology, 56*(2), 135–148

Suomi, S. J., & Harlow, H. F. (1972). Social rehabilitation of isolate-reared monkeys. *Developmental Psychology, 6,* 487–496.

Suomi, S. J., Harlow, H. F., & McKinny, W. T., Jr. (1972). Monkey psychiatrists. *American Journal of Psychiatry, 128,* 927–932.

Suomi, S. (1995). Influences of attachment theory on ethological studies of biobehavioral development in nonhuman primates. In S. Goldberg & R. Muir & J. Kerr (Eds.), *Attachment theory: Social, developmental, and clinical perspectives* (pp. 185–202). Hillsdale, NJ: Analytic Press.

Super, C. M., & Harkness, S. (1972). The infant's niche in rural Kenya and metropolitan America. In L. Adler (Ed.), *Issues in cross-cultural research.* New York: Academic Press.

Super, C. M. (1976). Environmental effects on motor development: A case of African infant precocity. *Developmental Medicine and Child Neurology, 18,* 561–567.

Super, C. M., & Harkness, S. (1986). The developmental niche: A conceptualization at the interface of child and culture. *International Journal of Behavioral Development, 9,* 545–569.

Super, C. M., & Harkness, S. (1997). The cultural structuring of child development. In J. W. Berry & Y. H. Poortinga & J. Pandey (Eds.), *Handbook of cross-cultural psychology, Vol.1: Theory and method.* Boston: Allyn & Bacon.

Suppes, P. (1966). The Uses of Computers in Education. *Scientific American, 215*(3), 206–220.

Suppes, P. (1988). Computer-assisted instructions. In D. Unwin & R. McAllese (Eds.), *The encyclopedia of educational media, communication and technology* (2nd ed.). New York: Greenwood.

Sussman, E. J., Nottlemann, E. D., Inhoff-Germain, G. E., Dorn, L. D., Cutler, G. B., Jr., Loriaux, D. L., & Chrousos, G. P. (1985). The relation of development and social-emotional behavior in young adolescents. *Journal of Youth and Adolescence, 14*, 245–264.

Sutton, J., Smith, P. K., & Swettenham, J. (1999). Bullying and "theory of mind": A critique of the "social skills deficit" view of anti-social behavior. *Social Development, 8*(1), 117–127.

Sutton-Smith, B., & Roberts, J. M. (1973). The cross-cultural and psychological study of games. In B. Sutton-Smith (Ed.), *The folkgames of children.* Austen, TX: University of Texas Press.

Sutton-Smith, B. (1997). *The ambiguity of play.* Cambridge, MA: Harvard University Press.

Swain, I. V., Zelazo, P. R., & Clifton, R. K. (1993). Newborn infants' memory for speech sounds retained over 24 hours. *Developmental Psychology, 29*, 312–323.

Sweeney, J., & Bradbard, M., R. (1988). Mothers' and fathers' changing perceptions of their male and female infants over the course of pregnancy. *Journal of Genetic Psychology, 149*(3), 393–404.

Szkrubalo, J., & Ruble, D. N. (1999). "God made me a girl": Sex-category constancy judgments and explanations revisited. *Developmental Psychology, 35*(2), 392–402

Takahashi, K. (1990). Are the key assumptions of the "strange situation" procedure universal? *Human Development, 33*, 23–30.

Tallal, P., Miller, S., & Fitch, R. H. (1993). The neurobiological basis of speech: A case for the preeminence of temporal processing. In P. Tallal & A. M. Galaburdn & R. R. Llinas & C. van Euler (Eds.), *Annals of the New York Academy of Sciences* (Vol. 682, pp. 27–47).

Tallal, P., Merzenich, M., Miller, S., & Jenkins, W. (1998). Language learning impairment: Integrating research and remediation. *Scandanavian Journal of Psychology, 39*(3), 197–199.

Tamis-Lemonda, C. S., & Bornstein, M. H. (1994). Specificity in mother-toddler language-play relations across the second year. *Developmental Psychology, 30*, 283–292.

Tanner, J. M. (1978). *Fetus into man: Physical growth from conception to maturity.* Cambridge, MA: Harvard University Press.

Tanner, J. M. (1990). *Fetus into man: Physical growth from conception to maturity (revised).* Cambridge, MA: Harvard University Press.

Tappan, M. B. (1997). Language, culture, and moral development: A Vygotskian Perspective. *Developmental Review., 17*(1), 78–100.

Tardif, T., Shatz, M., & Naigles, L. (1997). Caregiver speech and children's use of nouns versus verbs: A comparison of English, Italian, and Mandarin. *Journal of Child Language, 24*(3), 535–565.

Tardif, T., Gelman, S. A., & Xu, F. (1999). Putting the "noun bias" in context: A comparison of English and Mandarin. *Child Development, 70*(3), 620–635.

Taylor, M., & Hort, B. C. (1990). Can children be trained to make the appearance reality distinction? *Cognitive Development, 5, 89–99.*

Taylor, H. G., Klein, N., Schatschneider, C., & Hack, M. (1998). Perdictors of early school age outcomes in very low birth weight children. *Journal of Developmental & Behavioral Pediatrics, 19*, 235–243.

Telzrow, R. W., Campos, J. J., Shepherd, A., Bertenthal, B. I., & Atwater, S. (1987). Spatial understanding in infants with motor handicaps. In K. Jaffe (Ed.), *Childhood powered mobility: Developmental, technical and clinical perspectives.*

Templin, M. C. (1957). *Certain language skills in children.* Minneapolis: University of Minnesota Press.

Terman, L. M. (1925). *Genetic studies of genius.* Stanford: Stanford University Press.

Teti, D. M., Gelfand, D. M., Messinger, D. S., & Isabella, R. (1995). Maternal depression and the quality of early attachment: An examination of infants, preschoolers, and their mothers. Special Section: Parental depression and distress: Implications for development. *Developmental Psychology, 31*, 364–376.

Thatcher, R. W. (1991). Maturation of the human frontal lobes: Physiological evidence for staging. *Developmental Neuropsychology, 7(3)*, 397–419.

Thatcher, R. W. (1994). Cyclic cortical reorganization. In G. Dawson & K. W. Fischer (Eds.), *Human behavior and the developing brain.* New York: Guilford Press.

Thatcher, R. W. (1997). Human frontal lobe development: A theory of cyclical cortical reorganization. In N. A. Krasnegor, G.R. Lyon, & P.S. Goldman-Rakic, (Ed.), *Developmentof the prefrontal cortex: Evolution, neurobiology, and behavior* (pp. 85–116). Baltimore, MD: Paul A. Brookes.

Thelen, E., Ulrich, B. D., & Jensen, J. L. (1989). The developmental origins of locomotion. In M. Woollacott & A. Shumway-Cook (Eds.), *The development of posture and gait across the lifespan.* Columbia, SC: University of South Carolina Press.

Thelen, E., & Ulrich, B. D. (1991). Hidden skills. *Monographs of the Society for Research in Child Development, 56*(1, Serial No. 223).

Thelen, E., Corbetta, D., Kamm, K., Spencer, J. P., Schneider, K., & Zernicke, R. F. (1993). The transition to reaching: Mapping intention and intrinsic dynamics. *Child Development, 64*, 1099–1110.

Thelen, E. (1995). Motor development: A new synthesis. *American Psychologist, 50, 79–95.*

Theut, S. K., & Mrazek, D. A. (1997). Infants and toddlers with medical conditions and their parents: Reactions to illness and hospitalization and models for intervention. In S. Greenspan & S. Widers & J. Osofsky (Eds.), *Handbook of child and adolescent psychiatry, Vol. 1: Infants and preschoolers: Development and syndromes* (pp. 328–338). New York: Wiley.

Thoman, E. (1999). *Some good habits to acquire.* Los Angeles: Center for Media Literacy. Available: http://www.medialit.org/ReadingRoom/childrenTV/goodTVhabits.htm

Thoman, E. B., & Ingersoll, E. W. (1993). Learning in premature infants. *Developmental Psychology, 29*(4), 692–700.

Thoman, E. B., Hammond, K., Affleck, G., & Desilva, H. N. (1995). The breathing bear with preterm infants: Effects on sleep, respiration, and affect. *Infant Mental Health Journal, 16*(3), 160–168.

Thomas, A., Chess, S., Birch, H. G., Hertzig, M. E., & Korn, S. (1963). *Behavioral individuality in early childhood.* New York: New York University Press.

Thomas, A., & Chess, S. (1977). *Temperament and Development.* New York: Bruner/Mazel.

Thomas, A., & Chess, S. (1984). Genesis and evaluation of behavioral disorders: From infancy to early adult life. *American Journal of Psychiatry, 141*, 1–9.

Thomas, A., & Chess, S. (1989). Temperament and personality. In G. A. Kohnstamm & J. E. Bates & M. K. Rothbart (Eds.), *Temperament in childhood.* New York: Wiley.

Thompson, J. E. (1990). Maternal stress, anxiety, and social support during pregnancy: Possible directions for prenatal intervention. In I. R. Merkatz & J. E. Thompson (Eds.), *New perspectives on prenatal care.* New York: Elsevier.

Thompson, R. A. (1998). Early sociopersonality development. In N. Eisenberg (Ed.), *Handbook of child psychology* (5th ed.), *Vol. 3: Social, emotional, and personality development* (pp. 25–104). New York: Wiley.

Thompson, G. B., & Nicholson, T. (Eds.). (1999). *Learning to read: Beyond phonics and whole language.* New York: Teachers College Press.

Thorkildsen, T. A. (1989). Pluralism in children's moral reasoning about social justice. *Child Development, 60*, 965–972.

Thorkildsen, T. A., & Schmahl, C. M. (1997). Conceptions of fair learning practices among low-income African American and Latin American children: Acknowledging diversity. *Journal of Educational Psychology, 89*(4), 719–727.

Thorndike, E. L. (1911). *Animal intelligence: Experimental studies.* New York: Macmillan.

Thorne, B., & Luria, Z. (1986). Sexuality and gender in children's daily worlds. *Social Problems, 33,* 176–190.

Thorne, B. (1993). *Gender play: Girls and boys in school.* New Brunswick, NJ: Rutgers University Press.

Thurstone, L. L. (1938). *Primary mental abilities.* Chicago, IL: University of Chicago Press.

Tietjen, A. M., & Walker, L. J. (1985). Moral reasoning and leadership among men in a Papua New Guinea society. *Child Development, 21,* 982–992.

Third International Mathematics and Science Survey (TIMSS) (1997). Washington, DC: U.S. Department of Education, National Center for Education Statistics and National Science Foundation.

Tincoff, R., & Jusczyk, P. W. (1999). Some beginnings of word comprehension in 6-month-olds. *Psychological Science, 10*(2), 172–175.

Tisak, M. S., & Turiel, E. (1988). Variation in seriousness of transgression and children's moral and conventional concepts. *Developmental Psychology, 24,* 352–357.

Tizard, B., & Rees, J. (1975). The effect of early institutional rearing on the behavioral problems and affectional relationship of four-year-old children. *Journal of Child Psychology and Psychiatry, 16,* 61–73.

Tizard, B., & Hodges, J. (1978). The effect of early institutional rearing on the development of eight-year-old children. *Journal of Child Psychology and Psychiatry, 19,* 99–118.

Tobin, J. J., Wu, D. Y. H., & Davidson, D. H. (1989). *Preschool in three cultures: Japan, China, and the United States.* New Haven: Yale University Press.

Tolchinsky, L., & Teberosky, A. (1998). The development of word segmentation and writing in two scripts. *Cognitive Development, 13*(1), 1–24.

Tomasello, M. (1992). The social bases of language acquisition. *Social Development, 1,* 67––87.

Tomasello, M., & Mannie, S. (1985). Pragmatics of sibling speech to one-year-olds. *Child Development, 56,* 911–917.

Tomasello, M. (2000). *The cultural origins of human cognition.* Cambridge, MA: Harvard University Press.

Tooby, J., & Cosmides, L. (1998). Evolutionizing the cognitive sciences: A reply to Shapiro and Epstein. *Mind & Language,* (13)2, 195-204.

Toran-Allerand, C. D. (1984). On the genesis of sexual differentiation of the central nervous system: Morphogenetic consequences of steroidal exposure and possible role of a-Fetoprotein. In G. J. D. Vries & J. P. C. Bruin & H. B. M. Uylings & M. A. Corner (Eds.), *Progress in Brain Research.* 61: 63–98.

Toranzo, N. C. (1996). Empathy development: A critical classroom tool. *Volta Review, 98*(3), 107–125.

Torney-Purta, J. (1990). Youth in relation to social institutions. In S. S. Feldman & G. R. Elliott (Eds.), *At the threshold: The developing adolescent.* Cambridge, MA: Harvard University Press.

Toth, S. L., & Cicchetti, D. (1993). Where do we go from here in our treatment of victims? In D. Cicchetti & S. L. Toth (Eds.), *Advances in applied developmental psychology series: Vol. 8. Child abuse, child development, and social policy.* Norwood, NJ: Ablex.

Trevarthen, C. (1980). The foundations of intersubjectivity: Development of interpersonal and cooperative understanding in infants. In D. Olson (Ed.), *The social foundations of language and thought.* New York: W. W. Norton.

Trevarthen, C. (1993). On the interpersonal origins of self-concept. In U. Neisser (Ed.), *The perceived self: Ecological and interpersonal sources of self-knowledge.* Cambridge, MA: Cambridge University Press.

Trevarthen, C. (1998). The concept and foundations of infant intersubjectivity. In S. Braten (Ed.), *Intersubjective communication and emotion in early ontogeny* (pp. 15-46). New York: Cambridge University Press.

Trevethen, S. D., & Walker, L. J. (1989). Hypothetical versus real-life moral reasoning among psychopathic and delinquent youth. *Development Psychopathology, 1,* 91–103.

Triandis, H. C., McCusker, C., & Hui, C. H. (1990). Multimethod probes of individualism and collectivism. *Journal of Personality & Social Psychology, 59*(5), 1006–1020.

Troiden, R. R. (1988). *Gay and lesbian identity: A sociological analysis.* Dix Hills, NY: General Hall.

Troiden, R. R. (1993). The formation of homosexual identities. In L. D. Garnets & D. C. Kimmel (Eds.), *Psychological perspectives on lesbian and gay male experiences* (pp. 191–217). New York: Columbia University Press.

Tronick, E. Z., Winn, S., & Morelli, G. A. (1985). Multiple caretaking in the context of human evolution: Why don't the Efe know the western prescription for child care? In M. Reite & T. Field (Eds.), *The psychobiology of attachment and separation.* Orlando, FL: Academic Press.

Troyer, L. R., & Parisi, V. M. (1994). Management of labor. In J. R. Scott & P. J. DiSaia & C. B. Hammond & W. N. Spellacy (Eds.), *Dansforth's obstetrics and gynecology* (7th ed.). Philadelphia: J.B. Lippincott.

Tsang, J. L., & Balistreri, W. F. (1993). *Growth factors in perinatal development.* New York: Raven Press.

Tschirgi, J. E. (1980). Sensible reasoning: A hypothesis about hypotheses. *Child Development, 51,* 1–10.

Tuchmann-Duplessis, H., David, G., & Haegel, P. (1971). *Illustrated human embryology* (Vol. 1). New York: Springer-Verlag.

Tuchmann-Duplessis, H. (1975). *Drug effects on the fetus.* Acton, MA: Publishing Science Group Inc.

Tulviste, P. (1991). *The cultural-historical development of verbal thinking.* Commack, NY: Nova Science Publishers.

Turiel, E. (1978). Social regulation and domains of social concepts. In W. Damon (Ed.), *Social cognition (New directions for child development,* No. 1*).* San Francisco: Jossey-Bass.

Turiel, E. (1983). *The development of social knowledge: Morality and convention.* Cambridge: Cambridge University Press.

Turiel, E., Killen, M., & Helwig, C. C. (1987). Morality: Its structure, functions, and vagaries. In J. Kagan & S. Lamb (Eds.), *The emergence of morality.* Chicago: Chicago University Press.

Turiel, E. (1990). Moral judgement, moral action, and development. In D. Schrader (Ed.), *The legacy of Lawrence Kohlberg: New Directions for Child Development.* No. 47: San Francisco: Jossey-Bass.

Turiel, E., & Wainryb, C. (1994). Social reasoning and the varieties of social experiences in cultural contexts. In H. W. Reese (Ed.), *Advances in child development and behavior* (pp. 289–326). San Diego, CA: Academic Press, Inc.

Turiel, E. (1998). The development of morality. In W. Damon & N. Eisenberg (Eds.), *Handbook of child psychology* (5th ed.), *Vol.3: Social, emotional, and personality development* (pp. 863–932). New York: Wiley.

Turner, R. (1991). Fear of contraceptives, wish for closer relationship are major reasons teenagers delay clinic. *Family Planning Perspectives, 23*(Nov/Dec), 287–288.

Turner, P. J., & Gervai, J. (1995). A multidimensional study of gender typing in preschool children and their parents: Personality, attitudes, preferences, behavior, and cultural differences. *Developmental Psychology, 31*(5), 759–772.

Turner-Bowker, D. M. (1996). Gender stereotyped descriptors in children's picture books: Does "curious Jane" exist in the literature? *Sex Roles, v35*(7–8), 461–488.

United Nations Childrens Fund/UNICEF. (1999). *The state of the world's children.* Oxford: Oxford University Press.

U. S. Bureau of the Census (1995). *Statistical abstract of the United States: 1995* (115th ed.). Washington, DC: U. S. Government Printing Office.

U. S. Department of Health and Human Services. (1991). *Healthy people 2000: National Health Promotions and Disease Prevention Objectives.* Washington, DC: Government Printing Office (DHHS Publication No. PH591–50212).

U. S. Office of Education. (1977). *Procedures for evaluating specific learning disabilities*: Federal Register 42. Washington, DC: U. S. Government Printing Office.

U.S. Bureau of the Census (1998). Who's minding our preschoolers. *Current Population Reports*, Series P70–53. Washington, DC: U. S. Government Printing Office.

U.S. Bureau of the Census. (1998). *Statistical abstract of the United States: 1998* (118th ed.). Washington, DC: U. S. Government Printing Office.

U.S. Bureau of the Census (1999). Child support for custodial mothers and fathers: 1995. *Current Population Reports.* Washington, DC: U. S. Government Printing Office.

U.S. Department of Education: National Commission on Excellence in Education. (1983). *A nation at risk: The imperative for educational reform.* Washington, DC: U.S. Government Printing Office.

U.S. Department of Health and Human Services. (1996). Teenage births in the United States: National and state trends, 1990–1996. *Monthly Vital Statistics Report, 45*(3).

Unger, R. K., & Crawford, M. (1993). Commentary: Sex and gender: The troubled relationship between terms and concepts. *Psychological Science, 4*(2), 122–124

Urberg, K. A., Degirmencioglu, S. M., & Tolson, J. M. (1998). Adolescent friendship selection and termination: The role of similarity. *Journal of Social & Personal Relationships, 15*(5), 703–710.

Uzgiris, I. C., & Hunt, J. (1975). *Assessment in infancy: Ordinal scales of psychological development.* Champaign: University of Illinois Press.

Valsiner, J. (1998). Editorial: Culture & Psychology on the move. *Culture & Psychology, 4*, 5–9.

Van Biljon, J. A., Tolmie, C. J., & Plessis, J. P. (1999). Magix – an ICAE system for problem-based learning. *Computers & Education, 32*, 65–81.

Van Den Bergh, B. R. H. (1992). Maternal emotions during pregnancy and fetal and neonatal behavior. In J. G. Nijhuis (Ed.), *Fetal behavior: Development and perinatal aspects.* New York: Oxford University Press.

Vander Linde, E., Morrongiello, B. A., & Rovee-Collier, C. (1985). Determinants of retention in 8-week-old infants. *Developmental Psychology, 21*(4), 601–613.

Van Evra, J. (1990). *Television and child development.* Hillsdale, NJ: Erlbaum.

Vasquez, O. A., Pease-Alvarez, L., & Shannon, S. M. (1994). *Pushing boundaries : language and culture in a Mexicano community.* New York: Cambridge University Press.

Vaughn, B. E., Kopp, C. B., & Krakow, J. B. (1984). The emergence and consolidation of self-control from eighteen to thirty months of age: Normative trends and individual differences. *Child Development, 55*(3), 990–1004.

Vaughn, B. E., Lefever, G. B., Seifer, R., & Barglow, P. (1989). Attachment behavior, attachment security, and temperament during infancy. *Child Development, 60*, 728–737.

Verny, T., & Kelly, J. (1981). *The secret life of the unborn child.* New York: Summit Books.

Vogt, L. A., Jordan, C., & Tharp, R. G. (1987). Explaining school failure, producing school success: Two cases. *Anthropology and Education Quarterly, 18(4)*, 276–286.

Von Hofsten, C., & Ronnqvist, L. (1988). Preparations for grasping an object: A developmental study. *Journal of Experimental Psychology, 14*, 610–621.

Von Hofsten, C., & Siddiqui, A. (1993). Using the mother's actions as a reference for object exploration in 6- and 12-month-old infants. *British Journal of Developmental Psychology, 11*, 61–74.

Von Hofsten, C. (1997). On the early development of predictive abilities. In C. Dent-Read & P. Zukow-Goldring (Eds.), *Evolving explanations of development: Ecological approaches to organism-environment systems.* (pp. 163–194). Washington DC: American Psychological Association.

Vorhees, C. V., & Mollnow, E. (1987). Behavior teratogenesis: Long-term influences on behavior. In J. D. Osofsky (Ed.), *Handbook of infant development* (2nd ed.). New York: Wiley.

Vurpillot, E. (1968). The development of scanning strategies and their relation to visual differentiation. *Journal of Experimental Child Psychology, 6*, 632–650.

Vygotksy, L. S. (1978). *Mind in Society.* Cambridge, MA: Harvard University Press.

Vygotsky, L. S. (1934/1987). Thinking and speech. In T. N. Minick (Ed.), *The collected works of L. S. Vygotsky: Vol. 1. Problems of general psychology.* New York: Plenum Press.

Waddington, C. H. (1947). *Organizers and genes.* Cambridge: Cambridge University Press.

Wagner, C. L., Katikaneni, L. D., Cox, T. H., & Ryan, R. M. (1998). The impact of prenatal drug exposure on the neonate. *Obstetrics and Gynecology Clinics of North America, 25*(1), 169–194.

Wagner, D. A. (1974). The development of short-term and incidental memory: A cross cultural study. *Child Development, 48*, 389–396.

Wagner, D. A. (1978). Memories of Morocco: The influence of age, schooling, and environment on memory. *Cognitive Psychology, 10*, 1–28.

Wainryb, C. (1995). Reasoning about social conflicts in different cultures: Druze and Jewish children in Israel. *Child Development, 66*(2), 390–401.

Walden, T. A., & Baxter, A. (1989). The effect of context and age on social referencing. *Child Development, 60*, 1511–1518.

Walden, T., Lemerise, E., & Smith, M. C. (1999). Friendship and popularity in preschool classrooms. *Early Education & Development, 10*(3), 351–371.

Walker, L. J. (1989). A longitudinal study of moral reasoning. *Child Development, 60*, 157–166.

Walker, L. J., Pitts, R. C., Henning, K. H., & Matsuba, M. K. (1995). Reasoning about morality and real-life moral problems. In M. Keller & D. Hart (Eds.), *Morality in everyday life.* Cambridge: Developmental Perspectives.

Ward, S. L., & Overton, W. F. (1990). Semantic familiarity relevance and the development of deductive reasoning. *Developmental Psychology, 26*, 488–493.

Ward, K. (1994). Genetics and prenatal diagnosis. In J. R. Scott & P. J. DiSaia & C. B. Hammond & W. N. Spellacy (Eds.), *Dansforth's obstetrics and gynecology* (7th ed.). Philadelphia: J.B. Lippincott.

Wark, G. R., & Krebs, D. L. (1996). Gender and dilemma differences in real-life moral judgment. *Developmental Psychology., 32*(2), 220–230.

Warren, M. P., Brooks-Gunn, J., Fox, R., Lancelot, C., Newman, D., & Hamilton, W. G. (1991). Lack of bone accretion and amenarchea in young dancers: Evidence for a relative osteopenia in weight bearing bones. *Journal of Clinical Endocrinology and Metabolism, 72*, 847–853.

Warren, A. R., & McCloskey, L. A. (1997). Language in social contexts. In J. B. Gleason (Ed.), *The development of language* (pp. 210–258). Boston, MA: Allyn & Bacon.

Waterman, A. S. (1985). Identity in the context of adolescent psychology. In A. S. Waterman (Ed.), *Identity in adolescence: Progress and contents: (New directions for child development, No. 30).* San Francisco: Jossey-Bass.

Watson, J. B. (1930). *Behaviorism.* Chicago: University of Chicago Press.

Watson, M. W., & Fischer, K. W. (1980). Development of social roles in elicited spontaneous behavior during the preschool years. *Developmental Psychology, 16*, 483–494.

Waxman, S. R., & Gelman, R. (1986). Preschoolers use of superordinate relations in classification. *Cognitive Development, 1*, 139–156.

Waxman, S. R., & Hall, G. D. (1993). The development of a linkage between count nouns and object categories: Evidence from fifteen- to twenty-one-month-old infants. *Child Development, 69*, 1242–1257.

Wechsler, D. (1939). *The measurement of adult intelligence.* Baltimore: Williams & Wilkins.

Wechsler, D. (1974). *Manual for the Wechsler intelligence scale for children.* New York: Psychology Corporation.

Weill, B. C. (1930). *Are you training your child to be happy? Lesson material in child management.* Washington, DC: U.S. Government Printing Office.

Weinberg, M. K., & Tronick, E. Z. (1997). Maternal depression and infant maladjustment: A failure of mutual regulation. In J. D. Noshpitz (Ed.), *Handbook of child and adolescent psychiatry. Vol 1. Infants and preschoolers: Development and syndromes.* New York: Wiley.

Weisenfeld, H. C., & Sweet, R. L. (1994). Perinatal infections. In J. R. Scott & P. J. DiSaia & C. B. Hammond & W. N. Spellacy (Eds.), *Dansforth's obstetrics and gynecology* (7th ed.). Philadelphia: J.B. Lippincott.

Weisfeld, G. (1999). *Evolutionary principles of human adolescence.* New York: Basic Books.

Weisner, T. S., & Wilson-Mitchell, J. (1990). Nonconventional family lifestyles and sex typing in six-year-olds. *Child Development, 62*, 1915–1933.

Weisner, T. S. (1996). The 5-to-7 transition as an eccocultural project. In A. J. Sameroff & M. M. Haith (Eds.), *Reason and responsibility: The passage through childhood.* Chicago: University of Chicago Press.

Weiss, B., Dodge, K., Bates, J., & Pettit, G. (1992). Some consequences of early harsh discipline: Child aggression and a maladaptive social information processing style. *Child Development, 63*, 1236–1250.

Weiss, M. (1997). Parents' rejection of their appearance-impaired newborns: Some critical observations regarding the social myth of bonding. *Marriage & Family Review, 27*(3–4), 191–209.

Welch-Ross, M. K., & Schmidt, C. R. (1996). Gender-schema development and chidren's constructive story memory: Evidence for a developmental model. *Child Development, 67*(3), 820–835.

Wellman, H., & Lempers, J. D. (1977). The naturalistic communication abilities of two-year-olds. *Child Development, 48*, 1052–1057.

Wellman, H. M., & Williams, E. M. (1998). Knowledge acquisition in foundational domains. In D. Kuhn & R. S. Siegler (Eds.), *Handbook of child psychology* (5th ed.), *Vol 2: Cognition, perception, and language* (pp. 523–574). New York: Wiley.

Wells, G. (1996). Using the tool-kit of discourse in the activity of learning and teaching. *Mind, Culture, and Activity, 3*(2), 74–101.

Wells, G. (1999). *Dialogic inquiry: Towards a sociocultural practice and theory of education.* New York: Cambridge University Press.

Wentzel, K. R., & Asher, S. R. (1995). The academic level of neglected, rejected, popular, and controversial children. *Child Development, 66*, 754–763.

Werker, J. F., & Tees, R. C. (1999). Influences on infant speech processing: Toward a new synthesis. *Annual Review of Psychology, 50*(509–535).

Werner, H. (1948). *Comparative psychology of mental development.* New York: International Universities Press.

Werner, E., & Smith, R. S. (1982). *Vulnerable but invincible: A longitudinal study of resilient children and youth.* New York: McGraw-Hill.

Werner, E. E., & Smith, R. S. (1992). *Overcoming the odds: High-risk children from birth to adulthood.* Ithaca: Cornell University Press.

Werner, L. A., & Vanden Boss, G. R. (1993). Developmental psychoacoustics: What infants and children hear. *Hospital and Community Psychiatry, 44(7)*, 624–626.

Wertsch, J. V. (1991). *Voices of the mind.* Cambridge, MA: Harvard University Press.

Westinghouse Learning Corporation. (1969). *The impact of Head Start: An evaluation of the effects of Head Start on children's cognitive and affectional development. Executive summary, Ohio University report to the Office of Economic Opportunity.* Washington, DC: Learning House for Federal Scientific and Technical Informations.

Whitaker, R. C., Wright , J. A., Pepe, M. S., Seidel, K. D., & Dietz, W. H. (1997). Predicting obesity in young adulthood from childhood and parental obesity. *New England Journal of Medicine, 337*(13), 869–873.

Whitam, F. L., Diamond, M., & Martin, J. (1993). Homosexual orientation in twins: A report on 61 pairs and 3 triplet sets. *Archives of Sexual Behavior, 22*, 187–206.

White, L. A. (1949). *The science of culture.* New York: Grove Press.

White, B. L., & Carew, J. C. (1973). *Experience and environment: Major influences on the development of the young child.* Englewood Cliffs, NJ: Prentice-Hall.

White, B. L. (1975). *The first three years of life.* Englewood Cliffs, NJ: Prentice-Hall.

White, M. (1987). *The Japanese education challenge: A commitment to children.* New York: Free Press.

White, S. H. (1996). The relationship of developmental psychology to social policy. In E. F. Zigler & S. L. Kagan (Eds.), *Children, families, and government: Preparing for the twenty-first century* (pp. 409–426). New York: Cambridge University Press.

Whitehurst, G. J., Arnold, D. S., Epstein, J. N., Angell, A. L., Smith, M., & Fischel, J. E. (1994). A picture book reading intervention in day-care and home for children from low-income families. *Developmental Psychology, 30*, 679–689.

Whitehurst, G. J., & Lonigan, C. J. (1998). Child development and emergent literacy. *Child Development, 69*(3), 848–872.

Whiting, B. B., & Whiting, J. W. M. (1975). *Children of six cultures: A psycho-cultural analysis.* Cambridge, MA: Harvard University Press.

Whiting, J. W. M., Burbank, V. K., & Ratner, M. S. (1986). The duration of maidenhood across cultures. In J. W. M. Whiting & V. K. Burbank & M. S. Ratner (Eds.), *School-age pregnancy and parenthood: Biosocial dimensions* (pp. 273–302). New York: Aldine de Gruyer.

Whiting, B. B., & Edwards, C. P. (1988). *Children of different worlds: The formation of social behavior.* Cambridge, MA: Harvard University Press.

Wichstrom, L. (1998). Self-concept development during adolescence: Do American truths hold for Norwegians? In E. E. A. Skoe & A. L. von der Lippe (Eds.), *Personality development in adolescence: A cross national and life span perspective* (pp. 98–122). New York: Routledge.

Wilcox, A. J., Baird, D. D., & Weinberg, C. R. (1999). Time of implantation of the conceptus and loss of pregnancy. *New England Journal of Medicine, 340*(23), 1796–1799.

Willats, J. (1987). Marr and pictures: An information processing account of children's drawings. *Archives de Psychologie, 55*, 105–125.

Willats, J. (1995). An information processing approach to drawing development. In C. Lange-Küttner & G. V. Thomas (Eds.), *Drawing and looking* (pp. 27–43). New York: Harvester Wheatsheaf.

Williams, T. M. (1986). *The impact of television: A natural experiment in three communities.* Orlando, FL: Academic Press.

Wilson, E. O. (1975). *Sociobiology: The new synthesis.* Cambridge, MA: Harvard University Press.

Wilson, J. D., George, F. W., & Griffin, J. E. (1981). The hormonal control of sexual development. *Science, 211*, 1278–1284.

Wilson, M. N. (1986). The black extended family: An analytical consideration. *Developmental Psychology, 22*, 246–258.

Wilson, M. N., & Saft, E. W. (1993). Child maltreatment in the African-American community. In D. Cicchetti & S. L. Toth (Eds.), *Child abuse, child development, and social policy: Advances in applied developmental psychology* (Vol. 8). Norwood, NJ: Ablex.

Wilson, M. N. (Ed.). (1995). *African American family life: Its structural and ecological aspects.* San Francisco, CA: Jossey-Bass.

Winchester, A. M. (1972). *Genetics.* Boston: Houghton Mifflin.

Wineberg, S. S. (1987). The self-fulfillment of the self-fulfilling prophecy. *Educational Researcher, 16*, 28–36.

Winner, E., McCarthy, M., Kleinman, S., & Gardner, H. (1979). First metaphors. In D. Wolfe (Ed.), *Early symbolization (New directions for child development, No. 3)*. San Francisco: Jossey-Bass.

Winnicott, D. W. (1971). *Playing and reality*. London: Tavistock Publications.

Witter, F. R., & Keith, L. G. (Eds.). (1993). *Textbook of prematurity: Antecedents, treatment, & outcome*. Boston: Little, Brown, & Company.

Wolf, A. W., Lozoff, B., Latz, S., & Paludetto, R. (1996). Parental theories in the management of young children's sleep in Japan, Italy, and the United States. In S. Harkness & C. M. Super (Eds.), *Parents' cultural belief systems: Their origins, expressions, and consequences* (pp. 364–384). New York: Guilford Press.

Wolfe, W. S., Campbell, C. C., Frongillo, E. A., Haas, J. D., & Melnik, T. A. (1994). Overweight schoolchildren in New York state: Prevalence and characteristics. *American Journal of Public Health, 84(5)*, 807–813.

Wolfenstein, M. (1953). Trends in infant care. *American Journal of Orthopsychiatry, 33*, 120–130.

Wolff, P. H. (1966). The causes, controls, and organization of behavior in the neonate. *Psychological Issues, 5*, 1–105.

Wolff, P. H. (1969). The natural history of crying and other vocalizations in infancy. In B. M. Foss (Ed.), *Determinants of infant behavior* (Vol. 4). London: Methuen.

Wong, B. L. (1996). *The ABC's of learning disablities*. San Diego: Academic Press.

Wong-Fillmore, L. (1985). Second language learning in children: A proposed model. In R. Eshch & J. Provinzano (Eds.), *Issues in English language development*. Rosslyn, VA.: National Clearing House for Bilingual Education.

Woodruff-Pak, D. S., Logan, C. G., & Thompson, R. F. (1990). Neurobiological substrates of classical conditioning across the life-span. *Annals of the New York Academy of Sciences, 608*, 150–178.

Woodward, A. L., & Markman, E. M. (1998). Early word learning. In D. Kuhn & R. S. Sigler (Eds.), *Handbook of child psychology* (5th ed.), *Vol 2: Cognition, perception, and language* (pp. 371–420). New York: Wiley.

Worchel, F. F., & Allen, M. (1997). Mother's ability to discriminate cry types in low-birthweight premature and full-term infants. *Children's Health Care, 26*(3), 183–195.

Worthman, C. M., & Whiting, J. W. M. (1987). Social change in adolescent sexual behavior, mate selection, and premarital pregnancy rates in a Kikuyu community. *Ethos, 15*, 145–165.

Wright, H. F. (1956). Psychological development in Midwest. *Child Development, 27*, 265–286.

Wright, J. C., Huston, A. C., Reitz, A. L., & Pienyat, S. (1994). Young children's perceptions of television reality: Determinants and developmental differences. *Developmental Psychology, 30*, 229–239.

Wright, D. B., & Loftus, E. F. (1998). How misinformation alters memories. *Journal of Experimental Child Psychology, 71*(2), 155–164.

Wynn, K. (1992). Addition and subtraction by human infants. *Nature, 358*, 749–750.

Wynn, K. (1996). Infants' individuation and enumeration of actions. *Psychological Science, 7*(3), 164–169.

Yarrow, M. R., Scott, P. M., & Waxler, C. Z. (1973). Learning concern for others. *Developmental Psychology, 8*, 240–260.

Yates, M., & Youniss, J. (1999). *Roots of civic identity: International perspectives on community service and activism in youth*. New York: Cambridge University Press.

Yerkes, R. M. (Ed.). (1921). *Psychological examining in the United States Army* (Vol. 15).

Yonas, A., & Hartman, B. (1993). Perceiving the affordance of contact in four- and five-month-old infants. *Child Development, 64*, 298–308.

Young, C. M., Sipin, S. S., & Roe, O. A. (1968). Density and skinfold measurements: Body composition of pre-adolescent girls. *Journal of the American Dietetic Association, 53*, 25–31.

Young, K. T. (1990). American conceptions of infant development from 1955 to 1984: What the experts are telling parents. *Child Development, 61*, 17–28.

Youniss, J., & Smollar, J. (1985). *Adolescent relations with mothers, fathers, and friends*. Chicago: University of Chicago Press.

Youniss, J., & Yates, M. (1999). Youth service and moral-civic identity: A case for everyday morality. *Educational Psychology Review., 11*(4), 361–376.

Yule, G. (1997). *Referential communication tasks*. Mahwah, NJ: Erlbaum.

Zahavi, S., & Asher, S. R. (1978). The effects of verbal instruction on preschool children's aggressive behavior. *Journal of School Psychology, 16*, 146–153.

Zahn-Waxler, C., Radke-Yarrow, M., & King, R. (1979). Child rearing and children's prosocial initiations toward victims of distress. *Child Development, 50*, 319–330.

Zahn-Waxler, C., & Radke-Yarrow, M. (1982). The development of altruism: Alternative research strategies. In N. Eisenberg (Ed.), *The development of prosocial behavior*. New York: Academic Press.

Zahn-Waxler, C., Radke-Yarrow, M., Wagner, E., & Chapman, M. (1992). Development of concern for others. *Developmental Psychology, 28*, 126–136.

Zarbatany, L., Hartmann, D. P., & Rankin, D. B. (1990). The psychological functions of preadolescent peer activities. *Child Development, 61*(4), 1067–1080.

Zech, L., Vye, N. J., Bransford, J. D., Goldman, S. R., & al., e. (1998). An introduction to geometry through anchored instruction. In R. Lehrer & D. Chazan (Eds.), *Designing learning environments for developing understanding of geometry and space.* (pp. 439–463). Mahwah, NJ: Erlbaum.

Zelazo, P. R. (1983). The development of walking: New findings and old assumptions. *Journal of Motor Behavior, 15, 99–137.*

Zeskind, P. S., Klein, L., & Marshall, T. R. (1992). Adults' perceptions of experimental modifications of durations of pauses and expiratory sounds in infant crying. *Developmental Psychology, 28*(6), 1153–1162.

Zeskind, P. S., Platzman, K., Coles, C. D., & Schuetze, P. A. (1996). Cry analysis detects subclinical effects of prenatal alcohol exposure in newborn infants. *Infant Behavior & Development, 19*(4), 497–500.

Zigler, E., & Hall, N. W. (1989). Physical child abuse in America: Past, present, and future. In D. Cicchetti & V. Carlson (Eds.), *Child maltreatment: Theory and research on the causes and consequences of child abuse and neglect*. New York: Cambridge University Press.

Zigler, E. F., & Finn-Stevenson, M. (1999). Applied developmental psychology. In M. H. Bornstein & M. E. Lamb (Eds.), *Developmental psychology: An advanced textbook* (4th ed.) (pp. 555–598). Mahwah, NJ: Erlbaum.

Zill, N. (1994). Understanding why children in stepfamilies have more learning and behavior problems than children in nuclear families. In A. Booth & J. Dunn (Eds.), *Stepfamilies: Who benefits? Who does not?* (pp. 97–106). Hillsdale, NJ: Erlbaum.

Zuckerman, M. (1990). The psychophysiology of sensation seeking. *Journal of Personality, 58*(1), 313–345.

Zukow, P. G. (1986). The relationship between interaction with the caregiver and the emergence of play activities during the one-word period. *British Journal of Developmental Psychology, 4*, 223–234.

Zukow-Goldring, P. (1995). Sibling caregiving. In M. Bornstein (Ed.), *Handbook of Parenting, Vol. 3, Status and social conditions of parenting*. Hillsdale, NJ: Erlbaum.

Illustration Credits

CHAPTER 1

Opener: Scott Barrow/International Stock; p. 2: *(top)* Jean-Loup Charmet, Paris; p. 2: *(bottom)* Jean-Loup Charmet, Paris; p. 4: Corbis-Bettmann; p. 5: Lewis W. Hine Collection, NYPL; p. 7: Kari Rene Hall, Los Angeles Times; p. 11: Nina Leen, Life magazone © Time Inc.; p. 17: Down House and the Royal College of Surgeons of England; p. 20: G.B. Trudeau. Reprinted with permission of UNIVERSAL PRESS SYDICATE. All Rights Reserved; p. 21: Enrico Ferorelli; p. 23: Monkmeyer/Merrim; p. 24: Benjamin Harris; p. 27: Courtesy of Margaret Beale Spencer; p. 28: Courtesy of Sheila Cole; p. 31: Lawrence Migdale/Photo Researchers; p. 33: Herb Gehr, Life magazine © Time Inc.; p. 35: *(top)* G. L. Engel, F. Reichman, V. T. Harway, D. W. Hess, Monica: Infant-feeding behavior of a mother gastric fistula-fed as an infant: A 30 year longitudinal study of enduring effects, pp. 29–90, in E.J. Anthony and G.H. Pollack (Eds.), Parental Influences in Health and Disease, Boston: Little, Brown & Co., 1985; p. 35: *(bottom)* G. L. Engel, F. Reichman, V. T. Harway, D. W. Hess, Monica: Infant-feeding behavior of a mother gastric fistula-fed as an infant: A 30 year longitudinal study of enduring effects, pp. 29–90, in E.J. Anthony and G.H. Pollack (Eds.), Parental Influences in Health and Disease, Boston: Little, Brown & Co., 1985; p. 36: Yves DeBraine/Black Star; p. 38: *(top)* Shawn G. Henry/Material World; p. 38: *(bottom)* Lindsay Hebberd/Woodfin Camp & Associates; p. 38: *(margin left)* Courtesy of Gita Vgotskaya; p. 39: *(top)* Macduff Everton; p. 39: *(bottom)* V. Chiasson/Gamma Liason.

PART I

Opener: Yorgos Nikas/Tony Stone; p. 46: Xinhua/The Liason Agency Network; p. 47: Copyright Lennart Nilsson, A Child Is Born, 1990 ed., Dell Publishing Company.

CHAPTER 2

Opener: Martin Weitz/The Everett Collection; p. 52: Julie Newdol, Computer Graphics Laboratory, UCSF Copyright © Regents University of California; p. 55: Moravian Museum, Brno; p. 56: *(bottom left)* Kathryn Abbe and Frances McLaughlin-Gill; p. 56: *(bottom center)* Kathryn Abbe and Frances McLaughlin-Gill; p. 56: *(bottom right)* Kathryn Abbe and Frances McLaughlin-Gill; p. 56: *(top)* Barbara Rogoff; p. 57: BioPhoto Associates/Science Source/Photo Researchers; p. 60: *(left)* Mike Yamashita/Woodfin Camp & Associates; p. 60: *(center)* Lindsay Hebberd/Woodfin Camp & Associates; p. 60: *(right)* Jack Fields/Photo Researchers; p. 62: The New Yorker Collection J.B. Handelsman from cartoonbank.com. All Rights Reserved; p. 69: *(top)* Custom Medical Stock Photo; p. 69: *(bottom)* Jose Carrillo/PhotoEdit.

CHAPTER 3

Opener: Petit Format/Nestle/Photo Researchers; p. 82: Copyright Lennart Nilsson, A Child Is Born, 1990 ed., Dell Publishing Company; p. 84: *(top)* Copyright Lennart Nilsson, Behold Man, Little, Brown & Co.; p. 84: *(bottom)* Copyright Lennart Nilsson, Behold Man, Little, Brown & Co.; p. 88: Copyright Lennart Nilsson, A Child Is Born, 1990 ed., Dell Publishing Company; p. 90: Erika Stone/Photo Researchers; p. 92: Melanie Spence, University of Texas; p. 96: Marie Dorigny/REA; p. 98: *(top)* George Steinmetz; p. 98: *(bottom)* from Ann Pytkowicz Streissguth et al. (18 July 1980), Teratogenic effects of alcohol in humans and laboratory animals, Science 209, 353–361, figs. 2, 3, 4. Copyright 1980 by the American Association for the Advancement of Science. Photographs courtesy of University of Washington, School of Medicine; p. 103: Aileen & W. Eugene Smith/Black Star; p. 107: Roger Tully/Tony Stone; p. 112: Jonathon Selig/Tony Stone; p. 113: Evelyn Thoman, Infant Studies Laboratory.

PART II

Opener: Ellen Senisi/Photosynthesis; p. 124: Tina Manley; p. 125: Michelle Burgess/Stock Boston.

CHAPTER 4

Opener: Elie Bernager/Tony Stone; p. 134: James Killkelly, Scientific American, 252, pp. 46–52; p. 136: From First Glances by Davida Y. Teller, Journal of Investigative Opthalmology and Visual Science, Vol. 38, 1997, pp. 2183–2203. Photographs copyright of Anthony Young; p. 137: David Linton, Scientific American, 204, pp. 66–72; p. 139: Courtesy of Jacob E. Steiner, The Hebrew University-Hadassah School of Dental Medicine, Jeruselem; p. 141: J. DaCunha/Petit Format/Photo Researchers; p. 142: Elizabeth Crews; p. 144: Carroll Izard; p. 147: Laura Dwight; p. 151: Elizabeth Crews; p. 152: Henning Christoph/DAS FOTOARCHIV; p. 154: E. Gamper (1926), Zeitschrift fur der gesamte Neurologie und Psychiatrie, 104, p. 65, fig. 14; p. 159: Enrico Ferorelli; p. 161: Courtesy of Einar R. Siqueland, Brown University; p. 164: Laura Dwight; p. 167: Bernard Wolff, UNICEF; p. 168: *(left)* Frans Lanting/Minden Pictures; p. 168: *(center)* David Turnley/Black Star; p. 168: *(right)* Spencer Grant/PhotoEdit; p. 171: Pascal Maitre Cosmos/Matrix; p. 172: D. G. Freedman, Human Infancy: An Evolutionary Perspective. Erlbaum. 1974; p. 173: William Hubbell/Woodfin Camp & Associates.

CHAPER 5

Opener: Myrleen Ferguson/PhotoEdit; p. 181: Penny Tweedie/Tony Stone Worldwide; p. 184: *(top)* Laura Dwight; p. 184: *(bottom)* Laura Dwight; p. 187: *(top)* Martha Cooper; p. 187: *(bottom)* Library of Congress; p. 188: Randy Taylor/Sygma; p. 192: D. Goodman/Monkmeyer; p. 194: Adele Diamond; p. 201: *(top left, second from bottom left, second from top right)* Creszentia and Ted Allen; p. 201: *(second from top left)* Herve Chanmeton Chamaliers; p. 201: *(bottom left)* Marc Henrie A.S.C., London; p. 201: *(top right)* Jal Duncan; p. 201: *(bottom right)* Karl Wolffram; p. 202: *(top)* Courtesy of Prof. Carolyn Rovee-Collier, Rutgers University; p. 202: *(bottom)* Jean Mandler and Laraine McDonough; p. 205: A. N. Meltzoff; p. 206: Thomas Heinser; p. 209: Ursula Markus/ Photo Researchers; p. 210: Laura Dwight.

CHAPTER 6

Opener: Elizabeth Crews/The Image Works; p. 220: Laura Dwight; p. 221: *(left)* Courtesy of Karen Adolph, Carnegie Mellon; p. 221: *(right)* Courtesy of Karen Adolph, Carnegie Mellon; p. 223: Laura Dwight; p. 224: Laura Dwight; p. 227: George S. Zimbal/Monkmeyer; p. 228: Laura Dwight; p. 233: Courtesy of Judy DeLoache; p. 235: Courtesy of Sheila Cole; p. 237: Martin Rogers/Tony Stone; p. 238: *(top and bottom)* Harlow Primate Laboratory, University of Wisconsin;

p. 240: Mary D. Ainsworth; p. 241: Will & Deni McIntyre/Photo Researchers; p. 242: Ituri Forest Peoples Fund; p. 245: Laura Dwight; p. 248: Laura Dwight.

CHAPTER 7

Opener: Agence France-Presse; p. 260: Jean-Michel Turpin/Gamma Liason; p. 261: Chiasson/Gamma Liason; p. 263: Christopher Morris/ Black Star; p. 264: Elizabeth Crews; p. 266: Anthony Suau/Black Star; p. 268: Saul Conklin/PhotoEdit; p. 272: April Saul/The Philadelphia Inquirer; p. 274: Wesley Bocxe/Photo Researchers; p. 279: Harlow Primate Laboratory, University of Wisconsin; p. 280: Harlow Primate Laboratory, University of Wisconsin; p. 282 Stephanie Maze/Woodfin Camp & Associates.

PART III

Opener: James Nelson/Tony Stone; p. 290: Marc Pokempner/Tony Stone; p. 291: Elizabeth Crews.

CHAPTER 8

Opener: Jose Luis Pelaez Inc./The Stock Market; p. 298: Dwayne Newton/PhotoEdit; p. 301: Pamela Duffy; p. 306: Joel Gordon; p. 310: Myrleen Ferguson/PhotoEdit; p. 311: Novosti from Sovfoto; p. 316: Michael Newman/PhotoEdit; p. 319: Enrico Ferorelli; p. 321: Ursula Bellugi, The Salk Institute for Biological Studies; p. 325: Erika Stone.

CHAPTER 9

Opener: B. Daemmrich/The Image Works; p. 337: Steve Rubin/The Image Works; p. 341: The Exploratorium, San Francisco; p. 349: Al Seib/Los Angeles Times; p. 357: Courtesy of Sheila Cole; p. 358: Guglielmo De'Micheli/Material World; p. 360: Miguel Luis Fairbanks/ Material World; p. 363: Elizabeth Crews; p. 365: Courtesy of Carrie Hogan; p. 367: Nadia's drawings from Nadia: A Case of Extraordinary Drawing Ability in an Autistic Child by Lorne Selfe, © 1977 Academic Press, plates 20 and 27; p. 368: Lawrence Migdale; p. 369: U.S. Committee for UNICEF.

CHAPTER 10

Opener: Lindsay Hebberd/Woodfin Camp & Associates; p. 375: Courtesy of Sheila Cole; p. 377: *(top)* Karen Kasmauski/Matrix; p. 377: *(bottom)* Steve Lehman/Tony Stone; p. 379: Austrian Press and Information Service; p. 381: Lynn Johnson/Black Star; p. 384: Cathy Cheney/Stock Boston; p. 385: Lindsay Hebberd/Woodfin Camp & Associates; p. 386: Courtesy of Jennifer Cole; p. 398: UPI/Bettmann; p. 401: Herlinde Koelbl/Betty Dornheim Picture Service; p. 402: Albert Bandura, Stanford University; p. 403: Film Study Center, Harvard; p. 405: Michael H. Francis; p. 406: UPI/Bettmann Newsphotos; p. 409 Janet Kelly/Eagle-Times, Reading Pennsylvania; p. 410: David M. Grossman; p. 411: Laura Dwight.

CHAPTER 11

Opener: Lori Adamski Peek/Tony Stone; p. 423: Arthur Pollack/ Boston Herald; p. 425: David Reed/Material World; p. 428: Sean Sprague/Stock Boston; p. 432: Myrleen Ferguson/PhotoEdit; p. 436: Peter Turnley/Black Star; p. 441: Peter Ginter/Material World; p. 442: Barbara Rios/Photo Researchers; p. 443: Courtesy of Sheila Cole; p. 447: John Maier, Jr./The Image Works; p. 452: Stephanie Maze/ Woodfin Camp & Associates; p. 453: J. Guichard/Sygma; p. 454: *(top)* Elizabeth Crews; p. 454: *(bottom)* Elizabeth Crews; p. 456: Laura Dwight; p. 457: Michael Newman/ PhotoEdit.

PART IV

Opener: Suzanne DeChillo/New York Times Pictures; p. 464: Ian Shaw/ Tony Stone; p. 465: Elizabeth Crews.

CHAPTER 12

Opener: Pierre Perrin/SYGMA; p. 469: *(left)* Lawrence Migdale; p. 469: *(right)* Shawn G. Henry/Material World; p. 472: Margaret Ross/Stock Boston; p. 483: Martha Cooper; p. 486: Kirk McRoy/Material World; p. 487: Macduff Everton; p. 496: Lawrence Migdale; p. 497: Mike Fisher/AP Photo.

CHAPTER 13

Opener: Bruce Ayres/Tony Stone; p. 505: Macduff Everton; p. 506: Gianni Dagli Orti/Corbis; p. 507: Bonnie Kamin; p. 508: Bernard Schoenbaum, © 1994, The New Yorker Magazine; p. 510: Bob Daemmrich/Stock Boston; p. 511: Ulrike Welsch/Photo Researchers; p. 513: Elizabeth Crews; p. 519: *(top left)* Monkmeyer/Forsyth; p. 519: *(top right)* Betty Press/Woodfin Camp & Associates; p. 519: *(bottom left)* Sygma; p. 519: *(bottom right)* D. Peter Menzel/Material World; p. 533: Sidney Harris; p. 538: Mary Kate Denny/PhotoEdit/PictureQuest; p. 540: Charles Gupton/ Stone; p. 541: Laura Dwight/Omni-Photo Communications; p. 547: Lawrence Migdale.

CHAPTER 14

Opener: F. Armstrong/Photo Network; p. 555: *(top)* Catherine Ursillo/ Photo Researchers; p. 555: *(bottom)* Frans Lanting/Minden Pictures; p. 557: Lauren Greenfiels/Sygma; p. 571: Jeff Isaac Greenberg/Photo Researchers; p. 574: Lawrence Migdale; p. 586: Lawrence Migdale/ Stock Boston; p. 585 M.K. Denny/PhotoEdit; p. 590: Elizabeth Crews/The Image Works.

PART V

Opener: Don Smetzer/Tony Stone; p. 599: Keren Su/Tony Stone; p. 600: Devendra M Singh/Agence France Presse.

CHAPTER 15

Opener: Mark Downey/Lucid Images/PictureQuest; p. 605: Mark Peterson/SABA; p. 611: Devendra M Singh/Agence France Presse; p. 613: Carter Smith/New York Times; p. 615: Joseph Rodriguez/Black Star; p. 618: Joanna B. Pinneo/Aurora; p. 620: Eastcott/The Image Works; p. 621: Spencer Grant/PhotoEdit; p. 625: Lauren Greenfield; p. 630: R. Hutchings/PhotoEdit; p. 631: Nicholas Kristof/NYT Pictures; p. 632: A. Lichtenstein/The Image Works; p. 637: Ron Levine/Black Star.

CHAPTER 16

Opener: Corey Lowenstein/AP Photo/News & Observer; p. 646: Russell D. Curtis/Photo Researchers; p. 656: Stephen Thomas, The Last Navigator, Henry Holt & Company, 1987; p. 659: M. Greenlar/ The Image Works; p. 661: *(top)* Momatiuk/ Eastcott/ Woodfin Camp & Associates; p. 661: *(bottom)* Michelle Gabel/The Image Works; p. 672: Laura Dwight; p. 673: Mark Lennihan/AP Photo; p. 674: Joel Gordon; p. 675: Esbin-Anderson/Emotions Photo Network; p. 677: Liliana Nieto Delrio/JB Pictures; p. 682: Jan Sonnenmair/NYT Pictures; p. 687: Kaluzny/Thatcher/Tony Stone.

Name Index

Subject Index

Page references followed by italic *t* indicate material in tables.